>**marketing**research

The McGraw-Hill/Irwin Series in Marketing

Alreck & Settle
The Survey Research Handbook
Third Edition

Alsem & Wittink
Strategic Marketing: A Practical Approach
First Edition

Anderson, Beveridge, Lawton, & Scott
Merlin: A Marketing Simulation
First Edition

Arens
Contemporary Advertising
Tenth Edition

Arnould, Price, & Zinkhan
Consumers
Second Edition

Bearden, Ingram, & LaForge
Marketing: Principles & Perspectives
Fourth Edition

Belch & Belch
Advertising & Promotion: An Integrated Marketing Communications Approach
Sixth Edition

Bingham & Gomes
Business Marketing
Third Edition

Cateora & Graham
International Marketing
Twelfth Edition

Cole & Mishler
Consumer and Business Credit Management
Eleventh Edition

Cooper & Schindler
Marketing Research
First Edition

Cravens & Piercy
Strategic Marketing
Eighth Edition

Cravens, Lamb, & Crittenden
Strategic Marketing Management Cases
Seventh Edition

Crawford & Di Benedetto
New Products Management
Eighth Edition

Duncan
Principles of Advertising and IMC
Second Edition

Dwyer & Tanner
Business Marketing
Third Edition

Eisenmann
Internet Business Models: Text and Cases
First Edition

Etzel, Walker, & Stanton
Marketing
Thirteenth Edition

Forrest
Internet Marketing Intelligence
First Edition

Futrell
ABC's of Relationship Selling
Eighth Edition

Futrell
Fundamentals of Selling
Ninth Edition

Gourville, Quelch, & Rangan
Cases in Health Care Marketing
First Edition

Hair, Bush, & Ortinau
Marketing Research
Third Edition

Hawkins, Best, & Coney
Consumer Behavior
Ninth Edition

Johansson
Global Marketing
Fourth Edition

Johnston & Marshall
Churchill/Ford/Walker's Sales Force Management
Eighth Edition

Johnston & Marshall
Relationship Selling and Sales Management
First Edition

Kerin, Hartley, & Rudelius
Marketing: The Core
First Edition

Kerin, Berkowitz, Hartley, & Rudelius
Marketing
Eighth Edition

Lehmann & Winer
Analysis for Marketing Planning
Sixth Edition

Lehmann & Winer
Product Management
Fourth Edition

Levy & Weitz
Retailing Management
Fifth Edition

Mason & Perreault
The Marketing Game!
Third Edition

McDonald
Direct Marketing: An Integrated Approach
First Edition

Mohammed, Fisher, Jaworski, & Paddison
Internet Marketing: Building Advantage in a Networked Economy
Second Edition

Molinari
Marketing Research Project Manual
First Edition

Monroe
Pricing
Third Edition

Mullins, Walker, & Boyd
Marketing Management: A Strategic Decision-Making Approach
Fifth Edition

Nentl & Miller
SimSeries Simulations:
  SimSell
  SimSales Management
  SimMarketing
  SimMarketing Research
  SimCRM
First Edition

Perreault & McCarthy
Basic Marketing: A Global Managerial Approach
Fifteenth Edition

Perreault & McCarthy
Essentials of Marketing: A Global Managerial Approach
Tenth Edition

Peter & Donnelly
A Preface to Marketing Management
Tenth Edition

Peter & Donnelly
Marketing Management: Knowledge and Skills
Seventh Edition

Peter & Olson
Consumer Behavior
Seventh Edition

Purvis & Burton
Which Ad Pulled Best?
Ninth Edition

Quelch, Rangan, & Lal
Marketing Management Text and Cases
First Edition

Rayport & Jaworski
Introduction to e-Commerce
Second Edition

Rayport & Jaworski
e-Commerce
First Edition

Rayport & Jaworski
Cases in e-Commerce
First Edition

Richardson
Internet Marketing
First Edition

Roberts
Internet Marketing: Integrating Online and Offline Strategies
First Edition

Spiro, Stanton, & Rich
Management of a Sales Force
Eleventh Edition

Stock & Lambert
Strategic Logistics Management
Fourth Edition

Ulrich & Eppinger
Product Design and Development
Third Edition

Walker, Boyd, Mullins, & Larreche
Marketing Strategy: A Decision-Focused Approach
Fifth Edition

Weitz, Castleberry, & Tanner
Selling: Building Partnerships
Fifth Edition

Zeithaml & Bitner
Services Marketing
Fourth Edition

>marketing research

Donald R. Cooper
Florida Atlantic University

Pamela S. Schindler
Wittenberg University

**McGraw-Hill
Irwin**

Boston Burr Ridge, IL Dubuque, IA Madison, WI New York San Francisco St. Louis
Bangkok Bogotá Caracas Kuala Lumpur Lisbon London Madrid Mexico City
Milan Montreal New Delhi Santiago Seoul Singapore Sydney Taipei Toronto

McGraw-Hill
Irwin

MARKETING RESEARCH

Published by McGraw-Hill/Irwin, a business unit of The McGraw-Hill Companies, Inc., 1221 Avenue of the Americas, New York, NY, 10020. Copyright © 2006 by The McGraw-Hill Companies, Inc. All rights reserved. No part of this publication may be reproduced or distributed in any form or by any means, or stored in a database or retrieval system, without the prior written consent of The McGraw-Hill Companies, Inc., including, but not limited to, in any network or other electronic storage or transmission, or broadcast for distance learning.

Some ancillaries, including electronic and print components, may not be available to customers outside the United States.

This book is printed on acid-free paper.

1 2 3 4 5 6 7 8 9 0 WCK/WCK 0 9 8 7 6 5

ISBN 0-07-283786-1

Editorial director: *John E. Biernat*
Publisher: *Andy Winston*
Sponsoring editor: *Barrett Koger*
Managing developmental editor: *Nancy Barbour*
Executive marketing manager: *Dan Silverburg*
Producer, Media technology: *Damian Moshak*
Project manager: *Laura Griffin*
Manager, New book production: *Heather D. Burbridge*
Senior designer: *Mary E. Kazak*
Senior photo research coordinator: *Jeremy Cheshareck*
Photo researcher: *Keri Johnson*
Lead media project manager: *Cathy L. Tepper*
Supplement producer: *Gina F. DiMartino*
Developer, Media technology: *Brian Nacik*
Cover/interior design: *Kiera C. Pohl*
Cover image: © *Getty Images*
Typeface: *10/12 Times Roman*
Compositor: *Cenveo Indianapolis*
Printer: *Quebecor World Versailles Inc.*

Library of Congress Cataloging-in-Publication Data

Schindler, Pamela S.
    Marketing research / Pamela S. Schindler, Donald R. Cooper.—1st. ed.
      p. cm.
    Includes bibliographical references and index.
    ISBN 0-07-283786-1 (alk. paper)
    1. Marketing research. I. Cooper, Donald R. II. Title.

  HF5415.2.S327 2006
  658.8'3—dc22

                        2004057811

www.mhhe.com

To my sons, Ryan and Paul Cooper, for their love and courage; in memory of my daughter Chrissy; and to my Li Xiaoying for her gentle spirit, endless devotion, and loving care.

Donald Cooper

In loving memory, to my father, Robert N. Clark, an entrepreneur who taught me the value of risk, who was my most enthusiastic cheerleader during this book's development, and who never failed to tell me how proud he was of the woman I'd become and the promise I'd fulfilled; and to my exceptional husband, Bill, who shouldered significant additional burdens in the last two years yet never failed to provide a seemingly inexhaustible supply of love and support in whatever form it was needed most.

Pamela S. Schindler

>**brief**contents

>contents

>**part II**

The Design of Marketing Research   189

>part III

The Sources and Collection of Data   335

Marketing Research is designed to share the stimulating, challenging, fascinating, and sometimes frustrating world of research-supported marketing decisions with undergraduate students preparing to be future marketers. We have used our research and teaching experience and our numerous research industry contacts to create a textbook full of practical examples and researcher insights. For undergraduate students just learning about marketing research or graduate students advancing their research knowledge in the marketing arena, *Marketing Research* is designed as a valued reference. Students who become marketers, as well as those who become research specialists, will find *Marketing Research* of current and future value.

An Approach Based on Demystifying the Research Process

There are several approaches to teaching marketing research. You could present the big picture and context first and then break down the overall process into its parts. Or you could start with techniques and build each into a phase of the overall process until at the end the overview is known. This book takes the approach that students need an overview first in order to appreciate the nuances and details of the specific techniques they will be asked to employ to develop high-quality information. This belief led us to develop the text in four parts. The first part presents the overview, while Parts 2, 3, and 4 provide the details on methodologies and techniques. Some teachers might prefer to jump into survey design in the beginning and then explain the research process through that one methodology. But our experience reveals that the technique-first approach leaves the student at a loss to understand why the survey is given so much importance when other techniques have different but equally valuable merits.

We Set the Stage for Ethical Issue Discussions—You Decide How Often You Discuss Them

Students are just like research practitioners when it comes to ethical dilemmas: Some don't see the ethical issues in any decision, while those that do may not have thought about them enough to take a stance. Only a few will have clearly drawn their ethical boundaries when it comes to either marketing or marketing research decisions. Now more than ever it is important to talk about ethical issues in our classrooms, but it is sometimes difficult for our students and us if we don't have the right foundation. Chapter 7 gives your student the foundation for discussing

ethics in marketing research. It ties those critical issues to the research process diagram. It will be obvious to them that they will need to understand their own ethical principles in order to make good decisions at each stage of the marketing research process.

We consciously chose not to feed our students "ethical" boxed examples in every chapter. Identifying the ethical dilemmas in this way makes it far too easy; they think that such dilemmas come complete with neon signs. In fact, the ethical dilemma is often under the surface, not clearly obvious and often below a researcher's personal radar. While we made sure that the research studies we profile have their share of ethical struggles, we believe you, the instructor, should guide the choice of how often and in what fashion you bring those issues to the attention of your students. Some of you may decide that reading Chapter 7 is sufficient; others will want to reinforce the dilemmas we overview in Chapter 7 in every subsequent chapter's discussion.

Online marketing and information privacy is currently the hot ethical topic. A 2004 Gallup Poll revealed that people are more worried about the onslaught of marketing messages resulting from sharing their personal information (especially their e-mail addresses through a survey, a marketing promotion, a purchase, etc.) than they are about identity fraud. Clearly if you want to cover only one ethical issue in depth, information privacy should be the one. We've given you some special discussion aids to help with this discussion: The Direct Marketing Association Information Security Guidelines in Appendix B, as well as an overview of the European Union's data privacy directive and the United States' safe harbor agreement in Chapter 7.

Theory with the Right Balance of "How-To"

There is a continuing struggle in our classrooms between how much theory to combine with practice. We think the adage expounded in medical education works well in our research classroom: Learn one, do one, teach one. Many of our reviewers reinforced this perception—they have designed their marketing research courses around a research project (real or hypothetical) or series of projects. Over the decades that we've been teaching research methodology, we've tried both approaches and find they work in different ways equally well. So how much "how-to" is enough? If students are going to learn about it in the text, we decided to offer them enough "how-to" to let them execute what they have learned.

There are several places where this balance is and needs to be most evident: the chapters devoted to research proposals, qualitative research, survey research, statistical analysis, and presenting results. The *request for proposal (RFP)* starts the research process for most large projects, yet most texts ignore it. We walk our students through the process and give them a full-fledged example to follow. You'll find the RFP for the Ogilvy Research Award–winning *Covering Kids* campaign project in an appendix to Chapter 6 and learn how the proposal process was managed from a Snapshot in the same chapter.

Marketing researchers, in their search for insights, are turning more frequently to the qualitative techniques. These tools took a back seat to the quantitative ones during the last 20 years, which may explain why many of our students think *research* is synonymous with *surveys*. To correct this misconception, we've given students the "what and why" of numerous qualitative techniques, not just the focus group. While the focus group is the most frequently used qualitative technique, it may also be the most abused. So we've given students something they have rarely had access to: a focus group discussion guide. Now you and your students can see how a 24-year veteran moderator structures a focus group. It's in Appendix A.

The core of most of our research courses, regardless of where we teach or at what level, is the survey. We offer Appendix 15a on crafting effective measurement questions following Chapter 15, as well as detailed chapters on survey processes, measurement approaches, and measurement scales. You'll even find the different types of measurement scales detailed for online and non-Web survey approaches.

There is no getting around the math when you teach research. But we don't all teach our courses at the same level when it comes to the statistical and analytical processes. Because in practice marketing research can cover everything from basic statistics to multivariate methods, we've divided this material so that no matter at what level you structure your course, your students will find everything they need, now and later.

Reviewers told us that research reporting is often shortchanged in their courses. Those who build their course around a project are often time-starved at the end of the term. What they need is a chapter requiring limited classroom coverage of material. One of our reviewers told us that our last chapter, "Presenting Insights and Findings," is so well done that he wouldn't need to cover the material. Of course, we know he will—at some level—as it is far too important a topic to rely on tired, stressed students extracting the right conclusions from what they read. However, what makes this chapter outstanding is something obvious but not often present: a complete, *annotated* management report. We've embedded the report for the main Behind the Scenes project, which is woven throughout several chapters. We want the student to be able to visualize what a report looks like. It's what both verbal and visual learners told us they needed so that they can create a professional-looking report for their own project or evaluate and critique one by a another student or—in the future—by another researcher.

Teachers, Students, and Researchers Influenced the Content and Its Design

Every pedagogical and content element is carefully crafted to give the student a rich, learning experience and to make teaching this complex subject easier for the instructor. Each chapter has several features, pictured in the Walk-Through that follows, so you will become familiar with their color and heading formats:

- **Behind the Scenes** is the student's glimpse into what is really going on in research. Much that is done in research is proprietary information. If marketers openly shared all their successes and failures, they would lose competitive leverage. This feature gives us the ability to share those stories that researchers couldn't or wouldn't share with their names attached. And it gives us an opportunity to share with the student that researchers and their research are subject to the foibles of human personality. These vignettes are perfect for discussion, and we've woven the projects and the characters involved throughout the chapters. Although names and brands are withheld to protect the firm, this doesn't mean the characters or story lines are any less real. We promise to keep these vignettes constant over several editions—to help reduce your class preparation time—unless you tell us one of them isn't working for you or we learn of another scenario that is just too good to keep to ourselves.

- **Snapshots** are mini–case studies, embedded within each chapter to entice the student to read about current marketing research. Other texts put these at the end of the chapter, but our research tells us that few students read beyond the chapter summary, unless specifically assigned to do so. We hope to entice them to read about the research that is actually being done in their environment, with firms and organizations they know or have heard about. These profiles are as timely as we could make them, many happening just months before publication. And they are detailed enough to share some aspect of methodology or process. Unlike examples found in competitive texts that are written only from details gleaned from periodicals, ours are based on firsthand information. We went straight to the source for our facts, interviewing researchers and marketers who daily make the difficult decisions about research projects. By talking with dozens of practitioners, we learned their perspectives on where marketing research, as an industry, is headed and the subtle changes taking place within the practice of research. As a mini-case, each Snapshot is designed for class discussion and specifically relates to concepts within the text of the chapter where it is located.

- **PicProfiles** are research stories with a memory visual. These may be about a controversy or about research driving an advertising campaign (like the one about Karastan and Andie MacDowell). In each case, the visual helps tell—and helps the student retain—the research story.

- **Pull quotes** share the insights of researchers, educators, industry icons, entrepreneurs, and managers. These are quick ideas, from noteworthy individuals—both contemporary and historical—that influence how we do research and how, as marketers, we interpret and use the research done by others. By their nature, each is the opinion of a single person, so many can be the foundation for argument or lively discussion.

- **Close-Ups** are in-depth profiles of a current research practice or an expansion of a marketing research concept. You'll find several within the text. One offers more advanced analytical techniques. Some offer a detailed execution of an example we start in a Behind the Scenes vignette or a Snapshot. We've separated them from the text to highlight the material in a special and extremely timely way. This separation gives the instructor the choice to include or exclude the material when assigning the chapter. But we hope you'll assign the material, as this feature permits us to tell a longer story or offer a deeper perspective, and each offers fertile ground for extensive class discussion.

- **Cases** offer an opportunity to tell research stories in more depth and detail. Of course it helps that we have research contacts with really interesting stories to tell. You'll find stories from Ogilvy Research Award winners on children's health care initiatives, and you'll learn about the American Heart Association's first paid advertising campaign and the research behind it, as well as how the U.S. Tennis Association is revitalizing its sport and, in the process, conducting the largest research project ever related to sports. You'll learn how State Farm conducts the study that identifies the most dangerous intersections in the United States and uses the data to improve our safety, and you'll see how Campbell-Ewald uses research to measure the construct of *respect*. You'll learn how one man with a vision can move airlines as you follow the research being done by the Open Doors Organization in its attempt to substantiate the growing economic power of travel-

ers with disabilities and how NetConversions helps Kelley Blue Book design the most powerful automotive site on the Web. You'll learn how Wirthlin Worldwide helped the American Red Cross use research to revitalize donations and how Starbucks, Bank One (now J.P Morgan Stanley), and Visa dreamed up a new financial product that won *BusinessWeek*'s outstanding product honor. And you'll learn how the low-carbohydrate diet craze inspired Donatos Pizza and how Yahoo! and ACNielsen moved Web metrics a giant leap forward. These are research projects just completed, or in several instances, ongoing.

- **End-of-chapter appendices** offer rich detail on a special topic. Depending on how you structure your course, or the level of preparation of your students, you may not need this developmental or advanced information. You'll find two appendices (Chapter 5) that offer hints on searching of bibliographic databases. Another (Chapter 6) offers a *request for proposal* (RFP). Two more (Chapter 15) delve more deeply into crafting effective measurement questions and various types of pretesting, while one (Chapter 12) explores more complex experimental designs. We've separated them from the text of the chapter so that you can choose whether your students would benefit from this material.

- **DVD supplemental texts** explore topics of interest but only if your students' projects and assignments move in a specific direction. You'll find these on the text DVD:
  - A Summary of Marketing Research to 1960 (Chapter 2)
  - Decision Theory Problem (3)
  - Marketing Information Sources (5)
  - Seagate Proposal (6)
  - Qualitative Research with Children (9)
  - Creative Legacy of Qualitative Research (9)
  - Measuring Attitudes on Sensitive Subjects (14)
  - Tips on Intercept Survey Design (15)
  - MindWriter and Simalto+Plus (22)
  - Palm Grove data set (22)
  - Citing Electronic Sources (23)

- **Icons** are used to depict a relationship. Usually these are small graphic symbols that appear in the headers of an exhibit, a Snapshot, or a Close-Up; sometimes, they will appear in the margins. We've used one to highlight award-winning research (it looks like a trophy), another for foundation marketing theory needed to understand a research methodology (the 4-Ps), another connects various Snapshots and appendices related to the *Covering Kids* research story that crosses several chapters and culminates in a video case (a doctor's medical symbol), another reveals the Lexus SC 430 research story (car keys), another spotlights possible ethical dilemmas (scales), and, finally, another (film reel) indicates a video case.

Visual Learners Get the Tools They Need

As teachers of long standing, we struggle with the shifting nature of the way students absorb material and learn. When we started teaching, our students were primarily verbal learners: They learned from listening, reading, and presenting. What we discover daily in our own classrooms—that now we have more visual learners than verbal ones—shapes a very important feature of this textbook. Visual learners need diagrams and memory visuals connected to written labels in order to grasp material. *Marketing Research* contains a *fully integrated* series of process diagrams (30 in all) that encourages the visual learner to follow the steps in the research process. The primary research process diagram, presented in Chapter 4, looks like a flowchart but with special use of color and shape to denote specific research stages and steps. Students who learn visually will appreciate the reinforcement of the colors and symbols as they progress through the course. And they get that reinforcement with "breakout" process elements. These are more detailed representations of the specific steps in a portion of the process that the student is studying in that chapter. You won't find a more integrated visual tool for learning in any other marketing research textbook on the market.

Visual learners appreciate video, so we scoured the McGraw-Hill video library to find films that would offer opportunities for discussion of research principles. In addition, we developed detailed video discussion guides to help make that discussion a fruitful teaching and learning exercise. Adapting a marketing story to tell a research story isn't as easy as we might sometimes like, so McGraw-Hill made us an important commitment. In preparing this textbook, if we discovered a rich research story, ripe for video translation, McGraw-Hill would make those videos. You'll find four custom-crafted video stories for use in your marketing research class. Both case videos and written cases are on the text DVD. This is another commitment fulfilled—students now have the opportunity to watch the videos in preparation for class. If you don't want to use the video during class time, or even if you do—visual learners tell us it helps to see a video story more than once to extract all its material—students can prepare cases more thoroughly for in-class discussion or in-class writing exercises. You won't need to lend your video to a student who missed class on the day a crucial video discussion takes place.

Verbal Learners Get the Detail They Crave

We still have verbal learners in our classes—thank goodness, since many of their instructors are themselves verbal learners—and we have text features for them too:

- **Key terms in the margins** help reinforce the definitions of key concepts. We need our students to learn the jargon of research so that they can follow us and their classmates during class discussions. Our reviewers tell us that this is the most important design element to facilitate that jargon transfer.

- **Marginal reference notes** refer students to something they read in a previous chapter that will help them grasp current material, call attention to something they are learning now that will help them understand subsequent material in a later chapter, or elaborate on a current concept to help make it *stick* in their minds. Verbal learners tell us that when they see something more than once, especially in different contexts, they are more likely to remember it.

- **Four types of discussion questions** offer the student the challenge to understand key terms and try marketing research decision making on their own. That's pretty standard fare for marketing research texts, but we decided to take review questions further. Every text author takes substantial time developing exhibits that expound on critical concepts. Yet how often do discussion questions encourage a student to spend time with an exhibit? Our students told us that they often skip the exhibits, considering them "extras." But we know they aren't extra; they are central to understanding course material. So we have discussion questions (From Concept to Practice) that ask the student to spend time with the exhibits. If you want them to do that too, just assign those particular questions. And remember how the Behind the Scenes vignettes are developed around teaching points? Now you have discussion questions that deal with these vignettes. If you want to use the vignette for class discussion, assign the Behind the Scenes discussion questions.

- **Web exercises** help students learn more about research. Most students think they know all there is to know about the Internet. But what many of them can't do well is find specific information when they need to or evaluate the quality of the information they find. They miss the distinction between *browsing* and *searching*. Our Chapter 5 appendices on search basics and advanced searching offer the tools necessary to convert browsers to searchers. Then subsequent chapters ask students to find something related to the topic—like a product tour on new qualitative content analysis software or a research firm that does a special type of research, such as a product taste test or mystery shopping. This is the type of searching they might do if they work as marketing managers or researchers.

Expect the Expected, but Anticipate— and Receive—More

- Do you want students to experience analyzing large-scale research projects? You'll find that some case studies on your text DVD come with extensive data sets. Your students can crank the numbers at whatever level you desire.

- Do your students need self-quizzing to help them grasp concepts? You'll find Web-based quizzes so that students can reinforce and test their knowledge.

- Do you use computer-supported lectures? You'll find PowerPoint slide sets for each chapter, with an important extra: Adobe PDF files of every text art exhibit. Now you have the text visuals you need to produce the visually rich classroom presentations and discussions that your visual learners need. Students will have these PowerPoint slide sets, too, so you won't need to distribute yours unless you customize your set.

- Do you use tests to evaluate student performance? You'll find a test bank with questions offering different levels of difficulty, so you can pick the ones appropriate for your teaching model.

- Do you want more information on a particular issue or topic than the text provides? Both you and your students will love the Marketing Information Sources supplement on your text DVD. Both electronic and print sources are covered because only a small portion of information that is valuable to a marketer is available on or through the Web.

- Do you cover decision theory as a model for valuing research? You'll find a complete decision theory problem on the DVD.

- Do you involve your students in an actual research project? Then they will love the complete student project that is on the DVD, as well as the complete professional proposal they will find there.

Collaboration Created a Better Product

To bring a text concept to life, you have to have help from many people. So we extend our sincere appreciation:

- To Judith Violette, Director, Helmke Library at Indiana University–Purdue University at Fort Wayne (In-

diana), who worked to develop the comprehensive marketing information sources files on the text DVD and whose knowledge of information search is the foundation for Appendices 5a and 5b, as well as the evaluation of Internet information within Chapter 5. She never fails to find more efficient and effective ways to help us search.

- To Dr. John "Rusty" Brooks Jr., Houston Baptist University, who so skillfully collaborated on the *Instructor's Resource Guide.*

- To Dr. Tracey Tuten Ryan, Virginia Commonwealth University, who developed our PowerPoint slide set, test bank, and web quizzes.

- To Jeff Stevens, in Florida Atlantic University's public administration doctoral program, for contributions on missing data, portions of the multivariate statistics chapter, and the Simalto+Plus learning resource.

- To Nicole Samuels, in Florida Atlantic University's MPA program, whose perspective and creative ideas vastly helped to improve the effectiveness of our case discussion guides.

- To several special Wittenberg University students:
  - Rebecca Torsell ('04), a wonderful faculty aide who developed comparative spreadsheets galore, tracked down research company ads, and researched companies and examples of research in action but, mostly, who freed us to write uninterrupted.
  - Erin Mowrey ('04) and Jim Kuklewski (Wittenberg, '05), student directors in Wittenberg's Center for Applied Management, who tackled the portfolio research and dealt with the day-to-day minutia so that we didn't have to.
  - Monica McDonald ('05), who worked diligently to make sure that the sources on the DVD and company URLs were as current as possible when we went to press.

- To all those marketing researchers, advertisers, product managers, and organization leaders who have shared their projects, ideas, perspectives, and the love of what they do during hours and hours of interviews.

- To those marketing and research professionals who helped us develop written and video cases:
  - Julie Grabarkewitz and Paul Herrera, American Heart Association; Holly Ripans, American Red Cross; Mike Bordner and Ajay Gupta, Bank One; Laurie Laurant Smith, Arielle Burgess, Jill Grech, David Lockwood, and Arthur Miller, Campbell Ewald; Francie Turk, Consumer Connections; Tom Krouse, Donatos Pizza; Annie Burns and

Aimee Seagal, GMMB; Laura Light and Steve Struhl, Harris Interactive; Emil Vicale, Herobuilders.com; Adrian Chiu, NetConversions; Eric Lipp, Open Doors Organization; Stuart Schear, Robert Wood Johnson Foundation; and Elaine Arkin, consultant to RWJF; Colette Courtion, Starbucks; Mark Miller, Team One Advertising; Rebecca Conway, The Taylor Research Group; Scott Staniar, United States Tennis Association; Danny Robinson, Vigilante; Maury Giles, Wirthlin Worldwide; and Ken Mallon, Yahoo!.

- To Nancy Barbour, a valued sounding board who has become so much more than a Managing Development Editor; and to our Sponsoring Editor, Barrett Koger, who has negotiated for this text far more than most first editions have a prayer of achieving; and to Linda Schreiber, our Publisher, who felt strongly enough about us as successful authors to enthusiastically support our proposal.

- To the remainder of our very special McGraw-Hill team, for making the book a priority:
  - Editorial Director: John Biernat
  - Marketing Manager: Dan Silverburg
  - Media Producer: Damian Moshak
  - Project Manager: Laura Griffin
  - Production Supervisor: Heather Burbridge
  - Designer: Mary Kazak
  - Photo Researcher: Keri Johnson
  - Photo Coordinator: Jeremy Cheshareck
  - Supplement Producer: Cathy Tepper

- To our faculty reviewers for their insights, suggestions, disagreements, and challenges:

Phipps Arabie
Rutgers University–Newark

Joe K. Ballenger
Austin State University

Gary Benson
Chadron State University

Greg Bonner
Villanova University

James Curran
Bryant College

Harold Daniel
University of Maine

Carol W. DeMoranville
Northern Illinois University

Rene Desborde
Kentucky State University

Pola B. Gupta
Wright State University

Philip Hurdle
Elmira College

Michael Hyman
New Mexico State University

Richard Kolbe
Kent State University

Frederick Langrehr
Valparaiso University

Aron M. Levin
Northern Kentucky University

Hector R. Lozada
Seton Hall University

Yuko Minowa
Long Island University

Rajan Nataraajan
Auburn University

Joseph Orsini
CSU–Sacramento

Deborah L. Owens
University of Akron

Wayne Roberts
Southern Utah University

Donald E. Stem Jr.
Washington State University

We are also indebted to dozens of students who read parts of the manuscript and pointed out areas of confusion so that we could make concepts more understandable and who revealed that much of marketing research is either misunderstood or operates below their radar. We accept the challenge of debunking their myths and making the truth more visible.

This book was 2½ years in the writing, but more than 25 years in the making. We hope you find it as teacher-friendly and as student-enriching as we designed it to be. We want our students—and yours—to be able to visualize what research is really like in the trenches and behind the scenes. Every text element, every exhibit, every photograph, every screenshot, every Excel chart or SPSS printout, and every supplement has been chosen with this idea in mind.

We also hope you and your students discover, or rediscover, how interesting marketing research can be.

Donald Cooper
Pamela Schindler

Walkthrough

Behind the Scenes reveals research in the trenches.

Much of research activity isn't obvious or visible. These opening vignettes are designed to take the student behind the door marked RESEARCH. Through the activities of the principals at Visionary Insights, students learn about research projects, many that were revealed to the authors *off the record*. The characters and names of companies are fictional, but the research activities they describe are real—and happening behind the scenes in hundreds of firms every day.

>**behind**the**scenes**

The questionnaire is the most common data collection instrument in marketing research. Crafting one is part science and part art. To start, a researcher needs to have a solid idea of what type of analysis will be done for the project. Based on this desired analysis plan, the researcher will need to know what type of scale is needed before a single question can be drafted. In Chapter 11, Visionary Insights had captured a new project for Albany Outpatient Laser Clinic. We join Jason Henry and Sara Armstrong as they proceed through the survey creation process for this new project.

"How is the Albany survey coming?" asks Jason as he enters Sara's office.

"The client approved the investigative questions this morning. So we are ready to choose the measurement questions and then write the questionnaire," shares Sara, glancing up from her computer screen. "I was just checking our bank of pretested questions. I'm looking for questions related to customer satisfaction in the

...ady searching for appropriate ques-
...e the analysis plan drafted. Let me
...les you developed," requests Jason,
...r while you're scanning."

...r a sheaf of pages. Each has one or
...ncing the desired information vari-
...indicates the statistical diagnostics
...ed to generate the table.

...r finishes processing, Sara scans the
...for appropriate matches to Albany's
... "At first glance, it looks like there
...le-choice scales and ranking ques-
...e. But I'm not seeing a rating scale
...tion. We may need to customize a
...bany."

"Custom designing a question is expensive. Before you make that choice," offers Jason, "run another query using *CardioQuest* as a keyword. Right after I joined Visionary, we did a study for that large cardiology specialty in Orlando. I'm sure it included an overall satisfaction scale. It might be worth considering."

Sara types *CardioQuest* and *satisfaction*, and then waits for the computer to process her request. "Sure enough, he's right again," murmurs Sara. "How do you remember all the details of prior studies done eons ago?" she asks, throwing the purely hypothetical question at Jason. But Sara swivels to face Jason, all senses alert when she hears his muffled groan.

Jason frowns as he comments, "You have far more analytical diagnostics planned than would be standard for a project of this type and size, Sara. For example, are Tables 2, 7, and 10 really necessary?" Jason pauses but doesn't allow time for Sara to answer. "To stay within budget, we are going to have to whittle down the analysis phase of the project to what is essential. Let's see if we can reduce the analysis plan to something that Chance will accept. Now, walk me through what you think you'll reveal by three-way cross-tabulating these two attitudinal variables with the education variable."

>**chapter 15**

Questionnaires and Instruments

>**learning**objectives

After reading this chapter, you should understand . . .

1. The link forged between the management dilemma and the communication instrument by the management–research question hierarchy.

2. The influence of the communication method on instrument design.

3. The three general classes of information and what each contributes to the instrument.

4. The influence of question content, question wording, response strategy, and preliminary analysis planning on question construction.

5. Each of the numerous question design issues influencing instrument quality, reliability, and validity.

6. Sources for measurement questions.

7. The importance of pretesting questions and instruments.

Learning Objectives serve as memory flags.

Learning objectives serve as a road map as students start their journey into the chapter. Read first, these objectives subconsciously encourage students to seek relevant material, definitions, and exhibits.

Special tools for today's visual learner.

A transformation is taking place in many of our classrooms. During the last decade, more and more of our students have become visual—not verbal—learners. Verbal learners learn primarily from reading text. Visual learners need pictures, diagrams, and graphs to clarify and reinforce what the text relates.

Integrated research process exhibits reveal a rich and complex process in an understandable way.

Every textbook has exhibits. We use these tables and line drawings to bring key concepts to life and make complex concepts more understandable.

Within our array of exhibits is a very special series of **30 fully integrated research process exhibits.** Each exhibit in this series shares symbols, shapes, and colors with others in the series.

Exhibit 4-1 is the overview exhibit of the research process, to which all other exhibits related to the process will link.

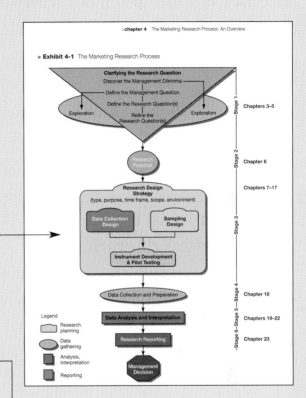

Subsequent exhibits (like this one for survey design) show more detail in a part of this process.

Another exhibit in the series might layer the main process exhibit with additional information (like this exhibit from the ethics chapter).

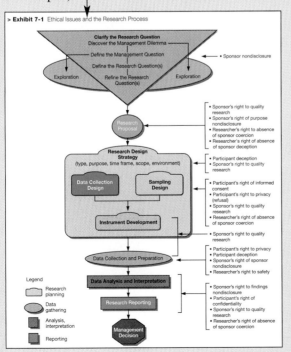

your preliminary analysis plan). In Phase 3 you must address topic and question sequencing. We discuss these topics sequentially, although in practice the process is not linear. For this discussion, we assume the questions are structured.

The order, type, and wording of the measurement questions, the introduction, the instructions, the transitions, and the closure in a quality communication instrument should accomplish the following:

- Encourage each participant to provide accurate responses.
- Encourage each participant to provide an adequate amount of information.
- Discourage each participant from refusing to answer specific questions.
- Discourage each participant from early discontinuation of participation.
- Leave the participant with a positive attitude about survey participation.

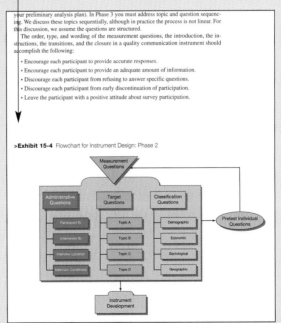

You'll find more than 260 exhibits to aid student understanding within this text.

Some topics deserve more attention—
with their own chapter!

Ethical issues get the attention they deserve.

Ethical issues abound in marketing research but may go un-
noticed by students who need a framework to discuss and
understand these issues. We devote a chapter to building that
framework. Then in subsequent chapters we highlight when
an ethical issue might be present with a special icon.

Help in moving from management dilemma to research design.

This is where talented people can steer research in the
wrong direction. We devote a chapter to this difficult
phase of research planning. And we introduce the student to a methodology for making the right decisions
more often.

Qualitative research steps out from the background.

Researchers are increasingly admitting that
quantitative research can't reveal all they need
to know to make smart marketing decisions. In
a special chapter, we capture the best of the
current qualitative methods and reveal where
and how they are used. Your students should
know the qualitative methods beyond the
perennial favorite—the focus group.

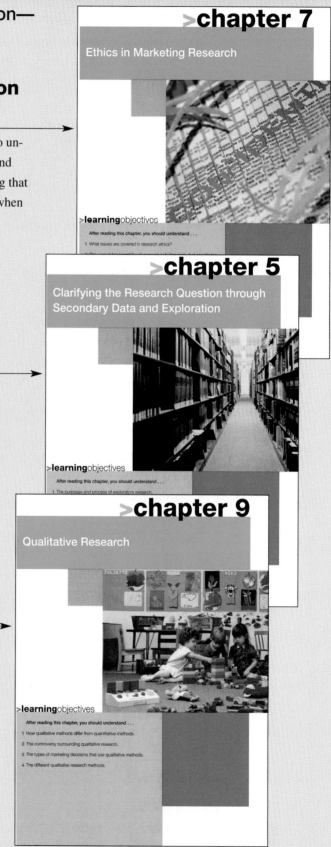

> **chapter 7**

Ethics in Marketing Research

> **learning**objectives

After reading this chapter, you should understand . . .

1 What issues are covered in research ethics?

> **chapter 5**

Clarifying the Research Question through
Secondary Data and Exploration

> **learning**objectives

After reading this chapter, you should understand . . .

1 The purposes and process of exploratory research.

> **chapter 9**

Qualitative Research

> **learning**objectives

After reading this chapter, you should understand . . .

1 How qualitative methods differ from quantitative methods.

2 The controversy surrounding qualitative research.

3 The types of marketing decisions that use qualitative methods.

4 The different qualitative research methods.

▸**snap**shot

Covering Kids: The Management-Research Question Hierarchy

Robert Wood Johnson Foundation (RWJF), a health care philanthropy, sponsors the Covering Kids initiative for one reason: millions of children in low- to moderate-income families who are eligible for the State Children's Health Insurance Program (SCHIP) are not enrolled. RWJF initially became involved because it was concerned that the federal government and the states were not actively or effectively publicizing Medicaid and SCHIP. The initial goal of RWJF's involvement was to make eligible families aware of SCHIP and Medicare and encourage enrollment. To this end, RWJF obtained the services of advertising agency GMMB, research firm Wirthlin Worldwide, and veteran social marketer Elaine Bratic Arkin.

The Foundation initially asked, "What must be done to enroll the largest percentage of eligible children in Medicaid and SCHIP?" Before GMMB could move forward, the team needed to determine whether the communication program needed to correct misconceptions, communicate benefits, overcome perceived process complexities, or some combination of these. Early exploratory research sought answers to, "What keeps eligible families from taking advantage of the prescription and doctor-visit programs of SCHIP and Medicaid?" The team also asked, "Is a negative stigma attached to participation in government health care programs?" When research indicated the answer to this question was "No," subsequent efforts focused on identifying other critical factors that discouraged families from enrolling. After research revealed that most working parents did not realize their children were eligible for a government program, the management question was refined to, "What must be communicated to parents of eligible children to get them to enroll their children in these programs?"

Ultimately a creative combination of research design and data analysis revealed: (1) the winning communications frame-

work: Being a good parent means raising happy, healthy children, and enrolling in a program offering low-cost or free health care is a smart choice for families, and (2) every communication must give working parents an easy, foolproof way to determine if their children were eligible while reinforcing the logic that making the call to enroll their children would address parents' innate desire to be good parents.

www.wirthlin.com; www.gmmb.com; www.rwjf.org.

> ▸ **We discuss the usefulness of various qualitative techniques, many of which are used during exploration, in Chapter 9.**

research question(s) the objective of the research study.

An unstructured exploration allows the researcher to develop and revise the management question and determine what is needed to secure answers to the proposed question.

The Research Question

Using his or her understanding of the basic theoretical concepts, the researcher's task is to assist the manager in formulating a research question that fits the need to resolve the management dilemma. A **research question** best states the objective of the marketing research study. It is a more specific management question that must be answered. It may be more than one question or just one. A marketing research process that answers this more specific question provides the manager with the information necessary to make the decision he or she is facing. Incorrectly defining the research question is the fundamental weakness in the marketing research process. Time and money can be wasted studying an alternative that won't help the manager rectify the original dilemma.

Students learn by and deserve the best examples.

Snapshots are research examples from the researcher's perspective.

Snapshots are like mini-cases: They help a student understand a concept in the text by giving a current example. As mini-cases they are perfect for lively class discussion. Each one focuses on a particular part of the research process as it applies to a particular firm and project. You'll find more than 80 of these timely research examples throughout the text, several in each chapter, some from well-known companies but many from research firms that until now you've had no reason to get to know.

Web addresses speed secondary data searches for additional information on an example.

Margin notes reinforce and link the text discussion to prior or subsequent material.

Icons help students link parts of a richer, more complex example, told over a series of chapters.

MindWriter

Some examples are so rich in detail that one Snapshot or exhibit just isn't sufficient. One of Visionary Insights' clients is MindWriter, a computer laptop manufacturer that prides itself on customer service, especially when it comes to laptop repair at its CompleteCare center. Each time you see this icon in the text, you'll be learning more about the customer satisfaction research that VI is doing for MindWriter.

Two award-winning research programs appear in several chapters and on the student DVD:

Covering Kids Research Program   *Lexus SC 430* Research Program

Other award-winning examples appear throughout the text.
Watch for this icon to recognize these examples.

The Close-Up offers a more in-depth examination of a key example.

Sometimes you just need more time and space to showcase all the detail of an example. This glimpse of the Close-Up from Chapter 23 reveals two pages from a complete annotated client research report.

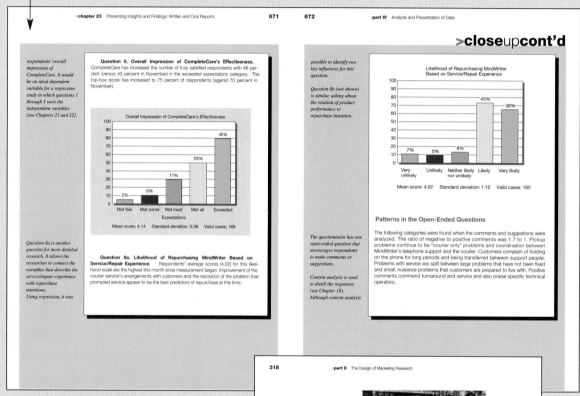

>**close**up**cont'd**

respondents' overall impression of CompleteCare. It would be an ideal dependent variable for a regression study in which questions 1 through 5 were the independent variables (see Chapters 21 and 22).

Question 6. Overall Impression of CompleteCare's Effectiveness. CompleteCare has increased the number of truly satisfied respondents with 46 percent (versus 43 percent in November) in the exceeded expectations category. The top-box score has increased to 75 percent of respondents (against 70 percent in November).

Overall Impression of CompleteCare's Effectiveness

Met few 2% Met some 6% Met most 17% Met all 29% Exceeded 46%
Expectations
Mean score: 4.14   Standard deviation: 0.98   Valid cases: 169

Question 8a is another question for more detailed research. It allows the researcher to connect the variables that describe the service/repair experience with repurchase intentions. Using regression, it was

Question 8a. Likelihood of Repurchasing MindWriter Based on Service/Repair Experience. Respondents' average scores (4.02) for this likelihood scale are the highest this month since measurement began. Improvement of the courier service's arrangements with customers and the resolution of the problem that prompted service appear to be the best predictors of repurchase at this time.

possible to identify two key influences for this question.

Question 8b (not shown) is similar, asking about the relation of product performance to repurchase intention.

Likelihood of Repurchasing MindWriter Based on Service/Repair Experience

Very unlikely 7% Unlikely 5% Neither likely nor unlikely 8% Likely 43% Very likely 38%

Mean score: 4.02   Standard deviation: 1.10   Valid cases: 165

Patterns in the Open-Ended Questions

The following categories were found when the comments and suggestions were analyzed. The ratio of negative to positive comments was 1.7 to 1. Pickup problems continue to be "courier only" problems and coordination between MindWriter's telephone support and the courier. Customers complain of holding on the phone for long periods and being transferred between support people. Problems with service are split between large problems that have not been fixed and small, nuisance problems that customers are prepared to live with. Positive comments commend turnaround and service and also praise specific technical operators.

The questionnaire has one open-ended question that encourages respondents to make comments or suggestions.

Content analysis is used to distill the responses (see Chapter 18). Although content analysis

---

PicProfile offers a memory visual to enhance an example.

In research, as in life, sometimes a picture is worth more than words. Sometimes you need to see what is being described to fully understand the foundation research principle. That's the case with the research for FloorGraphics. You need to see the ad to understand how the research guided its development. These visuals are offered as memory teasers, to help students remember the research example.

picprofile
Researchers know that as many as 60 percent of purchase decisions are made in the store. Thus marketers aggressively seek in-store space to place temporary displays, shelf-talkers, and instant coupons, as well as ceiling signs and banners. Even the floor is contested real estate. So the ability to demonstrate the effectiveness of promotional materials is critical. FLOORGraphics, Inc., uses a longitudinal design, tracking sales of products in matched groups of stores (test and control groups). After test stores receive the FLOORad, relative sales in both groups are again compared to pre-ad performance and to each other. Research shows the FLOORad effect (the percentage sales increase directly due to the FLOORad) can lift sales 20 to 40 percent depending on the product category. www.floorgraphics.com

In this design, we can deal with the seven major internal validity problems fairly well, although there are still some difficulties. Local history may occur in one group and not the other. Also, if communication exists between people in test and control groups, there can be rivalry and other internal validity problems.

Maturation, testing, and regression are handled well because one would expect them to be felt equally in experimental and control groups. Mortality, however, can be a problem if there are different dropout rates in the study groups. Selection is not a problem if random assignment is used.

The record of this design is not as good on external validity, however. There is a chance for a reactive effect from testing. This might be a substantial influence in attitude change where pretests introduce unusual topics and content. Nor does this design ensure against reaction between selection and the experimental variable. Even random selection may be defeated by a high decline rate among participants. This would result in using a disproportionate share of people who are essentially volunteers and who may not be typical of the population. If this occurs, we will need to replicate the experiment several times with other groups under other conditions before we can be confident of external validity.

Learning aids cement the concepts.

Discussion questions and Web exercises that go one step farther.

Four types of discussion questions reveal differing levels of understanding—from knowing a definition to applying a concept.

The Web exercise asks the student to search on the Web for something that they might need to do if they were acting the role of researcher.

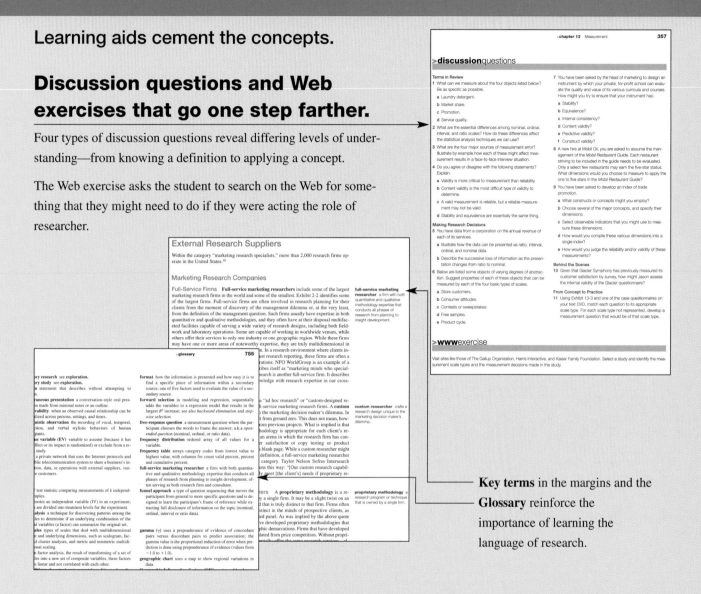

Key terms in the margins and the **Glossary** reinforce the importance of learning the language of research.

Supplements offer the tools students and faculty ask for . . . and more.

The student DVD with this text should be gold, as it contains that much value. Students will find everything from cases, video clips, and data sets to a directory of marketing information sources (with Web links), a research proposal, a sample student project, and supplemental material for many chapters.

Thirty-four cases are on the DVD, from one-page focused cases to full-coverage, comprehensive cases. Four very special video cases, filmed especially for this text, feature award-winning research programs and award-winning products and companies. You'll find 15 full-sized written cases providing an intensive look at some noteworthy research written especially to reveal the concepts in this text—10 of these are so new they reflect ongoing research programs or those conducted within the year before publication.

>part I

Research in Marketing

chapter 1

The Role of Research in Marketing

>**learning**objectives

After reading this chapter, you should understand . . .

1 What marketing research is and how it differs from marketing decision support systems and marketing intelligence systems.

2 The trends affecting marketing research and the emerging hierarchy of marketing decision makers.

3 The distinction between good marketing research and research that falls short of professional quality.

4 The value of learning marketing research process skills.

>**behind**the**scenes**

MindWriter

In each chapter of this book we will take you behind the scene at Visionary Insights (VI), Inc., a full-service marketing research firm. You'll meet several principals within Visionary Insights, including the VP of business development, Chance Bedford; the senior project manager, Jason Henry; and project specialist, Sara Armstrong. You'll also meet several of their clients, those whom VI is trying to capture as well as those whose research is in progress, as they interact with Visionary Insights. In this first vignette, a potential client, MindWriter, Inc., is in the final stages of screening potential marketing research firms to conduct its desired marketing research.

Myra Wines, director of consumer affairs for Mind-Writer, Inc., has been charged with the task of assessing MindWriter's CompleteCare program for servicing laptops. As a result, she sent several well-respected research firms a *request for proposal (RFP)*, and she and her team are interviewing the last of those firms, Visionary Insights.

Newly promoted to her position, Wines has a TV journalism and government public relations background. She has been a MindWriter laptop owner since it came on the market decades earlier and has never personally experienced a problem. She wants a research supplier from whom she can learn, as well as one whom she can trust to do appropriate, high-quality research.

The last interviewee is Jason Henry, senior project manager, Visionary Insights, Inc. VI comes highly recommended by a professional colleague in a different industry. VI has gained a reputation for merging traditional methodologies with some creative new approaches. Myra is interested in exploring the firm's methodology for customer satisfaction studies. As Wines approaches Henry in the waiting area, she extends her hand. "Welcome, to MindWriter, Jason, I'm Myra Wines."

Henry rises, clasping Wines's hand in a firm handshake. "Pleased to meet you, Myra."

Myra directs Jason's attention to a long corridor. "My team members are gathered in our conference room just down this hall. Let's join them, shall we?"

The interview process starts with Henry's short presentation on VI and its capabilities. As the interview progresses, Henry shares some impressive results accomplished for former clients in noncompetitive industries. The last slide in his presentation features a top industry award VI recently won for its customer satisfaction methodology.

During the Q&A that follows, Henry demonstrates current knowledge of the computer industry (he's obviously read numerous articles), confidence, and expertise, at a level that Wines initially had not expected given his relatively youthful appearance. At the conclusion of the interview, Wines is leaning toward hiring Visionary Insights but wants to confer with her team.

The next day, Myra calls Jason at his office. "We've chosen Visionary Insights for the MindWriter CompleteCare assessment contract. Congratulations."

"Thank you," accepts Jason. "You've made the right choice."

"I've got two seats on a flight to Austin next Wednesday," shares Myra. "Can you join me? This will be my first look at the CompleteCare facility and my first face-to-face contact with its manager. I'd like someone along who can lay the groundwork for the project and understand the number crunching that's already been done."

The phone goes silent as Jason pauses to consult his PDA. Two internal meetings will need to be shifted, but MindWriter is an important new client. "Yes, I can work that in as long as we're back by 7 p.m. I've got an evening commitment."

"Shouldn't be a problem," shares Myra. "Those seats I mentioned are on the corporate jet. We'll be back by 5:30. I'll meet you in the lobby at the county airstrip at 8 a.m. Wednesday then."

"A quick question," interrupts Jason before Myra can disconnect. "I need some idea of what's happening at this meeting."

"The meeting is to get you started. I'll introduce you to other people you will be working with and share more details about the concerns we have with the CompleteCare program," shares Myra.

"Fine. Can you arrange a third seat? It would be best to include Sara Armstrong from the very beginning. Her expertise will be crucial to the success of the assessment program."

"Yes, you mentioned her before. That shouldn't be a problem, but I'll check and get back to you."

"Then Wednesday Sara and I will plan on asking probing questions and listening to discover exactly what facts management has gathered, what the managers are concerned about, what the problem is from their point of view, what the problem really is at various levels of abstraction . . ."

"Listening to people. Discussing. Looking at things from different viewpoints. Those are things I am also very good at," shares Myra.

"Good. After we hear them out, we come to what VI is good at: Measurement. Scaling. Project design. Sampling. Finding elusive insights. May I assume we'll be collaborating on the report of results? . . ."

"Absolutely. I'll call you back within 10 minutes about that third seat."

> Why Study Marketing Research?

marketing research a systematic inquiry that provides information to guide marketing decisions.

You are about to begin your study of marketing research, both the process and the tools needed to reduce risk in marketing decision making. **Marketing research,** as we use it in this text, is a systematic inquiry that provides information to guide marketing decisions. More specifically, as expanded by the American Marketing Association (AMA), it is a process of determining, acquiring, analyzing and synthesizing, and disseminating relevant marketing data, information, and insights to decision makers in ways that mobilize the organization to take appropriate marketing actions that, in turn, maximize business performance.[1] A variety of different types of research projects are grouped under the label "marketing research," and we will explore them all later in this chapter.

Assume for the moment that you are the manager of your favorite full-service restaurant. You are experiencing significant turnover in your waiter/waitress pool, and some long-time customers have commented that the friendly atmosphere, which has historically drawn them to your door, is changing. Where will you begin in trying to solve this problem? Is this a problem for which marketing research should be used?

Try another decision-making scenario: You are talking with the head of the academic department in which you are majoring. This person chairs the committee that selects the textbook for the sales management course. Students have commented, on course evaluations, that the book currently being used is too difficult. Should the committee use additional marketing research to help evaluate its options?

Or maybe you are the head of your state's department of transportation, charged with determining which roads and bridges will be resurfaced or replaced in the next fiscal year. Usually you would look at the roads and bridges with the most traffic in combination with

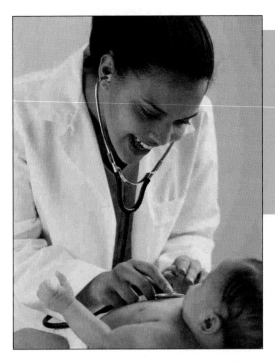

those representing the most economic disaster, if closed. However, the state's manager of public information has expressed concern about the potential for public outcry if work is once again directed to more affluent regions of the state. The manager suggests using marketing research to assist in making your decision, as the decision is one with numerous public relations ramifications. Should you authorize the recommended marketing research?

The American Marketing Association, the premier professional association in the marketing discipline, defines **marketing** as "an organizational function and a set of processes for creating, communicating, and delivering value to customers and for managing customer relationships in ways that benefit the organization and its stakeholders.[2] Obviously, many marketing decision makers can be found in consumer goods firms (like MindWriter, Inc.). However, a marketing decision maker also might be the pastor of a suburban church, a politician's election consultant, the director of a symphony, or the manager of a government assistance program. As the opening vignette and the early decision scenarios reveal, marketing decision makers can be found in every type of organization: businesses, not-for-profit organizations, and public agencies. Regardless of where these decision makers are found or whether their resources are abundant or limited, they all rely on information to make more efficient and effective use of their marketing budgets. Also, even those without typical marketing titles face decisions with marketing ramifications. Thus, in this book, we will take the broadest perspective of marketing and its resulting application to marketing research.

At no other time in our history has so much attention been placed on measuring and enhancing **return on marketing investment (ROMI).** At its most simplistic, when we measure ROMI we calculate the financial return for all marketing expenditures. Factoring into this calculation are several different types of returns including the number of qualified prospects, the rate of conversion of prospects to customers, the increase in buying frequency or amount by

marketing an organizational function and a set of processes for creating, communicating, and delivering value to customers and for managing customer relationships in ways that benefit the organization and its stakeholders.

return on marketing investment (ROMI) the calculation of the financial return for all marketing expenditures.

Covering Kids with Health Care

The Robert Wood Johnson Foundation (RWJF), established as a national philanthropy in 1972 and today the world's largest health foundation, is on a mission to improve the state of health care among American families. Many families cannot afford the co-payment of employer-sponsored health premiums or work for employers who cannot offer health benefits. RWJF makes grants to achieve three goals: (1) to ensure that all Americans have access to affordable health care, (2) to improve health care delivery services to people with chronic conditions, and (3) to promote health by reducing the harm caused by substance abuse from tobacco, alcohol, and illicit drugs. In 1997, RWJF developed its Covering Kids initiative. Its purpose was to generate state- and community-based programs that would design and simplify outreach programs to identify and enroll uninsured children from low-income families in the State Children's Health Insurance Program (SCHIP). SCHIP, a $24 billion program included in the federal Balanced Budget Act of 1997, provides payment for prescriptions and doctor visits. "We were going to expend significant resources, more than $47 million on an integrated communication campaign to reach a group of people that marketers spent very little time and effort serving. We wanted to be sure that what we were going to do was effective and would succeed

in enrolling the children of working families in SCHIP," shared communications officer Stuart Schear, the project's director. RWJF spent two years developing a coalition of government agencies and children's advocates to simplify enrollment forms and processes. People in the field feared that participation in government health care programs carried the negative stigma of welfare. Research was needed to determine why parents might or might not enroll their children. RWJF sought a collaborative partner that would use RWJF's extensive knowledge and understanding of working, low-income families at every stage of research design. The resulting research and its use to create advertising that enrolled kids in SCHIP earned RWJF, Wirthlin Worldwide (a strategic consulting and research provider with expertise in public issues), and GMMB (a strategic consulting firm specializing in public education and political campaigns) the 2002 David Ogilvy Research Award. This award is given for research contributing to highly successful advertising. In Snapshots throughout this text, we'll reveal the research and its results; watch for the Covering Kids icon.

www.rwjf.org, www.wirthlin.com, www.gmmb.com

---

customers, the retention of customers in the face of aggressive competition, the conversion of satisfied customers to advocates and their referral of other customers, and the increase in market share and market leadership. Increasingly organizational managers want to know what marketing strategies and tactics capture the most revenue. In the last dozen years, as technology has improved our measurement and tracking capabilities, marketers have realized they need a better understanding of customer behavior in order to influence the desired metrics. Marketing research plays an important role in this new measurement environment. Not only does it help marketers choose better strategies and tactics, but marketing research expenditures are increasingly scrutinized for their contribution to ROMI.

The marketing research course recognizes that students preparing to manage a marketing function—regardless of the setting—need training in a disciplined process for conducting an inquiry of a **management dilemma,** the problem or opportunity that requires a marketing decision. Several factors should stimulate your interest in studying marketing research:

management dilemma the problem or opportunity that requires a marketing decision.

1. *Explosive growth and influence of the Internet.* The explosive growth of company Web sites, e-commerce, and company publications brings extensive new amounts of information—but its quality and its credibility are increasingly suspect.

2. *Stakeholders demanding greater influence.* Customers, workers, shareholders, and the general public demand to be included in company decision making; armed with extensive information, they are more sensitive to their own self-interests than ever before and more resistant to marketing stimuli.

3. *More vigorous competition.* Competition, both global and domestic, is growing and often coming from unexpected sources; many organizations refocus on primary

Expected 2004 Marketing Research Budgets

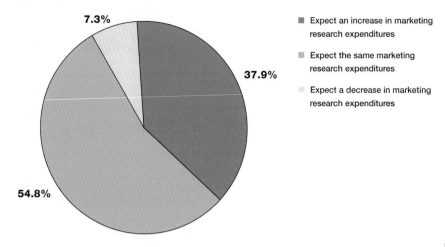

- ■ Expect an increase in marketing research expenditures
- ■ Expect the same marketing research expenditures
- ■ Expect a decrease in marketing research expenditures

7.3%

37.9%

54.8%

>**pic**profile

The American Marketing Association estimates that 2004 marketing plans will include more dollars spent on marketing research. It draws this conclusion from a survey of marketing professionals drawn from a panel of more than 800 members that was developed for the AMA by The Marketing Workshop Inc. Thirty-seven percent indicated their 2004 marketing budgets would reflect an increase for marketing research. The "Voice of the Marketer" is a continuing feature in *Marketing News,* a publication of the AMA. www.marketingpower.com; www.mwshop.com

competencies, while they seek to advance by reducing costs and converting customers to advocates.

4. *More government intervention.* Government continues to show concern with all aspects of society, becoming increasingly aggressive in protecting its various publics by posing restrictions on the use of marketing and marketing research tools.

5. *More complex marketing decisions.* Marketing managers have more variables to consider in every decision, increasing the manager's need for more and better information and for greater insights from that information.

6. *Maturing of marketing as a discipline.* The quality of theories and models to explain tactical and strategic results is improving, providing marketing managers with more knowledge.

7. *Greater computing power and speed.*
   - *More data, faster.* The power and ease of use of today's computers offers us the capability to analyze more data more quickly to deal with today's complex managerial problems.
   - *More integration of data.* Computer advances permit businesses to create and manage a **data warehouse,** an electronic storehouse where vast arrays of collected, integrated data are ready for mining.
   - *More meaningful knowledge from data.* Organizations increasingly practice **data mining,** applying mathematical models to extract meaningful knowledge from volumes of data contained within internal databases.
   - *Better visualization tools.* High-speed downloads of images allow us to help people visualize complex concepts; this enriches measurement capabilities.
   - *Powerful computations.* Sophisticated techniques of quantitative analysis are emerging to take advantage of increasingly powerful computing capabilities.

8. *New perspectives on established research methodologies.* Older tools and methodologies once limited to exploratory research are gaining wider acceptance in dealing with a broader range of marketing problems.

data warehouse electronic storehouse where vast arrays of collected, integrated data are ready for mining.

data mining applying mathematical models to extract meaningful knowledge from volumes of data contained within internal databases.

Yankelovich Delivers Sobering News to Marketers

In its 2004 Marketing Resistance Survey,* presented at the American Association of Advertising Agencies (AAAA) conference on April 15, 2004, Yankelovich Partners, Inc., revealed some sobering news to the nation's marketers: "Response to all forms of marketing is declining at precipitous rates." And negative attitudes once reserved for telemarketers have "gone mainstream."

Yankelovich Partners, Inc. (Yankelovich), has been conducting attitudinal studies on consumer value and lifestyle trends since the inception of the Yankelovich MONITOR© in 1971.[†] "MONITOR© was the first and remains the longest-running tracking of marketplace trends," shared Yankelovich president J. Walker Smith. It was no surprise to Yankelovich that attitudes toward advertising and marketing were increasingly negative. "We have been talking with our clients for some time about the challenge of marketing productivity. The traditional marketing model is facing increased resistance from consumers and clutter and intrusiveness are particular problems." Yankelovich works with marketers in an effort to adopt new practices that replace clutter and intrusiveness with more precision, relevance, power, and reciprocity—a fourfold set of principles that has become a mantra for Yankelovich consultants.

What follows are extractions from the 2004 Marketing Resistance Survey, a Yankelovich MONITOR© OmniPlus Study Topline Report. The data were drawn via 15-minute telephone surveys conducted between February 20 and February 29, 2004, among 601 empaneled 2003 MONITOR© respondents during one bimonthly MONITOR© OmniPlus survey. Data were weighted to ensure a nationally representative sample of consumers aged 16 and older.

Negative Attitudes about Marketing

Overwhelmingly, consumers express a negative opinion about the marketing and advertising they encounter today:

60% agree that their opinion of marketing and advertising has become much more negative than it was just a few years ago.

61% feel that the amount of marketing and advertising has gotten out of control.

70% tune out advertising more than they did just a few years ago.

45% say the amount of marketing and advertising they are exposed to detracts from their experience of everyday life.

46% say that their shopping experiences are less enjoyable because of all the pressure to buy.

53% say that spam has turned them off to all forms of marketing and advertising.

While the 2004 study did not use the same questions as an AAAA study conducted door-to-door via personal interviews in 1964, a comparison of the overall tone of the opinions expressed provides an indication of what has happened in marketing and advertising over the last 40 years. Consumers like marketing and advertising just as much, but they dislike clutter and intrusiveness much more.

To compute an overall measure of positive versus negative attitudes, four multipart, multidimensional scales were developed. Two scales measured positive attitudes: Positive Scale and Empowering Scale. Two scales measured negative attitudes: Annoyance Scale and Resistance Scale. People with high scores on both positive scales and low scores on both negative scales were counted as having a wholly positive view. People with high scores on both negative scales and low scores on both positive scales were counted as having a wholly negative view. See Exhibit CU 1-1. While a direct comparison of the results from these two studies is complicated by the differences in sampling, question wording, and scaling, the growth of negative opinions is unmistakable.

Worsening Intrusiveness

Consumers continue their love-hate relationship with advertising and marketing, valuing its information and the standard of living it affords, while decrying its intrusiveness (see Exhibit CU 1-2). During 2003, dissatisfaction with the most egregious marketing intrusions and annoyances resulted in the federal Do-Not-Call Registry, the HIPAA privacy rule, and the CAN-SPAM Act. Additionally, the attorneys general of New York, Missouri, and Virginia initiated widely publicized legal actions against spammers.

Marketing Resistance and Marketing Productivity

Negative opinions and concerns about intrusiveness give rise to consumer resistance to marketing. And the fervor with which consumers are resisting marketing suggests that the impact on marketing productivity is considerable:

> **Exhibit CU 1-1** 40-Year Attitude Comparison

1964 AAAA Study		2004 Yankelovich Marketing Resistance Survey	
View of Advertising		**View of Marketing and Advertising**	
Favorable	41%	28%	Wholly positive
Unfavorable	14%	36%	Wholly negative
Mixed	34%	36%	Neutral/mixed

60% describe themselves as a person who tries to resist or avoid being exposed to marketing and advertising.

69% say they are interested in products and services that enable them to block, skip, or opt out of being exposed to marketing and advertising.

54% say they avoid buying products that overwhelm them with marketing and advertising

In exchange for *no* advertising or commercials, they are willing to incur some costs:

60% say they would do more research themselves to find out what's on sale.

41% say they would pay for traditionally free media like network TV or radio.

33% say they would accept a slightly lower standard of living.

28% say they would pay a significantly greater amount for magazines.

More than half would like to see advertising eliminated entirely in e-mail (58%), public schools (51%), and mail (51%). And a significant portion would willingly eliminate advertising in faxes (43%), cable TV (40%), movie previews (39%), Web sites (38%), public TV (36%), network TV (34%), and concerts (30%).

Yankelovich's New Marketing Model—P&R[2]

There are four cornerstones to the new marketing model that will fit what tomorrow's consumers are going to want the most. Together these four actions provide a framework of collaboration, respect, and rapport that can reverse resistance and rebuild marketing productivity.

- *Precision in marketing.* 52% want less marketing and advertising; only 7% want more.
- *Relevance in marketing.* 59% say that most marketing and advertising have very little relevance to them.

- *Power for consumers.* 53% say that nothing has changed: Consumers are still at the mercy of marketers and advertisers.
- *Reciprocity for consumers.* 61% say that marketers and advertisers don't treat them with respect.

Permission-based marketing is an element of empowerment, but it does not change the nature of that marketing. If permission is used to continue to overwhelm consumers with more of the same saturation marketing, then consumers will realize that giving permission has changed nothing about their overall experience in the marketplace. This realization will breed even more resentment and resistance.

A new tool is needed to deliver what consumers want— reduced clutter through better targeting and messaging that responds to their new values by providing control and compensation. That tool is *addressable attitudes.* Historically, attitudes— needs, wants, motivations, intentions, and aspirations—have not been linked to a specific name and address. Hence, direct marketing that relied on data—usually demographics linked to behaviors—ignored attitudes. Brand marketing that relied on attitudinal data used demographic proxies to choose an audience for the message. The lack of addressable attitudes worsened clutter. Consumers were getting marketing that was misaddressed. Reaching consumers who are receptive—who possess the right attitudes to see value in the marketing and advertising— means getting attitudes scored into the transactional and media databases used to execute marketing tactics. Addressable attitudes represent the next big step forward in precision and relevance, and thus the best way to improve marketing productivity.‡

*Information in this Close-Up was extracted from conversations with principals at Yankelovich (J. Walker Smith, president) and the 2004 Marketing Resistance Survey, a Yankelovich MONITOR© OmniPlus Study Topline Report, April 15, 2004.
†Yankelovich MONITOR© is an ongoing survey of consumer value and lifestyle trends. In addition to a major trend study conducted each year, recontacts of respondents are made during the course of the year.
‡Yankelovich MindBase is a pioneering service that provides addressable attitudes for more productive database marketing.
www.yankelovich.com

> **Exhibit CU 1-2** 40-Year Benefits and Disadvantages Comparison

1964 AAAA Study		2004 Yankelovich Marketing Resistance Survey	
Benefits			**Benefits**
Advertising raises our standard of living	71%	75%	Marketing and advertising are good for the economy
Reasons people like advertising: Information	57%	68%	Gives me useful ideas about how to make my life better
Disadvantages			**Disadvantages**
Reasons people dislike advertising: Intrusiveness	40%	65%	Constantly bombarded with too much marketing and advertising

To do well in such an environment, you will need to understand how to identify quality information and to recognize the solid, reliable marketing research on which your high-risk decisions as a marketing manager can be based. You also will need to know how to conduct such research. Developing these skills requires understanding the scientific method as it applies to the marketing decision-making environment. This book addresses your needs as information collector, processor, evaluator, and user.

> Marketing Planning Drives Marketing Research

Marketers have access to information other than that generated by marketing research. Understanding the relationship between marketing research and these other information sources—marketing decision support systems and marketing intelligence—is critical for understanding how information drives marketing decisions: organizational mission, marketing goals, marketing strategies, and marketing tactics.

Marketing Goals

The pastor of a suburban church would have different marketing goals than would Dr. Robert Schuler, evangelist pastor of television's *Hour of Power,* just as a local bakery would have different goals than Nabisco. But each likely has goals related to sales (membership), market share, return on investment, profitability, customer acquisition, customer satisfaction, customer retention, or some combination of these—whether codified in a written marketing plan or detailed only in an entrepreneur's brain. To assist in making increasingly complex decisions on marketing goals, strategies, and tactics, marketers turn first to information drawn from the marketing decision support system, combined with that generated by marketing intelligence on competitive and environmental activity.

Marketing Decision Support

Every marketer is driven by the need to complete one or many exchanges with its prospective customers. Knowing that it costs less to retain a customer than to capture a new one, most modern marketers place a high value on keeping their customers buying repeatedly. No matter how we define an *exchange*—a purchase, a vote, attendance at a function, a donation to a cause—each exchange, along with the strategic and tactical activities designed to complete it, generates numerous elements of data. If organized for retrieval, collectively these data elements constitute a marketing **decision support system (DSS).** During the last two decades of the 20th century, the advances in computer technology made it possible to widely and quickly share this collected transactional data among an organization's decision makers. This is often done over an intranet or an extranet.

An **intranet** is a private network that is contained within an enterprise (not available to the public at large). It may consist of many interlinked local area networks and also use leased lines in the wide area network. Typically, an intranet includes connections through one or more computers to the outside Internet. The main purpose of an intranet is to share company information and computing resources among internal audiences. An intranet can also be used to facilitate working in groups and for teleconferences. An **extranet** is a private network that uses the Internet protocols and the public telecommunication system to share an organization's information, data, or operations with external suppliers, vendors, or customers. An extranet can be viewed as the external portion of a company's intranet. Through both intranets and extranets parties can access proprietary relational databases containing marketing-related information. Today, sophisticated marketers have developed DSSs where data can be accessed in real time (as transactions are completed). Catalog marketers (for example, casual clothing marketer Land's End, now a division of Sears) know

decision support system (DSS) numerous elements of data organized for retrieval and use in marketing decision making.

intranet a private network that is contained within an enterprise.

extranet a private network that uses the Internet protocols and the public telecommunication system to share an organization's information, data, or operations with external suppliers, vendors, or customers.

exactly what tactics generate a transaction from a particular individual within their prospect and customer databases, as well as just how profitable each customer is to the company—an estimate of that customer's lifetime value to the company. Such marketers have a distinct advantage in marketing planning over those without real-time access to transactional data.

Marketing Intelligence

As no marketing decision exists in a vacuum, the marketing decision maker must have a broad knowledge of the firm's environment. A **marketing intelligence system (MkIS)** is designed to provide the marketer with ongoing information about events and trends in the technological, economic, political and legal, demographic, cultural, social, and most critically, competitive arenas. Such information is amassed from a variety of sources, as is noted in Exhibit 1-1.

It is often data from a DSS or MkIS that stimulate the question: Should we do marketing research? In the MindWriter example, this might be data collected about laptop problems needing repair. Or for our restaurant whose friendliness quotient is changing, it might be customer comments collected by the wait staff. (See Exhibit 1-2.)

marketing intelligence system (MkIS) a system of ongoing information collection about events and trends in the technological, economic, political and legal, demographic, cultural, social, and competitive arenas.

Marketing Strategy

Many successful marketing organizations strive to maintain a lifetime association with their customers. However, other organizations exist—at least for short periods of time—that appear never to have heard of the **marketing concept.** This philosophy of marketing assumes that the primary strategy for achieving an organization's marketing goals is to

marketing concept the primary strategy for achieving an organization's marketing goals is to satisfy its customers and establish lifetime customer-organization relationships.

>**Exhibit 1-1** Some Sources of Marketing Intelligence

>**Exhibit 1-2** How Marketing Research Relates to the Marketing Planning Process

Stages or Processes within Marketing Planning	Appropriate Marketing Research
Situation Analysis • Identification of competitive strengths and weaknesses • Identification of trends (opportunities and threats)	• Competitive barrier analysis • Analysis of sources of competitive advantage • Trend analysis • Positioning analysis • Identification of publics and key issues concerns • Measure of market share
Selection of a Target Market • Analysis of the market • Selection of a target market	• Identification of segmentation bases • Market segmentation study • Needs assessment • Determination of purchase criteria • Buyer behavior analysis • Market demand estimation
Plan of the Marketing Mix • Product	• Product design assessment • Competitive product analysis • Competitive packaging assessment • Packaging trends assessment • Definition of brand image descriptors • Identification of brand name/symbol • New product ideation (concept development) • Package development or redesign
• Price	• Measure of price elasticity • Industry pricing patterns • Price-value perception analysis • Analysis of the effects of various price incentives
• Distribution	• Merchandising display assessment • Inventory management assessment • Location analysis (site analysis) • Market exposure assessment
• Promotion	• Message assessment • Content analysis • Copy testing • Media assessment • Media buy assessment
Marketing Control • Marketing audit	• Promotion effectiveness study • Assessment of effectiveness of marketing mix

continually satisfy its customers and, thus, establish lifetime customer-organization relationships. This strong interest in the marketing concept explains why customer satisfaction, customer loyalty, and customer assessment studies represent a significant portion of marketing research studies. As evidence of the importance of the marketing concept, Microsoft recently completed a major corporate restructuring. It decided to tie its 600 managers' compensation not to sales and profits but to levels of customer satisfaction as measured by periodic customer satisfaction surveys.[3]

marketing strategy the general approach an organization will follow to achieve its marketing goals.

A **marketing strategy** is defined as the general approach an organization will follow to achieve its marketing goals. In an earlier example, a restaurant was receiving comments that the friendly atmosphere was changing. This perception may have been the result of a change in strategy—a decision to switch from a restaurant where patrons were encouraged

>**Exhibit 1-4** Minute Maid and Marketing Research

Minute Maid's Consumer and Marketplace Knowledge team demonstrates that effective research doesn't end once the collected data are reported. Organizations in the top tier of research-based decision making see activation of strategies and tactics based on research-supported insights as the highest priority. **www.minutemaid.com**

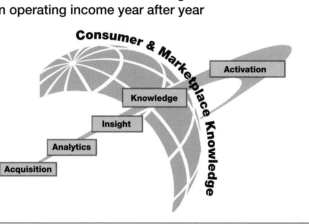

Minute Maid CMK Mission

Our Mission Is To . . .

* Leverage consumer, customer and marketplace knowledge to identify, develop and influence business strategies and tactics that will generate growth in operating income year after year

methodologies that proved themselves in the last several decades of the 20th century—surveys and focus groups. This tier is occupied by many large, medium, and small marketers of all types. Some of the firms newly arrived to this tier are in transition from the base tier. They have realized that failing to collect information prior to decision making or ignoring insights from information that has been collected puts them at a distinct competitive disadvantage.

Finally, the base tier comprises those marketers who primarily use instinct and intuition rather than formal marketing research to facilitate their decisions. These firms may or may not have sophisticated DSSs or MkISs. They believe themselves to be so close to

>**snap**shot

Mary Kay: Enticing Managers to Use Research-Based Decision Making

Cosmetics marketer Mary Kay, like many companies facing rapidly changing technology, is in transition—from relying on instinct, anecdotal evidence, and qualitative data to relying on quality quantitative information. When Teri Burgess moved from a product marketing position at Mary Kay to director of marketing analysis, her task was to create a database from mounds of consumer data. Now that the database is as user-friendly as demanded, she faces a new task, and one surprisingly familiar to marketing researchers worldwide: enticing marketing decision makers to rely on the insights available to them. "Part of the reluctance is cultural," shared Burgess. Without this information,

seasoned managers have made the hard decisions: to discontinue once-popular products, to introduce new fashion colors, to position stable products for alternative benefits. "And part of it may be lack of motivation. Until upper management demands that managers support their ideas and proposals with information from research and the decision support system, no amount of training—in how the system works and can be helpful—will make it happen."

www.marykay.com

> **We discuss the technological events and trends of the last half of the 20th century in Chapter 2.**

customers and distribution partners that they rarely need marketing research. When they do collect information, they use a limited amount of qualitative research, often in the form of an informal group discussion or individual interviews, to confirm their ideas. Especially in the business-to-business arena, they often rely on feedback filtered by their sales forces. Following guidelines for adequate sampling or other procedures of scientific inquiry is not fundamental to this group. Larger firms that occupy this tier are influenced as much by organizational culture as by resources. Many small companies find themselves in this tier not because of an unwillingness to use marketing research but based on a perception that any more formalized research is too expensive to employ and that their resources won't accommodate this mode of decision making.

" "People are 'erroneously confident' in their knowledge and underestimate the odds that their information or beliefs will be proved wrong. They tend to seek additional information in ways that confirm what they already believe. " "

Max Bazerman
Harvard University[7]

The trends of the past two decades, especially the technology that has been driving research methodologies of data collection and dissemination, make it likely that marketing managers who do not prepare to advance up the hierarchy will be at a severe competitive disadvantage.

> When is Research Unnecessary?

Marketing research has an inherent value only to the extent that it helps management make better decisions that help achieve organizational goals. Interesting information about consumers, competitors, or the environment might be pleasant to have, but its value is limited if the information cannot be applied to a critical decision. If a study does not help management select more effective, more efficient, less risky, or more profitable alternatives than otherwise would be the case, its use should be questioned. Alternatively, management may have insufficient resources (time, money, or skill) to conduct an appropriate study or may face a low level of risk associated with the decision at hand. In these situations, it is valid to avoid marketing research and its associated costs in time and money. Marketing research finds its justification in the contribution it makes to the decision maker's task and to the bottom line.

> When Is Research Essential?

Following are some examples of management problems involving marketing decision making based on information gathering. From each of these illustrations, we can abstract the essence of marketing research. How is it carried out? What can it do? What should it not be expected to do? As you read the four cases, be thinking about the possible range of situations for conducting marketing research, and try answering these questions:

1. What is the marketing decision-making dilemma facing the manager?
2. What must the researcher accomplish?

CHILDCO

You work for CHILDCO, a corporation that is considering growth through the acquisition of a toy manufacturer. The senior vice president for development asks you to head a task force to investigate six companies that are potential candidates. You assemble a cross-functional team composed of representatives from marketing, operations, human resources, and finance. Pertinent data are collected from public sources because of the sensitive nature of the project. You examine all of the following: company annual reports; articles in business journals, trade magazines, and newspapers; financial analysts' assessments; and company advertisements. The team members then develop summary profiles of the candidate firms based on the characteristics gleaned from the sources. The final report highlights the opportunities and problems that the acquisition of each target firm would bring to all areas of the business.

NUCMED

You are the business manager for NUCMED, a large group of physicians specializing in nuclear medicine and imaging. A prominent health insurance organization has contacted you promoting a new cost-containment program. The doctors' committee to whom you will make a recommendation will have a narrow enrollment window for their decision. If the doctors choose to join, they will agree to a reduced fee schedule in exchange for easier filing procedures, quicker reimbursement, and listing on a physicians' referral network. If they decline, they will continue to deal with their patients and the insurance carrier in the current manner. You begin your investigation by mining data from patient files to learn how many are using this carrier, frequency of care visits, complexity of filings, and so on. You then consult insurance industry data to discover how many potential patients in your area use this care plan, or similar care plans with alternative insurance carriers, and the likelihood of a patient's choosing or switching doctors to find one that subscribes to the proposed program. You attempt to confirm your data with information from professional and association journals. Based on this information, you develop a profile that details the number of patients, overhead, and potential revenue realized by choosing to join the plan.

ColorSplash

ColorSplash, a paint manufacturer, is having trouble maintaining profits. The owner believes inventory management is a weak area of the company's operations. In this industry, the many paint colors, types of paint, and container sizes make it easy for a firm to accumulate large inventories and still be unable to fill customer orders. The owner asks you to make recommendations. You look into the present warehousing and shipping operations and find excessive sales losses and delivery delays because of out-of-stock conditions. An informal poll of customers confirms your impression. You suspect the present inventory database and reporting system do not provide the prompt, usable information needed for appropriate production decisions.

Based on this supposition, you familiarize yourself with the latest inventory management techniques in a local college library. You ask the warehouse manager to take an accurate inventory, and you review the incoming orders for the last year. In addition, the owner shows you the production runs of the last year and his method for assessing the need for a particular color or paint type.

Modeling the last year of business using production, order, and inventory management techniques, you choose the method that provides the best theoretical profit. You run a pilot test using the new control methodology. After two months, the data show a much lower inventory and a higher order fulfillment rate. A measure of customer satisfaction—number of retailer complaints about out-of-stocks—indicates your retailers' satisfaction level is increasing. You recommend that the company adopt the new inventory method.

York College

You work for York College's alumni association. It is eager to develop closer ties with its aging alumni, to provide strong stimuli to encourage increased donations, and to induce older, nontraditional students to return to supplement enrollment. The president and board of directors are considering starting a retirement community geared toward university alumni and ask your association to assess the attractiveness of the proposal from an alumni viewpoint. Your director asks you to divide the study into four parts.

Phase 1

First you are to report on the number of alumni who are in the appropriate age bracket, the rate of new entries per year, and the actuarial statistics for the group. This information will permit the president to assess whether the project is worth continuing. Your *Phase 1 Report* reveals there are sufficient alumni to make the project feasible.

Phase 2

The next step in the study is to describe the social and economic characteristics of the target alumni group. You review gift statistics, analyze job titles, and assess home location and values. In addition, you review files from the last five years to see how alumni responded when they were asked about their income bracket. You are able to describe the alumni group for the president when you finish. It is evident from the *Phase 2 Report* that the target alumni can easily afford a retirement community as proposed.

Phase 3

The third phase of the study is to explain the characteristics of alumni who would be interested in a university-related retirement community. For this phase, you engage the American Association of Retired Persons (AARP) and a retirement community developer. In addition, you search for information on senior citizens from the federal government. From the developer you learn what characteristics of retirement community planning and construction are most attractive to retirees. From the AARP you learn about the main services and features that potential retirees look for in a retirement community. From government publications you become familiar with existing regulations and recommendations for operating retirement communities and uncover a full range of descriptive information on the typical retirement community dweller. You make an extensive report to both the alumni association director and the university president. The report covers the number of eligible alumni, their social and economic standings, and the characteristics of those who would be attracted by the retirement community.

Phase 4

The *Phase 3 Report* interests the college president. She asks for one additional phase to be completed. She needs to predict the number of alumni who would be attracted to the project so that she can adequately plan the size of the community. At this point, you call on the business school's marketing research class for help in designing a questionnaire for the alumni. By providing telephones and funding, you arrange for the class to conduct a survey among a random sample of the eligible alumni population. In addition, you have the class devise a second questionnaire for alumni who will become eligible in the next 10 years. Using the data collected, you can predict the initial demand for the community and estimate the growth in demand over the next 10 years. You submit your *Phase 4 Report* to the director and the president.

What Is the Dilemma Facing the Manager?

The manager's predicament is fairly well defined in the four cases. Let's see how carefully you read and understood them. In CHILDCO the senior vice president for development must make a proposal to the president or possibly the board of directors about whether to acquire a toy manufacturer and, if one is to be acquired, which one of the six under consideration is the best candidate. In NUCMED the physicians in the group must decide whether to join the proposed managed health care plan of one of their primary insurers. Their decision will directly affect pricing. In ColorSplash the owner of the paint manufacturer must decide whether to implement a new inventory management system in order to reverse customer dissatisfaction. At York College, the president must propose to the board of directors whether to fund the development of a retirement community. How did you do? If you didn't come to these same conclusions, reread the cases before proceeding, to catch what you missed.

In real life, management dilemmas are not always so clearly defined. In the case of MindWriter (the Behind the Scenes vignette), Myra Wines knows there is a concern about customer satisfaction, but her personal positive experience gives her no clue as to what is causing management's concern. Jason Henry has read at least one article in the business press that implies after-purchase service might be to blame.

In ColorSplash, rather than pinpointing the problem as one of inventory management, the paint manufacturer could have faced several interactive phenomena:

1. A strike by the teamsters, influencing inventory delivery to retail and wholesale customers.
2. The development of a new paint formula that offers superior coverage but requires a relatively scarce ingredient to manufacture, thereby affecting production rates.
3. A fire that destroys the primary loading dock of the main shipping warehouse in the Midwest, affecting delivery.
4. The simultaneous occurrence of all three events.

As the research process begins with a manager's decision-making task, accurately defining the dilemma is often difficult but paramount. We address this issue briefly in Chapter 4 and in more detail in Chapter 5.

What Types of Research Should Be Considered?

As we indicated earlier in this chapter, there are many types of studies that carry the label "marketing research." The different types of marketing research (summarized in Exhibit 1-5) represented by the four decision scenarios can be classified based on the use of theory as reporting, descriptive, explanatory, or predictive.

Reporting

At the most elementary level, a **reporting study** may be made only to provide an account or summation of some data or to generate some statistics. The task may be quite simple and the data readily available. At other times, the information may be difficult to find. A reporting study calls for knowledge of and skill with information sources and gatekeepers of information sources. (Refer to Exhibit 1-1, "Some Sources of Marketing Intelligence.") Such a study usually requires little inference or conclusion drawing. In CHILDCO the researcher needs to know what information should be evaluated in order to value a company. In the study of management, this knowledge would be acquired primarily in courses in financial management, accounting, and marketing. Knowing the type of information needed, the researcher in CHILDCO identifies sources of information, like trade press articles and annual reports. Because of the possible effect of the toy manufacturer evaluation on the stock prices of the conglomerate instigating the study and on each toy company, only public sources are used. Other reporting studies of a less sensitive nature might have the researcher interviewing source gatekeepers. In York College, for example, interviewing the

reporting study provides an account or summation of data, including descriptive statistics, on a particular topic.

> **CHILDCO and the first phase of York College each illustrates a reporting study.**

>Exhibit 1-5 Types of Marketing Studies

Type	Definition	Example
Reporting	Provides an account or summation of some marketing phenomenon.	• Determine the market share for each brand in a particular class of automobile. • Determine the current advertising themes for all competitors in a product class.
Descriptive	Discovers and reports the who, what, when, where, or how related to a specific marketing decision.	• Determine the market segment served by a particular concert series for a symphony orchestra. • Determine the geographic territory generating the strongest participation in a national contest.
Explanatory	Attempts to explain the reasons for a marketing phenomenon.	• Explain why attendance at a band's world tour concert was so drastically less this year than two years ago. • Discover why sales did not increase when the new bonus system for salesperson compensation was introduced.
Predictive	Attempts to forecast a marketing phenomenon.	• Estimate the demand for a new household electrical appliance. • Estimate the participation rate of a planned sweepstakes. • Estimate the effect on sales of a new pricing strategy.

director of local retirement facilities might have revealed other sources to include in the search. Such an expert is considered a gatekeeper. Early in your career, identifying gatekeepers within your firm and industry is critical to your success as a manager.

Purists claim that reporting studies do not qualify as research, although carefully gathered data can have great value. Others argue that at least one form, investigative reporting, has a great deal in common with widely accepted qualitative and clinical research.[8] A research design does not have to be complex and require inferences for a project to be called marketing research. In the early part of your career, you will likely be asked to perform a number of reporting studies. Many managers consider the execution of such studies an excellent way for new employees to become familiar with their employer and its industry.

Descriptive

descriptive study discovers answers to the questions *who, what, when, where,* and, sometimes, *how.*

research variable an event, act, or characteristic measured by research.

> NUCMED and the second phase of York College each illustrates a descriptive study.

A **descriptive study** tries to discover answers to the questions *who, what, when, where,* and, sometimes, *how.* The researcher attempts to describe or define a subject, often by creating a profile of a group of problems, people, or events. Such studies may involve the collection of data and the creation of a distribution of the number of times the researcher observes a single event, act, or characteristic (known as a **research variable**), or they may involve relating the interaction of two or more variables. In NUCMED, the researcher must present data that reveal who is affiliated with the insurer, who uses managed health care programs (both doctors and patients), the general trends in the use of imaging technology in diagnosing illness or injury severity, and the relationship of patient characteristics, doctor referrals, and technology use patterns.

Descriptive studies may or may not have the potential for drawing powerful inferences. Organizations that maintain databases of their employees, customers, and suppliers already have significant data to conduct descriptive studies using internal information. Yet many firms that have such data files do not mine them regularly for the decision-making insight they might provide. MindWriter's Myra Wines could mine numerous company databases for insight into the nature and number of service-related problems arising after purchase and, similarly, for information about product use inquiries. A database generated by warranty registration cards could reveal significant data concerning purchaser characteristics, as well as purchase location and product use behavior. A descriptive study, however, does not explain why an event has occurred or why the variables interact the way they do.

The descriptive study is popular in marketing research because of its versatility in numerous management dilemmas. In not-for-profit corporations and other organizations, descriptive investigations have a broad appeal to the administrator and policy analyst for planning, monitoring, and evaluating. In this context, *how* questions address issues such as quantity, cost, efficiency, effectiveness, and adequacy.[9]

Explanatory

Academics have debated the relationship between the next two types of studies, explanatory and predictive, in terms of which precedes the other. Both types of research are grounded in theory, and theory is created to answer *why* and *how* questions. For our purposes, an **explanatory study** goes beyond description and attempts to explain the reasons for the phenomenon that the descriptive study only observed. Research that studies the relationship between two or more variables is also referred to as a *correlational study*. In an explanatory study, the researcher uses theories, or at least hypotheses, to account for the forces that caused a certain phenomenon to occur. Think of a hypothesis as one plausible explanation that explains a result. In ColorSplash, believing the problem with paint stockouts is the result of poor inventory management, the owner asks the researcher to detail warehousing and shipping processes. This would be a descriptive study if it had stopped here. But if problems revealed in the processes could be linked with sales losses resulting from the company's inability to make timely deliveries to retail or wholesale customers, then an explanatory study would emerge. The researcher tests this hypothesis (plausible explanation) by modeling (creating a hypothetical picture of) the last year of business using the relationships between processes and results (stockout conditions).

> **explanatory study** attempts to explain an event, act, or characteristic measured by research.

> **ColorSplash and the third phase of York College each represents an explanatory study.**

Predictive

If discovering a plausible explanation for an event after it has occurred is valuable, it is even more desirable in marketing to be able to predict when and in what situations the event will occur. A **predictive study,** the fourth type, is just as rooted in theory as the explanatory study. Safety while flying has been a critical marketing issue for airlines. NATA, a national trade association for the aviation industry, may be interested in explaining the radiation risks from the sun and stars for flight crews and passengers. The variables might include altitude, proximity of air routes to the poles, time of year, and aircraft shielding. Perhaps the relations among the four variables explain the radiation risk variable. This type of study often calls for a high order of inference making. Why, for example, would a flight at a specified altitude at one time of year not produce so great a radiation risk to the airliner's occupants as the same flight in another season? The answer to such a question would be valuable in planning air routes, which might in turn adjust flight times, a critical decision criterion for many flying customers. It also would contribute to the development of a better theory of the phenomenon. In marketing research, prediction is found in studies conducted to evaluate specific courses of action or to forecast current and future values.

> **predictive study** attempts to predict when and in what situations an event, act, or characteristic will occur.

The researcher is asked to predict for the York College president the success of the proposed retirement facility. The prediction will be based on the number of applicants for residency the project will attract. This predictive study will be based on the explanatory hypothesis that alumni frequent programs and projects sponsored by the institution because of an association they maintain between their college experience and images of youthfulness and mental and physical stimulation.

> **The final phase of York College is an example of a predictive study.**

Finally, we would like to be able to control a phenomenon once we can explain and predict it. Being able to replicate a scenario and dictate a particular outcome is the objective of **control.** In York College, if we assume that the college proceeds with its retirement

> **control** the ability to replicate a scenario and dictate a particular outcome.

community and enjoys the predicted success, the president will find it attractive to be able to build a similar facility to serve another group of alumni and duplicate that success.

Control is a logical outcome of prediction. The complexity of the phenomenon and the adequacy of the prediction theory, however, largely decide success in a control study. At York College, if a control study were done of the various promotional approaches used with alumni to stimulate images of youthfulness, the promotional tactics that drew the largest number of alumni applications for residency could be identified. Once known, this knowledge could be used successfully with different groups of alumni *only if* the researcher could account for and control all other variables influencing applications.

> Is Marketing Research Always Problem-Solving Based?

applied research research that addresses existing problems or opportunities.

> Applied research is used to evaluate opportunities, as in CHILDCO and York College.

pure research (basic research) designed to solve problems of a theoretical nature with little direct impact on strategic or tactical decisions.

> One of the key purposes for marketing research is to improve our understanding of the marketing process.

> We discuss hypotheses in Chapter 3 and hypothesis testing in Chapter 20.

In the four marketing decision scenarios described above, researchers were asked to respond to "problems" that managers needed to solve. **Applied research** has a practical problem-solving emphasis, although the problem solving is not always generated by a negative circumstance. Whether the "problem" is negative, like rectifying an inventory system that is resulting in lost sales (ColorSplash), or positive, such as increasing stockholder wealth through acquiring another firm (CHILDCO), problem solving is prevalent in marketing research.

The problem-solving nature of applied research means it is conducted to reveal answers to specific questions related to action, performance, or policy needs. In this respect, all four examples appear to qualify as applied research. Pure, or basic, research is also problem-solving based, but in a different sense. It aims to solve perplexing questions (that is, problems) of a theoretical nature that have little direct impact on strategic or tactical decisions. **Pure research** or **basic research** in the marketing arena might involve a researcher for an advertising agency who is studying the results of the use of coupons versus rebates as demand stimulation tactics, but not in a specific instance or in relation to a specific client's product. In another pure-research scenario, researchers might study the influence on productivity of salesperson compensation systems that pay by number of transactions versus salary plus commission. Thus, both applied research and pure research are problem-solving based, but applied research is directed much more to making immediate marketing decisions.

The classical concept of basic research calls for a *hypothesis*—an explanation that is advanced for the purpose of testing its truth or falsity. In applied research such a narrow definition omits at least two types of investigation that are highly valued. First is the *exploratory study,* in which the investigator knows so little about the area of study that hypotheses have not yet emerged and the final research problem has not yet emerged. Equally important to marketing decision making is the *descriptive study.* "The very essence of description is to name the properties of things: You may do more, but you cannot do less and still have description. The more adequate the description, the greater is the likelihood that the units derived from the description will be useful in subsequent theory building."[10] One of the most fundamental research studies in marketing is the segmentation study. At its heart is the need to describe the relevant segments within the market.

In regard to the question posed at the beginning of this section, "Is marketing research always problem-solving based?" the answer is yes. Whether basic or applied, simple or complex, all marketing research should provide an answer to some question. If marketing managers always knew what was causing problems or offering opportunities in their realm of responsibility, there would be little need for applied research, pure research, or basic research; intuition would be all that was necessary to make quality decisions.

Any of the four types of studies—reporting, descriptive, explanatory, or predictive—can properly be called marketing research, as each provides information to solve a marketing problem or capitalize on an opportunity. This defines the bare minimum that any effort must meet to be called marketing research. A rough measure of the development of science in any field is the degree to which explanation and prediction have replaced reporting and description as research objectives. By this standard, marketing research is in a comparatively formative stage of development.

> What Is Good Research?

Good marketing research generates dependable data that are derived by professionally conducted practices and that can be used reliably for marketing decision making. In contrast, poor research is carelessly planned and conducted, resulting in data that a marketer can't use to reduce his or her decision-making risks. Good research follows the standards of the **scientific method,** systematic, empirically based procedures for generating replicable research.

scientific method
systematic, empirically based procedures for generating replicable research.

We list several defining characteristics of the scientific method in Exhibit 1-6 and discuss below the managerial dimensions of each.

1. *Purpose clearly defined.* The purpose of the marketing research—the problem involved or the decision to be made—should be clearly defined and sharply delineated in terms as unambiguous as possible. Getting this in writing is valuable even in instances where the same person serves as researcher and decision maker. The statement of the decision problem should include its scope, its limitations, and the precise meanings of all words and terms significant to the research. Failure of the researcher to do this adequately may

>**Exhibit 1-6** What Actions Guarantee Good Marketing Research?

Characteristics of Research	What a Manager Should Look For in Research Done by Others or Include in Self-Directed Research	Chapter
Purpose clearly defined	• Researcher distinguishes between symptom of organization's problem, the manager's perception of the problem, and the research problem.	4, 5
Research process detailed	• Researcher provides complete research proposal.	6
Research design thoroughly planned	• Exploratory procedures are outlined with constructs defined. • Sample unit is clearly described along with sampling methodology. • Data collection procedures are selected and designed.	4, 5, 8–17
High ethical standards applied	• Safeguards are in place to protect study participants, organizations, clients, and researchers. • Recommendations do not exceed the scope of the study. • The study's methodology and limitations sections reflect researcher's restraint and concern for accuracy.	7, 23
Limitations frankly revealed	• Desired procedure is compared with actual procedure in the report. • Desired sample is compared with actual sample in the report. • Impact on findings and conclusions is detailed.	8, 11, 12, 18–20, 23
Adequate analysis for decision maker's needs	• Sufficiently detailed findings are tied to collection instruments.	18–23
Findings presented unambiguously	• Findings are clearly presented in words, tables, and graphs. • Findings are logically organized to facilitate reaching a decision about the manager's problem. • Executive summary of conclusions is outlined. • Detailed table of contents is tied to the conclusions and findings presentation.	18–23
Conclusions justified	• Decision-based conclusions are matched with detailed findings.	18–23
Researcher's experience reflected	• Researcher provides experience/credentials with report.	23

raise legitimate doubts in the minds of research report readers as to whether the researcher has sufficient understanding of the problem to make a sound proposal attacking it. This characteristic is comparable to developing a strategic marketing plan for achieving an objective before developing a tactical plan or an action map.

> **The nine criteria summarized in Exhibit 1-6 profile desirable, decision-oriented research, especially when managers perform the research themselves. These criteria create barriers to adjusting research findings to meet desired ends.**

2. *Research process detailed.* The research procedures used should be described in sufficient detail to permit another researcher to repeat the research. Except when secrecy is imposed, research reports should reveal with candor the sources of data and the means by which they were obtained. Omission of significant procedural details makes it difficult or impossible to estimate the validity and reliability of the data and justifiably weakens the confidence of the reader in the research itself as well as any recommendations based on the research. This characteristic is comparable to developing a tactical plan.

3. *Research design thoroughly planned.* The procedural design of the research should be carefully planned to yield results that are as objective as possible. When a sampling of the population is involved, the report should include evidence concerning the degree of representativeness of the sample. A survey of opinions or recollections ought not to be used when more reliable evidence is available from documentary sources or by direct observation. Bibliographic searches should be as thorough and complete as possible. Experiments should have satisfactory controls. Direct observations should be recorded in writing as soon as possible after the event. Efforts should be made to minimize the influence of personal bias in selecting and recording data. This characteristic is comparable to developing detailed action plans for each marketing tactic.

> **We discuss ethical research issues at length in Chapter 7.**

> **Watch for this icon throughout the text.**

4. *High ethical standards applied.* Researchers often work independently and have significant latitude in designing and executing research projects. A research design that includes safeguards against causing mental or physical harm to participants and makes data integrity a first priority should be highly valued. Ethical issues in research reflect important moral concerns about the practice of responsible behavior in society.

Researchers frequently find themselves precariously balancing the rights of their subjects against the scientific dictates of their chosen method. When this occurs, they have a responsibility to guard the welfare of the participants in the studies and also the organizations to which they belong, their clients, their colleagues, and themselves. Careful consideration must be given to those research situations in which there is a possibility for physical or psychological harm, exploitation, invasion of privacy, and/or loss of dignity. The research need must be weighed against the potential for adverse effects. Typically, you can redesign a study, but sometimes you cannot. The researcher should be prepared for this dilemma.

5. *Limitations frankly revealed.* The researcher should report, with complete frankness, flaws in procedural design and estimate their effect on the findings. There are very few perfect research designs. Some of the imperfections may have little effect on the validity and reliability of the data; others may invalidate them entirely. A competent researcher should be sensitive to the effects of imperfect design. His or her experience in analyzing data should provide a basis for estimating the influence of design flaws. As a decision maker, you should question the value of research where no limitations are reported.

6. *Adequate analysis for decision maker's needs.* Analysis of the data should be extensive enough to reveal its significance, what marketers call insights. The methods of analysis used should be appropriate. The extent to which this criterion is met is frequently a good measure of the competence of the researcher. Adequate analysis of the data is the most difficult phase of research for the novice. The validity and reliability of data should be checked carefully. The data should be classified in ways that assist the researcher in reaching pertinent conclusions and clearly reveal the findings that have led to those conclusions. When statistical methods are used, the probability of error should be estimated and the criteria of statistical significance applied.

7. *Findings presented unambiguously.* Some evidence of the competence and integrity of the researcher may be found in the report itself. For example, language that is restrained, clear, and precise; assertions that are carefully drawn and hedged with appropriate reserva-

tions; and an apparent effort to achieve maximum objectivity tend to leave a favorable impression of the researcher with the decision maker. Generalizations that outrun the evidence on which they are based, exaggerations, and unnecessary verbiage tend to leave an unfavorable impression. Such reports are not valuable to managers wading through the minefields of marketing decision making. Presentation of data should be comprehensive, easily understood by the decision maker, and organized so that the decision maker can readily locate critical findings.

8. *Conclusions justified.* Conclusions should be limited to those for which the data provide an adequate basis. Researchers are often tempted to broaden the basis of induction by including personal experiences and their interpretations—data not subject to the controls under which the research data were gathered. Equally undesirable is the all-too-frequent practice of drawing conclusions from a study of a limited population and applying them universally. Researchers also may be tempted to rely too heavily on data collected in a prior study and use it in the interpretation of a new study. Such practice sometimes occurs among research specialists who confine their work to clients in a small industry. These actions tend to decrease the objectivity of the research and weaken readers' confidence in the findings. Good researchers always specify the conditions under which their conclusions seem to be valid.

9. *Researcher's experience reflected.* Greater confidence in the research is warranted if the researcher is experienced, has a good reputation in research, and is a person of integrity. Were it possible for the reader of a research report to obtain sufficient information about the researcher, this criterion perhaps would be one of the best bases for judging the degree of confidence a piece of research warrants and the value of any decision based upon it. For this reason the research report should contain information about the qualifications of the researcher.

In the chapters that follow, we discuss scientific research procedures and show their application to pragmatic problems of the marketing manager. At a minimum, our objective is to make you a more intelligent consumer of research products prepared by others as well as enable you to perform quality marketing research for your own decisions and those of others to whom you report.

>summary

1 Research is any organized inquiry carried out to provide information for solving problems. Marketing research is a systematic inquiry that provides information to guide marketing decisions. More specifically, it is a process of determining, acquiring, analyzing and synthesizing, and disseminating relevant marketing data, information, and insights to decision makers in ways that mobilize the organization to take appropriate marketing actions that, in turn, maximize business performance. Marketing research includes reporting, descriptive, explanatory, and predictive studies. We emphasize the last three in this book.

2 Not all marketers have established research as a priority in their process of decision making. Thus a hierarchy of marketing decision makers is emerging: The top tier contains those marketers who use research as a fundamental key step in all decisions and who use creative vision to establish proprietary methodologies; the middle tier is those marketers who occasionally turn to research but only rely on the tried-and-true methods; the bottom tier is those marketers who by choice or economic circumstance choose

to rely on intuition and judgment rather than marketing research.

3 The marketing managers of tomorrow will need to know more than any managers in history. Marketing research will be a major contributor to that knowledge. Marketing managers will find knowledge of research methods to be of value in many situations. They may need to conduct research either for themselves or for others. As buyers of research services marketers will need to be able to judge research quality. Finally, they may become marketing research specialists themselves.

4 What characterizes good research? Generally, one expects good research to be purposeful, with a clearly defined focus and plausible goals, with defensible, ethical, and repeatable procedures, and with evidence of objectivity. The reporting of procedures—their strengths and weaknesses—should be complete and honest. Appropriate analytical techniques should be used; conclusions drawn should be limited to those clearly justified by the findings; and reports of findings and conclusions should be clearly presented and

professional in tone, language, and appearance. Marketers should always choose a researcher who has an established reputation for quality work. The research objective and its

benefits should be weighed against potentially adverse effects.

>**key**terms

applied research 22	intranet 10	predictive study 21
basic research 22	management dilemma 6	pure research (basic research) 22
control 21	marketing 5	reporting study 19
data mining 7	marketing concept 11	research variable 20
data warehouse 7	marketing intelligence system (MkIS) 11	return on marketing investment (ROMI) 5
decision support system (DSS) 10		
descriptive study 20	marketing research 4	scientific method 23
explanatory study 21	marketing strategy 12	
extranet 10	marketing tactics 13	

>**discussion**questions

Terms in Review

1   What is marketing research? Why should there be any question about the definition of research?

2   What is the difference between applied research and basic or pure research? Use a decision about how a salesperson is to be paid, by commission or salary, and describe the question that would guide applied research versus the question that would guide pure research.

Making Research Decisions

3   A sales force manager needs to have information in order to decide whether to create a custom motivation program or purchase one offered by a consulting firm. What are the dilemmas the manager faces in selecting either of these alternatives?

4   You are the marketing manager of the retail division of a major corporation. Your firm has 35 stores scattered over four states. Corporate headquarters asks you to conduct an investigation to determine whether any of these stores should be closed, expanded, moved, or reduced. Is there a possible conflict between your roles as researcher and manager? Explain.

5   Advise each of the following persons on a specific research study that he or she might find useful. Classify each proposed study as reporting, descriptive, explanatory, or predictive.

   a When the management decision problem is known:

     (1) Manager of a full-service restaurant with high employee turnover.

     (2) Head of an academic department committee charged with selecting a research methods textbook.

   b When the management decision problem has not yet been specified:

     (1) Manager of a restaurant.

     (2) Director of Big Brothers/Big Sisters in charge of sponsor recruiting.

     (3) Data analyst with ACNielsen research.

     (4) Director of admissions at a university.

     (5) Product manager of the Ford Explorer.

     (6) Family services officer for your county.

     (7) Office manager for a pediatrician.

6   The new president of an old, established company is facing a problem. The company is currently unprofitable and is, in the president's opinion, operating inefficiently. The company sells a wide line of equipment and supplies to the dairy industry. Some items it manufactures, and many it wholesales to dairies, creameries, and similar plants. Because the industry is changing in several ways, survival will be more difficult in the future. In particular, many equipment companies are bypassing the wholesalers and selling directly to dairies. In addition, many of the independent dairies are being taken over by large food chains. How might marketing research help the new president make the right decisions?

7   You have received a marketing research report done by a consultant for your firm, a life insurance company. The

study is a survey of customer satisfaction based on a sample of 600. You are asked to comment on its quality. What will you look for?

8   As area sales manager for a company manufacturing and marketing outboard engines, you have been assigned the responsibility of conducting a research study to estimate the sales potential of your products in the domestic (U.S. or Canadian) market. Discuss key issues and concerns arising from the fact that you, the manager, are also the researcher.

Behind the Scenes

9   In what type(s) of study is Myra Wines of MindWriter interested (applied or basic/pure research; reporting, descriptive, explanatory, or predictive study)?

10   What evidence is presented in the Behind the Scenes vignette of data warehousing? Of data mining?

From Concept to Practice

11   Apply the principles in Exhibit 1–6 to the research scenario in question 8.

># **www**exercise

Visit the Advertising World portal (sponsored by Leo Burnett and housed at the University of Texas), **http://advertising.utexas.edu/ world/index.asp.** Choose "marketing research", and then link to one or more of the research companies listed on the site. How do they demonstrate the quality of their experience or their high ethical standards—two of the characteristics of good research summarized in Exhibit 1-6?

># **cases** *

HeroBuilders.com

   Data Development Inc.

* All cases, both written and video, are on the text DVD. The film icon indicates a video case. Check the DVD Index to determine whether a case has data, the research instrument, or other supplementary material.

chapter 2

The Marketing Research Industry

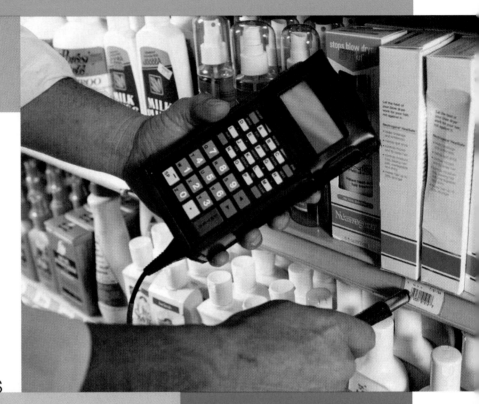

>learningobjectives

After reading this chapter, you should understand . . .

1 Recent historical events shaping marketing research.

2 The contribution of technology in enhancing marketing research and industry effectiveness.

3 The different categories of firms and their functions in the industry.

It is not unusual for marketing research companies to be working on several projects at one time. It is also not unusual for a single researcher or research team within a research company to be working on different stages of different research projects at one time. This is the normal circumstance for Visionary Insights, Inc. We again join Jason Henry to see what other projects occupy his time and to learn a little about how the marketing research industry works.

Jason Henry's immediate superior at Visionary Insights, "Chance" Bedford, sticks his head inside Jason's office and sees Jason pouring over data summary reports.

"How's it going, Jason?"

Jason looks up, his annoyance at being interrupted clearly visible on his face.

"Is that the initial data from the MSI biennial membership survey?"

Hoping to ward off a lengthy interruption, Jason responds with a curt "Yes" and then lowers his head again. However, his signal is ignored, as Chance grins and takes the chair opposite Jason's desk.

"Give me the scoop, Jason. Are any research priorities surfacing that we might be interested in pursuing?"

The Marketing Science Institute, one of the premier marketing trade associations, sets research priorities for collaboration between business and academic researchers. These research priorities are determined by a balloting of MSI trustees and serve as a blueprint for research organizations, guiding decisions on research projects. VI is one of the firms conducting the MSI membership research. Using focus groups at conferences of senior-level marketing executives, VI discovered several areas of research interest. This was followed by an extensive membership survey, the data from which Jason is just now starting to study.

"I've just now gotten the frequencies," grumbled Jason. "You'll know when I know."

Chance chuckles, well aware that Jason can be totally tunnel-visioned when he is immersed in data. As he levers himself from the chair and walks to the door, he pauses, looking back over his shoulder. "That's good." After a significant pause during which Jason assumes he has departed, Chance interrupts him again. "Don't forget to join us in the conference room when the Kraft team arrives—in 10 minutes."

Jason groans, but raises his head in time to return Chance's smile. "I'll be there."

This chapter begins with a summary of events that influenced how the marketing research field developed and then describes the structure of the marketing research industry. Our focus is on recent events. Students of marketing research who are acquainted with its history, and the trends that impact the structure of the industry, have a better grasp generally of how the industry has evolved—its corporate structures, offerings, and performance—and therefore better understand its challenges today.

The history of marketing research can be divided into roughly four periods: early history, emergence of the field from the Industrial Revolution to 1925, improvement in poll and survey methodology (1925–1960), and the Information Revolution (1960–present). From a brief look at the first three periods, it is apparent that early marketing research occurred before the twentieth century and was grounded in personal relationships between business owners and their customers as the information source for understanding needs and demand. In the industrial period, the producer was distanced from the individual consumer, and marketing research was primarily market analysis and distribution research. This period had notable academic pioneers and the creation of commercial research departments.

> **The first three periods are developed in greater detail on the text DVD.** In the subsequent period of polling and research methods improvement (1925–1960), survey research expanded, sampling improved, specifications for fieldwork were written, and the polling industry was born. During the 1940s, progress was made in methodology and systematic data analysis. The media developed along with rapid growth of communications technology. The latter established the mechanisms for mass marketing. Postwar years ushered in a time of prosperity, with significant expansion of marketing research expenditures and an interest in advertising and consumer (motivational) research. As marketing research entered the 1960s, the first high-speed computers came into use and changed the industry forever. Thus, we will start a more in-depth analysis with this period.

> Information Revolutionizes the Industry

Although the Information Revolution (roughly 1960–present) began technically with the invention of the computer in the late 1940s, noted management author Peter Drucker argues that the Information Revolution has only transformed processes that were already here and that the real impact has not yet been felt in the form of revolutionizing "information."[1] In business and government, for example, the way decision making occurs has changed little. But the amount of information available to make decisions, conduct research, and create strategy has benefited vastly from technology, which has routinized traditional processes in a myriad of ways.

With the potential to alter profoundly the structure of industries and markets, the Internet emerged as a major global distribution channel for goods and services. Despite the bursting bubble of dot-coms, the Information Revolution is not dead, at least not in a historical sense:

> It took automobiles from about 1890 to the 1940s—half a century of development—to reach amenity. Needed were paved roads, reliable brakes, ignition systems, safe tires, and a thousand other things. The information revolution is not radically different from previous revolutions. The Internet has had its boom and crash, and there is no reason to suppose that history will be negated: full use of the technology will arrive eventually. It always has. But this will require that the technology become workable for the user, and that businesses re-architect themselves to make use of it. This will happen gradually during the next 10 to 20 years as the missing components of the technology's use structure are put in place.[2]

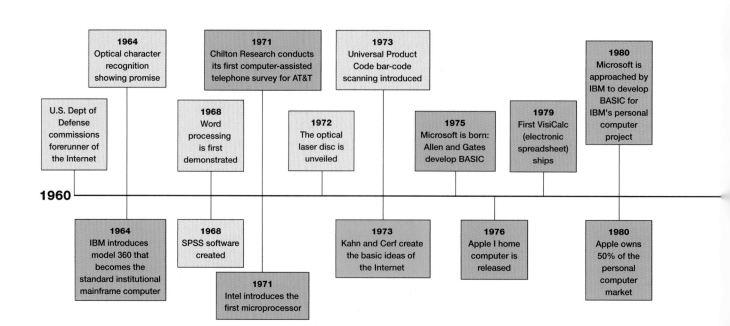

In the last 40 years (see the timeline below) we have shifted to a technology-based society. In 1946, the ENIAC computer weighed 30 tons, had 17,468 vacuum tubes, and occupied a space as large as a railroad boxcar.[3] Today, many handheld calculators have equivalent computing power for a few dollars. Today most people have a PDA, mobile, or desktop computer with more computing power than thought possible just a few years ago. Truly, the computer helps manage knowledge as the amount of information expands exponentially. But information technology transforms itself every 10 years, so the ways we have chosen to define the Information Revolution—large-scale computers, software development, PCs, Web-based interconnection—will likely be eclipsed by something new.

Data Collection Accelerates[4]

During this technology-rich era, marketing researchers have profited from new ways of speeding up data entry. Originally, keyboarding was the means for researchers to create a data file immediately and store it in a minimal space on a variety of media. Statistical packages like Minitab, SAS, and SPSS (often associated with their vast data analysis capabilities) now include full-screen editors, where an entire data file can be edited or browsed. The same software makes accessing data from databases, spreadsheets, data warehouses, or data marts comparatively effortless. For large projects, database programs serve as valuable data entry devices. These programs allow users to define data fields and link files so that storage, retrieval, and updating are simplified. Other entry devices include PC image scanners, with optical character recognition programs that transfer printed text into files. Optical scanning readers can process over 8,000 forms per hour and have been adopted by designers for data entry and preprocessing. Optical mark recognition (OMR) uses a spreadsheet-style interface to read and process user-created forms.

Other advances include direct-response entry, of which touch screens, voice recognition and response systems, and telephone keypads are some examples. Field interviewers use portable computers or electronic notebooks with a built-in communications modem or cellular link, sending files directly to another computer in the field or to a remote site. Bar code technology is used to simplify the interviewer's role as a data recorder. The interviewer passes a bar code wand over the appropriate codes and data are recorded in a small, lightweight unit for translation later. In the large-scale processing project Census 2000, the Census Data Capture Center used bar codes to identify residents. Point-of-sale terminals and scanners aid electronic data collection for numerous marketing objectives.

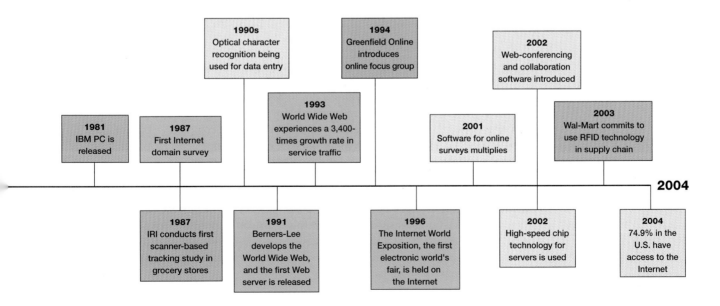

>**pic**profile

Many research companies offer proprietary services for different types of research. This ad is for an Internet-based concept testing methodology called Conceptor™ by Decision Analyst, Inc. A representative sample of 150 consumers is selected from Decision Analyst's Internet panel and invited to the company's encrypted Web server to view the new product concept. Each participant completes a battery of questions and diagnostic ratings. From the results, the concept's SuccessScore® is calculated using a mathematical model that factors in trial interest, purchase intent, expected frequency of purchase, uniqueness, pricing reactions, perceptions of value, and category rating. www.decisionanalyst.com

The novelty and convenience of communicating by computer led researchers to cyberspace in search of abundant sources of data. Computer-*assisted* telephone interviewing (CATI) is used in research organizations throughout the world. CATI works with a software-based telephone number management system to select numbers, dial the sample, and enter responses. Unlike CATI, there is no interviewer with the computer-*administered* telephone survey. A computer calls the phone number, conducts the interview, places data into a file for later tabulation, and terminates the contact. The questions are voice-synthesized, and the participant's answer and computer timing trigger continuation or disconnect.

Computer-delivered self-administered questionnaires use organizational intranets, the Internet, or online services to reach their participants. Participants may be targeted (as when an online e-business sends an e-mail to a registered e-purchaser to participate in a survey) or self-selecting (as when a computer screen pop-up window offers a survey to an individual who clicks on a particular Web site or when a potential participant responds to an inquiry looking for participants).

The computer-delivered surveys are crafted conventionally or developed with computer-aided research design (CARD) software that enables the user to design the questionnaire interactively. Such a survey may use preliminary notification via e-mail, and the return mechanism is usually the click of a mouse or a single keystroke. Computer technology also makes color and visually appealing designs possible within a survey—including photographs and video clips. The delivery of monetary and other incentives has been simplified with the use of e-currencies.

In exploratory research, the use of e-mail, Web sites, Usenet newsgroups, or an Internet chat room approximates group dynamics. Online focus groups make it possible to do "live" voice chats online, reducing or eliminating the cost associated with telephone focus groups. Videoconferencing focus groups also provide significant savings. Traditional focus groups and those using newer technologies employ video and audio recording for analysis of the interview. The recorded results are summarized using software programs that analyze the content of the written response.

Finally, geographic information systems (GISs), systems of hardware and software for spatially referenced data, are an outgrowth of technological advances. A marketing researcher might use a GIS to answer questions about sales targeting, health care or hospital network placement, real estate site selection, or customer locations. We discuss these applications for the market researcher and other new developments throughout this book.

Marketing Information Management

Previously, companies used four methods to obtain marketing information: marketing research projects, marketing intelligence, marketing information systems, and decision support systems. Each is used to make better decisions and reduce risk. The late 1970s and early 1980s saw the development and adoption of marketing information systems (MISs) and decision support systems (DSSs). The technologies of the information revolution facilitated accumulation of a vast knowledge base of customer behavior. According to MIS pioneers at Quaker Oats, Procter & Gamble, Citibank, Borden, Colgate-Palmolive, and Maytag, the competitive advantage belongs to the marketing organizations best able to exploit these technologies and, in the process, to bring value to their customers.[5] Several characteristics of the information value chain are:

> **We defined marketing intelligence systems and marketing decision support systems in Chapter 1.**

- *Data collection and transmission.* Computers and telecommunications lowered the costs of data collection, drastically changing knowledge about consumers both at store and household levels.

- *Data management.* The quantity of collected raw data overwhelms users, necessitating a means to manage it. Early efforts to provide a flow of information to marketers used MIS systems. As time passed, the challenge of database management from an MIS perspective included removing obstacles like resistance to use, reluctance of managers to disclose fully their information needs and decision criteria, costs of single-user report generation, system design time, slow adaptation to changing organization structures, and decision relevance (standard versus tailored reports).

- *Decision support systems.* A DSS integrates data management techniques, models, and analytical tools to support decision making. Such systems allow users to dialogue or interact with them.

- *Models.* Enormous quantities of marketing research data are reduced to relatively straightforward equations with statistical models. Expert systems, an outgrowth of artificial intelligence, and data mining entered the 21st century as important tools for marketing research. Advanced analytical tools are available to answer a variety of research questions. Traditional topics open to modeling—market share, price elasticity, and the cannibalization of one product's sales by the introduction of another product, to name a few—create decision support models that reflect the behavior of individuals, households, and industries.

> **We discuss data mining and its applications in Chapter 10.**

- *Data interpretation.* While routine MIS reports are useful for well-structured problems and those amenable to a standardized set of procedures, data must be more than timely and standardized; it must be meaningful to the user. Programs that combine modeling and decision support systems evolved in the latter part of the 20th century to provide the most utility to users. Common features now recognizable in data interpretation include menu-driven interfaces, accommodation of real-time requests, ability to model ill-defined problems, graphic representation tools and displays, and the means to adapt to different market environments.

> How the Industry Works

The picture of the marketing research industry is one of extremes. Very large suppliers account for the largest portion of the sales in the industry, but smaller firms and one-person shops dominate when you look at the number of research firms. Exhibit 2-1 provides an overview of the suppliers within the research industry.

> 66 For a long time, research companies have offered efficient collection of data, as well as timely and accurate reporting as their primary value propositions to clients. However, clients no longer view operational excellence as a value proposition, but rather as a basic expectation. 99
>
> *Rick Garlick*
> *Maritz Research*

For budget, equipment, facilities, and expertise reasons, the trend in the industry is clearly not to staff large internal research departments. In poor economic times, many firms eliminate their internal research operations altogether, feeling that such services are expendable or are readily available from external suppliers. In some ways the growth in prominence of the role of information technology manager or officer in many companies has forced the marketing researcher to an even more subordinate staff role. Regardless, the two functions—marketing research and information technology management—have little directly to do with one another.

>**Exhibit 2-1** Who Conducts Marketing Research?

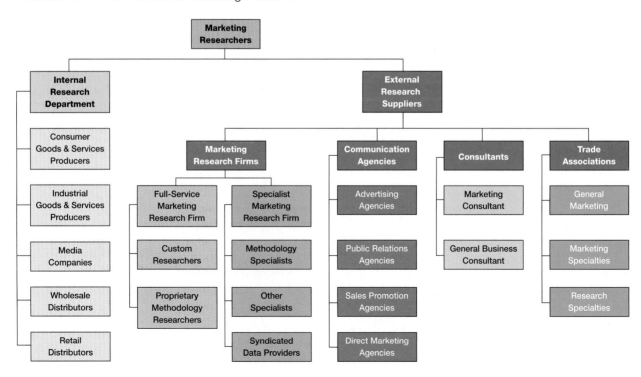

For Eastman Kodak, having a world-class marketing research department meant completely restructuring the department and redefining the department's responsibilities. Restructuring created three focus specialties within the department: performance management (research to help deliver long-term success and enhance the reliability of demand forecasting for products and services), research innovation, and consumer insights (research on consumer trends and motivations, as well as translation of the data into product and service ideas for commercial testing). Now researchers are judged not only on how data are collected but on how well the research factors into marketing decisions. The restructured marketing research function was tested in launching the new Kodak Plus Digital. Within its first year, this one-time-use camera that provides digital pictures on CD generated sales of $80 million. www.kodak.com

Internal Research Suppliers[6]

As we discussed in Chapter 1, not all marketers rely on research to make decisions. Only those firms that do are likely to have an internal research department or individual who coordinates marketing research initiatives. All types of research-based decision makers have internal research operations, but the structure and scope of these operations is as diverse as the products, services, and markets that they research. They range from one-person operations, where the individual primarily coordinates the hiring of external research suppliers, to small-staffed operations that do some survey or qualitative studies, to large-staffed divisions that more closely approximate the structures of research companies.

Historically, in the 1960s, as marketing research entered a new era of quantification and respectability, the number of firms with internal research departments grew. The marketing research function gained acceptance as a formal part of the organization. But growth and recognition did not always accord corporate respectability. When the decade of the 1970s arrived, researchers were known as the marketing research department, worked for the marketing function, and reported to marketing executives. Their freedom was constrained by brand managers and a rather narrow definition of their role—which primarily involved operating as order takers and reacting to the demand for projects and reports.

In the 1980s, marketing researchers experienced an identity crisis of sorts. Senior management's perception of the order taker remained. Consultants were asked frequently to assist the organization, and the sales function started to encroach on marketing's turf. Executives questioned the marketing research department's strategic role. Departments were downsized and restructured. The credibility crisis prompted the Advertising Research Foundation (ARF) to convene the first industrywide Leaders Forum in 1988.

During the 1990s, management wanted everything cheaper, faster, and with fewer people. Information overload and a crisis mode of operation were a daily occurrence. Consultants again addressed strategic issues. The Research Industry Leader's Forum (sponsored by ARF, AMA, CASRO, and MRA) was officially created in 1992 to address these problems. The results of an ARF study in 1999 indicated that "according to the CEOs surveyed,

Television programs, like *CourtTV,* are expected to know the composition of their viewing audiences. The media buyer relies on the accuracy of this information for recommending media buys to advertising clients. Most such information comes from audited audience data. Nielsen Media Research provides such services for TV programs in 40 countries, while Audit Bureau of Circulations provides a similar service for magazines. **www.nielsenmedia.com**

the accuracy and actionability of the information provided by research was thought to be low." [7]

The advent of the 21st century brought encouraging signs. Researchers made substantial strides expanding the scope of the field. Research proceeded in advertising and media, brand evaluation and choice, buyer and consumer behavior, channels of distribution, new products, pricing, sales force analysis, strategy and planning, measurement and scaling methods, and statistical methods. In a 2001 quantitative study conducted with the aid of the Cambridge Group, ARF sought to identify ways to redefine the research function, thereby making it more relevant to senior management. The opinions of CEOs, senior-level marketers, and market researchers at over 100 Fortune 500 companies were solicited to discover the core competencies possessed by an ideal management decision support function and to learn which decisions and activities were most important for marketing research support. The results from executives revealed a generally positive rating for marketing research, although a gap existed between the perceptions of researchers and those of senior-level marketers and CEOs (who viewed the importance of certain core competencies differently). Based on the executives' responses, marketing research began to expand into such areas as providing actionable insights, reducing risk in marketplace actions, and improving return on investment.[8] This is consistent with marketing scholar Philip Kotler's contention that as marketing costs rise, CEOs and board members demand greater accountability for marketing decisions and expenditures.[9]

External Research Suppliers

Within the category "marketing research specialists," more than 2,000 research firms operate in the United States.[10]

Marketing Research Companies

Full-Service Firms

Full-service marketing researchers include some of the largest marketing research firms in the world and some of the smallest. Exhibit 2-2 identifies some of the largest firms. Full-service firms are often involved in research planning for their clients from the moment of discovery of the management dilemma or, at the very least, from the definition of the management question. Such firms usually have expertise in both quantitative and qualitative methodologies, and they often have at their disposal multifaceted facilities capable of serving a wide variety of research designs, including both fieldwork and laboratory operations. Some are capable of working in worldwide venues, while others offer their services to only one industry or one geographic region. While these firms may have one or more areas of noteworthy expertise, they are truly multidimensional in terms of both research planning and execution. In a research environment where clients increasingly demand marketing insights, not just research reporting, these firms are often a combination of research and consulting operations. NFO WorldGroup is an example of a full-service marketing research firm. It describes itself as "marketing minds who specialize in research."[11] Taylor Nelson Sofres Intersearch is another full-service firm. It describes its approach as, "We combine category knowledge with research expertise in our cross-functional research teams."[12]

full-service marketing researcher a firm with both quantitative and qualitative methodology expertise that conducts all phases of research from planning to insight development.

Custom Researchers

Such phrases as "ad hoc research" or "custom-designed research" are often used to describe custom full-service marketing research firms. A **custom researcher** crafts a research design unique to the marketing decision maker's dilemma. In essence, such research firms start each project from ground zero. This does not mean, however, that they fail to apply lessons learned from previous projects. What is implied is that such firms do not assume that a given methodology is appropriate for each client's research, even if the research to be done is in an arena in which the research firm has considerable expertise, for example, customer satisfaction or copy testing or product evaluation research. Each project starts with a blank page. While a custom researcher might not always be a full-service research firm, by definition, a full-service marketing researcher would always fit into the custom research category. Taylor Nelson Sofres Intersearch (TNS) describes its custom research operations this way: "[Our custom research capability] allows us to design approaches that truly meet [the client's] needs if proprietary research solutions do not."[13]

custom researcher crafts a research design unique to the marketing decision maker's dilemma.

Proprietary Methodology Researchers

A **proprietary methodology** is a research program or technique that is owned by a single firm. It may be a slight twist on an established methodology or may be a method that is truly distinct to that firm. Firms often brand these methodologies to keep them distinct in the minds of prospective clients, as ACNielsen did with its Homescan® syndicated panel. As was implied by the above quote from TNS, some full-service researchers have developed proprietary methodologies that they apply across industries or across geographic demarcations. Firms that have developed such methodologies are often somewhat insulated from price competition. Without proprietary methodologies, all research firms essentially offer the same research services—although we accept that some perform such services with far more skill and expertise than others. Proprietary methodologies often grow from significant expertise in a given methodology or a given industry, developed over many years and thousands of client projects.

proprietary methodology a research program or technique that is owned by a single firm.

With the development of its customer engagement methodology, The Gallup Organization has reinvented itself using the proprietary research model, moving from public opinion

>**Exhibit 2-2** Some of the World's Largest and Best-Known Marketing Research Firms

Organization	Type of Research	Research Revenues, 2002*	
		United States (millions)	Worldwide (millions)
VNU Inc. www.vnu.com	A global leader in market research, providing measurement and analysis of marketplace dynamics and consumer behavior, as well as audience measurement for several leading brands, including ACNielsen market data	$1,300.0	$2,400.0
IMS Health Inc. imshealth.com	Provides information solutions to the pharmaceutical and health care industries	469.0	1,171.0
Information Resources Inc. www.infores.com	Provides UPC scanner-based business solutions to the consumer packaged goods industry	420.3	555.9
The Kantar Group www.kantargroup.com	Provides worldwide media research and measurement for media owners, agencies, and advertisers	299.1	962.3
Westat Inc. www.westat.com	Provides research to agencies of the U.S. government, as well as businesses, foundations, and state and local governments	285.8	285.8
Arbitron Inc. www.arbitron.com	Provides information services used to develop the local marketing strategies of the electronic media and their advertisers and agencies	219.6	227.5
NOP World US www.nopworld.com	Provides both custom and syndicated research, as well as research-based consulting, and analytic customer relationship management (CRM) services around the world; noted for its RoperASW and MediaMark divisions, with specialties in media audience measurement	206.6	224.1
NFO WorldGroup www.nfow.com	Provides results-oriented insights so that clients may develop stronger brands and market more successful products and services	163.0	452.9
Synovate (formerly Market Facts, Inc.) www.synovate.com	Provides global marketing research and consulting to businesses, governments, and associations	156.2	189.7
Taylor Nelson Sofres USA www.tnsofres.com	Provides custom research, omnibus studies, attitudinal polling, and drug sample monitoring in a variety of industries	150.5	166.9
Maritz Research www.maritzresearch.com	Provides large-scale, custom-designed research studies that produce critical marketing information in the areas of customer choice, customer experience, and customer loyalty	127.1	181.7
Ipsos www.ipsos.com	Explores market potential and market trends, tests products and advertising, studies audiences and their perceptions of various media, and measures public opinion trends around the globe	112.9	204.3

(continued)

>**Exhibit 2-2** Some of the World's Largest and Best-Known Marketing Research Firms *(concluded)*

Organization	Type of Research	Research Revenues, 2002* United States (millions)	Worldwide (millions)
J.D. Power and Associates jdpa.com	Conducts independent surveys of customer satisfaction, quality, and buyer behavior; best known for its marketing information for the automotive and hospitality industries	$ 109.3	$ 128.0
Opinion Research Corp. www.opinionresearch.com	Provides a combination of fact-based intelligence, strategic advisory services, and information technology to give clients a richer understanding of their customers and other constituencies to measure their actions and progress; does marketing and social issue research in more than 100 countries	91.4	133.6
The NPD Group Inc. www.npd.com	Provides tracking studies (comprehensive overview of product movement and consumer behavior) in numerous industries, including apparel, fashion, beauty, home, and electronics	88.7	101.7
Harris Interactive Inc. www.harrisinteractive.com	A worldwide market research and consulting firm, best known for *The Harris Poll* and for its pioneering use of the Internet to conduct scientifically accurate market research	64.9	75.4
C&R Research Service Inc. www.crresearch.com	Provides qualitative and ethnographic studies; known for its KidsEyez panel and research with Latino market segments	43.6	43.6
Wirthlin Worldwide www.wirthlin.com	Specializes in research used to develop communication and marketing strategy, including image and reputation enhancement, brand equity and positioning, and political campaign strategy; four-time winner of the David Ogilvy Research Award	39.6	46.8
Burke Inc. www.burke.com	Provides full-service research and consulting services in customer satisfaction, quality, and employee engagement; its Burke Institute provides continuing education for those in the research industry	34.3	45.5
Total		$4,381.9	$7,596.4
Total Top 50		5,033.1	8,318.2
All other (130 CASRO companies not included in the top 50)[†]		510.6	563.1
Total (180 companies)[‡]		$5,543.7	$8,881.3

*U.S. and worldwide and non-U.S. revenues that include nonresearch activities for some companies are significantly higher. This information is given in the individual company profiles.
[†]Rate of growth from year to year has been adjusted so as not to include revenue or losses from acquisitions or divestitures. See company profiles for example.
[‡]Total revenues of top 50 firms plus 130 survey research firms—beyond those in the top 50—that provide financial information, on a confidential basis, to the Council of American Surveys Research Organizations (CASRO).
Source: Data were developed from the companies' Web sites and from "Honomichl Top 50," *Marketing News* (American Marketing Association), June 9, 2003 (http://data.ama.org/publications/honomichl/display2.php).

>**snap**shot

Direct-to-Consumer Ads under Heavy Fire

Direct-to-consumer (D-to-C) pharmaceutical ads have drawn a lot of criticism since 1997 FDA regulations permitted such tactics. Proponents of legislation to disallow such practices fear such ads "unfairly influence important health care decisions" by causing patients to pressure doctors and thus encouraging doctors to prescribe unnecessary medications. The chairman of the American Medical Association believes such advertising may create an adversarial relationship between doctor and patient. He wants to know if such ads "improve the quality of care enough to make it worth the increased costs of the medicines being advertised." One democratic legislator believes "taxpayers should not have to subsidize excessive advertising that leads to higher prices at the pharmacy counter."

Ipsos-NPD tracks this issue for the pharmaceutical industry with its monthly PharmTrends® panel comprising 16,000 U.S. households. Panel members are measured for ad recall, pre-

scriptions filled, physician recommendations for over-the-counter (OTC) products, and OTC products purchased, as well as condition being treated. Its findings reveal that advertising "has encouraged higher levels of script fulfillment per year among consumers who reported that they were aware of advertising." Additionally, such advertising is credited with reminding patients to refill prescriptions. In its February InstaVue omnibus mail survey of 26,000 adults, 47 percent had seen pharmaceutical advertising in the past year, 25 percent indicated D-to-C ads encouraged them to call/visit their doctor to discuss the pharmaceutical advertised, and 15 percent reported asking for the specific drug advertised. Does this research confirm or refute that pharmaceutical ads undermine quality of care?

www.ipsos-npd.com

---

pollster and custom researcher to research-based consulting firm. While Gallup is capable of doing and still does custom research, it captures a significant portion of its revenue from management consulting based on proprietary methodologies. One of its proprietary methodologies is called Q12. This survey methodology uses 12 scaled questions to measure customer engagement. Gallup uses these same questions with all clients, so Q12 serves as a benchmark diagnostic for its subsequent consulting work. Gallup has copyrighted its questions and the survey instrument that incorporates them to guarantee that its intellectual property remains protected. Having a proprietary research methodology allows Gallup to charge its clients significant premiums for its research and consulting services.[14]

specialty marketing researcher establishes expertise in one or a few research methodologies.

Specialty Marketing Research Firms   **Specialty marketing researchers** represent the largest number of research firms and tend to dominate the small research firms operated by a single researcher or a very small staff. These firms may establish a specialty in one or several different arenas:

- *Methodology.* The firms may conduct only one type of research (for example, survey research, customer satisfaction research, ad copy testing, packaging evaluation, focus groups, retail mystery shopping, or retail design research).
- *Process.* The firms usually contribute to only a portion of the research process (for example, sample recruiting, telephone interviewing, or fielding a Web survey).
- *Industry.* The firms become experts in one or a few industries (for example, pharmaceutical research or entertainment research or telecommunications research).
- *Participant group.* The firms become experts in a particular participant group (for example, Latino-Americans, or children, or doctors, or country club golfers).
- *Geographic region.* The firms may operate in only one region of a country—as is true for many mystery shopping firms—or a single country or group of countries.

Methodology Specialists   A methodology specialist focuses its services on a particular research methodology. Usually the specialization is motivated by a skill set necessary to do the research or by specialized facilities or equipment needed to do the research.

>**snap**shot

Yahoo!: Banner Ads Move CPG

Product managers of consumer packaged goods (CPG) are facing increasing pressure for strong return-on-investment metrics for media buys, yet they still heavily rely on advertising recall or click stream analysis. "The thinking is that no one goes online to search out information on paper towels. But that doesn't mean that Internet ads can't significantly lift in-store sales," explained Ken Mallon, Yahoo's director of insights products. What was needed were new metrics that could showcase Internet ads' targeting efficiency and sales responsiveness. Yahoo teamed its extensive database of Internet visitors with the ACNielsen Homescan™ panel (126,000 global households that provide extensive demographic and lifestyle data and allow their purchases to be tracked). What resulted is *Yahoo!® Consumer Direct Powered by ACNielsen*. More than 40 percent of active Internet users use broadband or high-speed Internet access. This enables such households to be tested for exposure to standard media banner ads and also to the more interactive *rich-media* ads that are increasing on the Internet. For each advertiser, *Consumer Direct* tracks two metrics on each test group: effectiveness of ad targeting (Are the visitors being exposed to the ads most likely to purchase?) and persuasiveness of the advertising (What per-

centage of households exposed to the advertising actually purchase the advertised product?). Yahoo then compares this information to that on a group not exposed to the banner ads. Yahoo, with the assistance of Dynamic Logic, also provides advertisers with five more metrics critical for CPG success: ad awareness, brand awareness, brand favorability, message association with advertiser, and purchase intent.

"Using the browsing patterns of high-purchase households in the *Consumer Direct* research to model behavior, we then apply this knowledge to the Yahoo! database to identify 10 million households that exhibit similar browsing behavior," explained Mallon. These Yahoo visitors see ads to which they are most likely to respond. Every *Consumer Direct* CPG client has experienced sales lift.

www.yahoo.com; www.acnielsen.com; www.dynamiclogic.com

Learn more about this research by reading the case on your text DVD: "Yahoo!®: Consumer Direct Marries Purchase Metrics to Banner Ads."

One large group in this category includes firms that specialize in conducting focus groups. These firms not only offer the trained moderators who manage the small-group discussions, many of whom hold a Ph.D. in psychology, but also provide the sample screening procedures, the specially designed facilities, and the technical communications equipment for making this qualitative research as insightful as possible.

Another distinct specialty comprises firms doing observation studies. These researchers are often found studying retail shoppers, tracing their footsteps or recording the amount of time a shopper spends reading labels or interacting with displays. Envirosell and Design Forum both do retail observation studies.

Ethnography is a type of study that uses both observation and communication methodologies. The Context-Based Research Group describes itself as "an ethnographic research and consulting firm." It combines the backgrounds and skills of cultural anthropologists (more than 3,000 around the world) with the communications and business strategy of marketing experts to serve a diverse client base, including retailers, software manufacturers, food manufacturers, hotels, pharmaceutical companies, and even proponents of social causes.[15]

Firms providing Web page optimization research and Web performance metrics are an emerging group of methodology specialists. Such firms as Yahoo!, NetIQ (with WebTrends), and NetConversions are examples of methodology specialists in metrics related to Web content development.

Other Specialty Research Suppliers   The group of specialty research suppliers assist other research firms to complete projects. One large group in this category is sampling specialists. These firms provide the screening and recruiting of probability samples for a wide range of survey studies, as well as studies employing in-depth interviews, laboratory and in-home product testing, laboratory experiments, home ethnographies, and so on. These specialists usually are recruited by custom researchers or other specialty marketing researchers when help is needed in a large study, when a study needs to be completed quickly, or when special, difficult-to-recruit participants are needed. Survey Sampling Inc. is one of the largest suppliers of samples for telephone, mail, and online surveys and also offers specialty samples for industrial and health care research.[16] Greenfield Online specializes in assisting research firms by providing online samples that fulfill a variety of characteristics. Greenfield claims to have compiled the largest panel of opt-in participants in the online community. It has also partnered with Microsoft to build recruited online samples drawn from MSN.com membership.[17]

Specialty research suppliers may also specialize in a subset of a methodology specialty. For example, numerous firms offer focus group moderators but not the focus group facilities. Others provide the recruiting of focus group participants and the facilities but not the moderators.

Specialty research suppliers are too numerous to list here, but firms specialize in every subset of the research process, including Internet survey design and management, intercept interviewing in shopping malls, mechanically recorded observation studies, data entry, computer-assisted personal interviewing (CAPI), survey instrument design, and data description and summarization, to name a few. With the increase of online research, many researchers—especially internal research departments and small custom research firms—want to offer this methodology but do not have the capability to field such a study themselves. Qualtrics Labs, with its array of software and service products (surveypro.com for designing and fielding simple surveys, QuestionPro.com for more complex surveys, PerfectSurveys.com for intranet and e-mail surveys) promises researchers without online capabilities the ability to deliver professional-quality online survey results.[18] Training Technologies, Inc., also designs, fields, tracks, and posts survey results for those researchers without the necessary technical capabilities.[19]

Syndicated Data Providers

syndicated data provider
tracks the change of one or more measures over time, usually in a given industry.

Syndicated Data Providers   When marketers want comparative performance and opinion data, pitting themselves against their competitors in sales, market share, and share of voice, they turn to researchers that are syndicated data providers. For a substantial fee, often millions of dollars per year, marketers subscribe to receive the periodic data as well as the interpretation of these data. A **syndicated data provider** tracks the change of one or more measures over time, usually in a given industry. Such firms may track product movements through various retail outlets and wholesale environments. The tracking of sales performance measures during promotional events like coupon drops, distribution of product samples, special events, and advertising is often the key to successful strategic marketing planning. These research firms are also responsible for providing marketing decision makers with measures of price elasticity. In consumer packaged goods marketing, the first research company to provide scanner-based tracking through grocery outlets was Information Resources Inc. (IRI), in 1987.[20] Other firms providing syndicated research are noted in Exhibit 2-3.

Each syndicated data provider determines the frequency of data collection and reporting based on the needs of the members in the syndicate. While some studies provide data monthly or weekly, not all such studies are done as frequently as sales tracking studies. Some syndicated data are collected only once per year or once every few years. Other syndicated data are collected several times per year during designated collection periods. One example is the tracking of media consumption. Nielsen Media Research is well known for its *People Meter* research that mechanically records and then reveals the viewing habits of a panel of television watchers. Data are collected four times per year during so-called sweep weeks. These are periods of time when the TV networks often substitute special programming for their regular shows, thus increasing viewership. Advertising rates for the whole season of advertising slots are determined by a show's audience size and composition during sweep week. Arbitron collects similar data on radio listening habits. Typically the firm subscribing to the syndicate has full access to its data and the composite data, but not to an individual competitor's data.

>**Exhibit 2-3** Some Syndicated Data Providers

Company	Syndicated Service	What It Measures
ACNielsen www.acnielsen.com	Scantrack	Provides sales tracking across grocery, drug, and mass merchandisers
	Homescan	Provides consumer panel service for tracking retail purchases and motivations
Yahoo! and ACNielsen www.yahoo.com	Internet Confidence Index	Measures (quarterly) the confidence levels in Internet products and services.
Scarborough Research (a service of Arbitron, Inc., and VNU) www.scarborough.com		Provides a syndicated study to print and electronic media, new media companies, outdoor media, sports teams and leagues, agencies, advertisers, and Yellow Pages on local, regional, and national levels—including local market shopping patterns, demographics, media usage, and lifestyle activities.
Millward Brown www.millwardbrown.com	IntelliQuest www.intelliquest.com	Provides studies enabling clients to understand and improve the position of their technology, brands, products, media, or channels.
Information Resources www.infores.com	BehaviorScan	Collects store tracking data used with consumer panel data to track advertising influence in consumer packaged goods.
Nielsen Media Research www.nielsenmedia.com	National People Meter	Provides audience estimates for all national program sources, including broadcast networks, cable networks, Spanish-language networks, and national syndicators.
NOP World www.nopworld.com	Starch Ad Readership Studies	Provides raw readership scores collected via individual depth interview; records the percent of readers who saw the ad and read the copy. The ad is ranked not only against other ads in the issue but also against other ads in its product category over the last two years.
CSA TMO www.csa-fr.com	OPERBAC	Provides continuous tracking of banking insurance and credit purchases in European markets.
DoubleClick www.doubleclick.com	Diameter	Provides online audience measurement services for Web publishers, advertisers, and agencies.
Nielsen//NetRatings www.nielsen-netratings.com		Measures audience data using actual click-by-click Internet user behavior measured through a comprehensive real-time meter installed on individual computers worldwide (home and work).
Taylor Nelson Sofres Intersearch www.tns-i.com	Global eCommerce	Measures e-commerce activity in 27 countries, providing insights into 37 marketplaces via interviews.
		Provides a global customer service delivery and satisfaction benchmark for the hotel and hospitality industry.
J.D. Power Associates www.jdpower.com	PowerReport, PowerGram, etc.	Publishes in-depth analytical reports on automotive, travel, health, and other industries.
MediaMark www.mediamark.com		Supplies multimedia audience research to magazines, television, radio, Internet, and other media, leading national advertisers, and over 450 advertising agencies, including 90 of 100 agencies in the U.S.
Simmons (SMRB) www.smrb.com	National	Provides telephone research that covers important markets critical to advertisers, agencies and media alike—from Kids to Teens, Adults and Hispanics, to Households. 20,000 adults 18+

Sources: This table was constructed from descriptions published on each company's Web site.

Omnibus Researchers   Sometimes the marketing decision maker needs the answer to one or a few questions to make a quick tactical decision, such as when it faces a crisis caused by a product recall. Within the world of survey research, several research firms provide such a service, some even with a 24- to 48-hour turnaround. Exhibit 2-4 offers some examples. An **omnibus researcher** fields research studies, often by survey, at regular, predetermined intervals. An **omnibus study** combines one or a few questions from several marketing decision makers who need information from the same population. Typically, the marketer pays by the number of questions, usually between $700 and $1,500 per question. Many omnibus studies are still done by phone, but as online participants increasingly mirror the general population, an increasing number are being offered via the Internet. NOP World (NOP) uses a representative sample of 1,000 adults for its Telebus study.[21] NOP contacts participants during the weekend and provides the decision maker with feedback on Monday morning. For a firm facing a public relations crisis, the quick turnaround is invaluable, and the data are a fraction of the cost of a custom-designed study. NOP does omnibus studies with automobile drivers, parents, youth, and other population segments in Great Britain, using telephone and online surveys as well as face-to-face interviews. Medical Marketing Research Inc. conducts omnibus studies with physicians in all the medical specialties, while TNS offers the PhoneBus survey, interviewing 1,000 to 2,000 participants, twice per week, with results within four days.[22]

omnibus researcher fields research studies, often by survey, at regular, predetermined intervals.

omnibus study combines one or a few questions from several marketing decision makers who need information from the same population.

Communication Agencies

It is difficult for an advertising agency to recommend advertising in a particular medium (for example, television) or on a particular program (for example, *Survivor* or *CSI*) without fully understanding the demographics and lifestyles of the viewing audiences of each show. This explains why advertising, public relations, sales promotion, and direct marketing agencies are heavy users of syndicated research data, especially from media industry suppliers. It is even more difficult to develop a creative strategy without research on target

>**Exhibit 2-4** Some Omnibus Studies

Company	Sample Size	Sample Characteristics	Turnaround (from question to delivery)	Details
Lightspeed Research *Online Omnibus* www.lightspeedresearch.com	2,000	Adults	8 days	No more than 5 questions, with overall survey size = 15–20 questions; $750 per question
Business Advantage *Online Omnibus* www.bmrb.co.uk	500	CAD/CAM users; Great Britain	NA	£695
JupiterDirect Research *Online Omnibus* www.jupiterdirect.com	Up to 80,000	IT/IS experts	NA	$1,995 for up to 5 questions
TNSIntersearchNCompass™ *International Phone Omnibus* www.tns-i.com	—	Adults, any combination drawn from 80 countries	2 weeks	
Market Facts *TeenNation™ Online Omnibus* www.marketfacts.com	500	12- to 17-year-olds	1 week	$1,500 per question
Market Facts *Data Gage™ Mail Omnibus* www.marketfacts.com	5,000 up to 150,000 (increments of 5,000)	Panel participants	2 weeks	Monthly, questions to fill 3½ × 8½ card
ICM *Phone Omnibus (RDD)* www.icmresearch.co.uk	1,000	Persons 16 or 18 years old or older	3 days	Midweek and weekend; £400 per question, £800 for each free response question
AcuPoll Worldwide *Name testing; ad effectiveness omnibus* www.acupoll.com	—	Female heads of household, aged 18 and older	topline summary: 48 hours, full report: 7 days	Several times monthly
NFO WorldGroup *Online Omnibus* www.nfocfgroup.com	1,000	Online Canadians, aged 18 and older	7 days	Up to 6 questions; weekly

audience knowledge, motivations, attitudes, and behavior. So agencies are also voracious consumers and providers of custom and proprietary research. Within communication agency circles, there is some debate on whether a research division within an agency can maintain the objectivity needed to do custom research or whether, with conflicting demands from numerous clients, an internal research operation can be efficient and timely, so clients sometimes request that the research needed by these communication specialists be done by an external supplier.

Some agencies do extensive basic research to identify influences on ad recall and ad wear-out, on ad placement effectiveness, on the effectiveness of various creative approaches (for example, celebrity endorser versus animated product as spokesperson), on the effectiveness of communication strategies (for example, humor, violence, or sexuality in advertising), on the ROI for various media buys, and on the comparative effectiveness of different action stimulants (such as coupons versus samples), to name a few. For direct marketing agencies every single client's project is actually an experiment, with either the offer, the action stimulants, the creative strategy, or even the mailing envelope modified in split-sample tests. All agencies do extensive copy testing as a development tool in building a campaign and effectiveness testing with postplacement recall, knowledge, and behavior measures. Such measures combine custom research with syndicated research to explain why a campaign was a success.

Express Data at $750 per Question

During the controversy surrounding Napster and the music industry in 2000–2002, *American Demographics* wanted to run a story on intellectual property right violations. It turned to Taylor Nelson Sofres Intersearch (TNS) and its Express omnibus study to determine current attitudes on copyright violations. Each week, Wednesday through Sunday, the Express study reaches 1,000 carefully chosen males and females by phone. Express is not a panel; different participants are selected each week. *American Demographics* editor Rebecca Gardyn discussed with Intersearch the topic and the information the magazine wanted to know. "One question they had was whether respondents had appropriated copyrighted material without paying for it," shared Brenda Edwards, vice president of marketing communications for Intersearch.

Express follows the general rule of thumb that a particular client's questions not exceed two minutes of phone time on the omnibus. This translates to approximately six simple, standard questions (not complex multipart, multiscale, or branching questions). "A client receives the data pertaining to their questions from Express on Monday afternoon by 3:00 p.m.," explains Edwards. The data thus gathered provided substantiation for the *American Demographics* article published in September 2000. Eight percent of those responding "knew someone" who had copied computer software; 14 percent knew someone who had copied a prerecorded videocassette; 28 percent knew someone who had copied a prerecorded audiocassette or audio disk; 20 percent knew someone who had downloaded music free of charge from the Internet; and 46 percent knew someone who had photocopied pages from a book or magazine.

www.tns-i.com
www.americandemographics.com

Consultants

Both business and marketing consultants offer a wide range of services at the strategic and tactical levels. All are involved in doing extensive secondary data research for their clients. Such consultants may also be major influencers in research design, both of custom research and the selection of proprietary models. Even when they don't do the actual data collection themselves, they are often involved in the interpretation of results. Depending on the size of the firm, some consultancies conduct both qualitative studies (notably focus groups and expert interviews) and quantitative studies (usually through survey research) on knowledge, attitudes, opinions, and motivations as they seek new opportunities or solutions to their client's problems.

Trade Associations

Generally trade associations have as their purpose to promote, educate, and lobby for their members. While many commission research, not all conduct or supply research services. When they do, they are more likely to conduct basic as opposed to applied research—unless of course they are experiencing difficulty with their own marketing efforts, notably membership and PR.

General Marketing
The American Marketing Association and the Marketing Science Institute (MSI) are two organizations that conduct or sponsor and publish basic research on topics that affect marketing decision making. Every few years, the MSI publishes its list of research priorities. You'll find its top-tier priorities in Exhibit 2-5.

Marketing Specialties
Just as the discipline of marketing is divided into numerous categories, so too are the trade associations that serve those disciplines. Marketing research as a specialty has several trade associations that serve it:

>**Exhibit 2-5** Marketing Science Institute's Research Priorities, 2002–2004*

- *Assessing marketing productivity (return on marketing investment) and marketing metrics*[†]
- *Brands and branding* (including measuring and managing brand equity)
- *Managing customers* (including customer retention, customer expansion, and customer loyalty and engagement)
- *Growth, innovation, and new products* (including improving the metrics on new product introduction and product portfolio management)
- *Understanding customers* (including communication customer knowledge throughout the firm, exploring the customer experience)

*You can learn more about this nonprofit organization and its research priorities at www.msi.org.
[†]Marketing metrics are quantitative measures of marketing effectiveness. Ideally, every marketing decision maker needs a balanced set of measures to accurately assess marketing performance. These include such measures as a lead-to-sales conversion ratio, growth in customer value, customer retention rates, new product introduction-to-success ratios, etc. These measures vary from firm to firm and are based on the company's marketing goals, as well as its strategies and tactics. Other terms used to describe marketing metrics are *benchmarks* or *score-cards*. Marketing research professionals are more involved than ever before in helping firms generate and track these metrics.
Source: "2002–2004 Research Priorities," Marketing Science Institute, accessed July 20, 2004 (http://www.msi.org/msi/rp0204.cfm#Rank).

- *American Association of Public Opinion Researchers* publishes the *Public Opinion Quarterly,* which profiles research "studying the development and role of communication research, current public opinion, as well as the theories and methods underlying opinion research."[23]

- *Council of American Survey Research Organizations (CASRO)* conducts research on trends in survey research and on legislative issues affecting survey research, as well as monitors the standards with which research is conducted.[24]

- *Marketing Research Association (MRA)* provides education and serves as an advocate with appropriate government entities, other associations, and the public; what research it does relates to public opinion on issues of concern for the research industry.[25]

- *World Association of Opinion and Marketing Research Professionals (ESOMAR)* promotes the use of high-quality opinion and marketing research for improving decision making in business and society worldwide. Its primary research is on identifying legislative initiatives that will affect the marketing research industry.[26]

The communication specialties also have trade associations with research in their missions:

- *Advertising Research Foundation (ARF)* conducts or sponsors research to expand the research knowledge base by "developing new research tools, and impactful research studies."[27]

- *Association of National Advertisers (ANA)* conducts and compiles research on advertising trends, agency compensation, trends in corporate advertising, brand ROI, advertising clutter, and legislative and regulatory issues.[28]

- *Sales Research Trust (SRT) Ltd.* facilitates collaboration between practitioners and academics for research in the areas of selling and strategic customer account management.[29]

Media trade associations are also active in research activities:

- *Magazine Publishers of America (MPA)* conducts primary research studies and compiles secondary research reports to prove the effectiveness of magazine advertising. It also conducts a number of surveys that allow member companies to measure their performance against industry averages and to detect trends that may affect their magazine operations.[30]

- *National Association of Broadcasters (NAB)* conducts research in broadcast advertising trends, for example, the switch to digital programming and broadcasting. Through its Committee on Local Radio Audience Measurement and Committee on

Local Television Audience Measurement, it researches new ways to measure local radio listening and local television viewing.[31]

- *Newspaper Association of America (NAA)* compiles statistics on circulation, readership, audience, and advertising trends from its members.[32]
- *Point of Purchase Advertising International (POPAI)* conducts research—in partnership with the Advertising Research Foundation—to create audience metrics for point-of-purchase advertising, similar to those for broadcast and print media.[33]
- *Radio Advertising Bureau (RAB)* conducts research among its membership relating to advertising practices and sensitive issues, for example, the advertising of distilled spirits (hard liquor). It also conducts research on industry-specific buying behavior overall and within specific market segments.[34]

>summary

1 The history of marketing research spans different phases: its early history, the emergence of the field from the Industrial Revolution to 1925, improvement in poll and survey methodology (1925–1960), and the Information Revolution (1960–present). During the Information Revolution, technology's march from mainframe to personal computers fueled an amazing number of subtechnologies adopted by marketing researchers. Statistical packages reinvented the way data are entered, processed, and analyzed. Databases, spreadsheets, data warehouses, and data marts combined with data mining and expert systems to facilitate marketing intelligence, marketing information systems, and decision support systems. The Internet profoundly transformed the way we think about communication with participants, collection of data, and project speed.

2 In the present technology-rich era, electronics and software have transformed all phases of the research process. Computer-delivered questionnaires use organizational intranets, participants' e-mail, Web sites, Usenet newsgroups, or Internet chat rooms. Telecommunication technologies enhance videoconferencing and qualitative research. Devices and their software drivers have generated CATI, CAPI, CARD, and a host of other applications. Optical mechanisms, bar codes, point-of-sale terminals, GISs, and numerous other innovations have transformed the landscape of marketing research. By quickly adopting the technology as it becomes available, marketing researchers have made great strides ex-

panding the scope of the field. Research has proceeded in advertising and media, brand evaluation and choice, buyer and consumer behavior, channels of distribution, new products, pricing, sales force analysis, strategy and planning, measurement and scaling methods, and statistical methods. Practitioners of the art and science continually seek ways to improve professionalism and add value to their organizations, thereby making them more relevant to senior management. Current efforts center on how to make the marketing research function pivotal in setting corporate strategy.

3 The structure of the marketing research industry can be described in terms of internal or external suppliers to the firm. Internal research suppliers range from one-person operations, to small-staffed operations that do some survey or qualitative studies, to large-staffed divisions that more closely approximate the structures of external research companies. External research suppliers may be further categorized by the depth and scope of services they provide. This group is composed of full-service firms including custom and proprietary methodology researchers; specialty marketing research firms including methodology specialists, companies engaged in subsets of the research process, syndicated data providers, omnibus researchers, and communication agencies; consultants; and trade associations representing general marketing and marketing specialties. Each contributes in its own way to the overall industry and conducts or sponsors research to expand the client's knowledge base.

>**key**terms

custom researcher 37	omnibus study 44	syndicated data provider 42
full-service marketing researcher 37	proprietary methodology 37	
omnibus researcher 44	specialty marketing researcher 40	

>**discussion**questions

Terms in Review

1 What trends in marketing data management were apparent by the 1990s?

2 Describe the impact of computers from 1960 to the present.

3 Distinguish between omnibus studies and syndicated research studies.

4 Distinguish between full-service marketing researchers and specialty research suppliers.

Making Research Decisions

Appendix A

5 Factory owners and managers lost direct connections to their customer base as industrialization occurred. How would you have transformed mass marketing to one-to-one marketing if you were advising the owner of a textile plant?

Behind the Scenes

6 What advantages would accrue to an individual research firm for conducting research identified as a top-tier priority by the Marketing Science Institute?

From Concept to Practice

7 Select a state-of-the-research article from a marketing journal and create a timeline that reveals advances on a topical issue (e.g., consumer behavior, new product research, pricing research, sales force research) related to the MSI research priorities in Exhibit 2-5.

>**www**exercises

1 Ad Track is a weekly survey of how much consumers like or dislike a major advertising campaign compared with other ads. Who sponsors this poll, and who collects the data?

2 Visit one of the omnibus researcher Web sites and learn how the company's omnibus study is conducted.

>**chapter 3**

Thinking Like a Researcher

>**learning**objectives

After reading this chapter, you should understand . . .

1 The need for sound reasoning to enhance marketing research results.

2 The terminology used by professional researchers employing scientific thinking.

3 What you need to formulate a solid research hypothesis.

>behindthescenes

Truly effective research is more likely to result when a marketing research supplier works collaboratively with its client throughout the research process. However, not all clients are trained in research methodology, and some come from backgrounds other than marketing. The supplier needs to understand the client's background in order to effectively develop the collaboration. We rejoin Visionary Insights, Inc., as Jason Henry strives to profile the research knowledge, if any, of his client's representative—Myra Wines— the individual with whom he will be working on the MindWriter CompleteCare laptop servicing assessment project.

"Myra, have you had any experience with research suppliers?" asks Jason.

"Some. Actually, I worked for one of your competitors for a short time after college, on a project with the U.S. Army. That project helped me decide that research wasn't my life's work—not that it wasn't and isn't an important field and an important part of my new responsibilities."

"No need to apologize. Some of us have what it takes and others don't."

"Actually, there wasn't anything missing in my ability to observe data, or build rapport with study participants, or find insights," shares Myra. "The project made all the papers; you probably read about it."

"Refresh my memory."

"The death rate near one Army munitions testing area was unexplainably high. Local activists were trying to shut it down, fearing it was an environmental hazard. The Army had a vested interest in keeping it open. Besides, it didn't think the civilian deaths had anything to do with the firing range. U.S. Senator Sly forced the Army to investigate. Since the Army thought it had a public relations job on its hands, my firm was a logical choice; PR campaigns were a specialty.

"The firing range was a played-out mine, stripmined until it was worse than a moonscape. The area had once been a prosperous mining region, where the people were known for fearlessly and proudly going out to dig and produce. The nearest town was so severely economically depressed that, for the pitifully few jobs the Army provided, the folks welcomed the military in to bomb their backyard to cinders.

"The cannon the Army was testing was impressive. Troops armed it with 3-inch shells, put on ear protectors and goggles, and lobbed shells into the range. There would be a tremendous flash and boom, and the shells would go roaring and soaring out of sight. We would soon hear a tremendous boom coming back to us and see dust and ash kicked up several hundred feet. We were all very happy not to be downrange. When we went downrange later, we found a huge crater and a fused puddle of iron, but nothing else but slag and molten rocks.

"There was one problem. About every 20th shell would be a dud. It would fly off and land, and maybe kick up some dust, but explode it would not.

"On paper, this was not supposed to be a problem. The Army sent an officious second lieutenant to brief us. He showed us reports that the Army had dropped such duds from hundred-foot platforms, from helicopters, had applied torches to them—everything—and had discovered them to be completely inert. The only thing he claimed would ignite one of these duds was to drop another, live bomb on it.

"Regrettably, this proved not to be the case. My team had barely finished its initial briefing, when in the middle of the night we heard one of these so-called duds explode. We rushed out at dawn, and, sure enough, found a new crater, molten slag, molten rock, and so forth. It was quite a mystery.

"Our team took shifts doing an all-night observation study. During my two-hour stint, my partner and I saw people with flashlights moving around in there.

"We didn't know if the people were military or civilian. We learned later that locals were coming in at night, intending to crack open the bombs and scavenge for copper wire or anything they thought was salvageable. Except, of course, their actions occasionally ignited one of the beauties and erased any evidence of a crime being committed by vaporizing the perpetrators on the spot.

"Part of our research was to measure public sentiment about the firing range among the locals. During our stay in the area, we discovered the locals were involved in every kind of thrill sport. It was not unusual to see a 50-mile auto race with four ambulances on hand on the edge of the oval, to cart off the carnage to the surgical hospital in the next county. I saw men leap into cars with threadbare tires, loose wheels, malfunctioning brakes, with brake fluid and transmission fluid drooling all over the track. They could wheel their cars out onto the track on a tire they knew was thin as tissue, and if it blew out and put them in the hospital, their reaction was 'Some days you can't win for losin'.' Nobody thought anything of this. If we asked, their answer was, 'I'll go when my number is up,' or 'It's not in my hands.'

"Their attitude made sense, from a cultural-economic view. That attitude had permitted the men to go down in the mines year after year. Even the local sheriff wouldn't stop their daredevil behavior. 'They are going to die anyway,' he was overheard remarking. 'We all are going to die. People die every month that never go out on that dirt track.' Of course, unlike driving a car, messing with a potentially live bomb didn't leave much to skill but left everything to chance.

"The Army had considered an educational campaign to keep the scavengers out but, given our findings, decided it couldn't deal with such thinking by applying logic. Instead, it changed its procedure. The troops would now fire the shells in the morning and spend the afternoon finding the duds, to which they attached kerosene lanterns. At dusk, a fighter-bomber would fly over the area and bomb the lanterns—and the duds—to a molecular state. It was neat and it worked. And the death rate of the locals dropped dramatically."

As Myra finished her story, Jason asks, "It sounds like a successful project. By studying the locals' attitudes and behavior, you could discard the alternative of the education campaign. Why did you decide research wasn't for you?"

"My boss didn't like the idea that I broke confidentiality and told a local reporter what the locals were doing. I'd seen someone's dad or brother blown to pieces and felt I had to act. My dismissal taught me one of the rules of good research—the client always gets to choose whether to use, or release, the findings of any study."

> Marketing Research and the Scientific Method

sound reasoning the basis of sound research, based on finding correct premises, testing connections between facts and assumptions, and making claims based on adequate evidence.

Good marketing research is based on sound reasoning. Competent researchers and astute managers alike practice thinking habits that reflect **sound reasoning** —finding correct premises, testing the connections between their facts and assumptions, making claims based on adequate evidence. In the reasoning process, induction and deduction, observation, and hypothesis testing can be combined in a systematic way. In this chapter we illustrate how this works and why careful reasoning is essential for producing scientific results.

The scientific method, as practiced in business and marketing research, guides our approach to problem solving. The essential tenets of the scientific method are:

- Direct observation of phenomena.
- Clearly defined variables, methods, and procedures.
- Empirically testable hypotheses.
- The ability to rule out rival hypotheses.
- Statistical rather than linguistic justification of conclusions.
- The self-correcting process.

An important term in this list is *empirical*. Empirical testing or **empiricism** is said "to denote observations and propositions based on sensory experience and/or derived from such experience by methods of inductive logic, including mathematics and statistics."[1] Researchers using this approach attempt to describe, explain, and make predictions by relying on information gained through observation. This book is fundamentally concerned with empiricism—with the design of procedures to collect factual information about hypothesized relationships that can be used to decide if a particular understanding of a marketing problem and its possible solution are correct.

> **empiricism** observations and propositions based on sensory experience and/or derived by inductive logic.

The scientific method, and scientific inquiry generally, is described as a puzzle-solving activity.[2] For the researcher, puzzles are solvable problems that may be clarified or resolved through reasoning processes. The steps that follow represent one approach to assessing the validity of conclusions about observable events.[3] They are particularly appropriate for marketing researchers whose conclusions result from empirical data. The researcher:

1. Encounters a curiosity, doubt, barrier, suspicion, or obstacle.
2. Struggles to state the problem—asks questions, contemplates existing knowledge, gathers facts, and moves from an emotional to an intellectual confrontation with the problem.
3. Proposes hypotheses to explain the facts that are believed to be logically related to the problem.
4. Deduces outcomes or consequences of the hypotheses—attempts to discover what happens if the results are in the opposite direction of that predicted or if the results support the expectations.
5. Formulates several rival hypotheses.
6. Devises and conducts a crucial empirical test with various possible outcomes, each of which selectively excludes one or more hypotheses.
7. Draws a conclusion (an inductive inference) based on acceptance or rejection of the hypotheses.
8. Feeds information back into the original problem, modifying it according to the strength of the evidence.

Clearly, reasoning is pivotal to much of the researcher's success: gathering facts consistent with the problem, proposing and eliminating rival hypotheses, deducing outcomes, developing crucial empirical tests, and deriving the conclusion.

Sound Reasoning for Useful Answers

Every day we reason with varying degrees of success and communicate our meaning in ordinary language or, in special cases, in symbolic, logical form. Our meanings are conveyed through one of two types of discourse: exposition or argument. **Exposition** consists of statements that describe without attempting to explain. **Argument** allows us to explain, interpret, defend, challenge, and explore meaning. Two types of argument of great importance to research are deduction and induction.

> **exposition** statement that describes without attempting to explain.
>
> **argument** statement that explains, interprets, defends, challenges, or explores meaning.

Deduction

deduction a form of reasoning in which the conclusion must necessarily follow from the premises given.

Deduction is a form of argument that purports to be conclusive—the conclusion must necessarily follow from the reasons given. These reasons are said to imply the conclusion and represent a proof. This is a much stronger and different bond between reasons and conclusions than is found with induction. For a deduction to be correct, it must be both true and valid:

- Premises (reasons) given for the conclusion must agree with the real world (true).
- The conclusion must necessarily follow from the premises (valid).

A deduction is valid if it is impossible for the conclusion to be false if the premises are true. Logicians have established rules by which one can judge whether a deduction is valid. Conclusions are not logically justified if one or more premises are untrue or the argument form is invalid. A conclusion may still be a true statement, but for reasons other than those given. For example, consider the following simple deduction:

All employees at Visionary Insights can be trusted to observe the ethical code.	*(Premise 1)*
Sara is an employee of Visionary Insights.	*(Premise 2)*
Sara can be trusted to observe the ethical code.	*(Conclusion)*

If we believe that Sara can be trusted, we might think this is a sound deduction. But this conclusion cannot be accepted as a sound deduction unless the form of the argument is valid and the premises are true. In this case, the form is valid, and premise 2 can be confirmed easily. However, more than a billion dollars each year in confirmed retail employee theft will challenge the premise: "All employees can be trusted to observe an ethical code." And instances of employee fraud among professionals make any specific instance questionable. If one premise fails the acceptance test, then the conclusion is not a sound deduction. This is so even if we still have great confidence in Sara's honesty. Our conclusion, in this case, must be based on our confidence in Sara as an individual rather than on a general premise that all employees of Visionary Insights are ethical.

> 66 If we ignore supernatural inspiration, intuition is based on two things: experience and intelligence. The more experience I have with you, the more likely I am to encounter repetition of activities and situations that help me learn about you. The smarter I am, the more I can abstract from those experiences to find connections and patterns among them. 99
>
> *Jeffrey Bradshow*
> *Creator of the software that searches databases*

As marketing researchers, we may not recognize how much we use deduction to understand the implications of various acts and conditions. For example, in planning a survey, we might reason as follows:

Inner-city household interviewing is especially difficult and expensive.	*(Premise 1)*
This survey involves substantial inner-city household interviewing.	*(Premise 2)*
The interviewing in this survey will be especially difficult and expensive.	*(Conclusion)*

On reflection, it should be apparent that a conclusion that results from deduction is, in a sense, already "contained in" its premises.[4]

Induction

Inductive argument is radically different. There is no such strength of relationship between reasons and conclusions in induction. In **induction** you draw a conclusion from one or more particular facts or pieces of evidence. The conclusion explains the facts, and the facts support the conclusion. To illustrate, suppose your firm spends $1 million on a regional promotional campaign and sales do not increase. This is a fact—sales did not increase during or after the promotional campaign. Under such circumstances, we ask, "Why didn't sales increase?"

induction a form of reasoning that draws a conclusion from one or more particular facts or pieces of evidence.

One likely answer to this question is a conclusion that the promotional campaign was poorly executed. This conclusion is an induction because we know from experience that regional sales should go up during a promotional event. Also we know from experience that if the promotion is poorly executed, sales will not increase. The nature of induction, however, is that the conclusion is only a hypothesis. It is one explanation, but there are others that fit the facts just as well. For example, each of the following hypotheses might explain why sales did not increase:

- Regional retailers did not have sufficient stock to fill customer requests during the promotional period.
- A strike by the employees of our trucking firm prevented stock from arriving in time for the promotion to be effective.
- A category-five hurricane closed all our retail locations in the region for the 10 days during the promotion.

In this example, we see the essential nature of inductive reasoning. The inductive conclusion is an inferential jump beyond the evidence presented—that is, although one

These young men are part of a toy testing study. They are being observed playing with a kit that makes paper airplanes. Apply deductive and inductive reasoning to this image and develop your own conclusions concerning what will happen when they send their paper airplanes flying.

conclusion explains the fact of no sales increase, other conclusions also can explain the fact. It may even be that none of the conclusions we advanced correctly explain the failure of sales to increase.

For another example, let's consider the situation of Tracy Nelson, a salesperson at the Square Box Company. Tracy has one of the poorest sales records in the company. Her unsatisfactory performance prompts us to ask the question: "Why is she performing so poorly?" From our knowledge of Tracy's sales practices, the nature of box selling, and the market, we might conclude (hypothesize) that her problem is that she makes too few sales calls per day to build a good sales record. Other hypotheses might also occur to us on the basis of available evidence. Among these hypotheses are the following:

- Tracy's territory does not have the market potential of other territories.
- Tracy's sales-generating skills are so poorly developed that she is not able to close sales effectively.
- Tracy does not have authority to lower prices and her territory has been the scene of intense price-cutting by competitive manufacturers, causing her to lose many sales to competitors.
- Some people just cannot sell boxes, and Tracy is one of those people.

Each of the above hypotheses is an induction we might base on the evidence of Tracy's poor sales record, plus some assumptions or beliefs we hold about her and the selling of boxes. All of them have some chance of being true, but we would probably have more confidence in some than in others. All require further confirmation before they gain our confidence. Confirmation comes with more evidence. The task of research is largely to (1) determine the nature of the evidence needed to confirm or reject hypotheses and (2) design methods by which to discover and measure this other evidence.

Combining Induction and Deduction

Induction and deduction are used together in research reasoning. Dewey describes this process as the "double movement of reflective thought."[5] Induction occurs when we observe a fact and ask, "Why is this?" In answer to this question, we advance a tentative explanation (hypothesis). The hypothesis is plausible if it explains the event or condition (fact) that prompted the question. Deduction is the process by which we test whether the hypothesis is capable of explaining the fact. The process is illustrated in Exhibit 3-1:

1. You promote a product but sales don't increase. (Fact$_1$)
2. You ask the question: "Why didn't sales increase?" (Induction)
3. You infer a conclusion (hypothesis) to answer the question: The promotion was poorly executed. (Hypothesis)
4. You use this hypothesis to conclude (deduce) that the sales will not increase during a poorly executed promotion. You know from experience that ineffective promotion will not increase sales. (Deduction$_1$)

This example, an exercise in circular reasoning, points out that one must be able to deduce the initiating fact from the hypothesis advanced to explain that fact. A second critical point is also illustrated in Exhibit 3-1. To test a hypothesis, one must be able to deduce from it other facts that can then be investigated. This is what research is all about. We must deduce other specific facts or events from the hypothesis and then gather information to see if the deductions are true. In this example, we deduce:

5. A well-executed promotion will result in increased sales. (Deduction$_2$)
6. We run an effective promotion, and sales increase. (Fact$_2$)

>**Exhibit 3-1** Why Didn't Sales Increase?

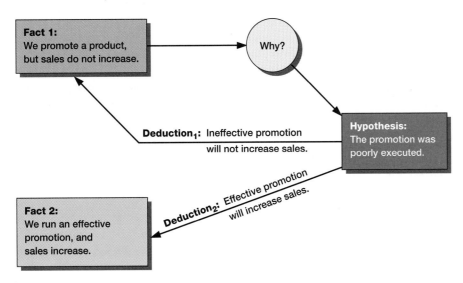

How would the double movement of reflective thought work when applied to Tracy Nelson's problem? The process is illustrated in Exhibit 3-2. The initial observation (fact$_1$) leads to hypothesis$_1$ that Tracy is lazy. We deduce several other facts from the hypothesis. These are shown as fact$_2$ and fact$_3$. We use research to find out if fact$_2$ and fact$_3$ are true. If they are found to be true, they confirm our hypothesis. If they are found to be false, our hypothesis is not confirmed, and we must look for another explanation.

In most research, the process may be more complicated than these examples suggest. For instance, we often develop multiple hypotheses by which to explain the problem in question. Then we design a study to test all the hypotheses at once. Not only is this more efficient, but it is also a good way to reduce the attachment (and potential bias) of the researcher for any given hypothesis.

>**Exhibit 3-2** Why is Tracy Nelson's Performance so Poor?

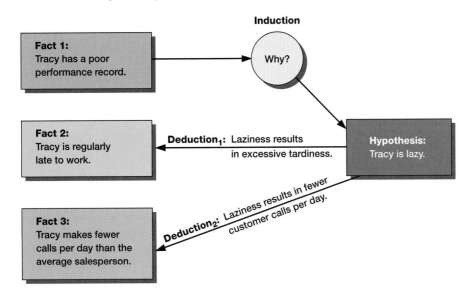

> The Language of Research

When we do research, we seek to know *what is* in order to understand, explain, and predict phenomena. We might want to answer the question: "What will be the marketing department's reaction to the new flexible work schedule?" or "Why did the stock market price surge higher when all normal indicators suggested it would go down?" When dealing with such questions, we must agree on definitions. Which members of the marketing department: clerical or professional? What kind of reaction? What are normal indicators? These questions require the use of concepts, constructs, and definitions. These and other terms are used by researchers to converse about applied and theoretical marketing problems.

Concepts

concept a bundle of meanings or characteristics associated with certain concrete, unambiguous events, objects, conditions, situations, or behaviors.

To understand and communicate information about objects and events, there must be a common ground on which to do it. Concepts serve this purpose. A **concept** is a generally accepted collection of meanings or characteristics associated with certain events, objects, conditions, situations, and behaviors. Classifying and categorizing objects or events that have common characteristics beyond any single observation creates concepts. When you think of a spreadsheet or a warranty card, what comes to mind is not a single example but your collected memories of all spreadsheets and warranty cards, from which you abstract a set of specific and definable characteristics.

We abstract such meanings from our experiences and use words as labels to designate them. For example, we see a man passing and identify that he is running, walking, skipping, crawling, or hopping. These movements all represent concepts. We also have abstracted certain visual elements by which we identify that the moving object is an adult male, rather than an adult female or a truck or a horse. We use numerous concepts daily in our thinking, conversing, and other activities.

Sources of Concepts

Concepts that are in frequent and general use have been developed over time through shared language usage. We acquire them through personal experience. Ordinary concepts make up the bulk of communication even in research, but we often run into difficulty trying to deal with an uncommon concept or a newly advanced idea. One way to handle this problem is to borrow from other languages (for example, *gestalt*) or to borrow from other fields (for example, from art, *impressionism*). The concept of gravitation is borrowed from physics and used in marketing in an attempt to explain why people shop where they do. The concept of distance is used in attitude measurement to describe degree of variability between the attitudes of two or more persons. Threshold is used effectively to describe a concept about the way we perceive.

Sometimes we need to adopt new meanings for words (make a word cover a different concept) or develop new labels for concepts. The recent broadening of the meaning of *model* is an example of the first instance; the development of concepts such as *sibling* and *status-stress* are examples of the second. When we adopt new meanings or develop new labels, we begin to develop a specialized jargon or terminology. Jargon no doubt contributes to efficiency of communication among specialists, but it excludes everyone else.

Importance to Research

In research, special problems grow out of the need for concept precision and inventiveness. We design hypotheses using concepts. We devise measurement concepts by which to test these hypothetical statements. We gather data using these measurement concepts. The

ITE: Raising Questions about Danger

State Farm recently published its third list of the most dangerous intersections in the United States. The nation's largest auto insurer has been studying its proprietary accident claims data for detailed patterns since 1998. In that year it discovered that one-third of all accidents involving State Farm–insured motorists took place in intersections. Prior studies in Michigan, Canada, and Australia indicated that low-cost changes could improve the safety of motorists in intersections—moving or improving signs or remounting traffic lights, improving light timing, and making lane markings more visible. For its study, State Farm analysts define an intersection as two roadways that intersect, excluding overpass crossings and interstate ramps. In the first study, a dangerous intersection was defined as one with the most auto crashes during the preceding year, with accident severity not a criterion. Estimated crashes were determined by weighting actual crash claims made to State Farm by a factor based upon the percentage of cars insured by State Farm in the metropolitan area where the intersection is located.

One organization, the Institute of Transportation Engineers (ITE), while complimenting the proactive stance of the auto insurer, has taken exception to the research methodology of State Farm in publishing its third annual list. In a press release, ITE has expressed its concern that "the State Farm Dangerous Intersection Initiative fails to adequately recognize ongoing efforts by the traffic engineering professionals in these jurisdictions." Because State Farm selected intersections based on its internal data of State Farm motorists and ignored publicly available traffic volume and police accident data, ITE claims that State Farm's list is inaccurate. ITE further adds that engineers often do not have the budgets to implement the desired solutions even when they know a traffic hazard exists. How do the concepts and constructs measured here influence the intersections on the list? What is the nature of the conflicts here between researcher and information user?

www.ite.org; www.statefarm.com

success of research hinges on (1) how clearly we conceptualize and (2) how well others understand the concepts we use. For example, when we survey people on the question of customer loyalty, the questions we use need to tap faithfully the attitudes of the participants. Attitudes are abstract, yet we must attempt to measure them using carefully selected concepts.

The challenge is to develop concepts that others will clearly understand. We might, for example, ask participants for an estimate of their family's total income. This may seem to be a simple, unambiguous concept, but we will receive varying and confusing answers unless we restrict or narrow the concept by specifying:

- Time period, such as weekly, monthly, or annually.
- Before or after income taxes.
- For head of family only or for all family members.
- For salary and wages only or also for dividends, interest, and capital gains.
- Income in kind, such as free rent, employee discounts, or food stamps.

Constructs

Concepts have progressive levels of abstraction—that is, the degree to which the concept does or does not have something objective to refer to. *Table* is an objective concept. We can point to a table and we have images of the characteristics of all tables in our mind. An abstraction like *personality* is much more difficult to visualize. Such abstract concepts are often called constructs. A **construct** is an image or abstract idea specifically invented for a given research and/or theory-building purpose. We build constructs by combining the simpler, more concrete concepts, especially when the idea or image we intend to convey is not subject to direct observation. When Jason and Myra tackle MindWriter's research study, they will struggle with the construct of *satisfied service customer*.

construct an image or idea specifically invented to represent an abstract phenomenon for a given research project.

Concepts and constructs are easily confused. Consider this example: Heather is a marketing researcher at PharmaLife, a pharmaceutical company that manufactures and distributes minoxidil-based products to combat hair loss. Although she has a very practical, applied problem, she must venture into the realm of psychological theory to solve this problem. We join her as she is preparing for a meeting with the company's ad agency. She has seen the storyboards for an upcoming campaign:

> A 30-something male, standing in his bathroom, is staring in the mirror. He sees his scalp through his thinning black hair. He begins conversing with himself—actually with three personas: his real self, the balding self, and the ideal self who has a full head of hair. The bald self has low self-esteem, is fearful, and is negative. The ideal self is well adjusted, successful, and self-confident. The real self resolves to do something. He must act before becoming completely bald and does not like the behavior he sees in the fearful self.

For this ad to successfully appeal to male self-esteem, it must elicit a sense of improved appearance by showing how the product will elevate the buyer's position socially: looking younger, more attractive, stronger, healthier, and so forth. Our researcher is confused about the components of self-esteem, particularly the consequences of low self-esteem, and worries that, if improperly targeted, the ad might backfire by eliciting complex negative responses. She searches the literature and begins to map out specific characteristics of this central aspect of psychological well-being.

Exhibit 3-3 illustrates some of the concepts and constructs she has found. The concepts at the bottom of the exhibit (father's death, divorce, hospitalizations, and worry over school grades) are the most concrete and easily measured. Concepts most likely to be connected to low-self-esteem males in the ad's message are hospitalizations (implying poor images of health and strength) and worry over grades (suggesting lack of achievement). The literature

>**Exhibit 3-3** Self-Esteem Constructs and Their Concepts

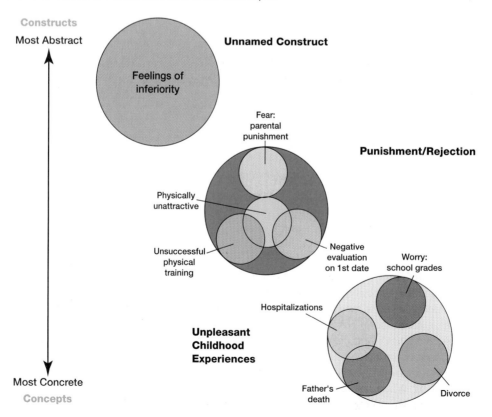

suggests that these concepts constitute a construct called "unpleasant childhood experiences" and also affect low self-esteem in later life. As Heather continues to map her findings, she discovers three more concepts: feelings of unattractiveness, negative experiences in dating, and lack of success in physical fitness training. Notice that these are shown in the exhibit as overlapping and all of these concepts, if overstated, would negatively affect her company's communication. Also note that they are more abstract (higher in the diagram) and would be more difficult to define and measure than, say, number of hospitalizations. The last concept in this group is very high on our abstraction index and may even qualify as a unique construct. The fear of parental punishment has numerous deep-seated sources but is *unlikely* to be associated with her ad's message. This cluster takes its name from the overall context: "punishment and rejection." Punishment and rejection is a nonexistent entity; it is a "constructed type" used in this research example to communicate the combination of meanings presented by the four components. The analyst uses it merely as a label so that the concepts she has discovered can be empirically related.

Heather has little information on the most abstract construct, which comprises a variety of feelings of being inferior to others. It is the least observable and most difficult to measure because it is composed of numerous concepts. It is also not mentioned in the research literature as being well connected to low self-esteem. Researchers sometimes refer to such entities as **hypothetical constructs** because they can be inferred only from the data; thus, they are presumed to exist but must await further testing to see what they actually consist of. If research shows the concepts and constructs in this example to be interrelated, and if their connections can be supported, then Heather will have the beginning of a **conceptual scheme.** In graphic form, it would depict the relationships among the characteristics of low self-esteem that our researcher wants to balance with high self-esteem needed in her company's message.

hypothetical construct construct inferred only from data; its presumption must be tested.

conceptual scheme the interrelationships between concepts and constructs.

Definitions

Confusion about the meaning of concepts can destroy a research study's value without the researcher or client even knowing it. If words have different meanings to the parties involved, then the parties are not communicating well. Definitions are one way to reduce this danger.

Researchers struggle with two types of definitions: dictionary definitions and operational definitions. In the more familiar dictionary definition, a concept is defined with a synonym. For example, a customer is defined as a patron; a patron, in turn, is defined as a customer or client of an establishment; a client is defined as one who employs the services of any professional and, loosely, as a patron of any shop.[6] Circular definitions may be adequate for general communication but not for research. In research, we measure concepts and constructs, and this requires more rigorous definitions.

Operational Definitions

An **operational definition** is a definition stated in terms of specific criteria for testing or measurement. These terms must refer to empirical standards (that is, we must be able to count, measure, or in some other way gather the information through our senses). Whether the object to be defined is physical (e.g., a can of soup) or highly abstract (e.g., achievement motivation), the definition must specify the characteristics and how they are to be observed. The specifications and procedures must be so clear that any competent person using them would classify the objects in the same way.

During her research project with the military, Myra observed numerous shells that, when fired, did not explode on impact. She knew the Army attached the operational definition "a shell that does not explode on impact" to the construct dud shell. But if asked, Myra would have applied the operational term *dud shell* only to "a shell that, once fired from a cannon, could not be made to explode by any amount of manipulation, human or

operational definition defines a variable in terms of specific measurement and testing criteria.

> **What operational definition did the Army use for "dud" ordnance? What operational definition did Myra and her research colleagues use?**

>**snap**shot

Marriott: What Is Concierge Service?

Marriott International, Inc., is a leading hospitality company with more than 1,800 properties in 53 countries and territories under various brand names (Marriott, Fairfield Inn, Residence Inn, Courtyard, TownePlace Suites, Fairfield Suites, Renaissance, and ExecuStay). Due to its diverse operations, when managers in this company want to deliver global consistency, they turn to its sophisticated internal research division. "We wanted to know what level of service the terms *concierge, club,* or *executive level* implied. We also needed to know which term generated feelings of belonging and appreciation. We need a term that promises a level of superior service that we can deliver consistently in every property both in the United States and throughout the world," shared manager of marketing research Brenda Roth. The task then was to find a global term for the special services floor found in the Marriott and Renaissance properties. First "pulse groups"

were conducted in the United States. Then a study was conducted involving 40 hotel intercept interviews in Hong Kong, London, and Frankfurt. Interviewers were bilingual, doing their interviews in the domestic language while recording responses in English to speed data processing and analysis. While most guests shared some common interpretations of the terms, "one possible German connotation of *concierge* was as a building superintendent similar to a custodian. Certainly not a desired interpretation." What operational definition would you develop for *concierge service*?

www.marriott.com

mechanical." Based on her operational definition, the town's residents rarely encountered "duds" during their excursions onto the firing range.

Suppose college undergraduates are to be classified by class. No one has much trouble understanding such terms as *freshman, sophomore*, and so forth. But the task may not be that simple if you must determine which students fall in each class. To do this, you need operational definitions.

Operational definitions may vary, depending on your purpose and the way you choose to measure them. Here are two different situations requiring different definitions of the same concepts:

1. You conduct a survey among students and wish to classify their answers by their class levels. You merely ask them to report their class status, and you record it. In this case, class is freshman, sophomore, junior, or senior, and you accept the answer each respondent gives as correct. This is a rather casual definition process but nonetheless an operational definition. It is probably adequate even though some of the respondents report inaccurately.

2. You make a tabulation of the class level of students from the university registrar's annual report. The measurement task here is more critical, so your operational definition needs to be more precise. You decide to define class levels in terms of semester hours of credit completed by the end of the spring semester and recorded in each student's record in the registrar's office:

Freshman	Fewer than 30 hours' credit
Sophomore	30 to 59 hours' credit
Junior	60 to 89 hours' credit
Senior	More than 90 hours' credit

Those examples deal with relatively concrete concepts, but operational definitions are even more critical for treating abstract ideas. Suppose one tries to measure a construct called "consumer socialization." We may intuitively understand what this means, but to attempt to measure it among consumers is difficult. We would probably develop questions on skills, knowledge, and attitudes, or we may use a scale that has already been developed and validated by someone else. This scale then operationally defines the construct.

Whether you use a definitional or operational definition, its purpose in research is basically the same—to provide an understanding and measurement of concepts. We may need to provide operational definitions for only a few critical concepts, but these will almost always be the definitions used to develop the relationships found in hypotheses and theories.

Variables

In practice, the term **variable** is used as a synonym for construct or the property being studied. In this context, a variable is a symbol of an event, act, characteristic, trait, or attribute that can be measured and to which we assign categorical values.[7]

For purposes of data entry and analysis, we assign numerical value to a variable based on the variable's properties. For example, some variables, said to be *dichotomous,* have only two values, reflecting the presence or absence of a property: employed-unemployed or male-female have two values, generally 0 and 1. When Myra Wines observed the cannon shells, they were exploded or unexploded. Variables also take on values representing added categories, such as the demographic variables of race or religion. All such variables that produce data that fit into categories are said to be *discrete,* since only certain values are possible. An automotive variable, for example, where "Chevrolet" is assigned a 5 and "Honda" is assigned a 6, provides no option for a 5.5.

Income, temperature, age, or a test score are examples of *continuous* variables. These variables may take on values within a given range or, in some cases, an infinite set. Your test score may range from 0 to 100, your age may be 23.5, and your present income could be $35,000.

variable an event, act, characteristic, trait, or attribute that can be measured and to which we assign categorical values.

> **The procedure for assigning values to variables is described in detail in Chapter 18.**

Independent and Dependent Variables

Researchers are most interested in relationships among variables. For example, does a newspaper coupon (independent variable) influence product purchase (dependent variable), or can a salesperson's ethical standards influence her ability to maintain customer relationships? As one writer notes:

> There's nothing very tricky about the notion of independence and dependence. But there is something tricky about the fact that the relationship of independence and dependence is a figment of the researcher's imagination until demonstrated convincingly. Researchers hypothesize relationships of independence and dependence: They invent them, and then they try by reality testing to see if the relationships actually work out that way.[8]

Many textbooks use the term *predictor variable* as a synonym for **independent variable (IV).** This variable is manipulated by the researcher, and the manipulation causes an effect on the dependent variable. We recognize that there are often several independent variables and that they are probably at least somewhat "correlated" and therefore not independent among themselves. Similarly, the term *criterion variable* is used synonymously with **dependent variable (DV).** This variable is measured, predicted, or otherwise monitored and is expected to be affected by manipulation of an independent variable. Exhibit 3-4 lists some terms that have become synonyms for *independent variable* and *dependent variable.*

independent variable, IV (predictor variable) the variable manipulated by the researcher, thereby causing an effect on the dependent variable.

dependent variable, DV (criterion variable) a measured, predicted, or otherwise monitored variable expected to be affected by manipulation of an independent variable.

>**Exhibit 3-4** Independent and Dependent Variables: Synonyms

Independent Variable	Dependent Variable
Predictor	Criterion
Presumed cause	Presumed effect
Stimulus	Response
Predicted from . . .	Predicted to . . .
Antecedent	Consequence
Manipulated	Measured outcome

Moderating Variables

In each relationship, there is at least one independent variable and a dependent variable. It is normally hypothesized that in some way the IV "causes" the DV to occur. For simple relationships, all other variables are considered extraneous and are ignored. Myra sets out to discover why the locals are scavenging salvageable materials from the unexploded cannon shells. She hypothesizes:

> Locals' conviction that predetermined fate dictates time and place of death (IV) leads them to undertake life-threatening behaviors—scavenging on the firing range (DV).
>
> If locals could be warned of the danger (IV) of their actions, they would change their nocturnal behavior (DV).

The sheriff's overheard remarks ultimately convince Myra and her research team that only a change in Army procedure will bring about the decline in shell-induced deaths caused by the nocturnal scavenging.

In actual study situations, for example, in a typical sales office, a simple one-on-one relationship needs to be revised to take other variables into account. Often we use another type of explanatory variable here—the moderating variable. A **moderating variable (MV)** is a second independent variable that is included because it is believed to have a significant contributory or contingent effect on the originally stated IV-DV relationship. For example, one might hypothesize:

moderating variable (MV) a second independent variable, believed to have a significant contributory or contingent effect on the originally stated IV-DV relationship.

> The switch to commission from a salary compensation system (IV) will lead to increased sales productivity (DV) per worker, especially among younger workers (MV).

In this case, there is a differential pattern of relationship between the compensation system and productivity that is the result of age differences among the workers.

Whether a given variable is treated as an independent or as a moderating variable depends on the hypothesis. If Myra had been a reporter (rather a researcher assigned to the Army project) viewing the local death and injury statistics, she might have arrived at a different hypothesis:

> The loss of mining jobs (IV) leads to acceptance of higher-risk behaviors to earn a family-supporting income—race-car driving or nocturnal scavenging (DV)— especially due to the proximity of the firing range (MV) and the limited education (MV) of the residents.

Extraneous Variables

extraneous variable (EV) a variable to assume or exclude from a research study.

An almost infinite number of **extraneous variables (EVs)** exist that might conceivably affect a given relationship. Some can be treated as independent or moderating variables, but most must either be assumed or excluded from the study. Fortunately, these variables have little or no effect on a given situation. Most can be safely ignored. Others may be important, but their impact occurs in such a random fashion as to have little effect. Using the example of the effect of a coupon on sales of cereal, one would normally think the imposition of a local sales tax, the election of a new mayor, a three-day rainy spell, and thousands of similar events and conditions would have little effect on cereal sales.

However, there may be other extraneous variables to consider as possible confounding variables to our hypothesized IV-DV relationship. For example, Myra might think that level of education as it impacts job skills might have an effect on the selection of income-producing activity by the locals. This notion might lead to our introducing an extraneous variable as the **control variable,** one introduced to help interpret the relationship between variables. For example:

control variable a variable introduced to help interpret the relationship between variables.

Among residents with less than a high school education (EV-control), the loss of high-income mining jobs (IV) leads to acceptance of higher-risk behaviors to earn a family-supporting income—race-car driving or nocturnal scavenging (DV)—especially due to the proximity of the firing range (MV).

Alternatively, one might think that the *type of customers* would have an effect on a compensation system's impact on sales productivity. This might lead to our introducing a control variable as follows:

With new customers (EV-control), a switch to commission from a salary compensation system (IV) will lead to increased sales productivity (DV) per worker, especially among younger workers (MV).

In our salesperson compensation example, we would attempt to control for type of customers by studying the effect of the switch in compensation within groups having different types of customers (new versus established). In a similar way, Myra would attempt to control for employable job skills by studying the education patterns and prior employment of the scavengers who lost their lives.

Intervening Variables

The variables mentioned with regard to causal relationships are concrete and clearly measurable; they can be seen, counted, or observed in some way. Sometimes, however, one may not be completely satisfied by the explanations they offer. An intervening variable is a conceptual mechanism through which the IV and MV might affect the DV. The **intervening variable (IVV)** may be defined as "that factor which theoretically affects the observed phenomenon but cannot be seen, measured, or manipulated; its effect must be inferred from the effects of the independent and moderator variables on the observed phenomenon."[9]

In the case of the compensation hypothesis, one might view the intervening variable to be job satisfaction, giving a hypothesis such as:

The switch to a commission compensation system (IV) will lead to higher sales productivity (DV) by increasing overall compensation (IVV).

Here are additional examples illustrating the relationships involving independent, moderating, controlled extraneous, and dependent variables. The management of a bank wishes to study the effect of promotion on savings. It might advance the following hypothesis:

A promotion campaign (IV) will increase savings activity (DV), especially when free prizes are offered (MV), but chiefly among smaller savers (EV-control). The results come from enhancing the motivation to save (IVV).

Myra's research for the army hypothesizes:

Marking dud shells with kerosene lanterns for same-evening detonation (IV) will reduce nocturnal scavenging (DV) among poorly educated local residents (MV) by eliminating the profit motive for such behavior (IVV).

Propositions and Hypotheses

We define a **proposition** as a statement about observable phenomena (concepts) that may be judged as true or false. When a proposition is formulated for empirical testing, we call it a **hypothesis.** As a declarative statement, a hypothesis is of a tentative and conjectural nature.

Hypotheses have also been described as statements in which we assign variables to cases. A **case** is defined in this sense as the entity or thing the hypothesis talks about. The variable is the characteristic, trait, or attribute that, in the hypothesis, is imputed to the case.[10] For example, we might create the following hypothesis:

Brand Manager Jones (case) has a higher-than-average achievement motivation (variable).

intervening variable (IVV) a factor that affects the observed phenomenon but cannot be measured or manipulated.

proposition a statement about observable phenomena that may be judged as true or false.

hypothesis a proposition formulated for empirical testing.

case the entity or thing the hypothesis talks about.

>**snap**shot

Forrester Research: Can an Auto Dealership Go Lean?

Not all research is driven by a specific client problem. Some firms specialize in researching emerging issues when the issue is more idea than reality. Forrester Research is one such research firm. As senior analyst Mark Bunger explains, research problems often come from taking an issue in one field and transplanting it into another arena. "The genesis of Forrester's 'Making Auto Retail Lean' study was a book I was reading by James Womack and Daniel Jones, *Lean Thinking: Banish Waste and Create Wealth in Your Corporation*." In their book the authors describe lean thinking as the "elimination of unnecessary waste in business" and explain that if lean principles are applied to the whole product cycle, from suppliers to customers, firms can demonstrate significant increases in productivity and sales. "I knew lean principles were being applied in the manufacturing of cars. I wondered if such principles were applied at the level of the auto dealership and with what effect." Bunger's question led Forrester to launch a study that had Bunger and his team of research associates conducting hour-long phone interviews with vendors of products and services related to supply chain enhancement (e.g., IBM), followed by a 15-minute, 20-question phone survey of 50 auto dealer CEOs. Bunger also visited dealers in his immediate area to flesh out ideas from the phone interviews. Data revealed that "dealers have the wrong cars 40 percent of the time." Yet if they

applied the lean principles so effective for car manufacturers, they could lower their demand chain–related costs up to 53 percent.

The Forrester study followed a fairly standard model for the firm: approximately two weeks to define and refine the problem—a stage that involves significant secondary data analysis; two to four weeks for data collection—a stage that involves selecting at least two sample segments (usually "experts" and users; for this study, vendors and dealers); and two to thirty hours to prepare a brief or report. Forrester's research is purchased by subscription. Subscribing companies related to the automotive industry have "whole-view" access to any report on any study that Forrester develops at an approximate cost of $7,000 per *seat*. When a subscriber wants numerous people to have direct access to Forrester research, a firm's subscription could be worth several million dollars.

Should auto dealers go lean? What reasoning approaches did you use to reach your conclusion? What concepts and constructs are embedded in this example? What hypotheses could you form from this example?

www.forrester.com

> **A checklist for developing strong hypotheses is presented in Exhibit 3-5, p. 69.**

If our hypothesis were based on more than one case, it would be a *generalization*. For example:

> Brand Managers in Company Z (cases) have a higher-than-average achievement motivation (variable).

Descriptive Hypotheses

descriptive hypothesis a statement about the existence, size, form, or distribution of a variable.

Both of the above hypotheses are examples of **descriptive hypotheses.** They state the existence, size, form, or distribution of some variable. Researchers often use a research question rather than a descriptive hypothesis. For example:

Descriptive Hypothesis Format	*Research Question Format*
• In Detroit (case), our potato chip market share (variable) stands at 13.7 percent.	• What is the market share for our potato chips in Detroit?
• American cities (case) are experiencing budget difficulties (variable).	• Are American cities experiencing budget difficulties?
• Eighty percent of Company Z stockholders (case) favor increasing the company's cash dividend (variable).	• Do stockholders of Company Z favor an increased cash dividend?
• Seventy percent of the high school–educated males (case) scavenge in the Army firing range for salvageable metals (variable).	• Do a majority of high school–educated male residents scavenge in the Army firing range for salvageable metals?

Either format is acceptable, but the descriptive hypothesis format has several advantages:

- It encourages researchers to crystallize their thinking about the likely relationships to be found.
- It encourages them to think about the implications of a supported or rejected finding.
- It is useful for testing statistical significance.

Relational Hypotheses

The research question format is less frequently used with a situation calling for **relational hypotheses.** These are statements that describe a relationship between two variables with respect to some case. For example, "Foreign (variable) cars are perceived by American consumers (case) to be of better quality (variable) than domestic cars." In this instance, the nature of the relationship between the two variables ("country of origin" and "perceived quality") is not specified. Is there only an implication that the variables occur in some predictable relationship, or is one variable somehow responsible for the other? The first interpretation (unspecified relationship) indicates a *correlational* relationship; the second (predictable relationship) indicates an *explanatory,* or *causal, relationship.*

relational hypothesis a statement about the relationship between two variables with respect to some case.

Correlational hypotheses state that the variables occur together in some specified manner without implying that one causes the other. Such weak claims are often made when we believe there are more basic causal forces that affect both variables or when we have not developed enough evidence to claim a stronger linkage. Here are three sample correlational hypotheses:

correlational hypothesis a statement indicating that variables occur together in some specified manner without implying that one causes the other.

> Young women (under 35 years of age) purchase fewer units of our product than women who are 35 years of age or older.
>
> The number of suits sold varies directly with the level of the business cycle.
>
> People in Atlanta give the president a more favorable rating than do people in St. Louis.

By labeling these as correlational hypotheses, we make no claim that one variable causes the other to change or take on different values.

With **explanatory (causal) hypotheses,** there is an implication that the existence of or a change in one variable causes or leads to a change in the other variable. As we noted previously, the causal variable is typically called the independent variable (IV) and the other the dependent variable (DV). Cause means roughly to "help make happen." So the IV need not be the sole reason for the existence of or change in the DV. Here are four examples of explanatory hypotheses:

explanatory (causal) hypothesis a statement that describes a relationship between two variables in which one variable leads to a specified effect on the other variable.

> An increase in family income (IV) leads to an increase in the percentage of income saved (DV).
>
> Exposure to the company's messages concerning industry problems (IV) leads to more favorable attitudes (DV) by employees toward the company.
>
> Loyalty to a particular grocery store (IV) increases the probability of purchasing the private brands (DV) sponsored by that store.
>
> An increase in the price of salvaged copper wire (IV) leads to an increase in scavenging (DV) on the Army firing range.

In proposing or interpreting causal hypotheses, the researcher must consider the direction of influence. In many cases, the direction is obvious from the nature of the variables. Thus, one would assume that family income influences savings rate rather than the reverse case. This also holds true for the Army example. Sometimes our ability to identify the direction of influence depends on the research design. In the worker attitude hypothesis, if the exposure to the message clearly precedes the attitude measurement, then the direction of exposure to attitude seems clear. If information about both exposure and attitude was collected at the same time, the researcher might be justified in saying that different attitudes led to selective message perception or nonperception. Store loyalty and purchasing of store brands appear to be interdependent. Loyalty to a store may increase the probability of buying the store's private brands, but satisfaction with the store's private brand may also lead to greater store loyalty.

The Role of the Hypothesis

In research, a hypothesis serves several important functions:

- It guides the direction of the study.
- It identifies facts that are relevant and those that are not.
- It suggests which form of research design is likely to be most appropriate.
- It provides a framework for organizing the conclusions that result.

Unless the researcher curbs the urge to include additional elements, a study can be diluted by trivial concerns that do not answer the basic questions posed by the management dilemma. The virtue of the hypothesis is that, if taken seriously, it limits what shall be studied and what shall not. To consider specifically the role of the hypothesis in determining the direction of the research, suppose we use this:

> Husbands and wives agree in their perceptions of their respective roles in purchase decisions.

The hypothesis specifies who shall be studied (married couples), in what context they shall be studied (their consumer decision making), and what shall be studied (their individual perceptions of their roles).

The nature of this hypothesis and the implications of the statement suggest that the best research design is a communication-based study, probably a survey or interview. We have at this time no other practical means to ascertain perceptions of people except to ask about them in one way or another. In addition, we are interested only in the roles that are assumed in the purchase or consumer decision-making situation. The study should not, therefore, involve itself in seeking information about other types of roles husbands and wives might play. Reflection upon this hypothesis might also reveal that husbands and wives disagree on their perceptions of roles, but these differences may be explained in terms of additional variables, such as age, social class, background, personality, and other factors not associated with their difference in gender.

What Is a Strong Hypothesis?   A strong hypothesis should fulfill three conditions:

- Adequate for its purpose.
- Testable.
- Better than its rivals.

The conditions for developing a strong hypothesis are developed more fully in Exhibit 3-5.

Theory

Hypotheses play an important role in the development of theory. How theory differs from hypothesis may cause confusion. We make the general distinction that the difference between theory and hypothesis is one of degree of complexity and abstraction. In general, theories tend to be complex, be abstract, and involve multiple variables. Hypotheses, on the other hand, tend to be more simple, limited-variable statements involving concrete instances.

A person not familiar with research uses the term *theory* to express the opposite of *fact.* In this sense, theory is viewed as being speculative or "ivory tower." One hears that managers

>**Exhibit 3-5** Checklist for Developing a Strong Hypothesis

Criteria	Interpretation
Adequate for Its Purpose	❏ Does the hypothesis reveal the original problem condition? ❏ Does the hypothesis clearly identify facts that are relevant and those that are not? ❏ Does the hypothesis clearly state the condition, size, or distribution of some variable in terms of values meaningful to the research problem (descriptive)? ❏ Does the hypothesis explain facts that gave rise to the need for explanation (explanatory)? ❏ Does the hypothesis suggest which form of research design is likely to be most appropriate? ❏ Does the hypothesis provide a framework for organizing the conclusions that result?
Testable	❏ Does the hypothesis use acceptable techniques? ❏ Does the hypothesis require an explanation that is plausible given known physical or psychological laws? ❏ Does the hypothesis reveal consequences or derivatives that can be deduced for testing purposes? ❏ Is the hypothesis simple, requiring few conditions or assumptions?
Better Than Its Rivals	❏ Does the hypothesis explain more facts than its rivals? ❏ Does the hypothesis explain a greater variety or scope of facts than its rivals? ❏ Is the hypothesis one that informed judges would accept as being the most likely?

need to be less theoretical or that some idea will not work because it is too theoretical. This is an incorrect picture of the relationship between fact and theory to the researcher. In truth, fact and theory are each necessary for the other to be of value. Our ability to make rational decisions, as well as to develop scientific knowledge, is measured by the degree to which we combine fact and theory. We all operate on the basis of theories we hold. In one sense, theories are the generalizations we make about variables and the relationships among them. We use these generalizations to make decisions and predict outcomes. For example, it is midday and you note that the outside natural light is dimming, dark clouds are moving rapidly in from the west, the breeze is freshening, and the air temperature is cooling. Would your understanding of the relationship among these variables (your weather theory) lead you to predict that something decidedly wet will probably occur in a short time?

A **theory** is a set of systematically interrelated concepts, definitions, and propositions that are advanced to explain and predict phenomena (facts). In this sense, we have many theories and use them continually to explain or predict what goes on around us. To the degree that our theories are sound and fit the situation, we are successful in our explanations and predictions.

In marketing, the product life cycle describes the stages that a product category goes through in the marketplace.[11] The generalized product life cycle has four stages (although the length and shape of product life cycles differ): introduction, growth, maturity, and decline (Exhibit 3-6). In each stage, many concepts, constructs, and hypotheses describe the influences that change revenue and profit. Definitions are also needed for communicating about the claims of the theory and its consistency in testing to reality.

For example, in the growth stage, companies spend heavily on advertising and promotion to create product awareness. In the early period of this stage these expenditures may be made to fuel *primary demand* (construct), improving product class awareness rather

theory a set of systematically interrelated concepts, definitions, and propositions that are advanced to explain or predict phenomena.

>**Exhibit 3-6** Traditional Product Life Cycle

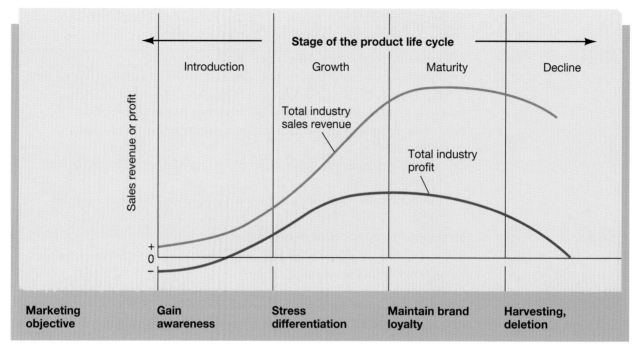

Source: Adapted from Roger Kerin, Eric Berkowitz, Steven Hartley, and William Rudelius, *Marketing,* 7th ed. (New York: McGraw-Hill, 2003), p. 295.

than brand awareness. Also, high pricing may reflect *skimming* (concept) to help the company recover developmental costs. The product manager may alternatively use low pricing, or *penetration pricing* (concept), to build unit volume. In the growth stage, sales increase rapidly because many consumers are trying or actually using the product; and those who tried, were satisfied, and bought again—*repeat purchasers* (concept)—are swelling the ranks. If the company is unable to attract repeat purchasers, this usually means death for the product (proposition). The maturity stage is a good time for the company in terms of generating cash (proposition). The costs of developing the product and establishing its position in the marketplace are paid and it tends be profitable. Firms will often try to use *extension strategies* (constructs). These are attempts to delay the decline stage of the product life cycle by introducing new versions of the product. In the decline stage, "products will consume a disproportionate share of management time and financial resources relative to their potential future worth"[12] (hypothesis). To make this hypothesis fully testable, we would need operational definitions for disproportionate share, time, resources, and future worth.

The challenge for market research in this example is to build more comprehensive theories to explain and predict how modifying the product and other marketing mix variables will benefit the firm.

Models

model a representation of a system constructed to study some aspect of that system or the system as a whole.

The term *model* is used in marketing research and other fields of business to represent phenomena through the use of analogy. A **model** is defined here as a representation of a system that is constructed to study some aspect of that system or the system as a whole. Models differ from theories in that a theory's role is explanation whereas a model's role is representation.

Early marketing models (and even those created as recently as the 1990s for mainframe computers) were enormously expensive and often incomprehensible to all but their developers. Modeling software, such as Excel, has made modeling more inexpensive and accessible.

>**Exhibit 3-7** A Consumer Behavior Model

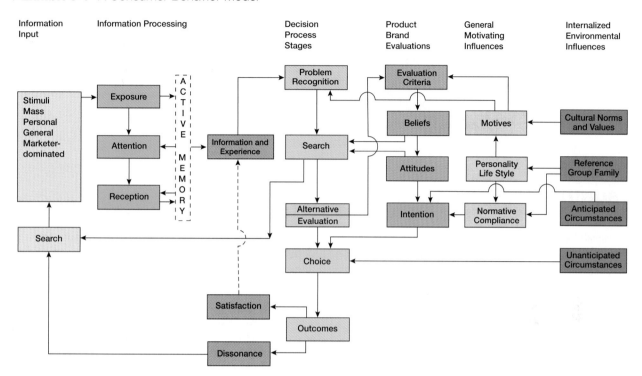

Source: Adapted from James F. Engle, Rodger D. Blackwell, and David T. Kollat, *Consumer Behavior,* 3d ed. Copyright © 1978 by the Dryden Press. Reprinted by permission of Holt, Rinehart and Winston, Inc.

Marketing models allow researchers and marketing managers to characterize present or future conditions: the effect of advertising on consumer awareness or intention to purchase, a product distribution channel, brand switching, redistribution of market share, and many other aspects of the marketing mix. A model's purpose is to increase our understanding, prediction, and control of the complexities of the marketing environment.

Exhibit 3-7 provides an example of a large-scale consumer behavior model. Such models allow researchers to specify hypotheses about the nature, relationship, and direction of causality among variables.

Descriptive, predictive, and normative models are found in marketing research.[13] *Descriptive* models are used frequently for more complex systems, such as the one in Exhibit 3-7. They allow visualization of numerous variables and relationships. *Predictive* models forecast future events and thereby facilitate market planning (see, for example, the Nike–Air Jordan New Product Case, in which Nike used the Fourt and Woodlock model to forecast basketball shoes for a market segment).[14] *Normative* models are used chiefly for control, informing us about what actions should be taken. Models may also be static, representing a system at one point in time, or dynamic, representing the evolution of a system over time.

Marketing models are developed through the use of inductive and deductive reasoning, which we suggested previously is integral to accurate conclusions about market behavior. As illustrated in Exhibit 3-8, a marketing model may originate from empirical observations about market behavior based on researched facts and relationships among variables. Inductive reasoning allows the modeler to draw conclusions from the facts or evidence in planning the dynamics of the model. The modeler may also use existing theory, managerial experience, judgment, or facts deduced from known laws of nature. In this case, deductive reasoning serves to create particular conclusions derived from general premises.

Marketing models are an important means of advancing marketing theories and aiding decision makers. Because the inputs are often unknown, imprecise, or temporal estimates of complex marketing mix variables, creating and using models in the marketing decision-making process can be a time-consuming endeavor.

▷**Exhibit 3-8** The Role of Reasoning in Model Development

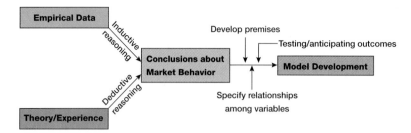

▷summary

1 Scientific inquiry is grounded in the inference process. This process is used for the development and testing of various propositions largely through the double movement of reflective thinking. Reflective thinking consists of sequencing induction and deduction in order to explain inductively (by hypothesis) a puzzling condition. In turn, the hypothesis is used in a deduction of further facts that can be sought to confirm or deny the truth of the hypothesis.

Researchers think of the doing of science as an orderly process that combines induction, deduction, observation, and hypothesis testing into a set of reflective thinking activities. Although the scientific method consists of neither sequential nor independent stages, the problem-solving process that it reveals provides insight into the way research is conducted.

2 Scientific methods and scientific thinking are based on concepts, the symbols we attach to bundles of meaning that we hold and share with others. We invent concepts to think about and communicate abstractions. We also use higher-level concepts—constructs—for specialized scientific explanatory purposes that are not directly observable. Concepts, constructs, and variables may be defined descriptively or operationally. Operational definitions must specify adequately the empirical information needed and how it will be collected. In addition, they must have the proper scope or fit for the research problem at hand.

Concepts and constructs are used at the theoretical levels; variables are used at the empirical level. Variables accept numerals or values for the purpose of testing and measurement. They may be classified as explanatory, independent, dependent, moderating, extraneous, and intervening.

3 Propositions are of great interest in research because they may be used to assess the truth or falsity of relationships among observable phenomena. When we advance a proposition for testing, we are hypothesizing. A hypothesis describes the relationships between or among variables. A good hypothesis is one that can explain what it claims to explain, is testable, and has greater range, probability, and simplicity than its rivals.

Sets of interrelated concepts, definitions, and propositions that are advanced to explain and predict phenomena are called theories. Models differ from theories in that models are analogies or representations of some aspect of a system or of the system as a whole. Models are used for description, prediction, and control.

▷**key**terms

>discussionquestions

Terms in Review

1 Distinguish among the following sets of items, and suggest the significance of each in a research context:

  a Concept and construct.

  b Deduction and induction.

  c Operational definition and dictionary definition.

  d Concept and variable.

  e Hypothesis and proposition.

  f Theory and model.

  g Scientific method and scientific attitude.

2 Describe the characteristics of the scientific method.

3 Here are some terms commonly found in a marketing setting. Are they concepts or constructs? Give two different operational definitions for each.

  a Store manager

  b Customer loyalty

  c Advertising campaign

  d Brand equity

  e Market share

  f Price leadership

  g Price-earnings ratio

  h Public opinion

  i Ethical standards

4 In your company's management development program, there was a heated discussion between some people who claimed, "Theory is impractical and thus no good," and others who claimed, "Good theory is the most practical approach to problems." What position would you take and why?

5 An automobile manufacturer observes the demand for its brand increasing as per capita income increases. Sales increases also follow low interest rates, which ease credit conditions. Buyer purchase behavior is seen to be dependent on age and gender. Other factors influencing sales appear to fluctuate almost randomly (competitor advertising, competitor dealer discounts, introductions of new competitive models).

  a If sales and per capita income are positively related, classify all variables as dependent, independent, moderating, extraneous, or intervening.

  b Comment on the utility of a model based on the hypothesis.

Making Research Decisions

6 You observe the following condition: "Our female sales representatives have lower customer defections than do our male sales representatives."

  a Propose the concepts and constructs you might use to study this phenomenon.

  b How might any of these concepts and/or constructs be related to explanatory hypotheses?

7 You are the office manager of a large firm. Your company prides itself on its high-quality customer service. Lately complaints have surfaced that an increased number of incoming calls are being misrouted or dropped. Yesterday, when passing by the main reception area, you noticed the receptionist fiddling with his hearing aid. In the process, a call came in and would have gone unanswered if not for your intervention. This particular receptionist had earned an unsatisfactory review three months earlier for tardiness. Your inclination is to urge this 20-year employee to retire or to fire him, if retirement is rejected, but you know the individual is well liked and seen as a fixture in the company.

  a Pose several hypotheses that might account for dropped or misrouted incoming calls.

  b Using the double movement of reflective thought, show how you would test these hypotheses.

8 The Institute of Transportation Engineers, a nationwide trade association with thousands of members, was dissatisfied with the way that State Farm arrived at its dangerous intersection list.

  a If ITE were to conduct a study of its own, what constructs and concepts would ITE define differently?

  b What hypotheses would ITE formulate to guide its version of the dangerous intersection study?

Behind the Scenes

9 Identify and classify all the variables in the Army's dud shell research.

10 What was Myra's hypothesis for the Army's dud shell research? What was the Army's hypothesis?

From Concept to Practice

11 Using Exhibits 3-2 and 3-3 as your guides, graph the inductions and deductions in the following statements. If there are gaps, supply what is needed to make them complete arguments.

  a Repeated studies indicate that economic conditions vary with—and lag 6 to 12 months behind—the changes in the national money supply. Therefore, we may conclude the money supply is the basic economic variable.

b Research studies show that heavy smokers have a higher rate of lung cancer than do nonsmokers; therefore, heavy smoking causes lung cancer.

c Show me a person who goes to church regularly, and I will show you a reliable worker.

>**www**exercise

Draw a conclusion via either induction or deduction about something happening at your school. Visit your school's Web site to determine if you can find evidence to support your conclusion.

>**cases***

Campbell-Ewald: R-E-S-P-E-C-T Spells Loyalty

Hero Builders.com

Open Doors: Extending Hospitality to Travelers with Disabilities

* All cases, both written and video, are on the text DVD. Check the DVD Index to determine whether a case has data, the research instrument, or other supplementary material.

>chapter 4

The Marketing Research Process:
An Overview

>learningobjectives

After reading this chapter, you should understand . . .

1 Research is decision- and dilemma-centered.

2 The clarified research question is the result of careful exploration and analysis and sets the direction for the research project.

3 How value assessments and budgeting influence the process for proposing research and, ultimately, research design.

4 What is included in research design, data collection, and data analysis.

5 Research process problems to avoid.

We rejoin Visionary Insights' Jason Henry as he works on the MindWriter CompleteCare customer satisfaction project. At this stage in the MindWriter research process, Jason Henry's task is to help MindWriter's project director, Myra Wines, define the correct information to collect. Henry and Wines have just spent the day at the CompleteCare facility in Austin and with other MindWriter managers who are influential to CompleteCare's success. They spent much of their time with Gracie Uhura, MindWriter's marketing manager.

On the return flight from Austin, Visionary Insights' Jason Henry and MindWriter's Myra Wines are discussing their trip. "That went really well," she says.

"There are going to be a few problems," disagrees Jason. "Gracie, like most marketing managers, wants the sun, the sky, and the moon. She wants to know the demographic characteristics of her users . . . their job descriptions . . . their salaries . . . their ethnicities . . . their education; wants to know their perception of MindWriter . . . of the quality of MindWriter's specific models; wants to know their satisfaction with the purchase channel and with the CompleteCare service, too."

"And your point is?" asks Myra.

"You and Gracie need to keep your eye on the bottom line. You can bet someone will want to know how you and Gracie can justify asking all these questions. They will ask, 'What is going to be the payoff in knowing the ethnicity of customers?' And if you or Gracie can't explain the justification for needing the information, if one of you can't establish that the dollar benefit of knowing is at least as great as the dollar cost of finding out, the question will get struck from the developing research."

"Is there no way we can justify knowing everything Gracie wants to know?" inquires Myra.

"We can draft a survey and do a pilot study of a few hundred customers and see if the ethnic background, or the salary level, or any other item that Gracie cares about is a good indicator of satisfaction, willingness to make a repeat purchase, postpurchase service satisfaction, and so forth. If it is, maybe collecting that information can be justified."

"So you feel we need to propose a pilot study to whittle down the information needed to critical items, followed by a larger study later?"

"A pilot study could help in other ways, too. Gracie wants to know the customers' perception of MindWriter's overall quality. But we have to ask ourselves, 'Are these customers really qualified to form independent opinions, or will they simply be parroting what they have read in the computer magazines or what a dealer told them?' A pilot study of a few hundred users can help determine if it is really useful to ask them their overall impression of the product.

"However, with the repair problem we can be reasonably sure that the CompleteCare customers know their own minds when it comes to evaluating their firsthand experience with MindWriter's service department."

"Today's tour of the CompleteCare facility really helped me understand the context of management's concerns," comments Myra. "Did you or Sara have a chance to look over any of the customer letters from the service department?"

Jason digs into his briefcase and extracts a small sheaf of photocopies. "Yes, and Sara reviewed transcriptions, too, on service center phone conversations. She pulled a few for us. One person writes, 'My MindWriter was badly damaged on arrival. I could not believe its condition when I unpacked it.' And here, 'The service technicians seemed to be unable to understand my complaint, but once they understood it, they performed immediate repairs.' You and I will collaborate to boil down these, and possibly dozens more like them, to a couple of representative questions that can be pilot-tested for clarity, consistency, and representativeness. You don't want MindWriter to pay for everything Gracie says she wants, just what she wants that has a payoff and is researchable."

> The Marketing Research Process

Writers usually treat the research task as a sequential process involving several clearly defined steps. No one claims that research requires completion of each step before going to the next. Recycling, circumventing, and skipping occur. Some steps are begun out of sequence, some are carried out simultaneously, and some may be omitted. Despite these variations, the idea of a sequence is useful for developing a project and for keeping the project orderly as it unfolds.

Exhibit 4-1 models the sequence of stages in the **research process**. We refer to it often as we discuss each stage and step in subsequent chapters. Our discussion of the questions that guide project planning and data gathering is incorporated into the model (see the elements within the inverted pyramid in Exhibit 4-1 and compare them with the elements in Exhibit 4-2). Exhibit 4-1 also organizes this chapter and introduces the remainder of the book.

research process various decision stages involved in a research project and the relationship between those stages.

The research process begins much as the opening vignette suggests. A management dilemma triggers the need for a decision. For MindWriter, a growing number of complaints about postpurchase service started the process. In other situations, a controversy arises, a major commitment of resources is called for, or conditions in the environment signal the need for a decision. For MindWriter, the critical event could have been a competitor's introduction of new technology. Such events cause managers to reconsider their purposes or objectives, define a problem for solution, or develop strategies for solutions they have identified.

The primary purpose of research is to reduce the level of risk of a marketing decision. Knowing that most new product introductions fail, this humorous ad from Greenfield Online suggests that not all new product ideas are worthy of consideration and that well-executed research can save a firm from a costly mistake. www.greenfieldonline.com

In our view of the research process, the management question—its origin, selection, statement, exploration, and refinement—is the critical activity in the sequence. Throughout the chapter we emphasize problem-related steps. A familiar quotation from Albert Einstein, no less apt today than when it was written, supports this view:

DON'T THROW GOOD MONEY AT A BAD IDEA.

Before you launch your new product, see if anyone wants it.

Pretest your new concept—online—with the company that pioneered marketing research on the Internet. Our panel of more than one million consumers from all across the Internet, the largest of its kind, includes exactly the people you want to reach.

Join the Research Revolution!™ Contact the world's most experienced Internet marketing research company for studies online, on time, on target and on budget.

www.greenfield.com 888.291.9997

Greenfield Online
Leading the Research Revolution®

> **Exhibit 4-1** The Marketing Research Process

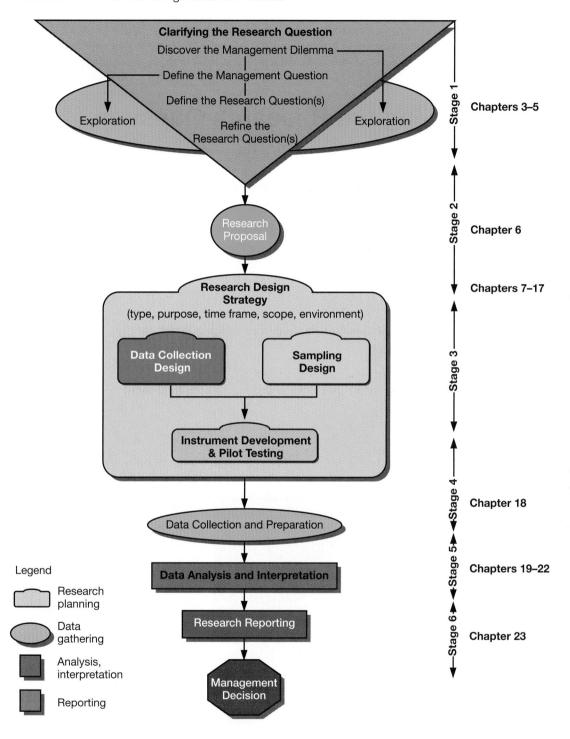

The formulation of a problem is far more often essential than its solution, which may be merely a matter of mathematical or experimental skill. To raise new questions, new possibilities, to regard old problems from a new angle requires creative imagination and marks real advance in science.[1]

Whether the researcher is involved in basic or applied research, a thorough understanding of the management question is fundamental to success in the research enterprise.

> Stage 1: Clarifying the Research Question

A useful way to approach the research process is to state the basic dilemma that prompts the research and then try to develop other questions by progressively breaking down the original question into more specific ones. You can think of the this process as the **management-research question hierarchy**. You can follow the research process as it develops for MindWriter in Exhibit 4-2.

management-research question hierarchy process of sequential question formulation that leads a manager or researcher from management dilemma to investigative questions.

management dilemma the problem or opportunity that requires a marketing decision.

The process begins at the most general level with the **management dilemma.** This is usually a symptom of an actual problem, such as:

- Rising costs.
- The discovery of an expensive chemical compound that would increase the efficacy of a drug.
- Increasing tenant move-outs from an apartment complex.
- Declining sales.
- A larger number of product defects during the manufacture of an automobile.
- An increasing number of letters and phone complaints about postpurchase service (as at MindWriter).

The management dilemma can also be triggered by an early signal of an opportunity or growing evidence that a fad may be gaining staying power—like the growing interest in low-carbohydrate diets indicated by the number of broadcast news segments and print news stories over an extended period of time.

Identifying management dilemmas is rarely difficult (unless the organization fails to track its performance factors—like sales, profits, employee turnover, manufacturing output and defects, on-time deliveries, customer satisfaction, etc.). However, choosing one dilemma on which to focus may be difficult. Choosing incorrectly will direct valuable resources (time, manpower, money, and equipment) on a path that may not provide critical decision-making information (the purpose of good research). As a marketing manager, only practice makes you proficient at identifying which are real problems and which are not, as well as correctly discerning the scope of the dilemma to be researched. For new managers, or established managers facing new responsibilities, developing several management-research question hierarchies, each starting with a different

> **Exhibit 4-2** Formulating the Research Question for MindWriter

To move from the management dilemma to the management question and subsequent research questions takes exploratory research. Such research may include examining previous studies, reviewing published studies and organizational records, and interviewing experts or information gatekeepers.

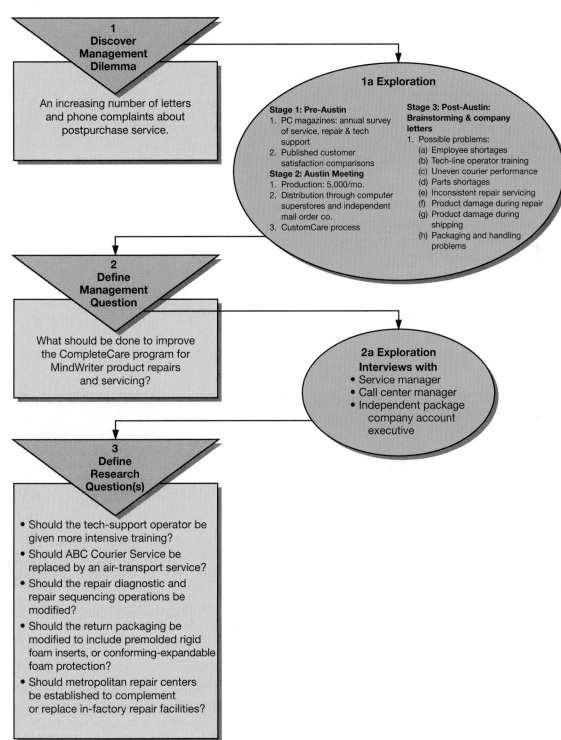

1
Discover Management Dilemma

An increasing number of letters and phone complaints about postpurchase service.

1a Exploration

Stage 1: Pre-Austin
1. PC magazines: annual survey of service, repair & tech support
2. Published customer satisfaction comparisons

Stage 2: Austin Meeting
1. Production: 5,000/mo.
2. Distribution through computer superstores and independent mail order co.
3. CustomCare process

Stage 3: Post-Austin: Brainstorming & company letters
1. Possible problems:
   (a) Employee shortages
   (b) Tech-line operator training
   (c) Uneven courier performance
   (d) Parts shortages
   (e) Inconsistent repair servicing
   (f) Product damage during repair
   (g) Product damage during shipping
   (h) Packaging and handling problems

2
Define Management Question

What should be done to improve the CompleteCare program for MindWriter product repairs and servicing?

2a Exploration Interviews with
• Service manager
• Call center manager
• Independent package company account executive

3
Define Research Question(s)

• Should the tech-support operator be given more intensive training?
• Should ABC Courier Service be replaced by an air-transport service?
• Should the repair diagnostic and repair sequencing operations be modified?
• Should the return packaging be modified to include premolded rigid foam inserts, or conforming-expandable foam protection?
• Should metropolitan repair centers be established to complement or replace in-factory repair facilities?

>**snap**shot

A Love-Match between Lexus and Research

If your product earns rave reviews for dependability/reliability, quality workmanship, and manufacturer reputation, that's good, right? If your firm delivers on the promise of your long-held promotional tagline—the "Pursuit of Perfection"—that's great, right? "Not good enough," claims Mark Miller, associate director of strategic planning, Team One Advertising, "when Toyota is determined to infuse the Lexus brand with passion."

Toyota faced some troubling statistics in the 1997–1999 model years. While the Lexus brand was setting sales records and overall the luxury coupe category was growing, its Lexus coupe sales were declining. And while Lexus scored well on the rational motivators, it lacked the emotional motivators deemed critical for luxury coupe success, especially against Corvette, Porsche, and Mercedes. Toyota engineers had developed a concept car in Japan, the SC 430. This car was Toyota's first luxury convertible and sported a technologically advanced, retractable hard top rather than the more usual soft "rag" top.

Team One was charged with developing the communications program to launch the SC 430. Understanding that this car was and needed to be a departure from traditional Lexus brand imagery, Team One needed information to accomplish Toyota's more aggressive agenda: "(1) evolve the Lexus brand using the

SC 430 convertible as the emotional flagship, (2) stimulate desire for the Lexus brand, as well as desire for the SC 430 convertible, (3) make a connection with luxury convertible buyers beyond the rational, and (4) inject more passion into our Pursuit of Perfection." Using syndicated tracking studies by Allison-Fisher and innovative quantitative research by Diagnostic Research Inc., along with strategic marketing clinic research by the Lexus team, and data mining Toyota's Consolidated Dynamic Study, Team One created its innovative French-language American-aired campaign. The *Cabriolet Nouveau* campaign married the association of the French with seduction, love, and romance to the "stylish, sophisticated, sexy" Lexus SC 430. The results were award-winning in numerous ways, including earning the 2002 David Ogilvy Research Award in the durables category.

Using the management-research question hierarchy, identify the management dilemma, management question(s), and research question(s) that would drive this research. Watch for the special icon that indicates a continuation of this research story example.

www.lexus.com; www.teamoneadv.com; www.diagnostic.com; www.allison-fisher.com

dilemma, will assist in the choice process. In all figures related to the research process model, in this and subsequent chapters, we use an inverted pyramid to represent the management-research question hierarchy.

Subsequent stages of the hierarchy take the marketer and his or her research collaborator through various brainstorming and exploratory research exercises to define the following:

- **Management question**—a restatement of the marketer's dilemma(s) in question form.

- **Research question(s)**—the hypothesis that best states the objective of the research; the question(s) that focuses the researcher's attention.

WASSUP? from Donatos Pizza

In the food business, strategic windows remain open for limited periods of time. "Restaurants are influenced by many factors. Some include product, message, weather, reputation, and competition," shared Donatos' chief concept officer, Tom Krouse. In Donatos *WASSUP?* meetings, each employee brings knowledge of an element from popular culture and the group discusses its possible effect on the company's 184 restaurants. Exposure comes from articles, movies, books, TV, and daily living. Donatos filters this less formal exploration with syndicated research. "By late July, we had research that showed 26 percent of adult eaters were carb-aware." And Donatos had evidence that adults were incorporating low-carb habits into their diets. In its own restaurants, diners were eating the toppings from their favorite meat-loaded pizza but leaving the crust behind. On this accumulated evidence, Donatos decided it wanted to own the low-carb position in pizza.

Donatos' first step was to compact its normal new product development process into less than six months—to be ready for the traditional postholiday increase in dieting. Taste tests told Donatos that the low-carb crust options available sacrificed taste—and choosing that route would have jeopardized its premium pizza flavor positioning, which was reinforced by its Edge-to-Edge™ toppings. Instead, Donatos chose a more expensive, but true-to-positioning, product that incorporated protein crisps and tested well with pizza eaters. Following the discovery of a high-heat-resistant paper that could serve as both baking and serving plate, the company did in-store trials in two restaurants. In-store postpurchase surveys of diners told Donatos its *No Dough* pizza was a winner. Donatos rolled out the *No Dough* pizza to its 184 restaurants in January 2004. The menu board now shows three crust versions: original crispy, traditional, or *No Dough*. Diners simply choose their favorite pizza toppings and choose the *No Dough* option. Increased visits from Atkin's dieters and purchases from a hidden segment, gluten avoiders, propelled sales increases. Coverage in numerous local papers and TV segments, on the *Today* show, and in the *New York Times* helps Donatos own the low-carb position in pizza in its markets.

www.donatos.com

To learn more, read the case on your DVD: "Donatos: Finding the New Pizza."

choices will be discussed here, although the same approach can be used with more than two choices. You'll find an example of decision theory on this book's DVD.

Two possible actions (A_1 and A_2) may represent two different ways to promote a company, support a cause, design a product, and so forth. The manager chooses the action that affords the best outcome—the action choice that meets or exceeds whatever criteria are established for judging alternatives. Each criterion is a combination of a **decision rule** and a **decision variable.** The decision variable might be "new customers captured," "contribution to profits," "time required for completion of the project," and so forth. For MindWriter, the decision variable might be number of "postservice complaints" or the level of "postservice satisfaction." Usually the decision variable is expressed in a quantifiable measure, often in dollars, representing sales, costs, or some form of profits. The decision rule may be "Choose the course of action with the lowest loss possibility" or, perhaps, "Choose the alternative that provides the greatest number of retained customers." For MindWriter, the decision rule might be "Choose the alternative that provides the highest level of postservice satisfaction."

The alternative selected (A_1 versus A_2) depends on the decision variable chosen and the decision rule used. The evaluation of alternatives requires that (1) each alternative is explicitly stated, (2) a decision variable is defined by an outcome that may be measured, and (3) a decision rule is determined by which outcomes may be compared.

decision rule criterion for judging the attractiveness of two or more alternatives when using a decision variable.

decision variable a quantifiable characteristic, attribute, or outcome on which a choice decision will be made.

Prior or Interim Evaluation
Some research projects are sufficiently unique that managerial experience provides little aid in evaluating the research proposal. Additionally, the management information need may be so great as to ensure that the research is approved. In such cases, managers may decide to control the research expenditure risk by doing a study in stages. They can then review costs and benefits at the end of each stage and give or withhold further authorization.

Ex Post Facto Evaluation
If there is any measurement of the value of research, it is usually an after-the-fact event. Using an estimate of alternative decision choices, the

preresearch likelihood that a decision choice would be selected, and a postresearch projection of the implemented decision's contribution to profitability (or some other decision variable), a researcher can estimate the contribution value of a research project. One such study using one manufacturer's research activities reported that 40 percent of the research actually directed the manager to the appropriate decision. Using data on profitability contribution and on direct research costs only, the researcher calculated a 3½-fold return on the manufacturer's investment.[4] While the postresearch effort at cost-benefit comes too late to guide a current research decision, such analysis may sharpen the manager's ability to make judgments about future research proposals.

The Research Proposal

Exhibit 4-1 depicts the research proposal as an activity that incorporates decisions made during early project planning phases of the study, including the management-research question hierarchy and exploration. The proposal process thus incorporates the choices the investigator makes in the preliminary steps, as depicted in Exhibit 4-3.

A written proposal is often required when a study is being suggested. This is especially true if an outside research supplier will be contracted to conduct the research. The written proposal ensures that the parties concur on the project's purpose, the proposed methods of investigation, the extent of analysis, and the timing of each phase as well as of delivery of results. Budgets are spelled out, as are other responsibilities and obligations. The proposal may serve the purpose of a legally binding contract.

A research proposal also may be oral, where all aspects of the research are discussed but not codified in writing. This is more likely when a manager directs his or her own research or the research activities of subordinates.

We describe detailed research proposals in Chapter 6, and you'll find a sample proposal on your text DVD.

> Stage 3: Designing the Research Project

Research Design

research design the blueprint for fulfilling research objectives and answering questions.

The **research design** is the blueprint for fulfilling objectives and providing the insight to answer management's dilemma. The field of marketing research offers a large variety of methods, techniques, procedures, and protocols. For example, you may decide on reviewing published records (a secondary data study), or studying one particular example in great detail (a case study), or conducting a survey, an experiment, or a computer simulation. If a survey is selected, should it be administered by mail, computer, telephone, the Internet, or personal interview? Should all relevant data be collected at one time or at several different points in time? What kind of structure will the questionnaire or interview guide possess? What question wording should be employed? Should the responses be scaled ("Please evaluate each of the following criteria for selecting a store for product X on a scale of 1 to 5, where 5 is critically important and 1 is not important.") or open-ended ("What is most important to you when choosing a store for product X?")? How will you ensure that the data you collect will accurately and precisely answer the manager's dilemma? Will characteristics of the interviewer influence responses to the measurement questions? What kind of training should the data collectors receive? Is a sample or a census to be taken? What types of sampling should be considered? These questions represent only a few of the decisions that have to be made when just one method is chosen.

While selecting an appropriate design may be complicated by this range of options, the creative researcher actually benefits from this confusing array of options. The numerous combinations spawned by the abundance of tools may be used to construct alternative perspectives on the same problem. By creating a research project using diverse methodologies, researchers are able to achieve greater insight than if they adopted the most frequently

> **snap**shot

Grilled Cheese Sandwiches and the Dairy Fairy

If you were Kraft and discovered that, while sales of sliced cheese were increasing, your brand's sales were decreasing, you might turn to advertising to reverse the slide. But just what would you say—and how? Faced with this situation, Kraft sent ethnographers from Strategic Frameworking to talk with moms aged 25 to 64 who were fixing sandwiches in their kitchens. Focus groups then reinforced that moms feel good about giving their kids cheese because of its nutritional value. Focus groups also revealed that even though their kids preferred Kraft slices, a price difference could persuade moms to purchase a competitive brand. A subsequent phone survey by Market Facts revealed moms would buy the pricier Kraft slices due to extra calcium. Next came TV-commercial tests for two spots featuring the "good-taste-plus-the-calcium-they-need" message. A spot featuring a straightforward message didn't score as high as one featuring kids scarfing down gooey grilled cheese sandwiches, but the male-voice-delivered "two-out-of-five-kids-don't-get-enough-calcium" message generated guilt, not positive purchase intentions. A revised commercial featured the cheese-scarfing kids while the Dairy Fairy (an animated cow) delivered the calcium message. Subsequently, Millward Brown Group discovered through copy testing research that the dual message had finally gotten through. The TV commercial aired, delivering an 11.8 percent increase in sales and a 14.5 percent increase in base volume. Sixty-five percent of the growth in sales was attributed to the campaign.

www.kraft.com; www.strategicframeworking.com; www.synovate.com; www.millwardbrown.com; www.jwt.com

used method or the method receiving the most attention in the media. Although pursuing research on a single research problem from a multimethod, multistudy strategy is not currently the norm, such designs are getting increasing attention from marketing researchers and winning numerous industry awards for effectiveness. The advantages and disadvantages of several competing designs should be considered before settling on a final one.

Jason's preference for MindWriter is to collect as much information as possible from an exploration of company records, interviews with company managers of various departments, and multiple phone surveys with CompleteCare service program users. Financial constraints, however, might force MindWriter to substitute a less expensive methodology: a self-administered survey in the form of a postcard questionnaire sent to each CompleteCare service program user with his or her returned laptop, followed by phone contact only with those who don't return the postcard.

We discuss identifying and classifying various research designs in Chapter 8, while in Chapters 9 through 15 we provide information on specific methodologies.

Sampling Design

Another step in planning the research project is to identify the target population (those people, events, or records that have the desired information and can answer the measurement questions) and then determine whether a sample or a census is desired. Taking a **census** requires that the researcher examine or count all elements in a target population. A **sample** examines a portion of the target population, and the portion must be carefully selected to represent that population. If sampling is chosen, the researcher must determine which and how many people to interview, which and how many events to observe, or which and how many records to inspect. When researchers undertake sampling studies, they are interested in estimating one or more population values (such as the percent of satisfied service customers who will buy new MindWriter laptops when the need arises) and/or testing one or more statistical hypotheses (for example, that highly satisfied CompleteCare service customers will be far more likely to repurchase the MindWriter brand of laptops).

If a study's objective is to predict repeat purchase of laptop brands, then the target population might be defined as all laptop computer owners. In the MindWriter example, given the speed with which technology changes, terms like *laptop* would need to be defined. Would

census a count of all elements in a population.

sample a group of cases, participants, events, or records constituting a portion of the target population, carefully selected to represent that population.

handheld and notebook computers be included or excluded? The researcher might also want to restrict the study to owners of the major laptop brands or to owners who reside in certain parts of the world. Because the research is designed to predict a population value from a sample of users, a probability sampling plan would need to be developed.

If a probability sampling design is chosen, the process for choosing the sample must then give every person within the target population a known nonzero chance of selection. If there is no feasible alternative, a nonprobability sampling approach may be used. Jason knows that his target population comprises MindWriter customers who have firsthand experience with the CompleteCare laptop servicing program. Given that a list of CompleteCare program users (a sample frame) is readily available each month, drawing a probability sample is feasible.

We describe types of samples, sample frames, how samples are drawn, and the determination of sample size in Chapters 16 and 17.

Pilot Testing

Given that thousands of dollars and hundreds of hours can be committed to a research project, the last step in research design is often a pilot test. The researcher may opt to skip pilot testing to condense the project time frame.

pilot test trial collection of data to detect weaknesses in the design or instrument and provide proxy data for probability sampling.

A **pilot test** is conducted to detect weaknesses in research methodology and the data collection instrument, as well as to provide proxy data for selection of a probability sample. It should, therefore, draw subjects from the target population and simulate the procedures and protocols that have been designated for data collection. If the study is a survey to be executed by mail, in the pilot test the questionnaire should be mailed. If the design calls for human observation, then a trained observer should collect the data with the appropriate observation checklist. The size of the pilot group may range from 25 to 100 subjects, depending on the research method to be tested, but the participants do not have to be statistically selected. In very small populations or special applications, pilot testing runs the risk of exhausting the supply of respondents and sensitizing them to the purpose of the study. This risk is generally overshadowed by the improvements made to the design by a trial run.

Pilot testing has saved countless survey studies from disaster by using the suggestions of the participants to identify and change confusing, awkward, or offensive questions and techniques. Using pilot testing in an interview study for EducTV, an educational television consortium, a disaster was averted. The pilot test revealed that the wording of nearly two-thirds of the questions was unintelligible to the target group, later found to have a median eighth-grade education. The revised instrument incorporated the respondents' own language and was successful. We discuss one of pilot testing's most common variations, the pretesting of survey instruments, in Chapter 15 and Appendix 15b.

> Stage 4: Data Collection and Preparation

The gathering of data may range from a simple observation at one location to a grandiose survey of multinational corporations at sites in different parts of the world. The method selected will largely determine how the data are collected. Questionnaires, standardized tests, and observational forms (called *checklists*) are among the devices used to record raw data.

But what are data? In the previous chapter, we described the relationship of facts to conclusions. One writer defines data as the facts presented to the researcher from the study's environment. Data may be further characterized by their abstractness, verifiability, elusiveness, and closeness to the phenomenon.[5] First, as abstractions, data are more metaphorical than real. For example, the growth in GDP cannot be observed directly; only the effects of it may be recorded. Second, data are processed by our senses—often limited in comparison to the senses of other living organisms. When sensory experiences consistently produce the same result, our data are said to be trustworthy because they may be verified. Third, capturing data is elusive, complicated by the speed at which events occur and the time-bound nature of observation. Opinions, preferences, and attitudes vary from one milieu to another and with the passage of time. For example, during presidential elections the incumbent president is often scrutinized and voters' favorability ratings are tracked with greater frequency. George W. Bush had the highest ratings ever recorded for a sitting president since Dwight Eisenhower immediately following the terrorist-retaliation bombing of Afghanistan.[6] However, as events in Iraq progressed, and as the election campaign year of 2003–2004 got under way and voters began questioning the advisability of remaining in Iraq, his approval ratings started to fall.[7] Finally, data reflect their truthfulness by closeness to the phenomena. **Secondary data** (data originally collected to address a problem other than the one that requires the manager's attention at the moment) have had at least one level of interpretation inserted between the event and its use for marketing decision making. **Primary data** (data the manager collects to address the specific problem at hand—the research question) are sought for their proximity to the truth and control over error. These cautions remind us to use care in designing data collection procedures and generalizing from results. We use a summary definition for **data** as information collected from participants, by observation, or from secondary sources.

Data are edited to ensure consistency across respondents and to locate omissions. In the case of a survey, editing reduces errors in the recording, improves legibility, and clarifies unclear and inappropriate responses. Edited data are then put into a form that makes analysis possible. Because it is impractical to place raw data into a report, alphanumeric codes are used to reduce the responses to a more manageable system for processing and storage. The codes follow various decision rules that the researcher has devised to assist with sorting, tabulating, and analyzing. Personal computers have made it possible to merge editing, coding, and data entry into fewer steps even when the final analysis may be run on a larger system. We address data collection in detail in Part III.

secondary data data originally collected to address a problem other than the one that requires the manager's attention at the moment.

primary data data the researcher collects to address the specific problem at hand—the research question.

data information collected from participants, by observation, or from secondary sources.

A focus group is one data collection methology. This group interview generates primary data.

>**snap**shot

Taking the Mystery Out of Mystery Shopping

When a retail salesperson receives a visit from a mystery shopper, it's all about processes. Amy Davidoff, president of MarketVoice Consulting, designs a mystery shopping study by starting with a clear understanding of the client's process priorities. Then she partners with the client to develop a shopper form, the detailed checklist of observations that will be recorded, as well as plenty of space for extensive written comments about the experience in general and for all items that received scores below a pre-specified level. While a shopper might target a particular sales associate within a retail environment—based, for example, on an accumulation of consumer complaints—more often a retail manager contracts for periodic shoppings over a specified time. "For one food and entertainment facility," shares Davidoff, "the shop form was 14 pages, covering a 2-hour shopping experience. (A more typical shop form is 5 to 7 pages.) The shop started when the shopper entered the door, included food

purchases at two different locations within the facility, restroom checks, specific types of interactions with the facility staff and merchandise purchases." During the shop, the researcher will determine if dozens of processes took place and at what level each was performed against specification. In the overall evaluation, the shop can add weight to more critical processes—those that contribute most to the customer experience and enhance customer loyalty. Taking multiple measures over time reveals weaknesses in training, flaws in operations and sales processes, and the occasional employee theft. "And if it's done correctly," claims Davidoff, "the sales associate may never know they participated in marketing research."

Mystery shopping takes place in many different arenas including stores, restaurants, and catalog operations. College students are often employed as mystery shoppers.

> Stage 5: Data Analysis and Interpretation

data analysis editing, reducing, summarizing, looking for patterns, and applying statistical techniques to data.

Managers need information and insights, not raw data, to make appropriate marketing decisions. Researchers generate information and insights by analyzing data after their collection. **Data analysis** usually involves reducing accumulated data to a manageable size, developing summaries, looking for patterns, and applying statistical techniques. Researchers then interpret their findings in light of the manager's research question or determine if the results are consistent with their hypotheses and theories. Increasingly, managers are asking research specialists to make recommendations based on their interpretation of the data. We address data analysis and interpretation in Chapters 18 to 22.

A modest example involves a market research firm that polls 2,000 people from its target population for a new generation of wallet-sized portable telephones. Each respondent will be asked four questions:

1. "Do you prefer the convenience of Pocket-Phone over existing cellular telephones?"
2. "Are there transmission problems with Pocket-Phone?"
3. "Is Pocket-Phone better suited to worldwide transmission than your existing cellular phone?"
4. "Would cost alone persuade you to purchase Pocket-Phone?"

The answers will produce 8,000 (2,000 $\times$ 4) pieces of raw data. Reducing the data to a workable size will yield eight statistics: the percentages of yes and no answers to each question. When the researcher adds a half-dozen demographic questions about the participants, the total amount of data easily triples. If the researcher scaled the four key questions (asking the participants to provide a number from 1 to 5 for each question) rather than eliciting yes-no responses, the analysis would likely require more powerful statistical analysis than summarization.

> Stage 6: Reporting the Results

Finally, it is necessary to prepare a report and transmit the findings, insights, and recommendations to the manager for the intended purpose of decision making. The researcher adjusts the style and organization of the report according to the target audience, the occasion, and the purpose of the research. As a result, most marketing researchers emphasize the need to make the research report manager-friendly, avoiding technical jargon. The results of applied research may be communicated via conference call, letter, written report, oral presentation, Webcast, or some combination of any or all of these methods. Reports should be developed from the manager's or information user's perspective. The sophistication of the research design and sampling plan or the software used to analyze the data may help to establish the researcher's credibility, but in the end the manager's foremost concern is solving the management dilemma. Thus, the researcher must accurately assess the manager's needs throughout the research process and incorporate this understanding into the final product, the research report.

The management decision maker occasionally shelves the research report without taking action. Inferior communication of results is a primary reason for this outcome. With this possibility in mind, a research supplier should strive for:

- Insightful adaptation of the information to the client's needs.

- Careful choice of words in crafting interpretations, conclusions, and recommendations.

Especially when research is contracted to an outside supplier, managers and researchers increasingly collaborate to develop appropriate reporting of project results and information.

Occasionally, organizational and environmental forces beyond the researcher's control argue against the implementation of results. Such was the case in a study conducted for the Association of American Publishers, which needed an ad campaign to encourage people to read more books. The research project, costing $125,000, found that only 13 percent of Americans buy general-interest books in stores. When the time came to commit $14 million to the campaign to raise book sales, the membership's interest had faded and the project died.[8] We cover the research report in Chapter 23.

At a minimum, a research report should contain the following:

- An executive summary consisting of a synopsis of the problem, findings, and recommendations.

- An overview of the research: the problem's background, a summary of exploratory findings drawn from secondary data sources, the actual research design and procedures, and conclusions.

- A section on implementation strategies for the recommendations.

- A technical appendix with all the materials necessary to replicate the project.

> Research Process Problems

Although it is desirable for research to be thoroughly grounded in management decision priorities, studies can wander off target or be less effective than they should be. As research progresses through its various stages, the researcher needs to remain objective.

The Favored-Technique Syndrome

Some researchers are method-bound. They recast the management question so it is amenable to their favorite methodology—a survey, for example. Others might prefer to emphasize the case study, while still others wouldn't consider either approach. Not all researchers are comfortable with experimental designs. Due to their wide range of experience and educational

> **It is the role of the manager sponsoring the research to spot an inappropriate-technique-driven research proposal.**

training, researchers are rarely well versed in every possible methodology. Out of a need for control or comfort, some will rely only on methods with which they have experience.

Persons knowledgeable about and skilled in some techniques but not in others may be blinded by their special competencies. Their concern for technique dominates the decisions concerning what will be studied (both investigative and measurement questions) and how (research design). The availability of technique is an important factor in determining how research will be done or whether a given study can be done. The marketing decision maker sponsoring the research should be wary of inappropriate-technique-driven research proposals. We discuss research techniques and when each is appropriate in Chapters 9 through 17.

In the MindWriter research, for example, numerous, standardized customer satisfaction questionnaires are available to researchers. Jason may have done studies using these instruments for any number of his clients. Myra should be cautious. She must not let Jason encourage her acceptance of an instrument he has developed for another client, even though he might be very persuasive about its success in the past. Such a technique might not be appropriate for MindWriter's search to resolve postpurchase service dissatisfaction.

Company Database Strip-Mining

> **We discussed decision support systems in Chapter 2.**

The existence of a pool of information or a database can distract a manager, seemingly reducing the need for other research. As evidence of the research-as-expense-not-investment mentality mentioned in Chapter 1, managers frequently hear from superiors, "We should use the information we already have before collecting more." Modern marketing information systems are capable of providing massive volumes of data. This is not the same as saying modern marketing information systems provide substantial knowledge or decision-making insights.

Each field in a database was originally created for a specific reason, a reason that may or may not be compatible with the management question facing the organization. The Mind-Writer service department's database, for example, probably contains several fields about the type of problem, the location of the problem, the remedy used to correct the problem, and so forth. Jason and Myra can accumulate facts concerning the service, and they can match each service problem with a particular MindWriter model and production sequence (from a production database), and, using yet another database (generated from warranty registration), they can match each problem to a name and address of an owner. But, having done all that, they still aren't likely to know how a particular owner uses his or her laptop or how satisfied an owner was with MindWriter's postpurchase service policies and practices.

Mining marketing information databases is fashionable, and all types of organizations increasingly value the ability to extract meaningful information. While such data mining is often a starting point in decision-based research, rarely will this activity answer all management questions related to a particular management dilemma. In this text, we emphasize research projects that tend to be nonroutine, nonrecurring, and complex, rather than those that rely solely on database management.

Unresearchable Questions

Not all management questions are researchable, and not all research questions are answerable. To be researchable, a question must be one for which observation or other data collection can provide the answer. Many questions cannot be answered on the basis of information alone.

Unresearchable questions include those for which past experience of the researcher or experience of the greater research industry has revealed that the information does not exist or cannot be gathered. An example is a study in which purchase information dating back 30 or more years is needed and no such records exist. It is unrealistic to assume purchasers can recall purchase behavior that long ago with sufficient accuracy or in sufficient detail to be useful.

Just as human memory can be faulty, when we seek motivations from participants, we may run into unresearchable questions. Sometimes customers and other participants simply don't know why they do what they do.

Questions of value and policy often must be weighed in management decisions. The multiple facets of the deliberations make many such questions unresearchable. During the early and mid-1980s several product-tampering incidents of over-the-counter drug products resulted in deaths. Asking "Should products be withdrawn if even one death is associated with its prescribed use, even if no fault for the tampered product accrues to the manufacturer?" might qualify as an unresearchable question. While information can be brought to bear on this question, such additional considerations as "safety to society" or "fairness to stockholders" or "an appropriate response to terrorist activity" may be important value debates that add to the decision. While we might be able to estimate a company's reputation or standing among its stakeholders in a similar hypothetical situation, only after the fact could we determine what people really felt about a company that was not responsive. When the managers responsible for Tylenol faced such a question, even though they had feedback within 24 hours of the first reported death, it was impossible to predict people's reaction to a second death until it was reported. Johnson & Johnson's decision to replace Tylenol capsules with solid Tylenol caplets ultimately was based on senior-level debate of such issues, not on direction provided by research that indicated that the public did not hold the manufacturer responsible for the deaths.[9]

Even if a question can be answered by facts alone, it might not be researchable because currently accepted and tested procedures or techniques are inadequate. The development of new techniques and methodologies is often the result of researchers' frustration with unresearchable problems. Such problems become the motivation for innovation in methodology.

Ill-Defined Management Problems

Some categories of problems are so complex, value-laden, and bound by constraints that they prove to be intractable to traditional forms of analysis. These questions have characteristics that are virtually the opposite of those of well-defined problems. Solving well-defined problems involves navigating from a starting point to the solution using natural transitions in the problem sequence to shift from one problem state to another. An **ill-defined problem** is one that addresses complex issues and cannot be expressed easily, concisely, or completely. Ill-defined problems pose a dilemma for researchers because a solution sequence cannot be plotted if little is understood about the path or the final outcome. Certain complex puzzles (see reference note 10) illustrate ill-defined problems when the components of their problem sequences are not fully specified, the problem description lacks concreteness, and the goal cannot be visualized.[10]

Ill-defined research questions in marketing are least susceptible to attack from quantitative research methods because such problems have too many interrelated facets for measurement to handle with accuracy.[11] Moreover, there are some research questions of this type for which methods do not presently exist; even if the methods were to be invented, they still might not provide the data necessary to solve them.[12] Novice researchers should avoid ill-defined problems. Even seasoned researchers will want to conduct a thorough exploratory study before proceeding with the latest approaches.

ill-defined problem one that addresses complex issues and cannot be expressed easily or completely.

Politically Motivated Research

It is important to remember that a manager's motivations for seeking research are not always obvious. Managers might express a genuine need for specific information on which to base a decision. This is the ideal scenario for quality research. Sometimes, however, a research study may not really be desirable but is authorized anyway, chiefly because its presence may win approval for a certain manager's pet idea. At other times, research may be authorized as a measure of personal protection for a decision maker in case he or she is criticized later. In these less-than-ideal cases, the researcher may find it more difficult to win the manager's support for an appropriate research design.

>summary

1 Research originates in the decision process. A manager needs specific information for setting objectives, defining tasks, finding the best strategy by which to carry out the tasks, or judging how well the strategy is being implemented.

    A dilemma-centered emphasis—the problem's origin, selection, statement, exploration, and refinement—dominates the sequence of the research process. A decision to do research can be inappropriately driven by the availability of coveted tools and databases. To be researchable, a problem must be subject to observation or other forms of empirical data collection.

2 How one structures the research question sets the direction for the project. A management problem or opportunity can be formulated as a hierarchical sequence of questions. At the most general level is the management dilemma. This is translated into a management question and then into a research question—the major objective of the study. In turn, the research question is further expanded into investigative questions. These questions represent the various facets of the problem to be solved, and they influence research design, including design strategy, data collection planning, and sampling. At the most specific level are measurement questions that are answered by respondents in a survey or answered about each subject in an observational study.

    Exploration of the problem is accomplished through familiarization with the available literature, interviews with experts, focus groups, or some combination. Revision of the management or research questions is a desirable outcome of exploration and enhances the researcher's understanding of the options available for developing a successful design.

3 Budgets and value assessments determine whether most projects receive necessary funding. Their thorough docu-

mentation is an integral part of the research proposal. Proposals are required for many research projects and should, at a minimum, describe the research question and the specific task the research will undertake.

4 Decisions concerning the type of study, the means of data collection, measurement, and sampling plans must be made when planning the design. Most researchers undertake sampling studies because of an interest in estimating population values or testing a statistical hypothesis. Carefully constructed delimitations are essential for specifying an appropriate probability sample. Nonprobability samples are also used.

    Pilot tests are conducted to detect weaknesses in the study's design, data collection instruments, and procedures. Once the researcher is satisfied that the plan is sound, data collection begins. Data are collected, edited, coded, and prepared for analysis.

    Data analysis involves reduction, summarization, pattern examination, and the statistical evaluation of hypotheses. A written report describing the study's findings is used to transmit the results and recommendations to the intended decision maker. By cycling the conclusions back into the original problem, a new research iteration may begin, and findings may be applied.

5 Several research process problems can diminish the value of research. Included in these are using a technique that is inappropriate for the information needed, just because it is familiar or the researcher has experience with it; attempting to substitute data mining for marketing research; focusing on an unresearchable question; failing to correctly define the management problem; and conducting politically motivated rather than management dilemma–motivated research.

>**key**terms

census 87

data 89

   primary data 89

   secondary data 89

data analysis 90

decision rule 85

decision variable 85

ill-defined problem 93

investigative questions 83

management dilemma 80

management question 82

management-research question hierarchy 80

measurement questions 83

pilot test 88

research design 86

research process 78

research question(s) 82

sample 87

>discussionquestions

Terms in Review

1 Some questions are answerable by research and others are not. Using some management problems of your choosing, distinguish between them.

2 Discuss the problems of trading off exploration and pilot testing under tight budgetary constraints. What are the immediate and long-term effects?

3 A retailer is experiencing a poor inventory management situation and receives alternative research proposals. Proposal 1 is to use an audit of last year's transactions as a basis for recommendations. Proposal 2 is to study and recommend changes to the procedures and systems used by the shipping/receiving department. Discuss issues of evaluation in terms of:

   a Ex post facto versus prior evaluation.

   b Evaluation using option analysis and decision theory.

Making Research Decisions

4 Believing that every employee contributes to marketing in an organization, the president of Oaks International Inc., when confronted by low productivity and rising customer complaints, is convinced by a research supplier to study job satisfaction in the corporation. What are some of the important reasons that this research project may fail to make an adequate contribution to the solution of management problems?

5 Based on an analysis of the last six months' sales, your boss notices that sales of beef products are declining in your chain's restaurants. As beef entrèe sales decline, so do profits. Fearing beef sales have declined due to several newspaper stories reporting *E. coli* contamination discovered at area grocery stores, he suggests a survey of area restaurants to see if the situation is pervasive.

   a What do you think of this research suggestion?

   b How, if at all, could you improve on your boss's formulation of the research question?

Behind the Scenes

6 What are the benefits to MindWriter if they implement the pilot study Jason recommends?

7 How can MindWriter's existing database be used to accumulate service problem information in advance of the proposed research? What information should be sought?

From Concept to Practice

8 Using Exhibit 4-1 and case examples from marketing firm's Web sites, discover how "favored technique" approaches to research design dominate many firms' strategies.

9 Refer to stage in Exhibit 4-1, then find a research example where a clear statement of the management dilemma leads to a precise and actionable research question.

>wwwexercise

Learn more about business intelligence from industry leader MicroStrategy. Visit its Web site and participate in a free Web seminar on a current case study. **(http://www.microstrategy.com/events/online_seminars/index.asp)**

>cases*

Calling Up Attendance	Mastering Teacher Leadership
Donatos: Finding the New Pizza	NCRCC: Teeing Up a New Strategic Direction
Goodyear's Aquatred	Outboard Marine Corporation
Inquiring Minds Want to Know—Now!	Ramada Demonstrates Its *Personal Best*™
KNSD, San Diego	State Farm: Dangerous Intersections

* All cases, both written and video, are on the text DVD. The film icon indicates a video case. Check the DVD Index to determine whether a case has data, the research instrument, or other supplementary material.

>chapter 5

Clarifying the Research Question through Secondary Data and Exploration

>learningobjectives

After reading this chapter, you should understand . . .

1 The purposes and process of exploratory research.

2 Two types and three levels of management decision-related secondary sources.

3 Five types of external information and the factors for evaluating the value of a source and its content.

4 The process of using exploratory research to understand the management dilemma and work through the stages of analysis necessary to formulate the research question (and ultimately investigative questions and measurement questions).

Jason Henry, Visonary Insights' senior project manager, presses the intercom button. "Sara, have you had a chance to summarize the transcripts from the CompleteCare call center?"

"Those, as well as the summary of the complaint letters," responds Sara as she strolls through the door to Jason's office.

Jason jerks at the closeness of her voice. "It's unnerving how you anticipate what I want before I ask for it."

"Not so tough," chuckles Sara, enjoying seeing the unflappable Jason look a little shaken. "You did tell me you wanted them first thing this morning. And it is 8:05."

"What about those articles on measuring customer satisfaction in technological products?"

"I'm human, Jason, not a robotic search engine. That's the next thing on my Palm to-do list."

"It seems logical that there might be special issues related to computers or other technical products when it comes to measuring satisfaction."

"But we both know that logic often doesn't have a thing to do with reality. Do you want me to brief you on what I've discovered from the complaint correspondence and the transcripts, or would you rather read the summary?"

"No, just leave it. I've set up an 8:30 phone interview with Sam Turnbull, the manager of the CompleteCare repair program. I need a few more minutes to review the questions I drafted last night."

"Fine. This call transcript was particularly interesting," shares Sara as she hands the transcript across the desk. "You might want to ask about this particular case. I'm sure he'll remember it.

"I'll just go start my search on whether technical products have differing measurement issues for satisfaction than the other industries we've studied."

"Um, hm . . ." Jason responds as he peruses the transcript. Then he glances up and stops Sara before she glides out the door. "While you are at it, see if there is an industrywide study on laptop satisfaction, something we might use as a benchmark. And anything you can find about the special problems associated with laptop construction, operation, use patterns, or repairs."

"I'm on it."

> A Search Strategy for Exploration

Exploration is particularly useful when researchers lack a clear idea of the problems they will meet during the study. Through exploration researchers develop concepts more clearly, establish priorities, develop operational definitions, and improve the final research design. Exploration may also save time and money. If the problem is not as important as first thought, more formal studies can be canceled.

Exploration serves other purposes as well. The area of investigation may be so new or so vague that a researcher needs to do an exploration just to learn something about the dilemma facing the manager. Important variables may not be known or thoroughly defined. Hypotheses for the research may be needed. Also, the researcher may explore to be sure it is practical to do a formal study in the area.

Despite its obvious value, researchers and managers alike give exploration less attention than it deserves. There are strong pressures for quick answers. Moreover, exploration is sometimes linked to old biases about qualitative research: subjectiveness, nonrepresentativeness, and nonsystematic design. More realistically, exploration may save both time and money and should not be slighted.

The exploratory phase search strategy usually comprises one or more of the following:

> **We explore the basics of data mining in Chapter 10.**

- Discovery and analysis of secondary sources:
    - Published studies (usually focused on the results of surveys or on case studies featuring one or a few incidents)
    - Document analysis
    - Retrieval of information from organization's database(s)

expert interview a discussion with someone knowledgeable about the problem or its possible solutions.

- Interviews with those knowledgeable about the problem or its possible solutions (called **expert interviews**)
- Interviews with individuals involved with the problem (called **individual depth interviews**, or IDIs)

individual depth interview (IDI) a type of interview that encourages the participant to talk extensively, sharing as much information as possible.

- Group discussions with individuals involved with the problem or its possible solutions (including informal groups, as well as formal techniques such as focus groups or brainstorming)

As the exploration process modeled with the management-research question hierarchy suggests (see Exhibit 5-1), exploration of secondary sources may be useful at any stage of the hierarchy. But most researchers find a review of secondary sources critical to moving from management question to research question. In moving from management question to research question, the researcher uses both internal and external secondary sources. While most marketers would explore their internal archives first, here we will address external sources first.

exploratory research research to expand understanding of an issue, problem, or topic.

In this **exploratory research** phase of your project, your objective is to accomplish the following:

- Expand your understanding of the management dilemma by looking for ways others have addressed and/or solved problems similar to your management dilemma or management question.
- Gather background information on your topic to refine the research question.
- Identify information that should be gathered to formulate investigative questions.
- Identify sources for and actual questions that might be used as measurement questions.
- Identify sources for and actual sample frames (lists of potential participants) that might be used in sample design.

literature search a review of books, articles, research studies, or Web-published materials related to the proposed study.

In most cases the exploration phase will begin with a **literature search**—a review of books as well as articles in journals or professional literature that relate to your management dilemma. Increasingly, this may include Web-published materials. A literature search requires the use of the library's online catalog and one or more bibliographic databases or

> **Exhibit 5-1** Integration of Secondary Data into the Research Process

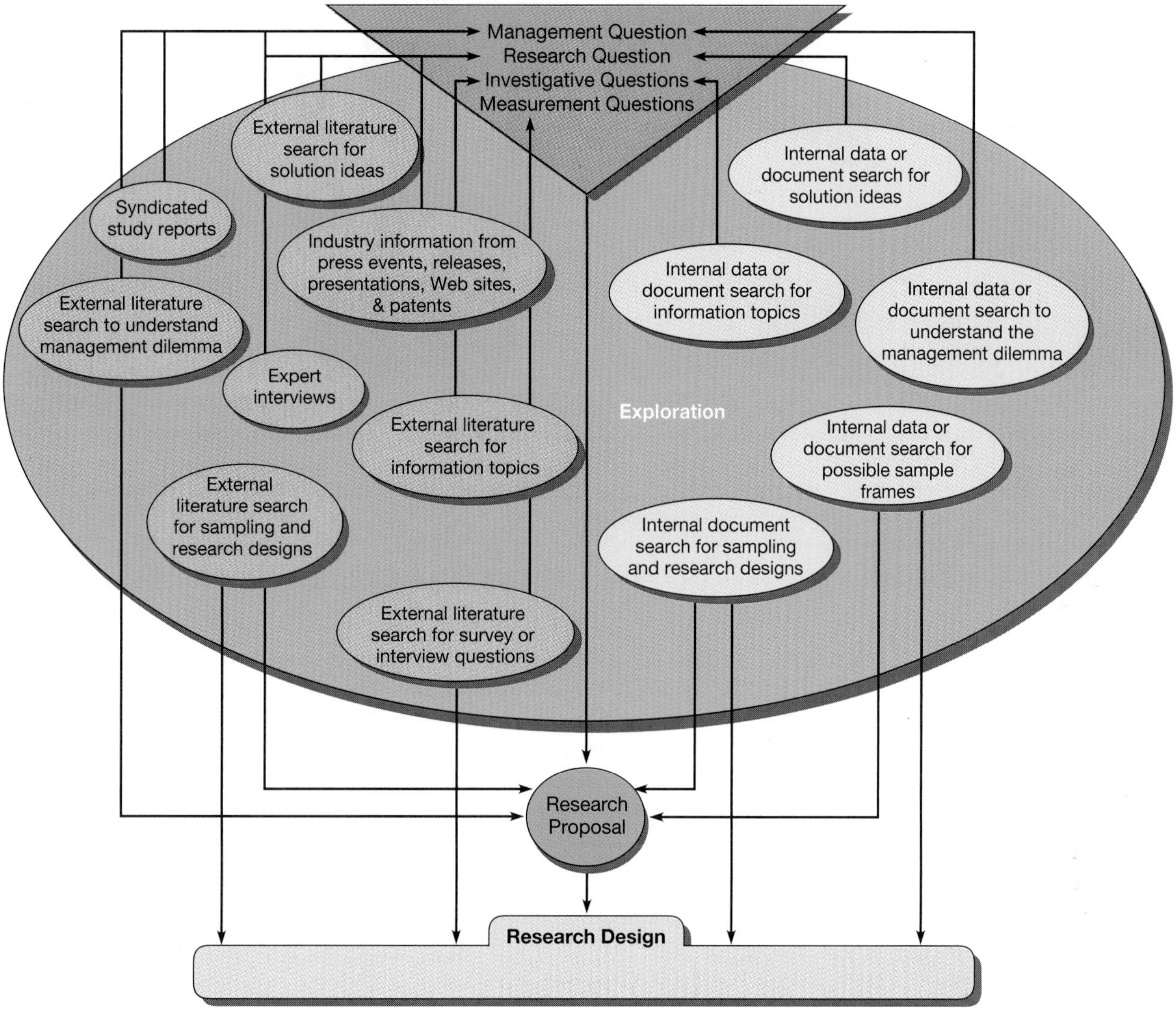

indexes. For some topics, it may be useful to consult a handbook or specialized encyclopedia first to establish a list of key terms, people, or events that have influenced your topic and also to determine what the major publications are and who the foremost authors are. Other reference materials will be incorporated into your search strategy as needed. In general, this literature search has five steps:

1. Define your management dilemma or management question.

2. Consult encyclopedias, dictionaries, handbooks, and textbooks to identify key terms, people, or events relevant to your management dilemma or management question.

3. Apply these key terms, names of people, or events in searching indexes, bibliographies, and the Web to identify specific secondary sources.

4. Locate and review specific secondary sources for relevance to your management dilemma.

5. Evaluate the value of each source and its content.

The result of your literature search may be a solution to the management dilemma. In such a case, no further research is necessary. Often, however, the management question remains unresolved, so the decision to proceed generates a research proposal (see Chapter 6).

> **pic**profile

Researchers often meet to discuss symptoms when developing the management-research question hierarchy. Whiteboard technology makes this phase of the research planning easier. With this technology, researchers can combine computer projected images and data with handwritten notations. This combination encourages full participant involvement in the discussion as the whiteboard captures detailed brainstorming ideas and conclusions. At the end of the discussion, each researcher walks away with the same record of the event.

The resulting proposal covers at minimum a statement of the research question and a brief description of the proposed research methodology. The proposal summarizes the findings of the exploratory phase of the research, usually with a bibliography of secondary sources that have led to the decision to propose a formal research study.

In this chapter we will concentrate on the exploration phase of the project and focus on finding, selecting, and evaluating information in both printed and electronic formats. In some instances, marketers will discover the answer to their management dilemma in the results of a secondary search. A great exploration of secondary sources pays dividends—big ones—if a costly research project is deemed unnecessary.

Levels of Information

As you explore your problem or topic, you may consider many different types of information sources, some much more valuable than others. Information sources are generally categorized into three levels: (1) primary sources, (2) secondary sources, and (3) tertiary sources.

primary sources original works of research or raw data without interpretation or pronouncements that represent an official opinion or position.

Primary sources are original works of research or raw data without interpretation or pronouncements that represent an official opinion or position. Included among the primary sources are memos, letters, complete interviews or speeches (in audio, video, or written transcript formats), laws, regulations, court decisions or standards, and most government data, including census, economic, and labor data. Primary sources are always the most authoritative because the information has not been filtered or interpreted by a second party. Other internal sources of primary data are inventory records, personnel records, purchasing requisition forms, statistical process control charts, and similar data.

secondary sources interpretations of primary data.

Secondary sources are interpretations of primary data. Encyclopedias, textbooks, handbooks, magazine and newspaper articles, and most newscasts are considered secondary information sources. Indeed, nearly all reference materials fall into this category. Internally, sales analysis summaries and investor annual reports would be examples of secondary sources, as they are compiled from a variety of primary sources. To an outsider, however, the annual report is viewed as a primary source, as it represents the official position of the corporation. A firm searching for secondary sources can search either internally or externally, as Exhibit 5-2 depicts.

>**snap**shot

Political Marketing Discovers Data Mining

The political advertising battle of the 2004 presidential election was one of the most contentious and longest in recent history. If you were then Senator John Kerry, aspiring democratic nominee for president, who would you have targeted to receive an inspiring political message? By some estimates, the uncommitted "swing" vote that would decide the election was less than 10 percent of the electorate. And to whom—or what—would you turn for help in reaching undecided voters? Kerry, being a savvy politician, knew about Datamart (just as G. W. Bush knew about Voter Vault). Datamart is the Democratic National Committee's venture into data warehousing and data mining. In the last presidential election year it was estimated to hold electronic files on 158 million Americans. The Republican National Committee's counterpart, Voter Vault, boasted files on 165 million Americans.

Just what tidbits might you find in these databases? While specifics vary by individual, almost all had name, address, phone number, elections voted, party registration, and whether or not the individual has donated to a political campaign. Matching with U.S. census data could supplement the voting data with marital status, children (presence, number), income, and education.

County records could add residence value. Door-to-door and phone canvassers could add media readership, catalog purchase behavior, and issues of interest (like a voter's stance on law enforcement, education, and the environment). According to DNC party chairman, Terry McAuliffe, Datamart contained 306 pieces of information attached to every name.

So how would you, as consultant to John Kerry, have used such information? One way would have been to identify workers forced into unemployment during the G. W. Bush administration. Then employ banner ads on Internet job search and employment sites to direct those individuals to the Kerry Web site (JohnKerry.com) and his plan for improving America's job market. Kerry's election consultant Voter Interactive might have used the database to send e-mails to such individuals. Kerry's use of Web banner advertising in both the Iowa and the New Hampshire primaries was considered a test of the effectiveness of Internet advertising to increase visitors to his Web site.

www.voterinteractive.com; www.dnc.org; www.rnc.org; www.JohnKerry.com

> **Exhibit 5-2** Secondary Sources for Developing the Question Hierarchy

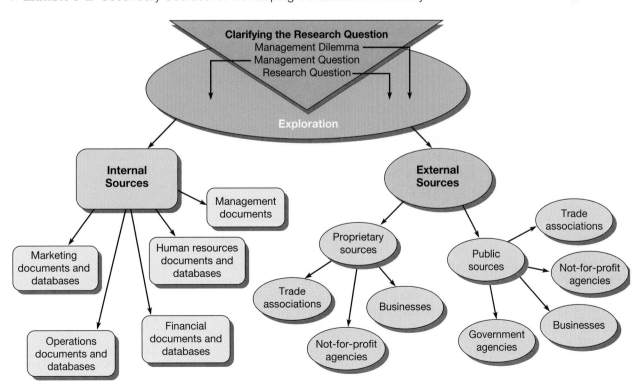

The U.S. Government is the world's largest source of data and information used by managers in all types of organizations.
www.pueblo.gsa.gov

Find your birth certificate.
Buy surplus government property.
Send a Presidential birthday greeting.
Contact your representative in Congress.
Get a flag from the Capitol. Protect your privacy.
Buy a Treasury note. See about an FHA mortgage.
Enlist in the military. Check on safe travel abroad.
Start a small business. Get info on immigration laws.
File for Social Security.   Reserve a campsite.
Check postage rates.   Buy Savings Bonds.
Find military personnel.   Find a Federal job.
Get help on tax issues.   Get your passport.
                              Visit a national park.
                           Apply for a gov't grant.
                          Report unsafe products.
                         Trace your family tree.
                        Register a trademark.
                        Get Medicare benefits.
                        Write the President.
                        Plan for college.
                        Buy a HUD home.
                        File your taxes.
                        Fly the U.S. flag.

Get the answers you can trust from the Federal Consumer Information Center. You've written to our Pueblo, CO address for years. Now you can call us toll-free for answers to your questions about all kinds of federal government programs, benefits and services.

We'll answer your questions directly or get you to the person who can. Recorded information is also available around the clock.

Now the only question left is how to reach us. Simple. Just call toll-free:

1-800-FED-INFO
(That's 1-800-333-4636)
Monday through Friday 8 a.m. to 8 p.m. Eastern Time
or visit www.pueblo.gsa.gov/call

A public service of this publication and the U.S. General Services Administration's Federal Consumer Information Center

tertiary sources aids to discover primary or secondary sources or an interpretation of a secondary source.

Tertiary sources may be interpretations of a secondary source but generally are represented by indexes, bibliographies, and other finding aids (e.g., Internet search engines).

From the beginning, it is important to remember that all information is not of equal value. As the source levels indicate, primary sources have more value than secondary sources, and secondary sources have more value than tertiary sources. In the opening vignette, Sara has read the MindWriter CompleteCare call center transcripts (a primary source), and Jason suggests that she also check for articles related to laptop manufacture, repair, and satisfaction (all secondary sources). Sara's summary of the transcript and letters is a secondary source. Visionary Insights' program for MindWriter will hinge on Jason's understanding of the current laptop repair scenario. If the information is essential to solving the management dilemma, it is wise to verify it in a primary source. That's why Sara wants Jason to ask CompleteCare's manager (primary source) for his take on the facts related to the disturbing call transcript she found.

Types of Information Sources

There are dozens of types of information sources, each with a special function. In this section we describe five of the information types used most by researchers at this phase of the project.

Indexes and Bibliographies

index secondary data source that helps identify and locate a single book, journal article, author, etc., from among a large set.

bibliography an information source that helps locate a single book, article, photograph, etc.

Indexes and **bibliographies** are the mainstay of any library because they help you identify and locate a single book or journal article from among the millions published. The single

Marketing Intelligence Is Crucial

How does a total communications agency providing clients with support in all aspects of media advertising, marketing/sales promotion, and public relations keep abreast of trends in its own and clients' industries? Andy Marken, president/CEO of Marken Communications, has a proven method: "We read—a lot!" Each month Marken and his staff read more than 50 different monthly magazines in their clients' areas of interest, as well as general business publications. They also skim or skip-read a dozen weekly business and trade publications and receive daily between six and eight online newsletters to skim or file. Additionally, they use observation and communication methodologies. Each year they attend client-related conventions as well as one- and two-day conferences to track competitive developments. "And we talk—face to face, on the phone, and via e-mail. If we gather nuggets of information from two disparate sources we practice free association to produce a successful conclusion." Then Marken Communications follows its discoveries with more secondary research—government offices, industry analyst groups, and financial institutions generate reams of reports that help it develop meaningful ideas and information for clients like Mitsubishi Chemical, Verbatim, Panasonic, Matsushita, Pinnacle Systems, LaCie, and other international firms.

www.markencom.com

most important bibliography in any library is its online catalog. As with all other information types, there are many specialized indexes and bibliographies unique to marketing topics. These can be very useful in a literature search to find authors and titles of prior works on the topic of interest.

Skill in searching bibliographic databases is essential for the marketing researcher. For the novice or less skilled, we provide two appendices at the end of this chapter. The first, "Bibliographic Database Searches," reviews the process of searching. The second, "Advanced Searches," reveals the more advanced techniques of skilled searchers.

> **We provide a list of key marketing information sources on your text DVD.**

Dictionaries

Dictionaries are so ubiquitous they probably need no explanation. We all use them to verify spelling or grammar usage or to define terms. In marketing, as in every field, there are many specialized dictionaries that define words, terms, or jargon unique to a discipline. Most of these specialized dictionaries include in their word lists information on people, events, or organizations that shape the discipline. They are also an excellent place to find acronyms. A growing number of dictionaries and glossaries (terms in a specialized field, area, or topic plus their definitions) are now available on the Web. Information from dictionaries and glossaries may be used to identify key terms for a search of an online or printed database.

dictionary secondary source that defines words, terms, or jargon unique to a discipline; may include information on people, events, or organizations that shape the discipline; an excellent source of acronyms.

Encyclopedias

Marketers use an **encyclopedia** to find background or historical information on a topic or to find names or terms that can enhance search results in other sources. For example, you might use an encyclopedia to find the date that Microsoft introduced Windows and then use that date to draw more information from an index to the time period. Encyclopedias are also helpful in identifying the experts in a field and the key writings on any topic. One example of an encyclopedia is the *Online TDM Encyclopedia* published by the Victoria Transportation Policy Institute.

encyclopedia a secondary source that provides background or historical information on a topic.

The *Online TDM Encyclopedia* is the most comprehensive source of information available anywhere in the world concerning innovative management solutions to transportation problems. The Encyclopedia provides detailed information on dozens of Transportation Demand Management (TDM) strategies, plus chapters on their planning, evaluation and implementation. It can help you view transportation problems from a new perspective, and expand the range of possible solutions to apply.[1]

Another example drawn from the area of distribution is the *PRTM Channels Encyclopedia*, published by Pittiglio Rabin Todd & McGrath (PRTM), a high-technology consultancy specializing in channel analysis. PRTM's encyclopedia describes the basic distribution channels used in the United States.[2]

Handbooks

handbook a secondary source used to identify key terms, people, or events relevant to the management dilemma or management question.

A **handbook** is a collection of facts unique to a topic. Handbooks often include statistics, directory information, a glossary of terms, and other data such as laws and regulations essential to a field. The best handbooks include source references for the facts they present. The *Statistical Abstract of the United States* is probably the most valuable and frequently used handbook available. It contains an extensive variety of facts, an excellent and detailed index, and a gateway to even more in-depth data for every table included. One handbook with which students and marketers alike are familiar is the *Occupational Outlook Handbook* published by the U.S. Bureau of Labor Statistics. In it you can find details about many marketing occupations.[3] Many handbooks are quite specialized, such as the one published by the Potato Association of America. It reveals not only consumption patterns but also potato growing and processing statistics.[4]

One of the most important handbooks, especially for business-to-business marketing, is the *North American Industry Classification System, United States (NAICS)*. Jointly designed with Canada and Mexico to provide comparability in business statistics throughout North America, especially as new businesses and new business sectors develop, this classification system of all businesses replaced the Standard Industrial Classification in 1997. Its next revision is in 2007.[5]

Directories

directory a reference source used to identify contact information.

Directories are used for finding names and addresses as well as other data. While many are available and useful in printed format, directories in digitized format that can be searched by certain characteristics or sorted and then downloaded are far more useful. Many are available free through the Web, but the most comprehensive directories are proprietary (that is, must be purchased). An especially useful directory available in most libraries in either print or electronic format is the *Encyclopedia of Associations* (called *Associations Unlimited* on the Web), which provides a list of public and professional organizations plus their locations and contact numbers. New York AMA Communications Services, Inc., publishes the *Green Book, a Worldwide Directory of Marketing Research Companies and Services*, as well as the *Green Book, a Worldwide Directory of Focus Group Companies and Services*.[6]

Evaluating Information Sources

source evaluation the five-factor process for evaluating a secondary source.

A researcher using secondary sources, especially if drawn from the Internet, will want to conduct a **source evaluation**. Marketers should evaluate and select information sources based on five factors that can be applied to any type of source, whether printed or electronic. These are:

- *Purpose*—the explicit or hidden agenda of the information source.
- *Scope*—the breadth and depth of topic coverage, including time period, geographic limitations, and the criteria for information inclusion.
- *Authority*—the level of the data (primary, secondary, tertiary) and the credentials of the source author(s).

> **Exhibit 5-3** Evaluating Web Sites as Information Sources

Evaluation Factor	Questions to Answer
Purpose	• Why does the site exist? • How evident is the purpose it is trying to convey? • Does it achieve its purpose? • How does its purpose affect the type and bias of information presented?
Authority	• What are the credentials of the author or institution or organization sponsoring the site? • Does the site give you a means of contacting anyone for further information? • Who links to this site? • If facts are supplied, where do they come from?
Scope	• How old is the information? • How often is it updated? • How much information is available? • Is it selective or comprehensive? • What are the criteria for inclusion? • If applicable, what geographic area or time period or language does it cover? • How does the information presented compare with that on similar sites? • Is it a series of links only (a metasite), or is there added value? • What is the nature of the added value? • What information did you expect to find that was missing? • Is the site self-contained, or does it link to other Web sites?
Audience	• Whom does the site cater to? • What level of knowledge or experience is assumed? • How does the intended audience affect the type and bias of the information?
Format	• How quickly can you find needed information? • How easy is the site to use? Is it intuitive? • Does it load quickly? • Is the design appealing? • Are there navigation buttons? • Is there a site map or search button? • Is there an easily identifiable help button? • Is Help helpful? • Are pages in ASCII or graphic format? • Is the information downloadable into a spreadsheet or word processing program, if desired?

• *Audience*—the characteristics and background of the people or groups for whom the source was created.

• *Format*—how the information is presented and the degree of ease of locating specific information within the source.

Sara is about to embark on an Internet search for various types of information. Exhibit 5-3 summarizes the critical questions she should ask when applying these source evaluation factors to the evaluation of Internet sources she discovers.

The purpose of early exploration is to help the researcher understand the management dilemma and develop the management question. Later stages of exploration are designed to develop the research question and ultimately the investigative and measurement questions.

> The Question Hierarchy: How Ambiguous Questions Become Actionable Research

The process we call the management-research question hierarchy is designed to move the researcher through various levels of questions, each with a specific function within the overall marketing research process. This multistep process is presented in Exhibit 5-4 and in the example in Exhibit 5-5. The role of exploration in this process is depicted in Exhibit 5-6.

The Management Question

management question the management dilemma restated in question format.

Management questions are the restatement of the management dilemma in question form. The management questions that evolve from the management dilemma are too numerous to list, but we can categorize them (see Exhibit 5-7). No matter how the management question is defined, many research directions can be taken. A specific question can lead to many studies. Therefore, it is the joint responsibility of the researcher and the marketer to choose the most productive project.

Assume, for example, a marketing researcher is hired to help the new management of a bank. The president is concerned about erosion of the bank's profitability (the management dilemma) and wants to turn this situation around. BankChoice is the oldest and largest of three banks in a city with a population of about 80,000. Profits have stagnated in recent years. The president and the researcher discuss the problem facing the organization and settle on this management question: "How can we improve our profit picture?"

The management question does not specify what kind of marketing research is to be done. This question is strictly managerial in thrust. It implies that the bank's management faces the task of developing a strategy for increasing profits. The question is broad. Notice that it doesn't indicate whether management should increase profits via increased deposits, downsizing of personnel, outsourcing of the payroll function, or some other means.

> **Exhibit 5-4** Management-Research Question Hierarchy

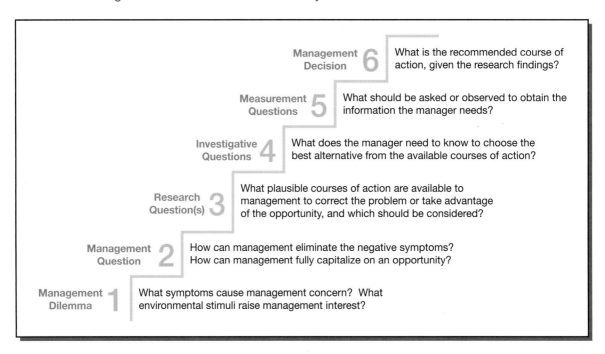

Further discussion between the bank president and the marketing researcher shows there are really two questions to be answered. The problem of low deposit growth is linked to concerns of a competitive nature. While lowered deposits directly affect profits, another part of the profit weakness is associated with negative factors within the organization that are increasing customer complaints. The qualified researcher knows that the management question as originally stated is too broad to guide a definitive marketing research project. As a starting point, the broadly worded question is fine, but BankChoice will want to refine its management question into these more specific subquestions:

- "How can we improve deposits?"
- "How can we improve internal operations that currently result in customer complaints?"

This separation of the management question into two subquestions may not have occurred without a discussion between the researcher and the manager.

Exploration

BankChoice has done no formal marketing research in the past. It has little specific information about competitors or customers and has not analyzed its internal operations. To

> **Exhibit 5-5** SalePro's Management-Research Question Hierarchy

Declining sales is one of the most common symptoms serving as a stimulus for a research project, especially a continuing pattern that is unexplained. SalePro, a large manufacturer of industrial goods, faces this situation. Exploration (1) reveals that sales, in fact, should not be declining in the South and Northeast. Environmental factors there are as favorable as in the growing regions. Subsequent exploration (2, 3) leads management to believe that the problem is in one of three areas; salesperson compensation, product formulation, or trade advertising. Further exploration (4) has SalePro management narrowing the focus of its research to alternative ways to alter the sales compensation system, which (5) leads to a survey of all sales personnel in the affected regions.

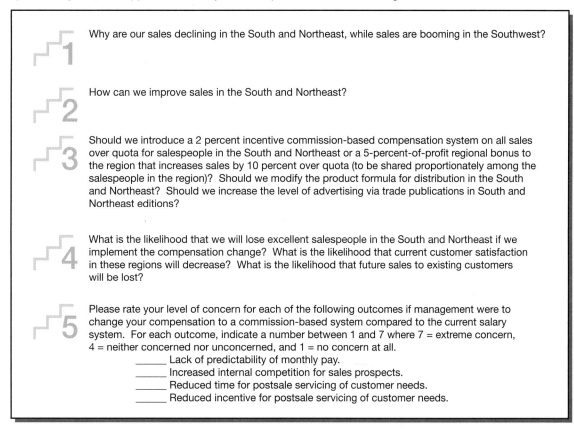

1 — Why are our sales declining in the South and Northeast, while sales are booming in the Southwest?

2 — How can we improve sales in the South and Northeast?

3 — Should we introduce a 2 percent incentive commission-based compensation system on all sales over quota for salespeople in the South and Northeast or a 5-percent-of-profit regional bonus to the region that increases sales by 10 percent over quota (to be shared proportionately among the salespeople in the region)? Should we modify the product formula for distribution in the South and Northeast? Should we increase the level of advertising via trade publications in South and Northeast editions?

4 — What is the likelihood that we will lose excellent salespeople in the South and Northeast if we implement the compensation change? What is the likelihood that current customer satisfaction in these regions will decrease? What is the likelihood that future sales to existing customers will be lost?

5 — Please rate your level of concern for each of the following outcomes if management were to change your compensation to a commission-based system compared to the current salary system. For each outcome, indicate a number between 1 and 7 where 7 = extreme concern, 4 = neither concerned nor unconcerned, and 1 = no concern at all.
    _____ Lack of predictability of monthly pay.
    _____ Increased internal competition for sales prospects.
    _____ Reduced time for postsale servicing of customer needs.
    _____ Reduced incentive for postsale servicing of customer needs.

> **Exhibit 5-6** Formulating the Research Question

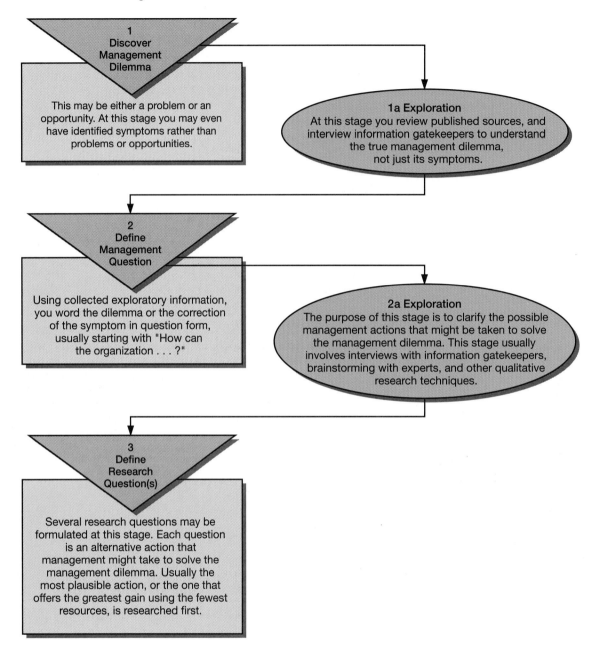

move forward in the management-research question hierarchy and define the research question, the client needs to collect some exploratory information on:

- What factors are contributing to the bank's failure to achieve a stronger growth rate in deposits?
- How well is the bank doing regarding customer satisfaction and financial condition compared to industry norms and competitors?

Small-group discussions are conducted among employees and managers, and trade association data are acquired to compare financial and operating statistics from company annual reports and end-of-year division reports. From the results of these two exploratory activities, it is obvious that BankChoice's operations are not as progressive as its competitors' but it has its costs well in line. So the revised management question becomes, "What

> **Exhibit 5-7** Types of Management Questions

Categories	General Question	Sample Management Questions
Choice of Purpose or Choice of Objectives	• What do we want to achieve?	• Should we reposition brand X as a therapeutic product from its current cosmetic positioning? • What goals should XYZ try to achieve in its next round of distributor negotiations?
Generalization and Evaluation of Solutions (choices between concrete actions to solve problems or take advantage of opportunities)	• How can we achieve the ends that we seek?	• How can we achieve our 5-year goal of doubling sales and profits? • What should be done to improve the CompleteCare program for product repairs and servicing?
Troubleshooting or Control (monitoring or diagnosing ways an organization is failing to meet its goals)	• How well is our marketing program meeting its goals? • Why is our marketing program not meeting its goals?	• What is our product line's sales-to-promotion cost ratio? • Why does our department have the lowest sales-to–Web page visit ratio? • Why does our product line have the lowest off-shelf display occasions in the industry?

should be done to make the bank more competitive?" The process of exploration will be critical in helping BankChoice identify its options.

> **BankChoice ultimately decides to conduct a survey of local residents. Two hundred residents complete questionnaires, and the information collected is used to guide repositioning of the bank.**

In addition to solving problems, marketers are likely to be looking for opportunities in the marketplace. So let's look at another case, TechByte. This company is interested in enhancing its position in a given technology that appears to hold potential for future growth. This interest or need might quickly elicit a number of questions:

• How fast might this technology develop?

• What are the likely applications of this technology?

• What companies now possess this technology, and which ones are likely to make a major effort to obtain the technology?

• How much will the new technology absorb in resources?

• What are the likely payoffs?

In the above exploration of opportunities, researchers would probably begin with specific books and periodicals. They would be looking only for certain aspects in this literature, such as recent developments, predictions by informed individuals about the prospects of the technology, identification of those involved in the area, and accounts of successful ventures or failures by others in the field. After becoming familiar with the literature, researchers might seek interviews with scientists, engineers, and product developers who are well known in the field. They would give special attention to those who represent the two extremes of opinion in regard to the prospects of the technology. If possible, they would talk with persons having information on particularly thorny problems in development and application. Of course, much of the information will be confidential and competitive. However, skillful investigation can uncover many useful indicators.

In the opening Visionary Insights' MindWriter vignette, Jason assigned his assistant Sara to discovering published PC industry studies on service and technical support, as well as published customer satisfaction comparisons among technical companies and products. Meanwhile, at MindWriter, Myra Wines is searching company archives for prior studies on customer satisfaction. Jason has realized from reviewing Sara's summary of customer correspondence that VI needs more knowledge on product design, CompleteCare's practices, and product handling, so Jason plans a second exploratory process starting with an expert interview with MindWriter's Sam Turnbull.

>**snap**shot

Covering Kids: The Management-Research Question Hierarchy

Robert Wood Johnson Foundation (RWJF), a health care philanthropy, sponsors the Covering Kids initiative for one reason: millions of children in low- to moderate-income families who are eligible for the State Children's Health Insurance Program (SCHIP) are not enrolled. RWJF initially became involved because it was concerned that the federal government and the states were not actively or effectively publicizing Medicaid and SCHIP. The initial goal of RWJF's involvement was to make eligible families aware of SCHIP and Medicare and encourage enrollment. To this end, RWJF obtained the services of advertising agency GMMB, research firm Wirthlin Worldwide, and veteran social marketer Elaine Bratic Arkin.

The Foundation initially asked, "What must be done to enroll the largest percentage of eligible children in Medicaid and SCHIP?" Before GMMB could move forward, the team needed to determine whether the communication program needed to correct misconceptions, communicate benefits, overcome perceived process complexities, or some combination of these. Early exploratory research sought answers to, "What keeps eligible families from taking advantage of the prescription and doctor-visit programs of SCHIP and Medicaid?" The team also asked, "Is a negative stigma attached to participation in government health care programs?" When research indicated the answer to this question was "No," subsequent efforts focused on identifying other critical factors that discouraged families from enrolling. After research revealed that most working parents did not realize their children were eligible for a government program, the management question was refined to, "What must be communicated to parents of eligible children to get them to enroll their children in these programs?"

Ultimately a creative combination of research design and data analysis revealed: (1) the winning communications frame-

work: Being a good parent means raising happy, healthy children, and enrolling in a program offering low-cost or free health care is a smart choice for families, and (2) every communication must give working parents an easy, foolproof way to determine if their children were eligible while reinforcing the logic that making the call to enroll their children would address parents' innate desire to be good parents.

www.wirthlin.com; www.gmmb.com; www.rwjf.org.

> **We discuss the usefulness of various qualitative techniques, many of which are used during exploration, in Chapter 9.**

An unstructured exploration allows the researcher to develop and revise the management question and determine what is needed to secure answers to the proposed question.

The Research Question

Using his or her understanding of the basic theoretical concepts, the researcher's task is to assist the manager in formulating a research question that fits the need to resolve the management dilemma. A **research question** best states the objective of the marketing research study. It is a more specific management question that must be answered. It may be more than one question or just one. A marketing research process that answers this more specific question provides the manager with the information necessary to make the decision he or she is facing. Incorrectly defining the research question is the fundamental weakness in the marketing research process. Time and money can be wasted studying an alternative that won't help the manager rectify the original dilemma.

research question(s) the objective of the research study.

>**snap**shot

Cooling Opportunities Discovered through Research

Paul Vanderburgh, of TARK, Inc., returned to his engineering roots when he joined his family's firm to head the marketing effort for technology that provides the cooling for X-ray machines. He brought with him extensive marketing research experience, having served as director of research for Design Forum, the research-driven retail design firm. In his new role, Vanderburgh's first task was to discover if TARK's X-ray cooling technology had application elsewhere in the industry. "The Internet made the task incredibly easier than it would have been just a few years earlier," shared Vanderburgh. "Before the Internet, I would have used the *Thomas Register*, and then called companies that appeared to have some relationship to what we do to learn product specifications, their customers, and more. I'd have relatively little information to start with. Today, *Thomas* is online and links me to target companies, many of which have detailed product specifications online. This allows me to reduce the number of companies that we contact personally while at the same time I'm increasing the likelihood of a successful partnership." Once Van-

derburgh narrows the field of possibilities with his Internet search, he shifts his research methodology, contacting each prospect company by phone. These "information interviews" are an in-depth extraction of critical data points about the prospect's current dilemmas. By talking engineer to engineer, TARK discovers whether it can solve any of those problems. "These interviews tell us whether a particular industry offers 'low hanging fruit'—a new application for our existing products and a new market segment." Such a discovery would kick TARK's marketing and sales efforts into high gear. That's just what happened when TARK discovered that power transformers found on telephone transmission poles needed similar cooling and that the current solution required maintenance every 4 months compared to every 12 to 18 months for TARK patented technology. Finding that TARK could save the communications industry money and maintenance effort was an important research discovery.

www.tarkinc.com

Meanwhile, at BankChoice the president has agreed to have the marketing research be guided by the following research question: "Should BankChoice position itself as a modern, progressive institution (with appropriate changes in services and policies) or maintain its image as the oldest, most reliable institution in town?"

Fine-Tuning the Research Question

The term *fine-tuning* might seem to be an odd usage for research, but it creates an image that most researchers come to recognize. Fine-tuning the question is precisely what a skillful practitioner must do after the exploration is complete. At this point, a clearer picture of the management and research questions be-

> 6 6 The most serious mistakes are not being made as a result of wrong answers. The truly dangerous thing is asking the wrong questions. 9 9
>
> *Peter Drucker*
> *Author*

gins to emerge. After a preliminary review of the literature, a brief exploratory study, or both, the project begins to crystallize in one of two ways:

1. It is apparent the question has been answered and the process is finished.

2. A question different from the one originally addressed has appeared.

The research question does not have to be materially different, but it will have evolved in some fashion. This is not cause for discouragement. The refined research question(s) will have better focus and will move the marketing research forward with more clarity than the initially formulated question(s).

In addition to fine-tuning the original question, other research question–related activities should be addressed in this phase to enhance the direction of the project:

1. Examine the variables to be studied. Are they satisfactorily defined? Have operational definitions been used where appropriate?

2. Review the research questions with the intent of breaking them down into specific second- and third-level questions.

3. If hypotheses (tentative explanations) are used, be certain they meet the quality tests mentioned in Chapter 3.

4. Determine what evidence must be collected to answer the various questions and hypotheses.

5. Set the scope of the study by stating what is not a part of the research question. This will establish a boundary to separate contiguous problems from the primary objective.

Investigative Questions

investigative questions questions the researcher must answer to satisfactorily arrive at a conclusion about the research question.

Investigative questions represent the information that the marketing decision maker needs to know; they are the questions the researcher must answer to satisfactorily arrive at a conclusion about the research question. To study the market, the researcher working on the BankChoice project develops two major investigative questions. Each question has several subquestions. These questions provide insight into the lack of deposit growth:

1. What is the public's position regarding financial services and their use?
    a. What specific financial services are used?
    b. How attractive are various services?
    c. What bank-specific and environmental factors influence a person's use of a particular service?

2. What is the bank's competitive position?
    a. What are the geographic patterns of our customers and of our competitors' customers?
    b. What demographic differences are revealed among our customers and those of our competitors?
    c. What descriptive words or phrases does the public (both customers and noncustomers) associate with BankChoice? With BankChoice's competitors?
    d. How aware is the public of BankChoice's promotional efforts?
    e. What opinion does the public hold of BankChoice and its competitors?
    f. How does growth in services compare among competing institutions?

Return again to the MindWriter situation. What does management need to know to choose among the different packaging specifications? As you develop your information needs, think broadly. In developing your list of investigative questions, include:

- *Performance considerations* (like the relative costs of the options, the speed of packing serviced laptops, and the arrival condition of test laptops packaged with different materials).
- *Attitudinal issues* (like perceived service quality based on packaging materials used).
- *Behavioral issues* (like employees' ease of use in packing with the considered materials).

predesigned measurement questions questions that have been formulated and tested previously by other researchers.

custom-designed measurement questions questions formulated specifically for the project at hand.

Predesigned measurement questions are questions that have been formulated and tested previously by other researchers, are recorded in the literature, and may be applied literally or be adapted for the project at hand. Some studies lend themselves to the use of these readily available measurement devices. Such questions provide enhanced validity and can reduce the cost of the project. Often, however, the measurement questions must be custom-tailored to the investigative questions. The resources for developing **custom-designed measurement questions**—questions formulated specifically for the project at hand—are the collective insights from all the activities in the marketing research process completed to this point, particularly insights from exploration. Later, during the pilot testing phase of the research process, these custom-designed questions will be refined.

>**close**up

MindWriter Exploration

Two days after their Austin trip, at 1 p.m. sharp, Sara ushers Myra into a round Visionary Insights' conference room.

Inside, Jason has posted paper to the curved walls.

Across the top of the first sheet, Sara has written, "Satisfaction with the service department." Today they focus on the easiest task and leave the customer profile pilot study for later. Besides, Gracie Uhura, marketing manager for MindWriter, is pressed for answers on whether the CompleteCare repair program enhances customer satisfaction and thus brand loyalty. If she is responsive on the smaller project, Visionary Insights is sure it will get the OK for the more ambitious one.

Jason and Myra pull two chairs in front of the first blank panel, at first staring in silence at its blankness.

As Jason begins to talk, Sara summarizes his ideas on the panels. He has learned a lot about MindWriter. Beginning with a visit to the Internet and an intense search through MindWriter's archives before their Austin trip, followed by the meetings in Austin, he knows the product is sold through computer superstores and independent mail-order companies. He also has learned that MindWriter ships about 5,000 portable/laptop computers per month. The product is successful yet constrained by the same supply shortages as the rest of the industry. Personal computer magazines have been consulted for their annual surveys on service, repair, and technical support. Overall customer satisfaction comparisons have been obtained from published sources.

Myra approaches the second blank panel and summarizes the information learned from the Austin trip under the label "CompleteCare Process." When customers experience a malfunction, they call an 800 number. The call center answers service, support, and ordering questions. Technical representatives are trained to:

- Take the name, phone, address, and MindWriter model number.
- Listen to the customer and ask questions to detect the nature of the problem.
- Attempt to resolve the problem if they can walk the customer through corrective steps.

If unable to resolve the problem, the representative provides a return authorization code and dispatches a package courier to pick up the unit before 5 p.m. The unit is delivered to Austin for service the next morning. The CompleteCare repair facility calls the customer if the repair information is incomplete. The unit is repaired by the end of that day and picked up by the courier. The call center then updates its database with service record information. If all goes well, the customer receives the repaired unit by 10:00 a.m. the following morning, 48 hours after MindWriter received the customer's original problem call.

As Myra sits down, Jason begins to rough out the known "problems" on a third panel. There are employee shortages at the call center and difficulties getting the new technical repre-

sentatives trained. The courier is inconsistent in executing its pickup and delivery contract. MindWriter is experiencing parts availability problems for some models. And, occasionally, units are returned to the customer either not fixed or damaged in some way. Jason brainstorms that the service area is not doing an adequate job. But Myra asserts that problems could be in the original packing, in handling, or even from activities related to taking the boxes on and off the shipping pallets.

Their brainstorming results in a restatement of the management question: "What should be done to improve the CompleteCare program (MindWriter's program for product repairs and servicing)?" After further discussion, Myra, Sara, and Jason brainstorm the following research and investigative questions.

Research Questions

1. Should the technical representative be given more intensive training?
2. Should ABC Courier Service be replaced with an overnight air-transport service?
3. Should the repair-diagnostic and repair-sequencing operations be modified?
4. Should the return packaging be modified to include premolded rigid foam inserts, conforming-expanding foam protection, or some other configuration?
5. Should metropolitan repair centers be established to complement or replace in-factory repair facilities?

Investigative Questions

1. How well is the call center helping the customers? Is it helping the customers with instructions? What percentage of customers' technical problems is the center solving without callbacks? How long do customers wait on the phone?
2. How good is the transportation company? Does it pick up and deliver the laptops responsively? How long do customers wait for pickup? Delivery? Are the laptops damaged due to package handling? What available packaging alternatives are cost-effective?
3. How good is the repair group? What is the sequencing of the repair program, diagnostics through completion? Is the repair complete? Are customers' problems resolved? Are new repair problems emerging? Are customers' repair-time expectations being met?
4. (Do this set of questions on your own. See Discussion Question 8 at the end of this chapter.)
5. What is the overall satisfaction with CompleteCare and with the MindWriter product?

Myra now has enough information to go back to Gracie Uhura at MindWriter. In particular, Myra wants to know whether she and Jason have translated Gracie's management question in a way that will adequately fulfill Gracie's need for information.

Even though Jason had a phone interview with Sam Turnbull, MindWriter's service manager, Myra and Jason may also want to interview the call center manager and the independent package company's account executive to determine if they are on the right track with their investigative questions. These people will be able to answer some investigative questions. The rest of the investigative questions will need to be translated into measurement questions to ask customers. If Myra and Jason are comfortable with the additional information from their interviews (and any additional customer letters), VI can then develop a questionnaire for CompleteCare customers.

Jason, Sara, and Myra wrap up their session discussing preliminary plans and timing. Jason wants a pilot test with a limited number of customers. Afterward, he will revise the questions, set up the logistics, and then roll out the marketing research program. Sampling will be a critical matter. If Gracie's budget is large, they can use a probability sample from the customer list that MindWriter generates every week. This will make telephone interviews possible. If a less expensive alternative is needed, however, they can propose that a questionnaire postcard survey be included with every laptop as it is returned to the customer. They also would do random sampling from the list of customers who do not respond. Nonresponders would be interviewed on the telephone. This way Myra and Jason can be assured of a cost-effective questionnaire with correction for nonresponse bias (an error that develops when an interviewer cannot locate or involve the targeted participant).

Myra, Sara, and Jason devise a tentative schedule (see Exhibit 5-8) before calling to arrange the follow-up interviews. They want to give Gracie target dates for completion of the exploratory phase and the instrument and pilot test, as well as a deadline for the first month's results.

> **Exhibit 5-8** A Gantt Chart of the MindWriter Project

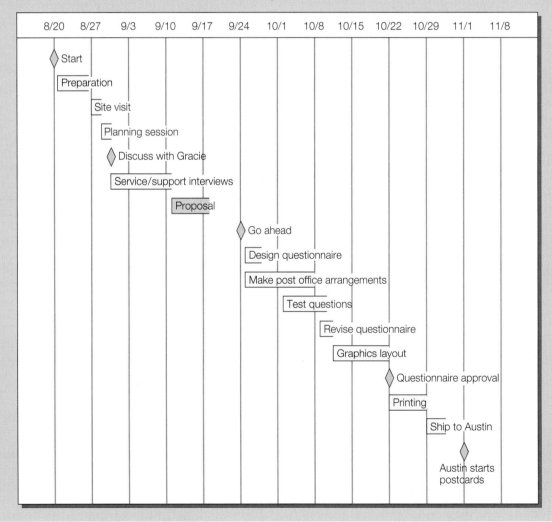

Measurement Questions

Measurement questions are the actual questions that researchers use to collect data in a study. They could become questions on a survey or elements on an observation checklist.

Measurement questions should be outlined by the completion of the project planning activities but usually await pilot testing for refinement. Two types of measurement questions are common in marketing research:

- Predesigned, pretested questions.
- Custom-designed questions.

> **measurement questions**
> the questions asked of
> participants or the
> observations that must
> be recorded.

> > **We discuss measure-
> ment questions only
> briefly here, as a more
> complete discussion
> begins in Chapter 13.**

>summary

1 The exploratory phase of the research process uses information to expand understanding of the management dilemma, look for ways others have addressed and/or solved problems similar to the management dilemma or management question, and gather background information on the topic to refine the research question. Exploration of the problem is accomplished through familiarization with the available literature, interviews with experts and other individual depth interviews, and group discussions or some combination of these. Revision of the management or research questions is a desirable outcome of exploration and enhances the researcher's understanding of the options available for developing a successful design.

2 Researching secondary sources is complex and challenging. There are two categories of sources available (external and internal) and three types of sources (primary, secondary, and tertiary). Primary sources are original works of research or raw data without interpretation. Secondary sources are interpretations of primary data. Tertiary sources may be interpretations of secondary sources or, more commonly, finding aids such as indexes, bibliographies, and Internet search engines.

3 There are generally five types of information sources used in most literature searches, including indexes and bibliographies, dictionaries, encyclopedias, handbooks, and directories. Each is useful to an exploratory phase literature search in a variety of ways. One of the harder tasks associated with using secondary sources is evaluating the quality of the information. Five factors to consider when evaluating the quality of the source are purpose, scope, authority, audience, and format.

4 How one structures the research question sets the direction for the project. A management problem or opportunity can be formulated as a hierarchical sequence of questions. At the base level is the management dilemma. This is translated into a management question and then into a research question—the major objective of the study. In turn, the research question is further expanded into investigative questions. These questions represent the various facets of the problem to be solved, and they influence research design, including design strategy, data collection planning, and sampling. At the most specific level are measurement questions that are answered by respondents in a survey or answered about each subject in an observational study.

>keyterms

>**discussion**questions

Terms in Review

1 Explain how each of the five evaluation factors for a secondary source influences its management decision-making value.

   a Purpose

   b Scope

   c Authority

   d Audience

   e Format

2 Define the distinctions between primary, secondary, and tertiary sources in a secondary search.

3 What problems of secondary data quality must researchers face? How can they deal with them?

Making Research Decisions

4 Below are a number of requests that a research staff assistant might receive. What specific tools or services would you expect to use to find the requisite information? (Hint: Use the appendices at the end of this chapter and the sources list on the DVD that accompanies this text.)

   a Has the FTC published any recent statements (within the last year) concerning its position on quality stabilization?

   b I need a list of the major companies located in Greensboro, North Carolina.

   c Please get me a list of the directors of General Motors, Microsoft, and Morgan Stanley & Co.

   d Is there a trade magazine that specializes in the flooring industry?

   e I would like to track down a study of small-scale service franchising that was recently published by a bureau of business research at one of the southern universities. Can you help me?

5 Confronted by low sales, the president of Oaks International Inc. asks a research company to study the activities of the customer relations department in the corporation. What are some of the important reasons that this research project may fail to make an adequate contribution to the solution of management problems?

6 You have been approached by the editor of *Gentlemen's Magazine* to carry out a research study. The magazine has been unsuccessful in attracting shoe manufacturers as advertisers. When the sales reps tried to secure advertising from shoe manufacturers, they were told men's clothing stores are a small and dying segment of their business. Since *Gentlemen's Magazine* goes chiefly to men's clothing stores, the manufacturers reasoned that it was, therefore, not a good vehicle for their advertising. The editor believes that a survey (via mail questionnaire) of men's clothing stores in the United States will probably show that these stores are important outlets for men's shoes and are not declining in importance as shoe outlets. He asks you to develop a proposal for the study and submit it to him. Develop the management-research question hierarchy that will help you to develop a specific proposal.

7 Develop the management-research question hierarchy for a management dilemma you face at work or with an organization to which you volunteer.

Behind the Scenes

8 Using the MindWriter postservicing packaging alternative as the research question, develop appropriate investigative questions within the management-research question hierarchy by preparing an exhibit similar to Exhibit 5-6.

9 Using Exhibits 5-4, 5-6, 5b-1, and 5b-2, state the research question and describe the search plan that Jason should have conducted before his brainstorming sessions with Myra Wines. What government sources should be included in Jason's search?

10 Using the "uneven courier performance" problem or the "product damaged during repair" problem (see the Closeup on page 113), develop some exploration activities that would let Jason or Myra proceed to develop a more refined research question dealing with this problem.

From Concept to Practice

11 Develop the management-research question hierarchy (Exhibits 5-4 and 5-6), citing marketing dilemma, management question, and research question(s), for each of the following:

   a The president of a home health care services firm.

   b The vice president of investor relations for an auto manufacturer.

   c The retail advertising manager of a major metropolitan newspaper.

   d The chief of police in a major city.

>**www**exercises

1 *Quirk's* magazine is one of the most respected for research reporting. Visit the Quirks.com site on the Web and select an article. Tie the content of the article to one or more concepts within the first five chapters of this text.

2 Use the material in chapter Appendices 5a and 5b to discover information about servicing computers that might be helpful on the MindWriter project.

>**cases**[*]

Agri Comp	**NCRCC: Teeing Up and New Strategic Direction**
BBQ Product Crosses over the Lines of Varied Tastes	**Overdue Bills**
Calling Up Attendance	**Ramada Demonstrates Its *Personal Best*™**
Donatos: Finding the New Pizza	**Retailers Unhappy with Displays from Manufacturers**
HeroBuilders.com	**State Farm: Dangerous Intersections**
Inquiring Minds Want to Know—NOW!	**Sturgel Division**
Mastering Teacher Leadership	**T-Shirt Designs**

McDonald's Tests Catfish Sandwich

* All cases, both written and video, are on the text DVD. Check the DVD Index to determine whether a case has data, the research instrument, or other supplementary material.

Bibliographic Database Searches

Searching a Bibliographic Database

In a **bibliographic database**, each record is a bibliographic citation to a book or a journal article. In your university library, the online catalog is an example of a bibliographic database.

There are several bibliographic databases available to business researchers. (See your text DVD.) Some of the more popular and comprehensive business bibliographic databases are:

- ABI/Inform (from Proquest Information and Learning).
- Business and Industry (from Gale Group).
- Business Source (from EBSCO).
- Dow Jones Interactive.
- Lexis-Nexis Universe (from a division of Reed Elsevier).

Most of the above databases offer numerous purchase options both in the amount and type of coverage. Some include abstracts, short summaries of the articles cited. Nearly all of the above databases include the contents of around two-thirds of the indexed journals in full text, although the amount and the specific titles may vary widely from database to database. Full-text options vary from an exact image of the page to ASCII text only or text plus graphics. Search options also vary considerably from database to database. It is for these reasons that most libraries supporting business programs offer more than one business periodical database.

The process of searching bibliographic databases and retrieving results is basic to all databases.

1. Select a database appropriate to your topic.
2. Construct a **search query** (also called a *search statement*).
   - Review and evaluate search results.
   - Modify the search query, if necessary.
3. Save the valuable results of your search.
4. Retrieve articles not available in the database.
5. Supplement your results with information from Web sources.

Select a Database Most of us select the most convenient database without regard to its scope, but considering the database contents and its limitations and criteria for inclusion at the beginning of your search will probably save you time in the long run. Remember that a library's online catalog is a bibliographic database that will help identify books and perhaps other media on a topic. While journal or periodical titles are listed in a library's online catalog, periodical or journal articles are rarely included. Use books for older, more comprehensive information. Use periodical articles for more current information or for information on very specific topics. A librarian can suggest one or more appropriate databases for the topic you are researching.

Save Results of Search While the temptation to print may be overwhelming, remember that if you download your results, you can cut and paste quotations, tables, and other information into your proposal without rekeying. In either case, make sure you keep the bibliographic information for your footnotes and bibliography. Most databases offer the choice of marking the records and printing or downloading them all at once or printing them one by one.

Retrieve Articles For articles not available in full text online, retrieval will normally require the additional step of searching the library's online catalog (unless there is a link from the database to the catalog) to determine if the desired issue is available and where it is located. Many libraries offer a document delivery service for articles not available. Some current articles may be available on the Web or via a fee-based service.

Searching the World Wide Web for Information

The World Wide Web is a vast information, business, and entertainment resource that would be difficult, if not foolish, to overlook. Millions of pages of data are publicly available, and the size of the Web doubles every few months.[1] But searching and retrieving reliable information on the Web is a great deal more problematic than searching a bibliographic database. There are no standard database fields, no carefully defined subject hierarchies (called

> **Exhibit 5a-1** Web Search Process Compared to Bibliographic Search Process

Bibliographic Search Process	Web Search Process
1. Select a database appropriate to your topic.	1. Select a search engine or directory.*
2. Construct a search query.	2. Determine your search options.*
• Review and evaluate search results.	3. Construct a search query.*
• Modify the search query, if necessary.	• Review and evaluate search results.
3. Save the valuable results of your search.	• Modify the search query, if necessary.
4. Retrieve articles not available in the database.	4. Save the valuable results of your search.*
5. Supplement your results with information from Web sources.	5. Supplement your results with information from non-Web sources.*

* Denotes a variation.

controlled vocabulary), no cross-references, no synonyms, no selection criteria, and, in general, no rules. There are dozens of search engines and they all work differently, but how they work is not always easy to determine. Nonetheless, the convenience of the Web and the extraordinary amount of information to be found on it are compelling reasons for using it as an information source.

As you can see in Exhibit 5a-1, the basic steps to searching the Web are similar to those outlined for searching a bibliographic database. As you approach the Web, you start at the same point: focusing on your management question. Are you looking for a known item (for example, IBM's Web site or that of the American Marketing Association)? Are you looking for information on a specific topic? If you are looking for a specific topic, what are its parameters? For example, if your topic is managed health care, are you hoping to find statistics, marketing ideas, public policy issues, accounting standards, or evidence of its impact on small business?

There are perfectly legitimate reasons to browse for information, and with its hypertext linking system, the Web is the ultimate resource for browsing. The trick is to browse and still stay focused on the topic at hand. In the browse mode you do not have any particular target. You follow hypertext links from site to site for the sheer joy of discovery. This is somewhat analogous to window shopping at the mall or browsing the bookshelves in the library. It may or may not be fruitful. And browsing is not likely to be efficient. Researchers often work on tight deadlines, as managers often cannot delay critical decisions. Therefore, researchers rarely have the luxury of undirected browsing.

Below we detail those steps in the Web search process that pose altered behavior for searches.

Select a Search Engine or Directory

A search for specific information or for a specific site that will help you solve your management question requires a great deal more skill and knowledge than browsing. Start by selecting one or more Internet search engines. Web search engines vary considerably in the following ways:

- The types of Internet sources they cover (http, telnet, Usenet, ftp, etc.).
- The way they search Web pages (every word? titles or headers only?).
- The number of pages they include in their indexes.
- The search and presentation options they offer.
- The frequency with which they are updated.

Furthermore, some information publicly indexable via the Web is not retrievable at all using current Web search engines. Among the material open to the public, but not indexed by search engines, are the following:[2]

- Pages that are proprietary (that is, fee-based) and/or password-protected, including the contents of bibliographic and other databases. Some password-protected databases, such as the Thomas Register, are actually free and available to the public after initial registration.

- Pages accessible only through a search form (databases), including such highly popular Web resources as library catalogs, e-commerce catalogs (such as Lands' End, Amazon.com, and similar offerings), and the Security and Exchange Commission's EDGAR catalog of SEC filings. If you want to find the price of a book at Amazon.com, you first will have to find the Amazon.com page and then search the database for the title.

- Poorly designed framed pages.

- Some non-HTML or non-plain-text pages, especially PDF graphics files, for which no text alternative is offered. These pages cannot be retrieved using any current search engine.

• Pages excluded by the Robots Exclusion Standard (usually implemented with a robots.txt file). This standard is used by Web administrators to tell indexing robots that certain pages are off-limits. An outstanding example of this is the U.S. government's extensive information resource called GPO Access (described below).

The search engine, portal, or directory you select may well be determined by how comprehensive you want your results to be.[3] If you want to use some major sites only, then start with a directory such as Yahoo!® If, however, you are interested in gathering comments and opinions that are the focus of usenet groups, then use a more inclusive search engine such as Northern Light®. At least within the publicly indexable pages, one approach emphasizes selectivity, and the other, comprehensiveness. If you are interested in comprehensiveness, use more than one search engine. You are likely to yield very different and perhaps better results using additional search engines.

What is the difference between a search engine, a portal, and a directory? Directories rely on human intervention to select, index, and categorize Web contents. Subject directories build an index based on Web pages or Web sites, but not on words within a page. Presenting a series of subject categories that are then further subdivided, Yahoo!® (**http://www.yahoo.com/**) was the first Web subject directory and is still one of the most popular choices for finding information on the Web. This is because most users are satisfied with a few good sites rather than a long list of possibilities.

A search engine's different software components allow it to search and retrieve Web pages. These include:

• Software that automatically sends robots, sometimes called "spiders," out to comb the Web, going from server to server to build an index of the words, pages, and files that are publicly indexable.

• Algorithms that determine how those pages will be selected and prioritized for display.

• User interface software that determines the search options available to the user.

Robots may be sent to roam the Web on a daily basis or on a six-week basis, so it is possible that some newer pages may not be included in the index developed by a particular search engine. Most search engines try for at least a monthly update of their indexes. Some robots may search only the upper-level pages and totally ignore valuable pages buried within a site.

The algorithm used by the search engine can have an enormous impact on the type and quantity of information retrieved. Search algorithms determine whether every word is to be included or only the top 50 or so words, whether more weight will be given to words in metadata or titles or in words used frequently, and so on. The possi-

bilities are limitless and are the major reason that results from one search may vary considerably from those of another search.

A **portal** is, as the name suggests, a gateway to the Web. A portal often includes a directory, a search engine, and other user features such as news and weather. Most Internet service providers (ISPs) are portals to the Web. The AOL® homepage is an example. This portal uses information based on past user search behavior to determine what to offer on the opening screen. Therefore, some valuable search engines, indexes, directories, and more may be relegated to an "other search aids" category. If as a researcher your behavior differs from the majority pattern, you have to be more knowledgeable about search strategies to bypass the frontline strategies offered by the portal. Several ISP portals now offer subscribers the option of customizing the portal with user-chosen search engines and secondary sources. Most of the major search engines are now actually portals to the Web that include their own search engine. Specialized portals are increasingly popular. An industry portal, one type of specialized portal, lists many different resources about a specific industry. Competia Express, the competitive intelligence site (**http://www.competia.com/express/index.html**), offers industry portals for many different industries.

Determine Search Options Nearly all search services have a Help button that will lead you to information about the search protocols and options of that particular search engine. How does the search engine work? Can you combine terms using Boolean operators (AND, OR, NOT) or other connectors? How do you enter phrases? Truncate terms? Determine output display? Limit by date or other characteristic? Some search engines provide a basic and an advanced search option. How do they differ?

Construct a Search Query and Enter Search Term(s) The Web is not a database, nor does it have a controlled vocabulary. Therefore, you must be as specific as possible, using the keywords in your management question and any variations you can think of. It is up to you to determine synonyms, variant spellings, and broader or narrower terms that will help you retrieve the information you need. This may involve some trial and error. For instance, a general term (such as *business*) would be useless in a search engine that purports to index every word in every document.

Save Results of Search If you have found good information, you will want to keep it for future reference so that you can cite it in your proposal or refer to it later in the development of your investigative questions. If you do not keep documents, you may have to reconstruct your search. At a future time, given that some portion of the

Web is revised and updated daily, those same documents may no longer be available.

Supplement Results with Information from Non-Web Sources

There is still a great deal of information in books, journals, and other print sources that is not available on the Web. While many novice researchers start and end here, the more sophisticated researcher knows a Web search is just one of many important options.

Searching for Specific Types of Information on the Web

Once you have defined your topic and established your search terms, you need to determine whether you are looking for a specific site (known item) or an address of a person or institution (who), a geographic place name and location (where), or a topic (what).

Known-Item Searches

In the same way that search protocols for the library's online catalog vary between a known-item (author or exact title) and a more general keyword search, the way you query the Web for an exact item also varies from a more general query. A trend among search engines is to establish algorithms that will yield more precise results. One of the first to follow this trend was the search engine Google® (**http://www. google.com/**), which debuted in 1998. Google and others like it help you retrieve the most precise results from known-item searches by creating an algorithm that interprets a link to a site as a vote for that site. The sites that receive the most votes (links) rise to the top of the results list in a known-item search. The Google® system also emphasizes the importance of the linking page in its algorithm.

Who Searches

In the "who" searches, you are looking for an e-mail address, a phone number, a street address, or a Web address of a person or institution. For this type of information you will first need to identify a database containing the information you need and then search that database according to its search protocols. At this writing, almost all Web search engines and portal sites partner with infoUSA® (**http://www.infoUSA.com/**) to supply the phone number databases for their white and yellow page services.[4]

Where Searches

A "where" option comprises the mapping services that help you locate an address on a map or discover the route from one place to another. Mapping services are databases tied to geographic information systems (GISs). Popular sites are Lycos® Roadmaps (**http://www.lycos.com/roadmap.html**) and MapQuest® (**http:// www.mapquest.com**).

What Searches

As we have already noted, search engines vary considerably in the way they work and in their size. If you are searching for a very unusual term, select one of the more comprehensive search engines, such as Northern Light® (**http://www.northernlight.com/**) or AltaVista® (**http://altavista.com/**). Generally, it is more efficient to start with a directory such as Yahoo!® or one of the more specialized directories on the Web. Some especially good specialized sites are the Argus Clearinghouse (**http://www.clearinghouse.net/**), featuring subject guides on dozens of topics prepared by librarians and other specialists, and INFOMINE® Scholarly Internet Resource Collections from the University of California housed at University of California–Riverside (**http:// infomine.ucr.edu/**). See Exhibit 5a-2 or your text DVD for a selection of marketing-related Web sites.

Since the Web was introduced to the world in 1992, Web technology has been seeking ways to make the contents more accessible. The dynamic nature of the Web, its lightning growth rate, the ephemeral nature of some Web pages, the different skill levels and interests of users, and the lack of standards make this an enormous challenge. Trends indicate that the Web will continue to grow and that we will continue to apply new technologies to tapping the information available on this vast and unique resource.[5] Already some search engines are better able to identify key resources. Efforts are under way to adopt standardized metatags in the coding to describe the contents of Web pages. Some search engines are using expert systems to learn more about the information requester. This is already being used extensively to target advertisements and is being used more frequently to "select" from among several options the information source that will be delivered to the requester. More efforts are being made to index a larger portion of the Web content; at the same time, efforts are also under way to improve the relevancy of the results delivered for any one search.

Government Information

Government publications, especially those of the U.S. government, are mandatory resources for many business research projects. The agencies of the U.S. government, considered as a whole, are the largest publishing body in the world. The government collects and provides access to a wide variety of social, economic, and demographic data. In addition, government laws and regulations, court decisions, policy papers, and studies all have a potential impact on business. Additionally, the government provides directories, maps, and other information sources. Specialists are available throughout the government to provide individual assistance.

Searching for government information is a complicated task that usually requires some knowledge of how

> **Exhibit 5a-2** Selected Web Sites for Marketing Research

Site ID	URL	Sponsor
Ad*Access	http://scriptorium.lib.duke.edu/adaccess/	Duke University Library
Advertising World (ad industry Portal)	http://advertising.utexas.edu/world	University of Texas, Dept. of Advertising
American Demographics	http://www.demographics.com	American Demographics
American Factfinder	http://factfinder.census.gov	U.S. Bureau of the Census
Competia Express (industry portal)	http://www.competia.com/express/	Competia
Global Edge	http://www.demographics.com	Michigan State University Center for International Business Education and Research
Kerlins.net Qualitative Research Bibliography	http://kerlins.net/bobbi/research/qualresearch/bibliography/	Bobbi Kerlin, PhD, Queen's University, Ontario
KnowThis.com Marketing Virtual Library	http://knowthis.com	Paul Christ, PhD, West Chester University of Pennsylvania
Marketing and Research Library	http://www.mrlibrary.com/	Sorensen Associates
MarketingPower.com	http://marketingpower.com	American Marketing Association
North American Industry Classification System (NAICS)	http://www.census.gov/epcd/www/naics.html	U.S. Office of Management and Budget
Stat-USA	http://www.stat-usa.gov	U.S. Dept. of Commerce

Some Proprietary Sources (with some free information)

Site ID	URL	Sponsor
Gallup Poll	http:/www.gallup.com/poll/	The Gallup Organization
Harris Poll	http://www.harrisinteractive.com/harris_poll/	Harris Interactive
The Polling Report	http://www.pollingreport.com/	The Polling Report
Public Opinion	http://europa.eu.int/comm./public_opinion/	European Commission
Public Agenda	http://www.publicagenda.org/	Public Agenda
Roper Center for Public Opinion Research	http://www.ropercenter.uconn.edu	University of Connecticut
Poll Question Database	http://www.irss.unc.edu/data_archive/pollsearch.html	The Odum Institute, University of North Carolina at Chapel Hill
Forrester Research Reports	http://forrester.com	Forrester Research
Roper Reports	http://www.nopworld.com	NOP World
JD Power Satisfaction Studies	http://www.jdpower.com	J.D. Power and Associates
Quirk's Marketing Research Review	http://www.quirks.com	Quirk Enterprises, Inc.
Ad Forum	http://www.adforum.com	Maydream
BizMiner	http://www.bizminer.com	

Trade Associations (a rich source of information but too numerous to list here)

government functions. In recent years, the U.S. government has been working aggressively to make its information available, not only through the Depository Library Program but also through the development of electronic resources. As a result, information that used to be tucked into the farthest corners of the library is now readily available and searchable on the Web. In many libraries, the entire government documents collection is included in the library's catalog, with links to Internet resources. In the remainder of this appendix, we examine three of the most useful government information types. A list of selected government resources on the Web is included in Exhibit 5a-3.

Government Organization Two of the most useful resources regarding government organization are:

- *U.S. Government Manual* (published annually); **http://www.gpoaccess.gov/gmanual/** (updated annually).
- *Congressional Directory* (published annually); **http://www.gpoaccess.gov/cdirectory/** (updated regularly).

The *U.S. Government Manual* describes the functions of every government agency and is particularly useful for identifying key personnel and agency contacts, including

> **Exhibit 5a-3** Selected Government Sources

Source	URL
American Factfinder	http://factfinder.census.gov/
Economics Statistics Briefing Room	http://www.whitehouse.gov/fsbr/esbr.html
EDGAR Database of Corporate Information (SEC filings)	http://www.sec.gov/edgar.shtml
FedStats	http://www.fedstats.gov/
GPO Access	http://www.gpoaccess.gov/
Stat-USA	http://www.stat-usa.gov/
U.S. Bureau of Labor Statistics	http://www.bls.gov/
U.S. Bureau of the Census	http://www.census.gov/
U.S. Dept. of Commerce	http://www.commerce.gov/
U.S. Small Business Administration	http://www.sbaonline.sba.gov/
U.S. Patent and Trademark Office	http://www.uspto.gov/
CBDNet (Commerce Business Daily)—government procurement, sales, and contract awards	http://cbdnet.access.gpo.gov

those at the local and regional levels. Generally very knowledgeable and helpful, these people are invaluable in any research project for their ability to cut through red tape and to answer questions pertinent to their agencies.

The *Congressional Directory* lists members of Congress and congressional committees, as well as key personnel throughout the U.S. government.

Laws, Regulations, and Court Decisions Government information regarding these key areas and other legal information can be obtained by consulting GPO Access (**http://www.gpoaccess.gov/**). GPO Access is the government's official and real-time site for finding government information. Included at this site is the complete *Monthly Catalog of U.S. Government Publications.* Use it to identify the full range of government publications, printed and electronic, issued in or after 1994.

Especially valuable on GPO Access are the databases covering laws, regulations, and congressional debates and publications. The key databases for laws and regulations are:

- *Congressional Bills*—provides texts of varying versions of bills. Only a small portion of this collection ever becomes law, but the topics can reveal trends of interest to business researchers.

- *Public Laws*—provides the texts of laws as they are passed; covers 1994 to the present. The printed version of this source is called *U.S. Statutes at Large.*

- *U.S. Code*—a codification of laws currently in effect and as revised over time. It is also available in libraries as a printed document.

- *Federal Register*—"the official daily publication for rules, proposed rules, and notices of federal agencies and organizations, as well as executive orders and other presidential documents"[6]; covers 1995 to the present. It is also available in libraries as a printed or microfiche document.

- *Code of Federal Regulations (CFR)*—"a codification of the general and permanent rules originally published in the *Federal Register* by the executive departments and agencies of the federal government."[7] A printed version is available in libraries.

GPO Access includes other valuable databases, including the Supreme Court decisions from 1937 to the present, the *Economic Report of the President,* the U.S. Budget, *Commerce Business Daily* (CBDNet), and GAO reports. New databases are added regularly.

Many libraries have created local gateways to GPO Access that help speed information retrieval (**http://www.gpoaccess.gov/**). GPO Access offers dozens of fields to search, and they can be searched independently or together. Searching each database independently provides more flexibility and more precise searching options because there are some fields that are unique to a particular database. In general, search options are similar to those for other databases. Use the search hints for each file for more details and special search possibilities.

Government Statistics Information regarding government statistics may be obtained by consulting the following sources:

- *Statistical Abstract of the United States* (**http://www.census.gov/prod/www/statistical-abstract-us.html**).

- FedStats (**http://www.fedstats.gov**).

- U.S. Bureau of the Census (**http://www.census.gov/**).

The government collects statistics on just about every topic imaginable—from crimes to hospital beds, from teachers to tax revenue, from steel production to flower imports. For any statistical inquiry, start with the *Statistical Abstract of the United States.* This annual compendium compiles statistics issued by nearly every government agency as well as additional data from selected nongovernment organizations. Many are time-series tables covering several years or even decades. All tables indicate the source of the statistics. These sources can then be consulted if desired for even more comprehensive data. Check the library's catalog, or ask the librarian to find these more specialized resources. Some may be available via FedStats.

FedStats is an online compilation of statistics provided by more than 70 U.S. agencies, including the Census Bureau, the Bureau of Labor Statistics, and the Federal Bureau of Investigation. Use the search option or the directory option to find the needed statistical tables. An especially useful feature of FedStats is the state and regional statistical data option.

No discussion of government statistical information would be complete without an examination of the U.S. Bureau of the Census. The Census Bureau is probably most well known for the Decennial Census of Population and Housing. The first such census was taken in 1790 to meet the constitutional mandate for apportioning seats in Congress. It has been taken in every year ending in zero since that date. Now it is used not only to apportion seats in the House of Representatives but also for allocation of federal aid to states and for a myriad of other purposes. The decennial census asks a certain core of questions of everyone. These are known as the "100 percent questions." While these questions may vary slightly from census to census, data on age, race, gender, relationship, and Hispanic origin are fairly constantly collected. A longer questionnaire is sent to a sample of the population. Data from its additional questions, used in conjunction with the data from the 100 percent questions, are used by government agencies at all levels, local planners, business and industry, schools, and social service agencies, among others,

for planning, grant writing, economic development, and many other purposes.

To make census information easier to understand, the Census Bureau, in cooperation with local planning agencies, has created a multilevel mapping system. The entire country is mapped into small units called *blocks.* Data from the 100 percent questions are available for all blocks, but sample data are not. Both 100 percent–question data and sample data are available for census tracts (groups of blocks) and for larger mapped units such as cities, metropolitan statistical areas, counties, and states. Tracts are especially valuable to local-level researchers because their boundaries remain mostly constant from census to census, thus allowing comparison. In cases where there is population growth, tracts may be split from one census to another and therefore may need to be added together to achieve comparable statistics. Metropolitan statistical areas, defined by the Office of Management and Budget, consist of a large population nucleus together with adjacent communities having a high degree of social and economic integration with that core. Metropolitan statistical areas comprise one or more entire counties, except in New England, where cities and towns are the basic geographic units.

In addition to the decennial census, the Census Bureau conducts the economic census in years ending in two and seven, covering all areas of the economy from the national to the local level. Both the decennial census and the economic census are supplemented by numerous survey reports, including the new American Community Survey, initiated to provide more up-to-date information on American communities. In fact, the Census Bureau has proposed using the American Community Survey—instead of the long (sample) questionnaire used through 2000—in the next decennial census. For an overview of the many report topics available, see the "Subjects A–Z" listing on the Census Bureau Web site (**http://www.census.gov/**).

Advanced Searches

In advanced searches, you use your knowledge of the database to make the search more productive.

The Search Query

Use the keywords from your management question to prepare a query for the databases. Bibliographic databases, including the library's online catalog, all have similar search options, usually a basic keyword search, an advanced search, and a way to choose a subject from a browse list. Like all databases, bibliographic databases consist of several standard fields.

Standard Search Fields for Monographs	
• Author	• Publisher
• Title	• Series
• Subject headings	

Limiters in Book Catalogs	
• Language	• Type of publication
• Date of publication	• Format (book, video, etc.)

In most bibliographic databases, all searches are keyword searches, but it is possible to search for a specific author or title or series (a known-item search) by limiting your results to a specific field of the bibliographic record. This is especially important if you are researching a prolific author such as Peter Drucker, who may have many works both by and about him. If you do not limit or narrow your search to a specific field, then you will do a general keyword search of all the records in the database. Because of the size of most databases, single-word searches generally yield results that are not very useful unless the single word is very unique. Instead, examine your management question for all relevant keywords and variations and establish a more precise search query using the connectors described as follows.

Standard Search Fields for Periodical Databases	
• Author	• Publisher
• Title	• Abstract
• Subject headings	• Company name
	• NAICS code

Limiters in Periodical Databases	
• Date	• Periodical title
• Full text	• Peer review (scholarly journals)

The most important thing to remember about search engines for the Web or for databases is that they do not all work alike. In fact, they have widely varying search protocols. What you do not know can act against you. So, if finding good information is important to you, take a couple of minutes to determine what special features and search options are used. For instance, if you enter a multi-word term, what happens? Does the database search your term as a phrase? Or does it insert a connector such as *AND* or *OR* between each word? How does it handle stopwords (*the, in,* and other similar small words)? The results will vary considerably in these three scenarios.

Search Strategy Options

Basic Searches   If you have a unique term, try a basic search with that term. Most bibliographic databases will present the results list in reverse date order; that is, the most recently published items will appear first. Review the list of items your search has retrieved. Are there too many? Not enough? Very relevant or not very relevant? If they meet the Goldilocks test of "just right," then you can move on to the next step (saving results).

Advanced Searches   If you have retrieved too few or no relevant items, or if you have retrieved hundreds of items, you should consider modifying your search query. Start with the most relevant items you find in the results list. Then do one of the following:

- Search for the cited works (the bibliography) of the full-text articles.
- Search for other works by the author or authors of the relevant citations.
- Check the subject headings assigned to the articles. Are there any more precise terms or synonyms that would improve your search results? More importantly, are there pairs of terms that appear in all of the most relevant items? Is there a thesaurus with the database that defines or expands the terminology used in the subject headings?

125

> **Exhibit 5b-1** Review of Advanced Search Options

Expanding Your Search	Narrowing Your Search	
OR	**AND**	**Phrases**
Use OR to search for plurals, synonyms, or spelling variations. Either or both terms will be present in results. • woman OR women • business OR corporation • International OR foreign	Use AND to require that all terms you specify be present in the results. • child AND advertising	Use a term consisting of two or more words. Some databases require that double quotes enclose the phrase, while others do not. • marketing research • "marketing research"
Truncation	**NOT**	**ADJ**
Symbols (?, *, !) can replace one or more characters or letters in a word or at the end of a word. • electr* (retrieves electricity, electric, electrical) • child? (retrieves children, childish, child's)	Use NOT to eliminate terms from your search. But use NOT with care. It is easy to eliminate the good with the unwanted. • advertising NOT advertorial	ADJ requires that the first term specified immediately precede the last term specified. • marketing ADJ research
	Limiters	
	Conditions (date, publication type, language) can limit your search. Most databases also offer field limiting, limiting the occurrences of your search to a specific database field, such as the author field, title field, etc. Some bibliographic databases offer the convenience of limiting the search results to peer-reviewed articles or to articles available only in full text. Use the latter with care, as some significant articles may be overlooked even though they are available in the library.	

> **Exhibit 5b-2** Advanced Searching Process

Step 1: Build a list of synonyms for each concept in the management question.

Concept A	Operator	Concept B	Operator	Concept C
online	AND	*commerce	AND	apparel
Web Internet electronic		retail* business *tailing .com		cloth* *wear lingerie

Step 2: Create and search with a concept group by combining each term in a column with OR. Put each concept group in parentheses. Then combine each concept group with AND.

(online OR web OR internet OR electronic) AND (*commerce OR retail* OR business OR *tailing OR .com) AND (apparel OR cloth* OR *wear OR lingerie)

As a result of your examination of the relevant citations and any background preparation you have done in other sources such as encyclopedias, you should now have one or more concepts and synonyms for each concept. You can now use Boolean operators or connectors (see Exhibit 5b-1) to combine terms or sets of terms to expand or narrow your search. There are four basic Boolean operators or connectors: OR, AND, NOT, and ADJ.

Think of your management question as a series of key concepts. For example, your management question might be "How can I design an appropriate online commerce environment for my apparel business?" In this example, con-

cept A would be *online;* concept B would be *commerce;* concept C would be *apparel.* In the most basic of keyword searches, you could use a keyword search with the operator AND to combine them:

online AND commerce AND apparel

If your search results are inadequate, you might need to expand your search statement with synonyms connected with the operator OR. For our sample management question, your search would look like Exhibit 5b-2. If your search results are too numerous, you'd need to limit your search.

chapter 6

The Marketing Research Request and Proposal Process

>**learning**objectives

After reading this chapter, you should understand . . .

1 The purpose of the request for proposal and the research proposal and how they are used by the marketing researcher and management decision maker.

2 The variations on each and their contents.

3 The processes for evaluating the quality of proposals and when each is used.

Marketing researchers are much in demand in professional associations because they have unique skills possessed by relatively few managers. Florida's chapter of the Marketing Research Society recognizes this and encourages its members to participate in various community organizations. Sara Armstrong, a Visionary Insights project manager, volunteers on the Economic Development Council for Palm Beach. As we join her, Sara has just arrived at the monthly meeting of the Economic Development Council, on which she represents the Florida chapter of the Marketing Research Society.

"Sara, I'm glad you've finally arrived," comments council president Craig Bowen, as he propels her across the dining room by grasping her elbow. "Come meet Robert Buffet."

"Robert, meet Sara Armstrong, with Visionary Insights." Sara recognizes his name; Buffet is the manager of the local office of a national management consulting firm specializing in the hospitality industry.

"Hello, Robert," she says as she extends her hand. Sara's initial impression is of brightly shined black shoes and razor-cut hair.

"And what a pleasure it is to meet you," he says in a ripe baritone voice, smiling with his lips but not his eyes, which are reluctantly drawn from a prominent banker who is chatting across the room with a competing consultant to focus on Sara.

"Here's the situation, Sara," says Bowen. "The state commerce secretary has been concerned for some time about the extent to which various counties' tourism efforts are really attracting additional visitors to the state. Robert's firm was chosen as one of the finalists and has been asked to submit a more detailed proposal to study the situation in five counties, assess actual economic development as a result of the separate tourism efforts, and ultimately report this back to Tallahassee."

"Am I right in suspecting that the governor is worried that individual county efforts might be counterproductive—that he would prefer evidence to support a more coordinated program?"

"Basically, that is the concern, Sara. The governor has asked our council to interview the firms submitting proposals and, once we've made a choice to do the research project, to assure the business community it is in their best interests to cooperate."

"And you want me on the team that critically examines these proposals and chooses the firm to receive the contract."

"Actually, I need you to head the review team. And I need your recommendation, by two weeks from Friday, please," says Bowen, smiling sheepishly. "Here is a copy of the RPF."

"And here is a copy of our proposal," says Robert, his attention now totally focused on Sara, having realized her importance to new business. "If you have questions, you may contact me at either of the numbers on my business card, but I'd be happy to give you an overview of the proposal over dinner."

But before Sara has a chance to respond, Bowen responds with a smile, "That might give you an unfair advantage, Robert." Then he turns his attention to Sara as he propels her away, commenting, "I want to introduce you to the rest of the team—so that you can set up your initial meeting—and to the other companies that are submitting proposals."

> Proposing Research

Many students and some marketing researchers view the proposal process as unnecessary work. In actuality, the more inexperienced a researcher is, the more important it is to have a well-planned and adequately documented proposal. The proposal process, Exhibit 6-1, in marketing research uses two primary documents: the *request for proposal* (RFP) and the *research proposal*. When the organization has research specialists on the payroll, the internal research proposal is often all that is needed. Often, however, companies do not have adequate capacity, resources, or the specialized talents in-house to execute a project, so they turn to outside research suppliers (including marketing and business research specialists, universities, research centers, and consulting firms). We will explore the second scenario first.

> The Request for Proposal (RFP)

request for proposal (RFP)
a formal bid request for research to be done by an outside supplier of research services.

The **request for proposal (RFP)** is the formal document issued by a corporate marketing research department, a marketing decision maker, or some other sponsor (such as the Economic Development Council in the opening vignette) to solicit services from research suppliers. Developing a well-written RFP takes time and planning. However, the benefit to the sponsoring organization is an opportunity to formalize the process of documenting, justi-

> **Exhibit 6-1** The Research Proposal Process

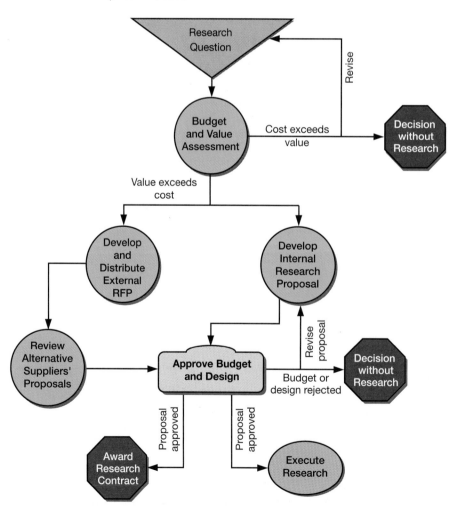

fying, and authorizing the procurement of research. RFPs also provide a chance to evaluate different solutions and offer the means of establishing, monitoring, and controlling the performance of the winning supplier.

The marketing researcher invites a qualified supplier to submit a proposal in accordance with a specific, detailed format—delivered by a deadline. Prescribing a common format makes comparison of competing proposals much easier. Each firm has its own requirements, and these are reflected not only in the form of the RFPs but in how they're distributed. The government, for example, is required by law to publicly announce RFPs. Private firms may limit supplier invitations to bidders that they have solicited before, to vendors that have provided past services, or to a single bidder (sole source). Both technical merit and the supplier's estimate of project cost determine how contracts are awarded.

Marketing research suppliers consider RFPs an important source of future business. Thus, they must be vigilant to retain credibility with current and past clients and must seek to achieve positive word of mouth. Professional guides or business listing services (such as the trade associations discussed in Chapter 2) promote the supplier's visibility. Companies sometimes avoid the formal RFP as a means of contacting suppliers. They may invite you to propose a project during a conversation and later ask you to formalize it in writing. Moreover, not all projects are conducive to the RFP process. However, in the next section, we will discuss how an organization requests state-of-the-art proposals for dealing with complex marketing research problems.

Creating the RFP

The first step is to define and understand fully the problem being addressed. In formal RFP processes, internal experts define the problem. They may be brand managers, new product specialists, or representatives from other functions. Alternatively, an expert or a group of experts may be retained to assist in defining the problem and then writing the RFP. In the tourism study, members of the commerce department and experts in the hospitality, travel, advertising, and entertainment fields would have participated at the request of the governor. Once the problem is defined, the technical section of the RFP can be written.

> **We discussed techniques for problem definition and clarification in Chapters 4 and 5.**

Besides defining the technical requirements of the desired research, critical components of the RFP include project management, pricing, and contract administration. These sections allow the potential research supplier to understand and meet the expectations of the sponsoring management team for the contracted services. Also, a section on proposal administration, including important dates, is included.

An important activity that precedes this is qualifying potential suppliers. Sponsors must determine which vendors have the capability to complete the project on time. When the process is not open to all bidders, criteria such as industry experience, reputation, geographic location, quality of previous work, size of staff, and strategic alliances with other vendors determine which bidders will be eligible to receive the RFP.

Although RFPs differ somewhat from firm to firm, the general components are:

• Proposal administration information.
• Summary statement of the problem.
• Technical section.
• Management section.
• Contracts and license section.
• Pricing section.

Proposal Administration

This section is an overview of important information on the administration of the project itself. It establishes the dates of the RFP process—when the RFP is released, when the RFP

Covering Kids—the RFP

The Robert Wood Johnson Foundation (RWJF) knew it wanted a collaborative partner to do the research for its Covering Kids initiative. Elaine Arkin, a social issues marketing specialist, was recruited to develop the request for proposal (RFP). The RFP described the Covering Kids initiative, as well as the type of marketing research needed, but stopped short of specifying the methodology. "We knew we needed to talk with low-income parents," shared Arkin. "And we wanted some baseline information, as well as some pre-testing of advertising." The RWJF team put together a search list by contacting firms that had managed large communication initiatives in the past. These contacts recommended a dozen firms that were then asked to describe their capabilities to do quantitative and qualitative research, as well as their experience with social issue research and with minority and low-income populations. In all, six firms were asked to submit detailed research proposals. A committee consisting of RWJF staffers, the team from GMMB (the agency charged with developing the campaign), and several research specialists reviewed all six proposals. "We were working on a very tight deadline. The research would need to be started and finished quickly, with the results incorporated into the GMMB-designed campaign—all in less than three months," indicated RWJF senior communications officer Stuart Schear. Each firm's proposal was reviewed for the feasibility of the methodology and the cost, as well as the firm's ability to meet the time constraints. "Two firms could not meet the constraints, and another two were deemed too small to deliver the quantitative and qualitative research needed," explained Arkin. Less than one week after receipt of the proposals, the review committee selected Wirthlin Worldwide to provide the research. Wirthlin started the research immediately.

www.rwjf.org; www.wirthlinworldwide.com; www.gmmb.com

team is available for questions, the date the proposal is expected, and the dates of the evaluation and supplier selections. It includes all requirements for preparing the proposal and describes how proposals will be evaluated. Contact names, addresses, and relevant telephone and fax numbers are listed. In the opening vignette, Sara Armstrong has been recruited to head the proposal review team but was not part of the team that created the RFP.

Summary Statement of the Problem

The summary statement can be an abstract of the technical section, or it can be included as the first page of the technical section. It often takes the form of a letter introducing the organization that issued the RFP and explaining its needs. As an example, let's use a problem statement from Visionary Insights' client, MindWriter, that deals with a customer satisfaction issue:

> The call center in MindWriter's new CompleteCare facility currently operates without an automated recording and monitoring process. We have 10 dedicated reviewers sustaining this function. In addition, our call center supervisors spend six hours per month monitoring the quality of our reviewers. The reviewers rely on a manually generated schedule to select representatives and times for monitoring. When representatives are on active calls during the monitoring schedule, it is problematic to trace them. However, reviewers have access to the online scheduling software. Thus, they can view the account screens selected by the representative using our own software tool.
>
> The quality of our customer service and the resulting satisfaction are of vital importance to MindWriter. We need to significantly increase the efficiency of our customer call monitoring through automation and a recorded database for agent review. We also need to discover the extent to which these technical changes to our process improve customer perceptions of service.

Technical Section

Technical information needed by the supplier to create the proposal is presented in this section. It begins by describing the problem(s) to be addressed and the technical detail of each requirement. It loosely describes the services to be performed and the equipment, software, and documentation required. This section should be neither too specific nor too general to allow the suppliers reasonable flexibility and creativity in research design but should also restrict them in meeting the needs of the sponsor. Typically, the following would be included:

- Problem statement.
- Description of functional requirements (what actual phases will be included in the research).
- Identification of constraints (what might limit research design creativity).

The sponsor's functional requirements assist suppliers in testing the comprehensiveness of their proposed solutions. Often, sponsors ask the proposed researcher to answer questions. In MindWriter's RFP, the writers have considered a wide range of functional issues:

Recording

- What proportion of calls does your proposed solution record?
- To what degree is your proposed system scalable?
- Can the representatives detect that they are being recorded?

System Integration and Retrieval

- Can you integrate multiple sources of information to the recording platform?
- Does your proposed solution offer redundancy in the event of a failure?
- Does your proposed solution store conversations along with their corresponding call-tag data in a single database?
- Can the recorded calls be replayed immediately?
- How does your proposed solution search calls for replay?
- What volume of long-term archived storage is available?

Evaluation and Analysis

- Can call data be displayed visually for analysis?
- How are calls selected for evaluation/scoring?
- Can values be assigned to each question and "rep performance" or "rep skill" category?
- Does your solution offer data mining capabilities?
- In what ways does your solution support managerial analysis of operations and business performance?
- How does your solution support the CompleteCare customer satisfaction philosophy at MindWriter?

Strategies for dealing with constraints include specifying what is anticipated. If the sponsor requires that the supplier offer creative solutions, the RFP describes the constraints within which solutions must work. A client of Visionary Insights provides an example, below, of sampling constraints in its RFP. The client is interested in using the benchmarks from previous studies and thus needs consistency in its current project.

- The sample sizes and breakdowns for various markets are:
  - Europe: 500 completed surveys.
  - Asia: 500 completed surveys.
  - United States: 300 completed surveys.
    - Regional differences.
    - Differentiation by segment and brand.

Luth Research is a full-service research provider, doing online focus groups as well as mail and phone surveys with extensive CATI facilities. A full-service provider is able to adapt its methodologies to the RFP at hand. When an RFP specifies a range of research services, a full-service provider may be able to fulfill all a firm's requirements. In this ad, Luth showcases its *SurveySavvy* online panel, a service that helps clients involve specific participants that are necessary for a research project—even IT professionals who wear earrings.
www.luthresearch.com

- Proposed sample proportion for distributors/resellers:
  - Resellers = 90–95% of respondents.
  - Distributors = 5–10%.

Building technical quality control into the RFP will subsequently strengthen the project. When the technical section contains thorough specifications and clear criteria for evaluating proposals, even low bidders must provide the requisite quality for consideration. In addition, when the RFP requires that the supplier provide technical reports during the project, project management is less costly for the firm. When a thorough understanding of the constraints is unknown, sponsors may schedule a planning meeting with possible researchers prior to their RFP response to clarify and examine options.

Management Section

Each project requires some level of management. The sponsor's timing on schedules, plans, and reports is included in this section. The management section also lists the requirements for implementation schedules, training and reporting schedules, quality control, and other documentation. If specific supplier qualifications are needed, they should be shown here. References from the supplier's customers may also be requested. Increasingly, detailed documentation Web sites are used to provide additional information to those invited to submit proposals. These Web site URLs are documented in the RFP.

Contracts and License Section

The types of contracts the supplier is expected to sign and any nondisclosure agreements are included in this section. The research supplier of marketing research is often privy to marketing strategies and tactics long before such competitive moves are undertaken. The supplier is also aware of challenges facing the marketer and actions being considered to address those challenges. Nondisclosure of such information is therefore critical. It is in this context that the sponsor should discuss the safeguarding of intellectual property and the use of copyrights. Terms of payment and required benchmarks are also set forth here. Typically, a sample purchase contract would be included. Since the RFP document is usually a part of the final contract, it should be worded precisely to avoid problems of interpretation. If a task is not described in the RFP or during contract negotiations, the firm may not be able to require that the supplier complete it.

Pricing Section

To cost the proposal, all information needed by the supplier must be provided. By using a format that lists all anticipated activities, proposals with different approaches can be compared on cost. The following list shows examples of items that could be included:

- Services
- Data collection
- Data analysis
- Meetings with client
- Travel
- Respondent survey incentives
- Mail and telephone costs
- Design meetings
- Internet design and activation
- Facilities and equipment
- Extensions to work agreements
- Pilot tests

- Report preparations
- Computer models
- Project management
- Questionnaire and reproduction costs
- Manpower costs
- Deliverables:
  - Training
  - Brochures/literature
  - Videotapes
  - Reports
  - Promotionals

Ethical standards are integral to designing the pricing section. For example, a sponsor would not send a vendor an RFP to (1) help the sponsor plan its project budget, (2) estimate costs and ideas for a project the sponsor intends to execute in-house, or (3) create the impression of a competitive bid when the sponsor intends to sole-source the project.

> **We discuss the sponsor's ethical requirements in Chapter 7.**

Format

The format requirements for RFPs differ widely. The sections above reflect informational requirements rather than an RFP outline. A typical format might contain the following elements:

- Instructions to bidders
- Background
  - Overview or profile of the buyer's company
  - Project overview
  - Project requirements
- Vendor information
  - Company profile
  - History and description
  - Legal summary (active lawsuits or pending litigation)
  - Partnerships and alliances
  - References
- Proposed solution
- Services and support
- Cost proposal
  - Services pricing
  - Maintenance pricing
  - Contractual terms and conditions

> **Exhibit 6-2** Checklist for Qualifying Research Suppliers

Research Supplier

❑ Research experience and industry status, including appropriate accreditation

   ❑ Scope/type of research performed (quantitative vs. qualitative vs. both; advertising creative development, product testing, site location, etc.)

      ❑ Knowledge of specific research methodologies (e.g. research with children, visual ethnography, conjoint analysis)

   ❑ Types of clients

      ❑ Knowledge of specific markets

         ❑ International links or associations, if needed

      ❑ No conflicts of interest

❑ Code of ethical performance

Research Supplier's Staff

❑ Skill and experience to manage the project

❑ Skill and experience to conduct desired research

   ❑ Specialist skills, when needed (psychologists, anthropologists, Internet technologists, etc.)

❑ Understanding of marketing

Research Supplier's Facilities, Procedures, and Quality Management

❑ Compatible project management system

❑ Compatible contractual arrangements, including billing

❑ Compatible client complaint and satisfaction handling procedures

❑ Desired quality assurance procedures

❑ Desired organization, procedures, and appropriate facilities

   ❑ Data collection (interviewers, interviewer training, CATI, CAPI, proprietary methodologies, etc.)

      ❑ Field operations

      ❑ Lab settings (taste testing, product testing, etc.)

   ❑ Data handling (internal or subcontracted, software used, etc.)

   ❑ Developing/drawing samples

❑ Compatible standard reporting procedures and guidelines

❑ Desired results presentation practices

Source: This checklist was developed from recommendations of industry practitioners and material on the ESOMAR Web site: http://www.esomar.nl/guidelines/CommissioningResearch.htm.

As each marketing research project is often unique, industry practices suggest that careful consideration should be used when qualifying potential research suppliers. Exhibit 6-2 offers a checklist developed from recommendations of industry practitioners and associations.

To recap, the marketer, marketing research department, or other research sponsor should achieve several objectives in the RFP process: qualify potential vendors, write and distribute the RFP eight to ten weeks before the requested date, be available to answer supplier questions or hold prebidding conferences, evaluate submissions on known criteria, award contracts and start the project on published dates, and provide a critique to all suppliers who submitted proposals. The latter will help unsuccessful bidders become competitive in the future and maintain your goodwill for future projects.

> **Exhibit 6-3** Modifications to Strengthen the RFP Process

Modifications	Features
Enhance the existing process.	• Send shorter RFPs by investing time up front to decide specific, desirable outcomes. • Use site visits and demonstrations to be certain the suppliers' designs or systems can meet their claims. • Automate the process to reduce time and cost of preparation. • Strategic Systems Solutions International offers Product Analyzer™ software to simplify objective supplier evaluation through various scoring algorithms. • Pragmatech Software, Inc., provides a suite of software products including The RFP Machine® (to build, edit, and maintain a central repository of company, product, and service information required for automated RFP and RFI creation); The Proposal Assembler™ (enables the design document templates to automatically create a complex, tailored proposal); and e-Proposals™ (which combine benefits of traditional proposals with the power, flexibility, and ubiquity of the Web).
Add the *request for information (RFI)* as the first step in overall RFP development.	The RFI lets a supplier know you are gathering information but are not prepared to purchase a good or service. It provides the company with an opportunity to more carefully define its requirements and alerts suppliers to the opportunity to respond to its requirements. There are several advantages to RFIs. An RFI: • Is an accepted method for determining if the techniques and methods are available, if cost estimates are reasonable, and if solutions exist. • Requires in-house people to agree on the requirements and set minimal expectations. • Eliminates supplier surprise, thereby helping suppliers to build a better response. • Requires a formal written response that may later be incorporated into the contract. • Provides a qualified list of suppliers and eliminates those who could not have responded to the RFP.
Replace the RFP with a *request for application (RFA)*.	An RFA consists of: • An overview of the requesting firm's organizational structure. • Business objectives. • Basic operational procedures. • Problems that the supplier's bid should address.
Replace the RFP with a *request for recommendation (RFR)*.	An RFR contains a clear statement of the problem and is sent to a small number of credible suppliers. The suppliers' responses would: • Be limited to a 10-page reply. • Contain ballpark prices for the information to be provided. • Include supplier recommendations with brief descriptions of solutions and support that can be offered. • Be due in three to four weeks (saving the cost of a consultant to prepare an RFP and leaving the firm with the flexibility to maintain control of the project's ultimate direction). Suppliers (usually no more than six) would be invited to visit the firm and make a two-hour presentation. The firm's statement of work would then be refined and the supplier list narrowed.

A well-written RFP allows an organization to request high-quality proposals for dealing with complex problems. When not done properly, the RFP process will take longer, cost more, and not provide a complete long-term solution. Therefore, when a marketer decides to put a marketing research project to bid using an RFP, it is essential that time and effort be invested at the beginning.

Modifications to the traditional RFP process can help the company achieve flexibility and maintain good vendor relations. For example, a *request for information* (RFI) lets a supplier know you are gathering information but are not prepared to purchase a good or service. This modification, shown in Exhibit 6-3, is a worthwhile first step to decide how to proceed with the creation of a full-fledged RFP. A *request for recommendation* (RFR) is an alternative that many firms prefer. It asks suppliers for recommendations with brief descriptions of solutions and support that they can offer. A *request for application* (RFA) provides organizational context so that the supplier can address the problem with more insight and propose solutions that will be compatible with the organization's culture and business strategy. Clear communications with suppliers through a coherent RFP process will result in a well-managed project with long-term benefits.

Now, let's say as a marketing researcher you have received an RFP. What is next? First, you decide if creating a proposal is worth your investment of time and effort. Even if you are not responding to the RFP, becoming familiar with proposals can be helpful. As a marketing researcher, you might consider producing all of your projects using a structure or template similar to the proposal format.

> The Research Proposal

proposal a work plan, prospectus, outline, statement of intent, or draft plan for a research project, including a proposed budget.

A **proposal** is an individual's or company's offer to produce a product or render a service to a potential buyer or sponsor. The purpose of the research proposal is:

1. To present the management question to be researched and relate its importance.
2. To discuss the research efforts of others who have worked on related questions.
3. To suggest the data necessary for solving the management's question and suggest how the data will be gathered, treated, and interpreted.

In addition, a research proposal must present the researcher's plan, services, and credentials in the best possible way to encourage the proposal's selection over competitors. In contract research, the survival of companies depends on their ability to develop winning proposals.[1] A proposal is also known as a *work plan, prospectus, outline, statement of intent, or draft plan.*[2] The proposal tells us what, why, how, where, and to whom the research will be done. It must also show the benefit of doing the research.[3]

The research proposal is essentially a road map, showing clearly the location from which a journey begins, the destination to be reached, and the method of getting there. Well-prepared proposals include potential problems that may be encountered along the way and methods for avoiding or working around them, much as a road map indicates alternate routes for a detour.

Sponsor Uses

All research has a sponsor in one form or another. The student researcher is responsible to the class instructor. In a corporate setting, whether the research is being done in-house by a research department or under contract to an external research firm, management sponsors the research. University-, government-, or corporate-sponsored (grant) research uses grant committees to evaluate the work.

A research proposal allows the sponsor to assess the sincerity of the researcher's purpose, the clarity of his or her design, the extent of his or her relevant background material, and the researcher's fitness for undertaking the project. Depending on the type of research and the sponsor, various aspects of a standard proposal design are emphasized. The proposal displays the researcher's discipline, organization, and logic. It thus allows the research sponsor to assess both the researcher and the proposed design, to compare them

>**snap**shot

Austin Kelley Helps Karastan Make a Statement

While Karastan has long been a brand leader in floor coverings, research showed that it was not connecting with rising, young, affluent consumers. Karastan, perceived as too formal for their active lifestyles, was seen as their "parents' brand."

In developing the best positioning for the brand, Karastan conducted a series of in-home focus groups in order to gather insight into its target consumer. Focus groups were held in the homes of women who were current and potential Karastan consumers. Each focus group consisted of 10 women whose ages ranged from midthirties to late forties. The in-home setting was selected to ensure the comfort level of the participants and to match the tone of the brand. Depending on their age, the focus group participants represented two groups: Brand Loyals and Rising Affluents. Throughout each two-hour session, participants engaged in open discussion, viewed product samples, and reacted to brand positioning lines. Moderators directed the conversation with questions such as, "What motivates you to decorate?" and "How does the concept of the home manifest itself for you?" Both groups conveyed a passion for decorating and an emotional connection with the home. In choosing floor coverings, it was the styles and colors that had the greatest impact on women's decorating choices. This insight, that women viewed decorating as a means of self-expression, helped to develop the positioning tagline: "Make a Statement. Your Own."

Karastan was poised to select a celebrity spokesperson who appealed to the interests of the target market. Actress/model/mother Andie MacDowell was selected to launch the campaign.

The campaign, which is presented in a Q&A format similar to a celebrity profile, is Karastan's first to target a younger, more contemporary audience than its traditional consumer. The effort positions the company's high-end carpets and rugs as fashion

brands for "decorating divas"—women who use their homes to make a unique and personal statement. Although MacDowell was the launch, the campaign will expand over the next few years to feature a diverse group of celebrities who make similar style statements.

www.karastan.com; www.austinkelley.com; www.slingshotstrategy.com

Can you envision the internal proposal for this research project?

---

against competing proposals on current organizational, scholastic, or scientific needs, and to make the best selection for the project.

Comparison of the research project results with the proposal is also the first step in the process of evaluating the overall research. By comparing the final product with the stated objectives, it is easy for the sponsor to decide if the research goal—a better decision on the management question—has been achieved.

Another benefit of the proposal is the discipline it brings to the sponsor. Many managers, requesting research from an internal research department, may not adequately define the problem they are addressing. The research proposal acts as a catalyst for discussion between the person conducting the research and the manager. The researcher translates the management question, as described by the manager, into the research question and outlines the objectives of the study. Upon review, the manager may discover that the interpretation of the problem does not encompass all the original symptoms. The proposal, then, serves as the basis for additional discussion between the manager and the researcher until all aspects of the management question are understood. Parts of the management question may not be researchable, or at least not subject to empirical study. An alternate design, such as

> **A poorly planned, poorly written, or poorly organized proposal damages the researcher's reputation more than would the decision not to submit a proposal.**

> **Exhibit 6-4** Proposal Development

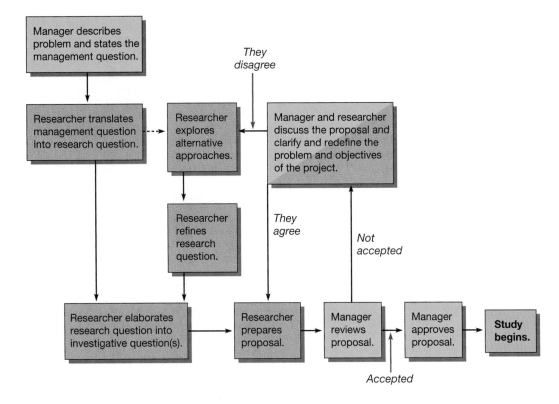

a qualitative or policy analysis study, may need to be proposed. Upon completion of the discussions, the sponsor and researcher should agree on a carefully worded research question. As Exhibit 6-4 reveals, proposal development can work in an iterative fashion until the sponsor authorizes the research to proceed.

For an outside research contract, proposals are usually submitted in response to an RFP. The researcher may wish to convince the sponsor that his or her approach to the research question differs from that indicated by the management question specified in the initial RFP. In this way, the researcher can show superior understanding of the management dilemma compared to researchers submitting competing proposals.

Researcher Benefits

A proposal is even more beneficial for the researcher than for the sponsor. The process of writing a proposal encourages the researcher to plan and review the project's logical steps. Related management and research literature should be examined in developing the proposal. This review prompts the researcher to assess previous approaches to similar management questions and revise the research plan accordingly. Additionally, developing the proposal offers the opportunity to spot flaws in the logic, errors in assumptions, or even management questions that are not adequately addressed by the objectives and design.

The in-house or contract researcher uses the approved research proposal as a guide throughout the investigation. Progress can be monitored and milestones noted. At completion, the proposal provides an outline for the final research report.[4]

> **Researchers often develop Gantt charts of the logical research steps, similar to the one in Exhibit 5-7 in Chapter 5, as working documents when developing responses to RFPs.**

Like any other professional, a contract researcher makes his or her profit from correctly estimating costs and pricing the research project appropriately. An in-house researcher is also held to a fiscal standard that includes living within a budget. A thorough proposal process is likely to reveal all possible cost-related activities, thus making cost estimation more accurate. As many of these cost-associated activities are related to time, a proposal benefits a researcher by forcing a time estimate for the project. These time and cost estimates encourage the researcher to plan the project so that work progresses steadily toward

>snapshot

USTA: Come Out Swinging

Some of you may be avid tennis players, but, statistically, odds are you aren't. The United States Tennis Association plans to change that, and to do so, they launched one of the more aggressive sports research programs in history.

Think large sample, very large sample, and you still might not envision the 25,503 households in the United States, British Columbia, Puerto Rico, and the U.S. Virgin Islands that were interviewed by The Taylor Research and Consulting Group, Inc., for the 2003 Tennis Participation Study. This telephone survey, large enough to provide statistically relevant data for all 17 *sections* of the USTA's membership, was followed by the use of a proprietary qualitative study, called *Street Spies,* by advertising and marketing agency Vigilante. The latter phase of the research was designed to help the USTA determine the appropriate message to get tennis swinging again as a sport.

"Tennis has everything a sport should have," shared marketing specialist Scott Staniar, whose job it is to reposition and relaunch tennis. "You can play it no matter your age; it's great for keeping you healthy and fit; it's a great way to meet people; and it's fun." But graphically tennis participation can be represented by a flat line. Tennis is losing as many players as it is gaining, often due to the time constraints of dual-income baby boomers. In order for tennis to grow, it needs to aggressively market itself as relevant to an increasingly culturally diverse youth population facing a myriad of recreational choices, not all of them physical—such as computer games and the Internet. "Even though players like Serena and Venus Williams have helped attract African-Americans and Hispanic Americans in greater numbers," says Kurt Kamperman, USTA chief executive, "tennis is still perceived by many as a country club sport." The *Come Out Swinging* campaign is designed to reinvigorate the sport with the spirit and vitality that is the game. The research led Vigilante to use celebrities who appeal to a wide range of ethnic audience segments.

Daisy Fuentes
VJ, News Anchor,
Talk Show Host,
Model, Actress,
Tennis Player

TENNIS. COME OUT SWINGING."

Each has his or her own gritty, urban, go-all-out competitive image that matches the sport. The campaign directs those who are interested to visit one of more than 3,500 Tennis Welcome Centers or tenniswelcomecenter.com. Tracking that behavior is just one way USTA will measure success. Can you envision the external proposal for this research?

www.usta.com; www.tenniswelcomecenter.com; www.vigilantenyc.com; www.thetaylorgroup.com.

To learn more about this research, read the case "USTA: Come Out Swinging" on your text DVD.

the deadline. Since many people are inclined to procrastinate, having a schedule helps them work methodically toward the completion of the project.

Types of Research Proposals

In general, research proposals can be divided between those generated for internal and those for external audiences. An internal proposal is done by staff specialists or by the research department within the firm. External proposals sponsored by university grant committees, government agencies, government contractors, not-for-profit organizations, or corporations can be further classified as either solicited or unsolicited. With few exceptions, the larger the project, the more complex the proposal. In public sector work, the complexity is generally greater than in a comparable private sector proposal.

There are three general levels of complexity: exploratory studies, small-scale studies, and large-scale studies. These are noted in Exhibit 6-5. The exploratory study generates the most

> **Exhibit 6-5** Proposal Complexity

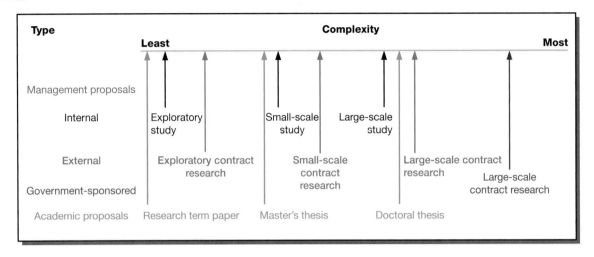

simple research proposal. More complex and common in business is the small-scale study—either an internal study or an external contract research project. The large-scale professional study, worth up to several million dollars, is the most complex proposal we deal with here. Government agency large-scale project RFPs usually generate proposals running several hundred pages and use the modules that we discuss next. However, each agency has unique requirements, but such specific coverage is beyond the scope of this text.

Exhibit 6-6 displays a set of modules for building a proposal. Their order can represent an outline for a proposal. Based on the type of proposal you are writing, you may choose the appropriate modules for inclusion. This is a general guide, and sometimes more or less than what is shown here is appropriate for a specific purpose. For example, most small-scale studies do not require a glossary of terms. Terms are defined within the body of the proposal. However, if the proposal deals with an esoteric subject that is not familiar to management, it is appropriate to add a glossary. For a solicited study, the RFP will indicate both the content headings and their order.

> **Take some time to review Exhibit 6-6. Compare the proposal modules suggested for each type of study. This will increase your understanding of proposals.**

Internal Proposals

Internal proposals are more succinct than external ones. At the least complex end of the continuum in Exhibit 6-6, a one- to three-page memo from the researcher to management outlining the problem statement, study objectives, research design, and schedule is enough to start an exploratory study. Privately and publicly held businesses are concerned with how to solve a particular problem, make a decision, or improve an aspect of their business. Seldom do businesses begin research studies for other reasons. Regardless of the intended audience, in the small-scale proposal, the literature review and bibliography are consequently not stressed and can often be stated briefly in the research design. Since management insists on brevity, an executive summary is mandatory for all but the most simple of proposals (projects that can be proposed in a two-page memo do not need an executive summary). Schedules and budgets are necessary for funds to be committed. For the smaller-scale projects, descriptions are not required for facilities and special resources, nor is there a need for a glossary. Since managers familiar with the problem sponsor small projects, the associated jargon, requirements, and definitions should be included directly in the text. Also, the measuring instrument and project management modules are not required. Managers will typically leave this detail for researchers.

External Proposals

solicited proposal proposal developed in response to an RFP.

An external proposal is either solicited or unsolicited. A **solicited proposal** is often in response to an RFP. The proposal is likely competing against several others for a contract or

> **Exhibit 6-6** Modules to Include in Proposals

Proposal Types / Proposal Modules	Management Internal			Management External			Government	Academic		
	Exploratory Study	Small-Scale Study	Large-Scale Study	Exploratory Contract	Small-Scale Contract	Large-Scale Contract	Large-Scale Contract	Term Paper	Master's Thesis	Doctoral Thesis
Executive summary		✔	✔	✔	✔	✔	✔			
Problem statement	✔	✔	✔	✔	✔	✔	✔	✔	✔	✔
Research objectives	✔	✔	✔	✔	✔	✔	✔	✔	✔	✔
Literature review			✔			✔	✔		✔	✔
Importance/ benefits of study			✔	✔	✔	✔	✔			✔
Research design	✔	✔	✔	✔	✔	✔	✔		✔	✔
Data analysis						✔	✔			✔
Nature and form of results		✔	✔		✔	✔	✔		✔	✔
Qualification of researchers				✔	✔	✔	✔			
Budget		✔	✔	✔	✔	✔	✔			
Schedule	✔	✔	✔	✔	✔	✔	✔			✔
Facilities and special resources			✔	✔	✔	✔	✔		✔	✔
Project management			✔			✔	✔			
Bibliography			✔			✔	✔	✔	✔	✔
Appendices/ glossary of terms			✔			✔	✔		✔	✔
Measurement instrument			✔			✔	✔			✔

grant. An **unsolicited proposal** is a suggestion by a contract researcher for research that might be done. An example of such a proposal is a consulting firm's proposing a research project to a client that has retained the consultancy for other purposes. Another example of an unsolicited proposal is a research firm's proposing an omnibus study to a trade association to address problems arising from a change in the cultural or political-legal environments. The unsolicited proposal has the advantage of not competing against others but the disadvantage of having to speculate on the ramifications of a management dilemma facing the firm's management. In addition to being an outsider assessing an internal problem, the writer of an unsolicited proposal must decide to whom the document should be sent. Such proposals are often time-sensitive, so the window of opportunity might close before a redirected proposal finds its appropriate recipient.

unsolicited proposal a suggestion by a contract researcher for research that might be done.

> **We offer a sample of an external proposal on your text DVD.**

The most important sections of the external proposal are the objectives, design, qualifications, schedule, and budget. In contract research, the results and objectives sections are the standards against which the completed project is measured. The executive summary of an external proposal may be included within the letter of transmittal. As the complexity of the project increases, more information is required about project management and the facilities and special resources. As we move toward government-sponsored research, particular attention must be paid to each specification in the RFP. To ignore or not meet any specification is to automatically disqualify your proposal as "nonresponsive."[5]

> **You might find it valuable to revisit the management-research question hierarchy and the research process model in Chapters 4 and 5 prior to reading this section.**

Structuring the Research Proposal

Consider again Exhibit 6-6. Using this reference, you can put together a set of modules that tailors your proposal to the intended audience. Each of the following modules is flexible, so its content and length may be adapted to specific needs.

Executive Summary

executive summary (proposal) an informative abstract providing the essentials of the proposal without the details.

The **executive summary** allows a busy manager or sponsor to understand quickly the thrust of the proposal. It is essentially an informative abstract, giving executives the chance to grasp the essentials of the proposal without having to read the details.[6] The goal of the summary is to secure a positive evaluation by the executive who will pass the proposal on to the staff for a full evaluation. As such, the executive summary should include brief statements of the management dilemma and management question, the research objectives/research question(s), and the benefits of your approach. If the proposal is unsolicited, a brief description of your qualifications is also appropriate.

Problem Statement

This section needs to convince the sponsor to continue reading the proposal. You should capture the reader's attention by stating the management dilemma, its background, its consequences, and the resulting management question. The importance of answering the management question should be emphasized here if a separate module on the importance/

benefits of the study is not included later in the proposal. In addition, this section should include any restrictions or areas of the management question that will not be addressed.

Problem statements too broadly defined cannot be addressed adequately in one study. It is important that the management question distinguish the primary problem from related problems clearly. Be sure your problem statement is clear without the use of idioms or clichés. After reading this section, the potential sponsor should know the management dilemma and the question, its significance, and why something should be done to change the status quo.[7]

Research Objectives

This module addresses the purpose of the investigation. It is here that you lay out exactly what is being planned by the proposed research. In a descriptive study, the objectives can be stated as the research question. Recall that the research question is then translated into investigative questions. If the proposal is for a causal study, then the objectives can be restated as a hypothesis.

The objectives module flows naturally from the problem statement, giving the sponsor specific, concrete, and achievable goals. It is best to list the objectives either in order of importance or in general terms first, moving to specific terms (i.e., research question followed by underlying investigative questions). The research question(s) (or hypotheses, if appropriate) should be separated from the flow of the text for quick identification.

The research objectives section is the basis for judging the remainder of the proposal and, ultimately, the final report. Verify the consistency of the proposal by checking to see that each objective is discussed in the research design, data analysis, and results sections.

Literature Review

The **literature review** section examines recent (or historically significant) research studies, company data, or industry reports that act as a basis for the proposed study. Begin your discussion of the related literature and relevant secondary data from a comprehensive perspective, moving to more specific studies that are associated with your problem. If the problem has a historical background, begin with the earliest references.

Avoid the extraneous details of the literature; do a brief review of the information, not a comprehensive report. Always refer to the original source. If you find something of interest in a quotation, find the original publication and ensure you understand it. In this way, you will avoid any errors of interpretation or transcription. Emphasize the important results and conclusions of other studies, the relevant data and trends from previous research, and particular methods or designs that could be duplicated or should be avoided. Discuss how the literature applies to the study you are proposing; show the weaknesses or faults in the design, discussing how you would avoid similar problems. If your proposal deals solely with secondary data, discuss the relevance of the data and the bias or lack of bias inherent in it.

The literature review may also explain the need for the proposed work to appraise the shortcomings and/or informational gaps in secondary data sources. This analysis may go beyond scrutinizing the availability or conclusions of past studies and their data to examining the accuracy of secondary sources, the credibility of these sources, and the appropriateness of earlier studies.

Close the literature review section by summarizing the important aspects of the literature and interpreting them in terms of your problem. Refine the problem as necessary in light of your findings.

Importance/Benefits of the Study

In this section you describe explicit benefits that will accrue from your study. The importance of "doing the study now" should be emphasized. Usually, this section is not more than a few paragraphs. If you find it difficult to write, then you have probably not adequately

literature review an examination of recent or historically significant research studies, company data, or industry reports that act as the basis for the proposed study.

> A literature review might reveal that the sponsor can answer the management question with a secondary data search rather than the collection of primary data. We discussed this more fully in Chapter 5.

clarified the management dilemma. Return to the analysis of the problem and ensure, through additional discussions with your sponsor or your research team or by a reexamination of the literature, that you have captured the essence of the problem.

This section also requires that you understand what is most troubling to your sponsor. If your sponsor is troubled by a perceived negative product image, you cannot promise that conducting a customer survey will enhance that product's image. You can, however, show the importance of this information and its implications. This survey allows management to show interest in and respond to customer concerns about the product and use the information to enhance product redesign.

The importance/benefits section is particularly important to the unsolicited external proposal. You must convince the sponsoring organization that your plan will meet its needs.

Research Design

> **> In Chapter 8, we discuss design strategies.**

Up to now, you have told the sponsor what the problem is, what your study goals are, and why it is important that you do the study. The proposal has presented the study's value and benefits. The design module describes what you are going to do in technical terms. This section should include as many subsections as needed to show the phases of the project. Provide information on your proposed design for tasks such as sample selection and size, data collection method, instrumentation, procedures, and ethical requirements. When more than one way exists to approach the design, discuss the methods you have rejected and explain why your selected approach is superior.

Data Analysis

> **> When there is no statistical or analytical expertise in the company, sponsors are more likely to hire professional help to interpret the soundness of this section.**

A brief section on the methods used for analyzing the data is appropriate for large-scale contract research projects and doctoral theses. With smaller projects, the proposed data analysis would be included within the research design section. It is in this section that you describe your proposed handling of the data and the theoretical basis for using the selected techniques. The object of this section is to assure the sponsor you are following correct assumptions and using theoretically sound data analysis procedures.

This module is often an arduous section to write. You can make it easier to write, read, and understand your data analysis by using sample or "dummy" charts and tables such as the example below (sometimes featuring hypothetical or "dummy" data):

Household Income	Likelihood to Enroll Child for Health Insurance		
	Will Enroll	**Might Enroll**	**Will Not Enroll**
$30,000–35,000			
$25,000–29,999			
$20,000–24,999			
$15,000–19,999			
Less than $15,000			

The data analysis section is so important to evaluating contract research proposals that the researcher should contact an expert to review the latest techniques available for use in the particular research study and compare them to the proposed techniques.

Nature and Form of Results

Upon finishing this section, the sponsor should be able to go back to the statement of the management question and research objectives and discover that each goal of the study has been covered. The researcher should also specify the types of data to be obtained and the interpretations that will be made in the analysis. If the data are to be turned over to the sponsor for proprietary reasons, make sure this is reflected. Alternatively, if the report will go to more than one sponsor, that should be noted.

This section also contains the contractual statement telling the sponsor exactly what types of information will be received. Statistical conclusions, applied findings, recommendations, action plans, models, strategic plans, and so forth, are examples of the forms of results.

Qualifications of Researchers

This section should begin with information on the principal investigator and then provide similar information on all individuals involved with the project. Two elements are critical:

1. Professional research competence (relevant research experience, the highest academic degree held, and memberships in business and technical societies).

2. Relevant management experience.[8]

> **Look for these elements in a proposal when hiring a contract researcher.**

With so many individuals, research specialty firms, and general consultancies providing marketing research services, the sponsor needs assurance that the researcher is professionally competent. Past research experience is the best barometer of competence, followed by the highest academic degree earned. To document relevant research experience, the researcher provides concise descriptions of similar projects. Highest degree usually follows the person's name (e.g., "S. Researcher, PhD in Statistics"). Society memberships provide some evidence that the researcher is cognizant of the latest methodologies and techniques. They follow the relevant research experience as a string or bulleted list, with organization name followed by term of membership and any relevant leadership positions.

> ❝If we knew what it was we were doing, it would not be called research, would it?❞
>
> *Albert Einstein*

Researchers are increasingly in the business of providing advice, not just research services. And businesses are looking for quality advice. Comparatively, the researcher who demonstrates relevant management or industry experience will be more likely to receive a favorable nod to his or her proposal. The format of this information should follow that used for relevant research experience. The entire curriculum vitae of each researcher need not be included unless required by the RFP. However, researchers often place complete vitae information in an appendix for review by interested sponsors.

Research companies often subcontract specific research activities to firms or individuals that specialize or offer specific resources or facilities. This is especially true for studies involving qualitative research techniques such as in-depth personal interviews and focus groups. Usually brief profiles of these companies are provided in this section only if their inclusion enhances the credibility of the researcher. Otherwise, profiles of such subcontractors are included in an appendix of the final report, rather than in the proposal.

Budget

The budget should be presented in the form the sponsor requests. For example, some organizations require secretarial assistance to be individually budgeted, whereas others insist it be included in the research director's fees or the overhead of the operation. In addition, limitations on travel, per diem rates, and capital equipment purchases can change the way in which you prepare a budget.

Typically, the budget should be no more than one to two pages. Exhibit 6-7 shows one format that can be used for small contract research projects. Additional information, backup details, quotes from vendors, and hourly time and payment calculations should be put into an appendix if required or kept in the researcher's file for future reference.

The budget statement in an internal research proposal is based on employee and overhead costs. The budget presented by an external research organization is not just the wages or salaries of its employees but the person-hour price that the contracting firm charges.

The detail the researcher presents may vary depending on both the sponsor's requirements and the contracting research company's policy. Some research companies,

Bissell: Small Budget Generates Powerful Direction

When CEO Mark Bissell returned from a European business trip with a prototype appliance, a steam cleaner named Steam Gun, he challenged the marketing research director to determine the marketing for the new product within a one-month time frame. With a full-scale research project out of the question, the research director chose a small-scale ethnography study using real-world observations of people's interactions with the product. He approached a local Parent Teacher Association, a ready source of female respondents, which distributed the Steam Gun to 20 volunteers. He followed up the test with in-home visits. Within 30 days, the research director knew the name must be changed and that those in the "serious cleaner" target segment would need to be convinced that steam cleaning with chemical-free water would be effective. He delivered a marketing program in the requisite time for the newly named Bissell® Steam 'n Clean®. The primary budget item in the research was a $1,500

donation to the PTA, proving that research budgets for successful decision making come in all sizes.

www.bissell.com

particularly in database and computerized analysis areas, quote on the basis of "person-machine hours" involved in a project. The person-machine hour is the hourly fee charged for a person with computer hardware and organizational resources. Here, rather than separating the "other costs" of Exhibit 6-7, these costs are embedded in a combined rate. One reason why external research agencies avoid giving detailed budgets is the possibility that disclosure of their costing practices will make their calculations public knowledge, reduc-

> **Exhibit 6-7** Sample Proposal Budget

Budget Items	Rate	Total Hours	Charge
A. Salaries			
1. Research director, Jason Henry	$200/hr	20 hours	$ 4,000
2. Associate	100/hr	10 hours	1,000
3. Research assistants (2)	20/hr	300 hours	6,000
4. Secretarial (1)	12/hr	100 hours	1,200
Subtotal			$12,200
B. Other costs			
5. Employee services and benefits			
6. Travel			$ 2,500
7. Office supplies			100
8. Telephone			800
9. Rent			
10. Other equipment			
11. Publication and storage costs			100
Subtotal			$ 3,500
C. Total of direct costs			$15,700
D. Overhead support			5,480
E. Total funding requested			$21,180

Understanding budgeting concerns is critical to a research specialist like Scientific Telephone Samples (STS). It provides random digit, listed, and business samples to firms conducting telephone and online surveys.
www.stssamples.com

ing their negotiating flexibility. Since budget statements embody a work strategy depicted in financial terms that could be used by the recipient of the proposal to develop a replicate research plan, vendors are often doubly careful.

The budget section of an external research contractor's proposal states the total fee payable for the assignment. When it is accompanied by a proposed schedule of payment, this is frequently detailed in a purchase order. As with other large-ticket-price services delivered over time in stages (e.g., building a home), payments can be paid at stages of completion. Sometimes a retainer is paid at the beginning of the contract, then a percentage at an intermediate stage, and the balance on completion of the project.

It is extremely important that you retain all information you use to generate your budget. If you use quotes from external contractors, get the quotation in writing for your file. If you estimate time for interviews, keep explicit notes on how you made the estimate. When the time comes to do the work, you should know exactly how much money is budgeted for each particular task.[9]

Some costs are more elusive than others. Do not forget to build the cost of proposal writing into your fee. Publication and delivery of final reports can be a last-minute expense that may be easily overlooked in preliminary budgets.

Schedule

Your schedule should include the major phases of the project, their timetables, and the milestones that signify completion of a phase. For example, major phases may be (1) exploratory interviews, (2) final research proposal, (3) questionnaire revision, (4) field interviews, (5) editing and coding, (6) data analysis, and (7) report generation. Each of these phases should have an estimated time schedule and people assigned to the work.

It may be helpful to you and your sponsor if you chart your schedule. You can use a Gantt chart, shown in Chapter 5, Exhibit 5-8. Alternatively, if the project is large and complex, a **critical path method (CPM)** of scheduling may be included.[10] In a CPM chart, the nodes represent major milestones, and the arrows suggest the work needed to get to the milestone. More than one arrow pointing to a node indicates all those tasks must be completed before the milestone has been met. Usually a number is placed along the arrow showing the number of days or weeks required for that task to be completed. The pathway from start to end that takes the longest time to complete is called the critical path, because any delay in an activity along that path will delay the end of the entire project. An example

critical path method (CPM) a scheduling tool for complex or large research proposals that cites milestones and time involved between milestones.

> **Exhibit 6-8** CPM Schedule

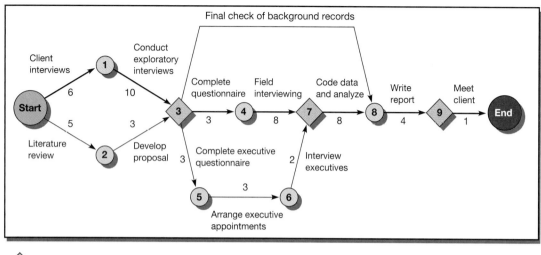

Milestones:
3 Proposal approval
7 Interviews completed
9 Final report completed

Critical Path:
S–1–3–4–7–8–9–E

Time to Completion:
40 working days

of a CPM chart is shown in Exhibit 6-8. Software programs designed for project management simplify scheduling and charting the schedule. Most are available for personal computers.

Facilities and Special Resources

Often, projects will require special facilities or resources that should be described in detail. For example, a contract exploratory study may need specialized facilities for focus group sessions. Computer-assisted telephone or other interviewing facilities may be required. Alternatively, your proposed data analysis may require sophisticated computer algorithms, and therefore you need access to an adequate system. These requirements will vary from study to study. The proposal should carefully list the relevant facilities and resources that will be used. The costs for such facility use should be detailed in your budget.

Project Management

project management the process of planning and managing a detailed project, through tables and charts that detail responsibilities and deadlines.

The purpose of the **project management** section is to show the sponsor that the research team is organized in a way to do the project efficiently. A master plan is required for complex projects to show how all the phases will be brought together. The plan includes:

- The research team's organization.
- Management procedures and controls for executing the research plan.
- Examples of management and technical reports.
- The research team's relationship with the sponsor.
- Financial and legal responsibility.
- Management competence.

Tables and charts are most helpful in presenting the master plan. The relationships between researchers and assistants need to be shown when several researchers are part of the team. Sponsors must know that the director is an individual capable of leading the team and acting as a useful liaison to the sponsor. In addition, procedures for information processing, record control, and expense control are critical to large operations and should be shown as part of the management procedures.

The type and frequency of progress reports should be recorded so that the sponsor can expect to be kept up to date and the researchers can expect to be left alone to do research. The sponsor's limits on control during the process should be delineated.

This section also discusses any details such as printing facilities, clerical help, or information processing capabilities to be provided by the sponsor rather than the researcher. In addition, rights to the data, the results, and authority to speak for the researcher and for the sponsor are included.

Payment frequency and timing are also covered in the master plan. Finally, proof of financial responsibility and overall management competence is provided.

Bibliography

For all projects that require a literature review, a bibliography is necessary. Use the bibliographic format required by the sponsor. If none is specified, a standard style manual will provide the details necessary to prepare the bibliography.[11] Many of these sources also offer suggestions for successful proposal writing.

Appendices

Glossary   The researcher should include a glossary of terms whenever there are many words unique to the research topic and not understood by the general management community. This is a simple section consisting of terms and definitions, similar in format to the glossary in this textbook. Also, the researcher should define any acronyms used, even if they are defined within the text (e.g., *CATI* for "computer-assisted telephone interviewing").

Measurement Instrument   For large projects, it is appropriate to include samples of the measurement instruments if they are available when you assemble the proposal. This allows the sponsor to discuss particular changes in one or more of the instruments. If the proposal includes the development of a custom-designed measurement instrument, omit this appendix section.

Other   Any detail that reinforces the body of the proposal can be included in an appendix. This includes researcher vitae, profiles of firms or individuals to which work will be subcontracted, budget details, and lengthy descriptions of special facilities or resources.

To see how some of these elements were incorporated in the MindWriter research proposal, see Exhibit 6-9.

Evaluating the Research Proposal

Proposals are subject to either formal or informal reviews. *Formal reviews* are regularly done for solicited proposals. The formal review process varies, but typically includes:

- Development of review criteria, using RFP guidelines.
- Assignment of points to each criterion, using a universal scale.
- Assignment of a weight for each criterion, based on importance of each criterion.
- Generation of a score for each proposal, representing the sum of all weighted criterion scores.

The sponsor should assign the criteria, the weights, and the scale to be used for scoring each criterion before the proposals are received. The proposal then should be evaluated with this checklist of criteria in hand. Points are recorded for each criterion reflecting the sponsor's

> **Exhibit 6-9** Visionary Insights' Proposal for MindWriter CompleteCare Satisfaction Research

When last we checked, Sara and Jason had completed an evening session to finish preparing a proposal for Myra Wines at MindWriter Corporation.

MindWriter | Myra requested that Jason exclude the executive summary for two reasons: the proposal is short and the essentials will be contained in the cover letter. The proposal follows the components discussed in this chapter. It is an appropriate adaptation for an internal, small-scale study. The module "qualification of researcher" was not needed because Myra, as a MindWriter employee, solicited the proposal; Myra had prejudged the researcher's (Visionary Insights') qualifications.

Repair Process Satisfaction Proposal
MindWriter Corporation CompleteCare Program

Problem Statement

MindWriter Corporation has recently created a service and repair program, CompleteCare, for its portable/laptop/notebook computers. This program promises to provide a rapid response to customers' service problems.

MindWriter is currently experiencing a shortage of trained technical operators in its telephone center. The package courier, contracted to pick up and deliver customers' machines to CompleteCare, has provided irregular execution. MindWriter has also experienced parts availability problems for some machine types.

Recent phone logs at the call center show complaints about CompleteCare; it is unknown how representative these complaints are and what implications they may have for satisfaction with MindWriter products.

Management desires information on the program's effectiveness and its impact on customer satisfaction to determine what should be done to improve the CompleteCare program for MindWriter product repair and servicing.

Research Objectives

The purpose of this research is to discover the level of satisfaction with the CompleteCare service program. Specifically, we intend to identify the component and overall levels of satisfaction with CompleteCare. Components of the repair process are important targets for investigation because they reveal:

(1) How customer tolerance levels for repair performance affect overall satisfaction, and

(2) Which process components should be immediately improved to elevate overall satisfaction of MindWriter customers experiencing product failures.

We will also discover the importance of types of product failure on customer satisfaction levels.

Importance/Benefits

High levels of user satisfaction translate into positive word-of-mouth product endorsements. These endorsements influence the purchase outcomes for (1) friends and relatives and (2) business associates.

Critical incidents, such as product failures, have the potential to either undermine existing satisfaction levels or preserve and even increase the resulting levels of product satisfaction. The outcome of the episode depends on the quality of the manufacturer's response.

An extraordinary response by the manufacturer to such incidents will preserve and enhance user satisfaction levels to the point that direct and indirect benefits derived from such programs will justify their costs.

This research has the potential for connecting to ongoing MindWriter customer satisfaction programs and measuring the long-term effects of CompleteCare (and product failure incidents) on customer satisfaction.

Research Design

Exploration: Qualitative   We will augment our knowledge of CompleteCare by interviewing the service manager, the call center manager, and the independent package company's account executive. Based on a thorough inventory of CompleteCare's internal and external processes, we propose to develop a mail survey.

Questionnaire Design   A self-administered questionnaire (postcard size) offers the most cost-effective method for securing feedback on the effectiveness of CompleteCare. The introduction on the postcard will be a variation of MindWriter's current advertising campaign.

Some questions for this instrument will be based on the investigative questions we presented to you previously, and others will be drawn from the executive interviews. We anticipate a maximum of 10 questions. A new five-point expectation scale, compatible with your existing customer satisfaction scales, is being designed.

Although we are not convinced that open-ended questions are appropriate for postcard questionnaires, we understand that you and Mr. Malraison like them. A comments/suggestions question will be included. In addition, we will work out a code block that captures the call center's reference number, model, and item(s) serviced.

Logistics   The postal arrangements are: box rental, permit, and "business reply" privileges to be arranged in a few days. The approval for a reduced postage rate will take one to two weeks. The budget section itemizes these costs.

> **Exhibit 6-9** Concluded

Pilot Test   We will test the questionnaire with a small sample of customers using your tech-line operators. This will contain your costs. We will then revise the questions and forward them to our graphics designer for layout. The instrument will then be submitted to you for final approval.

Evaluation of Nonresponse Bias   A random sample of 100 names will be secured from the list of customers who do not return the questionnaire. Call center records will be used for establishing the sampling frame. Nonresponders will be interviewed on the telephone and their responses compared statistically to those of the responders.

Data Analysis

We will review the postcards returned and send you a weekly report listing customers who are dissatisfied (score a "1" or "2") with any item of the questionnaire or who submit a negative comment. This will improve your timeliness in resolving customer complaints. Each month, we will provide you with a report consisting of frequencies and category percentages for each question. Visual displays of the data will be in bar chart/histogram form. We propose to include at least one question dealing with overall satisfaction (with CompleteCare and/or MindWriter). This overall question would be regressed on the individual items to determine each item's importance. A performance grid will identify items needing improvement with an evaluation of priority. Other analyses can be prepared on a time and materials basis.

The open-ended questions will be summarized and reported by model code. If you wish, we also can provide content analysis for these questions.

Results: Deliverables

1. Development and production of a postcard survey. MindWriter employees will package the questionnaire with the returned merchandise.
2. Weekly exception reports (transmitted electronically) listing customers who meet the dissatisfied customer criteria.
3. Monthly reports as described in the data analysis section.
4. Master Spreadsheets and data files with each month's data shipped to Austin by the fifth working day of each month.

Budget

Card Layout and Printing   Based on your card estimate, our designer will lay out and print 2,000 cards in the first run ($500). The specifications are as follows: 7-point Williamsburg offset hi-bulk with one-over-one black ink. A gray-scale layer with a MindWriter logo or CompleteCare can be positioned under the printed material at a nominal charge. The two-sided cards measure 4 1/4 by 5 1/2.

This allows us to print four cards per page. The opposite side will have the business reply logo, postage paid symbol, and address.

Cost Summary

Interviews	$1,550.00
Travel costs	2,500.00
Questionnaire development	1,850.00
Equipment/supplies	1,325.00
Graphics design	800.00
Permit fee (annual)	75.00
Business reply fee (annual)	185.00
Box rental (annual)	35.00
Printing costs	500.00
Data entry (monthly)	430.00
Monthly data files (each)	50.00
Monthly reports (each)	1,850.00
Total start-up costs	$11,150.00
Monthly run costs	$1,030.00*

*An additional fee of 0.21 per card will be assessed by the post office for business reply mail. At approximately a 30 percent return rate, we estimate the monthly cost to be less than $50.

> **Exhibit 6-10** Informal Proposal Review

Sara Armstrong
200 ShellPoint Tower
Palm Beach, Florida 33480

Mr. Harry Shipley, President
Economic Development Council
1800 Pink Flamingo Way
Palm Beach, Florida 33480

Dear Harry:

I have reviewed Robert Buffet's proposal for an investigation of the job creation practices of local companies and, in short, I am very much concerned with several aspects of the "proposal." It is not really a proposal at all, as it lacks sufficient detail.

First let me mention that I shared Buffet's proposal with my colleague, Jason Henry, a project director at Visionary Insights. I have worked with Jason on several projects and trust his opinion. Mr. Buffet and his organization may one day represent competition for Visionary Insights, and you must therefore be aware of a potential conflict of interest and perhaps discount the opinions stated here. Since I am delivering this letter to you in two days rather than the two weeks you requested, you may wish to discuss my comments with others.

What you and Mr. Buffet gave me is an abbreviated research plan for our county, but since it lacks many features found in a comprehensive proposal, I immediately saw it was not the full proposal that had been funded by the state commerce secretary. I called Tallahassee and reached a young woman who hemmed and hawed and refused to say if she was authorized to mail me the full proposal. Finally, I gave up arguing and gave her your address and told her she could mail it to you if she experienced an outbreak of belief in government-in-the-sunshine.

I then made several calls to people in Tallahassee. Did you know that this research idea is being floated by our senior U.S. senator, who is eager to throw a monkey wrench into the president's tax incentives plan? The senator whispered it to the governor and the governor whispered it to her commerce secretary, and here we are.

The problem statement is rather long and convoluted, but, in short, it poses the questions, "Are new high-tech companies creating jobs for residents of our county? Or are they bringing technical and manufacturing workers from outside the state and bypassing the local work force? Or are they doing research in these companies with a low level of manufacturing job creation? Or are they investing in 'smart' capital equipment that does not create jobs?" If you cut through the verbiage, I think you can see the project hits the mark with its questions.

The research objectives section is fairly straightforward. Buffet's people are going to identify all the companies in this county in the NAICS code groups associated with "high tech" and collect information on the number of locally hired employees in various job categories, chiefly in production, and also collect data on capital investments, debt, and other financial data, which Mr. Henry says makes good sense to collect and ought to be easy to do.

There is a section called Importance of the Study, which is full of platitudes and does not get around to mentioning the pending tax legislation. But at least the platitudes are brief.

I become nervous in the Design section. It calls for Mr. Buffet's group to go on site with a "team" and conduct individual depth interviews with the chief operating officer (COO), treasurer, and comptroller of each company and enter the data into a spreadsheet. I have double-checked this with Jason and also with a banker friend, and both of them assure me that a simple questionnaire might be mailed to the COO. There is no need whatsoever to send in a team to conduct unstructured open-ended interviews. While there might be a noncompliance problem associated with filling out a form, this might appropriately be addressed by pointing out the auspices—the state commerce secretary and your Economic Development Council—with an interview request as a last resort.

The proposal contains no budget and no specific list of researchers who will comprise the team. The firm would have carte blanche to go in with anyone on their payroll and try to induce the subjects to stray beyond the stated research objectives to talk about anything at all. Obviously such license would be a marketing tool and might allow the researchers to collect a list of researchable problems not related to the secretary's needs, as stated in the problem section.

I strongly advise you to tell Mr. Buffet to collect the information through a simple mail survey. Offer to send it out under your council's letterhead, or see if you can get the commerce office or even the governor's office to send it out. But do not subject your local business community to unstructured, free-ranging visits, which are clearly not justified by the research objectives.

Sincerely,

Sara

assessment of how well the proposal meets the company's needs relative to that criterion (e.g., 1 through 10, with 10 being the largest number of points assigned to the best proposal for a particular criterion). After the review, the weighted criterion scores are added to provide a cumulative total. The proposal with the highest number of points wins the contract.

Several people, each of whom may be assigned to a particular section, typically review long and complex proposals. The formal method is most likely to be used for competitive government, university, or public sector grants and also for large-scale contracts.

Small-scale contracts are more prone to informal evaluation. In an *informal review*, the project needs, and thus the criteria, are well understood but are not usually well documented. In contrast to the formal method, a system of points is not used and the criteria are not ranked. The process is more qualitative and impressionistic. Exhibit 6-10 shows Sara Armstrong's informal review of the proposal discussed in the opening vignette.

> **Exhibit 6-2 provides examples of some criteria for review.**

In practice, many factors contribute to a proposal's acceptance and funding. Primarily, the content discussed above must be included to the level of detail required by the sponsor's RFP. Beyond the required modules, other factors can quickly eliminate a proposal from consideration or improve the sponsor's reception of the proposal, among them:

- Neatness.
- Organization, in terms of being both logical and easily understood.
- Completeness in fulfilling the RFP's specifications, including budget and schedule.
- Appropriateness of writing style.
- Submission within the RFP's timeline.

Although a proposal produced on a word processor and bound with an expensive cover will not overcome design or analysis deficiencies, a poorly presented, unclear, or disorganized proposal will not get serious attention from the reviewing sponsor. Given that multiple reviewers may be evaluating only a specific section, the reviewer should be able to page through the proposal to any section of interest.

In terms of the technical writing style of the proposal, the sponsor must be able to understand the problem statement, the research design, and the methodology. The sponsor should clearly understand why the proposed research should be funded and the exact goals and concrete results that will come from the study.

The proposal also must meet specific RFP guidelines set by the sponsoring company or agency, including budgetary restrictions and schedule deadlines. A schedule that does not meet the expected deadlines will disqualify the proposal. A budget that is too high for the allocated funds will be rejected. Conversely, a low budget compared to competing proposals suggests that something is missing or there is something wrong with the researchers.

Finally, a late proposal will not be reviewed. While current project disqualification due to lateness may appear to be the worst result here, there is a possible longer-term effect created. Lateness communicates a level of disrespect for the sponsor—that the researcher's schedule is more important than the sponsor's. A late proposal also communicates a weakness in project management, which raises an issue of professional competence. This concern about competence may continue to plague the researcher during future project proposal reviews.

>summary

1 The request for proposal (RFP) and the research proposal are essential elements for marketing research planning. The RFP is a formal document issued by a corporate marketing research department to solicit services from research suppliers. The RFP process is a vehicle for qualifying potential vendors, writing and distributing a request for research services,

answering supplier questions, conducting a criteria-based bid evaluation, awarding contracts, and providing a critique to suppliers.

A proposal is an offer from a research supplier to produce a research product or service for the buyer or sponsor. It is often in direct response to the RFP. The research proposal presents a problem, discusses related research efforts, outlines the data needed for solving the problem, and shows the design used to gather and analyze the data.

Both RFPs and proposals provide benefits for the marketing researcher. For the company, the RFP is an opportunity to formalize the process of documenting, justifying, and authorizing the procurement of research. Vendor solutions are evaluated and project performance is monitored and controlled. The supplier's proposal becomes the guide for the investigation as well as the outline for contractual services. The proposal is also a useful tool to ensure that the sponsor and investigator agree on the research question and the direction of the project.

2 The RFP has modifications (requests for information, application, and recommendation) that make it more suitable for different user needs. Two types of proposals are covered: internal and external. Internal and external proposals have a problem-solving orientation. The staff of a company generates internal proposals. External proposals are prepared by an outside firm to obtain contract research. External proposals emphasize qualifications of the researcher, special facilities and resources, and project management aspects such as budgets and schedules. Within each type of proposal there are varying degrees of complexity; a proposal can vary in length from a two-page memo to more than 100 pages, from a telephone conversation to a multimedia presentation.

Proposals can be written with a set of sections or modules. The difference in type of proposal and level of project complexity determines which modules should be included.

3 Proposals can be formally or informally evaluated. The formal process uses a list of criteria and an associated point scale. The informal process is more qualitative. Important aspects beyond content include presentation style, timeliness, and credibility.

>**key**terms

>**discussion**questions

Terms in Review

1 What is an RFP, and how does it differ from a research proposal?

2 What, if any, are the differences between solicited and unsolicited proposals?

Making Research Decisions

3 You are the new manager of market intelligence in a rapidly expanding software firm. Many product managers and corporate officers have requested market surveys from you on various products. Design a form for a research proposal that can be completed easily by your research staff and the sponsoring manager. Discuss how your form improves communication of the research objectives between the manager and the researcher.

4 Consider the new trends in desktop publishing, multimedia computer authoring and display capabilities, and inexpensive videotaping and playback possibilities. How might they be used to enhance research proposals? Give several examples of appropriate use.

5 You are the manager of a research department in a large department store chain. Develop a list of criteria for evaluating the types of research activities listed below. Include a point scale and weighting algorithm.

a Market research.

b Advertising effectiveness.

c Retail site selection research

Behind the Scenes

6 If Sara had been asked to prepare a more formal evaluation of Buffet's response to the Economic Development Council's RFP, what content sections should the evaluation contain?

From Concept to Practice

7 Select a research report from a management journal. Outline a proposal for the research as if it had not yet been performed. Make estimates of time and costs. Generate a CPM schedule for the project following the format in Exhibit 6-8.

8 Using Exhibit 6-6 as your guide, what modules would you suggest be included in a proposal for each of the following cases?

a A bank interested in evaluating the effectiveness of its community contributions in dollars and loaned executive time.

b A manufacturer of leather custom-designed teacher development portfolios evaluating the market potential among teachers, who are now legally required to execute a professional development plan every three years.

c A university studying the possible calendar change from three 11-week quarters to two 16-week semesters.

d A dot-com that monitors clicks on banner ads and is interested in developing a different pricing structure for its service.

9 Review the Seagate proposal on the text DVD. Using Exhibit 6-6 as your guide, comment on what is or what is not contained therein.

>**www**exercises

1 Several marketing research firms offer newsletters and white papers as a part of their customer service and as a way to demonstrate their ability to do quality research. Decision Analyst offers this service on its Web site. Can you find a white paper on buying research services or RFPs on its site? **http://www.decisionanalyst.com**

2 Check out the demonstration software for MarketResearchPRO. Would such software help you put a marketing research proposal together? **http://www.marketresearchpro.com**

>**cases**[*]

Agri Comp	Inquiring Minds Want to Know—NOW!
BBQ Product Crosses Over the Lines of Varied Tastes	Mastering Teacher Leadership
Calling Up Attendance	McDonald's Tests Catfish Sandwich
Covering Kids with Health Care	NCRCC: Teeing Up and New Strategic Direction
Donatos: Finding the New Pizza	Ramada Demonstrates Its *Personal Best*™
Goodyear's Aquatred	Retailers Unhappy with Displays from Manufacturers
KNSD San Diego	State Farm: Dangerous Intersections
Outboard Marine	Sturgel Division
Pebble Beach Co.	T-Shirt Designs
HeroBuilders.com	

[*] All cases, both written and video, are on the text DVD. The film icon indicates a video case. Check the DVD Index to determine whether a case has data, the research instrument, or other supplementary material.

Covering Kids RFP

Wirthlin Worldwide earned the Ogilvy Research Award for creative and effective research instrumental in the development of the Covering Kids advertising campaign. This RFP from sponsor Robert Wood Johnson Foundation started the process that resulted in enrolling more than one million additional children for a health insurance initiative.

March 13, 2000

Name
Firm
Address
City, State Zip code

Dear XXXX:

As you know, we are working with GMMB&A to support the national Covering Kids Initiative (CKI). We appreciate your recent response to a proposal to support this effort's marketing research requirements. Since that time, we have further refined our requirements. We hope that you will be willing to review this request, and revise your previous proposal in any ways needed to meet these altered needs.

The Covering Kids Initiative is a $47 million national program of the Foundation that works to enroll eligible children in Medicaid and the Federal-state Children's Health Insurance Programs (SCHIP). Three-year grants for the Covering Kids Initiative support coalitions in 49 states and the District of Columbia. These coalitions conduct outreach initiatives and work to simplify and coordinate the enrollment processes for health coverage programs for low-income children. In its first two years of activity, the CKI has focused largely on simplifying the enrollment process. During the second year, in addition to continuing a focus on simplification and coordination, there will be target marketing campaigns to encourage adults to enroll eligible children in both the SCHIP and Medicaid programs.

The Foundation will work with its Covering Kids communications contractor to support these CKI coalitions in marketing, advertising, public relations, coalition building, and cause-related partnerships at the national and state levels. The tasks described here will help provide direction for the strategic development of communications and provide support for testing and measuring communications campaigns in six markets prior to introduction nationwide.

Background

There are approximately five million uninsured children in the US eligible for either SCHIP or Medicaid. While income eligibility requirements in the federally funded SCHIP programs vary from state-to-state, they all generally cover children in households of four with incomes up to $33,400 (higher in some states). About half of the eligible-uninsured Americans are non-Hispanic white, about 30% are African-American, another 20% are Hispanic/Latino. Although the numbers are much smaller, a large proportion of Native-Americans are also eligible but not covered.

There are many reasons why so many eligible children are not enrolled. Some primary barriers to enrollment are: lack of awareness of the availability of health programs, especially SCHIP; lack of knowledge of eligibility criteria for these programs; complicated/onerous application processes; a stigma attached to government-funded health care programs (especially for working parents); the lack of outreach experience and expertise (most states have never conducted outreach for programs like Medicaid).

The primary challenge for this project is to create a nationwide campaign to enroll children—yet the "fulfillment mechanisms" (the state SCHIP and Medicaid programs) vary from state to state. Many states have developed their own distinct marketing and branding campaigns, so that the SCHIP programs in Connecticut (HUSKY B) and in Georgia (PeachCare) and in Illinois (KidsCare) resemble traditional private health plans more than they do government programs based on income eligibility. A national 1-877-KIDS-NOW phone number is in use that seamlessly routes calls through to the appropriate state program office. We will likely use that toll-free number as a marketing and fulfillment mechanism for this effort.

The communications campaign will target specific groups of parents and other adults who could play a key role in enrolling eligible children in existing programs. Specific messages will be tested for use with subsets of low income Americans, including African-Americans, Hispanic/Latino, Native Americans and others. The Campaigns will first be tested and measured in six regional markets before national advertising begins. Ad buys and other communications activities will be coupled with local enrollment events. Communications activities and enrollment events will likely intensify twice annually, during the back-to-school and winter cold and flu seasons.

Contractual Needs

Requirements for market research and evaluation support are described in the two tasks below.

Task 1. MARKET RESEARCH. Design, conduct, analyze, and provide conclusions relevant to communications planning.

Task 1a. Develop an in-depth comprehensive profile (through a series of in-depth interviews) of the families of eligible-but-uninsured children—who are they, where are they, why are they not enrolled, the most effective messages/concepts to move individuals in specific groups to enroll in SCHIP/Medicaid, what messages/words/concepts are definite turn-offs among specific groups, etc.
Of particular interest:

- Hispanic/Latino rural/urban
- African-American rural/urban
- Native-American rural/urban
- White rural/urban

- Parents of children enrolled in SCHIP
- Parents of children enrolled in Medicaid
- Parents of uninsured children eligible for SCHIP and/or Medicaid who haven't applied
- Parents of uninsured children eligible for SCHIP and/or Medicaid who have applied but are not enrolled

Level of effort: approximately 120 in-depth interviews. [Alternative suggestions invited.]

Task 1b. Qualitative research among opinion leaders: their perceptions of SCHIP; their definition of success/failure, etc. These might include federal and state legislative staff, regulatory staff, child health advocates, constituency group leaders, and media gatekeepers.
Level of effort: approximately 25 in-depth interviews. [Alternative suggestions invited.]

Evaluation Task

Task 1. A comprehensive national survey. This survey will: help direct communications development; provide content for news placement; provide a pre-campaign benchmark (baseline data). We anticipate repeating this survey in the future to help gauge change and progress. However, at this time we are interested only in one benchmark survey.

We are considering two options for survey sampling: a) a national sample including oversamples of lower-income families as described above, or b) a sample consisting of lower-income families with sufficient subsets (described above) to be statistically reliable. We are interested in receiving recommendations regarding which option to pursue as well as a description of how this work would be done.

Task 2.   An evaluation of the media campaign in 6 test markets. Because the national advertising and public relations components of the communication campaign will be large in scope and level of effort, this test market phase will be used to test and refine media messages, techniques, and decisions. The test market evaluation is critical to decision making for this effort.

Six mid-sized media markets will be selected to obtain a mix of the targeted demographic groups and geographic diversity. The Foundation will provide the list of selected sites to the contractor. The advertising and public relations test phase will span 4–6 weeks, planned for late-August–early September 2000. The market test will be planned and executed through close collaboration with the communications contractor, the Covering Kids National Program Office and coalitions in the target markets, and the Foundation. It will be designed to gauge heightened awareness, perceptions of target audiences, willingness to apply, and impact of campaign on overcoming any attitudinal barriers to applying.

This market test will include

Task 2a.   Benchmark survey—a random sample telephone survey with oversamples of target audiences. To include both benchmarking questions (such as awareness, attitude, intention measures) and message development questions (such as questions about message concepts, language).

Task 2b.   Post-campaign survey—a brief telephone follow up survey using same sampling; to include questions to assess recall/awareness, attitudes, intentions.

Task 2c.   Tracking of callers to the promoted toll-free number—the Foundation/National Program Office will provide a liaison to the toll-free manager(s). At this time it is not clear whether this will include only the national toll-free number or/and some state operated numbers. This task will include both compiling and analyzing call data and identifying ways to re-contact callers to assess further actions.

Task 2d.   Follow up with callers—brief telephone survey to identify any questions taken. Phone numbers will be provided through the liaison described above. [Alternative method of assessment may be needed.]

Alternative suggestions for test market evaluation, with approximately the same level of effort required, are acceptable.

Anticipated Time Schedule

April 2000	contract awarded begin development of all tasks
May 2000	conduct national survey
June 2000	conduct research with potential beneficiaries, opinion leaders conduct benchmark survey in 6 test markets
August 2000	begin ads in test markets begin telephone tracking
September 2000	conduct testing market post-test surveys begin follow up with telephone callers
October 2000	present findings of national survey present findings from caller callbacks

Proposal Instructions

We invite you to submit a proposal addressing one or both of the tasks described above. Your proposal should address:

- your approach to conducting the work
- any alternative methods or procedures you would like to suggest for accomplishing the work described (optional)

- a discussion of any anticipated challenges to completing these tasks, and how you would propose handling the challenges
- comments on methodology and other recommendations for producing the needed information
- specific work to be performed, description of the deliverables to be provided, and all costs (included out-of-pocket costs), by task
- relevant experience and expertise
- references

The Foundation is not seeking lengthy or elaborate proposals. Rather proposals should succinctly provide information that will permit a review using the criteria listed below.

Review Criteria

In reviewing proposals, we will consider:

- your approach to the needs and tasks described here, including recommended methodology
- anticipated problems and how these would be handled
- company and staff experience in conducting similar market research and evaluation
- company and staff experience in conducting qualitative and quantitative research with a similar population
- company and staff experience with a health insurance or similar health care issue
- personnel, task and time line, project management
- proposed budget
- ability to respond to time schedule.

In addition we will expect that your company has no conflicts of interest with the Foundation.

Proposals will be due no later than COB Monday, March 27, delivered to

Stuart Schear (Four Copies)
Senior Communications Officer
The Robert Wood Johnson Foundation
Address
City, State   Zip code
Phone

David Smith (Four Copies)
GMMB&A
Address
City, State   Zip code
Phone

Kristine Hartvigsen (Three Copies)
Covering Kids National Program Office
Address
City, State   Zip code
Phone

Elaine Bratic Arkin (One Copy)
Address
City, State   Zip code
Phone

We anticipate notifying those who submit proposals of our decision no later than April 1, 2000. I am available by e-mail @ smr@rwjf.org to answer any questions you might have. The following websites offer a wealth of information as well:

> **<http://www.coveringkids.org>**—the website for "Covering Kids," the RWJF-funded initiative that these tasks will support

> **<http://www.insurekidsnow.gov>**—the HHS/HCFA website for the CHIP programs

> **<http://www.cbpp.org>**—the Center on Budget and Policy Priorities

Thank you for your thoughtful consideration of this request.

If you wish to speak with someone about this project, please call me at 609-951-5799. Either Elaine Arkin, a consultant to the Foundation, or I would be happy to speak with you.

Sincerely

Stuart Schear
Senior Communications Officer

chapter 7

Ethics in Marketing Research

>**learning**objectives

After reading this chapter, you should understand . . .

1 What issues are covered in research ethics?

2 The goal of "no harm" for all research activities and what constitutes no harm for participant, researcher, and research sponsor.

3 The differing ethical dilemmas and responsibilities of researchers, sponsors, and research assistants.

4 The role of ethical codes of conduct in professional associations.

Jason Henry has returned to the office following a proposal presentation designed to capture a research project from a potential new business. Chance, Jason's superior, and Jason had worked together on the project proposal. Both had hopes that the project would represent an entrée to significant new business for Visionary Insights.

"How did the proposal meeting go with MicroPeripheral this morning," inquires Chance as Jason drops into a chair across from Chance's desk.

"It didn't," flatly states Jason.

"Well, we had a good proposal, but we can't win every contract," commiserates Chance. "Do we know why?"

"Oh, we could have had the contract," claims Jason. "I just decided the contract wasn't right for Visionary Insights."

"Now you've got my attention," says Chance, leaning forward. "That would have been a small piece of business now, but being a research supplier to such a large computer peripheral manufacturer showed definite possibilities for a lucrative long-term relationship. What went wrong?"

"According to its president, Bill Henderson," explains Jason as he and Chance walk back to Jason's office, "MicroPeripheral (MP) has taken a near-lead position in peripherals for laptop computing, but peripherals are volatile. Peripherals grow smaller every month and have to be sold more cheaply. Henderson needs a detailed market report, which MP can very well afford to pay for, but he really wants something we can't deliver."

"The proposal we developed is for a detailed market study," puzzles Chance.

"Yes, but he has in mind an entirely different study than we proposed. He proposed hiring a headhunter to set up interviews for a mythical senior diversification manager position within a mythical company—he called it a disguised study. He wanted us to provide the focus group facility for the interviews, so we could use our sophisticated equipment to record every interview."

"I fail to see how this will give him the market data he needs," stated Chance, now clearly puzzled.

"According to Henderson, another CEO had tried this ploy and been able to attract competitors' employees to be interviewed. Every interview added greatly to the firm's understanding of the competition and the market. But then they hit the jackpot. One of the candidates was a key exec from the major competitor. On the basis of that interview and the information the duped executive innocently revealed, the company decided to shut down its California production line and open production in Mexico for a smaller, faster, cheaper version of its main product. The advance notice permitted the firm to steal significant market share."

"He had the gall to suggest we participate in this fraud?"

"Henderson assured me that it wasn't illegal, but I didn't stick around to hear more. I literally grabbed our proposal from the desktop—the one with the Visionary Insights logo boldly marked on the front—and walked out."

"So I imagine you've been on the phone since you returned," surmises Chance.

"I called every single research firm whose logo was visible in the array of proposals on Henderson's desk. They were all most appreciative," says Jason, smiling for the first time.

"And it's likely," smiles Chance, "that Henderson will soon find all his other proposals will be withdrawn."

> **What Are Research Ethics?**

ethics norms or standards of behavior that guide moral choices about research behavior.

As in other aspects of business, all parties in marketing research should exhibit ethical behavior. **Ethics** are norms or standards of behavior that guide moral choices about our behavior and our relationships with others. The goal of ethics in research is to ensure that no one is harmed or suffers adverse consequences from research activities. This objective is usually achieved. However, unethical activities are pervasive and include violating nondisclosure agreements, breaking participant confidentiality, misrepresenting results, deceiving participants or sponsors, invoicing for time, personnel, or expenses not used on a project, avoiding legal liability, and more.

For some researchers, ethical and legal norms are the same. We maintain the position in this text that legal constraints are the minimum standard for ethical behavior in research, not the ideal standard.

The recognition of ethics as a problem for economic organizations was revealed in a survey where 80 percent of the responding organizations reported the adoption of an ethical code. Surprisingly, the evidence that this effort has improved ethical practices is questionable. The same study reports limited success for codes of conduct that attempt to restrain improper behavior.[1]

There is no single approach to ethics. One approach, *deontology*, advocates that ethical behavior should be directed by "duties" regardless of the positive circumstances that might result from behavior that is in contradiction to the duty. An example of a duty might be "Do not lie" even though positive consequences might result. Advocating strict adherence to a set of laws or duties is difficult because of the unforeseen constraint put on researchers. Because of Germany's war history, for example, the government forbids many types of medical research. Consequently, the German people do not benefit from many advances in biotechnology and may have restricted access to genetically altered drugs in the future. Alternatively, relying on each individual's personal sense of morality, *ethical relativism*, is equally problematic. Consider the clash between those who believe death is deliverance from a life of suffering and those who value life to the point of preserving it indefinitely through mechanical means. Each value system claims superior knowledge of moral correctness.

Clearly, a middle ground between being completely law-governed and relying on ethical relativism is necessary. The foundation for that middle ground is an emerging consensus on ethical standards for researchers. In March 2003, the membership of the Marketing Research Association approved its expanded, 48-page *Code*

>**pic**profile

In April 2001, Procter & Gamble notified its competitor Unilever that more than 80 discarded documents detailing Unilever's three-year marketing plans for its hair care business had been collected by independent information agents hired by a P&G supplier. P&G voluntarily returned the documents, indicating that competitive intelligence gathering involving documents taken from trash receptacles was a violation of its ethical standards. Unilever believed that additional information was obtained by deception, with information gatherers claiming to be market analysts. Believing its hair care business had been irreparably compromised, Unilever sought financial restitution and restrictions on P&G's marketing activities in the hair care business. By September these hair care powerhouses had reached an out-of-court settlement. Unilever's hair care brands in the United States include Suave, Finesse, ThermaSilk, Salon Selectives, Rave, and Aqua Net. P&G markets Pert and Head and Shoulders. www.pg.com; www.unilever.com

of Marketing Research Standards.[2] Two other examples of research codes of conduct are those of the Council for American Survey Research Organizations (CASRO) and the American Marketing Association. Additionally, review boards and peer groups help researchers examine their research proposals for ethical dilemmas. Many design-based ethical problems can be eliminated by careful planning and constant vigilance. In the end, responsible research anticipates ethical dilemmas and attempts to adjust the design, procedures, and protocols during the planning process rather than treating them as an afterthought. Ethical research requires personal integrity from the researcher, the project manager, and the research sponsor.

Because integrity in research is vital, we are discussing its components early in this book and emphasizing ethical behavior throughout our coverage. Our objective is to stimulate an ongoing exchange about values and practical research constraints in the chapters that follow. This chapter is organized around the theme of ethical treatment of participants, clients or research sponsors, and other researchers. We also highlight appropriate laws and codes, resources for ethical awareness, and cases for application. Exhibit 7-1 relates each ethical issue under discussion to the research process introduced in Chapter 4.

> **When you see this icon, challenge yourself to identify the ethical issue.**

> Ethical Treatment of Participants

When ethics are discussed in research design, we often think first about protecting the rights of the participant, respondent, or subject. Whether data are gathered in an experiment, interview, observation, or survey, the participant has many rights to be safeguarded. In general, research must be designed so that a participant does not suffer physical harm, discomfort, pain, embarrassment, or loss of privacy. To safeguard against these, the researcher should follow three guidelines:[3]

1. Explain study benefits.
2. Explain participant rights and protections.
3. Obtain informed consent.

Benefits

Whenever direct contact is made with a participant, the researcher should discuss the study's benefits, being careful to neither overstate nor understate the benefits. An interviewer should begin an introduction with his or her name, the name of the research organization, and a brief description of the purpose and benefit of the research. This puts participants at ease, lets them know to whom they are speaking, and motivates them to answer questions truthfully. In short, knowing why one is being asked questions improves cooperation through honest disclosure of purpose. Inducements to participate, financial or otherwise, should not be disproportionate to the task or presented in a fashion that results in coercion.

Sometimes the actual purpose and benefits of your study or experiment must be concealed from the participants to avoid introducing bias. The need for concealing objectives leads directly to the problem of deception.

Deception

Deception occurs when the participants are told only part of the truth or when the truth is fully compromised. One form of deception relates to disguising nonresearch activities as opinion or marketing research. Examples of such deception are the use of research to (1) collect data that are used to compile lists or registers for fund-raising or selling merchandise or services, (2) perform industrial, commercial, or other forms of espionage or competitive intelligence, or (3) collect personal information for fraudulent or illegal

deception when truth is compromised to prevent biasing participants or protect sponsor confidentiality.

> Exhibit 7-1 Ethical Issues and the Research Process

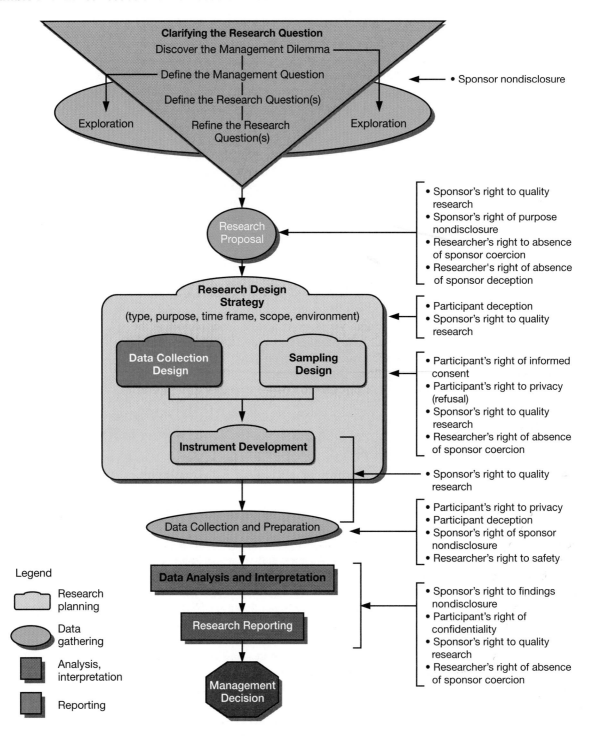

purposes (e.g., falsify credit reports, steal identities, collect debts, or coerce voting or purchase behavior).[4] Researchers abhor this type of deception as it undermines the professionalism of the industry and increases research refusal rates. Clearly, Jason withdrew Visionary Insights' proposal when he discovered that deception for nonresearch purposes was the basis of the desired research design. Jason believed Visionary Insights' ethical standards would have been violated and his firm's submission of a nondeceptive design was evidence that alternative designs were available.

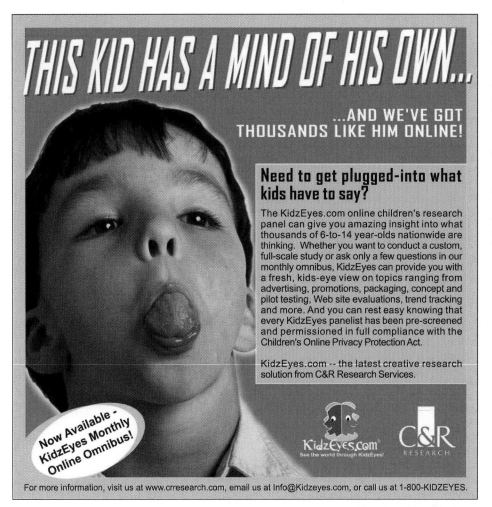

Marketing researchers have special ethical responsibilities when using children as participants. Besides providing informed consent, parents are often interviewed during the selection process to assure that if their child is chosen that he or she is mature enough to handle the activities planned, and has the verbal and physical capabilities necessary. Researchers that work with children want the child to perceive participation as an enjoyable—and sometimes even an exciting—experience. **www.cr-interactive.com**

Another type of deception is research design–based. It involves camouflaging true research objectives or the identity of the sponsor. There are two reasons for this latter type of deception: (1) to prevent biasing the respondents before the survey, observation exercise, or experiment and (2) to protect the confidentiality of a third party (e.g., the sponsor).

Some believe, however, that design-based deception should never occur. It is generally accepted in the industry that deception used only to improve participation rates should not be used. The benefits to be gained by appropriate design-based deception should be balanced against the risks to the participants. When possible, an experiment or interview should be redesigned to reduce reliance on deception. In addition, the participants' rights and well-being must be adequately protected. In instances where deception in an experiment could produce anxiety, a subject's medical condition should be checked to ensure that no adverse physical harm follows. The American Psychological Association's Ethics Code states that the use of deception is inappropriate unless deceptive techniques are justified by the study's expected scientific, educational, or applied value and equally effective alternatives that do not use deception are not feasible.[5] And, finally, the participants must have given their informed consent before participating in the research.

Informed Consent

Securing **informed consent** from participants is a matter of fully disclosing the procedures of the proposed survey or other research design before requesting permission to proceed with the study. There are exceptions that argue for a signed consent form. When dealing

informed consent
participant gives full consent to participation after receiving full disclosure of the procedures of the proposed survey.

> **Exhibit 7-2** Informed Consent Procedures for Surveys

CONTENT

Surveys conducted by the Indiana University Center for Survey Research contain the following informed consent components in their introductions:

1. Introduce ourselves—interviewer's name and Indiana University Center for Survey Research.
2. Briefly describe the survey topic (e.g., barriers to health insurance).
3. Describe the geographic area we are interviewing (e.g., people in Indiana) or target sample (e.g., aerospace engineers).
4. Tell who the sponsor is (e.g., National Endowment for the Humanities).
5. Describe the purpose(s) of the research (e.g., satisfaction with services received/provided by a local agency).
6. Give a "good-faith" estimate of the time required to complete the interview.
7. Promise anonymity and confidentiality (when appropriate).
8. Tell the respondent the participation is voluntary.
9. Tell the respondent that item nonresponse is acceptable.
10. Ask permission to begin.

Sample Introduction
Hello, I'm [fill in NAME] from the Center for Survey Research at Indiana University. We're surveying Indianapolis area residents to ask their opinions about some health issues. This study is sponsored by the National Institutes of Health and its results will be used to research the effect of community ties on attitudes toward medical practices. The survey takes about 40 minutes. Your participation is anonymous and voluntary, and all your answers will be kept completely confidential. If there are any questions that you don't feel you can answer, please let me know and we'll move to the next one. So, if I have your permission, I'll continue.

Sample Conclusion
The respondent is given information on how to contact the principal investigator. For example: John Kennedy is the principal investigator for this study. Would you like Dr. Kennedy's address or telephone number in case you want to contact him about the study at any time?

Source: "Telephone Surveys," Indiana University Center for Survey Research, accessed October 22, 2004 (http://www.indiana.edu/~csr/phone_surveys.html).

with children, it is necessary to have a parent or another person with legal standing sign a consent form. When doing research with medical or psychological ramifications, it is also wise to have a consent form. If there is a chance the data could harm the participant or if the researchers offer only limited protection of confidentiality, a signed form detailing the types of limits should be obtained. For most marketing research, oral consent is sufficient. An example of how informed consent procedures are implemented is shown in Exhibit 7-2. In this example, a university research center demonstrates how it adheres to the highest ethical standards for survey procedures.[6]

Federal, state, and local governments have laws, policies, and procedures in place to regulate research on human beings. In 1966 the U.S. government began a process that covers all research having federal support: Institutional Review Boards (IRBs). These evaluating panels engage in a risk assessment and benefit analysis review of proposed research. The Department of Health and Human Services (HHS) translated the federal regulations into policy. Most other federal and state agencies follow the HHS-developed guidelines.

Since 1981, the review requirement has been relaxed so that research that is routine no longer needs to go through the complete process.[7] Each institution receiving funding from Health and Human Services or doing research for HHS is required to have its own Institutional Review Board to review research proposals. Many institutions require that all research, whether funded or unfunded by the government, undergo review by the local

>**snap**shot

Engendering Trust Online

With the Internet a growing source of marketing research information, participants in such research deserve to know how the information they share will be used. According to Truste.org, "As an Internet user, you have a right to expect online privacy and the responsibility to exercise choice over how your personal information is collected, used, and shared by Web sites." Truste.org is especially interested in information collected from children under 13 years of age. "A Web site displaying the Children's Seal is committed to obtaining prior verifiable parental consent when and if information will be collected, as well as giving parental notice of how that information will be used." Truste.org offers its trustmarks to Internet sites that follow its privacy guidelines:

- *Adoption and implementation of a privacy policy* that takes into account consumer anxiety over sharing personal information online.
- *Notice and disclosure* of information collection and use practices.
- *Choice and consent,* giving users the opportunity to exercise control over their information.
- *Data security and quality and access* measures to help protect the security and accuracy of personally identifiable information.

www.truste.org

Institutional Review Board. The IRBs concentrate on two areas. First is the guarantee of obtaining complete, informed consent from participants. This can be traced to the first of 10 points in the Nuremberg Code.[8] Complete informed consent has four characteristics:

1. The participant must be competent to give consent.
2. Consent must be voluntary, free from coercion, force, requirements, and so forth.
3. Participants must be adequately informed to make a decision.
4. Participants should know the possible risks or outcomes associated with the research.

The second item of interest to the Institutional Review Board is the risk assessment and benefit analysis review. In the review, risks are considered when they add to the normal risk of daily life. Significantly, the only benefit considered is the immediate importance of the knowledge to be gained. Possible long-term benefits from applying the knowledge that may be gained in the research are not considered.[9]

Debriefing Participants

In situations where participants are intentionally or accidentally deceived, they should be debriefed once the research is complete. **Debriefing** involves several activities following the collection of data:

- Explanation of any deception.
- Description of the hypothesis, goal, or purpose of the study.
- Poststudy sharing of results.
- Poststudy follow-up medical or psychological attention.

First, the researcher shares the truth of any deception with the participants and the reasons for using deception in the context of the study's goals. In cases where severe reactions occur, follow-up medical or psychological attention should be provided to continue to ensure the participants remain unharmed by the research. Sometimes to ensure participation, the researcher may offer to share results of the study with participants. Depending on the study, this may be done immediately following participation or after data analysis.

Even when research does not deceive the participants, it is a good practice to offer them follow-up information. This retains the goodwill of the participant, providing an incentive

debriefing describes the goals of the research, as well as the truth and reasons for any deception.

to participate in future research projects. For surveys and interviews, participants can be offered a brief report of the findings. Usually, they will not request additional information. Occasionally, however, the research will be of particular interest to a participant. A simple set of descriptive charts or data tables can be generated for such an individual.

For experiments, all participants should be debriefed in order to put the experiment into context. Debriefing usually includes a description of the hypothesis being tested and the purpose of the study. Participants who were not deceived still benefit from the debriefing session. They will be able to understand why the experiment was created. The researchers also gain important insight into what the participants thought about during and after the experiment. This may lead to modifications in future research designs. Like survey and interview participants, participants in experiments and observational studies should be offered a report of the findings.

To what extent do debriefing and informed consent reduce the effects of deception? Research suggests that the majority of participants do not resent temporary deception and may have more positive feelings about the value of the research after debriefing than those who didn't participate in the study.[10] Nevertheless, deception is an ethically thorny issue and should be addressed with sensitivity and concern for research participants.

Right to Privacy

All individuals have a right to privacy, and researchers must respect that right. U.S. federal legislation that governs or influences the ways in which research is carried out are the Right to Privacy laws. Public Law 95-38 is the Privacy Act of 1974. This was the first law guaranteeing Americans the right to privacy. Public Law 96-440, the Privacy Protection Act of 1980, carries the right to privacy further. These two laws are the basis for protecting the privacy and confidentiality of the participants and the data in research. In 1999, the Gramm-Leach-Bliley Financial Modernization Act was passed. It affords individuals special privacy measures for freedom from disclosure of financial information.[11] Of special interest to researchers who specialize in working with children or those who conduct research online is the Children's Online Privacy Protection Act of 1998 (COPPA) passed October 23, 1998, which became effective in 2000. In addition to other stipulations, this rule requires posting of privacy policies on child-oriented Web sites, requires verifiable parental consent before collecting information from children, and gives parents access to and deletion authority over the information provided by their children younger than 13 years of age.[12]

The importance of the right to privacy is illustrated with this example: An employee of MonsterVideo, a large video company, is also a student at the local university. For a research project, this student and his team members decide to compare the video-viewing habits of a sample of customers by using telephone interviews. After inquiring about people's viewing habits and the frequency of rentals versus purchases, the students transition to the types of films people watch. They find that most participants answer questions about their preferences for children's shows, classics, best sellers, mysteries, and science fiction. But the cooperation ceases when the students question the viewing frequency of pornographic movies. Without the guarantee of privacy, most people will not answer these kinds of questions truthfully, if at all. The study then loses key data.

The privacy guarantee is important not only to retain validity of the research but also to protect participants. In the previous example, imagine the harm that could be caused by releasing information on the viewing habits of certain citizens. Clearly, the confidentiality of survey answers is an important aspect of the participants' right to privacy. There are also more subtle variations of this violation. Imagine participating in such a study and then beginning to receive e-mails, direct mail, and telephone solicitations for every new drama (or comedy or science fiction film) as it is released on DVD. Some unethical marketers still think research is a legitimate avenue to build a list of sales leads. Legitimate marketing researchers consider this a violation of privacy and confidentiality. They've even given it a derogatory name, "sugging," for *sales under the guise of research.*

> **Exhibit 7-3** Sample Standard for Participant Confidentiality

1. Fully preserve the confidentiality of participant-identifiable information from third parties, clients, and the public except:
   a. To validate interviews.
   b. To determine an additional fact of analytical importance to the study.

2. Disclose participant-identifiable information to the client *only* after obtaining written testament that the client:
   a. Will conduct the validation or recontact in a fully professional manner.
   b. Will use the information only for legitimate and ethical survey research purposes or to respond to participant complaints.
   c. Will use the information only for model building, internal (research organization) analysis, or the like and not for individual marketing efforts (e.g., lead generation).
   d. Will take no action toward an individual participant that is not taken toward the segment or group of individuals that the participant by chance has been chosen to represent.

3. Disclose participant-identifiable information to other researchers only when such organizations are conducting different phases of a multistage study (e.g., a trend analysis).

4. Secure agreement to preserve participant identity from clients or others present during the data collection phase of research.

5. Secure the following safeguards:
   a. Research staff do not use or discuss participant-identifiable data or information except for legitimate internal purposes.
   b. Subcontractors and consultants agree to maintain and respect participant confidentiality.
   c. Participant-identifiable information is deleted from completed questionnaires before providing access by clients or others.
   d. Only visible identification numbers are used on questionnaires, accompanied by an explanation that identifiers are used for control purposes and that participant confidentiality will not be compromised.
   e. Confidentiality is maintained even when survey results are requested for a legal proceeding.

Source: The above statements are extracted or derived from "CASRO Code of Standards and Ethics for Survey Research," from the CASRO Web site (http://www.casro.org/codeofstandards.cfm), downloaded November 30, 2002.

Once the guarantee of **confidentiality** is given, protecting that confidentiality is essential. Exhibit 7-3 offers a sample standard with respect to confidentiality. The researcher protects participant confidentiality in several ways:

confidentiality a privacy guarantee to retain validity of the research and protect participants.

- Obtaining signed nondisclosure documents.
- Restricting access to participant identification.
- Revealing participant information only with written consent.
- Restricting access to data instruments where the participant is identified.
- Nondisclosure of data subsets.

Researchers should restrict access to information that reveals names, telephone numbers, addresses, or other identifying features. Only researchers who have signed nondisclosure, confidentiality forms should be allowed access to the data. Links between the data or database and the identifying information file should be weakened. Individual interview response sheets should be inaccessible to everyone except the editors and data entry personnel. Occasionally, data collection instruments should be destroyed once the data are in a data file. Data files that make it easy to reconstruct the profiles or identification of individual participants should be carefully controlled. For very small groups, data should not be made available because it is often easy to pinpoint a person within the group. The U.S. government follows this guideline with respect to census data. Given the link between customer satisfaction and employee performance, more firms are using employee research as one source of data relating to marketing performance. Employee-satisfaction survey feedback in small units can be easily used to identify an individual through descriptive statistics alone. These last two protections—of individuals and small groups—are particularly important in human resources research.[13]

But privacy is more than confidentiality. A **right to privacy** means one has the right to refuse to be interviewed or to refuse to answer any question in an interview. Potential participants have a right to privacy in their own homes, including not admitting researchers and not answering telephones. And they have the right to engage in private behavior in

right to privacy the participant's right to refuse to be interviewed or answer specific questions in an interview.

Privacy Policy Turns JetBlue Red

Is enhanced Homeland Security justification for violating customers' privacy rights? JetBlue Airlines thought so in September 2002 when it provided more than 1.5 million customer itineraries and private personal information to a defense contractor, Torch Concepts, for a test of a proposed airline screening project to identify likely terrorists.

The Transportation Security Administration of the U.S. federal government is charged in a petition brought to the Federal Trade Commission with facilitating the information transfer to Torch Concepts. Torch Concepts supplemented the provided information with matching information including social security numbers, occupations, vehicle ownership, number of children, and income and other personal information purchased from Acxiom. Torch Concepts presented at a February 25, 2003, technology conference a study entitled "Homeland Security—Airline Passenger Risk Assessment." Data contained in the presentation referenced personal information from JetBlue customers. The presentation was later posted to the conference sponsor's Web site until it was removed September 16, 2003.

"The Privacy Act of 1974 regulates the government's collection, maintenance, use, and dissemination of personal information, and specifically provides protection for the Social Security number." The Electronic Information Center (EIC), a nonprofit, public service research organization, decried JetBlue's violation of its own privacy policy, which prohibits the sharing of customer information for any reason. On September 22, 2003, EIC filed a *Complaint and Request for Injunction, Investigation and for Other Relief* with the Federal Trade Commission. It charged "JetBlue Airways Corporation and Acxiom Corporation [as having] engaged in deceptive trade practices affecting commerce by disclosing consumer personal information to Torch Concepts Inc., an information mining company with its principal place of business in Huntsville, Alabama, in violation of 15 U.S.C. § 45(a)(1)." In an apologetic e-mail sent to angry customers, JetBlue chief executive David Neeleman concluded, "This was a mistake on our part."

www.jetblue.com; www.epic.org; www.acxiom.com; www.torchconcepts.com

---

private places without fear of observation. To address these rights, ethical researchers do the following:

- Inform participants of their right to refuse to answer any questions or participate in the study, to give the participants control of their levels of privacy.
- Obtain prior permission to interview or observe participants.
  - Preschedule personal and phone interviews.
  - Restrict observation to *public behavior in public places* when participants are not asked for prior permission. (Observe behavior outside the home or residence, the workplace, or any other place where confidentiality is ensured—doctors' and lawyers' offices during patient or client consultations, church confessionals, etc.)
- Limit the time required for participation, to limit the amount of information collected to only that which is deemed critical.

Data Collection in Cyberspace

Some ethicists argue that the very conduct that results in resistance from participants—interference, invasiveness in their lives, denial of privacy rights—has encouraged researchers to investigate topics online that have long been the principal commodity of offline investigation. The novelty and convenience of communicating by computer has led researchers to cyberspace in search of abundant sources of data. Whether we call it the "wired society," "digital life," "computer-mediated communication," or "cyberculture," the growth of cyberstudies causes us to question how we gather data online, deal with participants, and present results.

In a special ethics issue of *Information Society*, scholars involved in cyberspace research concluded:

>**snap**shot

Google: Tracking Search Patterns

According to data from Nielsen//NetRatings and SearchEngineWatch.com, Internet users in the United States spent about 15.1 million hours in August 2002 searching at Google. Additionally, more than 150 million inquiries a day flow to the Internet through Google's search engine. Google tracks a search by time of day, originating IP address, and sites on which the user clicked. Even though queries come from more than 100 countries, according to Greg Rae, a member of the Google team that logs those inquiries, patterns emerge. "It's amazing how similar people are all over the world based on what they are searching for." Google provides some of these patterns on its Web site Google Zeitgeist, but it protects its raw data from prying eyes due to privacy concerns. It knows, for example, that Britney Spears has become a benchmark of sorts based on the large number of inquiries that include her name and that major events—like September 11, 2001—or even minor ones—like a question posed on ABC's *Millionaire*—can cause spikes in inquiries. But what makes Google a marketing gold mine is its ability to predict future trends as well as mirror them. Marketers are interested not only for these predictive capabilities but also because searches reveal things about individuals that they wouldn't willingly talk about with researchers. So while Google publishes some of its aggregate trends on its Web site, it is just beginning to explore how or whether to use its data for marketing purposes.

www.google.com/press/zeitgeist.html
www.nielsen-netratings.com

All participants agree that research in cyberspace provides no special dispensation to ignore ethical precepts. Researchers are obligated to protect human subjects and "do right" in electronic venues as in more conventional ones. Second, each participant recognizes that cyberspace poses complex ethical issues that may lack exact analogs in other types of inquiry. The ease of covert observation, the occasional blurry distinction between public and private venues, and the difficulty of obtaining the informed consent of subjects make cyber-research particularly vulnerable to ethical breaches by even the most scrupulous scholars. Third, all recognize that because research procedures or activities may be permissible or not precluded by law or policy, it does not follow that they are necessarily ethical or allowable. Fourth, all agree that the individual researcher has the ultimate responsibility for assuring that inquiry is not only done honestly, but done with ethical integrity.[14]

Issues relating to cyberspace in research also relate to data mining. The information collection devices available today were once the tools of the spy, the science fiction protagonist, or the superhero. Smart cards, biometrics (finger printing, retinal scans, facial recognition), electronic monitoring (closed circuit television, digital camera monitoring), global surveillance, and genetic identification (DNA) are just some of the technological tools being used by today's organizations to track and understand employees, customers, and suppliers. The data mining of all this information, collected from advanced and not necessarily obvious sources, such as spyware, offers infinite possibilities for research abuse.

Data Mining Ethics

The primary ethical data mining issues in cyberspace are privacy-related: consent to information collection and control of information dissemination. Smart cards, those ubiquitous credit-card-sized devices that imbed personal information on a computer chip that is then matched to purchase, employment, or other behavior data, offer the researcher implied consent to participant surveillance. But the benefits of card use may be enough to hide from an unsuspecting user the data-mining purpose of the card.

Retailers, wholesalers, medical and legal service providers, schools, government agencies, and resorts, to name a few, use smart cards or their equivalent. The bottom line for these organizations is that collecting the information gains a major benefit: better customer understanding that can be the basis for competitive advantage. Participants in some of these programs provide—either enthusiastically or grudgingly—the personal information requested during enrollment procedures. But in others, a participant's consent is mandatory—as when smart cards are used with those convicted of crimes and sentenced to municipal or state correction facilities or with persons attending specific schools. In some instances, mandatory sharing of information is initially for personal welfare and safety— like when you admit yourself for a medical procedure and provide detailed information about medication or prior surgery. But in others, enrollment is for less critical but potentially attractive monetary benefits—for example, The Kroger Co., one of the largest grocers in the United States, offers significant discounts for enrollment in its Kroger Plus Shopper's Card program.[15]

> 66In the new e-frontier, one set of protagonists—merchants—would like to be cowboys, free to roam the range, and continue to share, rent or sell information they've collected about citizens without any fences or conditions.99
>
> *Robert E. Litan,*
> *Director, AEI-Brookings Joint Center*

Whether consent is willingly or hesitantly given, most participants want assurances that the information provided will be used by the organization for the purposes specified and not given or sold to other firms for entirely different—and potentially unapproved—purposes. As a result, legitimate data miners publicly post their information security policies. It is, however, up to the potential participant to read and respond appropriately to these policies by withholding or providing requested information.

European Union

General privacy laws may not be sufficient to protect the unsuspecting in the cyberspace realm of data collection. The 15 European Union (EU) countries started the new century by passing the European Commission's data protection directive. Under the directive, commissioners can prosecute companies and block Web sites that fail to live up to its strict privacy standards (see Exhibit 7-4). Specifically, the directive prohibits the transmission of names, addresses, ethnicity, and other personal information to any country that fails to provide adequate data protection. This includes direct mail lists, hotel and travel reservations, medical and work records, and orders for products, among a host of others.[16] U.S. industry and government agencies have resisted regulation of data flow. But the EU insists that it is the right of every citizen to find out what information about them is in a database and correct any mistakes. It is feared that few U.S. companies would willingly offer such access due to the high cost.[17] A perfect example of this reluctance is the difficulty individuals have correcting erroneous credit reports, even when such information is based on stolen personal identity or credit card transactions.

Yet questions remain regarding the definition of specific ethical behaviors for cyber-research, the sufficiency of existing professional guidelines, and the issue of ultimate responsibility for participants. If researchers are responsible for the ethical conduct of their research, are they solely responsible for the burden of protecting participants from every conceivable harm?

> Ethics and the Sponsor

There are also ethical considerations to keep in mind when dealing with the research client or sponsor. Whether undertaking product, market, or other marketing research, a sponsor has the right to receive ethically conducted research.

Confidentiality

Some sponsors wish to undertake research without revealing themselves. They have a right to several types of confidentiality (nondisclosure), including sponsor nondisclosure, purpose nondisclosure, and findings nondisclosure.

>snapshot

HP: Data's Safe Harbor

The European Union's data protection directive was adopted October 25, 1998. It sets strict standards for companies sending, sharing, or receiving data within EU member countries. On November 1, 2000, the voluntary U.S. Safe Harbor guidelines for transferring personal data between the United States and member countries of the European Union took effect. Claiming that "consumer confidence will be enhanced by ensuring customer privacy rights on- and off-line," Hewlett-Packard's customer privacy manager Barbara Lawler announced February 12, 2001, that HP would be the first high-tech company "to participate in the 'safe harbor' agreement between the U.S. Department of Commerce and European Union Data Protection Authorities."

HP's privacy policy directly addresses globally recognized fair information practices, including notifying customers about data collection, giving customers a choice for marketing contact and data sharing, allowing customers to access and modify collected data, and providing strong security and third-party oversight. The safe-harbor provisions provide legal protection and a framework allowing for the safe transfer of personal information from European Union countries to the United States. As of 2003, 267 U.S. organizations had certified their compliance with the safe-harbor principles.

www.hp.com

> **Exhibit 7-4** The Seven Basic Principles of the U.S. Safe Harbor Agreement

Companies that comply with this voluntary U.S. data privacy pact are granted immunity from legal action under the EU's data protection directive.

- *Notice.* Companies must notify consumers/participants about what information is being collected, how that information will be used, who that information will be shared with, and how individuals can contact the organization with any inquiries or complaints.

- *Choice.* Consumers/participants must be provided with an opt-out mechanism for any secondary uses of data and for disclosures to third parties. For sensitive information, participants must opt in before providing data that will be shared.

- *Access.* Individuals must have access to personal information about themselves that an organization holds and be able to correct, amend, or delete that information where it is inaccurate, except where the burden or expense of providing access would be disproportionate to the risks to the individual's privacy.

- *Security.* Organizations must take reasonable precautions to protect personal information from loss, misuse, and unauthorized access, disclosure, alteration, and destruction.

- *Onward transfer.* Companies disclosing personal data to a third party must, with certain exceptions, adhere to the notice and choice principles. A third party must subscribe to the safe-harbor principles.

- *Data integrity.* Reasonable steps must be taken to ensure that data collected are reliable, accurate, complete, and current.

- *Enforcement.* Companies must ensure there are readily available and affordable independent mechanisms to investigate consumer complaints, obligations to remedy problems, procedures to verify compliance with safe-harbor principles, and sufficiently rigorous sanctions to ensure compliance.

Source: Diane Bowers, "Privacy and the Research Industry in the U.S.," *ESOMAR Research World,* no. 7, July/August 2001, pp. 8–9 (http://www.esomar.nl/PDF/DataPrivacyUpdateUSA.pdf); Lori Enos, "Microsoft to Sign EU Privacy Accord," www.EcommerceTimes.com, May 16, 2001 (http://www.newsfactor.com/perl/story/9752.html); U.S. Department of Commerce, "Safe Harbor Overview" (http://www.export.gov/safeharbor/sh_overview.html), accessed November 30, 2002.

Companies have a right to dissociate themselves from the sponsorship of a research project. This type of confidentiality is called **sponsor nondisclosure.** Due to the sensitive nature of the management dilemma or the research question, sponsors may hire an outside consulting or research firm to complete research projects. This is often done when a company is testing a new product idea, to avoid potential consumers from being influenced by the company's current image or industry standing. Or if a company is contemplating entering a new market, it may not wish to reveal its plans to competitors. In such cases, it is the responsibility of the researcher to respect this desire and devise a plan that safeguards the identity of the research sponsor.

sponsor nondisclosure
when the sponsor of the research restricts revealing of its sponsorship.

Information can make or break a business on one of the world's busiest avenues, Wall Street. That's why you need a researcher that can extract information while keeping results strictly confidential. Seaport Surveys is one such firm. It specializes in executive recruiting, as well as business-to-business interviewing and executive focus groups in the greater New York area. **www.seaportsurveys.com**

purpose nondisclosure
when the sponsor camouflages the true research objective of the study.

Purpose nondisclosure involves protecting the purpose of the study or its details. A research sponsor may be testing a new idea that is not yet patented and may not want the competition to know of its plans. It may be investigating customer complaints and may not want to instigate legal activity. Or the sponsor might be contemplating a new store location and advance disclosure would spark the interest of government authorities and land speculators, potentially costing the firm thousands or millions of additional dollars. Finally, even if a sponsor feels no need to hide its identity or the study's purpose, most sponsors want the research data and findings to be confidential, at least until the management decision is made. Thus sponsors usually demand and receive **findings nondisclosure** between themselves or their researchers and any interested but unapproved parties.

findings nondisclosure
when the sponsor restricts the researcher from discussing the findings of the research project.

right to quality the sponsor's right to an appropriate, value-laden research design and data handling and reporting techniques.

Right to Quality Research

An important ethical consideration for the researcher and the sponsor is the sponsor's **right to quality** research. This right entails:

- Providing a research design appropriate for the research question.
- Maximizing the sponsor's value for the resources expended.
- Providing data handling and reporting techniques appropriate for the data collected.

From the proposal through the design to data analysis and final reporting, the researcher guides the sponsor on the proper techniques and interpretations. Often sponsors will have heard about a sophisticated data handling technique and will want it used even when it is inappropriate for the problem at hand. The researcher should guide the sponsor so that this does not occur. The researcher should propose the design most suitable for the problem. The researcher should not propose activities designed to maximize researcher revenue or minimize researcher effort at the sponsor's expense.

> **As you learn about research design, sampling, statistics, and reporting techniques, you'll learn the various conditions that must be met for results to be valid.**

Mark Twain popularized a statement generally attributed to Benjamin Disraeli, "There are three kinds of lies: lies, damn lies, and statistics."[18] It is the researcher's responsibility to prevent statistically distorted information. The ethical researcher always follows the analytical rules and conditions for generating valid results. The ethical researcher reports findings in ways that minimize the drawing of false conclusions. The ethical researcher also uses charts, graphs, and tables to show the data objectively—regardless of the results a sponsor might prefer to see.

An employee at Coca-Cola, fearing a test market of the sales stimulus of frozen Coke at Burger King was doing poorly, hired a man to treat numerous people to Burger King meals that included frozen Coke. It took a formal apology from Coke's president and a cash incentive to rectify this incident and preserve a longtime partnership.
www.cocacola.com;
www.bk.com

Design-Based Ethical Issues

Occasionally, research specialists may be asked by sponsors to participate in unethical behavior. Visionary Insights experienced just such a request in the opening vignette. Compliance by the researcher would be a breach of ethical standards. Some examples to be avoided are:

- Violating participant confidentiality.
- Changing data or creating false data to meet a desired objective.
- Changing data presentations or interpretations.
- Interpreting data from a biased perspective.
- Omitting sections of data analysis and conclusions.
- Making recommendations beyond the scope of the data collected.

> **Short cases in the Discussion Questions section at the end of this chapter are designed to have you articulate your own ethical standards as you respond to real ethical dilemmas.**

Let's examine the effects of complying with coercion to breach ethical standards. Some sponsors may coerce with the promise of punishment; for example, a sponsor may threaten to fire the researcher or tarnish the researcher's reputation. Alternatively, a sponsor may offer a reward: promotion, future contracts, or a larger payment for the existing research contract. For some researchers, a request may seem trivial and the reward high. But imagine, for a moment, what will happen to the researcher who falsifies research results at the request of a sponsor. Although there is a promise of future research, can the sponsor ever trust that researcher again? If the researcher's ethical standards are *for sale,* which sponsor might be the highest bidder next time? Although the promise of future contracts seems enticing, the sponsor is unlikely to keep such a promise due to lack of trust. The rewards of such unethical conduct are illusory. And any threat to one's professional reputation cannot be carried out effectively by a sponsor who has tried to coerce a researcher's unethical behavior. Giving in to coercion, whether framed as a reward or punishment, has an equally poor outcome: research that won't lead to a better decision.

What's the ethical course? Often, it requires confronting the sponsor's demand and taking the following actions:

- Educate the sponsor to the purpose of research.
- Explain the researcher's role in fact finding versus the sponsor's role in decision making.

- Explain how distorting the truth or breaking faith with participants leads to future problems.
- Failing moral suasion, terminate the relationship with the sponsor.

Deception

The sponsor also behaves unethically when it issues an RFP after it has already determined a research supplier or when it intends to conduct the research itself and issues the request only to obtain free research advice. Both of these actions are shortsighted, as the sponsor is unlikely to get the desired response to future RFPs once it becomes known for deceptive proposal-generating practices.

> Researchers and Team Members

Another ethical responsibility of researchers is their team's safety as well as their own. In addition, the responsibility for ethical behavior rests with the researcher who, along with assistants, is charged with protecting the anonymity of both the sponsor and the participant.

Safety

right to safety the right of interviewers, surveyors, experimenters, observers, and participants to be protected from any threat of physical or psychological harm.

It is the researcher's responsibility to design a project so that the safety of all interviewers, surveyors, experimenters, or observers is protected. Several factors may be important to consider in ensuring a researcher's **right to safety.** Some urban areas and undeveloped rural areas may be unsafe for research assistants. If, for example, the researcher must personally interview people in a high-crime district, it is reasonable to provide a second team member to protect the researcher. Alternatively, if an assistant feels unsafe after visiting a neighborhood by car, an alternate researcher should be assigned to the destination.[19] It is unethical to require staff members to enter an environment where they feel physically threatened. Researchers who are insensitive to these concerns face both research and legal risks—the least of which involves having interviewers falsify data.

Ethical Behavior of Assistants or Subcontractors

Researchers should require ethical compliance from team members just as sponsors expect ethical behavior from researchers. Marketing researchers are often specialists, so subcontracting portions of a large research project is likely. Subcontractors are hired to develop samples, conduct telephone or personal interviewing, enter data, and sometimes even analyze data and write reports. Assistants or subcontractors are expected to carry out the designated sampling plan, to interview or observe participants without bias, and to accurately record all necessary data. Unethical behavior, such as filling in an interview sheet without having asked the participant the questions, sometimes labeled "curb stoning," cannot be tolerated. The behavior of the assistants is under the direct control of the responsible researcher or field supervisor. While the behavior of subcontractors is not under the direct control of the researcher, their performance is the responsibility of the contracting researcher. If an assistant or subcontractor behaves improperly in an interview or shares a participant's interview sheet with an unauthorized person, this is the researcher's responsibility. Consequently, all assistants should be well trained and supervised, and all subcontractors should be carefully screened, including checking references for prior performance.

> **Exhibit 7-5** Summary of Ethical Issues by Category

	Sponsor	Researcher/ Research Supplier	Participant
Privacy	• Nondisclosure of purpose • Nondisclosure of findings or results • Nondisclosure of sponsorship	• Protection of proprietary methodologies	• Explanation of rights and protections • Securance of informed consent • Explanation of right of refusal
Motivation		• Absence of issuance of RFP when research will be done internally • Absence of issuance of RFP when supplier has been selected	• Explanation of intended data uses • Explanation of and delivery of benefits of participation • Debriefing following participation
Quality	• Absence of falsified data interviewers (curb stoning) • Fulfillment of sampling procedures • Provision of trained interviewers/data collectors • Appropriate design for the research question • Accurate accounting of expenses • Accurate invoice • Appropriate data handling and analytical procedures • Absence of researcher bias in interpreting data • Confinement of recommendations to scope of research collected	• Absence of sponsor coercion in design • Absence of sponsor coercion in reporting	
Safety		• Avoidance of designs that jeopardize personal safety of data collectors	• Preservation of participant confidentiality from third parties, sponsors, and public • Absence of participant deception • Right to confidentiality of source • Debriefing of participant—do no harm

Protection of Anonymity

As discussed previously, researchers and assistants protect the confidentiality of the sponsor's information and the anonymity of the participants. Each researcher handling data should be required to sign a confidentiality and nondisclosure statement.

We summarize these ethical issues in Exhibit 7-5.

> **Professional Standards**

Various standards of ethics exist for the professional researcher. Many corporations, professional associations, and universities have a **code of ethics.** The impetus for these policies and

code of ethics an organization's codified set of norms or standards of behavior that guide moral choices about research behavior.

Moral Myopia is Food for Thought

Much of our discussion of ethical concerns in marketing research has to do with living within codes of ethics required of members by professional associations, as well as abiding by the growing body of law relating to privacy issues and the exacting scientific standards with respect to data mining and data analysis. We also accept the need to address long-term consequences of research in the steps we take to protect the mental and physical well-being of participants and researchers—the *do-no-harm* standard. But, as researchers, should we be asking other questions?

If, as a researcher, you are asked to test a product concept, should you be asking a question other than "Is the methodology appropriate to the task" (right of quality)? What about asking, "Is doing the research that might support introducing this product in the best interests of the customer or society?"

An alcoholic milkshake was put on the market in the late 1970s to appeal to younger drinkers who didn't like the taste of hard liquor. Research factored into the development of the product and the development of the messaging used in its advertising. In the face of increasing concerns about alcohol abuse among youth, should the researcher today respond differently to an RFP for such research? A reduced-smoke cigarette was introduced in the 1980s; it carried an increased health hazard to the smoker while it purportedly addressed the ills of secondhand smoke. Should ethical warnings have sounded for researchers assigned to research the marketing of this product? As researchers assume a more consultative role, should the ethical dimensions researchers address increase proportionately?

An alternative approach to the subject of ethical research concerns—and a potentially stimulating discussion—might be to follow the path forged by Minette Drumwright and Patrick Murphy. In their article on moral myopia discovered via a qualitative study of professionals within advertising agencies, they raise concerns that could apply equally to research professionals. The questions their study findings raise are especially troubling when we consider the significant amount of marketing research done by advertising agencies or their affiliated research divisions.

Moral myopia is defined as a failure to identify ethical issues, not because they don't exist but because our perceptors are faulty or distorted. You might see how you could miss different ethical standards embodied within an unfamiliar culture—for example, while planning research in another country. But could you miss the ethical dilemmas posed within familiar surroundings, behaviors, and expectations?

Using content analysis of hours of taped interviews with advertising agency professionals, Drumwright and Murphy found a troubling level of moral myopia. Their study attempts to understand the possible reasons for this myopia. When translated into the arena of marketing research, these same hypothetical reasons reflect at least some current research practices:

- *Legal-as-ethical argument.* What researchers do must be perceived as ethical if what they do complies with current laws.
- *Ethical-code-as-highest-standard argument.* What researchers do must be perceived as ethical if their practices meet accepted research codes of ethics.
- *Smart-customer-in-control argument.* What researchers do must be perceived as ethical because their ever-vigilant, highly ethical research sponsors wouldn't tolerate unethical behavior from a research supplier.
- *Just-a-sheep, not-the-shepard argument.* What researchers do must be perceived as ethical because they follow accepted methodologies that have been used for years by trained researchers without overt negative consequences.
- *Ignorance-is-bliss argument.* What researchers do must be ethical because no one has told them differently or told them to stop.

The good news from the Drumwright-Murphy study is that they found that the work organization and its culture play an important role in encouraging or discouraging moral myopia. They also found pockets of moral imagination in the 29 agencies whose executives they interviewed. These agencies set and followed high ethical standards and used creativity to perform their services within those highly ethical frameworks—or they walked away from client assignments that, in good conscience, they could not perform.

These study findings—and the arguments Drumwright and Murphy used to try to explain them—are offered here as food for thought as you develop or reinforce your own ethical code that you will follow as a research sponsor or research supplier.

Source: The material in this Close-Up relies on an advance copy of Minette E. Drumwright and Patrick E. Murphy's "How Advertising Practitioners View Ethics: Moral Muteness, Moral Myopia, and Moral Imagination," to be published in the summer 2004 issue of *Journal of Advertising,* and on correspondence with Dr. Drumwright.

standards can be traced to two documents: the Belmont Report of 1979 and the *Federal Register* of 1991.[20] Society or association guidelines include ethical standards for the conduct of research. One comprehensive source contains 51 official codes of ethics issued by 45 associations in business, health, and law.[21] We list below several organizations that have codes of ethics.

Accounting—American Institute of Certified Public Accountants.

Advertising—American Association of Advertising Agencies; Direct Marketing Association.

Banking—American Bankers Association.

Engineering—American Association of Engineering Societies; National Society of Professional Engineers.

Financial planning—Association for Investment Management and Research; Certified Financial Planner Board of Standards/Institute of Certified Financial Planners; International Association for Financial Planning.

Human resources—American Society for Public Administration; Society for Human Resource Management.

Insurance—American Institute for Chartered Property Casualty Underwriters; American Society of Chartered Life Underwriters and Chartered Financial Consultants.

Management—Academy of Management; The Business Roundtable.

Marketing—American Marketing Association (AMA); Direct Marketing Association (DMA).

Marketing Research—Council for American Survey Research Organizations (CASRO); American Association for Public Opinion Research; Marketing Research Association (MRA).

Real estate—National Association of Realtors.

Other professional associations' codes have detailed research sections: the American Political Science Association, the American Sociological Association, and the Society of Competitive Intelligence Professionals. These associations update their codes frequently. You'll find a copy of the Direct Marketing Association's Information Security Guidelines in Appendix B.

We commend professional societies and business organizations for developing standards. However, without enforcement, standards are ineffectual. Effective codes (1) are regulative, (2) protect the public interest and the interests of the profession served by the code, (3) are behavior-specific, and (4) are enforceable. A study that assessed the effects of personal and professional values on ethical consulting behavior concluded:

> The findings of this study cast some doubt on the effectiveness of professional codes of ethics and corporate policies that attempt to deal with ethical dilemmas faced by business consultants. A mere codification of ethical values of the profession or organization may not counteract ethical ambivalence created and maintained through reward systems. The results suggest that unless ethical codes and policies are consistently reinforced with a significant reward and punishment structure and truly integrated into the business culture, these mechanisms would be of limited value in actually regulating unethical conduct.[22]

> Resources for Ethical Awareness

There is optimism for improving ethical awareness. According to the Center for Business Ethics at Bentley College, over a third of Fortune 500 companies have ethics officers. Almost 90 percent of business schools have ethics programs, up from a handful several years ago.[23] Exhibit 7–6 provides a list of recommended resources for students, researchers, and managers. The Center for Ethics and Business at Loyola Marymount University provides an online environment for discussing issues related to the necessity, difficulty, costs, and rewards of conducting business ethically. Its Web site offers a comprehensive list of business and research ethics links.[24]

> **Exhibit 7-6** Resources for Ethical Awareness

Journals and Magazines			
Business Ethics	*Business Ethics Quarterly*	*Ethikos*	*Journal of Business Ethics*

Research, Training, and Conferences

Applied Research Ethics National Association (ARENA), Boston, MA (617-423-4412; www.primr.org/).

Business ethics conferences, The Conference Board, New York, NY (212-759-0900; www.conference-board.org).

Center for Ethics and Business, Loyola Marymount University, Los Angeles, CA (310-338-2700; www.ethicsandbusiness.org).

Centre for Research Ethics, Göteborg University, Göteborg, Sweden (46 31 973 49 22; www.cre.gu.se/).

Center for the Study of Ethics in the Professions, Illinois Institute of Technology, Chicago, IL (312-567-3017; www.iit.edu/departments/csep/).

Council of American Survey Research Organizations (CASRO), Port Jefferson, NY (631-928-6954; www.casro.org).

Electronic Privacy Information Center, Washington, DC (202-483-1140; www.epic.org).

Ethics Corps Training for Business Leaders, Josephson Institute of Ethics, Marina del Rey, CA (310-306-1868; www.josephsoninstitute.org).

Ethics Resource Center, Washington, DC (202-737-2258; www.ethics.org).

European Business Ethics Network, Breukelen, The Netherlands (32 016 32 37 79; www.eben.org).

Graduate Research Ethics Education Workshop, Association of Practical and Professional Ethics, Indiana University, Bloomington, IN (812-855-6450; www.indiana.edu/nappe/gree.html).

Institute for Business and Professional Ethics, DePaul University, Chicago, IL (312-362-6624; http://commerce.depaul.edu/ethics/index.shtml).

Marketing Research Association, Rocky Hill, CT (860-257-4008; www.mra-net.org)

Teaching Research Ethics, Poynter Center, Indiana University, Bloomington, IN (812-855-0261; www.indiana.edu/~poynter/index.html).

The Beard Center for Leadership in Ethics, A. J. Palumbo School of Business Administration, Duquesne University, Pittsburgh, PA (412-396-5475; www.bus.duq.edu/Beard/).

The Center for Business Ethics, Bentley College, Waltham, MA (781-891-2981; http://ecampus.bentley.edu/dept/cbe/ethicscenters/domestic.html).

The Center for Professional and Applied Ethics, University of North Carolina, Charlotte, NC (704-687-3542; www.uncc.edu/colleges/arts_and_sciences/philosophy/center.html).

The Ethics Institute, Dartmouth College, Hanover, NH (603-646-1263; www.dartmouth.edu/~ethics/).

The Program in Ethics and the Professions, Harvard University, Cambridge, MA (617-495-1336; www.ethics.harvard.edu).

The Wharton Ethics Program, University of Pennsylvania, Philadelphia, PA (215-898-5847; http://ethics.wharton.upenn.edu/).

World Association of Public Opinion Research (WAPOR), Lincoln, NE (402-458-2030; www.unl.edu/WAPOR).

World Association of Research Professionals, Amsterdam, The Netherlands (31 20 664 21 41; www.esomar.nl)

>summary

1 Ethics are norms or standards of behavior that guide moral choices about our behavior and our relationships with others. Ethics differ from legal constraints, in which generally accepted standards have defined penalties that are universally enforced. The goal of ethics in research is to ensure that no one is harmed or suffers adverse consequences from research activities.

As research is designed, several ethical considerations must be balanced:

- Protect the rights of the participant or subject.

- Ensure the sponsor receives ethically conducted and reported research.
- Follow ethical standards when designing research.
- Protect the safety of the researcher and team.
- Ensure the research team follows the design.

2 In general, research must be designed so that a participant does not suffer physical harm, discomfort, pain, embarrassment, or loss of privacy. Begin data collection by explaining to participants the benefits expected from the research. Explain that their rights and well-being will be adequately protected and say how that will be done. Be certain that interviewers obtain the informed consent of the participant. The use of deception is questionable; when it is used, debrief any participant who has been deceived.

3 Many sponsors wish to undertake research without revealing themselves. Sponsors have the right to demand and receive confidentiality between themselves and the researchers. Ethical researchers provide sponsors with the research design

needed to solve the managerial question. The ethical researcher shows the data objectively, despite the sponsor's preferred outcomes.

The research team's safety is the responsibility of the researcher. Researchers should require ethical compliance from team members in following the research design, just as sponsors expect ethical behavior from researchers.

4 Many corporations and research firms have adopted a code of ethics. Several professional associations have detailed research provisions. Of interest are the American Association for Public Opinion Research, the Council of American Survey Research Organizations, the American Marketing Association, the American Political Science Association, the American Psychological Association, and the American Sociological Association. Federal, state, and local governments have laws, policies, and procedures in place to regulate research on human beings.

>**key**terms

code of ethics 181

confidentiality 173

debriefing 171

deception 167

ethics 166

informed consent 169

nondisclosure 177

findings 178

purpose 178

sponsor 177

right to privacy 173

right to quality 178

right to safety 180

>**discussion**questions

Terms in Review

1 Distinguish between confidentiality and privacy.

Making Research Decisions

2 *A competitive coup in the in-flight magazine.* When the manager for market intelligence of AutoCorp, a major automotive manufacturer, boarded the plane in Chicago, her mind was on shrinking market share and late product announcements. As she settled back to enjoy the remains of a hectic day, she reached for the in-flight magazine. It was jammed into the seat pocket in front of her.

Crammed into this already tiny space was a report with a competitor's logo, marked "Confidential—Restricted Circulation." It contained a description of new product announcements for the next two years. Not only was it intended for a small circle of senior executives, but it also answered the questions she had recently proposed to an external research firm.

The proposal for the solicited research could be canceled. Her research budget, already savaged, could be saved. She was home free, legally and careerwise.

She foresaw only one problem. In the last few months, AutoCorp's newly hired ethicist had revised the firm's Business Conduct Guidelines. They now required company employees in possession of a competitor's information to return it or face dismissal. But it was still a draft and not formally approved. She had the rest of the flight to decide whether to return the document to the airline or slip it into her briefcase.

a What are the most prudent decisions she can make about her responsibilities to herself and others?

b What are the implications of those decisions even if there is no violation of law or regulation?

3 *Free waters in Miro Beach: Boaters Inc. versus City Government.*[25] The city commissioners of Miro Beach proposed limits on boaters who anchor offshore in waterfront areas of the

St. Lucinda River adjoining the city. Residents had complained of pollution from the live-aboard boaters. The parking lot of boats created an unsightly view.

The city based its proposed ordinance on research done by the staff. It was not known if staff members were competent to conduct research. The staff requested a proposal from a team of local university professors who had conducted similar work in the past. The research cost was $10,000. After receiving the proposal, the staff chose to do the work itself and not expend resources for the project. Through an unidentified source, the professors later learned their proposal contained enough information to guide the city's staff and suggested data collection areas that might provide information that could justify the boaters' claims.

Based on the staff's one-time survey of waterfront litter, "pump-out" samples, and a weekly frequency count of boats, an ordinance was drafted and a public workshop was held. Shortly after, a group of concerned boat owners formed Boaters Inc., an association to promote boating, raise funds, and lobby the commission. The group's claims were that the boaters (1) spent thousands of dollars on community goods and services, (2) did not create the litter, and (3) were being unjustly penalized because the commission's fact finding was flawed.

With the last claim in mind, the boaters flooded the city with public record requests. The clerks reported that some weeks the requests were one per day. Under continued pressure, the city attorney hired a private investigator (PI) to infiltrate Boaters Inc. to collect information. He rationalized this on the grounds that the boaters had challenged the city's grant applications in order to "blackmail the city into dropping plans to regulate the boaters."

The PI posed as a college student and worked for a time in the home of the boater organization's sponsor while helping with mailings. Despite the PI's inability to corroborate the city attorney's theory, he recommended conducting a background investigation on the organization's principal, an employee of a tabloid newspaper. (The FBI, on request of city or county police organizations, generally performs background investigations.)

The PI was not a boating enthusiast and soon drew suspicion. Simultaneously, the organization turned up the heat on the city by requesting what amounted to 5,000 pages of information—"studies and all related documents containing the word 'boat.'" Failing to get a response from Miro Beach, the boaters filed suit under the Florida Public Records Act. By this time, the city had spent $20,000.

The case stalled, went to appeal, and was settled in favor of the boaters. A year later, the organization's principal filed an invasion-of-privacy and slander suit against the city attorney, the PI, and the PI's firm. After six months, the suit was amended to include the city itself and sought $1 million in punitive damages.

a What are the most prudent decisions the city can make about its responsibilities to itself and others?

b What are the implications of those decisions even if there is no violation of law or regulation?

4 *The high cost of organizational change.* Avionics Inc. needed help creating an organizational assessment survey prior to proceeding with the analysis of several possible business acquisition and product discontinuation decisions. It hired a faculty member from the nearby university to do the assessment. The young academic quickly discovered that in the 25-year history of Avionics Inc., there had never been an internal assessment of mission, vision, and employee engagement. Management repeatedly had shown a lack of concern for employee complaints over working conditions. Government inspectors had reported the number of heads down at desks as an index of questionable performance on government contracts. Avionics' engineers were secretly organizing for a unionization effort. Promising anonymity and honesty in data reporting, the academic earned the enthusiastic participation of Avionics' 500 employees.

The researcher began to feel the change in environment early on in his research effort. Headquarters dispatched staffers to monitor the development of the questionnaire, but the data collection was textbook perfect. No one asked to preview the findings, however, or showed any particular interest in the pending analysis. In the fifth week, the researcher boarded the corporate jet with the VP and senior manager to make a presentation at headquarters. Survey participants at the headquarters location had been invited to attend.

Behind the scenes, management had learned of the pending unionization effort and was intent on heading it off by using the research results to demonstrate that its underpinnings were the complaints of "a few disgruntled engineers." Management had also promised to engage a select few participants in action planning over the next few days.

An hour into the flight, the Avionics Inc. VP turned from his reading to the young researcher and surprised him by saying, "We have seen your results, and we would like you to change two key findings. They are not all that critical to this round of fixing the 'bone orchard,' and you'll have another crack at it as a consultant in the fall."

"But that would mean breaking faith with your employees . . . people who trust me to present the results objectively. It's what I thought you wanted . . . "

"Yes, well, look at it this way," replied the VP. "All of your findings we can live with except these two. They're an embarrassment to senior management. Let me put it plainly. We have government contracts into the foreseeable future. You could retire early with consulting income from this place. Someone will meet us on the runway with new slides. What do you say?"

a What are the most prudent decisions Avionics Inc. can make about its responsibilities to itself and others?

b What are the implications of those decisions even if there is no violation of law or regulation?

5 *Data mining ethics and company growth square off.* SupplyCo. is a supplier to a number of firms in an industry. This industry has a structure that includes suppliers, manufacturers, distributors, and consumers. Several companies are involved in the manufacturing process—from processed parts to creation of the final product—with each firm adding some value to the product.

By carefully mining its customer data warehouse, SupplyCo. reveals a plausible new model for manufacturing and distributing industry products that would increase the overall efficiency of the industry system, reduce costs of production (leading to greater industry profits and more sales for SupplyCo.), and result in greater sales and profits for some of the industry's manufacturers (SupplyCo.'s customers). The scenario in the Cummins Engines video case has some of the same properties as this ethical dilemma.

On the other hand, implementing the model would hurt the sales and profits of other firms that are also SupplyCo.'s customers but that are not in a position (due to manpower, plant, or equipment) to benefit from the new manufacturing/distribution model. These firms would lose sales, profits, and market share and potentially go out of business.

Does SupplyCo. have an obligation to protect the interests of all its customers and to take no action that would harm any of them, since SupplyCo. had the data within its warehouse only because of its relationship with its customers? (It would betray some of its customers if it were to use the data in a manner that would cause these customers harm.) Or does it have a more powerful obligation to its stockholders and employees to aggressively pursue the new model that research reveals would substantially increase its sales, profits, and market share against competitors?

a What are the most prudent decisions SupplyCo. can make about its responsibilities to itself and others?

b What are the implications of those decisions even if there is no violation of law or regulation?

Behind the Scenes

6 Assuming that MicroPeripheral's proposed methodology isn't fraudulent, is what the firm proposes to Visionary Insights unethical? Develop the arguments for both sides of this issue.

7 Is Jason's action, calling competitive firms to alert them to the situation he perceives as unethical, ethical? Identify the ethical issues involved in this situation, take a stand, and defend it.

From Concept to Practice

8 Reveal any conflicts among these responsibilities: nondisclosure of findings, nondisclosure of sponsor, nondisclosure of purpose, and debriefing of a deceived participant.

>**www**exercises

1 Do research-focused trade associations or research companies have special ethical guidelines for research involving children? Use a Web search engine to find out. What key words would you use in such a search?

2 Visit at least two of the Web sites of research trade associations and compare their codes of ethics. Are these codes identical? If not, what differences do you perceive?

>**case***

 Cummins Engines

* All cases, both written and video, are on the text DVD. The film icon indicates a video case. Check the DVD Index to determine whether a case has data, the research instrument, or other supplementary materials.

>part II

The Design of Marketing Research

chapter 8

Research Design: An Overview

>**learning**objectives

After reading this chapter, you should understand . . .

1 The major descriptors of research design.

2 The major types of research design.

3 The relationships that exist between variables in causal designs and the steps for evaluating those relationships.

Visionary Insights' Jason Henry and Sara Armstrong are working late. They have been finalizing their proposal for the MindWriter project. **Mind**Writer

They are taking a much deserved break.

Jason Henry tosses his empty paper coffee cup into the break lounge trash receptacle. "These anchors on cable news are totally unscientific," he comments, seemingly to no one in particular.

"She's an inexperienced kid getting her first break," states Sara as she surveys the remnants of that morning's bagels, "at an hour when no sane person is watching TV anyway, let alone subjecting it to scientific criticism."

"It is terrifically unscientific," he says, "to make unsubstantiated conclusions as she did."

"I thought she did an amusing job interviewing that psychiatrist," observes Sara. "He was a beautiful choice. With his accent and a beard, he reminded me of Freud himself. And don't you agree he was effective presenting his theory of hurricane-induced anger causing people to lash out at business."

"That's not the issue, Sara, and you know it. The fact is, she should not have claimed that when the recent hurricane brushed Galveston, it caused a rash of complaints against auto dealerships."

"But you have to admit that adorable young couple picketing the Mercedes dealership—the girl in a mink jacket and her husband in Gucci loafers, and both of them complaining they were powerless against big business—really helped make her point."

"As entertainment it was admirable. But as news supported with evidence, it was rotten science. She had no before-after comparison. I want to know how many people had complaints against dealerships before the hurricane hit. Pretty clearly, she not only had no file footage of before the hurricane, but she also had no statistics. For all I know the complaint behavior has not changed."

"Do you really believe, Jason, that anyone would have the foresight to collect such information?"

"Why not? The newspapers and TV stations on the Gulf are continually hyping the threat of hurricanes. They must make a fortune selling commercial time at inflated rates during hurricane season. So, yes, they knew a hurricane was due sometime in the near future, or was at least possible, and if they were responsible they would have done baseline measurements . . . "

"Not really feasible . . . "

" . . . or at least refrain from such pseudoscientific bunkum."

"Is that it? Is that your complaint?"

"That's part of it. The other part is that the hurricane brushed Galveston and then skittered out into the Gulf. Forty miles away, Houston was barely touched. Did she bother to check if complaint behavior in Houston was also elevated? Because if it was, that would debunk her theory that the hurricane caused the complaint behavior. You can't blame something that occurred in one location and not in the other for causing behavior seen in both locations. Can you?"

"I guess not."

"Got ya, Sara!" he exclaims, with his characteristic quirky grin firmly in place.

Sara groaned good-naturedly, realizing Jason has once again suckered her into an argument on his most favorite topic—the abuse of causality and logical reasoning—and she had fallen into the trap.

> What Is Research Design?

The topics covered by the term *research design* are wide-ranging, as depicted in Exhibit 8-1. This chapter introduces a classification of research designs and provides an overview of the most important design types (exploratory, descriptive, and causal). We refer you to subsequent chapters for a more thorough coverage of the unique features of qualitative studies, observational studies, surveys, and experiments. Our objective here is not for you to acquire the details of research design in one reading but for you to understand its scope and to get a glimpse of the available options for tailoring a design to your particular research needs.

There are many definitions of research design, but no single definition imparts the full range of important aspects.

- Research design constitutes the blueprint for the collection, measurement, and analysis of data.

- Research design aids the researcher in the allocation of resources by posing crucial choices in methodology.[1]

- Research design is the plan and structure of investigation so conceived as to obtain answers to research questions. The plan is the overall scheme or program of the research. It includes an outline of what the investigator will do from writing hypotheses and their operational implications to the final analysis of data.[2]

- A structure is the framework, organization, or configuration of . . . the relations among variables of a study. A research design expresses both the structure of the research problem and the plan of investigation used to obtain empirical evidence on relations of the problem.[3]

> **Exhibit 8-1** Design in the Research Process

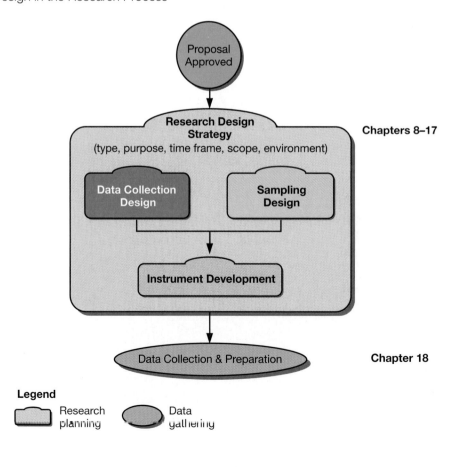

Chapters 8–17

Chapter 18

Legend

Research planning

Data gathering

These definitions differ in detail, but together they give the essentials. **Research design** is:

- An activity- and time-based plan.
- A plan always based on the research question.
- A guide for selecting sources and types of information.
- A framework for specifying the relationships among the study's variables.
- A procedural outline for every research activity.

research design the blueprint for fulfilling research objectives and answering questions.

> Classification of Designs

Early in any research study, one faces the task of selecting the specific design to use. Although there is not a simple classification to describe all design variations, Exhibit 8-2 organizes research designs into eight categories.[4] In practice, the distinctions among the category descriptors blur somewhat. But a brief discussion of each will illustrate its nature and use in designing research.

Degree of Research Question Crystallization

A study may be viewed as exploratory or formal. The essential distinctions between these two options are the degree of structure and the immediate objective of the study. **Exploratory studies** tend toward loose structures with the objective of expanding understanding of a topic, providing insights and possible explanations, or discovering future research tasks. The immediate purpose of exploration is usually to develop hypotheses or questions for further research. The **formal study** begins where the exploration leaves off— it begins with a hypothesis or research question and involves precise procedures and data source specifications. The goal of a formal research design is to test the hypotheses or answer the research questions posed.

exploratory study (exploration) loosely structured study or a phase in a research project designed to expand understanding of a topic, provide insights and possible explanations, or discover future research tasks.

formal study research question–driven process involving precise procedures for data collection and interpretation.

> **Exhibit 8-2** Descriptors of Research Design

Category	Options
The degree to which the research question has been crystallized	• Exploratory study • Formal study
The topical scope—breadth and depth— of the study	• Case • Statistical study
The purpose of the study	• Descriptive • Causal
The power of the researcher to produce effects in the variables under study	• Experimental • Ex post facto
The method of data collection	• Monitoring • Questioning/communication
The time dimension	• Cross-sectional • Longitudinal
The research environment	• Field setting • Laboratory setting • Simulation
The participants' perceptions of research activity	• Actual routine • Modified routine

> You may find it helpful to revisit Exhibit 4-1 as we discuss these descriptors.

The exploratory-formal study dichotomy recognizes that all studies have elements of exploration in them and few studies are completely uncharted. The sequence discussed in Chapter 4 (see Exhibit 4-1) suggests that more formalized studies contain at least an element of exploration before the final choice of design. More detailed consideration of exploratory research is found later in this chapter.

The Topical Scope

statistical study attempts to capture a population's characteristics by making inferences from a sample's characteristics and then testing resulting hypotheses.

Statistical studies differ from case studies in several ways. A **statistical study** is designed for breadth rather than depth. It attempts to capture a population's characteristics by making inferences from a sample's characteristics. Hypotheses are tested quantitatively. Generalizations about findings are presented based on the representativeness of the sample and the validity of the design. The MindWriter project discussed throughout the book is a statistical study.

case study a full contextual analysis of a few events or conditions and their interrelations.

A **case study** places more emphasis on a full contextual analysis of a few events or conditions and their interrelations. Although hypotheses are often used, the reliance on qualitative data makes support or rejection more difficult. An emphasis on detail provides valuable insight for problem solving, evaluation, and strategy. This detail is secured from multiple sources of information. It allows evidence to be verified and avoids missing data. Remember the proposed monitoring study for MindWriter? If MindWriter tracked one or more laptops, this could serve as a case study of the CompleteCare program. Discovering new hypotheses to correct postservice complaints would be the major advantage of tracking damaged MindWriter laptops with a case study design.

> We discuss the case study as a qualitative research methodology in Chapter 9.

Although case studies have been maligned as "scientifically worthless" because they do not meet minimal design requirements for comparison,[5] they have a significant scientific and marketing role. It is known that "important scientific propositions have the form of universals, and a universal can be falsified by a single counterinstance."[6] Thus, a single, well-designed case study can provide a major challenge to a theory and provide a source of new hypotheses and constructs simultaneously. Past experiences in product development, product launch, advertising, and customer acceptance are among a few examples where case studies aid marketing research.

The Purpose of the Study

The essential difference between descriptive and causal studies lies in their objectives. If the research is concerned with finding out *who, what, where, when,* or *how much,* then it is a **descriptive study**. If it is concerned with learning *why*—that is, how one variable produces changes in another—it is causal. Research on promotion is descriptive when it measures the types of promotions executed, how often, when, where, and by which competitor. In a **causal study**, we try to explain relationships among variables—for instance, why the coupon response rate is higher in city A than in city B.

descriptive study discovers answers to the questions who, what, when, where, or how much.

causal study attempts to reveal a causal relationship between variables.

Researcher Control of Variables

experiment a study involving manipulation of one or more variables to determine the effect on another variable.

The researcher's ability to manipulate variables is divided typically between experimental and ex post facto designs. In an **experiment**, the researcher attempts to control and/or manipulate the variables in the study. Sophisticated direct marketers use *split tests* on mailings. Rather than sending the same offer to all target customers, they split a mailing to test a particular variable, for example, the featured item on the cover. Part of the mailing would feature one item, while a second segment of the target audience would receive a catalog with a different featured item on the cover. In another example, e-mail invitations sent to potential online purchasers can feature a different offer for each group of prospects: free shipping; a $30 savings on an order of more than $100; buy one, get one free; and so on.

Experimental design is appropriate when one wishes to discover whether certain variables produce effects in other variables. For the catalog marketer, the experiment would measure number of orders, relative size of orders, and the speed of prospect response generated by one catalog cover versus another. The e-marketer would evaluate the click-through rate to the Web site, the speed of response, whether an order was placed, and the value of the order. Experimentation provides the most powerful support possible for a hypothesis of causation: was one cover or one e-mail invitation more powerful in generating desired buying behavior than another?

With an **ex post facto study**, investigators have no control over the variables in the sense of being able to manipulate them. They can only report what has happened or what is happening. An example is a study on retail store design. Meijer, the Michigan-based mass merchandiser, recently started renovating its stores in order to better compete with Target. An ex post facto design could have been used to evaluate the better of two store designs: the new one with a center focus for clothing and other soft goods and with aisles radiating out like spokes on a wheel or the traditional design featuring a straight-aisle grid pattern throughout the store. It is important that researchers using the ex post facto design not influence the variables; otherwise, they introduce bias. The researcher is limited to holding factors constant by selecting subjects according to strict sampling procedures and by statistical manipulation of findings. In Meijer, this would involve selecting matched stores with the new and old designs—stores with similar sales, profits, and shopper demographics—and monitoring shopper movement patterns to determine whether shoppers more readily progressed through the store in the desired pattern in one design versus another or whether shoppers more readily moved past preplanned promotional locations in one design versus another.

> **ex post facto design** after-the-fact report on what happened to the measured variable.

Method of Data Collection

This classification distinguishes between **monitoring** and communication processes. The former includes studies in which the researcher inspects the activities of a subject or the nature of some material without attempting to elicit responses from anyone. Traffic counts at an intersection as part of a retail site analysis, license plates recorded in a restaurant parking lot to determine the draw of a particular promotion, a search of the library collection to identify and evaluate competitor activity, an observation of the actions of a group of marketing decision makers in the process of evaluating new product ideas as part of a process audit, the State Farm Dangerous Intersection Study—all are examples of monitoring. In each case the researcher notes and records the information available from observations.

Monitoring for MindWriter might include "following" a computer through the repair process, documenting each activity or interaction between CompleteCare and call center employees and the damaged laptop.

In the **communication study**, the researcher asks questions of the subjects and collects their responses by personal or impersonal means. The collected data may result from (1) interview or telephone conversations, (2) self-administered or self-reported instruments sent through the mail, left in convenient locations, or transmitted electronically or by other means, or (3) instruments presented before and/or after a treatment or stimulus condition in an experiment. Jason and Sara propose a communication study for MindWriter that involves using a postcard questionnaire inserted in the packaging of laptops returned after CompleteCare servicing.

> **monitoring** a study in which the researcher inspects the activities of a participant or the nature of some material without eliciting responses from the participant.

> > **We use the term** *communication* **to contrast with** *monitoring* **because collecting data by questioning encompasses more than the survey method.**

> **communication study** the researcher questions the participants and collects their responses by personal or impersonal means.

The Time Dimension

Cross-sectional studies are carried out once and represent a snapshot of one point in time. **Longitudinal studies** are repeated over an extended period. The advantage of a longitudinal study is that it can track changes over time. Jason and Myra's proposal describes a

> **cross-sectional study** the study is conducted only once and reveals a snapshot of one point in time.

> **longitudinal study** a study that includes repeated measures over an extended period of time.

Claria Measures Effectiveness of Pepsi Sponsorship

Is sponsorship of the Super Bowl a wise promotional investment? It certainly looks promising. In its annual report, *The Final Score: 2004 Big Game Ad Effectiveness Study,* Claria Corporation reveals that sponsor Pepsi experienced the highest unaided awareness score of any advertiser and experienced a significant increase in traffic to its pepsiworld.com Web site. During the five weeks leading to the 2004 Super Bowl, pepsiworld.com experienced a 294 percent increase in visits. The visitors were drawn from the more than 480,000 superbowl.com visitors who clicked directly from Pepsi's ad on superbowl.com. Unprompted by a listing of advertisers, more than 40 percent of survey participants cited seeing a Pepsi ad on superbowl.com, six times the level of awareness of the next cited advertiser. When prompted with a list of advertisers, the number of participants citing they had seen a Pepsi ad rose to 52 percent.

So what was the research design? First, using Web analytics, Claria tracked GAIN Network volunteers as they browsed the Internet between December 1, 2003, and February 1, 2004, using

search terms like *super bowl, NFL, Patriots, Saints,* and so on. The Claria GAIN Network comprises 45 million Internet users who have agreed to receive advertising based on their browsing behavior (Claria indicates that GAIN Network members share the same demographics as other online users). Then Claria's Feedback Research division presented a pop-up invitation to participate in a Web survey to a sample of visitors to superbowl.com. More than 500 completed this first survey between January 9 and January 28, 2004. Finally, on Monday, February 2, 2004—the day following the big game—Feedback Research again recruited GAIN Network participants with a pop-up invitation to respond to a Web survey to reveal how they watched and reacted to Super Bowl ads; 900 people participated in this second survey.

www.claria.com; www.pepsiworld.com

To learn more, you may download the study report from the Claria Web site (**www.claria.com/companyinfo/press/feb04report/**).

---

longitudinal study, with satisfaction measurements taken continuously over several months and with monthly reports.

In longitudinal studies of the panel variety, the researcher may study the same people over time. In marketing, panels are set up to report consumption data on a variety of products. These data, collected from national samples, provide a major databank on relative market share, consumer response to new products, and new promotional methods. Other longitudinal studies, such as cohort groups, use different participants for each sequenced measurement. The service industry might have looked at the needs of aging baby boomers by sampling 40- to 45-year-olds in 1990 and 50- to 55-year-olds in 2000. Although each sample would be different, the population of 1945- to 1950-cohort survivors would remain the same.

> **❝One of the greatest challenges facing marketing research is the steady decline in response rates.❞**
>
> *Wally Balden*
> *Director of Internet Research, Maritz Research*

Some types of information once collected cannot be collected a second time from the same person without the risk of bias. The study of public awareness of an advertising campaign over a six-month period would require different samples for each measurement. In this type of study, the same survey or measurement instrument is used.

While longitudinal research is important, the constraints of budget and time impose the need for cross-sectional analysis. Some benefits of a longitudinal study can be revealed in a cross-sectional study by adroit questioning about past attitudes, history, and future expectations. However, responses to these kinds of questions should be interpreted with care.

field conditions the actual environmental conditions where the dependent variable occurs.

laboratory conditions studies that occur under conditions that do not simulate actual environmental conditions.

The Research Environment

Designs also differ as to whether they occur under actual environmental conditions (**field conditions**), under arbitrary conditions designed not to imitate reality but to facilitate measurement (**laboratory conditions**), or under conditions created to imitate reality

>**snap**shot

Targeting Billboard Ads to Passing Motorists' Demographics

Tom Langeland, a Sacramento-based entrepreneur and chief executive of the Alaris Media Network, intends to compile demographic information from the radio stations drivers listen to as they drive by. His company's 10 billboards are now in Louisville, Texas, and in Los Angeles, San Francisco, Sacramento, and Mantica, California. Alaris expects four more in the San Jose area soon.

The billboards use new technology with sensors that identify radio frequencies of passing vehicles and match them against demographic information. The billboards display both video and text and can be remotely programmed with modifications occurring as often as once an hour, based on radio-listening patterns. The billboards display messages and images based on income,

sex, race, and buying habit data. For example, if a high proportion of rush-hour drivers are tuned to a radio station known to have affluent or educated listeners, the billboard advertisements would target them.

The technology was created by Alaris's partner, MobilTrak, of Chandler, Arizona. Alaris and MobilTrak use syndicated data from Media Audit, which studies demographic patterns of radio listeners. Phyllis R. Neill, chief operating officer of the company, said, "We can tell you the percentage of people who drove past that were married, shop at Petsmart, that make over $100,000."

www.mobiltrak.com; www.themediaaudit.com; www.alaris.net

(**simulations**). If we were to test the ease of preparation of a new convenience food, the ideal test would be in a participant's home (field conditions). Since assigning researchers to view preparations in numerous homes—or setting up cameras to observe the preparation—is both time-consuming and costly, we might choose to bring participants to a central location, like a research test kitchen or a church kitchen (laboratory conditions). Hypothetically, if that mock kitchen could be changed to reflect the actual kitchen gadgets, dishes, and space-appliance configuration of every participant's kitchen, we would have a simulation. Simulations are specialized environments increasingly used in research, especially in conjunction with modeling. To simulate is to replicate the essence of a system or process. A simulation for MindWriter might involve an arbitrarily damaged laptop being tracked through the call center and the CompleteCare program, monitoring results at each workstation. The major characteristics of various conditions and relationships in actual situations are often represented in mathematical models. Role playing (like mystery shopping in a retail store) and other behavioral designs are also viewed as simulations.

simulation a study in which the conditions of a system or process are replicated.

> **See our example of marketing models in Chapter 3.**

Participants' Perceptions

The usefulness of a research design is reduced when people in a disguised study perceive that research is being conducted. Participants' perceptions influence the outcomes of the research in subtle ways or more dramatically, as was learned from the pivotal Hawthorne studies of the late 1920s. (In the findings of the first set of studies at the Hawthorne plant of the Western Electric Company, it was discovered that participants reacted favorably to receiving special attention—causing a rise in productivity.) Although there is no widespread evidence of attempts by participants or respondents to please researchers through successful hypothesis guessing and no evidence of the prevalence of sabotage, when participants believe that something out of the ordinary is happening, they behave less naturally. There are three levels of perception to consider:

1. Participants perceive no deviations from everyday routines.

2. Participants perceive deviations but see them as unrelated to the researcher.

3. Participants perceive deviations as researcher-induced.[7]

Mystery shopping may sometimes provide an example of the third level of perception. *Mystery shopping* involves individuals who pose as customers and visit retail or service organizations to observe and measure specific behaviors or circumstances. If a retail sales associate knows she is being observed and evaluated on actual execution versus how well standards are being met—with consequences in future compensation, scheduling, or work assignment—she is likely to modify her performance. In all research environments and control situations, researchers need to be vigilant about effects that may alter their conclusions. The potential for variations in participants' perceptions reminds us to consider the strengths and weaknesses of various study types before selecting a design.

> Exploratory Studies

Exploration is particularly useful when researchers lack a clear idea of the problems they will meet during the study. Through exploration researchers develop concepts more clearly, establish priorities, develop operational definitions, and improve the final research design. Exploration may also save time and money. If the problem is not as important as first thought, more formal studies can be canceled.

Exploration serves other purposes as well. The area of investigation may be so new or so vague that a researcher needs to do an exploration just to learn something about the dilemma facing the manager. Important variables may not be known or thoroughly defined. Hypotheses for the research may be needed. Also, the researcher may explore to be sure it is practical to do a formal study later. Snack-food giant Frito-Lay is often lauded for its success in new product development. A recent example is its introduction of Go Snacks: bite-sized versions of its market-favorite snacks packaged in hand-friendly, ergonomically styled containers designed to fit in car cupholders. A frozen food manufacturer might propose that research be done on the new product development processes of various successful companies, like Frito-Lay. An exploration might discover whether food company executives would reveal how their companies come up with new product ideas and the processes used to evaluate those ideas. A high degree of candid and clear information about this phase of marketing decision making would be essential for the study's success.

Despite its potential for saving time and money, researchers and managers alike give exploration less attention than it deserves because of pressures for quick answers and old biases about subjectiveness, nonrepresentativeness, and nonsystematic design.

Exploratory Techniques

qualitative techniques
nonquantitative data collection used to increase understanding of a topic.

The objectives of exploration may be accomplished with qualitative and quantitative techniques, although exploration relies more heavily on **qualitative techniques**. One author differentiates the two this way: "Quality is the essential character or nature of something; quantity is the amount. Quality is the what; quantity the how much. Qualitative refers to the meaning, the definition or analogy or model or metaphor characterizing something, while quantitative assumes the meaning and refers to a measure of it."[8]

A variety of approaches are adaptable for exploratory investigations of management questions:

- Interviewing (usually conversational rather than structured).
- Participant observation (to perceive firsthand what participants in the setting experience).

- Films, photographs, and videotape (to capture the life of the group under study).
- Projective techniques and psychological testing (such as a Thematic Apperception Test, projective measures, games, or role playing).
- Case studies (for an in-depth contextual analysis of a few events or conditions).
- Street ethnography (to discover how a cultural subgroup describes and structures its world at the street level).
- Elite or expert interviewing (for information from influential or well-informed people in an organization or community).
- Document analysis (to evaluate historical or contemporary confidential or public records, reports, government documents, and opinions).
- Proxemics and kinesics (to study the use of space and body-motion communication, respectively).[9]

> **We explore these techniques in detail in Chapter 9.**

An exploratory study is finished when the researchers have achieved the following:

- Established the range and scope of possible management decisions.
- Established the major dimensions of the research task.
- Defined a set of subsidiary investigative questions that can be used as guides to a detailed research design.

secondary data studies done by others and for different purposes than the one for which the data are being reviewed.

primary data original research where the data being collected are designed specifically to answer the research question.

> **We provide a detailed description of secondary data resources in Chapter 5 and on the text DVD.**

Delve, a full-service marketing research firm, admonishes its potential clients to remember that "face-to-face interaction is still one of the best ways to learn about people's experiences and impressions." www.delve.com

- Developed several hypotheses about possible causes of a management dilemma.
- Learned that certain other hypotheses are such remote possibilities that they can be safely ignored in any subsequent study.
- Concluded additional research is not needed or is not feasible.

Three exploratory techniques have wide applicability for the marketing researcher:

1. Secondary data analysis.
2. Experience surveys (one type within the category of individual interviews).
3. Focus groups (one type within the category of group interviews).

Secondary Data Analysis

The first step in an exploratory study is a search of secondary sources, sometimes called a *literature search*. Studies made by others for their own purposes represent **secondary data** to a researcher reviewing those studies to glean fresh insights for his or her own problem. If management could make an appropriate marketing decision based on those insights, it would be inefficient to discover anew through the collection of **primary data** (original research) what has already been discovered and reported.

Within secondary data exploration, a researcher should start first with an organization's own data archives. Reports of prior research studies often reveal extensive historical data or decision-making patterns. By reviewing prior studies, you can identify methodologies that proved successful and unsuccessful. Solutions that didn't receive attention in the past due to different environmental circumstances are revealed as potential ideas for further study. The researcher needs to avoid duplication in instances where prior collected data can provide sufficient information for resolving the current decision-making dilemma. Although MindWriter's CompleteCare program is new, one or more studies of the previous servicing practices are likely to reveal customer attitudes on which MindWriter based CompleteCare's current design.

The second source of secondary data is published documents prepared by authors outside the sponsor organization. There are tens of thousands of periodicals and hundreds of thousands of books on all aspects of marketing. Special catalogs, subject guides, and electronic indexes—available through most libraries—will help in this search. In many cases you can conduct a search online. Regarding MindWriter, thousands of articles have been written on customer service, and an Internet search using the keywords *customer service* and *computer repair* reveals thousands of hits.

A creative search of secondary sources will supply excellent background information as well as many good leads. Yet, if we confine the investigation to obvious subjects in bibliographic sources, we often miss much of the best information. Suppose the Point of Purchase Advertising Institute is interested in estimating the outlook for

in-store advertising over the next 10 years. We could search through the literature under the headings "in-store advertising," "point of sale," and "point of purchase." However, a search of these topics is restricting. When a search of the point-of-purchase industry is undertaken creatively, useful information also turns up under the following reference headings: "floor ads," "shelf talkers," "wobblers" (designed to attract shoppers' attention and trigger impulse sales as they dangle from store shelves), "register tapes," "in-store sampling," and "in-store coupons," just to name a few.

Experience Survey

Published data are seldom more than a fraction of the existing knowledge in a field. A significant portion of what is known on a topic, while in writing, may be proprietary to a given organization and thus unavailable to an outside searcher. Also, internal data archives are rarely well organized, making secondary sources, even when known, difficult to locate. Thus, tapping the collective memories and experiences of persons experienced in the area of study provides profitable information.

When we do a semistructured or unstructured interview with experts on a topic or a dimension of a topic, sometimes called an *expert interview* or *key informant survey*, we are conducting an **experience survey**. Don't be misled by the term *survey* here. This is not a scenario where an expert is checking off boxes next to predetermined responses on a questionnaire; it is an individual interview designed to extract as much information as possible from the expert's collective memory bank. We seek ideas about important issues or aspects of the subject to discover what is important across the subject's range of knowledge. The investigative format is usually flexible enough to explore various avenues that emerge during the interview. Broad questions, like those below, guide the discussion:

experience survey
semistructured or unstructured interviews with experts on a topic or dimension of a topic.

- What is being done?
- What has been tried in the past without success? With success?
- How have things changed? What are the change-producing elements of the situation?
- Who is involved in decisions? What role does each person play?
- What problem areas and barriers can be seen?
- What are the costs of the processes under study?
- Whom can we count on to assist and/or participate in the research?
- What are the priority areas?

The product of such questioning may be a new hypothesis, the discarding of old notions, or information about the practicality of doing the study. Probing may show whether certain facilities are available, what factors need to be controlled and how, and who will cooperate in the study.

Discovery is more easily carried out if the researcher can analyze cases that provide special insight. In exploration, we are less interested in getting a representative cross section than getting information from sources that might be perceptive. Assume we create an exploratory study of StarAuto's advertising. It has a history of executing creative, rule-bending approaches. People who might provide insightful information and could be identified for an experience survey include:

- *Potential car buyers*—those who recently began shopping for a car and thus are selectively perceptive to automobile advertising.
- *Dealer sales representatives*—persons whose job success is influenced by the success or failure of the advertising designed to draw prospects into a showroom.
- *Advertising columnists*—those with knowledge of what it takes to follow and break the rules in advertising; someone like Bob Garfield, the advertising columnist for *Advertising Age,* or Stuart Elliot, who writes for *The New York Times.*

- *Automotive industry analysts*—those who can provide perspective on how StarAuto is performing in the marketplace comparative to other brands.
- *Advertising industry analysts*—those who can provide insight into extreme examples of advertising and which advertising agencies are doing the work.
- *Advertising agency creative directors*—those charged with generating ideas for their clients that will stand out from the clutter.
- *Product or brand managers of automobile brands*—persons who can put StarAuto's advertising practices into the perspective of the overall marketing of automobiles.

During the early phase of their research for MindWriter, Jason and Sara plan to interview managers with expertise in three functions: (1) the service facility, (2) the call center, and (3) the contract courier service. Their emphasis will be on discovering not only what has been done in the past but also what change is feasible. For example, while exploration might indicate problems are a result of a staffing issue at the courier, MindWriter has no authority to hire or fire particular courier employees; it can only recommend terminating the contract with that particular courier service if resolution of the problem isn't forthcoming. Jason and Sara might want to expand the interviews to include long-term employees of the various departments, as their views are likely to be different from those of their managers. Because postpurchase service problems might be directly related to product design, expanding the experience survey to individuals associated with engineering and production could also be considered.

Focus Groups

focus group a discussion on a topic involving a small group of participants led by a trained moderator.

Focus groups became widely used in marketing research during the 1980s and are used for increasingly diverse research applications today.[10] A **focus group** is a group of people (typically made up of 6 to 10 participants), led by a trained moderator, who meet for 90 minutes to 2 hours. The facilitator or moderator uses group dynamics principles to focus or guide the group in an exchange of ideas, feelings, and experiences on a specific topic.

> **As the focus group is the most used qualitative research methodology, we study it in detail in Chapter 9.**

One topical objective of a focus group is a new product or product concept. The basic output of the session is a list of ideas and behavioral observations, with recommendations by the moderator. These ideas and observations are often used for later quantitative testing. As a group interview tool, focus groups have applied-research potential for other areas of marketing, particularly where the generation and evaluation of ideas or the assessment of needs is indispensable. In exploratory research, the qualitative data that focus groups produce may be used for enriching all levels of research questions and hypotheses and comparing the effectiveness of design options. The most common application of focus group research continues to be in the consumer arena. However, corporations are using focus group results for diverse exploratory applications.

> Descriptive Studies

In contrast to exploratory studies, more formalized studies are typically structured with clearly stated hypotheses or investigative questions. Formal studies serve a variety of research objectives:

1. Descriptions of phenomena or characteristics associated with a subject population (the *who, what, when, where*, and *how* of a topic).
2. Estimates of the frequency of appearance and the proportion of the population that has these characteristics.
3. Discovery of associations among different variables.

correlation the relationship by which two or more variables change together, such that systematic changes in one accompany systematic changes in the other.

The third study objective is sometimes labeled a correlational study, a subset of descriptive studies. **Correlation** is the relationship by which two or more variables change together,

Kool-Aid Regains Its Smile

What do you do when a venerable brand enjoying 100 percent awareness among moms and kids starts losing sales—even when it's still selling 500 million gallons per year? You call Sun Research Corp. (SRC) to reveal a strategy to stop the decline. SRC moderated 11 focus groups. Participants for each group were chosen to represent a market segment based on product usage. The focus groups revealed that heavy Kool-Aid users (those who use Kool-Aid at least 12 times a year) "aren't content to just add water to their Kool-Aid powder . . . [but] customize Kool-Aid by adding oranges, grapes, pineapples, fruit juice, and club soda. They also drink Kool-Aid year-round, and all family members drink it—it's not perceived as a beverage just for kids. In contrast, light/lapsed users are more likely to head out of the house for socializing."

A second round of five focus groups involving African-American households defined as heavy users and six more involving general-market and light/lapsed users were conducted by MLN Research (North Carolina), Mindy Goldberg & Associates (Philadelphia), and Marketing Resources (Maryland) to test the resulting ad campaigns. The heavy-user ad campaign, sporting the tagline "How do you like your Kool-Aid?" generated a 3 percent rise in sales among African-American households. A second campaign, for general and light/lapsed users and featuring Kool-Aid consumed from a portable thermos at a dog wash fund-raiser, helped generate a 2 percent sales rise in the overall market. The makers of Kool-Aid were all smiles at their 2.7 percent increase in market share during 2000.

www.kraftfoods.com

such that systematic changes in one accompany systematic changes in the other. The relationship is measured statistically with an index that represents how closely two variables covary—in unison or opposition. For example, young boys who play little-league baseball may be more likely to watch baseball games broadcast on TV or attend minor-league baseball games played in their home town stadium than are young men who do not play baseball.

A descriptive study may be simple or complex; it may be done in many settings. Whatever the form, a descriptive study can be just as demanding of research skills as the causal study, and we should insist on the same high standards for design and execution.

The simplest descriptive study concerns a question or hypothesis in which we ask or state something about the size, form, distribution, or existence of a variable. In the ongoing study at BankChoice, we are interested in understanding how well the bank is doing regarding customer satisfaction with their "personal banker" service. The research question might be, "What percentage of customers rate their satisfaction with BankChoice's 'personal banker' service as 'satisfied' or 'very satisfied'?" Using the hypothesis format we might predict, "80 percent or more of the customers rate their satisfaction with BankChoice's 'personal banker' service as 'satisfied' or 'very satisfied'."

> **The BankChoice example was first introduced in Chapter 5.**

We may also be interested in securing information about other variables related to perceptions of individualized service, such as the relative size of accounts, the number of accounts opened within the last six months, and the amount of activity (number of deposits and withdrawals per year) in accounts. Data on each of these variables, by themselves, may have value for management decisions. More complex relationships between these or other variables may be of even greater interest. Cross-tabulations between satisfaction ratings and account activity may suggest that differential rates of activity are related to personal attention. A cross-tabulation of account size and gender of account owner may also show a relationship. Such findings do not imply a causal relationship. In fact, our task is to determine if the variables are independent (or unrelated) and, if they are not, then to determine the strength or magnitude of the relationship. Neither procedure tells us which variable is the cause. For example, we might be able to conclude that gender and account size are related but not that gender is a causal factor in account size.

Descriptive studies are often much more complex than this example. One study of bank customers began as described and then went into much greater depth. Part of the study included an observation of account records that revealed highly satisfied customers had accounts that were typically larger and more active than those of customers who were neutral

The Woes of Cyber Shopping

Imagine that you walk into your favorite store and see dozens—even hundreds—of full shopping carts abandoned in the checkout aisles. You perceive that something is very wrong, but what? This is just the scenario online catalog vendors face. According to a Boston Consulting Group study, 65 percent of online shoppers abandon merchandise in their carts. Hanover Brands oversees 12 catalog operations including *International Male* and *The Company Store*. Telephone orders obtain a conversion rate of 99 percent, but online rates are far lower. The conversion rate indicates what percent of those calling to inquire about an item actually purchase the item. You might assume that a higher abandonment rate might be expected because the Internet encourages browsing. But Hanover wanted a higher online conversion rate without resorting to a button on its sites that connected the shopper to an expensive, live order taker. It set out to understand what caused abandonment and discover ways to eliminate such carts. First it used its database of e-mail addresses to conduct an e-mail survey. Then it conducted focus groups for more in-depth analysis. Finally, it hired BizRate to invite all online shoppers when logging off the site to evaluate the Web site, including the ordering experience, via an Internet survey. The research led to Hanover's antiabandonment program. Several early changes increased conversion rates of some sites by one-third. What did Hanover learn? Ditch the jargon of e-ordering and use the jargon of store shopping; add pictures to the cart (if a blue shirt is ordered, show the blue shirt) to reinforce selection and reduce cognitive dissonance; and if a customer abandons a cart before ordering, hold the cart with its merchandise—like a wish list—and encourage the shopper to return. Most, but not every, abandonment is based on a technical failure. Sometimes the shopper is just vacillating, needs to touch the merchandise, or wants reassurance that his or her credit card number will not be broadcast through cyberspace.

www.bcg.com; www.hanoverdirect.com; merchant.bizrate.com

about the personal banker services. A sample survey of customers provided information on stages in the family life cycle, attitudes toward savings, family income levels, and other matters. Correlation of this information with known satisfaction data showed that women owned larger accounts. Further investigation suggested that women with larger accounts were often widowed or working single women who were older than the average account holder. They called or visited the bank more frequently and spent more time with their personal banker than did males. Information about their attitudes, transaction practices, and account characteristics led to new business strategies at the bank.

Now let's look at the shopping behavior portion of the BankChoice study, where some evidence collected led to causal questions. The correlation between nearness to the office and the probability of having an account at the office suggested the question, "Why would people who live far from the office have an account there?" In this type of question a hypothesis makes its greatest contribution by pointing out directions that the research might follow. It might be hypothesized that:

1. Distant savers (operationally defined as those with addresses more than 2 miles from the office) have accounts at the office because they once lived near the office; they were near when the account decision was made.

2. Distant savers actually live near the office, but the address on the account is outside the 2-mile radius; they are near, but the records do not show this.

3. Distant savers work near the office; they are near by virtue of their work location.

4. Distant savers are not normally near the office but responded to a promotion that encouraged savers to bank via computer; this is another form of "nearness" in which this concept is transformed into one of "convenience."

When these hypotheses were tested, it was learned that a substantial portion of the distant savers could be accounted for by hypotheses 1 and 3. The conclusion: Location was closely related to saving at a given association. The determination of cause is not so simple, however, and these findings still fall within the definition of a descriptive study.

MindWriter could benefit from a descriptive study that profiles satisfied service customers versus dissatisfied ones. Service customer characteristics could then be matched with specific types of service problems—for example, geographic location with equipment overheating, or high humidity rates with corrosion damage, or gender with keyboard malfunctions—which could lead to identifying changes in product design or customer service policies.

> Causal Studies

The correlation between satisfaction with BankChoice's personal bankers and low probability of switching to another bank looks like strong evidence to some, but the researcher with scientific training will argue that correlation is not causation. Because two things change together does not imply a cause-and-effect relationship. For example, the stork population and human birth rate have both declined in Europe for the last 50 years; the number of telephone poles in a metropolitan area correlates with the number of heart attacks; and the marriage rate in the United States falls to its lowest level in January, when the national death rate peaks. In these instances, no one claims storks bring babies, or telephone poles cause heart attacks, or people die when they decide not to marry.

The essential element of **causation**, found in experimentation, is that some external factor "produces" a change in the dependent variable. A "produces" B or A "forces" B to occur. But that is an artifact of language, not what really happens. Empirically, we never demonstrate an A-B causality with certainty because we do not prove causal linkages deductively. Empirical research conclusions are inferences—inductive conclusions. These conclusions are probability statements, based on what we observe and measure and what we conclude is likely to happen. Many marketing studies seek to know not only *how* variables change in a descriptive fashion but *why*. The goal in such studies is to derive inferences about the *cause-and-effect* relationships in order to better understand, explain, or predict.

If we consider the possible relationships that can occur between two variables, we can conclude there are three possibilities:

- Symmetrical
- Reciprocal
- Asymmetrical[11]

A **symmetrical relationship** is one in which two variables vary together but we assume the changes in neither variable are due to changes in the other. Symmetrical conditions are most often found when two variables are alternate indicators of another cause or independent variable. We might conclude that a correlation between low sales contest involvement and low sales productivity is the result of (dependent on) another factor, such as poor or inadequate sales training.

A **reciprocal relationship** exists when two variables mutually influence or reinforce each other. This could occur if the reading of an advertisement leads to the use of a brand of product. The usage, in turn, sensitizes the person to notice and read more of the advertising of that particular brand.

Most research analysts look for **asymmetrical relationships**. With these we postulate that changes in one variable (the *independent variable, or IV*) are responsible for changes in another variable (the *dependent variable, or DV*). The identification of the IV and DV is often obvious, but sometimes the choice is not clear. In the latter cases we evaluate independence and dependence on the basis of:

1. *The degree to which each variable may be altered.* The relatively unalterable variable is the independent variable (e.g., age, social status, present packaging design).

2. *The time order between the variables.* The independent variable precedes the dependent variable.

causation situation where one variable leads to a specified effect on the other variable.

> **You may find it valuable to refer to Exhibit 3-2 as you read this section.**

symmetrical relationship when two variables vary together but without causation.

reciprocal relationship when two variables mutually influence or reinforce each other.

asymmetrical relationship when a change in one variable (IV) is responsible for a change in another variable (DV).

> **Definitions of the various types of variables are found in Chapter 3.**

> **Exhibit 8-3** Four Types of Asymmetrical Causal Relationships

Relationship Type	Nature of Relationship	Examples
Stimulus-Response	An event or change results in a response from some object.	• A change in commission structure leads to a higher level of agent sales. • A change in government economic policy restricts corporate financial decisions. • A price increase results in fewer unit sales.
Property-Disposition	An existing property causes a disposition.	• Age and attitudes about saving. • Gender and attitudes about financial services. • Social class and opinions about value of a college education.
Disposition-Behavior	A disposition causes a specific behavior.	• Favorable opinion about a brand and its purchase. • Job satisfaction and worker sales level. • Moral values and shoplifting.
Property-Behavior	An existing property causes a specific behavior.	• Stage of the family life cycle and purchase of furniture. • Social class and family savings patterns. • Age and sports participation.

Definitions
A *stimulus* is an event or force (e.g., drop in temperature, crash of stock market, product recall, or explosion in a factory). A *response* is a decision or reaction. A *property* is an enduring characteristic of a subject that does not depend on circumstances for its activation (e.g., age, gender, religious affiliation, ethnic group, physical condition). A *disposition* is a tendency to respond in a certain way under certain circumstances (e.g., attitudes, opinions, habits, values, and drives). A *behavior* is an action (e.g., consumption practices, work performance, interpersonal acts).

Exhibit 8-3 describes the four types of asymmetrical relationships: stimulus-response, property-disposition, disposition-behavior, and property-behavior. Experiments usually involve stimulus-response relationships. Property-disposition relationships are often studied in business and social science research. Much of ex post facto research involves relationships between properties, dispositions, and behaviors.

Testing Causal Hypotheses

When testing causal hypotheses, we seek three types of evidence:

1. Covariation between A and B.
   - Do we find that A and B occur together in the way hypothesized?
   - When A does not occur, is there also an absence of B?
   - When there is more or less of A, does one also find more or less of B?
2. Time order of events moving in the hypothesized direction.
   - Does A occur before B?
3. No other possible causes of B.
   - Can one determine that C, D, and E do not covary with B in a way that suggests possible causal connections?

Causation and Experimental Design

To be convincing, inferences from experimental designs must meet two other requirements, in addition to the three listed. The first is referred to as **control**. All factors, with the exception of the independent variable, must be held constant and must not be confounded with another variable that is not part of the study. The second requirement is that each person in the study must have an equal chance for exposure to each level of the independent variable. This is accomplished through **random assignment** of subjects to groups.

In this example, assume you wish to conduct a survey of York College's alumni to enlist their support for a new program. There are two different appeals, one largely emotional and the other much more logical in its approach. Before mailing out appeal letters to 50,000 alumni, you conduct an experiment to see whether the emotional or the rational appeal will draw the greater response. You choose a sample of 300 names from the alumni list and divide them into three groups of 100 each. Two of these groups are designated as experimental groups. One gets the emotional appeal and the other gets the logical appeal. The third group is the **control group** and it receives no appeal.

Covariation in this case is expressed by the percentage of alumni who respond in relation to the appeal used. Suppose 50 percent of those who receive the emotional appeal respond, while only 35 percent of those receiving the logical appeal respond. Control group members, unaware of the experiment, respond at a 5 percent rate—maybe they hear about the appeal from a friend, but not from the university. We would conclude that using the emotional appeal enhances response probability.

The time sequence of events was not a problem. There could be no chance that the alumni support led to sending the letter requesting support. Could some confounding factor (other than the appeal) have produced the same results? One can anticipate that certain factors are particularly likely to confound the results and can control these factors. If the question studied is of concern only to alumni who attended the university as undergraduates, those who attended only graduate school should be excluded, thus controlling this factor.

A second approach to control uses **matching**. There might be reason to believe that different ratios of alumni support will come from various age groups. To control by matching, we ensure all groups are essentially equal with respect to the variable of influence—that age distribution of alumni is the same in all three groups.

Even after using such controls, however, one cannot match or exclude other possible confounding variables. These are dealt with through random assignment of participants to each group.

Randomness must be secured in a carefully controlled fashion according to strict rules of assignment so that each group of alumni receives its fair share of different known factors. The researcher, using statistical significance tests, can estimate the probable effect of chance variations on the DV and can then compare this estimated effect of extraneous variation to the actual differences found in the DV in the experimental and control groups.

We emphasize that random assignment of subjects to experimental and control groups is the *basic technique* by which the two groups can be made equivalent. Matching and other control forms are supplemental ways of improving the quality of measurement. In a sense, matching and controls reduce the extraneous "noise" in the measurement system and in this way improve the sensitivity of measurement of the hypothesized relationship.

Causation and Ex Post Facto Design

Prior to the incidents following September 11, 2001, researchers at the Centers for Disease Control (CDC) in Atlanta did not have the ability to conclude that anthrax spores delivered via a letter carried by the United States Postal Service (USPS) would be capable of causing inhalation anthrax. Contracting this fatal disease was considered possible only if one were exposed to a large concentration of spores. An unrealistic research design would involve

control when all factors but the IV are held constant and not confounded with another variable that is not part of the study.

random assignment uses a randomized list of participants for assigning participants to test groups.

control group a group of participants that is measured but not exposed to the independent variable being studied.

matching an equalizing process for assigning participants to experimental and control groups.

> **Experimentation is covered in detail in Chapter 12.**

the assignment of people to two groups—one to receive anthrax spores via letter and one to receive no exposure to anthrax spores. This would test a hypothesis about the consequences of inhalation. However, after several deaths resulting from suspicious mail deliveries, causation was assumed although the CDC could not link at least one inhalation anthrax death to the USPS handling of a suspicious letter. Does this mean that the causal conclusion of the CDC drawn from facts collected after the deaths (that one or more letters contaminated with anthrax spores caused the deaths of several individuals) cannot be supported?

Many research studies cannot be carried out experimentally by manipulating variables. Yet we still are interested in the question of causation. Instead of manipulating and/or controlling exposure to an experimental variable, we study subjects who have been exposed to the independent factor and those who have not.

Consider the situation in which some Winn-Dixie grocery shoppers have developed a pattern of high coupon redemption. In searching for hypotheses to explain this phenomenon, we discover that most of these shoppers are members of a shopping club. Has membership in the shopping club caused increased coupon redemption at Winn-Dixie? It is not practical or realistic to structure an experiment. This would require that we assign participants to join the shopping club and then determine whether this affects their coupon redemption. Since the shopping club sells several of the product categories that Winn-Dixie sells, it isn't likely that Winn-Dixie managers would want to send low-redemption Winn-Dixie customers to its competitors to test their hypothesis.

The better approach would be to collect shopping club membership information during the process of enrolling shoppers in the Winn-Dixie savings program (Winn-Winn at Winn-Dixie!). Then there are two groups to monitor: those with shopping club membership and those without. Their coupon redemption data might look something like those in Exhibit 8-4. The data suggest that membership in the shopping club might be reflected by higher coupon redemption when the members shop at Winn-Dixie. Certainly the covariation evidence is consistent with this conclusion. But is there other evidence to give us even greater confidence in our conclusion?

What about the time order of events? If high redemption were found only after joining the club, this would be good evidence in support of our hypothesis. If high redemption occurs before joining the shopping club, the time order does not support our hypothesis as well.

> **Exhibit 8-4** Data on Shopping Club Membership

Coupon Redemption	Shopping Club Membership	
	Yes	No
High	280	10
Low	40	40

> **Exhibit 8-5** Cross-Tabulated Data on Shopping Club Membership

Household Size	Shopping Club Member		Not a Shopping Club Member	
	High Redemption	Low Redemption	High Redemption	Low Redemption
2 or fewer	48	30	6	36
3 or 4	117	35	4	4
5 or more	115	5	0	0

Of course, other factors could be causing the high redemption among the club members. Using control techniques will improve our ability to draw firm conclusions. First, in drawing a sample of non–shopping club members, we can choose a random sample from the files of all Winn-Dixie shoppers. Then we can gather information about potentially confounding factors and use these data to make cross-classification comparisons. Assume we also gather family size data on the shoppers under study and introduce this as a cross-classification variable; the results might look like those in Exhibit 8-5 on previous page. Shoppers with larger families are more likely to be among the high redeemers of coupons. Part of the high redemption rate among club members seems to be associated with the fact that most club members have larger families. Within family size groupings, it is also apparent that shopping club members have a higher incidence of high coupon redemption than nonmembers with the same family size. So does shopping club membership cause higher redemption of coupons at Winn-Dixie?

> **More will be said about the analysis of cross tabulation and the interpretation of relationships in Chapter 22.**

The ex post facto design is widely used in marketing research and often is the only approach feasible. In particular, one seeks causal explanations between variables that are impossible to manipulate and subjects that usually cannot be assigned to treatment and control groups. Thorough testing, validating of multiple hypotheses, and controlling for confounding variables are essential with ex post facto designs.

>summary

1 A research design is the strategy for a study and the plan by which the strategy is to be carried out. It specifies the methods and procedures for the collection, measurement, and analysis of data. Some major descriptors of designs are:

- Exploratory versus formalized.
- Observational versus interrogation/communication.
- Experimental versus ex post facto.
- Descriptive versus causal.
- Cross-sectional versus longitudinal.
- Case versus statistical.
- Field versus laboratory versus simulation.
- Subjects' perceptions: no deviations, some deviations, or researcher-induced deviations.

2 Exploratory research is appropriate for the total study in topic areas where the developed data are limited. In most other studies, exploration is the first stage of a project and is used to orient the researcher and the study. The objective of exploration is the development of hypotheses, not testing.

Formalized studies, including descriptive and causal, are those with substantial structure, specific hypotheses to be tested, or research questions to be answered. Descriptive studies are those used to describe phenomena associated

with a subject population or to estimate proportions of the population that have certain characteristics. Causal studies seek to discover the effect that a variable(s) has on another (or others) or why certain outcomes are obtained.

3 The relationships that occur between two variables may be symmetrical, reciprocal, or asymmetrical. Of greatest interest to the research analyst are asymmetrical relationships, which may be classified as any of the following types:

- Stimulus-response
- Property-disposition
- Disposition-behavior
- Property-behavior

We test causal hypotheses by (1) measuring the covariation among variables, (2) determining the time order relationships among variables, and (3) ensuring that other factors do not confound the explanatory relationships. Where possible, we try to achieve the ideal of experimental design with random assignment of subjects, matching of subject characteristics, and manipulation and control of variables. Using these methods and techniques, we measure relationships as accurately and objectively as possible.

>**key**terms

asymmetrical relationship 205	causation 205	control group 207
case study 194	communication study 195	correlation 202
causal study 194	control 207	cross-sectional study 195

>**discussion**questions

Terms in Review

1 Distinguish between the following:

   a Exploratory and formal studies.

   b Experimental and ex post facto research designs.

   c Descriptive and causal studies.

2 Establishing causality is difficult, whether conclusions have been derived inductively or deductively.

   a Explain and elaborate on the implications of this statement.

   b Why is ascribing causality more difficult when conclusions have been reached through induction?

   c Correlation does not imply causation. Illustrate this point with examples from business.

3 Using yourself as the subject, give an example of each of the following asymmetrical relationships:

   a Stimulus-response

   b Property-disposition

   c Disposition-behavior

   d Property-behavior

4 Why not use more control variables rather than depend on randomization as the means of controlling extraneous variables?

5 Researchers seek causal relationships by either experimental or ex post facto research designs.

   a In what ways are these two approaches similar?

   b In what ways are they different?

Making Research Decisions

6 You have been asked to determine how hospitals prepare and train volunteers. Since you know relatively little about this subject, how will you find out? Be as specific as possible.

7 You are the administrative assistant for a division chief in a large holding company that owns several hotels and theme parks. You and the division chief have just come from the CEO's office, where you were informed that the guest complaints related to housekeeping and employee attitude are increasing. Your on-site managers have mentioned some tension among the workers but have not considered it unusual. The CEO and your division chief instruct you to investigate. Suggest at least three different types of research that might be appropriate in this situation.

8 Propose one or more hypotheses for each of the following variable pairs, specifying which is the IV and which is the DV. Then develop the basic hypothesis to include at least one moderating variable or intervening variable.

   a The Index of Consumer Confidence and the business cycle.

   b Level of worker output and closeness of worker supervision.

   c Student GPA and level of effort in a class required by student's major.

Behind the Scenes

9 Using the eight design descriptors, profile the MindWriter CompleteCare satisfaction study as described in this and preceding chapters.

From Concept to Practice

10 Use the eight design descriptors in Exhibit 8-2 to profile the research described in the chapter Snapshots.

>**www**exercise

As a market, China has not yet delivered on its vast potential. Assume your firm is considering marketing a food product there and discovered during exploration the China Health and Nutrition Study (**http://www.cpc.unc.edu/china/**). This was a joint project of The Carolina Population Center at the University of North Carolina at Chapel Hill, the Institute of Nutrition and Food Hygiene, and the Chinese Academy of Preventive Medicine. Describe the research design of this study.

>**cases**[*]

Calling Up Attendance

Campbell-Ewald: R-E-S-P-E-C-T Spells Loyalty

Donatos: Finding the New Pizza

Gathering Marketing Information

Goodyear's Aquatred

Inquiring Minds Want to Know—NOW!

John Deere and Company

McDonald's Tests Catfish Sandwich

Open Doors: Extending Hospitality to Travelers with Disabilities

Overdue Bills

Ramada Demonstrates Its *Personal Best*™

State Farm: Dangerous Intersections

Sturgel Division

Volkswagen's Beetle

Yahoo!: *Consumer Direct* Marries Purchase Metrics to Banner Ads

* All cases, both written and video, are on the text DVD. The film icon indicates a video case. Check the DVD Index to determine whether a case has data, the research instrument, or other supplementary material.

chapter 9

Qualitative Research

>learningobjectives

After reading this chapter, you should understand . . .

1 How qualitative methods differ from quantitative methods.

2 The controversy surrounding qualitative research.

3 The types of marketing decisions that use qualitative methods.

4 The different qualitative research methods.

Researchers, as they gain experience and progress up the ranks within a research firm, acquire a variety of specialized skills. At Visionary Insights, Sara Armstrong's prior experience as a focus group moderator made her a natural to serve as a replacement when one of the moderators couldn't handle a client group due to a schedule conflict. Sara has just returned from her stint as a group moderator.

"Welcome back," Chance Bedford, Visionary Insights senior VP, comments as he stops just outside Sara Armstrong's office. "Any problems?"

"Thanks. Glad to be back. Moderating the Atlanta HealthPlus frozen-food groups was rather like slipping on comfortable shoes. While I hadn't planned to moderate any sessions this time, I was involved in developing the discussion guide. And I observed the Webcast of the San Francisco and Detroit groups just last week, so it was easy to step in. We'll be starting the report preparation for HealthPlus shortly."

"Sara, we're lucky to have someone on staff with the extensive qualitative research experience that you have," compliments Chance.

"Thanks," smiles Sara. "Jason stopped me on the way in. He said the transcripts were delivered Friday for the San Francisco group and the Detroit ones should be ready this afternoon, with Atlanta arriving by Wednesday. I'm just unearthing my observation notes from San Francisco now, so I can compare them with the transcripts.

"We captured some critical comments that I'm sure will be helpful in developing the new HealthPlus ad campaign," shares Sara as she extracts the desired transcripts from the file folders on her desk. From the size of the stack, she'd be doing a fair amount of reading in the next few days. "HealthPlus was right when it surmised that consumers are skeptical that something healthy can taste good. But we've also learned there are some triggers we can use in the advertising to get them to embrace the idea of eating healthy."

"HealthPlus certainly seems well positioned given the growing concern over rampant obesity, especially among youth," observes Chance. "I'll look forward to seeing your insights."

"Do you know if Sam has started NUD*IST yet?" asks Sara.

"Is NUD*IST the software that provides the preliminary analysis on the focus group transcripts' content?" asks Chance. At Sara's affirmative nod, he responds, "Then, yes, he has the San Francisco transcript in process. This is the first time I had the opportunity to see the process in action. NUD*IST is impressive."

"It saves us a lot of time," comments Sara. "By the way, the Atlanta facility was equipped with the newest version of FocusVision's VideoMarker, for marking the focus group video. That's the first time I've used the marking feature as a moderator. They promised me the marked CD by early next week. It's going to save a lot of time in preparing the client presentation."

Chance smiles. Sara's enthusiasm is always strong for anything digital or electronic. "Well, it looks like you have things well in hand, as usual, Sara. I'll want you with the team for the preliminary project meeting with LeapFrog at 4:00."

"Right," comments Sara as she looks up from sorting note files and transcripts, "the learning-toy producer that wants concept testing—I'll be there."

(Quantitative vs. Qualitative)

> What Is Qualitative Research?

Marketers basically do marketing research to understand how and why things happen. If the marketer needs to know only what happened, or how often things happened, quantitative research methodologies would serve the purpose. But to understand the different meanings that people place on their experiences often requires research techniques that delve more deeply into people's hidden interpretations, understandings, and motivations. Qualitative research is designed to tell the researcher how (process) and why (meaning) things happen as they do.

❝ Most of what influences what we say and do occurs below the level of awareness. That's why we need new techniques: to get at hidden knowledge—to get at what people don't know they know. ❞

Jerry Zaltman
Harvard University (creator of ZMET methodology)

qualitative research
interpretive techniques that seek to describe, decode, translate, and otherwise come to terms with the meaning, not the frequency, of certain phenomena.

> **Observation as a methodology deserves special attention and is covered in detail in Chapter 10.**

Qualitative research includes an "array of interpretive techniques which seek to describe, decode, translate, and otherwise come to terms with the meaning, not the frequency, of certain more or less naturally occurring phenomena in the social world."[1] Qualitative techniques are used at both the data collection and data analysis stages of a research project. At the data collection stage, the array of techniques includes focus groups, individual depth interviews (IDIs), case studies, ethnography, grounded theory, action research, and observation. During analysis, the qualitative researcher uses content analysis of written or recorded materials drawn from personal expressions by participants, behavioral observations, and debriefing of observers, as well as the study of artifacts and trace evidence from the physical environment.

Qualitative research aims to achieve an in-depth understanding of a situation, whether it explains why a person entering a Kroger grocery proceeds down each aisle in turn or heads for the rear of the store and chooses only alternate aisles thereafter or explains why some advertisements make us laugh and contribute to our commitment to a brand while others generate outrage and boycotts. Judith Langer, a noted qualitative researcher, indicates that qualitative research is ideal if you want to extract feelings, emotions, motivations, perceptions, consumer "language," or self-described behavior.[2] Exhibit 9-1 offers some examples of appropriate uses of qualitative research in marketing.

Qualitative research draws data from a variety of sources, including the following:[3]

• People (individuals or groups)
• Organizations or institutions
• Texts (published, including virtual ones)
• Settings and environments (visual/sensory and virtual material)
• Objects, artifacts, media products (textual/visual/sensory and virtual material)
• Events and happenings (textual/visual/sensory and virtual material)

In this chapter we will focus on the qualitative methods that draw data from people and organizations. The next chapter focuses on observation studies, which many authors consider an important contribution to qualitative data and which also contribute to the last four categories above.

> Qualitative versus Quantitative Research

The Controversy

Qualitative research methodologies have roots in a variety of disciplines, including anthropology, sociology, psychology, linguistics, communication, economics, and semiotics. Historically, qualitative methodologies have been available much longer—some as early as the 19th century—than the quantitative tools marketers rely on so heavily. Possibly because of

>**snap**shot

Dreamworks: Qualitative Research Reveals Futuristic Effects

Imagine you are Stephen Spielberg. You are in the planning stages of a movie that takes place in 2054, when "technology has advanced to the point where crimes can be detected before they are committed." So where do you start? What will the future be like? What special effects will seem plausible, yet stimulating, to today's audience? What special effects will help move the story line of a police officer hunted for a crime he hasn't yet committed?

Spielberg invited 23 of the best futuristic minds to join him for a three-day retreat. Each brought expertise in a special area: entertainment, transportation, the environment, social issues, law enforcement, even advertising. Between them they conceived

hundreds of mind-pictures that Spielberg's creative genius turned into special effects, hundreds of which he was convinced the audience would never even perceive as they watched *Minority Report*, starring Tom Cruise. The movie debuted on June 21, 2002, with an opening box office weekend generating $35.6 million. Within the first 73 days it had grossed $130.6 million. By the end of December, the worldwide gross for *Minority Report* had reached $342 million. The special effects are all the more real for their basis in present-day facts shared by those futurists via qualitative research sessions with Spielberg.

www.dreamworks.com; www.foxmovies.com

>**Exhibit 9-1** Some Appropriate Uses for Qualitative Research

Marketing Arena	Question to Be Answered
Market Segmentation	• Why does one demographic or lifestyle group use our product more than another? • Who are our customers, and how do they use our product to support their lifestyle? • What is the influence of culture on product choice?
Advertising Concept Development	• What images should we use to connect with our target customer?
New Product Development	• What would our current market think of a proposed product idea? • We need new products, but what should they be to take advantage of our existing customer-perceived strengths? • How will consumers embrace a new technology within their home? What are their future intentions?
Sales Analysis	• Why have once-loyal customers stopped buying?
Sales Development	• What actions could we take to boost industry sales?
Package Design	• How do customers use our package? How will considered modifications influence their perception of our product? How will considered modifications influence their use of our product?
Brand Image	• How does our brand image compare to our competitors' images? What could we do to make our product more distinctive? • What adds value to our brand?
Positioning	• Should we project our new car as a power symbol or an aid for sexual attraction and social acceptance? How should we talk about our product to distinguish it from competitors'?
Retail Design	• How do consumers prefer to shop in our store? Do they shop with a defined purpose, or are they affected by other motives?
Process Understanding	• What steps are involved in cleaning a wood floor? How is our product perceived or involved in this process?

their origins, qualitative methods don't enjoy the unqualified endorsement of upper management. Many senior managers maintain qualitative data are too subjective and susceptible to human error and bias in data collection and interpretation. They believe such research provides an unstable foundation for expensive and critical marketing decisions. The fact that results cannot be generalized from a qualitative study to a larger population is considered a fundamental weakness.

Increasingly, however, marketers are returning to these techniques as quantitative techniques fall short of providing the insights needed to make those ever-more-expensive marketing decisions. Marketers deal with the issue of trustworthiness of qualitative data through exacting methodology:[4]

- Carefully using literature searches to build probing questions.
- Thoroughly justifying the methodology or combination of methodologies chosen.
- Executing the chosen methodology in its natural setting (field study) rather than a highly controlled setting (laboratory).
- Choosing sample participants for relevance to the breadth of the issue rather than how well they represent the target population.
- Developing and including questions that reveal the exceptions to a rule or theory.
- Carefully structuring the data analysis.
- Comparing data across multiple sources and different contexts.
- Conducting peer-researcher debriefing on results for added clarity, additional insights, and reduced bias.

The Distinction

quantitative research the precise count of some behavior, knowledge, opinion, or attitude.

To understand the distinctions between qualitative and quantitative methodologies, let's define the latter. **Quantitative research** attempts precise measurement of something. In marketing research, quantitative methodologies usually measure consumer behavior, knowledge, opinions, or attitudes. Such methodologies answer questions related to how much, how often, how many, when, and who. While the survey is not the only methodology of the quantitative researcher, it is considered a dominant one.

The purpose of qualitative research is based on "researcher immersion in the phenomenon to be studied, gathering data which provide a detailed description of events, situations and interaction between people and things, [thus] providing depth and detail."[5] Quantitative research is often used for theory testing (Will a $1-off instant coupon or a $1.50 mail-in rebate generate more sales for Kellogg's Special K?), requiring that the researcher maintain a distance from the research so as not to bias the results. Qualitative research—sometimes labeled *interpretive research* because it seeks to develop understanding through detailed description—often builds theory but rarely tests it.

> 66 Polls and focus groups do a good job on issues where people have made up their minds, but there are a number of gridlock issues laden with complex trade-offs that people haven't thought out. 99
>
> *Daniel Yankelovich*
> *Creator of Yankelovich Monitor and ViewPoint Learning*

Besides the purpose of the research, this process sets up several key distinctions between qualitative and quantitative research, elaborated in Exhibit 9-2, including level of researcher involvement; sampling methodology and size; data collection processes, including participant preparation and researcher and research sponsor involvement; data type and preparation; data analysis and timing; processes for reaching insights and meaning; time frame of insight discovery; and the level of data security.[6]

Unlike the case with quantitative data, both the researcher and research sponsor often have more significant involvement in collecting and interpreting qualitative data. The

>**Exhibit 9-2** Qualitative versus Quantitative Research

	Qualitative	Quantitative
Focus of Research	• Understanding and interpretation	• Describe, explain, and predict
Researcher Involvement	• High—researcher is participant or catalyst	• Limited; controlled to prevent bias
Research Purpose	• In-depth understanding; theory building	• Describe or predict; build and test theory
Sample Design	• Nonprobability: purposive	• Probability
Sample Size	• Small	• Large
Research Design	• May evolve or adjust during the course of the project • Often uses multiple methodologies simultaneously or sequentially • Consistency is not expected • Involves longitudinal approach	• Determined before commencing the project • Uses single or mixed method • Consistency is critical • Involves either a cross-sectional or a longitudinal approach
Participant Preparation	• Pretasking is common	• No preparation desired to avoid biasing the participant
Data Type and Preparation	• Verbal or pictorial descriptions • Reduced to verbal codes (sometimes with computer assistance)	• Verbal descriptions • Reduced to numerical codes for computerized analysis
Data Analysis	• Human analysis following computer or human coding; primarily nonquantitative • Forces researcher to see the contextual framework of the phenomenon being measured—distinction between facts and judgments less clear • Always ongoing during the project	• Computerized analysis—statistical and mathematical methods dominate • Analysis may be ongoing during the project • Maintains clear distinction between facts and judgments
Insights and Meaning	• Deeper level of understanding is the norm; determined by type and quantity of free-response questions • Researcher participation in data collection allows insights to form and be tested during the process	• Limited by the opportunity to probe respondents and the quality of the original data collection instrument • Insights follow data collection and data entry, with limited ability to reinterview participants
Research Sponsor Involvement	• May participate by observing research in real time or via taped interviews	• Rarely has either direct or indirect contact with participant
Feedback Turnaround	• Smaller sample sizes make data collection faster for shorter possible turnaround • Insights are developed as the research progresses, shortening data analysis	• Larger sample sizes lengthen data collection; Internet methodologies are shortening turnaround but inappropriate for many studies • Insight development follows data collection and entry, lengthening research process; interviewing software permits some tallying of responses as data collection progresses
Data Security	• More absolute given use of restricted access facilities and smaller sample sizes	• Act of research in progress is often known by competitors; insights may be gleaned by competitors for some visible, field-based studies

Source: This exhibit was developed from material extracted from Judith Langer, *The Mirrored Window: Focus Groups from a Moderator's Point of View* (Ithaca, NY: Paramount Market Publishing, 2001); Hy Mariampolski, *Qualitative Market Research: A Comprehensive Guide* (Thousand Oaks, CA: Sage Publications, 2001); and David Carson, Audrey Gilmore, Chad Perry, and Kjell Gronhaug, *Qualitative Marketing Research* (Thousand Oaks, CA: Sage Publications, 2001).

>**Exhibit 9-3** Qualitative Research and the Research Process

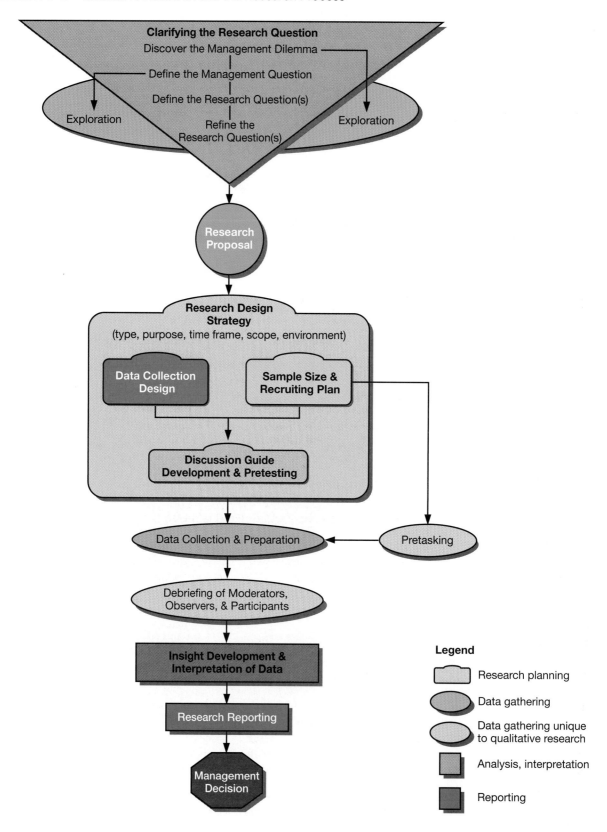

researcher may serve as a participant or a catalyst, as a participant observer, or as a group interview moderator. The research sponsor may observe (in some cases via Webcast of interviews directly to the sponsor's desktop computer), influence interview questions, and add interpretations and insights during the process. By contrast, with large quantitative studies, the researcher who interprets the data and draws conclusions from it is rarely the data collector and often has no contact at all with the participant.

Since researchers are immersed in the participant's world, any knowledge they gain can be used to adjust the data extracted from the next participant. In quantitative research, identical data are desired from all participants, so evolution of methodology is not acceptable.

Quantitative data often consist of participant responses that are coded, categorized, and reduced to numbers so that these data may be manipulated for statistical analysis. One objective is the quantitative tally of events or opinions, called *frequency of response.* Qualitative data are all about texts. Detailed descriptions of events, situations, and interactions, either verbal or visual, constitute the data. Data may be contained within transcriptions of interviews or video focus groups, as well as in notes taken during those interactions. But by definition they generate reams of words that need to be coded and analyzed by humans for meaning. While computer software is increasingly used for the coding process in qualitative research, at the heart of the qualitative process is the researcher—and his or her experience—framing and interpreting the data.[7]

Qualitative studies with their smaller sample sizes offer an opportunity for faster turnaround of findings. While speed should never be the primary reason for choosing a methodology, qualitative data may be especially useful to support a low-risk decision that must be made quickly.

Multimillion-dollar marketing strategies may lose their market persuasiveness if the competitor reacts too quickly. Data security is therefore of increasing concern. Both group and individual interviewing, the mainstay techniques of qualitative research, can be conducted in highly secure environments. In comparison, once a quantitative survey or field observation or experiment is started, it is quickly common knowledge among a research sponsor's competitors. While the data might not be known, the area of inquiry often can be determined. For example, in a test market—an experimental quantitative design—a research sponsor's competitors can often observe and extract insights right along with the sponsor.

> The Process of Qualitative Research

The process of developing a qualitative project is similar to the research process introduced in Chapter 4. However, three key distinctions suggested in the previous sections do affect the research process: (1) the level of question development in the management-research question hierarchy prior to the commencing of qualitative research, (2) the preparation of the participant prior to the research experience, and (3) the nature and level of data that come from the debriefing of interviewers or observers.

The qualitative researcher starts with an understanding of the marketer's problem, but the management-research question hierarchy is rarely developed prior to the design of research methodology. Rather, the research is guided by a broader question more similar in structure to the management question. Exhibit 9-3 introduces the modifications to the research process.

Much of qualitative research involves the deliberate preparation of the participant, called preexercises or **pretasking**. This step is important due to the desire to extract detail and meaning from the participant. A variety of creative and mental exercises draw participants' understanding of their own thought processes and ideas to the surface. Some of these include:

pretasking exercises to prepare participants for individual or group interviews on a topic.

- Placing the product or medium for in-home use (with instructions to use the product or medium—e.g., a magazine—repeatedly over the preparation period before the interview).

- Having the participants bring visual stimuli (e.g., family photos of areas or rooms in their homes that they hate to clean or have trouble decorating, or a favorite item of clothing).

- Having the participants prepare a visual collage (e.g., taking pictures over several weeks, with a one-time-use camera, of their children's favorite outfits for different purposes or situations or cutting pictures out of magazines that reflect how they feel when using a particular product or brand).

- Having the participants keep detailed diaries of behavior and perceptions (e.g., a record of their step-by-step experience preparing a meal using a particular product).

- Having the participants draw a picture of an experience (e.g., what they felt like when they last shopped in a particular store).

- Having the participants write a dialog of a hypothetical experience (e.g., how a conversation between the participant and a sales associate would progress when a complaint was not resolved).[8]

Pretasking is rarely used in observation studies and is considered a major source of error in quantitative studies.

In quantitative research unless a researcher is collecting his or her own data, interviewers or data collectors are rarely involved in the data interpretation or analysis stages. While data collectors contribute to the accuracy of data preparation, their input is rarely, if ever, sought in the development of data interpretations. In qualitative studies, due to the higher level of involvement of both the sponsor and the interviewer/data collector, these parties in the process are often debriefed or interviewed, with their insight adding richness to the interpretation of the data. Exhibit 9-4 provides an example of research question formation for a qualitative project.

> Qualitative Research Methodologies

The researcher chooses a qualitative methodology based on the project's purpose; its schedule, including the speed with which insights are needed; its budget; the issue(s) or topics(s) being studied; the types of participants needed; and the researcher's skill, personality, and preferences.

The Internet has made a world of difference in qualitative research, especially to the IDI and focus group. Invoke Solutions' Dynamic Survey methodology, which combines quantitative and qualitative techniques, won the 2004 American Marketing Association EXPLOR award for technical excellence in online research. With Dynamic Survey, a moderator coordinates responses of up to 200 participants in a single live online session that lasts between 60 and 90 minutes.
www.invoke.com

>**Exhibit 9-4** Formulating the Qualitative Research Question

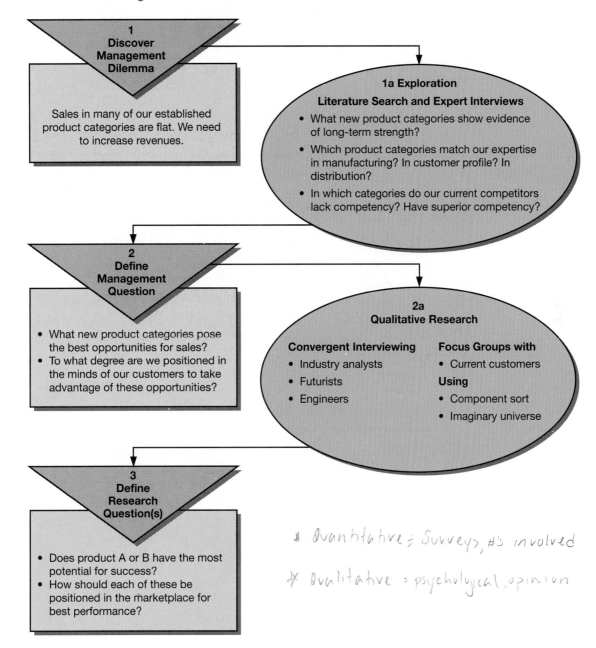

1
Discover
Management
Dilemma

Sales in many of our established product categories are flat. We need to increase revenues.

1a Exploration
Literature Search and Expert Interviews

- What new product categories show evidence of long-term strength?
- Which product categories match our expertise in manufacturing? In customer profile? In distribution?
- In which categories do our current competitors lack competency? Have superior competency?

2
Define
Management
Question

- What new product categories pose the best opportunities for sales?
- To what degree are we positioned in the minds of our customers to take advantage of these opportunities?

2a
Qualitative Research

Convergent Interviewing
- Industry analysts
- Futurists
- Engineers

Focus Groups with
- Current customers
Using
- Component sort
- Imaginary universe

3
Define
Research
Question(s)

- Does product A or B have the most potential for success?
- How should each of these be positioned in the marketplace for best performance?

Quantitative = Surveys, #'s involved

Qualitative = psychological, opinion

Sampling

Sample sizes for qualitative research vary by technique but are generally small. A study might include just two or three focus groups or a few dozen individual depth interviews. However unusual, one AT&T study, conducted to develop its 800 Reasons ad campaign for using AT&T long-distance service, used thousands of structured interviews in dozens of cities over several weeks. These interviews provided numerous reasons why businesses used the AT&T 800 service, and each of these "reasons" became the focus of a television and/or magazine ad in the multi-ad campaign.[9]

>Exhibit 9-5 A Comparison of Individual Depth Interviews and Group Interviews

Individual Interview	Group Interview
Research Objective • Explore life of individual in depth • Create case histories through repeated interviews over time • Test a survey	• Orient the researcher to a field of inquiry and the language of the field • Explore a range of attitudes, opinions, and behaviors • Observe a process of consensus and disagreement • Add contextual detail to quantitative findings
Topic Concerns • Detailed individual experiences, choices, biographies • Sensitive issues that might provoke anxiety	• Issues of public interest or common concern • Issues where little is known or of a hypothetical nature
Participants • Time-pressed participants or those difficult to recruit (e.g., elite or high-status participants) • Participants with sufficient language skills (e.g., those older than seven) • Participants whose distinctions would inhibit participation	• Participants whose backgrounds are similar or not so dissimilar as to generate conflict or discomfort • Participants who can articulate their ideas. • Participants who offer a range of positions on issues.

May or May Not

nonprobability sampling
selection of research participants where no attempt is made to generate a statistically representative sample.

> The general sampling guideline for qualitative research is: keep sampling as long as your breadth and depth of knowledge of the issue under study is expanding; stop when you gain no new knowledge or insights.

unstructured interview
customized IDI that starts with a participant narrative, with no specific questions or order of topics.

semistructured interview
participants are asked specific questions as well as probes of tangents revealed by their answers.

structured interview IDI using detailed interview guide for question order but using open-ended questions.

Qualitative research involves **nonprobability sampling**—where little attempt is made to generate a representative sample. Several types of nonprobability sampling are common:

• **Purposive sampling** (researchers choose participants arbitrarily for their unique characteristics or their experiences, attitudes, or perceptions; as conceptual or theoretical categories of participants develop during the interviewing process, researchers seek new participants to challenge emerging patterns).

• **Snowball sampling** (participants refer researchers to others who have characteristics, experiences, or attitudes similar to or different from their own).

• **Convenience sampling** (researchers select any readily available individuals as participants).

Interviews

The interview is the primary data collection technique for gathering data in qualitative methodologies. Interviews vary based on the number of people involved during the interview, the level of structure, the proximity of the interviewer to the participant, and the number of interviews conducted during the research.

An interview can be conducted individually (individual depth interview, or IDI) or in groups. Exhibit 9-5 compares the individual and the group interview as a research methodology. Both have a distinct place in qualitative research.

The researcher chooses either an **unstructured interview** (no specific questions or order of topics to be discussed, with each interview customized to each participant; generally starts with a participant narrative) or a **semistructured interview** (generally starts with a few specific questions and then follows the individual's tangents of thought with interviewer probes) or a **structured interview** (often uses a detailed interview guide similar to a questionnaire to guide the question order and the specific way the questions are asked, but the questions generally remain open-ended). Structured interviews permit more direct comparability of responses; question variability has been eliminated and thus answer variability is assumed to be real. Also, in the structured interview, the interviewer's neutrality has been maintained.

Most qualitative research relies on the unstructured or semistructured interview. The unstructured and semistructured interviews used in qualitative research are distinct from the structured interview in several ways. They:

- Rely on developing a dialog between interviewer and participant.
- Require more interviewer creativity.
- Use the skill of the interviewer to extract more and a greater variety of data.
- Use interviewer experience and skill to achieve greater clarity and elaboration of answers.

Many interviews are conducted face-to-face, with the obvious benefit of being able to observe and record nonverbal as well as verbal behavior. An interview, however, can be conducted by phone or online. Phone and online interviews offer the opportunity to conduct more interviews within the same time frame and draw participants from a wider geographic area. These approaches also save the travel expenses of moving trained interviewers to participants, as well as the travel fees associated with bringing participants to a neutral site. Using interviewers who are fresher and more comfortable in conducting an interview—often from their home or office—should increase the quality of the interview. Also, depending on the group from which participants are drawn, there may be insufficient numbers to conduct group interviews in any one market, forcing the use of phone or online techniques.

Comm. Approach to Data collection
- survey the people.

Projective Techniques

Because researchers are often looking for hidden or suppressed meanings, **projective techniques** can be used within the interview structures. Some of these techniques include:[10]

• **Word or picture association.**	Participants are asked to match images, experiences, emotions, products and services, even people and places, to whatever is being studied. *"Tell me what you think of when you think of Kellogg's Special K cereal."*
• **Sentence completion.**	Participants are asked to complete a sentence. *"Complete this sentence: People who buy over the Internet . . ."*
• **Cartoons or empty balloons.**	Participants are asked to write the dialog for a cartoonlike picture. *"What will the customer comment when she sees the salesperson approaching her in the new-car showroom."*
• **Thematic Apperception Test.**	Participants are confronted with a picture (usually a photograph or drawing) and asked to describe how the person in the picture feels and thinks.
• **Component sorts.**	Participants are presented with flash cards containing component features and asked to create new combinations.
• **Sensory sorts.**	Participants are presented with scents, textures, and sounds, usually verbalized on cards, and asked to arrange them by one or more criteria.
• **Laddering or benefit chain.**	Participants are asked to link functional features to their physical and psychological benefits, both real and ideal.

projective techniques qualitative methods that encourage the participant to reveal hidden or suppressed attitudes, ideas, emotions, and motives.

- **Imagination exercises.**   Participants are asked to relate the properties of one thing/person/brand to another. *"If Crest toothpaste were a college, what type of college would it be?"*
  - **Imaginary universe.**   Participants are asked to assume that the brand and its users populate an entire universe; they then describe the features of this new world.
  - **Visitor from another planet.**   Participants are asked to assume that they are aliens and are confronting the product for the first time; they then describe their reactions, questions, and attitudes about purchase or retrial.
  - **Personification.**   Participants are asked to imagine inanimate objects with the traits, characteristics and features, and personalities of humans. *"If brand X were a person, what type of person would brand X be?"*
  - **Authority figure.**   Participants are asked to imagine that the brand or product is an authority figure and to describe the attributes of the figure.
  - **Ambiguities and paradoxes.**   Participants are asked to imagine a brand as something else (e.g., a Tide dog food or Marlboro cereal), describing its attributes and position.
- **Semantic mapping.**   Participants are presented with a four-quadrant map where different variables anchor the two different axes; they then spatially place brands, product components, or organizations within the four quadrants.
  - **Brand mapping.**   Participants are presented with different brands and asked to talk about their perceptions, usually in relation to several criteria. They may also be asked to spatially place each brand on one or more semantic maps.

Paper-based exercises often draw out less verbal members of a group. Projective techniques can dissipate tension caused by sensitive topics or can be useful when a change of focus in the interview is imminent. A well-trained interviewer is required if the research demands that one or more of these techniques be included within an individual depth interview or group interview. These techniques are also time-consuming to apply, lengthening the time frame of the individual or group interview. They also lengthen the data analysis time.

Interviewer Qualifications

moderator a trained interviewer used for group interviews such as focus groups.

Interviewing requires a trained interviewer (often called a **moderator** for group interviews) or the skills gained from experience. These skills include making respondents comfortable, probing for detail without making the respondent feel harassed, remaining neutral while encouraging the participant to talk openly, listening carefully, following a participant's train of thought, and extracting insights from hours of detailed descriptive dialogue. Skilled interviewers learn to use their personal similarities with *or* differences from their interviewee to mine for information; similarities are used to convey sympathy and understanding, while differences are used to demonstrate eagerness to understand and empathize.

In quantitative research we are more interested in the data collector's following a prescribed procedure, whereas in qualitative research the individual conducting the interview needs a fuller understanding of the marketer's dilemma and how the insights will be used. So a skilled interviewer must be a "quick-study," someone who can grasp an understanding of an issue without necessarily having prior experience with the product or service or being a technical expert.

interview guide (discussion guide) a list of topics to be discussed or questions to be asked and in what order.

The interviewer needs to be able to extract information from a willing participant who often is not consciously aware that he or she possesses the information desired. The actual interviewer is usually responsible for generating the **interview** or **discussion guide,** the list

>**Exhibit 9-6** The Interview Question Hierarchy

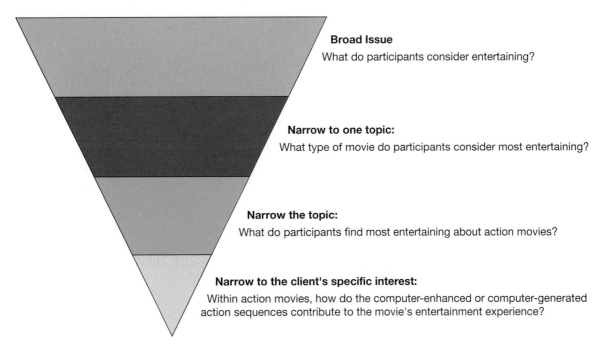

Broad Issue
What do participants consider entertaining?

Narrow to one topic:
What type of movie do participants consider most entertaining?

Narrow the topic:
What do participants find most entertaining about action movies?

Narrow to the client's specific interest:
Within action movies, how do the computer-enhanced or computer-generated action sequences contribute to the movie's entertainment experience?

Source: This graphic was adapted from one developed by Judith Langer and published in *The Mirrored Window: Focus Groups from a Moderator's Point of View* (Ithaca, NY: Paramount Market Publishing, 2001), **www.paramountbooks.com.**

of topics to be discussed (unstructured interview) or the questions to be asked (semistructured) and in what order (structured). In building this guide, many interviewers employ a hierarchical questioning structure, depicted in Exhibit 9-6 above. Broader questions start the interview, designed to put participants at ease and give them a sense that they have a lot to contribute, followed by increasingly more specific questions to draw out detail.

The interviewer is often responsible for generating the screening questions used to recruit participants for the qualitative research. This preinterview uses a device similar to a questionnaire, called a **recruitment screener.** Exhibit 9-7 provides the various elements necessary for a comprehensive recruitment screener. Each question is designed to reassure the researcher that the person who has the necessary information and experiences, as well as the social and language skills to relate the desired information, is invited to participate. Data gathered during the recruitment process are incorporated into the data analysis phase of the research, as recruitment data provide additional context for participants' expressions.

In general, then, the interviewer is a consultant with wide-ranging responsibilities:[11]

recruitment screener
semistructured or structured interview guide designed to assure the interviewer that the prospect will be a good participant for the planned qualitative research.

• Recommends the topics and questions.

• Controls the interview, but also plans—and may manage—the locations and facilities for the study.

• Proposes the criteria for drawing the sample participants.

• Writes the recruitment screener and may recruit participants.

• Develops the various pretasking exercises.

• Prepares any research tools (e.g., picture sorts or written exercises) to be used during the interview.

• Supervises the transcription process.

• Helps analyze the data and draw insights.

• Writes or directs the writing of the client report, including extracting video clips for the oral report.

>**Exhibit 9-7** What Is Included in a Recruitment Screener?

For best effect, qualitative research takes creative, articulate, expressive individuals. Finding appropriate participants is the task of the researcher. Here are some common elements addressed at this phase of the research.

Type of Information	Description
Heading	Include project name, date of interviews, identity of screener.
Screening requirements	Specify conditions that must be met to extend a prospect an offer to participate; may include quotas for various demographic, lifestyle, attitudinal, or usage questions.
Identity information	Include name of prospect, address, phone, e-mail.
Introduction	Describe purpose of study in a motivational way. Completely "blind" studies do not motivate participation.
Security questions	Reveal possible participant overparticipation or conflicts of interest; similar information on spouse or immediate family members.
Demographic questions	Determine match for age, gender, ethnicity or race, income, geography, employment status, or occupation.
Product/brand usage/purchase questions	Establish frequency of use, purchase, loyalty, etc.
Lifestyle questions	Establish the participant's daily life experiences, as well as those of the person with whom the participant shares his or her life.
Attitudinal and knowledge questions	Look for breadth in perceptions, attitudes, opinions, knowledge.
Articulation and creative questions	Seek evidence that participant can articulate his or her ideas and form and express opinions; scenarios might include problem/solution questions or ask participant to confront an unusual challenge. ("What could you do with a brick?")
Offer/termination	Invite participation, discuss compensation and pretasking, set up interview, or indicate that the person is not right for the current study but may be right for future studies.

Individual Depth Interviews

individual depth interview (IDI) an extensive, one-on-one, objective-driven, orchestrated conversation between researcher and participant.

An **individual depth interview (IDI)** is an interaction between an individual interviewer and a single participant. Individual depth interviews generally take between 20 minutes (telephone interviews) and 2 hours (prescheduled, face-to-face interviews) to complete, depending on the issues or topics of interest and the contact method used. Some techniques such as *life histories* may take as long as five hours. Participants are usually paid to share their insights and ideas; $1 per minute is the budgeting rule of thumb for general consumers, but much higher rates are demanded by participants representing highly skilled professionals.[12]

Interviewees are often provided with advance materials via mail, fax, or the Internet. Recently, advances in technology have encouraged the use of detailed visual and auditory aids during interviews, creating the methodology known as **computer-assisted personal interviews (CAPIs).** CAPIs often use a structured or semistructured individual depth interview.

computer-assisted personal interview (CAPI) IDI using detailed computer-generated visual and auditory aids.

Several unstructured individual depth interviews are common in marketing research, including oral histories, cultural interviews, life histories, critical incident technique, and sequential (or chronologic) interviewing. Exhibit 9-8 describes these techniques and provides examples.

Managing the Individual Depth Interview

Participants for individual depth interviews are usually chosen not because their opinions are representative of the dominant opinion but because their experiences and attitudes will reflect the full scope of the issue under study. Participants for individual depth interviews

>**Exhibit 9-8** Types of Research Using IDIs

Types	How Research Is Conducted	How Research Is Used
Oral history (*narrative*)	Ask participants to relate their personal experiences and feelings related to historical events or past behavior.	To develop products, for example, books. [*September 11, 2001: Stories from 55 Broad Street* by Eddie T. Deerfield and Thomas T. Noland Jr. (editors); *One Nation: America Remembers September 11, 2001* by Rudolph W. Giuliani; *An Album of Memories: Personal Histories from the Greatest Generation* by Tom Brokaw.]
Cultural interviews	Ask a participant to relate his or her experiences with a culture or subculture, including the knowledge passed on by prior generations and the knowledge participants have or plan to pass on to future generations.	To determine product positioning or advertising creation. (E.g., how people use baking soda leads to positioning the product as not just a baking ingredient but also a deodorizer, toothpaste substitute, etc.)
Life histories	Extract from a single participant memories and experiences from childhood to the present day regarding a product or service category, brand, or firm. Participants are encouraged to share how the significant people in their lives talked about or used the product or brand, how their tastes or preferences have changed over their lives with respect to the product or brand, and how their perceptions and preferences have been altered by their various life experiences.	To determine advertising development and positioning. (E.g., Frosted Flakes and Tony the Tiger—ad spots where adults feel they must appear in disguise because they eat a "child's cereal.")
Critical incident technique	The participant describes: • What led up to the incident. • Exactly what he or she did or did not do that was especially effective or ineffective. • The outcome or result of this action and why this action was effective or what more effective action might have been expected.	To study promotions that have failed or been highly successful, to evaluate public relations programs, personal sales and telemarketing sales programs, sales compensation or incentive programs, or other management-related incidents.
Convergent interviewing (*convergent and divergent interviewing*)	Experts serve as participants in a sequential series of IDIs; researcher refines the questions with each interview in order to converge on the central issues or themes in a topic area.	To develop appropriate questions for all types of research (in exploratory research).
Sequential interviewing (*chronologic interviewing*)	Approach the participant with questions formed around an anticipated series of activities that did or might have happened, in order to have the participant recall the detail of his or her own experience.	To determine store design, advertising development, and product design; it is used to extract details related to shopping behavior, advertising consumption behavior, and product use behavior.
Ethnography	Interviewer and participant collaborate in a field-setting participant observation and unstructured interview.	To determine product redesign, advertising development, positioning, distribution selection.
Grounded theory	Using a structured interview, each subsequent interview is adjusted based on the findings and interpretations from each previous interview, with the purpose to develop general concepts or theories with which to analyze the data.	To determine product design or redesign and advertising and promotion development.

Source: This exhibit was developed from Hy Mariampolski, *Qualitative Market Research: A Comprehensive Guide* (Thousand Oaks, CA: Sage Publications, 2001) p. 53; David Carson, Audrey Gilmore, Chad Perry, and Kjell Gronhaug, *Qualitative Marketing Research* (Thousand Oaks, CA: Sage Publications, 2001) pp. 84–89 and pp. 152–157; Strauss and Corbin's *Basics of Qualitative Research: Techniques and Procedure for Producing Grounded Theory,* 1990.

IBM's High-Touch Strategy Is Research-Driven

When Samuel Palmisano became chairman and chief executive of IBM, industry analysts didn't expect this 30-year IBM loyalist to rock the boat. But he started a research program that resulted in a very aggressive reorganization. The IBM strategy isn't quite so novel—create a strong connection between IBM and its customer—as is the extensive research behind it. Palmisano wanted his employees to talk to customers about their most troubling business problems. Rather than send the sales force to do that job, IBM formed teams: the sales executive in charge of the corporate account, a representative from the services division, a person from the software unit, and someone from the IBM research labs. These teams became known as "four in a box." But what each team was asked to do was think outside the box: fig-

ure out how IBM might help customers solve their pesky problems. And what resulted from all those customer interviews? A reorganization of the $89 billion company into 12 industry groups (e.g., banking, insurance, automobiles, utilities, consumer packaged goods, telecommunications, life sciences, etc.) rather than its previous three divisions (software, services, and research). The shift is under way to make IBM an executive-level consulting firm rather than a technology services company. The reorganization has IBM's labs, which used to focus on making machines calculate faster and more efficiently, refocusing on modeling patterns of human behavior to help solve business problems.

www.ibm.com

---

also need to be verbally articulate, in order to provide the interviewer with the richness of desired detail. Primary Insights Inc. developed its *CUE* methodology to help marketers understand the performance cues that consumers use to judge a product. It uses purposive sampling to recruit individuals "with a specific interest in and aptitude for analytical thinking and discovering how things work." *CUE* combines in-home product use with a diary preexercise, followed by individual depth interviews that extract what the participant saw, felt, heard, smelled, and sensed when interacting with the product. What evolves is a hierarchy of sensory cues that clients may use when modifying products to improve customer satisfaction.[13]

Individual depth interviews are usually recorded (audio and/or video) and transcribed to provide the researcher with the rich detail that the methodology is used for. Interviewers are also themselves debriefed to get their personal reactions to participant attitudes, insights, and the quality of the interview. Individual depth interviews use extensive amounts of interviewer time, in both conducting interviews and evaluating them, as well as facility time when premises are occupied for interviews. And while some respondents feel more comfortable discussing sensitive topics or sharing their own observations, behaviors, and attitudes with a single person, others are more forthcoming in group situations.

Group Interviews

group interview a single interviewer simultaneously interviews more than one research participant.

A **group interview** is a data collection method using a single interviewer with more than one research participant. Group interviews can be described by the group's size or its composition.

Group interviews vary widely in size: *dyads* (2 people), *triads* (3 people), *mini-groups* (2 to 6 people), small groups (focus groups—6 to 10 people—unarguably the most well known of group interview techniques), or *supergroups* (up to 20 people). The smaller groups are usually used when the overall population from which the participants are drawn is small, when the topic or concept list is extensive or technical, or when the research calls for greater intimacy. Dyads also are used when the special nature of a friendship or other relationship (e.g., spouses, superior-subordinate, siblings) is needed to stimulate frank discussion on a sensitive topic. Dyads and triads are also used frequently with young children who have lower levels of articulation or more limited attention spans and are thus more difficult to control in large groups. A supergroup is used when a wide range of ideas is needed

> **Check your text DVD for "Qualitative Research with Children."**

Hamilton Beach: Right Blend(er) for Mexico, but Not for Europe

Hamilton Beach/Proctor Silex (HB/PS) is a small-kitchen-appliance powerhouse in the United States. HB/PS sold one in every four such appliances in the United States, and more than 40 million appliances last year, so a global marketing strategy seemed a logical extension. But focus groups told the company differently. In Mexico, focus groups confirmed that the brand was considered quality and that the criteria American consumers used to select an appliance would be mirrored by the Mexicans. But the story was very different in Europe. There, focus groups revealed that HB/PS's lack of brand awareness wouldn't be nearly as much of a problem as its "clunky," "sturdy" designs. Europeans wanted aesthetically pleasing shapes and color in the appliances they chose for their homes, not the "professional," "institutional," or "large-capacity" products that Americans were buying.

BGIGlobal, part of SYNOVATE, the 9th largest research firm in the world, coordinated the focus groups in Europe. Product displays similar to those found in European retailers encouraged arriving participants to explore the products that would later be discussed and dissected. During the group interview, participants were encouraged to provide a detailed narrative of their last purchase within the small-kitchen-appliance category. HB/PS needed to understand the criteria driving the process and where decisions took place. The discussion guide driving the focus groups in both countries was similar. But in Europe, the first group reinforced for David Israel, HB/PS's international marketing manager, the value of the focus group methodology—its flexibility. As participants raised each new, startling issue, notes began flowing to the moderator, encouraging participants to travel down paths that the discussion guide hadn't anticipated. The focus groups helped HB/PS understand that it wasn't ready for the European market—at least not until its product designers redefined the product lines.

www.bgiglobal.com; www.hamiltonbeach.com

in a short period of time and when the researcher is willing to sacrifice a significant amount of participant interaction for speed.

In terms of composition, groups can be **heterogeneous** (consisting of different individuals; variety of opinions, backgrounds, actions) or **homogeneous** (consisting of similar individuals; commonality of opinions, backgrounds, actions). Groups also can comprise **experts** (individuals exceptionally knowledgeable about the issues to be discussed) or **nonexperts** (those who have at least some desired information but at an unknown level).

Driven by the belief that the data extracted will be richer because of the interaction, group interviews are one of the few research techniques in which the participants are encouraged to interact. However, given time constraints, group interviews permit spending only limited time extracting detail from each participant.[14] This problem is magnified when a group interview is structured to cover numerous questions or topics.

Another drawback of the group interview is the increased difficulty recruiting, arranging, and coordinating group discussions. But this aggravation—which can be subcontracted to a specialist research supplier—is deemed a small price to pay for the insights that often are revealed by group interaction.

Interviewers are tested by the challenge of managing the group's conversation while avoiding interjecting themselves into the group's process. It is also the moderator's job to control the extrovert or dominant personality and ensure meaningful contributions from all others, including the most introverted or private thinkers. When control is not maintained, some members' opinions may be suppressed and valuable insights lost. Sometimes an individual will be more honest with a neutral interviewer than with a group of peers. One example is a group of small-business owners being unwilling to divulge competitive strengths and weaknesses. A skilled researcher can anticipate which topics are more likely to obtain good results with an individual or a group interview.

A group interview's structure and process include moderator interaction with the group and probing of the group to clarify responses. As a result, the moderator may create bias in the results by sending verbal and nonverbal signals that some responses are more favorable

heterogeneous group participant group consisting of individuals with a variety of opinions, backgrounds, and actions relative to a topic.

homogeneous group participant group consisting of individuals with similar opinions, backgrounds, and actions relative to a topic.

expert group group consisting of individuals exceptionally knowledgeable on a particular topic or issue.

nonexpert group participants in a group interview with some unknown level of information about a topic.

than others. The moderator might also direct discussion down paths that are least likely to help the client. Only training, and subsequent experience, can overcome these potential weaknesses of group interviews.

The skilled researcher helps the sponsor determine an appropriate number of group interviews to conduct. The number of groups is determined by:

- The *scope* of the issue(s) being studied: The broader the issue(s), the more groups needed.
- The number of *distinct market segments* of interest: The larger the number and the greater the distinctions, the more groups needed.
- The *number of new ideas or insights* desired: The larger the number, the more groups needed.
- The *level of detail* of information: The greater the level of detail, the more groups needed.
- The *level of geographic or ethnic distinctions* in attitudes or behavior: The greater these influences, the more groups needed.
- The *homogeneity of the groups:* The less homogeneity, the more groups needed.

The general rule is: Keep conducting group interviews until no new insights are gained. Often a limited number of groups will suffice, or sometimes the number might grow to 8 or even 12.

It is often preferable, depending on the topic, to run separate group interviews for different subsets of the target population. For example, a study on nutritional advice may begin with separate consumer and physician groups to determine the best ways to provide the advice. This type of homogeneous grouping tends to promote more intense discussion and freer interaction.[15]

Researchers caution against forming groups solely on demographic descriptors, favoring "natural'" groups (like families, co-workers, church members, etc.) where the participants share an affinity base.[16] For customer groups, however, consideration should be given to such factors as gender, ethnicity, employment status, and education, as culture is a primary determinant of perception. In a recent exploratory study of discount shoppers, the attitudes about the economy and personal finances expressed by East Coast respondents and West Coast respondents diverged widely. The research sponsor was able to use information from group interviews to build a marketing strategy tailored to each geographic area.[17]

Regardless of group composition, it is the moderator who sets the tone of the group. Homogenous groups often discover their similarities early and get along well. But with heterogeneous groups, the moderator must provide the ice-breaker activities that get the participants interacting with each other. As with individual depth interviews, the moderator is responsible for developing the recruitment screener and the group discussion guide. Exhibit 9-9 summarizes the facilitators and inhibitors of individual participation in group interviews.

A closer look at one of the best known of group interviews, the focus group, may clarify these distinctions.

Focus Groups

focus group a discussion on a topic involving a small group of participants led by a trained moderator.

The **focus group,** introduced in Chapter 8, is a panel of people (typically made up of 6 to 10 participants), led by a trained moderator, who meet for 90 minutes to 2 hours. The facilitator or moderator uses group dynamics principles to focus or guide the group in an exchange of ideas, feelings, and experiences on a specific topic.

> **The term *focus group* was first coined by R. K. Merton in his 1956 book, *The Focused Interview*.**

Focus groups are often unique in research due to the research sponsor's involvement in the process. Most facilities permit the sponsor to observe the group and its dynamics in real time, drawing his or her own insights from the conversations and nonverbal signals he or she observes. Many facilities also allow the client to supply the moderator with new topics

>**Exhibit 9-9** Factors Influencing Participant Contributions in Group Interviews

As humans we seek pleasure over pain, comfort over discomfort, and acceptance over alienation. Both moderators and participants can influence behavior of group members.

Positive/Facilitators	
Recognition/ego enhancement	Moderator's expressed appreciation for participant contributions that contribute to issue understanding; participant's open agreement with other participant comments
Personal contribution	Participant's desire to be, and perception that his or her contributions are, helpful
Validation	Participant's need to have his or her feelings, attitudes, or ideas validated
Catharsis/load-sharing	Participant's need to share something negative or bothersome with others
Personal growth	Participant's desire to increase knowledge or understanding through new perspectives; participant's desire for new experiences
Socialization	Participant's desire to meet new people and make new friends in a "safe" environment
Expectations	Participant's accurate understanding of the purpose of the group discussion
Extrinsic rewards	Participant's value perception of fee for participation
Negative/Inhibitors	
Use of abstract terminology	Moderator or participant's use of terminology or unfamiliar jargon
Ego threats	Participant's challenging another participant's knowledge of the subject
Political correctness	Participant's withholding comments for fear that his or her contributions might be perceived as disrespectful of another's knowledge or opinions
Ego defense	Participant's withholding a comment for fear that it will make him or her appear unintelligent or that the opinion will be unpopular with the group
Memory decay	Participant's failure to remember incidents or details of incidents
Embellishment	Participant's creative additions to memories of behaviors in order to participate fully or inflate status
Inarticulation/rambling accounts	Participant's inability to express ideas quickly or concisely
Confusion	Participant's lack of understanding of the issue under discussion
Reticence	Participant's need to be invited to participate (rather than actively volunteering comments)
Time	Participant's concern about other obligations
Dominating/monopolizing	Participant's attempting to take leadership or the spotlight, thus blocking contributions of others

or questions that are generated by those observing in real time. This option is generally not available in an individual depth interview, other group interviews, or survey research.

Focus groups typically last about two hours but may run from one to three hours. Facilities usually provide for the group to be isolated from distractions. Thus the famous, or infamous, mirrored window allows those who are interested to observe the group while they avoid interfering with the group dynamics. Some facilities allow for product preparation and testing, as well as other creative exercises.

Fewer and lengthier focus groups are becoming common. As sessions become longer, activities are needed to bring out deeper feelings, knowledge, and motivations. Besides the creativity sessions (described in Chapter 8) that employ projective techniques or involve the participants in writing or drawing sessions, or creating visual compilations, other common activities within focus groups include:[18]

> **You'll find a sample focus group discussion guide in Appendix A.**

- *Free association.* "What words or phrases come to mind when you think of X?"
- *Picture sort.* Participants sort brand labels or carefully selected images related to brand personality on participant-selected criteria.
- *Photo sort.* Photographs of people are given to the group members, who are then asked: "Which of these people would . . .?" or "Which of these people would not . . .?"
- *Role play.* Two or more members of the group are asked to respond to questions from the vantage point of their personal or assigned role.

Focus groups are often used as an exploratory technique but may be a primary methodology. In two such cases, a small college used focus groups to develop a plan to attract more freshmen applications, and a blood center used a focus group to improve blood donations.[19] Focus groups are especially valuable in the following scenarios:[20]

> **When facing a high-risk decision, researchers rarely rely solely on focus group data, as the sample is too small and often not chosen to be representative.**

- Obtaining general background about a topic or issue.
- Generating research questions to be explored via quantitative methodologies.
- Interpreting previously obtained quantitative results.
- Stimulating new ideas for products and programs.
- Highlighting areas of opportunity for specific marketers to pursue.
- Diagnosing problems that marketers need to address.
- Generating impressions and perceptions of brands and product ideas.
- Generating a level of understanding about influences in the participant's world.

Groups best enable the exploration of surprise information and new ideas. Agendas can be modified as the research team moves on to the next focus group. Even within an existing focus group, an adept facilitator can build on the ideas and insights of previous groups, getting to a greater depth of understanding. However, because they are qualitative devices, with limited sampling accuracy, results from focus groups should not be considered a replacement for quantitative analyses.

In the opening vignette, Visionary Insights was involved in conducting and analyzing focus groups for a frozen-food manufacturer. Visionary Insights is also involved with assessing the CompleteCare service program for MindWriter. For the latter project VI could use focus groups involving employees (of the call center and service departments) to determine suggestions for improvements and provide an analysis of proposed improvements. MindWriter may want focus groups with CompleteCare customers (both dissatisfied and satisfied customers but restricted to separate groups) to reveal the scope of attitudes and experiences not documented within complaints.

Other Venues for Focus Group Interviews

While the following venues are most frequently used with focus groups, they can be used with other sizes and types of group interviews.

Telephone Focus Groups
In traditional focus groups, participants meet face-to-face, usually in specialized facilities that enable respondents to interact in a comfortable setting while being observed by a sponsoring client. However, often there is a need to reach people that face-to-face groups cannot attract. With modern telephone conferencing facilities, **telephone focus groups** can be particularly effective in the following situations:

telephone focus group
group participants are connected to the moderator and each other by teleconferencing equipment.

- When it is difficult to recruit desired participants—members of elite groups and hard-to-find respondents such as experts, professionals, physician specialists, high-level executives, and store owners.
- When target group members are rare, "low incidence," or widely dispersed geographically—directors of a medical clinic, celebrities, early adopters, and rural practitioners.

- When issues are so sensitive that anonymity is needed but respondents must be from a wide geographic area—people suffering from a contagious disease, people using nonmainstream products, high-income individuals, competitors.

- When you want to conduct only a couple of focus groups but want nationwide representation.

Telephone focus groups are usually shorter than traditional groups, averaging about one hour. Participants could be in their own offices or homes or be brought to a central location with the necessary equipment. Telephone focus groups are usually less expensive than face-to-face focus groups—by up to 40 percent.

In contrast to face-to-face groups, heterogeneous telephone groups can be productive. People in traditional superior-subordinate roles can be mixed as long as they are not from the same city. A telephone focus group is less likely to be effective under the following conditions:

- When participants need to handle a product.
- When an object of discussion cannot be sent through the mail in advance.
- When sessions will run long.
- When the participants are groups of young children.

Online Focus Groups   An emerging technique for exploratory research is to approximate group dynamics using e-mail, Web sites, Usenet newsgroups, or an Internet chat room. It is possible to do "live" voice chats online, reducing or eliminating the cost associated with telephone focus groups. Posting questions to a newsgroup with an interest in the research problem can generate considerable discussion. However, online discussions are not confidential unless they take place on an intranet. Although online forum discussions are unlikely to reflect the average participants, they can be a good way of getting in touch with populations that have special interests (e.g., BMW club members, little-league coaches, or "power computer users"). **Online focus groups** have also proved to be effective with teens and young adults, as well as technically employed segments of the market, those essentially comfortable with computer use. They are especially valuable when a computer-based application, such as software or a game, is the topic of group discussion. The technology permits use of visual images of materials (e.g., ads or product concepts) but retains the barrier between the group and the moderator. Online focus groups are a trade-off. What you gain in speed and access you give up in insights extracted from group dynamics, the flexibility to use nonverbal language as a source of data, and the moderator's ability to use physical presence to influence openness and depth of response.

A company's first venture into online focus groups doesn't have to be as traumatizing as a baby's first steps. Itracks is positioning itself as a specialty service provider to those who want to do online focus groups. It uses the reputations of its customers—Harris Interactive and Ipsos—to cement its credibility as a qualitative research company. **www.itracks.com**

online focus group participants use the technology of the Internet to approximate the interaction of a face-to-face focus group.

Hallmark: Qualitative Research Enriches Sinceramente Hallmark

Hallmark began offering Spanish-language cards in the mid-1980s. The 2000 United States census data show a sharp rise in the number of people who identify themselves as Hispanic, including many households where Spanish is the primary language spoken at home. Today 35.3 million people are included in this group, a 58% increase over the 1990 census figure. To better reflect the specific needs of today's Latino consumers, Hallmark enhanced its commitment to the Hispanic market and launched a new brand of culturally relevant greeting cards called *Hallmark en Español* in 1999. In February 2003, Hallmark expanded its commitment by launching *Sinceramente Hallmark,* a line of more than 2,500 cards for everyday occasions and holidays.

Hallmark's early research used online focus groups to create new messages for the line extension. The creative team, which includes Hispanic artists and writers, talked extensively to Hispanic consumers to gain insights into relevant designs and messages. While the extensive line includes year-round products for birthdays, love, weddings, and anniversaries, it also contains cards for special days of celebration, like *Quinceañera* (a special celebration of a girl's 15th birthday) and Dia de los Reyes (a celebration of the arrival of the three wise men in Bethlehem), among others. *Sinceramente Hallmark* includes bilingual cards, combining Spanish and English words—reflecting how many Hispanics speak—as well as digital cards available from the Hallmark Web site. The top five markets for Hispanic card sales are: (1) Los Angeles, (2) Miami, (3) Chicago, (4) New York, and (5) San Francisco.

www.hallmark.com

Cover: May God bless you, Quinceañera. Let your light shine before men in such a way that they may see your good works, and glorify your Father who is in heaven. Matthew 5:16 (NASB).
Inside: You have the light of the Lord within you . . . the light that can be seen in everything about you . . . And today you begin the radiant life of a lovely woman! Happy Birthday.

Videoconferencing Focus Groups Videoconferencing is another technology used with group interviews. Many researchers anticipate growth for this methodology. Like telephone focus groups, videoconferencing enables significant savings. By reducing the travel time for the moderator and the client, coordinating such groups can be accomplished in a shorter time. However, videoconferencing retains the barrier between the moderator and participants, although less so than the telephone focus group. Since large corporations and universities are more likely to have their own internal videoconferencing facilities, most videoconferencing focus groups will tend to occur within this setting, thus reducing the breadth of participants to those who can access these specialized facilities.

Recording, Analyzing, and Reporting Group Interviews

In face-to-face settings, some moderators use large sheets of paper on the wall of the group room to record trends; others use a personal notepad. Facility managers produce both video- and audiotapes to enable a full analysis of the interview. The verbal portion of the group interview is transcribed along with moderator debriefing sessions and added to mod-

>**snap**shot

FocusVision's VideoMarker

Extracting insights from data, conveying those insights to marketing decision makers, and implementing strategies and tactics based on those insights is a constant challenge for most marketing researchers. "The power to convince decision-makers is often locked in the footage of such interviews," shares Peter Houlahan, president and COO of FocusVision. FocusVision, a company that provides more than 280 facilities worldwide with services for videoconference focus groups and individual depth interviews (IDIs), developed new technology for this purpose: *VideoMarker*. Clients plug in their laptop (in a viewing room or their office via videostreaming technology). While watching the event, when they see footage they want to mark they click on the "VideoMark" button above the video area on their PC. A pop-up textbox allows the client to enter a note. The note is automatically coded with a time mark and the name of its creator. When the event is complete, video of the entire project and all notes are archived for immediate access (by password) and recorded on a CD-ROM that is sent to the client. Researchers can then create video clips to share with colleagues via e-mail, embed in documents or PowerPoint presentations, or group together into highlight reels. "The capability to show actual footage when presenting research results is especially relevant when clients aren't present to watch behind a one-way mirror or when they participate

via videoconferencing or videostreaming," offers Houlahan. One pharmaceutical company arranged to interview patients in more than seven hours of focus groups. With *VideoMarker*, researchers captured the highlights, which were then—with the patients' consent—incorporated into IDI research with physicians. "These research highlights were the key motivational tool used to persuade doctors to change how they prescribed the company's product."

www.focusvision.com

---

erator notes. These are analyzed across several focus group sessions using **content analysis.** This analytical process provides the research sponsor with a qualitative picture of the respondents' concerns, ideas, attitudes, and feelings. The preliminary profile of the content of a group interview is often done with computer software in content analysis (for example, NUD*IST, mentioned in the Behind the Scenes vignette). Such software searches for common phrasing and words, context, and patterns of expression on digitized transcripts.

content analysis process for measuring semantic content of a communication.

> **We discuss content analysis in Chapter 18.**

> Combining Qualitative Methodologies

Case Study[21]

The **case study,** also referred to as the *case history*, is a powerful research methodology that combines individual and (sometimes) group interviews with record analysis and observation. Researchers extract information from company brochures, annual reports, sales receipts, and newspaper and magazine articles, along with direct observation (usually done in the participant's "natural" setting), and combine it with interview data from participants. The objective is to obtain multiple perspectives of a single organization, situation, event, or process at a point in time or over a period of time. Case study methodology—or the written report from such a research project, often called a *case analysis* or *case write-up*—can be used to understand particular marketing processes. For example, one study might evaluate new product development processes for similarities, especially the use of outside

case study (case history) combines individual or group interviews with record analysis and observation.

consultants, ideation techniques, and computer simulation. Another study might examine in detail the purchaser's response to a marketing stimulus like a display. The results of the research could be used to experiment with modifications of the new product development process or with display selection and placement processes to generate higher-value transactions. The research problem is usually a how and why problem, resulting in a descriptive or explanatory study.

Researchers select the specific organizations or situations to profile because these examples or subjects offer critical, extreme, or unusual cases. Researchers most often choose multiple subjects, rather than a single subject, to study because of the opportunity for cross-case analysis. In studying multiple subjects, a deeper understanding of the subject emerges. When multiple units are chosen, it is because they offer similar results for predictable reasons (literal replication) or contrary results for predictable reasons (theoretical replication). While theoretical sampling seems to be common, a minimum of 4 cases with a maximum of 15 seems to be favored.

In the case study, interview participants are invited to tell the story of their experience, with those chosen representing different levels within the same organization or different perspectives of the same situation or process to permit depth of perspective. The flexibility of the case study approach and the emphasis on understanding the context of the subject being studied allow for a richness of understanding sometimes labeled *thick description*.

During analysis, a single case analysis is always performed before any cross-case analysis is conducted. The emphasis is on what differences occur, why, and with what effect. Prescriptive inferences about best practices are concluded after completing case studies on several organizations or situations and are speculative in nature.

Marketing students are quite familiar with studying marketing cases as a means of learning marketing principles. *In Search of Excellence*, a book by Tom Peters and Robert Waterman, was developed using case study methodology.[22] Other similar studies profiled in books written on Procter & Gamble and Disney have also used this methodology. In the marketing arena, such case studies have examined changes in new product development, sales processes, and promotion processes in the marketing arena.

Action Research

action research
brainstorming, followed by sequential trial-and-error attempts, until desired results are achieved.

Marketers conduct research in order to gain insights to make decisions in specific scenarios. **Action research** is designed to address complex, practical problems about which little is known—thus no known heuristics exist. So the scenario is studied; a corrective action is determined, planned, and implemented; the results of the action are observed and recorded; and the action is assessed as effective or not. The process is repeated until a desired outcome is reached, but along the way much is learned about the processes and about the prescriptive actions being studied. Action researchers investigate the effects of applied solutions. Whatever theories are developed are validated through practical application.[23]

Suppose a restaurant that had never received a customer complaint earns its first challenge by a disgruntled diner. If no general rule existed about how to treat unhappy patrons, the organization could study the situation and come up with alternative actions. It might:

• Ignore the problem. (Its lack of experience would prevent it from knowing that negative word of mouth—negative buzz—would be the likely result.)

• Apply the marketing concept, doing whatever is necessary to replace the unsatisfactory meal within the shortest period of time.

• Accept the current circumstance as uncorrectable, apologize to the customer, and remedy the situation by picking up the table's full dining tab and offering the customer a free meal to get him or her back in the restaurant another day.

In action research, one of those alternatives would be chosen and implemented, and then the results recorded. Was the customer happy when he or she left? Did the customer return to dine another evening or never return again? Over the next three months, what was the customer's full revenue value? If the customer didn't return, the next time a disgruntled customer voiced dissatisfaction a different action would be chosen, implemented, and then assessed in comparison to the first option's results.

> Merging Qualitative and Quantitative Methodologies

Triangulation is the term used to describe the combining of several qualitative methods or combining qualitative with quantitative methods. Because of the controversy described earlier, qualitative studies may be combined with quantitative ones to increase the perceived quality of the research, especially when a quantitative study follows a qualitative one and provides validation for the qualitative findings. Four strategies for combining methodologies are common in marketing research:[24]

triangulation research design that combines several qualitative methods or quantitative with qualitative methods.

1. Qualitative and quantitative studies can be conducted simultaneously.
2. A qualitative study can be ongoing while multiple waves of quantitative studies are done, measuring changes in behavior and attitudes over time.
3. A qualitative study can precede a quantitative study, and a second qualitative study then might follow the quantitative study, seeking more clarification.
4. A quantitative study can precede a qualitative study.

An example of the first strategy would be the combination of a public opinion poll at the time focus groups are being held to discover ways to sway a particular public's opinion. For the second strategy, we might collect life histories while multiple waves of questionnaires are measuring the response to differing promotional tactics. For the third, we could perform a qualitative study to identify peoples' behaviors and perceptions with respect to furniture shopping processes and interior decorating; then we could use that information to develop a quantitative study to measure the actual frequency of behaviors and attitudes. And, fourth, we might survey people's behavior and attitudes toward a brand and find we need some IDIs to explain findings that are unclear.

Many marketers recognize that qualitative research compensates for the weaknesses of quantitative research and vice versa. These forward thinkers believe that the methodologies complement rather than rival each other.

>summary

1 Qualitative research includes an array of interpretive techniques that seek to describe, decode, translate, and otherwise come to terms with the meaning, not the frequency, of certain more or less naturally occurring phenomena in the social world. Qualitative research methodologies differ from quantitative methodologies based on the focus of the research; its purpose; researcher involvement; sampling design; sample size; research design, including participant pretasking; data source, type, and preparation; methods of data analysis; level of insights and meaning extracted; research sponsor involvement; speed of the research; and data security. A qualitative methodology may be used alone to address marketing problems or in combination with other qualitative or quantitative methodologies.

2 While qualitative research is being used increasingly because of the methodologies' ability to generate deeper understanding, it still is perceived by many senior-level executives as a stepchild of quantitative data collection. This is primarily due to qualitative research's use of nonprobability sampling, the smaller sample sizes involved, and the nonprojectability of the results to a broader, target population.

3 Qualitative research is designed to tell the researcher how (process) and why (meaning) things happen as they do. In marketing planning and decision making, qualitative methodologies are used in market segmentation; advertising creative development; new product development, especially concept testing; sales analysis; sales development; package

design; brand development and assessment, especially understanding brand value; positioning; retail design; and understanding various processes, including consumers' decision-making processes. In data analysis, qualitative research uses content analysis of written or recorded materials drawn from personal expressions by participants, behavioral observations, and debriefing of observers, as well as the study of artifacts and trace evidence from the physical environment.

4 Qualitative methodologies used in marketing decision making evolved from techniques used in anthropology, sociology, psychology, linguistics, communication, economics, and semiotics. Common among these strategies are the individ-

ual depth interview (IDI) and the group interview, as well as observation, ethnography, action research, and grounded theory. Within group interviews, the focus group is the most widely used methodology.

Qualitative research often uses projective techniques, designed to encourage the participant to reveal in detail deeply suppressed attitudes, opinions, feelings, and experiences. Among these techniques are word or picture association, sentence completion, cartoons or empty balloons, the Thematic Apperception Test, imagination exercises, and sorting exercises. Participant preparation and the actual qualitative sessions themselves often include various creativity sessions and exercises.

>**key**terms

>**discussion**questions

Terms in Review

1 How does qualitative research differ from quantitative research?

2 How does data from qualitative research differ from data in quantitative research?

3 Why do senior executives feel more comfortable relying on quantitative data than qualitative data? How might a qualitative research company lessen the senior-level executive's skepticism?

4 Distinguish between structured, semistructured, and unstructured interviews.

Making Research Decisions

5 Assume you are a manufacturer of small kitchen electrics, like Hamilton Beach/Proctor Silex, and you want to determine if some innovative designs with unusual shapes and colors developed for the European market could be successfully marketed in the U.S. market. What qualitative research would you recommend, and why?

6 Assume you are Hallmark. (See the Snapshot on page 234.) You have identified four new themes for your Hispanic-targeted cards, *Sinceramente Hallmark*. You now need research to help your card designers create cards that correctly execute those themes. What research should you do now?

From Concept to Practice

7 Use Exhibit 9-7 to develop the recruitment screener for the research you described in your answer to question 5.

8 Conduct a focus group among students in your class on one of the following topics:

a Your department's problems offering requirements and electives essential for meeting your graduation expectations.

b Entertainment sponsored by your university to bring the community on campus.

Behind the Scenes

9 What dilemma does HealthPlus face, and why has the company turned to focus groups for insights?

>**www**exercise

Brunswick Corporation hired Doyle Research associates to do ideation/imagination activities as it sought to reverse the decline in bowling's popularity and to revitalize bowling alleys as an entertainment venue. Viz-a-Bowling was developed as a result of this research. Visit the Cosmic Bowling Web site. What qualitative techniques would you use to find the next generation of Cosmic Bowling innovations? **http://www.viz-a-ball.com/game/vizagame.htm**

>**cases***

Campbell-Ewald: R-E-S-P-E-C-T Spells Loyalty	Ramada Demonstrates Its *Personal Best*™
✷ Lexus SC 430	State Farm: Dangerous Intersections
Mastering Teacher Leadership	✷ Starbucks, Bank One, and Visa Launch Starbucks Card Duetto Visa
NCRCC: Teeing Up a New Strategic Direction	✷ USTA: Come Out Swinging
Open Doors: Extending Hospitality to Travelers with Disabilities	

* All cases, both written and video, are on the text DVD. The film icon indicates a video case. Check the DVD Index to determine whether a case has data, the research instrument, or other supplementary material.

>chapter 10

Observation Studies

>learningobjectives

After reading this chapter, you should understand . . .

1 When observation studies are most useful.

2 The distinctions between monitoring nonbehavioral and behavioral activities.

3 The strengths of the observation approach in research design.

4 The weaknesses of the observation approach in research design.

5 The three perspectives from which the observer-participant relationship may be viewed in observation studies.

6 The various designs of observation studies.

7 What is involved in internal data mining and how internal data mining techniques differ from literature searches.

Jason Henry and Sara Armstrong have been assigned to work on a project involving customer dissatisfaction with a superstore. An extensive survey is in progress, but the client has decided it needs an observation study as well. We join Sara, as she is getting prepared to leave for an exploratory investigation of her client's closest superstore, a preliminary step to developing an observation checklist for the larger observation study, when her vice president, Chance Bedford, intercepts her.

How's the HomeExtravaganza project coming," asks Chance Bedford as he steps into Sara Armstrong's office at Visionary Insights.

"We've just finished reviewing the proposals and have selected MarketViews as the subcontractor to do the observation study," responds Sara. "MarketViews will start a week after the checklist is finalized—that's the next step."

"You've obviously determined how the observation study will interact with the larger shopper motivation study we're doing. Fill me in."

"Yes. We'll be finished next week with the first measure in the motivation study. Early survey feedback is that customer confusion related to merchandise location and availability may be a contributing factor to declining repeat visits and sales. The observation study will identify specific types of shopper confusion in the store and the sales associates' response to that confusion."

"I was in the store in Boca just this month for the first time," remarks Chance. "The extensive product display is impressive, but a little overwhelming—and the store is mammoth, as well. I was certainly wishing I'd worn my Nikes!"

"HomeExtravaganza uses greeters and its advertising promises lots of helpful associates, but the motiva-

tion study is logging complaints that the associates aren't as helpful as they need to be," explains Sara. "MarketViews recommends participant observation, to determine just what form associate help is taking."

"We've used MarketViews before with good results."

"We're meeting with MarketViews' project director this afternoon to rough out the checklist. So we're taking an early lunch and plan to visit the store one more time," explains Sara as she moves from behind her desk. "We want to select specific locations for the interactions to take place and specific behaviors . . . like walking the customer to the aisle location versus giving directions to the location, finding the item in the aisle versus leaving the customer at the aisle entry. And I've come prepared," says Sara as she comes from behind her desk wearing her Reebok running shoes.

"Making another fashion statement, I see," comments Jason Henry as he enters Sara's office. "You are obviously ready to join me in an exploration of Home-Extravaganza."

"I'll leave you two to your own observation study then," remarks Chance as he turns to depart the office.

> **The Uses of Observation**

Much of what we know comes from observation. We notice a family member's reaction to a new product or an advertisement on the Super Bowl broadcast, co-workers' reactions to political intrigue, the sounds in a shopping mall, the smell of perfume, the taste of Krispy Kreme donuts or Starbucks coffee, the smoothness of the vice president's marble desk, and a host of other stimuli. While such observation may be a basis for knowledge, the collection processes are often haphazard.

Marketing managers often use observation as part of the exploratory phase of a research project. Such data collection is known as **simple observation.** Its practice is not standardized, as one would expect, because of the discovery nature of exploratory research.

Observation may also be the primary methodology to answer a research question when it is systematically planned and executed, uses proper controls, and provides a consistently dependable (reliable) and accurate and authoritative (valid) account of what happened. The decision to use observation as the major data collection method may be made as early as the moment the researcher moves from research questions to investigative questions. The latter specify the outcomes of the study—the specific questions the researcher must answer

simple observation
unstructured and exploratory observation of participants or objects.

>**Exhibit 10-1** Observation and the Research Process

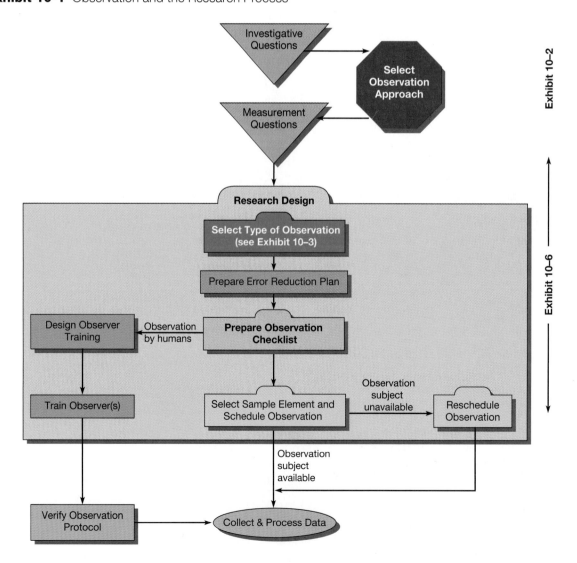

with collected data. If the study is to be something other than exploratory, **systematic observation** employs standardized procedures, trained observers, schedules for recording, and other devices for the observer that reflect the scientific procedures of other primary data methods. Systematic observation studies vary in the emphasis placed on recording and encoding observational information:

> At one end of the continuum are methods that are unstructured and open-ended. The observer tries to provide as complete and nonselective a description as possible. On the other end of the continuum are more structured and predefined methods that itemize, count, and categorize behavior. Here the investigator decides beforehand which behavior will be recorded and how frequently observations will be made. The investigator using structured observation is much more discriminating in choosing which behavior will be recorded and precisely how [it is] to be coded.[1]

Besides collecting data visually, observation involves listening, reading, smelling, and touching. Behavioral scientists define observation in terms of animal or human behavior, but this too is limiting. The versatility of observation makes it an indispensable primary method and a supplement for other methods. To relegate observation to a minor technique of field data collection is to ignore its potential for forging marketing decisions and denies its historic stature as a creative means of obtaining primary data. Exhibit 10-1 depicts the use of observation in the research process.

Research designs are classified by the approach used to gather primary data: We can observe, or we can communicate. Exhibit 10-2 describes the conditions under which observation is an appropriate method for data collection. It also contrasts those conditions with the communication modes discussed in Chapter 11—surveys and interviews.

systematic observation structured study using standardized procedures to observe participants or objects.

>**Exhibit 10-2** Selecting the Data Collection Method

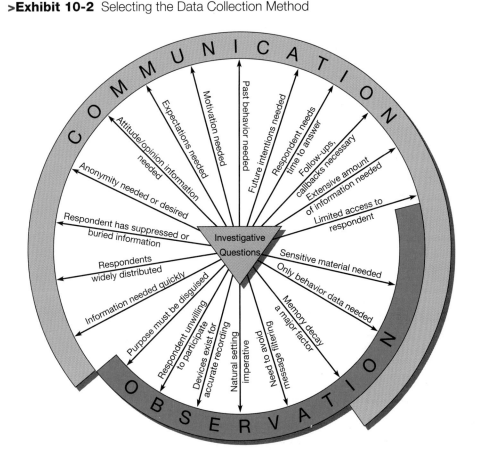

As used in this text, observation includes the full range of monitoring behavioral and nonbehavioral activities and conditions, which, as shown in Exhibit 10-3, can be classified roughly as follows:

Behavioral Observation

- Nonverbal behavior
- Linguistic behavior
- Extralinguistic behavior
- Spatial behavior

Nonbehavioral Observation

- Physical condition analysis
- Process or activity analysis
- Record analysis

>**Exhibit 10-3** Selecting an Observation Data Collection Approach

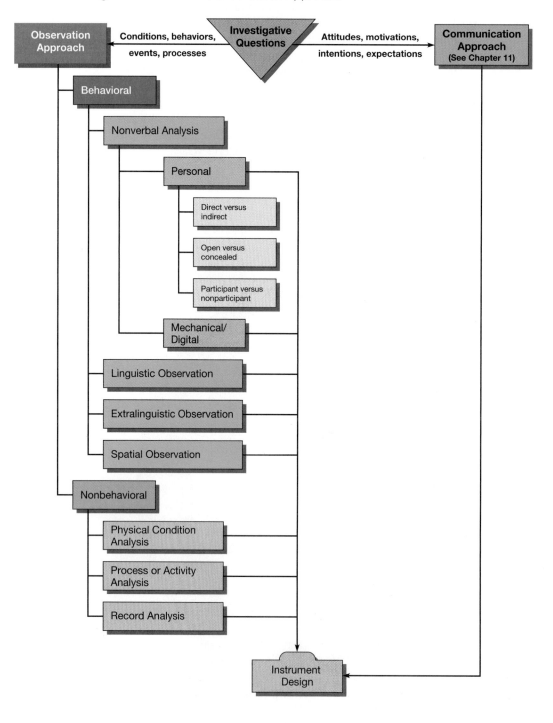

> Behavioral Observation

Types of Behavioral Observation

An observation study of persons can be classified into four major categories: nonverbal, linguistic, extralinguistic, and spatial.[2] **Nonverbal observation** is the most prevalent of these and includes recording physical actions or movements, such as body movement, motor expressions, and even exchanged glances. Both people and machines can perform the

nonverbal observation
recording of physical actions or movements of participants.

initial stage of a nonverbal observation study, the recording of behavior. At the level of gross body movement, one might study how a salesperson travels a territory. At a fine level, one can study the body movements of a retail worker packing a shipment for delivery or can time-sample the activity of a customer relations department's workforce to discover the share of time each worker spends on the phone with disgruntled customers. More abstractly, one can study body movement as an indicator of interest or boredom, or anger or pleasure, in a certain environment.

6 6 We noticed people scraping the toppings off our pizza crusts. We thought at first there was something wrong, but they said, 'We love it, we just don't eat the crust anymore.' 9 9

Tom Santor
Donatos Pizza

Motor expressions such as facial movements can be observed as a sign of emotional states. Eye blink rates are studied as indicators of interest in advertising messages. Exchanged glances are of interest in studies of interpersonal behavior.

Mechanical/Digital Observation[3]

Researchers use machines for recording behaviors for various reasons. Events and details of behavior often happen in such rapid sequence that the human eye doesn't prove adequate as the recording device. Additionally, human researchers must stop observing while they record previously seen behavior, missing unknown behaviors in the process. The research design may require extremely detailed observation (large number of behavioral events within a single observation) or observation of more than one participant at a time (as might be the case with a retail shopping observation). Due to the inability of a human researcher to observe and accurately record or recall so many events, such designs would require the use of mechanical or digital devices. Finally, trained human observers are expensive. One might be able to reduce the cost of a research project by using mechanical/digital devices at the recording stage.

By far the most commonly used mechanical/digital devices are the video camera and the audio recorder. These devices can be used to generate actual counts and descriptions of behaviors. Both devices can be used in natural or laboratory observations. They are used extensively in retail customer tracking studies and retail design development, to monitor nonverbal behavior in focus groups or individual depth interviews, to evaluate candidate performance during a debate within a political campaign, and even to monitor people taking surveys to determine their degree of seriousness, attention, or distraction.

Although not extensively but with some regularity, other devices have been employed in observational studies. These include the galvanometer, the tachistoscope (T-scope), the eye camera, and the pupilometer. Most often the researcher must obtain participants' willing compliance prior to using these devices. Thus they cannot easily be used in a disguised study. Each device's use may be part of a two-stage study that involves observation coupled with a postobservation communication study.

The *galvanometer* is a device that measures excitement, arousal, fear, or heightened physiological response to stimuli. It does this by measuring electrical activity in the participant's skin. If you are a fan of mysteries, or crime dramas, you are familiar with the galvanometer as a lie detector. The machine is the same; however, rather than asking the participant questions, in an observation study the researcher shows the participant still pictures or video in a planned sequence for a predetermined time. Galvanometers have been used most in advertising research, studying people's responses to images that affect attention, perceived benefits, and brand positioning.

The *eye camera* and *pupilometer* are devices that attach to a person's forehead. When a participant is shown various stimuli, the researcher can measure the movement of the eye and the dilation of the pupil in the eye, respectively. For example, during an episode of a television program or an advertisement you can match the eye movement precisely to what the participant is watching on the screen. And the physiological response to images, color, people, characters, locations, or logo types can be measured. These devices are used most in advertising, product development, and packaging research.

The *tachistoscope* is a timed shutter device that exposes a participant to some stimulus for a controlled period of time. Today's tachistoscope may be controlled by computer for very precise image exposure. Historically, its use has been associated with researchers' attempts to substantiate the effectiveness of *subliminal advertising* (the communication of promotional messages at a level below conscious recognition). Today, it is most often used to evaluate what a package communicates and its shelf impact, as well as the effectiveness of displays for generating attention and brand recognition. For example, a researcher might expose a participant to a series of photographs that simulate the customer's varying perspectives of a package. The exposures would be timed to 1/500 of a second, 1/200 of a second, 1/100 of a second, and so on. The package design that captures participants' attention in the shortest exposure time would be considered the stronger design in a comparative test.[4]

The use of these devices in designing research for Marlboro cigarettes is legendary. Marlboro, first introduced in the 1920s to society women looking for a mild smoke, was repositioned

PHILIP MORRIS
USA

>**snap**shot

Getting Full Value from Trade Shows

Increasingly, exhibitors at trade shows are driven by marketing return-on-investment (MROI) considerations. They need data to convince upper management that trade show participation is worth the time and effort. Observation techniques used at the retail level have crossed over to these trade show venues. Specifically, video ethnography and show traffic flow analysis can reveal that a trade show booth was located too close to the entrance, that display graphics lacked the attraction appeal of a competitor's booth, that space use discouraged involvement with personnel or display material, and even that more men than women ventured into a booth. Video ethnography typically involves multiple cameras used to continuously monitor participants and specific booths or spaces within booths over the multiple days of the show. Researchers then watch hours of tape to calculate booth-specific metrics. With traffic flow analysis, researchers track individual participants through the maze of booths from entrance to exit. To heighten understanding, additional researchers may interview tracked participants as they leave a particular booth to get motivation and attitude information to add to the behavioral data. Or participants might be enticed by prize lotteries or free passes for entertainment venues to carry PDAs that transmit specific questions about specific booths as they exit those booths—data that are beamed to a receiver and tallied as the show progresses, allowing adaptation of booth activities. So, the next time you attend a trade show watch for researchers. They will surely be watching you.

and reintroduced in 1954 as a filtered cigarette for men. The timing coincided with two events: the revelation of health concerns with smoking and the return of servicemen from Korea, where they acquired the smoking habit. The research tested consumer response to several new package designs to see what participants noticed and the nature of their responses. In a second phase, participants were interviewed to determine what they remembered. The bright-red ribbonlike element and the Philip Morris crest, still part of today's Marlboro package design, were originally designed to evoke the image of a medal, reminiscent of medals earned by soldiers in war.[5]

Other Behavioral Observation

Linguistic observation, the recording of human verbal behavior, is a second frequently used form of behavior observation. One simple type familiar to most students is the tally of "ahs" or other annoying sounds or words a professor makes or uses during a class. More serious applications are the study of a sales presentation's content or the study of what, how, and how much information is conveyed in an advertisement. A third form of linguistic behavior involves interaction processes that occur between two people or in small groups.

linguistic observation the observation of human verbal behavior during conversation, presentation, or interaction.

Behavior also may be analyzed on an extralinguistic level. Sometimes **extralinguistic observation** is as important a means of communication as linguistic observation. One author has suggested there are four dimensions of extralinguistic activity.[6] They are (1) vocal, including pitch, loudness, and timbre; (2) temporal, including the rate of speaking, duration of utterance, and rhythm; (3) interaction, including the tendencies to interrupt, dominate, or inhibit; and (4) verbal stylistic, including vocabulary and pronunciation peculiarities, dialect, and characteristic expressions. These dimensions could add substantial insight to the linguistic content of the interactions between salespeople and customers. Elections have frequently been influenced by such behavior, especially when debates are used as a means of getting a candidate's message to the voting public. Ronald Reagan was lauded for his command of extralinguistic behavior, and many credit his command with influencing his election as the 40th U.S. president.

extralinguistic observation the recording of vocal, temporal, interaction, and verbal stylistic behaviors of human participants.

A fourth type of behavior study, **spatial observation,** records how a person relates physically to others. One form of this study, *proxemics*, concerns how people organize the territory about them and how they maintain discrete distances between themselves and others.

spatial observation the recording of how humans physically relate to one another.

A study of how salespeople physically approach customers and a study of the effects of merchandise crowding in a retail environment are examples of this type of observation. What is viewed as acceptable in spatial relationships varies by culture, so an observation study in Asia would be different from one done in the United States.

Often in a study, the researcher will be interested in two or more of these types of information and will require more than one observer. In such forms of behavior study, it is important to consider the relationship between observers and participants.

> Evaluation of the Observation Method

The strengths and limitations of observation as a data collection method include:

Strengths

- Securing information about people or activities that cannot be derived from experiments or surveys.
- Avoiding participant filtering and forgetting.
- Securing environmental context information.
- Optimizing the naturalness of the research setting, to avoid influencing behavior.
- Reducing obtrusiveness (uninvited intrusion into a participant's life).

Limitations

- Enduring long periods to capture the relevant phenomena.
- Incurring higher expense of trained observers and specialized equipment.
- Having lower reliability of inferences from surface indicators.
- Quantifying data.
- Keeping disproportionately large records.
- Being limited on presenting activities and inferences about cognitive processes.

Observation is the only method available to gather certain types of information. The study of records, mechanical processes, and young children, as well as other inarticulate participants (for example, animals), falls into this category.

The observation study of trace evidence and records analysis permits a far more accurate depiction of past behavior than does a survey or other communication study. One successful television show, *CSI* on CBS, is based on this concept of accuracy of trace evidence as compared to data collected by communication. Our court system also puts more weight on factual systematic observation (collection of physical evidence) than it does on eyewitness testimony (participant recall through communication). Every participant filters information no matter how well intentioned he or she is. Forgetting occurs, and there are reasons why the respondent may not want to report fully and accurately. One value of observation is that we can collect the original data at the time they occur. We need not depend on reports by others. Observation overcomes many of these deficiencies, the same deficiencies associated with surveys and interviews.

Another strength of observation is that we can secure information that most participants would ignore either because it is so common and expected or because it is not seen as relevant. For example, if you are observing buying activity in a store, there may be conditions important to the research study that the shopper does not notice or consider important, such as: What is the weather? What is the day of the week or the time of the day? How heavy is customer traffic? What is the level of promotional activity in competing stores? We can expect to learn only a few of the answers to these questions by communicating with most participants.

Another advantage of observation is that it alone can capture the whole event as it occurs in its natural environment. Whereas the environment of an experiment may seem contrived to participants, and the number and types of questions limit the range of responses gathered from participants in communication studies, observation is less restrictive than

Lexus: The Winning Reaction

Observation should be a critical component in research even when it isn't the primary study design. The Team One/Lexus group had this point hammered home when the automaker unveiled its Lexus SC 430 retractable hardtop convertible at the New York Auto Show. Lexus had made exploratory communication studies a standard of its visits to the show, sending its agency team into the crowd to talk cars with luxury buyers clustering in and around competitor's booths. It was from these exploratory conversations the year before that Lexus learned that the primary motivations of the luxury-car segment were changing. One memory of the unveiling that remains crystal clear for account manager Adrian Barrow was the attendees' reaction. "They were drawn to the car, with that jaw-dropping-to-their-

knees look." Lexus, revered for its engineering, dependability, and reliability, didn't typically draw the same crowd as Jaguar and Maserati did at the show. So when attendees saw the car, their surprise was evident. "They couldn't get close enough to the car, or touch it or stroke it enough. You didn't need to talk to them; you could see the visceral reaction." That had to be a sweet sight for Team One and Lexus. The automaker's newest car, the one that had been crafted for looks and then performance ("from the skin in"), had just confirmed—before a single conversation was recorded—that it had the opportunity to add the desired passion to the *Pursuit of Perfection*.

www.teamoneadvertsing.com; www.lexus.com

most primary collection methods. Also, the limitations on the length of data collection activities imposed by surveys or experiments are relaxed for observation. For example, one may be interested in all the conditions surrounding an interaction between a potential customer entering HomeExtravaganza and the employees assigned to provide assistance and direction. Questioning could seldom provide the insight of observation for many aspects—body language, facial expression, tone of message delivery, directional pointing or accompanying the customer on her or his search, speed of walking—of the observational process.

Observation participants seem to accept an observational intrusion better than they respond to the intrusion of survey takers or interviewers. Individuals are under constant observation in today's culture. Cameras at the ATM or gasoline pump or traffic intersection, watchers observing life from a park bench, security personnel in our shopping malls, even TV shows like *Survivor* and *The Apprentice*—all have desensitized us to observation. Also, many observation studies are *concealed*—the participant doesn't know he or she is being observed. So observation is less demanding of participants and normally has a less biasing effect on their behavior than does questioning. With the use of video, it is possible to conduct *disguised* (the participant doesn't know the purpose of the observation) and unobtrusive observation studies much more easily than disguised questioning during an interview or a survey.

The observational method has some research limitations. A marketer may learn *what*, *where*, *who*, and *how*, and sometimes *with what effect*, but not *why* the people we observe behave as they do. It is difficult to gather information on such topics as intentions, attitudes, opinions, or preferences with observation.

Observation is a slow and expensive process that requires either human observers or costly surveillance equipment. The observer normally must be present at the scene of the event when it takes place, either in person or by some electronic means. Yet it is often impossible to predict where and when the event will occur. One way to guard against missing an event is to observe for prolonged periods until it does occur—a time-consuming process. And if behavior is videotaped, this approach leaves the researcher with hours of video or audio to review—adding more time before a decision can be reached. Even the observation of Web site activity can be a long process if a significant sample size is needed and participants visit a site or page infrequently or enter a site infrequently from a particular sponsor page of interest.

Observation is limited as a way to learn what is happening presently at some distant place or several widely separated places. Moving trained observers around or training several observers to record similar activities or their effects is, again, time-consuming and costly.

Observation may be at either a factual or an inferential level. Observation is most reliable when results are restricted to information that can be learned by overt action or surface indicators *(factual observation)*. To go below the surface, the observer must make inferences *(inferential observation)*. Inferences drawn from observation of customers in a retail store might be the use of a smile to infer that the customer is satisfied, feels comfortable in the environment, or feels welcomed. Two observers will probably agree on the nature of the surface event (a smile), but the inferences they draw from such data are much more variable. For some observers, a smile might infer that the customer just had a pleasant memory stimulated by a display of merchandise or that the salesperson seemed uncomfortable with the customer's question and the customer was trying to put the novice salesperson at ease. None of these inferences may be wrong, but neither may any be correct.

Exhibit 10-4 shows how we could separate the factual and inferential components of a salesperson's presentation. This table is suggestive only. It does not include many other variables that might be of interest, including data on customer purchase history; company, industry, and general economic conditions; the order in which sales arguments are presented; and specific words used to describe certain product characteristics. The particular content of observation will also be affected by the nature of the observation setting.

The observation environment is more suited to subjective assessment and recording of data than to controls and quantification of events. When control is exercised through active intervention by the researchers, their participation may threaten the validity of what is being assessed. Control is exercised through significant observer training and by use of a structured **observation checklist,** a measurement instrument for recording data in an observation study. The checklist provides the means for the observer to record the same observations for each participant or event. The structure itself—excluding some behaviors or effects of behaviors because they could not be anticipated—may threaten validity.

observation checklist the measurement instrument for recording data in an observation study.

>**Exhibit 10-4** Content of Observation: Factual versus Inferential

Factual	Inferential
Introduction/identification of salesperson and customer.	• Credibility of salesperson. Qualified status of customer.
Time and day of week.	• Convenience for the customer. Welcoming attitude of the customer.
Product presented.	• Customer interest in product.
Selling points presented per product.	• Customer acceptance of selling points per product.
Number of customer objections raised per product.	• Customer concerns about features and benefits.
Salesperson's rebuttal of objection.	• Effectiveness of salesperson's rebuttal attempts.
Salesperson's attempt to restore controls.	• Effectiveness of salesperson's control attempt. • Consequences for customer who prefers interaction.
Length of interview.	• Customer's/salesperson's degree of enthusiasm for the interview.
Environmental factors interfering with the interview.	• Level of distraction for the customer.
Customer purchase decision.	• General evaluation of sales presentation skill.

> The Observer-Participant Relationship

Communication with a participant presents a clear opportunity for interviewer bias. The problem is less pronounced with observation but is still real. The relationship between observer and participant may be viewed from three perspectives:

- Whether the observation is direct or indirect.
- Whether the observer's presence is known or unknown to the participant (concealment).
- What role the observer plays in the events or effects of events recorded.

Directness of Observation

Direct observation occurs when the observer is physically present and personally monitors what takes place. This approach is very flexible because it allows the observer to react to and report subtle aspects of events and behaviors as they occur. He or she is also free to shift places, change the focus of the observation, or concentrate on unexpected events if they occur. A weakness of this approach is that observers' perception circuits may become overloaded as events move quickly, and observers must later try to reconstruct what they were not able to record. Also, observer fatigue or boredom and distracting events can reduce the accuracy and completeness of direct observation.

direct observation when the observer is physically present and personally monitors and records the behavior of the participant.

   Indirect observation occurs when the recording is done by mechanical, photographic, or electronic means. For example, a special camera that takes one frame every second may be mounted in a department of a large store to study customer and employee movement. Indirect observation, while less flexible than direct observation, is also much less biasing and may be less erratic in accuracy. Another advantage of indirect observation is that the permanent record can be reanalyzed to include many different aspects of an event. Electronic recording devices, which have improved in quality and declined in cost, are being used more frequently in observation research.

indirect observation when the recording of data is done by mechanical, photographic, or electronic means.

Concealment

A second factor affecting the observer-participant relationship concerns whether the participant should know of the observer's presence or whether the observer's presence is concealed from the participant. When the observer is known, there is a risk of atypical activity by the participant. For example, an observed shopper might pick up a product and appear to be considering its purchase, whereas, if the shopper were not being observed, that product might not be among her or his normal consideration set. The initial entry of an observer into a situation often upsets the activity patterns of the participants, but this influence usually dissipates quickly, especially when participants are engaged in some absorbing activity or the presence of observers offers no potential threat to the participants' self-interest. The potential bias from participant awareness of observers is always a matter of concern, however.

   Observers use **concealment** to shield themselves from the object of their observation. Often, technical means such as mirrored windows, hidden cameras, or microphones are used. These methods reduce the risk of observer bias but bring up a question of ethics. Hidden observation is considered by some an invasion of privacy. In assessing the ethics, the propriety of concealment must be weighed against the resulting higher accuracy of information and an understanding that no harm must come to the participant. Once the observation is completed, debriefing the unsuspecting participant is a way to ensure no harm. When research involves child participants, researchers obtain prior parental consent to address these ethical issues.

concealment where the observer is shielded from the participant to avoid error caused by the observer's presence.

People Meters Go Personal

Television networks and stations measure audience viewing patterns to assist in making numerous decisions, among them program continuation or discontinuation, program location on the schedule, and advertising rates. They share this viewer data with advertisers, who then use the data to make network, station, and program selections. Nielsen Media Research partially collects its television viewer data for both broadcast and cable with electronic devices labeled "people meters." The people meter measures three things: the tuning state of the TV set (on, off, time); what channel/station is being tuned; and who is watching (via assigned code buttons). Additionally, households in the 53 largest markets have set-tuning meters that measure and transmit set-tuning data on a daily basis. There are 5,000 households in the national sample and more than 20,000 households in various local samples used to represent more than 102 million TV households in the United States. To supplement the people meter data, more than 1.6 million households provide written viewership diaries during four measurement periods known as "sweeps." Sweeps, usually two weeks long, occur in November, February, May, and July of each year.

As a result of an increase in media consumption outside the home, since May 2000 Nielsen Media Research and Arbitron have been testing a Portable People Meter (PPM system), pictured here, for media measurement in radio, television, and cable TV. People who accept an invitation to join a panel agree to carry a PPM with them wherever they go throughout the day. Media companies send out an inaudible signal attached to each program, which the PPM accepts. When a panel member returns home, he or she puts the PPM in a docking station for transmis-

sion. The various performance tests will be completed in the fall of 2004.

Participants are known to modify behavior when undisguised and unconcealed observation is used. Adaptations to normal behavior are rarely sustained over time. So Nielsen Media extends the time of observation to reduce this error source. Which part of Nielsen's research design employs observation techniques?

www.nielsenmedia.com; www.arbitron.com

A modified approach involves partial concealment. The presence of the observer is not concealed, but the objectives and participant of interest are. A study of selling methods may be conducted by sending an observer with a salesperson who is making calls on customers. However, the observer's real purpose may be hidden from both the salesperson and the customer (e.g., the researcher may pretend to be analyzing the display and layout characteristics of the stores they are visiting, when she or he is actually measuring linguistic behavior of a sales associate).

Sometimes a study involves phases where the research is concealed and others where it is not. Each year researchers from Digital Research, Inc., on behalf of *FamilyFun* magazine, use observation research as part of the selection of the annual Toy of the Year (TOY) awards. The participating companies receive invitations based on researchers' observation of toys in February at New York City's American International Toy Fair, where toy makers first unveil their best and brightest prospects for the end-of-year holiday season. Researchers then arrange play sessions for more than 100 local children in an elementary school. They use the children's play enjoyment to select the finalists, which are put to the play test again in 18 KinderCare locations around the country. Each day a new toy category is introduced at each center. During approximately three weeks, children play with the 71 finalists and then choose their favorite in each toy category in their age group as well as one favorite toy overall. The annual TOY awards have the ability to influence future toy design, as well as nearer-term marketing efforts.[7]

Participation

The third observer-participant issue is whether the observer should participate in the situation while observing. A more involved arrangement, **participant observation,** exists when the observer enters the social setting and acts as both an observer and a participant. Sometimes he or she is known as an observer to some or all of the participants; at other times the true role is concealed, as in a retail store when sales associates are evaluated by mystery shoppers. While reducing the potential for bias, this again raises an ethical issue. Often participants will not have given their consent and will not have knowledge of or access to the findings. After being deceived and having their privacy invaded, what further damage could come to the participants if the results became public? This issue needs to be addressed when concealment and covert participation are used.

Participant observation makes a dual demand on the observer. Recording can interfere with participation, and participation can interfere with recording. The observer's role may influence the way others act. Because of these problems, participant observation is used less in business research than, say, in anthropology or sociology. It is typically restricted to cases where nonparticipant observation is not practical—for example, a study of the functioning of a traveling auditing team.

participant observation
when the observer is physically involved in the research situation and interacts with the participant to influence some observation measures.

> **You may wish to revisit the snapshot on mystery shopping in Chapter 4, on page 90.**

> Conducting an Observation Study

The Type of Study

One author classifies observation studies by the degree of structure in the environmental setting and the amount of structure imposed on the environment by the researcher.[8] As reflected in Exhibit 10-5, observation studies can be divided into four classifications: (1) unstructured/natural, (2) unstructured/laboratory, (3) structured/natural, and (4) structured/laboratory. Each classification is used for a different research purpose; the first three are generally used to generate a hypothesis, while the fourth is used to test a hypothesis.

In a *structured observation,* very specific behaviors and effects are recorded, the same for every participant. In an *unstructured observation,* the researcher attempts to record all effects and behavior that occur with a specific participant in the context of a specific event. Structured observation requires a measuring instrument, an observation checklist, which is analogous to a questionnaire. Checklists should possess a high degree of precision in defining relevant behavior or acts and have mutually exclusive and exhaustive categories. Exhibit 10-6 shows the checklist development process.

A *natural study* occurs where the behavior or effect naturally takes place. A *laboratory study* attempts to simulate a natural environment but allows the researcher to manipulate and control variables being studied, actions often not possible in a natural setting. The researcher uses the facilities of a laboratory—videotape recording, mirrored windows, props, and stage sets—to introduce more control into the environment while simultaneously reducing the time needed for observation. In a laboratory setting, the participant groups being observed must be comparable and the laboratory conditions identical, just as in an experiment.

> **Exhibit 10-10 offers a sample of an observation checklist.**

>**Exhibit 10-5** Classification of Observation Studies

Research Class	Environment	Purpose	Research Tool	Example
1. Completely unstructured	Natural setting	Generate hypotheses	Recorded notes	Jason and Sara's exploratory trip to HomeExtravaganza to identify possible locations and behaviors to observe in the full-scale study.
2. Unstructured	Laboratory	Generate hypotheses	Pen-paper notes or electronically recorded	Videotaping participants as they maneuver through a "store" set up within a laboratory and recording their use of signage.
3. Structured	Natural setting	Generate hypotheses	Observation checklist	The full observation study that MarketViews will conduct for Visionary Insights, Inc., on client HomeExtravaganza.
4. Completely structured	Laboratory	Test hypotheses	Observation checklist; probably also electronic record of events	A follow-up study on HomeExtravaganza where a particpant will see computer-altered signage designs and placement. Modifications will reflect the direction provided by the earlier study.

>**Exhibit 10-6** Flowchart for Observation Checklist Design

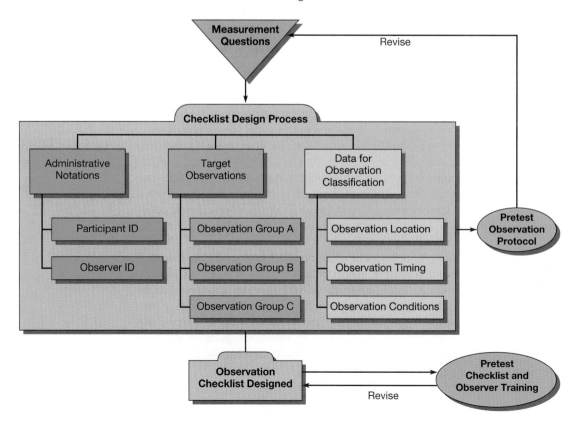

Content Specification

Specific conditions, events, or activities that we want to observe determine the observation reporting system (and correspond to measurement questions). To specify the observation content, we should include both the major variables of interest and any other variables that may affect them. From this cataloging, we then select those items we plan to observe. For each variable chosen, we must provide an operational definition if there is any question of concept ambiguity or special meanings. Even if the concept is a common one, we must make certain that all observers agree on the measurement terms by which to record results. Additionally, as we discussed earlier, observation data may be factual or inferential. For example, we may agree that variable W will be reported by count (factual), while for variable Y the observer will both record the count (factual) and judge qualitatively the effectiveness of its use (inferential).

Observer Training

There are a few general guidelines for the qualification and selection of observers:

- *Concentration*—ability to function in a setting full of distractions.
- *Detail-oriented*—ability to remember details of an experience.
- *Unobtrusive*—ability to blend with the setting and not be distinctive.
- *Experience level*—ability to extract the most from an observation study.

An obviously attractive observer may be a distraction in some settings but ideal in others. The same can be said for the characteristics of age or ethnic background.

For studies using direct observation with a simple checklist or coding system, prior experience is less important. Inexperience may even be an advantage if there is a risk that experienced observers may have preset convictions about the topic or if prior observations will influence what is perceived in a current observation—a condition called the **halo effect.** The observer can introduce error in other ways. Observers are subject to fatigue, and **observer drift,** which refers to a decay in consistency and accuracy over time that affects the coding of categories.[9] Only intensive videotaped training relieves these problems.

The observers should be thoroughly versed in the requirements of the specific study. Each observer should be informed of the outcomes sought and the precise content elements to be studied. Observer trials with the instrument and sample videotapes should be used until a high degree of reliability is apparent in the observers' observations. When there are interpretative differences between observers, they should be reconciled.

halo effect error caused when prior observations influence perceptions of current observations.

observer drift error caused by decay in consistency and accuracy on recorded observations over time, affecting categorization.

Research Design

The data collection plan specifies the details of the task. In essence it answers the questions who, what, when, how, and where.

Who?

Several questions related to people's responsibilities fall within this section of a plan. First, the plan must specify what qualifies a person to participate as a subject of the observation. This might be that the prospective participant meets a particular criterion (for example, be female) or initiates a specific action (for example, walks through the door of a store).

The plan must also indicate various responsibilities on the research side. Who will do the observing (for example, in a street ethnography)? Who might serve as an intermediary to help introduce an observer into an environment? Who serves as an emergency contact if conditions change or trouble develops? Who has primary responsibility for the various aspects of the study? Who fulfills ethical responsibilities (informed consent, debriefing) to the participants?

What?

The characteristics of the observation must be set as sampling elements and units of analysis. This is achieved when event-time dimension and "act" terms are defined. In **event sampling,** the researcher selects certain elements, behavioral acts, or conditions to record that answer the investigative questions. In **time sampling,** the researcher must choose among a time-point sample, continuous real-time measurement, or a time-interval sample. For a time-point sample, recording occurs at fixed points for a specified length. With continuous measurement, behavior or the elapsed time of the behavior is recorded. Like continuous measurement, time-interval sampling records every behavior in real time but counts the behavior only once during the interval.[10]

Assume the observer is instructed to observe a concession stand operation for 10 minutes out of each hour. Over a prolonged period, if the samples are drawn randomly, time sampling can give a good estimate of the pattern of activities. In a time-interval sampling of retail sales associates in a department store, the outcome may be a judgment of how well the workers are being supervised. In a study of sales presentations using continuous real-time sampling, the research outcome may be an assessment of a given salesperson's effectiveness or the effectiveness of different types of persuasive messages.

Other important dimensions are defined by acts. What constitutes an act is established by the needs of the study. It is the basic unit of observation. Any of the following could be defined as an act for an observation study:

- A single expressed thought.
- A physical movement.
- A facial expression.
- A motor skill.

Although acts may be well defined, they often present difficulties for the observer. A single statement from a sales presentation may include several thoughts about product advantages, a rebuttal to an objection about a feature, or some remark about a competitor. The observer is hard-pressed to sort out each thought, decide whether it represents a separate unit of observation, and then record it quickly enough to follow continued statements.

When?

Is the time of the study important, or can any time be used? In a study of out-of-stock conditions in a supermarket, the exact times of observation may be important. Inventory is shipped to the store on certain days only, and buying peaks occur on other days. The likelihood of a given product's being out of stock is a function of both time-related activities.

How?

Will the data be directly observed? If there are two or more observers, how will they divide the task? How will the results be recorded for later analysis? How will the observers deal with various situations that may occur—when expected actions do not take place or when someone challenges the observer in the setting?

Where?

Within a spatial confine, where does the act take place? In a retail traffic pattern study, the proximity of a customer's pause space to a display or directional sign might be recorded. Must the observation take place in a particular location within a larger venue? The location of the observation, such as a sales approach observation within a chain of retail stores, can significantly influence the acts recorded.

>**pic**profile

Few observation studies can approach the sheer size and comprehensiveness of SizeUSA, a digital observation study designed to make apparel, furniture, and car shopping more enjoyable. With obesity on the rise (20 percent of U.S. adults meet the government's definition for *obese,* with two-thirds being "overweight"), it's not surprising that manufacturers and retailers from Liz Claiborne to Steelcase to Ford to JCPenney's might need new insights. This may be in part because manufacturer's sizing was previously based on a 1941 study. But it was technology that made the three-dimensional scanning of American bodies possible. The Body Measurement System uses four cameras to register more than 200,000 data points on a body. These data points become coordinates for measuring from one data point to another. The resulting 200 body measurements take less than one minute. By September 2003, the study, sponsored by more than 30 manufacturers, retailers, and universities, scanned more than 10,000 adults. As a result, apparel manufacturers are reassessing garment specifications. Will it be long before car seats take on new dimensions, booths in restaurants expand for those with more ample proportions, casket builders redesign their products, or buying patterns for stocking retail shelves show a new understanding of regional differences in body shape? www.sizeusa.tc2.com

Observers face unlimited variations in conditions. Fortunately, most problems do not occur simultaneously. When the plans are thorough and the observers well trained, observation research is quite successful.

> Nonbehavioral Observation

Up to this point, our discussion has focused on direct observation as a traditional approach to data collection. Like surveys and experiments, some observation studies—particularly *participant observation*—require that the observer be physically involved in the research situation, interacting with the participant. This contributes to a **reactivity response,** a source of error where participants alter their true behavior in response to the researcher. For example, a salesperson might exhibit unexpected behavior if a participant observer portraying a customer challenges the accuracy of the salesperson's knowledge. Nonbehavioral observation, as its name implies, is an observation not of the behavior of a person but of the effects or traces of prior actions or of nonhuman activity. It is generally of three types: physical condition analysis, process or activity analysis, and record analysis.

reactivity response error introduced when participants alter their true behavior due to the presence of the observer.

Physical Condition Analysis

physical condition analysis the recording of observations of current conditions resulting from prior decisions.

Physical condition analysis is the observation of the effects of prior decisions. It is typified by store audits of merchandise availability or analysis of inventory conditions. Apparel retailers have long used physical condition analysis as a means of telling what merchandise is grabbing shopper attention. This can often be seen in the disarray of round rings of merchandise or the disruption of displays. While sales data captured at the register show what is selling, they don't fully reveal what captured shoppers' interest. Interest without purchase might be an indication of a possible future purchase, such as in a jumbled winter coat display in July. Or it could be an absence of value in the shopper's mind or an indication of defective merchandise, such as when a customer rejects apparel because it doesn't fit correctly or because the zipper is faulty. Like other observation studies, physical condition analysis cannot reveal the *motivation* behind a condition.

unobtrusive measures creative and imaginative forms of indirect observation, archival searches, and simple and contrived observation.

physical trace indirect observation that collects measures of erosion and measures of deposit.

Webb and his colleagues have given us an insight into some very innovative observational procedures that can be both nonreactive and inconspicuously applied. Called **unobtrusive measures,** these approaches encourage creative and imaginative forms of indirect observation, archival searches, and variations on simple and contrived observation.[11] Of particular interest are measures involving indirect observation based on **physical traces** that include *erosion* (measures of wear) and *accretion* (measures of deposit).

Natural *erosion measures* are illustrated by the frequency of replacement of vinyl floor tile in front of museum exhibits as an indicator of exhibit popularity. The study of wear and tear on book pages is a measure of library book use. Counting the remaining brochures in a car dealer's display rack after a favorable magazine review suggests consumer interest and traffic in the showroom.

Physical traces also include natural *accretion* such as discovering the listenership of radio stations by observing car radio settings as autos are brought in for service. Another type of unobtrusive study involves estimating liquor and magazine consumption by collecting and analyzing family trash. An interesting application compared beer consumption reports acquired through interviews with the findings of sampled trash. If the interview data were valid, the consumption figures for the area were at 15 percent. However, the validity was questioned when the beer can count from trash supported a 77 percent consumption rate.[12]

William Rathje is a professor of archaeology at the University of Arizona and founder of the Garbage Project in Tucson. His study of trash, refuse, rubbish, and litter resulted in the subdiscipline that the *Oxford English Dictionary* has termed *garbology.* By excavating landfills, he has gained insight into human behavior and cultural patterns—sometimes sorting the contents of up to 150 coded categories. His previous studies have shown that "people will describe their behavior to satisfy cultural expectations, like the mothers in Tucson who unanimously claimed they made their baby food from scratch, but whose garbage told a very different tale."[13]

Physical trace methods present a strong argument for use based on their ability to provide low-cost access to frequency, attendance, and incidence data without contamination from other methods or reactivity from participants. They offer excellent methods for validation. Thus, they work well as supplements to other methods. Designing an unobtrusive study can test a researcher's creativity, and one must be especially careful about inferences made from the findings. Erosion results may have occurred because of wear factors not considered, and accretion material may be the result of selective deposit or survival.

Process or Activity Analysis

process (activity) analysis observation by a time study of stages in a process, evaluated on both effectiveness and efficiency.

Process (or **activity**) **analysis** involves the time study of stages in a process, evaluating both effectiveness and efficiency. The stages might be sales transaction processes, traffic flows in a distribution system, paperwork flows related to contest participation, or order fulfillment steps in a cataloger's warehouse. While process or activity analysis might have behavioral components if the process is executed by people, it is the movement of the mer-

>**snap**shot

Wal-Mart Boosts RFID Technology for Observation

A consortium of 36 consumer packaged-goods (CPG) manufacturers, research companies, and universities has been working to change the way consumers generate and deliver purchase and consumption information, as well as how this information is integrated with detailed supply chain management information. If the Auto ID Center gets its way, all future CPGs will contain radio frequency identification (RFID) smart labels that will send signals to Internet databases and track a specific product unit from manufacturing through warehousing, retail display, and storage and potentially through consumer storage and consumption and the recycling center. Wal-Mart recently gave the new technology a boost by directing its 100 top suppliers to start using RFID technology as early as January 2005. By its sheer size, Wal-Mart's dictate could transform how observation studies in CPG are done. Goodyear, the world's largest tire manufacturer, also announced that its tires shipped to Wal-Mart in 2005 would contain an RFID microchip within the tire itself, which could also relay tire information to drivers about inflation and wear to improve vehicle safety.

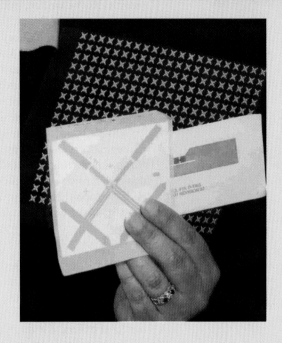

From a research perspective the opportunities seem enormous. Store shelf and display locations could be evaluated for promotional effectiveness, especially when combined with shopper card information. Average age of inventory could be known to the day or hour by matching the RFID location information with shipping and receiving documents. Product recalls could be handled with efficiency. While bar codes currently provide similar information to that promised by RFID tags, they must be scanned to be read. RFID tags need no such intervention but transmit continuously until disabled. Technically, if the tag on the product is not disabled at the time of purchase, the RFID tag could transmit location information from a consumer's car, home, or refrigerator. Such signals broadcast from a consumer's home or car would require compliance, similar to the way consumers volunteer to be part of ACNielsen's *Homescan* panel today. But according to Katherine Albrecht, founder of consumer action group CASPIAN, "Supermarket cards and retail surveillance devices are merely the opening volley of the marketers' war against consumers. If consumers fail to oppose these practices now, our long-term prospects may look like something from a dystopian science fiction novel."

The main driver of the RFID movement is supply chain savings. According to one analyst, Wal-Mart could save $8.4 billion a year by 2007 by perfecting its inventory management with the information provided by the tags. It also has the possibility of reducing theft, which is another large savings.

www.wal-martstores.com; www.goodyear.com; www.nocards.org; www.acnielsen.com; http://trolleyscan.com

chandise or the document, or the steps or subprocesses of a machine, that is of interest. In a day when instant photos and eyeglasses "in about an hour" are the norm, one dry cleaner was losing business to competitors over failure to meet the one-hour standard by 15 minutes. It tracked the source of the problem by a process analysis following a sample of garments. One step in the process related to customer care provisions. As a first-class operation, the dry cleaner resewed buttons that were loose or rehemmed pants or skirts—even if the garments were delivered to the store with these deficiencies. By demonstrating the extra value of this service, a value unknown to the customer, a small delay in availability was viewed as acceptable. The cleaner added a tag to the hanger that had a checklist of the "special customer care features" of its service and extended the promised time by the 15 minutes needed. In other examples, a retailer might want to study the processing of an order from merchandise delivery at a warehouse to sales floor in a mall, and an advertising agency might want to track the approval process of an ad storyboard.

Record Analysis

record analysis the extraction of data from current or historical records.

The most prevalent form of nonbehavioral observation research is **record analysis.** This may involve reviewing historical or current records and public or private records. The records may be written, printed, sound-recorded, photographed, videotaped, or digital.

An organization's own internal historical data are often an underutilized source of information in the exploratory or later phase of a research project. Due to employee turnover, the researcher may lack knowledge that such historical data exist or, based on time or budget constraints and the lack of an organized archive, the researcher may choose to ignore such data. The researcher using record analysis is basically a detective. Guided by a research question, the goal is to find patterns of information that offer sufficient insight to solve a problem or capture an opportunity.

While digging through data archives can be as simplistic as sorting through a file containing past patient records or inventory shipping manifests or rereading company reports (for example, financial statements or annual reports) and management-authored memos that have grown dusty with age, we will concentrate the remainder of our discussion here on more sophisticated structures and techniques.

Data Mining

data mining applying mathematical models to extract meaningful knowledge from integrated databases.

The term **data mining** describes the process of discovering knowledge from databases stored in data marts or data warehouses. An understanding of statistics is essential to the data mining process. Data mining tools perform exploratory and confirmatory statistical analysis to discover and validate relationships. The complex algorithms used in data mining have existed for more than two decades. The U.S. government has employed customized data mining to spot tax fraud, eavesdrop on foreign communications, and process satellite imagery.[14] Until recently, these tools have been available only to very large corporations or agencies due to their high costs. However, this is rapidly changing. In the evolution from *business data* to *information*, each new step built on previous ones. The four stages listed in Exhibit 10-7 were revolutionary because each allowed new management questions to be answered accurately and quickly.[15]

> See the "State Farm: Dangerous Intersections" case on your text DVD.

The process of extracting information from data has been done in some industries for years. Insurance companies often compete by finding small market segments where the premiums paid greatly outweigh the risks. They then issue specially priced policies to a particular segment with profitable results. However, two problems have limited the effectiveness of this process: Getting the data has been both difficult and expensive, and processing it into information has taken time—making it historical rather than predictive.

>**Exhibit 10-7** The Evolution of Data Mining

Evolutionary Step	Investigative Question	Enabling Technologies	Characteristics
Data collection (1960s)	"What was my average total revenue over the last five years?"	Computers, tapes, disks.	Retrospective, static data delivery.
Data access (1980s)	"What were unit sales in California last December?"	Relational databases (RDBMSs), structured query language (SQL), Open Database Connectivity (ODBC).	Retrospective, dynamic data delivery at the record level.
Data navigation (1990s)	"What were unit sales in California last December? Now drill down to Sacramento . . ."	Online analytic processing (OLAP), multidimensional databases, data warehouses.	Retrospective, dynamic data delivery at multiple levels.
Data mining (2000s)	"What's likely to happen to Sacramento unit sales next month? Why?"	Advanced algorithms, multiprocessor computers, massive databases.	Prospective, proactive information delivery.

In the recent past marketing databases maintained only the most current data necessary for decision support. Today's technology, however, allows organizations to maintain large archives containing historical information as well. Some researchers consider mining of these internal databases as part of a thorough secondary search.

We treat data mining here as a sophisticated method for producing marketing intelligence using the newest tools applied to the methodology of record analysis. While the subject of how data mining is done is better left to a management information systems or advanced statistics course, here we will look at how a researcher lays the foundation for such a research project.

A **data warehouse** is an electronic repository for databases that organizes large volumes of data into categories to facilitate retrieval, interpretation, and sorting by end users. The data warehouse provides an accessible archive to support dynamic organizational intelligence applications. The key words here are *dynamic* and *accessible*. Data warehouses that offer archaic methods for data retrieval are seldom used. Data in a data warehouse must be continually updated to ensure that managers have access to data appropriate for real-time decisions. In a data warehouse, the contents of departmental computers are duplicated in a central repository where standard architecture and consistent data definitions are applied. These data are available directly to departments or cross-functional teams for direct analysis or data may be available through intermediate storage facilities or **data marts** that compile locally required information. The entire system must be constructed for integration and compatibility among the different data marts. For decades Frito-Lay has used its extensive data warehouse to wedge new products into the crowded snack-food aisle by understanding the movement of snack foods through grocery stores, convenience stores, drugstores, and mass merchandisers. It is Frito-Lay's ability to use the predictive power of data mining that convinces store managers nationwide to modify stocking conditions in the snack-food aisle as well as on even more choice store real estate—the end-cap display.

The more accessible the databases that constitute the data warehouse, the more likely a researcher will use such databases to reveal patterns. Thus researchers are more likely to mine electronic databases than paper ones. It will be useful to remember that data in a data warehouse were once primary data, collected for a specific purpose. When researchers data-mine a company's data warehouse, all the data have become secondary data. The patterns revealed will be used for purposes other than those originally intended. It was State Farm Insurance's ability to mine its extensive nationwide database of accident locations and conditions at intersections where accidents occur that allowed it to identify high-risk intersections and then plan a primary data study to help communities determine alternatives to modify such intersections. Another example is an archive of sales invoices. In such invoices we have a wealth of data about what was sold, how much of each item or service was sold, at what price level, to whom, and where and when and how the products were shipped. Initially the company generated the sales invoice to facilitate the processes of billing and shipping. When a researcher mines that sales invoice archive, the search is for patterns of sales, by product, category, region of the country or world, price level, shipping methods, and so on. Therefore, data mining forms a bridge between primary and secondary data.

Traditional database queries are unidimensional and historical—for example, "How much beer was sold during December 2005 in the Sacramento area?" In contrast, data mining attempts to discover patterns and trends in the data and to infer rules from these patterns. For example, an analysis of retail sales by Sacramento FastShop identified products that are often purchased together—like beer and diapers—although they may appear to be unrelated. With the rules discovered from the data mining, a manager is able to support, review, and/or examine alternative courses of action for solving a management dilemma, alternatives that may later be studied further in the collection of new primary data.

Therefore, the purpose of data mining is to identify valid, novel, useful, and ultimately understandable patterns in data.[16] Similar to traditional mining, where we search beneath the surface for valuable ore, data mining searches large databases for information for managing an organization. Both require sifting a large amount of material to discover a profitable vein.

data warehouse electronic storehouse where vast arrays of collected, integrated data are ready for mining.

data mart intermediate storage facility that compiles locally required information.

Data mining technology provides two unique capabilities to the researcher or manager: pattern discovery and prediction.

Pattern Discovery   Data mining tools can be programmed to sweep regularly through databases and identify previously hidden patterns. An example of pattern discovery is the detection of stolen credit cards based on analysis of credit card transaction records. MasterCard processes 12 million transactions daily and uses data mining to detect fraud.[17] Other uses include finding retail purchase patterns (used for inventory management), identifying call center volume fluctuations (used for staffing), and locating anomalous data that could represent data entry errors (used to evaluate the need for training, employee evaluation, or security).

>Exhibit 10-8 Sample Data Mining Applications

Company	Use of Data Mining
Blue Cross Blue Shield	Mines data on member and provider questions about insurance claims and patient history, as well as inquiry/call history to improve call center staffing and training.
BMW	Uses data mining in the execution of its "stochastic crash-simulation technology," enabling "design improvements to the crashworthiness and safety of automobiles" while reducing product design cycle time.
Coca-Cola FEMSA	A Mexican bottler and distributor to Mexico, Argentina, and Latin America, uses data mining to decrease stockouts, reduce inventory, minimize variability in operations, and manage promotions.
Colgate-Palmolive	Operating in more than 200 countries, uses data mining to improve forecasts, production plans, and customer order fulfillment, as well as reduce overall order cycle times and costs.
Dow Chemical	In its data warehouse, stores news articles about clients, as well as a complete purchase history; uses data mining to improve sales visit effectiveness.
Hewlett-Packard	Used data mining to identify every World Trade Center customer and its systems and components at the time of the September 11, 2001, collapse. These components were matched with on-hand inventory in warehouses, in preparation for replacing destroyed systems.
IBM	Helps biologists make sense of the drastically increased amount of data that can be brought to bear on any biological or medical question. Its GeneMine was "designed to help scientists rapidly infer, validate, and propose experimental tests for the likely functions of unknown genes."
Meineke Discount Muffler Shops	A 900-plus franchised nationwide retail service provider, adds more than 5,000 customer and service records each week to an extensive data warehouse it then mines using MapInfo's MapMarker to make more effective advertising decisions and identify new franchise locations.
State Farm Insurance	Used observation as a way of verifying or negating patterns of behavior at intersections; documented the 10 worst intersections for auto claims and then used the results to plan a public relations grant program to help cities correct the problem.
Gillette	Partnered with PricewaterhouseCoopers, uses data mining to plan on-location promotional store displays for its German retailers.
Wal-Mart Stores	Uses data mining to design and modify store layouts to reduce shoplifting and theft.

Source: "Software to Track Customers' Needs Helped Firms React," *New York Times on the Web,* Oct. 1, 2001 http://www.nytimes.com/2001/10/01/technology/01CRM.html; the supply chain management special advertising section, *BusinessWeek,* Oct. 8, 2001; "SAP Customer Success Stories," http://www.mysap.com/solutions/crm/customersuccesses.asp/Gillette_50050088.pdf; "The GeneMine System for Genome/Proteome Annotation and Collaborative Data Mining," *IBM Systems Journal* 40, no. 2, 2001 http://www.research.ibm.com/journal/sj/402/lee.html; Silicon Graphics Inc.,"BMW Pioneers Stochastic Crash Simulation for Improved Vehicle Safety," http://www.sgi.com/manufacturing/success/bmw.html; "NCR More than Doubles Data Warehouse for World's Leading Retailer to over 100 Terabytes," http://hpcwire.com/dsstart/99/0824/100966.html; S. Reese, "Bad Mufflers Make Good Data," *American Demographics,* November 1998, pp. 42–44.

Predicting Trends and Behaviors   A typical example of a predictive problem is targeted marketing. Using data from past promotional mailings to identify the targets most likely to maximize return on investment, future mailings can be more effective. Bank of America and Mellon Bank both use data mining software to pinpoint marketing programs that attract high-margin, low-risk customers. Bank of America focuses on credit lines and retail lending; Mellon Bank has used data mining to optimize its home equity line of credit marketing to existing customers.[18] Other predictive problems include forecasting bankruptcy and loan default and finding population segments with similar responses to a given stimulus. Data mining tools also can be used to build risk models for a specific market, such as discovering the top 10 most significant buying trends each week. Exhibit 10-8 reveals how several organizations are using data mining.

The Data Mining Process   Data mining, as depicted in Exhibit 10-9, involves a five-step process:[19]

- *Sample.* Decide between census data (using all the records in a database) and sample data (using a portion of the records in the database).[20]
- *Explore.* Identify relationships within the data.
- *Modify.* Modify or transform data.
- *Model.* Develop a model that explains the data relationships.
- *Assess.* Test the model's accuracy.

Sample.   If the data set in question is not large, if the processing power of the computing is high, or if it is important to understand patterns for every record in the database, sampling should not be done. However, if the data set is very large (for example,

>**Exhibit 10-9** Data-Mining Process

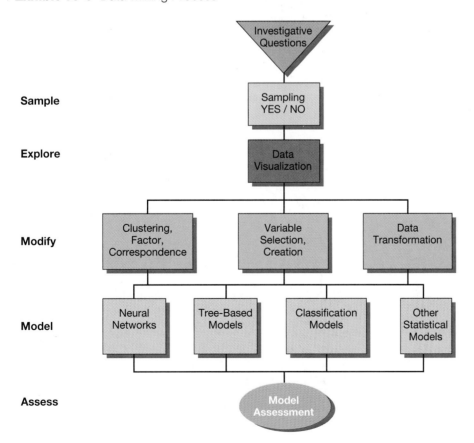

Designing the Observation Study

The design of a behavioral observation study follows the same pattern as other research. Once the researcher has specified the investigative questions, it is often apparent that the best way to conduct the study is through observation. Guidance for conducting a behavioral observation and translating the investigative question(s) into an observational checklist is the subject of this Close-Up. We first review the procedural steps and then explain how to create a checklist.

Most studies that use behavioral observation follow a general sequence of steps that parallel the research process. (See Exhibit 10-1.) Here we adapt those steps to the terminology of the observational method:

- Define the content of the study.
- Develop a data collection plan that identifies the observational targets, sampling strategy, and acts (operationalized as a checklist or coding scheme).
- Secure and train observers.
- Collect the data.
- Analyze the data.

In this chapter's Behind the Scenes, we recount an incident in which Visionary Insights is subcontracting a behavioral observation study to MarketViews, a specialty research firm. VI's client, HomeExtravaganza, is experiencing declining repeat visits at its new superstore units. Preliminary results from a periodic survey indicate that customer confusion in the megastore is discouraging customers from returning, so an observation study is planned to see how employees and store design elements contribute to or solve the problem. The research questions might be:

- What do employees do to reduce or eliminate customer confusion?
- What do employees do that contributes to customer confusion?
- Which design elements diffuse customer confusion?
- Which design elements contribute to customer confusion?

Futher assume that the survey indicates that customers who feel confused and cited this confusion as their reason for not returning had entered the store looking for a variety of merchandise, stocked in various locations throughout the vast store. They described their hopelessness as evolving from the experience of not knowing where to start the process of searching. Such customers showed no particular similarities or differences in terms of ethnic background, age, or education level. Some had the assistance of greeters or floor assistance associates, while others did not.

The observation targets will be twofold: shoppers entering the store through the main entrance and employees serving as greeters and floor assistance associates. Customers who request assistance from the main-entrance greeter or who consult the directional location signs will be the primary target. If they approach a floor assistance associate, the employee will also become a target.

Survey research reveals some inconsistency by time of day and type of merchandise sought, so MarketViews plans to sample during four primary day parts—early morning, midday, afternoon, and early evening—as well as at all three "directional locations," where signage describing the store and the shopper's current "You are here" location is noted.

Notes taken by Jason and Sara during a tour of the store help to identify the acts to record. During their subsequent meeting, it is decided that MarketViews will record the customer's seeking of assistance, either personal or signage; his or her consulting of the directional signage and its location; the customer's path to the desired merchandise; and whether a purchase is completed. The assistance acts of the floor assistance associate will also be recorded. These are determined to be assistance versus no assistance, pointing plus verbal direction, verbal direction only, providing the customer with a store copy-sheet directional map on which the associate marks the location of the merchandise and the path to get there, inquiry to other staff for location assistance, passing the customer to another floor assistance associate, accompanying the customer to the correct aisle, accompanying the customer to actual merchandise shelf location, and providing verbal assistance to selection of the appropriate product from the array of products provided.

It is determined that a checklist will be created and tested by MarketViews, with any necessary changes occurring after the test. The checklist developed is shown in Exhibit 10-10. The foremost concern is that either the customer or the associate will discover that he or she is being observed and will change behavior. Human observers will be used to trace the path of observational targets. By means of the store's security cameras, researchers will record customers flowing through the main entrance and past the greeter location and stopping at directional location signs. Counts of brochure store maps distributed from the directional signage locations and copy-sheet directional maps used by floor assistance associates will also be used as a measure of customers seeking directional assistance.

>**Exhibit 10-10** Sample Checklist for HomeExtravaganza Study

Time_____ Day: M T W Th F Sa Su Date_____ Store No. _____ Observer #_____

Target Customer Interception Location: ❑ Main Entry ❑ Directional Location Sign: ❑ #1
❑ #2
❑ #3

Target Shopper Characteristics: ❑ Male ❑ Female
❑ Child ❑ Child-teen+ ❑ Adult ❑ Senior

Shopper Companion(s): ❑ Alone ❑ With others: ❑ other adult No. ___ M No. ___ F
❑ child/children No. ___

Shopping Cart Used: ❑ No ❑ Yes

Greeter verbal interaction with target: ❑ No ❑ Yes Greeter No. _____
Action ❑ Point to directional sign
❑ Verbal directions

Floor Assistance Associate Interaction: ❑ No ❑ Yes Interception location: Aisle# _____ Crossway# _____
Associate # _____
Assistance given: ❑ No ❑ Yes Action: ❑ Verbal direction only
❑ Verbal direction plus pointing
❑ Store directional copy-map with marked mdse location
❑ Store directional copy-map with mdse location & path
❑ Inquire of other staff
❑ Pass customer to another FAA
❑ Accompany customer to aisle location
❑ Accompany customer to mdse shelf location
❑ Product selection assistance offered

Directional Sign Interaction: ❑ No ❑ Yes Sign location: ❑ #1
❑ #2
❑ #3

Purchase: ❑ No ❑ Yes: Item Sought Assistance For: ❑ No ❑ Yes

Customer Path:

> **For an appropriate sampling technique, choose from among those described in Chapter 16.**

Wal-Mart's data warehouse is estimated to contain terabytes of data), the processing power is limited, or speed is more important than complete analysis, it is wise to draw a sample. In some instances, researchers may use a subset of the data, for example, local data that are appropriate for their geography or data from one store versus the whole chain. Alternatively, researchers may select an appropriate sampling technique. Since fast turnaround for decisions is often more important than absolute accuracy, sampling is appropriate.

If general patterns exist in the data as a whole, these patterns will be found in the sample. If a niche is so tiny that it is not represented in a sample yet is so important that it influences the big picture, it will be found using exploratory data analysis (EDA).

> **We explore EDA techniques in Chapter 18.**

Explore.   After the data are sampled, the next step is to explore them visually or numerically for trends or groups. Both visual and statistical exploration (data visualization) can be used to identify trends. The researcher also looks for outliers—data that are unusual—to see if the data need to be cleaned, cases need to be dropped, or a larger sample needs to be drawn.

Modify.   Based on the discoveries in the exploration phase, the data may require modification. Several sophisticated statistical techniques are completed during this phase as appropriate. A data reduction program, such as factor analysis, correspondence analysis, or clustering, may be used (see Chapter 21). Sometimes during this phase, new constructs are discovered. During modification new factors may be introduced to categorize the data into groups. In addition, variables based on combinations of existing variables may be added, recoded, transformed, or dropped.

At times, finding descriptive segments within the data is all that is required to answer the investigative question. However, if a complex predictive model is needed, the researcher will move to the next step of the process.

Model.   Modeling techniques in data mining include the use of sophisticated multivariate techniques. The purpose of discovering a model within the records being analyzed is to be able to predict or estimate future behavior based on past behavior.

Assess.   The final step in data mining is to assess the model to estimate how well it performs. A common method of assessment involves applying the model to a portion of data that was not used during the sampling stage. If the model is valid, it will work for this "holdout" sample. Another way to test a model is to run the model against known data. For example, if you know which customers in a file have high loyalty and your model predicts techniques that are designed to create loyalty, you can check to see whether the model will select these customers accurately.

>summary

1 Observation is one of the few options available for studying records, mechanical processes, small children, and complex interactive processes. We can gather data as the event occurs and can come closer to capturing the whole event than is possible with communication. On the other hand, we have to be present to catch the event or have some recording device on the scene to do the job.

2 Observation includes a variety of monitoring situations that cover nonbehavioral and behavioral activities.

3 The strengths of observation as a data collection method include:

- Securing information about people or activities that cannot be derived from experiments or surveys.

- Avoiding participant filtering and forgetting.

- Securing environmental context information.

- Optimizing the naturalness of the research setting.

- Reducing obtrusiveness.

4 Observation may be limited by:

- The difficulty of waiting for long periods to capture the relevant phenomena.

- The expense of observer costs and equipment.

- The reliability of inferences from surface indicators.

- The problems of quantification and disproportionately large records.

- The limitation on presenting activities and inferences about cognitive processes.

5 We can classify observation in terms of the observer-participant relationship. This relationship may be viewed from three perspectives: (a) Is the observation direct or indirect?

(b) Is the observer's presence known or unknown? (c) Is the observer a participant or nonparticipant?

6 The design of an observation study follows the same general pattern as other research. Observational studies fall into four general types based on the degree of structure and the nature of the observational environment. The researcher must define the content of the study; develop a data collection plan that identifies participants, sampling strategy, and "acts" (often operationalized as a checklist or coding scheme); secure and train observers; and launch the study.

Unobtrusive measures offer an unusual and creative approach to reducing reactivity in observational research by indirect observation and other methods. Measures of erosion and accretion serve as ways to confirm the findings from other methods or operate as singular data sources.

7 Managers faced with current decisions requiring immediate attention often overlook internal data in a company's data warehouse. Data mining is the process of discovering knowledge from databases. Data mining technology provides two unique capabilities to the researcher or manager: pattern discovery and the prediction of trends and behaviors. Data mining tools perform exploratory and confirmatory statistical analyses to discover and validate relationships. These tools even extend confirmatory statistical approaches by allowing the automated examination of large numbers of hypotheses. Data mining involves a five-step process: sample, explore, modify, model, and assess.

>**key**terms

concealment 251	observation	observation checklist 250
data mart 261	direct 251	observer drift 255
data mining 260	extralinguistic 247	physical condition analysis 258
data warehouse 261	indirect 251	physical trace 258
event sampling 256	linguistic 247	process (activity) analysis 258
halo effect 255	nonverbal 245	reactivity response 257
	participant 253	record analysis 260
	simple 242	time sampling 256
	spatial 247	unobtrusive measures 258
	systematic 243	

>**discussion**questions

Terms in Review

1 Compare the advantages and disadvantages of the communication study to those of observation. Under which circumstances could you make a case for using observation?

2 What ethical risks are involved in observation? In the use of unobtrusive measures?

3 Based on present or past work experience, suggest problems that could be resolved by using observation-based data.

4 Distinguish between the following:

  a The relative value of communication and observation.

  b Nonverbal, linguistic, and extralinguistic analysis.

  c Factual and inferential observation.

Making Research Decisions

5 The observer-participant relationship is an important consideration in the design of observation studies. What kind of relationship would you recommend in each of the following cases?

  a Observations of professional conduct in the classroom by the student author of a course evaluation guide.

  b Observation of retail shoppers by a researcher who is interested in determining customer purchase time by type of goods purchased.

  c Observation of a focus group interview by a client.

6 Assume you are the manufacturer of modular office systems and furniture as well as office organization elements (desktop and wall organizers, filing systems, etc.). Your company has been asked to propose an observation study to examine the use of office space by white-collar and managerial workers for a large insurance company. This study will be part of a project to improve office efficiency and paperwork flow. It is expected to involve the redesign of office space and the purchase of new office furniture and organization elements.

a What are the varieties of acts that might be observed?

b Select a limited number of content areas for study, and operationally define the observation acts that should be measured.

7 Develop a checklist to be used by observers in the previous study.

a Determine how many observers you need, and assign two or three to a specific observation task.

b Compare the results of your group members' checklists for stability of recorded perceptions.

8 You wish to analyze the pedestrian traffic that passes a given store in a major shopping center. You are interested in determining how many shoppers pass by this store, and you would like to classify these shoppers on various relevant dimensions. Any information you secure should be obtainable from observation alone.

a What other information might you find useful to observe?

b How would you decide what information to collect?

c Devise the operational definitions you would need.

d What would you say in your instructions to the observers you plan to use?

e How might you sample this shopper traffic?

Behind the Scenes

9 Develop the investigative questions that might have guided MarketViews' observation study at HomeExtravaganza.

From Concept to Practice

10 Using Exhibit 10-3, identify the type of study described in each of the Snapshots featured in this chapter.

>**www**exercise

One of the longest ongoing observation studies is the garbage project at the University of Arizona. If you manufactured packaging materials for food and personal care products, how might you use what the researchers have learned? To get started, try **bara.arizona.edu/gs.htm.**

>**cases**[*]

 Envirosell

Retailer Unhappy with Manufacturer Displays

NetConversions Influences Kelley Blue Book

State Farm: Dangerous Intersections

* All cases, both written and video, are on the text DVD. The film icon indicates a video case. Check the DVD Index to determine whether a case has data, the research instrument, or other supplementary material.

chapter 11

Surveys and Interviews

>**learning**objectives

After reading this chapter, you should understand . . .

1 The process for selecting the appropriate and optimal communication approach.

2 What factors affect participation in communication studies.

3 The major sources of error in communication studies and how to minimize them.

4 The major advantages and disadvantages of the three communication approaches.

5 Why an organization might outsource a communication study.

Visionary Insights has been asked by Albany Outpatient Laser Clinic Inc. to develop a survey to assess patient satisfaction. As part of the exploratory phase, Sara Armstrong has been reviewing documentation provided by the clinic. Complaint letters were included in the documentation.

"Jason, you'll enjoy this one," Sara comments as she arrives for their meeting to discuss the Albany Outpatient Laser Clinic patient satisfaction project. She extends the letter and smiles widely.

"Is that the letter that clinic administrator George Bowlus promised he'd send over this morning?"

Sara nods as she passes it across the desk

Edna Koogan, P. A., Attorney at Law
P. O. Box 8219-2767
Albany, New York 12212-2767

Dr. Edith Coblenz, M.D.
3456 Barshoot Building
Albany, New York 12212

Dear Edith,

I want you to have my side of this morning's incident at the Albany Outpatient Laser Clinic Inc. I am sure you have by now heard from the business manager and the admissions director and possibly the anesthetist. You are a stockholder in the center, I know, and as your former lawyer and current patient, I thought I owed you a warning and explanation.

You told me to report to the center at 7 a.m. for a workup in preparation for eye surgery tomorrow. I caught a cab and was there at 6:55 promptly. I identified myself as your patient, and at once the receptionist called someone from the back room and said, "Ms. Koogan's personal physician is Dr. Coblenz," which is, of course, not true, as you are my eye doctor. But I was too cold to argue since they had left us standing in the snow until 7:10.

A fellow insisted on taking my glasses and medications with him "for a workup." As soon as he disappeared with my glasses a second admissions clerk appeared and handed me a "questionnaire" to fill out. It appeared to be a photocopy of a photocopy of a photocopy and was very faintly printed in small gray type on a light gray sheet. When I pointed out that I was about to be admitted for treatment of glaucoma, a leading cause of blindness, she told me, "Do the best you can." When I objected emphatically, she seemed taken aback. I suppose most of her 80-year-old patients are more compliant, but I guess I am an intractable old attorney.

Was I wrong to object to the questionnaire being too faint and the type too small? Am I the first glaucoma patient who has ever been treated at the Laser Center? One would think they would understand you can't ask someone blind in one eye to fill out such a questionnaire, especially without her glasses. The clerk finally, grudgingly, asked me to sit by her side, so she could help me.

There were several questions about my name, address, age, and occupation. Then she wanted to know the name of the admitting physician and then the phone number (but not the name) of the physician who was most familiar with my health. I said the admitting physician was an eye doctor and the physician most familiar with my health was a GP, and asked, which did she want the phone number for, the eye doctor or the GP? She admonished me to try and "get over that bad attitude." Then she told me to go fill out the form as best I could.

A very nice patient (hemorrhoids, no vision problems) offered to help me. She began reading the questionnaire and came to the item "Past Medical History: Yes or No." She didn't think this made any sense, and neither did I, because everyone has a past medical history, and no one

Dr. Edith Coblenz, M.D.   Page 2

would answer no; but after a while we decided that it meant I should answer yes or no to all of the questions underneath, such as: Did I have diabetes? Did I have heart disease? When we came to "Have you ever had or been treated for the flu?" we could not decide if it meant, have I ever had the flu? Or have I had flu recently (I had flu six months ago, but is that "recent"?) so we asked the receptionist. She became almost speechless and said she would get me some help.

After a while the "help" appeared—a nurse who wanted to measure my blood pressure and induce me to take a blue pill, which she said would be good for my "nerves." I refused and pointed out rather curtly that this was not a gulag but an admissions department, a place of business, for crying out loud, where they ought to be able to handle a little criticism from someone trained to elicit accurate information.

By then several nice people had pitched in to help me with the questionnaire. But this made it even harder to decide on the answers, because we understood so many of the questions differently and couldn't agree. When we came to "Are all your teeth intact?" One man thought it meant, "Do you have false teeth?" And another thought it meant, "Do you have any broken dentures?" But a woman who assured me her son is a dentist said it meant, "Do you have any loose teeth?" We couldn't decide how to settle this issue.

Then there was the question "Do you have limited motion of your neck?" and by then everyone was enjoying the incongruity of these questions. Of course I have limited motion of the neck. Doesn't everyone? We decided to save that question for later clarification.

After all of the yes-no questions there came various other stumpers, such as "Please list your current medications." The problem is, of course, that I have purple eye drops and yellow eye drops, but the young man had taken them away from me "for a workup," so I had no way of accurately answering the questions. I was pretty sure one of them was glucagon, so I guessed and put that down, but then I had second thoughts and scratched it out. (When I got home, I checked and it was betagan, not glucagon.)

There were four of us working on the questionnaire by then, and we were laughing and crowing and having a high time and discharging our anxieties, which further annoyed the admissions clerk. So she called the anesthetist, a stuck-up young fellow who said he had written the questionnaire himself and had never had any problems with it. That is when I told him, if he had not had any problems with this questionnaire, this proved it was better to be lucky than smart.

He said he was going to overlook my "attitude" because he knew I was old and anxious about the coming operation. I told him I was going to take my business somewhere else because of the bilaterality problem. "What is that?" he asked. I said, I have two eyes, and if anyone as dumb as him went after me with a laser, he would probably cut the wrong eye.

I caught a cab and sent my neighbor back for my glasses. As your lawyer, I urge you not to further involve yourself with such fools.

Edna

"It would seem that Albany Clinic might need help with questionnaire development," comments Jason.

Sara responds sarcastically, "You think?"

> Characteristics of the Communication Approach

Research designs can be classified by the approach used to gather primary data. There are two alternatives. We can observe conditions, behavior, events, people, or processes. Or we can *communicate* with people about various topics, including participants' attitudes, motivations, intentions, and expectations. The researcher determines the appropriate data collection approach largely by identifying the types of information needed—investigative questions the researcher must answer. As marketers we learn much about opinions and attitudes by communication-based research; observation techniques are incapable of revealing such critical elements. This is also true of intentions, expectations, motivations, and knowledge. Information about past events is often available only through surveying or interviewing people who remember the events. Thus, the choice of a communication versus an observation approach may seem an obvious one, given the directions in which investigative questions may lead. The characteristics of the sample unit—specifically, whether a participant can articulate his or her ideas, thoughts, and experiences—also play a role in the decision. Part A of Exhibit 11-1 shows the relationship of these decisions to the research process detailed in Chapter 4. Part B indicates how the researcher's choice of a communication approach affects the following:

- The creation and selection of the measurement questions (to be explored in Chapters 13 and 14).

- Instrument design (to be discussed in Chapter 15), which incorporates attempts to reduce error and create participant-screening procedures.

- Sampling issues (explored in Chapters 16 and 17), which drive contact and callback procedures.

- Data collection processes, which create the need for follow-up procedures (when self-administered instruments are used) and possible interviewer training (when personal or telephone surveying methods are used).

In this chapter we focus on the choices the researcher must make once the communication approach has been chosen (Exhibit 11-2). We discuss the characteristics and applications of the various communication approaches as well as their individual strengths and weaknesses (summarized in Exhibit 11-5).

The **communication approach** involves surveying or interviewing people and recording their responses for analysis. A **survey** is a measurement process used to collect information during a highly structured interview—sometimes with a human interviewer and other times without. Questions are carefully chosen or crafted, sequenced, and precisely asked of each participant. The goal of the survey is to derive comparable data across subsets of the chosen sample so that similarities and differences can be found. When combined with statistical probability sampling for selecting participants, survey findings and conclusions are projectable to large and diverse populations.

The great strength of the survey as a primary data collecting approach is its versatility. Abstract information of all types can be gathered by questioning others. Additionally, a few well-chosen questions can yield information that would take much more time and effort to gather by observation. A survey that uses the telephone, mail, a computer, e-mail, or the Internet as the medium of communication can expand geographic coverage at a fraction of the cost and time required by observation. The bad news for communication research is all communication research has some error. Understanding the various sources of error helps researchers avoid or diminish such error.

communication approach a design involving surveying or interviewing people.

survey a measurement process using a highly structured interview.

> **The communication approach differs significantly from the observation approach discussed in Chapter 10. You might wish to revisit Exhibit 10-2 where the methods are compared.**

Error in Communication Research

As depicted in Exhibit 11-3, there are three major sources of error in communication research: measurement questions and survey instruments, interviewers, and participants. Researchers cannot help a marketing decision maker answer a research question if they (1) select or craft inappropriate questions, (2) ask them in an inappropriate order, or (3) use inappropriate transitions and instructions to elicit information. We will spend considerable time in Chapters 13, 14, and 15 discovering ways to avoid these sources of error.

>**Exhibit 11-1** Data Collection Approach: Impact on the Research Process

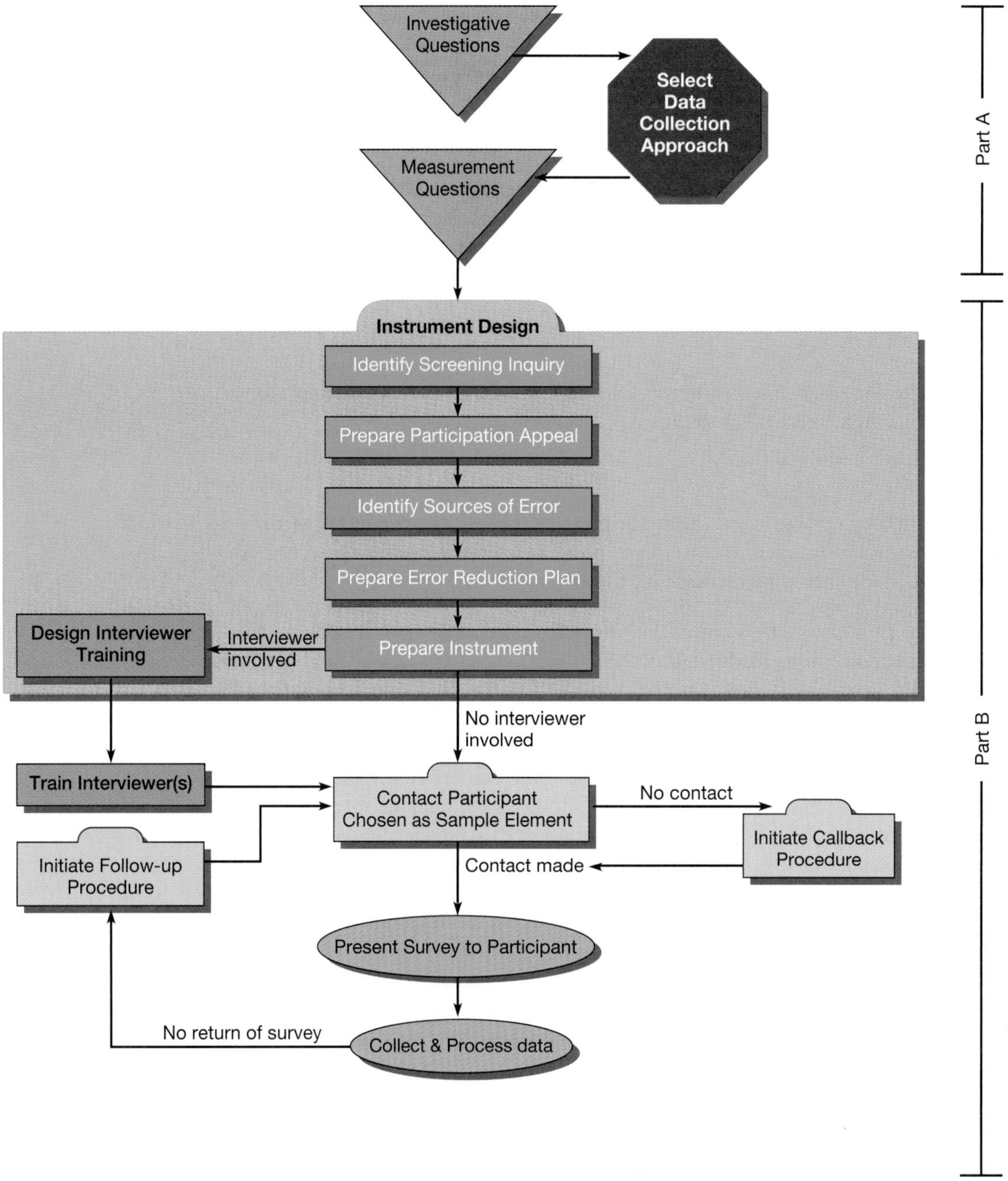

Interviewer Error

interviewer error error that results from interviewer influence of the participant.

From the introduction to the conclusion of the interview, there are many points where the interviewer's control of the process can affect the quality of the data. **Interviewer error,** a major source of sampling error and response bias, is caused by numerous actions:

• *Failure to secure full participant cooperation (sampling error).* The sample is likely to be biased if interviewers do not do a good job of enlisting participant cooperation. While instrument error was evident in the Albany clinic study, there is also a question of whether the distributor of the survey (the receptionist) contributed to the lack of data quality in the data collected from Edna. Toward the end of the communica-

>**Exhibit 11-2** Selecting a Communication Data Collection Method

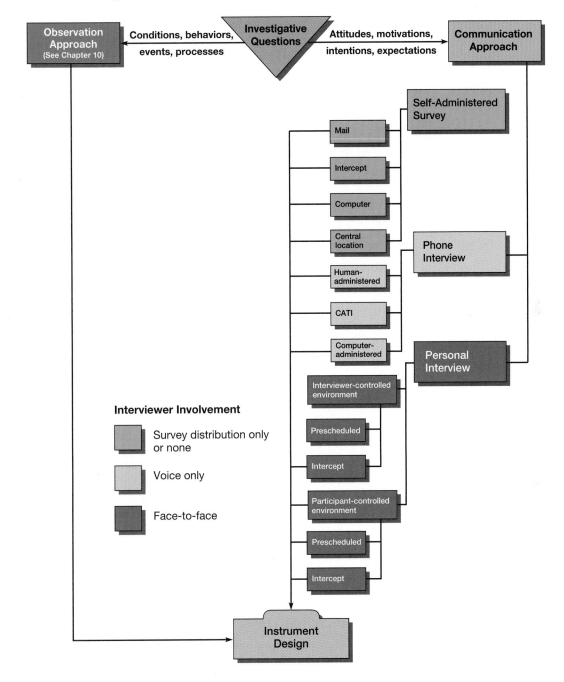

tion, there is some doubt about the seriousness with which questions were answered. Stressing the importance of the information for the upcoming surgery and having a receptionist trained to serve as question interpreter/prober could reduce this type of error.

• *Failure to record answers accurately and completely (data entry error).* Error may result from an interview recording procedure that forces the interviewer to summarize or interpret participant answers or that provides insufficient space to record verbatim answers as provided by the participant.

• *Failure to consistently execute interview procedures.* The precision of survey estimates will be reduced and there will be more error around estimates to the extent that

>**Exhibit 11-3** Sources of Error in Communication Research

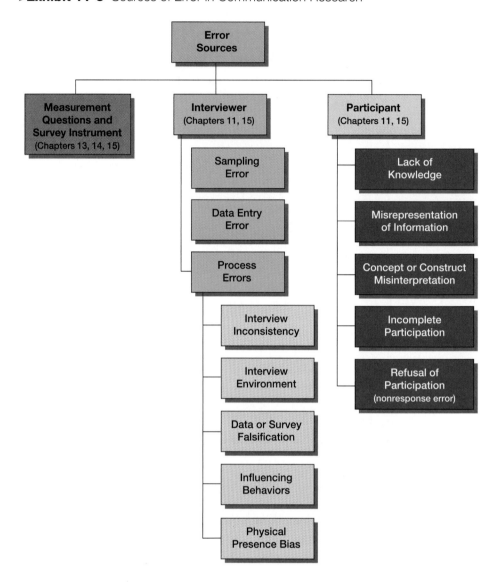

interviewers are inconsistent in ways that influence the data. In the Albany clinic study, providing different definitions (of diseases) to different clinic patients completing the medical history would create bias.

- *Failure to establish appropriate interview environment.* Answers may be systematically inaccurate or biased when interviewers fail to appropriately train and motivate participants or fail to establish a suitable interpersonal setting.[1] Since the Albany clinic study asked for factual rather than attitudinal data, interviewer-injected bias would have been limited. If the clinic had required the admissions clerk (who insulted Edna by referring to her negative attitude) to also conduct a postsurgery interview on patient satisfaction, the results of the latter study may have been influenced by interviewer bias.

- *Falsification of individual answers or whole interviews.* Perhaps the most insidious form of interviewer error is cheating. Surveying is difficult work, often done by part-time employees, usually with only limited training and under little direct supervision. At times, falsification of an answer to an overlooked question is perceived as an easy solution to counterbalance the incomplete data. This easy, seemingly harmless first step can be followed by more pervasive forgery. It is not known how much of this occurs, but it should be of constant concern to research directors as they develop their data collection design and to those organizations that outsource survey projects.

- *Inappropriate influencing behavior.* It is also obvious that an interviewer can distort the results of any survey by inappropriate suggestions, directions, or verbal probes; by word emphasis and question rephrasing; by tone of voice; or by body language, facial reaction to an answer, or other nonverbal signals. These activities, whether premeditated or merely due to carelessness, are widespread. This problem was investigated using a simple questionnaire and participants who then reported on the interviewers. The conclusion was, "The high frequency of deviations from instructed behavior is alarming."[2]

- *Physical presence bias.* Interviewers can influence participants in unperceived subtle ways. Older interviewers are often seen as authority figures by young participants, who modify their responses accordingly. Some research indicates that perceived social distance between interviewer and participant has a distorting effect, although the studies do not fully agree on just what this relationship is.[3]

In light of the numerous studies on the various aspects of interview bias, the safest course for researchers is to recognize the constant potential for response error.

Participant Error

Three broad conditions must be met by participants to have a successful survey:

- The participant must possess the information being targeted by the investigative questions.
- The participant must understand his or her role in the interview as the provider of accurate information.
- The participant must have adequate motivation to cooperate.

Thus participants cause error in two ways: whether they respond (willingness) and how they respond.

Participation-Based Errors   Three factors influence participation:[4]

- The participant must believe that the experience will be pleasant and satisfying.
- The participant must believe that answering the survey is an important and worthwhile use of his or her time.
- The participant must dismiss any mental reservations that he or she might have about participation.

Whether the experience will be pleasant and satisfying depends heavily on the interviewer in personal and telephone surveys. Typically, participants will cooperate with an interviewer whose behavior reveals confidence and who engages people on a personal level. Effective interviewers are differentiated not by demographic characteristics but by these interpersonal skills. By confidence, we mean that most participants are immediately convinced they will want to participate in the study and cooperate fully with the interviewer. An engaging personal style is one where the interviewer instantly establishes credibility by adapting to the individual needs of the participant. For the survey that does not employ human interpersonal influence, convincing the participant that the experience will be enjoyable is the task of a prior notification device or the study's written introduction.

For the participant to think that answering the survey is important and worthwhile, some explanation of the study's purpose is necessary, although the amount of disclosure will vary based on the sponsor's objectives. In personal or phone surveys the researcher will provide the interviewer with instructions for discovering what explanation is needed and supplying it. Usually, the interviewer states the purpose of the study, tells how the information will be used, and suggests what is expected of the participant. Participants should feel that their co-operation will be meaningful to themselves and to the survey results. When this is achieved, more participants will express their views willingly.

As depicted in Exhibit 11-4, the quality and quantity of information secured depend heavily on the ability and willingness of participants to cooperate. Potential participants often have reservations about being interviewed that must be overcome. They may suspect the interviewer has an illegitimate purpose. They may view the topic as too sensitive and thus the interview as potentially embarrassing or intrusive. Or they may feel inadequate or fear the questioning will belittle them. Previous encounters with marketers who have attempted to disguise their sales pitch or fund-raising activities as a research survey can also erode participants' willingness to cooperate. In personal and phone interviews, participants often react more to their feelings about the interviewer than to the content of the questions.

At the core of a survey or interview is an interaction between two people or between a person and a questionnaire. In the interaction the participant is asked to provide information. While he or she has hope of some minimal personal reward—in the form of compensation for participation or enhanced status or knowledge—he or she has little hope of receiving any immediate or direct benefit from the data extracted. Thus participant motivation is a responsibility of the researcher and the interviewer. Studies of reactions to many surveys show that participants can be motivated to participate in personal and phone interviews and, in fact, can even enjoy the experience. In one study, more than 90 percent of participants said the interview experience was interesting, and three-fourths reported they were willing to be interviewed again.[5] In intercept/self-administered studies, the interviewer's primary role is to encourage participation as the participant completes the questionnaire on his or her own. Taking away Edna's glasses, along with the natural anxiety associated with eye surgery, would not have encouraged Edna's participation. However, the "required" nature of the information (we assume surgery would not commence without prior completion of the questionnaire) guaranteed Edna's participation, no matter how grudgingly given.

>**Exhibit 11-4** Factors Influencing Participant Motivation

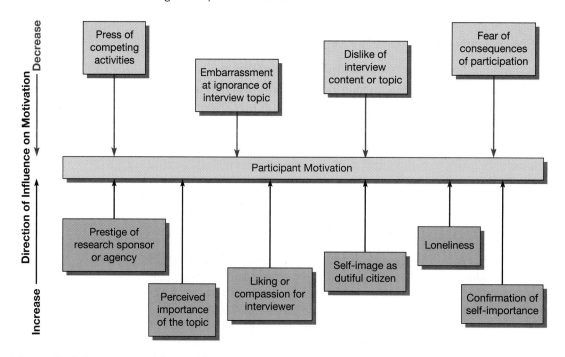

Source: Influenced by Robert L. Kahn and Charles F. Cannell, "Interviewing," in David L. Sills, ed., *International Encyclopedia of the Social Sciences,* vol. 8, p. 153. Copyright © 1968 by Crowell Collier and Macmillan, Inc.

It Raises Understanding—and Also the Dead

Launching a new television series can be gut-wrenching. Networks spend millions developing new shows only to have them rejected in one or two episodes by the viewers. But some shows have an edge—or more specifically a dial. MSInteractive invented its Perception Analyzer™ technology more than 20 years ago. Each spring in cities across the country, samples of viewers watch pilot episodes of potential new shows, responding with Perception Analyzer's handheld dial to everything they see. Don't like a character? The viewer turns the dial to a number below 50 (the neutral point). A particular bit makes the viewer laugh, and he or she turns the dial to 80. "We collect data every second on what the viewer is feeling," shared David Paull, director of business development and marketing. "At the end of a 30-minute sit-com pilot, we have 1,800 data points for every member of the sample." To familiarize the sample with the dial, each participant is asked a series of questions up front. Some researchers will quiz participants on discrete choices like their gender (dial 1 for male, 2 for female); others will query them on an intensity scale using 0 to 100 for a question like "How much of a fan are you of

situation comedies?" All the data can be summarized on bar charts and tables, but the power of Perception Analyzer™ is its ability to superimpose a continuously generated line graph over the show itself. "The network can see precisely what appealed—or didn't appeal—not only to the audience as a whole, but also to specific demographic segments." Moderators in follow-up focus groups or personal interviews use the data to formulate questions to probe for understanding of participant reactions. "This approach generates real-time, anonymous, and accurate data to help researchers ask the right questions to gain true market insight." In the tested pilot episode of *ER,* actress Julianna Margolies commits suicide and dies. However, by the time this award-winning show actually aired, Julianna is rescued by George Clooney's character and proceeds to enjoy five seasons of health, including the birth of twins. "Understanding how the audience felt about Julianna's character was the insight that led to the change."

www.perceptionanalyzer.com

By failing to respond or refusing to respond, participants create a nonrepresentative sample for the study overall or for a particular item or question in the study. In surveys, **nonresponse error** occurs when the responses of participants differ in some systematic way from the responses of nonparticipants. This occurs when the researcher (1) cannot locate the person (the predesignated sample element) to be studied or (2) is unsuccessful in encouraging that person to participate. This is an especially difficult problem when you are using a probability sample of subjects. Many studies have shown that better-educated individuals and those more interested in the topic participate in surveys. A high percentage of those who reply to a given survey have usually replied to others, while a large share of those who do not respond are habitual nonparticipants.[6]

nonresponse error error that develops when an interviewer cannot locate or involve the targeted participant.

Researchers are not without actions to avoid or diminish the error discussed above. We will explore these options in detail in Chapters 13 to 17. Despite its challenges, communicating with research participants—and the use of the survey—is the principal method of marketing research.

Response-Based Errors   **Response error** is generated in two ways: when the participant fails to give a correct answer or fails to give the complete answer. The interviewer can do little about the participant's information level. Screening questions qualify participants when there is doubt about their ability to answer. The most appropriate applications for communication research are those where participants are uniquely qualified to provide the desired information. Questions can be used to inquire about characteristics of a participant, such as his or her household income, age, sexual preference, ethnicity, or family life-cycle stage. Questions can also be asked that reveal information exclusively internal to the participant. We include here items such as the participant's lifestyle, attitudes, opinions, expectations, knowledge, motivations, and intentions.

response error when the participant fails to give a correct or complete answer.

If we ask participants to report on events that they have not personally experienced, we need to assess the replies carefully. If our purpose is to learn what the participant understands to be the case, it is legitimate to accept the answers given. But if our intent is to learn what the event or situation actually was, we must recognize that the participant is reporting secondhand data and the accuracy of the information declines.

In the Visionary Insights study of MindWriter's CompleteCare program, only those individuals who have experienced difficulty with their laptops and gone through the program have direct knowledge of the service process. Although some associates and family members are likely to have some secondhand knowledge of the experience, no one but the actual laptop owners is likely to give Visionary Insights as clear a picture of what works and what doesn't with CompleteCare. The laser patient, Edna, on the other hand, had a totally different experience when she went for surgery to correct her vision. Answers to many questions on the patient survey might have been known by a caregiver, especially since Edna was experiencing eye problems serious enough to warrant surgery. And the clinic's admissions department could have been confident that such information was as accurate as it would have been if given by Edna herself. Since inaccuracy is a correctable source of error, a family or group member should not be asked about another member's experience unless there is no other way to get the information directly. We should not depend on secondhand sources if a more direct source can be found.

Participants also cause error by responding in such a way as to unconsciously or consciously misrepresent their actual behavior, attitudes, preferences, motivations, or intentions (*response bias*). Participants create response bias when they modify their responses to be socially acceptable or to save face or reputation with the interviewer (*social desirability bias*), and sometimes even in an attempt to appear rational and logical.

One major cause of response bias is *acquiescence*—the tendency to be agreeable. On the participant's part, acquiescence may be a result of lower cognitive skills or knowledge related to a concept or construct, language difficulties, or perceived level of anonymity. However, researchers can contribute to acquiescence by the speed with which they ask questions (the faster questions are asked, the more acquiescence) and the placement of questions in an interview (the later the question, the more acquiescence.)[7]

Sometimes participants may not have an opinion on the topic of concern. Under this circumstance, their proper response should be "don't know" or "have no opinion." Some research suggests that most participants who chose the "don't know" response option actually possess the knowledge or opinion that the researcher seeks.[8] Participants may choose the option to shorten the time spent in the participation process, be ambivalent or have conflicting opinions on the topic, feel they have insufficient information to form a judgment—even though they actually have taken a position—don't believe that the response choices match their position, or don't possess the cognitive skills to understand the response options. If they choose the "don't know" option for any of these reasons, studies suggest that probing for their true position will increase both reliability and validity of the data. However, forcing a participant to express some opinion he or she does not hold by withholding a "don't know" option makes it difficult for researchers to know the reliability of the answers.

Participants may also interpret a question or concept differently from what was intended by the researcher. This occurs when the researcher uses words that are unfamiliar to the participant. Thus, the individual answers a question that is different from the one the researcher intended to ask. This problem is reflected in Edna's letter concerning the clinic's survey.

Regardless of the reasons, each source of participant-initiated error diminishes the value of the data collected. It is difficult for a researcher to identify such occasions. Thus, communicated responses should be accepted for what they are—statements by individuals that reflect varying degrees of truth and accuracy.

Choosing a Communication Method

Once the sponsor or researcher has determined that surveying or interviewing is the appropriate data collection approach, various means may be used to secure information from individuals. A researcher can conduct a semistructured interview or survey by personal

>**Exhibit 11-5** Comparison of Communication Approaches

	Self-Administered Survey	Telephone Interview	Personal Interview
Description	Questionnaires are: • Mailed, faxed, or couriered to be self-administered—with return mechanism generally included (denoted below as a). • Computer-delivered via intranet, Internet, and online services—computer stores/forwards completed instruments automatically (denoted below as b). • People are intercepted in a central location and studied via paper or computerized instrument—without interviewer assistance; e.g., restaurant and hotel comment cards (denoted below as c).	People selected to be part of the sample are interviewed on the telephone by a trained interviewer.	People selected to be part of the sample are interviewed in person by a trained interviewer.
Advantages	• Allows contact with otherwise inaccessible participants (e.g., CEOs). • Incentives may be used to increase response rate. • Often lowest-cost option. • Expanded geographic coverage without increase in costs (a). • Requires minimal staff (a). • Perceived as more anonymous (a). • Allows participants time to think about questions (a). • More complex instruments can be used (b). • Fast access to the computer-literate (b). • Rapid data collection (b, c). • Participant who cannot be reached by phone (voice) may be accessible (b, c). • Sample frame lists viable locations rather than prospective participants (b, c). • Visuals may be used (b, c).	• Lower costs than personal interview. • Expanded geographic coverage without dramatic increase in costs. • Uses fewer, more highly skilled interviewers. • Reduced interviewer bias. • Fastest completion time. • Better access to hard-to-reach participants through repeated callbacks. • Can use computerized random dialing. • CATI—computer-assisted telephone interviewing: Responses can be entered directly into a computer file to reduce error and cost.	• Good cooperation from participants. • Interviewer can answer questions about survey, probe for answers, use follow-up questions, and gather information by observation. • Special visual aids and scoring devices can be used. • Illiterate and functionally illiterate participants can be reached. • Interviewer can prescreen participant to ensure he or she fits the population profile. • CAPI—computer-assisted personal interviewing: Responses can be entered into a portable microcomputer to reduce error and cost.
Disdvantages	• Low response rate in some modes. • No interviewer intervention available for probing or explanation (a). • Cannot be long or complex (a). • Accurate mailing lists needed (a). • Often participants returning survey represent extremes of the population—skewed responses (a). • Anxiety among some participants (b). • Directions/software instruction needed for progression through the instrument (b). • Computer security (b). • Need for low-distraction environment for survey completion (c).	• Response rate is lower than for personal interview. • Higher costs if interviewing geographically dispersed sample. • Interview length must be limited. • Many phone numbers are unlisted or not working, making directory listings unreliable. • Some target groups are not available by phone. • Responses may be less complete. • Illustrations cannot be used.	• High costs. • Need for highly trained interviewers. • Longer period needed in the field collecting data. • May be wide geographic dispersion. • Follow-up is labor-intensive. • Not all participants are available or accessible. • Some participants are unwilling to talk to strangers in their homes. • Some neighborhoods are difficult to visit. • Questions may be altered or participant coached by interviewers.

interview or telephone or can distribute a self-administered survey by mail, fax, computer, e-mail, the Internet, or a combination of these. As noted in Exhibit 11-5, while there are commonalities among these approaches, several considerations are unique to each.

In the last two decades of the 20th century, a revolution—albeit a quiet one—was under way in survey research. Driven by changing technology and the need to make research more responsible to the bottom line and MROI objectives, the paper-and-pencil survey standard of the prior 60 years was replaced by a new computerized standard. Whether it goes by the name of "computer-assisted data collection" (CADAC), "computer-assisted survey information collection" (CASIC), or "computer-assisted interviewing" (CAI), the trend is growing. While less obvious in the public sector (the U.S. government is the largest survey researcher in the world, and paper-and-pencil approaches still hold prominence there), in the private sector of survey research with households and organizations, the computer's influence on this methodology is far-reaching. It influences all the various data collection practices.

> Self-Administered Surveys

self-administered questionnaire an instrument completed by the participant without additional contact with an interviewer beyond delivery.

mail survey self-administered study, both delivered and returned by mail.

The **self-administered questionnaire** is ubiquitous in modern living. You have experienced service evaluations of hotels, restaurants, car dealerships, and transportation providers. Often a short questionnaire is left to be completed by the participant in a convenient location or is packaged with a product. User registrations, product information requests in magazines, warranty cards, the MindWriter CompleteCare study, and the Albany clinic study are examples of self-administered surveys. Self-administered **mail surveys** are delivered not only by the U.S. Postal Service but also via fax and courier service. Other delivery modalities include *computer-delivered* and *intercept* studies.

Evaluation of the Self-Administered Survey

computer-assisted self-interview (CASI) computer-delivered questionnaire that is self-administered by the participant.

disk-by-mail (DBM) survey a type of computer-assisted self-interview where the survey and its management software, on computer disk, are delivered by mail to the participant.

Nowhere has the computer revolution been felt more strongly than in the area of the self-administered survey. Computer-delivered self-administered questionnaires (also labeled **computer-assisted self-interviews**, or **CASIs**) use organizational intranets, the Internet, or online services to reach their participants. Participants may be targeted (as when BizRate, an online e-business rating service, sends an e-mail to a registered e-purchaser to participate in a survey following the completion of their order) or self-selecting (as when a computer screen pop-up window offers a survey to an individual who clicks on a particular Web site or when a potential participant responds to a postcard or e-mail inquiry looking for participants). The questionnaire and its managing software may be resident on the computer or its network, or both may be sent to the participant by mail—**disk-by-mail (DBM) survey**. A 2001 Gartner Research Dataquest survey found that 61 percent of U.S. households are actively online and, once connected, 91 percent are likely to continue their Internet subscription.[9] Is it any wonder, then, that marketing researchers have embraced computer-delivered self-administered surveys? See Exhibit 11-6.

Intercept surveys—at malls, conventions, state fairs, vacation destinations, even busy city street corners—may use a traditional paper-and-pencil questionnaire or a computer-delivered survey via a kiosk. The respondent participates without interviewer assistance, usually in a predetermined environment, such as a room in a shopping mall. All modes have special problems and unique advantages (as shown in Exhibit 11-5).

As computer-delivered surveys, especially those delivered via the Internet, are in their infancy, much of what researchers know about self-administered surveys has been learned from experiments conducted with mail surveys and from personal experience. So as we explore the strengths and weaknesses of the various self-administered survey methods, we will start with this body of knowledge.

>**Exhibit 11–6** The Web as a Survey Research Venue

Web Advantages	Example
Short turnaround of results; results are tallied as participants complete surveys.	A soft-drink manufacturer got results from a Web survey in just five days.
Ability to use visual stimuli.	Florida's tourism office used eye movement tracking to enhance its Web site and improve its billboard and print ads.
Ability to do numerous surveys over time.	A printer manufacturer did seven surveys in six months during the development of one of its latest products.
Ability to attract participants who wouldn't participate in another research project, including international participants.	An agricultural equipment manufacturer did a study using two-way pagers provided free to farmers to query users about its equipment—participants usually unavailable by phone or PC.
Participants feel anonymous.	Anonymity was the necessary ingredient for a study on impotence conducted by a drug manufacturer.
Shortened turnaround from questionnaire draft to execution of survey.	A Hewlett-Packard survey using Greenfield Online's QuickTake took two weeks to write, launch, and field—not the standard three months using non-Web venues.
Experiences unavailable by other means.	• One major advertising agency is conducting Web research using virtual super-market aisles that participants wander through, reacting to client products and promotions. • LiveWorld has developed a packaging study showing more than 75 images of labels and bottle designs.
Web Disadvantages **(and emerging solutions)**	**Example**
Recruiting the right sample is costly and time-consuming; unlike phone and mail sample frames, no lists exist. (Firms like Greenfield Online and Survey Samples, Inc., now provide samples built from panels of Internet users who have indicated an interest in participating in online surveys.)	TalkCity, working for Whitton Associates and Fusion5, set up a panel of 3,700 teens for a survey to test new packaging for a soft-drink using phone calls, referrals, e-mail lists, banner ads, and Web site visits. It drew a sample of 600 for the research. It cost more than $50,000 to set up the list.
Converting surveys to the Web can be expensive. (Firms like Qualtric Labs with its SurveyPro software and Apian with its Perseus software for wireless surveys and intranet surveys have made the process of going from paper to Internet much easier.)	LiveWorld's teen study cost $50,000 to $100,000 to set up, plus additional fees with each focus group or survey. The total price tag was several hundred thousand dollars.
It takes technical as well as research skill to field a Web survey. (Numerous firms now offer survey hosting services.)	A 10- to 15-minute survey can take up to five days of technical expertise to field and test.
While research is more compatible with numerous browsers, the technology isn't perfect. (Some survey hosting services use initial survey screen questions that identify the browser and system specifications and deliver the survey in the format most compatible with the participant's system.)	A well-known business magazine did a study among a recruited sample only to have the survey abort on question 20 of a larger study.

Source: These examples are drawn from the personal experience of the authors, as well as from Noah Shachtman, "Why the Web Works as a Market Research Tool," *AdAge.com,* Summer 2001 (http://adage.com/tools2001).

Costs

Self-administered surveys of all types typically cost less than surveys via personal interviews. This is true of mail surveys, as well as of both computer-delivered and intercept surveys. Telephone and mail costs are in the same general range, although in specific cases either may be lower. The more geographically dispersed the sample, the more likely it is that self-administered surveys via computer or mail will be the low-cost method. A mail or computer-delivered study can cost less because it is often a one-person job. And computer-delivered studies (including those that employ interviewer-participant interaction) eliminate the cost of printing surveys, a significant cost of both mail studies and personal interviewing employing paper-and-pencil surveys. The most significant cost savings with computer-delivered surveys involve the much lower cost of pre- and postnotification (often done by mail or phone when other self-administered surveys are involved), as well as the lower per-participant survey delivery cost of very large studies.[10]

Sample Accessibility

One asset to using mail self-administered surveys is that researchers can contact participants who might otherwise be inaccessible. Some groups, such as major corporate executives and physicians, are difficult to reach in person or by phone, as gatekeepers (secretaries, office managers, and assistants) limit access. But researchers can often access these special participants by mail or computer. When the researcher has no specific person to contact—say, in a study of corporations—the mail or computer-delivered survey may be routed to the appropriate participant. Additionally, the computer-delivered survey can often reach samples that are identified in no way other than their computer and Internet use, such as the users of a particular online game or those who have shopped with a particular online retailer.

Time Constraints

While intercept studies still pressure participants for a relatively quick response, in a mail survey the participant can take more time to collect facts, talk with others, or consider replies at length than is possible in a survey employing the telephone or in a personal interview. Computer-delivered studies, especially those accessed via e-mail links to the Internet, often have time limitations on both access and completion once started. And once started, computer-delivered studies usually cannot be interrupted by the participant to seek information not immediately known. One recent computer-delivered study sponsored by

Procter & Gamble, however, asked of participants (who used skin moisturizers) the actual duration of time that the participant spent applying the product to various skin areas following a bath or shower. These questions came in the middle of a fairly lengthy survey. The participant was encouraged to discontinue the survey, time his or her moisturizer application following the next bath or shower, and return to the survey via a link and personal code with detailed responses.[11]

Anonymity

Mail surveys are typically perceived as more impersonal, providing more anonymity than the other communication modes, including other methods for distributing self-administered questionnaires. Computer-delivered surveys still enjoy that same perceived anonymity, although increased concerns about privacy may erode this perception in the future.[12]

Topic Coverage

A major limitation of self-administered surveys concerns the type and amount of information that can be secured. Researchers normally do not expect to obtain large amounts of information and cannot probe deeply into topics. Participants will generally refuse to cooperate with a long and/or complex mail, computer-delivered, or intercept questionnaire unless they perceive a personal benefit. Returned mail questionnaires with many questions left unanswered testify to this problem, but there are also many exceptions. One general rule of thumb is that the participant should be able to answer the questionnaire in no more than 10 minutes—similar to the guidelines proposed for telephone studies. On the other hand, one study of the general population delivered more than a 70 percent response to a questionnaire calling for 158 answers.[13] Several early studies of computer-delivered surveys show that participants indicate some level of enjoyment with the process, describing the surveys as interesting and amusing.[14] The novelty of the process, however, is expected to decline with experience, and recent declines in Web and e-mail survey response rates seem to be supporting this expectation.

Maximizing Participation in the Self-Administered Survey

To maximize the overall probability of response, attention must be given to each point of the survey process where the response may break down.[15] For example:

- The wrong address, e-mail or postal, can result in nondelivery or nonreturn.
- The envelope or fax cover sheet may look like junk mail and be discarded without being opened, or the subject line on e-mail may give the impression of spam and not encourage that the e-mail be opened.
- Lack of proper instructions for completion may lead to nonresponse.
- The wrong person may open the envelope or receive the fax or e-mail and fail to call it to the attention of the right person.
- A participant may find no convincing explanation or inducement for completing the survey and thus discard it.
- A participant may temporarily set the questionnaire aside or park it in his or her e-mail in-box and fail to complete it.
- The return address may be lost, so the questionnaire cannot be returned.

Thus, efforts should be directed toward maximizing the overall probability of response. One approach, the Total Design Method (TDM), suggests minimizing the burden on participants by designing questionnaires that:[16]

- Are easy to read.
- Offer clear response directions.
- Include personalized communication.
- Provide information about the survey via advance notification.
- Encourage participants to respond.[17]

More than 200 methodological articles have been published on efforts to improve response rates. Few approaches consistently showed positive response rates.[18] However, several practical suggestions emerge from the conclusions:[19]

- Preliminary or advance notification of the delivery of a self-administered questionnaire increases response rates.
- Follow-ups or reminders after the delivery of a self-administered questionnaire increase response rates.
- Clearly specified return directions and devices (e.g., response envelopes, especially postage-stamped) improve response rates.
- Monetary incentives for participation increase response rates.
- Deadline dates do not increase response rates but do encourage participants to respond sooner.
- A promise of anonymity, while important to those who do respond, does not increase response rates.
- An appeal for participation is essential.

Self-Administered Survey Trends

Computer surveying is surfacing at trade shows, where participants complete questionnaires while making a visit to a company's booth. Continuous tabulation of results provides a stimulus for attendees to visit a particular exhibit as well as gives the exhibitor detailed information for evaluating the productivity of the show. This same technology easily transfers to other situations where large groups of people congregate.

Companies are now using intranet capabilities to evaluate employee policies and behavior. Ease of access to electronic mail systems makes it possible for both large and small organizations to use computer surveys with both internal and external participant groups. Many techniques of traditional mail surveys can be easily adapted to computer-delivered questionnaires (e.g., follow-ups to nonparticipants are more easily executed and are less expensive).

It is not unusual to find registration procedures and full-scale surveying being done on World Wide Web sites. University sites are asking prospective students about their interests, and university departments are evaluating current students' use of online materials. A short voyage on the Internet reveals organizations using their sites to evaluate customer service processes, build sales-lead lists, evaluate planned promotions and product changes, determine supplier and customer needs, discover interest in job openings, evaluate employee attitudes, and more. Advanced and easier-to-use software for designing Web questionnaires is no longer a promise of the future—it's here.

Web-based questionnaire
a measurement instrument both delivered and collected via the Internet.

> You will find a useful Web questionnaire tutorial at http://www. surveypro.com/.

The **Web-based questionnaire,** a measurement instrument both delivered and collected via the Internet, has the power of computer-assisted telephone interview systems, but without the expense of network administrators, specialized software, or additional hardware. As a solution for Internet or intranet Web sites, you need only a personal computer and Web access. Most products are browser-driven with design features that allow custom survey creation and modification.

Two primary options are proprietary solutions offered through research firms and off-the-shelf software designed for researchers who possess the knowledge and skills we describe here and in Chapter 15. With fee-based services, you are guided (often online) through problem formulation, questionnaire design, question content, response strategy, and wording and sequence of questions. The supplier's staff generates the questionnaire HTML code, hosts the survey at their server, and provides data consolidation and reports. Off-the-shelf software is a strong alternative. *PC Magazine* reviewed six packages containing well-designed user interfaces and advanced data preparation features.[20] The advantages of these software programs are:

- Questionnaire design in a word processing environment.
- Ability to import questionnaire forms from text files.
- A coaching device to guide you through question and response formatting.
- Question and scale libraries.
- Automated publishing to a Web server.
- Real-time viewing of incoming data.
- Ability to edit data in a spreadsheet-type environment.
- Rapid transmission of results.
- Flexible analysis and reporting mechanisms.

Ease of use is not the only influence pushing the popularity of Web-based instruments. Cost is a major factor. A Web survey is much less expensive than conventional survey research. Although fees are based on the number of completions, the cost of a sample of 100 might be one-sixth that of a conventional telephone interview. Bulk mailing and e-mail data collection have also become more cost-effective because any instrument may be configured as an e-mail questionnaire.

The computer-delivered survey has made it possible to use many of the suggestions for increasing participation. Once the computer-delivered survey is crafted, the cost of redelivery via computer is very low. Preliminary notification via e-mail is both more timely and less costly than notification for surveys done by phone or mail. The click of a mouse or a single keystroke returns a computer-delivered study. Many computer-delivered surveys use color, even color photographs, within the survey structure. This is not a cost-effective option with paper surveys. And video clips—never an option with a mail survey—are possible with a computer-delivered survey. In addition, e-currencies have simplified the delivery of monetary and other incentives. However, employing all the stimulants for participation cannot overcome technology snafus. These glitches are likely to continue to plague participation as long as researchers and participants use different computer platforms, operating systems, and software.

While Web- and e-mail-based self-administered surveys have certainly caught the lion's share of business attention in the last few years, the tried-and-true methods of telephone and personal interviews still have their strengths—and their advocates in the research community.

> Survey via Telephone Interview

The survey via **telephone interview** is still the workhorse of survey research. With the high level of telephone service penetration in the United States and the European Union, access to participants through low-cost, efficient means has made telephone interviewing a very attractive alternative for marketing researchers. Nielsen Media Research uses thousands of calls each week to determine television viewing habits, and Arbitron does the same for radio listening habits. Pollsters working with political candidates use telephone surveys to assess the power of a speech or a debate during a hotly contested campaign. Numerous firms field phone omnibus studies each week. Individual questions in these studies are used to capture everything from people's feeling about the rise in gasoline prices to the power of a celebrity spokesperson in an advertising campaign or the latest teenage fashion trend.

telephone interview a study conducted wholly by telephone contact between participant and interviewer.

In the September 4, 2003, Harris Poll, 42 percent of adults erroneously thought registering for the national Do Not Call registry would ban telephone survey calls as well. While researchers are aggressively exploring online research, the phone survey still plays an important role in marketing research.

computer-assisted telephone interviewing (CATI) a telephone survey with computer sequenced questions and real-time data entry.

computer-administered telephone survey a telephone survey via voice-synthesized computer questions.

noncontact rate ratio of noncontacts to all potential contacts.

refusal rate ratio of participants who decline the interview to all eligible contacts.

Evaluation of the Telephone Interview

Of the advantages that telephone interviewing offers, probably none ranks higher than its moderate cost. One study reports that sampling and data collection costs for telephone surveys can run from 45 to 64 percent lower than costs for comparable personal interviews.[21] Much of the savings comes from cuts in travel costs and administrative savings from training and supervision. When calls are made from a single location, the researcher may use fewer, yet more skilled, interviewers. Telephones are especially economical when callbacks to maintain precise sampling requirements are necessary and participants are widely scattered. Long-distance service options make it possible to interview nationally at a reasonable cost.

Telephone interviewing can be combined with immediate entry of the responses into a data file by means of terminals, personal computers, or voice data entry. This brings added savings in time and money. **Computer-assisted telephone interviewing (CATI)** is used in research organizations throughout the world. A CATI facility consists of acoustically isolated interviewing carrels organized around supervisory stations. The telephone interviewer in each carrel has a personal computer or terminal that is networked to the phone system and to the central data processing unit. A software program that prompts the interviewer with introductory statements, qualifying questions, and precoded questionnaire items drives the survey. These materials appear on the interviewer's monitor. CATI works with a telephone number management system to select numbers, dial the sample, and enter responses. One facility, the Survey Research Center at the University of Michigan, consists of 60 carrels with 100 interviewers working in shifts from 8 a.m. to midnight (EST) to call nationwide. When fully staffed, it produces more than 10,000 interview hours per month.[22]

Another means of securing immediate response data is the **computer-administered telephone survey.** Unlike CATI, there is no human interviewer. A computer calls the phone number, conducts the interview, places data into a file for later tabulation, and terminates the contact. The questions are voice-synthesized, and the participant's answers and computer timing trigger continuation or disconnect. Several modes of computer-administered surveys exist, including *touch-tone data entry (TDE); voice recognition (VR),* which recognizes a limited vocabulary, usually yes/no responses; and *automatic speech recognition (ASR)* for recognizing and recording a wide range of verbal responses. CATI is often compared to the self-administered questionnaire and offers the advantage of enhanced participant privacy. One study showed that the noncontact rate for this electronic survey mode is similar to that for other telephone interviews when a random phone list is used. It also found that rejection of this mode of data collection affects the refusal rate (and thus nonresponse error) because people hang up more easily on a computer than on a human.[23] The **noncontact rate** is a ratio of potential but unreached contacts (no answer, busy, answering machine or voice mail, and disconnects but not refusals) to all potential contacts.

The **refusal rate** refers to the ratio of contacted participants who decline the interview to all potential contacts. New technology, notably call-filtering systems where the receiver

RTI International Call Center Services employs over 400 interviewers, institutional contactors, quality control monitors, team leaders, and supervisors in its two state-of-the-art call centers located in Greenville and Raleigh, North Carolina. The call centers typically conduct between 10 and 30 different data collection efforts concurrently, with staff members completing more than 100,000 telephone interviews annually. Call center staff come from all walks of life—many are students or others who work as interviewers part-time in the evenings and on weekends. RTI International conducts rigorous training with all telephone staff on standardized interviewing techniques, strategies for gaining participant cooperation, and the use of its computer-assisted telephone interviewing system. **www.rti.org**

can decide whether a call is answered based on caller identity, is expected to increase the noncontact rate associated with telephone surveys. The 2003 CMOR Respondent Cooperation and Industry Image Study reported that while survey refusal rates have been growing steadily over several years, the rate "took a sharper than usual increase" this year. The study also noted that "positive attitudes [about participating in surveys] are declining, while negative perceptions are increasing."[24]

When compared to either personal interviews or mail self-administered surveys, the use of telephones brings a faster completion of a study, sometimes taking only a day or so for the fieldwork. When compared to personal interviewing, it is also likely that interviewer bias, especially bias caused by the physical appearance, body language, and actions of the interviewer, is reduced by using telephones.

> 66 The ubiquity of cell phones and the rapid and continuing development of the Internet have completely altered the way we talk to each other, the way marketers talk to customers, the way customers shop and the way the media research their audiences. 99
>
> *Alain Tessier*
> *Founder, Mediamark Research, Inc.*

Finally, behavioral norms work to the advantage of telephone interviewing. If someone is present, a ringing phone is usually answered, and it is the caller who decides the purpose, length, and termination of the call.[25]

There are also disadvantages to using the telephone for research. A skilled researcher will evaluate the use of a telephone survey to minimize the effect of these disadvantages:

• Inaccessible households (no telephone service or no/low contact rate).

• Inaccurate or nonfunctioning numbers.

- Limitation on interview length (fewer measurement questions).
- Limitations on use of visual or complex questions.
- Ease of interview termination.
- Less participant involvement.
- Distracting physical environment.

Inaccessible Households

Approximately 94 percent of all U.S. households have access to telephone service.[26] On the surface, this should make telephone surveys a prime methodology for communication studies. However, several factors reduce such an enthusiastic embrace of the methodology. Rural households and households with incomes below the poverty line remain underrepresented in telephone studies, with phone access below 75 percent.[27] More households are using filtering devices and services to restrict access, including caller ID, privacy manager, Tele-Zapper, and unlisted numbers (estimated between 22 and 30 percent of all household phone numbers).[28] Meanwhile, the number of inaccessible individuals continues to increase as cellular/wireless phone use increases. From 1985 to 2002, the number of U.S. wireless telecommunication subscribers grew from 203.6 thousand to 134.5 million.[29] Many of these numbers are unlisted or possess screening or filtering services. Additionally, people's use of phone modems to access the Internet makes household lines ring busy for long periods of time. Recent FCC filings indicate that fewer than 15 percent of U.S. households have second telephone lines, required for simultaneous Internet access.[30] Effective May 2004 federal wireless local-number portability legislation made it possible for subscribers to take their wired phone number to their wireless phone service (or the reverse) or to shift their wireless service between carriers without losing their wireless number. Thus the guidelines for identifying the physical location of a phone by its number—and, in turn, the location of its owner—no longer apply.[31]

These causes of variations in participant availability by phone can be a source of bias. A random dialing procedure is designed to reduce some of this bias. **Random dialing** normally requires choosing phone exchanges or exchange blocks and then generating random numbers within these blocks for calling.[32] Of course, just reaching a household doesn't guarantee its participation.

random dialing
computerized process that chooses phone exchanges or exchange blocks and generates random numbers within these blocks for telephone surveys.

Inaccurate or Nonfunctioning Numbers

One source says the highest incidence of unlisted numbers is in the West, in large metropolitan areas, among nonwhites, and for persons between 18 and 34 years of age.[33] Several methods have been developed to overcome the deficiencies of directories; among them are techniques for choosing phone numbers by using random dialing or combinations of directories and random dialing.[34] However, increasing demand for multiple phone lines by both households and individuals has generated new phone area codes and local exchanges. This too increases the inaccuracy rate.

Limitation on Interview Length

A limit on interview length is another disadvantage of the telephone survey, but the degree of this limitation depends on the participant's interest in the topic. Ten minutes has generally been thought of as ideal, but interviews of 20 minutes or more are not uncommon. One telephone survey sponsored by Kraft lasted approximately 30 minutes. It was designed to judge the willingness of sample issue recipients to subscribe to a prototype magazine, *food&family*. The survey also measured the effectiveness of the sample issue of the magazine to deliver purchase intent for Kraft products featured in the recipes contained therein.[35] In another study, interviews ran for one and a half hours in a survey of long-distance services.[36]

Limitations on Use of Visual or Complex Questions

The telephone survey limits the complexity of the survey and the use of complex scales or measurement techniques that is possible with personal interviewing, CASI, or WWW surveys. For example, in personal interviews, participants are sometimes asked to sort or rank an array of cards containing different responses to a question. For participants who cannot visualize a scale or other measurement device that the interview is attempting to describe, one solution has been to employ a nine-point scaling approach and to ask the participant to visualize it by using the telephone dial or keypad.[37] In telephone interviewing it is difficult to use maps, illustrations, and other visual aids. In some instances, however, interviewers have supplied these prior to a prescheduled interview via fax, e-mail, or the Internet.

Ease of Interview Termination

Some studies suggest that the response rate in telephone studies is lower than that for comparable face-to-face interviews. One reason is that participants find it easier to terminate a phone interview. Telemarketing practices may also contribute. Public reaction to investigative reports of wrongdoing and unethical behavior within telemarketing activities places an added burden on the researcher, who must try to convince a participant that the phone interview is not a pretext for soliciting contributions (labeled *frugging*—fund-raising under the guise of research) or selling products (labeled *sugging*—sales under the guise of research).

Less Participant Involvement

Telephone surveys can result in less thorough responses, and persons interviewed by phone find the experience to be less rewarding than a personal interview. Participants report less rapport with telephone interviewers than with personal interviewers. Given the growing costs and difficulties of personal interviews, it is likely that an even higher share of surveys will be by telephone in the future. Thus, it behooves marketing researchers using telephone surveys to attempt to improve the enjoyment of the interview. One authority suggests:

> We need to experiment with techniques to improve the enjoyment of the interview by the participant, maximize the overall completion rate, and minimize response error on specific measures. This work might fruitfully begin with efforts at translating into verbal messages the visual cues that fill the interaction in a face-to-face interview: the smiles, frowns, raising of eyebrows, eye contact, etc. All of these cues have informational content and are important parts of the personal interview setting. We can perhaps purposefully choose those cues that are most important to data quality and participant trust and discard the many that are extraneous to the survey interaction.[38]

Changes in the Physical Environment

Replacement of home or office phones with cellular and wireless phones also raises concerns. In regard to telephone surveys, researchers are concerned about the changing environment in which such surveys might be conducted, the resulting quality of data collected under possibly distracting circumstances—at a busy intersection, in the midst of weekly shopping in a congested grocery aisle, at the local high school basketball tournament—and the possible increase in refusal rates.

Telephone Survey Trends

Future trends in telephone surveying bear watching. Answering machines or voice-mail services pose potentially complex response rate problems since they are estimated to have substantial penetration in American households. Previous research discovered that most such households are accessible; the subsequent contact rate was greater in answering-machine households than in no-machine households and about equal with busy-signal

households. Other findings suggested that (1) individuals with answering machines were more likely to participate, (2) machine use was more prevalent on weekends than on weekday evenings, and (3) machines were more commonplace in urban than in rural areas.

Voice-mail options offered by local phone service providers have less market penetration but are gaining increasing acceptance. Questions about the sociodemographics of users and nonusers and the relationship of answering-machine/voice-mail technology to the rapid changes in the wireless market remain to be answered.[39] Caller identification technology, the assignment of facsimile machines or computer modems to dedicated phone lines, and technology that identifies computer-automated dialers and sends a disconnect signal in response are all expected to have an impact on the noncontact rate of phone interviews.

The variations among the 60 telephone companies' services and the degree of cooperation that will be extended to researchers are also likely to affect noncontact rates. There is also concern about the ways in which random dialing can be made to deal with nonworking and ineligible numbers.[40] But arguably no single threat poses greater danger than the government-facilitated Do Not Call registry initiated in 2003 by the Federal Trade Commission. More than 50 million U.S. household and cell numbers, a third of all U.S. households, were registered in its initial wave of enrollment.[41] While currently survey researchers are exempt from its restrictions, customer confusion about the distinction between research and telemarketing is likely to cause an increase in the nonresponse rate. Telemarketers might be the catalyst, but legitimate research will suffer.

> Survey via Personal Interview

personal interview a two-way communication initiated by an interviewer to obtain information from a participant.

A survey via **personal interview** is a two-way conversation between a trained interviewer and a participant. With her poor eyesight and the problems of question clarity, a personal interview, rather than the intercept/self-administered questionnaire, might have been a preferable communication method for Edna at the Albany Outpatient Laser Clinic.

Evaluation of the Personal Interview

> **We discuss the individual depth interview at length in Chapter 9.**

There are real advantages as well as clear limitations to surveys via personal interview. The greatest value lies in the depth of information and detail that can be secured. It far exceeds

>**snap**shot

Aleve: Personal Interviews Provide Relief

Bayer Consumer Care inherited Aleve, a long-duration over-the-counter painkiller, from Procter & Gamble in 1996. Since its launch in 1994, P&G hadn't been able to move Aleve beyond a 6 percent market share. Bayer chose CLT Research Associates to identify potential Aleve users. CLT conducted in-home interviews with a random sample of 800 men and women aged 18 to 75 who had used a nonprescription pain reliever in the past year. The research revealed that 24 percent of those interviewed could be defined as "pain-busters" (heavy users of analgesics who were likely to try new products to gain relief). More than one-third of those identified as pain-busters had tried Aleve. Bayer's task was to use the research to identify a strategy to get pain-busters to choose Aleve when they faced their analgesic-stocked medicine cabinet.

First, Moskowitz Jacobs, Inc., had 249 participants rate various statements about Aleve. Statements that promised "control over pain" or "freedom to do the things you want" were discov-

ered as important emotional triggers for consumers interested in minimizing the number of pills they took to relieve pain—Aleve's differential benefit. Next Bayer managers analyzed syndicated data from Medioscope, Nielsen Panel Data, MRI, and Simmons and conducted a series of focus groups moderated by Viewpoints Consulting, Inc., to flesh out findings. The sum of this research revealed Aleve users were more likely to suffer from arthritis and back pain than the average analgesic user. This helped Bayer define the benefit of Aleve as "liberation from tough pain, making a dramatic difference in the quality of life." The resulting Dramatic Difference ad campaign boosted the subsequent year's sales by 16 percent, with a rise in market share to 7 percent, its highest ever.

www.aleve.com; www.cltresearch.com; www.smrb.com; http://acnielsen.com

the information secured from telephone and self-administered studies via mail or computer (both intranet and Internet). The interviewer can also do more things to improve the quality of the information received than is possible with another method.

The absence of assistance in interpreting questions in the Albany clinic study was a clear weakness that would have been improved by the presence of an interviewer. Interviewers can note conditions of the interview, probe with additional questions, and gather supplemental information through observation. Edna was obviously in good spirits and very relaxed after she and her fellow patients had critiqued the questionnaire. This attitude would have been observed and noted by an interviewer. Of course, we're hopeful that the interviewer would correctly interpret laughter as a sign of humor and not as a negative attitude, as did the admissions clerk.

Human interviewers also have more control than other kinds of communication studies. They can prescreen to ensure the correct participant is replying, and they can set up and control interviewing conditions. They can use special scoring devices and visual materials, as is done with **computer-assisted personal interviewing (CAPI)**. Interviewers also can adjust the language of the interview as they observe the problems and effects the interview is having on the participant.

With such advantages, why would anyone want to use any other survey method? Probably the greatest reason is that personal interviewing is costly, in terms of both money and time. A survey via personal interview may cost anywhere from a few dollars to several hundred dollars for an interview with a hard-to-reach person. Costs are particularly high if the study covers a wide geographic area or has stringent sampling requirements. An exception to this is the survey via **intercept interview** that targets participants in centralized locations such as retail malls or, as with Edna, in a doctor's office. Intercept interviews reduce costs associated with the need for several interviewers, training, and travel. Product and service demonstrations also can be coordinated, further reducing costs. Their cost-effectiveness, however, is offset when representative sampling is crucial to the study's outcome. The intercept survey would have been a possibility in the Albany clinic study, although more admissions clerks would likely have been needed if volunteers were not available to perform this task.

Costs have risen rapidly in recent years for most communication methods because changes in the social climate have made personal interviewing more difficult. Many people today are reluctant to talk with strangers or to permit strangers to visit in their homes. Interviewers are

Computer-assisted personal interviewing (CAPI) a personal interview with computer-sequenced questions capable of employing visualization techniques.

intercept interview a face-to-face communication that targets participants in a centralized location.

> **You will find tips on intercept surveys on the text DVD.**

Does Permission Marketing Extend to Research?[42]

In the best-seller, *Permission Marketing: Turning Strangers into Friends, and Friends into Customers,* Seth Godin and Don Peppers focused marketers' attention on two business practices, which they defined as interruption marketing and permission marketing. In the most popular e-book ever, *Unleashing the Ideavirus,* Godin discusses the power of amplified word of mouth. Both these manifests offer lessons for researchers.

INTERRUPTION MARKETING

Godin claims that interruption marketing is what most marketers do and have been doing for centuries: They yell out their benefits as we pass by their exhibit; they interrupt our dinner with their telemarketing calls; they interrupt our movies, radio, or television shows with commercials; they interrupt our stock news with Internet pop-up ads. Interruption marketing needs to rely increasingly on creativity—or even shock—to get our attention. The more marketers do this, the more immune to interruption we become. Godin claims that the interruption model worked as long as there was not an overabundance of interruptions. But the model isn't working as well as it used to in an environment where we are bombarded with more than 3,000 marketing messages a day. The evidence? As customers, you and I are opting to *pay* to avoid interruptions. Weren't you willing to pay $2.99 just last weekend to rent that classic movie from Blockbuster even though you could have watched it on commercial-loaded TV? Or maybe you purchased *Lord of the Rings* or *Matrix* so that you could watch it again and again without interruption.

PERMISSION MARKETING

Permission marketing operates on a different premise. The marketer gives its customer the right, the encouragement, and the power to engage in a conversation with the company, as well as with other prospects and customers. The customer controls whether to maintain the conversation or discontinue it. Customers give permission for interaction because they perceive a reward. If the marketer fails to deliver the reward, the customer will withdraw the permission—the first step in severing a relationship. If a potential customer ignores a firm's ad or denies a salesperson entrance, the marketer has effectively been told, "I'm not interested." The marketer can decide to send a barrage of new messages at that disengaged individual, but the more it interrupts, the more it is likely to gain an enduring enemy rather than a partner. Godin considers e-mail the ultimate conversational medium and a powerful one when married with Internet content. "If you get permission to use e-mail to deliver marketing messages, and if people agree to pay attention to those messages, you've changed the game." The power of permission is that the marketer is not faced with disinterest or animosity every time it attempts a conversation with a prospect or customer.

In one *FastCompany* article, Godin noted three major anticipated shifts in marketing's future: (1) that conversations between a marketer and its customers would become increasingly less visible to competitors and noncustomers, (2) that benefits exchanged between marketer and customer would need to become increasingly tangible, and (3) that customers would increasingly subscribe to the information they thought had value in order to exclude interruptions they thought had none.

reluctant to visit unfamiliar neighborhoods alone, especially for evening interviewing. Finally, results of surveys via personal interviews can be affected adversely by interviewers who alter the questions asked or in other ways bias the results. As Edna and her friends discussed the Albany clinic survey, they each applied their own operational definitions to the concepts and constructs being asked. This confusion created a bias that might have been eliminated by a well-trained interviewer. Interviewer bias, identified as one of the three major sources of error in Exhibit 11-3, was discussed earlier in this chapter. If we are to overcome these deficiencies, we must appreciate the conditions necessary for interview success.

> Selecting an Optimal Survey Method

The choice of a communication method is not as complicated as it might first appear. By comparing your research objectives with the strengths and weaknesses of each method, you will be able to choose one that is suited to your needs. The summary of advantages and disadvantages of personal interviews, telephone interviews, and self-administered questionnaires presented in Exhibit 11-5 should be useful in making such a comparison.

PERMISSION RESEARCH

While Godin's book is focused on what advertisers have to do to gain our attention, there are valuable lessons for survey researchers as well. The logical research extension of Godin's argument is that marketers should offer customers or receptive prospects the opportunity to participate in survey research. This is exactly what several companies are doing. Greenfield Online has built an e-mail database of individuals who are willing to participate in surveys for a large and varied group of companies. Procter & Gamble has amassed a permission survey population to test new concepts and anticipate the effects of attitude and lifestyle changes on current products and their marketing. *BusinessWeek* invited its subscriber group to join a survey panel, which it later queried about the attractiveness of a possible new venture: *BusinessWeek,* the television show. And such surveys don't have to be delivered via e-mail or the Internet, although increasingly they are. Once the participant has given permission for the research company to ask for involvement, this is an indication that the survey—or the panel diary—can be delivered by a variety of media.

As refusal rates rise, *permission surveying*—the act of surveying prospects or customers who have given permission for such engagement—should become increasingly attractive. One recent study reported in the *Journal of Advertising Research* noted that salience of an issue to the sampled population has strong positive correlation with response rates, regardless of the survey delivery method.[43] Marketing decisions are increasingly complex in an environment of product proliferation and lack of true product distinction. The survey remains the researcher's process for extracting large amounts of detailed information from willing participants. So what if we could turn a willing participant into an enthusiastic one? Using Godin's approach, survey researchers should be able to marry the doctrine of mutual benefit and participant enthusiasm to engage the participant in longer surveys or more complex exercises that are more likely to reveal true motivations or buried attitudes.

Discontinuations/disconnects are also troublesome in survey research. Participants discontinue surveys when their life interrupts. Discontinuation would be reduced and surveys should be returned more quickly in a permission surveying environment.

Most marketers would prefer that their survey activity be invisible to their competition. Competitors can use survey activity to reveal what their rival is considering. In some instances those same marketers can use their newfound knowledge to preempt a competitive move. One recent permission survey explored a new product concept for a dairy product that has visible cosmetic effects: radiant, even skin tone and shinier hair. A survey was used to determine whether the promise of the new product was believable and embraceable or would be rejected. The more surveys are used to glean understanding that is applied to making strategic and tactical decisions, the more attractive the invisibility of permission surveying will become.

Godin believes that free content on the Internet is waning and that what free content exists after the inevitable Internet shakeout will be the lure to get an idea virus (amplified word of mouth) started. He's convinced that marketers who use customers as "sneezers" (those who gain status for sharing valuable new ideas with others) will be the true beneficiaries of an idea virus, and those customers will opt in for other types of behaviors that give them ideas to spread. Participating in a survey is but one more way sneezers can enhance their position: They will know things that others don't or know them long before most others will.

www.sethgodin.com

When your investigative questions call for information from hard-to-reach or inaccessible participants, the telephone interview, mail survey, or computer-delivered survey should be considered. However, if data must be collected very quickly, the mail survey would likely be ruled out because of lack of control over the returns. Alternatively, you may decide your objective requires extensive questioning and probing; then the survey via personal interview should be considered.

If none of the choices turns out to be a particularly good fit, it is possible to combine the best characteristics of two or more alternatives into a mixed mode survey. Although this decision will incur the costs of the combined modes, the flexibility of tailoring a method to your unique needs is often an acceptable trade-off.

In the MindWriter study, Visionary Insights plans to insert a postcard questionnaire (a self-administered survey delivered via courier) in each laptop returned by the Complete-Care repair service. But this plan is not without problems. Not all customers will return their questionnaires, creating nonresponse bias. The postcard format doesn't permit much space for encouraging customer response. Alerting customers to the importance of returning the response card by phone (to announce courier delivery of a repaired laptop) might improve the research design, but it would be too costly when 10,000 units are processed monthly. Participants would not be in the best frame of mind if they received a damaged laptop; dissatisfaction could lead to a decreased response rate and an increase in call center contacts. Visionary Insights' proposal contains a follow-up procedure—telephoning nonparticipants to obtain their answers when response cards are not returned. This will likely decrease nonresponse error. Where most of the study participants are answering measurement questions without assistance, telephone interviewing creates the possibility of interviewer bias at an unknown level for at least part of the data.

In the Albany clinic study, the researcher could have taken several actions to improve the quality of the data. Distributing the questionnaire to the patient's eye doctor or to the patient (by mail) prior to arrival would have increased the accuracy of identifying medications, diagnoses, hospitalizations, and so forth. The patient's eye doctor was in the best position to encourage compliance with the collection process but was not consulted. Having the patient bring the completed questionnaire to the admissions procedure, where the admissions clerk could review the completed instrument for accuracy and completeness, would have given the researcher the opportunity to clarify any confusion with the questions, concepts, and constructs. Finally, pretesting the instrument with a sample of patients would have revealed difficulties with the process and operational definitions. Edna's concerns could have been eliminated before they surfaced.

Ultimately, all researchers are confronted by the practical realities of cost and deadlines. As Exhibit 11-5 suggests, on the average, surveys via personal interview are the most expensive communication method and take the most field time unless a large field team is used. Telephone surveys are moderate in cost and offer the quickest option, especially when CATI is used. Questionnaires administered by e-mail or the Internet are the least expensive. When your desired sample is available via the Internet, the Internet survey may prove to be the least expensive communication method with the most rapid (simultaneous) data availability. The use of the computer to select participants and reduce coding and processing time will continue to improve the cost-to-performance profiles of this method in the future.

Most of the time, an optimal method will be apparent. However, managers' needs for information often exceed their internal resources. Such factors as specialized expertise, a large field team, unique facilities, or a rapid turnaround prompt managers to seek assistance from research vendors of survey-related services.

Outsourcing Survey Services

> **Types of research suppliers were discussed in Chapter 2.**

Commercial suppliers of research services vary from full-service operations to specialty consultants. When confidentiality is likely to affect competitive advantage, the manager or staff will sometimes prefer to bid only a phase of the project. Alternatively, the organization's staff members may possess such unique knowledge of a product or service that they must fulfill a part of the study themselves. Regardless, the exploratory work, design, sampling, data collection, or processing and analysis may be contracted separately or as a whole. Most organizations use a request for proposal (RFP) to describe their requirements and seek competitive bids (see the sample RFP in Chapter 6).

Research firms also offer special advantages that their clients do not typically maintain in-house. Centralized-location interviewing or computer-assisted telephone facilities may be particularly desirable for certain research needs. A professionally trained staff with considerable experience in similar management problems is another benefit. Data processing and statistical analysis capabilities are especially important for some projects. Other vendors have specially designed software for interviewing and data tabulation.[44] Panel suppliers provide another type of research service, with emphasis on longitudinal survey work.[45]

By using the same participants over time, a **panel** can track trends in attitudes toward issues or products, product adoption or consumption behavior, and a myriad of other research interests. Suppliers of panel data can secure information from personal and telephone interviewing techniques as well as from the mail, the Web, and mixed-modes surveys. Diaries are a common means of chronicling events of research interest by the panel members. These are mailed back to the research organization. Point-of-sale terminals and scanners aid electronic data collection for panel-type participant groups. And mechanical devices placed in the homes of panel members may be used to evaluate media usage. ACNielsen, Yankelovich Partners, The Gallup Organization, and Harris Interactive all manage extensive panels.

panel group of potential participants who have indicated a willingness to participate in research studies.

>summary

1 The communication approach involves surveying or interviewing people and recording their responses for analysis. Communication is accomplished via personal interviews, telephone interviews, or self-administered surveys, with each method having its specific strengths and weaknesses. The optimal communication method is the one that is instrumental for answering your research question and dealing with the constraints imposed by time, budget, and human resources. The opportunity to combine several survey methodologies makes the use of the mixed mode desirable in many projects.

2 Successful communication requires that we seek information the participant can provide and that the participant understand his or her role and be motivated to play that role. Motivation, in particular, is a task for the interviewer. Good rapport with the participant should be established quickly, and then the technical process of collecting data should begin. The latter often calls for skillful probing to supplement the answers volunteered by the participant. Simplicity of directions and instrument appearance are additional factors to consider in encouraging response in self-administered communication studies.

3 Two factors can cause bias in interviewing. One is nonresponse. It is a concern with all surveys. Some studies show that the first contact often secures less than 20 percent of the designated participants. Various methods are useful for increasing this representation, the most effective being making callbacks until an adequate number of completed interviews have been secured. The second factor is response error, which occurs when the participant fails to give a correct or complete answer. The interviewer also can contribute to response error. The interviewer can provide the main solution for both of these two types of errors.

4 The self-administered questionnaire can be delivered by the U.S. Postal Service, facsimile, a courier service, a computer, or an intercept. Computer-delivered self-administered questionnaires use organizational intranets, the Internet, or online services to reach their participants. Participants may be targeted or self-selecting. Intercept studies may use a traditional questionnaire or a computerized instrument in environments where interviewer assistance is minimal.

Telephone interviewing remains popular because of the diffusion of telephone service in households and the low cost of this method compared with personal interviewing. Long-distance telephone interviewing has grown. There are also disadvantages to telephone interviewing. Many phone numbers are unlisted, and directory listings become obsolete quickly. There is also a limit on the length and depth of interviews conducted using the telephone.

The major advantages of personal interviewing are the ability to explore topics in great depth, achieve a high degree of interviewer control, and provide maximum interviewer flexibility for meeting unique situations. However, this method is costly and time-consuming, and its flexibility can result in excessive interviewer bias.

5 Outsourcing survey services offers special advantages to managers. A professionally trained research staff, centralized-location interviewing, focus group facilities, and computer-assisted facilities are among them. Specialty firms offer software and computer-based assistance for telephone and personal interviewing as well as for mail and mixed modes. Panel suppliers produce data for longitudinal studies of all varieties.

>**key**terms

>**discussion**questions

Terms in Review

1 Distinguish among response error, interviewer error, and nonresponse error.

2 How do environmental factors affect response rates in personal interviews? How can researchers overcome these environmental problems?

Making Research Decisions

3 Assume you are planning to interview shoppers in a shopping mall about their views on increased food prices and what the federal government should do about them. In what different ways might you try to motivate shoppers to cooperate in your survey?

4 In recent years, in-home personal interviews have grown more costly and more difficult to complete. Suppose, however, you have a project in which you need to talk with people in their homes. What might you do to hold down costs and increase the response rate?

5 In the following situations, decide whether you would use a personal interview, telephone survey, or self-administered questionnaire. Give your reasons.

a A survey of the residents of a new subdivision on why they happened to select that area in which to live. You also wish to secure some information about what they like and do not like about life in the subdivision.

b A poll of students at Metro University on their preferences among three candidates who are running for president of the student government.

c A survey of 58 wholesale grocery companies, scattered over the eastern United States, on their equipment for warehouse inventory management.

d A survey, for your business magazine, of financial officers of the Fortune 500 corporations to learn their predictions for the economic outlook in their industries in the next year.

e A study of applicant requirements, job tasks, and performance expectations as part of a job analysis of student work-study jobs on a college campus of 2,000 students, where 1,500 are involved in the work-study program; information will be used to develop a jobs-source magazine.

6 You decide to conduct a survey of 40 families in the 721-phone exchange. You want an excellent representation of all subscribers in the exchange area. Explain how you will carry out this study.

7 You plan to conduct a mail survey of the traffic managers of 1,000 major manufacturing companies across the country. The study concerns their company policies regarding the payment of buy-in/stocking allowances for obtaining retail distribution for new products. What might you do to improve the response rate of such a survey?

8 A major restaurant chain is experiencing a decline in female patronage, especially during the lunch trade. It fears that female employees' concerns of sexual harassment have leaked to the public. It wants to determine the cause of the decline in patronage. How would you handle the following issues: *talk to everyone in the workplace*

a Sample selection. *talk to someone in community.*

b The communication approach (self-administered, telephone, personal interview, and/or mixed).

c The purpose: fact-finding, awareness, relationship building, and/or change.

d Minimization of response and nonresponse error.

Behind the Scenes

9 Define the appropriate communication study for the Albany Outpatient Laser Clinic.

From Concept to Practice

10 Using Exhibit 11-1 as your guide, graph the communication study you designed in question 9.

>**www**exercise

Find a study that compares two methodologies, for example, telephone survey and Internet survey, or self-administered mail and Web survey. What does this study say about the effectiveness of the research methodologies being compared. One such study is at http://www.mcic.org/reports_newsletters/year2001/FINAL_SPRING_Y01.pdf.

>**cases**[*]

Can Research Rescue the Red Cross?

Covering Kids with Health Care

Cummins Engines

Data Development

Donatos: Finding the New Pizza

Endries Fasteners

Envirosell

Inquiring Minds Want to Know—NOW!

Lexus SC 430

Mastering Teacher Leadership

NCRCC: Teeing Up and New Strategic Direction

Ramada Demonstrates Its *Personal Best*™

Starbucks, Bank One, and Visa Launch Starbucks Duetto Visa

Sturgel Division

USTA: Come Out Swinging

* All cases, both written and video, are on the text DVD. The film icon indicates a video case. Check the DVD Index to determine whether a case has data, the research instrument, or other supplementary material.

chapter 12

Experiments and Test Markets

After reading this chapter, you should understand . . .

1 The uses for experimentation.

2 The advantages and disadvantages of the experimental method.

3 The seven steps of a well-planned experiment.

4 Internal and external validity with experimental research designs.

5 The three types of experimental designs and the variations of each.

6 The functions and types of test marketing used in experimenting with new marketing products and services.

Jason slides into a seat next to Chance at the conference lunch table. Chance glances his way and nods briefly but keeps his attention on the man to his left. He is describing some of the finer details of the Point of Purchase Advertising Institute's groundbreaking experiment to put display materials on a directly comparative basis with other audited advertising and sales promotion activities. Chance had just attended his presentation during the morning session of the conference.

As he stops speaking, Chance introduces Jason, "Doug Adams, I'd like you to meet my colleague, Jason Henry. Jason, Doug is vice president and co-founder of Prime Consulting Group, Inc. [Prime]."

Jason extends his hand across Chance's plate, "Pleased to meet you, Doug. Prime took the lead on that POP industry experiment, right? Sorry I missed your presentation, but the boss," Jason nodded to Chance, "had us divide and conquer—to cover more sessions."

Doug returns Jason's smile and handshake. "It seems to be the topic of conversation at this table at the moment, so maybe you'll get some of the content here," welcomes Doug. "I was just explaining how we needed a methodology that could separate out other sales influencers, like price, local advertising, media-delivered coupons, or a secondary stocking location in order to measure the sales lift generated by the POP material. For example, if Frito-Lay offered Doritos at $2.49, reduced from $2.99, plus it stocked a secondary location near the soft-drink aisle, Frito-Lay could track the sales lift. If sales increased even more when a Doritos sign was posted over the secondary stock location, then the power of the POP could be determined."

"Your session was generating all the buzz as I entered the dining room," comments Jason. "How many types of POP were assessed?"

"Ultimately, 20 different types," shares Doug. "Several different message types—for example, brand name, photo, price, retail savings, thematic . . . like a movie tie-in . . . or generic . . . like the summer barbeque season—and numerous locations."

"Like regular shelf stocking location, end-cap, front lobby . . . ?" asks Jason. At Doug's affirmative nod Jason asks, "How did you keep the manufacturers from distorting the experiment?"

To give Doug a chance to take a bite, Chance supplies, "Prime used a double-blind audit tracking procedure using observation, coupled with sales tracking through more than 250 supermarkets from the IRI panel of stores and 120 convenience stores from six retailers with Nielsen's Market Decisions program. The manufacturers didn't know which stores were involved."

"And did the POP create the sales lift the retailers expected?" asks Jason.

"Not only were we able to calculate sales lift for each type of promotion," shares Doug, "but we were also able to calculate a full cost-per-thousand [CPM] estimate, including the cost of manufacturing, delivering, and installing the point-of-purchase material. TV, radio, and in-store ads are still quoting CPM exposures without the cost of the ad."

"If grocery and convenience stores buy in, this will be a large piece of business for one or several firms," comments Chance. "What's been the reaction?"

"When a retailer, who has been relying on his gut instinct to accept or reject POP materials for his store,

sees that that same material can cause a 20 to 40 percent lift in store sales, he's bound to be receptive. We think it's going to be a major new research initiative," smiles Doug. "Are you interested?"

> What Is Experimentation?

Why do events occur under some conditions and not under others? Research methods that answer such questions are called *causal* methods. (Recall the discussion of causality in Chapter 8.) Ex post facto research designs, where a researcher interviews respondents or observes what is or what has been, also have the potential for discovering causality. The distinction between these methods and experimentation is that the researcher is required to accept the world as it is found, whereas an experiment allows the researcher to alter systematically the variables of interest and observe what changes follow.

In this chapter, we define experimentation and discuss its advantages and disadvantages. We present an outline for the conduct of an experiment as a vehicle to introduce important concepts. Questions of validity are also examined: Does the experimental treatment determine the observed difference, or was some extraneous variable responsible? And how can one generalize the results of the study across times, settings, and persons? The most widely accepted designs are presented along with a section on test marketing that describes how these test methods assist marketing managers introduce new products or services or relaunch enhanced versions of established brands.

An **experiment** is a study involving intervention by the researcher beyond that required for measurement. The usual intervention is to manipulate some variable in a setting and observe how it affects the participants or subjects being studied (e.g., people or physical entities). The researcher manipulates the independent or explanatory variable and then observes whether the hypothesized dependent variable is affected by the intervention.

An example of such an intervention is a retail experiment based on a famous study of bystanders and thieves.[1] In this experiment, participants are invited to come to a new store where they have an opportunity to see someone steal the purse of another customer looking at merchandise on a nearby display. Confederates of the experimenter, of course, act the roles of the accosted shopper and the thief. As in the original study, the major hypothesis concerns whether people observing a theft are more likely to report it (1) if they are alone when they observe the crime or (2) if they are in the company of someone else.

There is at least one **independent variable (IV)** and one **dependent variable (DV)** in a causal relationship. We hypothesize that in some way the IV "causes" the DV to occur. The independent, explanatory, or *predictor* variable in our example is the state of either being alone when observing the theft or being in the company of another person. The dependent variable, or *criterion* variable, is whether the participants report observing the crime. The results of the earlier study would suggest that bystanders are more likely to report the theft if they observe it alone rather than in another person's company.

On what grounds did the researchers conclude that people who are alone are more likely to report theft observed than people in the company of others? Three types of evidence form the basis for this conclusion. First, there must be an *agreement between independent*

> **You may wish to revisit our discussion of causality in Chapter 8.**

experiment study involving manipulation of one or more variables to determine the effect on another variable.

independent variable (IV) the variable manipulated by the researcher, thereby causing an effect on the dependent variable.

dependent variable (DV) a measured, predicted, or otherwise monitored variable expected to be affected by manipulation of an IV.

and *dependent variables*. The presence or absence of one is associated with the presence or absence of the other. Thus, more reports of the theft (DV) would come from lone observers (IV_1) than from paired observers (IV_2).

Second, beyond the correlation of independent and dependent variables, we consider the *time order of the occurrence of the variables*. The effect on the dependent variable should not precede the manipulation of the independent variable. The effect and manipulation may occur simultaneously, or the manipulation may occur before the effect. In our bystanders and thieves experiment, this requirement is of little concern since it is unlikely that people could report a theft before observing it.

The third important support for the conclusion comes when researchers are confident that other *extraneous variables did not influence the dependent variable*. To ensure that these other variables are not the source of influence, researchers control their ability to confound the planned comparison. In a laboratory test, researchers arrange standardized conditions for control. The theft observation experiment could occur in a laboratory set up as a store. The entire event would be staged for the participants' benefit. Both the accosted shopper and the thief would be instructed to speak and act in a specific way. Only the accosted shopper, the thief, and the participants would be in the simulated store. The same process would be repeated with each trial of the experiment. (And, of course, as we learned earlier, since the experimenter employed deception, he would debrief the unsuspecting participant at the end of each observation.)

While such controls are important, further precautions are needed so that the results achieved reflect only the influence of the independent variable on the dependent variable.

> 66 Your success in life isn't based on your ability to simply change. It is based on your ability to change faster than your competition, customers and business. 99
>
> *Mark Sanborn*
> *Founder, Speakers Roundtable*

> An Evaluation of Experiments

Advantages

When we elaborated on the concept of cause in Chapter 8, we said causality could not be proved with certainty but the probability of one variable's being linked to another could be established convincingly. The experiment comes closer than any primary data collection method to accomplishing this goal. The foremost advantage is the researcher's ability to manipulate the independent variable. Consequently, the probability that changes in the dependent variable are a function of that manipulation increases. Also, a control group (a group not exposed to the experimental treatment) serves as a comparison to assess the existence and potency of the manipulation.

The second advantage of the experiment is that contamination from extraneous variables can be controlled more effectively than in other designs. This helps the researcher isolate experimental variables and evaluate their impact over time. Third, the convenience and cost of experimentation are superior to those of other methods. These benefits allow the experimenter opportunistic scheduling of data collection and the flexibility to adjust variables and conditions that evoke extremes not observed under routine circumstances. In addition, the experimenter can assemble combinations of variables for testing rather than having to search for their fortuitous appearance in the study environment.

Fourth, **replication**—repeating an experiment with different participant groups and conditions—leads to the discovery of an average effect of the independent variable across people, situations, and times. Fifth, researchers can use naturally occurring events and, to some extent, **field experiments** (a study of the dependent variable in actual environmental conditions) to reduce participants' perceptions of the researcher as a source of intervention or deviation in their everyday lives.

replication the process of repeating an experiment with different participant groups and conditions to determine the average effect of the IV across people, situations, and times.

field experiment a study of the dependent variable in actual environmental conditions.

Unicast's Video Ad Outperforms TV Ad

Advertising on the Internet has experienced mixed results, and as a result most advertisers still rely heavily on television ads. But Unicast, an online advertising provider to more than 1,400 Web partners and 650 ad agencies and advertisers, has the research to prove its newest Internet advertising technology—a full-motion, full-sound video commercial—can deliver on the most important ad effectiveness metrics.

For a six-week period (January 19 through February 29, 2004) Unicast tested its proprietary video commercial format with ads from five advertisers, including AT&T, Honda, Pepsi, Vonage, and Warner Brothers. The ads aired on 15 sites and were tested on 6 sites including ABCnews.com, ESPN.com, Lycos, About.com, and MSN.com. During the test, 3,592 Internet users received a pop-up invitation to participate in a Web survey; 1,748 had experienced a one-time exposure to one of the video commercial ads, while 1,844 were not exposed to any of the ads. Dynamic Logic conducted the research and measured the results against its *AdIndex MarketNorms* (calculated on ads tested through fourth quarter 2003, $n = 1,234,195$). "We've been monitoring annoyance with online ads for three years," shared Unicast marketing director Annette Mullin, "so initially we were concerned that annoyance might increase with a 30-sec

ad." The survey reports that while 28 percent found the video ads annoying, this is significantly less than the 38 percent who find television ads annoying, and overwhelmingly less than the 78.3 percent of consumers who find pop-up ads very annoying. More importantly, the video commercial format vastly outperformed conventional online ads (banners, pop-ups, etc.) on metrics like brand awareness, message association, brand favorability, and purchase intent.

Unicast's video commercial plays 30-second ads in broadcast quality (30 frames per second). It is precached (downloads fully before seen by the viewer) and interactive (can contain click-through options from the ad). "Vonage, the advertiser in the test that had the lowest awareness going in and the most to gain," explained Mullin, "experienced high percentage increases across all metrics." Advertisers were pleasantly surprised by the results. As a result more Web sites and advertisers have signed up to use the video format ads that 69 percent of test participants indicated were "like watching a TV ad" on their computer.

Visit Unicast's Web site gallery to see different types of Internet ads and the research that supports their use by advertisers.

www.unicast.com; www.dynamiclogic.com

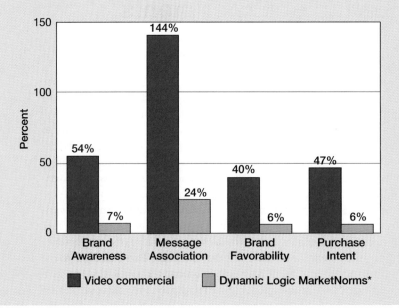

Disadvantages

First, the artificiality of the laboratory is arguably the primary disadvantage of the experimental method. However, many participants' perceptions of a contrived environment can be improved by investment in the facility. Second, when we generalize the results from a sample that is not representative of its population, there are problems despite the use of random assignment. The extent to which a study can be generalized from college students to managers or executives is open to question. And when an experiment is unsuccessfully disguised, volunteer participants are often those with the most interest in the topic. Third, despite the low costs of experimentation, many applications of experimentation far outrun the budgets for other primary data collection methods. Fourth, experimentation is most effectively targeted at problems of the present or immediate future. Experimental studies of the past are not feasible, and studies about intentions or predictions are difficult. Finally, marketing research is often concerned with the study of people. There are limits to the types of manipulation and controls that are ethical.

> Conducting an Experiment²

In a well-executed experiment, researchers complete a series of activities to carry out their craft successfully. Although the experiment is the premier scientific methodology for establishing causation, the resourcefulness and creativeness of the researcher are needed to make the experiment live up to its potential. In this section, and as we introduce Exhibit 12-1, we provide an overview of seven activities the researcher must accomplish to make the endeavor successful:

1. Select relevant variables.
2. Specify the level(s) of the treatment.
3. Control the experimental environment.
4. Choose the experimental design.
5. Select and assign the participants.
6. Pilot-test, revise, and test.
7. Analyze the data.

Selecting Relevant Variables

Throughout the book we have discussed the idea that a research problem can be conceptualized as a hierarchy of questions starting with a management problem. The researcher's task is to translate an ambiguous problem into the question or hypothesis that best states the objectives of the research. Depending on the complexity of the problem, investigative questions and additional hypotheses can be created to address specific facets of the study or data that need to be gathered. Further, we have previously described a **hypothesis** as a tentative descriptive statement that describes a relationship between two or more variables. It must also be **operationalized**, a term we used earlier in discussing how concepts are transformed into variables to make them measurable and subject to testing.

Consider the following research question as we work through the seven points listed above:

> Does a sales presentation that describes product benefits in the introduction of the message lead to improved retention of product knowledge?

hypothesis a tentative descriptive statement of the relationship between variables.

operationalized the process of transforming concepts and constructs into measurable variables suitable for testing.

>**Exhibit 12-1** Experimentation in the Research Process

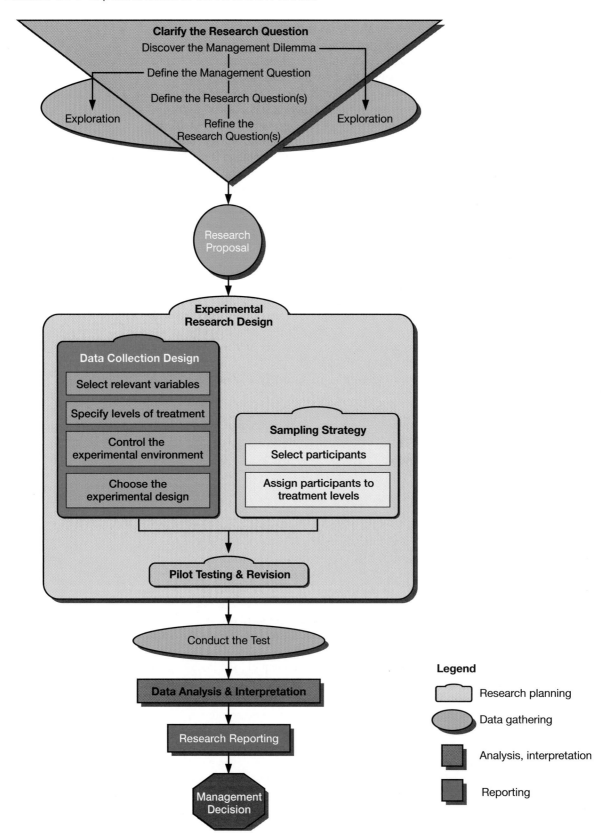

Since a hypothesis is a tentative statement—a speculation—about the outcome of the study, it might take this form:

> Sales presentations in which the benefits module is placed in the introduction of a 12-minute message produce better retention of product knowledge by the customer than those where the benefits module is placed in the conclusion.

The researchers' challenges at this step are to:

1. Select variables that are the best operational definitions of the original concepts.
2. Determine how many variables to test.
3. Select or design appropriate measures for the chosen variable(s).

The researchers would need to select variables that best operationalize the concepts *sales presentation, product benefits, retention,* and *product knowledge.* The product's classification and the nature of the intended audience should also be defined. In addition, the term *better* could be operationalized by specifying the statistical criteria that must be met (greater than or less than an average number on a measurement scale). The number of variables in an experiment is constrained by the project budget, the time allocated, the availability of appropriate controls, and the number of participants being tested. For statistical reasons, there must be more participants than variables.[3]

The selection of measures for testing requires a thorough review of the available literature and instruments. In addition, measures must be adapted to the unique needs of the research situation without compromising their intended purpose or original meaning.

Specifying Treatment Levels

In an experiment, participants experience a manipulation of the independent variable, called the **experimental treatment.** The **treatment levels** are the arbitrary or natural groups the researcher makes within the independent variable. For example, if age of the actors in an advertisement is hypothesized to have an effect on consumers' awareness of the ad, the actors selected might be divided into high, middle, and low age ranges to represent three levels of the independent variable.

> **experimental treatment** the manipulated independent variable(s).

> **treatment levels** the arbitrary or natural groupings within the independent variable in an experiment.

The treatment levels assigned to an independent variable should be based on simplicity and common sense. In the sales presentation example, the experimenter should not select 8 minutes and 10 minutes as the starting points to represent the two treatment levels if the average message about the product is 12 minutes long. Similarly, if the benefits module is in the first and second minute of the presentation, observable differences may not occur because the levels are too close together. Thus, in the first trial, the researcher is likely to position the midpoint of the benefits module at the same interval from the end of the introduction as from the end of the conclusion (see Exhibit 12-2).

Under an entirely different hypothesis, several levels of the independent variable may be needed to test order-of-presentation effects. Here we use only two. Alternatively, a **control group** could provide a base level for comparison. The control group is composed of participants who are not exposed to the independent variable(s), in contrast to those who receive the experimental treatment.

> **control group** a group of participants that is measured but not exposed to the independent variable being studied.

Controlling the Experimental Environment

In our sales presentation experiment, extraneous variables can appear as differences in age, gender, race, dress, communications competence, and many other characteristics of the presenter, the message, or the situation. These have the potential for distorting the effect of the treatment on the dependent variable and must be controlled or eliminated. However, at this stage, we are principally concerned with **environmental control,** holding constant the physical environment of the experiment. The introduction of the experiment to the participants

> > **Chapter 3 discussed the nature of extraneous variables and the need for their control.**

> **environmental control** holding constant the physical environment of the experiment.

>**Exhibit 12-2** Experiment of Placement of Benefits Module within Sales Presentation

Hypothesis: Sales presentations in which the benefits module is placed in the introduction of a 12-minute message produce better retention of product knowledge by the customer than those where the benefits module is placed in the conclusion.

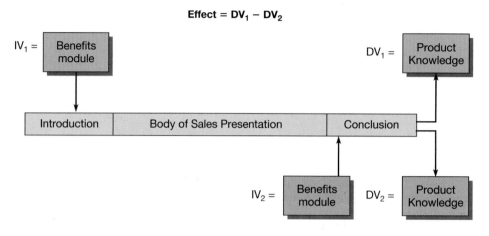

blind when participants do not know if they are being exposed to the experimental treatment.

double-blind when neither the researcher nor the participant knows when a participant is exposed to the experimental treatment.

> **The POP study in the opening vignette was a double-blind study.**

> **Many of the experimental designs are diagrammed and described later in this chapter.**

and the instructions would likely be videotaped for consistency. The arrangement of the room, the time of administration, the experimenter's contact with the participants, and so forth, must all be consistent across each administration of the experiment.

Other forms of control involve participants and experimenters. When participants do not know if they are receiving the experimental treatment, they are said to be **blind.** When neither the researcher nor the participant knows when a subject is being exposed to the experimental treatment, the experiment is said to be **double-blind.** Both approaches control unwanted complications such as participants' reactions to expected conditions or experimenter influence.

Choosing the Experimental Design

Unlike the general descriptors of research design that were discussed in Chapter 8, experimental designs are unique to the experimental method. They serve as positional and statistical plans to designate relationships between experimental treatments and the experimenter's observations or measurement in the temporal scheme of the study. In the conduct of the experiment, the researchers apply their knowledge to select one design that is best suited to the goals of the research. Judicious selection of the design improves the probability that the observed change in the dependent variable was caused by the manipulation of the independent variable and not by another factor. It simultaneously strengthens the generalizability of results beyond the experimental setting.

Selecting and Assigning Participants

The participants selected for the experiment should be representative of the population to which the researcher wishes to generalize the study's results. This may seem self-evident, but we have witnessed several decades of experimentation with college sophomores that contradict that assumption. In the sales presentation example, corporate buyers, purchasing managers, or others in a decision-making capacity would provide better generalizing power than undergraduate college students *if* the product in question was targeted for industrial use rather than to the consumer.

The procedure for random sampling of experimental participants is similar in principle to the selection of respondents for a survey. The researcher first prepares a sampling frame (a list of sampling units such as individuals, geographic areas, firms) and then assigns each participant to a group using a randomization technique. Systematic sampling (e.g., every

>snapshot

Effect of Magazine Advertising on Sales

For the first time, the Magazine Publishers of America (MPA) has a definitive study demonstrating that magazine advertising does positively affect not only the incidence of sales but also the dollar value and quantity of sales. ACNielsen sent 50,000 households in its Household Scanner Panel™ a four-color questionnaire featuring the covers of April, May, and June issues of 14 magazines. Panelists scanned the bar codes of the covers of the magazines they had read. The scanned information was uploaded to ACNielsen, where demographically matched panels of 4,000 households each were constructed. Half of each panel had been

exposed to magazine ads for 1 of the 10 brands being tracked, while the other half had not. Actual sales data drawn from records of scanned purchases were compared. Households exposed to magazine ads were more likely to purchase those brands, and dollar sales also increased among 8 of the 10 brands studied. You can learn more about the ACNielsen Household Scanner Panel™ from the ACNielsen Web site.

www.magazine.org; www.acnielsen.com

10th element on a population list) may be used if the sampling frame is free from patterns that parallel the sampling ratio. For example, if every 10th firm on the list is a large organization but small, medium, and large organizations exist in equal proportion in the population of firms, the researcher has a problem. Since the sampling frame is often small, experimental participants are recruited; thus they are a self-selecting sample. However, if randomization is used, those assigned to the experimental group are likely to be similar to those assigned to the control group. **Random assignment** to the groups is required to make the groups as comparable as possible with respect to the dependent variable. Randomization does not guarantee that if a pretest of the groups was conducted before the treatment condition, the groups would be pronounced identical; but it is an assurance that any differences remaining are randomly distributed. In our example, we would need three randomly assigned groups—one for each of the two treatments and one for the control group.

When it is not possible to randomly assign participants to groups, matching may be used. **Matching** employs a nonprobability quota sampling approach. The object of matching is to have each experimental and control participant matched on every characteristic used in the research. This becomes more cumbersome as the number of variables and groups in the study increases. Since the characteristics of concern are only those that are correlated with the treatment condition or the dependent variable, they are easier to identify, control, and match.[4] In the sales presentation experiment, if a large part of the sample was composed of businesswomen who had recently completed communication training, we would not want the characteristics of gender, business experience, and communication training to be disproportionately assigned to one group.

Some authorities suggest a **quota matrix** as the most efficient means of visualizing the matching process.[5] In Exhibit 12-3, one-third of the participants from each cell of the matrix would be assigned to each of the three groups. If matching does not alleviate the assignment problem, a combination of matching, randomization, and increasing the sample size would be used.

random assignment uses a randomized sample frame for assigning participants to experimental and control groups.

matching an equalizing process for assigning participants to experimental and control groups.

quota matrix a means of visualizing the matching process.

> We discuss random sampling in Chapter 16.

Pilot Testing, Revising, and Testing

The procedures for this stage are similar to those for other forms of primary data collection. Pilot testing is intended to reveal errors in the design and improper control of extraneous or environmental conditions. Pretesting the instruments permits refinement before the final test. This is the researcher's best opportunity to revise scripts, look for control problems with laboratory conditions, and scan the environment for factors that might confound the results. In field experiments, researchers are sometimes caught off guard by events that have a dramatic effect on participants: The test marketing of a competitor's product is

>**Exhibit 12-3** Quota Matrix Example

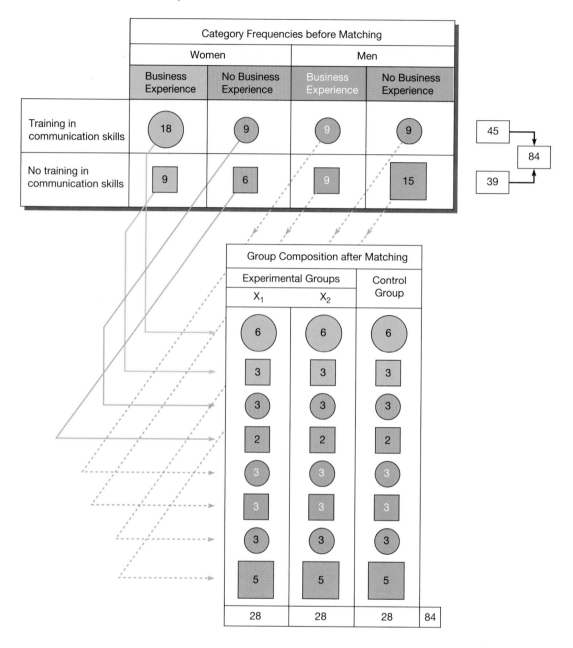

announced by the media before the experiment begins, the test market city is flooded with coupons, or a reorganization of a store's layout disrupts normal shopping patterns of test consumers. The experiment should be timed so that participants are not sensitized to the independent variable by factors in the environment.

Analyzing the Data

If adequate planning and pretesting have occurred, the experimental data will take an order and structure uncommon to surveys and unstructured observational studies. It is not that data from experiments are easy to analyze; they are simply more conveniently arranged because of the levels of the treatment condition, pretests and posttests, and the group structure. The choice of statistical techniques is commensurately simplified.

>**close**up

An Experiment on the Impact of Streaming Media Ads
MILLWARD BROWN Research Report: Millward Brown, 800.COM, and RealNetworks Inc.

MILLWARD BROWN RESEARCH REPORT

In order to determine the brand building effectiveness of streaming media advertising, RealNetworks in conjunction with 800.COM contracted Millward Brown, a noted online and offline brand research company, to conduct a *BrandImpact* study of an 800.COM streaming media ad. The dramatic results from this study are below.

THE BRAND IMPACT STUDY OBJECTIVES

Was the 800.COM ad noticed and remembered in connection with the brand?

Did the ad increase awareness for the 800.COM brand?

Did the ad impact consumers' perceptions of the 800.COM brand?

RESEARCH METHODOLOGY

A small percentage of users are sampled. Of those sampled, random assignments between control and test groups are made. The control group sees the control (decoy) ad and the test group sees the test ad (800.COM). The same survey is then administered to both groups measuring overall brand and advertising awareness. Image ratings for 800.COM are performed by both control and test members. Differences in advertising and brand awareness as well as in image attribute ratings are attributed to the impact of the test ad.

Fielded:

March 29 through March 31, 1999

Ad Placement Location:

Ads ran just prior to RealChannels and Presets on the RealPlayer

Cooperation Rates:

	CLICKTHROUGH	COMPLETES	RATE
Control Group	3% (3149)	47% (1492)	1.5%
Test Group	1% (2524)	47% (1180)	.5%

STUDY RESULTS

Brand Awareness:

Q. Did the ad increase awareness of the 800.COM brand?
A. Yes

ELECTRONIC RETAILERS	CONTROL	TEST	% INCREASE
On/offline Retailers	15%	36%	140%
Online only Retailers	15%	39%	160%

Brand Perception:

POSITIVE STATEMENT	CONTROL AD	TEST AD	OTHER BRANDS
Is growing more popular	10%	22%	13%
Makes it easy to shop online	07%	16%	12%
Is growing more popular	10%	22%	13%
Provides good value at a great price	06%	15%	13%
Is cool and cutting edge	05%	14%	10%
Provides a one-stop shopping environment	06%	13%	12%
Offers differ from competition	03%	11%	10%
Meets your needs	05%	10%	14%
Sets the standard for others to follow	03%	09%	09%

NEGATIVE STATEMENT	CONTROL AD	TEST AD	OTHER BRANDS
Is better than other online retailers	03%	09%	05%

MILLWARD BROWN CONCLUSIONS

Building an online brand requires marketers to leverage continuously the medium beyond the status quo.

- Consumers are overloaded by a constant barrage of communication messaging.
- Cutting through the clutter requires effective creative.
- Delivery must be in a format that catches the consumer off guard and captures their attention.

What made the 800.COM ad work, across all of the levels measured, is the combination of powerful rich media delivery and strong creative messaging.

Source: MILLWARD BROWN, www.realnetworks.com/products/advertising/ sales/Millward%20Brown_summary.html; **www.millwardbrown.com.**

Researchers have several measurement and instrument options with experiments. Among them are:

> **Chapters 18 to 21 provide comprehensive coverage of data analysis.**

• Observation techniques and coding schemes.

• Paper-and-pencil tests.

• Self-administered instruments with open-ended or closed questions.

• Scaling techniques (e.g., Likert scales, semantic differentials, Q-sort).

• Physiological measures (e.g., galvanic skin response, EKG, voice pitch analysis, eye dilation).

> Validity in Experimentation

internal validity when the conclusion(s) drawn about a demonstrated experimental relationship truly implies cause.

external validity when an observed causal relationship can be generalized across persons, settings, and times.

Even when an experiment is the ideal research design, it is not without problems. There is always a question about whether the results are true. We have previously defined validity as whether a measure accomplishes its claims. While there are several different types of validity, here only the two major varieties are considered: **internal validity**—do the conclusions we draw about a demonstrated experimental relationship truly imply cause?—and **external validity**—does an observed causal relationship generalize across persons, settings, and times?[6] Each type of validity has specific threats we need to guard against.

Internal Validity

Among the many threats to internal validity, we consider the following seven:

• History

• Maturation

• Testing

• Instrumentation

• Selection

• Statistical regression

• Experimental mortality

History

> **See Exhibit 12-4, p. 316, for a more detailed explanation of symbols.**

During the time that an experiment is taking place, some events may occur that confuse the relationship being studied. In many experimental designs, we take a control measurement (O_1) of the dependent variable before introducing the manipulation (X). After the manipulation, we take an after-measurement (O_2) of the dependent variable. Then the difference between O_1 and O_2 is the change that the manipulation has caused.

A company's management may want to test the hypothesis that its employees are poorly informed about its product lines. To assess the value of such an effort, managers give employees a test on their knowledge of the company's products (O_1). Then they present the educational campaign (X) to these employees, after which they again measure the employees' knowledge level (O_2). This design, known as a *preexperiment* because it is not a very strong design, can be diagrammed as follows:

$$O_1 \qquad\qquad X \qquad\qquad O_2$$
Pretest   Manipulation   Posttest

The effect would measure the difference between O_1 and O_2. Between O_1 and O_2, however, many events could occur that confound the effects of the education effort. A newspaper article might appear about the company's new product offerings, a departmental meeting or luncheon conversation might occur at which this topic is discussed, or another occurrence could distort the effects of the company's education test.

Maturation

Changes also may occur within the participant that are a function of the passage of time and are not specific to any particular event. These are of special concern when the study covers a long time, but they may also be factors in tests that are as short as an hour or two. A participant can become hungry, bored, or tired in a short time, and this condition can affect response results.

Testing

The process of taking a test can affect the scores of a second test. The mere experience of taking the first test can have a learning effect that influences the results of the second test.

Instrumentation

This threat to internal validity results from changes between observations in either the measuring instrument or the observer. Using different questions at each measurement is an obvious source of potential trouble, but using different observers or interviewers also threatens validity. There can even be an instrumentation problem if the same observer is used for all measurements. Observer experience, boredom, fatigue, and anticipation of results can all distort the results of separate observations.

Selection

An important threat to internal validity is the selection of participants for experimental and control groups. Validity considerations require that the groups be equivalent in every respect. If participants are randomly assigned to experimental and control groups, this selection problem can be largely overcome. Additionally, matching the members of the groups on key factors can enhance the equivalence of the groups. Comparing the two processes based on their effects on internal validity, randomization, when possible, is the preferred method.

Statistical Regression

This factor operates especially when groups have been selected by their extreme scores. Suppose we measure the output of all sales representatives in a department for a few days before an experiment and then conduct the experiment with only those whose productivity scores are in the top 25 percent and bottom 25 percent. No matter what is done between O_1 and O_2, there is a strong tendency for the average of the high scores at O_1 to decline at O_2 and for the low scores at O_1 to increase. This tendency results from imperfect measurement that, in effect, records some persons abnormally high and abnormally low at O_1. In the second measurement, members of both groups score more closely to their long-run mean scores.

Experimental Mortality

This occurs when the composition of the study groups changes during the test. Attrition is especially likely in the experimental group, and with each dropout the group changes. Because members of the control group are not affected by the testing situation, they are less likely to withdraw. In a compensation incentive study, some employees might not like the change in compensation method and may withdraw from the test group; this action could distort the comparison with the control group that has continued working under the established system, perhaps without knowing a test is under way.

The threats mentioned to this point are generally, but not always, dealt with adequately in experiments by random assignment. Control through the use of sophisticated control group designs is also used. Five additional threats to internal validity are independent of whether or not one randomizes.[7] The first three have the effect of equalizing experimental and control groups.

1. *Diffusion or imitation of treatment.* If people in the experimental and control groups talk, then those in the control group may learn of the treatment, eliminating the difference between the groups.

2. *Compensatory equalization.* Where the experimental treatment is much more desirable, there may be an administrative reluctance to deprive the control group members. Actions that compensate the control group may confound the experiment.

3. *Compensatory rivalry.* This may occur when members of the control group know they are in the control group. This may generate competitive pressures, causing the control group members to try harder.

4. *Resentful demoralization of the disadvantaged.* When the treatment is desirable and the experiment is conspicuous, control group members may become resentful that they are deprived and lower their cooperation and output.

5. *Local history.* The regular history effect already mentioned impacts both experimental and control groups alike. However, when one assigns all experimental persons to one group session and all control people to another, there is a chance for some peculiar event to confound results. This problem can be handled by administering treatments to individuals or small groups that are randomly assigned to experimental or control sessions.

External Validity

Internal validity factors cause confusion about whether the experimental treatment (X) or extraneous factors are the source of observed differences. In contrast, external validity is concerned with the interaction of the experimental treatment with other factors and the resulting impact on the ability to generalize to (and across) times, settings, or persons. Among the major threats to external validity are the following interactive possibilities:

• Reactivity of testing on X

• Interaction of selection and X

• Other reactive factors

Reactivity of Testing on X

The reactive effect refers to sensitizing participants via a pretest so that they respond to the experimental stimulus (X) in a different way. A before-measurement of a participant's knowledge about the brand repositioning plans of a company will often sensitize the participant to various experimental communication efforts that might be made about the company. This before-measurement effect can be particularly significant in experiments where the IV is a change in attitude or knowledge.

Interaction of Selection and X

The process by which test participants are selected for an experiment may be a threat to external validity. The population from which one selects participants may not be the same as the population to which one wishes to generalize results. Suppose you use a selected group of consumers in a mall for a test of product awareness. The question remains as to whether you can extrapolate the results to all consumers frequenting the mall. Or consider a study in which you ask a cross section of a population to participate in an experiment but a substantial number refuse. If you conduct the experiment only with those who agree to participate (self-selection), can the results be generalized to the total population?

Other Reactive Factors

The experimental settings themselves may have a biasing effect on a participant's response to X. An artificial setting can obviously produce results that are not representative of larger populations. Suppose the mall consumers in a test are moved to a vacant store to separate them from the control group. These new conditions alone could create a strong reactive condition.

If participants know they are participating in an experiment, there may be a tendency to role-play in a way that distorts the effects of X. Another reactive effect is the possible interaction between X and participant characteristics. Coupon incentives may be more effective with persons in one age group, in one household position, or with a certain personality trait.

Problems of internal validity can be solved by the careful design of experiments, but this is less true for problems of external validity. External validity is largely a matter of generalization, which, in a logical sense, is an inductive process of extrapolating beyond the data collected. In generalizing, we estimate the factors that can be ignored or will interact with the experimental variable. Assume that the closer two events are in time, space, and measurement, the more likely they are to follow the same laws. As a rule of thumb, first seek internal validity. Try to secure as much external validity as is compatible with the internal validity requirements by making experimental conditions as similar as possible to conditions under which the results will apply.

> Experimental Research Designs

The many experimental designs vary widely in their power to control contamination of the relationship between independent and dependent variables. The most widely accepted designs are based on this characteristic of control: (1) preexperiments, (2) true experiments, and (3) field experiments (see Exhibit 12-4).

Preexperimental Designs

All three preexperimental designs are weak in their scientific measurement power—that is, they fail to control adequately the various threats to internal validity. This is especially true of the after-only case study.

After-Only Case Study

This may be diagrammed as follows:

$$X \qquad\qquad\qquad O \qquad\qquad\qquad (1)$$

| Treatment or manipulation of independent variable | Observation or measurement of dependent variable |

An example is a media campaign about a product's features without a prior measurement of target consumer knowledge. Results would reveal only how much target consumers know

>Exhibit 12-4 Key to Design Strategies

X	An *X* represents the introduction of an experimental stimulus to a group. The effects of this independent variable(s) are of major interest.
O	An *O* identifies a measurement or observation activity.
R	An *R* indicates that the group members have been randomly assigned to a group.
E	An *E* represents the effect of the experiment and is presented as an equation.

The *X*'s and *O*'s in the diagram are read from left to right in temporal order.

X's and *O*'s vertical to each other indicate that the stimulus and/or observations take place simultaneously.

Parallel rows that are not separated by dashed lines indicate that comparison groups have been equalized by the randomization process.

Those separated with a dashed line have not been so equalized.

after the media campaign, but there is no way to judge the effectiveness of the campaign. How well do you think this design would meet the various threats to internal validity? The lack of a pretest and control group makes this design inadequate for establishing causality.

One-Group Pretest-Posttest Design

This is the design used earlier in the educational example. It meets the various threats to internal validity better than the one-shot case study, but it is still a weak design. How well does it control for history? Maturation? Testing effect? The others?

$$O_1 \qquad\qquad X \qquad\qquad O_2 \qquad\qquad (2)$$
$$\text{Pretest} \qquad \text{Manipulation} \qquad \text{Posttest}$$

Static Group Comparison

This design provides for two groups, one of which receives the experimental stimulus while the other serves as a control. Imagine this scenario: A brand is being repositioned,

>**snap**shot

A Nose for Problem Odors

Ever wonder how consumer product companies test the effectiveness of their creations? At Hill Top Research, Inc., founded in 1947 and the largest consumer product testing firm in the world, researchers use a variety of devices—including the human nose. In one deodorant study participants are brought to a test site that contains a hot room. Researchers apply the product being tested to each participant's armpit, followed by the insertion of a cotton pad under each arm, which participants retain by pressing their arms to their sides. Researchers then lead participants to the hot room—where temperatures are warm enough to make anyone sweat. When the participants exit the room after the de-

fined period of time, the cotton pad is removed for analysis. Then the odor detective does his or her job: A cup with a small hole in the bottom is placed against the participant's armpit (to ensure uniform distance between nose and pit), and the detective positions her or his nose near the hole and inhales. With a successful formulation, the odor detective does not detect a strong or offensive odor. What are some of the variables a researcher would need to control in this study? What sources of error must be controlled?

www.hill-top.com

and an ad is run in one-fourth of the 210 Designated Market Areas (DMAs) in the United States. After the ad airs, those who remember seeing it would be in the experimental group (X). Those who have no recall of the ad would be in the control group. The attitudes of each group toward the brand would be measured. A pretest before the ad treatment might be possible, but not on a large scale. Moreover, timing of the pretest would be problematic.

$$X \qquad\qquad O_1 \qquad\qquad (3)$$
$$\overline{} \qquad \overline{}$$
$$O_2$$

The addition of a comparison group creates a substantial improvement over the other two designs. Its chief weaknesses are that there is no way to be certain that the two groups are equivalent or that the individuals assigned to experimental and control groups are representative.

True Experimental Designs

The major deficiency of the preexperimental designs is that they fail to provide comparison groups that are truly equivalent. The way to achieve equivalence is through random assignment and, supplementally, through matching. With randomly assigned groups, we can employ tests of statistical significance to assess the observed differences.

Pretest-Posttest Control Group Design

This design consists of adding a control group to the one-group pretest-posttest design and assigning the participants to either of the groups by a random procedure (R). The diagram is:

$$R \qquad O_1 \qquad X \qquad O_2 \qquad\qquad (4)$$
$$R \qquad O_3 \qquad\qquad O_4$$

The effect of the experimental variable is

$$E = (O_2 - O_1) - (O_4 - O_3)$$

>**pic**profile

Researchers know that as many as 60 percent of purchase decisions are made in the store. Thus marketers aggressively seek in-store space to place temporary displays, shelf-talkers, and instant coupons, as well as ceiling signs and banners. Even the floor is contested real estate. So the ability to demonstrate the effectiveness of promotional materials is critical. FLOORgraphics, Inc., uses a longitudinal design, tracking sales of products in matched groups of stores (test and control groups). After test stores receive the FLOORad, relative sales in both groups are again compared to pre-ad performance and to each other. Research shows the FLOORad effect (the percentage sales increase directly due to the FLOORad) can lift sales 20 to 40 percent depending on the product category. www.floorgraphics.com

In this design, we can deal with the seven major internal validity problems fairly well, although there are still some difficulties. Local history may occur in one group and not the other. Also, if communication exists between people in test and control groups, there can be rivalry and other internal validity problems.

Maturation, testing, and regression are handled well because one would expect them to be felt equally in experimental and control groups. Mortality, however, can be a problem if there are different dropout rates in the study groups. Selection is not a problem if random assignment is used.

The record of this design is not as good on external validity, however. There is a chance for a reactive effect from testing. This might be a substantial influence in attitude change where pretests introduce unusual topics and content. Nor does this design ensure against reaction between selection and the experimental variable. Even random selection may be defeated by a high decline rate among participants. This would result in using a disproportionate share of people who are essentially volunteers and who may not be typical of the population. If this occurs, we will need to replicate the experiment several times with other groups under other conditions before we can be confident of external validity.

Posttest-Only Control Group Design

In this design, the pretest measurements are omitted. Pretests are well established in classical research design but are not really necessary when it is possible to randomize. The design is

$$R \qquad X \qquad O_1 \qquad\qquad\qquad\qquad (5)$$
$$R \qquad\qquad\quad O_2$$

The experimental effect is measured by the difference between O_1 and O_2.

$$E = (O_2 - O_1)$$

The simplicity of this design makes it more attractive than the pretest-posttest control group design. Internal validity threats from history, maturation, selection, and statistical regression are controlled adequately by random assignment. Since the participants are measured only once, the threats of testing and instrumentation are reduced, but different mortality rates between experimental and control groups continue to be a potential problem. The design reduces the external validity problem of testing interaction effect.

Field Experiments:
Quasi- or Semi-Experiments[8]

Direct marketers, with their large, detailed databases on customer response to offers, as well as their propensity to make every offer with a split test (control group), are clearly moving themselves toward the realm of true experimental designs done under field conditions. Most marketers, however, cannot control enough of the extraneous variables or the experimental treatment under field conditions to use a true experimental design. Because the stimulus condition occurs in a natural environment, a field quasi- or semi-experiment is required.

A modern version of the bystander and thief field experiment, mentioned at the beginning of the chapter, involves the use of electronic article surveillance to prevent shrinkage due to shoplifting. In a proprietary study, a shopper came to the optical counter of an upscale mall store and asked to be shown special designer frames. The salesperson, a confederate of the experimenter, replied that she would get them from a case in the adjoining department and disappeared. The "thief" selected two pairs of sunglasses from an open display, deactivated the security tags at the counter, and walked out of the store.

Thirty-five percent of the participants (store customers) reported the theft upon the return of the salesperson. Sixty-three percent reported it when the salesperson asked about the shopper. Unlike the case in previous studies, the presence of a second customer did not reduce the willingness to report a theft.

This study was not possible with a control group, a pretest, or randomization of customers, but the information gained was essential and justified a compromise of true experimental designs. We use the preexperimental designs previously discussed or quasi-experiments to deal with such conditions. In a quasi-experiment, we often cannot know when or to whom to expose the experimental treatment. Usually, however, we can decide when and whom to measure. A quasi-experiment is inferior to a true experimental design but is usually superior to preexperimental designs. In this section, we consider a few common quasi-experiments.

Nonequivalent Control Group Design

This is a strong and widely used quasi-experimental design. It differs from the pretest-posttest control group design, because the test and control groups are not randomly assigned. The design is diagrammed as follows:

$$O_1 \qquad X \qquad O_2 \qquad\qquad (6)$$
$$\overline{}$$
$$O_3 \qquad\qquad O_4$$

There are two varieties. One is the *intact equivalent design,* in which the membership of the experimental and control groups is naturally assembled. For example, with teenage participants, we may use different classes in a school, membership in similar clubs, or customers from similar stores. Ideally, the two groups are as alike as possible. This design is especially useful when any type of individual selection process would be reactive.

The second variation, the *self-selected experimental group design,* is weaker because volunteers are recruited to form the experimental group, while nonvolunteer participants are used for control. Such a design is likely when participants believe it would be in their interest to be a participant in an experiment—say, an experimental training program.

Comparison of pretest results $(O_1 - O_3)$ is one indicator of the degree of equivalence between test and control groups. If the pretest results are significantly different, there is a real question about the groups' comparability. On the other hand, if pretest observations are similar between groups, there is more reason to believe internal validity of the experiment is good.

Separate Sample Pretest-Posttest Design

This design is most applicable when we cannot know when and to whom to introduce the treatment but we can decide when and whom to measure. The basic design is

$$R \qquad O_1 \qquad (X) \qquad\qquad (7)$$
$$R \qquad\qquad X \qquad O_2$$

The parenthesized treatment (X) is irrelevant to the purpose of the study but is shown to suggest that the experimenter cannot control the treatment.

This is not a strong design because several threats to internal validity are not handled adequately. History can confound the results but can be overcome by repeating the study at other times in other settings. In contrast, the design is considered superior to true experiments in external validity. Its strength results from its being a field experiment in which the samples are usually drawn from the population to which we wish to generalize our findings.

We would find this design more appropriate if the population were large, if a before-measurement were reactive, or if there were no way to restrict the application of the treatment. Assume a company is planning an intense campaign to enhance consumer attitudes toward energy conservation. It might draw two random samples of consumers, one of which is interviewed about energy use attitudes before the information campaign. After the campaign the other group is interviewed.

Group Time Series Design

A time series design introduces repeated observations before and after the treatment and allows participants to act as their own controls. The single treatment group design has before-after measurements as the only controls. There is also a multiple design with two or more comparison groups as well as the repeated measurements in each treatment group.

$$R \qquad O_1 \qquad O_2 \qquad O_3 \qquad X \qquad O_4 \qquad O_5 \qquad O_6 \qquad\qquad (8)$$

Is Current Test Marketing Representative?

With 70 percent of new product introductions failing, the test market, a long-standing experimental research tradition in the marketing research of consumer goods, is under attack. A test market involves placing a new product in a sample of stores, usually in two or more cities, and then monitoring sales performance under different promotion, pricing, and physical placement conditions. Nonproponents claim the racial diversity of the U.S. population is not well reflected in several U.S. cities often chosen to provide crucial evidence of product viability. Cedar Rapids (Iowa), Columbus (Ohio), Little Rock (Arkansas), and Evansville (Indiana), four popular test market locations, are primarily populated by non-Hispanic white households. Yet, 22.9 percent of U.S. households claimed a different ethnic background in the Census Bureau's 2000 decennial census. Information Resources, Inc. (IRI), whose *BehaviorScan* syndicated

research uses similar cities, claims household demographics are only one criterion for site choice. Valerie Skala, IRI's vice president of Analytic Product Management and Development, claims "category and brand purchase patterns, as well as representative retail development," are more important. Test marketing site choice is also determined by cost and availability of retailers willing to stock the new product. IRI and VNU's ACNielsen Market Decisions have contracts with retailers that facilitate immediate placement, eliminating the need to negotiate placement with each store's corporate office. Does the absence of comparable demographics in test markets render the test market methodology faulty?

www.vnu.com; www.iri.com

The time series format is especially useful where regularly kept records are a natural part of the environment and are unlikely to be reactive. The time series approach is also a good way to study unplanned events in an ex post facto manner. If the federal government were to suddenly begin price controls, we could still study the effects of this action on gasoline prices later if we had regularly collected records for the period before and after the advent of price control.

The internal validity problem for this design is history. To reduce this risk, we keep a record of possible extraneous factors during the experiment and attempt to adjust the results to reflect their influence.

> Test Marketing

This section examines traditional and emerging designs for test marketing including the characteristics of six test market types and the strengths and weaknesses of each type.

A **test market** is a controlled experiment conducted in a carefully chosen marketplace (e.g., Web site, store, town, or other geographic location) to measure marketplace response and predict sales or profitability of a product. The objective of a market test study is to assist marketing managers introduce new products or services, add products to existing lines, identify concepts with potential, or relaunch enhanced versions of established brands. By testing the viability of a product, managers reduce the risks of failure. Complex experimental designs are often required to meet the controlled experimental conditions of test markets. They also are used in other marketing research where control of extraneous variables is essential. We describe the extensions of true experimental designs in this chapter's appendix.

The successful introduction of new products is critical to a firm's financial success. Failures not only create significant losses for companies but also hurt the brand and company reputation. According to ACNielsen, the failure rate for new products approaches 70 percent.[9] Estimates from other sources vary between 40 and 90 percent depending on whether the products are in consumer or industrial markets. Product failure may be attributable to

test market a controlled experiment conducted in a carefully chosen marketplace to measure and predict sales or profitability of a product.

many factors, especially inadequate marketing research. Test-marketed products, typically evaluated in consumer industries, enjoy a significantly higher success rate because managers can reduce their decision risk through reality testing. They gauge the effectiveness of pricing, packaging, promotions, distribution channels, dealer response, advertising copy, media usage patterns, and other aspects of the marketing mix. Test markets also help managers evaluate improved versions of existing products and services.

Test Market Selection

There are several criteria to consider when selecting test market locations. As we mentioned earlier, one of the primary advantages of a carefully conducted experiment is external validity or the ability to generalize to (and across) times, settings, or persons. The location and characteristics of participants should be *representative* of the market in which the product will compete. This requires consideration of the product's target competitive environment, market size, patterns of media coverage, distribution channels, product usage, population size, housing, income, lifestyle attributes, age, and ethnic characteristics. Not even "typical" all-American cities are ideal for all market tests. Kimberly-Clark's Depend and Poise brand products for bladder control could not be adequately tested in a college town. Cities that are overtested create problems for market selection because savvy participants' prior experiences cause them to respond atypically.

Multiple locations are often required for optimal demographic balance. Sales may vary by region, necessitating test sites that have characteristics equivalent to those of the targeted national market. Several locations may also be required for experimental and control groups.

Media coverage and *isolation* are additional criteria for locating the test. Although the test location may not be able to duplicate precisely a national media plan, it should adequately represent the planned promotion through print and broadcast coverage. Large metropolitan areas produce media spillover that may contaminate the test area. Advertising is

wasted as the media alerts distributors, retailers, and consumers in adjacent areas about the product. Competitors are warned more quickly about testing activities and the test loses it competitive advantage. In 2002, Dairy Queen (DQ) Corp., which has 5,700 stores throughout the world, began testing electronic irradiated burgers at the Hutchinson and Spicer locations in Minnesota. No quick-service restaurant chains provide irradiated burgers, although McDonald's and Burger King also researched this option. DQ originally focused information about the test at the store level rather than with local media. When the *Minneapolis Star Tribune* ran a story about the test, DQ had to inform all Minnesota store operators about the article, although all operators had known about the planned test. The article created awareness for anti-irradiation activists and the potential for demonstrations—an unplanned consequence of the test market.[10] Although relatively isolated communities are more desirable because their remoteness aids controlling critical promotional features of the test, in this instance media spillover and unintended consequences of unplanned media coverage became a concern.

The *control of distribution* affects test locations and types of test markets. Cooperation from distributors is essential for market tests conducted by the product's manufacturer. The distributor should sell exclusively in the test market to avoid difficulties arising from out-of-market warehousing, shipping, and inventory control. When distributors in the city are either unavailable or uncooperative, a controlled test, where the research firm manages distribution, should be considered.

Types of Test Markets

There are six major types of test markets: standard, controlled, electronic, simulated, virtual, and Web-enabled. In this section, we discuss their characteristics, advantages and disadvantages, and future uses.

Standard Test Markets

The **standard test market** is a traditional test of a product and/or marketing mix variables on a limited geographic basis. It provides a real-world test for evaluating products and marketing programs on a smaller, less costly scale. The firm launching the product selects specific sales zones, test market cities, or regions that have characteristics comparable to those of the intended consumers of the product. The firm performs the test through its existing distribution channels, using the same elements as used in a national rollout. Exhibit 12-5 shows some U.S. cities commonly used as test markets.

> **standard test market** real-time test of a product through existing distribution channels.

Standard test markets benefit from using actual distribution channels and discovering the amount of trade support necessary to launch and sustain the product. High costs ($1 million is typical, ranging upward to $30 million) and long time (12 to 18 months for a go/no-go decision) are disadvantages. The loss of secrecy when the test exposes the concept to the competition further complicates the usefulness of traditional tests.

In March 2000, in an affluent suburb of Indianapolis, Shell Oil Co. test-marketed the first robotic gas pump that allows drivers to serve themselves without leaving their cars.

>**Exhibit 12-5** Test Market Cities

Source: Acxiom Corporation, a database services company, released its first "Mirror on America," May 24, 2004, ranking America's top 150 Metropolitan Statistical Areas (MSAs) on overall consumer test market characteristics. "Which American City Provides the Best Consumer Test Market?" http://www.acxiom.com/default.aspx?ID=2521&Country_Code=USA. Also see: http://www.bizjournals.com/phoenix/stories/2000/11/20/daily5.html and http://celebrity-network.net/trc/business.htm

The innovation, which uses a combination of robotics, sensors, and cameras to guide the fuel nozzle into a vehicle's gas tank, took eight years to develop. Its features allow a parent to stay with children while pumping gas and enable a driver to avoid exposure to gas fumes or the risk of spillage, static fire, or even bad weather. Unfortunately, the product requires a coded computer chip containing vehicle information that must be placed on the windshield and a special, spring-loaded gas cap, which costs $20. The introduction could hardly have been more ill-timed. Just as gasoline prices began their upward advance and the end of winter removed the incentive for staying behind the wheel, Shell planned to charge an extra $1 per fill-up.[11]

The SmartPump is a robotic gas pump that dispenses fuel without the customer ever getting out of the car. Customers pay an additional $1 for the service.
www.shell.com

controlled test market
real-time test of a product through arbitrarily selected distribution partners.

> **Consumer packaged goods are consumer goods packaged by manufacturers and not sold unpackaged (in bulk) at the retail level (e.g., food, drinks, personal care products).**

Controlled Test Markets

The term **controlled test market** refers to real-time forced distribution tests conducted by a specialty research supplier that guarantees distribution of the test product through outlets in selected cities. The test locations represent a proportion of the marketer's total store sales volume. The research firm typically handles the retailer sell-in process and all distribution activities for the client during the market test. The firm offers financial incentives for distributors to obtain shelf space from nationally prominent retailers and provides merchandising, inventory, pricing, and stocking control. Using scanner-based, survey, and other data sources, the research service gathers sales, market share, and consumer demographics data, as well as information on first-year volumes.

Companies such as ACNielsen Market Decisions and Information Resources, Inc., give consumer packaged-goods (CPG) manufacturers the ability to evaluate sales potential while reducing the risks of new or relaunched products prior to a national rollout. Market Decisions, for example, has over 25 small to medium-size test markets available nationwide. Typically, consumers experience all the elements associated with the first-year marketing plan, including media advertising and consumer and trade promotions. Manufacturers with a substantial commitment to a national rollout also have the opportunity to "fast-track" products during a condensed time period (three to six months) before launch.[12]

Controlled test markets cost less than traditional ones (although they may reach several million dollars per year). They reduce the likelihood of competitor monitoring and provide a streamlined distribution function through the sponsoring research firm. Their drawbacks include the number of markets evaluated, the use of incentives—which distort trade cost estimates—and the evaluation of advertising.

Electronic Test Markets

electronic test market test that combines store distribution, consumer scanner panel data, and household-level media delivery.

An **electronic test market** is a test system that combines store distribution services, consumer scanner panels, and household-level media delivery in specifically designated markets. Retailers and cable TV operators have cooperative arrangements with the research firm in these markets. Electronic test markets, previously used with consumer packaged-goods brands, have the capability to measure marketing mix variables that drive trial and repeat purchases by demographic segment for both CPG and non-CPG brands. Information Resources Inc. (IRI), for example, offers a service called BehaviorScan, which is also known as a *split-cable test* or *single-source test* that combines scanner-based consumer panels with sophisticated broadcasting systems. IRI uses a combination of Designated

Market Area–level cut-ins on broadcast networks and local cable cut-ins to assess the effect of the advertising that the household panel views. IRI and ACNielsen collect supermarket, drugstore, and mass merchandiser scanner data used in such systems. The BehaviorScan service makes use of these data with respondents who are then exposed to different commercials with various advertising weights.[13]

IRI's TV system operates as a within-market TV advertising testing service. The five BehaviorScan markets are Eau Claire, Wisconsin; Cedar Rapids, Iowa; Midland, Texas; Pittsfield, Massachusetts; and Grand Junction, Colorado. As small markets, with populations of 75,000 to 215,000, they provide lower marketing support costs than other test markets and offer appropriate experimental controls over the test conditions. Although several thousand households may be used, by assigning every local cable subscriber a cell, the service can indiscernibly deliver different TV commercials to each cell and evaluate the effect of the advertising on the panelists' purchasing behavior. For a control, nonpanelist households in the cable cell are interviewed by telephone.

BehaviorScan tracks the actual purchases of a household panel through bar-coded products at the point of purchase. Participants show their identification card at a participating store and are also asked to "report purchases from non-participating retailers, including mass merchandisers and supercenters, by using a handheld scanner at home."[14] Computer programs link the household's purchases with television viewing data to get a refined estimate (± 10 percent) of the product's national sales potential in the first year. Consider the observation of a Frito-Lay senior vice president:

> BehaviorScan is a critical component of Frito-Lay's go-to-market strategy for a couple of reasons. First, it gives us absolutely the most accurate read on the sales potential of a new product, and a well-rounded view of consumer response to all elements of the marketing mix. Second, BehaviorScan TV ad testing enables us to significantly increase our return on our advertising investment.[15]

The advantages of electronic test markets are apparent from the quality of strategic information provided but suffer from an artifact of their identification card data collection strategy: participants may not be representative.

Simulated Test Markets

A **simulated test market (STM)** occurs in a laboratory research setting designed to simulate a traditional shopping environment using a sample of the product's consumers. STMs do not occur in the marketplace but are often considered a pretest before a full-scale market test. STMs are designed to determine consumer response to product initiatives in a compressed time period. A computer model, containing assumptions of how the new product would sell, is augmented with data provided by the participants in the simulation.

STMs have common characteristics: (1) Consumers are interviewed to ensure that they meet product usage and demographic criteria; (2) they visit a research facility where they are exposed to the test product and may be shown commercials or print advertisements for target and competitive products; (3) they shop in a simulated store environment (often resembling a supermarket aisle); (4) those not purchasing the product are offered free samples; (5) follow-up information is collected to assess product reactions and to estimate repurchase intentions; and (6) researchers combine the completed computer model with consumer reactions in order to forecast the likely trial purchase rates, sales volume, and adoption behavior prior to market entry.

When in-store variations are used, research suppliers select three to five cities representing the market where the product will be launched. They choose a mall with a high frequency of targeted consumers. In the mall, a simulated store in a vacant facility is stocked with products from the test category. Intercept interviews qualify participants for a 15-minute test during which participants view an assortment of print or television advertisements and are asked to recall salient features. Measures of new product awareness are obtained. With "dollars" provided by the research firm, participants may purchase the test product or any of the competing products. Advertising awareness, packaging, and adoption

simulated test market test of a product conducted in a laboratory setting designed to simulate a traditional shopping environment.

are assessed with a computer model, as in the laboratory setting. Purchasers may be offered additional opportunities to buy the product at a reduced price in the future.

STMs were widely adopted in the 1970s by global manufacturers as an alternative to standard test markets, which were considered more expensive, slower, and less protected. Although STM models continue to work somewhat well in today's mass-market world, their effectiveness will diminish in the next decade as the one-to-one marketing environment becomes more diverse. To obtain forecast accuracy at the individual level, not just trial or repeat probabilities, STMs require individualized marketing plans to estimate different promotional and advertising factors for each person.[16]

M/A/R/C Research, Inc., has what it calls its *Assessor* model with many features that address the deficiencies of previous STM forecasting models. For example, instead of a comparison of consumer reactions to historical databases, individual consumer preferences and current experiences with existing brands help to define the fit for the new product environment. A competitive context pertinent to each consumer's unique set of alternatives plays a prominent role in new product assessment. Important user segments (e.g., parent brand users, heavy users, or teenagers) are analyzed separately to capture distinct behaviors. According to M/A/R/C, the results of three different models (attitudinal preference models; a trial, repeat, depth-of-repeat model; and a behavioral decision model) are merged to reduce the influence of bias. From an accuracy standpoint, over 90 percent of the validated Assessor forecasts are within 10 percent of the actual, in-market sales volume figures.[17] Realistically, plus or minus 10 percent represents a level of precision that many firms are not willing to accept.

STMs offer several benefits. The costs ($50,000 to $150,000) is one-tenth of the cost of a traditional test market, competitor exposure is minimized, time is reduced to six to eight months, and modeling allows the evaluation of many marketing mix variables. The inability to measure trade acceptance and its lack of broad-based consumer response are its drawbacks.

Virtual Test Markets

virtual test market a test of a product using a computer simulation of an interactive shopping experience.

A **virtual test market** uses a computer simulation and hardware to replicate the immersion of an interactive shopping experience in a three-dimensional environment. Essential to the immersion experience is the system's ability to render realistically product offerings in real time. Other features of interactive systems are the ability to explore (navigate in the virtual world) and manipulate the content in real time. In virtual test markets, the participants move through a store and display area containing the product. They handle the product by touching its image and examine it dimensionally with a rotation device to inspect labels, prices, usage instructions, and packaging. Purchases are made by placing the product in a shopping cart. Data collected include time spent by product category, frequency and time with product manipulation, and order quantity and sequence, as well as video feedback of participant behavior.

An example of a virtual environment application reveals it as an inexpensive marketing research tool:

> Goodyear conducted a study of nearly 1,000 people. . . . Each respondent took a trip through a number of different virtual tire stores stocked with a variety of brands and models. . . . Goodyear found the results of the test valuable on several fronts. First, the research revealed the extent to which shoppers in different market segments valued the Goodyear brand over competing brands. Second, the test suggested strategies for repricing the product line.[18]

Virtual test markets are part of a family of virtual technology techniques dating back to the early 1990s. The term *Virtual Shopping*® was registered by Allison Research Technologies (ART) in the mid-90s.[19] ART's interfaces create a detailed virtual environment (supermarket, bar/tavern, convenience store, fast-food restaurant, drugstore, computer store, car dealership, and so forth) for participant interaction. Consumers use a display interface to point out what products are appealing or what they might purchase. Products, in CPG and non-CPG categories, are arrayed just as in an actual store. Data analysis includes the current range of sophisticated marketing research techniques and simulated test market methodologies.[20] Improvements in virtual reality technology are creating opportunities for multisensory shopping. Current visual and auditory environments are being augmented with additional modes of sensory perception such as touch, taste, and smell.

A hybrid market test that bridges virtual environments and Internet platforms begins to solve the difficult challenge of product design teams: concept selection. A traditional reliance on expensive physical prototypes may be resolved with virtual prototypes. Virtual prototypes were discovered to provide results comparable to those of physical ones, cost less to construct, and allow Web researchers to explore more concepts. In some cases, however, the computer renderings make virtual prototypes look better in virtual reality and score lower in physical reality—especially when comparisons are made with commercially available products.[21]

Web-Enabled Test Markets

Manufacturers have found an efficient way to test new products, refine old ones, survey customer attitudes, and build relationships. **Web-enabled test markets** are product tests using online distribution. They are primarily used by large CPG manufacturers that seek fast, cost-effective means for estimating new product demand. Although they offer less control than traditional experimental design, Procter & Gamble test-marketed Dryel, the home dry-cleaning product, for more than three years on 150,000 households in a traditional fashion while Drugstore.com tested the online market before its launch in 1999, taking less than a week and surveying about 100 people. Procter & Gamble now conducts 40 percent of its 6,000 product tests online. The company's annual research budget is about $140 million, but it believes that figure can be halved by shifting research projects to the Internet.[22]

Web-enabled test market test of a product using online distribution.

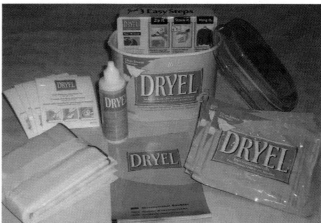

In 2000, when P&G geared up to launch Crest Whitestrips, a home tooth-bleaching kit, its high retail price created uncertainty. After an eight-month campaign offering the strips solely through the product's dedicated Web site, it sold 144,000 whitening kits online. Promoting the online sale, P&G ran TV spots, placed advertisements in lifestyle magazines, and sent e-mails to customers who signed up to receive product updates (12 percent of whom subsequently made a purchase). Retailers were convinced to stock the product, even at the high price. By timing the introduction with additional print and TV ad campaigns, P&G sold nearly $50 million worth of Crest Whitestrips kits three months later.[23] P&G's success has been emulated by its competitors and represents a growing trend. General Mills, Quaker, and a number of popular start-ups have followed, launching online test-marketing projects of their own.

>summary

1 Experiments are studies involving intervention by the researcher beyond that required for measurement. The usual intervention is to manipulate a variable (the independent variable) and observe how it affects the participants being studied (the dependent variable).

An evaluation of the experimental method reveals several advantages: (a) the ability to uncover causal relationships, (b) provisions for controlling extraneous and environmental variables, (c) convenience and low cost of creating test situations rather than searching for their appearance in business situations, (d) the ability to replicate findings and thus rule out idiosyncratic or isolated results, and (e) the ability to exploit naturally occurring events.

2 Some advantages of other methods that are liabilities for the experiment include (a) the artificial setting of the laboratory, (b) generalizability from nonprobability samples, (c) disproportionate costs in select business situations, (d) a focus restricted to the present and immediate future, and (e) ethical issues related to the manipulation and control of human participants.

3 Consideration of the following activities is essential for the execution of a well-planned experiment:

a Select relevant variables for testing.

b Specify the levels of treatment.

c Control the environmental and extraneous factors.

d Choose an experimental design suited to the hypothesis.

e Select and assign participants to groups.

f Pilot-test, revise, and conduct the final test.

g Analyze the data.

4 We judge various types of experimental research designs by how well they meet the tests of internal and external validity. An experiment has high internal validity if one has confidence that the experimental treatment has been the source of change in the dependent variable. More specifically, a design's internal validity is judged by how well it meets seven threats. These are history, maturation, testing, instrumentation, selection, statistical regression, and experimental mortality.

External validity is high when the results of an experiment are judged to apply to some larger population. Such an experiment is said to have high external validity regarding that population. Three potential threats to external validity are testing reactivity, selection interaction, and other reactive factors.

5 Experimental research designs include (a) preexperiments, (b) true experiments, and (c) quasi-experiments. The main distinction among these types is the degree of control that the researcher can exercise over validity problems.

Three preexperimental designs were presented in the chapter. These designs represent the crudest form of experimentation and are undertaken only when nothing stronger is possible. Their weakness is the lack of an equivalent comparison group; as a result, they fail to meet many internal validity criteria. They are the (a) after-only control study, (b) one-group pretest-posttest design, and (c) static group comparison.

Two forms of the true experiment were also presented. Their central characteristic is that they provide a means by which we can ensure equivalence between experimental and control groups through random assignment to the groups.

These designs are (a) pretest-posttest control group and (b) posttest-only control group.

The classical two-group experiment can be extended to multigroup designs in which different levels of the test variable are used as controls rather than the classical nontest control. In addition, the true experimental design can be extended into more sophisticated forms that use blocking. We discuss two such forms, the randomized block and the Latin square, in Appendix 12, along with the factorial design in which two or more independent variables are accommodated.

Between the extremes of preexperiments, with little or no control, and true experiments, with random assignment, there is a gray area in which we find quasi-experiments. These are useful designs when some variables can be controlled but equivalent experimental and control groups usually cannot be established by random assignment. There are many quasi-experimental designs, but only three were covered in this chapter: (a) nonequivalent control group design, (b) separate sample pretest-posttest design, and (c) group time series design.

6 Test marketing is a controlled experimental procedure conducted in a carefully selected marketplace to test a product or service to predict sales and profit outcomes. Marketing managers use test marketing to introduce new products or services, add products to existing lines, identify concepts with potential, or relaunch enhanced versions of established brands. There are six major types of test markets. A standard test market is a traditional test of a product and/or marketing mix variables on a limited geographic basis. It provides a real-world test on a smaller, less costly scale. The firm selects test market cities or regions comparable to those of the intended consumers of the product and tests it through its existing distribution channels. Controlled test markets are "live" forced distribution tests conducted by a specialty research supplier that guarantees distribution of the test product through outlets in selected cities. An electronic test market is a test system that combines store distribution services, consumer scanner panels, and household-level media delivery in specifically designated markets. Retailers and cable TV operators have cooperative arrangements with the research firm in these tests. A simulated test market (STM), often a pretest before a full-scale market test, occurs in a laboratory setting designed to simulate a traditional shopping environment using a sample of the product's consumers. STMs use computer models and data provided by participants in the simulation. A virtual test market uses a computer simulation and hardware to replicate the immersion of an interactive shopping experience in a virtual, three-dimensional environment. Web-enabled test markets are a growing trend for large consumer packaged-goods manufacturers that seek fast, cost-effective means to test new products, refine old ones, survey customer attitudes, and build relationships.

>**key**terms

blind 308	external validity 312	replication 303
control group 307	field experiment 303	simulated test market (STM) 325
controlled test market 324	hypothesis 305	standard test market 323
dependent variable (DV) 302	independent variable (IV) 302	test market 321
double-blind 308	internal validity 312	treatment levels 307
electronic test market 324	matching 309	virtual test market 326
environmental control 307	operationalized 305	Web-enabled test market 327
experiment 302	quota matrix 309	
experimental treatment 307	random assignment 309	

>**discussion**questions

Terms in Review

1 Distinguish between the following:

  a Internal validity and external validity.

  b History and maturation.

  c Random sampling, randomization, and matching.

  d Active factors and blocking factors.

  e Environmental variables and extraneous variables.

  f Traditional test markets and simulated test markets.

2 Compare the advantages of experiments with the advantages of survey and observational methods.

3 Why would a noted marketing researcher say, "It is essential that we always keep in mind the model of the controlled experiment, even if in practice we have to deviate from an ideal model"?

4 What ethical problems do you see in conducting experiments with human participants?

5 What essential characteristics distinguish a true experiment from other research designs?

Making Research Decisions

6 A lighting company seeks to study the percentage of defective glass shells arriving on shelves. Theoretically, the percentage of defectives is dependent on temperature, humidity, and the level of artisan expertise. Complete historical data are available for the following variables on a daily basis for a year. How should this study be conducted?

  a Temperature (high, normal, low).

  b Humidity (high, normal, low).

  c Artisan expertise level (expert, average, mediocre).

7 Describe how you would operationalize variables for experimental testing in the following research question: What are the performance differences between 10 microcomputers connected in a local area network (LAN) and one minicomputer with 10 terminals?

8 A pharmaceuticals manufacturer is testing a drug developed to treat cancer. During the final stages of development the drug's effectiveness is being tested on individuals for different dosage conditions and age groups. One of the problems is patient mortality during experimentation. Justify your design recommendations through a comparison of alternatives and in terms of external and internal validity.

  a Recommend the appropriate design for the experiment.

  b Explain the use of control groups, blinds, and double-blinds if you recommend them.

9 You are asked to develop an experiment for a study of the effect that financial incentives have on the participation rates secured from intercept interview participants. This study will involve 300 people, who will be assigned to one of the following conditions: no compensation, $1 compensation, and $3 compensation. A number of sensitive issues will be explored concerning various social problems, and the 300 people will be drawn from the adult population. Describe how your design would be set up if it were (a) a completely randomized design, (b) a randomized block design, (c) a Latin square, and (d) a factorial design (suggest another active variable to use). Which would you use? Why?

10 What type of experimental design would you recommend in each of the following cases? Suggest in some detail how you would design each study:

  a A study of the effects of various levels of advertising effort and price reduction on the sale of specific branded grocery products by a retail grocery chain.

b A study to determine whether it is true that the use of fast-paced music played over a supermarket's sound system will speed the shopping rate of customers without an adverse effect on the amount spent per customer.

11 What advantages do simulated test markets and virtual test markets have over traditional test markets? What are their disadvantages?

Behind the Scenes

12 Using the symbols in Exhibit 12-4, design the experiment that is being discussed at the trade association luncheon.

What are the strengths and weaknesses of the design as you have drafted it?

From Concept to Practice

13 Using Exhibit 12-4, diagram an experiment described in one of the Snapshots featured in this chapter using research design symbols.

>**www**exercise

Use a search engine to find an experiment described on the Web. Remember that experiments sometimes go by other names, like "taste test" in consumer food products or "beta test" in software products. Also, use terms introduced in this chapter. What experiment could you do that would use the same methodology?

>**cases**[*]

McDonald's Tests Catfish Sandwich

Retailers Unhappy with Displays from Manufacturers

* All cases, both written and video, are on the text DVD. Check the DVD Index to determine whether a case has data, the research instrument, or other supplementary material.

>appendix12a

Complex Experimental Designs

Earlier in the chapter, we discussed true experimental designs in their most frequently used forms, but researchers often require an extension of the basic design for sophisticated experiments and market tests. Extensions differ from the traditional designs in (1) the number of different experimental stimuli that are considered simultaneously by the experimenter and (2) the extent to which assignment procedures are used to increase precision.

Before we consider the types of variations, there are some commonly used terms that should be defined. *Factor* is widely used to denote an independent variable. Factors are divided into treatment levels, which represent various subgroups. A factor may have two or more levels, such as (1) male and female; (2) large, medium, and small; or (3) no training, brief training, and extended training. These levels should be defined operationally.

Factors also may be classified by whether the experimenter can manipulate the levels associated with the participant. *Active factors* are those the researcher can manipulate by causing a participant to receive one level or another. Treatment is used to denote the different levels of active factors. With the second type, the *blocking factor,* the experimenter can only identify and classify the participant on an existing level. Gender, age group, customer status, and ethnicity are examples of blocking factors, because the participant comes to the experiment with a pre-existing level of each.

Up to this point, the assumption is that experimental participants are people, but this is often not so. A broader term is *test unit;* it can refer equally well to an individual, product type, geographic market, medium of information dissemination, and innumerable other entities.*

Completely Randomized Design

The basic form of the true experiment is a completely randomized design. To illustrate its use, and that of more complex designs, consider a decision now facing the pricing manager at the Top Cannery. He would like to know what the ideal difference in price is between Top's private

*Check this Web site for examples of industrial experiments:
http://www.statsoft.com/textbook/stathome.html.

brand of canned vegetables and national brands such as Del Monte and Stokely's.

It is possible to set up an experiment on price differentials for canned green beans. Eighteen company stores and three price spreads (treatment levels) of 7 cents, 12 cents, and 17 cents between the company brand and national brands are used for the study. Six of the stores are assigned randomly to each of the treatment groups. The price differentials are maintained for a period, and then a tally is made of the sales volumes and gross profits of the canned green beans for each group of stores.

This design can be diagrammed as follows:

$$
\begin{array}{llll}
R & O_1 & X_1 & O_2 \\
R & O_3 & X_3 & O_4 \qquad \text{(A1)} \\
R & O_5 & X_5 & O_6
\end{array}
$$

Here, O_1, O_3, and O_5 represent the total gross profits for canned green beans in the treatment stores for the month before the test. X_1, X_3, and X_5 represent 7-cent, 12-cent, and 17-cent treatments, while O_2, O_4, and O_6 are the gross profits for the month after the test started.

We assume that the randomization of stores to the three treatment groups was sufficient to make the three store groups equivalent. When there is reason to believe this is not so, we must use a more complex design.

Randomized Block Design

If there is a single major extraneous variable, the randomized block design is used. Random assignment is still the basic way to produce equivalence among treatment groups, but the researcher may need additional assurances. First, if the sample being studied is very small, it is risky to depend on random assignment alone to guarantee equivalence. Small samples, such as the 18 company stores, are typical in field experiments because of high costs or because few test units are available. Another reason for blocking is to learn whether treatments bring different results among various groups of participants.

Consider again the canned green beans pricing experiment. Assume there is reason to believe that lower-income families are more sensitive to price differentials than are higher-income families. This factor could seriously distort our results unless we stratify the stores by customer income. Therefore, each of the 18 stores is assigned to one of three income blocks and randomly assigned, within blocks, to the price difference treatments. The design is shown in the following table.

Active Factor: Price Difference		Blocking Factor: Customer Income		
		High	Medium	Low
7 cents	R	X_1	X_1	X_1
12 cents	R	X_2	X_2	X_2
17 cents	R	X_3	X_3	X_3

(A2)

Note: The O's have been omitted. The horizontal rows no longer indicate a time sequence, but various levels of the blocking factor. However, before-and-after measurements are associated with each of the treatments.

In this design, one can measure both main effects and interaction effects. The *main effect* is the average direct influence that a particular treatment of the independent variable (IV) has on the dependent variable (DV), independent of other factors. The *interaction effect* is the influence of one factor or variable on the effect of another. The main effect of each price difference is discovered by calculating the impact of each of the three treatments averaged over the different blocks. Interaction effects occur if you find that different customer income levels have a pronounced influence on customer reactions to the price differentials. (See Chapter 20, "Hypothesis Testing.")

Whether the randomized block design improves the precision of the experimental measurement depends on how successfully the design minimizes the variation within blocks and maximizes the variation between blocks. If the response patterns are about the same in each block, there is little value to the more complex design. Blocking may be counterproductive.

Latin Square Design

The Latin square design may be used when there are two major extraneous factors. To continue with the pricing example, assume we decide to block on the size of store and on customer income. It is convenient to consider these two blocking factors as forming the rows and columns of a table. We divide each factor into three levels to provide nine groups of stores, each representing a unique combination of the two blocking variables. Treatments are then randomly assigned to these cells so that a given treatment appears only once in each row and column. Because of this restriction, a Latin Square must have the same number of rows, columns, and treatments. The design looks like the following table.

Store Size	Customer Income		
	High	Medium	Low
Large	X_3	X_1	X_2
Medium	X_2	X_3	X_1
Small	X_1	X_2	X_3

(A3)

Treatments can be assigned by using a table of random numbers to set the order of treatment in the first row. For example, the pattern may be 3, 1, 2 as shown above. Following this, the other two cells of the first column are filled similarly, and the remaining treatments are assigned to meet the restriction that there can be no more than one treatment type in each row and column.

The experiment takes place, sales results are gathered, and the average treatment effect is calculated. From this, we can determine the main effect of the various price spreads on the sales of company and national brands. The cost information allows us to discover which price differential produces the greatest margin.

A limitation of the Latin square is that we must assume there is no interaction between treatments and blocking factors. Therefore, we cannot determine the interrelationships among store size, customer income, and price spreads. This limitation exists because there is not an exposure of all combinations of treatments, store sizes, and customer income groups. Such an exposure would require a table of 27 cells, while this one has only 9. If one is not especially interested in interaction, the Latin square is much more economical.

Factorial Design

One commonly held misconception about experiments is that the researcher can manipulate only one variable at a time. This is not true; with factorial designs, you can deal with more than one treatment simultaneously. Consider again the pricing experiment. The president of the chain might also be interested in finding the effect of posting unit prices on the shelf to aid shopper decision making. The following table can be used to design an experiment that includes both the price differentials and the unit pricing.

Unit Price Information?	Price Spread		
	7 cents	12 cents	17 cents
Yes	$X_1 Y_1$	$X_1 Y_2$	$X_1 Y_3$
No	$X_2 Y_1$	$X_2 Y_2$	$X2 Y_3$

(A4)

This is known as a 2 × 3 factorial design in which we use two factors: one with two levels and one with three levels of intensity.[†] The version shown here is completely randomized, with the stores being randomly assigned to one of six treatment combinations. With such a design, it is possible to estimate the main effects of each of the two independent variables and the interactions between them. The results can help to answer the following questions:

1. What are the sales effects of the different price spreads between company and national brands?

2. What are the sales effects of using unit-price marking on the shelves?

3. What are the sales effect interrelations between price spread and the presence of unit-price information?

[†]We describe factorial designs used with conjoint analysis in Chapter 22.

Covariance Analysis

We have discussed direct control of extraneous variables through blocking. It is also possible to apply some degree of indirect statistical control on one or more variables through analysis of covariance. Even with randomization, one may find that the before-measurement shows an average knowledge-level difference between experimental and control groups. With covariance analysis, one can adjust statistically for this before-difference. Another application might occur if the canned green beans pricing experiment were carried out with a completely randomized design, only to reveal a contamination effect from differences in average customer income levels. With covariance analysis, one can still do some statistical blocking on average customer income after the experiment has been run.[†]

[†]We discuss the statistical aspects of covariance analysis with analysis of variance (ANOVA) in Chapter 19.

>part III

The Sources and Collection of Data

chapter 13

Measurement

> **learning**objectives

After reading this chapter, you should understand . . .

1 The distinction between measuring objects, properties, and indicants of properties.

2 The similarities and differences between the four scale types used in measurement and when each is used.

3 The four major sources of measurement error.

4 The criteria for evaluating good measurement.

Researchers often capture new business based on referrals. Sometimes when the client is important enough, they will take on additional tasks even if these offer little opportunity for increased new business. We join Jason Henry, a project director with Visionary Insights in charge of the MindWriter CompleteCare assessment project. At MindWriter's request, Jason is conferring with a symphony director. This symphony, and its success, is a special philanthropic project of MindWriter.

The executive director of Glacier Symphony gestures broadly at the still snowcapped Canadian Rockies. "It has been three very happy years for me here, though not easy ones since I let corporate America intrude on our idyllic existence."

"You mean the MindWriter people?" prompts Jason Henry. "The ones who flew me up here? My clients and your benefactor?"

"Please, don't misunderstand," says the executive director as she propels Jason across a manicured lawn toward the refreshment tent. "When I rented them a part of our compound for use in corporate education, they quite generously insisted that I avail myself of some of their training for midlevel managers."

"They said you were having trouble with attendance?" ventures Jason. "Tell me what you do here."

"We offer one of the most outstanding summer music festivals in the country—maybe the continent. We present several concerts each week, all summer long, with evening performances on both Friday and Saturday. During the week, rehearsals are open to music patrons and students. And, of course, our skilled musicians enhance their own skills by networking with each other.

"During the winter my artistic directors prepare the next summer's program and hire the musicians, coordinating closely with me on the budget. This is quite complicated, as most of our musicians spend only two weeks with us. Fully 600 performing artists from many parts of the continent are part of this orchestra over the course of a summer festival.

"Colleges in British Columbia send me their music scholarship students for summer employment as dishwashers, waiters, cleaners, and the like. It is a special opportunity for them, rubbing shoulders with their idols and learning to enhance their own performance skills in the process.

"So your problems is…?" urges Jason again.

"My problem is patronage, specifically the lack of commitment of the local residents of Glacier to consistently support their Glacier Symphony Festival. Do you realize how rare it is for a town this size to have more than 600 performing musicians in a summer? You would think the residents would be as ecstatic as our dishwashers!"

"Do you know why they are less than supportive?" inquires Jason, glad they have finally arrived at the reason MindWriter had asked him to divert his homebound flight from San Francisco to British Columbia.

"Well, some of the residents have communicated with us informally," comments the director, somewhat hesitantly.

"And they said . . . ?" urges Jason, more than a little impatiently, remembering why he so values Sara Armstrong for usually handling this phase of exploratory research.

"One commented: 'I've never heard this music before—why can't the performers play something I'll recognize.' Another, 'Where were the video screens? And the special visual effects?' And another: 'Why would I want to spend more than an hour watching a stage full of people sitting in chairs?'"

"Hold on," says Jason, making a note in his Palm-Pilot. "I can see your orchestra is striking a sour note." Jason smiles, chuckling at his own wit, while the director remains stoic. "MindWriter uses an extensive program for measuring customer satisfaction, and . . ."

"Ah, yes, measuring customer satisfaction," interrupts the director, "second only to cash flow for the MindWriter folks. The care and frequency with which they measure customer satisfaction in the MindWriter seminars here dumbfounds me. Throughout each seminar they host here, morning, afternoon, or evening, everyone breaks for coffee and is required to fill out a critique of the speaker. The results are tabulated by the time the last coffee cup has been collected, and the seminar leader has been given feedback. Is he or she presenting material too slowly or too quickly? Are there too many jokes or not enough? Are concrete examples being used often enough? Do the participants want a hard copy of the slides? They measure attitudinal data six times a day and even query you about the meals, including taste, appearance, cleanliness and speed, friendliness, and accuracy of service."

"Understandable," observes Jason. "Your scholarship students have frequent contact with the residents, both here and in town, right? We might use them to collect some more formal data," brainstorms Jason to himself.

"Jason," interjects the director, "were you ever a musician?"

"No," explains Jason, "my interests ran more toward statistics than Schubert."

"Then you wouldn't realize that while musicians could talk about music—and the intricacies of performing music—for hours with each other, once a resident exclaims little or no interest, our scholarship students would likely tune them out."

"It is just as well," comments Jason, now resigned to getting more involved in Glacier Symphony's problem than he had first assumed would be necessary. "Untrained interviewers and observers can be highly unreliable and inaccurate in measuring and reporting behavior," says Jason. "Have you tried a suggestion box?"

"No, but I do send reminder postcards for each concert."

"Not quite the same thing," murmurs Jason as he hands the director his business card. "As a devotee of the MindWriter way, I'm sure you have a current satisfaction survey for concert goers in your files." At her nod, Jason continues, "Send it to me. At MindWriter's request and at its expense, I'll revise it for you. I'll work out the collection and analysis details on my flight home and be in touch next week."

The director, smiling and shaking Jason's hand, responds, "I'll ask one of our scholarship students to drive you back to the community airport, then. You're bound to have a lot in common."

> The Nature of Measurement

In everyday usage, measurement occurs when an established index verifies the height, weight, or other feature of a physical object. How well you like a song, a painting, or the personality of a friend is also a measurement. To measure is to discover the extent, dimensions, quantity, or capacity of something, especially by comparison with a standard. We measure casually in daily life, but in research the requirements are rigorous.

Measurement in research consists of assigning numbers to empirical events, objects or properties, or activities in compliance with a set of rules. This definition implies that measurement is a three-part process:

1. Selecting observable empirical events.

2. Developing a set of **mapping rules**: a scheme for assigning numbers or symbols to represent aspects of the event being measured.

3. Applying the mapping rule(s) to each observation of that event.[1]

You recall the term *empirical*. Researchers use an empirical approach to describe, explain, and make predictions by relying on information gained through observation.

Assume you are studying people who attend an auto show where prototypes for new models are on display. You are interested in learning the male-to-female ratio among attendees. You observe those who enter the show area. If a person is female, you record an F; if male, an M. Any other symbols such as 0 and 1 or # and % also may be used if you know what group the symbol identifies. Exhibit 13-1 uses this example to illustrate the above components.

Researchers might also want to measure the styling desirability of a new concept car at this show. They interview a sample of visitors and assign, with a different mapping rule, their opinions to the following scale:

> **measurement** assigning numbers to empirical events in compliance with a mapping rule.

> **mapping rule** a scheme for assigning numbers to aspects of an empirical event.

What is your opinion of the styling of the Speedbird?

Very desirable   5   4   3   2   1   Very undesirable

All measurement theorists would call the rating scale in Exhibit 13-1 a form of measurement, but some would challenge whether classifying males and females is a form of measurement. Their argument is that measurement must involve quantification—that is, "the assignment of numbers to objects to represent amounts or degrees of a property possessed by all of the objects."[2] This condition was met when measuring opinions of car styling. Our approach endorses the more general view that "numbers as symbols within a mapping rule" can reflect both qualitative and quantitative concepts.

The goal of measurement—indeed, the goal of "assigning numbers to empirical events in compliance with a set of rules"—is to provide the highest-quality, lowest-error data for testing hypotheses, estimation or prediction, or description. Researchers deduce from a hypothesis that certain conditions should exist. Then they measure for these conditions in the real world. If found, the data lend support to the hypothesis; if not, researchers conclude the hypothesis is faulty. An important question at this point is, "Just what does one measure?"

The object of measurement is a *concept*, the symbols we attach to bundles of meaning that we hold and share with others. We invent higher-level concepts—*constructs*—for specialized scientific explanatory purposes that are not directly observable and for thinking about and communicating abstractions. Concepts and constructs are used at theoretical levels; variables are used at the empirical level. *Variables* accept numerals or values for the purpose of testing and measurement. Concepts, constructs, and variables may be defined descriptively or operationally. An *operational definition* defines a variable in terms of specific measurement and testing criteria. It must specify adequately the empirical information needed and how it will be collected. In addition, it must have the proper scope or fit for the research problem at hand. We review these terms with examples in Exhibit 13-2.

> **You may want to revisit Chapter 3 for a thorough discussion of these research terms.**

>**Exhibit 13-1** Characteristics of Measurement

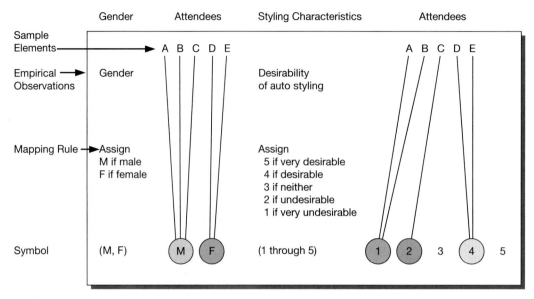

Attendees A, B, and C are male, and find the auto's styling to be undesirable.
Attendees D and E are female and find the auto's styling desirable.

What Is Measured?

objects concepts defined by ordinary experience.

properties characteristics of objects that are measured.

Variables being studied in research may be classified as objects or as properties. **Objects** include the concepts of ordinary experience, such as tangible items like furniture, laundry detergent, people, or automobiles. Objects also include things that are not as concrete, such as genes, attitudes, and peer-group pressures. **Properties** are the characteristics of the object. A person's *physical properties* may be stated in terms of weight, height, and posture, among others. *Psychological properties* include attitudes and intelligence. *Social properties* include leadership ability, class affiliation, and status. These and many other properties of an individual can be measured in a research study.

In a literal sense, researchers do not measure either objects or properties. They measure indicants of the properties or indicants of the properties of objects. It is easy to observe that A is taller than B and that C participates more than D in a group process. Or suppose you are analyzing members of a sales force of several hundred people to learn what personal properties contribute to sales success. The properties are age, years of experience, and number of calls made per week. The indicants in these cases are so accepted that one considers the properties to be observed directly.

In contrast, it is not easy to measure properties of constructs like "lifestyles," "opinion leadership," "distribution channel structure," and "persuasiveness." Since each property cannot be measured directly, one must infer its presence or absence by observing some indicant or pointer measurement. When you begin to make such inferences, there is often disagreement about how to develop an operational definition for each indicant.

Not only is it a challenge to measure such constructs, but a study's quality depends on what measures are selected or developed and how they fit the circumstances. The nature of measurement scales, sources of error, and characteristics of sound measurement are considered next.

66 If you can't measure it, you can't manage it. 99

Bob Donath, Consultant,
Bob Donath and Co., Inc.

>**Exhibit 13-2** Review of Key Terms

Concept: a bundle of meanings or characteristics associated with certain events, objects, conditions, situations, or behaviors.

Classifying and categorizing objects or events that have common characteristics beyond any single observation creates concepts. When you think of a spreadsheet or a warranty card, what comes to mind is not a single example but your collected memories of all spreadsheets and warranty cards from which you abstract a set of specific and definable characteristics.

Construct: an image or idea specifically invented for a given research and/or theory-building purpose.

We build constructs by combining the simpler, more concrete concepts, especially when the idea or image we intend to convey is not subject to direct observation. When Jason and Sara prepare the measurement instrument for MindWriter's research study, they will wrestle with the construct of a "satisfied service customer " and its meaning.

Variable: an event, act, characteristic, trait, or attribute that can be measured and to which we assign numerals or values; a synonym for the construct or the property being studied.

The numerical value assigned to a variable is based on the variable's properties. For example, some variables, said to be *dichotomous,* have only two values, reflecting the presence or absence of a property: employed-unemployed or male-female have two values, generally 0 and 1. Variables also take on values representing added categories, such as the demographic variables of race and religion. All such variables that produce data that fit into categories are *discrete* variables, since only certain values are possible. An automotive variable, for example, where "Chevrolet" is assigned a 5 and "Honda" is assigned a 6, provides no option for a 5.5. Income, temperature, age, and a test score are examples of *continuous* variables. These variables may take on values within a given range or, in some cases, an infinite set. Your test score may range from 0 to 100, your age may be 23.5, and your present income could be $35,000.

Operational definition: a definition for a construct stated in terms of specific criteria for testing or measurement; refers to an empirical standard (we must be able to count, measure, or gather information about the standard through our senses).

Researchers deal with two types of definitions: dictionary definitions and operational definitions. In the more familiar dictionary definition, a concept is defined with a synonym. For example, a customer is defined as a patron; a patron, in turn, is defined as a customer or client of an establishment. When we measure concepts and constructs, we require the more rigorous definition offered by an operational definition. Whether the object being defined is physical (e.g., a can of soup) or highly abstract (e.g., an attitude toward packaging), the operational definition must specify the characteristics and how they are to be observed or counted. The specifications and procedures must be so clear that any competent person using them would classify the objects in the same way. For example: *For our study, a can of peaches will be any container—metal, glass, plastic, or composite—that weighs at least 12 ounces and is purchased at a grocery, drug, convenience, or mass merchandiser within the Detroit, Michigan, Consolidated Metropolitan Statistical Area (CMSA).*

> Measurement Scales

In measuring, one devises some mapping rule and then translates the observation of property indicants using this rule. For each concept or construct, several types of measurement are possible; the appropriate choice depends on what you assume about the mapping rules. Each one has its own set of underlying assumptions about how the numerical symbols correspond to real-world observations.

>Exhibit 13-3 Measurement Scales

Type of Data	Characteristics of Data	Basic Empirical Operation	Example
Nominal	Classification (mutually exclusive and collectively exhaustive categories), but no order, distance, or natural origin	Determination of equality	Gender (male, female)
Ordinal	Classification and order, but no distance or natural origin	Determination of greater or lesser value	Doneness of meat (well, medium well, medium rare, rare)
Interval	Classification, order, and distance, but no natural origin	Determination of equality of intervals or differences	Temperature in degrees
Ratio	Classification, order, distance, and natural origin	Determination of equality of ratios	Age in years

Mapping rules have four characteristics:

1. *Classification.* Numbers are used to group or sort responses. No order exists.
2. *Order.* Numbers are ordered. One number is greater than, less than, or equal to another number.
3. *Distance.* Differences between numbers are ordered. The difference between any pair of numbers is greater than, less than, or equal to the difference between any other pair of numbers.
4. *Origin.* The number series has a unique origin indicated by the number zero. This is an absolute and meaningful zero point.

Combinations of these characteristics of classification, order, distance, and origin provide four widely used classifications of measurement scales:[3] (1) nominal, (2) ordinal, (3) interval, and (4) ratio. Let's preview these measurement scales before we discuss their technical details. Suppose your marketing professor asks a student volunteer to taste-test six candy bars. The student begins by evaluating each on a chocolate–not chocolate scale; this is a nominal measurement. Then the student ranks the candy bars from best to worst; this is an ordinal measurement. Next, the student uses a 7-point scale that has equal distance between points to rate the candy bars with regard to some taste criterion (e.g., crunchiness); this is an interval measurement. Finally, the student, considers another taste dimension and assigns 100 points among the six candy bars; this is a ratio measurement.

The characteristics of these measurement scales are summarized in Exhibit 13-3. Deciding which type of data is appropriate for your research needs should be seen as a part of the research process, as seen in Exhibit 13-4.

nominal scale scale with mutually exclusive and collectively exhaustive categories, but without the properties of order, distance, or origin.

Nominal Scales

In marketing research, nominal data are widely used. With **nominal scales**, you are collecting information on a variable that naturally or by design can be grouped into two or more categories that are mutually exclusive and collectively exhaustive. If data were collected from the symphony patrons at the Glacier compound, patrons could be classified by whether they had attended prior symphony performances or this was their first time. Every patron would fit into one of the two groups within the variable *attendance*.

The counting of members in each group is the only possible arithmetic operation when a nominal scale is employed. If we use numerical symbols within our mapping rule to identify categories, these numbers are recognized as labels only and have no quantitative value. The number 23, we

>**Exhibit 13-4** Moving from Investigative to Measurement Questions

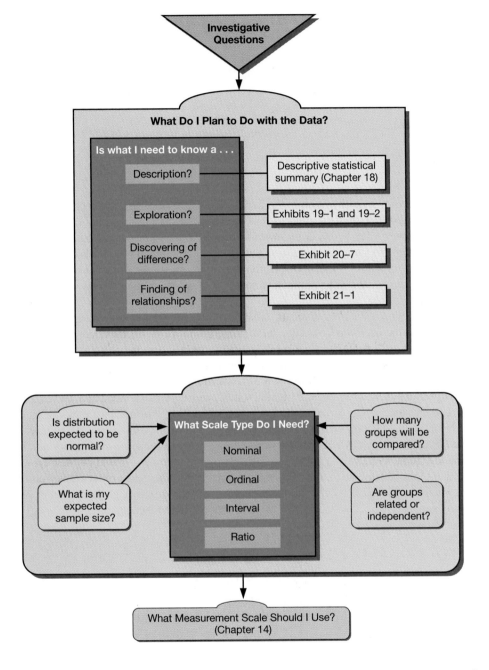

know, does not imply a sequential count of players or a skill level; it is only a means of identification. Of course, you might want to argue about a jersey number representing a skill level if it is LeBron James wearing jersey 23.

Nominal classifications may consist of any number of separate groups if the groups are mutually exclusive and collectively exhaustive. Thus, one might classify the students in a course according to their expressed religious preferences. Mapping rule A given in the table on the next page is not a sound nominal scale because its categories are not mutually exclusive or collectively exhaustive. Mapping rule B meets the minimum requirements; it covers all the major religions and offers an "other" option. Nominal scales are the least powerful of the four data types. They suggest no order or distance relationship and have no arithmetic origin. The scale wastes any information a sample element might share about varying degrees of the property being measured.

Religious Preferences	
Mapping Rule A	**Mapping Rule B**
1 = Baptist	1 = Christian
2 = Catholic	2 = Muslim
3 = Protestant	3 = Hindu
4 = Scientology	4 = Buddhist
5 = Unitarian-Universalist	5 = Jewish
6 = Jewish	6 = Other
7 = Secular/nonreligious/agnostic/atheist	

> **We discuss significance tests and measures of association in Chapters 20 and 21. Several tests for statistical significance may be used with nominal data; the most common is the chi-square test.**

Since the only quantification is the number count of cases in each category (the frequency distribution), the researcher is restricted to the use of the mode as the measure of central tendency.[4] The *mode* is the most frequently occurring value. You can conclude which category has the most members, but that is all. There is no generally used measure of *dispersion* for nominal scales. Dispersion describes how scores cluster or scatter in a distribution. By cross-tabulating nominal variables with other variables, you can begin to discern patterns in data.

While nominal data are statistically weak, they are still useful. If no other scale can be used, one can almost always classify a set of properties into a set of equivalent classes. Nominal measures are especially valuable in exploratory work where the objective is to uncover relationships rather than secure precise measurements. This type of scale is also widely used in survey and other research when data are classified by major subgroups of the population. Classifications such as respondents' marital status, gender, political orientation, and exposure to a certain experience provide insight into important demographic data patterns.

Jason visited Glacier because of his familiarity with MindWriter's extensive research into customer satisfaction. His visit revealed Glacier's need for some exploratory nominal data on symphony patrons. Patrons could be divided into groups—based on their appreciation of the conductor (favorable, unfavorable), on their attitude toward facilities (suitable, not suitable), on their perception of the program (clichéd, virtuoso), on their level of symphony support (financial support, no financial support)—and then analyzed.

Ordinal Scales

ordinal scale scale with mutually exclusive and collectively exhaustive categories, as well as the property of order, but not distance or unique origin.

Ordinal scales include the characteristics of the nominal scale plus an indication of order. Ordinal data require conformity to a logical postulate, which states: If *a* is greater than *b* and *b* is greater than *c*, then *a* is greater than *c*.[5] The use of an ordinal scale implies a statement of "greater than" or "less than" (an equality statement is also acceptable) without stating how much greater or less. While ordinal measurement speaks of greater-than and less-than measurements, other descriptors may be used—"superior to," "happier than," "poorer than," or "important than." Like a rubber yardstick, an ordinal scale can stretch varying amounts at different places along its length. Thus, the real difference between ranks 1 and 2 on a satisfaction scale may be more or less than the difference between ranks 2 and 3. An ordinal concept can be extended beyond the three cases used in the simple illustration of *a* > *b* > *c*. Any number of cases can be ranked.

> **Correlational analysis of ordinal data is restricted to various ordinal techniques. Measures of statistical significance are technically confined to a body of statistics known as *nonparametric methods*, synonymous with *distribution-free statistics*.[6]**

Another extension of the ordinal concept occurs when there is more than one property of interest. We may ask a taster to rank varieties of carbonated soft drinks by flavor, color, carbonation, and a combination of these characteristics. We can secure the combined ranking either by asking the respondent to base his or her ranking on the combination of properties or by constructing a combination ranking of the individual rankings on each property.

Examples of ordinal data include attitude and preference scales. (In the next chapter, we provide detailed examples of attitude scales.) Because the numbers used with ordinal scales

>**snap**shot

Color-Coded Terror-Alert System: How Do You Measure Normal?

In March 2002, the Homeland Security Advisory System was announced as a threat-level system to publicize information about the risk of terrorist attacks to federal, state, and local authorities, and to the American people. The five-rank, color-coded system begins at the lowest level, green, and moves upward through blue, yellow, orange, and red ranks. Each color represents a threat level (low, guarded, elevated, high, severe) and is accompanied by security criteria in each category. Officials compare the alert levels to the color-coded system used during World War II.

The system was designed to be a comprehensive and effective communications structure based on a terror-measurement system. As a public relations communication initiative it has been less successful. It has caused confusion and consternation when government spokespeople explain the reasons for raising and lowering threat levels—which are essentially based on changing threat assessments by intelligence analysts. The Homeland Security secretary, Tom Ridge, contends that the five-level system gives government and industry a "common vocabulary" and concrete suggestions for preparing against terrorist attacks. Private citizens find that as a measurement system it provides little

concrete evidence or advice for preparation, as evidenced by nearly three weeks in February 2003 when an orange alert caused anxious Americans to stock up on water, food, duct tape, and plastic sheeting. The frustration with this measurement system was summed up by one editorial writer: "If it's normal to be 'elevated,' being higher inevitably will be alarming. And if the color coordinators can't say anything about the nature or location of the threat that's changing the color, they will frighten people everywhere."

www.whitehouse.gov; www.gopbi.com

have only a rank meaning, the appropriate measure of central tendency is the median. The *median* is the midpoint of a distribution. A percentile or quartile reveals the dispersion.

Researchers differ about whether more powerful tests are appropriate for analyzing ordinal measures. Because nonparametric tests are abundant, simple to calculate, have good statistical power,[7] and do not require that the researcher accept the assumptions of parametric testing, we advise their use with nominal and ordinal data. It is understandable, however, that because parametric tests (such as the *t*-test or analysis of variance) are versatile, accepted, and understood, they will continue to be used with ordinal data when those data approach the characteristics required for interval measurement.

Interval Scales

Interval scales have the power of nominal and ordinal data plus one additional strength: They incorporate the concept of equality of interval (the scaled distance between 1 and 2 equals the distance between 2 and 3). Calendar time is such a scale. For example, the elapsed time between 3 and 6 a.m. equals the time between 4 and 7 a.m. One cannot say, however, 6 a.m. is twice as late as 3 a.m., because "zero time" is an arbitrary zero point. Centigrade and Fahrenheit temperature scales are other examples of classical interval scales. Both have an arbitrarily determined zero point, not a unique origin.

Researchers treat many attitude scales as interval, as we illustrate in the next chapter. When a scale is interval and the data are relatively symmetric with one mode, you use the arithmetic mean as the measure of central tendency. You can compute the average time of a TV promotional message or the average attitude value for different age groups in a market test. The standard deviation is the measure of dispersion.

interval scale scale with the properties of order and equal distance between points and with mutually exclusive and exhaustive categories.

> **The product-moment correlation, *t*-tests, *F*-tests, and other parametric tests are the statistical procedures of choice for interval data.[8]**

When the distribution of scores computed from interval data lean in one direction or the other (skewed right or left), we use the median as the measure of central tendency and the interquartile range as the measure of dispersion. The reasons for this are discussed in Chapter 18.

Ratio Scales

ratio scale a scale with the properties of categorization, order, equal intervals, and unique origin.

Ratio scales incorporate all of the powers of the previous scales plus the provision for absolute zero or origin. Ratio data represent the actual amounts of a variable. Measures of physical dimensions such as weight, height, distance, and area are examples. In the behavioral sciences, few situations satisfy the requirements of the ratio scale—the area of psychophysics offering some exceptions. In marketing research, we find ratio scales in many areas. There are money values, population counts, distances, return rates, productivity rates, and amounts of time (e.g., elapsed time in seconds before a customer service representative answers a phone inquiry).

Swatch's *BeatTime*—a proposed standard global time introduced at the 2000 Olympics that may gain favor as more of us participate in cross-time-zone chats (Internet or otherwise)—is a ratio scale. It offers a standard time with its origin at 0 beats (12 midnight in Biel, Switzerland, at the new Biel Meridian timeline). A day is composed of 1,000 beats, with a "beat" worth 1 minute, 26.4 seconds.[9]

With the Glacier project, Jason could measure a customer's age, the number of years he or she has attended, and the number of times a selection has been performed in the Glacier summer festival. These measures all generate ratio data. For practical purposes, however, the analyst would use the same statistical techniques as with interval data.

All statistical techniques mentioned up to this point are usable with ratio scales. Other manipulations carried out with real numbers may be done with ratio-scale values. Thus, multiplication and division can be used with this scale but not with the others mentioned. Geometric and harmonic means are measures of central tendency, and coefficients of variation may also be calculated for describing variability.

Researchers often encounter the problem of evaluating variables that have been measured on different scales. For example, the choice to purchase a product by a consumer is a nominal variable, and cost is a ratio variable. Certain statistical techniques require that the measurement levels be the same. Since the nominal variable does not have the characteristics of order, distance, or point of origin, we cannot create them artificially after the fact. The ratio-based salary variable, on the other hand, can be reduced. Rescaling product cost into categories (e.g., high, medium, low) simplifies the comparison. This example may be extended to other measurement situations—that is, converting or rescaling a variable involves reducing the measure from the more powerful and robust level to a lesser one.[10] The loss of measurement power with this decision means that lesser-powered statistics are then used in data analysis, but fewer assumptions for their proper use are required.

In summary, higher levels of measurement generally yield more information. Because of the measurement precision at higher levels, more powerful and sensitive statistical procedures can be used. As we saw with the candy bar example, when moving from a higher measurement level to a lower one, there is always a loss of information. Finally, when we collect information at higher levels, we can always convert, rescale, or reduce the data to arrive at a lower level.

> Sources of Measurement Differences

The ideal study should be designed and controlled for precise and unambiguous measurement of the variables. Since complete control is unattainable, error does occur. Much error is systematic (results from a bias), while the remainder is random (occurs erratically). One authority has pointed out several sources from which measured differences can come.[11]

Assume you are conducting an ex post facto study of corporate citizenship of a multi-national manufacturer. The company produces family, personal, and household care products. The participants are residents of a major city. The study concerns the Prince Corporation, a large manufacturer with its headquarters and several major facilities located in the city. The objective of the study is to discover the public's opinions about the company's approach to health, social welfare, and the environment. You also want to know the origin of any generally held adverse opinions.

> **The Prince Corporation image study starts here and is used throughout this chapter.**

Ideally, any variation of scores among the respondents would reflect true differences in their opinions about the company. Attitudes toward the firm as an employer, as an ecologically sensitive organization, or as a progressive corporate citizen would be accurately expressed. However, four major error sources may contaminate the results: (1) the respondent, (2) the situation, (3) the measurer, and (4) the data collection instrument.

Error Sources

The Respondent

Opinion differences that affect measurement come from relatively stable characteristics of the respondent. Typical of these are employee status, ethnic group membership, social class, and nearness to manufacturing facilities. The skilled researcher will anticipate many of these dimensions, adjusting the design to eliminate, neutralize, or otherwise deal with them. However, even the skilled researcher may not be as aware of less obvious dimensions. The latter variety might be a traumatic experience a given participant had with the Prince Corporation, its marketing programs, or its employees. Respondents may be reluctant to express strong negative (or positive) feelings, may purposefully express attitudes that they perceive as different from those of others, or may have little knowledge about Prince but be reluctant to admit ignorance. This reluctance to admit ignorance of a topic can lead to an interview consisting of "guesses" or assumptions, which, in turn, create erroneous data.

Respondents may also suffer from temporary factors like fatigue, boredom, anxiety, hunger, impatience, or general variations in mood or other distractions; these limit the ability to respond accurately and fully. Designing measurement scales that engage the participant for the duration of the measurement is crucial.

Situational Factors

Any condition that places a strain on the interview or measurement session can have serious effects on the interviewer-respondent rapport. If another person is present, that person can distort responses by joining in, by distracting, or by merely being there. If the respondents believe anonymity is not ensured, they may be reluctant to express certain feelings. Curbside or intercept interviews are unlikely to elicit elaborate responses, while in-home interviews more often do.

The Measurer

The interviewer can distort responses by rewording, paraphrasing, or reordering questions. Stereotypes in appearance and action introduce bias. Inflections of voice and conscious or unconscious prompting with smiles, nods, and so forth, may encourage or discourage certain replies. Careless mechanical processing—checking of the wrong response or failure to record full replies—will obviously distort findings. In the data analysis stage, incorrect coding, careless tabulation, and faulty statistical calculation may introduce further errors.

The Instrument

A defective instrument can cause distortion in two major ways. First, it can be too confusing and ambiguous. The use of complex words and syntax beyond participant comprehension is typical. Leading questions, ambiguous meanings, mechanical defects (inadequate space for

>snapshot

Measuring Attitudes about Copyright Infringement

In the midst of the Napster file-swapping controversy, and in connection with an issue centering on privacy issues, the editors of *American Demographics* hired TNS Intersearch to conduct a study of adults regarding their behavior and attitudes relating to copyright infringement. The survey instrument for the telephone study asked 1,051 adult respondents several questions about activities that might or might not be considered copyright infringement. The lead question asked about specific copyright-related activities:

Do you know someone who has done or tried to do any of the following?

1. Copying software not licensed for personal use.
2. Copying a prerecorded videocassette such as a rental or purchased video.
3. Copying a prerecorded audiocassette or compact disc.
4. Downloading music free of charge from the Internet.
5. Photcopying pages from a book or magazine.

A subsequent question asked respondents, "In the future, do you think that the amount of (ACTIVITY) will increase, decrease, or stay the same?" where "(ACTIVITY)" relates to one of the five numbered elements. Also, each respondent was asked to select a phrase from a list of four phrases "that best describes how you feel about (ACTIVITY)," and to select a phrase from a list of four phrases that "best describes what you think may happen as a result of (ACTIVITY)." The last content question asked the degree to which respondents would feel favorably toward a company that provided "some type of media content for free": more favorable, less favorable, or "it wouldn't impact your impression of the company." As you might expect, younger adults had different behaviors and attitudes compared to older adults on some indicants. What measurement issues were involved in this study?

www.americandemographics.com;
www.intersearch.tnsofres.com

replies, response-choice omissions, and poor printing), and multiple questions suggest the range of problems. Many of these problems are the direct result of operational definitions that are insufficient, resulting in an inappropriate scale being chosen or developed.

A more elusive type of instrument deficiency is poor selection from the universe of content items. Seldom does the instrument explore all the potentially important issues. The Prince Corporation study might treat company image in areas of employment and ecology but omit the company management's civic leadership, its support of local education programs, its philanthropy, or its position on minority issues. Even if the general issues are studied, the questions may not cover enough aspects of each area of concern. While we might study the Prince Corporation's image as an employer in terms of salary and wage scales, promotion opportunities, and work stability, perhaps such topics as working conditions, company management relations with organized labor, and retirement and other benefit programs should also be included.

> The Characteristics of Good Measurement

What are the characteristics of a good measurement tool? An intuitive answer to this question is that the tool should be an accurate counter or indicator of what we are interested in measuring. In addition, it should be easy and efficient to use. There are three major criteria for evaluating a measurement tool: validity, reliability, and practicality.

- *Validity* is the extent to which a test measures what we actually wish to measure.
- *Reliability* has to do with the accuracy and precision of a measurement procedure.
- *Practicality* is concerned with a wide range of factors of economy, convenience, and interpretability.[12]

In the following sections, we discuss the nature of these qualities and how researchers can achieve them in their measurement procedures.

Validity

Many forms of validity are mentioned in the research literature, and the number grows as we expand the concern for more scientific measurement. This text features two major forms: external and internal validity.[13] The *external validity* of research findings is the data's ability to be generalized across persons, settings, and times; we discussed this in reference to experimentation in Chapter 12, and more will be said in Chapter 16 on sampling.[14] In this chapter, we discuss only internal validity. **Internal validity** is further limited in this discussion to the ability of a research instrument to measure what it is purported to measure. Does the instrument really measure what its designer claims it does?

One widely accepted classification of validity consists of three major forms: (1) content validity, (2) criterion-related validity, and (3) construct validity (see Exhibit 13-5).[15]

internal validity ability of a research instrument to measure what it is purposed to measure.

Content Validity

The **content validity** of a measuring instrument is the extent to which it provides adequate coverage of the investigative questions guiding the study. If the instrument contains a representative sample of the universe of subject matter of interest, then content validity is good. To evaluate the content validity of an instrument, one must first agree on what elements constitute adequate coverage. In the Prince Corporation study, we must decide what knowledge and attitudes are relevant to the measurement of corporate public image and then decide which forms of these opinions are relevant positions on these topics. In the Glacier study, Jason must first determine what factors are influencing customer satisfaction before determining if published indexes can be of value. If the data collection instrument adequately covers the topics that have been defined as the relevant dimensions, we conclude the instrument has good content validity.

A determination of content validity involves judgment. First, the designer may determine it through a careful definition of the topic, the items to be scaled, and the scales to be used. This logical process is often intuitive and unique to each research designer.

content validity the extent to which measurement scales provide adequate coverage of the investigative questions.

> **The management-research question hierarchy discussed in Chapter 5 helps to reduce research questions into specific investigative and measurement questions that have content validity.**

>**Exhibit 13-5** Summary of Validity Estimates

Type	What Is Measured	Methods
Content	Degree to which the content of the items adequately represents the universe of all relevant items under study.	• Judgmental • Panel evaluation with content validity ratio
Criterion-related	Degree to which the predictor is adequate in capturing the relevant aspects of the criterion.	• Correlation
Concurrent	Description of the present; criterion data are available at the same time as predictor scores	• Correlation
Predictive	Prediction of the future; criterion data are measured after the passage of time.	• Correlation
Construct	Answers the question, "What accounts for the variance in the measure?"; attempts to identify the underlying construct(s) being measured and determine how well the test represents it (them).	• Judgmental • Correlation of proposed test with established one • Convergent-discriminant techniques • Factor analysis • Multitrait-multimethod analysis

A second way is to use a panel of persons to judge how well the instrument meets the standards. The panel independently assesses the test items for an instrument as essential, useful but not essential, or not necessary. "Essential" responses on each item from each panelist are evaluated by a content validity ratio, and those meeting a statistical significance value are retained. In both informal judgments and this systematic process, "content validity is primarily concerned with inferences about test construction rather than inferences about test scores."[16]

It is important not to define content too narrowly. If you were to secure only superficial expressions of opinion in the Prince Corporation attitude survey, it would probably not have adequate content coverage. The research should delve into the processes by which these attitudes came about. How did the respondents come to feel as they do, and what is the intensity of feeling? The same would be true of MindWriter's evaluation of service quality and satisfaction. It is not enough to know a customer is dissatisfied. The manager charged with enhancing or correcting the program needs to know what processes, employees, parts, and time sequences within the CompleteCare program have led to that dissatisfaction.

Criterion-Related Validity

criterion-related validity
the success of a measurement scale for prediction or estimation.

Criterion-related validity reflects the success of measures used for prediction or estimation. You may want to predict an outcome or estimate the existence of a current behavior or condition. These are *predictive* and *concurrent* validity, respectively. They differ only in a time perspective. An attitude scale that correctly forecasts the outcome of a purchase decision has predictive validity. An observational method that correctly categorizes families by current income class has concurrent validity. While these examples appear to have simple and unambiguous validity criteria, there are difficulties in estimating validity. Consider the problem of estimating family income. There is a knowable true income for every family, but we may find the figure difficult to secure. Thus, while the criterion is conceptually clear, it may be unavailable.

A researcher may want to develop a preemployment test that will predict sales success. There may be several possible criteria, none of which individually tells the full story. Total sales per salesperson may not adequately reflect territory market potential, competitive conditions, or the different profitability rates of various products. One might rely on the sales manager's overall evaluation, but how unbiased and accurate are such impressions? The researcher must ensure that the validity criterion used is itself "valid." Any criterion measure must be judged in terms of four qualities: (1) relevance, (2) freedom from bias, (3) reliability, and (4) availability.[17]

A criterion is *relevant* if it is defined and scored in the terms we judge to be the proper measures of salesperson success. If you believe sales success is adequately measured by dollar sales volume achieved per year, then it is the relevant criterion. If you believe success should include a high level of penetration of large accounts, then sales volume alone is not fully relevant. In making this decision, you must rely on your judgment in deciding what partial criteria are appropriate indicants of salesperson success.

Freedom from bias is attained when the criterion gives each salesperson an equal opportunity to score well. The sales criterion would be biased if it did not show adjustments for differences in territory potential and competitive conditions.

A *reliable* criterion is stable or reproducible. An erratic criterion (using monthly sales, which are highly variable from month to month) can hardly be considered a reliable standard by which to judge performance on a sales employment test. Finally, the information specified by the criterion must be *available*. If it is not available, how much will it cost and how difficult will it be to secure? The amount of money and effort that should be spent on development of a criterion depends on the importance of the problem for which the test is used.

> **Chapter 20 describes statistical techniques used to find correlation between variables.**

Once there are test and criterion scores, they must be compared in some way. The usual approach is to correlate them. For example, you might correlate test scores of 40 new salespeople with first-year sales achievements adjusted to reflect differences in territorial selling conditions.

>snapshot

Can Eureka!Ranch's Merwyn Predict Success?

Most new products fail. That's a fact that many marketers only grudgingly accept as inevitable. The Eureka!Ranch (E!R) founder, Doug Hall, wasn't willing to accept those odds. Using an extensive database of new product metrics gathered from 5,000 new product introductions—both failures and successes—E!R developed *Merwyn,* a simulation that replaces the more traditional concept testing, a methodology that relies on potential customers' projection of purchase intention. "Research on focus groups used for concept testing shows that participants can totally change their perceptions of a product concept—from dislike to preference—within the 2 hour time frame," shared Justin Beck, Merwyn's technology manager. Beck hypothesizes that if customers could deliberate in a store aisle for the same duration, they might have a similar transformation. Yet the average customer deliberates just a few seconds over every such decision.

Early success records are impressive. The Merwyn process starts with a company developing a written description of a new product. The company then completes a short inventory of questions that adds depth to the product concept. This information is digested by Merwyn, and the result is provided to a panel of three specially trained "experts." The experts are consumers,

trained by E!R to evaluate certain key factors in analyzing the idea, a process that takes these trained analysts as little as 15 minutes. The results of the expert analysis are fed again to Merwyn, and a probability of success is one of the metrics revealed. The typical product concept evaluated by your typical man-on-the-street would average a 27; the E!R average is 37. If the product concept earns above a 50 on a 100 scale, the idea has a high probability of success. Bill Wise of Wise Consumer Products is one such success story. His initial concept for a household cleaner of garbage disposals earned only a 29 on the tough Merwyn barometer. But after modifying several factors to make the product's overt promise more believable and capable of demonstrating a dramatic difference over its competition, the product concept's Merwyn score jumped into the 60s. Wise developed the product and recently earned the right to market his "SpringAgain" from what some think is the harshest product critic in the world, Wal-Mart stores. SpringAgain has shelf exposure throughout Wal-Mart this fall.

www.eurekaranch.com

Construct Validity

In attempting to evaluate **construct validity,** we consider both the theory and the measuring instrument being used. If we were interested in measuring the effect of trust in relationship marketing, the way in which "trust" was operationally defined would have to correspond to an empirically grounded theory. If a known measure of trust in relationship marketing was available, we might correlate the results obtained using this measure with those derived from our new instrument. Such an approach would provide us with preliminary indications of *convergent* validity (the degree to which scores on one scale correlate with scores on other scales designed to assess the same construct). If Jason were to develop a customer satisfaction index for Glacier and, when compared, the results revealed the same indications as a predeveloped, established index, Jason's instrument would have convergent validity. Similarly, if Jason and Sara developed an instrument to measure satisfaction with the CompleteCare program and the derived measure could be confirmed with a standardized customer satisfaction measure, convergent validity would exist.

Returning to our example above, another method of validating the trust construct would be to separate it from other constructs in the theory or related theories. To the extent that trust could be separated from bonding, reciprocity, and empathy, we would have completed the first steps toward *discriminant* validity (the degree to which scores on a scale *do not* correlate with scores from scales designed to measure different constructs).

We discuss the three forms of validity separately, but they are interrelated, both theoretically and operationally. Predictive validity is important for a test designed to predict product success. In developing such a test, you would probably first list the factors (constructs) that provide the basis for useful prediction. For example, you would advance a theory about the variables in product success—an area for construct validity. Finally, in developing the

construct validity a measurement scale that demonstrates both convergent validity and discriminant validity.

> **An example of factor analysis is described in Chapter 22.**

>**Exhibit 13-6** Understanding Validity and Reliability

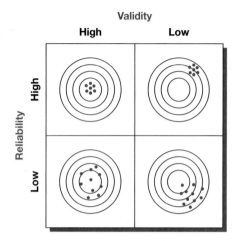

Let's use an archer's bow and target as an analogy.

High reliability means that repeated arrows shot from the same bow would hit the target in essentially the same place—although not necessarily the intended place (first row of the graphic). If we had a bow with high validity as well, then every arrow would hit the bull's-eye (upper left panel). If reliability is low or decreases for some reason, arrows would be more scattered (lacking similarity or closeness, like those shown in the second row).

High validity means that the bow would shoot true every time. It would not pull to the right or send an arrow careening into the woods. Arrows shot from a high-validity bow will be clustered around a central point (the bull's eye), even when they are dispersed by reduced reliability (lower left graphic). Low-validity shots are distorted, rather like a flawed bow pulling our arrows to the right (second column of the graphic). We wouldn't hit the bull's-eye we were aiming at because the low-validity bow—like the flawed data collection instrument—would not perform as planned. When low validity is compounded by low reliability, the pattern of arrows is not only off the bull's-eye but also dispersed (lower right graphic).

specific items for inclusion in the success prediction test, you would be concerned with how well the specific items sample the full range of each construct (a matter of content validity). Looking at Exhibit 13-6, we can better understand the concepts of validity and reliability by using an archer's bow and target as an analogy.

Reliability

reliability a characteristic of measurement concerned with accuracy, precision, and consistency.

A measure is reliable to the degree that it supplies consistent results. **Reliability** is a necessary contributor to validity but is not a sufficient condition for validity. The relationship between reliability and validity can be simply illustrated with the use of a bathroom scale. If the scale measures your weight correctly (using a concurrent criterion such as a scale known to be accurate), then it is both reliable and valid. If it consistently overweighs you by 6 pounds, then the scale is reliable but not valid. If the scale measures erratically from time to time, then it is not reliable and therefore cannot be valid. So if a measurement is not valid, it hardly matters if it is reliable—because it does not measure what the designer needs to measure in order to solve the research problem. In this context, reliability is not as valuable as validity, but it is much easier to assess.

Reliability is concerned with estimates of the degree to which a measurement is free of random or unstable error. Reliable instruments can be used with confidence that transient and situational factors are not interfering. Reliable instruments are robust; they work well at different times under different conditions. This distinction of time and condition is the basis for frequently used perspectives on reliability—stability, equivalence, and internal consistency (see Exhibit 13-7).

Stability

stability a characteristic of a measurement scale if it provides consistent results with repeated measures.

A measure is said to possess **stability** if you can secure consistent results with repeated measurements of the same person with the same instrument. An observation procedure is stable if it gives the same reading on a particular person when repeated one or more times. It is often possible to repeat observations on a subject and to compare them for consistency. When there is much time between measurements, there is a chance for situational factors to change, thereby affecting the observations. The change would appear incorrectly as a drop in the reliability of the measurement process.

Stability measurement in survey situations is more difficult and less easily executed than in observational studies. While you can observe a certain action repeatedly, you usually can

>**snap**shot

Surfing for the Perfect Measurement

When Web banner ads, and the newer superstitial ads or interactive marketing units (IMUs)—larger ads with voice and motion in pop-up windows, similar to TV commercials—were first aired, they were heralded as the first truly measurable advertising medium. With a measurement called the *click-through rate,* advertisers could track the number of potential customers who saw an ad, clicked on the ad, arrived at the advertiser's Web site, and then bought a product online. But while Web advertising has grown faster than any other medium, to an estimated $5.4 billion, advertisers are no longer sure whether the click-through rate measures anything meaningful. "Click-through rates are a misleading statistic—they aren't indicative of raised awareness or of consumer interest," says Scot McLernon, who is executive vice president for ad sales at MarketWatch.com. While advertisers can compute cost measures (cost per click or cost per conversion to purchase from ad click), Web advertising has substantiated rather than disproved a well-known adage: Response to advertising is often delayed and certainly not direct. Some firms,

like MarketWatch.com, aren't counting click-through rates at all, hoping to persuade "the advertising industry to view online ads as tools for branding rather than direct marketing." Others, like Interactive Advertising Bureau (IAB), demonstrate that advertisers are resorting to tried-and-true, but far less exacting, ad effectiveness measures: conducting online surveys among those who recall having seen ads and measuring brand awareness, product association with message, purchase intent, and brand favorability. In its latest study by "Dynamic Logic, [IAB] found that the new larger ad units (IMUs) are 25 percent more effective in lifting key brand metrics such as brand awareness and message association—even at one exposure." What type of data and what measurement scales have firms involved with Web advertising been using to measure effectiveness? What should advertisers use?

www.cbs.marketwatch.com; www.dynamiclogic.com; www.iab.net

>**Exhibit 13-7** Summary of Reliability Estimates

Type	Coefficient	What Is Measured	Methods
Test-retest	Stability	Reliability of a test or instrument inferred from examinee scores; same test is administered twice to same subjects over an interval of less than six months.	Correlation
Parallel forms	Equivalence	Degree to which alternative forms of the same measure produce same or similar results; administered simultaneously or with a delay. Interrater estimates of the similarity of judges' observations or scores.	Correlation
Split-half, KR20, Cronbach's alpha	Internal consistency	Degree to which instrument items are homogeneous and reflect the same underlying construct(s).	Specialized correlational formulas

resurvey only once. This leads to a test-retest arrangement—with comparisons between the two tests to learn how reliable they are. Some of the difficulties that can occur in the test-retest methodology and cause a downward bias in stability include:

- *Time delay between measurements*—leads to situational factor changes (also a problem in observation studies).
- *Insufficient time between measurements*—permits the respondent to remember previous answers and repeat them, resulting in biased reliability indicators.

- *Respondent's discernment of a study's disguised purpose*—may introduce bias if the respondent holds opinions related to the purpose but not assessed with current measurement questions.
- *Topic sensitivity*—occurs when the respondent seeks to learn more about the topic or form new and different opinions before the retest.

A suggested remedy is to extend the interval between test and retest (from two weeks to a month). While this may help, the researcher must be alert to the chance that an outside factor will contaminate the measurement and distort the stability score. Consequently, stability measurement through the test-retest approach has limited applications. More interest has centered on equivalence.

Equivalence

A second perspective on reliability considers how much error may be introduced by different investigators (in observation) or different samples of items being studied (in questioning or scales). Thus, while stability is concerned with personal and situational fluctuations from one time to another, **equivalence** is concerned with variations at one point in time among observers and samples of items. A good way to test for the equivalence of measurements by different observers is to compare their scoring of the same event. An example of this is the scoring of Olympic figure skaters by a panel of judges.

In studies where a consensus among experts or observers is required, the similarity of the judges' perceptions is sometimes questioned. How does a panel of supervisors render a judgment on merit raises, a new product's packaging, or future business trends? *Interrater reliability* may be used in these cases to correlate the observations or scores of the judges and render an index of how consistent their ratings are. In Olympic figure skating, a judge's relative positioning of skaters (determined by establishing a rank order for each judge and comparing each judge's ordering for all skaters) is a means of measuring equivalence.

The major interest with equivalence is typically not how respondents differ from item to item but how well a given set of items will categorize individuals. There may be many differences in response between two samples of items, but if a person is classified the same way by each test, then the tests have good equivalence.

One tests for item sample equivalence by using alternative or *parallel forms* of the same test administered to the same persons simultaneously. The results of the two tests are then correlated. Under this condition, the length of the testing process is likely to affect the subjects' responses through fatigue, and the inferred reliability of the parallel form will be reduced accordingly. Some measurement theorists recommend an interval between the two tests to compensate for this problem. This approach, called *delayed equivalent forms,* is a composite of test-retest and the equivalence method. As in test-retest, one would administer form X followed by form Y to half the examinees and form Y followed by form X to the other half to prevent "order-of-presentation" effects.[18]

The researcher can include only a limited number of measurement questions in an instrument. This limitation implies that a sample of measurement questions from a content domain has been chosen and another sample producing a similar number will need to be drawn for the second instrument. It is frequently difficult to create this second set. Yet if the pool is initially large enough, the items may be randomly selected for each instrument. Even with more sophisticated procedures used by publishers of standardized tests, it is rare to find fully equivalent and interchangeable questions.[19]

Internal Consistency

A third approach to reliability uses only one administration of an instrument or test to assess the **internal consistency** or homogeneity among the items. The *split-half* technique can be used when the measuring tool has many similar questions or statements to which the participant can respond. The instrument is administered and the results are separated by

equivalence when an instrument secures consistent results with repeated measures by the same investigator or different samples.

internal consistency a characteristic of an instrument in which the items are homogeneous.

item into even and odd numbers or into randomly selected halves. When the two halves are correlated, if the results of the correlation are high, the instrument is said to have high reliability in an internal consistency sense. The high correlation tells us there is similarity (or homogeneity) among the items. The potential for incorrect inferences about high internal consistency exists when the test contains many items—which inflates the correlation index.

The Spearman-Brown correction formula is used to adjust for the effect of test length and to estimate reliability of the whole test. [20]

Practicality

The scientific requirements of a project call for the measurement process to be reliable and valid, while the operational requirements call for it to be practical. **Practicality** has been defined as *economy, convenience, and interpretability*.[21] While this definition refers to the development of educational and psychological tests, it is meaningful for marketing measurements as well.

practicality a characteristic of sound measurement concerned with factors of economy, convenience, and interpretability.

Economy

Some trade-off usually occurs between the ideal research project and the budget. Data are not free, and instrument length is one area where economic pressures dominate. More items give more reliability, but in the interest of limiting the interview or observation time (and therefore costs), we hold down the number of measurement questions. The choice of data collection method is also often dictated by economic factors. The rising cost of personal interviewing first led to an increased use of telephone surveys and subsequently to the current rise in Internet surveys. In standardized tests, the cost of test materials alone can be such a significant expense that it encourages multiple reuse. Add to this the need for fast and economical scoring, and we see why computer scoring and scanning are attractive.

Convenience

A measuring device passes the convenience test if it is easy to administer. A questionnaire or a measurement scale with a set of detailed but clear instructions, with examples, is easier to complete correctly than one that lacks these features. In a well-prepared study, it is not uncommon for the interviewer instructions to be several times longer than the interview questions. Naturally, the more complex the concepts and constructs, the greater is the need for clear and complete instructions. We can also make the instrument easier to administer by giving close attention to its design and layout. While reliability and validity dominate our choices in design of scales here and later in Chapter 15, administrative difficulty should play some role. A long completion time, complex instructions, participant's perceived difficulty with the survey, and their rated enjoyment of the process also influence design. Layout issues include crowding of material, poor reproductions of illustrations, and the carryover of items from one page to the next or the need to scroll the screen when taking a web survey. Both design and layout issues make completion of the instrument more difficult.

Interpretability

This aspect of practicality is relevant when persons other than the test designers must interpret the results. It is usually, but not exclusively, an issue with standardized tests. In such cases, the designer of the data collection instrument provides several key pieces of information to make interpretation possible:

- A statement of the functions the test was designed to measure and the procedures by which it was developed.
- Detailed instructions for administration.

- Scoring keys and instructions.
- Norms for appropriate reference groups.
- Evidence about reliability.
- Evidence regarding the intercorrelations of subscores.
- Evidence regarding the relationship of the test to other measures.
- Guides for test use.

>summary

1 While people measure things casually in daily life, research measurement is more precise and controlled. In measurement, one settles for measuring properties of the objects rather than the objects themselves. An event is measured in terms of its duration. What happened during it, who was involved, where it occurred, and so forth, are all properties of the event. To be more precise, what are measured are indicants of the properties. Thus, for duration, one measures the number of hours and minutes recorded. For what happened, one uses some system to classify types of activities that occurred. Measurement typically uses some sort of scale to classify or quantify the data collected.

2 There are four scale types. In increasing order of power, they are nominal, ordinal, interval, and ratio. Nominal scales classify without indicating order, distance, or unique origin. Ordinal data show magnitude relationships of more than and less than but have no distance or unique origin. Interval scales have both order and distance but no unique origin. Ratio scales possess classification, order, distance, and unique origin.

3 Instruments may yield incorrect readings of an indicant for many reasons. These may be classified according to error

sources: (a) the respondent or participant, (b) situational factors, (c) the measurer, and (d) the instrument.

4 Sound measurement must meet the tests of validity, reliability, and practicality. Validity reveals the degree to which an instrument measures what it is supposed to measure to assist the researcher in solving the research problem. Three forms of validity are used to evaluate measurement scales. Content validity exists to the degree that a measure provides an adequate reflection of the topic under study. Its determination is primarily judgmental and intuitive. Criterion-related validity relates to our ability to predict some outcome or estimate the existence of some current condition. Construct validity is the most complex and abstract. A measure has construct validity to the degree that it conforms to predicted correlations of other theoretical propositions.

A measure is reliable if it provides consistent results. Reliability is a partial contributor to validity, but a measurement tool may be reliable without being valid. Three forms of reliability are stability, equivalence, and internal consistency. A measure has practical value for the research if it is economical, convenient, and interpretable.

>keyterms

>**discussion**questions

Terms in Review

1 What can we measure about the four objects listed below? Be as specific as possible.

  a Laundry detergent.

  b Market share.

  c Promotion.

  d Service quality.

2 What are the essential differences among nominal, ordinal, interval, and ratio scales? How do these differences affect the statistical analysis techniques we can use?

3 What are the four major sources of measurement error? Illustrate by example how each of these might affect measurement results in a face-to-face interview situation.

4 Do you agree or disagree with the following statements? Explain.

  a Validity is more critical to measurement than reliability.

  b Content validity is the most difficult type of validity to determine.

  c A valid measurement is reliable, but a reliable measurement may not be valid.

  d Stability and equivalence are essentially the same thing.

Making Research Decisions

5 You have data from a corporation on the annual revenue of each of its services.

  a Illustrate how the data can be presented as ratio, interval, ordinal, and nominal data.

  b Describe the successive loss of information as the presentation changes from ratio to nominal.

6 Below are listed some objects of varying degrees of abstraction. Suggest properties of each of these objects that can be measured by each of the four basic types of scales.

  a Store customers.

  b Consumer attitudes.

  c Contests or sweepstakes.

  d Free samples.

  e Product cycle.

7 You have been asked by the head of marketing to design an instrument by which your private, for-profit school can evaluate the quality and value of its various curricula and courses. How might you try to ensure that your instrument has:

  a Stability?

  b Equivalence?

  c Internal consistency?

  d Content validity?

  e Predictive validity?

  f Construct validity?

8 A new hire at Mobil Oil, you are asked to assume the management of the *Mobil Restaurant Guide.* Each restaurant striving to be included in the guide needs to be evaluated. Only a select few restaurants may earn the five-star status. What dimensions would you choose to measure to apply the one to five stars in the *Mobil Restaurant Guide?*

9 You have been asked to develop an index of trade promotion.

  a What constructs or concepts might you employ?

  b Choose several of the major concepts, and specify their dimensions.

  c Select observable indicators that you might use to measure these dimensions.

  d How would you compile these various dimensions into a single index?

  e How would you judge the reliability and/or validity of these measurements?

Behind the Scenes

10 Given that Glacier Symphony has previously measured its customer satisfaction by survey, how might Jason assess the internal validity of the Glacier questionnaire?

From Concept to Practice

11 Using Exhibit 13-3 and one of the case questionnaires on your text DVD, match each question to its appropriate scale type. For each scale type not represented, develop a measurement question that would be of that scale type.

>**www**exercise

Visit sites like those of The Gallup Organization, Harris Interactive, and Kaiser Family Foundation. Select a study and identify the measurement scale types and the measurement decisions made in the study.

>cases*

Campbell-Ewald: R-E-S-P-E-C-T Spells Loyalty

Data Development

Donatos: Finding the New Pizza

Endries Fasteners

NCRCC: Teeing Up and New Strategic Direction

NetConversions Influences Kelley Blue Book

Pebble Beach Co.

Ramada Demonstrates Its *Personal Best*™

USTA: Come Out Swinging

Yahoo!: *Consumer Direct* Marries Purchase Metrics to Banner Ads

* All cases, both written and video, are on the text DVD. The film icon indicates a video case. Check the DVD Index to determine whether a case has data, the research instrument, or other supplementary material.

chapter 14

Measurement Scales

>learningobjectives

After reading this chapter, you should understand . . .

1 The nature of attitudes and their relationship to behavior.

2 The critical decisions involved in selecting an appropriate measurement scale.

3 The characteristics and use of rating, ranking, sorting, and other preference scales.

Visionary Insights' VP, Chance Bedford, recently captured a new client interested in a major study dealing with teens' online shopping attitudes and behavior. Jason Henry and Sara Armstrong are the project coordinators. Chance is interested in their progress on this valuable piece of new business.

"How's the survey coming?" asks Chance as he finds Jason and Sara taking a break in Jason's office.

"The mind of a 17-year-old is fascinating," grins Jason.

"Did you know the 24-year-old is just entering the peak of his or her coolness quotient?" contributes Sara.

"Glad to see this new project has you in such good spirits," Chance says dryly.

"Oh, we're making progress," shares Jason. "The focus groups provided great insight into these young adults and what they think is cool. Of course, it wasn't so very long ago that I was one of them, so I could have accurately guessed what they would say. Sara and I are just reviewing various scales we might use to tap into their attitudes about online shopping."

Sara rolls her eyes upward and comments to Chance, "He has jeans older than some of the participants.

"But, seriously," she continues, "our literature search revealed a comprehensive AOL phone study done by Roper Starch on teens' online behavior and their influence on family choices to go online. The researcher used a scale to determine how frequently teens use the Internet for a variety of online behaviors— 'very often, pretty often, only once in a while, and never.' We are debating scales for our study when we ask teens about their attitudes and behavior related to shopping."

"They also asked participants for responses to several hypothetical situations to extract nominal data related to their interest in online behavior," comments Jason. "I especially liked: 'If you and your family had to be stranded alone on an island for a long period of time, would you prefer to have a telephone, a television, or a computer connected to the Internet? Assume you could have only one.' Sara and I have drafted some hypothetical scenarios. The fact that AOL used similar questions confirms their likely success with the age group."

"We've also developed alternative measurement questions for some issues, including Likert and constant-sum scales. And we'll soon have a Q-sort to show you," shares Sara.

"Good. I really stopped by," explains Chance, "to drop off this journal article on scaling. The researcher has estimated the psychological distance between various scale points. Pretty interesting reading. You might want to see where that puts the 'very often, pretty often, only once in a while, never' scale in terms of its usefulness."

This chapter covers procedures that will help you understand measurement scales so that you might select or design measures that are appropriate for your research. We concentrate here on the problems of measuring more complex constructs, like attitudes. Conceptually, we start this process by revisiting the research process (see Exhibit 14-1) to understand where the act of scaling fits in the process.

Scales in marketing research are generally constructed to measure behavior, knowledge, and attitudes. Attitude scales are among the most difficult to construct, so we will use attitudes to develop your understanding of scaling.

>**Exhibit 14-1** The Scaling Process

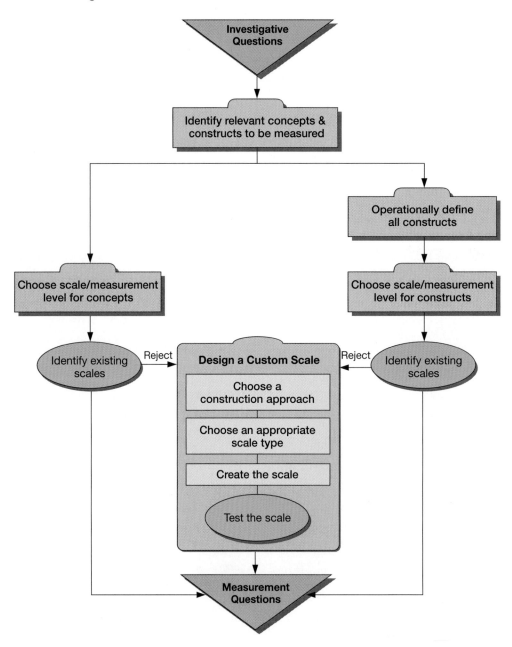

> **The Nature of Attitudes**

Sara and Jason are properly concerned about attitude measurement for their study of teenage online shopping. But what is an attitude? There are numerous definitions, but one seems to capture the essence: An **attitude** is a learned, stable predisposition to respond to oneself, other persons, objects, or issues in a consistently favorable or unfavorable way.[1] Important aspects of this definition include the learned nature of attitudes, their relative permanence, and their association with socially significant events and objects. Because an attitude is a *predisposition,* it would seem that the more favorable one's attitude is toward a product or service, the more likely that the product or service will be purchased. But, as we will see, that is not always the case.

attitude a learned, stable predisposition to respond to oneself, other persons, objects, or issues in a consistently favorable or unfavorable way.

Let's use Sara as an example to illustrate the nature of attitudes:

1. She is convinced that Visionary Insights has great talent, terrific clients, and superior opportunities for growth in the marketing research business.

2. She loves working at VI.

3. She expects to stay with the firm and work hard to achieve rapid promotions for greater visibility and influence.

The first statement is an example of a *cognitively* based attitude. It represents Sara's memories, evaluations, and beliefs about the properties of the object, Visionary Insights. A *belief* is an estimate (probability) about the truth of something. In this case, it is the likelihood that the characteristics she attributes to her work environment are true. The statement "I think the cellular market will expand rapidly to incorporate radio and video" is also derived from cognition and belief. The second statement above is an *affectively* based attitude. It represents Sara's feelings, intuition, values, and emotions toward the object. "I love the Yankees" or "I hate corn flakes" are other examples of emotionally oriented attitudes. Finally, researchers recognize a third component, *conative* or *behaviorally* based attitudes. The concluding statement reflects Sara's expectations and behavioral intentions toward her firm and the instrumental behaviors necessary to achieve her future goals.

The Relationship between Attitudes and Behavior

The attitude-behavior relationship is not straightforward, although there may be close linkages. Attitudes and behavioral intentions do not always lead to actual behaviors; and while attitudes and behaviors are expected to be consistent with each other, that is not always the case. Moreover, behaviors can influence attitudes. For example, marketers know that a positive experience with a product or service reinforces a positive attitude or makes a customer question a negative attitude. This is one reason that restaurants where you have a bad dining experience may give you a coupon for a free meal on your next visit. They know a bad experience contributes mightily to formation of negative attitudes.

Marketing researchers treat attitudes as *hypothetical constructs* because of their complexity and the fact that they are inferred from the measurement data, not actually observed. These qualifications cause researchers to be cautious about the ways certain aspects of measured attitudes predict behavior. Several factors have an effect on the applicability of attitudinal research for marketing:

- Specific attitudes are better predictors of behavior than general ones.

- Strong attitudes (strength is affected by *accessibility* or how well the object is remembered and brought to consciousness, how extreme the attitude is, or the degree of confidence in it) are better predictors of behavior than weak attitudes composed of little intensity or topical interest.

- Direct experiences with the attitude object (when the attitude is formed, during repeated exposure, or through reminders) produce behavior more reliably.
- Cognitive-based attitudes influence behaviors better than affective-based attitudes.
- Affective-based attitudes are often better predictors of consumption behaviors.
- Using multiple measurements of attitude or several behavioral assessments across time and environments improves prediction.
- The influence of reference groups (interpersonal support, urges of compliance, peer pressure) and the individual's inclination to conform to these influences improves the attitude-behavior linkage.[2]

Marketers measure and analyze the attitudes of customers because attitudes offer insights about behavior. Many of the attitude measurement scales that marketers use have been tested for reliability and validity, but often we craft unique scales that don't share those standards. An example is an instrument that measures attitudes about a particular tourist attraction, product, or candidate, as well as the person's intention to visit, buy, or vote. Neither the attitude nor the behavioral intent instrument, alone or together, is effective in predicting the person's actual behavior if it has not been designed carefully. Nevertheless, marketing managers know that the measurement of attitudes is an important aspect of marketing strategy and often the best tool available because attitudes reflect past experience and shape future behavior.

Attitude Scaling

scaling the assignment of numbers or symbols to a property of objects according to value or magnitude.

Attitude scaling is the process of assessing an attitudinal disposition using a number that represents a person's score on an attitudinal continuum ranging from an extremely favorable disposition to an extremely unfavorable one. **Scaling** is the "procedure for the assignment of numbers (or other symbols) to a property of objects in order to impart some of the characteristics of numbers to the properties in question."[3] Procedurally, we assign numbers to indicants of the properties of objects. Thus, one assigns a number scale to the various levels of heat and cold and calls it a thermometer. To measure the temperature of the air, you know that a property of temperature is that its variation leads to an expansion or contraction of mercury. A glass tube with mercury provides an indicant of temperature change by the rise or fall of the mercury in the tube. Similarly, your attitude toward your university could be measured on numerous scales that capture indicators of the different dimensions of your awareness, feelings, or behavioral intentions toward the school.

> Selecting a Measurement Scale

Selecting and constructing a measurement scale requires the consideration of several factors that influence the reliability, validity, and practicality of the scale:

- Research objectives
- Response types
- Data properties
- Number of dimensions
- Balanced or unbalanced
- Forced or unforced choices
- Number of scale points
- Rater errors

Research Objectives

Researchers' objectives are too numerous to list (including, but not limited to, studies of attitude, attitude change, persuasion, awareness, purchase intention, cognition and action, actual and repeat purchase). Researchers, however, face two general types of scaling objectives:

- To measure characteristics of the participants who participate in the study.
- To use participants as judges of the objects or indicants presented to them.

Assume you are conducting a study of customers concerning their attitudes toward a change in corporate identity (a company logo and peripherals). With the first study objective, your scale would measure the customers' orientation as favorable or unfavorable. You might combine each person's answers to form an indicator of overall orientation. The emphasis in this first study is on measuring attitudinal differences among people. With the second objective, you might use the same data, but you are now interested in how satisfied people are with different design options. Each participant is asked to choose the object he or she favors or the preferred solution. Participants judge which object has more of some characteristic or which design solution is closest to the company's stated objectives.

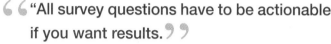

"All survey questions have to be actionable if you want results."

Frank Schmidt, Senior Scientist
The Gallup Organization

Response Types

Measurement scales fall into one of four general types: rating, ranking, categorization, and sorting. A **rating scale** is used when participants score an object or indicant without making a direct comparison to another object or attitude. For example, they may be asked to evaluate the styling of a new automobile on a 7-point rating scale. **Ranking scales** constrain the study participant to making comparisons and determining order among two or more properties (or their indicants) or objects. Participants may be asked to choose which one of a pair of cars has more attractive styling. A *choice* scale requires that participants choose one alternative over another. They could also be asked to rank-order the importance of comfort, ergonomics, performance, and price for the target vehicle. **Categorization** asks participants to put themselves or property indicants in groups or categories. Asking auto show attendees to identify their gender or ethnic background or to indicate whether a particular prototype design would appeal to a youthful or mature driver would require a category response strategy. **Sorting** requires that participants sort cards (representing concepts or constructs) into piles using criteria established by the researcher. The cards might contain photos or images or verbal statements of product features such as various descriptors of the car's performance.

rating scale a scale that scores an object or property without making a direct comparison to another object or property.

ranking scale a scale that scores an object or property by making a comparison and determining order among two or more objects or properties.

categorization participants put themselves or property indicants into groups or categories.

sorting participants sort cards (representing concepts or constructs) into piles using criteria established by the researcher.

Data Properties

Decisions about the choice of measurement scales are often made with regard to the data properties generated by each scale. In Chapter 13, we said that we classify scales in increasing order of power; scales are nominal, ordinal, interval, or ratio. Nominal scales classify data into categories without indicating order, distance, or unique origin. Ordinal data show relationships of *more than* and *less than* but have no distance or unique origin. Interval scales have both order and distance but no unique origin. Ratio scales possess all four properties' features. The assumptions underlying each level of scale determine how a particular measurement scale's data will be analyzed statistically.

Number of Dimensions

unidimensional scale
seeks to measure only one
attribute of the participant or
object.

multidimensional scale
seeks to simultaneously
measure more than one
attribute of the participant or
object.

Measurement scales are either *unidimensional* or *multidimensional*. With a **unidimensional scale,** one seeks to measure only one attribute of the participant or object. One measure of an actor's star power is his or her ability to "carry" a movie. It is a single dimension. Several items may be used to measure this dimension and by combining them into a single measure, an agent may place clients along a linear continuum of star power. A **multidimensional scale** recognizes that an object might be better described with several dimensions than on a unidimensional continuum. The actor's *star power* variable might be better expressed by three distinct dimensions—ticket sales for last three movies, speed of attracting financial resources, and column-inch/amount-of-TV coverage of the last three films.

Balanced or Unbalanced

balanced rating scale has
an equal number of categories
above and below the midpoint,
or an equal number of
favorable/unfavorable response
choices.

unbalanced rating scale
has an unequal number of
favorable and unfavorable
response choices.

A **balanced rating scale** has an equal number of categories above and below the midpoint. Generally, rating scales should be balanced, with an equal number of favorable and unfavorable response choices. However, scales may be balanced with or without an indifference or midpoint option. A balanced scale might take the form of "very good—good—average—poor —very poor." An **unbalanced rating scale** has an unequal number of favorable and unfavorable response choices. An example of an unbalanced scale that has only one unfavorable descriptive term and four favorable terms is "poor—fair—good—very good—excellent." The scale designer expects that the mean ratings will be near "good" and that there will be a symmetrical distribution of answers around that point, but the scale does not allow participants who are unfavorable to express the intensity of their attitude.

The use of an unbalanced rating scale can be justified in studies where researchers know in advance that nearly all participants' scores will lean in one direction or the other. Raters are inclined to score attitude objects higher if the objects are very familiar and if they are ego-involved.[4] Brand-loyal customers are also expected to respond favorably. When researchers know that one side of the scale is not likely to be used, they try to achieve precision on the side that will most often receive the participant's attention. Unbalanced scales are also considered when participants are known to be either "easy raters" or "hard raters." An unbalanced scale can help compensate for the error of *leniency* created by such raters.

Forced or Unforced Choices

forced-choice rating scale
requires that participants select
from available alternatives.

**unforced-choice rating
scale** provides participants
with an opportunity to express
no opinion when they are
unable to make a choice
among the alternatives offered.

An **unforced-choice rating scale** provides participants with an opportunity to express no opinion when they are unable to make a choice among the alternatives offered. A **forced-choice scale** requires that participants select one of the offered alternatives. Marketing researchers often exclude the response choice "no opinion," "undecided," "don't know," "uncertain," or "neutral" when they know that most participants have an attitude on the topic. It is reasonable in this circumstance to constrain participants so that they focus on alternatives carefully and do not idly choose the middle position. However, when many participants are clearly undecided and the scale does not allow them to express their uncertainty, the forced-choice scale biases results. Researchers discover such bias when a larger percentage of participants express an attitude than did so in previous studies on the same issue. Some of this bias is attributable to participants providing meaningless responses or reacting to questions about which they have no attitudes (see Chapter 15). This affects the statistical measures of the mean and median, which shift toward the scale's midpoint, making it difficult to discern attitudinal differences throughout the instrument.[5] Understanding neutral answers is a challenge for marketing researchers. In a customer satisfaction study that focused on the overall satisfaction question with a company in the electronics industry, an unforced scale was used. Study results, however, revealed that 75

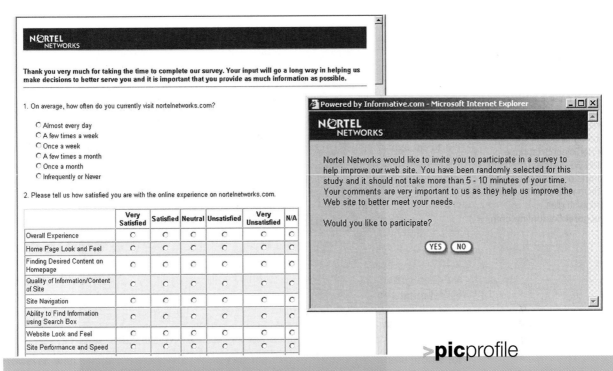

Online surveys are increasingly common due in large part to their speed in data collection. They also offer versatility for use with various types of measurement scales; flexibility in containing not only verbal but graphical, photographic, video, and digital elements; access to difficult-to-contact or inaccessible participants; and lower cost of large-sample completion. The visual appearance of the measurement scale is very important in getting the participant to click through to completion. This invitation from Nortel Networks and the opening screen of the questionnaire are designed to encourage participation. Informative, Inc., fielded this survey for Nortel Networks (designed to evaluate their website). The first screen of the questionnaire indicates two strategies: a multiple-choice/single response strategy incorporating forced choice, and a multi-item rating grid which does not force choice (notice the NA column). If you look closely, you can also see a scroll bar on the first screen. Some designers will put only one question to a screen in Web questionnaires believing that participants who have to scroll may not fully complete the survey. This survey was designed for a technical audience, so that was not as much a concern. www.nortelnetworks.com; www.informative.com

percent of those in the "neutral" participant group could be converted to brand loyalists if the company excelled (received highly favorable ratings) on only 2 of the 26 other scaled questions in the study.[6] Thus, the participants in the neutral group weren't truly neutral, and a forced-choice scale would have revealed the desired information.

Number of Scale Points

What is the ideal number of points for a rating scale? Academics and practitioners often have dogmatic reactions to this question, but the answer is more practical: A scale should be appropriate for its purpose. For a scale to be useful, it should match the stimulus presented and extract information proportionate to the complexity of the attitude object, concept, or construct. A product that requires little effort or thought to purchase, is habitually bought, or has a benefit that fades quickly (low-involvement products) can be measured generally with a simple scale. A 3-point scale (better than average—average—worse than average) is probably sufficient for a deodorant, a fast-food burger, gift-wrapping, or a snack. There is little support for choosing a scale with 5 or more points in this instance. But when the product is complex, plays an important role in the consumer's life, and is costly (e.g., financial services, luxury goods, automobiles, and other high-involvement products), a scale with 5 to 11 points should be considered.

>Exhibit 14-5 Adapting SD Scales for Retail Store Image Study

Convenience of Reaching the Store from Your Location		
Nearby	___: ___: ___: ___: ___: ___: ___:	Distant
Short time required to reach store	___: ___: ___: ___: ___: ___: ___:	Long time required to reach store
Difficult drive	___: ___: ___: ___: ___: ___: ___:	Easy drive
Difficult to find parking place	___: ___: ___: ___: ___: ___: ___:	Easy to find parking place
Convenient to other stores I shop	___: ___: ___: ___: ___: ___: ___:	Inconvenient to other stores I shop

Products Offered		
Wide selection of different kinds of products	___: ___: ___: ___: ___: ___: ___:	Limited selection of different kinds of products
Fully stocked	___: ___: ___: ___: ___: ___: ___:	Understocked
Undependable products	___: ___: ___: ___: ___: ___: ___:	Dependable products
High quality	___: ___: ___: ___: ___: ___: ___:	Low quality
Numerous brands	___: ___: ___: ___: ___: ___: ___:	Few brands
Unknown brands	___: ___: ___: ___: ___: ___: ___:	Well-known brands

Source: Robert F. Kelly and Ronald Stephenson, "The Semantic Differential: An Information Source for Designing Retail Patronage Appeals," *Journal of Marketing* 31 (October 1967), p. 45.

>Exhibit 14-6 Steps in Constructing an SD Scale

1. Select the concepts: nouns, noun phrases, or nonverbal stimuli such as visual sketches. Concepts are chosen by judgment and reflect the nature of the investigative question. In the MindWriter study, one concept might be "Call Center accessibility."

2. Select bipolar word pairs or phrase pairs appropriate to your needs. If the traditional Osgood adjectives are used, several criteria guide your selection:

   - Three bipolar pairs are required when using evaluation, potency, and activity. Scores on these individual items can be averaged, by factor, to improve their reliability.

   - The scale should be relevant to the concepts being judged. Choose adjectives that allow connotative perceptions to be expressed. Irrelevant concept-scale pairings yield neutral midpoint values that convey little information.

   - Scales should be stable across raters and concepts. A pair such as "large–small" may be interpreted as denotative when judging a physical object such as "automobile" but may be used connotatively with abstract concepts such as "product quality."

   - Scales should be linear between polar opposites and pass through the origin. A pair that fails this test is "rugged–delicate," which is nonlinear on the evaluation dimension. When used separately, both adjectives have favorable meanings.*

3. Create the scoring system and assign a weight to each point on the scale. The negative signs in the original scoring procedure ($-3, -2, -1, 0, +1, +2, +3$) were found to produce coding errors, and the 0 point is arbitrary. Most SD scales have 7 points: 7, 6, 5, 4, 3, 2, and 1.

4. As with Likert scales, about half of the adjective pairs are randomly reversed to minimize the halo effect.

*Charles E. Osgood, G. J. Suci, and P. H. Tannenbaum, *The Measurement of Meaning* (Urbana: University of Illinois Press, 1957).

In Exhibit 14-7 we see a scale used by a consulting firm to help a movie production company evaluate actors for the leading role of a risky film venture. The selection of concepts is driven by the characteristics they believe the actor must possess to produce box office financial targets; there are three actor candidates, plus a fourth—the ideal candidate. Based on the producer's requirements, we choose 10 scales to score the candidates. The letters along the left side, which show the relevant factor, would be omitted from the actual scale, as would the numerical values shown. Also note that the evaluation, potency, and activity scales are mixed. To analyze the results, the set of evaluation (E) values is averaged, as are those for the potency (P) and activity (A) dimensions.

The data are plotted in a "snake diagram" in Exhibit 14-8. Here the adjective pairs are reordered so evaluation, potency, and activity descriptors are grouped together, with the ideal factor reflected by the left side of the scale. Profiles of the three actor candidates may be compared to each other and to the ideal.

>**Exhibit 14-7** SD Scale for Analyzing Actor Candidates

Analyze (candidate) for current position:

(E)	Sociable	(7):	____:	____:	____:	____:	____:	____:	____:	(1)	Unsociable
(P)	Weak	(1):	____:	____:	____:	____:	____:	____:	____:	(7)	Strong
(A)	Active	(7):	____:	____:	____:	____:	____:	____:	____:	(1)	Passive
(E)	Progressive	(7):	____:	____:	____:	____:	____:	____:	____:	(1)	Regressive
(P)	Yielding	(1):	____:	____:	____:	____:	____:	____:	____:	(7)	Tenacious
(A)	Slow	(1):	____:	____:	____:	____:	____:	____:	____:	(7)	Fast
(E)	True	(7):	____:	____:	____:	____:	____:	____:	____:	(1)	False
(P)	Heavy	(7):	____:	____:	____:	____:	____:	____:	____:	(1)	Light
(A)	Hot	(7):	____:	____:	____:	____:	____:	____:	____:	(1)	Cold
(E)	Unsuccessful	(1):	____:	____:	____:	____:	____:	____:	____:	(7)	Successful

>**Exhibit 14-8** Graphic Representation of SD Analysis

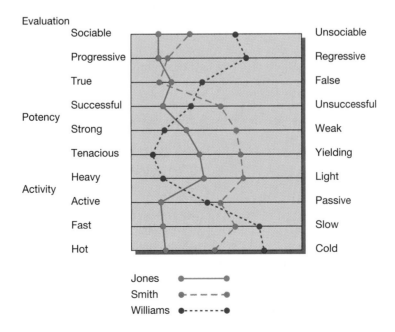

Jones
Smith
Williams

Numerical/Multiple Rating List Scales

numerical scale interval scale using numeric scale points between verbal anchors.

Numerical scales have equal intervals that separate their numeric scale points, as shown in Exhibit 14-2. The verbal anchors serve as the labels for the extreme points. Numerical scales are often 5-point scales but may have 7 or 10 points. The participants write a number from the scale next to each item. If numerous questions about a product's performance were included in the example, the scale would provide both an absolute measure of importance and a relative measure (ranking) of the various items rated. The scale's linearity, simplicity, and production of ordinal or interval data make it popular for managers and researchers. When evaluating a new product concept, purchase intent is frequently measured with a 5- to 7-point numerical scale, with the anchors being "definitely would buy" and "definitely would not buy."

multiple rating list scale a single interval or ordinal numerical scale where raters respond to a series of objects.

A **multiple rating list scale** (Exhibit 14-2) is similar to the numerical scale but differs in two ways: (1) It accepts a circled response from the rater and (2) the layout facilitates visualization of the results. The advantage is that a mental map of the participant's evaluations is evident to both the rater and the researcher. This scale produces interval data.

Stapel Scales

Stapel scale a numerical scale with up to 10 categories where the central position is a named attribute.

The **Stapel scale** is used as an alternative to the semantic differential, especially when it is difficult to find bipolar adjectives that match the investigative question. In the example in Exhibit 14-2 there are three attributes of corporate image. The scale is composed of the word (or phrase) identifying the image dimension and a set of 10 response categories for each of the three attributes.

Fewer response categories are sometimes used. Participants select a plus number for the characteristic that describes the attitude object. The more accurate the description, the larger is the positive number. Similarly, the less accurate the description, the larger is the negative number chosen. Ratings range from $+5$ to -5, where participants select a number that describes the store very accurately to very inaccurately. Like the Likert, SD, and numerical scales, Stapel scales usually produce interval data.

Constant-Sum Scales

constant-sum scale participant allocates points to more than one attribute or property indicant, such that they total a constant sum, usually 100 or 10.

A scale that helps the researcher discover proportions is the **constant-sum scale.** With a constant-sum scale, the participant allocates points to more than one attribute or property indicant, such that they total a constant sum, usually 100 or 10. In the Exhibit 14-2 example, two categories are presented that must sum to 100. In the restaurant example, the participant distributes 100 points among four categories:

> You have 100 points to distribute among the following characteristics of the Dallas Steakhouse. Indicate the relative importance of each attribute:
>
> ____ Food Quality
>
> ____ Atmosphere
>
> ____ Service
>
> ____ Price
>
> 100 TOTAL

Up to 10 categories may be used, but both participant precision and patience suffer when too many stimuli are proportioned and summed. A participant's ability to add is also taxed in some situations; thus this is not a response strategy that can be effectively used with children or the uneducated. The advantage of the scale is its compatibility with percent (100 percent) and the fact that alternatives that are perceived to be equal can be so scored—

unlike the case with most ranking scales. The scale is used to record attitudes, behavior, and behavioral intent. The constant-sum scale produces interval data.

Graphic Rating Scales

The **graphic rating scale** was originally created to enable researchers to discern fine differences. Theoretically, an infinite number of ratings are possible if participants are sophisticated enough to differentiate and record them. They are instructed to mark their response at any point along a continuum. Usually, the score is a measure of length (millimeters) from either endpoint. The results are treated as interval data. The difficulty is in coding and analysis. This scale requires more time than scales with predetermined categories.

Never   _____X_____   Always

Other graphic rating scales (see Exhibit 14-2) use pictures, icons, or other visuals to communicate with the rater and represent a variety of data types. Graphic scales are often used with children, whose more limited vocabulary prevents the use of scales anchored with words.

> # Ranking Scales

In ranking scales, the participant directly compares two or more objects and makes choices among them. Frequently, the participant is asked to select one as the "best" or the "most preferred." When there are only two choices, this approach is satisfactory, but it often results in ties when more than two choices are found. For example, assume participants are asked to select the most preferred among three or more models of a product. In response, 40 percent choose model A, 30 percent choose model B, and 30 percent choose model C. Which is the preferred model? The analyst would be taking a risk to suggest that A is most preferred. Perhaps that interpretation is correct, but 60 percent of the participants chose some model other than A. Perhaps all B and C voters would place A last, preferring either B or C to A. This ambiguity can be avoided by using some of the techniques described in this section.

Using the **paired-comparison scale,** the participant can express attitudes unambiguously by choosing between two objects. Typical of paired comparisons would be the sports car preference example in Exhibit 14-9. The number of judgments required in a paired

graphic rating scale participant places his or her response along a line or continuum.

paired-comparison scale a participant chooses a preferred object within a pair of objects for a series of pairs, resulting in a rank order of objects.

Assume you are asked by Galaxy Department Stores to study the shopping habits and preferences of teen girls. Galaxy is seeking a way to compete with specialty stores that are far more successful in serving this market segment. Galaxy is considering the construction of an intrastore boutique catering to these teens. What measurement issues would determine your construction of measurement scales?

>**Exhibit 14-9** Ranking Scales

Paired-Comparison Scale
data: ordinal

"For each pair of two-seat sports cars listed, place a check beside the one you would most prefer if you had to choose between the two."

___ BMW Z4   ___ Chevrolet Corvette
___ Porsche Boxster   ___ Porsche Boxster

___ Chevrolet Corvette   ___ Porsche Boxster
___ BMW Z4   ___ Dodge Viper

___ Chevrolet Corvette   ___ Dodge Viper
___ Dodge Viper   ___ BMW Z4

Forced Ranking Scale
data: ordinal

"Rank the radar detection features in your order of preference. Place the number 1 next to the most preferred, 2 by the second choice, and so forth."

___ User programming
___ Cordless capability
___ Small size
___ Long-range warning
___ Minimal false alarms

Comparative Scale
data: ordinal

"Compared to your previous hair dryer's performance, the new one is:"

SUPERIOR		ABOUT THE SAME		INFERIOR
1	2	3	4	5

comparison is $[(n)(n-1)/2]$, where n is the number of stimuli or objects to be judged. When four cars are evaluated, the participant evaluates six paired comparisons $[(4)(3)/2 = 6]$.

In another example we might compare packaging design proposals considered by a brand manager (see Exhibit 14-10). Generally, there are more than two stimuli to judge, resulting in a potentially tedious task for participants. If 15 suggestions for design proposals are available, 105 paired comparisons would be made.

Reducing the number of comparisons per participant without reducing the number of objects can lighten this burden. You can present each participant with only a sample of the stimuli. In this way, each pair of objects must be compared an equal number of times. Another procedure is to choose a few objects that are believed to cover the range of attractiveness at equal intervals. All other stimuli are then compared to these few standard objects. If 36 automobiles are to be judged, four may be selected as standards and the others divided into four groups of eight each. Within each group, the eight are compared to each other. Then the 32 are individually compared to each of the four standard automobiles. This reduces the number of comparisons from 630 to 240.

Paired comparisons run the risk that participants will tire to the point that they give ill-considered answers or refuse to continue. Opinions differ about the upper limit, but five or six stimuli are not unreasonable when the participant has other questions to answer. If the data collection consists only of paired comparisons, as many as 10 stimuli are reasonable. A paired comparison provides ordinal data.

The **forced ranking scale,** shown in Exhibit 14-9, lists attributes that are ranked relative to each other. This method is faster than paired comparisons and is usually easier and more motivating to the participant. With five items, it takes 10 paired comparisons to complete

forced ranking scale the participant orders several objects or properties of objects.

># >**snap**shot

Paired Comparison Increases Hospitality

Should Northwest Airlines, Marriott, or Alaskan Airlines attempt to attract the business of Americans with disabilities? If so, what would it take to capture the segment? Eric Lipp, executive director of the Open Doors Organization (ODO), an advocacy organization for those with disabilities, sponsored a study to find out. High on his agenda was providing an incentive to the travel industry to make accommodations to attract the 22 million adults with disabilities who have traveled in the last two years on 63 million trips—and who may want to travel more. "We now estimate that Americans with disabilities currently spent $13.2 billion in travel expenditures and that amount would at least double [to $27.2 billion] if travel businesses were more attuned to the needs of those with disabilities."

ODO hired Harris Interactive, a global market research and consulting firm best known for The Harris Poll and for pioneering the Internet method to conduct scientifically accurate market research. Harris Interactive conducted a hybrid study via both online and phone surveys to determine the magnitude of the disability travel segment, its purchasing power, and the accommodations the segment needed to increase travel. "Those with disabilities can't all be reached with one method," explained Laura Light, project director with Harris Interactive. "The nature of their physical limitation might preclude one method or the

other." And how did the firm evaluate all the possible accommodations—from Braille safety cards on airplanes to a designated person to handle problems in a hotel? Harris Interactive used its proprietary COMPASS™ methodology, which uses paired comparisons as a measurement tool. COMPASS™ saves the participant time and energy," explained Light. "Even with a long list, COMPASS™ can be done quickly." In the ODO study, COMPASS™ was used twice: once to measure 17 possible airline accommodations and once to measure 23 possible hotel accommodations. By having each participant evaluate only a portion of the large number of accommodation pairs rather than the full list (136 for airline accommodations and 253 for hotel accommodations), each question was answered in under four minutes. By using this process with all members of the sample, Harris Interactive is able to rank order the items and measure the magnitude of difference between items. This makes it easier for Delta, Marriott, or Alaskan Airlines to make the right choices about accommodations for those with disabilities.

www.opendoorsnfp.org; www.harrisinteractive.com

To learn more about this research, read the case "Open Doors: Extending Hospitality to Travelers with Disabilities" on your text DVD.

>**Exhibit 14-10** Response Patterns of 200 Heavy Users' Paired Comparisons on 5 Alternative Package Designs

Paired-comparison data may be treated in several ways. If there is substantial consistency, we will find that if A is preferred to B, and B to C, then A will be consistently preferred to C. This condition of transitivity need not always be true but should occur most of the time. When it does, take the total number of preferences among the comparisons as the score for that stimulus. Assume a brand manager is considering five distinct packaging designs. The marketer would like to know how heavy users would rank these designs. One option would be to ask a sample of the heavy-users segment to pair-compare the packaging designs. With a rough comparison of the total preferences for each option, it is apparent that B is the most popular.

	Designs				
	A	**B**	**C**	**D**	**E**
A	—	164*	138	50	70
B	36	—	54	14	30
C	62	146	—	32	50
D	150	186	168	—	118
E	130	170	150	82	—
Total	378	**666**	510	178	268
Rank order	3	**1**	2	5	4

*Interpret this cell as 164 of 200 customers preferred suggested design B (column) to design A (row).

New researchers often want to draft questions immediately. Their enthusiasm makes them reluctant to go through the preliminaries that make for successful surveys. Exhibit 15-1 is a suggested flowchart for instrument design. The procedures followed in developing an instrument vary from study to study, but the flowchart suggests three phases. Each phase is discussed in this chapter, starting with a review of the research question hierarchy.

> Revisiting the Research Question Hierarchy

The management–research question hierarchy is the foundation of the research process and also of successful instrument development (see Exhibit 15-2). By this stage in a research project, the process of moving from the general management dilemma to specific measurement questions has traveled through the first three question levels:

> **This section relates to Phase 1 on Exhibit 15-1.**

1. *Management question*—the dilemma, stated in question form, that the manager needs resolved.

2. *Research question(s)*—the fact-based translation of the question the researcher must answer to contribute to the solution of the management question.

3. *Investigative questions*—specific questions the researcher must answer to provide sufficient detail and coverage of the research question. Within this level, there may be several questions as the researcher moves from the general to the specific.

4. *Measurement questions*—questions participants must answer if the researcher is to gather the needed information and resolve the management question.

> **We discussed how to refine a management dilemma and take it through the research process in Chapter 5 and depicted the process in Exhibit 5-4.**

In the Albany Outpatient Laser Clinic study, the eye surgeons would know from experience the types of medical complications that could result in poor recovery. But they might be far less knowledgeable about what medical staff actions and attitudes affect client recovery and perception of well-being. Coming up with an appropriate set of information needs in this study will take the guided expertise of the researcher. Significant exploration would likely have preceded the development of the investigative questions. In Visionary Insights' project for MindWriter, exploration was limited to several interviews and

>**Exhibit 15-1** Flowchart for Instrument Design

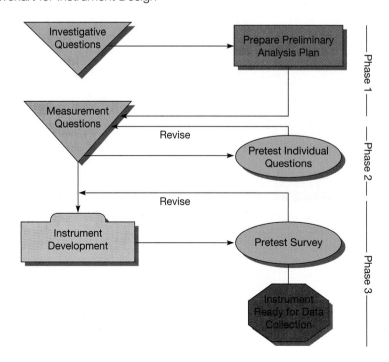

>**Exhibit 15-2** Flowchart for Instrument Design: Phase 1

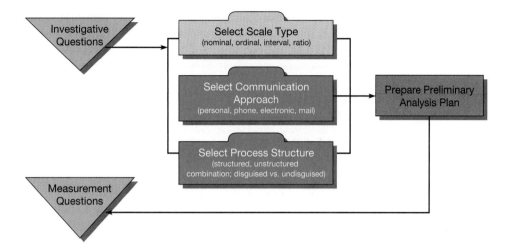

data mining of company service records because the concepts were not complicated and the researchers had experience in the industry.

Normally, once the researcher understands the connection between the investigative questions and the potential measurement questions, a strategy for the survey is the next logical step. This proceeds to getting down to the particulars of instrument design. The following are prominent among the strategic concerns:

> **The Close-Up at the end of this chapter reveals the thinking that led to the final questionnaire in the MindWriter CompleteCare project.**

1. What type of scale is needed to perform the desired analysis to answer the management question?
2. What communication approach will be used?
3. Should the questions be structured, unstructured, or some combination?
4. Should the questioning be undisguised or disguised? If the latter, to what degree?

Technology has also affected the survey development process, not just the method of the survey's delivery. Today's software, hardware, and Internet and intranet infrastructures allow researchers to (1) write questionnaires more quickly by tapping question banks for appropriate, tested questions, (2) create visually driven instruments that enhance the process for the participant, (3) use questionnaire software that eliminates separate manual data entry, and (4) build questionnaires that save time in data analysis.[1]

> **WebSurveyor is the software featured in the opening chapter photo.**

Type of Scale for Desired Analysis

The analytical procedures available to the researcher are determined by the scale types used in the survey. As Exhibit 15-2 clearly shows, it is important to plan the analysis before developing the measurement questions. Chapter 13 discussed nominal, ordinal, interval, and ratio scales and explained how the characteristics of each type influence the analysis (statistical choices and hypothesis testing). We demonstrate how to code and extract the data from the instrument, select appropriate descriptive measures or tests, and analyze the results in Chapters 18 to 22. In this chapter, we are most interested in asking each question in the right way and in the right order to collect the appropriate data for desired analysis.

Communication Approach

As discussed in Chapter 11, communication-based research may be conducted by personal interview, telephone, mail, computer (intranet and Internet), or some combination of these (called *hybrid studies*). Decisions regarding which method to use as well as where to interact

> **You'll find tips for intercept questionnaire design on your text DVD.**

with the participant (at home, at a neutral site, at the sponsor's place of business, etc.) will affect the design of the instrument. In personal interviewing and computer surveying, it is possible to use graphics and other questioning tools more easily than it is in questioning done by mail or phone. The different delivery mechanisms result in different introductions, instructions, instrument layout, and conclusions. For example, researchers may use intercept designs, conducting personal interviews with participants at central locations like shopping malls, stores, sports stadiums, amusement parks, or county fairs. The intercept study poses several instrument challenges.

In the MindWriter example, these decisions were easy. The dispersion of participants, the necessity of a service experience, and budget limitations all dictated a mail survey where the participant received the instrument either at home or at work. Using a telephone survey, which in this instance is the only way to follow up with nonparticipants, could, however, be problematic. This is due to memory decay caused by the passage of time between return of the laptop and contact with the participant by telephone.

Visionary Insights has several options for the Albany study. Clearly a self-administered study is possible, as all the participants are congregating in a centralized location for scheduled surgery. But given the importance of some of the information to medical recovery, a survey conducted via personal interview might be an equally valid choice. We need to know the methodology before we design the questionnaire, as some measurement scales are difficult to answer without the visual aid of seeing the scale.

Disguising Objectives and Sponsors

disguised question a measurement question designed to conceal the question's and study's true purpose.

Another consideration in communication instrument design is whether the purpose of the study should be disguised. A **disguised question** is designed to conceal the question's true purpose. Some degree of disguise is often present in survey questions, especially to shield the study's sponsor. We disguise the sponsor and the objective of a study if the researcher believes that participants will respond differently than they would if both or either was known.

The accepted wisdom among researchers is that they must disguise the study's objective or sponsor in order to obtain unbiased data. The decision about when to use disguised questions within surveys may be made easier by identifying four situations where disguising the study objective is or is not an issue:

- Willingly shared, conscious-level information.
- Reluctantly shared, conscious-level information.
- Knowable, limited-conscious-level information.
- Subconscious-level information.

In surveys requesting conscious-level information that should be willingly shared, either disguised or undisguised questions may be used, but the situation rarely requires disguised techniques.

Example: Have you attended the showing of a foreign language film in the last six months?

In the MindWriter study, the questions revealed in Exhibit 15-13 ask for information that the participant should know and be willing to provide.

> **You might wish to review the projective techniques discussed in Chapter 9.**

Sometimes the participant knows the information we seek but is reluctant to share it for a variety of reasons. When we ask for an opinion on some topic on which participants may hold a socially unacceptable view, we often use projective techniques. In this type of disguised question the survey designer phrases the questions in a hypothetical way or asks how other people in the participant's experience would answer the question. We use projective techniques so that participants will express their true feelings and avoid giving stereotyped answers. The assumption is that responses to these questions will indirectly reveal the participant's opinions.

Example: Have you downloaded copyrighted music from the Internet without paying for it? (nonprojective)

Example: Do you know people who have downloaded copyrighted music from the Internet without paying for it? (projective)

Not all information is at the participant's conscious level. Given some time—and motivation—the participant can express this information. Asking about individual attitudes when participants know they hold the attitude but have not explored why they hold the attitude may encourage the use of disguised questions. A classic example is a study of government bond buying during World War II.[2] A survey sought reasons why, among people with equal ability to buy, some bought more war bonds than others. Frequent buyers had been personally solicited to buy bonds, while most infrequent buyers had not received personal solicitation. No direct *why* question to participants could have provided the answer to this question because participants did not know they were receiving differing solicitation approaches.

Example: What is it about air travel during stormy weather that attracts you?

In assessing buying behavior, we accept that some motivations are subconscious. This is true for attitudinal information as well. Seeking insight into the basic motivations underlying attitudes or consumption practices may or may not require disguised techniques. Projective techniques (such as sentence completion tests, cartoon or balloon tests, and word association tests) thoroughly disguise the study objective, but they are often difficult to interpret.

Example: Would you say, then, that the comment you just made indicates you would or would not be likely to shop at Galaxy Stores? (survey probe during personal interview)

In the MindWriter study, the questions were direct and undisguised, as the specific information sought was at the conscious level. Customers knew they were evaluating their experience with the service and repair program at MindWriter; thus the purpose of the study and its sponsorship were also undisguised. While the sponsor of the Albany clinic study was obvious, any attempt by a survey to reveal psychological factors that might affect recovery and satisfaction might need to use disguised questions. The survey would not want to unnecessarily upset a patient before or immediately following surgery, as that might in itself affect attitude and recovery.

> **The MindWriter questionnaire is Exhibit 15-13 p. 419.**

Preliminary Analysis Plan

Researchers are concerned with adequate coverage of the topic and with securing the information in its most usable form. A good way to test how well the study plan meets those needs is to develop "dummy" tables that display the data one expects to secure. Each **dummy table** is a cross-tabulation between two or more variables. For example, in the biennial study of what Americans eat conducted by *Parade* magazine,[3] we might be interested to know whether age influences the use of convenience foods. The dummy table shown in Exhibit 15-3 would match the age ranges of participants with the degree to which they use convenience foods. The preliminary analysis plan serves as a check on whether the planned measurement questions (for example, the rating scales on use of convenience foods and on age) meet the data needs of the research question. This also helps the researcher determine the type of scale needed for each question (for example, ordinal data on frequency of use and on age)—a preliminary step to developing measurement questions for investigative questions.

dummy table displays data one expects to secure during data analysis.

In the opening vignette, Visionary Insights used the development of a preliminary analysis plan to determine whether the project could be kept on budget. The number of hours spent on data analysis is a major cost of any survey. Too expansive an analysis plan can reveal unnecessary questions. *The guiding principle of survey design is always to ask only what is needed.*

> **You might find it useful to review Exhibit 11-1, "Data Collection Approach," in Chapter 11.**

>**Exhibit 15-3** Dummy Table for American Eating Habits

| Age | Use of Convenience Foods | | | | |
	Always Use	Use Frequently	Use Sometimes	Rarely Use	Never Use
18–24					
25–34					
35–44					
45–54					
55–64					
65+					

>**snap**shot

A Survey Cold as Ice

In December 2002, 1.5 million North Carolinians lost power due to a storm that covered the state with more than an inch of ice that coated tree limbs and brought down power lines. After seven years of repeated natural disasters (two hurricanes, a record-setting flood, a major snowstorm, and drought), North Carolina needed to assess the true cost of this latest disaster and see how the state's residents used weather predictions to prepare for it. It is the state's responsibility to determine the marketing effectiveness of its communication initiatives. The state decided to use a survey.

Odum Institute (at the University of North Carolina–Chapel Hill—maintains one of the nation's largest archives of polling data) and RTI International (a nonprofit "dedicated to conducting research that improves the human condition") stepped in. They conducted a telephone survey of 457 households in 36 counties—those counties included in North Carolina's application for federal disaster assistance. The goal was to give decision makers and the public information that would be useful in preparing for the state's next natural disaster.

RTI knew its analysis plan needed to reveal not only the direct costs of dealing with the disaster but also the indirect costs, like missed work, damage to residences, spoiled food, or hotel accommodations. It also knew that residents' satisfaction with emergency response would influence their actions during the next disaster. And RTI needed to measure attitudes about prevention. Would willingness to prevent a reoccurrence of lost power by burying power lines increase with number of days of power lost?

Shown in the right column is one dummy table for the RTI study for North Carolina, including the aggregate data that was collected. What types of measurement scales would be necessary to complete this table?

> Overall Satisfaction

| Days without power | Power Supplier Response Satisfaction Rating | | |
	Municipal Power	Duke Power	Progress Energy
	7.6	6.6	6.5
1			
2			
3			
Etc.			

Eighty percent of households indicated a willingness to take preventive actions—including 47 percent that were willing to pay extra on their monthly bill to bury power lines. But one of the more significant findings was that the municipal power companies responded more quickly and earned a higher performance rating from customers than did Duke Power and Progress Energy. On a 10-point satisfaction scale ("I was satisfied with my electric power company's response to the ice storm") where 5 was "neither agree nor disagree," municipals earned a 7.6 while the nonmunicipal electric providers earned 6.6 and 6.5, respectively. Each day without power led to a decline in the household's satisfaction level—and the governor and local politicians suffered a similar fate. This survey had a margin of error of ± 4.7 percent.

www.rti.com

> Constructing and Refining the Measurement Questions

Drafting or selecting questions begins once you develop a complete list of investigative questions and decide on the collection processes to be used. The creation of a survey question is not a haphazard or arbitrary process. It is exacting and requires paying significant attention to detail and simultaneously addressing numerous issues. Whether you create or borrow or license a question, in Phase 2 (see Exhibit 15-4) you generate specific measurement questions considering subject content, the wording of each question (influenced by the degree of disguise and the need to provide operational definitions for constructs and concepts), and response strategy (each producing a different level of data as needed for your preliminary analysis plan). In Phase 3 you must address topic and question sequencing. We discuss these topics sequentially, although in practice the process is not linear. For this discussion, we assume the questions are structured.

> **This section relates to Phase 2 on Exhibit 15-1.**

The order, type, and wording of the measurement questions, the introduction, the instructions, the transitions, and the closure in a quality communication instrument should accomplish the following:

• Encourage each participant to provide accurate responses.

• Encourage each participant to provide an adequate amount of information.

• Discourage each participant from refusing to answer specific questions.

• Discourage each participant from early discontinuation of participation.

• Leave the participant with a positive attitude about survey participation.

>**Exhibit 15-4** Flowchart for Instrument Design: Phase 2

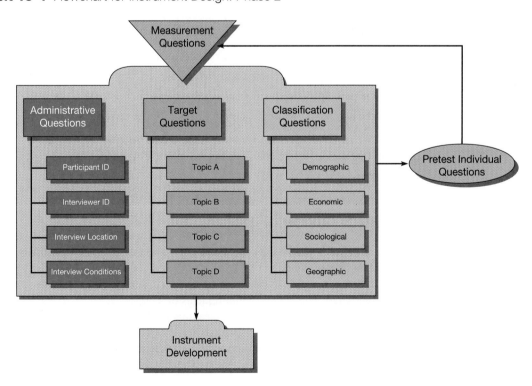

Question Categories and Structure

Questionnaires and **interview schedules** (an alternative term for the questionnaires used in personal interviews) can range from those that have a great deal of structure to those that are essentially unstructured. Questionnaires contain three categories of measurement questions:

- Administrative questions.
- Classification questions.
- Target questions (structured or unstructured).

Administrative questions identify the participant, interviewer, interview location, and conditions. These questions are rarely asked of the participant but are necessary for studying patterns within the data and identify possible error sources. **Classification questions** usually cover sociological-demographic variables that allow participants' answers to be grouped so that patterns are revealed and can be studied. These questions usually appear at the end of a survey (except for those used as *filters* or *screens,* questions that determine whether a participant has the requisite level of knowledge to participate). **Target questions** address the investigative questions of a specific study. These are grouped by topic in the survey. Target questions may be **structured** (they present the participants with a fixed set of choices; often called *closed questions*) or **unstructured** (they do not limit responses but do provide a frame of reference for participants' answers; sometimes referred to as *open-ended questions*).

At the Albany clinic, some questions will need to be unstructured because anticipating medications and health history for a wide variety of individuals would be a gargantuan task for a researcher and would take up far too much paper space.

Question Content

Question content is first and foremost dictated by the investigative questions guiding the study. From these questions, questionnaire designers craft or borrow the target and classification questions that will be asked of participants. Four questions, covering numerous issues, guide the instrument designer in selecting appropriate question content:

- Should this question be asked (does it match the study objective)?
- Is the question of proper scope and coverage?
- Can the participant adequately answer this question as asked?
- Will the participant willingly answer this question as asked?

Exhibit 15-5 summarizes these issues related to constructing and refining measurement questions that are described below and detailed in the Appendix 15a: "Crafting Effective Measurement Questions."

Question Wording

It is frustrating when people misunderstand a question that has been painstakingly written. This problem is partially due to the lack of a shared vocabulary. The difficulty of understanding long and complex sentences or involved phraseology aggravates the problem further. Our dilemma arises from the requirements of question design (the need to be explicit, to present alternatives, and to explain meanings). All contribute to longer and more involved sentences.[4]

The difficulties caused by question wording exceed most other sources of distortion in surveys. They have led one social scientist to conclude:

>**Exhibit 15-5** A Summary of the Major Issues Related to Measurement Questions

Issue Category	Fundamental Issue
Question Content	
1. Purposeful versus interesting	Does the question ask for data that will be merely interesting or truly useful in making a marketing decision?
2. Incomplete or unfocused	Will the question reveal what the marketing decision maker needs to know?
3. Double-barreled questions	Does the question ask the participant for too much information? Would the desired single response be accurate for all parts of the question?
4. Precision	Does the question ask precisely what the marketing decision maker needs to know?
5. Time for thought	Is it reasonable to assume that the participant can frame an answer to the question?
6. Participation at the expense of accuracy	Does the question pressure the participant for a response regardless of knowledge or experience?
7. Presumed knowledge	Does the question assume the participant has knowledge he or she may not have?
8. Recall and memory decay	Does the question ask the participant for information that relates to thoughts or activity too far in the participant's past to be remembered?
9. Balance (general vs. specific)	Does the question ask the participant to generalize or summarize behavior that may have no discernable pattern?
10. Objectivity	Does the question omit or include information that will bias the participant's response?
11. Sensitive information	Does the question ask the participant to reveal embarrassing, shameful, or ego-related information?
Question Wording	
12. Shared vocabulary	Does the question use words that have no meaning or a different meaning for the participant?
13. Unsupported assumption	Does the question assume a prior experience, a precondition, or prior knowledge that the participant does not or may not have?
14. Frame of reference	Is the question worded from the participant's, rather than the researcher's, perspective?
15. Biased wording	Does the question contain wording that implies the researcher's desire for the participant to respond in one way versus another?
16. Personalization	Is it necessary for the participant to reveal personal attitudes and behavior, or may the participant project these attitudes and behaviors to someone like him or her?
17. Adequate alternatives	Does the question provide a mutually exhaustive list of alternatives to encompass realistic or likely participant attitudes and behaviors?
Response Strategy Choice	
18. Objective of the study	Is the question designed to classify or label attitudes, conditions, and behaviors or to reveal them?
19. Thoroughness of prior thought	Has the participant developed an attitude on the issue being asked?
20. Communication skill	Does the participant have sufficient command of the language to answer the question?
21. Participant motivation	Is the level of motivation sufficient to encourage the participant to give thoughtful, revealing answers?

To many who worked in the Research Branch it soon became evident that error or bias attributable to sampling and to methods of questionnaire administration were relatively small as compared with other types of variations—especially variation attributable to different ways of wording questions.[5]

While it is impossible to say which wording of a question is best, we can point out several areas that cause participant confusion and measurement error. The diligent question designer will put a survey question through many revisions before it satisfies these criteria:[6]

- Is the question stated in terms of a shared vocabulary?
- Does the question contain vocabulary with a single meaning?
- Does the question contain unsupported or misleading assumptions?
- Does the question contain biased wording?
- Is the question correctly personalized?
- Are adequate alternatives presented within the question?

In the vignette, Sara's study of the prior survey used by the Albany laser clinic illustrated several of these problems. One question asked participants to identify their "referring physician" and the "physician most knowledgeable about your health." This question was followed by one requesting a single phone number. Participants didn't know which doctor's phone number was being requested. By offering space for only one number, the data collection instrument implied that both parts of the question might refer to the same doctor. Further, the questions about past medical history did not offer clear directions. One question asked participants about whether they had "had the flu recently," yet made no attempt to define whether *recently* was within the last 10 days or the last year. Another asked "Are your teeth intact?" Prior participants had answered by providing information about whether they wore false teeth, had loose teeth, or had broken or chipped teeth—only one of which was of interest to the doctor performing surgery. To another question ("Do you have limited motion of your neck?"), all respondents answered yes. Sara could only conclude that a talented researcher did not design the clinic's previously used questionnaire. While the Albany outpatient Laser Clinic survey did not reveal any **leading questions,** these can inject significant error by inferring that one response should be favored over another. One classic hair care study asked, "How did you like Brand X when it lathered up so nicely?" Obviously, the participant was supposed to factor in the richness of the lather in evaluating the shampoo.

The MindWriter questionnaire (see Exhibit 15-13) simplified the process by using the same response strategy for each factor the participant was asked to evaluate. The study basically asks, "How did our CompleteCare service program work for you when you consider each of the following factors?" It accomplishes this by setting up the questioning with "Take a moment to tell us how well we've served you." Because the sample includes CompleteCare users only, the underlying assumption that participants have used the service is acceptable. The language is appropriate for the participant's likely level of education. And the open-ended question used for "comments" adds flexibility to capture any unusual circumstances not covered by the structured list.

> **leading question** a measurement question whose wording suggests to the participant the desired answer.

> 66 By using the Internet, you can show consumers pictures, show them packaging and even play videos. 99
>
> *Gordon Black*
> *Founder, Harris Interactive*

Target questions need not be constructed solely of words. Computer-assisted, computer-administered, and Web surveys and interview schedules, and to a lesser extent printed surveys, often incorporate visual images as part of the questioning process.

Response Strategy

> **unstructured response** where participant's response is limited only by space, layout, instructions, or time.

> **structured response** participant's response is limited to specific alternatives provided.

A third major decision area in question design is the degree and form of structure imposed on the participant. The various response strategies offer options that include **unstructured response** (or *open-ended response,* the free choice of words) and **structured response** (or *closed response,* specified alternatives provided). Free responses, in turn, range from those in which the participants express themselves extensively to those in which participants' latitude is restricted by space, layout, or instructions to choose one word or phrase, as in a fill-in question. Closed responses typically are categorized as dichotomous, multiple-choice, checklist, rating, or ranking response strategies.

Several situational factors affect the decision of whether to use open-ended or closed questions.[7] The decision is also affected by the degree to which these factors are known to the interviewer. The factors are:

- Objectives of the study.
- Participant's level of information about the topic.
- Degree to which participant has thought through the topic.
- Ease with which participant communicates.
- Participant's motivation level to share information.

Response Strategies Illustrated

Examples of the strategies described in this section are found in Exhibit 15-6.

Free-Response Strategy

Free-response questions, also known as *open-ended questions,* ask the participant a question and either the interviewer pauses for the answer (which is unaided) or the participant records his or her ideas in his or her own words in the space provided on a questionnaire. Survey researchers usually try to reduce the number of such questions as they pose significant problems in interpretation and are costly in terms of data analysis.

free-response question
measurement question where the participant chooses the words to frame the answer.

Dichotomous Response Strategy

A topic may present clearly dichotomous choices: Something is a fact or it is not; a participant can either recall or not recall information; a participant attended or didn't attend an event. **Dichotomous questions** suggest opposing responses, but this is not always the case. One response may be so unlikely that it would be better to adopt the middle-ground alternative as one of the two choices. For example, if we ask participants whether a product is underpriced or overpriced, we are not likely to get many selections of the former choice. The better alternatives to present to the participant might be "fairly priced" or "overpriced."

dichotomous question a measurement question that offers two mutually exclusive and exhaustive alternatives.

In many two-way questions, there are potential alternatives beyond the stated two alternatives. If the participant cannot accept either alternative in a dichotomous question, he or she may convert the question to a multiple-choice or rating question by writing in his or her desired alternative. For example, the participant may prefer an alternative such as "don't know" to a yes-no question or prefer "no opinion" when faced with a favor-oppose option. In other cases, when there are two opposing or complementary choices, the participant may prefer a qualified choice ("yes, if X doesn't occur," or "sometimes yes and sometimes no," or "about the same"). Thus, two-way questions may become multiple-choice or rating questions, and these additional responses should be reflected in your revised analysis plan. Dichotomous questions generate nominal data.

Multiple-Choice Response Strategy

Multiple-choice questions are appropriate where there are more than two alternatives or where we seek gradations of preference, interest, or agreement; the latter situation also calls for rating questions. While such questions offer more than one alternative answer,

multiple-choice question a measurement question that poses more than two category responses but seeks a single answer.

>**Exhibit 15-6** Alternative Response Strategies

Free Response	What factors influenced your enrollment in Metro U?
Dichotomous Selection	Did you attend either of the "A Day at College" programs at Metro U? ❑ Yes ❑ No
Paired-Comparison (Dichotomous Selection)	In your decision to attend Metro U, which was more influential: the semester calendar or the many friends attending from your hometown? ❑ Semester calendar. ❑ Many friends attending from hometown.
Multiple Choice	Which one of the following factors was most influential in your decision to attend Metro U? ❑ Good academic reputation. ❑ Specific program of study desired. ❑ Enjoyable campus life. ❑ Many friends from home attend. ❑ High quality of the faculty.
Checklist	Which of the following factors encouraged you to apply to Metro U? (Check all that apply.) ❑ Tuition cost. ❑ Specific program of study desired. ❑ Parents' preferences. ❑ Opinion of brother or sister. ❑ Many friends from home attend. ❑ High school counselor's recommendation. ❑ High quality of the faculty. ❑ Good academic reputation. ❑ Enjoyable campus life. ❑ Closeness to home. ❑ Opportunity to play collegiate sports.
Rating	Each of the following factors has been shown to have some influence on a student's choice in applying to Metro U. Using your own experience, for each factor please tell us whether the factor was "strongly influential," "somewhat influential," or "not at all influential."

	Strongly Influential	Somewhat Influential	Not at All Influential
Good academic reputation	❑	❑	❑
Enjoyable campus life	❑	❑	❑
Many friends from home attend	❑	❑	❑
High quality of the faculty	❑	❑	❑
Semester calendar	❑	❑	❑

Ranking	Please rank-order your top three factors from the following list based on their influence in encouraging you to apply to Metro U. Use 1 to indicate the most encouraging factor, 2 the next most encouraging factor, etc. _____ Opportunity to play collegiate sports. _____ Closeness to home. _____ Enjoyable campus life. _____ Good academic reputation. _____ High quality of the faculty. _____ High school counselor's recommendation. _____ Many friends from home attend. _____ Opinion of brother or sister. _____ Parents' preferences. _____ Specific program of study desired. _____ Tuition cost.

Managers may sometimes need information quickly to resolve a problem or take advantage of a brief window of opportunity. RTI International, an industry leader in the development and use of state-of-the-art software systems to improve the quality of survey data, formed a strategic alliance with Knowledge Networks to use its probability-based panel of U.S. households to conduct fast-turnaround studies. The Web-enabled panel offers clients access to a statistically valid random sample of households (not just Internet users) who participate in studies via the Internet from their homes. "It's proved a great way for researchers to get very quick access to many (or just a few) sample members," claims Tim Gabel, RTI's director of research computing. **www.rti.org; www.knowledgenetworks. com**

they request that the participant make a single choice. Multiple-choice questions can be efficient, but they also present unique design and analysis problems.

One type of problem occurs when one or more responses have not been anticipated. Assume we ask whether retail mall security and safety rules should be determined by the (1) store managers, (2) sales associates who work at the mall, (3) federal government, or (4) state government. The union has not been mentioned in the alternatives. Many participants might combine this alternative with "sales associates," but others will view "unions" as a distinct alternative. Exploration prior to drafting the measurement question attempts to identify the most likely choices.

A second problem occurs when the list of choices is not exhaustive. Participants may want to give an answer that is not offered as an alternative. This may occur when the desired response is one that combines two or more of the listed individual alternatives. Many participants may believe the store management *and* the sales associates acting jointly should set store safety rules, but the question does not include this response. When the researcher tries to provide for all possible options, choosing from the list of alternatives can become exhausting. We guard against this by discovering the major choices through exploration and pretesting (discussed in detail in Appendix 15b). We may also add the category "other (please specify)" as a safeguard to provide the participant with an acceptable alternative for all other options. In our analysis of responses to a pretested, self-administered questionnaire we may create a combination alternative.

Yet another problem occurs when the participant divides the question of store safety into several questions, each with different alternatives. Some participants may believe rules dealing with air quality in stores should be set by a federal agency while those dealing with aisle obstructions or displays should be set by store management and union representatives. Still others may want store management in conjunction with a sales associate committee to make rules. To address this problem, the instrument designer would need to divide the question. Pretesting should reveal if a multiple-choice question is really a **double-barreled question**.

double-barreled question a measurement question that includes two or more questions in one that the participant might need to answer differently.

Another challenge in alternative selection occurs when the choices are not mutually exclusive (the participant thinks two or more responses overlap). In a multiple-choice question that asks students, "Which one of the following factors was most influential in your decision to attend Metro U?" these response alternatives might be listed:

1. Good academic reputation.
2. Specific program of study desired.
3. Enjoyable campus life.
4. Many friends from home attend.
5. High quality of the faculty.
6. Opportunity to play collegiate-level sports.

Some participants might view items 1 and 5 as overlapping, and some may see items 3 and 4 in the same way.

It is also important to seek a fair balance in choices when a participant's position on an issue is unknown. One study showed that an off-balance presentation of alternatives biases the results in favor of the more heavily offered side.[8] If four gradations of alternatives are on one side of an issue and two are offered reflecting the other side, responses will tend to be biased toward the better-represented side. However, researchers may have a valid reason for using an unbalanced array of alternatives. They may be trying to determine the degree of positive (or negative) response, already knowing which side of an issue most participants will choose based on the selection criteria for participation.

It is necessary in multiple-choice questions to present reasonable alternatives—particularly when the choices are numbers or identifications. If we ask, "Which of the following numbers is closest to the number of students enrolled in American colleges and universities today?" these choices might be presented:

1. 75,000
2. 750,000
3. 7,500,000
4. 25,000,000
5. 75,000,000

It should be obvious to most participants that at least three of these choices are not reasonable, given general knowledge about the population of the United States and about the colleges and universities in their hometowns. (The estimated 2003 U.S. population is 290.8 million based on the 2000 census of 281.4 million. The Ohio State University has more than 50,000 students.)

The order in which choices are given can also be a problem. Numeric alternatives are normally presented in order of magnitude. This practice introduces a bias. The participant assumes that if there is a list of five numbers, the correct answer will lie somewhere in the middle of the group. Researchers are assumed to add a couple of incorrect numbers on each side of the correct one. To counteract this tendency to choose the central position, put the correct number at an extreme position more often when you design a multiple-choice question.

Order bias with nonnumeric response categories often leads the participant to choose the first alternative (**primacy effect**) or the last alternative (**recency effect**) over the middle ones. Primacy effect dominates in visual surveys—self-administered via Web or mail— while recency effect dominates in oral surveys—phone and personal interview surveys.[9] Using the *split-ballot technique* can counteract this bias: different segments of the sample are presented alternatives in different orders. To implement this strategy in face-to-face interviews, the researcher would list the alternatives on a card to be handed to the participant when the question is asked. Cards with different choice orders can be alternated to ensure positional balance. The researcher would leave the choices unnumbered on the card so that the participant replies by giving the response category itself rather than its identifying number. It is a good practice to use cards like this any time there are four or more choice alter-

primacy effect order bias where the participant tends to choose the first alternative.

recency effect order bias where the participant tends to choose the last alternative.

natives. This saves the interviewer reading time and ensures a more valid answer by keeping the full range of choices in front of the participant. With computer-assisted surveying, the software can be programmed to rotate the order of the alternatives so that each participant receives the alternatives in randomized order (for nonordered scales) or in reverse order (for ordered scales).

In most multiple-choice questions, there is also a problem of ensuring that the choices represent a one-dimensional scale—that is, the alternatives to a given question should represent different aspects of the same conceptual dimension. In the college selection example, the list included features associated with a college that might be attractive to a student. This list, while not exhaustive, illustrated aspects of the concept "college attractiveness factors within the control of the college." The list did not mention other factors that might affect a school attendance decision. Parents and peer advice, local alumni efforts, and one's high school adviser may influence the decision, but these represent a different conceptual dimension of "college attractiveness factors"—those not within the control of the college.

Multiple-choice questions usually generate nominal data. When the choices are numeric alternatives, this response structure may produce at least interval and sometimes ratio data. When the choices represent ordered but unequal, numerical ranges (for example, a question on family income: <$20,000; $20,000–$100,000; >$100,000) or a verbal rating scale (for example, a question on how you prefer your steak prepared: well done, medium well, medium rare, or rare), the multiple-choice question generates ordinal data.

Checklist Response Strategy

When you want a participant to give multiple responses to a single question, you will ask the question in one of three ways: the checklist, rating, or ranking strategy. If relative order is not important, the **checklist** is the logical choice. Questions like "Which of the following factors encouraged you to apply to Metro U? (Check all that apply)" force the participant to exercise a dichotomous response (yes, encouraged; no, didn't encourage) to each factor presented. Of course, you could have asked for the same information with a series of dichotomous selection questions, one for each individual factor, but this would have been both time- and space-consuming. Checklists are more efficient. Checklists generate nominal data.

checklist a measurement question that poses numerous alternatives and encourages multiple unordered responses.

Rating Response Strategy

Rating questions ask the participant to position each factor on a companion scale, either verbal, numeric, or graphic. "Each of the following factors has been shown to have some influence on a student's choice to apply to Metro U. Using your own experience, for each factor please tell us whether the factor was 'strongly influential,' 'somewhat influential,' or 'not at all influential.'" Generally, rating-scale structures generate ordinal data; some carefully crafted scales generate interval data.

It is important to remember that the researcher should represent only one response dimension in rating-scale response options. Otherwise, effectively, you present the participant with a double-barreled question with insufficient choices to reply to both aspects.

> ❝Every time you return a DVD, Netflix asks you to rate it on a scale of one to five. With this information, the service figures out precisely what sorts of films appeal to you, and lets you know about them.❞
> *Craig Tomashoff*
> *(a NetFlix customer)*

rating question a question that asks the participant to position each property or object on a verbal, numeric, or graphic continuum.

Example A: How likely are you to enroll at Metro University?

(Responses with more than one dimension, ordinal scale)

(a) extremely likely to enroll

(b) somewhat likely to enroll

(c) not likely to apply

(d) will not apply

Example B: How likely are you to enroll at Metro University?

(Responses within one dimension, interval scale)

(a) extremely likely to enroll

(b) somewhat likely to enroll

(c) neither likely nor unlikely to enroll

(d) somewhat unlikely to enroll

(e) extremely unlikely to enroll

Ranking Response Strategy

ranking question a measurement question that asks the participant to compare and order two or more objects or properties using a numeric scale.

When relative order of the alternatives is important, the **ranking question** is ideal. "Please rank-order your top three factors from the following list based on its influence in encouraging you to apply to Metro U. Use 1 to indicate the most encouraging factor, 2 the next most encouraging factor, etc." The checklist strategy would provide the three factors of influence, but we would have no way of knowing the importance the participant places on each factor. Even in a personal interview, the order in which the factors are mentioned is not a guarantee of influence. Ranking as a response strategy solves this problem.

One concern surfaces with ranking activities. How many presented factors should be ranked? If you listed the 15 brands of potato chips sold in a given market, would you have the participant rank all 15 in order of preference? In most instances it is helpful to remind yourself that while participants may have been selected for a given study due to their experience or likelihood of having desired information, this does not mean that they have knowledge of all conceivable aspects of an issue, but only of some. It is always better to have participants rank only those elements with which they are familiar. For this reason, ranking questions might appropriately follow a checklist question that identifies the objects of familiarity. If you want motivation to remain strong, avoid asking a participant to rank more than seven items even if your list is longer. Ranking generates ordinal data.

All types of response strategies have their advantages and disadvantages. Several different strategies are often found in the same questionnaire, and the situational factors mentioned earlier are the major guides in this matter. There is a tendency, however, to use closed questions instead of the more flexible open-ended type. Exhibit 15-7 summarizes some important considerations in choosing between the various response strategies.

>**Exhibit 15-7** Characteristics of Response Strategies

Characteristic	Dichotomous	Multiple Choice	Checklist	Rating	Rank Ordering	Free Response
Type of Scale	Nominal	Nominal, ordinal, or ratio	Nominal	Ordinal or interval	Ordinal	Nominal or ratio
Usual Number of Answer Alternatives Provided	2	3 to 10	10 or fewer	3 to 7	10 or fewer	None
Desired Number of Participant Answers	1	1	10 or fewer	1 per item	7 or fewer	1
Used to Provide . . .	Classification	Classification, order, or specific numerical estimate	Classification	Order or distance	Order	Classification (of idea), order, or specific numerical estimate

Response Strategies and the Web Questionnaire

All of the above strategies are available for use on Web questionnaires. However, with the Web survey you are faced with slightly different layout options for response than those noted in Exhibit 15-6. For the multiple-choice or dichotomous response strategy, the designer chooses between radio buttons and drop-down boxes. For the checklist or multiple response strategy, the designer must use the checkbox. For rating scales, designers may use pop-up windows that contain the scale and instructions, but the response option is usually the radio button. For ranking questions, designers use radio buttons, drop-down boxes, and textboxes. For the open-ended question, the designer chooses either the one-line textbox or the scrolled textbox. Web surveys and other computer-assisted surveys can return a participant to a given question or prompt them to complete a response when they click the "submit" button; this is especially valuable for checklists, rating scales, and ranking response strategies. Exhibit 15-8 shows these layout options.

Sources of Existing Questions

The tools of data collection should be adapted to the problem, not the reverse. Thus, the focus of this chapter has been on crafting an instrument to answer specific investigative questions. But inventing, refining, and pretesting questions demands considerable time and effort. For some topics, a careful review of the related literature and an examination of existing instrument sourcebooks can shorten this process. Increasingly, companies that specialize in survey research maintain a question bank of pretested questions. In the opening vignette, Sara was accessing Visionary Insights' question bank.

A review of literature will reveal instruments used in similar studies that may be obtained by writing to the researchers or, if copyrighted, may be purchased through a clearinghouse. Instruments also are available through compilations and sourcebooks. While these tend to be oriented to social science applications, they are a rich source of ideas for tailoring questions to meet a marketer's needs. Several compilations are recommended; we have suggested them in Exhibit 15-9.[10]

Borrowing items from existing sources is not without risk. It is quite difficult to generalize the reliability and validity of selected questionnaire items or portions of a questionnaire

>**Exhibit 15-8** Internet Survey Response Options

Where have you seen advertising for MindWriter laptop computers?

Free Response/Open Question
using textbox

Dichotomous Selection
using radio buttons
(may also use pull-down box)

I plan to purchase a MindWriter laptop in the next 3 months.

◎ Yes
◎ No

My next laptop computer will have . . .

◎ More memory.
◎ More processing speed.

Paired Comparison
using radio buttons
(may also use pull-down box)

Closed Question–Single Response
using radio buttons
(may also use pull-down box
or checkbox)

What ONE magazine do you read most often for computing news?

◎ PC Magazine
◎ Wired
◎ Computing Magazine
◎ Computing World
◎ PC Computing
◎ Laptop

that have been taken out of the original context. Researchers whose questions or instruments you borrow may not have reported sampling and testing procedures needed to judge the quality of the measurement scale. Just because Visionary Insights has a satisfaction scale in its question bank used for the CardioQuest survey does not mean the question will be appropriate for the Albany Outpatient Laser Clinic. Sara would need to know the intended purpose of the CardioQuest study and the time of construction, as well as the results of pretesting, to determine the reliability and validity of its use in the Albany study. Even then she would be wise to pretest the question in the context of her Albany survey.

Language, phrasing, and idioms can also pose problems. Questions tend to age or become outdated and may not appear (or sound) as relevant to the participant as freshly worded questions. Integrating previously used and customized questions is problematic. Often adjacent questions in one questionnaire are relied on to carry context. If you select one question from a contextual series, the borrowed question is left without its necessary meaning.[11] Whether an instrument is constructed with designed questions or adapted with questions borrowed or licensed from others, pretesting is expected.

> Drafting and Refining the Instrument

As depicted in Exhibit 15-10, Phase 3 of instrument design—drafting and refinement—is a multistep process:

> **This section reflects Phase 3 in Exhibit 15-1.**

1. Develop the participant-screening process (done especially with personal or phone surveys, but also with early notification procedures with e-mail and Web surveys), along with the introduction.

>**Exhibit 15-8** Continued

What ONE magazine do you read most often for computing news?

Please select your answer ∨
- PC Magazine
- Wired
- Computing Magazine
- **Computing World**
- PC Computing
- Laptop

Closed Question–Single Response
using pull–down box

Which of the following computing magazines did you look at in the last 30 days?
- ☐ PC Magazine
- ☐ Wired
- ☐ Computing Magazine
- ☐ Computing World
- ☐ PC Computing
- ☐ Laptop

Closed Question–Multiple Response
using checkbox
(may also use radio buttons)

Please indicate the importance of each of the characteristics in choosing your next laptop. [Select one answer in each row. Scroll to see the complete list of options.]

	Very Important		Neither Important nor Unimportant		Not at all Important	
Fast reliable repair service	◉	○	○	○	○	∨
Service at my location	○	○	◉	○	○	
Maintenance by the manufacturer	◉	○	○	○	○	
Knowledgeable technicians	◉	○	○	○	○	
Notification of upgrades	○	○	○	○	◉	∧

Rating Grid
Requires a single response per line The longer the list, the more likely the participant must scroll.
(may also use checkboxes)

From the list below, please choose the three most important service options when choosing your next laptop.

Fast reliable repair service	— ∨
Service at my location	—
Maintenance by the manufacturer	1
Knowledgeable technicians	2
	3
Notification of upgrades	— ∨

Ranking Question
using pull-down box
(may also use textboxes, in which ranks are entered)
[This question asks for a limited ranking of only three of the listed elements.]

2. Arrange the measurement question sequence:
    a. Identify groups of target questions by topic.
    b. Establish a logical sequence for the question groups and questions within groups.
    c. Develop transitions between these question groups.
3. Prepare and insert instructions—for the interviewer or participant—including termination instructions, skip directions, and probes.
4. Create and insert a conclusion, including a survey disposition statement.
5. Pretest specific questions and the instrument as a whole.

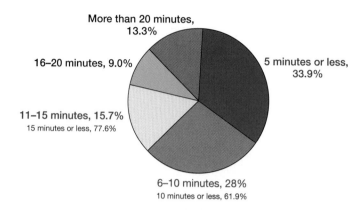

Maximum Online Survey Length Prior to Abandonment

More than 20 minutes, 13.3%

16–20 minutes, 9.0%

11–15 minutes, 15.7%
15 minutes or less, 77.6%

5 minutes or less, 33.9%

6–10 minutes, 28%
10 minutes or less, 61.9%

>**pic**profile

As marketing resistance rises and survey cooperation declines, survey length is of increasing concern. InsightExpress studied the Web survey process and revealed that people taking Web surveys prefer shorter to longer surveys, consistent with what we know about phone and intercept survey participants. While 77 percent were likely to complete a survey that took 15 minutes or less, almost one in three participants needed a survey to be 5 minutes or less for full completion. As participating in on-line surveys loses its novelty, prospective participants are likely to become even more reluctant to give significant time to the survey process. Therefore, it is critical that researchers ask only what is necessary. www.insightexpress.com

>**snap**shot

Does Direct-Response TV Influence Purchase Behavior?

The year 2004 marked the 20th anniversary of the infomercial, so the Electronic Retailing Association (ERA) decided the time was right for a tracking study. Three types of direct-response television (DRTV) tempt viewers to purchase products directly: the direct-response commercial (30- to 120-second TV commercial), the infomercial (30-minute paid program), and live shopping shows (like *QVC, Home Shopping Network, Shop at Home,* and *ShopNBC*). According to a 300-participant telephone survey conducted by Leisure Trends Group for ERA, since 1996 the percentage of those 16 or older viewing the three types of DRTV has declined 11 percent but now reaches 63 percent. This translates to 136.2 million viewers annually. Among 16- to 24-year-olds, viewership has increased compared to that in the previous year. ERA sees this as good news given that television viewing

overall by persons in this group is declining as they turn increasingly to the Internet for entertainment. Overall, 37 percent of Americans say they have been enticed to buy a product they saw advertised on TV—39 percent of infomercial viewers, 34 percent of live shopping show viewers, and 32 percent of direct-response commercial viewers. These percentages are all lower than they were in a comparative study in 1994. Of those who purchased, 76 percent purchased from a store or the Internet, while 59 percent dialed the phone number given on the TV. If you were considering DRTV as a distribution option, would this study convince you to use DRTV?

www.retailing.org; www.leisuretrends.com

Introduction and Participant Screening

screen question (filter question) a question to qualify the participant's knowledge about the target questions of interest or experience necessary to participate.

The introduction must supply the sample unit with the motivation to participate in the study. It must reveal enough about the forthcoming questions, usually by revealing some or all of the topics to be covered, for participants to judge their interest level and their ability to provide the desired information. In any communication study, the introduction also reveals the amount of time participation is likely to take. The introduction also reveals the research organization or sponsor (unless the study is disguised) and possibly the objective of the study. In personal or phone interviews as well as in e-mail and Web surveys, the introduction usually contains one or more **screen questions** or filter questions to determine if

>**Exhibit 15-9** Sources of Questions

Author(s)	Title	Source
William Bearden and R. Netemeyer	Handbook of Marketing Scales: Multi-Item Measures for Marketing and Consumer Behavior Research	London: Sage Publications, Inc., 2001
Alec Gallup and George H. Gallup, eds.	The Gallup Poll Cumulative Index: Public Opinion, 1935–1997	Wilmington, DE: Scholarly Resources, 1999
John P. Robinson, Philip R. Shaver, and Lawrence S. Wrightsman	Measures of Personality and Social-Psychological Attitudes	San Diego, CA: Academic Press, 1990, 1999
John Robinson and L. Wrightsman	Measures of Political Attitudes	San Diego, CA: Academic Press, 1999
George H. Gallup Jr., ed.	The Gallup Poll: Public Opinion 1998	Wilmington, DE: Scholarly Resources, 1998
Gordon Bruner and Paul Hensel	Marketing Scales Handbook: A Compilation of Multi-Item Measure V.II	Chicago, IL: American Marketing Association, 1996, 1998
Elizabeth H. Hastings and Philip K. Hastings, eds.	Index to International Public Opinion 1986–1987	Westport, CT: Greenwood Publishing Group, September 1988
Elizabeth Martin, Diana McDuffee, and Stanley Presser	Sourcebook of Harris National Surveys: Repeated Questions 1963–1976	Chapel Hill, NC: Institute for Research in Social Science, 1981
Philip E. Converse, Jean D. Dotson, Wendy J. Hoag, and William H. McGee III, eds.	American Social Attitudes Data Sourcebook, 1947–1978	Cambridge, MA: Harvard University Press, 1980
Philip K. Hastings and Jessie C. Southwick, eds.	Survey Data for Trend Analysis: An Index to Repeated Questions in the U.S. National Surveys Held by the Roper Public Opinion Research Center	Williamsburg, MA: Roper Public Opinion Center, 1975
National Opinion Research Center	General Social Surveys 1972–2000: Cumulative Code Book	Ann Arbor, MI: ICPSR, 2000
John P. Robinson, Robert Athanasiou, and Kendra B. Head	Measures of Occupational Attitudes and Occupational Characteristics	Ann Arbor, MI: Institute for Social Research, University of Michigan, 1968
Web Sources		
Interuniversity Consortium for Political and Social Research (general social survey)	www.icpsr.umich.edu/8080/GSS/index.html	
iPoll (contains more than 380,000 questions in its searchable database)	www.ropercenter.uconn.edu/poll.htm	
Online Survey Research/Public Opinion Centers (a world listing)	www.ku.edu/cwis/units/coms2/po/	
Survey Research Library, Florida State University	www.fsu.edu/~survey/surveys.htm	
The Odum Institute (houses the Louis Harris Opinion Polls)	www.irss.unc.edu	

the potential participant has the knowledge or experience necessary to participate in the study. At a minimum, a phone or personal interviewer will introduce himself or herself to help establish critical rapport with the potential participant. Exhibit 15-11 provides a sample introduction and other components of a telephone study of nonparticipants to a self-administered mail survey.

>**Exhibit 15-10** Flowchart for Instrument Design: Phase 3

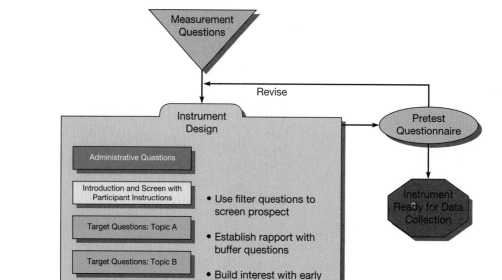

Measurement Question Sequencing

branched question a
measurement question
sequence determined by the
participant's previous answers.

The design of survey questions is influenced by the need to relate each question to the others in the instrument. Often the content of one question (called a **branched question**) assumes other questions have been asked and answered. The psychological order of the questions is also important; question sequence can encourage or discourage commitment and promote or hinder the development of researcher-participant rapport.

The basic principle used to guide sequence decisions is this: The nature and needs of the participant must determine the sequence of questions and the organization of the interview schedule. Four guidelines are suggested to implement this principle:

1. The question process must quickly awaken interest and motivate the participant to participate in the interview. Put the more interesting topical target questions early. Leave classification questions (e.g., age, family size, income) not used as filters or screens to the end of the survey.

2. The participant should not be confronted by early requests for information that might be considered personal or ego-threatening. Put questions that might influence the participant to discontinue or terminate the questioning process near the end.

3. The questioning process should begin with simple items and then move to the more complex, as well as move from general items to the more specific. Put taxing and challenging questions later in the questioning process.

4. Changes in the frame of reference should be small and should be clearly pointed out. Use transition statements between different topics of the target question set.

>**Exhibit 15-11** Sample Components of Communication Instruments

Component	Example
Introduction	Good evening. May I please speak with (name of participant)? Mr. (participant's last name), I'm (your name), calling on behalf of MindWriter Corporation. You recently had your MindWriter laptop serviced at our CompleteCare Center. Could you take five minutes to tell us what you thought of the service provided by the center?
Transition	The next set of questions asks about your family and how you enjoy spending your nonworking or personal time.
Instructions for . . . a. Terminating (following filter or screen question)	I'm sorry, today we are only talking with individuals who eat cereal at least three days per week, but thank you for speaking with me. (Pause for participant reply.) Good-bye.
b. Participant discontinue	Would there be a time I could call back to complete the interview? (Pause; record time.) We'll call you back then at (repeat day, time). Thank you for talking with me this evening. Or: I appreciate your spending some time talking with me. Thank you.
c. Skip directions (between questions or groups of questions)	3. Did you purchase boxed cereal in the last 7 days? ❑ Yes ❑ No (skip to question 7)
d. Disposition instructions	A postage-paid envelope was included with your survey. Please refold your completed survey and mail it to us in the postage-paid envelope.
Conclusion a. Phone or personal interview	That's my last question. Your insights and the ideas of other valuable customers will help us to make the CompleteCare program the best it can be. Thank you for talking with us this evening. (Pause for participant reply). Good evening.
b. Self-administered (usually precedes the disposition instructions)	Thank you for sharing your ideas about the CompleteCare program. Your insights will help us serve you better.

Awaken Interest and Motivation

We awaken interest and stimulate motivation to participate by choosing or designing questions that are attention-getting and not controversial. If the questions have human-interest value, so much the better. It is possible that the early questions will contribute valuable data to the major study objective, but their major task is to overcome the motivational barrier.

Sensitive and Ego-Involving Information

Regarding the introduction of sensitive information too early in the process, two forms of this error are common. Most studies need to ask for personal classification information about participants. Participants normally will provide these data, but the request should be made at the end of the survey. If made at the start of the survey, it often causes participants to feel threatened, dampening their interest and motivation to continue. It is also dangerous to ask any question at the start that is too personal. For example, participants in one survey were asked whether they suffered from insomnia. When the question was asked immediately after the interviewer's introductory remarks, about 12 percent of those interviewed admitted to having insomnia. When a matched sample was asked the same question after two **buffer questions** (neutral questions designed chiefly to establish rapport with the participant), 23 percent admitted suffering from insomnia.[12]

buffer question neutral measurement question designed chiefly to establish rapport with the participant.

2. Which of the following attributes do you like about the automobile you just saw? (Select all that apply)
- ☑ Overall appeal
- ☑ Headroom
- ☐ Design
- ☐ Color
- ☑ Height from the ground
- ☐ Other [＿＿＿＿＿＿]
- ☐ None of the above

[Next Question]

3. For those items that you selected, how important is each? (Provide one answer for each attribute)

	Extremely important		Neither important nor not important		Not at all important	Don't know
a) Overall appeal	○	○	○	○	○	○
b) Height from the ground	○	○	○	○	○	○
c) Headroom	○	○	○	○	○	○

>picprofile

One of the attractions of using a Web survey is the ease with which participants follow branching questions immediately customized to their response patterns. In this survey, participants were shown several pictures of a prototype vehicle. Those who responded to question 2 by selecting one or more of the attributes in the checklist question were sequenced to a version of question 3 that related only to their particular responses to question 2. Note also that in question 3 the researcher chose not to force an answer, allowing the participant to indicate he or she had no opinion ("Don't know") on the issue of level importance.

Simple to Complex

Deferring complex questions or simple questions that require much thought can help reduce the number of "don't know" responses that are so prevalent early in interviews.

General to Specific

The procedure of moving from general to more specific questions is sometimes called the *funnel approach*. The objectives of this procedure are to learn the participant's frame of reference and to extract the full range of desired information while limiting the distortion effect of earlier questions on later ones. This process may be illustrated with the following series of questions:

1. How do you think this country is getting along in its relations with other countries?
2. How do you think we are doing in our relations with Iran?
3. Do you think we ought to be dealing with Iran differently than we are now?
4. (If yes) What should we be doing differently?
5. Some people say we should get tougher with Iran and others think we are too tough as it is; how do you feel about it?[13]

The first question introduces the general subject and provides some insight into the participant's frame of reference. The second question narrows the concern to a single country, while the third and fourth seek views on how the United States should deal with Iran. The fifth question illustrates a specific opinion area and would be asked only if this point of toughness had not been covered in earlier responses. Question 4 is an example of a

>**Exhibit 15-12** Question Sequencing

Question	Percent Answering Yes	
	A. Asked First	**B. Asked First**
A. Should the United States permit its citizens to join the French and British armies?	45%	40%
B. Should the United States permit its citizens to join the German army?	31	22

branched question; the response to the previous question determines whether or not question 4 is asked of the participant.

There is also a risk of interaction whenever two or more questions are related. Question-order influence is especially problematic with self-administered questionnaires, because the participant is at liberty to refer back to questions previously answered. In an attempt to "correctly align" two responses, accurate opinions and attitudes may be sacrificed. Computer-administered and Web surveys have largely eliminated this problem.

The two questions shown in Exhibit 15-12 were asked in a national survey at the start of World War II.[14] Apparently, some participants who first endorsed enlistment with the Allies felt obliged to extend this privilege to joining the German army. Where the decision was first made against joining the German army, a percentage of the participants felt constrained from approving the option to join the Allies.

> **You might find it valuable to refer to Exhibit 9-6 "The Interview Question Hierarchy," page 225.**

Question Groups and Transitions

The last question-sequencing guideline suggests arranging questions to minimize shifting in subject matter and frame of reference. Participants often interpret questions in the light of earlier questions and miss shifts of perspective or subject unless they are clearly stated. Participants fail to listen carefully and frequently jump to conclusions about the import of a given question before it is completely stated. Their answers are strongly influenced by their frame of reference. Any change in subject by the interviewer may not register with them unless it is made strong and obvious. Most questionnaires that cover a range of topics are divided into sections with clearly defined transitions between sections to alert the participant to the change in frame of reference. Exhibit 15-13 provides a sample of a transition in the MindWriter CompleteCare study when measurement questions changed from service-related questions to personal and family-related questions.

Instructions

Instructions to the interviewer or participant attempt to ensure that all participants are treated equally, thus avoiding building error into the results. Two principles form the foundation for good instructions: clarity and courtesy. Instruction language needs to be unfailingly simple and polite.

Instruction topics include those for:

• *Terminating an unqualified participant*—defining for the interviewer how to terminate an interview when the participant does not correctly answer the screen or filter questions.

• *Terminating a discontinued interview*—defining for the interviewer how to conclude an interview when the participant decides to discontinue.

• *Moving between questions on an instrument*—defining for an interviewer or participant how to move between questions or topic sections of an instrument (*skip directions*) when movement is dependent on the specific answer to a question or when branched questions are used.

  • *Disposing of a completed questionnaire*—defining for an interviewer or partici-
    pant completing a self-administered instrument how to submit the completed
    questionnaire.

In a self-administered questionnaire, instructions must be contained within the survey instrument. Personal interviewer instructions sometimes are in a document separate from the
questionnaire (a document thoroughly discussed during interviewer training) or are dis-
tinctly and clearly marked (highlighted, printed in colored ink, or boxed on the computer
screen or in a pop-up window) on the data collection instrument itself. Sample instructions
are presented in Exhibit 15-11.

Conclusion

The role of the conclusion is to leave the participant with the impression that his or her involvement has been valuable. Subsequent researchers may need this individual to participate in new studies. If every interviewer or instrument expresses appreciation for
participation, cooperation in subsequent studies is more likely. A sample conclusion is
shown in Exhibit 15-11.

Overcoming Instrument Problems

There is no substitute for a thorough understanding of question wording, question content,
and question sequencing issues. However, the researcher can do several things to help improve survey results, among them:

  • Build rapport with the participant.
  • Redesign the questioning process.
  • Explore alternative response strategies.
  • Use methods other than surveying to secure the data.
  • Pretest all the survey elements.

> **See Appendix 15b on
pretesting for coverage
of these final two
bullets.**

Build Rapport with the Participant

Most information can be secured by direct undisguised questioning if rapport has been developed. Rapport is particularly useful in building participant interest in the project, and the
more interest participants have, the more cooperation they will give. One can also overcome participant unwillingness by providing some material compensation for cooperation.
This approach has been especially successful in mail surveys and is increasingly used in
Web surveys.

The assurance of confidentiality also can increase participants' motivation. One approach is to give discrete assurances, both by question wording and interviewer comments
and actions, that all types of behavior, attitudes, and positions on controversial or sensitive
subjects are acceptable and normal. Where you can say so truthfully, guarantee that participants' answers will be used only in combined statistical totals (aggregate data), not
matched to an individual participant. If participants are convinced that their replies contribute to some important purpose, they are more likely to be candid, even about taboo topics. If a researcher's organization uses an Institutional Review Board to review surveys
before use, the board may require an instruction indicating that any response—in fact, participation—is voluntary. This is especially important where surveys are used with internal
marketing publics (employees).

Redesign the Questioning Process

You can redesign the questioning process to improve the quality of answers by modifying the administrative process and the response strategy. We might show that confidentiality is indispensable to the administration of the survey by using a group administration of questionnaires, accompanied by a ballot-box collection procedure. Even in face-to-face interviews, the participant may fill in the part of the questionnaire containing sensitive information and then seal the entire instrument in an envelope. While this does not guarantee confidentiality, it does suggest it.

We can also develop appropriate questioning sequences that will gradually lead a participant from "safe" questions to those that are more sensitive. As already noted in our discussion of disguised questions, indirect questioning (using projective techniques) is a widely used approach for securing opinions on sensitive topics. The participants are asked how "other people" or "people around here" feel about a topic. It is assumed the participants will reply in terms of their own attitudes and experiences, but this outcome is hardly certain. Indirect questioning may give a good measure of the majority opinion on a topic but fail to reflect the views either of the participant or of minority segments.

With certain topics, it is possible to secure answers by using a proxy code. When we seek family income groups, we can hand the participant a card with income brackets like these:

A. Under $25,000 per year.

B. $25,000 to $49,999 per year.

C. $50,000 to $74,999 per year.

D. $75,000 and over per year.

The participant is then asked to report the appropriate bracket as either A, B, C, or D. For some reason, participants are more willing to provide such an obvious proxy measure than to verbalize actual dollar values.

Explore Alternative Response Strategies

When drafting the original question, try developing positive, negative, and neutral versions of each type of question. This practice dramatizes the problems of bias, helping you to select question wording that minimizes such problems. Sometimes use an extreme version of a question rather than the expected one.

Minimize nonresponses to particular questions by recognizing the sensitivity of certain topics. In a self-administered instrument, for example, asking a multiple-choice question about income or age, where incomes and ages are offered in ranges, is usually more successful than using a free-response question (such as "What is your age, please? _____").

> **We discussed the use of similar unobtrusive measures in Chapter 10.**

The Value of Pretesting

The final step toward improving survey results is **pretesting,** the assessment of questions and instruments before the start of a study (see Exhibits 15-1, 15-2, and 15-10). There are abundant reasons for pretesting individual questions, questionnaires, and interview schedules: (1) discovering ways to increase participant interest, (2) increasing the likelihood that participants will remain engaged to the completion of the survey, (3) discovering question content, wording, and sequencing problems, (4) discovering target question groups where researcher training is needed, and (5) exploring ways to improve the overall quality of survey data.

pretesting the assessment of questions and instruments before the start of a study.

> **We discuss various methods of pretesting in Appendix 15b, "Pretesting Options and Discoveries."**

> Most of what we know about pretesting is prescriptive. According to contemporary authors, there are no general principles of good pretesting, no systematization of practice, no consensus about expectations, and we rarely leave records for each other. How a pretest was conducted, what investigators learned from it, how they redesigned their questionnaire on the basis of it—these matters are reported only sketchily in research reports, if at all.[15]

Nevertheless, pretesting not only is an established practice for discovering errors but also is useful for training the research team. Ironically, professionals who have participated in scores of studies are more likely to pretest an instrument than is a beginning researcher hurrying to complete a project. Revising questions five or more times is not unusual. Yet inexperienced researchers often underestimate the need to follow the design-test-revise process.

Instrument Design for MindWriter

Replacing an imprecise management question with specific measurement questions is an exercise in analytical reasoning. We described that process incrementally in the MindWriter features in Chapters 4, 6, and 14. In Chapter 4, Sara's and Jason's fact finding at MindWriter resulted in their ability to state the management dilemma in terms of management, research, and investigative questions. Adding context to the questions allowed them to construct the proposal described in Chapter 6. In Chapter 14, they returned to the list of investigative questions and selected one question to use in testing their scaling approach. Here is a brief review of the steps Jason and Sara have taken so far and the measurement questions that have resulted.

SYNOPSIS OF THE PROBLEM

MindWriter Corporation's new service and repair program for laptop computers, CompleteCare, was designed to provide a rapid response to customers' service problems. Management has received several complaints, however. Management needs information on the program's effectiveness and its impact on customer satisfaction. There is also a shortage of trained technical operators in the company's telephone center. The package courier is uneven in executing its pickup and delivery contract. Parts availability problems exist for some machine types. Occasionally, customers receive units that either are not fixed or are damaged in some way.

> *Management question:* What should be done to improve the CompleteCare program for MindWriter laptop repairs and servicing to enhance customer satisfaction?

RESEARCH QUESTIONS

1 Should the technical representatives be given more intensive training?

2 Should ABC Courier Service be replaced by an overnight air transport?

3 Should the repair diagnostic and repair sequencing operations be modified?

4 Should the return packaging be modified to include premolded rigid foam inserts, conforming-expanding foam protection, or neither?

5 Should metropolitan repair centers be established to complement or replace in-factory repair facilities?

INVESTIGATIVE QUESTIONS

a Are customers' expectations being met in terms of the time it takes to repair the systems? What is the customers' overall satisfaction with the CompleteCare service program and the MindWriter product?

b How well is the call center helping customers? Is it helping them with instructions? What percentage of customers' technical problems is it solving without callbacks or subsequent repairs? How long must customers wait on the phone?

c How good is the transportation company? Does it pick up and deliver the system responsively? How long must customers wait for pickup and delivery? Are the laptops damaged due to package handling?

d How good is the repair group? What problems are most common? What repair processes are involved in fixing these problems? For what percentage of laptops is the repair completed within the promised time limit? Are customers' problems fully resolved? Are there new problems with the newer models? How quickly are these problems diagnosed?

e How are repaired laptops packaged for return shipping? What is the cost of alternative rigid foam inserts and expandable-foam packaging? Would new equipment be required if the packaging were changed? Would certain shipping-related complaints be eliminated with new packaging materials?

The extensive scope of the research questions and resulting measurement questions forced MindWriter to reassess the scope of the desired initial research study, to determine where to concentrate its enhancement efforts. Management chose a descriptive rather than a prescriptive scope.

MEASUREMENT QUESTIONS

The measurement questions used for the self-administered package insert instrument are shown in Exhibit 15-13.[16] The first investigative question in (a), above, is addressed in survey items 3, 5, and 8a, while the second question is addressed in items 6 and 8a. Of the investigative questions in (b), the first two are addressed as "responsiveness" and "technical competence" with telephone assistance in the questionnaire. The second two investigative questions in (b) may be answered by accessing the company's service database. The questionnaire's three-part question on courier service parallels investigative question (c). Specific service deficiencies will be recorded in the "Comments/Suggestions" section. Investigative questions under (d) and (e) are covered with questionnaire items 3, 4, and 5. Since service deficiencies reflected in item 5 may be attributed to both the re-

pair facility and the courier, the reasons (items 1, 2, 3, 4, and comments) will be cross-checked during analysis. Questionnaire item 6 uses the same language as the last investigative question in (a). Questionnaire item 7 is an extension of item 6 but attempts to secure an impression of behavioral intent to use CompleteCare again. Finally, the last item will make known the extent to which change is needed in CompleteCare by revealing repurchase intention as linked to product and service experience.

> **Exhibit 15-13** Measurement Questions for the MindWriter Study

	Met **few** expectations	Met **some** expectations	Met **most** expectations	Met **all** expectations	**Exceeded** expectations
MindWriter personal computers offer you ease of use and maintenance. When you need service, we want you to rely on **CompeteCare,** wherever you may be. That's why we're asking you to take a moment to tell us how well we've served you.	1	2	3	4	5

1. Telephone assistance with your problem:
    a. Responsiveness   1   2   3   4   5
    b. Technical competence   1   2   3   4   5
2. The courier service's effectiveness:
    a. Arrangements   1   2   3   4   5
    b. Pickup speed   1   2   3   4   5
    c. Delivery speed   1   2   3   4   5
3. Speed of the overall repair process.   1   2   3   4   5
4. Resolution of the problem that prompted service/repair.   1   2   3   4   5
5. Condition of your MindWriter on arrival.   1   2   3   4   5
6. Overall impression of CompleteCare's effectiveness.   1   2   3   4   5
7. Likelihood of using CompleteCare on another occasion.
    (1 = very unlikely   3 = neither likely nor unlikely   5 = very likely)   1   2   3   4   5
8. Likelihood of repurchasing a MindWriter based on:
    (1 = very unlikely   3 = neither likely nor unlikely   5 = very likely)
    a. Service/repair experience   1   2   3   4   5
    b. Product performance   1   2   3   4   5

Comments/Suggestions: _____

How may we contact you to follow up on any problems you have experienced?

Last Name   First Name   (_____) _____ Phone

City   State   Zip

Service Code

Source: ©Cooper Research Group, Inc., 1993. Used by permission. See reference note 16.

>summary

1 The instrument design process starts with a comprehensive list of investigative questions drawn from the management–research question hierarchy. Instrument design is a three-phase process with numerous issues within each phase: (a) developing the instrument design strategy, (b) constructing and refining the measurement questions, and (c) drafting and refining the instrument.

2 Several choices must be made in designing a communication study instrument. Surveying can be a face-to-face interview, or it can be much less personal, using indirect media and self-administered questionnaires. The questioning process can be unstructured, as in an IDI, or the questions can be clearly structured. Responses may be unstructured and open-ended or structured with the participant choosing from a list of possibilities. The degree to which the objectives and intent of the questions should be disguised must also be decided.

3 Instruments obtain three general classes of information. Target questions address the investigative questions and are the most important. Classification questions concern participant characteristics and allow participants' answers to be grouped for analysis. Administrative questions identify the participant, interviewer, and interview location and conditions.

4 Question construction involves three critical decision areas. They are (a) question content, (b) question wording, and (c) response strategy. Question content should pass the following tests: Should the question be asked? Is it of proper scope? Can and will the participant answer adequately?

Question wording difficulties exceed most other sources of distortion in surveys. Retention of a question should be confirmed by answering these questions: Is the question stated in terms of a shared vocabulary? Does the vocabulary have a single meaning? Does the question contain misleading assumptions? Is the wording biased? Is it correctly personalized? Are adequate alternatives presented?

The study's objective and participant factors affect the decision of whether to use open-ended or closed questions. Each response strategy generates a specific level of data, with available statistical procedures for each scale type influencing the desired response strategy. Participant factors include level of information about the topic, degree to which the topic has been thought through, ease of communication, and motivation to share information. The decision is also affected by the interviewer's perception of participant factors.

Both dichotomous response and multiple-choice questions are valuable, but on balance the latter are preferred if only because few questions have only two possible answers. Checklist, rating, and ranking strategies are also common.

5 Question sequence can drastically affect participant willingness to cooperate and the quality of responses. Generally, the sequence should begin with efforts to awaken the participant's interest in continuing the interview. Early questions should be simple rather than complex, easy rather than difficult, nonthreatening, and obviously germane to the announced objective of the study. Frame-of-reference changes should be minimal, and questions should be sequenced so that early questions do not distort replies to later ones.

6 Sources of questions for the construction of questionnaires include the literature on related research and sourcebooks of scales and questionnaires. Borrowing items has attendant risks, such as time and situation-specific problems or reliability and validity. Incompatibility of language and idiom also needs to be considered.

>**key**terms

administrative question 398	dummy table 395	rating question 405
branched question 412	free-response question 401	recency effect 404
buffer question 413	interview schedule 398	screen question (filter question) 410
checklist 405	leading question 400	structured response 400
classification question 398	multiple-choice question 401	target question 398
dichotomous question 401	pretesting 417	structured, 398
disguised question 394	primacy effect 404	unstructured, 398
double-barreled question 403	ranking question 406	unstructured response 400

>**discussion**questions

Terms in Review

1 Distinguish between:

  a Direct and indirect questions.

  b Open-ended and closed questions.

  c Research, investigative, and measurement questions.

  d Alternative response strategies.

2 Why is the survey technique so popular? When is it not appropriate?

3 What special problems do open-ended questions have? How can these be minimized? In what situations are open-ended questions most useful?

4 Why might a researcher wish to disguise the objective of a study?

5 One of the major reasons why survey research may not be effective is that the survey instruments are less useful than they should be. What would you say are the four possible major faults of survey instrument design?

6 Why is it desirable to pretest survey instruments? What information can you secure from such a pretest? How can you find the best wording for a question on a questionnaire?

7 One design problem in the development of survey instruments concerns the sequence of questions. What suggestions would you give to researchers designing their first questionnaire?

8 One of the major problems facing the designer of a survey instrument concerns the assumptions made. What are the major "problem assumptions"?

Making Research Decisions

9 Below are six questions that might be found on questionnaires. Comment on each as to whether or not it is a good question. If it is not, explain why. (Assume that no lead-in or screening questions are required. Judge each question on its own merits.)

a Do you read *National Geographic* magazine regularly?

b What percentage of your time is spent asking for information from others in your organization?

c When did you first start chewing gum?

d How much discretionary buying power do you have each year?

e Why did you decide to attend Big State University?

f Do you think the president is doing a good job now?

10 In a class project, students developed a brief self-administered questionnaire by which they might quickly evaluate a professor. One student submitted the following instrument. Evaluate the questions asked and the format of the instrument.

Professor Evaluation Form

1. Overall, how would you rate this professor?
   ☐ Good   ☐ Fair   ☐ Poor

2. Does this professor
   a. Have good class delivery? _____
   b. Know the subject? _____
   c. Have a positive attitude toward the subject? _____
   d. Grade fairly? _____
   e. Have a sense of humor? _____
   f. Use audiovisuals, case examples, or other classroom aids? _____
   g. Return exams promptly? _____

3. What is the professor's strongest point? _____
4. What is the professor's weakest point? _____
5. What kind of class does the professor teach? _____
6. Is this course required? _____

7. Would you take another course from this professor? _____

11 Assume the American Society of Training Directors is studying its membership in order to enhance member benefits and attract new members. Below is a copy of a cover letter and mail questionnaire received by a member of the society. Please evaluate the usefulness and tone of the letter and the questions and format of the instrument.

Dear ASTD Member:

The ASTD is evaluating the perception of value of membership among its members. Enclosed is a short questionnaire and a return envelope. I hope you will take a few minutes and fill out the questionnaire as soon as possible, as the sooner the information is returned to me, the better.

Sincerely,

Director of Membership

Questionnaire

Directions: Please answer as briefly as possible.

1. With what company did you enter the field of training? _____
2. How long have you been in the field of training? _____
3. How long have you been in the training department of the company with which you are presently employed? _____
4. How long has the training department in your company been in existence? _____
5. Is the training department a subset of another department? If so, what department? _____
6. For what functions (other than training) is your department responsible? _____
7. How many people, including yourself, are in the training department of your company (local plant or establishment)? _____
8. What degrees do you hold and from what institutions? _____
   Major _____   Minor _____
9. Why were you chosen for training? What special qualifications prompted your entry into training? _____
10. What experience would you consider necessary for an individual to enter into the field of training with your company? Include both educational requirements and actual experience. _____

Behind the Scenes

12 Design the introduction of the Albany Outpatient Laser Clinic survey, assuming it will continue to be a self-administered questionnaire.

13 To evaluate whether presurgery patient attitudes affect recovery and ultimate patient satisfaction with the Albany Outpatient Laser Clinic, design a question for the self-administered survey. (You may wish to review the Behind the Scenes vignettes in this chapter and Chapter 11.)

From Concept to Practice

14 Using Exhibits 15-1, 15-4, and 15-10, develop the flowchart for the Albany Outpatient Laser Clinic study in the opening vignette.

>**www**exercises

1 Volunteer to participate in a survey on the Web. You can use a search engine to find such sites (Keyword: *survey panel*), or visit http://www.dreamwater.org/surveys/ and click on the links provided to such panels as Greenfield Online and NFO. What questionnaire design decisions were made for the survey you took?

2 You can experience a sample Web survey by visiting the InsightExpress shared surveys Web page (http://www.insightexpress.com). Look for "Topline Reports," and click on "access results now."

>**cases***

Can Research Rescue the Red Cross?	Starbucks, Bank One, and Visa Launch Starbucks Duetto Visa
Inquiring Minds Want to Know—NOW!	
	T-Shirt Designs
KNSD San Diego	USTA: Come Out Swinging
Mastering Teacher Leadership	
	Volkswagen's Beetle
NCRCC: Teeing Up and New Strategic Direction	
Pebble Beach Co.	

* All cases, both written and video, are on the text DVD. The film icon indicates a video case. Check the DVD Index to determine whether a case has data, the research instrument, or other supplementary material.

Crafting Effective Measurement Questions

Numerous issues influence whether the questions we ask on questionnaires generate the decision-making data that marketing decision-makers sorely need. Each of the issues summarized in Exhibit 15-5 is developed more fully here.

Question Content

Should This Question Be Asked?

Purposeful versus Interesting   Questions that merely produce "interesting information" cannot be justified on either economic or research grounds. Challenge each question's function. Does it contribute significant information toward answering the research question? Will its omission limit or prevent the thorough analysis of other data? Can we infer the answer from another question? A good question designer knows the value of learning more from fewer questions.

Is the Question of Proper Scope and Coverage?

Incomplete or Unfocused   We can test this content issue by asking, "Will this question reveal all we need to know?" We sometimes ask participants to reveal their motivations for particular behaviors or attitudes by asking them, "Why?" This simple question is inadequate to probe the range of most causal relationships. When studying product use behavior, for example, we learn more by directing two or three questions on product use to the heavy-use consumer and only one question to the light user.

Questions are also inadequate if they do not provide the information you need to interpret responses fully. If you ask about the Albany clinic's image for quality patient care, do different groups of patients or those there for the first versus the third time have different attitudes? To evaluate relative attitudes, do you need to ask the same question about other companies? In the original Albany clinic survey, participants were asked, "Have you ever had or been treated for a recent cold or flu?" If participants answer yes, what exactly have they told the researcher that would be of use to the eye surgeon? Wouldn't it be likely that the surgeon is interested in medication taken to treat colds or flu within, say, the prior 10 days? This question also points to two other problems of scope and coverage: the double-barreled question and the imprecise question.

Double-Barreled Questions   Does the question request so much content that it should be broken into two or more questions? While reducing the overall number of questions in a study is highly desirable, don't try to ask double-barreled questions. The Albany clinic question about flu ("Have you ever had or been treated for a recent cold or flu?") fires more than two barrels. It asks four questions in all (Ever had cold? Ever had flu? Been treated for cold? Been treated for flu?).

Here's another common example posed to menswear retailers: "Are this year's shoe sales and gross profits higher than last year's?" Couldn't sales be higher with stagnant profits, or profits higher with level or lower sales? This second example is more typical of the problem of double-barreled questions.

A less obvious double-barreled question is the question we ask to identify a family's or a group's TV station preference. Since a single station is unlikely, a better question would ask the station preference of each family member separately or, alternatively, screen for the group member who most often controls channel selection on Monday evenings during prime time. Also, it's highly probable that no one station would serve as an individual's preferred station when we cover a wide range of time (8 to 11 p.m.). This reveals another problem, the imprecise question.

Precision   To test a question for precision, ask, "Does the question ask precisely what we want and need to know?" We sometimes ask for a participant's income when we really want to know the family's total annual income before taxes in the past calendar year. We ask what a participant purchased "last week" when we really want to know what he or she purchased in a "typical 7-day period during the past 90 days." The Albany clinic's patients were asked for cold and flu history during the time frame "ever." It is hard to imagine an adult who has never experienced a cold or flu and equally hard to assume an adult hasn't been treated for one or both at some time in his or her life.

A second precision issue deals with common vocabulary between researcher and participant. To test your question for this problem, ask, "Do I need to offer operational definitions of concepts and constructs used in the question?"

Can the Participant Answer Adequately?

Time for Thought   Although the question may address the topic, is it asked in such a way that the participant will be able to frame an answer, or is it reasonable to assume that the participant can determine the answer? This is also a question that drives sample design, but once the ideal sample unit is determined, researchers often assume that participants who fit the sample profile have all the answers, preferably on the tips of their tongues. To frame a response to some questions takes time and thought; such questions are best left to self-administered questionnaires.

Participation at the Expense of Accuracy   Participants typically want to cooperate in interviews; thus they assume giving any answer is more helpful than denying knowledge of a topic. Their desire to impress the interviewer may encourage them to give answers based on no information. A classic illustration of this problem occurred with the following question:[1] "Which of the following statements most closely coincides with your opinion of the Metallic Metals Act?" The response pattern shows that 70 percent of those interviewed had a fairly clear opinion of the Metallic Metals Act; however, there is no such act. The participants apparently assumed that if a question was asked, they should provide an answer. Given reasonable-sounding choices, they selected one even though they knew nothing about the topic.

To counteract this tendency to respond at any cost, *filter* or *screen questions* are used to qualify a participant's knowledge. If the MindWriter service questionnaire is distributed via mail to all recent purchasers of MindWriter products, we might ask, "Have you required service for your laptop since its purchase?" Only those for whom service was provided could supply the detail and scope of the responses indicated in the investigative question list. If such a question is asked in a phone interview, we would call the question a *screen,* because it is being used to determine whether the person on the other end of the phone line is a qualified sample unit. This same question asked on a computer-administered questionnaire would likely *branch* or *skip* the participant to a series of classification questions.

Assuming that participants have prior knowledge or understanding may be risky. The risk is getting many answers that have little basis in fact. The Metallic Metals Act illustration may be challenged as unusual, but in another case a Gallup report revealed that 45 percent of the persons surveyed did not know what a "lobbyist in Washington" was and 88 percent could not give a correct description of "jurisdictional strike."[2] This points to the need for operational definitions as part of question wording.

Presumed Knowledge   The question designer should consider the participants' information level when determining the content and appropriateness of a question. In some studies, the degree of participant expertise can be substantial, and simplified explanations are inappropriate and discourage participation. In asking the public about gross margins in menswear stores, we would want to be sure the "general-public" participant understands the nature of "gross margin." If our sample unit were a merchant, explanations might not be needed. A high level of knowledge among our sample units, however, may not eliminate the need for operational definitions. Among merchants, gross margin per unit in dollars is commonly accepted as the difference between cost and selling price; but when offered as a percentage rather than a dollar figure, it can be calculated as a percentage of unit selling price or as a percentage of unit cost. A participant answering from the "cost" frame of reference would calculate gross margin at 100 percent; another participant, using the same dollars and the "selling price" frame of reference, would calculate gross margin at 50 percent. If a construct is involved and differing interpretations of a concept are feasible, operational definitions may still be needed.

Recall and Memory Decay   The adequacy problem also occurs when you ask questions that overtax participants' recall ability. People cannot recall much that has happened in their past, unless it was dramatic. Your mother may remember everything about your arrival if you were her first child: the weather, time of day, even what she ate prior to your birth. If you have several siblings, her memory of subsequent births may be less complete. If the events surveyed are of incidental interest to participants, they will probably be unable to recall them correctly even a short time later. An unaided recall question, "What radio programs did you listen to last night?" might identify as few as 10 percent of those individuals who actually listened to a program.[3]

Balance (General versus Specific)   Answering adequacy also depends on the proper balance between generality and specificity. We often ask questions in terms too general and detached from participants' experiences. Asking for average annual consumption of a product may make an unrealistic demand for generalization on people who do not think in such terms. Why not ask how often the product was used last week or last month? Too often participants are asked to recall individual use experiences over an extended time and to average them for us. This is asking participants to do the researcher's work and encourages substantial response errors. It may also contribute to a higher refusal rate and higher discontinuation rate.

There is a danger in being too narrow in the time frame applied to behavior questions. We may ask about movie attendance for the last seven days, although this is too short a time span on which to base attendance estimates. It may be better to ask about attendance, say, for the last 30 days. There are no firm rules about this generality-specificity problem. Developing the right level of general-

>**Exhibit 15a-1** A Test of Alternative Response Strategies

A. What is your favorite brand of ice cream? _____

B. Some people have a favorite brand of ice cream, while others do not have a favorite brand. In which group are you? (please check)

    ❑ I do not have a favorite brand of ice cream.

    ❑ I have a favorite brand of ice cream.

What is your favorite (if you have a favorite)? _____

>**Exhibit 15a-2** Results of Alternative Response Strategies Test

Response	Version A	Version B
Named a favorite brand	77%*	39%*
Named a favorite flavor rather than a brand	19	18
Had no favorite brand	4	43
Total	100%	100%
	n = 57	*n* = 56

*Significant difference at the 0.001 level.

ity depends on the subject, industry, setting, and experience of the question designer.

Objectivity The ability of participants to answer adequately is also often distorted by questions whose content is biased by what is included or omitted. The question may explicitly mention only the positive or negative aspects of the topic or make unwarranted assumptions about the participant's position. Consider Exhibit 15a-1, an experiment in which two forms of a question were asked. Fifty-seven randomly chosen graduate business students answered version A, and 56 answered version B. Their responses are shown in Exhibit 15a-2. The probable cause of the difference in level of brand preference expressed is that A is an unsupported assumption. It assumes and suggests that everyone has a favorite brand of ice cream and will report it. Version B indicates the participant need not have a favorite.

A deficiency in both versions is that about one participant in five misinterpreted the meaning of the term *brand*. This misinterpretation cannot be attributed to low education, low intelligence, lack of exposure to the topic, or quick or lazy reading of the question. The subjects were students who had taken at least one course in marketing in which branding was prominently treated.*

*Word confusion difficulties are discussed later in this appendix.

Will the Participants Answer Willingly?

Sensitive Information Even if participants have the information, they may be unwilling to give it. Some topics are considered too sensitive to discuss with strangers. These vary from person to person, but one study suggests the most sensitive topics concern money matters and family life.[4] More than one-fourth of those interviewed mentioned these as the topics about which they would be "least willing to answer questions." Participants of lower socioeconomic status also included political matters in this "least willing" list.

Participants also may be unwilling to give correct answers for ego reasons. Many exaggerate their incomes, the number of cars they own, their social status, and the amount of high-prestige literature they read. They also minimize their age and the amount of low-prestige literature they read. Many participants are reluctant to try to give an adequate response. Often this will occur when they see the topic as irrelevant to their own interests or to their perception of the survey's purpose. They participate halfheartedly, often answer with "don't know," give negative replies, give stereotypical responses, or refuse to be interviewed.

You can learn more about crafting questions dealing with sensitive information by reading the DVD Close-up "Measuring Attitudes on Sensitive Subjects."

Question Wording

Shared Vocabulary Because surveying is an exchange of ideas between interviewer and participant, each must understand what the other says, and this is possible only if the vocabulary used is common to both parties.[5] Two problems arise. First, the words must be simple enough to allow adequate communication with persons of limited education. This is dealt with by reducing the level of word difficulty to simple English words and phrases (more is said about this in the section on word clarity).

Technical language is the second issue. Even highly educated participants cannot answer questions stated in unfamiliar technical terms. Technical language also poses difficulties for interviewers. In one study of how corporation executives handled various financial problems, interviewers had to be conversant with technical financial terms. This necessity presented the researcher with two alternatives—hiring people knowledgeable in finance and teaching them interviewing skills or teaching financial concepts to experienced interviewers.[6] This vocabulary problem also exists where similar or identical studies are conducted in different countries and multiple languages.

A great obstacle to effective question wording is the choice of words. Questions to be asked of the public should be restricted to the 2,000 most common words in the English language.[7] Even the use of simple words is not enough. Many words have vague references or meanings that must be gleaned from their context. In a repair study, technicians were asked, "How many radio sets did you repair last month?" This question may seem unambiguous, but participants interpreted it in two ways. Some viewed it as a question of them alone; others interpreted "you" more inclusively, as referring to the total output of the shop. There is also the possibility of misinterpreting "last month," depending on the timing of the questioning. Using "during the last 30 days" would be much more precise and unambiguous. Typical of the many problem words are these: *any, could, would, should, fair, near, often, average,* and *regular.* One author recommends that after stating a question as precisely as possible, we should test each word against this checklist:

- Does the word chosen mean what we intend?
- Does the word have multiple meanings? If so, does the context make the intended meaning clear?
- Does the word chosen have more than one pronunciation? Is there any word with similar pronunciation with which the chosen word might be confused?
- Is a simpler word or phrase suggested or possible?[8]

We cause other problems when we use abstract concepts that have many overtones or emotional qualifications.[9] Without concrete referents, meanings are too vague

for the researcher's needs. Examples of such words are *business, government,* and *society.*

Shared vocabulary issues are addressed by using the following:

- Simple rather than complex words.
- Commonly known, unambiguous words.
- Precise words.
- Interviewers with content knowledge.

Unsupported Assumptions Unwarranted assumptions contribute to many problems of question wording. A metropolitan newspaper, *Midwest Daily,* conducted a study in an attempt to discover what readers would like in its redesigned lifestyle section. One notable question asked readers: "Who selects your clothes? You or the man in your life?" In this age of educated, working, independent women, the question managed to offend a significant portion of the female readership. In addition, *Midwest Daily* discovered that many of its female readers were younger than researchers originally assumed and the only man in their lives was their father, not the spousal or romantic relationship alluded to by the questions that followed. Once men reached this question, they assumed that the paper was interested in serving only the needs of female readers. The unwarranted assumptions built into the questionnaire caused a significantly smaller response rate than expected and caused several of the answers to be uninterpretable.

Frame of Reference Inherent in word meaning problems is also the matter of a frame of reference. Each of us understands concepts, words, and expressions in light of our own experience. The U.S. Bureau of the Census wanted to know how many people were in the labor market. To learn whether a person was employed, it asked, "Did you do any work for pay or profit last week?" The researchers erroneously assumed there would be a common frame of reference between the interviewer and participants on the meaning of *work.* Unfortunately, many persons viewed themselves primarily or foremost as homemakers or students. They failed to report that they also worked at a job during the week. This difference in frame of reference resulted in a consistent underestimation of the number of people working in the United States.

In a subsequent version of the study, this question was replaced by two questions, the first of which sought a statement on the participant's major activity during the week. If the participant gave a nonwork classification, a second question was asked to determine if he or she had done any work for pay besides this major activity. This revision increased the estimate of total employment by more than 1 million people, half of them working 35 hours or more per week.[10]

The frame of reference can be controlled in two ways. First, the interviewer may seek to learn the frame of refer-

> **Exhibit 15a-3** Split Test of Alternative Question Wording

Should the United States do any of the following at this time?

    A. Increase our armed forces further, even if it means more taxes.

Should the United States do any of the following at this time?

    B. Increase our armed forces further, even if you have to pay a special tax.

Eighty-eight percent of those answering question A thought the armed forces should be increased, while only 79 percent of those answering question B favored increasing the armed forces.

Source: Hadley Cantril, ed. *Gauging Public Opinion* (Princeton, NJ: Princeton University Press, 1944), p. 48.

ence used by the participant. When asking participants to evaluate their reasons for judging a retail store as unattractive, the interviewer must learn the frames of reference they use. Is the store being evaluated in terms of its particular features and layout, the failure of management to respond to a complaint made by the participant, the preference of the participant for another store, or the participant's recent difficulty in returning an unwanted item?

Second, it is useful to specify the frame of reference for the participant. In asking for an opinion about the new store design, the interviewer might specify that the question should be answered based on the participant's opinion of the layout, the clarity and placement of signage, the ease of finding merchandise, or another frame of reference.

Biased Wording Bias is the distortion of responses in one direction. It can result from many of the problems already discussed, but word choice is often the major source. Obviously such words or phrases as *politically correct* or *fundamentalist* must be used with great care. Strong adjectives can be particularly distorting. One alleged opinion survey concerned with the subject of preparation for death included the following question: "Do you think that decent, low-cost funerals are sensible?" Who could be against anything that is *decent* or *sensible?* There is a question about whether this was a legitimate survey or a burial service sales campaign, but it shows how suggestive an adjective can be.

Congressional representatives have been known to use surveys as a means of communicating with their constituencies. Questions are worded, however, to imply the issue stance that the representative favors. Can you tell the representative's stance in the following question?

Example: Would you have me vote for a balanced budget if it means higher costs for the supplemental Social Security benefits which you have already earned?

We can also strongly bias the participant by using prestigious names in a question. In a historic survey on whether

the war and navy departments should be combined into a single defense department, one survey said, "General Eisenhower says the army and navy should be combined," while the other version omitted his name. Given the first version (name included), 49 percent of the participants approved of having one department; given the second version, only 29 percent favored one department.[11] Just imagine using Michael Jordan's or Shaq O'Neill's name in a survey question asked of teen boys interested in basketball. The power of aspirational reference groups to sway opinion and attitude is well established in advertising; it shouldn't be underestimated in survey design.

We also can bias response through the use of superlatives, slang expressions, and fad words. These are best excluded unless they are critical to the objective of the question. Ethnic references should also be stated with care.

Personalization How personalized should a question be? Should we ask, "What would you do about . . . ?" Or should we ask, "What would people with whom you work do about . . . ?" The effect of personalization is shown in a classic example reported by Cantril.[12] A split test—where a portion of the sample received one question, with another portion receiving a second question—was made of a question concerning attitudes about the expansion of U.S. armed forces in 1940, as noted in Exhibit 15a-3.

These and other examples show that personalizing questions changes responses, but the direction of the influence is not clear. We cannot tell whether personalization or no personalization is superior. Perhaps the best that can be said is that when either form is acceptable, we should choose that which appears to present the issues more realistically. If there are doubts, then split survey versions should be used (one segment of the sample should get one question version, while a second segment should receive the alternative question version).

Adequate Alternatives Have we adequately expressed the alternatives with respect to the purpose of the question? It is usually wise to express each alternative

>**Exhibit 15a-4** Expressing Alternatives

The way a question is asked can influence the results. Consider these two alternative questions judging companies' images in the community in the face of layoffs:

A. Do you think most manufacturing companies that lay off workers during slack periods could arrange things to avoid layoffs and give steady work right through the year?

B. Do you think most manufacturing companies that lay off workers in slack periods could avoid layoffs and provide steady work right through the year, or do you think layoffs are unavoidable?

The Results

When Asked . . .	A	B
Company could avoid layoffs	63%	35%
Could not avoid layoffs	22	41
No opinion	15	24

Source: Hadley Cantril, ed. *Gauging Public Opinion* (Princeton, NJ: Princeton University Press, 1944), p. 48.

explicitly to avoid bias. This is illustrated well with a pair of questions that were asked of matched samples of participants.[13] The question forms that were used are noted in Exhibit 15a-4.

Often the above issues are simultaneously present in a single question. Exhibit 15a-5 reveals several questions drawn from actual mail surveys. We've identified the problem issues and suggest one solution for improvement. While the suggested improvement might not be the only possible solution, it does correct the issues identified. What other solutions could be applied to correct the problems identified?

Response Strategy

The objectives of the study; characteristics of participants, especially their level of information, level of motivation to participate, and ease of communication; the nature of the topic(s) being studied; the type of scale needed; and your analysis plan dictate the response strategy. Examples of the strategies described in Chapter 15 and discussed in detail in Chapters 13 and 14 are found in Exhibit 15-6.

Objective of the Study If the objective of the question is only to classify the participant on some stated point of view, then the closed question will serve well. Assume you are interested only in whether a participant approves or disapproves of a certain corporate policy. A closed question will provide this answer. This response strategy ignores the full scope of the participant's opinion and the events that helped shape the attitude at its foundation. If

the objective is to explore this wider territory, then an open-ended question (free-response strategy) is preferable.

Open-ended questions are appropriate when the objective is to discover opinions and degrees of knowledge. They are also appropriate when the interviewer seeks sources of information, dates of events, and suggestions or when probes are used to secure more information. When the topic of a question is outside the participant's experience, the open-ended question may offer the better way to learn his or her level of information. Closed questions are better when there is a clear frame of reference, the participant's level of information is predictable, and the researcher believes the participant understands the topic.

Open-ended questions also help to uncover certainty of feelings and expressions of intensity, although well-designed closed questions can do the same.

Thoroughness of Prior Thought If a participant has developed a clear opinion on the topic, a closed question does well. If an answer has not been thought out, an open-ended question may give the participant a chance to ponder a reply, and then elaborate on and revise it.

Communication Skill Open-ended questions require a stronger grasp of vocabulary and a greater ability to frame responses than do closed questions.

Participant Motivation Experience has shown that closed questions typically require less motivation and answering them is less threatening to participants. But the response alternatives sometimes suggest which answer is appropriate; for this reason, closed questions may be biased.

>Exhibit 15a-5 Reconstructing Questions

	Poor Measurement Question	Improved Measurement Question
Problems: Checklist appears to offer options that are neither exhaustive nor mutually exclusive. Also, it doesn't fully address the content needs of understanding why people choose a hotel when they travel for personal reasons versus business reasons. **Solution:** Organize the alternatives. Create subsets within choices; use color or shading to highlight subsets. For coding ease, expand the alternatives so the participant does not frequently choose "Other."	If your purpose for THIS hotel stay included personal pleasure, for what ONE purpose specifically? ❑ Visit friend/relative ❑ Weekend escape ❑ Sporting event ❑ Sightseeing ❑ Family event ❑ Vacation ❑ Other: _____	Which reason BEST explains your purpose for THIS personal pleasure hotel stay? ❑ Dining ❑ Shopping ❑ Entertainment 　. . . was this for a . . . ❑ Sport-related event? 　　　　　　　❑ Theater, musical, or other performance? 　　　　　　　❑ Museum or exhibit? ❑ Visit friend/relative 　. . . was this for a special event? ❑ YES ❑ NO ❑ Vacation 　. . . was this primarily for . . . ❑ Sightseeing? 　　　　　　　❑ Weekend escape? ❑ Other: _____
Problems: Double-barreled question; no time frame for the behavior; "frequently" is an undefined construct for eating behavior; depending on the study's purpose, "order" is not as powerful a concept for measurement as others (e.g., purchase, consume, or eat). **Solution :** Split the questions; expand the response alternatives; clearly define the construct you want to measure.	When you eat out, do you frequently order appetizers and dessert? ❑ YES　　❑ NO	Considering your personal eating experiences away from home in the last 30 days, did you purchase an appetizer or dessert more than half the time? 　　　　　　More Than　　Less Than 　　　　　　Half the Time　Half the Time Purchased 　an appetizer　　❑　　　　❑ 　a dessert　　　❑　　　　❑ ❑ Purchased neither appetizers nor desserts.
Problem: Nonspecific time frame; likely to experience memory decay; nonspecific screen (not asking what you really need to know to qualify a participant). **Solution :** Replace "ever" with a more appropriate time frame; screen for the desired behavior.	Have you ever attended a college basketball game? ❑ YES　　❑ NO	In the last six months, have you been a spectator at a basketball game played by college teams on a college campus? ❑ YES　　　❑ NO
Problem: Question faces serious memory decay as a coat may not be purchased each year; isn't asking if the coat was a personal purchase or for someone else; nor do you know the type of coat purchased; nor do you know whether the coat was purchased for full price or at a discount. **Solution:** Limit the time frame; specify the coat type.	How much did you pay for the last coat you purchased?	Did you purchase a dress coat for your personal use in the last 60 days? ❑ YES　　　❑ NO 　Thinking of this dress coat, how much did you pay? (to the nearest dollar) $ _____.00 　Was this coat purchase made at a discounted price? ❑ YES　　　❑ NO

While the open-ended question offers many advantages, closed questions are generally preferable in large surveys. They reduce the variability of response, make fewer demands on interviewer skills, are less costly to administer, and are much easier to code and analyze. After adequate exploration and testing, we can often develop closed questions that will perform as effectively as open-ended questions in many situations. Experimental studies suggest that closed questions are equal or superior to open-ended questions in many more applications than is commonly believed.[14]

Pretesting Options and Discoveries

Pretesting is a critical activity for successful development of a survey. We explore here the purposes and methods for effectively pretesting questions and instruments.

Pretesting Options

There are various types of pretesting that can be used to refine an instrument. They range from obtaining informal reviews by colleagues to creating conditions similar to those of the final study.

Researcher Pretesting

Designers typically test informally in the initial stages and build more structure into the tests along the way. Fellow instrument designers can do the first-level pretest. One way to accomplish this is to have researchers divided into teams. One team writes the survey, while the other critically reviews it. The reviewers' and researchers' many differences of opinion are likely to create numerous suggestions for improvement. Usually at least two or three drafts can be effectively developed by bringing research colleagues into the process.

Participant Pretesting

Participant pretests require that the questionnaire be field-tested by sample participants or participant surrogates (individuals with characteristics and backgrounds similar to those of the desired participants).

Field pretests involve distributing the test instrument exactly as the actual instrument will be distributed. Most studies use two or more pretests. National projects may use one trial to examine local reaction and another to check for regional differences. Although many researchers try to keep pretest conditions and times close to what they expect for the actual study, personal interview and telephone limitations make it desirable to test in the evenings or on weekends in order to interview people who are not available for contact at other times.

Test mailings are useful, but it is often faster to use a substitute procedure. In the MindWriter example, the managers who were interviewed in the exploratory study were later asked to review the pilot questionnaire. The interviewers left them alone and returned later. Upon their return, they went over the questions with each manager.

They explained that they wanted the manager's reactions to question clarity and ease of answering. After several such interviews, the instrument was revised and the testing process was repeated with customers. With minor revision, the questionnaire was reproduced and prepared for insertion into the computer packing material.

Collaborative Pretests

Different approaches taken by interviewers and the participants' awareness of those approaches affect the pretest. If the researcher alerts participants to their involvement in a preliminary test of the questionnaire, the participants are essentially being enlisted as collaborators in the refinement process. Under these conditions, detailed probing of the parts of the question, including phrases and words, is appropriate. Because of the time required for probing and discussion, it is likely that only the most critical questions will be reviewed. The participant group may therefore need to be conscripted from colleagues and friends to secure the additional time and motivation needed to cover an entire questionnaire. If friends or associates are used, experience suggests that they introduce more bias than strangers, argue more about wording, and generally make it more difficult to accomplish other goals of pretesting such as timing the length of questions or sections.[1]

Occasionally, a highly experienced researcher may improvise questions during a pretest. When this occurs, it is essential to record the interview or take detailed notes so that the questionnaire may be reconstructed later. Ultimately, a team of interviewers would be required to follow the interview schedule's prearranged sequence of questions. Only experienced investigators should be free to depart from the interview schedule during a pretest and explore participants' answers by adding probes.

Noncollaborative Pretests

When the researcher does not inform the participant that the activity is a pretest, it is still possible to probe for reactions but without the cooperation and commitment of time provided by collaborators. The comprehensiveness of the effort also suffers because of flagging cooperation. The virtue of this approach is that the questionnaire can be tested under conditions approaching those of the final study. This realism is similarly useful for training interviewers.

Pretesting Discoveries

Participant Interest   An important purpose of pretesting is to discover participants' reactions to the questions. If participants do not find the experience stimulating when an interviewer is physically present, how will they react on the phone or in the self-administered mode? Pretesting helps discover where repetitiveness or redundancy is bothersome or what topics were not covered that the participant expected. An alert interviewer will look for questions or groups of questions that the participant perceives to be sensitive or threatening or topics about which the participant knows nothing.

Meaning   Questions that we borrow or adapt from the work of others carry an authoritativeness that may prompt us to avoid pretesting them, but they are often most in need of examination. Are they still timely? Is the language relevant? Do they need context from adjacent questions? Newly constructed questions should be similarly checked for meaningfulness to the participant. Does the question evoke the same meaning as that intended by the researcher? How different is the researcher's frame of reference from that of the average participant? Words and phrases that trigger a "what do you mean?" response from the participant need to be singled out for further refinement.

Question Transformation   Participants do not necessarily process every word in the question. They also may not share the same definitions for the terms they hear. When this happens, participants modify the question to make it fit their own frame of reference or simply change it so that it makes sense to them. Probing is necessary to discover how participants have transformed the question when this is suspected.[2]

Continuity and Flow   In self-administered questionnaires, questions should read effortlessly and flow from one to another and from one section to another. In personal and telephone interviews, the sound of the question and its transition must be fluid as well. A long set of questions with 9-point scales that worked well in a mail instrument would not be effective on the telephone unless you were to ask participants to visualize the scale as the touch keys on their phone. Moreover, transitions that may appear redundant in a self-administered questionnaire may be exactly what needs to be heard in personal or telephone interviewing.

Question Sequence   Question arrangement can play a significant role in the success of the instrument. Research authorities recommend starting with stimulating questions and placing sensitive questions last. Since questions concerning income and family life are most likely to be refused, this is good advice for building trust before getting to classification questions that might lead to a refusal situation. However, interest-building questions need to be tested first to be sure they are stimulating. Pretesting with a large enough sample of participants permits some experimentation with question sequence.

Skip Instructions   In interviews and questionnaires, skip patterns and their contingency sequences may not work as envisioned on paper. Skip instructions are designed to route or sequence the participant to another question contingent on his or her answer to the previous question *(branched questions)*. Pretesting in the field helps to identify problems with skip instructions or symbols (e.g., box-and-arrow schematic) that the designers may not have thought of. By correcting these instructions in the revision stage, we also avoid problems with flow and continuity.

Variability   Making sure that question alternatives cover the range of possible participant answers is an important purpose of pretesting. With 25 to 100 participants in the pretest sample, statistical data on the proportion of participants answering yes or no or marking "strongly agree" to "strongly disagree" can supplement the qualitative assessment provided by the pretest interviewers. This information is useful for sample size calculations and for getting preliminary indications of reliability problems with scaled questions. When using a very small pretest sample of participants, pretesting cannot provide definitive quantitative conclusions. Small samples can, however, deliver an early warning about survey questions that may not discriminate among participants or can identify sections of the survey where meaningful subgrouping may occur in the final sample.

Length and Timing   Most draft questionnaires or interview schedules suffer from lengthiness. By timing each question and section, the researcher is in a better position to make decisions about modifying or cutting material. In personal and telephone interviews, labor is a project expense. Thus, if the budget influences the final length of the questionnaire, an accurate estimate of elapsed time is essential. Videotaped or audiotaped pretests may also be used for this purpose. Their function in reducing errors in data recording is widely accepted.

When Surveying Doesn't Work   Sometimes surveying will not secure the information needed. A classic example concerns a survey conducted to discover magazines read by participants. An unusually high rate was reported for prestigious magazines, and an unusually low rate was reported for tabloid magazines. The study was revised so that the subjects, instead of being interviewed, were asked to contribute their old magazines to a charity drive (an observation study). The collection gave a more realistic estimate of readership of both types of magazines.[3]

Most researchers have found that the survey is a very powerful tool in their research methods arsenal. It is only a matter of careful attention to detail and practice that will have you joining their ranks.

>chapter 16

Basic Sampling Concepts

>learningobjectives

After reading this chapter, you should understand . . .

1 The two premises on which sampling theory is based.

2 The characteristics of accuracy and precision for measuring sample validity.

3 The five questions that must be answered to develop a sampling plan.

4 The two categories of sampling techniques and the variety of sampling techniques within each category.

5 The various sampling techniques and when each is used.

Marketing research is a fairly small professional community. Within a given company, other than research specialists, few trained researchers may be found, making collaboration necessary. Researchers from different companies often share their experiences at professional conferences in an attempt to advance the industry as a whole. As a result, researchers are often privy to each other's successes as well as their failures. They use each other's mistakes to improve their own projects.

"The ideal participant is thoughtful, articulate, rational, and, above all, cooperative. Real people, however, are fractious, stubborn, ill-informed, and even perverse. Nevertheless they are who you have to work with," muses Jason as he and Sara hammer out the details of the Glacier Symphony sampling plan.

"Sam Champion, marketing director for CityBus," shares Sara, "certainly had sampling problems. He allowed a novice researcher—Eric Burbidge—to do the sampling to determine where the company could most effectively promote its new daily route schedule. Its big problem was a small budget and riders from two separate cities, where two different papers had substantial circulations—and just as substantial advertising rates. CityBus was hoping to advertise in only one paper. But the newspapers didn't have circulation figures by specific news vending boxes. Champion told the tale at the last MRA luncheon.

"It seems Burbidge was inexperienced enough to try to answer CityBus's question of which newspaper to use for ads by conducting a survey on one bus that runs between the two cities during evening rush hour. Burbidge boards the bus on route 99 and tells the driver he's from headquarters and there to do an official survey during the evening ride." Sara pauses for effect and lowers her voice to mimic a base frog. "I need to test my hypothesis that readership of newspapers on route 99 is equally divided between the *East City Gazette* and the *West City Tribune*."

Jason, now interested, interrupts, "He said that to a busload of passengers?"

"Well, no, the passengers hadn't yet boarded. The way Champion told the story, Burbidge barged his way to the front of the line and rapped his clipboard on the door to gain entry before any of the passengers could board. He said that to the driver.

"Anyway, Burbidge distributes his questionnaires, and the passengers diligently complete them and bring them forward to where Burbidge sits at the front of the bus. And then they start to play paper-ball hockey in the aisle of the bus."

"Paper-ball hockey?" questions Jason.

"Evidently they wad the newspapers they have been reading while waiting for the bus into balls and bat them through the legs of self-appointed goalies at each end of the bus aisle. Anyway, the driver tells Burbidge that since East City Club plays hockey that night that when he cleans out the bus most of the newspapers will be the *East City Gazette*. The riders evidently like to study the night's pro game in advance, so newsstand sales are brisk in the terminal, but only for the newspaper that does the better job of covering the sport *du jour*. Of course the next night, the riders would be buying the *West City Tribune* because it does a better job of covering pro basketball.

"Burbidge is upset and mumbles something about the survey asking for the paper most recently purchased. The driver tells him not to sweat it. 'They buy the *Gazette* before hockey and the *Trib* before basketball . . . but of course in the morning they bring the paper that is dropped on their doorstep.'

"Burbidge is now mumbling that by choosing route 99, and choosing hockey night, he has totally distorted his results.

"The driver, who is Champion's favorite dart opponent, is thoroughly enjoying Burbidge's discomfort because he was acting like such an ass at the beginning. So the driver tells Burbidge, 'I know from reading the CityBus newsletter that by the time you announce the new routes and schedules, we will be finished with hockey and basketball and into the baseball season. And, of course, most of these folks on the 5:15 bus are East City folks, while most on the 5:45 bus are West City folks, so your outcome will naturally be affected by choosing the 5:15 any time of the year.'

"Burbidge, fully exasperated, asks the driver, 'Is there anything else you would care to share with me?'

"The driver evidently couldn't hide his grin when he says, 'The riders on the 5:45 usually don't read the newspaper much at all. They've been watching sports in the terminal bar while waiting for the bus. Most aren't feeling any pain—if you get my meaning—and can't read the small newsprint as I don't turn on the overhead lights.'"

Sara pauses, allowing Jason to ask, "Is there a lesson to this story, Sara?"

"Well, we've been talking about having the student musicians distribute and collect surveys at each Friday evening's performance. I'm wondering if Glacier has any demographic data from previous surveys that might shed some light on concert attendees. I'd hate to systematically bias our sample, like Burbidge did. Since we won't be present to collect the data—like he was—we might never know."

> The Nature of Sampling

Most people intuitively understand the idea of sampling. One taste from a drink tells us whether it is sweet or sour. If we select a few ads from a magazine, we usually assume our selection reflects the characteristics of the full set. If some members of our staff favor a promotional strategy, we infer that others will also. These examples vary in their representativeness, but each is a sample.

sampling the process of selecting some elements from a population to represent that population.

population element the individual participant or object on which the measurement is taken.

population all elements about which we wish to make some inferences.

census a count of all the elements in a population.

sampling frame a list of elements in the population from which the sample is actually drawn.

The basic idea of **sampling** is that by selecting some of the elements in a population, we may draw conclusions about the entire population. A **population element** is the individual participant or object on which the measurement is taken. It is the unit of study. While an element may be a person, it can just as easily be something else. For example, each staff member questioned about an optimal promotional strategy is a population element, each advertising account analyzed is an element of an account population, and each ad is an element of a population of advertisements. A **population** is the total collection of elements about which we wish to make some inferences. All office workers in the firm compose a population of interest; all 4,000 files define a population of interest. A **census** is a count of all the elements in a population. If 4,000 files define the population, a census would obtain information from every one of them. We call the listing of all population elements from which the sample will be drawn the **sample frame**.

For CityBus, the population of interest is all riders of affected routes in the forthcoming route restructuring. In studying customer satisfaction with the CompleteCare service operation for MindWriter, the population of interest to Visionary Insights is all individuals who have had a laptop repaired while the CompleteCare program has been in effect. The population element is any one individual interacting with the service program.

Why Sample?

There are several compelling reasons for sampling, including (1) lower cost, (2) greater accuracy of results, (3) greater speed of data collection, and (4) availability of population elements.

Lower Cost

The economic advantages of taking a sample rather than a census are massive. Consider the cost of taking a census. In 2000, due to a Supreme Court ruling requiring a census rather than statistical sampling techniques, the U.S. Bureau of the Census increased its 2000 Decennial Census budget estimate by $1.723 billion, to $4.512 billion.[1] Is it any wonder that researchers in all types of organizations ask, "Why should we spend thousands of dollars interviewing all 4,000 employees in our company if we can find out what we need to know by asking only a few hundred?"

Greater Accuracy of Results

Deming argues that the quality of a study is often better with sampling than with a census. He suggests, "Sampling possesses the possibility of better interviewing (testing), more thorough investigation of missing, wrong, or suspicious information, better supervision, and better processing than is possible with complete coverage."[2] Research findings substantiate this opinion. More than 90 percent of the total survey error in one study was from nonsampling sources and only 10 percent or less was from random sampling error.[3] The U.S. Bureau of the Census, while mandated to take a census of the population every 10 years, shows its confidence in sampling by taking sample surveys to check the accuracy of its census. The U.S. Bureau of the Census knows that in a census, segments of the population are seriously undercounted. Only when the population is small, accessible, and highly variable is accuracy likely to be greater with a census than a sample.

Greater Speed of Data Collection

Sampling's speed of execution reduces the time between the recognition of a need for information and the availability of that information. For every disgruntled customer that the MindWriter CompleteCare program generates, several prospective customers will move away from MindWriter to a competitor's laptop. So fixing the problems within the CompleteCare program will not only keep current customers coming back but also discourage prospective customers from defecting to competitive brands due to negative word of mouth.

Availability of Population Elements

Some situations require sampling. Safety is a compelling marketing appeal for most vehicles. Yet we must have evidence to make such a claim. So we crash-test cars to test bumper strength or efficiency of airbags to prevent injury. In testing for such evidence, we destroy the cars we test. A census would mean complete destruction of all cars manufactured. Sampling is also the only process possible if the population is infinite.

Sample versus Census

The advantages of sampling over census studies are less compelling when the population is small and the variability within the population is high. Two conditions are appropriate for a census study: A census is (1) *feasible* when the population is small and (2) *necessary*

Sampling the Census

For the 2000 census, the U.S. Bureau of the Census proposed for the first time that the every-10-year census substitute statistical sampling to help adjust for the undercounting of some population segments. This undercounting includes renters, as well as immigrant and minority groups, who have been less responsive to past census requests for information. In January 1999, by a 5–4 decision, the U.S. Supreme Court banned sampling in census results for the purpose of federal apportionment but allowed it for counting population cohorts for business research purposes and for districting within states.

Before the 2010 census, Republicans hope to ban sampling altogether because undercounted groups traditionally vote as Democrats. However, Democrats could vote to change the wording of the Census Act as amended in 1976, thus incorporating sampling for all uses. Researchers are most concerned about whether the sampling procedure could incorporate errors in the results, rendering the results at least as flawed as the data now produced and making long-term comparative studies difficult.

Census results are used as a quality control in selecting units for sample cells. For the first time, the 2000 census allowed Americans to "identify themselves as more than one race, leaving the door open to seemingly endless combinations of racial and ethnic identities." According to early census releases, approximately 7 million people identify themselves as multiracial. While less than 3 percent of the overall U.S. population, these individuals are younger than the population as a whole—42 percent are under 18 years of age. Drawing a nationally representative sample using ethnicity as a descriptor will never be the same again. Visit the census site on the Internet to discover more.

www.census.gov

when the elements are quite different from each other.[4] When the population is small and variable, any sample we draw may not be representative of the population from which it is drawn. The resulting values we calculate from the sample are incorrect as estimates of the population values. Consider North American manufacturers of stereo components. Fewer than 50 companies design, develop, and manufacture amplifier and loudspeaker products at the high end of the price range. The size of this population suggests a census is feasible. The diversity of their product offerings makes it difficult to accurately sample from this group. Some companies specialize in speakers, some in amplifier technology, and others in compact-disc transports. Choosing a census in this situation is appropriate.

What Is a Good Sample?

The ultimate test of a sample design is how well it represents the characteristics of the population it purports to represent. In measurement terms, the sample must be valid. Validity of a sample depends on two considerations: accuracy and precision.

Accuracy

Accuracy is the degree to which bias is absent from the sample. When the sample is drawn properly, the measure of behavior, attitudes, or knowledge (the measurement variables) of *some* sample elements will be *less than* (thus, underestimate) the measure of those same variables drawn from the population. Also, the measure of the behavior, attitudes, or knowledge of *other* sample elements will be *more than* the population values (thus, overestimate them). Variations in these sample values offset each other, resulting in a sample value that is close to the population value. For these offsetting effects to occur, however, there must be enough elements in the sample, and they must be drawn in a way that favors neither overestimation nor underestimation.

For example, assume you were asked to test the level of brand recall of the "counting sheep" creative approach for the Serta mattress company. Hypothetically, you could mea-

sure via sample or census. You want a measure of brand recall in combination with message clarity: "Serta mattresses are *so comfortable* you'll feel the difference the minute you lie down." In the census, 52 percent of participants who are TV viewers correctly recalled the brand and message. Using a sample, 70 percent recalled the brand and correctly interpreted the message. With both results for comparison, you would know that your sample was biased, as it significantly overestimated the population value of 52 percent. Unfortunately, in most studies taking a census is not feasible, so we need an estimate of the amount of error.[5]

An accurate (unbiased) sample is one in which the underestimators offset the overestimators. **Systematic variance** has been defined as "the variation in measures due to some known or unknown influences that 'cause' the scores to lean in one direction more than another."[6] Homes on the corner of the block, for example, are often larger and more valuable than those within the block. Thus, a sample that selects only corner homes will cause us to overestimate home values in the area. Burbidge learned that in selecting bus route 99 for his newspaper readership sample, the time of the day, day of the week, and season of the year of the survey dramatically reduced the accuracy and validity of his sample.

systematic variance a variation that causes measurements to skew in one direction or another.

Increasing the sample size can reduce systematic variance as a cause of error. However, even the large size won't reduce error if the list from which you draw your participants is biased. The classic example of a sample with systematic variance was the *Literary Digest* presidential election poll in 1936, in which more than 2 million people participated. The poll predicted Alfred Landon would defeat Franklin Roosevelt for the presidency of the United States. Your memory is correct; we've never had a president named Alfred Landon. We discovered later that the poll drew its sample from telephone owners, who were in the middle and upper classes—at the time, the bastion of the Republican Party—while Roosevelt appealed to the much larger working class, whose members could not afford to own phones and typically voted for the Democratic Party candidate.

Precision

A second criterion of a good sample design is precision of estimate. Researchers accept that no sample will fully represent its population in all respects. However, to interpret the findings of research, we need a measure of how closely the sample represents the population. The numerical descriptors that describe samples may be expected to differ from those that describe populations because of random fluctuations inherent in the sampling process. This is called **sampling error** (or *random sampling error*) and reflects the influence of chance in drawing the sample members. Sampling error is what is left after all known sources of systematic variance have been accounted for. In theory, sampling error consists of random fluctuations only, although some unknown systematic variance may be included when too many or too few sample elements possess a particular characteristic. Let's say Visionary Insights draws a sample from an alphabetical list of MindWriter owners who are having their laptops currently serviced by the CompleteCare program. We insert a survey response card in a sample of returned laptops. Assume 80 percent of those surveyed had their laptops serviced by Max Jensen. Also assume from the exploratory study that Jensen had more complaint letters about his work than any other technician. Arranging the list of laptop owners currently being serviced in an alphabetical listing would have failed to *randomize* the sample frame. If Visionary Insights drew its sample from that listing, it would actually have increased its sampling error.

sampling error error created by the sampling process.

Precision is measured by the standard error of estimate, a type of standard deviation measurement; the smaller the standard error of estimate, the higher is the precision of the sample. The ideal sample design produces a small standard error of estimate. However, not all types of sample design provide estimates of precision, and samples of the same size can produce different amounts of error.

Types of Sample Design

The researcher makes several decisions when designing a sample. These are represented in Exhibit 16-1. The sampling decisions flow from two decisions made in the formation of the management-research question hierarchy: the nature of the management question and the specific investigative questions that evolve from the research question. These decisions are influenced by requirements of the project and its objectives, level of risk the marketer can tolerate, budget, time, available resources, and culture.

In the discussion that follows, we will use three examples:

- The CityBus study introduced in the vignette at the beginning of this chapter.
- The continuing Visionary Insights MindWriter CompleteCare customer satisfaction study.
- A study of the feasibility of starting a dining club near the campus of Metro University.

The researchers at Metro U are exploring the feasibility of creating a dining club whose facilities would be available on a membership basis. To launch this venture, they will need to make a substantial investment. Research will allow them to reduce many risks. Thus the research question is, "Would a membership dining club be a viable enterprise?" Some investigative questions that flow from the research question include:

>**Exhibit 16-1** Sampling Design within the Research Process

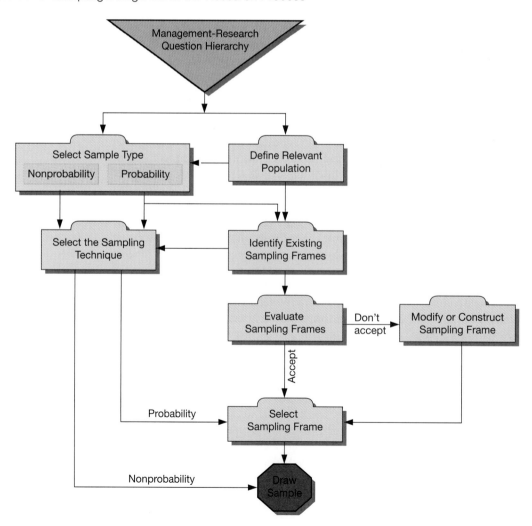

1. Who would patronize the club, and on what basis?
2. How many would join the club under various membership and fee arrangements?
3. How much would the average member spend per month?
4. What days would be most popular?
5. What menu and service formats would be most desirable?
6. What lunch times would be most popular?
7. Given the proposed price levels, how often per month would each member have lunch or dinner?
8. What percent of the people in the population say they would join the club, based on the projected rates and services?

We use the last three investigative questions for examples and focus specifically on questions 7 and 8 for assessing the project's risks. First, we will digress with other information and examples on sample design, coming back to Metro U in the next section.

In decisions of sample design, the representation basis and the element selection techniques, as shown in Exhibit 16-2, classify the different approaches.

Representation

The members of a sample are selected using probability or nonprobability procedures.

Nonprobability sampling is arbitrary and subjective; when we choose subjectively, we usually do so with a pattern or scheme in mind (e.g., only talking with young people or only talking with women). Each member of the population does not have a known chance of being included. Allowing interviewers during a mall-intercept study to choose sample elements "at random" (meaning "as they wish" or "wherever they find them") is not random sampling. While we are not told how Burbidge selected the riders of Bus route 99 as his sample, it's clear that he did not use probability sampling techniques.

Early Internet samples had all the drawbacks of nonprobability samples. Those individuals who frequented the Internet were not representative of most target markets or audiences, as far more young, technically savvy men frequented the Internet than did any other demographic group. As Internet use increases and gender discrepancies diminish, many such samples now closely approximate non-Internet samples. Of increasing concern, however, is what the Bureau of the Census labels the "great digital divide"—low-income and ethnic subgroups' underrepresentation in their use of the Internet compared to the general population. Additionally, many Internet samples were, and still are, drawn substantially from panels. These are composed of individuals who have self-selected to become part of a pool of individuals interested in participating in online marketing research. There is much discussion among professional researchers about whether Internet samples should be treated as probability or nonprobability samples. Some admit that any sample drawn from a panel is more appropriately treated as a nonprobability sample; others vehemently disagree, citing the success of such well-known panels as NielsenMedia's people meter panels for TV audience

nonprobability sampling
an arbitrary and subjective sampling procedure where each population element does not have a known, nonzero chance of being included.

>**Exhibit 16-2** Types of Sampling Designs

Element Selection	Representation Basis	
	Probability	**Nonprobability**
Unrestricted	Simple random	Convenience
Restricted	Complex random	Purposive
	Systematic	Judgment
	Cluster	Quota
	Stratified	Snowball
	Double	

Creating Samples: Then and Now

With more and more research being done via the Internet, what's the future of the probability sample? This is just one of the questions we asked Linda Piekarski, a 20-plus-year veteran with Survey Sampling, Inc. (SSI), a firm that compiles samples for probability and nonprobability research.

Sampling has changed a lot in the last 5 to 10 years, but it's all part of an evolution that firms like SSI have seen before. "In the 1950s probability samples were drawn based on addresses. Teams of female researchers would go door-to-door in neighborhoods, verifying that the address was occupied. And clients would get paper lists of addresses for their samples." But, gradually, those researchers didn't find people at home—they were off working at their own careers—so the telephone became the primary means of contact. "Today, because researchers haven't done a good job of educating the public about the value of research and the difference between research and telemarketing,

we are having the same problems with phone contact. People lead busy lives. More and more researchers have trouble making contact via phone. Even when they do, today's privacy technology (phone companies' privacy management and caller-ID services, answering machines, voice mail, and Tele-zappers) increasingly makes survey completion difficult." As a result, many researchers have turned to permission-based samples via the Internet. SSI has developed its own e-mail-based permission population composed of thousands of individuals for research purposes only. "And we protect their identities and their e-mail addresses so they don't get spammed." But Piekarski worries about the validity and reliability of the information drawn with such samples. "As accessible as these people are, it's still not a probability sample."

www.surveysampling.com

---

assessment and IRI's BehaviorScan panel for tracking consumer packaged goods. As you study the differences here, you should draw your own conclusion.

Key to the difference between nonprobability and probability samples is the term *random.* In the dictionary, random is defined as "without pattern" or as "haphazard." In sampling, random means something else entirely. **Probability sampling** is based on the concept of random selection—a controlled procedure that assures that each population element is given a known nonzero chance of selection. This procedure is never haphazard. Only probability samples provide estimates of precision. When a marketer is making a decision that will influence the expenditure of thousands, if not millions, of dollars, an estimate of precision is critical. Also, only probability samples offer the opportunity to generalize the findings to the population of interest from the sample population. While exploratory research does not necessarily demand this, explanatory, descriptive, and causal studies do.

probability sampling a controlled, randomized procedure that assures that each population element is given a known, nonzero chance of selection.

> 66 As we came out of the [2004] Super Bowl, the [moral] mood of the country seemed to have changed, and some of our ads got wrapped into that same controversy. . . . [We are] prepared to do better research . . . there's something going on we need to understand. 99
>
> *August A. Busch IV*
> *President, Anheuser-Busch Inc.*

Element Selection

Whether the elements are selected individually and directly from the population—viewed as a single pool—or additional controls are imposed, element selection may also classify samples. If each sample element is drawn individually from the population at large, it is an unrestricted sample. Restricted sampling covers all other forms of sampling.

> Steps in Sampling Design

There are several questions to be answered in securing a sample. Each requires unique information. While the questions presented here are sequential, an answer to one question often forces a revision to an earlier one.

1. What is the target population?
2. What are the parameters of interest?
3. What is the sampling frame?
4. What is the appropriate sampling method?
5. What size sample is needed?

What Is the Target Population?

The definition of the population may be apparent from the management problem or the research question(s), but often it is not. Is the population for the dining club study at Metro University defined as "full-time day students on the main campus of Metro U"? Or should the population include "all persons employed at Metro U"? Or should townspeople who live in the neighborhood be included? Without knowing the target market chosen for the new venture, it is not obvious which of these is the appropriate sampling population.

There also may be confusion about whether the population consists of individuals, households, or families, or a combination of these. If a communication study needs to measure income, then the definition of the population element as individual or household can make quite a difference. In an observation study, a sample population might be nonpersonal: displays within a store or any ATM a bank owns or all single-family residential properties in a community. Good operational definitions are critical in choosing the relevant population.

Assume the Metro University Dining Club is to be solely for the students and employees on the main campus. The researchers might define the population as "all currently enrolled students and employees on the main campus of Metro U." However, this does not include family members. They may want to revise the definition to make it "current students and employees of Metro U, main campus, and their families."

In the nonprobability sample, Burbidge seems to have defined his relevant population as any rider of the CityBus system. He presumes he has an equal need to determine newspaper readership of both regular and infrequent CityBus riders so that he might reach them with information about the new route structure, maps, and schedules. He can, however, easily reach regular riders by distributing information about the new routes via display racks on the bus for a period before the new routes are implemented. Infrequent riders, then, are the real population of interest of his newspaper readership study.

What Are the Parameters of Interest?

Population parameters are summary descriptors (e.g., incidence proportion, mean, variance) of variables of interest in the population. **Sample statistics** are descriptors of those same relevant variables computed from sample data. Sample statistics are used as estimators of population parameters. The sample statistics are the basis of our inferences about the population. Depending on how measurement questions are phrased, each may collect a different level of data. Each different level of data also generates different sample statistics. Thus choosing the parameters of interest will actually dictate the sample type and its size.

Asking Metro U affiliates to reveal their frequency of eating on or near campus (less than 5 times per week, greater than 5 but less than 10 times per week, or greater than 10 times per week) would provide an ordinal data estimator. Of course, we could ask the question differently and obtain an absolute count of eating experiences and that would generate ratio data. In MindWriter, the rating of service by CompleteCare on a 5-point scale would be an example of an interval data estimator. Asking the CityBus riders about their number of days of ridership during the past seven days would result in ratio data. Exhibit 16-3 indicates population parameters of interest for our three example studies.

When the variables of interest in the study are measured on interval or ratio scales, we use the sample mean to estimate the population mean and the sample standard deviation to

population parameters
summary descriptors of variables of interest in the population.

sample statistics
descriptors of the relevant variables computed from sample data.

> **We discuss data types in greater detail in Chapters 13 and 17.**

>Exhibit 16-3 Example Population Parameters

Study	Population Parameter of Interest	Data Level & Measurement Scale
CityBus	Frequency of ridership within 7 days	Ordinal (more than 10 times, 6 to 10 times, 5 or fewer times)
		Ratio (absolute number of rides)
MindWriter	Perceived quality of service	Interval (scale of 1 to 5, with 5 being "exceeded expectations")
	Proportion by gender of Laptop 9000 customers with problems	Nominal (percent female, male)
Metro U	Frequency of eating on or near campus within the last 30 days	Ratio (actual eating experiences)
	Proportion of students/employees expressing interest in dining club	Nominal (interested, not interested)

population proportion of incidence number of category elements divided by number of elements in the population.

> **We discuss proportion estimators in more detail in Chapter 17.**

Sampling from pools of special respondents, such as doctors and other professionals with time-starved occupations, often involves hiring firms that specialize in such recruiting.

estimate the population standard deviation. When the variables of interest are measured on nominal or ordinal scales, we use the sample proportion of incidence to estimate the population proportion and the pq to estimate the population variance. The **population proportion of incidence** "is equal to the number of elements in the population belonging to the category of interest, divided by the total number of elements in the population."[7] Proportion measures are necessary for nominal data and are widely used for other measures as well. The most frequent proportion measure is the percentage. In the Metro U study, examples of nominal data are the proportion of a population that expresses interest in joining the club (for example, 30 percent; therefore p is equal to 0.3 and q, those not interested, equals 0.7)

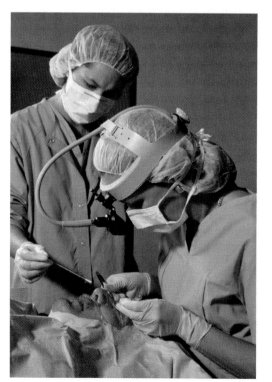

or the proportion of married students who report they now eat in restaurants at least five times a month. The City-Bus study seeks to determine whether East City or West City has the most riders on bus route 99. MindWriter might want to know if men or women have experienced the most problems with laptop model 9000. These measures for CityBus and MindWriter would result in nominal data.

There may also be important subgroups in the population about whom we would like to make estimates. For example, we might want to draw conclusions about the extent of dining club use that could be expected from married students versus single students, residential students versus commuter students, and so forth. Such questions have a strong impact on the nature of the sampling frame we accept (we would want the list organized by these subgroups or within the list each characteristic of each element would need to be noted), the design of the sample, and its size. Burbidge should be more interested in reaching infrequent rather than regular CityBus riders with the newspaper advertising he plans; to reach frequent riders CityBus could use on-bus signs or distribute paper schedules rather than using more expensive newspaper ads. And in the MindWriter study, Jason may be interested in comparing the responses of those who experienced poor service and those who experienced excellent service through the CompleteCare program.

What Is the Sampling Frame?

The sampling frame is closely related to the population. It is the list of elements from which the sample is actually drawn. Ideally, it is a complete and correct list of population members only. Jason should find limited problems obtaining a sampling frame of CompleteCare service users, as MindWriter has maintained a database of all calls coming into the Call Center and all serial numbers of laptops serviced.

As a practical matter, however, the sampling frame often differs from the theoretical population. For the dining club study, the Metro U directory would be the logical first choice as a sampling frame. Directories are usually accurate when published in the fall, but suppose the study is being done in the spring. The directory will contain errors and omissions because some people will have withdrawn or left since the directory was published, while others will have enrolled or been hired. Usually university directories don't mention the families of students or employees. Just how much inaccuracy one can tolerate in choosing a sampling frame is a matter of judgment. You might use the directory anyway, ignoring the fact that it is not a fully accurate list. However, if the directory is a year old, the amount of error might be unacceptable. One way to make the sampling frame for the Metro U study more representative of the population would be to secure a supplemental list of the new students and employees as well as a list of the withdrawals and terminations from Metro U's registrar and human resources databases. You could then add and delete information from the original directory. Or, if their privacy policies permit, you might just request a current listing from each of these offices and use these lists as your sampling frame.

A greater distortion would be introduced if a branch campus population were included in the Metro U directory. This would be an example of a too inclusive frame—that is, a frame that includes many elements other than the ones in which we are interested. A university directory that includes faculty and staff retirees is another example of a too inclusive sampling frame.

Often you have to accept a sampling frame that includes people or cases beyond those in whom you are interested. You may have to use a telephone directory to draw a sample of business telephone numbers. Fortunately, this is easily resolved. You draw a sample from the larger population and then use a screening procedure to eliminate those who are not members of the group you wish to study.

The Metro U dining club survey is an example of a sampling frame problem that is readily solved. Often one finds this task much more of a challenge. Suppose you need to sample the

A decade ago, Chinese families with a home telephone were envied. By 2004, China's fixed telephone users totaled 295 million and cellular telephone service rose above 305 million subscribers in a population of 1.3 billion. Business or personal listings are inadequate for developing sampling frames when in a six-month period 68 million households add services.

> **We discuss screening procedures in Chapter 15.**

members of an ethnic group, say, Asians residing in Little Rock, Arkansas. There is probably no directory of this population. While you may use the general city directory, sampling from this too inclusive frame would be costly and inefficient, as Asians represent only a small fraction of Little Rock's population. The screening task would be monumental. Since ethnic groups frequently cluster in certain neighborhoods, you might identify these areas of concentration and then use a reverse area telephone or city directory, which is organized by street address, to draw the sample. Burbidge had a definite problem, as no sample frame of CityBus riders existed. While some regular riders used monthly passes, infrequent riders usually paid cash for their fares. It might have been possible for Burbidge to anticipate this and to develop over time a listing of customers. Bus drivers could have collected relevant contact information over a month, but the cost of contacting customers via phone or mail would have been much more expensive than the self-administered intercept approach Burbidge chose for data collection. One sampling frame available to Burbidge was a list of bus routes. This list would have allowed him to draw a probability sample using a cluster sampling technique. We discuss more complex sampling techniques later in this chapter.

The sampling issues we have discussed so far are fairly universal. It is not until we begin talking about sampling frames and sampling methods that international research starts to deviate. International researchers often face far more difficulty in locating or building sample frames. Countries differ in how each defines its population; this affects census and relevant population counts.[8] Some countries purposefully oversample to facilitate the analysis of issues of particular national interest; this means we need to be cautious in interpreting published aggregate national figures.[9] These distinctions and difficulties may lead the researcher to choose nonprobability techniques or different probability techniques than they would choose if doing such research in the United States or other developed countries. In a study that is fielded in numerous countries at the same time, researchers may use different sampling methodologies, resulting in hybrid studies that will need care to be combined. It is common practice to weight sample data in cross-national studies to develop sample data that are representative.[10] Choice of sampling methods is often dictated by culture as much as by communication and technology infrastructure. Just as all advertising campaigns would not be appropriate in all parts of the world, all sampling techniques would not be appropriate in all subcultures. Our discussion in this text focuses more on domestic than international research. We believe it is easier to learn the principles of research in an environment that you know versus one in which many students can only speculate. Yet we also believe that ethnic and cultural sensitivity should influence every decision of researchers, whether they do research domestically or internationally. We will point out distinctions as we go.

What Is the Appropriate Sampling Method?

The researcher faces a basic choice: a probability or nonprobability sample. With a probability sample, a researcher can make probability-based confidence estimates of various parameters that cannot be made with nonprobability samples. Choosing a probability sampling technique has several consequences. A researcher must follow appropriate procedures, so that:

- Interviewers or others cannot modify the selections made.
- Only the selected elements from the original sampling frame are included.
- Substitutions are excluded except as clearly specified and controlled according to predetermined decision rules.

Despite all due care, the actual sample achieved will not match perfectly the sample that is originally drawn. Some people will refuse to participate, and others will be difficult, if not impossible, to find. Thus no matter how careful we are in replacing those who refuse or are never located, sampling error is likely to rise.

> **You may wish to review the discussions of error in Chapters 11 and 12.**

With personnel records available at a university and a population that is geographically concentrated, a probability sampling method is possible in the dining club study. University directories are generally available, and the costs of using a simple random sample would not be great here. Then, too, since the researchers are thinking of a major investment in the dining club, they would like to be highly confident they have a representative sample. The same analysis holds true for MindWriter: A sample frame is readily available, making a probability sample possible and likely.

While the probability cluster sampling technique was available to him, it is obvious that Burbidge chose nonprobability sampling, arbitrarily choosing bus route 99 as a judgment sample and attempting to survey everyone riding the bus during the arbitrary times in which he chose to ride. What drove him to this decision is likely what makes researchers turn to nonprobability sampling in other situations: ease, speed, and cost.

What Size Sample Is Needed?

Much folklore surrounds this question. The most pervasive myths are (1) a sample must be large or it is not representative and (2) a sample should bear some proportional relationship to the size of the population from which it is drawn. With nonprobability samples, researchers confirm these myths using the number of subgroups, rules of thumb, and budget considerations to settle on a sample size. In probability sampling, how large a sample should be is a function of the variation in the population parameters under study and the estimating precision needed by the researcher. Some principles that influence sample size include:

> **The process of determining the sample size is the subject of Chapter 17.**

- The greater the dispersion or variance within the population, the larger the sample must be to provide estimation precision.
- The greater the desired precision of the estimate, the larger the sample must be.
- The narrower or smaller the error range, the larger the sample must be.
- The higher the confidence level in the estimate, the larger the sample must be.
- The greater the number of subgroups of interest within a sample, the greater the sample size must be, as each subgroup must meet minimum sample size requirements.

Cost considerations influence decisions about the size and type of sample and the data collection methods. Almost all studies have some budgetary constraint, and this may encourage a researcher to use a nonprobability sample. Probability sample surveys incur list costs for sample frames, callback costs, and a variety of other costs that are not necessary when nonprobability samples are used. But when the data collection method is changed, the amount and type of data that can be obtained also change. Note the effect of a $2,000 budget on sampling considerations:

Simple random sampling: $25 per interview; 80 completed interviews.

Geographic cluster sampling: $20 per interview; 100 completed interviews.

Self-administered questionnaire: $12 per respondent; 167 completed instruments.

Telephone interviews: $10 per respondent; 200 completed interviews.[11]

For CityBus the cost of sampling riders' newspaper preferences to discover where to run the route-reconfiguration announcements must be significantly less than the cost of running ads in both East City and West City dailies. Thus the nonprobability judgment sampling procedure that Burbidge used was logical from a budget standpoint. The investment required to open the dining club at Metro U also justifies the more careful probability approach taken by the students. For MindWriter, an investment in CompleteCare has already been made; Jason needs to be highly confident that his recommendations to change CompleteCare procedures and policies are on target and thoroughly supported by the data collected. These considerations justify MindWriter's probability sampling approach.

> Probability Sampling

Simple Random Sampling

The unrestricted, simple random sample is the purest form of probability sampling. Since all probability samples must provide a known nonzero probability of selection for each population element, the **simple random sample** is considered a special case in which each population element has a known and equal chance of selection.

simple random sample a probability sample in which each element has a known and equal chance of selection.

$$\text{Probability of Selection} = \frac{\text{sample size}}{\text{population size}}$$

The Metro U dining club study has a population of 20,000. If the sample size is 300, the probability of selection is 1.5 percent (300/20,000 = .015). In this section, we use the simple random sample to build a foundation for understanding sampling procedures and choosing probability samples. The simple random sample is easy to implement with automatic dialing (random dialing) and with computerized voice response systems. However, it requires a list of population elements, can be time-consuming and expensive, and can require larger sample sizes than other probability methods. Exhibit 16-4 provides an overview of the steps involved in choosing a random sample.

Complex Probability Sampling

Simple random sampling is often impractical. Reasons include (1) it requires a population list (sampling frame) that is often not available; (2) it fails to use all the information about a population, thus resulting in a design that may be wasteful; and (3) it may be expensive to implement in both time and money. These problems have led to the development of alternative designs that are superior to the simple random design in statistical and/or economic efficiency.

A more efficient sample in a statistical sense is one that provides a given precision (standard error of the mean or proportion) with a smaller sample size. A sample that is economically more efficient is one that provides a desired precision at a lower dollar cost. We achieve this with designs that enable us to lower the costs of data collecting, usually through reduced travel expense and interviewer time.

In the discussion that follows, four alternative probability sampling approaches are considered: (1) systematic sampling, (2) stratified sampling, (3) cluster sampling, and (4) double sampling.

Systematic Sampling

systematic sampling probability sample drawn by applying a calculated skip interval to a sample frame.

skip interval interval between sample elements drawn from a sample frame in systematic sampling.

A versatile form of probability sampling is **systematic sampling**. In this approach, every kth element in the population is sampled, beginning with a random start of an element in the range of 1 to k. The kth element, or **skip interval**, is determined by dividing the sample size into the population size to obtain the skip pattern applied to the sampling frame. This

>**Exhibit 16-4** How to Choose a Random Sample

Selecting a *random sample* is accomplished with the aid of computer software, a table of random numbers, or a calculator with a random number generator. Drawing slips out of a hat or Ping-Pong balls from a drum serves as an alternative *if every element in the sampling frame has an equal chance of selection*. Mixing the slips (or balls) and returning them between every selection ensures that every element is just as likely to be selected as any other.

A table of random numbers (such as Appendix D, Exhibit D-10) is a practical solution when no software program is available. Random number tables contain digits that have no systematic organization. Whether you look at rows, columns, or diagonals, you will find neither sequence nor order. Exhibit D-10 in Appendix D is arranged into 10 columns of five-digit strings, but this is solely for readability.

Assume the researchers want a sample of 10 from a population of 95 elements. How will the researcher begin?

1. *Assign each element within the sampling frame a unique number* from 01 to 95.

2. *Identify a random start from the random number table* (drop a pencil point-first onto the table with closed eyes. Let's say the pencil dot lands on the eighth column from the left and 10 numbers down from the top of Exhibit D-10, marking the five digits 05067).

3. *Determine how the digits in the random number table will be assigned to the sampling frame* to choose the specified sample size (researchers agree to read the first two digits in this column downward until 10 are selected).

4. *Select the sample elements from the sampling frame* (05, 27, 69, 94, 18, 61, 36, 85, 71, and 83 using the above process. The digit 94 appeared twice and the second instance was omitted; 00 was omitted because the sampling frame started with 01).

Other approaches to selecting digits are endless: horizontally right to left, bottom to top, diagonally across columns, and so forth. Computer selection of a simple random sample will be more efficient for larger projects.

assumes that the sample frame is an accurate list of the population; if not, the number of elements in the sample frame is substituted for population size.

$$k = \text{skip interval} = \frac{\text{population size}}{\text{sample size}}$$

The major advantage of systematic sampling is its simplicity and flexibility. It is easier to instruct field workers to choose the dwelling unit listed on every kth line of a listing sheet than it is to use a random numbers table. With systematic sampling, there is no need to number the entries in a large personnel file before drawing a sample. To draw a systematic sample, do the following:

• Identify, list, and number the elements in the population.
• Identify the skip interval (k).
• Identify the random start.
• Draw a sample by choosing every kth entry.

Invoices or customer accounts can be sampled by using the last digit or a combination of digits of an invoice or customer account number. Time sampling is also easily accomplished. Systematic sampling would be an appropriate technique for MindWriter's CompleteCare program evaluation.

Systematic sampling can introduce subtle biases. A concern with systematic sampling is the possible *periodicity* in the population that parallels the sampling ratio. In sampling restaurant sales of dessert by drawing days of the year, a skip interval of 7 would bias results, no matter which day provides the random start. A less obvious case might involve a survey in an area of apartment buildings where the typical pattern is eight apartments per building. A skip interval of 8 could easily oversample some types of apartments and undersample others.

Another difficulty may arise when there is a *monotonic trend* in the population elements. That is, the population list varies from the smallest to the largest element or vice versa. Even a chronological list may have this effect if a measure has trended in one direction over time. Whether a systematic sample drawn under these conditions provides a biased estimate of the population mean or proportion depends on the initial random draw. Assume that a list of 2,000 commercial banks is created, arrayed from the largest to the smallest, from which a sample of 50 must be drawn for analysis. A skip interval of 40 beginning with a random start at 16 would exclude the 15 largest banks and give a small-size bias to the findings.

The only protection against these subtle biases is constant vigilance by the researcher. Some ways to avoid such bias include:

- Randomize the population before sampling (e.g., order the banks by name rather than size).
- Change the random start several times in the sampling process.
- Replicate a selection of different samples.

While systematic sampling has some theoretical problems, from a practical point of view it is usually treated as a simple random sample. When similar population elements are grouped within the sampling frame, systematic sampling is statistically more efficient than a simple random sample. This might occur if the listed elements are ordered chronologically, by size, by class, and so on. Under these conditions, the sample approaches a proportional stratified sample. The effect of this ordering is more pronounced on the results of cluster samples than for element samples and may call for a proportional stratified sampling formula.[12]

Stratified Sampling

stratified random sampling a probability sample that includes elements from each of the mutually exclusive strata within a population.

Most populations can be segregated into several mutually exclusive subpopulations, or strata. The process by which the sample is constrained to include elements from each of the segments is called **stratified random sampling**. University students can be divided by their class level, school or major, gender, and so forth. After a population is divided into the appropriate strata, a simple random sample can be taken within each stratum. The results from the study can then be weighted (based on the proportion of the strata to the population) and combined into appropriate population estimates.

There are three reasons why a researcher chooses a stratified random sample: (1) to increase a sample's statistical efficiency, (2) to provide adequate data for analyzing the various subpopulations or strata, and (3) to enable different research methods and procedures to be used in different strata.[13]

Stratification is usually more efficient statistically than simple random sampling and at worst it is equal to it. With the ideal stratification, each stratum is homogeneous internally and heterogeneous with other strata. This might occur in a sample that includes members of several distinct ethnic groups. In this instance, stratification makes a pronounced improvement in statistical efficiency.

It is also useful when the researcher wants to study the characteristics of certain population subgroups. Thus, if one wishes to draw some conclusions about activities in the different classes of a student body, stratified sampling would be used. Similarly, if a restaurant were interested in testing menu changes to attract younger patrons while retaining its older, loyal customers, stratified sampling using age and prior patronage as descriptors would be appropriate. Stratification is also called for when different methods of data collection are applied in different parts of the population, a research design that is becoming increasingly common. This might occur when we survey company employees at the home office with one method but must use a different approach with employees scattered throughout the country.

>**snap**shot

IRI's Wal-Mart Solution

The year 2001 ushered in a new era in retailing information for U.S. consumer packaged-goods (CPG) manufacturers. Prior to August 1, Information Resources, Inc. (IRI), which purchased point-of-sale data from Wal-Mart and resold it in numerous forms to manufacturers, was restricted by contract from providing a client manufacturer with specific competitors' data. When the contract expired, Wal-Mart decided it would no longer sell its point-of-sale data. So what does a syndicated research provider do when it loses access to the data of the world's largest retailer? It changes its sampling design.

In September 2001, IRI introduced its InfoScan Advantage service to monitor Wal-Mart activity with consumer panel data. However, IRI needed to change the design of its existing panel to better reflect Wal-Mart's customers. IRI expanded its panel almost 20 percent—to 65,000 households—added more Hispanic

and African-American households, and drew more households from rural counties. While the data will not be as detailed as in the past, Ed Kuehnle, IRI's group president of IRI North America, claims "InfoScan® Advantage will provide IRI customers [CPG manufacturers like Johnson & Johnson, PepsiCo, and Procter & Gamble] with the most comprehensive and in-depth information possible from the available data sources." IRI panelists record purchases with calculator-size scanners. IRI provides a view of food, drug, mass-merchandise, and Wal-Mart outlets in one integrated database. "This intelligence enhances the ability of IRI clients to reduce risk in new product introductions, optimize marketing investments and effectively execute [marketing plans] at retail."

www.infores.com

If data are available on which to base a stratification decision, how shall we go about it?[14] The ideal stratification would be based on the primary variable under study. If the major concern were to learn how often per month patrons would use the Metro U dining club, then one would like to stratify on this expected number of use occasions. The only difficulty with this idea is that if we knew this information, we would not need to conduct the study. We must, therefore, pick a variable for stratifying that we believe will correlate with the frequency of club use per month, something like days at work or class schedule as an indication of when a sample element might be near campus at mealtimes.

Researchers often have several important variables about which they want to draw conclusions. A reasonable approach is to seek some basis for stratification that correlates well with the major variables. It might be a single variable (class level), or it might be a compound variable (class by gender). In any event, we will have done a good stratifying job if the stratification base maximizes the difference among strata means and minimizes the within-stratum variances for the variables of major concern.

The more strata used, the closer you come to maximizing interstrata differences (differences between stratum) and minimizing intrastratum variances (differences within a given stratum). You must base the decision partially on the number of subpopulation groups about which you wish to draw separate conclusions. Costs of stratification also enter the decision. The more strata you have, the higher the cost of the research project due to the cost associated with more detailed sampling. There is little to be gained in estimating population values when the number of strata exceeds six.[15]

The size of the strata samples is calculated with two pieces of information: (1) how large the total sample should be and (2) how the total sample should be allocated among strata. In deciding how to allocate a total sample among various strata, there are proportionate and disproportionate options.

Proportionate versus Disproportionate Sampling   In **proportionate stratified sampling,** each stratum is properly represented so that the sample size drawn from the stratum is proportionate to the stratum's share of the total population. This approach is more popular than any of the other stratified sampling procedures. Some reasons for this include:

proportionate stratified sampling each stratum's size is proportionate to the stratum's share of the population.

- It has higher statistical efficiency than a simple random sample.

- It is much easier to carry out than other stratifying methods.

- It provides a self-weighting sample; the population mean or proportion can be estimated simply by calculating the mean or proportion of all sample cases, eliminating the weighting of responses.

On the other hand, proportionate stratified samples often gain little in statistical efficiency if the strata measures and their variances are similar for the major variables under study.

disproportionate stratified sampling each stratum's size is not proportionate to the stratum's share of the population.

Any stratification that departs from the proportionate relationship is **disproportionate**. There are several disproportionate allocation schemes. One type is a judgmentally determined disproportion based on the idea that each stratum is large enough to secure adequate confidence levels and error range estimates for individual strata. The table below shows the relationship between proportionate and disproportionate stratified sampling.

	Population	Proportionate Sample	Disproportionate Sample
Male	45%	45%	35%
Female	55	55	65

A researcher makes decisions regarding disproportionate sampling, however, by considering how a sample will be allocated among strata. One author states,

> In a given stratum, take a larger sample if the stratum is larger than other strata; the stratum is more variable internally; and sampling is cheaper in the stratum.[16]

If one uses these suggestions as a guide, it is possible to develop an optimal stratification scheme. When there is no difference in intrastratum variances and when the costs of sampling among strata are equal, the optimal design is a proportionate sample.

While disproportionate sampling is theoretically superior, there is some question as to whether it has wide applicability in a practical sense. If the differences in sampling costs or variances among strata are large, then disproportionate sampling is desirable. It has been suggested that "differences of several-fold are required to make disproportionate sampling worthwhile."[17]

The process for drawing a stratified sample is:

- Determine the variables to use for stratification.

- Determine the proportions of the stratification variables in the population.

- Select proportionate or disproportionate stratification based on project information needs and risks.

- Divide the sampling frame into separate frames for each stratum.

- Randomize the elements within each stratum's sampling frame.

- Follow random or systematic procedures to draw the sample from each stratum.

Cluster Sampling

cluster sampling divides the population into subgroups, then draws a sample from each subgroup.

In a simple random sample, each population element is selected individually. The population can also be divided into groups of elements with some groups randomly selected for study. This is **cluster sampling**. Cluster sampling differs from stratified sampling in several ways, as indicated in Exhibit 16-5.

Two conditions foster the use of cluster sampling: (1) the need for more economic efficiency than can be provided by simple random sampling and (2) the frequent unavailability of a practical sampling frame for individual elements.

>**Exhibit 16-5** Comparison of Stratified and Cluster Sampling

Stratified Sampling	Cluster Sampling
1. We divide the population into a *few* subgroups.	1. We divide the population into *many* subgroups.
• Each subgroup has *many* elements in it.	• Each subgroup has *few* elements in it.
• Subgroups are selected according to some criterion that is related to the variables under study.	• Subgroups are selected according to some criterion of ease or availability in data collection.
2. We try to secure *homogeneity* within subgroups.	2. We try to secure *heterogeneity* within subgroups.
3. We try to secure *heterogeneity* between subgroups.	3. We try to secure *homogeneity* between subgroups.
4. We randomly choose *elements* from within each subgroup.	4. We randomly choose several *subgroups* that we then typically study in depth.

Statistical efficiency for cluster samples is usually lower than for simple random samples chiefly because clusters often don't meet the need for heterogeneity and, instead, are homogeneous. For example, families in the same block (a typical cluster) are often similar in social class, income level, ethnic origin, and so forth. While statistical efficiency in most cluster sampling may be low, economic efficiency is often great enough to overcome this weakness. The criterion, then, is the net relative efficiency resulting from the trade-off between economic and statistical factors. It may take 690 interviews with a cluster design to give the same precision as 424 simple random interviews. But if it costs only $5 per interview in the cluster situation and $10 in the simple random case, the cluster sample is more attractive ($3,450 versus $4,240).

Area Sampling

Much research involves populations that can be identified with some geographic area. When this occurs, it is possible to use **area sampling**, the most important form of cluster sampling. This method overcomes the problems of both high sampling cost and the unavailability of a practical sampling frame for individual elements. Area sampling methods have been applied to national populations, county populations, and even smaller areas where there are well-defined political or natural boundaries.

area sampling cluster sampling technique applied to a population with well-defined political or geographic boundaries.

Suppose you want to survey the adult residents of a city. You would seldom be able to secure a listing of such individuals. It would be simple, however, to get a detailed city map that shows the blocks of the city. If you take a sample of these blocks, you are also taking a sample of the adult residents of the city.

A low-cost, frequently used method, the area cluster sample may use geographic sample units (e.g., city blocks).

Design   In designing cluster samples, including area samples, we must answer several questions:

1. How homogeneous are the resulting clusters?
2. Shall we seek equal-sized or unequal-sized clusters?
3. How large a cluster shall we take?
4. Shall we use a single-stage or multistage cluster?
5. How large a sample is needed?

1. When clusters are homogeneous, this contributes to low statistical efficiency. Sometimes one can improve this efficiency by constructing clusters to increase intracluster variance. In the dining club study, researchers might have chosen a course as a cluster, choosing to sample all students in that course if it enrolled students of all four class years. Or maybe they could choose a departmental office that had faculty, staff, and administrative positions as well as student workers. In area sampling to increase intracluster variance, researchers could combine into a single cluster adjoining blocks that contain different income groups or social classes.

2. A cluster sample may be composed of clusters of equal or unequal size. The theory of clustering is that the means of sample clusters are unbiased estimates of the population mean. This is more often true when clusters are naturally equal, such as households in city blocks. While one can deal with clusters of unequal size, it may be desirable to reduce or counteract the effects of unequal size. There are several approaches to this:

• Combine small clusters and split large clusters until each approximates an average size.
• Stratify clusters by size and choose clusters from each stratum.
• Stratify clusters by size and then subsample, using varying sampling fractions to secure an overall sampling ratio.[18]

3. There is no *a priori* answer to the ideal cluster size question. Comparing the efficiency of differing cluster sizes requires that we discover the different costs for each size and estimate the different variances of the cluster means. Even with single-stage clusters (where the researchers interview or observe every element within a cluster), it is not clear which size (say, 5, 20, or 50) is superior. Some have found that in studies using single-stage area clusters, the optimal cluster size is no larger than the typical city block.[19]

4. Concerning single-stage or multistage cluster designs, for most large-scale area sampling, the tendency is to use multistage designs. Several situations justify drawing a sample within a cluster, in preference to the direct creation of smaller clusters and taking a census of that cluster using one-stage cluster sampling:[20]

• Natural clusters may exist as convenient sampling units yet, for economic reasons, may be larger than the desired size.
• We can avoid the cost of creating smaller clusters in the entire population and confine subsampling to only those large natural clusters.
• The sampling of naturally compact clusters may present practical difficulties. For example, independent interviewing of all members of a household may be impractical.

5. The answer to how many subjects must be interviewed or observed depends heavily on the specific cluster design, and the details can be complicated. Unequal clusters and multistage samples are the chief complications, and their statistical treatment is beyond the scope of this book.[21] Here we will treat only single-stage sampling with equal-size clusters (called *simple cluster sampling*). It is analogous to simple random sampling. We can think of a population as consisting of 20,000 clusters of one student each, or 2,000 clusters of 10 students each, and so on. Assuming the same specifications for precision and confidence, we should expect that the calculation of a probability sample size would be the same for both clusters.

Double Sampling

It may be more convenient or economical to collect some information by sample and then use this information as the basis for selecting a subsample for further study. This procedure is called **double sampling, sequential sampling**, or **multiphase sampling**. It is usually found with stratified and/or cluster designs. The calculation procedures are described in more advanced texts.

Double sampling can be illustrated by the dining club example. You might use a telephone survey or another inexpensive survey method to discover who would be interested in joining such a club and the degree of their interest. You might then stratify the interested respondents by degree of interest and subsample among them for intensive interviewing on expected consumption patterns, reactions to various services, and so on. Whether it is more desirable to gather such information by one-stage or two-stage sampling depends largely on the relative costs of the two methods.

Because of the wide range of sampling designs available, it is often difficult to select an approach that meets the needs of the research question and helps to contain the costs of the project. To help with these choices, Exhibit 16-6 may be used to compare the various

double sampling (sequential sampling, multiphase sampling) a procedure for selecting a subsample from a sample.

>**Exhibit 16-6** Comparison of Probability Sampling Designs

Type	Description	Advantages	Disadvantages
Simple Random Cost: High Use: Moderate	Each population element has an equal chance of being selected into the sample. Sample drawn using random number table/generator.	Easy to implement with automatic dialing (random-digit dialing) and with computerized voice response systems.	Requires a listing of population elements. Takes more time to implement. Uses larger sample sizes. Produces larger errors.
Systematic Cost: Moderate Use: Moderate	Selects an element of the population at the beginning with a random start, and following the sampling skip interval selects every kth element.	Simple to design. Easier to use than the simple random. Easy to determine sampling distribution of mean or proportion.	Periodicity within the population may skew the sample and results. If the population list has a monotonic trend, a biased estimate will result based on the start point.
Stratified Cost: High Use: Moderate	Divides population into subpopulations or strata and uses simple random on each strata. Results may be weighted and combined.	Researcher controls sample size in strata. Increased statistical efficiency. Provides data to represent and analyze subgroups. Enables use of different methods in strata.	Increased error will result if subgroups are selected at different rates. Especially expensive if strata on the population have to be created.
Cluster Cost: Moderate Use: High	Population is divided into internally heterogeneous subgroups. Some are randomly selected for further study.	Provides an unbiased estimate of population parameters if properly done. Economically more efficient than simple random. Lowest cost per sample, especially with geographic clusters. Easy to do without a population list.	Often lower statistical efficiency (more error) due to subgroups being homogeneous rather than heterogeneous.
Double (sequential or multiphase) Cost: Moderate Use: Moderate	Process includes collecting data from a sample using a previously defined technique. Based on the information found, a subsample is selected for further study.	May reduce costs if first stage results in enough data to stratify or cluster the population.	Increased costs if indiscriminately used.

The Truth in Florida

In 1997, Florida Department of Health (FDOH) officials decided to do something about an alarming trend: Teen smoking was increasing; some estimates placed the increase at as much as 7 percent in the prior five years. They decided to launch a public service advertising campaign (PSA) aimed at youth as part of a larger control effort to include marketing and public relations initiatives. The $140 million in funding would come from the proceeds of Florida's $11.3 billion legal settlement with the tobacco companies. FDOH turned to Crispin Porter & Bogusky (CP&B) to develop edgy PSAs that would resonate with youth. These ads had names, like "liars," and "junk yard dogs." The creative strategy would be to rebrand smoking or, as CP&B's Neydy Gomez described, "to create a brand as strong and as powerful [as the cool brands the tobacco industry had created] to take the place of tobacco brands." CP&B called the campaign *Truth*.

CP&B involved youths at every step of the process. At a Teen Tobacco Summit, 600 high school students brainstormed approaches that would work with teens. CP&B created a 45-member youth sounding board to serve as marketing advisers. CP&B also involved representatives from Students Working Against Tobacco (SWAT). It also devoted significant resources to determine the impact of the advertising, test advertising effectiveness, and evaluate new concepts as the campaign aged.

After two years, the Florida *Truth* campaign had achieved unprecedented success:

- Cigarette use dropped 40 percent among middle school students (from 18.8 to 11.1 percent).
- Cigarette use dropped 21 percent among high school students (from 27.4 to 22.6 percent).
- Never-used-tobacco behavior rose 39.8 percent (from 56.4 to 69.3 percent) among middle school students.

- Never-used-tobacco behavior rose 26 percent (from 39.1 to 43.1 percent) among high school students.
- Florida teens' awareness of the "truth" brand stood at 94 percent.

Given such evidence of the success of the Florida *Truth* campaign, it should be no surprise that the American Legacy Foundation, a public health foundation created as a result of the November 1998 master settlement agreement between state attorneys general and the tobacco companies, signed on to fund the national extension of *Truth.* But the foundation would want data to substantiate national effectiveness. The Research Triangle Institute fielded the National Youth Tobacco Survey, a self-administered survey taken by 35,828 middle and high school students. A baseline was established in 1999, with the first formal post-*Truth* data collection in the spring of 2000. Additionally, the Legacy Media Tracking Survey, a longitudinal study conducted with periodic national telephone surveys of 12- to 24-year-olds, monitors youths' exposure to *Truth* and their tobacco-related beliefs, attitudes, and behaviors. Baseline was administered in fall 1999 and winter 2000 before the national *Truth* campaign was launched. A second round of random-dialed phone interviews was conducted from April to July 2001 with more than 20,000 youths.

You can see some of the *Truth* ads at the Crispin Porter & Bogusky Web site and the survey instruments and data sets are available at the American Legacy Web site. What sampling designs were used in this effort?

www.cpbgroup.com; www.americanlegacy.org

advantages and disadvantages of probability sampling. Nonprobability sampling techniques are covered in the next section. They are used frequently and offer the researcher the benefit of low cost. However, they are not based on a theoretical framework and do not operate from statistical theory; consequently, they produce selection bias and nonrepresentative samples. Despite these weaknesses, their widespread use demands their mention here.

> Nonprobability Sampling

Any discussion of the relative merits of probability versus nonprobability sampling clearly shows the technical superiority of the former. In probability sampling, researchers use a random selection of elements to reduce or eliminate sampling bias. Under such conditions, we can have substantial confidence that the sample is representative of the population from which it is drawn. In addition, with probability sample designs, we can estimate an error range within which the population parameter is expected to fall. Thus, we can not only reduce the chance for sampling error but also estimate the range of probable sampling error present.

With a subjective approach like nonprobability sampling, the probability of selecting population elements is unknown. There are a variety of ways to choose persons or cases to include in the sample. Often we allow the choice of subjects to be made by field workers on the scene. When this occurs, there is greater opportunity for bias to enter the sample selection procedure and to distort the findings of the study. Also, we cannot estimate any range within which to expect the population parameter. Given the technical advantages of probability sampling over nonprobability sampling, why would anyone choose the latter? There are some practical reasons for using the less precise methods.

Practical Considerations

We may use nonprobability sampling procedures because they satisfactorily meet the sampling objectives. While a random sample will give us a true cross section of the population, this may not be the objective of the research. If there is no desire or need to generalize to a population parameter, then there is much less concern about whether the sample fully reflects the population. Often researchers have more limited objectives. They may be looking only for the range of conditions or for examples of dramatic variations. This is especially true in exploratory research where one may wish to contact only certain persons or cases that are clearly atypical. Burbidge would have likely wanted a probability sample if the decision resting on the data was the actual design of the new CityBus routes and schedules. However, the decision of where and when to place advertising announcing the change is a relatively low-cost one in comparison.

Additional reasons for choosing nonprobability over probability sampling are cost and time. Probability sampling clearly calls for more planning and repeated callbacks to ensure that each selected sample member is contacted. These activities are expensive. Carefully controlled nonprobability sampling often seems to give acceptable results, so the investigator may not even consider probability sampling. Burbidge's results from bus route 99 would generate questionable data, but he seemed to realize the fallacy of many of his assumptions once he spoke with bus route 99's driver—something he should have done during exploration prior to designing the sampling plan.

While probability sampling may be superior in theory, there are breakdowns in its application. Even carefully stated random sampling procedures may be subject to careless application by the people involved. Thus, the ideal probability sampling may be only partially achieved because of the human element.

It is also possible that nonprobability sampling may be the only feasible alternative. The total population may not be available for study in certain cases. At the scene of a major event, it may be infeasible to attempt to construct a probability sample. A study of past correspondence between two companies must use an arbitrary sample because the full correspondence is normally not available.

In another sense, those who are included in a sample may select themselves. In mail surveys, those who respond may not represent a true cross section of those who receive the questionnaire. The receivers of the questionnaire decide for themselves whether they will participate. In Internet surveys those who volunteer don't always represent the appropriate cross section—that's why screening questions are used before admitting a participant to the sample. There is, however, some of this self-selection in almost all surveys because every respondent chooses whether to be interviewed.

Methods

Convenience

Nonprobability samples that are unrestricted are called **convenience samples**. They are the least reliable design but normally the cheapest and easiest to conduct. Researchers or field workers have the freedom to choose whomever they find, thus the name "convenience." Examples include informal pools of friends and neighbors, people responding to a

convenience samples
nonprobability sample where element selection is based on ease of accessibility.

newspaper's invitation for readers to state their positions on some public issue, a TV reporter's "person-on-the-street" intercept interviews, or the use of employees to evaluate the taste of a new snack food.

While a convenience sample has no controls to ensure precision, it may still be a useful procedure. Often you will take such a sample to test ideas or even to gain ideas about a subject of interest. In the early stages of exploratory research, when you are seeking guidance, you might use this approach. The results may present evidence that is so overwhelming that a more sophisticated sampling procedure is unnecessary. In an interview with students concerning some issue of campus concern, you might talk to 25 students selected sequentially. You might discover that the responses are so overwhelmingly one-sided that there is no incentive to interview further.

Purposive Sampling

A nonprobability sample that conforms to certain criteria is called *purposive sampling*. There are two major types—judgment sampling and quota sampling.

Judgment sampling occurs when a researcher selects sample members to conform to some criterion. In a study of labor problems, you may want to talk only with those who have experienced on-the-job discrimination. Another example of judgment sampling occurs when election results are predicted from only a few selected precincts that have been chosen because of their predictive record in past elections. Burbidge chose bus route 99 because the current route between East City and West City led him to believe that he could get a representation of both East City and West City riders.

When used in the early stages of an exploratory study, a judgment sample is appropriate. When one wishes to select a biased group for screening purposes, this sampling method is also a good choice. Companies often try out new product ideas on their employees. The rationale is that one would expect the firm's employees to be more favorably disposed toward a new product idea than the public. If the product does not pass this group, it does not have prospects for success in the general market.

Quota sampling is the second type of purposive sampling. We use it to improve representativeness. The logic behind quota sampling is that certain relevant characteristics describe the dimensions of the population. If a sample has the same distribution on these characteristics, then it is likely to be representative of the population regarding other variables on which we have no control. Suppose the student body of Metro U is 55 percent female and 45 percent male. The sampling quota would call for sampling students at a 55 to 45 percent ratio. This would eliminate distortions due to a nonrepresentative gender ratio. Burbidge could have improved his nonprobability sampling by considering time-of-day and day-of-week variations and choosing to distribute surveys to bus route 99 riders at various times, thus creating a quota sample.

In most quota samples, researchers specify more than one control dimension. Each should meet two tests: It should (1) have a distribution in the population that we can estimate and (2) be pertinent to the topic studied. We may believe that responses to a question should vary depending on the gender of the respondent. If so, we should seek proportional responses from both men and women. We may also feel that undergraduates differ from graduate students, so this would be a dimension. Other dimensions, such as the student's academic discipline, ethnic group, religious affiliation, and social group affiliation, also may be chosen. Only a few of these controls can be used. To illustrate, suppose we consider the following:

Gender: Two categories—male, female.

Class level: Two categories—graduate, undergraduate.

College: Six categories—Arts and Science, Agriculture, Architecture, Business, Engineering, other.

Religion: Four categories—Protestant, Catholic, Jewish, other.

judgment sampling purposive sampling where the researcher arbitrarily selects sample units to conform to some criterion.

quota sampling purposive sampling in which relevant characteristics are used to stratify the sample.

> **As we discussed in Chapter 9, qualitative research often uses purposive sampling.**

Fraternal affiliation: Two categories—member, nonmember.

Family social-economic class: Three categories—upper, middle, lower.

In an extreme case, we might ask an interviewer to find a male undergraduate business student who is Catholic, a fraternity member, and from an upper-class home. All combinations of these six factors would call for 288 such cells to consider. This type of control is known as *precision control.* It gives greater assurance that a sample will be representative of the population. However, it is costly and too difficult to carry out with more than three variables.

> **Review Exhibit 12-3 for a matrix application of quota sampling.**

When we wish to use more than three control dimensions, we should depend on *frequency* control. With this form of control, the overall percentage of those with each characteristic in the sample should match the percentage holding the same characteristic in the population. No attempt is made to find a combination of specific characteristics in a single person. In frequency control, we would probably find that the following sample array is an adequate reflection of the population:

	Population	Sample
Male	65%	67%
Married	15	14
Undergraduate	70	72
Campus resident	30	28
Independent	75	73
Protestant	39	42

Quota sampling has several weaknesses. First, the idea that quotas on some variables assume a representativeness on others is argument by analogy. It gives no assurance that the sample is representative of the variables being studied. Often, the data used to provide controls might be outdated or inaccurate. There is also a practical limit on the number of simultaneous controls that can be applied to ensure precision. Finally, the choice of subjects is left to field workers to make on a judgmental basis. They may choose only friendly looking people, people who are convenient to them, and so forth.

Despite the problems with quota sampling, it is widely used by opinion pollsters and marketing and other researchers. Probability sampling is usually much more costly and time-consuming. Advocates of quota sampling argue that while there is some danger of systematic bias, the risks are usually not that great. Where predictive validity has been checked (e.g., in election polls), quota sampling has been generally satisfactory.

Snowball

This design has found a niche in recent years in applications where respondents are difficult to identify and are best located through referral networks. It is also especially appropriate for some qualitative studies. In the initial stage of **snowball sampling**, individuals are discovered and may or may not be selected through probability methods. This group is then used to refer the researcher to others who possess similar characteristics and who, in turn, identify others. Similar to a reverse search for bibliographic sources, the "snowball" gathers subjects as it rolls along. Various techniques are available for selecting a nonprobability snowball with provisions for error identification and statistical testing. Let's consider a brief example.

snowball sampling
subsequent participants are referred by current sample elements.

The high end of the U.S. audio market is composed of several small firms that produce ultra-expensive components used in recording and playback of live performances. A risky new technology for improving digital signal processing is being contemplated by one firm. Through its contacts with a select group of recording engineers and electronics designers, the first-stage sample may be identified for interviewing. Subsequent interviewees are likely to reveal critical information for product development and marketing.

Variations on snowball sampling have been used to study drug cultures, teenage gang activities, power elites, community relations, insider trading, and other applications where respondents are difficult to identify and contact.

>summary

1 Sampling is based on two premises. One is that there is enough similarity among the elements in a population that a few of these elements will adequately represent the characteristics of the total population. The second premise is that while some elements in a sample underestimate a population value, others overestimate this value. The result of these tendencies is that a sample statistic such as the arithmetic mean is generally a good estimate of a population mean.

2 A good sample has both accuracy and precision. An accurate sample is one in which there is little or no bias or systematic variance. A sample with adequate precision is one that has a sampling error that is within acceptable limits for the study's purpose.

3 In developing a sample, five procedural questions need to be answered:

   a What is the target population?

   b What are the parameters of interest?

   c What is the sampling frame?

   d What is the appropriate sampling method?

   e What size sample is needed?

4 A variety of sampling techniques are available. They may be classified by their representation basis and element selection techniques as shown in the accompanying table.

	Representation Basis	
Element Selection	**Probability**	**Nonprobability**
Unrestricted	Simple random	Convenience
Restricted	Complex random	Purposive
	• Systematic	• Judgment
	• Cluster	• Quota
	• Stratified	Snowball
	• Double	

Probability sampling is based on random selection—a controlled procedure that ensures that each population element is given a known nonzero chance of selection. The simplest type of probability approach is simple random sampling. In this design, each member of the population has an equal chance of being included in a sample. In contrast, nonprobability selection is "not random." When each sample element is drawn individually from the population at large, this is unrestricted sampling. Restricted sampling covers those forms of sampling in which the selection process follows more complex rules.

5 Complex sampling is used when conditions make simple random samples impractical or uneconomical. The four major types of complex random sampling discussed in this chapter are systematic, stratified, cluster, and double sampling. Systematic sampling involves the selection of every kth element in the population, beginning with a random start between elements from 1 to k. Its simplicity in certain cases is its greatest value.

Stratified sampling is based on dividing a population into subpopulations and then randomly sampling from each of these strata. This method usually results in a smaller total sample size than would a simple random design. Stratified samples may be proportionate or disproportionate.

In cluster sampling, we divide the population into convenient groups and then randomly choose the groups to study. It is typically less efficient from a statistical viewpoint than the simple random because of the high degree of homogeneity within the clusters. Its great advantage is its savings in cost—if the population is dispersed geographically—or in time. The most widely used form of clustering is area sampling, in which geographic areas are the selection elements.

At times it may be more convenient or economical to collect some information by sample and then use it as a basis for selecting a subsample for further study. This procedure is called double sampling.

Nonprobability sampling also has some compelling practical advantages that account for its widespread use. Often probability sampling is not feasible because the population is not available. Then, too, frequent breakdowns in the application of probability sampling discount its technical advantages. You may find also that a true cross section is often not the aim of the researcher. Here the goal may be the discovery of the range or extent of conditions. Finally, nonprobability sampling is usually less expensive to conduct than is probability sampling.

Convenience samples are the simplest and least reliable forms of nonprobability sampling. Their primary virtue is low cost. One purposive sample is the judgmental sample, in which one is interested in studying only selected types of subjects. The other purposive sample is the quota sample. Subjects are selected to conform to certain predesignated control measures that secure a representative cross section of the population. Snowball sampling uses a referral approach to reach particularly hard-to-find respondents.

>**key**terms

>**discussion**questions

Terms in Review

1 Distinguish between:

  a Statistic and parameter.

  b Sample frame and population.

  c Restricted and unrestricted sampling.

  d Simple random and complex random sampling.

  e Convenience and purposive sampling.

  f Sample precision and sample accuracy.

  g Systematic and error variance.

  h Variable and attribute parameters.

  i Proportionate and disproportionate samples.

2 Under what kind of conditions would you recommend:

  a A probability sample? A nonprobability sample?

  b A simple random sample? A cluster sample? A stratified sample?

  c A disproportionate stratified probability sample?

3 You plan to conduct a survey using unrestricted sampling. What subjective decisions must you make?

4 Describe the differences between a probability sample and a nonprobability sample.

5 Why would a marketing researcher use a quota purposive sample?

Making Research Decisions

6 Your task is to interview a representative sample of attendees for the large concert venue where you work. The new season schedule includes 200 live concerts featuring all types of musicians and musical groups. Since neither the number of attendees nor their descriptive characteristics are known in advance, you decide on nonprobability sampling. Based on past seating configurations, you can calculate the number of tickets that will be available for each of the 200 concerts. Thus, collectively, you will know the number of possible attendees for each type of music. From attendance research conducted at concerts held by the Glacier Symphony during the previous two years, you can obtain gender data on attendees by type of music. How would you conduct a reasonably reliable nonprobability sample?

7 Your large firm is about to change to a customer-centered organization structure, where employees who have rarely had customer contact will now likely significantly influence customer satisfaction and retention. As part of the transition, your superior wants an accurate evaluation of the morale of the firm's large number of computer technicians. What type of sample would you draw if it was to be an unrestricted sample?

Behind the Scenes

8 Design an alternative nonprobability sample that will be more representative of infrequent and potential riders for the CityBus project.

9 How would you draw a cluster sample for the CityBus project?

From Concept to Practice

10 Using Exhibit 16-6 as your guide, for each sampling technique describe the sampling frame for a study of employers' skill needs in new hires using the industry in which you are currently working or wish to work.

>**www**exercise

Visit the Web site of the Henry J. Kaiser Family Foundation, a nonprofit organization that studies critical issues related to health and health services (www.kff.org). Select one of the foundation's studies and evaluate the sampling plan. If you were marketing a product or service related to the issue being studied, how would you adjust the sampling plan?

>**cases***

Calling Up Attendance

Campbell-Ewald: R-E-S-P-E-C-T Spells Loyalty

Can Research Rescue the Red Cross?

Goodyear's Aquatred

Inquiring Minds Want to Know—NOW!

KNSD San Diego

Outboard Marine

Pebble Beach Co.

Starbucks, Bank One, and Visa Launch Starbucks Duetto Visa

State Farm: Dangerous Intersections

USTA: Come Out Swinging

Volkswagen's Beetle

* All cases, both written and video, are on the text DVD. The film icon indicates a video case. Check the DVD Index to determine whether a case has data, the research instrument, or other supplementary material.

>chapter 17

Determining Sample Size

>learningobjectives

After reading this chapter, you should understand . . .

1 The process of organizing and summarizing data using descriptive statistics.

2 The role of normal and standardized normal distributions and their relationship to population estimates.

3 Computing point and interval population estimates through an understanding of population distribution, sample distributions, and the distribution of sample means.

4 How to estimate the appropriate sample size for samples when the question of interest involves means and proportions.

of elements in the distribution that met a criterion. In this case, the criterion is the origin of manufacture.

In Exhibit 17-2, the bell-shaped curve that is superimposed on the distribution of annual unit sales increases (percent) for LCD TV manufacturers is called the **normal distribution**. The distribution of values for any variable that has a normal distribution is governed by a mathematical equation. This distribution is a symmetrical curve and reflects a frequency distribution of many natural phenomena such as the height of people of a certain gender and age.

Many variables of interest that researchers will measure will have distributions that approximate a **standard normal distribution**. A standard normal distribution is a special case of the normal distribution in which all values are given standard scores. This distribution has a mean of 0 and a standard deviation of 1. For example, a manufacturer that had an annual unit sales increase of 7 percent would be given a standard score of zero since 7 is the mean of the LCD TV distribution. A **standard score** (or **Z score**) tells you how many

normal distribution a frequency distribution of many natural phenomena; graphically shaped like a symmetrical curve.

standard normal distribution the statistical standard for describing normally distributed sample data.

standard score (Z score) conveys how many standard deviation units a case is above or below the mean.

>**Exhibit 17-2** Histogram of Annual Unit Sales Increase (%)

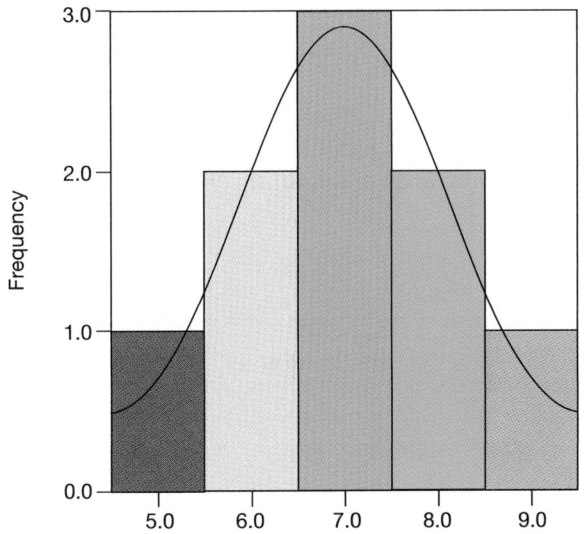

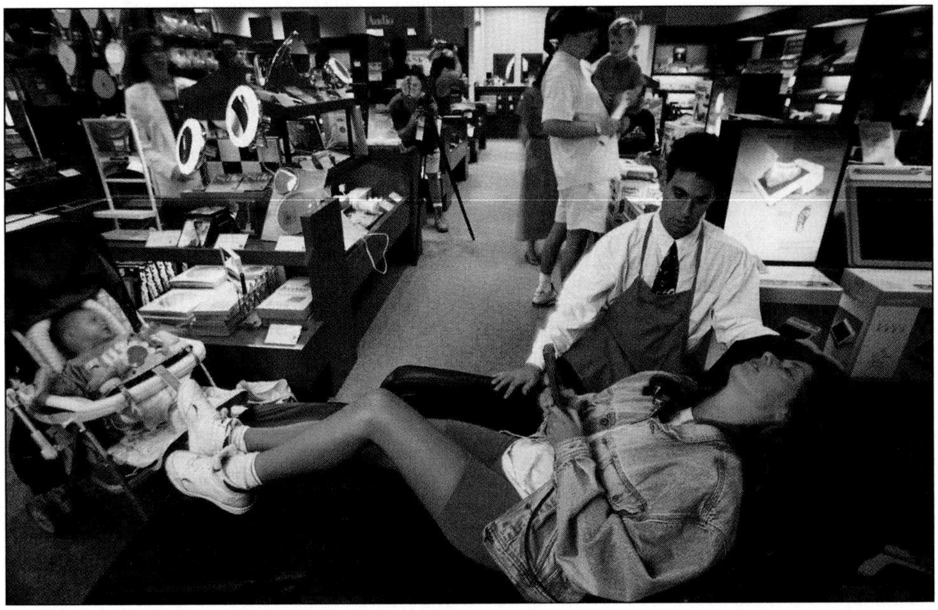

Recliners have had an appeal historically to only a subset of furniture buyers but have recently gained in popularity. The *proportion* is the percentage of elements in the population who would consider buying one.

> **The standard deviation
is defined and
illustrated in the next
section.**

units a case (a manufacturer in this example) is above or below the mean. The Z score, being standardized, allows us to compare the results of different normal distributions, something we do frequently in research. Assume that Zenith has an annual unit sales increase of 9 percent. To calculate a standard score for this manufacturer, you would find the difference between the value and the mean and divide by the standard deviation of the distribution shown in Exhibit 17-1:

$$\text{Zenith's standard score} = \frac{\text{value} - \text{mean}}{\text{standard deviation}} = \frac{9 - 7}{1.22} = 1.64$$

The standard normal distribution, shown in part A of Exhibit 17-3, is a standard of comparison for describing distributions of sample data. It is used with inferential statistics that assume normally distributed variables.

> **Refer to Exhibit 17-1
for the values of the
variable in these
examples.**

descriptive statistics
display characteristics of the
location, spread, and shape of
a data array.

We will come back to this exhibit in a moment. Now let's review some descriptive tools that reveal the important characteristics of distributions and will help us later with the determination of sample size. The characteristics of central tendency, variability, and shape are useful tools for summarizing distributions. Their definitions, applications, and formulas fall under the heading of **descriptive statistics**. The definitions will be familiar to most readers.

Measures of Central Tendency

Summarizing information such as that from our collected data of LCD TV manufacturers often requires the description of "typical" values. Suppose we want to know the typical percentage unit sales increase for these companies. We might define typical as the average

>**Exhibit 17-3** Characteristics of Distributions

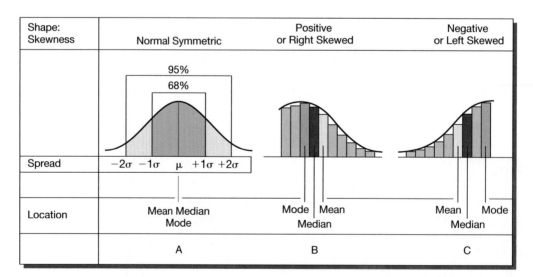

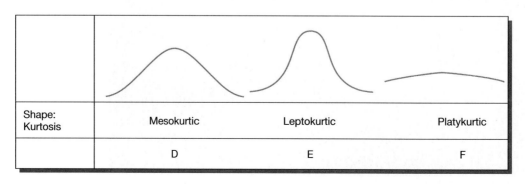

response (mean); the middle value, when the distribution is sorted from lowest to highest (median); or the most frequently occurring value (mode). The common measures of **central tendency** (or center) include the mean, median, and mode.

The **mean** is calculated by the formula below:

$$\bar{X} = \frac{\sum_{i=1}^{n} X_i}{n}$$

For the unit sales increase variable, the distribution of responses is 5, 6, 6, 7, 7, 7, 8, 8, 9. The arithmetic average, or mean (the sum of the nine values divided by 9) is

$$\frac{5 + 6 + 6 + 7 + 7 + 7 + 8 + 8 + 9}{9} = 7 \text{ (an average 7\% unit sales increase)}$$

The **median** is the midpoint of the distribution. Half of the observations in the distribution fall above and the other half fall below the median. When the distribution has an even number of observations, the median is the average of the two middle scores. The median is the most appropriate locator of center for ordinal data and has resistance to extreme scores, thereby making it a preferred measure for interval and ratio data when their distributions are not normal. The median is sometimes symbolized by *M* or *mdn*.

From the sample distribution for the percentage unit sales increase variable, the median of the nine values is 7:

5 6 6 7 **7** 7 8 8 9

If the distribution had 10 values, the median would be the average of the values for the fifth and sixth cases.

The **mode** is the most frequently occurring value. There may be *more than one* mode in a distribution. When there is more than one score that has the highest yet equal frequency, the distribution is bimodal or multimodal. There may be *no* mode in a distribution if every score has an equal number of observations. The mode is the location measure of central tendency for nominal data and a point of reference along with the median and mean for examining spread and shape of distributions. In our LCD TV percentage unit sales increase example, the most frequently occurring value is 7. As revealed in the frequency distribution in Exhibit 17-1, there are three companies that have unit sales increases of 7 percent.

Notice in Exhibit 17-3, part A, that the mean, median, and mode are the same in a normal distribution. When these measures of central tendency diverge, the distribution is no longer normal.

central tendency a measure of location (mean, median, mode)

mean the arithmetic average of a data distribution.

median the midpoint of a data distribution.

mode the most frequently occurring value in a distribution.

A sample of a multicultural population must be larger to account for differences in ethnicity.

Progressive Wants Your Autograph

Progressive Insurance, Inc., started near Cleveland in 1937 by two lawyers, has been shaking up the insurance industry for decades. But its maverick attitude has become increasingly evident during the last 10 years. Its impressive string of firsts includes 24-hour service, insurance over the Web, Immediate Response © (which settles claims within minutes rather than weeks using specialized technology-equipped sports utility vehicles), and free rate comparison service. Recently, some Texas drivers have been experiencing lower insurance rates due to a test of a patented information transfer process called *Autograph™*. Most drivers' insurance rates are determined based on a company's past realized losses with a classification of automobile and a classification of driver. *Autograph™* provides Progressive with detailed data about when, where, and how much the insured vehicle has been driven.

The data are reported periodically and automatically using cellular communication technology. Thus automobile insurance rates are based on current, not historic, driving patterns—if you drive less, you pay less. The *Autograph™* collection device is about the size of a videocassette. And this rate reducer also packs some special safety features: For an additional monthly fee, Progressive can track your vehicle if it's stolen, remotely unlock your doors, offer roadside and directional assistance, and even detect when your battery is low.

How large a sample of drivers would Progressive need to test its hypothesis that drivers who drive differently (when, where, and how much) deserve different rates?

www.progressive.com

Measures of Variability

variability another term for measures of spread or dispersion within a data set.

The common measures of **variability**, alternatively referred to as *dispersion* or *spread,* are the variance, standard deviation, range, interquartile range, and quartile deviation. They describe how scores cluster or scatter in a distribution.

variance a measure of score dispersion about the mean.

The **variance** is a measure of score dispersion about the mean. If all the scores are identical, the variance is 0. The greater the dispersion of scores, the greater the variance. Both the variance and the standard deviation are used with interval and ratio data. The symbol for the sample variance is s^2, and that for the population variance is the Greek letter sigma, squared (σ^2). The variance is computed by summing the squared distance from the mean for all cases and dividing the sum by the total number of cases minus 1:

$$\text{Variance} = s^2 = \frac{\text{sum of the squared distances from the mean for all cases}}{(\text{number of cases} - 1)}$$

$$S^2 = \frac{\sum_{i=1}^{n} (X_i - \bar{X})^2}{n-1}$$

For the percentage unit sales increase variable, we would compute the variance as

$$s^2 = \frac{(5-7)^2 + (6-7)^2 + (6-7)^2 + (7-7)^2 + (7-7)^2 + (7-7)^2 + (8-7)^2 + (8-7)^2 + (9-7)^2}{8} = 1.5$$

standard deviation a measure of spread; the positive square root of the variance.

The **standard deviation** summarizes how far away from the average the data values typically are. It is perhaps the most frequently used measure of spread because it improves interpretability by removing the variance's square and expressing deviations in their original units (e.g., sales in dollars, not dollars squared). It is also an important concept for descriptive statistics because it reveals the amount of variability within the data set. Like the mean, the standard deviation is affected by extreme scores. The symbol for the sample standard deviation is *s,* and that for a population standard deviation is σ. Alternatively, it is labeled *std. dev.* You calculate the standard deviation by taking the square root of the variance.

$$s = \sqrt{s^2}$$

The standard deviation for the percentage unit sales increase variable in our example is 1.22:

$$1.22 = \sqrt{1.5}$$

The **range** is the difference between the largest and smallest scores in the distribution. The percentage annual unit sales increase variable has a range of 4 (9 − 5 = 4). Unlike the standard deviation, the range is computed from only the minimum and maximum scores; thus, it is a very rough measure of spread. With the range as a point of comparison, it is possible to get an idea of the homogeneity (small std. dev.) or heterogeneity (large std. dev.) of the distribution. For a homogeneous distribution, the ratio of the range to the standard deviation should be between 2 and 6. A number above 6 would indicate a high degree of heterogeneity. In the percentage unit sales increase example, the ratio is 4/1.22 = 3.28. The range provides useful but limited information for all data. It is mandatory for ordinal data.

The **interquartile range (IQR)** is the difference between the first and third quartiles of the distribution. It is also called the *midspread*. Ordinal or ranked data use this measure in conjunction with the median. It is also used with interval and ratio data when asymmetrical distributions are suspected or for exploratory analysis. Recall the following relationships: The minimum value of the distribution is the 0 percentile; the maximum, the 100th percentile. The first quartile (Q_1) is the 25th percentile; the median, Q_2, is the 50th percentile. The third quartile (Q_3) is the 75th percentile. For the percentage unit sales increase data, the quartiles are:

$$
\begin{array}{ccccccccc}
5 & 6 & 6 & 7 & \mathbf{7} & 7 & 8 & 8 & 9 \\
& Q_1 & & Q_2 & & Q_3 & & Q_4 &
\end{array}
$$

The quartile deviation, or semi-interquartile range, is expressed as

$$Q = \frac{Q_1 - Q_3}{2}$$

The **quartile deviation** is always used with the median for ordinal data. It is helpful for interval and ratio data when the distribution is stretched (or skewed) by extreme values. In a normal distribution, the median plus one quartile deviation (Q) on either side encompasses 50 percent of the observations. Eight Qs cover approximately the range. Q's relationship with the standard deviation is constant ($Q = .6745s$) when scores are normally distributed. For our annual percentage unit sales increase example, the quartile deviation is 1 [(6 − 8)/2 = 1].

Measures of Shape

The measures of shape, skewness and kurtosis, describe departures from the symmetry of a distribution and its relative flatness (or peakedness), respectively. They use deviation scores ($X − \bar{X}$). **Deviation scores** show us how far any observation is from the mean. The company that posted a percentage unit sales increase of 9 has a deviation score of 2 (9 − 7). The measures of shape are often difficult to interpret when extreme scores are in the

One of the challenges for researchers in an increasingly diverse culture is selecting samples that reflect the population diversity. When a research project calls for a culturally diverse sample, many firms turn to specialists with expertise in recruiting different ethnic and cultural subgroups. **www.cheskin.com**

range the difference between the largest and smallest scores in the distribution.

interquartile range (IQR) measures the distance between the first and third quartiles of a distribution.

quartile deviation a measure of dispersion for ordinal data involving the median and quartiles.

deviation scores display distance of observation from the mean.

> **Refer to the graphics in Exhibit 17-3, parts B through F.**

skewness a measure of a distribution's deviation from symmetry.

distribution. Generally, shape is best communicated through visual displays. From a practical standpoint, the calculation of skewness and kurtosis is easiest with spreadsheet or statistics software.

Skewness is a measure of a distribution's deviation from symmetry. In a symmetrical distribution, the mean, median, and mode are in the same location. A distribution that has cases stretching toward one tail or the other is called *skewed*. As shown in Exhibit 17-3, part B, when the tail stretches to the right, to larger values, it is positively skewed. In part C, scores stretching toward the left, toward smaller values, skew the distribution negatively. Note the relationship between the mean, median, and mode in asymmetrical distributions. The symbol for skewness is *sk*.

$$sk = \frac{n}{(n-1)(n-2)} \sum \left(\frac{x_i - \bar{x}}{s}\right)^3$$

where *s* is the sample standard deviation (the unbiased estimate of sigma).

When a distribution approaches symmetry, *sk* is approximately 0. With a positive skew, *sk* will be a positive number; with negative skew, *sk* will be a negative number. The calculation of skewness for our annual percentage unit sales increase data produces an index of 0 and reveals no skew.

kurtosis a measure of a distribution's peakedness or flatness.

As illustrated in the lower portion of Exhibit 17-3, **kurtosis** is a measure of a distribution's peakedness (or flatness). Distributions that have scores that cluster heavily or pile up in the center (along with more observations than normal in the extreme tails) are peaked or *leptokurtic*. Flat distributions, with scores more evenly distributed and tails fatter than a normal distribution, are called *platykurtic*. Intermediate or *mesokurtic* distributions approach normal—neither too peaked nor too flat. The symbol for kurtosis is *ku*.

$$ku = \left[\frac{n(n+1)}{(n-1)(n-2)(n-3)} \sum \left(\frac{x_i - \bar{x}}{s}\right)^4\right] - \frac{3(n-1)^2}{(n-2)(n-3)}$$

where *s* is the sample standard deviation (the unbiased estimate of sigma).

The value of *ku* for a normal or mesokurtic distribution is close to 0. A leptokurtic distribution will have a positive value, and the platykurtic distribution will be negative. As with skewness, the larger the absolute value of the index, the more extreme is the characteristic. In the annual percentage unit sales increase example, the kurtosis is calculated as −.29, which suggests a very slight deviation from a normally shaped curve with some flattening contributed by smaller-than-expected frequencies of the value 7.

> ❝ In a recent Gallup 'poll on polls,' . . . when asked about the scientific sampling foundation on which polls are based . . . most said that a survey of 1,500–2,000 respondents—a larger than average sample size for national polls—cannot represent the views of all Americans. ❞
>
> *Frank Newport*
> *The Gallup Poll's Editor in Chief,*
> *The Gallup Organization*

Basic Concepts for Sampling

In the Metro University dining club study described in Chapter 16, we explored probability sampling and the various concepts used to design the sampling process.

Exhibit 17-4 shows the Metro U dining club study population ($N = 20,000$) consisting of five subgroups based on their preferred lunch times. The values 1 through 5 represent preferred lunch times, each a 30-minute interval, starting at 11:00 a.m., 11:30 a.m., 12:00 noon, 12:30 p.m., and 1:00 p.m. The frequency of response (*f*) in the population distribution, shown beside the population subgroup, is what would be found if a census of the elements was taken. Normally, population data are unavailable or are too costly to obtain. We are pretending omniscience about the population for the sake of the example.

>**Exhibit 17-4** Random Samples of Preferred Lunch Times

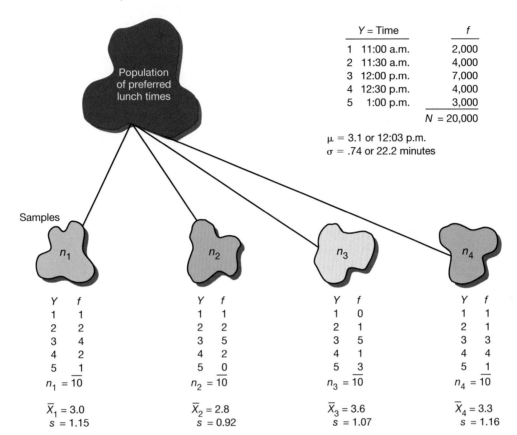

Y = Time	f
1 11:00 a.m.	2,000
2 11:30 a.m.	4,000
3 12:00 p.m.	7,000
4 12:30 p.m.	4,000
5 1:00 p.m.	3,000
	N = 20,000

μ = 3.1 or 12:03 p.m.
σ = .74 or 22.2 minutes

Y	f		Y	f		Y	f		Y	f
1	1		1	1		1	0		1	1
2	2		2	2		2	1		2	1
3	4		3	5		3	5		3	3
4	2		4	2		4	1		4	4
5	1		5	0		5	3		5	1
n_1 = 10			n_2 = 10			n_3 = 10			n_4 = 10	

$\overline{X}_1$ = 3.0 $\overline{X}_2$ = 2.8 $\overline{X}_3$ = 3.6 $\overline{X}_4$ = 3.3
s = 1.15   s = 0.92   s = 1.07   s = 1.16

Point Estimates

Now assume we sample 10 elements from this population without knowledge of the population's characteristics. We use a sampling procedure from a statistical software program, a random number generator, or the table of random numbers approach described in Chapter 16. Our first sample (n_1 = 10) provides us with the frequencies shown below the image of sample n_1 in Exhibit 17-4. We also calculate a mean score, $\overline{X}_1$ = 3.0, for this sample. This mean would place the average preferred lunch time at 12:00 noon. The mean is a **point estimate** and our best predictor of the unknown population mean (the arithmetic average of the population). Assume further that we return the first sample to the population and draw a second, third, and fourth sample by the same procedure. The frequencies, means, and standard deviations are as shown in Exhibit 17-4. As the data suggest, each sample shares some similarities with the population, but none is a perfect duplication because no sample perfectly replicates its population.

point estimate sample mean; our best predictor of the unknown population mean.

Interval Estimates

We cannot judge which estimate is the true mean (or accurately reflects the population mean). However, we can estimate the interval in which the true μ will fall by using any of the samples. This is accomplished by using a formula that computes the standard error of the mean:

$$\sigma_{\bar{X}} = \frac{\sigma}{\sqrt{n}}$$

where

$\sigma_{\bar{X}}$ = standard error of the mean or the standard deviation of all possible $\bar{X}$s

σ = population standard deviation

n = sample size

standard error of the mean the standard deviation of the distribution of sample means.

The standard deviation of the distribution of all possible sample means is estimated by the **standard error of the mean**. It varies directly with the standard deviation of the population from which it is drawn, as shown in Exhibit 17-5. If the standard deviation is reduced by 50 percent, the standard error will also be reduced by 50 percent. It also varies inversely with the square root of the sample size. If the square root of the sample size is doubled, the standard error is cut by one-half, provided the standard deviation remains constant.

Let's now examine what happens when we apply sample data (n_1) from Exhibit 17-4 to the formula. The sample standard deviation will be used as an unbiased estimator of the population standard deviation:

$$\sigma_{\bar{X}} = \frac{s}{\sqrt{n}}$$

where

s = standard deviation of the sample, n_1

$n_1 = 10$

$\bar{X} = 3.0$

$s_1 = 1.15$

Substituting into the equation:

$$\sigma_{\bar{X}} = \frac{s}{\sqrt{n}} = \frac{1.15}{\sqrt{10}} = .36$$

Estimating the Population Mean

interval estimate range of values within which the true population parameter is expected to fall.

How does this improve our prediction of μ from $\bar{X}$? The standard error creates an interval estimate that brackets the point estimate. The **interval estimate** is an interval or range of values within which the true population parameter is expected to fall. In this example, μ is

>Exhibit 17-5 Effects on Standard Error of Mean of Increasing Precision

	Reducing the Standard Deviation by 50%	Quadrupling the Sample
$\sigma_{\bar{X}} = \dfrac{s}{\sqrt{n}}$	$\sigma_{\bar{X}} = \dfrac{.74}{\sqrt{10}} = .234$	$\sigma_{\bar{X}} = \dfrac{.8}{\sqrt{25}} = .16$
	$\sigma_{\bar{X}} = \dfrac{.37}{\sqrt{10}} = .117$	$\sigma_{\bar{X}} = \dfrac{.8}{\sqrt{100}} = .08$

where
$\sigma_{\bar{X}}$ = standard error of the mean
s = standard deviation of the sample
n = sample size

Note: A 400% increase in sample size (from 25 to 100) would only yield a 200% increase in precision (from .16 to .08). Researchers are often asked to increase precision, but the question should be, "At what cost?" Each of those additional sample elements adds both time and cost to the study.

predicted to be 3.0 or 12:00 noon (the mean of n_1) $\pm$ .36. This range may be visualized on a continuum:

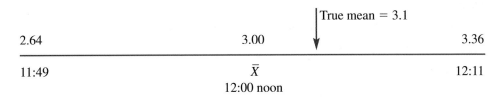

	True mean = 3.1	
2.64	3.00	3.36
11:49	$\overline{X}$ 12:00 noon	12:11

We would expect to find the true μ between 2.64 and 3.36—between 11:49 a.m. and 12:11 p.m. (If 2 = 11:30 a.m. and .64(30 minutes) = 19.2 minutes, then 2.64 = 11:30 a.m. + 19.2 minutes, or 11:49 a.m.) Since we assume omniscience in this illustration, we know the population average value is 3.1. Further, because standard errors have characteristics like other standard scores (a mean of 0 and a standard deviation of 1), we have 68 percent confidence in this estimate—that is, one standard error encompasses $\pm$ 1 Z, or 68 percent of the area under the normal curve (see Exhibit 17-6). Recall that the area under the curve also represents the confidence estimates that we make about our results. The combination of the interval range and the degree of confidence creates the confidence interval. A **confidence interval** is computed in a prescribed way to obtain a known probability of including the unknown population parameter. For example, $\mu = \overline{X} \pm$ sampling error with a *known probability.* If we want to improve our confidence from 68 to 95 percent, multiply the standard error of .36 by $\pm$1.96 (Z), since 1.96 Z covers 95 percent of the area under the curve (see Exhibits 17-6 and 17-7). Now, with 95 percent confidence, the interval in which we would find the true mean increases to $\pm$.70 (from 2.3 to 3.7, or from 11:39 a.m. to 12:21 p.m.).

> **confidence interval** the combination of interval range and degree of confidence.

Parenthetically, if we compute the standard deviation of the distribution of sample means in Exhibit 17-4 (3.0, 2.8, 3.6, 3.3), we will discover it to be .35. Compare this to the standard error from the original calculation (.36). The result is consistent with the definition of the standard error: *The standard deviation of the distribution of sample means (n_1, n_2, n_3, and n_4) equals the standard error.*

Now let's return to the dining club example and apply some of these concepts to the researchers' problem. If the researchers were to interview all the students and employees in the defined population, asking them, "How many times per month would you eat at the club?" they would get a distribution something like that shown in part A of Exhibit 17-8. The responses would range from zero to as many as 30 lunches per month, with a μ and σ as designated.

However, the researchers cannot take a census, so μ and σ remain unknown. By sampling 64 people, they find the mean to be 10.0 and the standard deviation to be 4.1 eating

>Exhibit 17-6 Confidence Levels and the Normal Curve

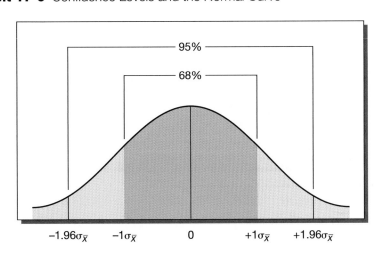

>**Exhibit 17-7** Standard Errors Associated with Areas under the Normal Curve

Standard Error (Z score)	Percent of Area*	Approximate Degree of Confidence
1.00	68.27	68%
1.65	90.10	90
1.96	95.00	95
3.00	99.73	99

*Includes both tails in a normal distribution.

>**Exhibit 17-8** A Comparison of Population Distribution, Sample Distribution, and Distribution of Sample Means for Metro U Dining Club Study

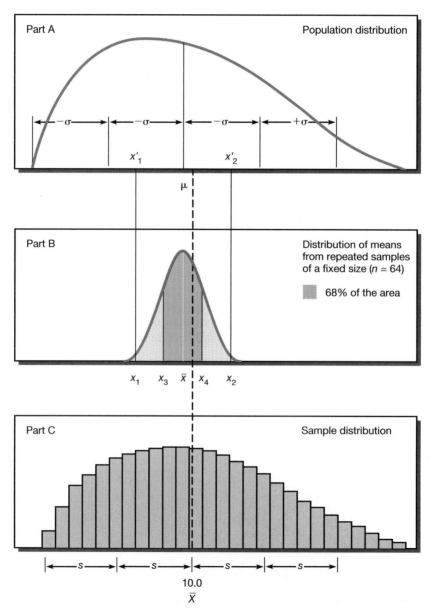

Note: The distributions in the figures are not to scale, but this fact is not critical to our understanding of the dispersion relationship depicted.

experiences (how often the participants would eat at the club per month). Turning to part C of Exhibit 17-8, three observations about this sample distribution are consistent with our earlier illustration. First, it is shown as a histogram; it represents a frequency distribution of empirical data, while the smooth curve of part A is a theoretical distribution. Second, the sample distribution (part C) is similar in appearance but is not a perfect duplication of the population distribution (part A). Third, the mean of the sample differs from the mean of the population.

If the researchers could draw repeated samples, as we did earlier, they could plot the mean of each sample to secure the solid-line distribution found in part B. According to the **central limit theorem**, for sufficiently large samples ($n = 30$), the sample means will be distributed around the population mean approximately in a normal distribution. Even if the population is not normally distributed, the distribution of sample means will be normal if there is a large enough set of samples.

> **central limit theorem** the sample means of repeatedly drawn samples will be distributed normally around the population mean.

Estimating the Interval for the Metro U Dining Club Sample

Any sample mean will fall within the range of the distribution extremes shown in part B of Exhibit 17-8. We also know that about 68 percent of the sample means in this distribution will fall between x_3 and x_4 and 95 percent will fall between x_1 and x_2.

If we project points x_1 and x_2 up to the population distribution (part A of Exhibit17-8) at points x'_1 and x'_2, we see the interval where any given mean of a random sample of 64 is likely to fall 95 percent of the time. Since we will not know the population mean from which to measure the standard error, we infer that there is also a 95 percent chance that the population mean is within two standard errors of the sample mean (10.0). This inference enables us to find the sample mean, mark off an interval around it, and state a confidence likelihood that the population mean is within this bracket.

Because the researchers are considering an investment in this project, they would want some assurance that the population mean is close to the figure reported in any sample they take. To find out how close the population mean is to the sample mean, they must calculate the standard error of the mean and estimate an interval range within which the population mean is likely to be.

Given a sample size of 64, they still need a value for the standard error. Almost never will one have the value for the standard deviation of the population (σ), so we must use a proxy figure. The best proxy for σ is the standard deviation of the sample (s). Here the standard deviation ($s = 4.1$) was obtained from a pilot sample of 64 cases:

$$\sigma_{\bar{X}} = \frac{s}{\sqrt{n}} = \frac{4.1}{\sqrt{64}} = .51$$

where

$\sigma_{\bar{X}}$ = standard error of the mean

s = standard deviation of the sample

n = sample size

If one standard error of the mean is equal to 0.51 visit, then 1.96 standard errors (95 percent) are equal to 1.0 visit. The researchers can estimate with 95 percent confidence that the population mean of expected visits is within 10.0 ± 1.0 visit, or from 9.0 to 11.0 meal visits per month.

> **We discuss pilot tests as part of the pretest phase in Chapter 15.**

Changing Confidence Intervals

The above estimate may not be satisfactory in two ways. First, it may not represent the degree of confidence the researchers want in the interval estimate, considering their financial

>**Exhibit 17-9** Estimates Associated with Various Confidence Levels in the Metro U Dining Club Study

Approximate Degree of Confidence	Z Score	Percent of Area*	Interval Range of Dining Visits per Month
68%	1.00	68.27	μ is between 9.48 and 10.52 visits
90	1.65	90.10	μ is between 9.14 and 10.86 visits
95	1.96	95.00	μ is between 8.98 and 11.02 visits
99	3.00	99.73	μ is between 8.44 and 11.56 visits

*Includes both tails in a normal distribution.

confidence level the probability that the results will be correct.

risk. The **confidence level** is a percentage that reflects the probability that the results will be correct. They might want a higher degree of confidence than the 95 percent level used here. For example, confidence levels of 80, 90, 95, and 99 percent or higher are chosen based on the consequences of error. We might be comfortable with a 90 percent probability (and a 10 percent risk of error) for a product launch within an established product category but require a 99.999 percent confidence in testing a drug for treatment of cystic fibrosis. By referring to a table of areas under the normal curve (a reflection of the normal distribution), researchers can find various other combinations of probability. Exhibit 17-9 summarizes some of those more commonly used. Thus, if the university researchers want a greater confidence in the probability of including the population mean in the interval range, they can move to a higher standard error, say, $\bar{X} \pm 3$ standard errors of the mean. When computed, the population mean now lies somewhere between $10.0 \pm 3(0.51)$, or from 8.47 to 11.53 visits per month. With 99.73 percent confidence, we can say this interval will include the population mean. The confidence interval estimate allows the researchers to estimate the market demand for the dining club within different ranges.

We might wish to have an estimate that will hold for a much smaller range, for example, 10.0 ± 0.2. To secure this smaller interval range, we must either (1) accept a lower level of confidence in the results or (2) take a sample large enough to provide this smaller interval with the higher desired confidence level.

If one standard error is equal to 0.51 visit, then 0.2 visit would be equal to 0.39 standard error $(0.2/0.51 = .39)$. Referring to a table of areas under the normal curve (Appendix D, Exhibit D-1), we find that there is a 30.3 percent chance that the true population mean lies within ± 0.39 standard error of 10.0. With a sample of 64, the sample mean would be subject to so much error variance that only 30 percent of the time could the researchers expect to find the population mean between 9.8 and 10.2. This is such a low level of confidence that the researchers would normally move to the second alternative; they would increase the sample size until they could secure the desired interval estimate and degree of confidence.

> Calculating the Sample Size for Questions Involving Means

Before we compute the desired sample size for the Metro U dining club study, let's review the information we will need:

> **Knowledge of these factors allows us to determine sample size accurately.**

1. The *precision* desired and how to quantify it:
   a. The *confidence level* we want with our estimate.
   b. The *size of the interval estimate.*
2. The expected *dispersion in the population* for the investigative question used.
3. Whether a finite population adjustment is needed.

>**Exhibit 17-10** Metro U Sampling Design Decisions on "Meal Frequency" and "Joining" Constructs

	Metro U Decisions	
Sampling Issues	**"Meal Frequency"** (interval, ratio data)	**"Joining"** (nominal, ordinal data)
1. The precision desired and how to quantify it:		
• The confidence researcher wants in the estimate (selected based on risk)	95% confidence ($Z = 1.96$)	95% confidence ($Z = 1.96$)
• The size of the interval estimate the researcher will accept (based on risk)	$\pm.5$ meal per month	$\pm.10$ (10 percent)
2. The expected range in the population for the question used to measure precision:	0 to 30 meals	0 to 100%
Measure of Central Tendency		
• Sample mean	10	
• Sample proportion of population with the given attribute being measured		30%
Measure of Dispersion		
• Standard deviation	4.1	
• Measure of sample dispersion		$pq = .30(.70) = .21$
3. Whether a finite population adjustment should be used	No	No
4. Estimate of standard deviation of population:		
• Standard error of mean	$.5/1.96 = 0.255$	
• Standard error of the proportion		$.10/1.96 = 0.051$
5. Sample size calculation	See formula (pg. 480)	See formula (pg. 482)
6. Calculated sample size	$n = 259^*$	$n = 81$

*Because both investigative questions were of interest, the researcher would use the larger of the two sample sizes calculated, $n = 259$, for the study.

The researchers have selected two investigative question constructs as critical—"frequency of patronage" and "interest in joining"—because they believe both to be crucial to making the correct decision on the Metro U dining club opportunity. The first requires a point estimate; the second, a proportion. The decisions needed and decisions made by the Metro U researchers are summarized in Exhibit 17-10.

Precision

Precision is measured by (1) the degree of confidence researchers and marketers wish to have in the estimate and (2) the interval range in which they expect to find the parameter estimate. The 95 percent confidence level is often used for precision, but more or less confidence may be needed in light of the risks of any given project. Similarly, the size of the interval estimate for predicting the population parameter from the sample data should be decided. When a smaller interval is selected, the researcher is saying that precision is vital, largely because inherent risks are high. For example, on a 5-point measurement scale, one-tenth of a point is a very high degree of precision in comparison to a 1-point interval. Given that a patron could eat up to 30 meals per month at the dining club (30 days times one meal per day), anything less than one meal per day would be asking for a high degree of precision in the Metro U study. The high risk of the Metro U study warrants the 0.5-meal precision selected. Of course, if the researchers are willing to accept a larger interval range (±1 meal), and thus a larger amount of risk, then they could reduce the sample size.

Population Dispersion

> **Refer to Exhibit 17-5 to see the effects of changes in precision.**

The next factor that affects the size of the sample for a given level of precision is the population dispersion or variability. The smaller the possible dispersion, the smaller will be the sample needed to give a representative picture of population members. If the population's number of meals ranges from 18 to 25, a smaller sample will give us an accurate estimate of the population's average meal consumption. However, with a population dispersion ranging from 0 to 30 meals consumed, a larger sample is needed for the same degree of confidence in the estimates. Since the true population dispersion of estimated meals per month eaten at the Metro University Dining Club is unknowable, the standard deviation of the sample is used as a proxy figure. Where do we get proxies of the population dispersion? Typically, this figure is based on any of the following:

- Previous research on the topic.
- A pilot test or pretest of the data instrument among a sample drawn from the population.
- A rule-of-thumb calculation (one-sixth of the range based on six standard deviations within 99.73 percent confidence).

If the range is from 0 to 30 meals, the rule-of-thumb method produces a standard deviation of 5 meals. The researchers in this study want more precision than the rule-of-thumb method provides, so they take a pilot sample of 25 and find the standard deviation to be 4.1 meals.

Size of the Population

A final factor affecting the size of a random sample is the size of the population. When the size of the calculated sample exceeds 5 percent of the population, the finite limits of the population constrain the sample size needed. A correction factor formula is available in that event. Applying this formula allows the researcher to achieve the same precision and confidence with a smaller sample. In the Metro U example, however, *as in most sample calculations,* population size does not have a major effect on sample size. Before determining if population size should be an issue, we must first calculate the sample size using our desired precision and confidence and dispersion estimates.

The sample size is computed for the first construct, meal frequency, as follows:

$$\sigma_{\bar{X}} = \frac{s}{\sqrt{n}}$$

$$\sqrt{n} = \frac{s}{\sigma_{\bar{X}}}$$

$$n = \frac{s^2}{\sigma_{\bar{X}}^2}$$

$$n = \frac{(4.1)^2}{(.255)^2}$$

$$n = 258.5, \text{ or } 259$$

where

$\sigma_{\bar{X}}$ = standard error of the mean = $(0.5/1.96) = 0.255$

s = standard deviation of the sample

n = sample size

If the population size is 20,000, then 5 percent is 1,000. As the calculated sample size (259) is less than 5 percent of the population (1,000), we would not need to make an adjustment

>**snap**shot

The Right Sample for Studying Sex Education

The Henry J. Kaiser Family Foundation (KFF), "an independent philanthropy focusing on the major health care issues facing the nation," is "primarily an operating organization that develops and runs its own research and communications programs." It recently released a study of principals, teachers, students, and their parents that challenges the "convention that Americans are reluctant to have sexual health issues taught in school; [rather] the surveys show that most parents, along with educators and students themselves, would expand sex education courses and curriculum."

How do you conduct a study on this sensitive topic? KFF chose Princeton Survey Research Associates to do several series of phone surveys. Interviews with "313 principals, 1,001 teachers of sex education classes, [and] 1,501 pairs of students and [their] parents were conducted February 2 through May 23, 1999." The principals and teachers were recruited to represent "all public, middle junior, and senior high schools enrolling grades 7 through 12 in the continental United States. They were ran-

domly and proportionately selected from a national database of public schools by type of school." Random dialing was used to identify households with children between 11 and 19 years of age who were enrolled in public schools in grades 7 through 12. Once the student was identified, the interviewer asked to speak with the male parent or guardian (followed by the female guardian, if the male guardian was unavailable). The parent was surveyed first, followed by the student, during the same contact if possible. "At least 15 attempts were made to complete an interview at every sample school or household." At the 95 percent confidence level, the error interval was ±3 percent for students-parents and teachers, and ±6 percent for principals. The participation rate was 54 percent for students-parents, 72 percent for teachers, and 41 percent for principals. What do you think of the sampling done for this study? You can link to a full study report from the KFF Web site.

www.kff.org; www.psra.com

for the population size. However, in cases where there is a very large population (such as the cellular phone user population of China), the correction factor would reduce the sample size and thus significantly reduce the cost of the study. Applying the correction formula only reduces the sample size needed in the Metro U study to 256 (compared to the original calculation of 259).

Finite population correction formula:

$$n = \frac{s^2}{\sigma_{\bar{X}}^2} \sqrt{\frac{(N - n)}{(N - 1)}}$$

where N = population size and n = sample size.

> Calculating the Sample Size for Questions Involving Proportions

The second key question concerning the dining club study was "What percentage of the population says it would join the dining club, based on the projected rates and services?" Another example is a CNN poll that projects the percentage of people who hold opinions for or against a proposition or a candidate. Such opinion polls are usually reported with a margin of error of ±5 percent. In marketing research, we often deal with proportion data— the proportion of prospects interested in purchasing a condominium property, the percentage who are likely to attend an event, the proportion who will fly on the Thanksgiving holiday weekend, the percentage having favorable attitudes about the musicians who use their concerts to support their favored political candidate.

In the Metro U study, a pretest answers this question using the same general procedure as before. But instead of the arithmetic mean, with proportions, it is p (the proportion of the population that has a given attribute)—in this case, interest in joining the dining club. And instead of the standard deviation, dispersion is measured in terms of $p \times q$ (in which q is the proportion of the population not having the attribute, and $q = (1 - p)$). The measure of dispersion of the sample statistic also changes from the standard error of the mean to the standard error of the proportion, σ_p.

We calculate a sample size based on these data by making the same two subjective decisions—deciding on an acceptable interval estimate and the degree of confidence. Assume that from a pilot test, 30 percent of the students and employees say they will join the dining club. We decide to estimate the true proportion in the population within 10 percentage points of this figure ($p = 0.30 \pm 0.10$). Assume further that we want to be 95 percent confident that the population parameter is within ± 0.10 of the sample proportion. The calculation of the sample size proceeds as before:

± 0.10 = desired interval range within which the population proportion is expected (subjective decision)

$1.96\ \sigma_p$ = 95 percent confidence level for estimating the interval within which to expect the population proportion (subjective decision)

$\sigma_p = 0.051$ = standard error of the proportion (0.10/1.96)

pq = measure of sample dispersion (used here as an estimate of the population dispersion)

n = sample size

$$\sigma_p = \sqrt{\frac{pq}{n}}$$

$$n = \frac{pq}{\sigma_p^2}$$

$$n = \frac{0.3 \times 0.7}{(.051)^2}$$

$$n = 81$$

where

σ_p = standard error of the proportion

pq = measure of dispersion

n = sample size

The sample size of 81 persons is based on an infinite population assumption. If the sample size is less than 5 percent of the population, there is little to be gained by using a finite population adjustment. The researchers interpreted the data found with a sample of 81 chosen randomly from the population as: "We can be 95 percent confident that 30 percent of the respondents would say they would join the dining club with a margin of error of ± 10 percent."

Previously, the researchers used pilot testing to generate the variance estimate for the calculation. Suppose this is not an option. Proportional data have a feature concerning the variance that is not found with interval or ratio data. The pq ratio can never exceed 0.25. For example, if $p = 0.5$, then $q = 0.5$, and their product is 0.25. If either p or q is greater than 0.5, then their product is smaller than 0.25 ($0.4 \times 0.6 = 0.24$, and so on). When we have no information regarding the probable p value, we can assume that $p = 0.5$ and solve for the sample size:

New Product Research Blind Spot

"There has always been a gap in new product research," claims Jim Lane, senior VP, Alliance Research, "between the time a new product is introduced and when it is possible to extract customer information." The reason? While new product marketers can track store sales audit data, locating purchasers to conduct attitudinal studies often lags as much as six months. Alliance Research combines its proprietary techniques for attitude measurement with parent company Catalina Marketing Corp.'s point-of-sale (POS) promotional system to develop a sample frame of purchasers of new products to participate in an interactive-voice-response (IVR) survey. Purchasers receive an invitation printed on the red-trimmed coupons that accompany their register receipts. For participation, Alliance compensates each respondent with up to $5, with current participation rates comparable to those for telephone studies. By inviting participants at the time of first purchase, the six-month wait for attitudinal data is history. Now this critical information is available to brand and marketing managers within weeks of a new product's hitting the shelf.

In what circumstances and why might immediate feedback not be an accurate measure of a new product's reception?

www.allianceresearch.com

$$n = \frac{pq}{\sigma_p^2}$$

$$n = \frac{(.50)\,(.50)}{(0.51)^2}$$

$$n = \frac{.25}{(0.051)^2}$$

$$n = 96$$

where

  pq = measure of dispersion

  n = sample size

If we use this maximum variance estimate in the dining club example, we find the sample size needs to be 96 persons in order to have an adequate sample for the question about joining the club.

When there are several investigative questions of strong interest, researchers calculate the sample size for each such variable—as we did in the Metro U study for "meal frequency" and "joining." The researcher then chooses the calculation that generates the largest sample. This ensures that all data will be collected with the necessary level of precision.

>summary

1 Marketing researchers make decisions about the sample sizes for interviews, experiments, product test markets, or Web surveys. A basic understanding of statistics is required for determining sample size. Statistical concepts and terminology allow us to understand the important characteristics of distributions. Descriptive statistics are used to summarize distributions. A frequency distribution summarizes data by arraying it in a frequency table. A proportion is the percentage of elements in the distribution that met a certain criterion. Summarizing the information from collected data often requires the description of "typical" values. The common measures of central tendency vary in application by scale or data and include the mean, median, and mode. Measures of variability describe how scores cluster or scatter in a

distribution. The variance, standard deviation, range, interquartile range, and quartile deviation are the indices of variability for metric (interval and ratio) data. The measures of distribution shape, skewness and kurtosis, describe departures from the symmetry and the distribution's relative flatness (or peakedness), respectively.

2 The distribution of values for any variable that has a normal distribution is governed by a mathematical equation. The normal distribution is a symmetrical, bell-shaped curve where the mean, median, and mode are all equal. Many variables of interest have distributions that approximate a standard normal distribution. The standard normal distribution is a standard of comparison for describing distributions of sample data and is used with inferential statistics that assume normally distributed variables. In a standard normal distribution, all values are given as standard scores. Standard scores tell us how many units an individual case is above or below the mean.

3 Techniques for computing population estimates were described in terms of point and interval estimates, the standard error of the mean, and the confidence level. Changing confidence intervals were also described. The central limit theorem informs us of the relationships between population and sampling distributions. Even if the population is not normally distributed, the distribution of sample means will be normal if there is a large enough set of samples.

4 To determine the sample size for questions involving means, we need the following information:

a The precision desired and how to quantify it:

(1) The confidence level we want with our estimate.

(2) The size of the interval estimate.

b The expected dispersion in the population for the investigative question used to measure precision.

c Whether a finite population adjustment is needed.

To compute the sample size for questions involving proportions, we use the same procedure—also deciding on an acceptable interval estimate and the degree of confidence—except we substitute p (the proportion of the population that has a given attribute) for the arithmetic mean and, instead of the standard deviation, dispersion is measured by $p \times q$ (in which q is the proportion of the population not having the attribute, and $q = (1 - p)$). The measure of dispersion of the sample statistic also changes from the standard error of the mean to the standard error of the proportion.

>**key**terms

central limit theorem 477	**interval estimate** 474	**range** 471
central tendency 469	**kurtosis** 472	**skewness** 472
confidence interval 478	**mean** 469	**standard deviation** 470
confidence level 475	**median** 469	**standard error of the mean** 474
descriptive statistics 468	**mode** 469	**standard normal distribution** 467
deviation scores 471	**normal distribution** 467	**standard score (Z score)** 467
frequency distribution 466	**point estimate** 473	**variability** 470
frequency table 466	**proportion** 466	**variance** 470
interquartile range (IQR) 471	**quartile deviation (Q)** 471	

>**discussion**questions

Terms in Review

1 Distinguish between:

a Frequency distribution, normal distribution, and standard normal distribution.

b Mean, median, and mode.

c Standard deviation and standard score.

d Point estimate and interval estimate.

2 What should be the ratio of the range to the standard deviation?

Making Research Decisions

3 You plan to conduct a survey using random sampling. What subjective decisions must you make?

4 You draw a random sample of 300 sales employee records from the personnel file and find that the average years of

service per employee is 6.3, with a standard deviation of 3.0 years.

a What percentage of the workers would you expect to have more than 9.3 years of service?

b What percentage would you expect to have more than 5.0 years of service?

5 A manufacturer of precision gaskets makes gaskets in two grades: military and consumer automobile. In military applications, the precise gasket thickness is far more critical than in consumer automobile applications. The production run for military applications is very small, whereas the production run for consumer applications is very large. Explain how these facts affect decisions in sample design, confidence intervals, and sample size.

6 You wish to take an unrestricted random sample of undergraduate students at Cranial University to ascertain their levels of spending per month for food purchased off campus and eaten on the premises where purchased. You ask a test sample of nine students about their food expenditures and find that on the average they report spending $20, with two-thirds of them reporting spending from $10 to $30. What size sample do you think you should take? (Assume your universe is infinite.)

7 You wish to adjust your sample calculations to reflect the fact that there are only 2,500 students in your population. How does this additional information affect your estimated sample size in question 6?

Behind the Scenes

8 Build a case against following Jason's advice: "Instead of just sampling 100 from your existing customer base, also do a separate survey of every 20th person from the Chamber of Commerce directory. You'll have one survey of customers and another of potential customers, and you'll still end up saving over $1,000."

From Concept to Practice

9 The researcher studying the Glacier Symphony patron problem wants to know how many phone numbers need to be obtained to complete a survey of attendees. Experience suggests that the city of Glacier has about 70 percent working listings. The percentage of people who attend the symphony's summer festival is estimated at 30 percent, and approximately 75 percent will be willing to complete the interview. What is the desired sample size? How many numbers should the researcher obtain?

>**www**exercises

1 Find some sample size calculators on the Web and identify which is the best of your sample. Compare it to the calculator at UCLA (**http://calculators.stat.ucla.edu/powercalc/**).

2 Visit The Gallup Organization and learn how it chooses a representative sample for The Gallup Poll. **http://www.gallup.com/help/FAQs/poll1.asp**

>**cases***

Calling Up Attendance	✸ **KNSD San Diego**
Campbell-Ewald: R-E-S-P-E-C-T Spells Loyalty	**Mastering Teacher Leadership**
Can Research Rescue the Red Cross?	**NCRCC: Teeing Up and New Strategic Direction**
✸ **Goodyear's Aquatred**	**NetConversions Influences Kelley Blue Book**
Inquiring Minds Want to Know—NOW!	**Open Doors: Extending Hospitality to Travelers with Disabilities**

Outboard Marine

Pebble Beach Co.

Starbucks Launches Duetto Visa

State Farm: Dangerous Intersections

USTA: Come Out Swinging

Volkswagen's Beetle

Yahoo!: *Consumer Direct* Marries Purchase Metrics to Banner Ads

* All cases, both written and video, are on the text DVD. The film icon indicates a video case. Check the DVD Index to determine whether a case has data, the research instrument, or other supplementary material.

>part IV

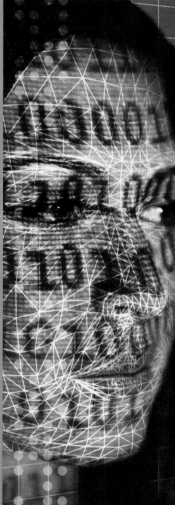

Analysis and Presentation of Data

chapter 18

Data Preparation and Description

After reading this chapter, you should understand . . .

1 The importance of editing the collected raw data to detect errors and omissions.

2 How coding is used to assign numbers and other symbols to answers and to categorize responses.

3 The use of content analysis to interpret and summarize open questions.

4 Problems and solutions for "don't know" responses and handling missing data.

5 The options for data entry and manipulation.

Laypeople often think that data need only to be tallied to be presented. But a trained researcher understands that data are rarely ready to be tallied after they are collected. Data entry, if it doesn't happen simultaneously with the survey process, adds days to the process, as does checking the data for accuracy. Myra Wines, MindWriter's primary contact with Visionary Insights, arrives early for a meeting she requested with Jason and interrupts a data session on another of Jason's projects. She has a vested interest in what Jason is working on, and she is about to offer VI a new project.

"Is my being early for our meeting a problem?" asks Myra as she slides past a pile of computer printouts stacked precariously high just inside the door to Jason's office. "Might the industrious team in your outer office be studying my MindWriter Project 2 data?"

"Not yet," comments Jason as he waves Myra to an empty chair. "Just give me one second." He quickly writes two notes on Post-its and slaps one on a pencil sketch of a graph and attaches the other to a histogram. "Sammye, you want to come get these?" Jason calls to one of the team members in the outer office.

Meanwhile, Myra chooses an available chair and waits. She is here to convince Jason to take on yet another project for MindWriter. This one has a short turnaround.

Turning his attention to Myra, Jason extracts a folder lying on the credenza behind him. "Actually those worker bees are new members of my staff, graduate students from the university. They're assigned to the City Center for Performing Arts project," shares Jason. "It's because of your recommendation that we got the job. I thought you knew."

"Of course I knew. I've been serving on CCPA's board for two years. Will you be presenting the preliminary analysis at the next meeting, this Friday?"

"As in day after tomorrow? Only in our dreams! The preliminary analysis you see them working on is strictly for us. While we may develop presentation charts that might be presented to the Center, it is just as likely that none of the material you see stacked here

will end up in the report as is. We are nowhere near ready to write the client report. We just finished cleaning the data file yesterday. This morning I ran a full set of frequencies. Jill, David, and Sammye started their preliminary analysis . . . uh, 90 minutes ago."

"So I guess I'll have to wait until you have something more solid to get even a briefing on what you've found so far?" inquires Myra, smiling.

"Ah," smiles Jason in return, "you've learned Visionary's process fairly well."

Myra grins and then modifies her position in the chair, leaning slightly toward Jason. Just before she speaks, Jason observes, "Oh, no! You're changing into your 'It's time to get down to business' posture. So what's the new project you want to discuss . . . and the impossible deadline you need me to meet?"

"Just hear me out, Jason. MindWriter's LT3000 product group has decided it needs to use 'superiority in custom-designed systems' as its claim in a new ad campaign, but legal says we don't have enough data to support the claim. The ad agency we have chosen has a short window of opportunity. We need supporting data within 10 days." Myra holds up her hand to stop the objection she anticipates from Jason. "We know you don't have time to collect new primary data and analyze it in 10 days . . . so I brought the next best thing. I've got three boxes of miscellaneous records in my trunk . . ."

"Let's go see what you brought me," Jason groans good-naturedly as he unfolds himself from his chair. "Then we'll see if this project is even feasible." As he passes through the outer office, Jason motions for one of the students to follow; then in an aside to Myra he says, "Myra, meet David Chesley. You're just lucky that my new interns are all so eager that they will enjoy juggling two projects at one time."

> Introduction

data preparation the processes that ensure the accuracy of data and their conversion from raw form into classified forms appropriate for analysis.

Once the data begin to flow, a researcher's attention turns to data analysis. This chapter focuses on the first phases of that process, data preparation and description. **Data preparation** includes editing, coding, and data entry and is the activity that ensures the accuracy of the data and their conversion from raw form to reduced and classified forms that are more appropriate for analysis. Preparing a descriptive statistical summary is another preliminary step leading to an understanding of the collected data. It is during this step that data entry errors may be revealed and corrected. Exhibit 18-1 reflects the steps in this phase of the research process.

>**Exhibit 18-1** Data Preparation in the Research Process

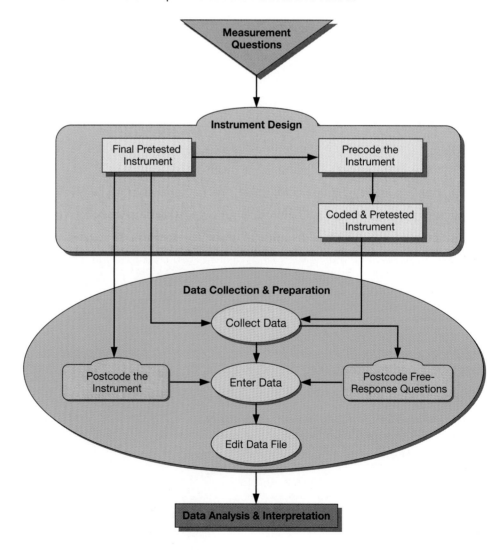

> Editing

The customary first step in analysis is to edit the raw data. **Editing** detects errors and omissions, corrects them when possible, and certifies that maximum data quality standards are achieved. The editor's purpose is to guarantee that data are:

editing process for detecting errors and data omissions, and correcting them when possible.

- Accurate.
- Consistent with the intent of the question and other information in the survey.
- Uniformly entered.
- Complete.
- Arranged to simplify coding and tabulation.

In the following question asked of adults 18 or older, one respondent checked two categories, indicating that he was a retired officer and currently serving on active duty.

Please indicate your current military status:

- ☑ Active duty
- ❑ National Guard
- ☑ Reserve
- ❑ Separated
- ❑ Retired
- ❑ Never served in the military

The editor's responsibility is to decide which of the responses is both consistent with the intent of the question or other information in the survey and most accurate for this individual participant.

Field Editing

In large projects, field editing review is a responsibility of the field supervisor. It, too, should be done soon after the data have been gathered. During the stress of data collection in a personal interview and paper-and-pencil recording in an observation, the researcher often uses ad hoc abbreviations and special symbols. Soon after the interview, experiment, or observation, the investigator should review the reporting forms. It is difficult to complete what was abbreviated or written in shorthand or noted illegibly if the entry is not caught that day. When entry gaps are present from interviews, a callback should be made rather than guessing what the respondent "probably would have said." Self-interviewing has no place in quality research.

A second important control function of the field supervisor is to validate the field results. This normally means he or she will reinterview some percentage of the respondents, at least on some questions, verifying that they have participated and that the interviewer performed adequately. Many research firms will recontact about 10 percent of the respondents in this process of data validation.

Western Wats, a data collection specialist, reminds us that speed without accuracy won't help a marketing decision maker choose the right direction. "After all, being quick on the draw doesn't do any good if you miss the mark." www.westernwats.com

Central Editing

At this point, the data should get a thorough editing. For a small study, the use of a single editor produces maximum consistency. In large studies, editing tasks should be allocated so that each editor deals with one entire section. Although the latter approach will not identify inconsistencies between answers in different sections, the problem can be handled by identifying questions in different sections that might point to possible inconsistency and having one editor check the data generated by these questions.

Sometimes it is obvious that an entry is incorrect—for example, when data clearly specify time in days (e.g., 13) when it was requested in weeks (you expect a number of 4 or less)—or is entered in the wrong place. When replies are inappropriate or missing, the editor can sometimes detect the proper answer by reviewing the other information in the data set. This practice, however, should be limited to the few cases where it is obvious what the correct answer is. It may be better to contact the respondent for correct information, if time and budget allow. Another alternative is for the editor to strike out the answer if it is inappropriate. Here an editing entry of "no answer" or "unknown" is called for.

Another problem that editing can detect concerns faking an interview that never took place. This "armchair interviewing" is difficult to spot, but the editor is in the best position to do so. One approach is to check responses to open-ended questions. These are most difficult to fake. Distinctive response patterns in other questions will often emerge if data falsification is occurring. To uncover this, the editor must analyze as a set the instruments used by each interviewer.

Here are some useful rules to guide editors in their work:

- Be familiar with instructions given to interviewers and coders.

- Do not destroy, erase, or make illegible the original entry by the interviewer; original entries should remain legible.

- Make all editing entries on an instrument in some distinctive color and in a standardized form.

- Initial all answers changed or supplied.

- Place initials and date of editing on each instrument completed.

Frequency distributions are arrayed via a table format when using SPSS for exploratory data analysis. The researcher here requested a frequency printout of all variables partially into data collection when 83 cases had been entered. SPSS presents them sequentially in one document. The left frame indicates all the variables included in this particular output file. Both variables Qual2 and Qual3 indicate 3 missing cases. This would be a cautionary flag to a good researcher. During editing the researcher would want to verify that these are true instances where participants did not rate the quality of both objects, rather than data entry errors. www.spss.com

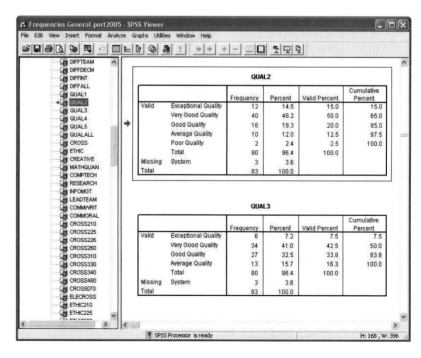

>**snap**shot

CBS: Some Labs Are Extraordinary

Visitors to Las Vegas have an opportunity to determine the direction of CBS programming by visiting the CBS Television City Research Center in the MGM Grand Hotel and Casino. According to Andrew Wing, president of ACNielsen Entertainment, what makes Las Vegas an ideal location for a research lab is the cross section of the American population and the large number of international citizens among its 36 million visitors each year. In a typical screening with 250 people, individuals represent more than 40 states and every conceivable lifestyle. Participants watch a 30- to 45-minute segment of a new or proposed program, without commercial interruptions, followed by a survey process lasting 15 minutes. Each seat is equipped with a computer touch screen linked to ACNielsen Entertainment's proprietary Nielsen ReelResearch Internet site. Participants share feedback on the show and personal demographics in real time, while network ex-

ecutives observe participants and their feedback from remote offices around the country. The facility, designed by GES, also provides focus group capabilities, used for follow-up interviews along with other research initiatives. Participants are compensated with a chance to win a home theater system and a $10 coupon that they may redeem on program-logo T-shirts, caps, pins, key chains, even computer software in the CBS Television City store. Arising out of a temporary test conducted in 1991, the research facility today operates 12 hours per day year-round. So on your next visit to the City of Lights, when the slots or big-name entertainers lose appeal, entertain yourself with research.

What are some of the advantages to having touch-screen data entry?

www.acnielsen.com; www.viad.com

> Coding

Coding involves assigning numbers or other symbols to answers so that the responses can be grouped into a limited number of categories. In coding, *categories* are the partitions of a data set of a given variable (for example, if the variable is *gender,* the partitions are *male* and *female*). *Categorization* is the process of using rules to partition a body of data. Both closed and open-ended questions must be coded.

> **coding** assigning numbers or symbols to responses so that they can be tallied and grouped into a limited number of categories.

The categorization of data sacrifices some data detail but is necessary for efficient analysis. In marketing research, most statistical and banner/table software programs work more efficiently in the *numeric* mode. Instead of entering the word *male* or *female* in response to a question that asks for the identification of one's gender, we would use numeric codes (for example, 0 for male and 1 for female). Numeric coding simplifies the researcher's task in converting a nominal variable, like gender, to a "dummy variable," a topic we discuss in Chapter 21. Statistical software also can use alphanumeric codes, as when we use M and F, or other letters, in combination with numbers and symbols for gender.

> 66 In the future, we'll stop moaning about the lack of perfect data and start using the good data with much more advanced analytics and data-matching techniques. 99
>
> *Kate Lynch*
> *Research Director,*
> *Leo Burnett's Starcom Media Unit*

Codebook Construction

A **codebook,** or *coding scheme,* contains each variable in the study and specifies the application of coding rules to the variable. It is used by the researcher or research staff to promote more accurate and more efficient data entry. It is also the definitive source for locating the positions of variables in the data file during analysis. In many statistical programs, the coding scheme is integral to the data file. Most codebooks—computerized or not—contain the question number, variable name, location of the variable's code on the

> **codebook** the coding rules for assigning numbers or other symbols to each variable.

input medium (e.g., spreadsheet or SPSS data file), descriptors for the response options, and whether the variable is alphabetic or numeric. An example of a paper-based codebook is shown in Exhibit 18-2. Pilot testing of an instrument provides sufficient information about the variables to prepare a codebook. A preliminary codebook used with pilot data may reveal coding problems that will need to be corrected before the data for the final study are collected and processed.

Coding Closed Questions

The responses to closed questions include scaled items for which answers can be anticipated. Closed questions are favored by researchers over open-ended questions for their efficiency and specificity. They are easier to code, record, and analyze. When codes are established in the instrument design phase of the research process, it is possible to precode the questionnaire during the design stage. With computerized survey design, and computer-assisted, computer-administered, or online collection of data, precoding is necessary as the software tallies data as they are collected. **Precoding** is particularly helpful for manual data entry (for example, from mail or self-administered surveys) because it makes the intermediate step of completing a *data entry coding sheet* unnecessary. With a precoded instrument, the codes for variable categories are accessible directly from the questionnaire. A participant, interviewer, field supervisor, or researcher (depending on the data collection method) is able to assign the appropriate code on the instrument by checking, circling, or printing it in the proper coding location.

precoding assigning codebook codes to variables in a study and recording them on the questionnaire.

Exhibit 18-3 shows questions in the sample codebook. When precoding is used, editing precedes data processing. Note question 4, where the respondent may choose between five categories of marital status and enter the number of the item best representing present status in the coding portion of the questionnaire. This code is later transferred to an input medium for analysis.

Coding Open-Ended Questions

One of the primary reasons for using open-ended questions is that insufficient information or lack of a hypothesis may prohibit preparing response categories in advance. Researchers are forced to categorize responses after the data are collected. Other reasons for using open-ended responses include the need to measure sensitive or disapproved behavior, discover salience or importance, or encourage natural modes of expression.[1] Also, it may be easier and more efficient for the participant to write in a known short answer rather than read through a long list of options. Whatever the reason for their use, analyzing enormous volumes of open-ended questions slows the analysis process and increases the opportunity for error. The variety of answers to a single question can be staggering, hampering postcollection categorization. Even when categories are anticipated and precoded for open-ended questions, once data are collected researchers may find it useful to reassess the predetermined categories. One example is a 7-point scale where the researcher offered the participant three levels of agreement, three levels of disagreement, and one neutral position. Once the data are collected, if these finer nuances of agreement do not materialize, the editor may choose to recategorize the data into three levels: one level of agreement, one level of disagreement, and one neutral position.

Exhibit 18-3, question 6, illustrates the use of an open-ended question for which advance knowledge of response options was not available. The answer to "What prompted you to purchase your most recent life insurance policy?" was to be filled in by the participant as a short-answer essay. After preliminary evaluation, response categories (shown in the codebook, Exhibit 18-2) were created for that item.

>**Exhibit 18-2** Sample Codebook of Questionnaire Items

Question	Variable Number	Code Description	Variable Name
_____	1	Record number	RECNUM
_____	2	Respondent number	RESID
1	3	5 digit zip code 99999 = Missing	ZIP
2	4	2 digit birth year 99 = Missing	BIRTH
3	5	Gender 1 = Male 2 = Female 9 = Missing	GENDER
4	6	Marital status 1 = Married 2 = Widow(er) 3 = Divorced 4 = Separated 5 = Never married 9 = Missing	MARITAL
5	7	Own–Rent 1 = Own 2 = Rent 3 = Provided 9 = Missing	HOUSING
6		Reason for purchase 1 = Mentioned 0 = Not mentioned	
	8	Bought home	HOME
	9	Birth of child	BIRTHCHD
	10	Death of relative or friend	DEATH
	11	Promoted	PROMO
	12	Changed job/career	CHGJOB
	13	Paid college expenses	COLLEXP
	14	Acquired assets	ASSETS
	15	Retired	RETIRED
	16	Changed marital status	CHGMAR
	17	Started business	STARTBUS
	18	Expanded business	EXPBUS
	19	Parent's influence	PARENT
	20	Contacted by agent	AGENT
	21	Other	OTHER

Coding Rules

Four rules guide the pre- and postcoding and categorization of a data set. The categories within a single variable should be:

- Appropriate to the research problem and purpose.
- Exhaustive.
- Mutually exclusive.
- Derived from one classification principle.

>Exhibit 18-3 Sample Questionnaire Items

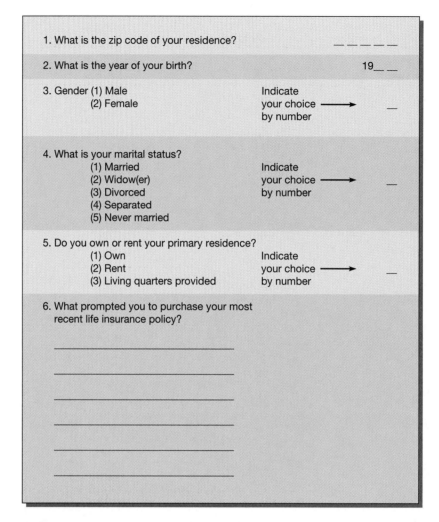

Researchers address these issues when developing or choosing each specific measurement question. One of the purposes of pilot testing of any measurement instrument is to identify and anticipate categorization issues.

Appropriateness

Appropriateness is determined at two levels: (1) the best partitioning of the data for testing hypotheses and showing relationships and (2) the availability of comparison data. For example, when actual age is obtained (ratio scale), the editor may decide to group data by age ranges to simplify pattern discovery within the data. The number of age groups and breadth of each range, as well as the endpoints in each range, should be determined by comparison data—for example, U.S. census age ranges, a customer database that includes age ranges, or the age data available from Fox TV used for making an advertising media buy.

Exhaustiveness

Researchers often add an "other" option to a measurement question because they know they cannot anticipate all possible answers. A large number of "other" responses, however, suggests the measurement scale the researcher designed did not anticipate the full range of information. The editor must determine if "other" responses appropriately fit into established categories, if new categories must be added, if "other" data will be ignored, or if some combination of these actions will be taken.

While the exhaustiveness requirement for a single variable may be obvious, a second aspect is less apparent. Does one set of categories—often determined before the data are collected—fully capture all the information in the data? For example, responses to an open-ended question about family economic prospects for the next year may originally be categorized only in terms of being "optimistic" or "pessimistic." It may also be enlightening to classify responses in terms of other concepts such as the precise focus of these expectations (income or jobs) and variations in responses between family heads and others in the family.

Mutual Exclusivity

Another important rule when adding categories or realigning categories is that category components should be mutually exclusive. This standard is met when a specific answer can be placed in one and only one cell in a category set. For example, in a survey, assume that you asked participants for their occupation. One editor's categorization scheme might include (1) professional, (2) managerial, (3) sales, (4) clerical, (5) crafts, (6) operatives, and (7) unemployed. As an editor, how would you code a participant's answer that specified "salesperson at Gap and full-time student" or maybe "elementary teacher and tax preparer"? According to census data, it is not unusual for adults in our society to have more than one job. Here, operational definitions of the occupations categorized as "professional," "managerial," and "sales" should help clarify the situation. But the editor facing this situation also would need to determine how the second-occupation data are handled. One option would be to add a second-occupation field to the data set; another would be to develop distinct codes for each unique multiple-occupation combination.

Single Dimension

The problem of how to handle an occupation entry like "unemployed salesperson" brings up a fourth rule of category design. The need for a category set to follow a single classificatory principle means every option in the category set is defined in terms of one concept or construct. Returning to the occupation example, the person in the study might be both a salesperson and unemployed. The "salesperson" label expresses the concept *occupation type;* the response "unemployed" is another dimension concerned with *current employment status* without regard to the respondent's normal occupation. When a category set encompasses more than one dimension, the editor may choose to split the dimensions and develop an additional data field; "occupation" now becomes two variables: "occupation type" and "employment status."

Using Content Analysis for Open Questions

Increasingly text-based responses to open-ended measurement questions are analyzed with content analysis software. **Content analysis** measures the semantic content or the *what* aspect of a message. Its breadth makes it a flexible and wide-ranging tool that may be used as a stand-alone methodology or as a problem-specific technique. Trend-watching organizations like the BrainReserve, the Naisbitt Group, SRI International, and Inferential Focus use variations on content analysis for selected projects, often spotting changes from newspaper or magazine articles before they can be confirmed statistically. The Naisbitt Group's content analysis of 2 million local newspaper articles compiled over a 12-year period resulted in the publication of *Megatrends.*

content analysis analytical process for measuring the semantic content of a communication.

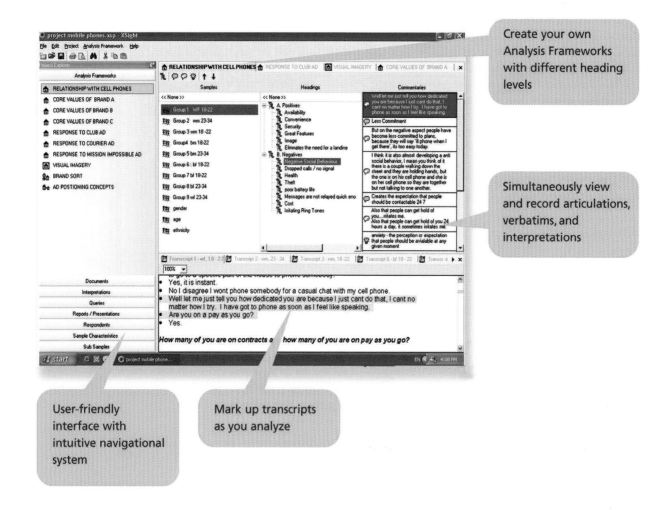

Create your own Analysis Frameworks with different heading levels

Simultaneously view and record articulations, verbatims, and interpretations

User-friendly interface with intuitive navigational system

Mark up transcripts as you analyze

QSR, the company that provided us with N6, the latest version of NUD*IST, and N-VIVO, introduced a commercial version of the content analysis software in 2004, XSight. XSight was developed for and with the input of researchers. **www.qsrinternational.com**

Types of Content

Content analysis has been described as "a research technique for the objective, systematic, and quantitative description of the manifest content of a communication."[2] Because this definition is sometimes confused with simply counting obvious message aspects such as words or attributes, more recent interpretations have broadened the definition to include latent as well as manifest content, the symbolic meaning of messages, and qualitative analysis. One author states:

> In any single written message, one can count letters, words, or sentences. One can categorize phrases, describe the logical structure of expressions, ascertain associations, connotations, denotations, elocutionary forces, and one can also offer psychiatric, sociological, or political interpretations. All of these may be simultaneously valid. In short, a message may convey a multitude of contents even to a single receiver.[3]

Content analysis follows a systematic process for coding and drawing inferences from texts. It starts by determining which units of data will be analyzed. In written or verbal texts, data units are of four types: syntactical, referential, propositional, or thematic. Each unit type is the basis for coding texts into mutually exclusive categories in our search for meaning.

- *Syntactical* units can be words, phrases, sentences, or paragraphs; words are the smallest and most reliable data units to analyze. While we can certainly count these

Georgia Pacific: This Research Was Brawny

When Atlanta-based Georgia-Pacific Corp. (G-P) acquired Brawny paper towels, Michael Burandt, G-P's executive vice president and president–North American consumer products, knew the company had a "truly competitive product." So G-P used product development research to make it better (incorporating a "through-air-dried" process) and marketing research to determine how best to communicate the new feature of absorbent strength embodied in a softer towel. Product testing research revealed that consumers perceived the new Brawny as better than the previous version. But how should G-P highlight the significant change? Georgia-Pacific launched the "Do You Know a Brawny Man?" contest and then used content analysis on the 4,000 essay and photo entries to define the traits of the icon. As a result, the company threw out the blond, mustached lumberjack used for more than 30 years and replaced him with a dark-haired, clean-shaven, sensitive male. In a second consumer test comparing the old with the new icon, 73 percent chose the new Brawny man. They thought he appeared stronger (66 percent) and well-rounded (68 percent) and was a better fit with the brand (64 percent). A few months later, the new Brawny man began appearing in print and TV advertising as the character endorser for the brand. In one tongue-in-cheek TV ad the new icon berates the former icon for his lack of sensitivity—implying this was the reason for the change. This print ad was a free-standing coupon insert appearing in newspapers.

www.gp.com

units, we are more interested in the meaning their use reveals. In content analysis we might determine the words that are most commonly used to describe product A versus its competitor, product B. We ask, "Are these descriptions for product A more likely to lead to favorable opinions and thus to preference and ultimately selection, compared to the descriptions used for product B?"

- *Referential* units are *described* by words, phrases, and sentences; they may be objects, events, persons, and so forth, to which a verbal or textual expression refers. Participants may refer to a product as a "classic," a "power performer," or "ranked first in safety"—each word or phrase may be used to describe different objects, and it is the object that the researcher codes and analyzes in relation to the phrase.

- *Propositional* units are *assertions* about an object, event, person, and so on. For example, a researcher assessing advertising for magazine subscriptions might conclude, "Subscribers who respond to offer A will save $15 over the single issue rate." It is the assertion of savings that is attached to the text of this particular ad claim.

- *Thematic* units are *topics* contained within (and across) texts; they represent higher-level abstractions inferred from the text and its context. The responses to an open-ended question about purchase behavior may reflect a temporal theme: the past ("I never purchased an alternative brand before you changed the package"), the present ("I really like the new packaging"), or the future ("I would buy the product more often if it came in more flavors"). We could also look at the comments as relating to the themes or topics of "packaging" versus a product characteristic, "flavors."

As with all other research methodologies, the analytical use of content analysis is influenced by decisions made prior to data collection. Content analysis guards against selective perception of the content, provides for the rigorous application of reliability and validity criteria, and is amenable to computerization.

What Content Is Analyzed?

Content analysis may be used to analyze written, audio, or video data from experiments, observations, surveys, and secondary data studies. The obvious data to be content-analyzed include transcripts of focus groups, transcripts of interviews, and open-ended survey responses. But marketing researchers also use content analysis on advertisements, promotional brochures, press releases, speeches, Web pages, historical documents, and conference proceedings, as well as magazine and newspaper articles. In competitive intelligence and the marketing of political candidates content analysis is a primary methodology.

Example

Let's look at an informal application of content analysis to a problematic open-ended question. In this example, which we are processing without the use of content analysis software, suppose employees in the sales department of a manufacturing firm are asked, "How might company–customer relations be improved?" A sample of the responses yields the following:

- We should treat the customer with more respect.
- We should stop trying to speed up the sales process when the customer has expressed objections or concerns.
- We should have software that permits real-time tracking of a customer's order.
- Our laptops are outdated. We can't work with the latest software or access information quickly when we are in the field.
- My [the sales department] manager is rude with customers when he gets calls while I'm in the field. He should be transferred or fired.
- Management should stop pressuring us to meet sales quotas when our customers have restricted their open-to-buy status.

> **These categories are called analysis frameworks in XSight. See the screenshot on page 498.**

The first step in analysis requires that the units selected or developed help answer the research question. In our example, the research question is concerned with learning who or what the sales force thinks is a source for improving company–customer relations. The first pass through the data produces a few general categories in one concept dimension: source of responsibility, shown in Exhibit 18-4. These categories are mutually exclusive. The use of "other" makes the category set exhaustive. If, however, many of the sample participants suggested the need for action by other parties—for example, the government or a trade association—then including all those responses in the "other" category would ignore much of the richness of the data. As with coding schemes for numerical responses, category choices are very important.

Since responses to this type of question often suggest specific actions, the second evaluation of the data uses propositional units. If we used only the set of categories in Exhibit 18-4, the analysis would omit a considerable amount of information. The second analysis produces categories for action planning:

- Human relations.
- Technology.
- Training.
- Strategic planning.
- Other action areas.
- No action area identified.

How can we categorize a response suggesting a combined training-technology process? Exhibit 18-5 illustrates a combination of alternatives. By taking the categories of the first

>**Exhibit 18-4** Open Question Coding Example (before revision)

Question: "How can company–customer relations be improved?"

Locus of Responsibility	Mentioned	Not Mentioned
A. Company	_____	_____
B. Customer	_____	_____
C. Joint Company-Customer	_____	_____
F. Other	_____	_____

>**Exhibit 18-5** Open Question Coding (after revision)

Question: "How can company–customer relations be improved?"

Locus of Responsibility	Frequency (*n* = 100)
A. Management	
1. Sales manager	10
2. Sales process	20
3. Other	7
5. No action area identified	3
B. Salesperson	
1. Training	15
C. Customer	
1. Buying processes	12
2. Other	8
3. No action area identified	5
D. Environmental conditions	
E. Technology	20
F. Other	

list of the action areas, it is possible to get an accurate frequency count of the joint classification possibilities for this question.

Using available software, the researcher can spend much less time coding open-ended responses and capturing categories. Software also eliminates the high cost of sending responses to outside coding firms. What used to take a coding staff several days may now be done in a few hours.

Content analysis software applies statistical algorithms to open-ended question responses. This permits stemming, aliasing, and exclusion processes. *Stemming* uses derivations of common root words to create aliases (e.g., using *searching, searches, searched,* for *search*). *Aliasing* searches for synonyms (*wise* or *smart* for *intelligent*). *Exclusion* filters out trivial words (*be, is, the, of*) in the search for meaning.[4]

When you are using menu-driven programs, an autocategorization option creates manageable categories by clustering terms that occur together throughout the textual data set. Then, with a few keystrokes, you can modify categorization parameters and refine your results. Once your categories are consistent with the research and investigative questions, you select what you want to export to a data file or in tab-delimited format. The output, in the form of tables and plots, serves as modules for your final report. Exhibit 18-6 shows a plot produced by a content analysis of the MindWriter complaints data. The distances between pairs of terms reveal how likely it is that the terms occur together, and the colors represent categories.

>**Exhibit 18-6** Proximity Plot of MindWriter Customer Complaints

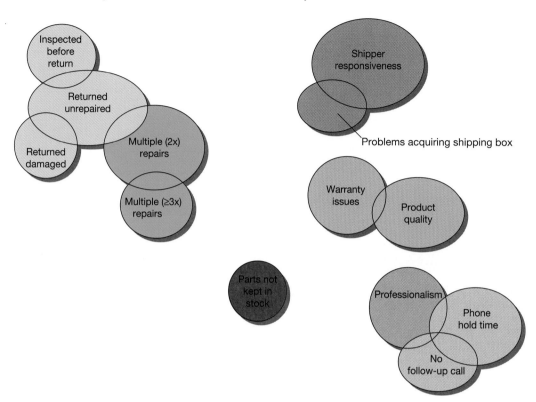

"Don't Know" Responses

**"don't know" (DK)
response** a response given
when a participant has
insufficient knowledge,
direction, or willingness to
answer a question.

The **"don't know" (DK) response** presents special problems for data preparation. When the DK response group is small, it is not troublesome. But there are times when it is of major concern, and it may even be the most frequent response received. Does this mean the question that elicited this response is useless? The answer is, "It all depends." Most DK answers fall into two categories.[5] First, there is the legitimate DK response when the respondent does not know the answer. This response meets our research objectives; we expect DK responses and consider them to be useful.

In the second situation, a DK reply illustrates the researcher's failure to get the appropriate information. Consider the following illustrative questions:

1. Who developed the Managerial Grid concept?
2. Do you believe the new president's fiscal policy is sound?
3. Do you like your present job?
4. Which of the various brands of chewing gum do you believe has the best quality?
5. How often each year do you go to the movies?

It is reasonable to expect that some legitimate DK responses will be made to each of these questions. In the first question, the respondents are asked for a level of information that they often will not have. There seems to be little reason to withhold a correct answer if known. Thus, most DK answers to this question should be considered as legitimate. A DK response to the second question presents a different problem. It is not immediately clear whether the respondent is ignorant of the president's fiscal policy or knows the policy but has not made a judgment about it. The researchers should have asked two questions: In the first, they would have determined the respondent's level of awareness of fiscal policy. If the interviewee passed the awareness test, then a second question would have secured judgment on fiscal policy.

>**Exhibit 18-7** Handling "Don't Know" Responses

Question: Do you have a productive relationship with your present salesperson?

Years of Purchasing	Yes	No	Don't Know
Less than 1 year	10%	40%	38%
1–3 years	30	30	32
4 years or more	60	30	30
Total	100%	100%	100%
	n = 650	*n =* 150	*n =* 200

In the remaining three questions, DK responses are more likely to be a failure of the questioning process, although some will surely be legitimate. The respondent may be reluctant to give the information. A DK response to question 3 may be a way of saying, "I do not want to answer that question." Question 4 might also elicit a DK response in which the reply translates to "This is too unimportant to talk about." In question 5, the respondents are being asked to do some calculation about a topic to which they may attach little importance. Now the DK may mean, "I do not want to do that work for something of so little consequence."

Dealing with Undesired DK Responses

The best way to deal with undesired DK answers is to design better questions at the beginning. Researchers should identify the questions for which a DK response is unsatisfactory and design around it. Interviewers, however, often inherit this problem and must deal with it in the field. Several actions are then possible. First, good interviewer-respondent rapport will motivate respondents to provide more usable answers. When interviewers recognize an evasive DK response, they can repeat the question or probe for a more definite answer. The interviewer may also record verbatim any elaboration by the respondent and pass the problem on to the editor.

If the editor finds many undesired responses, little can be done unless the verbatim comments can be interpreted. Understanding the real meaning relies on clues from the respondent's answers to other questions. One way to do this is to estimate the allocation of DK answers from other data in the questionnaire. The pattern of responses may parallel income, education, or experience levels. Suppose a question concerning whether customers like their present salesperson elicits the answers in Exhibit 18-7. The correlation between years of purchasing and the "don't know" answers and the "no" answers suggests that most of the "don't knows" are disguised "no" answers.

There are several ways to handle "don't know" responses in the tabulations. If there are only a few, it does not make much difference how they are handled, but they will probably be kept as a separate category. If the DK response is legitimate, it should remain as a separate reply category. When we are not sure how to treat it, we should keep it as a separate reporting category and let the research sponsor make the decision.

Missing Data

Missing data are information from a participant or case that is not available for one or more variables of interest. In survey studies, missing data typically occur when participants accidentally skip, refuse to answer, or do not know the answer to an item on the questionnaire. In longitudinal studies, missing data may result from participants dropping out of the study, or being absent for one or more data collection periods. Missing data also occur due to researcher error, corrupted data files, and changes in the research or instrument design after data were collected from some participants, such as when variables are dropped or

missing data information from a participant or case that is not available for one or more variables of interest.

added. The strategy for handling missing data consists of a two-step process: the marketing researcher first explores the pattern of missing data to determine the mechanism for *missingness* (the probability that a value is missing rather than observed) and then selects a missing data technique.

Mechanisms for Missing Data

In order to select a missing data technique, the researcher must first determine what caused the data to be missing. There are three basic mechanisms for this: data missing completely at random (MCAR); data missing at random (MAR); and data not missing at random (NMAR). If the probability of missingness for a particular variable is neither dependent on the variable itself nor any other variable in the data set, then data are MCAR. Data are considered MAR if the probability of missingness for a particular variable is dependent on another variable but not itself when other variables are held constant. The practical significance of this distinction is that the proper missing data technique can be selected that will minimize bias in subsequent analyses. The third type of mechanism, NMAR, occurs when data are not missing completely at random and they are not predictable from other variables in the data set. Data NMAR are considered *nonignorable* and must be treated on an improvised basis.

Missing Data Techniques

Three basic types of techniques can be used to salvage data sets with missing data: (1) listwise deletion; (2) pairwise deletion; and (3) replacement of missing values with estimated scores. *Listwise deletion,* or complete case analysis, is perhaps the simplest approach, and is the default option in most statistical packages like SPSS and SAS. With this method, cases are deleted from the sample if they have missing values on any of the variables in the analysis. Listwise deletion is most appropriate when data are MCAR. In this situation, no bias will be introduced because the subsample of complete cases is essentially a random sample of the original sample. However, if data are MAR but not MCAR, then a bias may be introduced, especially if a large number of cases are deleted. For example, if men were more likely than women to be responsible for missing data on the variable *shopping preference,* then the results would be biased towards women's shopping preferences.

Pair-wise deletion, also called available case analysis, assumes that data are MCAR. In the past, this technique was used frequently with linear models that are functions of means, variances, and covariances. Missing values would be estimated using all cases that had data for each variable or pair of variables in the analysis. Today most experts caution against pairwise deletion, and recommend alternative approaches.

The replacement of missing values with estimated values includes a variety of techniques. This option generally assumes that data are MAR, since the missing values on one variable are predicted from observed values on another variable. A common option available on many software packages is the replacement of missing values with a mean or other central tendency score. This is a simple approach, but has the disadvantage of reducing the variability in the original data, which can cause bias. Another option is to use a regression or likelihood-based method. Such techniques are found in specialty software packages and the procedures for using them are beyond the scope of this text.

> Data Entry

data entry the process of converting information gathered by secondary or primary methods to a medium for viewing and manipulation.

Data entry converts information gathered by secondary or primary methods to a medium for viewing and manipulation. Keyboarding remains a mainstay for researchers who need to create a data file immediately and store it in a minimal space on a variety of media. However, researchers have profited from more efficient ways of speeding up the research process, especially from bar coding and optical character and mark recognition.

VNS: A Black Eye for Research

A little before 8 p.m., November 7, 2000, major news sources declared Al Gore the winner of Florida's electoral votes. Two hours later they pulled their prediction, reverting to "too close to call." By 2:15 a.m. George W. Bush was declared the 43d president, and soon after Al Gore conceded the election. A month of Florida recounts gave the 2000 election its place in political, legal, news, and research history. Voter News Service (VNS), run by a consortium of ABC, NBC, CBS, CNN, FOX, and the Associated Press, was responsible for the exit polls. Exit polls, regarded as reliable indicators of voting results, conduct intercept interviews with voters as they leave voting booths. Voters provide whom they voted

for, why, and extensive demographic and psychographic information. How could an established polling organization and world-recognized news organizations' research fail so miserably? The answers are (1) a biased sample with too many surveys completed in heavily democratic precincts, (2) miscounted or misentered data in Duvall County (home of Jacksonville), and (3) a rush to judgment for the news value of any early "call" when statistically the margin between candidates was truly too close to decide. Antitrust advocates claim that collusion versus competition resulted in poor methodology and sought to break up VNS before another "campaign fiasco" occurs.

November 2000 Presidential Election: Timeline for Poll-Based Action

10:00 p.m. News organizations withdraw prediction of Al Gore as president-elect.

2:15 a.m. News organizations declare George W. Bush the next president.

4:15 a.m. News organizations withdraw prediction of Bush as president-elect.

— November 7, 2000 — — November 8, 2000 —

8:00 a.m. News organizations declare election for Al Gore.

2:30 a.m. Al Gore concedes election to George W. Bush.

3:00 a.m. Al Gore withdraws concession.

Alternative Data Entry Formats

Keyboarding

A full-screen editor, where an entire data file can be edited or browsed, is a viable means of data entry for statistical packages like SPSS or SAS. SPSS offers several data entry products, including Data Entry Builder™, which enables the development of forms and surveys, and Data Entry Station™, which gives centralized entry staff, such as telephone interviewers or online participants, access to the survey. Both SAS and SPSS offer software that effortlessly accesses data from databases, spreadsheets, data warehouses, or data marts.

Database Development For large projects, database programs serve as valuable data entry devices. A **database** is a collection of data organized for computerized retrieval. Programs allow users to define data fields and link files so that storage, retrieval, and updating are simplified. The relationship between *data fields, records, files,* and *databases* is illustrated in Exhibit 18-8. A company's orders serve as an example of a database. Ordering information may be kept in several files: salesperson's customer files, customer financial records, order production records, and order shipping documentation. The data are separated so that authorized people can see only those parts pertinent to their needs. However, the files may be linked so that when, say, a customer changes his or her shipping

database a collection of data organized for computerized retrieval.

▸Exhibit 18-8 Data Fields, Records, Files, and Databases

Data fields represent single elements of information (e.g., an answer to a particular question) from all participants in a study. Data fields can contain numeric, alphabetic, or symbolic information. A **record** is a set of data fields that are related to one case or participant (e.g., the responses to one completed survey). Records represent rows in a data file or spreadsheet program worksheet. **Data files** are sets of records (e.g., responses from all participants in a single study) that are grouped together for storage on diskettes, disks, tapes, CD-ROM, or optical disks. *Databases* are made up of one or more data files that are interrelated. A database might contain all customer survey information collected quarterly for the last 10 years.

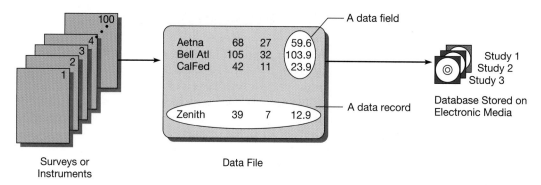

address, the change is entered once and all the files are updated. Another database entry option is e-mail data capture. It has become popular with those using e-mail-delivered surveys. The e-mail survey can be delivered to a specific respondent whose e-mail address is known. Questions are completed on the screen, returned via e-mail, and incorporated into a database.[6] An intranet can also capture data. When participants linked by a network take an online survey by completing a database form, the data are captured in a database in a network server for later or real-time analysis.[7] ID and password requirements can keep unwanted participants from skewing the results of an online survey.

Researchers consider database entry when they have large amounts of potentially linked data that will be retrieved and tabulated in different ways over time. Another application of a database program is as a "front-end" entry mechanism. A telephone interviewer may ask the question "How many children live in your household?" The computer's software has been programmed to accept any answer between 0 and 20. If a "P" is accidentally struck, the program will not accept the answer and will return the interviewer to the question. With a precoded online instrument, some of the editing previously discussed is done by the program. In addition, the program can be set for automatic conditional branching. In the example, an answer of 1 or greater causes the program to prompt the questioner to ask the ages of the children. A 0 causes the age question to be automatically skipped. Although this option is available whenever interactive computing is used, front-end processing is typically done within the database design. The database will then store the data in a set of linked files that allow the data to be easily sorted. Descriptive statistics and tables—the first steps in exploring data—are readily generated from within the database.

Spreadsheet   Spreadsheets are a specialized type of database for data that need organizing, tabulating, and simple statistics. They also offer some database management, graphics, and presentation capabilities. Data entry on a **spreadsheet** uses numbered rows and lettered columns with a matrix of thousands of cells into which an entry may be placed. Spreadsheets allow you to type numbers, formulas, and text into appropriate cells. Many statistics programs for personal computers and also charting and graphics applications have data editors similar to the Excel spreadsheet format shown in Exhibit 18-9. This is a convenient and flexible means for entering and viewing data.

Optical Recognition

If you use a PC image scanner, you probably are familiar with **optical character recognition (OCR)** programs that transfer printed text into computer files in order to edit and use

>Exhibit 18-9 Data Entry Using Spreadsheets

Each row is a record (a single participant's responses). Each column is a variable measured in the survey. In this survey, questions 1, 3, and 5 are nominal variables that have two response categories. Question 6 uses multiple columns as it is a multipart rating question using a 1-to-5 scale. This is a typical way of coding variables in a spreadsheet before they are imported by SPSS (assuming you are using a spreadsheet instead of the SPSS Data Editor to start your study). Note that each participant is assigned an identification number (case ID). After running preliminary frequencies, having a case ID data field enables you to quickly find and correct suspect data like odd value codes or missing cases.

Case ID	Q1	Q2	Q3	Q4	Q5	Q6a	Q6b	Q6c	Q6d	Q6e	Q6f
0001	1	2	1	10	2	1	2	1	1	4	4
0002	2	5	2	7	1	2	2	3	2	4	5
0003	1	2	1	6	2	2	4	3	4	4	4
0004	1	2	1	1	1	3	4	4	4	5	4
0005	2	6	2	8	2	3	5	4	2	5	1
0006	2	1	2	8	2	3	5	2	2	3	1
0007	1	3	1	8	1	2	5	3	5	3	3
0008	2	4	2	5	2	3	3	4	5	1	3
0009	1	2	1	9	1	3	2	4	5	2	5
0010	2	2	2	9	2	4	2	5	5	3	5
0011	2	5	2	9	1	4	1	1	3	1	5
0012	1	2	1	9	1	2	2	2	3	2	2
0013	2	1	2	3	2	5	3	3	4	2	1
0014	1	6	1	2	2	3	4	4	5	5	2
0015	2	4	2	3	1	1	4	3	1	5	3
0016	2	3	2	4	2	5	5	5	2	5	4
0017	1	3	1	6	1	5	5	2	1	1	4
0018	2	3	2	5	2	5	5	2	2	2	3

it without retyping. There are other, related applications. **Optical scanning** of instruments—the choice of testing services—is efficient for researchers. Examinees darken small circles, ellipses, or spaces between sets of parallel lines to indicate their answers. A more flexible format, **optical mark recognition (OMR)** uses a spreadsheet-style interface to read and process user-created forms. Optical scanners process the marked-sensed questionnaires and store the answers in a file. This method, most often associated with standardized and preprinted forms, has been adopted by researchers for data entry and preprocessing due to its speed (10 times faster than keyboarding), cost savings on data entry, convenience in charting and reporting data, and improved accuracy. It reduces the number of times data are handled, thereby reducing the number of errors that are introduced.

Other techniques include direct-response entry, of which voting procedures used in several states are an example. With a specially prepared punch card, citizens cast their votes by pressing a pen-shaped instrument against the card next to the preferred candidate. This opens a small hole in a specific column and row of the card. The cards are collected and placed directly into a card reader. This method also removes the coding and entry steps. Another governmental application is the 1040EZ form used by the Internal Revenue Service. It is designed for computerized number and character recognition. Similar character recognition techniques are employed for many forms of data collection. Again, both approaches move the response from the question to data analysis with little handling.

optical scanning a data entry process where answers are recorded on computer-readable forms and then scanned to form a data record.

optical mark recognition (OMR) software that uses a spreadsheet-style interface to read and process data from user-created forms.

Voice Recognition

The increase in computerized random dialing has encouraged other data collection innovations. **Voice recognition** and voice response systems are providing some interesting alternatives for the telephone interviewer. Upon getting a voice response to a randomly dialed number, the computer branches into a questionnaire routine. These systems are advancing quickly and will soon translate recorded voice responses into data files.

voice recognition computer systems programmed to record verbal answers to questions.

Digital

Telephone keypad response, frequently used by restaurants and entertainment venues to evaluate customer service, is another capability made possible by computers linked to telephone lines. Using the telephone keypad (touch tone), an invited participant answers questions by pressing the appropriate number. The computer captures the data by decoding the tone's electrical signal and storing the numeric or alphabetic answer in a data file. While not originally designed for collecting survey data, each of the software components within Microsoft Office XP includes advanced speech recognition functionality, enabling people to enter and edit data by speaking into a microphone.[8]

Field interviewers can use mobile computers or notebooks instead of clipboards and pencils. With a built-in communications modem, wireless LAN, or cellular link, their files can be sent directly to another computer in the field or to a remote site. This lets supervisors inspect data immediately or simplifies processing at a central facility. This is the technology that Nielsen Media is using with its portable people meter.

Bar Code Since adoption of the Universal Product Code (UPC) in 1973, the bar code has developed from a technological curiosity to a business mainstay. After a study by McKinsey & Company, the Kroger grocery chain pilot-tested a production system and bar codes became ubiquitous in that industry.[9]

Bar-code technology is used to simplify the interviewer's role as a data recorder. When an interviewer passes a bar-code wand over the appropriate codes, the data are recorded in a small, lightweight unit for translation later. In the large-scale processing project Census 2000, the Census Data Capture Center used bar codes to identify residents. Researchers studying magazine readership can scan bar codes to denote a magazine cover that is recognized by an interview participant.

VNS: This Hit Was the Knockout

After the fiasco of the 2000 presidential election when Voter News Service (VNS) exit polls resulted in miscalled election results, withdrawal of concession speeches, and a month of Florida recounts, VNS invested more than $10 million to upgrade its computing technology, including the installation of a voice recognition data entry system. But during the November 2002 congressional elections, the VNS consortium owners—ABC, CBS, CNN, Fox News, NBC, and the Associated Press—had to abandon their use of exit polls midstream. The technology overhaul had attempted (unsuccessfully) to merge two operating systems, get those systems to successfully integrate multiple databases, and launch the voice recognition data entry system without allowing sufficient testing time. Many of the more than 30,000 interviewers collecting exit-poll information were disconnected before they could finish inputting data over the phone. Others couldn't gain entry to the new system at all. Early exit polls proved just as inaccurate as the polls two years earlier. For example, in one highly visible contest, exit polls showed Elizabeth Dole being defeated for the North Carolina senatorial race when she was actually winning. Dole ultimately claimed her seat with a decisive 200,000-vote margin. This second right hook proved a knockout for VNS; on January 13, 2003, the news-research consortium conceded defeat and disbanded VNS.

The **bar code** is used in numerous applications: point-of-sale terminals, hospital patient ID bracelets, inventory control, product and brand tracking, promotional technique evaluation, shipment tracking, marathon runners, rental car locations (to speed the return of cars and generate invoices), and tracking of insects' mating habits. The military uses 2-foot-long bar codes to label boats in storage. The codes appear on business documents, truck parts, and timber in lumberyards. Federal Express shipping labels use a code called *Codabar*. Other codes, containing letters as well as numbers, have potential for researchers.

bar code technology employing labels containing electronically read vertical-bar data codes.

On the Horizon

Even with these time reductions between data collection and analysis, continuing innovations in multimedia technology are being developed by the personal computer business. The capability to integrate visual images, streaming video, audio, and data may soon replace video equipment as the preferred method for recording an experiment, interview, or focus group. A copy of the response data could be extracted for data analysis, but the audio and visual images would remain intact for later evaluation. Although technology will never replace researcher judgment, it can reduce data-handling errors, decrease time between data collection and analysis, and help provide more usable information.

>summary

1 The first step in data preparation is to edit the collected raw data to detect errors and omissions that would compromise quality standards. The editor is responsible for making sure the data are accurate, consistent with other data, uniformly entered, and ready for coding. In survey work, it is common to use both field and central editing.

2 Coding is the process of assigning numbers and other symbols to answers so that we can classify the responses into categories. Categories should be appropriate to the research problem, exhaustive of the data, mutually exclusive, and unidimensional. The reduction of information through coding requires that the researcher design category sets carefully,

using as much of the data as possible. Codebooks are guides to reduce data entry error and serve as a compendium of variable locations and other information for the analysis stage. Software developments in survey construction and design include embedding coding rules that screen data as they are entered, identifying data that are not entered correctly.

3 Closed questions include scaled items and other items for which answers are anticipated. Precoding of closed items avoids tedious completion of coding sheets for each response. Open-ended questions are more difficult to code since answers are not prepared in advance, but they do encourage disclosure of complete information. A systematic method for analyzing open-ended questions is content analysis. It uses preselected sampling units to produce frequency counts and other insights into data patterns.

4 "Don't know" replies are evaluated in light of the question's nature and the respondent. While many DKs are legitimate, some result from questions that are ambiguous or from an interviewing situation that is not motivating. It is better to re-

port DKs as a separate category unless there are compelling reasons to treat them otherwise. Missing data occur when respondents skip, refuse to answer, or do not know the answer to a questionnaire item, drop out of the study, or are absent for one or more data collection periods. Researcher error, corrupted data files, and changes to the instrument during administration also produce missing data. Researchers handle missing data by first exploring the data to discover the nature of the pattern and then selecting a suitable technique for replacing values by deleting cases (or variables) or estimating values.

5 Data entry is accomplished by keyboard entry from precoded instruments, optical scanning, real-time keyboarding, telephone pad data entry, bar codes, voice recognition, OCR, OMR, and data transfers from electronic notebooks and laptop computers. Database programs, spreadsheets, and editors in statistical software programs offer flexibility for entering, manipulating, and transferring data for analysis, warehousing, and mining.

>**key**terms

bar code 509	**data preparation** 490	**optical mark recognition (OMR)** 507
codebook 493	**database** 505	**optical scanning** 507
coding 493	**"don't know" (DK) response** 502	**precoding** 494
content analysis 497	**editing** 491	**record** 506
data entry 504	**missing data** 503	**spreadsheet** 506
data field 506	**optical character recognition (OCR)** 506	**voice recognition** 507
data file 506		

>**discussion**questions

Terms in Review

1 Define or explain:

  a Coding rules.

  b Spreadsheet data entry.

  c Bar codes.

  d Precoded instruments.

  e Content analysis.

  f Missing data.

  g Optical mark recognition.

2 How should the researcher handle "don't know" responses?

Making Research Decisions

3 A problem facing shoe store managers is that many shoes eventually must be sold at markdown prices. This prompts

us to conduct a mail survey of shoe store managers in which we ask, "What methods have you found most successful for reducing the problem of high markdowns?" We are interested in extracting as much information as possible from these answers to better understand the full range of strategies that store managers use. Establish what you think are category sets to code 500 responses similar to the 14 given below. Try to develop an integrated set of categories that reflects your theory of markdown management. After developing the set, use it to code the 14 responses.

  a Have not found the answer. As long as we buy style shoes, we will have markdowns. We use PMs on slow merchandise, but it does not eliminate markdowns. (*PM* stands for "push-money"—special item bonuses for selling a particular style of shoe.)

b Using PMs before too old. Also reducing price during season. Holding meetings with salespeople indicating which shoes to push.

c By putting PMs on any slow-selling items and promoting same. More careful check of shoes purchased.

d Keep a close watch on your stock, and mark down when you have to—that is, rather than wait, take a small markdown on a shoe that is not moving at the time.

e Using the PM method.

f Less advance buying—more dependence on in-stock shoes.

g Sales—catch bad guys before it's too late and close out.

h Buy as much good merchandise as you can at special prices to help make up some markdowns.

i Reducing opening buys and depending on fill-in service. PMs for salespeople.

j Buy more frequently, better buying, PMs on slow-moving merchandise.

k Careful buying at lowest prices. Cash on the buying line. Buying closeouts, FDs, overstock, "cancellations." (*FD* stands for "factory-discontinued" style.)

l By buying less "chanceable" shoes. Buy only what you need, watch sizes, don't go overboard on new fads.

m Buying more staple merchandise. Buying more from fewer lines. Sticking with better nationally advertised merchandise.

n No successful method with the current style situation. Manufacturers are experimenting, the retailer takes the markdowns—cuts gross profit by about 3 percent—keep your stock at lowest level without losing sales.

4 Select a small sample of class members, work associates, or friends and ask them to answer the following in a paragraph or two: "What are your career aspirations for the next five years?" Use one of the four basic units of content analysis to analyze their responses. Describe your findings as frequencies for the unit of analysis selected.

Behind the Scenes

5 What data preparation process was Jason doing during data entry?

6 Data entry followed data collection in the research profiled during the opening vignette. What should have concerned Jason about this process?

From Concept to Practice

7 Choose one of the cases on your text DVD that has an instrument (check the Cases section for a listing of all cases and an abstract for each). Code the instrument for data entry.

>**www**exercises

1 See what the next generation of qualitative research analysis can do. Visit the QRS Web site and take a product tour of XSight (**http://www.qsr.com.au/products/productoverview/XSight.htm**).

2 Visit the Internet home page of three of the world's biggest research companies (you'll find several of them mentioned in Exhibit 2-2 in Chapter 2). Do a content analysis of the three home pages. Be sure to look at all formats of content—text, pictures, video, and audio—and all four types of content: syntactical, referential, propositional, and thematic. How will you categorize the data? How will you create a data record for each company? What content elements are common to all? What elements are unique to a particular research company?

>**cases**[*]

Agri Comp

Inquiring Minds Want to Know—NOW!

Mastering Teacher Leadership

NCRCC: Teeing Up and New Strategic Direction

NetConversions Influences Kelley Blue Book

[*] All cases, both written and video, are on the text DVD. Check the DVD Index to determine whether a case has data, the research instrument, or other supplementary material.

>chapter 19

Exploring, Displaying, and Examining Data

>learningobjectives

After reading this chapter, you should understand . . .

1 That exploratory data analysis techniques provide insights and data diagnostics by emphasizing visual representations of the data.

2 How cross-tabulation is used to examine relationships involving categorical variables, serves as a framework for later statistical testing, and makes table-based analysis using one or more control variables an efficient tool for data visualization and later decision making.

Myra and Jason are wrapping up their review of the materials Myra delivered for MindWriter's latest partnership with Visionary Insights. Jason, knowing Myra is eager to hear any tidbits on the City Center for Performing Arts project, escorts her through the outer office, where his newest staff member, Sammye, is busy pouring over cross-tabs. He decides it's the perfect time to test Sammye on the rules of data confidentiality he broached with the interns last week.

"Sammye Grayson, meet Myra Wines from MindWriter. We'll be working with her on a short-turnaround project during the next week." Sammye rises to shake Myra's extended hand, as Jason asks, innocently, "Anything interesting on those initial cross-tabs?"

Myra smiles, raises an expressive eyebrow, and waits for Sammye's response.

Sammye hesitates and then, looking at Jason for some signal of why he asked the question in the presence of a different client, responds, "Three of the early cross-tabs appeared to show some support for the board's assumptions about the alcohol issue—on whether current patrons endorse the selling of beer and wine during intermissions. But we're not far enough into the data to say which of the board's assumptions are fully correct and which might have to be modified based on the patterns emerging within subgroups of the sample."

Jason raises a hand to stop the detailed answer to his question. Sammye knows from the look on his face that she's done something wrong.

"I shouldn't have answered your question," blurts Sammye. "I walked right into the trap you set, eyes wide open."

Myra jumps in before Jason can respond. "I've seen Jason do this once before to an intern, so you should feel like one of the team. And, no, you shouldn't have responded—confidentiality is rule number one at Visionary—and as a client, I appreciate it. No harm done this time, though. What Jason failed to tell you is I'm on CCPA's board and part of the project team.

Before Jason stopped you, things were getting interesting. Please continue."

Sammye, getting a nod from Jason, shares, "We'll probably have to do some recoding of the age and race variables for the patterns to emerge clearly. The team is also interested in the differences between ethnic groups in future performance preferences. We've also finished coding each patron's address with its GPS (Geographic Positioning System) code. The preliminary mapping begins tomorrow; Jason hired a master's candidate in geography to provide the mapping. I've scheduled a conference call for . . . (Sammye flips her desk calendar pages to the following week) . . . Friday of next week with Jackson Murray and other members of the CCPA project team."

"When the board approved your proposed analysis plan," queries Myra, "I don't remember seeing any reference to those boxlike diagrams with tails I see on that graph you just handed to Jason."

"Most of what the team will be doing the next three days," intervenes Jason, "involves more graphical displays than statistical ones. Right now we're just getting a sense of what the data are telling us. We'll decide what, if any, new analyses to add to the proposed plan by this Friday. It's this early work that lays the groundwork for the more sophisticated analyses that follow. There isn't anything glamorous about it, but without it we might miss some crucial findings."

Jason pauses for effect and then says, "By the way, that 'little diagram' is called a boxplot. I actually did several during the preliminary analysis phase for

MindWriter's CompleteCare study. I didn't give them to you because I would have had to explain how to interpret them and . . ."

". . . and anything you have to explain isn't clear enough," finishes Myra. "I learned Visionary's rule on reporting to clients very well on MindWriter-1." Smiling at Sammye, Myra shares, "I appreciate rule number two just as much as rule number one."

> Exploratory Data Analysis

The convenience of data entry via spreadsheet, optimal mark recognition (OMR), or the data editor of a statistical program makes it tempting to move directly to statistical analysis. That temptation is even stronger when the data can be entered and viewed in real time. Why waste time finding out if the data confirm the hypothesis that motivated the study? Why not obtain descriptive statistical summaries (based on our discussion in Chapter 17) and then test hypotheses?

Exploratory data analysis is both a data analysis perspective and a set of techniques. In this chapter, we will present unique and conventional techniques including graphical and tabular devices to visualize the data. Exhibit 19-1 reminds you of the importance of data visualization as an integral element in the data analysis process and as a necessary step prior to hypothesis testing. In Chapter 3, we said research conducted scientifically is a puzzle-solving activity as well as an attitude of curiosity, suspicion, and imagination essential to discovery. It is natural, then, that exploration and examination of the data would be an integral part of our data analysis perspective.

exploratory data analysis (EDA) patterns in the collected data guide the data analysis or suggest revisions to the preliminary data analysis plan.

confirmatory data analysis an analytical process guided by classical statistical inference in its use of significance and confidence.

In **exploratory data analysis (EDA)** the researcher has the flexibility to respond to the patterns revealed in the preliminary analysis of the data. Thus patterns in the collected data guide the data analysis or suggest revisions to the preliminary data analysis plan. This flexibility is an important attribute of this approach. When the researcher is attempting to prove causation, however, confirmatory data analysis is required. **Confirmatory data analysis** is an analytical process guided by classical statistical inference in its use of significance and confidence.[1]

One authority has compared exploratory data analysis to the role of police detectives and other investigators and confirmatory analysis to that of judges and the judicial system. The former are involved in the search for clues and evidence; the latter are preoccupied

As this Booth Research Services ad suggests, the researcher's role is to make sense of numerous data displays and thus assist the research sponsor in making an appropriate marketing decision. Great data exploration and analysis will distill mountains of data printouts into insightful and supportable conclusions.

We have 610 pages of research that all lead to one conclusion.

You'd rather not go through 610 pages of research to get a conclusion.

Cut to the chase.

Booth Research Services
1-800-727-2577 / www.boothresearch.com

©1999 Booth Research Services

>**Exhibit 19-1** Data Exploration, Examination, and Analysis in the Research Process

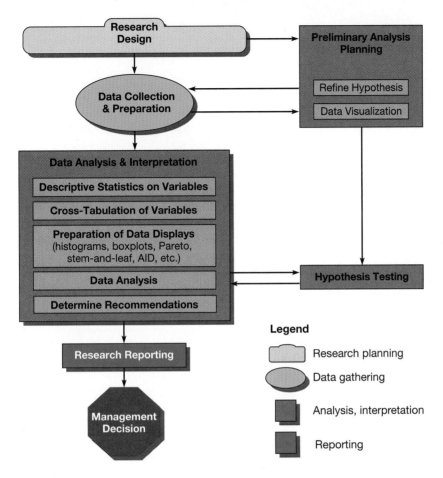

with evaluating the strength of the evidence that is found. Exploratory data analysis is the first step in the search for evidence, without which confirmatory analysis has nothing to evaluate.[2] Consistent with that analogy, EDA shares a commonality with exploratory designs, not formalized ones. Because it doesn't follow a rigid structure, it is free to take many paths in unraveling the mysteries in the data—to sift the unpredictable from the predictable.

A major contribution of the exploratory approach lies in the emphasis on visual representations and graphical techniques over summary statistics. Summary statistics, as you will see momentarily, may obscure, conceal, or even misrepresent the underlying structure of the data. When numerical summaries are used exclusively and accepted without visual inspection, the selection of confirmatory models may be based on flawed assumptions.[3] For these reasons, data analysis should begin with visual inspection. After that, it is not only possible but also desirable to cycle between exploratory and confirmatory approaches.

Frequency Tables, Bar Charts, and Pie Charts[4]

Several useful techniques for displaying data are not new to EDA. They are essential to any examination of the data. For example, a **frequency table** is a simple device for arraying data. An example is presented in Exhibit 19-2. It arrays data by assigned numerical value, with columns for percent, valid percent (percent adjusted for missing data), and cumulative percent. Ad recall, a nominal variable, describes the ads research participants

frequency table arrays category codes from lowest value to highest value, with columns for count, percent, valid percent, and cumulative percent.

The Media Outlook

Demand and economic forecasting are research staples for a marketer. Some firms like Wilkofsky Gruen (W&G) have built a business around developing such forecasts. Others, like auditor Pricewaterhouse Coopers (PWC), crafted their reputation as an industry expert by underwriting such forecasts. These two firms annually collaborate to develop the entertainment industry's *Global Entertainment and Media Outlook*. "W&G has developed a set of proprietary algorithms, which use information from a variety of sources—a special PWC data collection project in a particular country, government databases, and their own proprietary databases, for example," shared Deborah Scruby, marketing

director at PWC. "Once their draft report is prepared—it can be as large as 500 pages—we circulate it to experts and specialists around the world, who help interpret or find additional insights on various aspects of specific media and the entertainment industry." Together W&G and PWC collaborate to develop the final forecast, which is sold to financial analysts, large multinational media companies, universities and libraries, and the various media. "For us," explained Scruby, "the forecast is a marketing initiative, but it is crucial information for our clients."

www.pwcglobal.com; www.wilkofskygruen.com

>**Exhibit 19-2** A Frequency Table of Ad Recall

Value Label	Value	Frequency	Percent	Valid Percent	Cumulative Percent
TV program A	1	10	10.0	10.0	10.0
TV program B	2	8	8.0	8.0	18.0
TV program C	3	7	7.0	7.0	25.0
TV program D	4	13	13.0	13.0	38.0
Radio program A	5	24	24.0	24.0	62.0
Radio program B	6	4	4.0	4.0	66.0
Radio program C	7	11	11.0	11.0	77.0
Magazine A	8	6	6.0	6.0	83.0
Magazine B	9	7	7.0	7.0	90.0
Outdoor billboard	10	10	10.0	10.0	100.0
Total		100	100.0	100.0	

Valid cases 100   Missing cases 0

remembered seeing or hearing without being prompted by the researcher or the measurement instrument. Although there are 100 observations, the small number of media placements make the variable easily tabled. The same data are presented in Exhibit 19-3 using a pie chart and a bar chart. The values and percentages are more readily understood in this graphic format, and visualization of the media placements and their relative sizes is improved.

> ❝ It is precisely because the unexpected jolts us out of our preconceived notions, our assumptions, our certainties, that it is such a fertile source of innovation. ❞
>
> *Peter Drucker*
> *Author, Innovation and Entrepreneurship*

When the variable of interest is measured on an interval-ratio scale and is one with many potential values, these techniques are not particularly informative. Exhibit 19-4 is a condensed frequency table of the average annual purchases of PrimeSell's top 50 customers. Only two values, 59.9 and 66, have a frequency greater than 1. Thus, the primary contribution of this table is an ordered list of values. If the table were converted to a bar chart, it would have 48 bars of equal length and two bars with two occurrences. Bar charts do not reserve spaces for values

>**Exhibit 19-3** Nominal Variable Displays (Ad Recall)

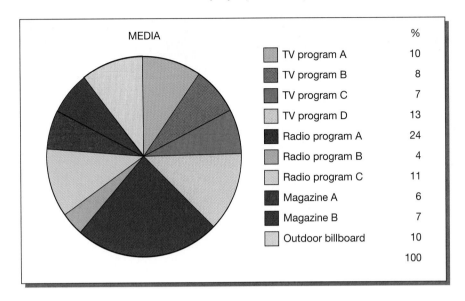

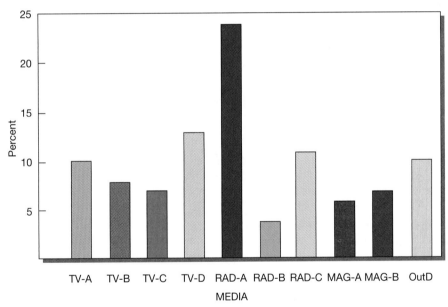

where no observations occur within the range. Constructing a pie chart for this variable would also be pointless.

Histograms

The histogram is a conventional solution for the display of interval-ratio data. **Histograms** are used when it is possible to group the variable's values into intervals. Histograms are constructed with bars (or asterisks) that represent data values, where each value occupies an equal amount of area within the enclosed area. Data analysts find histograms useful for (1) displaying all intervals in a distribution, even those without observed values, and (2) examining the shape of the distribution for skewness, kurtosis, and the modal pattern. When looking at a histogram, one might ask: Is there a single hump (a mode)? Are subgroups identifiable when multiple modes are present? Are straggling data values detached from the central concentration?[5]

histogram a graphical bar chart that groups continuous data values into equal intervals, with one bar for each interval.

>**Exhibit 19-4** Average Monthly Purchases of PrimeSell's Top 50 Customers

Value	Frequency	Percent	Cumulative Percent	Value	Frequency	Percent	Cumulative Percent
54.9	1	2	2	75.6	1	2	54
55.4	1	2	4	76.4	1	2	56
55.6	1	2	6	77.5	1	2	58
56.4	1	2	8	78.9	1	2	60
56.8	1	2	10	80.9	1	2	62
56.9	1	2	12	82.2	1	2	64
57.8	1	2	14	82.5	1	2	66
58.1	1	2	16	86.4	1	2	68
58.2	1	2	18	88.3	1	2	70
58.3	1	2	20	102.5	1	2	72
58.5	1	2	22	104.1	1	2	74
59.9	2	4	26	110.4	1	2	76
61.5	1	2	28	111.9	1	2	78
62.6	1	2	30	118.6	1	2	80
64.8	1	2	32	123.8	1	2	82
66.0	2	4	36	131.2	1	2	84
66.3	1	2	38	140.9	1	2	86
67.6	1	2	40	146.2	1	2	88
69.1	1	2	42	153.2	1	2	90
69.2	1	2	44	163.2	1	2	92
70.5	1	2	46	166.7	1	2	94
72.7	1	2	48	183.2	1	2	96
72.9	1	2	50	206.9	1	2	98
73.5	1	2	52	218.2	1	2	100
				Total	50	100	

The values for the average annual purchases variable presented in Exhibit 19-4 were measured on a ratio scale and are easily grouped. Other variables possessing an underlying order are similarly appropriate for histograms. A histogram would not be used for a nominal variable like ad recall (Exhibit 19-3) that has no order to its categories.

A histogram of the average annual purchases is shown in Exhibit 19-5. The midpoint for each interval for the variable of interest, average annual purchases, is shown on the horizontal axis; the frequency or number of observations in each interval, on the vertical axis. We erect a vertical bar above the midpoint of each interval on the horizontal scale. The height of the bar corresponds with the frequency of observations in the interval above which it is erected. This histogram was constructed with intervals 20 increments wide, and the last interval contains only two observations, 206.9 and 218.2. These values are found in PrimeSell's average annual purchases frequency table (Exhibit 19-4). Intervals with 0 counts show gaps in the data and alert the analyst to look for problems with spread. When the upper tail of the distribution is compared with the frequency table, we find three extreme values (183.2, 206.9, and 218.2). Along with the peaked midpoint and reduced number of observations in the upper tail, this histogram warns us of irregularities in the data.

Stem-and-Leaf Displays[6]

stem-and-leaf display a tree-type frequency distribution for each data value, without equal interval grouping.

The **stem-and-leaf display** is a technique that is closely related to the histogram. It shares some of the histogram's features but offers several unique advantages. It is easy to construct by hand for small samples or may be produced by computer programs. In contrast to histograms, which lose information by grouping data values into intervals, the stem-and-leaf presents actual data values that can be inspected directly, without the use of enclosed bars or asterisks as the representation medium. This feature reveals the distribution of val-

Wirthlin Worldwide Research Redesigns Red Cross Donations

September 11, 2001, elicited generous donations to the American Red Cross (RC) while it simultaneously raised questions and concerns about the Red Cross's fund-raising practices and processes, especially those related to the Liberty Fund. Realizing that confusion could erode trust, the RC hired Wirthlin Worldwide to assist it to improve its fund-raising messaging. Wirthlin conducted 12 focus groups in seven cities (Baltimore, Birmingham, Boston, Charleston, Houston, Minneapolis, and San Francisco)—to represent a range of urban and suburban populations, different degrees of local disasters and diversity, and city population sizes—followed by two nationwide public opinion polls. Two key segments were of interest in both surveys, each involving 1,000 adults: (1) prior Red Cross donors and (2) those who had never donated to the Red Cross. Survey participants were asked to listen to 30-second radio ads and asked questions that would test the clarity and persuasiveness of the revised messaging that

evolved out of the focus groups. Following the survey, the RC consulted nonprofit opinion leaders (e.g., Better Business Bureau, GuideStar, Association of Fundraising Professionals) to evaluate the proposed fund-raising changes that were indicated by the survey. A new fund-raising process—Donor DIRECT (Donor Intent Recognition Confirmation Trust)—was launched June 2002, receiving favorable publicity and positive subsequent polling feedback. The Colorado fires during the summer of 2002 provided the litmus test of the new process: the Red Cross saw an increase in undesignated donations to its Disaster Relief Fund. The Red Cross and Wirthlin Worldwide research earned *PRWeek*'s 2003 Technique Award: Best Use of Research or Measurement.

www.wirthlinworldwide.com; www.redcross.org

To learn more about this research, read the case on your text DVD: "Can Research Rescue the Red Cross?"

>**Exhibit 19-5** Histogram of PrimeSell's Top 50 Customers' Average Annual Purchases

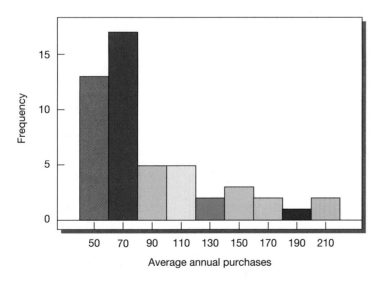

ues within the interval and preserves their rank order for finding the median, quartiles, and other summary statistics. It also eases linking a specific observation back to the data file and to the subject that produced it.

Visualization is the second advantage of stem-and-leaf displays. The range of values is apparent at a glance, and both shape and spread impressions are immediate. Patterns in the data—such as gaps where no values exist, areas where values are clustered, or outlying values that differ from the main body of the data—are easily observed.

To develop a stem-and-leaf display for the data in Exhibit 19-4, the first digits of each data item are arranged to the left of a vertical line. Next, we pass through the average annual purchases percentages in the order they were recorded and place the last digit for each item (the unit position, 1.0) to the right of the vertical line. Note that the digit to the right of the decimal point is ignored. The last digit for each item is placed on the horizontal row corresponding to its first digit(s). Now it is a simple matter to rank-order the digits in each row, creating the stem-and-leaf display shown in Exhibit 19-6.

Each line or row in this display is referred to as a *stem,* and each piece of information on the stem is called a *leaf.* The first line or row is

5 | 4 5 5 6 6 6 7 8 8 8 8 9

The meaning attached to this line or row is that there are 12 items in the data set whose first digit is five: 54, 55, 55, 56, 56, 56, 57, 58, 58, 58, 58, and 59. The second line,

6 | 1 2 4 6 6 7 9 9

shows that there are eight average annual purchase values whose first digit is six: 61, 62, 64, 66, 66, 67, 69, and 69.

When the stem-and-leaf display shown in Exhibit 19-6 is turned upright (rotated 90 degrees to the left), the shape is the same as that of the histogram shown in Exhibit 19-5.

>**Exhibit 19-6** A Stem-and-Leaf Display of PrimeSell's Average Annual Purchases Data

Stem	Leaf
5	4 5 5 6 6 6 7 8 8 8 8 9
6	1 2 4 6 6 7 9 9
7	0 2 2 3 5 6 7 8
8	0 2 2 6 8
9	
10	2 4
11	0 1 8
12	3
13	1
14	0 6
15	3
16	3 6
17	
18	3
19	
20	6
21	8

Pareto Diagrams

Pareto diagrams derive their name from a 19th-century Italian economist. In quality management, J. M. Juran first applied this concept by noting that only a vital few defects account for most problems evaluated for quality and that the trivial may explain the rest. Historically, this has come to be known as the 80/20 rule—that is, an 80 percent improvement in quality or performance can be expected by eliminating 20 percent of the causes of unacceptable quality or performance. Marketers often refer to this rule in relation to sales: that 80 percent of sales are generated by 20 percent of their customers.

Pareto diagram represents frequency data as a bar chart, ordered from most to least, overlayed with a line graph denoting the cumulative percentage at each variable level.

The **Pareto diagram** is a bar chart whose percentages sum to 100 percent. The data are derived from a multiple-choice–single-response scale, a multiple-choice–multiple-response scale, or frequency counts of words (or themes) from content analysis. The respondents' answers are sorted in decreasing importance, with bar height in descending order from left to right. The pictorial array that results reveals the highest concentration of improvement potential in the fewest number of remedies. An analysis of MindWriter customer complaints is depicted as a Pareto diagram in Exhibit 19-7. The cumulative frequency line in this exhibit shows that the top two problems (the repair did not resolve the customer's problem, and the product was returned multiple times for repair) accounted for 80 percent of the perceptions of inadequate repair service.

>**Exhibit 19-7** Pareto Diagram of MindWriter Repair Complaints

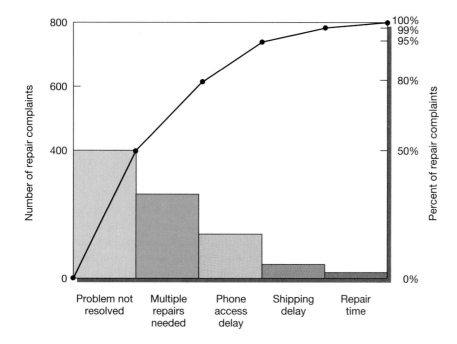

Boxplots[7]

The **boxplot,** or *box-and-whisker plot,* is another technique used frequently in exploratory data analysis.[8] A boxplot reduces the detail of the stem-and-leaf display and provides a different visual image of the distribution's location, spread, shape, tail length, and outliers. Boxplots are extensions of the **five-number summary** of a distribution. This summary consists of the median, the upper and lower quartiles, and the largest and smallest observations. The median and quartiles are used because they are particularly **resistant statistics.** *Resistance* is a characteristic that "provides insensitivity to localized misbehavior in data."[9] Resistant statistics are unaffected by outliers and change only slightly in response to the replacement of small portions of the data set.

Recall the discussion of the mean and standard deviation in Chapter 17. Now assume we take a data set [5,6,6,7,7,7,8,8,9] and calculate its mean. The mean of the set is 7; the standard deviation 1.22. If the 9 is replaced with 90, the mean becomes 16 and the standard deviation increases to 27.78. The mean is now 2 times larger than most of the numbers in the distribution, and the standard deviation is more than 22 times its original size. Changing only one of nine values has disturbed the location and spread summaries to the point where they no longer represent the other eight values. Both the mean and the standard deviation are considered **nonresistant statistics;** they are susceptible to the effects of extreme values in the tails of the distribution and do not represent typical values well under conditions of asymmetry. The standard deviation is particularly problematic because it is computed from the squared deviations from the mean.[10] In contrast, the median and quartiles are highly resistant to change. When we changed the 9 to 90, the median remained at 7 and the lower and upper quartiles stayed at 6 and 8, respectively. Because of the nature of quartiles, up to 25 percent of the data can be made extreme without perturbing the median, the rectangular composition of the plot, or the quartiles themselves. These characteristics of resistance are incorporated into the construction of boxplots.

boxplot visual image of the variable's distribution location, spread, shape, tail length, and outliers.

five-number summary the median, the upper and lower quartiles, and the largest and smallest observations of a variable's distribution.

resistant statistics statistical measures relatively unaffected by outliers within a data set.

nonresistant statistics a statistical measure that is susceptible to the effects of extreme values.

Boxplots may be constructed easily by hand or by computer programs. The basic ingredients of the plot are:

1. The rectangular plot that encompasses 50 percent of the data values.
2. A center line (or other notation) marking the median and going through the width of the box.
3. The edges of the box, called *hinges.*
4. The "whiskers" that extend from the right and left hinges to the largest and smallest values.[11]

interquartile range (IQR) measures the distance between the first and third quartiles of a distribution.

outliers data points that exceed +1.5 the interquartile range (IQR).

These values may be found within 1.5 times the **interquartile range (IQR)** from either edge of the box. These components and their relationships are shown in Exhibit 19-8.

When you are examining data, it is important to separate legitimate outliers from errors in measurement, editing, coding, and data entry. **Outliers,** data points that exceed +1.5 the interquartile range, reflect unusual cases and are an important source of information for the study. They are displayed or given special statistical treatment, or other portions of the data set are sometimes shielded from their effects. Outliers that are entry mistakes should be corrected or removed during editing.

Exhibit 19-9 summarizes several comparisons that are of help to the analyst. Boxplots are an excellent diagnostic tool, especially when graphed on the same scale. The upper two plots in the exhibit are both symmetric, but one is larger than the other. Larger box widths are sometimes used when the second variable, from the same measurement scale, comes from a larger sample size. The box widths should be proportional to the square root of the sample size, but not all plotting programs account for this.[12] Right- and left-skewed distributions and those with reduced spread are also presented clearly in the plot comparison. Finally, groups may be compared by means of multiple plots. One variation, in which a notch at the median marks off a confidence interval to test the equality of group medians, takes us a step closer to hypothesis testing.[13] Here the sides of the box return to full width at the upper and lower confidence intervals. When the intervals do not overlap, we can be confident, at a specified confidence level, that the medians of the two populations are different.

In Exhibit 19-10, multiple boxplots compare five sectors of PrimeSell's customers by their average annual purchases data. The overall impression is one of potential problems

>Exhibit 19-8 Boxplot Components

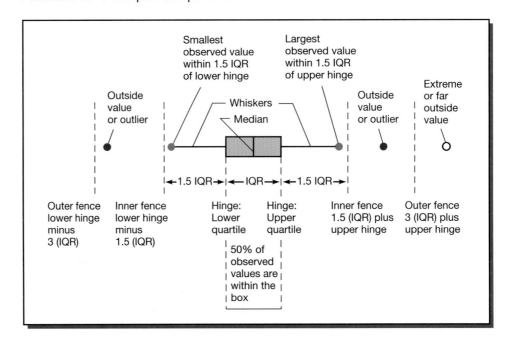

>**Exhibit 19-9** Diagnostics with Boxplots

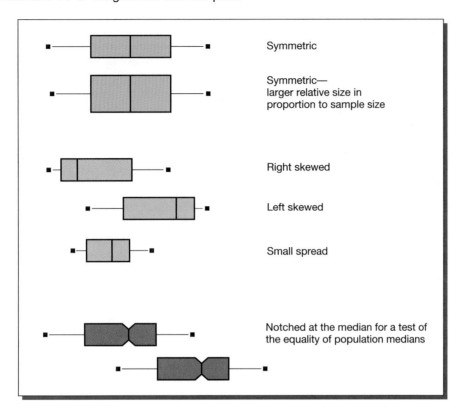

>**Exhibit 19-10** Boxplot Comparison of Customer Sectors

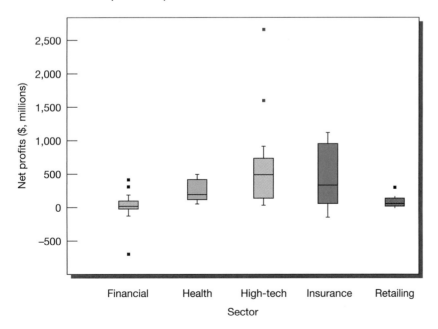

for the analyst: unequal variances, skewness, and extreme outliers. Note the similarities of the profiles of finance and retailing in contrast to the high-tech and insurance sectors. If hypothesis tests are planned, further examination of this plot for each sector would require a stem-and-leaf display and a five-number summary. From this, we could make decisions on the types of tests to select for confirmatory analysis (see Chapters 20, 21, and 22).

Mapping

Increasingly, participant data are being attached to their geographic dimension as Geographic Information System (GIS) software and coordinate measuring devices have become more affordable and easier to use. Essentially a GIS works by linking data sets to each other with at least one common data field (for example, a household's street address). The GIS allows the researcher to connect target and classification variables from a survey to specific geographic-based databases like U.S. Census data, to develop a richer understanding of the sample's attitudes and behavior. When radio frequency idenitification (RFID) data become more prevalent, much behavioral data will be able to connect with these new geographically rich databases.

> **We discussed RFID technology in Chapter 10.**

The most common way to display such data is with a map. Colors and patterns denoting knowledge, attitude, behavior, or demographic data arrays are superimposed over street maps (finest-level GIS), block-group maps, or county, state, or country maps to help identify the best locations for stores based on demographic, psychographic, and life-stage segmentation data. Florists array promotional response information geographically and use the map to plan targeted promotions. Consumer and business-to-business marketers use mapping of data on ownership, usage level, and price sensitivity in plotting geographic rollouts of new products, planning promotions, and making strategic pricing decisions. While this is an attractive option for exploratory analysis, it does take specialized software and hardware, as well as the expertise to operate it. Marketing students are often encouraged to take specialized courses on GIS to expand their skill set in this growing area.

Throughout this section we have exploited the visual techniques of exploratory data analysis to look beyond numerical summaries and gain insight into the patterns of the data. Few of the approaches have stressed the need for advanced mathematics, and all have an intuitive appeal for the analyst. When the more common ways of summarizing location,

Retail site selection is a research specialty that often uses mapping of data during exploratory data analysis. As this PCensus ad humorously reminds us, determining whether a site has the potential to attract sufficient members of a market and offers facilitating infrastructure and appropriate traffic patterns is often facilitated by mapping the demographics and other variables of interest, such as the level of interest in or anticipated use of the product. PCensus works with mapping software, U.S. Census data, and lifestyle data from Claritas to give a retailer a clear picture of where a new store should be located. Visit **www.pcensus.com** for a demonstration. **www.tetrad.com**

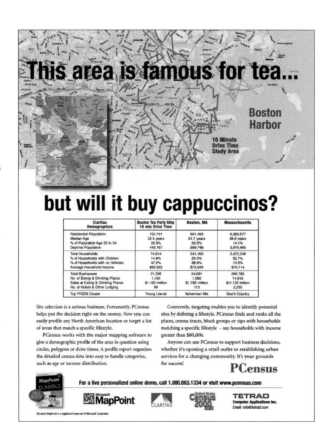

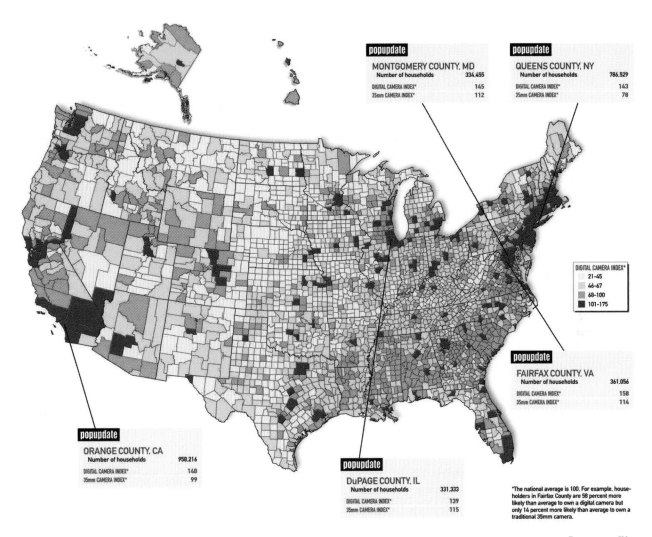

popupdate

MONTGOMERY COUNTY, MD
Number of households	334,455
DIGITAL CAMERA INDEX*	145
35mm CAMERA INDEX*	112

popupdate

QUEENS COUNTY, NY
Number of households	786,529
DIGITAL CAMERA INDEX*	143
35mm CAMERA INDEX*	78

DIGITAL CAMERA INDEX*	
	21–45
	46–67
	68–100
	101–175

popupdate

FAIRFAX COUNTY, VA
Number of households	361,056
DIGITAL CAMERA INDEX*	158
35mm CAMERA INDEX*	114

popupdate

ORANGE COUNTY, CA
Number of households	958,216
DIGITAL CAMERA INDEX*	140
35mm CAMERA INDEX*	99

popupdate

DuPAGE COUNTY, IL
Number of households	331,333
DIGITAL CAMERA INDEX*	139
35mm CAMERA INDEX*	115

*The national average is 100. For example, house-holders in Fairfax County are 58 percent more likely than average to own a digital camera but only 14 percent more likely than average to own a traditional 35mm camera.

>**pic**profile

Sometimes there is no better way to display data than with a map. In 2003, sales of digital cameras exceeded $3.1 billion, more than 10 times the level in 1998. That's bad news for companies like Kodak that once enjoyed significant revenue from repeat purchases of film. To find counties where ownership of digital cameras is above average, *American Demographics* teamed up with Claritas, a San Diego–based market research company, to design this map. At a quick glance you can tell where digital cameras have really captured the shutterbug's fancy and areas where penetration is limited. Photo Marketing Association International estimates U.S. household penetration at 42 percent in 2004 and forecasts sales of 25.8 million digital cameras in 2008. http://demographics.com; www.claritas.com; www.pmai.org.

spread, and shape have conveyed an inadequate picture of the data, we have used more resistant statistics to protect us from the effects of extreme scores and occasional errors. We have also emphasized the value of transforming the original scale of the data during preliminary analysis rather than at the point of hypothesis testing.

> **Location, spread, and shape were introduced in Chapter 17.**

> Cross-Tabulation

Depending on the management question, we can gain valuable insights by examining the data with cross-tabulation. **Cross-tabulation** is a technique for comparing data from two

cross-tabulation a technique for comparing data from two or more categorical variables.

Mapping Path of Online Buyers Reveals Four Car-Buying Segments

Is every hit on a car-related Web site a sale waiting to happen? Or are such hits just a means of starting the car search or the wanderings of a car buff? Forrester Research undertook a study of 78,000 car-site visitors with the assistance of comScore Networks. comScore Networks hosts a database of "more than 1.5 million global Internet users who have given comScore explicit permission to confidentially capture their Web-wide browsing, buying and other transaction behavior, including offline purchasing." Forrester Research looked for correlation in surfing patterns among the Internet users who visited 1 or more of 170 car-related Web sites in a three-month period. Then, through the use of a Web pop-up survey, Forrester determined whether these visitors purchased a car and what they bought. For each sample element, Forrester was able to trace the path of Web inquiry. Patterns of frequency and intensity and duration of research sessions, as well as cross-site visits for comparisons, proved to be strong short-term purchase indicators.

Roughly one in every four auto-site visitors buys a car within three months of the first visit. But not all surfers of car sites are equally likely to buy. After pouring over the data using SPSS statistical software, and refining the data with programs written within Excel, Forrester found that four segments emerged. More than half of "explorers" will buy, but they benefit from an explicit process where competitive advantages are detailed at each step. About one-third of "off-roaders" buy, but they have waded through mountains of intensive research by the time they act. "Drive-bys" visit fewer than five sites, and while they are the largest segment, only 20 percent buy in the short term. And frequent-visitor "cruisers" are more influencers than buyers (only 15 percent buy), as they are considered the true car buffs. "Web shoppers don't first visit information sites, then manufacturers' sites, then dealer sites as they move from awareness to interest to desire and action," shared senior analyst Mark Bunger. "Car buying online is a messier, more complex consideration process than previous conventional wisdom suggested."

www.forrester.com; www.comscore.com

>**Exhibit 19-11** SPSS Cross-Tabulation of Gender by Overseas Assignment Opportunity

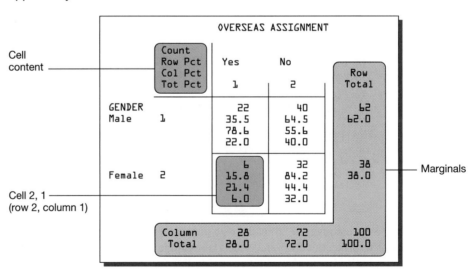

or more categorical variables such as gender and selection by one's company for an overseas marketing assignment. Cross-tabulation is used with demographic variables and the study's target variables (operationalized measurement questions). The technique uses tables having rows and columns that correspond to the levels or code values of each variable's categories. Exhibit 19-11 is an example of a computer-generated cross-tabulation. This table has two rows for gender and two columns for assignment selection. The combination of the variables with their values produces four cells. Each **cell** contains a count of the cases of the joint classification and also the row, column, and total percentages. The number of row cells and column cells is often used to designate the size of the table, as in this 2 × 2 table. The cells are individually identified by their row and column numbers, as illustrated. Row and column totals, called **marginals,** appear at the bottom and right "margins" of the table. They show the counts and percentages of the separate rows and columns.

Cross-tabulation is a first step for identifying relationships between variables. When tables are constructed for statistical testing, we call them **contingency tables,** and the test determines if the classification variables are independent of each other (see chi-square in Chapter 20). Of course, tables may be larger than 2 × 2.

cell a subgroup of a data table created by the intersection of two (or more) variables.

marginals a term for the column and row totals in a cross-tabulation.

contingency tables a cross-tabulation table constructed for statistical testing.

The Use of Percentages

Percentages serve two purposes in data presentation. First, they simplify the data by reducing all numbers to a range from 0 to 100. Second, they translate the data into standard form, with a base of 100, for relative comparisons. In a sampling situation, the number of cases that fall into a category is meaningless unless it is related to some base. A count of 28 overseas assignees has little meaning unless we know it is from a sample of 100. Using the latter as a base, we conclude that 28 percent of this study's sample has an overseas marketing assignment.

While the above is useful, it is even more useful when the research problem calls for a comparison of several distributions of data. Assume the previously reported data were collected five years ago and the present study had a sample of 1,500, of which 360 were selected for overseas assignments. By using percentages, we can see the relative relationships and shifts in the data (see Exhibit 19-12).

With two-dimension tables, the selection of a row or column will accentuate a particular distribution or comparison. This raises the question about which direction the percentages should be calculated. Most computer programs offer options for presenting percentages in both directions and interchanging the rows and columns of the table. But in situations where one variable is hypothesized to be the presumed cause, is thought to affect or predict a response, or is simply antecedent to the other variable, we label it the independent variable. Percentages should then be computed in the direction of this variable. Thus, if the independent variable is placed on the row, select row percentages; if it is on the column, select column percentages. In which direction should the percentages run in the

>**Exhibit 19-12** Comparison of Percentages in Cross-Tabulation Studies by Overseas Marketing Assignment

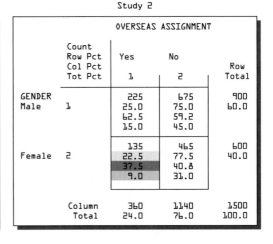

>**snap**shot

Extensive Research Launches Starbucks Card Duetto™ Visa

BusinessWeek recognized the Starbucks Card Duetto™ Visa as one of the important new products of 2003. In fact, it was the only financial product on the list. Starbucks Card Duetto™ Visa is a multifunction card that combines the features of a prepaid stored-value card, known as the Starbucks Card, with a regular credit card. Starbucks, in conjunction with Visa and Bank One, did extensive research to determine if the proposed new payment option had appeal. Focus groups were used to determine the level of potential consumer confusion with the multifunction card, determine card attractiveness, and refine messaging. A series of online surveys were conducted both before and after the launch of the product to determine market receptivity. A press release about the partnership about eight months before launch generated news coverage resulting in traffic to Starbucks' Web site. Early purchase intent was determined by those Starbucks customers who took initiative and signed up via the Web site to be prenotified by e-mail when the card became available. Among the postlaunch research questions guiding measurement of return on marketing investment (ROMI) are:

- Does the card enhance the Starbucks customer experience (how satisfied is each customer, and do customers feel appreciated)?
- Did the card prove valuable to all partners: Starbucks, Bank One, and Visa?
- Did card activity, which is linked to charitable donations, permit Starbucks to give back to the communities in which it operates in a significant way?

If you were in charge of this research, what would you be looking for during exploratory data analysis?

www.bankone.com; www.starbucks.com; www.visa.com

To learn more about this research, read the case and watch the video on your text DVD: "Starbucks, Bank One, and Visa Launch the Starbucks Card Duetto™ Visa."

---

previous example? If only the column percentages are reported, we imply that assignment status has some effect on gender. This is implausible. When percentages are reported by rows, the implication is that gender influences selection for overseas assignments.

Care should be taken in interpreting percentages from tables. Consider again the data in Exhibit 19-12. From the first to the second study, it is apparent that the percentage of females selected for overseas assignments rose from 15.8 to 22.5 percent of their respective samples. This should not be confused with the percentage within each sample who were women with overseas assignments, a number which increased from 6 percent (Study 1) to 9 percent (Study 2). Among all overseas selectees, in the first study 21.4 percent were women, while in the second study, 37.5 percent were women. Similar comparisons can be made for the other categories. The tables verify an increase in women with overseas assignments, but we cannot conclude that their gender had anything to do with the increase.

Percentages are used by virtually everyone dealing with numbers—but often incorrectly. The following guidelines, if used during analysis, will help to prevent errors in reporting:[14]

- *Averaging percentages.* Percentages cannot be averaged unless each is weighted by the size of the group from which it is derived. Thus, a simple average will not suffice; it is necessary to use a weighted average.

- *Use of too large percentages.* This often defeats the purpose of percentages—which is to simplify. A large percentage is difficult to understand and is confusing. If a 1,000 percent increase is experienced, it is better to describe this as a 10-fold increase.

- *Using too small a base.* Percentages hide the base from which they have been computed. A figure of 60 percent when contrasted with 30 percent would appear to suggest a sizable difference. Yet if there are only three cases in the one category and six in the other, the differences would not be as significant as they have been made to appear with percentages.

- *Percentage decreases can never exceed 100 percent.* This is obvious, but this type of mistake occurs frequently. The higher figure should always be used as the base or denominator. For example, if a price was reduced from $1 to $.25, the decrease would be 75 percent (75/100).

>**Exhibit 19-13** SPSS Cross-Tabulation with Control and Nested Variables

	Control Variable					
	Category 1			Category 2		
	Nested Variable			Nested Variable		
	cat 1	cat 2	cat 3	cat 1	cat 2	cat 3
Stub...	Cells...					

	SEX OF EMPLOYEE			
	MALES		FEMALES	
	MINORITY CLASSIFICATION		MINORITY CLASSIFICATION	
	WHITE	NONWHITE	WHITE	NONWHITE
EMPLOYMENT CATEGORY				
CLERICAL	16%	7%	18%	7%
OFFICE TRAINEE	7%	3%	17%	2%
SECURITY OFFICER	3%	3%		
COLLEGE TRAINEE	7%	0%	1%	
EXEMPT EMPLOYEE	6%	0%	0%	
MBA TRAINEE	1%	0%	0%	
TECHNICAL	1%			

Other Table-Based Analysis

The recognition of a meaningful relationship between variables generally signals a need for further investigation. Even if one finds a statistically significant relationship, the questions of why and under what conditions remain. The introduction of a **control variable** to interpret the relationship is often necessary. Cross-tabulation tables serve as the framework.

Statistical packages like Minitab, SAS, and SPSS have among their modules many options for the construction of *n*-way tables with provision for multiple control variables. Suppose you are interested in creating a cross-tabulation of two variables with one control. Whatever the number of values in the primary variables, the control variable with five values determines the number of tables. For some applications, it is appropriate to have five separate tables; for others, it might be preferable to have adjoining tables or have the values of all the variables in one. Management reports are of the latter variety. Exhibit 19-13 presents an example in which all three variables are handled under the same banner. Programs such as this one can handle far more complex tables and statistical information.[15]

An advanced variation on *n*-way tables is **automatic interaction detection (AID).** AID is a computerized statistical process that requires that the researcher identify a dependent variable and a set of predictors or independent variables. The computer then searches among up to 300 variables for the best single division of the data according to each predictor variable, chooses one, and splits the sample using a statistical test to verify the appropriateness of this choice.

Exhibit 19-14 shows the tree diagram that resulted from an AID study of customer satisfaction with MindWriter's CompleteCare repair service. The initial dependent variable is the overall impression of the repair service. This variable was measured on an interval scale of 1 to 5. The variables that contribute to perceptions of repair effectiveness were also measured on the same scale but were rescaled to ordinal data for this example (1–2 = poor, 3 = average, and 4–5 = excellent). The top box shows that 62 percent of the respondents rated the repair service as excellent (41% + 21%). The best predictor of repair effectiveness is "resolution of the problem."

control variable a variable introduced to help interpret the relationship between variables.

automatic interaction detection (AID) a data partitioning procedure that searches up to 300 variables for the single best predictor of a dependent variable.

>**Exhibit 19-14** Automatic Interaction Detection Example (MindWriter's Repair Satisfaction)

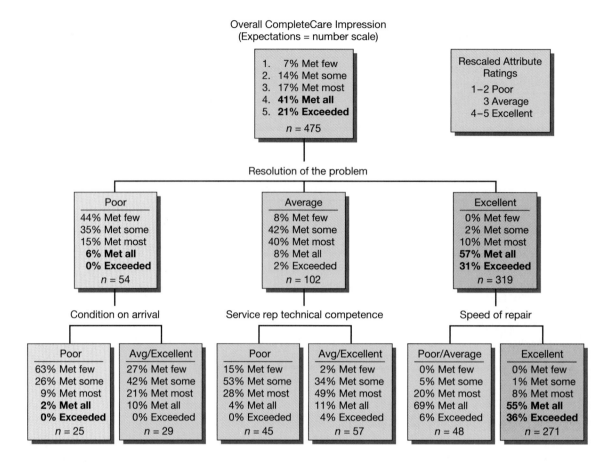

On the left side of the tree, customers who rated "resolution of the problem" as poor have fewer expectations being met or exceeded than the average for the sample (6 percent versus 62 percent). A poor rating on "condition on arrival" exacerbates this, reducing the total satisfied group to 2 percent. From this example you can see that the researcher separately studied (applied AID to) each subgroup to find the variable that when split again makes the next largest contribution to understanding the consumers' evaluation process—and to the reduction of unexplained variation in each subsample. This analysis alerts decision makers at MindWriter to the best- and worst-case scenarios for the CompleteCare service, how to recover during a problematic month, and which "key drivers," or independent variables influencing the process, should receive corrective resources.

>**summary**

1 Exploratory data analysis (EDA) provides a perspective and set of tools to search for clues and patterns in the data. EDA augments rather than supplants traditional statistics. In addition to numerical summaries of location, spread, and shape, EDA uses visual displays to provide a complete and accurate impression of distributions and variable relationships.

Frequency tables array data from lowest to highest values with counts and percentages. They are most useful for in-

specting the range of responses and their repeated occurrence. Bar charts and pie charts are appropriate for relative comparisons of nominal data. Histograms are optimally used with continuous variables where intervals group the responses. The Pareto diagram is a bar chart whose percentages sum to 100 percent. The causes of the problem under investigation are sorted in decreasing importance, with bar height descending from left to right. Stem-and-leaf displays and boxplots are EDA techniques that provide visual representations of distributions. The former present actual data values using a histogram-type device that allows inspection of spread and shape. Boxplots use the five-number summary to convey a detailed picture of a distribution's main body, tails, and outliers. Both stem-and-leaf displays and boxplots rely on resistant statistics to overcome the limitations of descriptive measures that are subject to extreme scores.

2 The examination of relationships involving categorical variables employs cross-tabulation. The tables used for this purpose consist of cells and marginals. The cells may contain combinations of count, row, column, and total percentages. The tabular structure is the framework for later statistical testing. Computer software for cross-classification analysis makes table-based analysis with one or more control variables an efficient tool for data visualization and later decision making. An advanced variation on *n*-way tables is automatic interaction detection (AID).

>**key**terms

automatic interaction detection (AID) 529	**cross-tabulation** 525	**marginals** 527
boxplot 521	**exploratory data analysis (EDA)** 514	**nonresistant statistics** 521
cell 527	**five-number summary** 521	**outliers** 522
confirmatory data analysis 514	**frequency table** 515	**Pareto diagram** 520
contingency table 527	**histogram** 517	**resistant statistics** 521
control variable 529	**interquartile range (IQR)** 522	**stem-and-leaf display** 518

>**discussion**questions

Terms in Review

1 Define or explain:

  a Marginals.

  b Pareto diagram.

  c Nonresistant statistics.

  d Lower control limit.

  e The five-number summary.

Making Research Decisions

2 Suppose you were preparing two-way tables of percentages for the following pairs of variables. How would you run the percentages?

  a Age and consumption of breakfast cereal.

  b Family income and confidence about the family's future.

  c Marital status and sports participation.

  d Crime rate and unemployment rate.

3 You study the attrition of entering college freshmen (those students who enter college as freshmen but don't stay to graduate). You find the following relationships between attrition, aid, and distance of home from college. What is your interpretation? Consider all variables and relationships.

	Aid		Home Near Receiving Aid		Home Far Receiving Aid	
	Yes (%)	No (%)	Yes (%)	No (%)	Yes (%)	No (%)
Drop Out	25	20	5	15	30	40
Stay	75	80	95	85	70	60

4 A local health agency is experimenting with two appeal letters, A and B, with which to raise funds. It sends out 400 of the A appeal and 400 of the B appeal (each subsample is divided equally among working-class and middle-class neighborhoods). The agency secures the results shown in the following table.

  a Which appeal is the best?

  b Which class responded better to which letter?

  c Is appeal or social class a more powerful independent variable?

	Appeal A		Appeal B	
	Middle Class (%)	Working Class (%)	Middle Class (%)	Working Class (%)
Contribution	20	40	15	30
No Contribution	80	60	85	70
	100	100	100	100

5 Assume you have collected data on sales associates of a large retail organization in a major metropolitan area. You analyze the data by type of work classification, education level, and whether the workers were raised in a rural or urban setting. The results are shown below. How would you interpret them?

Annual Retail Employee Turnover per 100 Employees

| | High Education | | Low Education | | | |
	Salaried	Hourly Wage	Salaried	Hourly Wage	Salaried	Hourly Wage
Rural	8	16	6	14	18	18
Urban	12	16	10	12	19	20

From Concept to Practice

6 Use the data in Exhibit 19-5 to construct a stem-and-leaf display.

   a Where do you find the main body of the distribution?

   b How many values reside outside the inner fence(s)?

Behind the Scenes

7 Identify the variables being cross-tabulated by Sammye. Identify some plausible reasons why such an exploration would be a good idea.

>**www**exercise

Your university likely has SPSS or SAS, or SPSS came bundled with your book. Visit these two companies' Web sites and compare their software's statistical analysis capabilities. If you were buying such software for your employer, which would you choose and why?

>**cases***

Agri Comp

NCRCC: Teeing Up and New Strategic Direction

Mastering Teacher Leadership

* All cases, both written and video, are on the text DVD. Check the DVD Index to determine whether a case has data, the research instrument, or other supplementary material.

chapter 20

Hypothesis Testing

After reading this chapter, you should understand . . .

1 The nature and logic of hypothesis testing.

2 What a statistically significant difference is.

3 The six-step hypothesis testing procedure.

4 The differences between parametric and nonparametric tests and when to use each.

5 The factors that influence the selection of an appropriate test of statistical significance.

6 How to interpret the various test statistics.

>behindthescenes

We rejoin Visionary Insight's Jason Henry as he and his interns are proceeding with the Center City for Performing Arts Association research. One of the critical issues driving the study is whether alcohol should be served during intermissions of concerts and other performances. While there appears to be a significant opportunity for additional revenue, costs and liability will also increase. There is also some danger that patrons may not want to expose their children to such an environment, and this could affect ticket sales to families. The Center City Symphony has recently instituted a similar policy and attendance by young unmarried adults has increased. CCPA doesn't want to miss the opportunity of attracting a younger audience.

"Sammye, I'd like to meet with you and David about verifying the gender and age differences on the alcohol issue for Center City for Performing Arts Association." Jason makes his way through the cluttered outer office, stepping around piles of printouts, topped with sketched graphs or detailed cross-tabulated tables with handwritten notes.

Sammye looks up as Jason disappears into his office. "David's working down in the conference room," she calls out. "I'll go grab him and be right there."

Moments later, Sammye and David return, carrying with them the cross-tabulated data to which Jason had referred.

Jason smiles, waiting for them to settle. "So what have you got?"

David jumps right in. "There is definitely a difference in attitude about serving alcohol during intermission at performances. But it doesn't appear to be quite what the CCPA board expected."

"How so?"

"Well, the younger patrons seem somewhat divided, while those between 35 and 54 are against and those 55 and over are strongly in favor."

"What was your original hypothesis?"

"Based on your meeting notes from the project session with the CCPA board, we formulated the hypothe-sis that there would be a difference on the alcohol issue based on age," shares Sammye. "But we assumed that the younger the patrons, the more in favor of alcohol they would be. The numbers just aren't supporting that. And I'm not so sure that age is the right variable to look at."

Jason extends his hand across his desk. "Let me see the statistics on age."

"And I've got the stats on gender too," offers Sammye.

"Are those in line with your hypothesis?"

"Not really," shares David. "Men and women are all over the place. We hypothesized that men would be in favor while women would be against. That's just not panning out."

Jason glances at the printout, mainly to be sure they had run the correct test. He is pleased to see that their interpretation of the statistics is correct. "Looks like you have some work yet, to determine the pockets of resistance. Since the sample split—wasn't it 57 percent in favor to 43 percent against?—we don't want to rec-ommend that CCPA proceed *without* being able to tell the board the likely direction of potential trouble.

"Sometimes our preliminary analysis plan can take us only so far," comments Jason. "Let's talk about what tests you plan to run now."

> Introduction

> **Induction and deduction were discussed in Chapter 3.**

In Chapters 18 and 19, we discussed the procedures for data preparation and preliminary analysis. The next step for many studies is hypothesis testing.

Just as your understanding of scientific reasoning was important in the last two chapters, recollection of the specific differences between induction and deduction is fundamental to hypothesis testing. Inductive reasoning moves from specific facts to general, but tentative, conclusions. We can never be absolutely sure that inductive conclusions are flawless. With the aid of probability estimates, we can qualify our results and state the degree of confidence we have in them. Statistical inference is an application of inductive reasoning. It allows us to reason from evidence found in the sample to conclusions we wish to make about the population.

inferential statistics includes the estimation of population values and the testing of statistical hypotheses.

Inferential statistics is the second of two major categories of statistical procedures, the other being descriptive statistics. We used descriptive statistics in Chapter 17 when describing distributions. Under the heading **inferential statistics,** two topics are discussed in this book. The first, estimation of population values, was used with sampling in Chapter 17, but we will return to it here briefly. The second, testing statistical hypotheses, is the primary subject of this chapter. There are more examples of hypothesis tests in this chapter than most students will need for a term project or early assignments in their marketing research careers. They are provided, like Appendix C, for later reference along with the readings for this chapter found at the end of the book.

> **A section on nonparametric techniques in Appendix C provides further study for readers with a special interest in nominal and ordinal variables.**

> Hypothesis Testing

Having detailed your hypotheses in your preliminary analysis planning, the purpose of hypothesis testing is to determine the accuracy of your hypotheses due to the fact that you have collected a sample of data, not a census. Exhibit 20-1 reminds you of the relationships among your design strategy, data collection activities, preliminary analysis, and hypothesis testing.

We evaluate the accuracy of hypotheses by determining the statistical likelihood that the data reveal true differences—not random sampling error. We evaluate the importance of a statistically significant difference by weighing the practical significance of any change that we measure.

classical statistics an objective view of probability in which the hypothesis is rejected, or not, based solely on the sample data collected.

Although there are two approaches to hypothesis testing, the more established is the classical or sampling-theory approach. **Classical statistics** are found in all of the major statistics books and are widely used in marketing research applications. This approach represents an objective view of probability in which the decision making rests totally on an analysis of available sampling data. A hypothesis is established; it is rejected or fails to be rejected, based on the sample data collected.

Bayesian statistics uses subjective probability estimates based on general experience rather than on collected data.

The second approach is known as **Bayesian statistics,** which are an extension of the classical approach. They also use sampling data, but they go beyond to consider all other available information. This additional information consists of subjective probability estimates stated in terms of degrees of belief. These subjective estimates are based on general experience rather than on specific collected data. Various decision rules are established, cost and other estimates can be introduced, and the expected outcomes of combinations of these elements are used to judge decision alternatives.

> ❝People are 'erroneously confident' in their knowledge and underestimate the odds that their information or beliefs will be proved wrong. They tend to seek additional information in ways that confirm what they already believe.❞
>
> *Max Bazerman*
> *Professor, Harvard University*

>**Exhibit 20-1** Hypothesis Testing and the Research Process

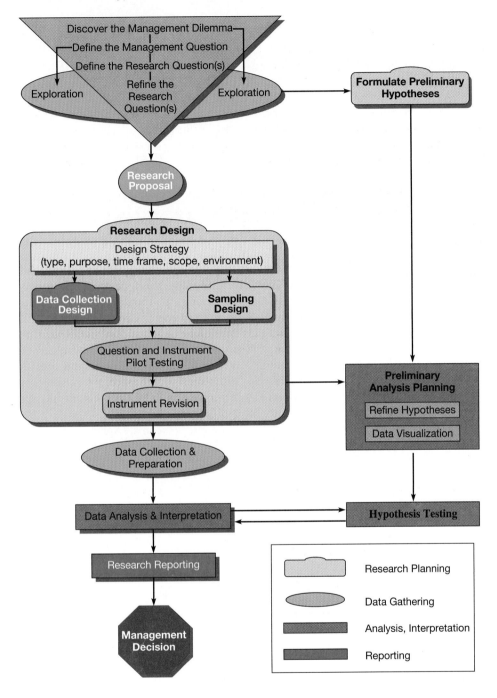

Discover the Management Dilemma

Define the Management Question

Define the Research Question(s)

Refine the Research Question(s)

Exploration

Exploration

Formulate Preliminary Hypotheses

Research Proposal

Research Design

Design Strategy
(type, purpose, time frame, scope, environment)

Data Collection Design

Sampling Design

Question and Instrument Pilot Testing

Instrument Revision

Preliminary Analysis Planning

Refine Hypotheses

Data Visualization

Data Collection & Preparation

Data Analysis & Interpretation

Hypothesis Testing

Research Reporting

Management Decision

Research Planning

Data Gathering

Analysis, Interpretation

Reporting

Statistical Significance

Following classical statistics approach, we accept or reject a hypothesis on the basis of sampling information alone. Since any sample will almost surely vary somewhat from its population, we must judge whether the differences are statistically significant or insignificant. A difference has **statistical significance** if there is good reason to believe the difference does not represent random sampling fluctuations only. For example, Honda, Toyota, DaimlerChrysler, Ford, and other auto companies produce hybrid vehicles using an advanced technology that combines a small gas engine with an electric motor. The vehicles

statistical significance an index of how meaningful the results of a statistical comparison are.

run on an electric motor at slow speeds but shift to both the gasoline motor and electric motor at city and higher freeway speeds. Their advertising strategies focus on fuel economy. Let's say that the hybrid Civic has maintained an average of about 50 miles per gallon (mpg) with a standard deviation of 10 mpg. Suppose researchers discover by analyzing all production vehicles that the mpg is now 51. Is this difference statistically significant from 50? Of course it is, because the difference is based on a *census* of the vehicles and there is no sampling involved. It has been demonstrated conclusively that the population average has moved from 50 to 51 mpg. While it is of statistical significance, whether it is of **practical significance** is another question. If a decision maker judges that this variation has no real importance, then it is of little practical significance.

> **practical significance**
> when a statistically significant difference has real importance to the decision maker.

Since it would be too expensive to analyze all of a manufacturer's vehicles frequently, we resort to sampling. Assume a sample of 25 cars is randomly selected and the average mpg is calculated to be 54. Is this statistically significant? The answer is not obvious. It is significant if there is good reason to believe the average mpg of the total population has moved up from 50. Since the evidence consists of only a sample, consider the second possibility: that this is only a random sampling error and thus is not significant. The task is to decide whether such a result from this sample is or is not statistically significant. To answer this question, one needs to consider further the logic of hypothesis testing.

The Logic of Hypothesis Testing

> **null hypothesis (H_0)**
> assumption that no difference exists between the sample parameter and the population statistic.

In classical tests of significance, two kinds of hypotheses are used. The **null hypothesis** is used for testing. It is a statement that no difference exists between the parameter (a measure taken by a census of the population or a prior measurement of a sample of the population) and the statistic being compared to it (a measure from a recently drawn sample of the population). Analysts usually test to determine whether there has been no change in the population of interest or whether a real difference exists. Why not state the hypothesis in a positive form? Why not state that any difference between the sample statistic and the population parameter is due to some reason? Unfortunately, this type of hypothesis cannot be tested definitively. Evidence that is consistent with a hypothesis stated in a positive form can almost never be taken as conclusive grounds for accepting the hypothesis. A finding that is consistent with this type of hypothesis might be consistent with other hypotheses too, and thus it does not demonstrate the truth of the given hypothesis.

For example, suppose a coin is suspected of being biased in favor of heads. The coin is flipped 100 times and the outcome is 52 heads. It would not be correct to jump to the conclusion that the coin is biased simply because more than the expected number of 50 heads resulted. The reason is that 52 heads is consistent with the hypothesis that the coin is fair.

On the other hand, flipping 85 or 90 heads in 100 flips would seem to contradict the hypothesis of a fair coin. In this case there would be a strong case for a biased coin.

In the hybrid-vehicle example, the null hypothesis states that the population parameter of 50 mpg has not changed. A second, **alternative hypothesis** holds that there has been a change in average mpg (i.e., the sample statistic of 54 indicates the population value probably is no longer 50). The alternative hypothesis is the logical opposite of the null hypothesis.

The hybrid-car example can be explored further to show how these concepts are used to test for significance:

- The null hypothesis (H_0): There has been no change from the 50 mpg average.

The alternative hypothesis (H_A) may take several forms, depending on the objective of the researchers. The H_A may be of the "not the same" or the "greater than" or "less than" form:

- The average mpg has changed from 50.
- The average mpg has increased (decreased) from 50.

These types of alternative hypotheses correspond with two-tailed and one-tailed tests. A **two-tailed test,** or *nondirectional test,* considers two possibilities: The average could be more than 50 mpg, or it could be less than 50. To test this hypothesis, the regions of rejection are divided into two tails of the distribution. A **one-tailed test,** or *directional test,* places the entire probability of an unlikely outcome into the tail specified by the alternative hypothesis. In Exhibit 20-2, the first diagram represents a nondirectional hypothesis, and the second is a directional hypothesis of the "greater than" variety.

Hypotheses for Exhibit 20-2 may be expressed in the following form:

Null	H_0:μ = 50 mpg
Alternative	H_A:$\mu \neq$ 50 mpg (not the same case)

Or

Null	H_0:$\mu \leq$ 50 mpg
Alternative	H_A:$\mu >$ 50 mpg (greater than case)

Or

Null	H_0:$\mu \geq$ 50 mpg
Alternative	H_A:$\mu <$ 50 mpg (less than case)

alternative hypothesis (H_A) that a difference exists between the sample parameter and the population statistic to which it is compared.

two-tailed test nondirectional test to reject the hypothesis that the sample statistic is either greater than or less than the population parameter.

one-tailed test a directional test of a null hypothesis assumes the sample parameter is not the same as the population statistic, but that the difference can be in only one direction.

>**Exhibit 20-2** One- and Two-Tailed Tests at the 5% Level of Significance

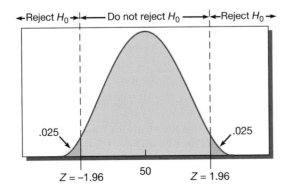

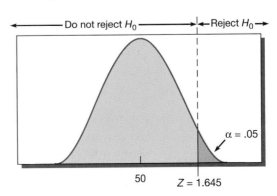

Direct-to-Consumer Ads under Heavy Fire

Direct-to-consumer (D-to-C) pharmaceutical ads have drawn a lot of criticism since 1997 Food and Drug Administration (FDA) regulations permitted such tactics. Proponents of legislation to disallow the practice fear such ads "unfairly influence important health care decisions" by causing patients to pressure doctors and thus encourage doctors to prescribe unnecessary prescriptions. The chairman of the American Medical Association believes such advertising may create an adversarial relationship between doctor and patient. He wants to know if the ads "improve the quality of care enough to make it worth the increased costs of the medicines being advertised." One democratic legislator believes "taxpayers would not have to subsidize excessive advertising that leads to higher prices at the pharmacy counter."

Ipsos-NPD tracks this issue for the pharmaceutical industry with its monthly PharmTrends® panel, comprising 16,000 U.S. households. Panel members are measured for ad recall, pre-

scriptions filled, physician recommendations for over-the-counter (OTC) products, and OTC products purchased, as well as condition being treated. Panel findings reveal that advertising "has encouraged higher levels of script fulfillment per year among consumers who reported that they were aware of advertising." Additionally, such advertising is credited with reminding patients to refill prescriptions. In its February InstaVue omnibus mail survey of 26,000 adults, 47 percent had seen pharmaceutical advertising in the past year, 25 percent indicated D-to-C ads encouraged them to call/visit their doctors to discuss the pharmaceutical advertised, and 15 percent reported asking for the very drug advertised.

How would you determine if this research confirmed or refuted that "pharmaceutical ads undermine quality of care"?

www.ipsos-npd.com

In testing these hypotheses, adopt this decision rule: Take no corrective action if the analysis shows that one cannot reject the null hypothesis. Note the language "cannot reject" rather than "accept" the null hypothesis. It is argued that a null hypothesis can never be proved and therefore cannot be "accepted." Here, again, we see the influence of inductive reasoning. Unlike deduction, where the connections between premises and conclusions provide a legitimate claim of "conclusive proof," inductive conclusions do not possess that advantage. Statistical testing gives only a chance to (1) disprove (reject) or (2) fail to reject the hypothesis. Despite this terminology, it is common to hear "accept the null" rather than the clumsy "fail to reject the null." In this discussion, the less formal *accept* means "fail to reject" the null hypothesis.

If we reject a null hypothesis (finding a statistically significant difference), then we are accepting the alternative hypothesis. In either accepting or rejecting a null hypothesis, we can make incorrect decisions. A null hypothesis can be accepted when it should have been rejected or rejected when it should have been accepted.

These problems are illustrated with an analogy to the American legal system.[1] In our system of justice, the innocence of an indicted person is presumed until proof of guilt beyond a reasonable doubt can be established. In hypothesis testing, this is the null hypothesis; there should be no difference between the presumption of innocence and the outcome unless contrary evidence is furnished. Once evidence establishes beyond reasonable doubt that innocence can no longer be maintained, a just conviction is required. This is equivalent to rejecting the null hypothesis and accepting the alternative hypothesis. Incorrect decisions or errors are the other two possible outcomes. We can unjustly convict an innocent person, or we can acquit a guilty person.

Exhibit 20-3 compares the statistical situation to the legal one. One of two conditions exists in nature—either the null hypothesis is true or the alternative hypothesis is true. An indicted person is innocent or guilty. Two decisions can be made about these conditions: One may accept the null hypothesis or reject it (thereby accepting the alternative). Two of these situations result in correct decisions; the other two lead to decision errors.

When a **Type I error** (α) is committed, a true null hypothesis is rejected; the innocent person is unjustly convicted. The α value is called *the level of significance* and is the prob-

Type I error (α) error when one rejects a true null hypothesis.

>**Exhibit 20-3** Comparison of Statistical Decisions to Legal Analogy

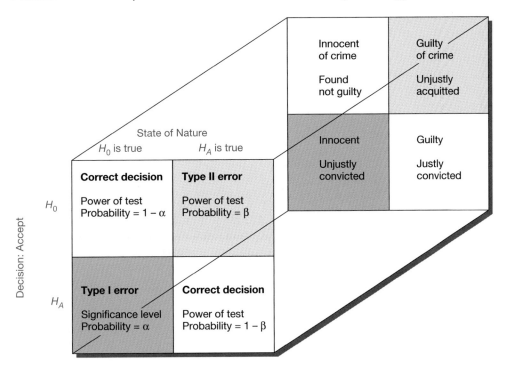

ability of rejecting the true null. With a **Type II error (β),** one fails to reject a false null hypothesis; the result is an unjust acquittal, with the guilty person going free. In our system of justice, it is more important to reduce the probability of convicting the innocent than that of acquitting the guilty. Similarly, hypothesis testing places a greater emphasis on Type I errors than on Type II errors. Next we shall examine each of these errors in more detail.

Type II error (β) error when one fails to reject a false null hypothesis.

Type I Error

Assume the hybrid manufacturer's problem is complicated by a consumer testing agency's assertion that the average mpg has changed. Assume the population mean is 50 mpg, the standard deviation of the population is 10 mpg, and the size of the sample is 25 vehicles. With this information, one can calculate the standard error of the mean ($\sigma_{\bar{X}}$) (the standard deviation of the distribution of sample means). This hypothetical distribution is pictured in Exhibit 20-4. The standard error of the mean is calculated to be 2 mpg:

$$\sigma_{\bar{X}} = \frac{\sigma}{\sqrt{n}} = \frac{10}{\sqrt{25}} = 2$$

If the decision is to reject H_0 with a 95 percent confidence interval ($\alpha = .05$), a Type I error of .025 in each tail is accepted (this assumes a two-tailed test). In part A of Exhibit 20-4, see the **regions of rejection** indicated by the shaded areas. The area between these two regions is known as the **region of acceptance.** The dividing points between the rejection and acceptance areas are called **critical values.** Since the distribution of sample means is normal, the critical values can be computed in terms of the standardized random variable,[2] where

Z = 1.96 (significance level = .05)

$\bar{X}_c$ = the critical value of the sample mean

μ = the population value stated in $H_0 = 50$

$\sigma_{\bar{X}}$ = the standard error of a distribution of means of samples of 25

region of rejection area beyond the region of acceptance set by the level of significance.

region of acceptance area between the two regions of rejection or above/below the region of acceptance at the chosen level of significance.

critical value the dividing point(s) between the region of acceptance and the region of rejection.

>**Exhibit 20-4** Probability of Making a Type I Error Given H_0 Is True

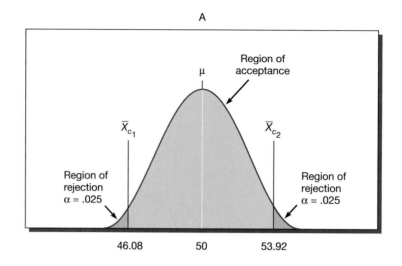

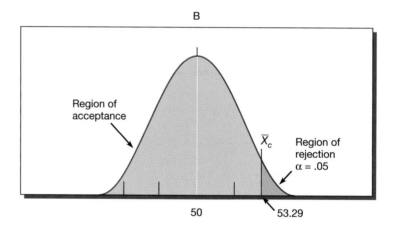

Thus the critical values for the test of the null hypothesis (that the mpg has not changed) are computed as follows:

$$Z = \frac{\bar{X} - \mu}{\sigma_{\bar{X}}}$$

$$-1.96 = \frac{\bar{X}_c - 50}{2}$$

$$\bar{X}_c = 46.08$$

$$1.96 = \frac{\bar{X}_c - 50}{2}$$

$$\bar{X}_c = 53.92$$

If the probability of a Type I error is 5 percent ($\alpha = .05$), the probability of a correct decision if the null hypothesis is true is 95 percent. By changing the probability of a Type I error, you move critical values either closer to or farther away from the assumed parameter of 50. This can be done if a smaller or larger α error is desired and critical values are moved to reflect this. You can also change the Type 1 error and the regions of acceptance by changing the size of the sample. For example, if you take a sample of 100, the critical values that provide a Type I error of .05 are 48.04 and 51.96.

The alternative hypothesis concerned a change in either direction from 50, but the manufacturer is interested only in increases in mpg. For this, one uses a one-tailed (greater than) H_A and places the entire region of rejection in the upper tail of the distribution. One can accept a 5 percent α risk and compute a new critical value (X_c). (See Appendix Exhibit D-1 to find the Z value of 1.645 for the area of .05 under the curve.) Substitute this in the Z equation and solve for $\bar{X}_c$:

$$Z = 1.645 = \frac{\bar{X}_c - 50}{2}$$

$$\bar{X}_c = 53.29$$

This new critical value, the boundary between the regions of acceptance and rejection, is pictured in part B of Exhibit 20-4.

Type II Error

The manufacturer would commit a Type II error (β) by accepting the null hypothesis ($\mu = 50$) when in truth it had changed. This kind of error is difficult to detect. The probability of committing a β error depends on five factors: (1) the true value of the parameter, (2) the α level we have selected, (3) whether a one- or two-tailed test was used to evaluate the hypothesis, (4) the sample standard deviation, and (5) the size of the sample. We secure a different β error if the new β moves from 50 to 54 rather than only to 52. We must compute separate β error estimates for each of a number of assumed new population parameters and $\bar{X}_c$ values.

To illustrate, assume μ has actually moved to 54 from 50. Under these conditions, what is the probability of our making a Type II error if the critical value is set at 53.29? (See Exhibit 20-5.) This may be expressed in the following fashion:

$P(A_2)S_1 = \alpha = .05$ (assume a one-tailed alternative hypothesis)

$P(A_1)S_2 = \beta = ?$

$$\sigma_{\bar{X}} = \frac{\sigma}{\sqrt{n}} = \frac{10}{\sqrt{25}} = 2$$

$$Z = \frac{\bar{X} - \mu}{\sigma_{\bar{X}}} = \frac{53.29 - 54}{2} = -.355$$

Using Exhibit D-1 in Appendix D, we interpolate between .35 and .36 Z scores to find the .355 Z score. The area between the mean and Z is .1387. β is the tail area, or the area below the Z, and is calculated as

$$\beta = .50 - .1387 = .36$$

This condition is shown in Exhibit 20-5. It is the percent of the area where we would *not* reject the null ($H_0: \mu = 50$) when, in fact, it was false because the true mean was 54. With an α of .05 and a sample of 25, there is a 36 percent probability of a Type II (β) error if the μ is 54. We also speak of the **power of the test**—that is (1 − β). For this example, the power of the test equals 64 percent (1 − .36)—that is, we will correctly reject the false null hypothesis with a 64 percent probability. A power of 64 percent is less than the 80 percent minimum percentage recommended by statisticians.

power of the test 1 minus the probability of committing a Type II error.

There are several ways to reduce a Type II error. We can shift the critical value closer to the original μ of 50; but to do this, we must accept a bigger α. Whether to take this action depends on the evaluation of the relative α and β risks. It might be desirable to enlarge the acceptable α risk because a worsening of the mileage would probably call for increased

>**Exhibit 20-5** Probability of Making a Type II Error

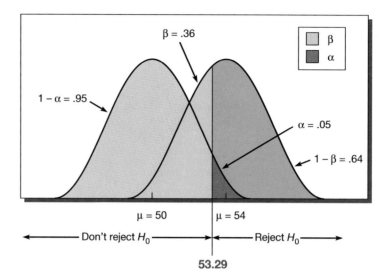

efforts to stimulate efficiency. Committing a Type I error would mean only that we engaged in efforts to stimulate efficiency when the situation had not worsened. This act probably would not have many adverse effects even if mpg had not increased.

A second way to reduce Type II error is to increase sample size. For example, if the sample were increased to 100, the power of the test would be much stronger:

$$\sigma_{\bar{X}} = \frac{\sigma}{\sqrt{n}} = \frac{10}{\sqrt{100}} = 1$$

$$Z = \frac{\bar{X} - \mu}{\sigma_{\bar{X}}} = \frac{53.29 - 54}{1} = -.71$$

$$\beta = .50 - .2612 = .24$$

This would reduce the Type II error to 24 percent and increase the power of the test to 76 percent.

A third method seeks to improve both α and β errors simultaneously and is difficult to accomplish. We know that measuring instruments, observations, and recording produce error. By using a better measuring device, tightening the observation and recording processes, or devising a more efficient sample, we can reduce the variability of observations. This diminishes the standard error of estimate and in turn reduces the sampling distributions' spread. The net effect is that there is less tail area in the error regions.

Statistical Testing Procedures

Testing for statistical significance follows a relatively well-defined pattern, although authors differ in the number and sequence of steps. One six-stage sequence is as follows:

1. *State the null hypothesis.* While the researcher is usually interested in testing a hypothesis of change or differences, the null hypothesis is always used for statistical testing purposes.

2. *Choose the statistical test.* To test a hypothesis, one must choose an appropriate statistical test. There are many tests from which to choose, and there are at least four criteria that can be used in choosing a test. One is the power efficiency of the test. A

more powerful test provides the same level of significance with a smaller sample than a less powerful test. In addition, in choosing a test, one can consider how the sample is drawn, the nature of the population, and (importantly) the type of measurement scale used. For instance, some tests are useful only when the sequence of scores is known or when observations are paired; other tests are appropriate only if the population has certain characteristics; still other tests are useful only if the measurement scale is interval or ratio. More attention is given to test selection later in the chapter.

3. *Select the desired level of significance.* The choice of the **level of significance** should be made before we collect the data. The most common level is .05, although .01 is also widely used. Other α levels such as .10, .025, or .001 are sometimes chosen. The exact level to choose is largely determined by how much α risk one is willing to accept and the effect that this choice has on β risk. The larger the α, the lower is the β.

> **level of significance** the probability of rejecting a true null hypothesis.

4. *Compute the calculated difference value.* After the data are collected, use the formula for the appropriate significance test to obtain the calculated value. Athough the computation typically results from a software program, we illustrate the procedures in this chapter to help you visualize what is being done.

5. *Obtain the critical test value.* After we compute the calculated t, χ^2, or other measure, we must look up the critical value in the appropriate table for that distribution (or it is provided with the software calculation). The critical value is the criterion that defines the region of rejection from the region of acceptance of the null hypothesis.

6. *Interpret the test.* For most tests if the calculated value is larger than the critical value, we reject the null hypothesis and conclude that the alternative hypothesis is supported (although it is by no means proved). If the critical value is larger, we conclude we have failed to reject the null.[3]

Probability Values (*p* Values)

According to the "interpret the test" step of the statistical test procedure, the conclusion is stated in terms of rejecting or not rejecting the null hypothesis based on a reject region selected before the test is conducted. A second method of presenting the results of a statistical test reports the extent to which the test statistic disagrees with the null hypothesis. This method has become popular because analysts want to know what percentage of the sampling distribution lies beyond the sample statistic on the curve, and most statistical computer programs report the results of statistical tests as probability values (*p* values). The ***p* value** is the probability of observing a sample value as extreme as, or more extreme than, the value actually observed, given that the null hypothesis is true. This area represents the probability of a Type I error that must be assumed if the null hypothesis is rejected. The *p* value is compared to the significance level (α), and on this basis the null hypothesis is either rejected or not rejected. If the *p* value is less than the significance level, the null hypothesis is rejected (if *p* value < α, reject the null). If *p* is greater than or equal to the significance level, the null hypothesis is not rejected (if *p* value > α, don't reject the null).

> ***p* value** probability of observing a sample value as extreme as, or more extreme than, the value actually observed, given that the null hypothesis is true.

Statistical data analysis programs commonly compute the *p* value during the execution of a hypothesis test. The following example will help illustrate the correct way to interpret a *p* value.

In part B of Exhibit 20-4 the critical value was shown for the situation where the manufacturer was interested in determining whether the average mpg had increased. The critical value of 53.29 was computed based on a standard deviation of 10, sample size of 25, and the manufacturer's willingness to accept a 5 percent α risk. Suppose that the sample mean equaled 55. Is there enough evidence to reject the null hypothesis? If the *p* value is less than .05, the null hypothesis will be rejected. The *p* value is computed as follows.

The standard deviation of the distribution of sample means is 2. The appropriate Z value is

$$Z = \frac{\bar{X} - \mu}{\sigma_{\bar{X}}}$$

$$Z = \frac{55 - 50}{2}$$

$$Z = 2.5$$

The p value is determined using the standard normal table. The area between the mean and a Z value of 2.5 is .4938. For this one-tailed test, the p value is the area above the Z value. The probability of observing a Z value at least as large as 2.5 is only .0062 (.5000 − .4938 = .0062) if the null hypothesis is true.

This small p value represents the risk of rejecting a true null hypothesis. It is the probability of a Type I error if the null hypothesis is rejected. Since the p value (p = .0062) is smaller than α = .05, the null hypothesis is rejected. The manufacturer can conclude that the average mpg has increased. The probability that this conclusion is wrong is .0062.

> Tests of Significance

This section provides an overview of statistical tests that are representative of the vast array available to the researcher. After a review of the general types of tests and their assumptions, the procedures for selecting an appropriate test are discussed. The remainder of the section contains examples of parametric and nonparametric tests for one-sample, two-sample, and k-sample cases. Readers needing a comprehensive treatment of significance tests are referred to the suggested readings for this chapter.

Types of Tests

parametric tests
significance tests for data from interval or ratio scales.

nonparametric tests
significance tests for data from nominal and ordinal scales.

There are two general classes of significance tests: parametric and nonparametric. **Parametric tests** are more powerful because their data are derived from interval and ratio measurements. **Nonparametric tests** are used to test hypotheses with nominal and ordinal data. Parametric techniques are the tests of choice if their assumptions are met. Assumptions for parametric tests include the following:

- The observations must be independent—that is, the selection of any one case should not affect the chances for any other case to be included in the sample.
- The observations should be drawn from normally distributed populations.
- These populations should have equal variances.
- The measurement scales should be at least interval so that arithmetic operations can be used with them.

normal probability plot
compares the observed values with those expected from a normal distribution.

The researcher is responsible for reviewing the assumptions pertinent to the chosen test. Performing diagnostic checks on the data allows the researcher to select the most appropriate technique. The normality of a distribution may be checked in several ways. We have previously discussed the measures of location, shape, and spread for preliminary analysis and considered graphic techniques for exploring data patterns and examining distributions. Another diagnostic tool is the **normal probability plot.** This plot compares the observed values with those expected from a normal distribution.[4] If the data display the characteristics of normality, the points will fall within a narrow band along a straight line. An example is shown in the upper left panel of Exhibit 20-6.

Testing a Hypothesis of Unrealistic Drug Use in Movies

Are American teens exposed to unrealistic drug usage or to unrealistic consequences from such use? Mediascope, a nonprofit organization concerned with responsible depictions of social and health issues in the media, recently completed for the Office of National Drug Control Policy a content analysis of the top 200 rental movies to determine their depiction of substance use. The researchers used the Video Software Dealers Association's most popular (top 100) home video titles based on rental income during two sequential years. Movies were categorized as follows: action adventure, comedy, or drama. Data were also collected on each title's Motion Picture Association of America (MPAA) rating (G, PG, PG-13, or R). Although technically teens should have been excluded from R-rated titles (which made up 48 percent of the overall sample), the study included all 20 of the most popular teen movies as identified in a prior independent study.

Trained coders watched all 200 movies, paying particular attention to alcohol, tobacco, illicit drugs, over-the-counter medicines, prescription medicines, inhalants, and unidentified pills. Coders ignored substances administered by medical personnel in a hospital or health-related scenario. Substance use included explicit portrayals of consumption. Substance appearance was noted when evidence of materials or paraphernalia was noted without any indication of use. Coders identified dominant messages about substance use and the consequences of use. Coders also noted scenes depicting illicit drug use or those depicting use by characters known to be under 18. Prevalence of use was determined by counting the characters in each movie and determining not only the percentage of characters using drugs but also whether the character had a major or minor role. Coders profiled characters by age, gender, and ethnicity, as well as other characteristics. Frequency of substance abuse was determined for each five-minute interval of each movie, with the presence or absence of various substances noted, starting with the completion of the title credits and ending when the final credits began. How would the last movie you watched have fared under this scrutiny?

www.mediacampaign.org; www.americacares.org; www.vsda.org

An alternative way to look at this is to plot the deviations from the straight line. These are shown in a "detrended" plot in the upper right panel of the figure. Here we would expect the points to cluster without pattern around a straight line passing horizontally through 0. In the bottom two panels of Exhibit 20-6, there is neither a straight line in the normal probability plot nor a random distribution of points about 0 in the detrended plot. Visually, the bottom two plots tell us the variable is not normally distributed. In addition, two separate tests of the hypothesis that the data come from normal distributions are rejected at a significance level of less than .01.[5]

If we wished to check another assumption—say, one of equal variance—a spread-and-level plot would be appropriate. Statistical software programs often provide diagnostic tools for checking assumptions. These may be nested within a specific statistical procedure, such as analysis of variance or regression, or provided as a general set of tools for examining assumptions.

Parametric tests place different emphasis on the importance of assumptions. Some tests are quite robust and hold up well despite violations. For others, a departure from linearity or equality of variance may threaten the validity of the results.

Nonparametric tests have fewer and less stringent assumptions. They do not specify normally distributed populations or equality of variance. Some tests require independence of cases; others are expressly designed for situations with related cases. Nonparametric tests are the only ones usable with nominal data; they are the only technically correct tests to use with ordinal data, although parametric tests are sometimes employed in this case. Nonparametric tests may also be used for interval and ratio data, although they waste much of the information available. Nonparametric tests are also easy to understand and use. Parametric tests have greater efficiency when their use is appropriate, but even in such cases nonparametric tests often achieve an efficiency as high as 95 percent. This means the nonparametric test with a sample of 100 will provide the same statistical testing power as a parametric test with a sample of 95.

>Exhibit 20-6 Probability Plots and Tests of Normality

>Exhibit 20-6 Probability Plots and Tests of Normality

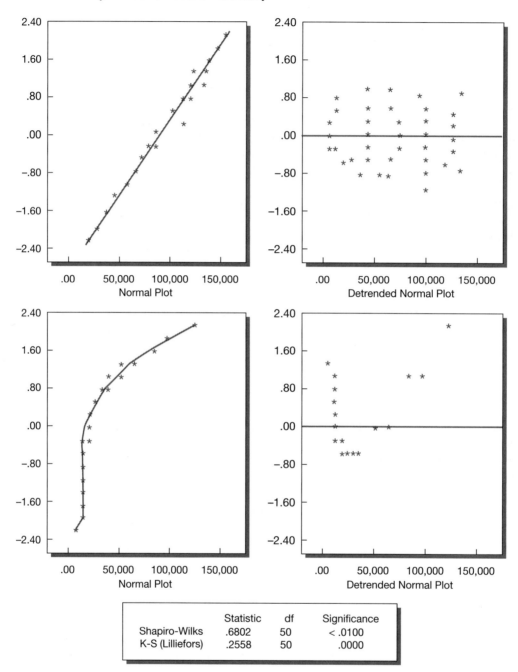

	Statistic	df	Significance
Shapiro-Wilks	.6802	50	< .0100
K-S (Lilliefors)	.2558	50	.0000

How to Select a Test

In attempting to choose a particular significance test, the researcher should consider at least three questions:

- Does the test involve one sample, two samples, or *k* (more than two) samples?
- If two samples or *k* samples are involved, are the individual cases independent or related?
- Is the measurement scale nominal, ordinal, interval, or ratio?

Additional questions may arise once answers to these are known: What is the sample size? If there are several samples, are they of equal size? Have the data been weighted? Have the data been transformed? Often such questions are unique to the selected technique. The answers can complicate the selection, but once a tentative choice is made, standard statistics textbooks will provide further details.

Decision trees provide a more systematic means of selecting techniques. One widely used guide from the Institute for Social Research starts with questions about the number of variables, nature of the variables (continuous, discrete, dichotomous, independent, dependent, and so forth), and level of measurement. It goes through a tree structure asking detailed questions about the nature of the relationships being searched, compared, or tested. Over 130 solutions to data analysis problems are paired with commonly asked questions.[6]

An expert system offers another approach to choosing appropriate statistics. Capitalizing on the power and convenience of personal computers, expert system programs provide a comprehensive search of the statistical terrain just as a computer search of secondary sources does. Most programs ask about your research objectives, the nature of your data, and the intended audience for your final report. When you are not 100 percent confident of your answers, you can bracket them with an estimate of the degree of your certainty. One such program, Statistical Navigator, covers various categories of statistics from exploratory data analysis through reliability testing and multivariate data analysis. In response to your answers, a report is printed containing recommendations, rationale for selections, references, and the statistical packages that offer the suggested procedure.[7] SPSS and SAS include coaching and help modules with their software.

Selecting Tests Using the Choice Criteria

In the next section, we use the three questions discussed in the last section (see bullets) to develop a classification of the major parametric and nonparametric tests and measures. Because parametric tests are preferred for their power when their assumptions are met, we discuss them first in each of the subsections: one-sample tests, two-sample tests, k- (more-than-two-) sample tests. This is shown in Exhibit 20-7.[8] To illustrate the application of the criteria to test selection, consider that your testing situation involves two samples, the samples are independent, and the data are interval. The figure suggests the t-test of differences as the appropriate choice. The most frequently used of the tests listed in Exhibit 20-7 are covered next. For additional examples see Appendix C.

One-Sample Tests

One-sample tests are used when we have a single sample and wish to test the hypothesis that it comes from a specified population. In this case we encounter questions such as these:

- Is there a difference between observed frequencies and the frequencies we would expect, based on some theory?
- Is there a difference between observed and expected proportions?
- Is it reasonable to conclude that a sample is drawn from a population with some specified distribution (normal, Poisson, and so forth)?
- Is there a significant difference between some measures of central tendency ($\bar{X}$) and its population parameter (μ)?

A number of tests may be appropriate in this situation. The parametric test is discussed first.

one-sample tests tests that involve measures taken from a single sample compared to a specified population.

>Exhibit 20-7 Recommended Statistical Techniques by Measurement Level and Testing Situation

Measurement Scale	One-Sample Case	Two-Samples Tests		k-Samples Tests	
		Related Samples	Independent Samples	Related Samples	Independent Samples
Nominal	• Binomial • χ^2 one-sample test	• McNemar	• Fisher exact test • χ^2 two-samples test	• Cochran Q	• χ^2 for k samples
Ordinal	• Kolmogorov-Smirnov one-sample test • Runs test	• Sign test • Wilcoxon matched-pairs test	• Median test • Mann-Whitney U • Kolmogorov-Smirnov • Wald-Wolfowitz	• Friedman two-way ANOVA	• Median extension • Kruskal-Wallis one-way ANOVA
Interval and Ratio	• t-test • Z test	• t-test for paired samples	• t-test • Z test	• Repeated-measures ANOVA	• One-way ANOVA • n-way ANOVA

Parametric Tests

Z test a parametric test to determine the statistical significance between a sample distribution mean and a population parameter.

t-test a parametric test to determine the statistical significance between a sample distribution mean and a population parameter.

Z distribution the normal distribution of measurements assumed for comparison.

t distribution a normal distribution with more tail area than that in a Z normal distribution.

The **Z test** or **t-test** is used to determine the statistical significance between a sample distribution mean and a parameter.

The **Z distribution** and **t distribution** differ. The t has more tail area than that found in the normal distribution. This is a compensation for the lack of information about the population standard deviation. Although the sample standard deviation is used as a proxy figure, the imprecision makes it necessary to go farther away from 0 to include the percentage of values in the t distribution necessarily found in the standard normal.

When sample sizes approach 120, the sample standard deviation becomes a very good estimate of the population standard deviation (σ); beyond 120, the t and Z distributions are virtually identical.

Some typical real-world applications of the one-sample test are:

• Finding the average monthly balance of credit card holders compared to the average monthly balance five years ago.

• Comparing the failure rate of computers in a 20-hour test of quality specifications.

• Discovering the proportion of people who would shop in a new district compared to the assumed population proportion.

• Comparing the average product revenues this year to last year's revenues.

Example   To illustrate the application of the t-test in the one-sample case, consider again the hybrid-vehicle problem mentioned earlier. With a sample of 100 vehicles, the researchers find that the mean miles per gallon for the car is 52.5 mpg, with a standard deviation of 14. Do these results indicate the population mean might still be 50?

In this problem, we have only the sample standard deviation (s). This must be used in place of the population standard deviation (σ). When we substitute s for σ, we use the t distribution, especially if the sample size is less than 30. We define t as

$$t = \frac{\bar{X} - \mu}{s/\sqrt{n}}$$

This significance test is conducted by following the six-step procedure recommended earlier:

1. *Null hypothesis.*

$$H_0: = 50 \text{ miles per gallon (mpg)}$$

$$H_A: > 50 \text{ mpg (one-tailed test)}$$

2. *Statistical test.* Choose the *t*-test because the data are ratio measurements. Assume the underlying population is normal and we have randomly selected the sample from the population of production vehilces.

3. *Significance level.* Let $\alpha = .05$, with $n = 100$.

4. *Calculated value.*

$$t = \frac{52.5 - 50}{14/\sqrt{100}} - \frac{2.5}{1.4} = 1.786 \qquad \text{d.f.} = n - 1 = 99$$

5. *Critical test value.* We obtain this by entering the table of critical values of *t* (see Appendix Exhibit D-2 at the back of the book), with 99 degrees of freedom (d.f.) and a level of significance value of .05. We secure a critical value of about 1.66 (interpolated between d.f. = 60 and d.f. = 120 in Exhibit D-2).

6. *Interpretation.* In this case, the calculated value is greater than the critical value (1.786 > 1.66), so we reject the null hypothesis and conclude that the average mpg has increased.

Nonparametric Tests

In a one-sample situation, a variety of nonparametric tests may be used, depending on the measurement scale and other conditions. If the measurement scale is nominal (classificatory only), it is possible to use either the binomial test or the chi-square (χ^2) one-sample test. The binomial test is appropriate when the population is viewed as only two classes, such as male and female, buyer and nonbuyer, and successful and unsuccessful, and all observations fall into one or the other of these categories. The binomial test is particularly useful when the size of the sample is so small that the χ^2 test cannot be used.

Chi-Square Test

Probably the most widely used nonparametric test of significance is the **chi-square (χ^2) test.** It is particularly useful in tests involving nominal data but can be used for higher scales. Typical are cases where persons, events, or objects are grouped in two or more nominal categories such as "yes-no," "favor-undecided-against," or class "A, B, C, or D."

Using this technique, we test for significant differences between the *observed* distribution of data among categories and the *expected* distribution based on the null hypothesis. Chi-square is useful in cases of one-sample analysis, two independent samples, or *k* independent samples. It must be calculated with actual counts rather than percentages.

In the one-sample case, we establish a null hypothesis based on the expected frequency of objects in each category. Then the deviations of the actual frequencies in each category are compared with the hypothesized frequencies. The greater the difference between them, the less is the probability that these differences can be attributed to chance. The value of χ^2 is the measure that expresses the extent of this difference. The larger the divergence, the larger is the χ^2 value.

The formula by which the χ^2 test is calculated is

$$\chi^2 = \sum_{i=1}^{k} \frac{(O_i - E_i)^2}{E_i}$$

chi-square (χ^2) test a test of significance used for nominal and ordinal measurements.

in which

> O_i = observed number of cases categorized in the ith category
>
> E_i = expected number of cases in the ith category under H_0
>
> k = the number of categories

There is a different distribution for χ^2 for each number of degrees of freedom (d.f.), defined as $(k - 1)$ or the number of categories in the classification minus 1:

$$\text{d.f.} = k - 1$$

With chi-square contingency tables of the two-samples or k-samples variety, we have both rows and columns in the cross-classification table. In that instance, d.f. is defined as rows minus 1 $(r - 1)$ times columns minus 1 $(c - 1)$.

$$\text{d.f.} = (r - 1)(c - 1)$$

In a 2×2 table there is 1 d.f., and in a 3×2 table there are 2 d.f. Depending on the number of degrees of freedom, we must be certain the numbers in each cell are large enough to make the χ^2 test appropriate. When d.f. = 1, each expected frequency should be at least 5 in size. If d.f. > 1, then the χ^2 test should not be used if more than 20 percent of the expected frequencies are smaller than 5 or when any expected frequency is less than 1. Expected frequencies can often be increased by combining adjacent categories. Four categories of freshmen, sophomores, juniors, and seniors might be classified into upper class and lower class. If there are only two categories and still there are too few in a given class, it is better to use the binomial test.

Assume a survey of student interest in the Metro University Dining Club (discussed in Chapter 17) is taken. We have interviewed 200 students and learned of their intentions to join the club. We would like to analyze the results by living arrangement (type and location of student housing and eating arrangements). The 200 responses are classified into the four categories shown in the accompanying table. Do these variations indicate there is a significant difference among these students, or are they sampling variations only? Proceed as follows:

Living Arrangement	Intend to Join	Number Interviewed	Percent (no. interviewed/200)	Expected Frequencies (percent × 60)
Dorm/fraternity	16	90	45	27
Apartment/rooming house, nearby	13	40	20	12
Apartment/rooming house, distant	16	40	20	12
Live at home	15	30	15	9
Total	60	200	100	60

1. *Null hypothesis.* H_0: $O_i = E_i$. The proportion in the population who intend to join the club is independent of living arrangement. In H_A: $O_i \neq E_i$, the proportion in the population who intend to join the club is dependent on living arrangement.

2. *Statistical test.* Use the one-sample χ^2 to compare the observed distribution to a hypothesized distribution. The χ^2 test is used because the responses are classified into nominal categories and there are sufficient observations.

3. *Significance level.* Let $\alpha = .05$.

>**snap**shot

Research beyond the Clip

You're McDonald's, and you just announced that you are closing 300 stores in the United States. How is this playing in newspapers across America? Is the reporting balanced? Or maybe you're BP (formerly British Petroleum), and you've just invested millions to change your corporate identification and logo and to reposition your firm as the "environmentally friendly" energy conglomerate through executive presentations and advertising. How is the press treating the story? Is the spin positive or negative? Where is the story appearing? Is your key message getting through? The Burrelle's Information Services division of Burrelle's/Luce (B/L) offers one of the longest established "clipping" services used by public relations managers to answer questions like these.

"The most basic research we provide clients is the ad-equivalent value of the news clips," shared Sharon Miller, account executive for B/L. The client notifies B/L that it plans to distribute a press release. Staff at B/L scan the desired print and Internet sources for news of the client—"clips." "For print and online publications, the actual space that the story occupies is physically measured. Then, that space is multiplied by the ad rate for identical space in that medium—the ad equivalent." Burrelle's also delivers an assessment of the coverage of key messages the client tried to convey, as well as the tone of the story and the firm's prominence in any story—did the firm get mentioned in the headline or the lead paragraph, or was it the focus of more than half of the article? Managers can obtain comparative analysis evaluating their firm's news coverage against that of other firms in their industry or against ROI investment criteria through online reporting via B/L's secure Insight platform. If you were a public relations professional, how would you test the hypothesis that your coverage for any given event was more positive than that of your competition?

www.burrellesluce.com

4. *Calculated value.*

$$\chi^2 = \sum_{i=1}^{k} \frac{(O_i - E_i)^2}{E_i}$$

Calculate the expected distribution by determining what proportion of the 200 students interviewed were in each group. Then apply these proportions to the number who intend to join the club. Then calculate the following:

$$\chi^2 = \frac{(16 - 27)^2}{27} + \frac{(13 - 12)^2}{12} + \frac{(16 - 12)^2}{12} + \frac{(15 - 9)^2}{9}$$

$$= 4.48 + 0.08 + 1.33 + 4.0$$

$$= 9.89$$

$$\text{d.f.} = (4 - 1)(2 - 1) = 3$$

5. *Critical test value.* Enter the table of critical values of χ^2 (see Exhibit D-3), with 3 d.f., and secure a value of 7.82 for $\alpha = .05$.

6. *Interpretation.* The calculated value is greater than the critical value, so the null hypothesis is rejected and we conclude that intending to join is dependent on living arrangement.

Two-Independent-Samples Tests

The need to use **two-independent-samples tests** is often encountered in marketing research. We might compare the purchasing predispositions of a sample of subscribers from two magazines to discover if they are from the same population. Similarly, a test of

two-independent-samples tests parametric and nonparametric tests used when the measurements are taken from two samples that are unrelated.

distribution methods from two channels or the market share movements from two competing products could be compared.

Parametric Tests

The Z and t-tests are frequently used parametric tests for independent samples, although the F test also can be used.

The Z test is used with large sample sizes (exceeding 30 for both independent samples) or with smaller samples when the data are normally distributed and population variances are known. The formula for the Z test is

$$Z = \frac{(\bar{X}_1 - \bar{X}_2) - (\mu_1 - \mu_2)0}{\sqrt{\dfrac{S_1^2}{n_1} + \dfrac{S_2^2}{n_2}}}$$

With small sample sizes, normally distributed populations, and the assumption of equal population variances, the t-test is appropriate:

$$t = \frac{(\bar{X}_1 - \bar{X}_2) - (\mu_1 - \mu_2)0}{\sqrt{S_p^2 \left(\dfrac{1}{n_1} + \dfrac{1}{n_2}\right)}}$$

where

$(\mu_1 - \mu_2)$ is the difference between the two population means.

S_p^2 is associated with the pooled variance estimate:

$$S_p^2 = \frac{(n_1 - 1) S_1^2 + (n_2 - 1)S_2^2}{n_1 + n_2 - 2}$$

To illustrate this application, consider a problem that might face a manager at KDL, a media firm that is evaluating account executive trainees. The manager wishes to test the effectiveness of two methods for training new account executives. The company selects 22 trainees, who are randomly divided into two experimental groups. One receives type A and the other type B training. The trainees are then assigned and managed without regard to the training they have received. At the year's end, the manager reviews the performances of employees in these groups and finds the following results:

	A Group	**B Group**
Average hourly sales	$X_1 = \$1,500$	$X_2 = \$1,300$
Standard deviation	$s_1 = 225$	$s_2 = 251$

Following the standard testing procedure, we will determine whether one training method is superior to the other:

1. *Null hypothesis.*

   H_0: There is no difference in sales results produced by the two training methods.

   H_A: Training method A produces sales results superior to those of method B.

2. *Statistical test.* The t-test is chosen because the data are at least interval and the samples are independent.

3. *Significance level.* $\alpha = .05$ (one-tailed test).

4. *Calculated value.*

$$t = \frac{(1{,}500 - 1{,}300) - 0}{\sqrt{\dfrac{(10)(225)^2 + (10)(251)^2}{20}\left(\dfrac{1}{11} + \dfrac{1}{11}\right)}}$$

$$= \frac{200}{101.63} = 1.97 \qquad \text{d.f.} = 20$$

There are $n - 1$ degrees of freedom in each sample, so total d.f. is

$$\text{d.f.} = (11 - 1) + (11 - 1) = 20$$

5. *Critical test value.* Enter Appendix Exhibit D-2 with d.f. = 20, one-tailed test, α = .05. The critical value is 1.725.

6. *Interpretation.* Since the calculated value is larger than the critical value ($1.97 > 1.725$), reject the null hypothesis and conclude that training method A is superior.

Nonparametric Tests

The chi-square (χ^2) test is appropriate for situations in which a test for differences between samples is required. It is especially valuable for nominal data but can be used with ordinal measurements. When parametric data have been reduced to categories, they are frequently treated with χ^2 although this results in a loss of information. Preparing to solve this problem is the same as presented earlier although the formula differs slightly:

$$\chi^2 = \sum_i \sum_j \frac{(O_{ij} - E_{ij})^2}{E_{ij}}$$

in which

O_{ij} = observed number of cases categorized in the ijth cell

E_{ij} = expected number of cases under H_0 to be categorized in the ijth cell

Suppose MindWriter is concerned about the optimal distribution channel for its new lightweight notebook. It has reason to believe that the age of the purchaser is a factor. Since the company has complete records of its previous laptop purchases, a sample was drawn from computer superstores and direct (online) sales. Purchases in both groups are interviewed by telephone to determine their postsale satisfaction and obtain their age.

The expected values have been calculated and are shown:

		Channel of Distribution		
	Cell Designation Count Expected Values	Superstore	Direct	Row Total
Age of Purchaser				
	20–34	1,1 12 8.24	1,2 4 7.75	16
	35–54	2,1 9 7.73	2,2 6 7.27	15
	55 or older	3,1 13 18.03	3,2 22 16.97	35
Column Total		34	32	66

The testing procedure is:

1. *Null hypothesis.*

   H_0: There is no difference in distribution channel for age categories of purchasers.

   H_A: There is a difference in distribution channel for age categories of purchasers.

2. *Statistical test.* χ^2 is appropriate. The measurement level is ordinal.

3. *Significance level.* $\alpha = .05$, with d.f. $= (3 - 1)(2 - 1) = 2$.

4. *Calculated value.* The expected distribution is provided by the marginal totals of the table. If there is no relationship between age and channel, there will be the same proportion of age groups in both online and superstore classes. The numbers of expected observations in each cell are calculated by multiplying the two marginal totals common to a particular cell and dividing this product by n. For example,

$$\frac{34 \times 16}{66} = 8.24, \text{ the expected value in cell } (1,1)$$

$$\chi^2 = \frac{(12 - 8.24)^2}{8.24} + \frac{(4 - 7.75)^2}{7.75} + \frac{(9 - 7.73)^2}{7.73} + \frac{(6 - 7.72)^2}{7.72}$$

$$+ \frac{(13 - 18.03)^2}{18.03} + \frac{(22 - 16.97)^2}{16.97}$$

$$= 7.01$$

5. *Critical test value.* Enter Appendix Exhibit D-3 and find the critical value 5.99 with $\alpha = .05$ and d.f. $= 2$.

6. *Interpretation.* Since the calculated value is greater than the critical value, the null hypothesis is rejected.

For chi-square to operate properly, data must come from random samples of multinomial distributions, and the expected frequencies should not be too small. We previously noted the traditional cautions that expected frequencies (E_i) below 5 should not compose more than 20 percent of the cells, and that no cell should have an E_i of less than 1. Some research has argued that these restrictions are too severe.[9]

In another type of χ^2, the 2×2 table, a correction known as *Yates' correction for continuity* is applied when sample sizes are greater than 40 or when the sample is between 20 and 40 and the values of E_i are 5 or more. (We use this correction because a continuous distribution is approximating a discrete distribution in this table. When the E_is are small, the approximation is not necessarily a good one.) The formula for this correction is

$$\chi^2 = \frac{n\left(|AD - BC| - \dfrac{n}{2}\right)^2}{(A + B)(C + D)(A + C)(B + D)}$$

where the letters represent the cells designated as

A	B
C	D

When the continuity correction is applied to the data shown in Exhibit 20-8, a χ^2 value of 5.25 is obtained. The observed level of significance for this value is .02192. If the level of significance had been set at .01, we would accept the null hypothesis. However, had we

>**Exhibit 20-8** Comparison of Corrected and Noncorrected Chi-Square Results Using SPSS Procedure Cross-Tab

```
                    INCOME BY POSSESSION OF MBA

                        MBA
              Count
                        Yes       No
                                                   Row
                         1         2             Total
        INCOME   ─────────────────────────────────────────

                 High 1      30        30          60
                                                   60.0

                 Low 2       10        30          40
                                                   40.0

                 Column      40        60         100
                 Total       40.0      60.0       100.0


Chi-Square                              Value      D.F.      Significance
─────────────────────────────────────────────────────────────────────────
Pearson                                6.25000      1          .01242
Continuity Correction                  5.25174      1          .02192
Likelihood Ratio                       6.43786      1          .01117
Mantel-Haenszel                        6.18750      1          .01287
Minimum Expected Frequency: 16.000
```

calculated χ^2 without correction, the value would have been 6.25, which has an observed level of significance of .01242. Some researchers may be tempted to reject the null at this level. (But note that the critical value of χ^2 at .01 with 1 d.f. is 6.64. See Appendix Exhibit D-3.) The literature is in conflict regarding the merits of Yates' correction, but if nothing else, this example suggests one should take care when interpreting 2×2 tables.[10] To err on the conservative side would be in keeping with our prior discussion of Type I errors.

The Mantel-Haenszel test and the likelihood ratio also appear in Exhibit 20-8. The former is used with ordinal data; the latter, based on maximum likelihood theory, produces results similar to Pearson's chi-square.

Two-Related-Samples Tests

The **two-related-samples tests** concern those situations in which persons, objects, or events are closely matched or the phenomena are measured twice. One might compare the consumption of husbands and wives, the performance of employees before and after vacations, or the effects of a marketing test stimulus when persons were randomly assigned to groups and given pretests and posttests. Both parametric and nonparametric tests are applicable under these conditions.

two-related-samples tests
parametric and nonparametric tests used when the measurements are taken from closely matched samples or the phenomena are measured twice from the same sample.

Parametric Tests

The *t*-test for independent samples would be inappropriate for this situation because one of its assumptions is that observations are independent. This problem is solved by a formula where the difference is found between each matched pair of observations, thereby reducing the two samples to the equivalent of a one-sample case—that is, there are now several differences, each independent of the other, for which one can compute various statistics.

In the following formula, the average difference, $\bar{D}$ corresponds to the normal distribution when the α difference is known and the sample size is sufficient. The statistic *t* with $(n - 1)$ degrees of freedom is defined as

$$t = \frac{\bar{D}}{S_D/\sqrt{n}}$$

where

$$\bar{D} = \frac{\Sigma D}{n}$$

$$S_D = \sqrt{\frac{\Sigma D^2 - \frac{(\Sigma D)^2}{n}}{n - 1}}$$

To illustrate, we use two years of *Forbes* sales data (in millions of dollars) from 10 companies, as listed in Exhibit 20-9.

1. *Null hypothesis.*

   H_0: $\mu = 0$; there is no difference between year 1 and year 2 sales.

   H_A: $\neq 0$; there is a difference between year 1 and year 2 sales.

2. *Statistical test.* The matched- or paired-samples *t*-test is chosen because there are repeated measures on each company, the data are not independent, and the measurement is ratio.

3. *Significance level.* Let $\alpha = .01$, with $n = 10$ and d.f. $= n - 1$.

4. *Calculated value.*

$$t = \frac{\bar{D}}{S_D/\sqrt{n}} = \frac{3{,}578.10}{570.98} = 6.28 \qquad \text{d.f.} = 9$$

5. *Critical test value.* Enter Appendix Exhibit D-2, with d.f. $= 9$, two-tailed test, $\alpha = .01$. The critical value is 3.25.

6. *Interpretation.* Since the calculated value is greater than the critical value (6.28 > 3.25), reject the null hypothesis and conclude there is a statistically significant difference between the two years of sales.

A computer solution to the problem is illustrated in Exhibit 20-10. Notice that an **observed significance level** is printed for the calculated *t* value (highlighted). With SPSS, this is often rounded and would be interpreted as significant at the .0005 level. The corre-

observed significance level the probability value compared to the significance level (e.g., .05) chosen for testing, and on this basis the null hypothesis is either rejected or not rejected.

>**Exhibit 20-9** Sales Data for Paired-Samples *t*-Test (dollars in millions)

Company	Sales Year 2	Sales Year 1	Difference D	D²
GM	126932	123505	3427	11744329
GE	54574	49662	4912	24127744
Exxon	86656	78944	7712	59474944
IBM	62710	59512	3192	10227204
Ford	96146	92300	3846	14791716
AT&T	36112	35173	939	881721
Mobil	50220	48111	2109	4447881
Du Pont	35099	32427	2632	6927424
Sears	53794	49975	3819	14584761
Amoco	23966	20779	3187	10156969
Total			$\Sigma D = 35781$	$\Sigma D^2 = 157364693$

>**Exhibit 20-10** SPSS Output for Paired-Samples *t*-Test (dollars in millions)

```
                     ---t-tests for paired samples---

                  Number                      Standard      Standard
     Variable    of Cases       Mean          Deviation       Error

     Year 2 Sales    10        62620.9        31777.649      10048.975
     Year 1 Sales    10        59038.8        31072.871       9836.104


     (Difference  Standard   Standard  |          2-tail  |   t    Degrees of  2-tail
       Mean)      Deviation    Error   |  Corr.    Prob.   | Value   Freedom    Prob.

       3582.1000  1803.159   570.209   |  .999     .000    | 6.28      9        .000
```

lation coefficient, to the left of the *t* value, is a measure of the relationship between the two pairs of scores. In situations where matching has occurred (such as husbands' and wives' scores), it reveals the degree to which the matching has been effective in reducing the variability of the mean difference.

Nonparametric Tests

The *McNemar test* may be used with either nominal or ordinal data and is especially useful with before-after measurement of the same subjects. Test the significance of any observed change by setting up a fourfold table of frequencies to represent the first and second set of responses:

	After	
Before	**Do Not Favor**	**Favor**
Favor	A	B
Do Not Favor	C	D

Since $A + D$ represents the total number of people who changed (B and C are no-change responses), the expectation under a null hypothesis is that $1/2 (A + D)$ cases change in one direction and the same proportion in the other direction. The McNemar test uses a transformation of the χ^2 test:

$$\chi^2 = \frac{(|A - D| - 1)^2}{A + D} \quad \text{with d.f.} = 1$$

The "minus 1" in the equation is a correction for continuity since the χ^2 is a continuous distribution and the observed frequencies represent a discrete distribution.

To illustrate this test's application, we use survey data from SteelShelf Corporation, whose marketing researchers decided to test a new concept in office seating with employees at the company's headquarters facility. Managers took a random sample of their employees before the test, asking them to complete a questionnaire on their attitudes toward the design concept. On the basis of their responses, the employees were divided into equal groups reflecting their favorable or unfavorable views of the design. After the campaign, the same 200 employees were asked again to complete the questionnaire. They were again classified as to favorable or unfavorable attitudes. The testing process is:

1. *Null hypothesis.*

$$H_0: P(A) = P(D)$$

$$H_A: P(A) \neq P(D)$$

2. *Statistical test.* The McNemar test is chosen because nominal data are used and the study involves before-after measurements of two related samples.
3. *Significance level.* Let $\alpha = .05$, with $n = 200$.
4. *Calculated value.*

$$\chi^2 = \frac{(|10 - 40| - 1)^2}{10 + 40} = \frac{29^2}{50} = 16.82 \qquad \text{d.f.} = 1$$

Before	After	
	Do Not Favor	**Favor**
Favor	$A = 10$	$B = 90$
Do Not Favor	$C = 60$	$D = 40$

5. *Critical test value.* Enter Appendix Exhibit D-3, and find the critical value to be 3.84 with $\alpha = .05$ and d.f. = 1.
6. *Interpretation.* The calculated value is greater than the critical value ($16.82 > 3.84$), indicating one should reject the null hypothesis, and conclude that the new concept had a signficant positive effect on employees' attitudes. In fact, χ^2 is so large that it would have surpassed an α of .001.

k-Independent-Samples Tests

k-independent-samples tests signficance tests when measurements are taken from three or more samples.

We often use **k-independent-samples tests** in marketing research when three or more samples are involved. Under this condition, we are interested in learning whether the samples might have come from the same or identical populations. When the data are measured on an interval-ratio scale and we can meet the necessary assumptions, analysis of variance and the *F* test are used. If preliminary analysis shows the assumptions cannot be met or if the data were measured on an ordinal or nominal scale, a nonparametric test should be selected.

As with the two-samples case, the samples are assumed to be independent. This is the condition of a completely randomized experiment when subjects are randomly assigned to various treatment groups. It is also common for an ex post facto study to require comparison of more than two independent sample means.

Parametric Tests

analysis of variance (ANOVA) tests the null hypothesis that the means of several independent populations are equal.

The statistical method for testing the null hypothesis that the means of several populations are equal is **analysis of variance (ANOVA)**. *One-way analysis of variance* is described in this section. It uses a single-factor, fixed-effects model to compare the effects of one *treatment* or *factor* (brands of coffee, varieties of residential housing, types of retail stores) on a continuous dependent variable (coffee consumption, hours of TV viewing, shopping expenditures). In a fixed-effects model, the levels of the factor are established in advance, and the results are not generalizable to other levels of treatment. For example, if coffee were Jamaican-grown, Colombian-grown, and Honduran-grown, we could not extend our inferences to coffee grown in Guatemala or Mexico.

> **We discussed factors in Chapter 12.**

To use ANOVA, certain conditions must be met. The samples must be randomly selected from normal populations, and the populations should have equal variances. In addition, the distance from one value to its group's mean should be independent of the distances of other values to that mean (independence of error). ANOVA is reasonably robust, and minor variations from normality and equal variance are tolerable. Nevertheless, the analyst should check the assumptions with the diagnostic techniques previously described.

Analysis of variance, as the name implies, breaks down or partitions total variability into component parts. Unlike the *t*-test, which uses sample standard deviations, ANOVA uses squared deviations of the variance so that computation of distances of the individual data points from their own mean or from the grand mean can be summed (recall that standard deviations sum to zero).

In an ANOVA model, each group has its own mean and values that deviate from that mean. Similarly, all the data points from all of the groups produce an overall *grand mean*. The total deviation is the sum of the squared differences between each data point and the overall grand mean.

The total deviation of any particular data point may be partitioned *into between-groups variance* and *within-groups variance*. The between-groups variance represents the effect of the treatment, or factor. The differences of between-groups means imply that each group was treated differently, and the treatment will appear as deviations of the sample means from the grand mean. Even if this were not so, there would still be some natural variability among subjects and some variability attributable to sampling. The within-groups variance describes the deviations of the data points within each group from the sample mean. This results from variability among subjects and from random variation. It is often called *error*.

Intuitively, we might conclude that when the variability attributable to the treatment exceeds the variability arising from error and random fluctuations, the viability of the null hypothesis begins to diminish. And this is exactly the way the test statistic for analysis of variance works.

The test statistic for ANOVA is the **F ratio.** It compares the variance from the last two sources:

> **F ratio** the *F* test statistic comparing measurements of *k* independent samples.

$$F = \frac{\text{between-groups variance}}{\text{within-groups variance}} = \frac{\text{mean square}_{\text{between}}}{\text{mean square}_{\text{within}}}$$

where

$$\text{Mean square}_{\text{between}} = \frac{\text{sum of squares}_{\text{between}}}{\text{degrees of freedom}_{\text{between}}}$$

$$\text{Mean square}_{\text{within}} = \frac{\text{sum of squares}_{\text{within}}}{\text{degrees of freedom}_{\text{within}}}$$

To compute the *F* ratio, the sum of the squared deviations for the numerator and denominator are divided by their respective degrees of freedom. By dividing, we are computing the variance as an average or mean, thus the term **mean square.** The degrees of freedom for the numerator, the mean square between groups, are one less than the number of groups ($k - 1$). The degrees of freedom for the denominator, the mean square within groups, are the total number of observations minus the number of groups ($n - k$).

> **mean square** the variance computed as an average or mean.

If the null hypothesis is true, there should be no difference between the population means, and the ratio should be close to 1. If the population means are not equal, the numerator should manifest this difference, and the *F* ratio should be greater than 1. The *F* distribution determines the size of ratio necessary to reject the null hypothesis for a particular sample size and level of significance.

To illustrate one-way ANOVA, consider *Travel Industry Magazine*'s reports from international travelers about the quality of in-flight service on various carriers from the United States to Europe. Before writing a feature story coinciding with a peak travel period, the magazine decided to retain a researcher to secure a more balanced perspective on

the reactions of travelers. The researcher selected passengers who had current impressions of the meal service, comfort, and friendliness of a major carrier. Three airlines were chosen and 20 passengers were randomly selected for each airline. The data, found in Exhibit 20-11,[11] are used for this and the next two examples. For the one-way analysis of variance problem, we are concerned only with the columns labeled "Flight Service Rating 1" and "Airline." The factor, airline, is the grouping variable for three carriers.

Again, we follow the procedure:

1. *Null hypothesis.*

H_0: $\mu_{A1} = \mu_{A2} = \mu_{A3}$

H_A: $\mu_{A1} \neq \mu_{A2} \neq \mu_{A3}$ (The means are not equal.)

2. *Statistical test.* The *F* test is chosen because we have *k* independent samples, accept the assumptions of analysis of variance, and have interval data.

>**Exhibit 20-11** Data Table: Analysis of Variance Examples*

| | Flight Service | | | | | Flight Service | | | |
	Rating 1	Rating 2	Airline†	Seat Selection‡		Rating 1	Rating 2	Airline†	Seat Selection‡
1	40	36	1	1	31	52	65	2	2
2	28	28	1	1	32	70	80	2	2
3	36	30	1	1	33	73	79	2	2
4	32	28	1	1	34	72	88	2	2
5	60	40	1	1	35	73	89	2	2
6	12	14	1	1	36	71	72	2	2
7	32	26	1	1	37	55	58	2	2
8	36	30	1	1	38	68	67	2	2
9	44	38	1	1	39	81	85	2	2
10	36	35	1	1	40	78	80	2	2
11	40	42	1	2	41	92	95	3	1
12	68	49	1	2	42	56	60	3	1
13	20	24	1	2	43	64	70	3	1
14	33	35	1	2	44	72	78	3	1
15	65	40	1	2	45	48	65	3	1
16	40	36	1	2	46	52	70	3	1
17	51	29	1	2	47	64	79	3	1
18	25	24	1	2	48	68	81	3	1
19	37	23	1	2	49	76	69	3	1
20	44	41	1	2	50	56	78	3	1
21	56	67	2	1	51	88	92	3	2
22	48	58	2	1	52	79	85	3	2
23	64	78	2	1	53	92	94	3	2
24	56	68	2	1	54	88	93	3	2
25	28	69	2	1	55	73	90	3	2
26	32	74	2	1	56	68	67	3	2
27	42	55	2	1	57	81	85	3	2
28	40	55	2	1	58	95	95	3	2
29	61	80	2	1	59	68	67	3	2
30	58	78	2	1	60	78	83	3	2

* All data are hypothetical.
† Airline: 1 = Delta; 2 = Lufthansa; 3 = KLM.
‡ Seat selection: 1 = economy; 2 = business.

3. *Significance level.* Let $\alpha = .05$, and d.f. = [numerator $(k - 1) = (3 - 1) = 2$], [denominator $(n - k) = (60 - 3) = 57$] = $(2, 57)$.

4. *Calculated value.*

$$F = \frac{MS_b}{MS_W} = \frac{5822.017}{205.695} = 28.304 \qquad \text{d.f. } (2, 57)$$

See summary in Exhibit 20-12.

5. *Critical test value.* Enter Appendix Exhibit D-8, with d.f. $(2, 57)$, $\alpha = .05$. The critical value is 3.16.

6. *Interpretation.* Since the calculated value is greater than the critical value $(28.3 > 3.16)$, we reject the null hypothesis and conclude there are statistically significant differences between two or more pairs of means. Note in Exhibit 20-12 that the p value equals .0001. Since the p value (.0001) is less than the significance level (.05), we have a second method for rejecting the null hypothesis.

The ANOVA model summary in Exhibit 20-12 is a standard way of summarizing the results of analysis of variance. This table contains the sources of variation, degrees of freedom, sum of squares, mean squares, and calculated F value. The probability of rejecting the null hypothesis is computed up to 100 percent α—that is, the probability value column reports the exact significance for the F ratio being tested.

>**Exhibit 20-12** Summary Tables for One-Way ANOVA Example*

Model Summary†					
Source	d.f.	Sum of Squares	Mean Square	F Value	p Value
Model (Airline)	2	11644.033	5822.017	28.304	0.0001
Residual (Error)	57	11724.550	205.694		
Total	59	23368.583			

Means Table				
	Count	Mean	Std. Dev.	Std. Error
Delta	20	38.950	14.006	3.132
Lufthansa	20	58.900	15.089	3.374
KLM	20	72.900	13.902	3.108

Scheffé's S Multiple Comparison Procedure‡					
	Vs.	Diff.	Crit. Diff.	p Value	
Delta	Lufthansa	19.950	11.400	0.0002	S
	KLM	33.950	11.400	0.0001	S
Lufthansa	KLM	14.000	11.400	0.0122	S

*All data are hypothetical.
† Factor: Airline; Dependent: Flight service rating 1.
‡ S = significantly different at the .05 level; significance level: .05.

A Priori Contrasts

When we compute a *t*-test, it is not difficult to discover the reasons why the null is rejected. But with one-way ANOVA, how do we determine which pairs are not equal? We could calculate a series of *t*-tests, but they would not be independent of each other and the resulting Type I error would increase substantially. This is not recommended. If we decided in advance that a comparison of specific populations was important, a special class of tests known as *a priori* **contrasts** could be used after the null was rejected with the *F* test (it is *a priori* because the decision was made before the test).[12]

A modification of the *F* test provides one approach for computing contrasts:

$$F = \frac{MS_{CON}}{MS_W}$$

The denominator, the within-groups mean square, is the same as the error term of the one-way's *F* ratio (recorded in the summary table, Exhibit 20-12). We have previously referred to the denominator of the *F* ratio as the error variance estimator. The numerator of the contrast test is defined as

$$MS_{CON} = SS_{CON} = \frac{\left(\sum_j C_j \bar{X}_j\right)^2}{\sum_j \frac{C_j^2}{n}}$$

where

C_j = the contrast coefficient for the group j

n_j = the number of observations recorded for group j

A contrast is useful for experimental and quasi-experimental designs when the researcher is interested in answering specific questions about a subset of the factor. For example, in a comparison of coffee products, we have a factor with six levels. The levels, blends of coffee, are meaningfully ordered. Assume we are particularly interested in two Central American–grown blends and one Colombian blend. Rather than looking at all possible combinations, we can channel the power more effectively by stating the comparisons of interest. This increases our likelihood of detecting differences if they really exist.

Multiple Comparison Tests

For the probabilities associated with the contrast test to be properly used in the report of our findings, it is important that the contrast strategy be devised ahead of the testing. In the airline study, we had no theoretical reason for an *a priori* contrast. However, when we examine the table of mean ratings (Exhibit 20-12), it is apparent that the airline means were quite different. Comparisons after the results are compared require *post hoc* tests or pairwise **multiple comparison tests** (or *range tests*) to determine which means differ. These tests find homogeneous subsets of means that are not different from each other. Multiple comparisons test the difference between each pair of means and indicate significantly different group means at an α level of .05, or another level that you specify. Multiple comparison tests use group means and incorporate the MS_{error} term of the *F* ratio. Together they produce confidence intervals for the population means and a criterion score. Differences between the mean values may be compared.

There are more than a dozen such tests with different optimization goals: maximum number of comparisons, unequal cell size compensation, cell homogeneity, reduction of Type I or Type II errors, and so forth. The merits of various tests have produced considerable debate among statisticians, leaving the researcher without much guidance for the selection of a test. In Exhibit 20-13, we provide a general guide. For the example in Exhibit

a priori contrasts a special class of tests used in conjunction with the *F* test specifically designed to test the hypotheses of the experiment or study (in comparison to post hoc or unplanned tests).

multiple comparison tests compare group means following the finding of a statistically significant *F* test.

>**Exhibit 20-13** Selection of Multiple Comparison Procedures

Test	Pairwise Comparisons	Complex Comparisons	Equal *n*'s Only	Unequal *n*'s	Equal Variances Assumed	Unequal Variances Not Assumed
Fisher LSD	x			x	x	
Bonferroni	x		x	x		
Tukey HSD	x		x		x	
Tukey-Kramer	x			x	x	
Games-Howell	x			x		x
Tamhane T2	x			x		x
Scheffé *S*		x		x	x	
Brown-Forsythe		x		x		x
Newman-Keuls	x		x		x	
Duncan	x		x		x	
Dunnett's T3						x
Dunnett's C						x

>**Exhibit 20-14** One-Way Analysis of Variance Plots

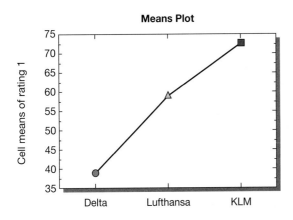

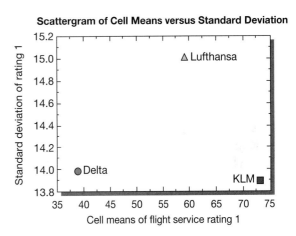

20-12, we chose Scheffé's *S*. It is a conservative test that is robust to violations of assumptions.[13] The computer calculated the critical difference criterion as 11.4; all the differences between the pairs of means exceed this. The null hypothesis for the Scheffé was tested at the .05 level. Therefore, we can conclude that all combinations of flight service mean scores differ from each other.

While the table in Exhibit 20-12 provides information for understanding the rejection of the one-way null hypothesis and the Scheffé null, in Exhibit 20-14 we use plots for the comparisons. The means plot shows relative differences among the three levels of the factor. The means by standard deviations plot reveals lower variability in the opinions recorded by the hypothetical Delta and KLM passengers. Nevertheless, these two groups are sharply divided on the quality of in-flight service, and that is apparent in the upper plot.

Exploring the Findings with Two-Way ANOVA

Is the airline on which the passengers traveled the only factor influencing perceptions of in-flight service? By extending the one-way ANOVA, we can learn more about the service ratings. There are many possible explanations. We have chosen to look at the seat selection of the travelers in the interest of brevity.

>**Exhibit 20-15** Summary Table for Two-Way ANOVA Example*

Model Summary†					
Source	d.f.	Sum of Squares	Mean Square	F Value	p Value
Airline	2	11644.033	5822.017	39.178	0.0001
Seat selection	1	3182.817	3182.817	21.418	0.0001
Airline by seat selection	2	517.033	258.517	1.740	0.1853
Residual	54	8024.700	148.606		

Means Table Effect: Airline by Seat Selection				
	Count	Mean	Std. Dev.	Std. Error
Delta economy	10	35.600	12.140	3.839
Delta business	10	42.300	15.550	4.917
Lufthansa economy	10	48.500	12.501	3.953
Lufthansa business	10	69.300	9.166	2.898
KLM economy	10	64.800	13.037	4.123
KLM business	10	81.000	9.603	3.037

*All data are hypothetical.
†Dependent: Flight service rating 1.

Recall that in Exhibit 20-11, data were entered for the variable seat selection: economy and business-class travelers. Adding this factor to the model, we have a *two-way* analysis of variance. Now three questions may be considered with one model:

- Are differences in flight service ratings attributable to airlines?
- Are differences in flight service ratings attributable to seat selection?
- Do the airline and the seat selection interact with respect to flight service ratings?

The third question reveals a distinct advantage of the two-way model. A separate one-way model on airlines averages out the effects of seat selection. Similarly, a single-factor test of seat selection averages out the effects of the airline choice. But an interaction test of airline by seat selection considers them *jointly*.

Exhibit 20-15 reports a test of the hypotheses for these three questions. The significance level was established at the .01 level. We first inspect the interaction effect, airline by seat selection, since the individual *main effects* cannot be considered separately if the factors interact. The interaction was not significant at the .01 level, and the null is accepted. Now the separate main effects, airline and seat selection, can be verified. As with the one-way ANOVA, the null hypothesis for the airline factor was rejected, and seat selection was also rejected (statistically significant at .0001).

Means and standard deviations listed in the table are plotted in Exhibit 20-16. We note a band of similar deviations for economy-class travelers and a band of lower variability for business class—with the exception of one carrier. The plot of cell means confirms visually what we already know from the summary table: There is no interaction between airline and seat selection ($p = .185$). If an interaction had occurred, the lines connecting the cell means would have crossed rather than displaying a parallel pattern.

Analysis of variance is an extremely versatile and powerful method that may be adapted to a wide range of testing applications. Discussions of further extensions in *n*-way and experimental designs may be found in the list of suggested readings.

>**Exhibit 20-16** Two-Way Analysis of Variance Plots

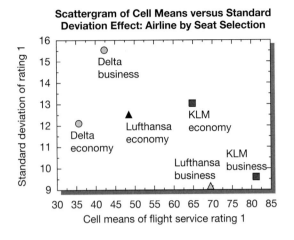

Scattergram of Cell Means versus Standard Deviation Effect: Airline by Seat Selection

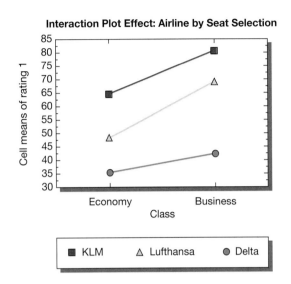

Interaction Plot Effect: Airline by Seat Selection

Nonparametric Tests

When there are k independent samples for which nominal data have been collected, the chi-square test is appropriate. It can also be used to classify data at higher measurement levels, but metric information is lost when reduced. The k-samples χ^2 test is an extension of the two-independent-samples cases treated earlier. It is calculated and interpreted in the same way.

The Kruskal-Wallis test is appropriate for data that are collected on an ordinal scale or for interval data that do not meet F-test assumptions, that cannot be transformed, or that for another reason prove to be unsuitable for a parametric test. Kruskal-Wallis is a one-way analysis of variance by ranks. It assumes random selection and independence of samples and an underlying continuous distribution.

Data are prepared by converting ratings or scores to ranks for each observation being evaluated. The ranks range from the highest to the lowest of all data points in the aggregated samples. The ranks are then tested to decide if they are samples from the same population. An application of this technique is provided in Appendix C.

k-Related-Samples Tests

Parametric Tests

A *k*-related-samples test is required for situations where (1) the grouping factor has more than two levels, (2) observations or subjects are matched or the same subject is measured more than once, and (3) the data are at least interval. In test marketing experiments or ex post facto designs with k samples, it is often necessary to measure subjects several times. These repeated measurements are called **trials.** For example, multiple measurements are taken in studies of stock prices, products evaluated by reliability, inventory, sales, and measures of product performance. Hypotheses for these situations may be tested with a univariate or multivariate general linear model. The latter is beyond the scope of this discussion.

The repeated-measures ANOVA is a special type of n-way analysis of variance. In this design, the repeated measures of each subject are related just as they are in the related t-test when only two measures are present. In this sense, each subject serves as its own control requiring a within-subjects variance effect to be assessed differently than the between-

k-related samples tests
compare measurements from more than two groups from the same sample or more than two measures from the same participant.

trials repeated measures taken from the same participant.

>**Exhibit 20-17** Summary Tables for Repeated-Measures ANOVA*

Model Summary†					
Source	**d.f.**	**Sum of Squares**	**Mean Square**	**F Value**	**p Value**
Airline	2	35527.550	17763.775	67.199	0.0001
Subject (group)	57	15067.650	264.345		
Ratings	1	625.633	625.633	14.318	0.0004
Ratings by air	2	2061.717	1030.858	23.592	0.0001
Ratings by subj	57	2490.650	43.696		

Means Table Ratings by Airline				
	Count	**Mean**	**Std. Dev.**	**Std. Error**
Rating 1, Delta	20	38.950	14.006	3.132
Rating 1, Lufthansa	20	58.900	15.089	3.374
Rating 1, KLM	20	72.900	13.902	3.108
Rating 2, Delta	20	32.400	8.268	1.849
Rating 2, Lufthansa	20	72.250	10.572	2.364
Rating 2, KLM	20	79.800	11.265	2.519

Means Table Effect: Ratings				
	Count	**Mean**	**Std. Dev.**	**Std. Error**
Rating 1	60	56.917	19.902	2.569
Rating 2	60	61.483	23.208	2.996

*All data are hypothetical.
†Dependent: Flight service ratings 1 and 2.

groups variance in a factor like airline or seat selection. The effects of the correlated measures are removed before calculation of the F ratio.

This model is an appropriate solution for the data presented in Exhibit 20-11. You will remember that the one-way and two-way examples considered only the first rating of in-flight service. Assume a second rating was obtained after one week by reinterviewing the same respondents. We now have two trials for the dependent variable, and we are interested in the same general question as with the one-way ANOVA, with the addition of how the passage of time affects perceptions of in-flight service.

Following the testing procedure, we state:

1. *Null hypotheses.*

    (1) Airline: H_0: $\mu_{A1} = \mu_{A2} = \mu_{A3}$

    (2) Ratings: H_0: $\mu_{R1} = \mu_{R2}$

    (3) Ratings $\times$ airline:

$$H_0: (\mu_{R2A1} - \mu_{R2A2} - \mu_{R2A3}) = (\mu_{R1A1} - \mu_{R1A2} - \mu_{R1A3})$$

    For the alternative hypotheses, we will generalize to the statement that not all the groups have equal means for each of the three hypotheses.

2. *Statistical test.* The F test for repeated measures is chosen because we have related trials on the dependent variable for k samples, accept the assumptions of analysis of variance, and have interval data.

>**Exhibit 20-18** Repeated-Measures ANOVA Plot

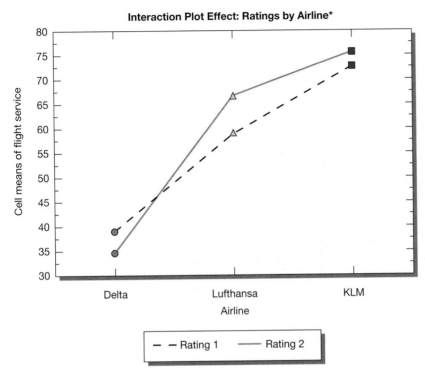

*All data are hypothetical.

3. *Significance level.* Let $\alpha = .05$ and d.f. = [airline (2, 57), ratings (1, 57), ratings by airline (2, 57)].

4. *Calculated values.* See summary in Exhibit 20-17.

5. *Critical test value.* Enter Appendix Exhibit D-8, with d.f. (2, 57), $\alpha = .05$ and (1, 57), $\alpha = .05$. The critical values are 3.16 (2, 57) and 4.01 (1, 57).

6. *Interpretation.* The statistical results are grounds for rejecting all three null hypotheses and concluding there are statistically significant differences between means in all three instances. We conclude the perceptions of in-flight service were significantly affected by the different airlines, the interval between the two measures had a significant effect on the ratings, and the measures' time interval and the airlines interacted to a significant degree.

The ANOVA summary table in Exhibit 20-17 records the results of the tests. A means table provides the means and standard deviations for all combinations of ratings by airline. A second table of means reports the differences between flight service ratings 1 and 2. In Exhibit 20-18, there is an interaction plot for these data. Note that the second in-flight service rating was improved in two of the three groups after one week, but for the third carrier, there was a decrease in favorable response. The intersecting lines in the interaction plot reflect this finding.

Nonparametric Tests

When the k related samples have been measured on a nominal scale, the Cochran Q test is a good choice.[14] This test extends the McNemar test, discussed earlier, for studies having more than two samples. It tests the hypothesis that the proportion of cases in a category is equal for several related categories.

When the data are at least ordinal, the Friedman two-way analysis of variance is appropriate. It tests matched samples, ranking each case and calculating the mean rank for each variable across all cases. It uses these ranks to compute a test statistic. The product is a two-way table where the rows represent subjects and the columns represent the treatment conditions.[15]

>summary

1 In classical statistics we make inferences about a population based on evidence gathered from a sample. Although we cannot state unequivocally what is true about the entire population, representative samples allow us to make statements about what is probably true and how much error is likely to be encountered in arriving at a decision. The Bayesian approach also employs sampling statistics but has an additional element of prior information to improve the decision maker's judgment.

2 A difference between two or more sets of data is statistically significant if it actually occurs in a population. To have a statistically significant finding based on sampling evidence, we must be able to calculate the probability that some observed difference is large enough that there is little chance it could result from random sampling. Probability is the foundation for deciding on the acceptability of the null hypothesis, and sampling statistics facilitate acquiring the estimates.

3 Hypothesis testing can be viewed as a six-step procedure:

1 Establish a null hypothesis as well as the alternative hypothesis. It is a one-tailed test of significance if the alternative hypothesis states the direction of difference. If no direction of difference is given, it is a two-tailed test.

2 Choose the statistical test on the basis of the assumption about the population distribution and measurement level. The form of the data can also be a factor. In light of these considerations, one typically chooses the test that has the greatest power efficiency or ability to reduce decision errors.

3 Select the desired level of confidence. While $\alpha = .05$ is the most frequently used level, many others are also used. The α is the significance level that we desire and is typically set in advance of the study. Alpha or Type I error is the risk of rejecting a true null hypothesis and represents a decision error. The β or Type II error is the decision error that results from accepting a false null hypothesis. Usually, one determines a level of acceptable α error and then seeks to reduce the β error by increasing the sample size, shifting from a two-tailed to a one-tailed significance test, or both.

4 Compute the actual test value of the data.

5 Obtain the critical test value, usually by referring to a table for the appropriate type of distribution.

6 Interpret the result by comparing the actual test value with the critical test value.

4 Parametric and nonparametric tests are applicable under the various conditions described in the chapter. They were also summarized in Exhibit 20-6. Parametric tests operate with interval and ratio data and are preferred when their assumptions can be met. Diagnostic tools examine the data for violations of those assumptions. Nonparametric tests do not require stringent assumptions about population distributions and are useful with less powerful nominal and ordinal measures.

5 In selecting a significance test, one needs to know, at a minimum, the number of samples, their independence or relatedness, and the measurement level of the data. Statistical tests emphasized in the chapter were the Z and t-tests, analysis of variance, and chi-square. The Z and t-tests may be used to test for the difference between two means. The t-test is chosen when the sample size is small. Variations on the t-test are used for both independent and related samples.

One-way analysis of variance compares the means of several groups. It has a single grouping variable, called a factor, and a continuous dependent variable. Analysis of variance (ANOVA) partitions the total variation among scores into between-groups (treatment) and within-groups (error) variance. The F ratio, the test statistic, determines if the differences are large enough to reject the null hypothesis. ANOVA may be extended to two-way, n-way, repeated-measures, and multivariate applications.

Chi-square is a nonparametric statistic that is used frequently for cross-tabulation or contingency tables. Its applications include testing for differences between proportions in populations and testing for independence. Corrections for chi-square were discussed.

>**key**terms

>**discussion**questions

Terms in Review

1 Distinguish between the following:

  a Parametric tests and nonparametric tests.

  b Type I error and Type II error.

  c Null hypothesis and alternative hypothesis.

  d Acceptance region and rejection region.

  e One-tailed tests and two-tailed tests.

  f Type II error and the power of the test.

2 Summarize the steps of hypothesis testing. What is the virtue of this procedure?

3 In analysis of variance, what is the purpose of the mean square between and the mean square within? If the null hypothesis is accepted, what do these quantities look like?

4 Describe the assumptions for ANOVA, and explain how they may be diagnosed.

Making Research Decisions

5 Suggest situations where the researcher should be more concerned with Type II error than with Type I error.

  a How can the probability of a Type I error be reduced? A Type II error?

  b How does practical significance differ from statistical significance?

  c Suppose you interview all the members of the freshman and senior classes and find that 65 percent of the fresh-men and 62 percent of the seniors favor a proposal to send Help Centers offshore. Is this difference significant?

6 What hypothesis testing procedure would you use in the following situations?

  a A test classifies applicants as accepted or rejected. On the basis of data on 200 applicants, we test the hypothesis that ad placement success is not related to gender.

  b A company manufactures and markets automobiles in two different countries. We want to know if the gas mileage is the same for vehicles from both facilities. There are samples of 45 units from each facility.

  c A company has three categories of marketing analysts: (1) with professional qualifications but without work experience, (2) with professional qualifications and with work experience, and (3) without professional qualifications but with work experience. A study exists that measures each analyst's motivation level (classified as high, normal, and low). A hypothesis of no relation between analyst category and motivation is to be tested.

  d A company has 24 salespersons. The test must evaluate whether their sales performance is unchanged or has improved after a training program.

  e A company has to evaluate whether it should attribute increased sales to product quality, advertising, or an interaction of product quality and advertising.

7 You conduct a survey of a sample of 25 members of this year's graduating marketing students and find that the average GPA is 3.2. The standard deviation of the sample is 0.4. Over the last 10 years, the average GPA has been 3.0. Is the GPA of this year's students significantly different from the long-run average? At what alpha level would it be significant?

8 You are curious about whether the professors and students at your school are of different political persuasions, so you take a sample of 20 professors and 20 students drawn randomly from each population. You find that 10 professors say they are conservative and 6 students say they are conservative. Is this a statistically significant difference?

9 You contact a random sample of 36 graduates of Western University and learn that their starting salaries averaged $28,000 last year. You then contact a random sample of 40 graduates from Eastern University and find that their average starting salary was $28,800. In each case, the standard deviation of the sample was $1,000.

   a Test the null hypothesis that there is no difference between average salaries received by the graduates of the two schools.

   b What assumptions are necessary for this test?

10 A random sample of students is interviewed to determine if there is an association between class and attitude toward corporations. With the following results, test the hypothesis that there is no difference among students on this attitude.

	Favorable	Neutral	Unfavorable
Freshmen	100	50	70
Sophomores	80	60	70
Juniors	50	50	80
Seniors	40	60	90

11 You do a survey of marketing students and liberal arts school students to find out how many times a week they read a daily newspaper. In each case, you interview 100 students. You find the following:

$\bar{X}_m$ = 4.5 times per week

S_m = 1.5

$\bar{X}_{la}$ = 5.6 times per week

S_{la} = 2.0

Test the hypothesis that there is no significant difference between these two samples.

12 One-Koat Paint Company has developed a new type of porch paint that it hopes will be the most durable on the market. The R&D group tests the new product against the two leading competing products by using a machine that scrubs until it wears through the coating. One-Koat runs five trials with each product and secures the following results (in thousands of scrubs):

Trial	One-Koat	Competitor A	Competitor B
1	37	34	24
2	30	19	25
3	34	22	23
4	28	31	20
5	29	27	20

Test the hypothesis that there are no differences between the means of these products (α = .05).

13 A computer manufacturer is introducing a new product specifically targeted at the home market and wishes to compare the effectiveness of three sales strategies: computer stores, home electronics stores, and department stores. Numbers of sales by 15 salespeople are recorded below:

   Electronics store: 5, 4, 3, 3, 3

   Department store: 9, 7, 8, 6, 5

   Computer store: 7, 4, 8, 4, 3

   a Test the hypothesis that there is no difference between the means of the retailers (α = .05).

   b Select a multiple comparison test, if necessary, to determine which groups differ in mean sales (α = .05).

14 The *Fortune* magazine annual list of the 40 richest self-made Americans under the age of 40 (*Fortune*, September 17, 2001), revealed some interesting changes. With the collapse of the dot-coms, the new super-rich from sports and entertainment joined the list.

Rank	Name	Company	Net Worth ($, millions)
1	Michael Dell	Dell Computer	16,300
2	Pierre Omidyar	eBay	4,390
3	Jeff Skoll	eBay	2,630
4	Ted Waitt	Gateway, Inc.	1,870
5	Jeff Bezos	Amazon.Com, Inc.	1,230
6	Vinny Smith	Quest Software	780
7	David Filo	Yahoo	730
8	Jerry Yang	Yahoo	721
9	Rob Glaser	RealNetworks	635
10	Dan Snyder	Washington Redskins	604
11	Greg Reyes	Brocade Communications Systems	518
12	Jen-Hsun Huang	Nvidia	507
13	Michael Jordan	Washington Wizards	398
14	Joe Liemandt	Trilogy Software	390
15	Jeanette Symons	Zhone Technologies	374
16	Pantas Sutardja	Marvell Technology	363
17	John Schnatter	Papa John's International	293

Rank	Name	Company	Net Worth ($, millions)
18	Sanjay Kumar	Computer Associates International, Inc.	270
19	Tom Cruise	Cruise/Wagner Productions	251
20	Percy Miller (Master P)	No Limit	249
21	James T. Demetriades	SeeBeyond Technology	239
22	Sean Combs (P. Diddy)	Bad Boy Entertainment	231
23	Jerry Greenberg	Sapient	225
24	J. Stuart Moore	Sapient	224
25	Sudhakar Ravi	SonicWALL	219
26	Sreekanth Ravi	SonicWALL	219
27	David Hitz	Network Appliance	202
28	John L. MacFarlane	Openwave Systems Inc.	198
29	Jeffrey Citron	Vonage	194
30	Raul Fernandez	Dimension Data North America	188
31	Eric Greenberg	Innovation Investments	187
32	Chris Klaus	Internet Security Systems	187
33	Anousheh Ansari	Sonus	180
34	Halsey Minor	12 Entrepreneuring	180
35	Michael Saylor	Microstrategy	180
36	Jim Carrey	Pit Bull Productions	171
37	Jonathan M. Rothberg	CuraGen	168
38	Marc Andreessen	Loudcloud	166
39	Nav Sooch	Silicon Laboratories	162
40	Tiger Woods	ETW	160

a Devise a grouping variable to classify the companies in the accompanying table (e.g., Internet, computers, celebrities).

b Using one-way analysis of variance, test the hypothesis that there is no difference in net worth among the groups.

15 A consumer testing firm is interested in testing two competing antivirus products for personal computers. It wants to know how many strains of virus will be removed. The data are:

Virus Removed by Anti-V?	Virus Removed by Q-Cure?	
	Yes	No
Yes	45	33
No	58	20

Are Anti-V and Q-Cure equally effective ($\alpha = .05$)?

16 A researcher for an auto manufacturer is examining preferences for styling features on larger sedans. Buyers were classified as "first time" and "repeat," resulting in the following table.

	Preference	
	European Styling	Japanese Styling
Repeat	40	20
First time	8	32

a Test the hypothesis that buying characteristic is independent of styling preference ($\alpha = .05$).

b Should the statistic be adjusted?

Behind the Scenes

17 If you were Sammye, what test would you propose should be run on the City Center for Performing Arts project?

From Concept to Practice

18 Using the data in Exhibit 20-11 for the variables flight service rating 2 and airline (2, 3), test the hypothesis of no difference between means.

>**www**exercise

Find a study reported on the Web and identify its likely hypothesis. How would you test this hypothesis given the data that was collected. (Hint: The Henry Kaiser Family Foundation Web site is a great source of fully cited research reports: **http://www.kff.org**.)

>**cases***

Inquiring Minds Want to Know—NOW!	NCRCC: Teeing Up a New Strategic Direction
Mastering Teacher Leadership	Yahoo!: *Consumer Direct* Marries Purchase Metrics to Banner Ads

* All cases, both written and video, are on the text DVD. Check the DVD Index to determine whether a case has data, the research instrument, or other supplementary material.

chapter 21

Measures of Association

>learningobjectives

After reading this chapter, you should understand . . .

1 How correlation analysis may be applied to study relationships between two or more variables.

2 The uses, requirements, and interpretation of the product moment correlation coefficient.

3 How predictions are made with regression analysis using the method of least squares to minimize errors in drawing a line of best fit.

4 How to test regression models for linearity and whether the equation is effective in fitting the data.

5 The nonparametric measures of association and the alternatives they offer when key assumptions and requirements for parametric techniques cannot be met.

Jason Henry is ensconced in his office, discussing one of his favorite topics—statistics—when Sara Armstrong arrives for a scheduled analysis meeting on the MindWriter project.

Sara arrives for an analysis meeting with Jason and finds a round, bald little man sitting at Jason's desk, studying the screen of a laptop computer, stroking his gray beard and smiling broadly.

"Sara," says Jason, "meet Jack Adams, rising political marketing consultant."

Jack, who seems to be caressing his laptop, grins broadly. "Hello, Sara," says Jack. "I wanted Jason to know this little computer has made me the marketing kingpin of the Boca Beach political scene."

"Jack sold his painting business on Long Island to his three boys and moved to Boca Beach after his wife passed away," offers Jason in explanation.

"For three months I played golf in the morning and sat by the pool and played cards in the afternoon. For three months, seven days, I did this. I was going crazy. Then my next-door neighbor Marty died and his wife gave me his MindWriter."

"Jason came through Boca Beach and stopped for a visit. He downloaded a statistical program, free from the Internet. I must say, statistics in college never generated as much excitement as they have recently," grins Jack. "We had a wise guy, Sandy Plover, a former electrical contractor in Jersey, who got himself into local politics. Being a natural-born troublemaker, he waited for his chance to agitate. As it happens, the sheriff released data to the newspaper that the incidence of arrests resulting from police calls to Oceanside—the richer of the two neighborhoods where the sheriff happens to live—is higher than in Gladeside."

Jack types the following:

Research hypothesis: Gladeside residents get special treatment when it comes to solving crimes and thus live in a safer environment due to their higher incomes and greater political power.

Null hypothesis: Gladeside and Oceanside receive the same attention from the police.

	Gladeside	Oceanside
Police calls without arrest	46	40
Police calls resulting in arrest	4	10
Total calls	50	50

"I doubt that Sandy would have paid attention, except that in both neighborhoods the total number of police calls happened to be 50, which made it easy for him to see that in Oceanside the rate of arrests was twice that in Gladeside."

"Actually," says Sara, "I'm surprised there would be any police calls in such an upscale community."

"We are old," says Jack, "but not dead."

"In any case, Sandy's finely honed political instincts told him he was going nowhere by trying to turn the community against the sheriff. It would be much, much better to turn voters of Oceanside against those in Gladeside. So he complained about the disparate impact of arrests. While both the communities are roughly the same size, in Oceanside folks are mostly from Brooklyn, and in Gladeside folks come from the Bronx."

"But the ethics . . ."

". . . meant nothing to Sandy. He told me, 'I think I'm gonna kick some butt and make a name for myself down here.' "

"The trouble with the police calls as an issue is that sheriffs' offices nowadays are well staffed with statistically educated analysts who know very well how to rebut oddball claims," interrupts Jason.

"While I personally miss the old days, I punched the numbers into this MindWriter here to double-check the stats. I did the obvious first, just what I supposed a police analyst would have done. I ran a cross-tabulation and a chi-square test of the hypothesis that the arrests in Oceanside were disproportionate to those in Gladeside."

"To an untrained observer it would appear that they are," contributes Sara as she peers over Jack's shoulder. "But then I'm not so easily hoodwinked."

"Good for you, Sara!" exclaims Jack. "What you have here is the 'eyeball' fallacy, as my dear old professor called it almost 50 years ago. As I explained to Sandy, 100 police encounters resulting in a few arrests is nothing, nada, not a large enough sample to trust a quick peek and a leap to a conclusion. You run it through the computer, and, sure enough, although the ratios seem to be out of whack, the difference is not statistically significant. You cannot support 'disparate impact.' No way."

"Granting that 10 arrests per 50 is bigger than 4 per 50," observes Jason, "Jack saw that a statistician would say that it is not disproportionate enough to convince a scientist that the police were acting differently in the two neighborhoods. A statistician would say, wait and see, let the story unfold, collect a bigger sample."

"How did Sandy accept your explanation, Jack?"

"He was ready to shoot the messenger, very much bothered, at first, that I would not support his political strategy. But I was pretty sure the sheriff would come roaring back with a statistical analysis to throw cold water over Sandy."

"Did you bring him around?"

"That jerk, come around? Never. He ran to the papers, and spilled his numbers and accusations in a letter to the editor that was printed on a Monday, and

Tuesday the sheriff came back with his experts and made Sandy look like a fool—on page one, if you can believe it. So Sandy was washed up, but he mentioned to the reporter that I had provided the same interpretation before he went to the paper, so I now have a new career: resident political marketing genius. What I do is look at the opponents' polling results and deny their validity for the newspapers and TV. If the opposing party is ahead by a few poll points, I scoff at the thinness of the margin. If their lead is wide, I belittle the size of the sample and intimate that any statistician would see through them."

"Jack is colorful, amusing, and good-natured in debunking his opponents' polls, and the newspaper writers have never challenged him to substantiate his claims or interpretations," contributes Jason. "What he learned from me is that statistics is so complicated, and scares so many people, that you can claim or deny anything. And he is usually right to debunk the polls, since for a preelection political poll to be taken seriously there has to be a large enough sample to produce significant results. And there has to be a big enough spread between winners and losers to protect against a last-minute shift in voter sentiment. In the small, closely contested voting precincts of condominium politics, hardly any poll can meet two such stringent criteria."

"So now I sit in my condo's clubhouse and people come over and want to know what I think about the Middle East, campaign reform, everything." Jack, rising, extends his hand to Sara, "I can tell you have things to do, so I'll move along. It was nice meeting you, Sara."

Sara watches Jack Adams give Jason a bear hug and then walk out the door.

"So, Sara, what did you think of Jack's knowledge of statistics?"

> Introduction

In the previous chapter, we emphasized testing hypotheses of difference. However, management questions in marketing frequently revolve around the study of relationships between two or more variables. Then, a *relational hypothesis* is necessary. In the research question "Are U.S. kitchen appliances perceived by American consumers to be of better quality than foreign kitchen appliances?" the nature of the relationship between the two variables ("country of origin" and "perceived quality") is not specified. The implication, nonetheless, is that one variable is responsible for the other. A correct relational hypothesis for this question would state that the variables occur together in some specified manner without implying that one causes the other.

Various objectives are served with correlation analysis. The strength, direction, shape, and other features of the relationship may be discovered. Or tactical and strategic questions may be answered by predicting the values of one variable from those of another. Let's look at some typical management questions:

> **You might want to review our discussion of relational hypotheses in Chapter 3.**

- In the mail-order business, excessive catalog costs quickly squeeze margins. Many mailings fail to reach receptive or active buyers. What is the relationship between mailings that delete inactive customers and the improvement in profit margins?

- Medium-sized companies often have difficulty attracting the cream of the MBA crop, and when they are successful, they have trouble retaining them. What is the relationship between the candidate's rank based on an executive interview and the rank obtained from testing or managerial assessment?

- Cigarette company marketing allocations shifted a few years ago as a result of multi-state settlements eliminating outdoor and transit advertising. More recently, advertising in magazines with large youth readerships came under scrutiny. During a given period, what is the relationship between point-of-sale expenditures and net profits?

- Aggressive U.S. high-tech companies have advertised heavily in the European chip market, and their sales have grown 20 percent over sales of the three largest European firms. Can we predict next year's sales based on present advertising?

All these questions may be evaluated by means of measures of association. And all call for different techniques based on the level at which the variables were measured or the intent of the question. The first three use nominal, ordinal, and interval data, respectively. The last one is answered through simple linear regression.

With correlation, one calculates an index to measure the nature of the relationship between variables. With regression, an equation is developed to predict the values of a dependent variable. Both are affected by the assumptions of measurement level and the distributions that underlie the data.

Exhibit 21-1 lists some common measures and their uses. The chapter follows the progression of the exhibit, first covering bivariate linear correlation, then examining simple regression, and concluding with nonparametric measures of association. Exploration of data through visual inspection and diagnostic evaluation of assumptions continues to be emphasized.

> Bivariate Correlation Analysis

Bivariate correlation analysis differs from nonparametric measures of association and regression analysis in two important ways. First, parametric correlation requires two continuous variables measured on an interval or ratio scale. Second, the coefficient does not distinguish between independent and dependent variables. It treats the variables symmetrically since the coefficient r_{xy} has the same interpretation as r_{yx}.

bivariate correlation analysis a correlation of two continuous variables measured on an interval or ratio scale.

>Exhibit 21-1 Commonly Used Measures of Association

Measurement	Coefficient	Comments and Uses
Interval and Ratio	Pearson (product moment) correlation coefficient	For continuous linearly related variables.
	Correlation ratio (eta)	For nonlinear data or relating a main effect to a continuous dependent variable.
	Biserial	One continuous and one dichotomous variable with an underlying normal distribution.
	Partial correlation	Three variables; relating two with the third's effect taken out.
	Multiple correlation	Three variables; relating one variable with two others.
	Bivariate linear regression	Predicting one variable from another's scores.
Ordinal	Gamma	Based on concordant-discordant pairs: $(P - Q)$; proportional reduction in error (PRE) interpretation.
	Kendall's tau b	$P - Q$ based; adjustment for tied ranks.
	Kendall's tau c	$P - Q$ based; adjustment for table dimensions.
	Somers's d	$P - Q$ based; asymmetrical extension of gamma.
	Spearman's rho	Product moment correlation for ranked data.
Nominal	Phi	Chi-square (CS) based for 2×2 tables.
	Cramer's V	CS based; adjustment when one table dimension > 2.
	Contingency coefficient C	CS based; flexible data and distribution assumptions.
	Lambda	PRE-based interpretation.
	Goodman & Kruskal's tau	PRE based with table marginals emphasis.
	Uncertainty coefficient	Useful for multidimensional tables.
	Kappa	Agreement measure.

Pearson's Product Moment Coefficient r

Pearson correlation coefficient an estimate of strength of linear association and its direction between interval or ratio variables.

The **Pearson** (product moment) **correlation coefficient** varies over a range of $+1$ through 0 to -1. The designation r symbolizes the coefficient's estimate of linear association based on sampling data. The coefficient ρ represents the population correlation.

Correlation coefficients reveal the magnitude and direction of relationships. The *magnitude* is the degree to which variables move in unison or opposition. The size of a correlation of $+.40$ is the same as one of $-.40$. The sign says nothing about size. The degree of correlation is modest. The coefficient's sign signifies the *direction* of the relationship. Direction tells us whether large values on one variable are associated with large values on the other (and small values with small values). When the values correspond in this way, the two variables have a positive relationship: As one increases, the other also increases. Family income, for example, is positively related to household food expenditures. As income increases, food expenditures increase. Other variables are inversely related. Large values on the first variable are associated with small values on the second (and vice versa). The prices of products and services are inversely related to their scarcity. In general, as products decrease in available quantity, their prices rise. The absence of a relationship is expressed by a coefficient of approximately zero.

> ❝ **"To truly understand consumers' motives and actions, you must determine relationships between what they think and feel and what they actually do.** ❞
>
> *David Singleton*
> *Vice President of Insights, Zyman Marketing Group*

Scatterplots for Exploring Relationships

Scatterplots are essential for understanding the relationships between variables. They provide a means for visual inspection of data that a list of values for two variables cannot. Both the direction and the shape of a relationship are conveyed in a plot. With a little practice, the magnitude of the relationship can be seen.

scatterplot a visual technique that depicts both the direction and the shape of a relationship between two variables.

Exhibit 21-2 contains a series of scatterplots that depict some relationships across the range r. The three plots on the left side of the figure have their points sloping from the upper left to the lower right of each x-y plot.[1] They represent different magnitudes of negative relationships. On the right side of the figure, the three plots have opposite patterns and show positive relationships.

When stronger relationships are apparent (for example, the ±.90 correlations), the points cluster close to an imaginary straight line passing through the data. The weaker relationships (±.40) depict a more diffuse data cloud with points spread farther from the line.

The shape of linear relationships is characterized by a straight line, whereas nonlinear relationships have curvilinear, parabolic, and compound curves representing their shapes. Pearson's r measures relationships in variables that are linearly related. It cannot distinguish linear from nonlinear data. Summary statistics alone do not reveal the appropriateness of the data for the model, which is why inspecting the data is important.

The need for data visualization is illustrated with four small data sets possessing identical summary statistics but displaying strikingly different patterns.[2] Exhibit 21-3 contains these data and Exhibit 21-4 plots them. In Plot 1 of the figure, the variables are positively related. Their points follow a superimposed straight line through the data. This example is well suited to correlation analysis. In Plot 2, the data are curvilinear in relation to the line, and r is an inappropriate measure of their relationship. Plot 3 shows the presence of an influential point that changed a coefficient that would have otherwise been a perfect +1.0. The last plot displays constant values of x (similar to what you might find in an animal or quality control experiment). One leverage point establishes the fitted line for these data.

We will return to these concepts and the process of drawing the line when we discuss regression. For now, comparing Plots 2 through 4 with Plot 1 suggests the importance of visually inspecting correlation data for underlying patterns to ensure linearity. Careful analysts make scatterplots an integral part of the inspection and exploration of their data. Although small samples may be plotted by hand, statistical software packages save time and offer a variety of plotting procedures.

The Assumptions of r

Like other parametric techniques, correlation analysis makes certain assumptions about the data. Many of these assumptions are necessary to test hypotheses about the coefficient.

The first requirement for r is **linearity.** All of the examples in Exhibit 21-2 with the exception of $r = 0$ illustrate a relationship between variables that can be described by a straight line passing through the data cloud. When $r = 0$, no pattern is evident that could be described with a single line. Parenthetically, it is also possible to find coefficients of 0 where the variables are highly related but in a nonlinear form. As we have seen, plots make such findings evident.

linearity the assumption that data can be described by a straight line passing through the data array.

>**Exhibit 21-2** Scatterplots of Correlations between Two Variables

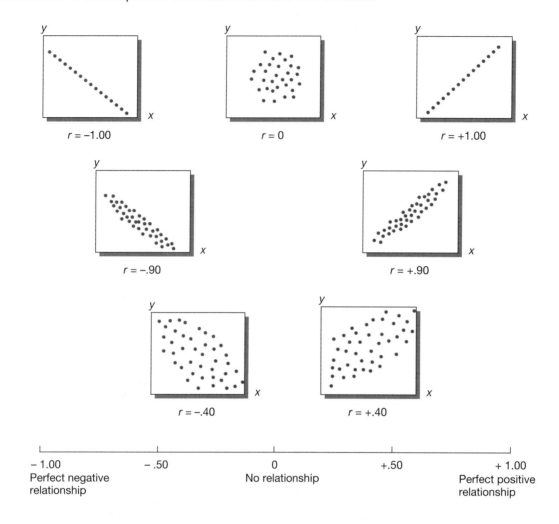

$r = -1.00$

$r = 0$

$r = +1.00$

$r = -.90$

$r = +.90$

$r = -.40$

$r = +.40$

-1.00	$-.50$	0	$+.50$	$+1.00$
Perfect negative relationship		No relationship		Perfect positive relationship

>**Exhibit 21-3** Four Data Sets with the Same Summary Statistics

S_s	X_1	Y_1	X_2	Y_2	X_3	Y_3	X_4	Y_4
1	10	8.04	10	9.14	10	7.46	8	6.58
2	8	6.95	8	8.14	8	6.77	8	5.76
3	13	7.58	13	8.74	13	12.74	8	7.71
4	9	8.81	9	8.77	9	7.11	8	8.84
5	11	8.33	11	9.26	11	7.81	8	8.47
6	14	9.96	14	8.10	14	8.84	8	7.04
7	6	7.24	6	6.13	6	6.08	8	5.25
8	4	4.26	4	3.10	4	5.39	19	12.50
9	12	10.84	12	9.13	12	8.15	8	5.56
10	7	4.82	7	7.26	7	6.42	8	7.91
11	5	5.68	5	4.74	5	5.73	8	6.89
Pearson's r		0.81642		0.81624		0.81629		0.81652
r^2		0.66654		0.66624		0.66632		0.66671
Adjusted r^2		0.62949		0.62916		0.62925		0.62967
Standard error		1.2366		1.23721		1.23631		1.2357

>**Exhibit 21-4** Different Scatterplots for the Same Summary Statistics

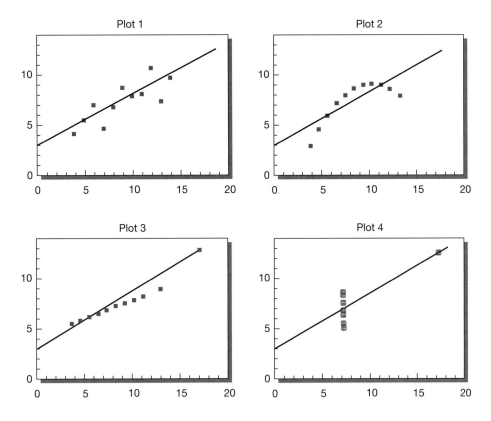

The second assumption for correlation is a **bivariate normal distribution**—that is, the data are from a random sample of a population where the two variables are normally distributed in a joint manner.

Often these assumptions or the required measurement level cannot be met. Then the analyst should select a nonlinear or nonparametric measure of association, many of which are described later in this chapter.

bivariate normal distribution data are from a random sample where two variables are normally distributed in a joint manner.

Computation and Testing of *r*

The formula for calculating Pearson's *r* is

$$r = \frac{\Sigma(X - \bar{X})(Y - \bar{Y})}{(n - 1)s_x s_y} \tag{1}$$

where

n = the number of pairs of cases

s_x, s_y = the standard deviations for X and Y

>Exhibit 21-5 Computation of Pearson's Product Moment Correlation

(1) Corporation	(2) Creative Spending ($, millions) X	(3) Creative Volume ($, millions) Y	(4) Deviations from Means $(X - \bar{X})x$	(5) $(Y - \bar{Y})y$	(6) xy	(7) x^2	(8) y^2
1	82.6	126.5	−93.84	−178.64	16763.58	8805.95	31912.25
2	89.0	191.2	−87.44	−113.94	9962.91	7645.75	12982.32
3	176.0	267.0	−0.44	−38.14	16.78	0.19	1454.66
4	82.3	137.1	−94.14	−168.04	15819.29	8862.34	28237.44
5	413.5	806.8	237.06	501.66	118923.52	56197.44	251602.56
6	18.1	35.2	158.34	−269.94	42742.3	25071.56	72867.60
7	337.3	425.5	160.86	120.36	19361.11	25875.94	14486.53
8	145.8	380.0	−30.64	74.86	−2293.71	938.81	5604.02
9	172.6	326.6	−3.84	21.36	−82.02	14.75	456.25
10	247.2	355.5	70.76	50.36	3563.47	5006.98	2536.13

$\bar{X} = 176.44$ $\bar{Y} = 305.14$ $\Sigma xy = 224777.23$
$s_x = 216.59$ $s_y = 124.01$ $\Sigma x^2 = 138419.71$
        $\Sigma y^2 = 422139.76$

Alternatively,

$$r = \frac{\Sigma xy}{\sqrt{(\Sigma x^2)(\Sigma y^2)}} \tag{2}$$

since

$$s_x = \sqrt{\frac{\Sigma x^2}{N}} \qquad s_y = \sqrt{\frac{\Sigma y^2}{N}}$$

If the numerator of equation (2) is divided by n, we have the *covariance*, the amount of deviation that the X and Y distributions have in common. With a positive covariance, the variables move in unison; with a negative one, they move in opposition. When the covariance is 0, there is no relationship. The denominator for equation (2) represents the maximum potential variation that the two distributions share. Thus, correlation may be thought of as a ratio.

Exhibit 21-5 contains a random subsample of 10 U.K. firms. The variables chosen to illustrate the computation of r are *creative spending* (how much the firms spend on creative print, broadcast, and digital materials and placement) and *creative volume* (the measure of new creative services business they capture as a result). Beneath each variable is its mean and standard deviation. In columns 4 and 5 we obtain the deviations of the X and Y values from their means, and in column 6 we find the product. Columns 7 and 8 are the squared deviation scores.

Substituting into the formula, we get

$$r = \frac{224777.23}{\sqrt{138419.71} \times \sqrt{422139.76}} = .9298$$

In this subsample, the variables are positively related and have a very high coefficient. As creative spending increases, creative volume increases; the opposite is also true. Linearity of the variables may be examined with a scatterplot such as the one shown in Exhibit 21-6. The data points fall along a straight line.

>**Exhibit 21-6** Plot of U.K. Firms' Creative Spending with Creative Volume

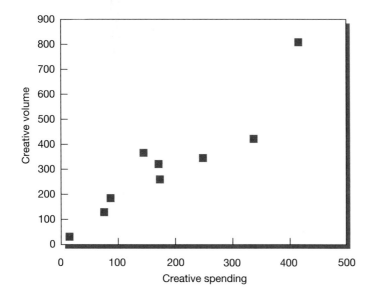

>**Exhibit 21-7** Diagram of Common Variance

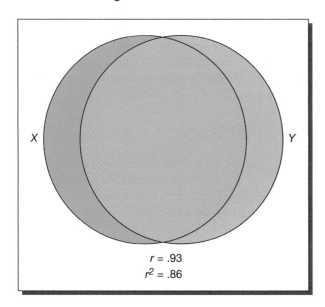

Common Variance as an Explanation

The amount of common variance in X (creative spending) and Y (creative volume) may be summarized by r^2, the **coefficient of determination.** As Exhibit 21-7 shows, the overlap between the two variables is the proportion of their common or shared variance.

The area of overlap represents the percentage of the total relationship accounted for by one variable or the other. So 86 percent of the variance in X is explained by Y, and vice versa.

coefficient of determination (r^2) amount of common variance in two variables in regression.

Testing the Significance of r

Is the coefficient representing the relationship between *creative spending* and *creative volume* real, or does it occur by chance? This question tries to discover whether our r is a chance deviation from a population p of zero. In other situations, the researcher may wish to know if significant differences exist between two or more rs. In either case, r's significance should be checked before r is used in other calculations or comparisons. For this test, we must have independent random samples from a bivariate normal distribution. Then the Z or t-test may be used for the null hypothesis, $p = 0$.

The formula for small samples is

$$t = \frac{r}{\sqrt{\dfrac{1 - r^2}{n - 2}}}$$

where

$r = .93$

$n = 10$

Substituting into the equation, we calculate t:

$$t = \frac{.93}{\sqrt{\dfrac{1 - .86}{8}}} = 7.03$$

With $n - 2$ degrees of freedom, the statistical program calculates the value of t (7.03) at a probability less than .005 for the one-tailed alternative, $H_A: p > 0$. We reject the hypothesis that there is no linear relationship between *creative spending* and *creative volume* in the population. The above statistic is appropriate when the null hypothesis states a correlation of 0. It should be used only for a one-tailed test.[3] However, it is often difficult to know in advance whether the variables are positively or negatively related, particularly when a computer removes our contact with the raw data. Software programs produce two-tailed tests for this eventuality. The observed significance level for a one-tailed test is half of the printed two-tailed version in most programs.

Interpretation of Correlations

> **You might want to review the nature of causation in Chapter 8.**

A correlation coefficient of any magnitude or sign, whatever its statistical significance, does not imply causation. Increased net profits may cause an increase in market value, or improved satisfaction may cause improved performance in certain situations, but correlation provides no evidence of cause and effect. Several alternate explanations may be provided for correlation results:

- *X* causes *Y*.
- *Y* causes *X*.
- *X* and *Y* are activated by one or more other variables.
- *X* and *Y* influence each other reciprocally.

Ex post facto studies seldom possess sufficiently powerful designs to demonstrate which of these conditions could be true. By controlling variables under an experimental design, we may obtain more rigorous evidence of causality.

artifact correlations where distinct subgroups in the data combine to give the impression of one.

Take care to avoid so-called **artifact correlations,** where distinct groups combine to give the impression of one. The upper panel of Exhibit 21-8 shows data from two business sectors. If all the data points for the *X* and *Y* variables are aggregated and a correlation is computed for a single group, a positive correlation results. Separate calculations for each sector (note that points for sector A form a circle, as do points for sector B) reveal *no* relationship between the *X* and *Y* variables. A second example, shown in the lower panel, contains a plot of data on assets and sales. We have enclosed and highlighted the data for the financial sector. This is shown as a narrow band enclosed by an ellipse. The companies in this sector score high on assets and low in sales—all are banks. When the data for banks are removed and treated separately, the correlation is nearly perfect (.99). When banks are returned to the sample and the correlation is recalculated, the overall relationship drops to the

>Exhibit 21-8 Artifact Correlations

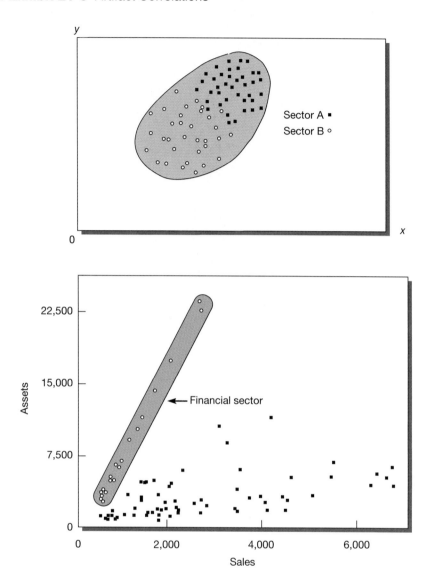

mid-.80s. In short, data hidden or nested within an aggregated set may present a radically different picture.

Another issue affecting interpretation of coefficients concerns practical significance. Even when a coefficient is statistically significant, it must be practically meaningful. In many relationships, other factors combine to make the coefficient's meaning misleading. For example, in nature we expect rainfall and the height of reservoirs to be positively correlated. But in states where water management and flood control mechanisms are complex, an apparently simple relationship may not hold. Techniques like partial and multiple correlation or multiple regression are helpful in sorting out confounding effects.

With large samples, even exceedingly low coefficients can be statistically significant. This "significance" only reflects the likelihood of a linear relationship in the population. Should magnitudes less than .30 be reported when they are significant? It depends. We might consider the correlations between variables such as cash flow, sales, market value, or net profits to be interesting revelations of a particular phenomenon whether they were high, moderate, or low. The nature of the study, the characteristics of the sample, or other reasons will be determining factors. *A coefficient is not remarkable simply because it is statistically significant.*

Envirosell: Studies Reveal Left-Hand Retail

World retailers collect and subscribe to numerous data sources, but they need knowledge from the data to craft their merchandising, staffing, and promotion strategies, as well as their store designs. Retail giants (e.g., The Gap, Limited, Starbucks, Radio Shack, McDonald's) turn to consultant Paco Underhill when they want to know how consumers buy what they do and what barriers prevent or discourage buying. Underhill describes himself as a "commercial researcher, which means I am part scientist, part artist, and part entrepreneur." His company, Envirosell, has offices in the United States, Milan, Sidney, and São Paulo. Envirosell concentrates on the third segment of retail information, drawn from observation (segment 1 is register data, and segment 2 is communication studies). In an ABC News live e-chat, Underhill said, "The principal differences in 1st world shopping patterns are governed more by education and income than by ethnicity . . . but the Brits and Aussies [do] tend to walk as they drive. This sets up some very peculiar retail [shopping] patterns, because their walking patterns set up a left-hand dominance, whereas in the U.S. and much of the rest of the world, our walking patterns set up a right-hand dominance." How would you set up an observation study to verify Underhill's conclusions?

www.envirosell.com

If you were Gap and about to design a store to open in London, how would you design a study to verify Paco Underhill's conclusions about left-hand dominance?

By probing the evidence of direction, magnitude, statistical significance, and common variance together with the study's objectives and limitations, we reduce the chances of reporting trivial findings. Simultaneously, the communication of practical implications to the reader will be improved.

> Simple Linear Regression[4]

In the previous section, we focused on relationships between variables. The product moment correlation was found to represent an index of the magnitude of the relationship, the sign governed the direction, and r^2 explained the common variance. Relationships also serve as a basis for estimation and prediction.

When we take the observed values of X to estimate or predict corresponding Y values, the process is called **simple prediction.**[5] When more than one X variable is used, the outcome is a function of multiple predictors. Simple and multiple predictions are made with a technique called **regression analysis.**

The similarities and differences of correlation and regression are summarized in Exhibit 21-9. Their relatedness would suggest that beneath many correlation problems is a regression analysis that could provide further insight about the relationship of Y with X.

simple prediction when we take the observed values of X to estimate or predict corresponding Y values.

regression analysis uses simple and multiple predictors to predict Y from X values.

>**Exhibit 21-9** Comparison of Bivariate Linear Correlation and Regression

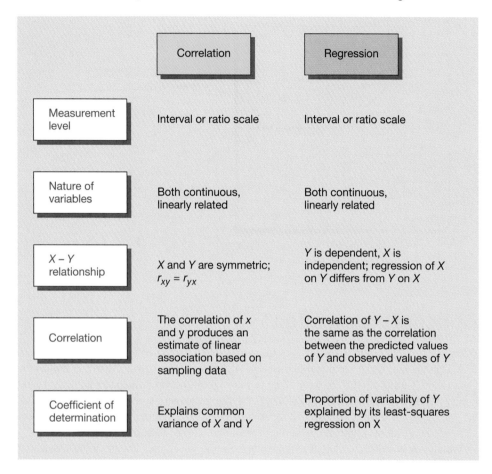

	Correlation	Regression
Measurement level	Interval or ratio scale	Interval or ratio scale
Nature of variables	Both continuous, linearly related	Both continuous, linearly related
$X - Y$ relationship	X and Y are symmetric; $r_{xy} = r_{yx}$	Y is dependent, X is independent; regression of X on Y differs from Y on X
Correlation	The correlation of x and y produces an estimate of linear association based on sampling data	Correlation of $Y - X$ is the same as the correlation between the predicted values of Y and observed values of Y
Coefficient of determination	Explains common variance of X and Y	Proportion of variability of Y explained by its least-squares regression on X

The Basic Model

A straight line is fundamentally the best way to model the relationship between two continuous variables. The bivariate linear regression may be expressed as

$$Y = \beta_0 + \beta_1 X_i$$

where the value of the dependent variable Y is a linear function of the corresponding value of the independent variable X_i in the ith observation. The slope and the Y intercept are known as **regression coefficients.** The **slope,** β_1, is the change in Y for a 1-unit change in X. It is sometimes called the "rise over run." This is defined by the formula

$$\beta_1 = \frac{\Delta Y}{\Delta X}$$

This is the ratio of change (Δ) in the rise of the line relative to the run or travel along the X axis. Exhibit 21-10 shows a few of the many possible slopes you may encounter.

The **intercept,** β_0, is the value for the linear function when it crosses the Y axis; it is the estimate of Y when $X = 0$. A formula for the intercept based on the mean scores of the X and Y variables is

$$\beta_0 = \overline{Y} - \beta_1 \overline{X}$$

regression coefficients the intercept and slope coefficients.

slope (β_1) the change in Y for a 1-unit change in X.

intercept (β_0) one of two regression coefficients, is the value for the linear function when it crosses the Y axis or the estimate of Y when X is zero.

>Exhibit 21-10 Examples of Different Slopes

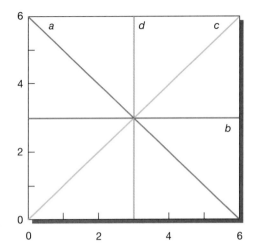

Line	Slope
a	−1
b	0
c	+1
d	∞

> The test for a 0 slope is described later, in "Testing the Goodness of Fit."

Concept Application

What makes Generation X-ers all over the world select a glass of wine rather than a beer, Jack Daniels and Coke, or Bacardi Breezer? A research report from Australia highlights Generation X attitudes toward wine. The results suggest the top influencers are friends and family, wine reviews, and visits to wineries.[6] From the winery's perspective, tasting from the barrel is not only a widespread sales tool but also a major determinant of market *en primeur* or futures contracts, which represent about 60 percent of the harvest.

Weather is widely regarded as responsible for pronouncements about a wine's taste and potential quality. A Princeton economist has elaborated on that notion. He suggested that just a few facts about local weather conditions may be better predictors of vintage French red wines than the most refined palates and noses.[7] The regression model developed predicts an auction price index for about 80 wines from winter and harvest rainfall amounts and average growing-season temperatures. Interestingly, the calculations suggested that the 1989 Bordeaux would be one of the best since 1893. French traditionalists reacted hysterically to these methods yet agreed with the conclusion.

Our first example will use one predictor with highly simplified data. Let X represent the average growing-season temperature in degrees Celsius and Y the price of a 12-bottle case in French francs (6.8 French francs = 1 euro). The data appear below.

X Average Termperature (Celsius)	*Y* Price per Case (FF)
12	2,000
16	3,000
20	4,000
24	5,000
$\bar{X} = 18$	$\bar{Y} = 3{,}500$

The plotted data in Exhibit 21-11 show a linear relationship between the pairs of points and a perfect positive correlation, $r_{yx} = 1.0$. The slope of the line is calculated:

$$\beta_1 = \frac{Y_i - Y_j}{X_i - X_j} = \frac{4{,}000 - 3{,}000}{20 - 16} = \frac{1{,}000}{4} = 250$$

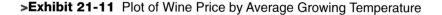

>**Exhibit 21-11** Plot of Wine Price by Average Growing Temperature

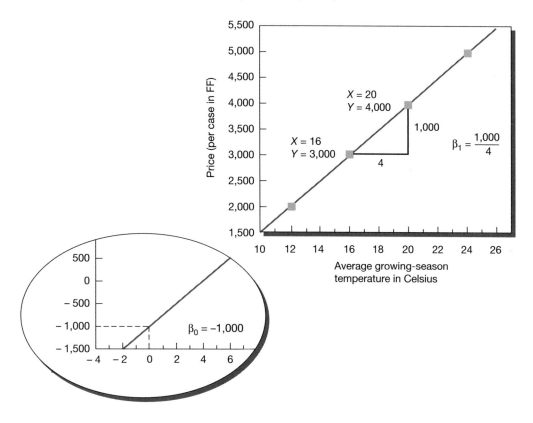

where the X_iY_i values are the data points (20, 4,000) and X_jY_j are points (16, 3,000). The intercept β_0 is $-1,000$, the point at which $X = 0$ in this plot. This area is off the graph and appears in an insert on the figure.

$$\beta_0 = \bar{Y} - \beta_1\bar{X} = 3,500 - 250(18) = -1,000$$

Substituting into the formula, we have the simple regression equation

$$Y = -1,000 + 250X_i$$

We could now predict that a warm growing season with 25.5°C temperature would bring a case price of 5,375 French francs. $\hat{Y}$ (called *Y-hat*) is the predicted value of *Y*:

$$\hat{Y} = -1,000 + 250(25.5) = 5,375$$

Unfortunately, one rarely comes across a data set composed of four paired values, a perfect correlation, and an easily drawn line. A model based on such data is *deterministic* in that for any value of *X*, there is only one possible corresponding value of *Y*. It is more likely that we will collect data where the values of *Y* vary for each *X* value. Considering Exhibit 21-12, we should expect a distribution of price values for the temperature $X = 16$, another for $X = 20$, and another for each value of *X*. The means of these *Y* distributions will also vary in some systematic way with *X*. These variabilities lead us to construct a *probabilistic* model that also uses a linear function.[8] This function is written

$$Y_i = \beta_0 + \beta_1X_i + \varepsilon_1$$

where ε symbolizes the deviation of the *i*th observation from the mean, $\beta_0 + \beta_1X_i$.

>Exhibit 21-12 Distribution of *Y* for Observations of *X*

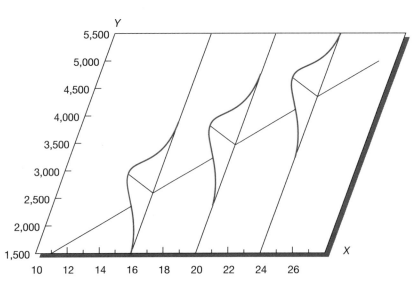

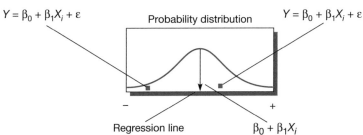

$Y = \beta_0 + \beta_1 X_i + \varepsilon$ Probability distribution $Y = \beta_0 + \beta_1 X_i + \varepsilon$

$\beta_0 + \beta_1 X_i$

Regression line

error term the deviations of values of *Y* from the regression line of *Y* for a particular value of *X*.

method of least squares a procedure for finding a regression line that keeps errors of estimate to a minimum.

France's Bordeaux Business School offers a master of business administration in the wine sector. Surprised? Business schools throughout Europe are increasingly tailoring their programs with innovative degrees that respond to the changing environment of business. In addition to wine, MBA specializations focus on the music industry, luxury brands, sports management, agribusiness, e-business, consulting, and public sector specialities. **www.iht.com**

As shown in Exhibit 21-12, the actual values of *Y* may be found above or below the regression line represented by the mean value of *Y* ($\beta_0 + \beta_1 X_i$) for a particular value of *X*. These deviations are the error in fitting the line and are often called the **error term.**

Method of Least Squares

Exhibit 21-13 contains a new data set for the wine price example. Our prediction of *Y* from *X* must now account for the fact that the *X* and *Y* pairs do not fall neatly along the line. Actually, the relationship could be summarized by several lines. Exhibit 21-14 suggests two

alternatives based on visual inspection—both of which produce errors, or vertical distances from the observed values to the line. The **method of least squares** allows us to find a regression line, or line of best fit, that will keep these errors to a minimum. It uses the criterion of minimizing the total squared errors of estimate. When we predict values of *Y* for each X_i, the difference between the actual Y_i and the predicted $\hat{Y}$ is the error. This error is squared

>**Exhibit 21-13** Data for Wine Price Study

	Y Price (FF)	X Temperature (C°)	XY	Y²	X²
1	1,813	11.80	21,393.40	3,286,969.00	139.24
2	2,558	15.70	40,160.60	6,543,364.00	246.49
3	2,628	14.00	36,792.00	6,906,384.00	196.00
4	3,217	22.90	73,669.30	10,349,089.00	524.41
5	3,228	20.00	64,560.00	10,419,984.00	400.00
6	3,629	20.10	72,942.90	13,169,641.00	404.01
7	3,886	17.90	69,559.40	15,100,996.00	320.41
8	4,897	23.40	114,589.80	23,980,609.00	547.56
9	4,933	24.60	121,351.80	24,334,489.00	605.16
10	5,199	25.70	133,614.30	27,029,601.00	660.49
Σ	35,988	196.10	748,633.50	141,121,126.00	4,043.77
Mean	3,598.80	19.61			
s	1,135.66	4.69			
Sum of squares (SS)	11,607,511.59	198.25	42,908.82		

>**Exhibit 21-14** Scatterplot and Possible Regression Lines Based on Visual Inspection: Wine Price Study

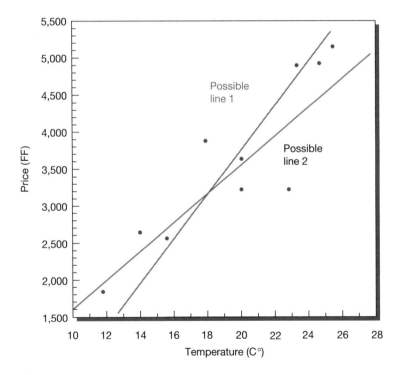

and then summed. The line of best fit is the one that minimizes the total squared errors of prediction.[9]

$$\sum_{i=1}^{n} e_i^2 \text{ minimized}$$

Regression coefficients β_0 and β_1 are used to find the least-squares solution. They are computed as follows:

$$\beta_1 = \frac{\Sigma XY - \dfrac{(\Sigma X)(\Sigma Y)}{n}}{\Sigma X^2 - \dfrac{(\Sigma X)^2}{n}}$$

$$\hat{\beta}_0 = \bar{Y} - \hat{\beta}_1 \bar{X}$$

>**Exhibit 21-15** Drawing the Least-Squares Line: Wine Price Study

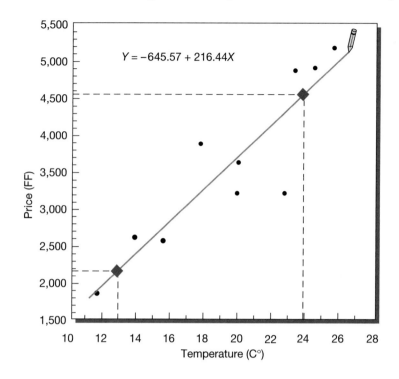

$$Y = -645.57 + 216.44X$$

Substituting data from Exhibit 21-13 into both formulas, we get

$$\beta_1 = \frac{748{,}633.5 - \dfrac{(196.1)(35{,}988)}{10}}{4{,}043.77 - \dfrac{(196.1)^2}{10}} = 216.439$$

$$\hat{\beta}_0 = 3{,}598.8 - (216.439)(19.61) = -645.569$$

The predictive equation is now $\hat{Y} = -645.57 + 216.44\,X_i$.

Drawing the Regression Line

Before drawing the regression line, we select two values of X to compute. Using values 13 and 24 for X_i, the points are

$$\hat{Y} = -645.57 + 216.44(13) = 2{,}168.15$$

$$\hat{Y} = 645.57 + 216.44(24) = 4{,}548.99$$

Comparing the line drawn in Exhibit 21-15 to the trial lines in Exhibit 21-14, one can readily see the success of the least-squares method in minimizing the error of prediction.

Residuals

residual the difference between the regression line value of Y and the real Y value.

We now turn our attention to the plot of standardized residuals in Exhibit 21-16. A **residual** is what remains after the line is fit or $(Y_i - \hat{Y}_i)$. When standardized, residuals are comparable

># >**snap**shot

What's a Marketing Education without Wine?

What do Harvard, Yale, UCLA, Columbia, the Kellogg School of Management at Northwestern, Pennsylvania's Wharton Business School, and Berkeley's Hass School of Business have in common? They are among a growing number of B-schools where wine clubs have flourished. Some have even added wine education to the business curriculum.

While medical research has shown that moderate drinking can reduce the risk of heart disease, that's not the appeal for students who believe that it can be an effective tool for shaping positive business relationships. Brian Scanlon of Harvard's Wine & Cuisine Society summed it up this way: "Wine knowledge is an indispensable skill in today's business environment. If you're at a crucial business dinner and you want to pick the perfect wine to create the right atmosphere, you need to know the vintages, the regions and the best winemakers."

Vineyard owners couldn't be more supportive. Jack Cakebread of Cakebread Cellars, on a promotional tour at business schools around the country, reported the relationship between age and visitation frequency at Cakebread's tasting room. Almost 70 percent of visitors are in their 20s and 30s. Although wine industry research forecasts a drop in wine enthusiasm by Generation X, the future corporate executives represent a radically different segment.

David Mogridge is on a student team at Berkeley that brings in lecturers on a wide range of topics like growing, shipping, legal issues, branding, and strategy. In an interview with Eric Zelko of *Wine Spectator,* Mogridge said playfully, "When I think about it, everything I learned in business school, I learned in wine class."

www.winespectator.com

>**Exhibit 21-16** Plot of Standardized Residuals: Wine Price Study

Case	−3.0	0.0	3.0	Y Price	Predicted Price	Residual
1		* .		1,813	1,908.4112	−95.4112
2		* .		2,558	2,752.5234	−194.5234
3		. *		2,628	2,384.5771	243.4229
4	*	.		3,217	4,310.8844	−1,093.8844
5	*	.		3,228	3,683.2112	−455.2112
6		*		3,629	3,704.8551	−75.8551
7		. *		3,886	3,228.6893	657.3107
8		. *		4,897	4,419.1039	477.8961
9		. *		4,933	4,678.8307	254.1693
10		. *		5,199	4,916.9137	282.0863

−3.0   0.0   3.0

to Z scores with a mean of 0 and a standard deviation of 1. In this plot, the standardized residuals should fall between 2 and −2, be randomly distributed about zero, and show no discernible pattern. All these conditions say the model is applied appropriately.

In our example, we have one residual at −2.2, a random distribution about zero, and few indications of a sequential pattern. It is important to apply other diagnostics to verify that the regression assumptions (normality, linearity, equality of variance, and independence of error) are met. Various software programs provide plots and other checks of regression assumptions.[10]

Predictions

If we wanted to predict the price of a case of investment-grade red wine for a growing season that averages 21°C, our prediction would be

$$\hat{Y} = -645.57 + 216.44(21) = 3{,}899.67$$

This is a *point prediction* of Y and should be corrected for greater precision. As with other confidence estimates, we establish the degree of confidence desired and substitute into the formula

$$\hat{Y} \pm t_{\alpha/2}s \sqrt{1 + \frac{1}{10} + \frac{(X - \bar{X})^2}{SS_x}}$$

where

$t_{\alpha/2}$ = the two-tailed critical value for t at the desired level (95 percent in this example)

s = the standard error of estimate (also the square root of the mean square error from the analysis of variance of the regression model) (see Exhibit 21-19).

SS_x = the sum of squares for X (Exhibit 21-13).

$$3{,}899.67 \pm (2.306)(538.559) \sqrt{1 + \frac{1}{10} + \frac{(21 - 19.61)^2}{198.25}}$$

$$3{,}899.67 \pm 1{,}308.29$$

We are 95 percent confident of our prediction that a case of investment-quality red wine grown in a particular year at 21°C average temperatures will be initially priced at 3,899.67 ± 1,308.29 French francs (FF), or from approximately 2,591 to 5,208 FF. The comparatively large band width results from the amount of error in the model (reflected by r^2), some peculiarities in the Y values, and the use of a single predictor.

It is more likely that we would want to predict the average price of *all* cases grown at 21°C. This prediction would use the same basic formula but omitting the first digit (the 1) under the radical. A narrower *confidence* band is the result since the average of all Y values is being predicted from a given X. In our example, the confidence interval for 95 percent is 3,899.67 ± 411.42, or from 3,488 to 4,311 FF.

The predictor we selected, 21°C, was close to the mean of X (19.61). Because the **prediction and confidence bands** are shaped like a bow tie, predictors farther from the mean have larger bandwidths. For example, X values of 15, 20, and 25 produce confidence bands of ±565, ±397, and ±617, respectively. This is illustrated in Exhibit 21-17. The farther one's selected predictor is from X, the wider is the prediction interval.

prediction and confidence bands bow-tie-shaped confidence interval around a predictor.

Testing the Goodness of Fit

With the regression line plotted and a few illustrative predictions, we should now gather some evidence of **goodness of fit**—how well the model fits the data. The most important test in bivariate linear regression is whether the slope, β_1, is equal to zero.[11] We have already observed a slope of zero in Exhibit 21-10, line *b*. Zero slopes result from various conditions:

goodness of fit a measure of how well the regression model is able to predict Y.

- Y is completely unrelated to X, and no systematic pattern is evident.
- There are constant values of Y for every value of X.
- The data are related but represented by a nonlinear function.

>**Exhibit 21-17** Prediction and Confidence Bands on Proximity to *X*

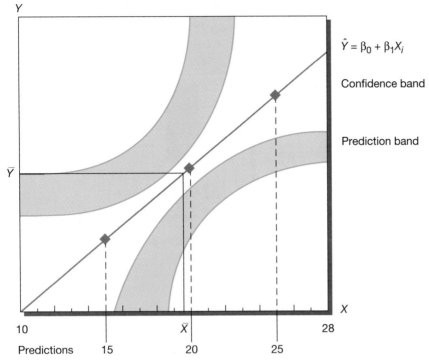

The *t*-Test

To test whether $\beta_1 = 0$, we use a two-tailed test (since the actual relationship is positive, negative, or zero). The test follows the *t* distribution for $n - 2$ degrees of freedom:

$$t = \frac{b_1}{s(b_1)} = \frac{216.439}{34.249} = 5.659$$

where

b_1 was previously defined as the slope β_1.

$s(b_1)$ is the standard error of β_1.[12]

We reject the null hypothesis, $\beta_1 = 0$, because the calculated *t* is greater than any *t* value for 8 degrees of freedom and $\alpha = .01$. Therefore, we conclude that the slope is not equal to zero.

The *F* Test

Computer printouts generally contain an analysis of variance (ANOVA) table with an *F* test of the regression model. In bivariate regression, *t* and *F* tests produce the same results since t^2 is equal to *F*. In multiple regression, the *F* test has an overall role for the model, and each of the independent variables is evaluated with a separate *t*-test. From the last chapter, recall that ANOVA partitions variance into component parts. For regression, it comprises explained deviations, $\hat{Y} - \bar{Y}$, and unexplained deviations, $Y - \hat{Y}$. Together they constitute the total deviation, $Y - \bar{Y}$. This is shown graphically in Exhibit 21-18. These sources of deviation are squared for all observations and summed across the data points.

In Exhibit 21-19, we develop this concept sequentially, concluding with the *F* test of the regression model for the wine data. Based on the results presented in that table, we find

>**Exhibit 21-18** Components of Variation

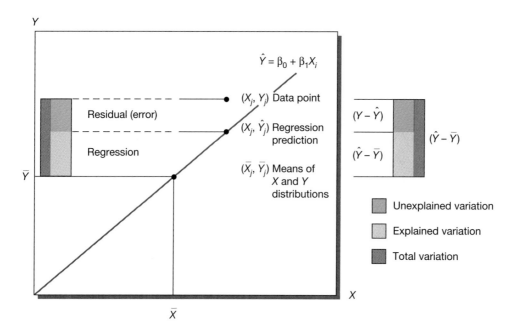

statistical evidence of a linear relationship between variables. The null hypothesis, $r^2 = 0$, is rejected with $F = 32.02$, d.f. (1, 8), $p < .005$. The alternative hypothesis is accepted. The null hypothesis for the F test had the same effect as $\beta_1 = 0$ since we could select either test. Thus, we conclude that X and Y are linearly related.

Coefficient of Determination

In predicting the values of Y without any knowledge of X, our best estimate would be $\bar{Y}$, its mean. Each predicted value that does not fall on Y contributes to an error of estimate, $Y - \bar{Y}$. The total squared error for several predictions would be $\Sigma (Y_i - \bar{Y})^2$. By introducing known values of X into a regression equation, we attempt to reduce this error even further. Naturally, this is an improvement over using $\bar{Y}$, and the result is $(\hat{Y} - \bar{Y})$. The total improvement based on several estimates is $\Sigma(\hat{Y}_i - \bar{Y})^2$, the amount of variation explained by the relationship between X and Y in the regression. Based on the formula, the *coefficient of determination* is the ratio of the line of best fit's error over that incurred by using Y. One purpose of testing, then, is to discover whether the regression equation is a more effective predictive device than the mean of the dependent variable.

As in correlation, the coefficient of determination is symbolized by r^2.[13] It has several purposes. As an index of fit, it is interpreted as the total proportion of variance in Y explained by X. As a measure of linear relationship, it tells us how well the regression line fits the data. It is also an important indicator of the predictive accuracy of the equation. Typically, we would like to have an r^2 that explains 80 percent or more of the variation. Lower than that, predictive accuracy begins to fall off. The coefficient of determination, r^2, is calculated like this:

$$r2 = \frac{\sum\limits_{i=1}^{n} (\hat{Y} - \bar{Y})^2}{\sum\limits_{i=1}^{n} (Y - \bar{Y})^2} = \frac{SS_r}{SS_e} = 1 - \frac{SS_e}{SS_t}$$

>**Exhibit 21-19** Progressive Application of Partitioned Variance Concept

General Concept				
$(\hat{Y} - \bar{Y})$	+	$(Y - \hat{Y})$	=	$(Y - \bar{Y})$
Explained Variation (the regression relationship between X and Y)		Unexplained Variation (cannot be explained by the regression relationship)		Total Variation

ANOVA Application		
$\sum_{i=1}^{n} (\hat{Y} - \bar{Y})^2$	$\sum_{i=1}^{n} (Y - \hat{Y})^2$	$\sum_{i=1}^{n} (Y - \bar{Y})^2$
SS_r Sum of Squares Regression	SS_e Sum of Squares Error	SS_t Sum of Squares Total

Contents of Summary Table

Source	Degrees of Freedom	Sum of Squares	Mean Square	F Ratio
Regression	1	SS_r	$MS_r = \dfrac{SS_r}{1}$	$\dfrac{MS_r}{MS_e}$
Error	$n - 2$	SS_e	$MS_e = \dfrac{SS_e}{n-2}$	
Total		SS_t		

ANOVA Summary Table: Test of Regression Model

Source	Degrees of Freedom	Sum of Squares	Mean Square	F Ratio
Regression	1	9,287,143.11	9,287,143.11	32.02
Residual (error)	8	2,320,368.49	290,046.06	
Total		11,607,511.60		

Significance of F = .0005

For the wine price study, r^2 was found by using the data from the bottom of Exhibit 21-19:

$$r^2 = 1 - \frac{2,320,368.49}{11,607,511.60} = .80$$

Eighty percent of the variance in price may be explained by growing-season temperatures. With actual data and multiple predictors, our results would improve.

> Nonparametric Measures of Association[14]

Measures for Nominal Data

Nominal measures are used to assess the strength of relationships in cross-classification tables. They are often used with chi-square or may be used separately. In this section, we provide examples of three statistics based on chi-square and two that follow the proportional reduction in error approach.

There is no fully satisfactory all-purpose measure for categorical data. Some are adversely affected by table shape and number of cells; others are sensitive to sample size or marginals. It is perturbing to find similar statistics reporting different coefficients for the same data. This occurs because of a statistic's particular sensitivity or the way it was devised.

Technically, we would like to find two characteristics with nominal measures:

- When there is no relationship at all, the coefficient should be 0.
- When there is a complete dependency, the coefficient should display unity, or 1.

This does not always happen. In addition to being aware of the sensitivity problem, analysts should be alert to the need for careful selection of tests.

Chi-Square-Based Measures

Exhibit 21-20 reports a 2×2 table showing the test of an advertising campaign involving 66 people. The variables are success of the campaign and whether direct mail was used. In this example, the observed significance level is less than the testing level ($\alpha = .05$), and the null hypothesis is rejected. A correction to chi-square is provided. We now turn to measures of association to detect the strength of the relationship. Notice that the exhibit also provides an approximate significance of the coefficient based on the chi-square distribution. This is a test of the null hypothesis that no relationship exists between the variables of direct mail and campaign success.

The first **chi-square-based measure** is applied to direct mail and campaign success. It is called **phi (ϕ).** Phi ranges from 0 to $+1.0$ and attempts to correct χ^2 proportionately to N. Phi is best employed with 2×2 tables like Exhibit 21-20 since its coefficient can exceed $+1.0$ when applied to larger tables. Phi is calculated

$$\phi = \sqrt{\frac{\chi^2}{N}} = \sqrt{\frac{6.616257}{66}} = .3056$$

Phi's coefficient shows a moderate relationship between marketing campaign success and direct mail. There is no suggestion in this interpretation that one variable causes the other, nor is there an indication of the direction of the relationship.

Cramer's V is a modification of phi for larger tables and has a range up to 1.0 for tables of any shape. It is calculated like this:

$$V = \sqrt{\frac{\chi^2}{N(k-1)}} = \sqrt{\frac{6.616257}{66(1)}} = .3056$$

where $k =$ the lesser number of rows or columns.
In Exhibit 21-20, the coefficient is the same as phi.

> **You may wish to review our discussion of chi-square in Chapter 19.**

chi-square-based measures tests to detect the strength of the relationship between the variables tested with a chi-square test.

phi (ϕ) used with chi-square, a measure of association for nominal, nonparametric variables.

Cramer's V used with chi-square, a measure of association for nominal, nonparametric variables with larger than 2×2 tables.

>**Exhibit 21-20** Chi-Square-Based Measures of Association

	Marketing Campaign Success		
Count	Yes	No	Row Total

Direct Mail		Yes	No
	Yes	21	10	31
	No	13	22	35
	Column Total	34	32	66

Chi-Square	Value	d.f.	Significance
Pearson	6.16257	1	.01305
Continuity correction	4.99836	1	.02537

Minimal expected frequency 15.030

Statistic	Value	Approximate Significance
Phi	.30557	.01305[*]
Cramer's V	.30557	.01305[*]
Contingency coefficient C	.29223	.01305[*]

[*]Pearson chi-square probability.

The **contingency coefficient** *C* is reported last. It is not comparable to other measures and has a different upper limit for various table sizes. The upper limits are determined as

$$\sqrt{\frac{k-1}{k}}$$

where *k* = the number of columns.

For a 2 × 2 table, the upper limit is .71; for a 3 × 3, .82; and for a 4 × 4, .87. Although this statistic operates well with tables having the same number of rows as columns, its upper-limit restriction is not consistent with a criterion of good association measurement. *C* is calculated as

$$C = \sqrt{\frac{\chi^2}{\chi^2 + N}} = \sqrt{\frac{6.616257}{6.616257 + 66}} = .2922$$

The chief advantage of *C* is its ability to accommodate data in almost every form: skewed or normal, discrete or continuous, and nominal or ordinal.

Proportional Reduction in Error

Proportional reduction in error (PRE) statistics are the second type used with contingency tables. Lambda and tau are the examples discussed here. The coefficient **lambda (λ)** is based on how well the frequencies of one nominal variable offer predictive evidence about the frequencies of another. Lambda is asymmetrical—allowing calculation for the direction of prediction—and symmetrical, predicting row and column variables equally.

The computation of lambda is straightforward. In Exhibit 21-21, we have results from an opinion survey with a sample of 400 shareholders in publicly traded advertising firms. Of the

contingency coefficient C used with chi-square, a measure of association for nominal, nonparametric variables.

proportional reduction in error (PRE) measures of association used with contingency tables to predict frequencies.

lambda (λ) a measure of how well the frequencies of one nominal variable predict the frequencies of another variable.

>**Exhibit 21-21** Proportional Reduction of Error Measures

What is your opinion about capping executives' salaries?

	Cell designation Count Row Pct.	Favor	Do Not Favor	Row Total
	Managerial	1,1 90 82.0	1,2 20 18.0	110
Occupational Class	White collar	2,1 60 43.0	2,2 80 57.0	140
	Blue collar	3,1 30 20.0	3,2 120 80.0	150
	Column Total	180 45.0%	220 55.0%	400 100.0%

Chi-Square	Value		d.f.	Significance
Pearson	98.38646		2	.00000
Likelihood ratio	104.96542		2	.00000

Minimum expected frequency 49.500

Statistic	Value	ASEI	T Value	Approximate Significance
Lambda:				
Symmetric	.30233	.03955	6.77902	
With occupation dependent	.24000	.03820	5.69495	
With opinion dependent	.38889	.04555	7.08010	
Goodman & Kruskal tau:				
With occupation dependent	.11669	.02076		.00000*
With opinion dependent	.24597	.03979		.00000*

*Based on chi-square approximation.

400 shareholders, 180 (45 percent) favor capping executives' salaries; 220 (55 percent) do not favor doing so. With this information alone, if asked to predict the opinions of an individual in the sample, we would achieve the best prediction record by always choosing the modal category. Here it is "do not favor." By doing so, however, we would be wrong 180 out of 400 times. The probability estimate for an incorrect classification is .45, $P(1) = (1 - .55)$.

Now suppose we have prior information about the respondents' occupational status and are asked to predict opinion. Would it improve predictive ability? Yes, we would make the predictions by summing the probabilities of all cells that are not the modal value for their rows [for example, cell (1, 2) is 20/400, or .05]:

$$P(2) = \text{cell } (1, 2) \ .05 + \text{cell } (2, 1) \ .15 + \text{cell } (3, 1) \ .075 = .275$$

Lambda is then calculated:

$$\lambda = \frac{P(1) - P(2)}{P(1)} = \frac{.45 - .275}{.45} = .3889$$

Note that the asymmetric lambda in Exhibit 21-21, where opinion is the dependent variable, reflects this computation. As a result of knowing the respondents' occupational classification, we improve our prediction by 39 percent. If we wish to predict occupational classification from opinion instead of the opposite, a λ of .24 would be secured. This means that 24 percent of the error in predicting occupational class is eliminated by knowledge of opinion on the executives' salary question. Lambda varies between 0 and 1, corresponding with no ability to eliminate errors to elimination of all errors of prediction.

Goodman and Kruskal's **tau** (τ) uses table marginals to reduce prediction errors. In predicting opinion on executives' salaries without any knowledge of occupational class, we would expect a 50.5 percent correct classification and a 49.5 percent probability of error. These are based on the column marginal percentages in Exhibit 21-21.

tau (τ) a measure of association that uses table marginals to reduce prediction errors.

Column Marginal		Column Percent		Correct Cases
180	*	45	=	81
220	*	55	=	121
				202

Total correct classification

Correct classification of the opinion variable = .505 = $\dfrac{202}{400}$

Probability of error, $P(1) = (1 - .505) = .495$

When additional knowledge of occupational class is used, information for correct classification of the opinion variable is improved to 62.7 percent with a 37.3 percent probability of error. This is obtained by using the cell counts and marginals for occupational class (refer to Exhibit 21-21), as shown below:

Row 1	$\left(\dfrac{90}{110}\right)90 + \left(\dfrac{20}{110}\right)20$	=	73.6364 + 3.6364	=	77.2727
Row 2	$\left(\dfrac{60}{140}\right)60 + \left(\dfrac{80}{140}\right)80$	=	25.7143 + 45.7142	=	71.4286
Row 3	$\left(\dfrac{30}{150}\right)30 + \left(\dfrac{120}{150}\right)120$	=	6.0 + 96.0	=	102.0000

Total correct classification (with additional information on occupational class) 250.7013

Correct classification of opinion variable = .627 = $\dfrac{250.7}{400}$

Probability of error, $P(2) = (1 - .627) = .373$

Tau is then computed like this:

$$\tau = \frac{P(1) - P(2)}{P(1)} = \frac{.495 - .373}{.495} = \boxed{.246}$$

Exhibit 21-21 shows that the information about occupational class has reduced error in predicting opinion to approximately 25 percent. The table also contains information on the test of the null hypothesis that tau = 0 with an approximate observed significance level and asymptotic error (for developing confidence intervals). Based on the small observed significance level, we would conclude that tau is significantly different from a coefficient of 0 and that there is an association between opinion on executives' salaries and occupational class in the population from which the sample was selected. We can also establish the confidence level for the coefficient at the 95 percent level as approximately .25 ± .04.

Speedpass is McD's Cashless Payment

Lots of people will be waving while visiting McDonald's in Chicago. And it won't be because they want to attract attention or be overly friendly. Instead, some Chicagoland McDonald's (as well as some in Boise, ID) are testing a cashless payment system based on RFID technology by FreedomPay. This system was first tested by McDonald's franchises in New York and Southern California and tested in 2001 by nine Chicago McDonald's restaurant owners. The system, called Speedpass, is activated when a customer waves a Speedpass device at a reader located either in the drive-thru or inside at the checkout counter. Most recently,

these devices are designed to dangle from keychains. The Speedpass system was originally introduced by ExxonMobil Corp. at its Mobil gas stations. Similar systems have been tested by Taco Bell and KFC.

How should this study be designed to measure the effectiveness of cashless payment systems? What relationships do you expect to find? Will they require parametric or nonparametric measures of association?

www.speedpass.com; www.mcdonalds.com; www.freedompay.com

Measures for Ordinal Data

ordinal measures measures of association between variables generating ordinal data.

When data require **ordinal measures,** there are several statistical alternatives. In this section we will illustrate:

- Gamma.
- Kendall's tau *b* and tau *c*.
- Somers's *d*.
- Spearman's rho.

All but Spearman's rank-order correlation are based on the concept of concordant and discordant pairs. None of these statistics require the assumption of a bivariate normal distribution, yet by incorporating order, most produce a range from -1.0 (a perfect negative relationship) to $+1.0$ (a perfect positive one). Within this range, a coefficient with a larger magnitude (absolute value of the measure) is interpreted as having a stronger relationship. These characteristics allow the analyst to interpret both the direction and the strength of the relationship.

Exhibit 21-22 presents data for 70 managerial employees of KeyDesign, a large industrial design firm. All 70 employees have been evaluated for coronary risk by the firm's health insurer. The management levels are ranked, as are the fitness assessments by the physicians. If we were to use a nominal measure of association with these data (such as Cramer's *V*), the computed value of the statistic would be positive since order is not present in nominal data. But using ordinal measures of association reveals the actual nature of the relationship. In this example, all coefficients have negative signs; therefore, lower levels of fitness are associated with higher management levels.

concordant when a participant that ranks higher on one ordinal variable also ranks higher on another variable.

The information in the exhibit has been arranged so that the number of concordant and discordant pairs of individual observations may be calculated. When a subject that ranks higher on one variable also ranks higher on the other variable, the pairs of observations are said to be **concordant.** If a higher ranking on one variable is accompanied by a lower ranking on the other variable, the pairs of observations are **discordant.** Let *P* stand for concordant pairs and *Q* stand for discordant. When concordant pairs exceed discordant pairs in a $P - Q$ relationship, the statistic reports a positive association between the variables under study. As discordant pairs increase over concordant pairs, the association becomes negative. A balance indicates no relationship between the variables. Exhibit 21-23 summarizes the procedure for calculating the summary terms needed in all the statistics we are about to discuss.[15]

discordant when a subject that ranks higher on one ordinal variable ranks lower on another variable.

gamma (γ) uses a preponderance of evidence of concordant pairs versus discordant pairs to predict association.

Goodman and Kruskal's **gamma (γ)** is a statistic that compares concordant and discordant pairs and then standardizes the outcome by maximizing the value of the denominator.

>**Exhibit 21-22** Tabled Ranks for Management and Fitness Levels at KeyDesign

Count		Management Level			
		Lower	Middle	Upper	
Fitness	High	14	4	2	20
	Moderate	18	6	2	26
	Low	2	6	16	24
		34	16	20	70

Statistic	Value[*]
Gamma	−.70
Kendall's tau b	−.51
Kendall's tau c	−.50
Somers's d	
Symmetric	−.51
With fitness dependent	−.53
With management-level dependent	−.50

[*]The t value for each coefficient is −5.86451.

It has a proportional reduction in error (PRE) interpretation that connects nicely with what we already know about PRE nominal measures. Gamma is defined as

$$\gamma = \frac{P - Q}{P + Q} = \frac{172 - 992}{172 + 992} = \frac{-820}{1164} = \boxed{-.70}$$

For the fitness data, we conclude that as management level increases, fitness decreases. This is immediately apparent from the larger number of discordant pairs. A more precise explanation for gamma takes its absolute value (ignoring the sign) and relates it to PRE. Hypothetically, if one was trying to predict whether the pairs were concordant or discordant, one might flip a coin and classify the outcome. A better way is to make the prediction based on the preponderance of concordance or discordance; the absolute value of gamma is the proportional reduction in error when prediction is done the second way. For example, you would get a 50 percent hit ratio using the coin. A PRE of .70 improves your hit ratio to 85 percent $(.50 \times .70) + (.50) = .85$.

With a γ of −.70, 85 percent of the pairs are discordant and 15 percent are concordant.[16] There are almost six times as many discordant pairs as concordant pairs. In situations where the data call for a 2 × 2 table, the appropriate modification of gamma is Yule's Q.[17]

Kendall's **tau** b (τ_b) is a refinement of gamma that considers tied pairs. A tied pair occurs when subjects have the same value on the X variable, on the Y variable, or on both. For a given sample size, there are $n(n-1)/2$ pairs of observations.[18] After concordant pairs and discordant pairs are removed, the remainder are tied. Tau b does not have a PRE interpretation but does provide a range of −1.0 to +1.0 for square tables. Its compensation for ties uses the information found in Exhibit 21-23. It may be calculated as

$$\tau_b = \frac{P - Q}{\sqrt{\left(\frac{n(n-1)}{2} - T_x\right)\left(\frac{n(n-1)}{2} - T_y\right)}}$$

$$= \frac{172 - 992}{\sqrt{(2{,}415 - 871)(2{,}415 - 791)}} = \boxed{.-.51}$$

tau b (τ_b) a refinement of gamma for ordinal data that considers "tied" pairs, not only discordant or concordant pairs, for square tables.

>**Exhibit 21-23** Calculation of Concordant (P), Discordant (Q), Tied (T_x, T_y), and Total Paired Observations: KeyDesign Example

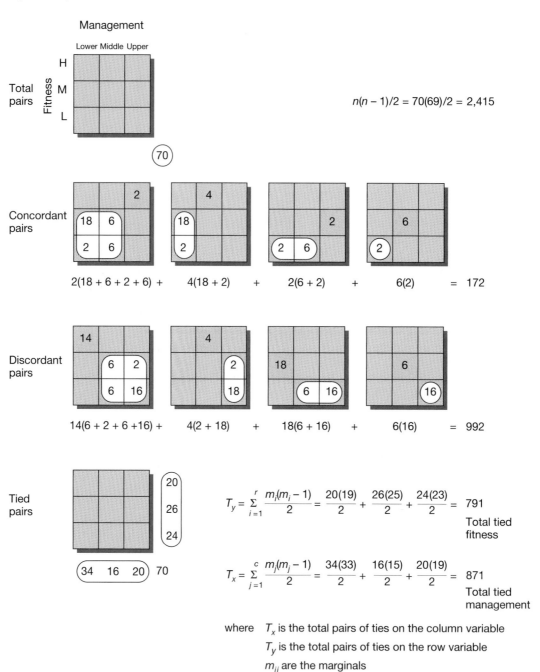

Management

Lower Middle Upper

Total pairs

Fitness H M L

$n(n-1)/2 = 70(69)/2 = 2{,}415$

(70)

Concordant pairs

$2(18 + 6 + 2 + 6) + \quad 4(18 + 2) \quad + \quad 2(6 + 2) \quad + \quad 6(2) \quad = 172$

Discordant pairs

$14(6 + 2 + 6 + 16) + \quad 4(2 + 18) \quad + \quad 18(6 + 16) \quad + \quad 6(16) \quad = 992$

Tied pairs

$$T_y = \sum_{i=1}^{r} \frac{m_i(m_i - 1)}{2} = \frac{20(19)}{2} + \frac{26(25)}{2} + \frac{24(23)}{2} = 791$$

Total tied fitness

$$T_x = \sum_{j=1}^{c} \frac{m_j(m_j - 1)}{2} = \frac{34(33)}{2} + \frac{16(15)}{2} + \frac{20(19)}{2} = 871$$

Total tied management

where T_x is the total pairs of ties on the column variable

T_y is the total pairs of ties on the row variable

m_{ij} are the marginals

tau c (τ_c) a refinement of gamma for ordinal data that considers "tied" pairs, not only discordant or concordant pairs, for any-size table.

    Kendall's **tau c** (τ_c) is another adjustment to the basic $P - Q$ relationship of gamma. This approach to ordinal association is suitable for tables of any size. Although we illustrate tau c, we would select tau b since the cross-classification table for the fitness data is square. The adjustment for table shape is seen in the formula

$$\tau_c = \frac{2m(P - Q)}{N^2(m - 1)} = \frac{2(3)(172 - 992)}{(70)^2(3 - 1)} = -.50$$

where m is the smaller number of rows or columns.

Somers's d, rounds out our coverage of statistics employing the concept of concordant-discordant pairs. This statistic's utility comes from its ability to compensate for tied ranks and adjust for the direction of the dependent variable. Again, we refer to the preliminary calculations provided in Exhibit 21-23 to compute the symmetric and asymmetric ds. As before, the symmetric coefficient (equation 1) takes the row and column variables into account equally. The second and third calculations show fitness as the dependent and management level as the dependent, respectively.

> **Somers's d** a measure of association for ordinal data that compensates for "tied" ranks and adjusts for direction of the independent variable.

$$d_{\text{sym}} = \frac{(P - Q)}{n(n - 1) - T_x T_y/2} = \frac{-820}{1,584} = -.51 \tag{1}$$

$$d_{y - x} = \frac{(P - Q)}{\dfrac{n(n - 1)}{2} - T_x} = \frac{-820}{2,415 - 871} = -.53 \tag{2}$$

$$d_{x - y} = \frac{(P - Q)}{\dfrac{n(n - 1)}{2} - T_y} = \frac{-820}{2,415 - 791} = -.50 \tag{3}$$

The **Spearman's rho (ρ)** correlation is a another ordinal measure. Along with Kendall's tau, it is used frequently with ordinal data. Rho correlates ranks between two ordered variables. Occasionally, researchers find continuous variables with too many abnormalities to correct. Then scores may be reduced to ranks and calculated with Spearman's rho.

> **Spearman's rho (ρ)** correlates ranks between two ordinal variables.

As a special form of Pearson's product moment correlation, rho's strengths outweigh its weaknesses. First, when data are transformed by logs or squaring, rho remains unaffected. Second, outliers or extreme scores that were troublesome before ranking no longer pose a threat since the largest number in the distribution is equal to the sample size. Third, it is an easy statistic to compute. The major deficiency is its sensitivity to tied ranks. Ties distort the coefficient's size. However, there are rarely too many ties to justify the correction formulas available.

To illustrate the use of rho, consider a situation where KDL, a media firm, is recruiting account executive trainees. Assume the field has been narrowed to 10 applicants for final evaluation. They arrive at the company headquarters, go through a battery of tests, and are interviewed by a panel of three executives. The test results are evaluated by an industrial psychologist who then ranks the 10 candidates. The executives produce a composite ranking based on the interviews. Your task is to decide how well these two sets of ranking

>**Exhibit 21-24** KDL Data for Spearman's rho

	Rank by			
Applicant	Panel x	Psychologist y	d	d²
1	3.5	6.0	−2.5	6.25
2	10.0	5.0	5.0	25.00
3	6.5	8.0	−1.5	2.25
4	2.0	1.5	0.5	0.25
5	1.0	3.0	−2	4.00
6	9.0	7.0	2.0	4.00
7	3.5	1.5	2.0	4.00
8	6.5	9.0	−2.5	6.25
9	8.0	10.0	−2	4.00
10	5.0	4.0	1.0	1.00
				57.00

Note: Tied ranks were assigned the average (of ranks) as if no ties had occurred.

agree. Exhibit 21-24 contains the data and preliminary calculations. Substituting into the equation, we get

$$r_s = 1 - \frac{6\Sigma d^2}{n^3 - n} = \frac{6(57)}{(10)^3 - 10} = .654$$

where n is the number of subjects being ranked.

The relationship between the panel's and the psychologist's rankings is moderately high, suggesting agreement between the two measures. The test of the null hypothesis that there is no relationship between the measures ($r_s = 0$) is rejected at the .05 level with $n - 2$ degrees of freedom.

$$t = r_s \sqrt{\frac{n - 2}{1 - r_s^2}} = \sqrt{\frac{8}{1 - .4277}} = 2.45$$

>summary

1 Management questions frequently involve relationships between two or more variables. Correlation analysis may be applied to study such relationships. A correct correlational hypothesis states that the variables occur together in some specified manner without implying that one causes the other.

2 Parametric correlation requires two continuous variables measured on an interval or ratio scale. The product moment correlation coefficient represents an index of the magnitude of the relationship: Its sign governs the direction and its square explains the common variance. Bivariate correlation treats X and Y variables symmetrically and is intended for use with variables that are linearly related.

Scatterplots allow the researcher to visually inspect relationship data for appropriateness of the selected statistic. The direction, magnitude, and shape of a relationship are conveyed in a plot. The shape of linear relationships is characterized by a straight line, whereas nonlinear relationships are curvilinear or parabolic or have other curvature. The assumptions of linearity and bivariate normal distribution may be checked through plots and diagnostic tests.

A correlation coefficient of any magnitude or sign, regardless of statistical significance, does not imply causation. Similarly, a coefficient is not remarkable simply because it is statistically significant. Practical significance should be considered in interpreting and reporting findings.

3 Regression analysis is used to further our insight into the relationship of Y with X. When we take the observed values of X to estimate or predict corresponding Y values, the process is called simple prediction. When more than one X variable is used, the outcome is a function of multiple predictors. Simple and multiple predictions are made with regression analysis.

A straight line is fundamentally the best way to model the relationship between two continuous variables. The method of least squares allows us to find a regression line, or line of best fit, that minimizes errors in drawing the line. It uses the criterion of minimizing the total squared errors of estimate. Point predictions made from well-fitted data are subject to error. Prediction and confidence bands may be used to find a range of probable values for Y based on the chosen predictor. The bands are shaped in such a way that predictors farther from the mean have larger bandwidths.

4 We test regression models for linearity and to discover whether the equation is effective in fitting the data. An important test in bivariate linear regression is whether the slope is equal to zero (i.e., whether the predictor variable X is a significant influence on the criterion variable Y). In bivariate regression, t-tests and F tests of the regression produce the same result since t^2 is equal to F.

5 Often the assumptions or the required measurement level for parametric techniques cannot be met. Nonparametric measures of association offer alternatives. Nominal measures of association are used to assess the strength of relationships in cross-classification tables. They are often used in conjunction with chi-square or may be based on the proportional reduction in error (PRE) approach.

Phi ranges from 0 to +1.0 and attempts to correct chi-square proportionately to N. Phi is best employed with 2×2 tables. Cramer's V is a modification of phi for larger tables and has a range up to 1.0 for tables of any configuration. Lambda, a PRE statistic, is based on how well the frequencies of one nominal variable offer predictive evidence about the frequencies of another. Goodman and Kruskal's tau uses table marginals to reduce prediction errors.

Measures for ordinal data include gamma, Kendall's tau b and tau c, Somers's d, and Spearman's rho. All but Spearman's rank-order correlation are based on the concept of concordant and discordant pairs. None of these statistics require the assumption of a bivariate normal distribution, yet by incorporating order, most produce a range from −1 to +1.

>**key**terms

>**discussion**questions

Terms in Review

1 Distinguish between the following:

  a Regression coefficient and correlation coefficient.

  b $r = 0$ and $\rho = 0$.

  c The test of the true slope, the test of the intercept, and $r^2 = 0$.

  d r^2 and r.

  e A slope of 0.

  f F and t^2.

2 Describe the relationship between the two variables in the four plots.

(a)

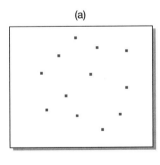

(b)

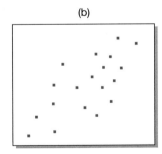

(c)

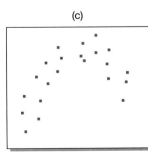

(d)

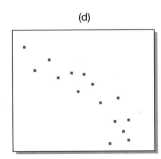

Making Research Decisions

3 A polling organization collected data on a sample of 60 registered voters regarding a tax on the market value of equity transactions as one remedy for the budget deficit.

	Education		
Opinion about Market Tax	**High School**	**College Grad.**	**MBA**
Favorable	15	5	0
Undecided	10	8	2
Unfavorable	0	2	18

 a Compute gamma for the table.

 b Compute tau b or tau c for the same data.

 c What accounts for the differences?

 d Decide which is more suitable for these data.

4 Using the table data in question 3, compute Somers's d symmetric and then use opinion as the dependent variable. Decide which approach is best for reporting the decision.

5 A research team conducted a study of soft-drink preferences among residents in a test market prior to an advertising campaign for a new cola product. Of the participants, 130 are teenagers and 130 are adults. The researchers secured the following results:

	Cola	Noncola
Teenagers	50	80
Adults	90	40

Calculate an appropriate measure of association, and decide how to present the results. How might this information affect the advertising strategy?

Behing the Scenes

6 What would the numbers of "police calls resulting in arrest" for Gladeside and Oceanside need to change to in order to support the conclusion of "disparate impact."

From Concept to Practice

7 Using the following data,

X	Y
3	6
6	10
9	15
12	24
15	21
18	20

 a Create a scatterplot.

 b Find the least-squares line.

 c Plot the line on the diagram.

 d Predict: Y if X is 10.

    Y if X is 17.

8 A home pregnancy test claims to be 97 percent accurate when consumers obtain a positive result. To what extent are the variables of "actual clinical condition" and "test readings" related?

 a Compute phi, Cramer's V, and the contingency coefficient for the table below. What can you say about the strength of the relationship between the two variables?

 b Compute lambda for these data. What does this statistic tell you?

Actual Clinical Condition * Test Readings of In-Vitro Diagnostic Cross-Tabulation

Count Actual clinical condition	Test Readings of In-Vitro Diagnostic		Total
	Positive	**Negative**	
Pregnant	451 accurate	36 inaccurate	487
Not pregnant	15 inaccurate	183 accurate	198
Total	466	219	685

9 Fill in the missing blocks for the ANOVA summary table on net profits and market value used with regression analysis.

ANOVA Summary Table

	d.f.	Sum of Squares	Mean Square	F
Regression	1	11,116,995.47		
Error			116,104.63	
Total	9	12,045,832.50		

 a What does the F tell you? (alpha $= .05$)

 b What is the t value? Explain its meaning.

Forbes 500 Random Subsample ($, millions)					
Assets	Sales	Market Value	Net Profit	Cash Flow	Number of Employees (thousands)
1,034.00	1,510.00	697.00	82.60	126.50	16.60
956.00	785.00	1,271.00	89.00	191.20	5.00
1,890.00	2,533.00	1,783.00	176.00	267.00	44.00
1,133.00	532.00	752.00	82.30	137.10	2.10
11,682.00	3,790.00	4,149.00	413.50	806.80	11.90
6,080.00	635.00	291.00	18.10	35.20	3.70
31,044.00	3,296.00	2,705.00	337.30	425.50	20.10
5,878.00	3,204.00	2,100.00	145.80	380.00	10.80
1,721.00	981.00	1,573.00	172.60	326.60	1.90
2,135.00	2,268.00	2,634.00	247.20	355.50	21.20

11 Secure Spearman rank-order correlations for the largest Pearson coefficient in the matrix from question 10. Explain the differences between the two findings.

12 Using the matrix data in question 10, select a pair of variables and run a simple regression. Then investigate the appropriateness of the model for the data using diagnostic tools for evaluating assumptions.

13 For the data below,

X	Y
25	5
19	7
17	12
14	23
12	20
9	25
8	26
7	28
3	20

a Calculate the correlation between X and Y.

b Interpret the sign of the correlation.

c Interpret the square of the correlation.

d Plot the least-squares line.

e Test for a linear relationship:

  (1) $\beta_1 = 0$.

  (2) $r = 0$.

  (3) An F test.

>**www**exercise

The University of Michigan's Institute of Social Research is one of the largest education-based survey facilities in the country. Visit its site and read the report on the *National Survey of American Life: Coping with Stress in the 21st Century* (**http://www.rcgd.isr.umich.edu/prba/survey.html**). Click on "questionnaires" and then on two segments of the sample (e.g., "adolescents," "adults"). What's the association of the two groups on any one question?

>cases*

Mastering Teacher Leadership   Overdue Bills

NCRCC: Teeing Up and New Strategic Direction

* All cases, both written and video, are on the text DVD. Check the DVD Index to determine whether a case has data, the research instrument, or other supplementary material.

>chapter 22

Multivariate Analysis: An Overview

>learningobjectives

After reading this chapter, you should understand . . .

1 How to classify and select multivariate techniques.

2 That multiple regression predicts a metric dependent variable from a set of metric independent variables.

3 That discriminant analysis classifies people or objects into categorical groups using several metric predictors.

4 How multivariate analysis of variance assesses the relationship between two or more metric dependent variables and independent classificatory variables.

5 How structural equation modeling explains causality among constructs that cannot be directly measured.

6 How conjoint analysis assists researchers to discover most importance attributes and the levels of desirable features.

7 How principal components analysis extracts uncorrelated factors from an initial set of variables and (exploratory) factor analysis reduces the number of variables to discover the underlying constructs.

8 The use of cluster analysis techniques for grouping similar objects or people.

9 How perceptions of products or services are revealed numerically and geometrically by multidimensional scaling.

We join the group from Visionary Insights at a local restaurant. Jason, Sara, and their new interns are sharing a very, very late lunch, having spent three days on exploratory data analysis for the Center City Performing Arts Association. They are discussing problems with one particular analysis as Henry Parker, a researcher with a competitive firm, approaches the table. Researchers are generally a collaborative professional group. Their understanding of sophisticated data analysis creates a common bond. As in any profession, however, there are those who don't meet the standards and who other professional researchers merely tolerate.

Parker drapes his arm across Sara's shoulder, before bending in close to breathe his greeting in her face. "Saw some of my favorite people from Visionary Insights and just had to stop by for a 'friendly hello.'"

Jason takes pity on Sara, drawing Parker's attention as Sara tries to shrug off his arm. "How's business, Henry?" Jason inquires, although he already knew Parker's firm had lost a proposed project to Visionary just that morning. He stands and extends his hand for a handclasp he really doesn't want, with a quick smile thrown Sara's way that says, "You owe me!"

Parker clasps Jason's extended hand and puts a lock on his right bicep as well. Now it is Sara's turn to commiserate the invading of Jason's personal space.

It was Parker's annoying practice, while holding you in his firm grip, to make amazingly improbable comparisons between people, groups, institutions, products, services, practices—anything and everything—by declaring the likes of "All things being equal, Mercury would seem to be a more congenial planet on which life might emerge than Earth." Meaning, if you allowed for its atmosphere being nonexistent, and its temperature being 1,380 degrees Fahrenheit, there was presumably something about its gravitational fields or length of day that fitted Parker's preferred cosmology. You cannot argue against that kind of pseudoscientific blather.

Now Parker is lecturing Jason about a project he was doing with the governing board of the public housing authority. "The best tenants are the Pantamarians," he declares. "All things being equal, they are the most law-abiding and hard-working tenants. These folks are from Pantamarie, all English-speakers from a little island in the Caribbean. Never heard of Pantamarie before I started this project, but, I tell you, they are the most law-abiding tenants . . ."

". . . all things being equal," echoes Jason ironically, as the very same words slip from Parker's mouth. Sara sees signs of Jason's increasing impatience, as he struggles to free himself from Parker's grasp.

"Do be more specific," urges Jason, yanking his arm from Parker's grasp none too gently. "Are you telling me that the Pantamarians have the lowest crime rate in the housing authority? You must have data—your project's funded by federal funds, right? So you must have data."

"Well," says Parker, evasively, "you have got to allow for these Pantamarians having very large families. And they did not get much schooling, back home."

"So what is not equal is their family size and education. What else is not equal?" Jason leans forward into Parker's space and stares icily into Parker's eyes.

Unbeknownst to Parker, he is saved from Jason's impending verbal attack by the arrival of the waiter carrying a loaded lunch tray.

"Well, I see lunch has arrived . . . nice to see you all . . . enjoy," smiles Parker as he turns and walks away.

"Parker wouldn't know how to prove his Pantamarian theory if Sammye or David ran the numbers for him," shares Jason to the table at large. "You can be sure that the authority staff has been keeping really good records—family size, education, age—the Federal Housing and Urban Development people won't give Parker's firm a penny without it. But I'm equally sure he hasn't accessed those data.

"So, David, what would you do to prove or disprove Parker's theory?"

David pauses in lifting the fork to his lips. "I'd set crime rate as the dependent variable and country of origin as the independent variable, and apply *analysis of covariance,* correcting for the effects of education, age, household size, whatever."

"Or," joins Sammye, "maybe he could do a *factor analysis* that includes Caribbean country of origin, the population count for 2005, GDP per capita, teacher ratios, female life expectancy, births and deaths, the infant mortality rate per 1,000 of the population, radios and phones per 100 people, hospital beds, age, and family size. Then he'd know which variables are worth studying."

"Better yet," contributes Sara, joining into the spirit of the exercise Jason has started for his interns, "Parker could take the results of Sammye's factor analysis and run a *multiple regression* with crime rate as the dependent variable and the new factors that we output from the factor analysis as predictors."

"What about this," Jason contributes with a grin. "Parker could take his famous Pantamarians and the same data for their neighboring countrymen and see if he could correctly classify them with a *discriminant analysis.* Voilà! His Pantamarians could be proved to be the most law-abiding tenants," Jason pauses for effect. "Or not—all things being equal!"

Jason grins at Sara. "I completely forgot to congratulate him on landing the public authority contract and losing the more lucrative one—to us!"

After pausing for effect, Sara asks, "Now, Sammye, what was that you were saying about your *multidimensional scaling* problem before Parker interrupted?"

> Introduction

In recent years, multivariate statistical tools have been applied with increasing frequency to research problems. This recognizes that many problems we encounter are more complex than the problems bivariate models can explain. Simultaneously, computer programs have taken advantage of the complex mathematics needed to manage multiple-variable relationships. Today, computers with fast processing speeds and versatile software bring these powerful techniques to researchers.

Throughout marketing, more and more problems are being addressed by considering multiple independent and/or multiple dependent variables. Sales managers base forecasts on various product history variables; marketing researchers consider the complex set of buyer preferences and preferred product options; and analysts classify levels of risk based on a set of predictors.

multivariate analysis
statistical techniques that focus upon and bring out in bold relief the structure of simultaneous relationships among three or more phenomena.

One author defines **multivariate analysis** as "those statistical techniques which focus upon, and bring out in bold relief, the structure of simultaneous relationships among three or more phenomena."[1] Our overview of multivariate analysis seeks to illustrate the meaning of this definition while building on your understanding of bivariate statistics from the last few chapters. Several common multivariate techniques and examples will be discussed.

Because a complete treatment of this subject requires a thorough consideration of the mathematics, assumptions, and diagnostic tools appropriate for each technique, our coverage is necessarily limited. Readers desiring greater detail are referred to the suggested readings for this chapter.

> Selecting a Multivariate Technique

Multivariate techniques may be classified as **dependency** and **interdependency techniques**. Selecting an appropriate technique starts with an understanding of this distinction. If criterion and predictor variables exist in the research question, then we will have an assumption of dependence. Multiple regression, multivariate analysis of variance (MANOVA), and discriminant analysis are techniques where criterion or dependent variables and predictor or independent variables are present. Alternatively, if the variables are interrelated without designating some as dependent and others independent, then interdependence of the variables is assumed. Factor analysis, cluster analysis, and multidimensional scaling are examples of interdependency techniques.

Exhibit 22-1 provides a diagram to guide in the selection of techniques. Let's take an example to show how you might make a decision. Every other year since 1978, the Roper organization has tracked public opinion toward business by providing a list of items that are said to be the responsibility of business. The respondents are asked whether business fulfills these responsibilities "fully, fairly well, not too well, or not at all well." The following issues make up the list:[2]

- Developing new products and services.
- Producing good-quality products and services.
- Making products that are safe to use.
- Hiring minorities.
- Providing jobs for people.
- Being good citizens of the communities in which they operate.
- Paying good salaries and benefits to employees.
- Charging reasonable prices for goods and services.
- Keeping profits at reasonable levels.
- Advertising honestly.
- Paying their fair share.
- Cleaning up their own air and water pollution.

You have access to data on these items and wish to know if they could be reduced to a smaller set of variables that would account for most of the variation among respondents. In response to the first question in Exhibit 22-1, you correctly determine there are no dependent variables in the data set. You then check to see if the variables are **metric** or **nonmetric measures**. In the exhibit, *metric* refers to ratio and interval measurements, and *nonmetric* refers to data that are nominal and ordinal. Based on the measurement scale, which appears to have equal intervals, and preliminary findings that show a linear relationship between several variables, you decide the data are metric. This decision leads you to three options: multidimensional scaling, cluster analysis, or factor analysis. *Multidimensional scaling* develops a perceptual map of the locations of some objects relative to others. This map specifies how the objects differ. *Cluster analysis* identifies homogeneous subgroups or clusters. *Factor analysis* looks for patterns among the variables to discover if an underlying combination of the original variables (a factor) can summarize the original set. Based on your research objective, you select factor analysis.

Suppose you are interested in predicting family food expenditures from family income, family size, and whether the family's location is rural or urban. Returning to Exhibit 22-1, you conclude there is a single dependent variable, family food expenditures. You decide this variable is metric since dollars are measured on a ratio scale. The independent variables, income and family size, also meet the criteria for metric data. However, you are not sure about the location variable since it appears to be a dichotomous nominal variable. According to the exhibit, your choices are automatic interaction detection (AID), multiple classification analysis (MCA), and multiple regression. You recall from Chapter 19 that AID was designed to locate the most important predictors in a set of

dependency techniques those techniques where criterion or dependent variables and predictor or independent variables are present.

interdependency techniques techniques where criterion or dependent variables and predictor or independent variables are not present.

metric measures statistical techniques using interval and ratio measures.

nonmetric measures statistical techniques using ordinal and nominal measures.

>**Exhibit 22-1** Selecting from the Most Common Multivariate Techniques

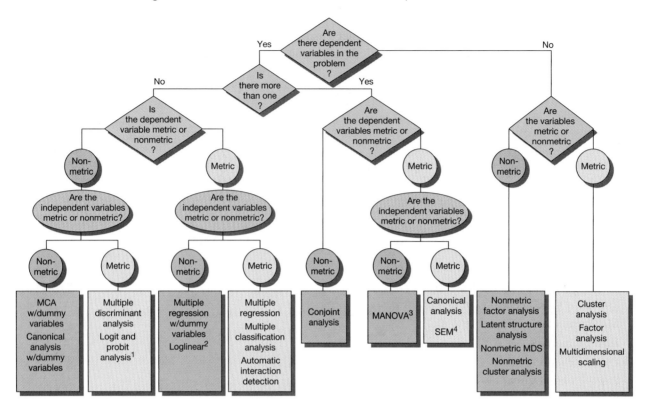

[1]The independent variable is metric only in the sense that a transformed proportion is used.
[2]The independent variable is metric only when we consider that the number of cases in the cross-tabulation cell is used to calculate the logs.
[3]Factors may be considered nonmetric independent variables in that they organize the data into groups. We do not classify MANOVA and other multivariate analysis of variance models.
[4]SEM refers to structural equation modeling for latent variables. It is a family of models appropriate for confirmatory factor analysis, path analysis, time series analysis, recursive and nonrecursive models, and covariance structure models. Because it may handle dependence and interdependence, metric and nonmetric, it is arbitrarily placed in this diagram.
Source: Partially adapted from T. C. Kinnear and J. R. Taylor, "Multivariate Methods in Marketing: A Further Attempt at Classification," *Journal of Marketing,* October 1971, p. 57; and J. F. Hair Jr., Rolph E. Anderson, Ronald L. Tatham, and Bernie J. Grablowsky, *Multivariate Data Analysis* (Tulsa, OK: Petroleum Publishing Co., 1979), pp. 10–14.

numerous independent variables and create a tree-like answer. MCA handles weak predictors (including nominal variables), correlated predictors, and nonlinear relationships. Multiple regression is the extension of bivariate regression. You believe that your data exceed the assumptions for the first two techniques and that by treating the nominal variable's values as 0 or 1, you could use it as an independent variable in a multiple regression model. You prefer this to losing information from the other two variables—a certainty if you reduce them to nonmetric data.

In the next two sections, we will extend this discussion as we illustrate dependency and interdependency techniques.

> Dependency Techniques

multiple regression
statistical tool used to develop a self-weighting estimating equation that predicts values for a dependent variable from the values of independent variables.

Multiple Regression

Multiple regression is used as a descriptive tool in three types of situations. First, it is often used to develop a self-weighting estimating equation by which to predict values for a criterion variable (DV) from the values for several predictor variables (IVs). Thus, we might try to predict company sales on the basis of new housing starts, new marriage rates, annual disposable income, and a time factor. Another prediction study might be one in which we estimate a student's academic performance in college from the variables of rank in high school class, SAT verbal scores, SAT quantitative scores, and a rating scale reflecting impressions from an interview.

Second, a descriptive application of multiple regression calls for controlling for confounding variables to better evaluate the contribution of other variables. For example, one might wish to control the brand of a product and the store in which it is bought to study the effects of price as an indicator of product quality.[3] A third use of multiple regression is to test and explain causal theories. In this approach, often referred to as **path analysis**, regression is used to describe an entire structure of linkages that have been advanced from a causal theory.[4] In addition to being a descriptive tool, multiple regression is also used as an inference tool to test hypotheses and to estimate population values.

> **path analysis** describes, through regression, an entire structure of linkages advanced by a causal theory.

Method

Multiple regression is an extension of the bivariate linear regression presented in Chapter 21. The terms defined in that chapter will not be repeated here. Although **dummy variables** (nominal variables coded 0, 1) may be used, all other variables must be interval or ratio. The generalized equation is

> **dummy variables** nominal variables converted for use in multivariate statistics.

$$Y = \beta_0 + \beta_1 X_1 + \beta_2 X_2 + \cdots + \beta_n X_n + \varepsilon$$

where

$\beta_0 =$ a constant, the value of Y when all X values are zero

$\beta_i =$ the slope of the regression surface (the β represents the regression coefficient associated with each X_i).

$\varepsilon \ =$ an error term, normally distributed about a mean of 0 (for purposes of computation, the ε is assumed to be 0).

The regression coefficients are stated either in raw score units (the actual X values) or as **standardized coefficients** (X values restated in terms of their standard scores). In either case, the value of the regression coefficient states the amount that Y varies with each unit change of the associated X variable when the effects of all other X variables are being held constant. When the regression coefficients are standardized, they are called **beta weights** (β), and their values indicate the relative importance of the associated X values, particularly when the predictors are unrelated. For example, in an equation where $\beta_1 = .60$ and $\beta_2 = .20$, one concludes that X_1 has three times the influence on Y as does X_2.

> **standardized coefficients** regression coefficients in standardized form (mean = 0) used to determine the comparative impact of variables that come from different scales.

> **beta weights** standardized regression coefficients where the size of the number reflects the level of influence X exerts on Y.

Example

In a Snapshot later in this chapter, we describe an e-business that uses multivariate approaches to understand its target market in the global "hybrid-mail" business. SuperLetter's basic service enables users to create a document on any PC and send it in a secure, encrypted mode over the Internet to a distant international terminal near the addressee, where it will be printed, processed, and delivered via a local postal service. Spread like a "fishnet" over the world's major commercial markets, the network connects corresponding parties, linking the world's "wired" with its "nonwired." The British Armed Forces and some U.S. military organizations have used it to speed correspondence between families and service members in Afghanistan and Iraq.

We use multiple regression in this example to evaluate the *key drivers* of customer usage for hybrid mail. Among the available independent or predictor variables, we expect some to better explain or predict the dependent or criterion variable than other (thus they are *key* to our understanding). The independent variables are customer perceptions of (1) cost/speed valuation, (2) security (limits on changing, editing, or forwarding a document and document privacy), (3) reliability, (4) receiver technology (hard copy for receivers with no e-mail or fax access), and (5) impact/emotional value (reducing e-mail spam clutter and official/important appearance). We have chosen the first three variables, all measured on 5-point scales, for this equation:

Y = customer usage

X_1 = cost/speed valuation

X_2 = security

X_3 = reliability

SPSS computed the model and the regression coefficients. Most statistical packages provide various methods for selecting variables for the equation. The equation can be built with all variables or specific combinations, or you can select a method that sequentially adds or removes variables (forward selection, backward elimination, and stepwise selection). **Forward selection** starts with the constant and adds variables that result in the largest R^2 increase. **Backward elimination** begins with a model containing all independent variables and removes the variable that changes R^2 the least. **Stepwise selection**, the most popular method, combines forward and backward sequential approaches. The independent variable that contributes the most to explaining the dependent variable is added first. Subsequent variables are included based on their incremental contribution over the first variable and on whether they meet the criterion for entering the equation (e.g., a significance level of .01). Variables may be removed at each step if they meet the removal criterion, which is a larger significance level than that for entry.

The standard elements of a stepwise output are shown in Exhibit 22-2. In the upper portion of the exhibit there are three models. In model 1, cost/speed is the first variable to enter the equation. This model consists of the constant and the variable cost/speed. Model 2 adds the security variable to cost/speed. Model 3 consists of all three independent variables. In the summary statistics for model 1, you see that cost/speed explains 77 percent of customer usage (see the "R^2" column). This is increased by 8 percent in model 2 when security is added (see "R^2 Change" column). When reliability is added in model 3, accounting for only 2 percent, 87 percent of customer usage is explained.

The other reported statistics have the following interpretations.

1. Adjusted R^2 for model 3 = .871. R^2 is adjusted to reflect the model's goodness of fit for the population. The net effect of this adjustment is to reduce the R^2 from .873 to .871, thereby making it comparable to other R^2s from equations with a different number of independent variables.

2. Standard error of model 3 = .4937. This is the standard deviation of actual values of Y about the estimated Y values.

3. Analysis of variance measures whether or not the equation represents a set of regression coefficients that, in total, are statistically significant from zero. The critical value for F is found in Appendix D (Exhibit D-8), with degrees of freedom for the numerator equaling k, the number of independent variables, and for the denominator, $n - k - 1$, where n for model 3 is 183 observations. Thus, d.f. = (3, 179). The equation is statistically significant at less than the .05 level of significance (see the column labeled "Sig. F Change").

4. Regression coefficients for all three models are shown in the lower table of Exhibit 22-2. The column headed "B" shows the unstandardized regression coefficients for the equation. The equation may now be constructed as

$$Y = -.093 + .448X_1 + .315X_2 + 254X_3$$

5. The column headed "Beta" gives the regression coefficients expressed in standardized form. When these are used, the regression Y intercept is zero. Standardized coefficients are useful when the variables are measured on different scales. The beta

---

forward selection sequentially adds the variable to a regression model that results in the largest R^2 increase.

backward elimination sequentially removes the variable from a regression model that changes R^2 the least.

stepwise selection a method for sequentially adding or removing variables from a regression model to optimize R^2.

>**Exhibit 22-2** Multiple Regression Analysis of Hybrid-Mail Customer Usage, Cost/Speed Valuation, Security, and Reliability

Model Summary

Model	R	R^2	Adjusted R^2	Std. Error of the Estimate	Change Statistics				
					R^2 Change	F Change	d.f.1	d.f.2	Sig. F Change
1	.879	.772	.771	.6589	.772	612.696	1	181	.000
2	.925	.855	.854	.5263	.083	103.677	2	180	.000
3	.935	.873	.871	.4937	.018	25.597	3	179	.000

1 Predictors: (constant), cost/speed.
2 Predictors: (constant), cost/speed, security.
3 Predictors: (constant), cost/speed, security, reliability.

Coefficients

Model		Unstandardized Coefficients		Standardized Coefficients	t	Sig.	Collinearity Statistics
		B	Std. Error	Beta			VIF
1	(Constant)	.579	.151		3.834	.000	
	Cost/speed	.857	.035	.879	24.753	.000	1.000
2	(Constant)	9.501E-02	.130		.733	.464	
	Cost/speed	.537	.042	.551	12.842	.000	2.289
	Security	.428	.042	.437	10.182	.000	2.289
3	(Constant)	−9.326E-02	.127		−.734	.464	
	Cost/speed	.448	.043	.460	10.428	.000	2.748
	Security	.315	.045	.321	6.948	.000	3.025
	Reliability	.254	.050	.236	5.059	.000	3.067

Dependent variable: Customer usage.

coefficients also show the relative contribution of the three independent variables to the explanatory power of this equation. The cost/speed valuation variable explains more than either of the other two variables.

6. Standard error is a measure of the sampling variability of each regression coefficient.

7. The column headed "t" measures the statistical significance of each of the regression coefficients.

Again compare these to the table of t values in Appendix Exhibit D-2, using degrees of freedom for one independent variable. All three regression coefficients are judged to be significantly different from zero. Therefore, the regression equation shows the relationship between the dependent variable, customer usage of hybrid mail, and three independent variables: cost/speed, security, and reliability. The regression coefficients are both individually and jointly statistically significant. The independent variable cost/speed influences customer usage the most, followed by security and then reliability.

Collinearity, where two independent variables are highly correlated—or **multicollinearity**, where more than two independent variables are highly correlated—can have damaging effects on multiple regression. When this condition exists, the estimated regression coefficients can fluctuate widely from sample to sample, making it risky to interpret the coefficients as an indicator of the relative importance of predictor variables. Just how high can acceptable correlations be between independent variables? There is no definitive

collinearity when two independent variables are highly correlated.

multicollinearity when more than two independent variables are highly correlated.

NCRCC: Teeing Up a New Strategic Direction

NCR Country Club (NCRCC) has undergone a dramatic transformation within the last three years with the construction of a multimillion-dollar clubhouse and dining facility, but the changes have been built on the long-standing tradition of fine golf and dining. Started in 1954 as an employee benefit of the National Cash Register Co. but now an open-membership club, this country club located near Dayton, Ohio, hosts two 18-hole golf courses. The NCRCC South course, a par-71 championship course of 6,824 yards of heavily wooded rolling countryside, has played host to the PGA Championship (1996), the U.S. Open (1986), and the U.S. Mid-Amateur (1998) and is consistently ranked by *Golf Digest* as one of the top 100 courses in the United States.

When its aging membership started to decrease and a one-year membership referral drive didn't dramatically reverse the trend, NCRCC turned to the McMahon Group, a research and strategic golf-course management specialist, for insight and direction. Through an extensive two-stage research design employing six focus groups of 10 to 15 people each, followed by 886 membership surveys, McMahon's research helped NCRCC design a new strategic direction. Sophisticated modeling and analysis led to new facilities for swimming and fitness that turned this proud golf and dining organization into a full-service club for 2,000 with amenities to serve its new target member (the under-46, golf-oriented household, with one or more children under 21 still living at home).

www.mcmahongroup.com; www.ncrcountryclub.com

> **We discuss the correlation matrix, which displays multiple combinations of two variable relationships, in Chapter 21.**

answer, but correlations at a .80 or greater level should be dealt with in one of two ways: (1) Choose one of the variables and delete the other, or (2) create a new variable that is a composite of the highly intercorrelated variables and use this new variable in place of its components. Making this decision with a correlation matrix alone is not always advisable. In the example just presented, Exhibit 22-2 contains a column labeled "Collinearity Statistics" that shows a *variable inflation factor (VIF)* index. This is a measure of the effect of the other independent variables on a regression coefficient. Large values, usually 10.0 or more, suggest collinearity or multicollinearity. With the three predictors in the hybrid-mail example, multicollinearity is not a problem.

Another difficulty with regression occurs when researchers fail to evaluate the equation with data beyond those used originally to calculate it. A practical solution is to set aside a portion of the data (from a fourth to a third) and evaluate the estimating equation. This is called a **holdout sample**. One uses the equation with the holdout data to calculate a new R^2 and compare it to the original R^2 to see how well the equation predicts beyond its data set.

holdout sample the portion of the sample excluded for later validity testing when the estimating equation is first computed.

Discriminant Analysis

Researchers often wish to classify people or objects into two or more groups. One might need to classify persons as either buyers or nonbuyers, good or bad credit risks, or to classify superior, average, or poor products in some market. The objective is to establish a procedure to find the predictors that best classify subjects. Discriminant analysis is frequently used in market segmentation research.

Method

discriminant analysis a technique using two or more independent interval or ratio variables to classify the observations in the categories of a nominal dependent variable.

Discriminant analysis joins a nominally scaled criterion or dependent variable with one or more independent variables that are interval- or ratio-scaled. Once the discriminant equation is found, it can be used to predict the classification of a new observation. This is done by calculating a linear function of the form

$$D_i = d_0 + d_1 X_1 + d_2 X_2 + \cdots + d_p X_p$$

where

D_i is the score on discriminant function i.

The d_is are weighting coefficients; d_0 is a constant.

The Xs are the values of the discriminating variables used in the analysis.

A single discriminant equation is required if the categorization calls for two groups. If three groups are involved in the classification, it requires two discriminant equations. If more categories are called for in the dependent variable, one needs $N - 1$ discriminant functions.

While the most common use for discriminant analysis is to classify persons or objects into various groups, it can also be used to analyze known groups to determine the relative influence of specific factors for deciding into which group various cases fall. Assume we have MindWriter service ratings that enable us to classify postpurchase service as successful or unsuccessful on performance. We might also be able to secure test results on three measures: motivation for working with customers (X_1), technical expertise (X_2), and accessibility to repair status information (X_3). Suppose the discriminant equation is

$$D = .06X_1 + .45X_2 + .30X_3$$

Since discriminant analysis uses standardized values for the discriminant variables, we conclude from the coefficients that motivation for working with customers is less important than the other two in classifying postpurchase service.[5]

Example

An illustration of the method takes us back to the problem in the last chapter where KDL, a media firm, is hiring MBAs for its account executives program. Over the years the firm has had indifferent success with the selection process. You are asked to develop a procedure to improve this. It appears that discriminant analysis is a perfect technique. You begin by gathering data on 30 MBAs who have been hired in recent years. Fifteen of these have been successful employees, while the other 15 have been unsatisfactory. The files provide the following information that can be used to conduct the analysis:

X_1 = years of prior work experience

X_2 = GPA in graduate program

X_3 = employment test scores

An algorithm determines how well these three independent variables will correctly classify those who are judged successful from those judged unsuccessful. The classification results are shown in Exhibit 22-3. This indicates that 25 of the 30 ($30 - 3 - 2 = 25$) cases have been correctly classified using these three variables.

The standardized and unstandardized discriminant function coefficients are shown in part B of Exhibit 22-3. These results indicate that X_3 (the employment test) has the greatest discriminating power. Several significance tests also may be computed. One, Wilk's lambda, has a chi-square transformation for testing the significance of the discriminant function. If computed for this example, it indicates that the equation is statistically significant at the $\alpha = .0004$ level. Using the discriminant equation,

$$D = .659X_1 + .580X_2 + .975X_3$$

you can now predict whether future candidates are likely to be successful account executives.

MANOVA

Multivariate analysis of variance, or **MANOVA**, is a commonly used multivariate technique. MANOVA assesses the relationship between two or more dependent variables and

multivariate analysis of variance (MANOVA) assesses the relationship between two or more dependent variables and classificatory variables or factors.

>**Exhibit 22-3** Discriminant Analysis Classification Results at KDL Media

A.

Actual Group		Number of Cases	Predicted Success 0	Predicted Success 1
Unsuccessful	0	15	13 86.70%	2 13.30%
Successful	1	15	3 20.00%	12 80.00%

Note: Percent of "grouped" cases correctly classified: 83.33%.

B.

	Unstandardized	Standardized
X_1	.36084	.65927
X_2	2.61192	.57958
X_3	.53028	.97505
constant	12.89685	

classificatory variables or factors. In marketing research, MANOVA can be used to test differences among samples of employees, customers, manufactured products, production parts, and so forth.

Method

MANOVA is similar to the univariate ANOVA described earlier, with the added ability to handle several dependent variables. If ANOVA is applied consecutively to a set of interrelated dependent variables, erroneous conclusions may result. MANOVA can correct this by simultaneously testing all the variables and their interrelationships. MANOVA uses special matrices [sums-of-squares and cross-products (SSCP) matrices] to test for differences among groups. The variance between groups is determined by partitioning the total SSCP matrix and testing for significance. The F ratio, generalized to a ratio of the within-group variance and total-group variance matrices, tests for equality among treatment groups.

> 6 6 Research is formalized curiosity. It is poking and prying with a purpose. 9 9
>
> *Zora Neale Hurston*
> *Anthropologist and Author*

centroid term used for the multivariate mean scores in MANOVA

MANOVA examines similarities and differences among the multivariate mean scores of several populations. The null hypothesis for MANOVA is that all of the **centroids** (multivariate means) are equal, $H_0: \mu_1 = \mu_2 = \mu_3 = \cdots \mu_n$. The alternative hypothesis is that the vectors of centroids are unequal, $H_A: \mu_1 \neq \mu_2 \neq \mu_3 \neq \cdots \mu_n$. Exhibit 22-4 shows graphically three populations whose centroids are unequal, allowing the researcher to reject the null hypothesis. When the null hypothesis is rejected, additional tests are done to understand the results in detail. Several alternatives may be considered:

1. Univariate F tests can be run on the dependent variables.

2. Simultaneous confidence intervals can be produced for each variable.

3. Stepdown analysis, like stepwise regression, can be run by computing F values successively. Each value is computed after the effects of the previous dependent variable are eliminated.

4. Multiple discriminant analysis can be used on the SSCP matrices. This aids in the discovery of which variables contribute to the MANOVA's significance.[6]

>**Exhibit 22-4** MANOVA Techniques Show These Three Centroids to be Unequal in the CalAudio Study

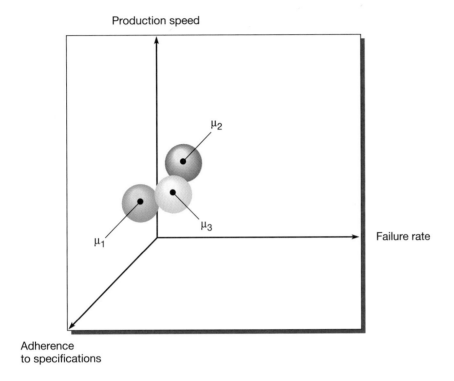

Before using MANOVA to test for significant differences, you must first determine that MANOVA is appropriate, that is, that the assumptions for its use are met.

Example

To illustrate, let's look at CalAudio, a firm that manufactures MP3 players. The marketing manager is concerned about brand loyalty and fears that the quality of the manufactured players may be affecting customers' repurchase decisions. The closest competitor's product appears to have fewer repair issues and higher satisfaction ratings. Two measures are used to assess quality in this example: adherence to product specifications and time before failure. Measured on a 0-to-100 scale, with 100 meeting all product specifications, the specification variable is averaging approximately 90. The mean time before failure is calculated in weeks; it is approximately 159 weeks, or three years.

Management asks the industrial engineering department to devise a modified manufacturing procedure that will improve the quality measures but not change the production rate significantly. A new method is designed that includes more efficient parts handling and "burn-in" time, when MP3 players are powered up and run at high temperatures.

Engineering takes a sample of 15 MP3 players made with the old manufacturing method and 15 made with the new method. The players are

>**Exhibit 22-5** MANOVA Cell Means and Standard Deviations in CalAudio Study

VARIABLE	FACTOR	LEVEL	MEAN	STD. DEV.
FAILURE				
	METHOD	1	158.867	4.998
	METHOD	2	181.067	5.994
	For entire sample		169.967	12.524
SPECIFICATIONS				
	METHOD	1	89.800	2.077
	METHOD	2	94.800	2.178
	For entire sample		92.300	3.292
SPEED				
	METHOD	1	2.126	.061
	METHOD	2	2.599	.068
	For entire sample		2.362	.249

measured for their adherence to product specifications and are stress-tested to determine their time before failure. The stress test uses accelerated running conditions and adverse environmental conditions to simulate years of use in a short time.

Exhibit 22–5 shows the mean and standard deviation of the dependent variables (failure, specifications, and manufacturing speed) for each level of method.[7] Method 1 represents the current manufacturing process, and method 2 is the new process. The new method extended the time before failure to 181 weeks, compared to 159 weeks for the existing method. The adherence to specifications is also improved, up to 95 from 90. But the manufacturing speed is slower by approximately 30 minutes (.473 hour).

We have used diagnostics to check the assumptions of MANOVA except for equality of variance. Both levels of the manufacturing method variable produce a matrix, and the equality of these two matrices must be determined (H_0: variances are equal). Exhibit 22-6 contains homogeneity-of-variance tests for separate dependent variables and a multivariate test. The former are known as *univariate tests*. The multivariate test is a comparable version that tests the variables simultaneously to determine whether MANOVA should proceed.

The significance levels of Cochran's C and Bartlett-Box F do not allow us to reject any of the tests for the dependent variables considered separately. This means the two methods have equal variances in each dependent variable. This fulfills the univariate assumptions for homogeneity of variance. We then consider the variances and covariances simultaneously with Box's M, also found in Exhibit 22-6. Again, we are unable to reject the homogeneity-of-variance assumption regarding the matrices. This satisfies the multivariate assumptions.

When MANOVA is applied properly, the dependent variables are correlated. If the dependent variables are unrelated, there would be no necessity for a multivariate test, and we could use separate F tests for failure, specifications, and speed, much like the ANOVAs in Chapter 20. Bartlett's test of sphericity helps us decide if we should continue analyzing MANOVA results or return to separate univariate tests. In Exhibit 22-7, we will look for a determinant value that is close to 0. This implies that one or more dependent variables are a linear function of another. The determinant has a chi-square transformation that simplifies testing for statistical significance. Since the observed significance is below that set for the model ($\alpha = .05$), we are able to reject the null hypothesis and conclude there are dependencies among the failure, specifications, and speed variables.

We now move to the test of equality of means that considers the three dependent variables for the two levels of manufacturing method. This test is analogous to a t-test or an F test for multivariate data. The sums-of-squares and cross-products matrices are used.

>**Exhibit 22-6** MANOVA Homogeneity-of-Variance Tests in the CalAudio Study

```
VARIABLE          TEST                        RESULTS

FAILURE

          Cochran's C (14,2) =        .58954, P = .506 (approx.)
          Bartlett-Box F (1,2352) =   .44347, P = .506

SPECIFICATIONS

          Cochran's C (14,2) =        .52366, P = .862 (approx.)
          Bartlett-Box F (1,2352) =   .03029, P = .862

SPEED

          Cochran's C (14,2) =        .55526, P = .684 (approx.)
          Bartlett-Box F (1,2352) =   .16608, P = .684

    Multivariate Test for Homogeneity of Dispersion Matrices

          Box's M =                   6.07877
          F with (6,5680) DF =         .89446, P = .498 (approx.)
          Chi-Square with 6 DF =      5.37320, P = .497 (approx.)
```

>**Exhibit 22-7** Bartlett's Test of Sphericity in the CalAudio Study

```
    Statistics for WITHIN CELLS correlations

    Log (Determinant) =                -3.92663
    Bartlett's test of sphericity =   102.74687 with 3 D.F.
    Significance =                       .000

    F(max) criterion =                7354.80161 with (3,28) D.F.
```

Exhibit 22-8 shows three tests, including the Hotelling T^2. All the tests provided are compared to the F distribution for interpretation. Since the observed significance level is less than $\alpha = .05$ for the T^2 test, we reject the null hypothesis that said methods 1 and 2 provide equal results with respect to failure, specifications, and speed. Similar results are obtained from the Pillai trace and Wilks's statistic.

Finally, to detect where the differences lie, we can examine the results of univariate F tests in Exhibit 22-9. Since there are only two methods, the F is equivalent to t^2 for a two-sample t-test. The significance levels for these tests do not reflect that several comparisons are being made, and we should use them principally for diagnostic purposes. This is similar to problems that require the use of multiple comparison tests in univariate analysis of variance. Note, however, that there are statistically significant differences in all three dependent variables resulting from the new manufacturing method. Techniques for further analysis of MANOVA results were listed at the beginning of this section.

> **See Chapter 20's discussion of multiple comparison procedures.**

Structural Equation Modeling[8]

Since the late 1980s, marketing researchers have relied increasingly on structural equation modeling to test hypotheses about the dimensionality of, and relationships among, latent

>**Exhibit 22-8** Multivariate Tests of Significance in the CalAudio Study

```
Multivariate Tests of Significance (S = 1, M = 1/2, N = 12)

Test Name        Value       Exact F    Hypoth. DF   Error DF   Sig. of F

Hotelling      51.33492    444.90268       3.00        26.00       .000
Pillai           .98089    444.90268       3.00        26.00       .000
Wilks            .01911    444.90268       3.00        26.00       .000
```

Note: F statistics are exact.

>**Exhibit 22-9** Univariate Tests of Significance in the CalAudio Study

```
Univariate F Tests with (1,28) D.F.

Variable   Hypoth. SS    Error SS   Hypoth. MS   Error MS          F    Sig. of F

FAILURE    3696.30000   852.66667   3696.30000   30.45238   121.37967     .000
SPECS       187.50000   126.80000    187.50000    4.52857    41.40379     .000
SPEED         1.67560      .11593      1.67560     .00414   404.68856     .000
```

Note: F statistics are exact.

structural equation modeling (SEM) uses analysis of covariance structures to explain causality among constructs.

and observed variables. **Structural equation modeling (SEM)** implies a structure for the covariances between observed variables, and accordingly it is sometimes called *covariance structure modeling.* More commonly, researchers refer to structural equation models as LISREL (linear structural relations) models—the name of the first and most widely cited SEM computer program.

SEM is a powerful alternative to other multivariate techniques, which are limited to representing only a single relationship between the dependent and independent variables. The major advantages of SEM are (1) that multiple and interrelated dependence relationships can be estimated simultaneously and (2) that it can represent unobserved concepts, or *latent variables,* in these relationships and account for measurement error in the estimation process. While the details of SEM are quite complex, well beyond the scope of this text, this section provides a broad conceptual introduction.

Method

Researchers using SEM must follow five basic steps:

1. *Model specification.* The first step in SEM is the *specification,* or formal statement, of the model's *parameters.* These parameters, constants that describe the relations between variables, are specified as either *fixed* or *free.* Fixed parameters have values set by the researcher, and are not estimated from the data. For example, if there is no hypothesized relationship between variables, the parameter would be fixed at zero. When there is a hypothesized, but unknown, relation between the variables, the parameters are set free to be estimated from the data. Researchers must be careful to consider all the important predictive variables to avoid **specification error**, a bias that overestimates the importance of the variables included in the model.

specification error an overestimation of the importance of the variables included in a structural model.

2. *Estimation.* After the model has been specified, the researcher must obtain estimates of the free parameters from the observed data. This is often accomplished using an *iterative method,* such as *maximum likelihood estimation (MLE).*

3. *Evaluation of fit.* Following convergence, the researcher must evaluate the goodness-of-fit criteria. *Goodness-of-fit tests* are used to determine whether the model should or should not be rejected. If the model is not rejected, the researcher will continue the analy-

sis and interpret the path coefficients in the model. Most, if not all, SEM computer software programs include several different goodness-of-fit measures, each of which can be categorized as one of three types of measures.

4. *Respecification of the model.* Model respecification usually follows the estimation of a model with indications of poor fit. Sometimes, the model is compared with competing or *nested* models to find the best fit among a set of models, and then the original model is respecified to produce a better fit. Respecifying the model requires that the researcher fix parameters that were formerly free or free parameters that were formerly fixed.

5. *Interpretation and communication.* SEM hypotheses and results are most commonly presented in the form of **path diagrams,** which are graphic illustrations of the measurement and structural models. The main features of path diagrams are ellipses, rectangles, and two types of arrows. The ellipses represent latent variables. Rectangles represent observed variables, which can be indicators of latent variables in the measurement model or of independent variables in the structural model. Straight arrows are pointed at one end and indicate the direction of prediction from independent to dependent variables or from indicators to latent variables. Curved arrows are pointed at both ends and indicate correlations between variables.

> **path diagram** presents predictive and associative relationships among constructs and indicators in a structural model.

In a research report, the path diagrams should illustrate the model originally specified and estimated by the researcher; the portion of the model for which parameter estimates were significant; and a model that resulted from one or more modifications and reestimations of the original model. The researcher should also take care to include the method of estimation, the fit criteria selected, and the parameter estimates.

Example

A marketing research consultant, hired by MindWriter, investigated the relationship between customer satisfaction and service quality, as well as the degree to which customer satisfaction and service quality predict customer purchase intention. The researcher used the *competing models strategy,* and proposed three possible relations among the variables. In model 1, satisfaction was proposed as an antecedent of service quality, and only service quality had a direct effect on purchase intention. In model 2, service quality was proposed as an antecedent of satisfaction, and only satisfaction had a direct effect on purchase intention. And in model 3, service quality and satisfaction were correlated, and both had a direct effect on purchase intention.

To collect the data, the researcher added three assumedly valid batteries of questions to the company's product and service warranty card. As soon as a large enough sample was obtained, the researcher specified the parameters of the proposed models and compared the implied structure with the covariance matrix of the data using maximum likelihood estimation as the iterative process.

The researcher finds that of the three proposed models, none of them have a satisfactory goodness of fit. However, of the three, model 2 seemed the most promising in that it yielded the lowest chi-square value and the highest value for the adjusted-goodness-of-fit index. After examining the second model's residual matrices and modification index, the researcher finds that the model could achieve a better fit if relation between service quality and purchase intention were not fixed. Accordingly, the researcher respecifies the model, freeing that parameter, and the implied matrix yields an acceptable goodness of fit. The implications of the results are that good service quality leads to customer satisfaction and that both variables have a direct effect on purchase intention (see Exhibit 22-10).

The example in Exhibit 22-10 illustrates the three measurement models, one for each latent variable, relative to the full structural model. The three latent variables are satisfaction, service quality, and purchase intention, and each latent variable has three indicators. The direction of the single-pointed arrows from service quality and satisfaction to purchase intention denotes that purchase intention is a dependent variable in its relation to both service quality and satisfaction. However, while satisfaction is independent in its relation to

>**Exhibit 22-10** Measurement Models Relative to the Full Structural Equation Model

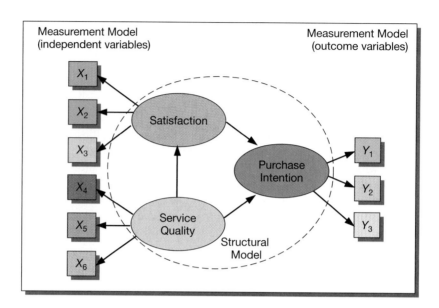

purchase intention, it is dependent in its relation to service quality. The ability to model all three relations simultaneously is one of the foremost advantages of using SEM over other multivariate techniques.

Conjoint Analysis

The most common applications for conjoint analysis are market research and product development. Consumers buying a MindWriter computer, for example, may evaluate a set of attributes to choose the product that best meets their needs. They may consider brand, speed, price, educational value, games, or capacity for work-related tasks. The attributes and their features require that the buyer make trade-offs in the final decision making.

Method

conjoint analysis measures complex decision making that requires multiattribute judgments.

Conjoint analysis typically uses input from nonmetric independent variables. Normally, we would use cross-classification tables to handle such data, but even multiway tables become quickly overwhelmed by the complexity. If there were three prices, three brands, three speeds, two levels of educational values, two categories for games, and two categories for work assistance, the model would have 216 decision levels ($3 \times 3 \times 3 \times 2 \times 2 \times 2$). A choice structure this size poses enormous difficulties for respondents and analysts. Conjoint analysis solves this problem with various optimal scaling approaches, often with loglinear models, to provide researchers with reliable answers that could not be obtained otherwise.

utility score a score in conjoint analysis used to represent each aspect of a product or service in a participant's overall preference ratings.

The objective of conjoint analysis is to secure **utility scores** (sometimes called *part-worths*) that represent the importance of each aspect of a product or service in the subjects' overall preference ratings. Utility scores are computed from the subjects' rankings or ratings of a set of cards. Each card in the deck describes one possible configuration of combined product attributes.

The first step in a conjoint study is to select the attributes most pertinent to the purchase decision. This may require an exploratory study such as a focus group, or it could be done by an expert with thorough market knowledge. The attributes selected are the independent variables, called *factors*. The possible values for an attribute are called *factor levels*. In the MindWriter example, the speed factor may have levels of 1.5 gigahertz and 3 gigahertz. Speed, like price, approaches linear measurement characteristics since consumers typically

>**snap**shot

Insider Information

PricewaterhouseCoopers (PWC), a consulting company based in New York, wanted to position itself as a telecommunications specialist. An alliance with PointCast Network (now InfoGate) was proposed in 1998 to launch a free, up-to-the-minute e-business providing specialized information to telecommunications decision makers. The result is TelecomInsider.

Why was PWC willing to foot the $50,000 in start-up capital? Through focus groups and surveys with PWC's desired target audience, telecommunications senior managers, PWC found executives were seeking convenience in accessing the information and premium content that would help them make business decisions. Analysis of multiple variables in its tracking research during October 1999 shows that of the 76,000 viewers to the TelecomInsider site, 24 percent of click-throughs from the TelecomInsider articles go to PWC's Web site. TelecomInsider is now patched into cell phones, Palm Pilots, and pagers so that users can have instant access to TelecomInsider's information.

www.pwcglobal.com; www.telecominsider.com

choose higher speeds and lower prices. Other factors like brand are measured as discrete variables.

After selecting the factors and their levels, a computer program determines the number of product descriptions necessary to estimate the utilities. SPSS procedures build a file structure for all possible combinations, generate the subset required for testing, produce the card descriptions, and analyze results. The command structure within these procedures provides for holdout sampling, simulations, and other requirements frequently used in commercial applications.[9]

Example

Watersports enthusiasts know the dangers of ultraviolet (UV) light. It fades paint and clothing; yellows surfboards, skis, and sailboards; and destroys sails. More important, UV damages the eye's retina and cornea. In the 1990s, Americans were spending $1.3 billion on 189 million pairs of sunglasses, most of which failed to provide adequate UV protection. Manufacturers of sunglasses for specialty markets have improved their products to such a degree that all of the companies in our example advertised 100 percent UV protection. Many other features influence trends in this market. For this example, we chose four factors from information contained in a review of sun protection products.[10]

Brand	Bolle	Hobbies	Oakley	Ski Optiks
Style*	A	A	A	A
	B	B	B	B
	C	C	C	C
Flotation	Yes	Yes	Yes	Yes
	No	No	No	No
Price	$100	$100	$100	$100
	$72	$72	$72	$72
	$60	$60	$60	$60
	$40	$40	$40	$40

*A = multiple color choices for frames, lenses, and temples.
B = multiple color choices for frames, lenses, and straps (no hard temples).
C = limited colors for frames, lenses, and temples.

This is a 4 (brand) $\times$ 3 (style) $\times$ 2 (flotation) $\times$ 4 (price) design, or a 96-option full-concept study. The algorithm selected 16 cards to estimate the utilities for the full concept. Combinations of interest that were not selected can be estimated later from the utilities. In addition, four holdout cards were administered to subjects but evaluated separately. The cards shown in Exhibit 22-11 were administered to a small sample ($n = 10$). Subjects were asked to order their cards from most to least desirable. The data produced the results presented in Exhibits 22-12 and 22-13.

Exhibit 22-12 contains the results of the eighth participant's preferences. This individual was an avid windsurfer, and flotation was the most important attribute for her, followed by style and price and then brand. From her preferences, we can compute her maximum utility score:

> **Exhibit 22-11** Concept Cards for Conjoint Sunglasses Study

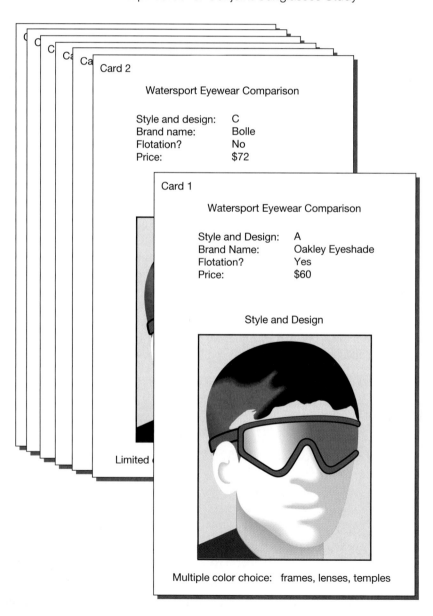

$$\text{(Style B) } 3.46 + \text{(Oakley brand) } 1.31 + \text{(flotation) } 20.75$$
$$+ \text{(price @ \$40) } 5.90 + \text{(constant)} - 8.21 = 23.21$$

If brand and price remain unchanged, a design that uses a hard temple with limited color choices (style C) and no flotation would produce a considerably lower total utility score for this respondent. For example:

$$\text{(Style C)} - 2.04 + \text{(Oakley brand) } 1.31 + \text{(no float) } 10.38$$
$$+ \text{(price @ \$40) } 5.90 + \text{(constant)} - 8.21 = 7.34$$

We could also calculate other combinations that would reveal the range of this individual's preferences. Our prediction that respondents would prefer less expensive prices did not hold for the eighth respondent, as revealed by the asterisk next to the price factor in Exhibit 22-12. She reversed herself once on price to get flotation. Other subjects also reversed once on price to trade off for other factors.

>**Exhibit 22-12** Conjoint Results for Participant 8, Sunglasses Study

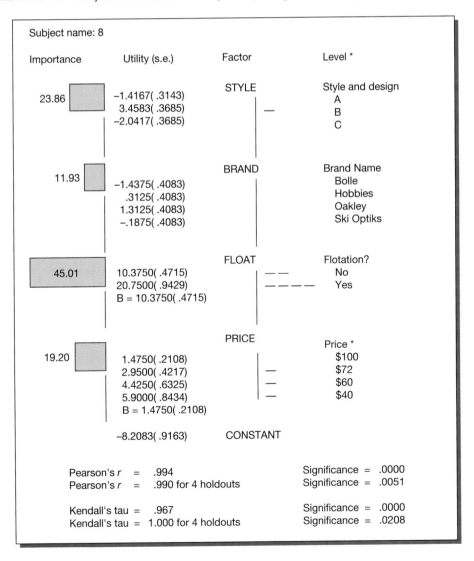

›Exhibit 22-13 Conjoint Results for Sunglasses Study Sample ($n = 10$)

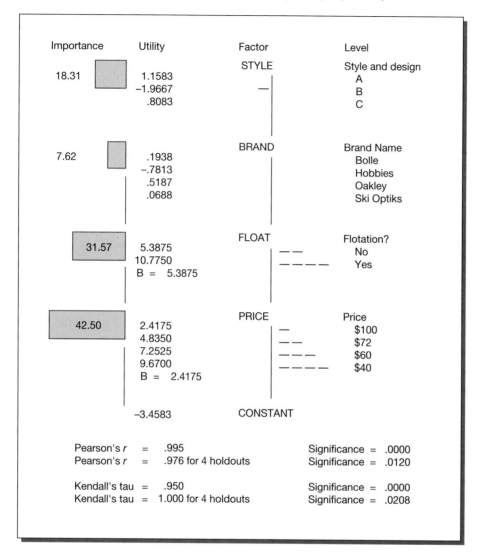

Importance	Utility		Factor	Level
18.31	1.1583 −1.9667 .8083	—	STYLE	Style and design A B C
7.62	.1938 −.7813 .5187 .0688		BRAND	Brand Name Bolle Hobbies Oakley Ski Optiks
31.57	5.3875 10.7750 B = 5.3875	— — — — —	FLOAT	Flotation? No Yes
42.50	2.4175 4.8350 7.2525 9.6700 B = 2.4175	— — — — — — — — — —	PRICE	Price $100 $72 $60 $40
	−3.4583		CONSTANT	

Pearson's r = .995   Significance = .0000
Pearson's r = .976 for 4 holdouts   Significance = .0120

Kendall's tau = .950   Significance = .0000
Kendall's tau = 1.000 for 4 holdouts   Significance = .0208

The results for the sample are presented in Exhibit 22-13. In contrast to individuals, the sample placed price first in importance, followed by flotation, style, and brand. Group utilities may be calculated just as we did for the individual. At the bottom of the printout we find Pearson's r and Kendall's tau. Each was discussed in Chapter 21. In this application, they measure the relationship between observed and estimated preferences. Since holdout samples (in conjoint, regression, discriminant, and other methods) are not used to construct the estimating equation, the coefficients for the holdouts are often a more realistic index of the model's fit.

Conjoint analysis is an effective tool used by researchers to match preferences to known characteristics of market segments and design or target a product accordingly. See your student DVD for a MindWriter example of conjoint analysis using Simalto+Plus.

The Mail as a "Super" E-Business

The world's postal system is projected to grow at a rate of 3.8 percent through 2005, according to its governing body, the Universal Postal Union (UPU). Hybrid mail will account for 6 percent, or 33 billion, of the world's 550 billion pieces of physical mail in 2005 according to the UPU. SuperLetter.com plans to be an e-business success story in this hybrid-mail sector. According to founder and successful entrepreneur Christopher Schultheiss, "We are establishing the world's first global 'hybrid mail' network enabling users to create letters or documents on their personal computers, send them like email in a secure encrypted mode over the Internet to remote printers near the recipients, where they will be printed, folded, enveloped, franked with postage and delivered in the local mail."

Using a variety of multiple-variable analytic techniques, SuperLetter specifically identified its target market as professional and financial service firms, not-for-profit organizations, educa-

tional groups, and immigrant/expatriate communities. SuperLetter will also draw from the $100 billion worldwide international courier market, like FedEx, UPS, and DHL, now experiencing strong growth rates (15 percent in international volumes relative to single-digit domestic growth). But the greatest source of messaging is likely to come from the Internet itself. Focused primarily on international correspondence, SuperLetter bridges the gap between conventional door-to-door postal services, which take from 5 to 10 days for overseas delivery, and private express/courier services, which may take from 2 to 3 days. SuperLetter's basic international service delivers a letter from desk to door in 2 to 3 days for about one-tenth of private express costs and under one-half of those costs for same-day services.

www.superletter.com

> Interdependency Techniques

Factor Analysis

Factor analysis is a general term for several specific computational techniques. All have the objective of reducing to a manageable number many variables that belong together and have overlapping measurement characteristics. The predictor-criterion relationship that was found in the dependence situation is replaced by a matrix of intercorrelations among several variables, none of which is viewed as being dependent on another. For example, one may have data on 100 employees with scores on six attitude scale items.

factor analysis a technique for discovering patterns among the variables to determine if an underlying combination of the original variables (a factor) can summarize the original set.

Method

Factor analysis begins with the construction of a new set of variables based on the relationships in the correlation matrix. While this can be done in a number of ways, the most frequently used approach is **principal components analysis**. This method transforms a set of variables into a new set of composite variables or principal components that are not correlated with each other. These linear combinations of variables, called **factors**, account for the variance in the data as a whole. The best combination makes up the first principal component and is the first factor. The second principal component is defined as the best linear combination of variables for explaining the variance *not* accounted for by the first factor. In turn, there may be a third, fourth, and *k*th component, each being the best linear combination of variables not accounted for by the previous factors.

The process continues until all the variance is accounted for, but as a practical matter it is usually stopped after a small number of factors have been extracted. The output of a principal components analysis might look like the hypothetical data shown in Exhibit 22-14.

principal components analysis one of the methods of factor analysis that transforms a set of variables into a new set of composite variables.

factors the result of transforming a set of variables into a new set of composite variables through factor analysis.

>**Exhibit 22-14** Principal Components Analysis from a Three-Variable Data Set

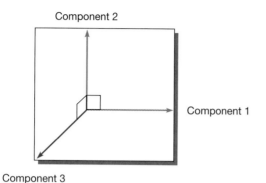

Component 2

Component 1

Component 3

Extracted Components	% of Variance Accounted For	Cumulative Variance
Component no. 1	63%	63%
Component no. 2	29	92
Component no. 3	8	100

>**Exhibit 22-15** Factor Matrices

| | A | | | B | |
| Variable | Unrotated Factors | | | Rotated Factors | |
	I	II	h^2	I	II
A	0.70	−.40	0.65	0.79	0.15
B	0.60	−.50	0.61	0.75	0.03
C	0.60	−.35	0.48	0.68	0.10
D	0.50	0.50	0.50	0.06	0.70
E	0.60	0.50	0.61	0.13	0.77
F	0.60	0.60	0.72	0.07	0.85
Eigenvalue	2.18	1.39			
Percent of variance	36.3	23.2			
Cumulative percent	36.3	59.5			

loadings the correlation coefficients that estimate the strength of the variables composing the factor.

eigenvalue the proportion of total variance in all the variables that is accounted for by a factor.

communality the estimate of the variance in each variable that is explained by the factors being studied.

rotation a technique used to provide a more simple and interpretable picture of the relationships between factors and variables.

Numerical results from a factor study are shown in Exhibit 22-15. The values in this table are correlation coefficients between the factor and the variables (.70 is the r between variable A and factor I). These correlation coefficients are called **loadings**. Two other elements in Exhibit 22-15 need explanation. **Eigenvalues** are the sum of the variances of the factor values (for factor I the eigenvalue is $.70^2 + .60^2 + .50^2 + .60^2 + .60^2$). When divided by the number of variables, an eigenvalue yields an estimate of the amount of total variance explained by the factor. For example, factor I accounts for 36 percent of the total variance. If a factor has a low eigenvalue, then it adds little to the explanation of variances in the variables and may be disregarded. The column headed "h^2" gives the **communalities**, or estimates of the variance in each variable that is explained by the two factors. With variable A, for example, the communality is $.70^2 + (−.40)^2 = .65$, indicating that 65 percent of the variance in variable A is statistically explained in terms of factors I and II.

In this case, the unrotated factor loadings are not informative. What one would like to find is some pattern in which factor I would be heavily loaded (have a high r) on some variables and factor II on others. Such a condition would suggest rather "pure" constructs underlying each factor. You attempt to secure this less ambiguous condition between factors and variables by **rotation**. This procedure allows choices between orthogonal and

>**Exhibit 22-16** Orthogonal Factor Rotations

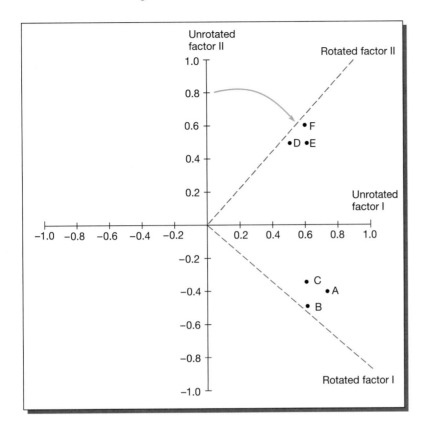

oblique methods. (When the factors are intentionally rotated to result in no correlation between the factors in the final solution, this procedure is called *orthogonal*; when the factors are not manipulated to be zero correlation but may reveal the degree of correlation that exists naturally, it is called *oblique*.) We illustrate an orthogonal solution here.

To understand the rotation concept, consider that you are dealing only with simple two-dimensional rather than multidimensional space. The variables in Exhibit 22-15 can be plotted in two-dimensional space as shown in Exhibit 22-16. Two axes divide this space, and the points are positioned relative to these axes. The location of these axes is arbitrary, and they represent only one of an infinite number of reference frames that could be used to reproduce the matrix. As long as you do not change the intersection points and keep the axes at right angles, when an orthogonal method is used you can rotate the axes to find a better solution or position for the reference axes. "Better" in this case means a matrix that makes the factors as pure as possible (each variable loads onto as few factors as possible). From the rotation shown in Exhibit 22-16, it can be seen that the solution is improved substantially. Using the rotated solution suggests that the measurements from six scales may be summarized by two underlying factors (see the rotated factors section of Exhibit 22-15).

The interpretation of factor loadings is largely subjective. There is no way to calculate the meanings of factors; they are what one sees in them. For this reason, factor analysis is largely used for exploration. One can detect patterns in latent variables, discover new concepts, and reduce data. Factor analysis is also applied to test hypotheses with confirmatory models using SEM.

Example

Student grades make an interesting example. The chairperson of Metro U's MBA program has been reviewing grades for the first-year students and is struck by the patterns in the data. His hunch is that distinct types of people are involved in the study of marketing, and he decides to gather evidence for this idea.

Suppose a sample of 21 grade reports is chosen for students in the middle of the GPA range. Three steps are followed:

1. Calculate a correlation matrix between the grades for all pairs of the 10 courses for which data exist.

2. Factor-analyze the matrix by the principal components method.

3. Select a rotation procedure to clarify the factors and aid in interpretation.

Exhibit 22-17 shows a portion of the correlation matrix. These data represent correlation coefficients between the 10 courses. For example, grades secured in V1 (Financial Accounting) correlated rather well (0.56) with grades received in course V2 (Managerial Accounting). The next best correlation with V1 grades is an inverse correlation ($-.44$) with grades in V7 (Production).

After the correlation matrix, the extraction of components is shown in Exhibit 22-18. While the program will produce a table with as many as 10 factors, you choose, in this

>**Exhibit 22-17** Correlation Coefficients, Metro U MBA Study

Variable	Course	V1	V2	V3	V10
V1	Financial Accounting	1.00	0.56	0.17	-.01
V2	Managerial Accounting	0.56	1.00	-.22	0.06
V3	Finance	0.17	-.22	1.00	0.42
V4	Marketing	-.14	0.05	-.48	-.10
V5	Human Behavior	-.19	-.26	-.05	-.23
V6	Organization Design	-.21	-.00	-.56	-.05
V7	Production	-.44	-.11	-.04	-.08
V8	Probability	0.30	0.06	0.07	-.10
V9	Statistical Inference	-.05	0.06	-.32	0.06
V10	Quantitative Analysis	-.01	0.06	0.42	1.00

>**Exhibit 22-18** Factor Matrix Using Principal Factor with Iterations, Metro U MBA Study

Variable	Course	Factor 1	Factor 2	Factor 3	Communality
V1	Financial Accounting	0.41	0.71	0.23	0.73
V2	Managerial Accounting	0.01	0.53	-.16	0.31
V3	Finance	0.89	-.17	0.37	0.95
V4	Marketing	-.60	0.21	0.30	0.49
V5	Human Behavior	0.02	-.24	-.22	0.11
V6	Organization Design	-.43	-.09	-.36	0.32
V7	Production	-.11	-.58	-.03	0.35
V8	Probability	0.25	0.25	-.31	0.22
V9	Statistical Inference	-.43	0.43	0.50	0.62
V10	Quantitative Analysis	0.25	0.04	0.35	0.19
Eigenvalue		1.83	1.52	0.95	
Percent of variance		18.30	15.20	9.50	
Cumulative percent		18.30	33.50	43.00	

case, to stop the process after three factors have been extracted. Several features in this table are worth noting. Recall that the communalities indicate the amount of variance in each variable that is being "explained" by the factors. Thus, these three factors account for about 73 percent of the variance in grades in the financial accounting course. It should be apparent from these communality figures that some of the courses are not explained well by the factors selected.

The eigenvalue row in Exhibit 22-18 is a measure of the explanatory power of each factor. For example, the eigenvalue for factor 1 is 1.83 and is computed as follows:

$$1.83 = (.41)^2 + (.01)^2 + \cdots + (.25)^2$$

The percent of variance accounted for by each factor in Exhibit 22-18 is computed by dividing eigenvalues by the number of variables. When this is done, one sees that the three factors account for about 43 percent of the total variance in course grades.

In an effort to further clarify the factors, a varimax (orthogonal) rotation is used to secure the matrix shown in Exhibit 22-19. The largest factor loadings for the three factors are as follows:

Factor 1		Factor 2		Factor 3	
Financial Accounting	0.84	Finance	0.90	Marketing	0.65
Managerial Accounting	0.53	Organization Design	−.56	Statistical Inference	0.79
Production	−.54				

Interpretation

The varimax rotation appears to clarify the relationship among course grades, but as pointed out earlier, the interpretation of the results is largely subjective. We might interpret the above results as showing three kinds of students, classified as the accounting, finance, and marketing types.

A number of problems affect the interpretation of these results. Among the major ones are these:

1. The sample is small and any attempt at replication might produce a different pattern of factor loadings.

2. From the same data, another number of factors rather than three can result in different patterns.

>**Exhibit 22-19** Varimax Rotated Factor Matrix, Metro U MBA Study

Variable	Course	Factor 1	Factor 2	Factor 3
V1	Financial Accounting	0.84	0.16	−.06
V2	Managerial Accounting	0.53	−.10	0.14
V3	Finance	−.01	0.90	−.37
V4	Marketing	−.11	−.24	0.65
V5	Human Behavior	−.13	−.14	−.27
V6	Organization Design	−.08	−.56	−.02
V7	Production	−.54	−.11	−.22
V8	Probability	0.41	−.02	−.24
V9	Statistical Inference	0.07	0.02	0.79
V10	Quantitative Analysis	−.02	0.42	0.09

3. Even if the findings are replicated, the differences may be due to the varying influence of professors or the way they teach the courses rather than to the subject content.

4. The labels may not truly reflect the latent construct that underlies any factors we extract.

This suggests that factor analysis can be a demanding tool to use. It is powerful, but the results must be interpreted with great care.

Cluster Analysis

cluster analysis identifies homogeneous subgroups of study objects or participants and then studies the data by these subgroups.

Unlike techniques for analyzing the relationships between variables, **cluster analysis** is a set of techniques for grouping similar objects or people. Originally developed as a classification device for taxonomy, its use has spread because of classification work in medicine, biology, and other sciences. Its visibility in those fields and the availability of high-speed computers to carry out the extensive calculations have sped its adoption in marketing. Understanding one's market very often involves classifying, or "segmenting," customers into homogeneous groups that have common buying characteristics or behave in similar ways. Such segments frequently share similar psychological, demographic, lifestyle, age, financial, or other characteristics.

Cluster analysis offers a means for segmentation research and other marketing problems where the goal is to classify similar groups. It shares some similarities with factor analysis, especially when factor analysis is applied to people (Q-analysis) instead of to variables. It differs from discriminant analysis in that discriminant analysis begins with a well-defined group composed of two or more distinct sets of characteristics in search of a set of variables to separate them. Cluster analysis starts with an undifferentiated group of people, events, or objects and attempts to reorganize them into homogeneous subgroups.

Method

Five steps are basic to the application of most cluster studies:

1. Selection of the sample to be clustered (e.g., buyers, medical patients, inventory, products, employees).

2. Definition of the variables on which to measure the objects, events, or people (e.g., market segment characteristics, product competition definitions, financial status, political affiliation, symptom classes, productivity attributes).

3. Computation of similarities among the entities through correlation, Euclidean distances, and other techniques.

4. Selection of mutually exclusive clusters (maximization of within-cluster similarity and between-cluster differences) or hierarchically arranged clusters.

5. Cluster comparison and validation.

Different clustering methods can and do produce different solutions. It is important to have enough information about the data to know when the derived groups are real and not merely imposed on the data by the method.

The example in Exhibit 22-20 shows a cluster analysis of individuals based on three dimensions: age, income, and family size. Cluster analysis could be used to segment the car-buying population into distinct markets. For example, cluster A might be targeted as potential minivan or sport-utility vehicle buyers. The market segment represented by cluster B might be a sports and performance car segment. Clusters C and D could both be targeted as buyers of sedans, but the C cluster might be the luxury buyer. This form of clustering or a hierarchical arrangement of the clusters may be used to plan marketing campaigns and develop strategies.

Example

Entertainment industry marketing is a complex business. A huge number of films are released each year internationally with some notable financial surprises. Paris offers one of the world's best selections of films and sources of critical review for predicting an international audience's acceptance. Residents of New York and Los Angeles are often surprised to discover their cities are eclipsed by Paris's average of 300 films per week shown in over 100 locations.

We selected ratings from 12 cinema reviewers using sources ranging from *Le Monde* to international publications sold in Paris. The reviews reputedly influence box-office receipts, and the entertainment business takes them seriously.

The object of this cluster example was to classify 19 films into homogeneous subgroups. The production companies were American, Canadian, French, Italian, Spanish, Finnish, Egyptian, and Japanese. Three genres of film were represented: comedy, dramatic comedy, and psychological drama. Exhibit 22-21 shows the data by film name, country of origin, and genre. The table also lists the clusters for each film using the **average linkage method**. This approach considers distances between all possible pairs rather than just the nearest or farthest neighbor.

The sequential development of the clusters and their relative distances are displayed in a diagram called a *dendogram.* Exhibit 22-22 shows that the clustering procedure begins with 19 films and continues until all the films are again an undifferentiated group. The solid vertical line shows the point at which the clustering solution best represents the data. This determination was guided by coefficients provided by the SPSS program for each stage of the procedure. Five clusters explain this data set.

The first cluster shown in Exhibit 22-22 has three French-language films and one Canadian film, all of which are dramatic comedies. Cluster 2 consists of comedy films. Two French and two other European films joined at the first stage, and then these two groups came together at the second stage. Cluster 3, composed of dramatic comedies, is otherwise diverse. It is made up of two American films with two Italian films adding to the group at

average linkage method evaluates the distance between two clusters by first finding the geometric center of each cluster and then computing distances between the two centers.

>**Exhibit 22-20** Cluster Analysis on Three Dimensions

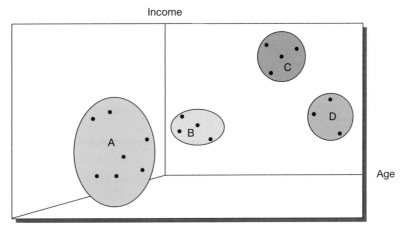

>Exhibit 22-21 Film, Country, Genre, and Cluster Membership

Film	Country	Genre	Case	Number of Clusters			
				5	4	3	2
Cyrano de Bergerac	France	DramaCom	1	1	1	1	1
Il y a des Jours	France	DramaCom	4	1	1	1	1
Nikita	France	DramaCom	5	1	1	1	1
Les Noces de Papier	Canada	DramaCom	6	1	1	1	1
Leningrad Cowboys . . .	Finland	Comedy	19	2	2	2	2
Storia de Ragazzi . . .	Italy	Comedy	13	2	2	2	2
Conte de Printemps	France	Comedy	2	2	2	2	2
Tatie Danielle	France	Comedy	3	2	2	2	2
Crimes and Misdem . . .	USA	DramaCom	7	3	3	3	2
Driving Miss Daisy	USA	DramaCom	9	3	3	3	2
La Voce della Luna	Italy	DramaCom	12	3	3	3	2
Che Hora E	Italy	DramaCom	14	3	3	3	2
Attache-Moi	Spain	DramaCom	15	3	3	3	2
White Hunter Black . . .	USA	PsyDrama	10	4	4	3	2
Music Box	USA	PsyDrama	8	4	4	3	2
Dead Poets Society	USA	PsyDrama	11	4	4	3	2
La Fille aux All . . .	Finland	PsyDrama	18	4	4	3	2
Alexandrie, Encore . . .	Egypt	DramaCom	16	5	3	3	2
Dreams	Japan	DramaCom	17	5	3	3	2

>Exhibit 22-22 Dendogram of Film Study Using Average Linkage Method

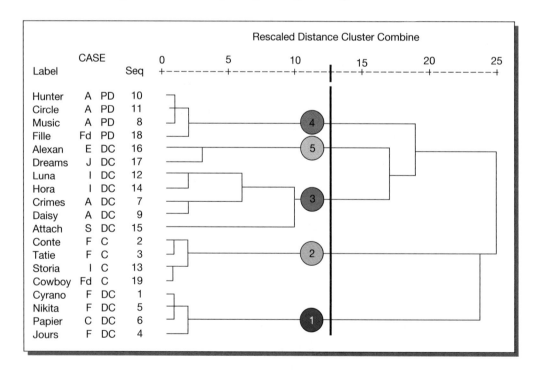

the fourth stage. Late in the clustering process, cluster 3 is completed when a Spanish film is appended. In cluster 4, we find three American psychological dramas combined with a Finnish film at the second stage. In cluster 5, two very different dramatic comedies are joined in the third stage.

Cluster analysis classified these productions based on reviewers' ratings. The similarities and distances are influenced by film genre and culture (as defined by the translated language).

>**Exhibit 22-23** Similarities Matrix of 16 Restaurants

	1	2	3	4	5	6	7	8	9	10	11	12	13	14	15	16
1	0															
2	3.9	0														
3	4.7	6.7	0													
4	4.4	2.8	4.7	0												
5	14.0	12.4	18.5	15.2	0											
6	4.9	6.9	0.2	4.9	18.7	0										
7	0.8	3.7	4.1	3.7	14.5	4.3	0									
8	6.0	2.1	8.5	4.0	11.8	8.7	5.8	0								
9	4.3	6.9	1.1	5.3	18.3	1.2	3.8	8.9	0							
10	8.2	4.9	8.5	4.1	15.3	8.6	7.6	3.9	9.3	0						
11	8.6	8.7	4.7	5.9	21.1	4.5	7.8	9.7	5.7	7.7	0					
12	2.2	3.7	6.9	5.5	11.8	7.1	2.8	5.5	6.5	8.5	10.5	0				
13	8.4	9.8	3.7	7.2	22.0	3.5	7.8	11.2	4.5	10.0	2.9	10.6	0			
14	12.8	13.4	8.2	10.6	25.8	8.1	12.1	14.4	9.1	12.0	4.7	14.9	4.6	0		
15	19.1	18.2	23.8	21.0	6.2	24.0	19.7	17.8	23.4	21.5	26.9	16.9	27.4	31.5	0	
16	2.6	5.2	2.1	4.0	16.5	2.3	2.0	7.2	1.9	8.0	6.3	4.8	5.8	10.3	21.7	0

Multidimensional Scaling

Multidimensional scaling (MDS) creates a special description of a respondent's perception about a product, service, or other object of interest on a *perceptual map*. This often helps the marketing researcher to understand difficult-to-measure constructs such as product quality or desirability. In contrast to variables that can be measured directly, many constructs are perceived and cognitively mapped in different ways by individuals. With MDS, items that are perceived to be similar will fall close together on the perceptual map, and items that are perceived to be dissimilar will be farther apart.

multidimensional scaling (MDS) a scaling technique to simultaneously measure more than one attribute of the participants or objects.

Method

We may think of three types of attribute space, each representing a multidimensional map. First, there is *objective space,* in which an object can be positioned in terms of its measurable attributes: its flavor, weight, and nutritional value. Second, there is *subjective space,* where perceptions of the object's flavor, weight, and nutritional value may be positioned. Objective and subjective attribute assessments may coincide, but often they do not. A comparison of the two allows us to judge how accurately an object is being perceived. Individuals may hold different perceptions of an object simultaneously, and these may be averaged to present a summary measure of perceptions. In addition, a person's perceptions may vary over time and in different circumstances; such measurements are valuable to gauge the impact of various perception-affecting actions, such as advertising programs.

With a third map we can describe respondents' preferences using the object's attributes. This represents their ideal; all objects close to this ideal point are interpreted as preferred by respondents to those that are more distant. Ideal points from many people can be positioned in this preference space to reveal the pattern and size of preference clusters. These can be compared to the subjective space to assess how well the preferences correspond to perception clusters. In this way, cluster analysis and MDS can be combined to map market segments and then examine products designed for those segments.

Example

We illustrate multidimensional scaling with a study of 16 restaurants in a resort area.[11] The restaurants chosen represent medium-price family restaurants to high-price gourmet restaurants. We created a metric algorithm measuring the similarities among the 16 restaurants by asking patrons questions on a 5-point metric scale about different dimensions of service quality and price. The matrix of similarities is shown in Exhibit 22-23. Higher numbers reflect the items that are more dissimilar.

>Exhibit 22-24 Positioning of Selected Restaurants

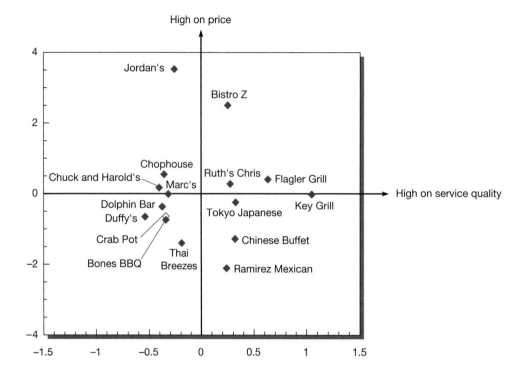

We might also ask participants to judge the similarities between all possible pairs of restaurants; then we produce a matrix of similarities using (nonmetric) ordinal data. The matrix would contain ranks with 1 representing the most similar pair and *n* indicating the most dissimilar pair.

A computer program is used to analyze the data matrix and generate a perceptual map.[12] The objective is to find a multidimensional spatial pattern that best reproduces the original order of the data. For example, the most similar pair (restaurants 3, 6) must be located in this multidimensional space closer together than any other pair. The least similar pair (restaurants 14, 15) must be the farthest apart. The computer program presents these relationships as a geometric configuration so that all distances between pairs of points closely correspond to the original matrix.

Determining how many dimensions to use is complex. The more dimensions of space we use, the more likely the results will closely match the input data. Any set of *n* points can be satisfied by a configuration of $n - 1$ dimensions. Our aim, however, is to secure a structure that provides a good fit for the data and has the fewest dimensions. MDS is best understood using two or at most three dimensions.

stress index an index used in multidimensional scaling that ranges from 1 (worst fit) to 0 (perfect fit).

Most software programs include the calculation of a **stress index** (*S*-stress or Kruskal's stress) that ranges from the worst fit (1) to the perfect fit (0). This study, for example, had a stress of .001. Another index, R^2, is interpreted as the proportion of variance of transformed data accounted for by distances in the model. A result close to 1.0 is desirable.

In the restaurants example, we conclude that two dimensions represent an acceptable geometric configuration, as shown in Exhibit 22-24. The distance between Crab Pot and Bones BBQ (3, 6) is the shortest, while that between Ramirez Mexican and Jordan's (14, 15) is the longest. As with factor analysis, there is no statistical solution to the definition of the dimensions represented by the *X* and *Y* axes. The labeling is judgmental and depends on the insight of the researcher, analysis of information collected from respondents, or another basis. Respondents sometimes are asked to state the criteria they used for judging the similarities, or they are asked to judge a specific set of criteria.

Consistent with raw data, Jordan's and Bistro Z have high price but service quality close to the sample mean. In contrast, Flagler and Key Grills generated a price close to the sample's average while providing higher service quality. We could hypothesize that the latter two restaurants may be more efficient to run—are smaller and less complex—but that would need to be confirmed with another study. The clustering of companies in attribute space shows that they are perceived to be similar along the dimensions measured.

MDS is most often used to assess perceived similarities and differences among objects. Using MDS allows the researcher to understand constructs that are not directly measurable. The process provides a spatial map that shows similarities in terms of relative distances. It is best understood when limited to two or three dimensions that can be graphically displayed.

>summary

1 Multivariate techniques are classified into two categories: dependency and interdependency. When a problem reveals the presence of criterion and predictor variables, we have an assumption of dependence. If the variables are interrelated without designating some as dependent and others independent, then interdependence of the variables is assumed. The choice of techniques is guided by the number of dependent and independent variables involved and whether they are measured on metric or nonmetric scales.

2 Multiple regression is an extension of bivariate linear regression. When a researcher is interested in explaining or predicting a metric dependent variable from a set of metric independent variables (although dummy variables may also be used), multiple regression is often selected. Regression results provide information on the statistical significance of the independent variables, the strength of association between one or more of the predictors and the criterion, and a predictive equation for future use.

3 Discriminant analysis is used to classify people or objects into groups based on several predictor variables. The groups are defined by a categorical variable with two or more values, whereas the predictors are metric. The effectiveness of the discriminant equation is based not only on its statistical significance but also on its success in correctly classifying cases to groups.

4 Multivariate analysis of variance, or MANOVA, is one of the more adaptive techniques for multivariate data. MANOVA assesses the relationship between two or more metric dependent variables and classificatory variables or factors. MANOVA is most commonly used to test differences among samples of people or objects. In contrast to ANOVA, MANOVA handles multiple dependent variables, thereby simultaneously testing all the variables and their interrelationships.

5 Marketing researchers have relied increasingly on structural equation modeling (SEM) to test hypotheses about the dimensionality of, and relationships among, latent and observed variables. Researchers refer to structural equation models as LISREL (linear structural relations) models. The major advantages of SEM are (1) that multiple and interrelated dependence relationships can be estimated simultaneously and (2) that it can represent unobserved concepts, or latent variables, in these relationships and account for measurement error in the estimation process. Researchers using SEM must follow five basic steps: (1) model specification, (2) estimation, (3) evaluation of fit, (4) respecification of the model, and (5) interpretation and communication.

6 Conjoint analysis is a technique that typically handles nonmetric independent variables. Conjoint analysis allows the researcher to determine the importance of product or service attributes and the levels or features that are most desirable. Respondents provide preference data by ranking or rating cards that describe products. These data become utility weights of product characteristics by means of optimal scaling and loglinear algorithms.

7 Principal components analysis extracts uncorrelated factors that account for the largest portion of variance from an initial set of variables. Factor analysis also attempts to reduce the number of variables and discover the underlying constructs that explain the variance. A correlation matrix is used to derive a factor matrix from which the best linear combination of variables may be extracted. In many applications, the factor matrix will be rotated to simplify the factor structure.

8 Unlike techniques for analyzing the relationships between variables, cluster analysis is a set of techniques for grouping similar objects or people. The cluster procedure starts with an undifferentiated group of people, events, or objects and attempts to reorganize them into homogeneous subgroups.

9 Multidimensional scaling (MDS) is often used in conjunction with cluster analysis or conjoint analysis. It allows a respondent's perception about a product, service, or other object of attitude to be described in a spatial manner. MDS helps the business researcher to understand difficult-to-measure constructs such as product quality or desirability, which are perceived and cognitively mapped in different ways by different individuals. Items judged to be similar will fall close together in multidimensional space and are revealed numerically and geometrically by spatial maps.

>**key**terms

>**discussion**questions

Terms in Review

1 Distinguish among multidimensional scaling, cluster analysis, and factor analysis.

2 Describe the differences between dependency techniques and interdependency techniques. When would you choose a dependency technique?

Making Research Decisions

3 How could discriminant analysis be used to provide insight into MANOVA results where the MANOVA has one independent variable (a factor with two levels)?

4 Describe how you would create a conjoint analysis study of off-road vehicles. Restrict your brands to three, and suggest possible factors and levels. The full-concept description should not exceed 256 decision options.

5 What type of multivariate method do you recommend in each of the following cases and why?

   a You want to develop an estimating equation that will be used to predict which applicants will come to your university as students.

   b You would like to predict family income using such variables as education and stage in family life cycle.

   c You wish to estimate standard labor costs for manufacturing a new dress design.

   d You have been studying a group of successful salespeople. You have given them a number of psychological tests. You want to bring meaning out of these test results.

6 Sales of a product are influenced by the salesperson's level of education and gender, as well as consumer income, ethnicity, and wealth.

   a Formulate this statement as a multiple regression model (form only, without parameter estimation).

   b Specify dummy variables.

   c If the effects of consumer income and wealth are not additive alone, and an interaction is expected, specify a new variable to test for the interaction.

7 What multivariate technique would you use to analyze each of the following problems? Explain your choice.

   a Employee job satisfaction (high, normal, low) and employee success (0–2 promotions, 3–5 promotions, 5+ promotions) are to be studied in three different departments of a company.

   b Consumers making a brand choice decision between three brands of coffee are influenced by their own income levels and the extent of advertising of the brands.

   c Consumer choice of color in fabrics is largely dependent on ethnicity, income levels, and the temperature of the geographic area. There is detailed areawide demographic data on income levels, ethnicity, and population, as well as the weather bureau's historical data on temperature. How would you identify geographic areas for selling dark-colored fabric? You have sample data for 200 randomly selected consumers: their fabric color choice, income, ethnicity, and the average temperature of the area where they live.

From Concept to Practice

8 An analyst sought to predict the annual sales for a home-furnishing manufacturer using the following predictor variables:

X_1 = marriages during the year

X_2 = housing starts during the year

X_3 = annual disposable personal income

X_4 = time trend (first year = 1, second year = 2, and so forth)

Using data for 24 years, the analyst calculated the following estimating equation:

$$Y = 49.85 - .068X_1 + .036X_2 + 1.22X_3 - 19.54X_4$$

The analyst also calculated an R^2 = .92 and a standard error of estimate of 11.9. Interpret the above equation and statistics.

9 You are working with a consulting group that has a new project for the Palm Grove School System. The school system of this large county has individuals with purchasing, service, and maintenance responsibilities. They were asked to evaluate the vendor/distribution channels of products that the county purchases. The evaluations were on a 10-point metric scale for the following variables:

Delivery speed—amount of time for delivery once the order has been confirmed.

Price level—level of price charged by the product suppliers.

Price flexibility—perceived willingness to negotiate on price.

Manufacturer's image—manufacturer or supplier's image.

Overall service—level of service necessary to preserve a satisfactory relationship between buyer and supplier.

Sales force—overall image of the manufacturer's sales representatives.

Product quality—perceived quality of a particular product.

The data are found on the text DVD.

Your task is to complete an exploratory factor analysis on the survey data. The purpose for the consulting group is twofold: (a) to identify the underlying dimensions of these data and (b) to create a new set of variables for inclusion into subsequent assessments of the vendor/distribution channels. Methodology issues to consider in your analysis are:

a Desirability of principal components versus principal axis factoring.

b Decisions on criteria for number of factors to extract.

c Rotation of the factors.

d Factor loading significance.

e Interpretation of the rotated matrix.

Prepare a report summarizing your findings and interpreting your results.

>**www**exercise

FRED II (Federal Reserve Economic Data of the Federal Reserve Bank of St. Louis) is a database of over 1,000 U.S. economic time series. Visit this Web site (**http://research.stlouisfed.org/fred2/**), and select one variable as the dependent variable. What other variables might you use in a multiple regression analysis?

>**cases**[*]

Mastering Teacher Leadership

NCRCC: Teeing Up and New Strategic Direction

* All cases, both written and video, are on the text DVD. Check the DVD Index to determine whether a case has data, the research instrument, or other supplementary material.

chapter 23

Presenting Insights and Findings: Written and Oral Reports

>learningobjectives

After reading this chapter, you should understand . . .

1 That a quality presentation of research findings can have an inordinate effect on a reader's or a listener's perceptions of a study's quality.

2 The contents, types, lengths, and technical specifications of research reports.

3 That the writer of a research report should be guided by questions of purpose, readership, circumstances/limitations, and use.

4 That while some statistical data may be incorporated in the text, most statistics should be placed in tables, charts, or graphs.

5 That oral presentations of research findings should be developed with concern for organization, visual aids, and delivery in unique communication settings. Presentation quality can enhance or detract from what might otherwise be excellent research.

>behindthescenes

For many researchers the culmination of a project is both exhilarating and depressing. Researchers have ownership of a project until the report is made to the marketer. Even if a marketer does his or her own research, once the report is finalized, there is no changing the content. We join Visionary Insights' MindWriter team as they reach the point of report finalization.

"Has it occurred to you that your draft of the Mind-Writer report has not been touched in the last two days? The stack of marked-up pages is right there on your desk, and you have been working around it."

Jason frowns and momentarily flicks his eyes to the stack of marked pages.

Sara plunges ahead with her complaint. "It's no big deal, you know. You promised to chop out three pages of methodology that nobody will care about but your fellow statistics jocks . . ."—Jason shoots her an aggrieved look—". . . and to remove your recommendations and provide them in a separate, informal letter so that Gracie Uhura or Myra Wines can distribute them under her name and claim credit for your 'brilliance.'"

"I think I have writer's block."

"No. Writer's block is when you can't write. You can't unwrite; that's the problem. You have unwriter's block. Look, some people do great research and then panic when they have to decide what goes in the report and what doesn't. Or they can't take all the great ideas running around in their heads and express their abstractions in words. Or they don't believe they are smart enough to communicate with their clients, or vice versa. So they freeze up. This isn't usually your problem. There is some sort of emotional link to this Mind-Writer report, Jason; face it."

"I love the MindWriter project."

"Ah, there's the problem," she says. "Jason, I have heard you say that you hate projects for other clients, and I have heard you say that you like projects. But this is the first time I have heard you say you love a project. There comes a time when, after you have nurtured something, you have to let go. Then it isn't yours. It is someone else's, or it is its own thing, but it is not yours."

"I guess you're right," Jason smiles sheepishly. "I'm a little too invested. This MindWriter project was my baby—well, yours and mine. If I chop three pages out of the report, it is finished. Then it belongs to Myra and Gracie. I don't own it anymore. I can't implement my recommendations. I can't change anything. I can't have second thoughts."

"Fix it, then. Send MindWriter an invoice. Write a proposal for follow-up work. Do something, Jason. Finish it. Let go and move on." Sara smiles and pauses as she is about to leave Jason's office. Jason had pulled the report to the center of his desk, a very good sign. "By the way, Custom Foods just awarded us the contract for its ideation work. I'd hate to work on that project without you, but . . ."

> Introduction

As part of the research proposal, the sponsor and the marketing researcher agree on what types of reporting will occur both during and at the end of the research project. Depending on the budget for the project, a formal oral presentation may not be part of the reporting. A research sponsor, however, is sure to require a written report. Exhibit 23-1 details the reporting phase of the research process.

> The Written Research Report

It may seem unscientific and even unfair, but a poor final report or presentation can destroy a study. Research technicians may appreciate the brilliance of badly reported content, but most readers will be influenced by the quality of the reporting. This fact should prompt researchers to make special efforts to communicate clearly and fully.

>**Exhibit 23-1** Sponsor Presentation and the Research Process

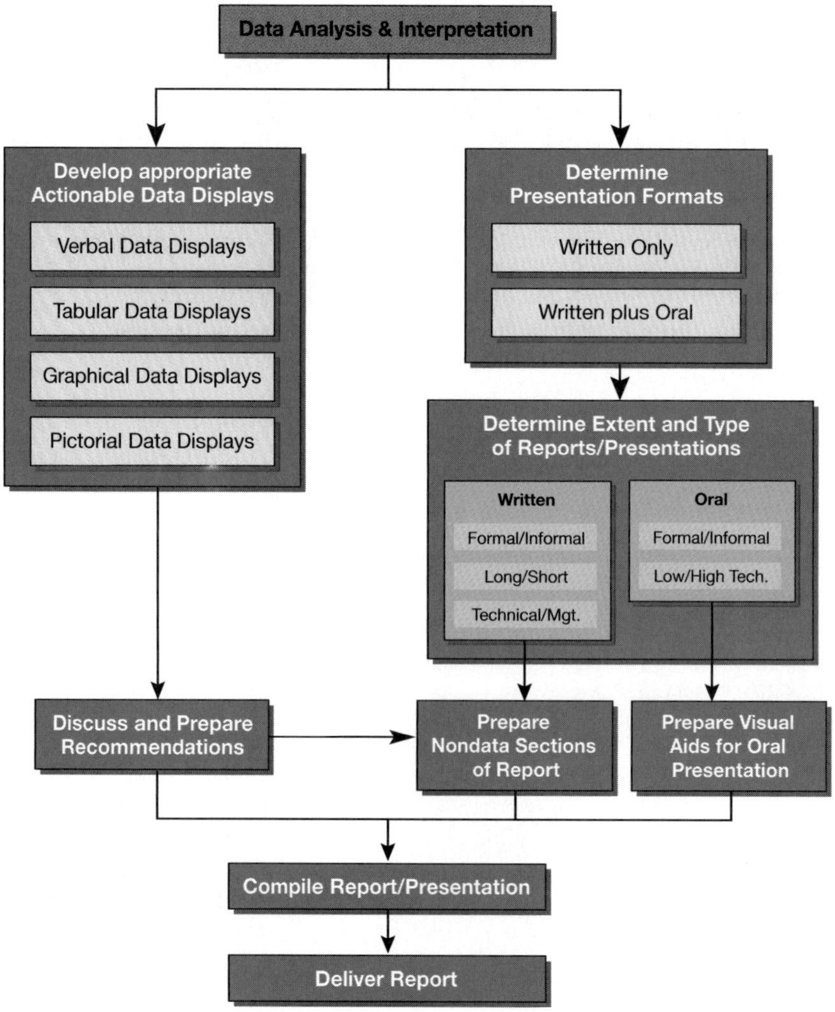

The research report contains findings, analyses of findings, interpretations, conclusions, and sometimes recommendations. The researcher is the expert on the topic and knows the specifics in a way no one else can. Because a written research report is an authoritative one-way communication, it imposes a special obligation for maintaining objectivity. Even if your findings seem to point to an action, you should demonstrate restraint and caution when proposing that course.

Reports may be defined by their degree of formality and design. The formal report follows a well-delineated and relatively long format. This is in contrast to the informal or short report.

Short Reports

Short reports are appropriate when the problem is well defined, is of limited scope, and has a simple and straightforward methodology. Most informational, progress, and interim reports are of this kind: a report of cost-of-living changes for upcoming labor negotiations or an exploration of filing "dumping" charges against a foreign competitor.

Short reports are about five pages. If used on a Web site, they may be even shorter. At the beginning, there should be a brief statement about the authorization for the study, the problem examined, and its breadth and depth. Next come the conclusions and recommendations, followed by the findings that support them. Section headings should be used.

A letter of transmittal is a vehicle to convey short reports. A five-page report may be produced to track sales on a quarterly basis. The report should be direct, make ample use of graphics to show trends, and refer the reader to the research department for further information. Detailed information on the research method would be omitted, although an overview could appear in an appendix. The purpose of this type of report is to distribute information quickly in an easy-to-use format. Short reports are also produced for clients with small, relatively inexpensive research projects.

The letter is a form of a short report. Its tone should be informal. The format follows that of any good business letter and should not exceed a few pages. A letter report is often written in personal style (*we, you*), although this depends on the situation.

Memorandum reports are another variety and follow the *To, From, Subject* format. These suggestions may be helpful for writing short reports:

• Tell the reader why you are writing (it may be in response to a request).

• If the memo is in response to a request for information, remind the reader of the exact point raised, answer it, and follow with any necessary details.

• Write in an expository style with brevity and directness.

• If time permits, write the report today and leave it for review tomorrow before sending it.

• Attach detailed materials as appendices when needed.

Long Reports

Long reports are of two types, the technical or base report and the management report. The choice depends on the audience and the researcher's objectives.

Many projects will require both types of reports: a **technical report,** written for an audience of researchers, and a **management report,** written for the nontechnically oriented manager or client. While some researchers try to write a single report that satisfies both needs, this complicates the task and is seldom satisfactory. The two types of audiences have different technical training, interests, and goals.

technical report a report written for an audience of researchers.

management report a report written for the nontechnically oriented manager or client.

E-Speed or No Speed

The Internet has forever transformed a marketing decision maker's expectations relating to speed of data results. The Internet has given marketers a taste of "e-time"—data tabulated and synthesized in real time. "While some marketer's realize that e-speed may sacrifice quality in research," shared Darcy Zwetko, manager–research services, Opinion Search, Inc. (Ottawa, Canada), "knowing the speed available with online surveys encouraged us to make our CATI survey results accessible in real time, directly via each client's computer." Opinion Search calls this industry first *dataCAP* for "Data Control and Access Portal." Among other opportunities, *dataCAP* provides:

- Real-time frequencies.
- Real-time cross-tabulation.
- Real-time open-ended verbatim responses.
- Real-time quota status.
- Daily status of your projects.
- Daily call disposition reports.

Besides being fast, *dataCAP* delivers encrypted information to protect data privacy. Speed without safety won't win a firm any clients. And speed that sacrifices quality won't have them coming back.

www.opinionsearch.com

The Technical Report

This report should include full documentation and detail. It will normally survive all working papers and original data files and so will become the major source document. It is the report that other researchers will want to see because it has the full story of what was done and how it was done.

While completeness is a goal, you must guard against including nonessential material. A good guide is that sufficient procedural information should be included to enable others to replicate the study. This includes sources of data, research procedures, sampling design, data gathering instruments, index construction, and data analysis methods. Most information should be attached in an appendix.

A technical report should also include a full presentation and analysis of significant data. Conclusions and recommendations should be clearly related to specific findings. Technical jargon should be minimized but defined when used. There can be brief references to other research, theories, and techniques. While you expect the reader to be familiar with these references, it is useful to include some short explanations, perhaps as footnotes or endnotes.

The short technical report covers the same items as the long technical report but in an abbreviated form. The methodology is included as part of the introduction and takes no more than a few paragraphs. Most of the emphasis is placed on the findings and conclusions. A memo or letter format covers only the minimum: what the problem is and what the research conclusions are.

The Management Report

In contrast to the technical report, the management report is for the nontechnical client. The reader has little time to absorb details and needs a prompt exposure to the most critical findings; thus the report's sections are in an inverted order. After the prefatory and introductory sections, the conclusions with accompanying recommendations are presented. Individual findings are presented next, supporting the conclusions already made. The appendices present any required methodological details. The order of the management report allows clients to grasp the conclusions and recommendations quickly, without much reading. Then, if they wish to go further, they may read on into the findings. The management report should make liberal use of visual displays.

Sometimes the client has no research background and is interested in results rather than in methodology. The major communication medium in this case is the management report. It is still helpful to have a technical report if the client later wishes to have a technical appraisal of the study.

The style of the report should encourage rapid reading and quick comprehension of major findings, and it should prompt understanding of the implications and conclusions. The report tone is journalistic and must be accurate. Headlines and underlining for emphasis are helpful; pictures and graphs often replace tables. Sentences and paragraphs should be short and direct. Consider liberal use of white space and wide margins. It may be desirable to put a single finding on each page. It also helps to have a theme running through the report and even graphic or animated characters designed to vary the presentation.

> Research Report Components

Research reports, long and short, have a set of identifiable components. Usually headings and subheadings divide the sections. Each report is individual; sections may be dropped or added, condensed or expanded to meet the needs of the audience. Exhibit 23-2 lists four types of reports, the sections that are typically included, and the general order of presentation. Each of these formats can be modified to meet the needs of the audience.

Prefatory Items

Prefatory materials do not have direct bearing on the research itself. Instead, they assist the reader in using the research report.

Letter of Transmittal

When the relationship between the researcher and the client is formal, a **letter of transmittal** should be included. This is appropriate when a report is for a specific client (e.g., the company president) and when it is generated for an outside organization. The letter should refer to the authorization for the project and any specific instructions or limitations placed on the study. It should also state the purpose and the scope of the study. For many internal projects, it is not necessary to include a letter of transmittal.

letter of transmittal the element of the final report that provides the purpose of, scope of, authorization for, and limitations of the study.

Title Page

The title page should include four items: the title of the report, the date, and for whom and by whom it was prepared. The title should be brief but include the following three elements: (1) the variables included in the study, (2) the type of relationship among the variables, and (3) the population to which the results may be applied.[1] Redundancies such as "A Report of" and "A Discussion of" add length to the title but little else. Single-word titles are also of little value. Here are three acceptable ways to word report titles:

Descriptive study:	The Five-Year Demand Outlook for Consumer Packaged Goods in the United States
Correlation study:	The Relationship between Relative National Inflation Rates and Household Purchases of Brand X in International Markets
Causal study:	The Effect of Various Motivation Methods on Retail Sales Associates' Attitudes and Performance

>Exhibit 23-2 Research Report Sections and Their Order of Inclusion

Report Modules	Short Report		Long Report	
	Memo or Letter	Short Technical	Management	Technical
Prefatory Information		1	1	1
Letter of transmittal		✓	✓	✓
Title page		✓	✓	✓
Authorization statement		✓	✓	✓
Executive summary		✓	✓	✓
Table of contents			✓	✓
Introduction	1	2	2	2
Problem statement	✓	✓	✓	✓
Research objectives	✓	✓	✓	✓
Background	✓	✓	✓	✓
Methodology		✓ (briefly)	✓ (briefly)	3
Sampling design				✓
Research design				✓
Data collection				✓
Data analysis				✓
Limitations		✓	✓	✓
Findings		3	4	4
Conclusions	2	4	3	5
Summary and conclusions	✓	✓	✓	✓
Recommendations	✓	✓	✓	✓
Appendices		5	5	6
Bibliography				7

Authorization Letter

When the report is sent to a public organization, it is common to include a letter of authorization showing the authority for undertaking the research. This is especially true for reports to federal and state governments and nonprofit organizations. The letter not only shows who sponsored the research but also delineates the original request.

Executive Summary

executive summary a concise summary of the major findings, conclusions, and recommendations.

An **executive summary** can serve two purposes. It may be a report in miniature (sometimes called a *topline report*), covering all the aspects in the body of the report but in abbreviated form. Or it may be a concise summary of the major findings and conclusions, including recommendations. Two pages are generally sufficient for executive summaries. Write this section after the rest of the report is finished. It should not include new information but may require graphics to present a particular conclusion. Expect the summary to contain a high density of significant terms since it is repeating the highlights of the report.

Table of Contents

As a rough guide, any report of several sections that totals more than 6 to 10 pages should have a table of contents. If there are many tables, charts, or other exhibits, they should also be listed after the table of contents in a separate table of illustrations.

Introduction

The introduction prepares the reader for the report by describing the parts of the project: the problem statement, research objectives, and background material.[2] In most projects, the introduction can be taken from the research proposal with minor editing.

Problem Statement

The problem statement contains the need for the research project. The problem is usually represented by a management question. It is followed by a more detailed set of objectives.

Research Objectives

The research objectives address the purpose of the project. These objectives may be research questions and associated investigative questions. In correlational or causal studies, the hypothesis statements are included. As we discussed in Chapter 3, hypotheses are declarative statements describing the relationship between two or more variables. They state clearly the variables of concern, the relationships among them, and the target group being studied. Operational definitions of critical variables should be included.

Background

Background material may be of two types. It may be the preliminary results of exploration from an experience survey, focus group, or another source. Alternatively, it could be secondary data from the literature review. A traditional organizational scheme is to think of the concentric circles of a target. Starting with the outside ring, the writer works toward the center. The bull's eye contains the material directly related to the problem. Sources and means for securing this information are presented in Chapter 5 and on your text DVD.

Previous research, theory, or situations that led to the management question are also discussed in this section. The literature should be organized, integrated, and presented in a way that connects it logically to the problem. The background includes definitions, qualifications, and assumptions. It gives the reader the information needed to understand the remainder of the research report.[3]

Background material may be placed before the problem statement or after the research objectives. If it is composed primarily of literature review and related research, it should follow the objectives. If it contains information pertinent to the management problem or the situation that led to the study, it can be placed before the problem statement (where it is found in many applied studies).

Methodology

In short reports and management reports, the methodology should not have a separate section; it should be mentioned in the introduction, and details should be placed in an appendix. However, for a technical report, the methodology is an important section, containing at least five parts.

Sampling Design

The researcher explicitly defines the target population being studied and the sampling methods used. For example, was this a probability or nonprobability sample? If probability, was it simple random or complex random? How were the elements selected? How was the size determined? How much confidence do we have, and how much error was allowed?

Explanations of the sampling methods, uniqueness of the chosen parameters, or other points that need explanation should be covered with brevity. Calculations should be placed in an appendix instead of in the body of the report.

Research Design

The coverage of the design must be adapted to the purpose. In an experimental study, the materials, tests, equipment, control conditions, and other devices should be described. In descriptive or ex post facto designs, it may be sufficient to cover the rationale for using one design instead of competing alternatives. Even with a sophisticated design, the strengths and weaknesses should be identified and the instrumentation and materials discussed. Copies of materials are placed in an appendix.

Data Collection

This part of the report describes the specifics of gathering the data. Its contents depend on the selected design. Survey work generally uses a team with field and central supervision. How many people were involved? What was their training? How were they managed? When were the data collected? How much time did it take? What were the conditions in the field? How were irregularities handled? In an experiment, we would want to know about subject assignment to groups, the use of standardized procedures and protocols, the administration of tests or observational forms, manipulation of the variables, and so forth.

Typically, you would include a discussion on the relevance of secondary data that guided these decisions. Again, detailed materials such as field instructions should be included in an appendix.

Online Reporting

Medical Radar International (MRI), a Swedish research company, works exclusively in the pharmaceutical field. It conducts its syndicated study—Radar Dynamics—on the use of pharmaceuticals by doctors across several European countries, by interviewing 150 to 300 physicians (depending on the size of the country) twice each year.

Using a variety of SPSS software products, including In2quest's In2data for database development, Quantum for fast data tabulation, and SmartViewer, MRI can report results quickly.

With SmartViewer Web server software, a pharmaceutical company participating in the syndicated study can view password-protected results from Medical Radar's own Web site, even customizing the data in tables that specifically suit its needs, while the underlying data are tamper-protected. Staffan Hallstram, systems manager at MRI, reports Web distribution is the "ideal method" for distributing its syndicated research reports.

www.medical-radar.com; www.spss.com

Data Analysis

This section summarizes the methods used to analyze the data. Describe data handling, preliminary analysis, statistical tests, computer programs, and other technical information. The rationale for the choice of analysis approaches should be clear. A brief commentary on assumptions and appropriateness of use should be presented.

Limitations

This topic is often handled with ambivalence. Some people wish to ignore the matter, feeling that mentioning limitations detracts from the impact of the study. This attitude is unprofessional and possibly unethical. Others seem to adopt a masochistic approach of detailing everything. The section should be a thoughtful presentation of significant methodology or implementation problems. An evenhanded approach is one of the hallmarks of an honest and competent investigator. All research studies have their limitations, and the sincere investigator recognizes that readers need aid in judging the study's validity.

Findings

This is generally the longest section of the report. The objective is to explain the data rather than draw interpretations or conclusions. When quantitative data can be presented, this should be done as simply as possible with charts, graphics, and tables.

The data need not include everything you have collected. The criterion for inclusion is, "Is this material important to the reader's understanding of the problem and the findings?" However, make sure to show findings unfavorable to your hypotheses as well as those that support them, as this reinforces the bond of trust that has developed between researcher and sponsor.

It is useful to present findings in numbered paragraphs or to present one finding per page with the quantitative data supporting the findings presented in a small table or chart on the same page (see Exhibit 23-3). While this arrangement adds to the bulk of the report, it is convenient for the reader.

❝❝No one, no group, no function, has an inherent right to exist in a company. You are creating value (where none existed before), adding value, maintaining value (status-quo), or draining it. Those who drain or maintain value are eventually cut.❞❞

Dave Marcum
Author, businessThink

>**Exhibit 23-3** Example of a Findings Page in Central City Bank Market Study

Findings:

1. In this city, *commercial banks are not the preferred savings medium.* Banks are in a weak third place behind money market accounts.

2. Customers of the Central City Bank have a *somewhat more favorable attitude toward bank savings* and less of a preference for government bonds.

Question:

Suppose that you have just received an extra $1,000 and have decided to save it. Which of the savings methods listed would be your preferred way to save it?
- ❏ Government bonds
- ❏ Savings and loan
- ❏ Bank savings
- ❏ Credit union
- ❏ Stock
- ❏ Other

Savings Method	Total Replies	Central City Bank Customers	Other Bank Customers
Government bonds	24%	20%	29%
Savings and loan	43	45	42
Bank	13	18	8
Credit union	9	7	11
Stock	7	8	5
Other	4	2	5
Total	100%	100%	100%
	n = 216	*n* = 105	*n* = 111

Conclusions

Summary and Conclusions

The summary is a brief statement of the essential findings. Sectional summaries may be used if there are many specific findings. These may be combined into an overall summary. In simple descriptive research, a summary may complete the report, because conclusions and recommendations may not be required.

Findings state facts; conclusions represent inferences drawn from the findings. A writer is sometimes reluctant to make conclusions and leaves the task to the reader. Avoid this temptation when possible. As the researcher, you are the one best informed on the factors that critically influence the findings and conclusions. Good researchers don't draw conclusions that go beyond the data related to the study.

Conclusions may be presented in a tabular form for easy reading and reference. Summary findings may be subordinated under the related conclusion statement. These may be numbered to refer the reader to pages or tables in the findings sections.

Recommendations

Increasingly, researchers are expected to offer ideas for corrective actions. In applied re-search the recommendations will usually be for managerial action, with the researcher sug-gesting one or several alternatives that are supported by the findings. Also, marketing researchers may recommend further research initiatives. In basic or pure research, recom-mendations are often suggestions for further study that broaden or test the understandings of a subject area.

Appendices

The appendices are the place for complex tables, statistical tests, supporting documents, copies of forms and questionnaires, detailed descriptions of the methodology, instructions to field workers, and other evidence important for later support. The reader who wishes to learn about the technical aspects of the study and to look at statistical breakdowns will want a complete appendix.

Bibliography

The use of secondary data requires a bibliography. Long reports, particularly technical ones, require a bibliography. A bibliography documents the sources used by the writer. Although bibliographies may contain work used as background or for further study, it is preferable to include only sources used for preparing the report.

> Writing the Report

Students often give inadequate attention to reporting their findings and conclusions. This is unfortunate. A well-presented study will often impress the reader more than a study with greater scientific quality but a weaker presentation. Judging a report as competently written is often the key first step to a manager's decision to use the findings in decision making and also to consider implementation of the researcher's recommendations. Report-writing skills are especially valuable to the junior executive or researcher who aspires to rise in an organization. A well-written study frequently enhances career prospects.

Prewriting Concerns

Before writing, one should ask again, "What is the purpose of this report?" Responding to this question is one way to crystallize the problem.

The second prewriting question is, "Who will read the report?" Thought should be given to the needs, temperament, and biases of the audience. You should not distort facts to meet these needs and biases but should consider them while developing the presentation. Knowing who will read the report may suggest its appropriate length. Generally, the higher the report goes in an organization, the shorter it should be.

Another consideration is technical background—the gap in subject knowledge between the reader and the writer. The greater the gap, the more difficult it is to convey the full findings meaningfully and concisely.

The third prewriting question is, "What are the circumstances and limitations under which I am writing?" Is the nature of the subject highly technical? Do you need statistics? Charts? What is the importance of the topic? A crucial subject justifies more effort than a minor one. What should be the scope of the report? How much time is available? Deadlines often impose limitations on the report.

Finally, "How will the report be used?" Try to visualize the reader using the report. How can the information be made more convenient? How much effort must be given to getting the attention and interest of the reader? Will the report be read by more than one person? If so, how many copies should be made? What will be the distribution of the report?

The Outline

Once the researcher has made the first analysis of the data, drawn tentative conclusions, and completed statistical significance tests, it is time to develop an outline. A useful system employs the following organizational structure:

   I. Major Topic Heading
      A. Major subtopic heading
         1. Subtopic

a. Minor subtopic
(1) Further detail
(a) Even further detail

Software for developing outlines and visually connecting ideas simplifies this once-onerous task. Two styles of outlining are widely used—the topic outline and the sentence outline. In the **topic outline**, a key word or two are used. The assumption is that the writer knows its significance and will later remember the nature of the argument represented by that word or phrase or, alternatively, the outliner knows that a point should be made but is not yet sure how to make it.

topic outline a report planning format using key words or phrases.

The **sentence outline** expresses the essential thoughts associated with the specific topic. This approach leaves less development work for later writing, other than elaboration and explanation to improve readability. It has the obvious advantages of pushing the writer to make decisions on what to include and how to say it. It is probably the best outlining style for the inexperienced researcher because it divides the writing job into its two major components—what to say and how to say it.

sentence outline a report planning format using complete sentences.

Here is an example of the type of detail found with each of these outlining formats:

Topic Outline	Sentence Outline

I. Demand
  A. How measured
    1. Voluntary error
    2. Shipping error
      a. Monthly variance
	I. Demand for refrigerators
	  A. Measured in terms of factory shipments as reported to the U.S. Department of Commerce.
	    1. Error is introduced into year-to-year comparisons because reporting is voluntary.
	    2. A second factor is variations from month to month because of shipping and invoicing patterns.
	      a. Variations up to 30 percent this year depending on whether shipments were measured by actual shipment data or invoice date.

The Bibliography

Style manuals provide guidelines on form, section and alphabetical arrangement, and annotation. Proper citation, style, and formats are unique to the purpose of the report. The instructor, program, institution, or client often specifies style requirements. The uniqueness of varying requirements makes detailed examples in this chapter impractical, although the endnotes and references in this book provide an example. As cited in Chapter 6 on the research proposal, we recommend the *Publication Manual of the American Psychological Association;* Kate L. Turabian, *A Manual for Writers of Term Papers, Theses, and Dissertations;* and Joseph Gibaldi and Walter S. Achtert, *MLA Handbook for Writers of Research Papers.*

Bibliographic retrieval software allows researchers to locate and save references from online services and translate them into database records. Entries can be further searched, sorted, indexed, and formatted into bibliographies of any style. Many retrieval programs are network-compatible and connect to popular word processors.

Writing the Draft

Once the outline is complete, decisions can be made on the placement of graphics, tables, and charts. Each should be matched to a particular section in the outline. While graphics might be added later or tables changed into charts, it is helpful to make a first approximation of the graphics before beginning to write. Choices for reporting statistics will be reviewed later in this chapter.

Each writer uses different mechanisms for getting thoughts into written form. Some will write in longhand, relying on someone else to transcribe their prose into word-processed format. Others are happiest in front of a word processor, able to add, delete, and move sections at will. Whichever works for you is the best approach to use.

Computer software packages check for spelling errors and provide a thesaurus for looking up alternative ways of expressing a thought. A CD-ROM can call up the 20-volume *Oxford English Dictionary,* believed to be the greatest dictionary in any language. Common word confusion (*there* for *their, to* for *too,* or *effect* for *affect*) will not be found by standard spelling checkers. Advanced programs will scrutinize your report for grammar, punctuation, capitalization, doubled words, transposed letters, homonyms, style problems, and readability level. The style checker will reveal misused words and indicate awkward phrasing. Exhibit 23-4 shows sample output from a commercial package used on one of this text's vignettes. The program shown writes comments to a text file, prepares a backup copy of the original, and generates a statistics report. The statistics summarize the program's evaluation of readability, grade level, and sentence structure. Comparisons to "reference" documents, or documents that you submit for comparison, may be made. The software cannot guarantee an error-free report but will greatly reduce your time in proofreading and enhance the style of the completed product.[4]

▶**Exhibit 23-4** Grammar and Style Proofreader Results

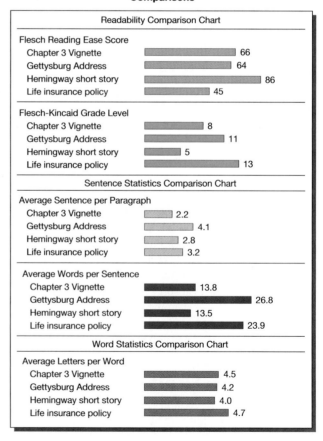

Statistics

Statistics for: Chapter 3 Vignette	Problems marked/detected: 8/8
Readability Statistics	
Flesch Reading Ease: 66	Flesch-Kincaid Grade Level: 8
Gunning's Fog Index: 11	

Paragraph Statistics	
Number of paragraphs: 25	Average length: 2.2 sentences

Sentence Statistics		
Number of sentences: 55	Passive voice:	4
Average length:	13.8 words	Short (< 12 words) : 39
End with ? :	2	Long (> 28 words) : 7
End with ! :	0	

Word Statistics		
Number of words:	759	Average length: 4.58 letters

Document Summary for: Chapter 3 Vignette	Problems detected: 8
Readability Statistics	Interpretation
Grade level: 8 (Flesch-Kincaid)	Preferred level for most readers.
Reading ease score: 66 (Flesch)	This represents 6 to 10 years of schooling.
Passive voice: 331	Writing may be difficult to read or ambiguous for this writing style.
Average sentence length: 13.8 words	Most readers could easily understand sentences of this length.
Average word length: 1.50 syl.	Vocabulary used in this document is understandable for most readers.
Average paragraph length: 2.2 sentences	Most readers could easily follow paragraphs of this length.

Comparisons

Readability Comparison Chart

Flesch Reading Ease Score

Chapter 3 Vignette	66
Gettysburg Address	64
Hemingway short story	86
Life insurance policy	45

Flesch-Kincaid Grade Level

Chapter 3 Vignette	8
Gettysburg Address	11
Hemingway short story	5
Life insurance policy	13

Sentence Statistics Comparison Chart

Average Sentence per Paragraph

Chapter 3 Vignette	2.2
Gettysburg Address	4.1
Hemingway short story	2.8
Life insurance policy	3.2

Average Words per Sentence

Chapter 3 Vignette	13.8
Gettysburg Address	26.8
Hemingway short story	13.5
Life insurance policy	23.9

Word Statistics Comparison Chart

Average Letters per Word

Chapter 3 Vignette	4.5
Gettysburg Address	4.2
Hemingway short story	4.0
Life insurance policy	4.7

Readability

Sensitive writers consider the reading ability of their audience to achieve high readership. You can obtain high readership more easily if the topic interests the readers and is in their field of expertise. In addition, you can show the usefulness of the report by pointing out how it will help the readers. Finally, you can write at a level that is appropriate to the audience's reading abilities. To test writing for difficulty level, use a standard **readability index.** The Flesch Reading Ease Score gives a score between 0 and 100. The lower the score, the harder the material is to read. The Flesch-Kincaid Grade Level and Gunning's Fog Index both provide a score that corresponds with the grade level needed to easily read and understand the document. Although it is possible to calculate these indexes by hand, some software packages will do it automatically. The most sophisticated packages allow you to specify the preferred reading level. Words that are above that level are highlighted to allow you to choose an alternative.

readability index measures the difficulty level of written material.

Advocates of readability measurement do not claim that all written material should be at the simplest level possible. They argue only that the level should be appropriate for the audience. They point out that comic books score about 6 on the Gunning scale (that is, a person with a sixth-grade education should be able to read that material). *Time* usually scores about 10, while *The Atlantic* is reported to have a score of 11 or 12. Material that scores much above 12 becomes difficult for the public to read comfortably. Such measures obviously give only a rough idea of the true readability of a report. Good writing calls for a variety of other skills to enhance reading comprehension.

Comprehensibility

Good writing varies with the writing objective. Research writing is designed to convey information of a precise nature. Avoid ambiguity, multiple meanings, and allusions. Take care to choose the right words—words that convey thoughts accurately, clearly, and efficiently. When concepts and constructs are used, they must be defined, either operationally or descriptively.

Words and sentences should be carefully organized and edited. Misplaced modifiers run rampant in carelessly written reports. Subordinate ideas mixed with major ideas make the report confusing to readers, forcing them to sort out what is important and what is secondary when this should have been done for them.

Finally, there is the matter of pace. **Pace** is defined as:

pace the rate at which the printed page presents information to the reader.

> The rate at which the printed page presents information to the reader. . . . The proper pace in technical writing is one that enables the reader to keep his mind working just a fraction of a second behind his eye as he reads along. It logically would be slow when the information is complex or difficult to understand; fast when the information is straightforward and familiar. If the reader's mind lags behind his eye, the pace is too rapid; if his mind wanders ahead of his eye (or wants to) the pace is too slow.[5]

If the text is overcrowded with concepts, there is too much information per sentence. By contrast, sparse writing has too few significant ideas per sentence. Writers use a variety of methods to adjust the pace of their writing:

- Use ample white space and wide margins to create a positive psychological effect on the reader.
- Break large units of text into smaller units with headings to show organization of the topics.
- Relieve difficult text with visual aids when possible.
- Emphasize important material and deemphasize secondary material through sentence construction and judicious use of italicizing, underlining, capitalization, and parentheses.
- Choose words carefully, opting for the known and short rather than the unknown and long. Graduate students, in particular, seem to revel in using jargon, pompous

constructions, and long or arcane words. Naturally, there are times when technical terms are appropriate. Scientists communicate efficiently with jargon, but the audiences for most applied research are not scientifically trained and need more help than many writers supply.

- Repeat and summarize critical and difficult ideas so that readers have time to absorb them.
- Make strategic use of service words. These are words that "do not represent objects or ideas, but show relationship. Transitional words, such as the conjunctions, are service words. So are phrases such as 'on the other hand,' 'in summary,' and 'in contrast.'"[6]

Tone

Review the writing to ensure the tone is appropriate. The reader can, and should, be referred to, but researchers should avoid referring to themselves. One author notes that the "application of the 'you' attitude . . . makes the message sound like it is written to the reader, not sent by the author. A message prepared for the reader conveys sincerity, personalization, warmth, and involvement on the part of the author."[7] To accomplish this, remove negative phrasing and rewrite the thought positively. Do not change your recommendations or your findings to make them positive. Instead, review the phrasing. Which of the following sounds better?

End users do not want the Information Systems Department telling them what software to buy.

End users want more autonomy over their computer software choices.

The messages convey the same information, but the positive tone of the second message does not put readers from the Information Systems Department on the defensive.

Final Proof

It is helpful to put the draft away for a day before doing the final editing. Go to the beach, ride a bicycle in the park, or see a movie—do anything that is unrelated to the research project. Then return to the report and read it with a critical eye. Does the writing flow smoothly? Are there transitions where they are needed? Is the organization apparent to the reader? Do the findings and conclusions adequately meet the problem statement and the research objectives? Are the tables and graphics displaying the proper information in an easy-to-read format? After assuring yourself that the draft is complete, write the executive summary.

Presentation Considerations

The final consideration in the report-writing process is production. Reports can be typed; printed on an ink-jet, laser, color, or other printer; or sent out for typesetting. Most student and small research reports are typed or produced on a computer printer. The presentation of the report conveys to the readers the professional approach used throughout the project. Care should be taken to use compatible fonts throughout the entire report. The printer should produce consistent, easy-to-read letters on quality paper. When reports are photocopied for more than one reader, make sure the copies are clean and have no black streaks or gray areas.

Overcrowding of text creates an appearance problem. Readers need the visual relief provided by ample white space. We define "ample" as 1 inch of white space at the top, bottom, and right-hand margins. On the left side, the margin should be at least 1¼ inches to provide room for binding or punched holes. Even greater margins will often improve report appearance and help to highlight key points or sections. Overcrowding also occurs when the report contains page after page of large blocks of unbroken text. This produces an unpleasant psychological effect on readers because of its formidable appearance. Overcrowded text, however, may be avoided in the following ways:

- Use shorter paragraphs. As a rough guide, any paragraph longer than half a page is suspect. Remember that each paragraph should represent a distinct thought.
- Indent parts of text that represent listings, long quotations, or examples.
- Use headings and subheadings to divide the report and its major sections into homogeneous topical parts.
- Use vertical listings of points (such as this list).

Inadequate labeling creates another physical problem. Each graph or table should contain enough information to be self-explanatory. Text headings and subheadings also help with labeling. They function as signs for the audience, describing the organization of the report and indicating the progress of discussion. They also help readers to skim the material and to return easily to particular sections of the report.

> Presentation of Statistics[8]

The presentation of statistics in research reports is a special challenge for writers. Four basic ways to present such data are in (1) a text paragraph, (2) semitabular form, (3) tables, or (4) graphics.

Text Presentation

This is probably the most common method of presentation when there are only a few statistics. The writer can direct the reader's attention to certain numbers or comparisons and emphasize specific points. The drawback is that the statistics are submerged in the text, requiring the reader to scan the entire paragraph to extract the meaning. The following material has a few simple comparisons but becomes more complicated when text and statistics are combined:

> Wal-Mart's continued ascendancy to the ranks of super-business is clearly visible in a comparison between it and the Forbes 500 top-ranked business, General Electric. While ranked 6th overall, Wal-Mart surpasses the number 1–ranked GE in overall sales (85.6% greater) and sales growth over the previous year (167.3% greater). In profit growth compared to the previous year, Wal-Mart's 20% profit growth demolishes GE's 7.1%. But GE is still the winner in overall profits where it counts the most; Wal-Mart earns only 53.1% of the manufacturing behemoth.

>close up

MindWriter Written Report

A written report is the culmination of the MindWriter project, which has illustrated the research process throughout the book. Visionary Insights' contract for the CompleteCare project requires a report about the size of a student term project. Although repetitive portions have been omitted to conserve space, it should give the reader some idea of how an applied project of this size is summarized. Descriptive statistics and simple graphics are used to analyze and present most of the data. References to chapters where specific details may be reviewed are shown in the marginal comments.

The presentation of findings follows the content specifications of Exhibit 23-2 for short reports. It falls between a memo/letter and a short technical report. The objective was to make it available quickly for feedback to the CompleteCare team. It was therefore set up as a PDF e-mail attachment.

The fax cover sheet acts as a temporary transmittal letter until the plain paper copies are sent.

It provides all necessary identification and contact information. The writer's and recipient's relationship makes using first names appropriate.

To:	Ms. Gracie Uhura	**From:**	Jason Henry
Company:	MindWriter Corp.	**Company:**	Visionary Insights, Inc.
Location:	Austin, TX Bldg 5	**Location:**	Palm Beach, FL
Telephone:	512.555.1234	**Telephone:**	407.555.4321
Fax:	512.555.1250	**Fax:**	407.555.4357

Total number of pages including this one: 11

January 5, 2005

Dear Gracie,

Authorization for the study. Scope of findings (month). Specific instructions for process issues.

This fax contains the CompleteCare December report requested by Mr. Malraison through Myra Wines. You may expect the plain paper copies tomorrow morning for distribution.

Request for follow-up by the client to reduce the study's limitations.

We hope that the Call Center will complete the nonrespondent surveys so that we can discover the extent to which these results represent all CompleteCare customers.

Progress update and feedback on improvements.

This month's findings show improvements in the areas we discussed last week by telephone. The response rate is also up. You will be delighted to know that our preliminary analysis shows improvements in the courier's ratings.

Best regards,

Jason

Title contains reference to a known survey and program. Descriptions of variables, relationships, and population are unnecessary.

The recipient of the report, corporation, and date appear next.

The report's preparer, location, and telephone number facilitate contact for additional information.

The information level identifies this as a restricted circulation document for in-house use only.

CompleteCare Customer Survey Results for December

Prepared for Ms. Gracie Uhura
MindWriter Corporation
January 2005

Visionary Insights, Inc
200 ShellPoint Tower
Palm Beach, Florida 33480

407.555.4321

MindWriter CONFIDENTIAL

Title repeated.

Section headings are used.
Introduction contains period of coverage for report, management question, and secondary research objective.

An overview of the report's contents allows readers to turn to specific section of interest.

The executive summary provides a synopsis of essential findings. It is the report in miniature—six paragraphs.

Both positive and negative results are capsulized.

Criteria for indexes are provided as reminders. The methodology,

MindWriter CompleteCare December Results

Introduction

This report is based on the December data collected from the MindWriter Complete-Care Survey. The survey asks customers about their satisfaction with the Complete-Care repair and service system. Its secondary purpose is to identify monthly improvement targets for management.

The findings are organized into the following sections: (1) an executive summary, (2) the methods used, (3) the Service Improvement Grid, (4) detailed findings for each question, and (5) patterns in the open-ended questions.

Executive Summary

The highest degrees of satisfaction with CompleteCare were found in the categories of "delivery speed" and "pickup speed." Average scores on these items were between 4.2 and 4.4 on a 5-point scale. "Speed of repair," "condition on arrival," and "overall impression of CompleteCare's effectiveness" also scored relatively well. They were above the *met all expectations* level (see appropriate charts).

Several questions were below the *met all expectations* level. From the lowest, "Call Center's responsiveness," to "Call Center's technical competence," and "courier service's arrangements," the average scores ranged from 2.0 to 3.9. In general, ratings have improved since November with the exception of "condition on arrival."

The three items generating the most negative comments are (1) problems with the courier's arrangements, (2) long telephone waits, and (3) transfer among many people at the Call Center. These same comments carry over for the last two months.

CompleteCare's criteria for Dissatisfied Customers consist of negative comments in the Comments/Suggestions section or ratings of less than three (3.0) on questions one through eight. Forty-three percent of the sample met these criteria, down from 56 percent last month. By counting only customers' comments (positive/negative or +/−), the percentage of Dissatisfied Customers would be 32 percent.

The ratio of negative to positive comments was 1.7 to 1, an improvement over November's ratio (2.3 to 1).

reported in brief, reminds the readers of the data collection method, nature and format of the questionnaire, scales used, and target measurement issues.

The sample, a self-selecting nonprobability sample, and the response rate are shown. With respondents' data from the postcards and the Call Center's files on nonrespondents, a future study on nonresponse bias is planned.

This section begins the Findings section. Findings consist of the action planning grid and detailed results sections. The headings were specified by the client.

The method for creating the planning grid and the grid's contents are highlighted.
The statistical technique

When the expectation-based satisfaction scores are adjusted for perceived importance, "Call Center responsiveness," "Call Center technical competence," and "courier arrangements" are identified as action items. "Repair speed" and "problem resolution" maintained high importance scores and are also rated above average.

Methodology

The data collection instrument is a postage-paid postcard that is packed with the repaired product at the time the unit is shipped back to the customer.

The survey consists of 12 satisfaction questions measured on five-point scales. The questions record the degree to which the components of the CompleteCare process (arrangements for receiving the customer's computer through return of the repaired product) meet customers' *expectations*. A final categorical question asks whether customers will use CompleteCare again. Space for suggestions is provided.

Sample

The sample consisted of 175 customers who provided impressions of Complete-Care's effectiveness. For the four-week period, the response rate was 35 percent with no incentive given. Nothing is yet known about the differences between respondents and nonrespondents.

Service Improvement Grid

The grid on page three compares the degree to which expectations were met along with the *derived importance* of those expectations. The average scores for both axes determine the dividing lines for the four quadrants. The quadrants are labeled to identify actionable items and to highlight those that bear watching for improvement or deterioration.

The **Concentrate Efforts** quadrant is the area where customers are marginally satisfied with service but consider service issues important. Question 1a, "Call Center's responsiveness," Question 1b, "Call Center's technical competence," and Question 2a, "courier arrangements," are found here. "Technical competence" was similarly rated last month. Its perceived importance was rated higher in previous months. "Courier arrangements" has increased in perceived importance over previous reports.

>**close**up**cont'd**

The statistical technique for producing the grid is correlation. A modification of scatterplots was used to create a plot with reference lines (see Chapter 21).

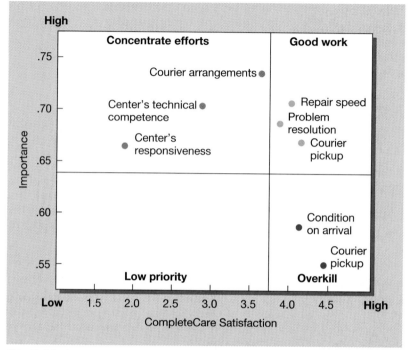

Note: Satisfaction scores are in the range of 1.0 to 5.0 and importance is in the range of 0 to 1.0.

The contents of each quadrant are described. Comparisons and connections to the next section are previewed.

In the **Good Work** quadrant, CompleteCare has, on average, *met all expectations* with the "repair speed" and "courier pickup" questions. Their mean scores are greater than 4.0 and considered important by respondents. "Problem resolution" has improved but remains a borderline concern.

There are no items in the **Low Priority** quadrant.

Overkill, the last quadrant, contains two questions. Question 5, "condition on arrival," has improved its ratings over last month but has dropped slightly on the importance scale because the average of importance scores (horizontal line) moved upward. Question 2c, "courier delivery speed," has a high satisfaction rating, but respondents considered this item to have lower importance than most issues in CompleteCare.

the results of individual questions. This section announces the two-part content and presents, briefly and in a direct style, the most pertinent outcomes.

This graphic gives the reader a three-month view of all the questions at a glance. Vertical bars are the simplest and easiest to read for the amount of space allocated. Horizontal grid lines guide the eye from the bar tops to the closest value on the mean score axis.

Charts similar to these may be produced by the same spreadsheet that handles data entry. Charting programs offer other options and will import the data from spreadsheets.
The first individual item is

Detailed Findings

The figures that follow provide (1) a comparison of the mean scores for each of the questions for the last three months and (2) individual question results. The latter contains frequencies for the scale values, percentages for each category, mean scores, standard deviations, and valid cases for each question. (See Appendix for question wording and placement.)

The three-month comparison (October, November, December) shows results for all scaled questions. December data bars (in blue) reveal improvements on all average scores (vertical axis) except Question 5, "condition on arrival." Most aspects of the service/repair process have shown improvement over the three-month period.

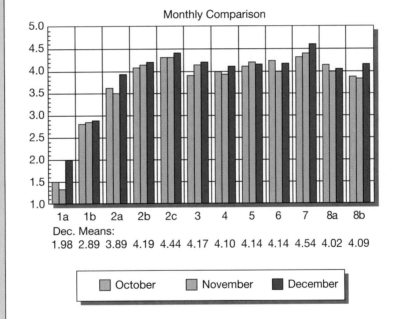

>closeupcont'd

The first individual item is reported with mean scores, percentages, and recommendations for improvement.

Question 1a. Call Center's Responsiveness. This question has the lowest mean score of the survey. Using a top-box method of reporting (combining the top two categories), 11 percent of the respondents felt that the Call Center met or exceeded their expectations for service responsiveness. This has improved only marginally since November and has significant implications for program targets. Based on our visit and recent results, we recommend that you begin immediately the contingency programs we discussed: additional training for Call Center operators and implementation of the proposed staffing plan.

This chart conveys the message of low responsiveness rather well but does not have a label for the vertical axis. It is easy to confuse percentages with the number of respondents (which it is supposed to represent).

Similar reporting formats are skipped.

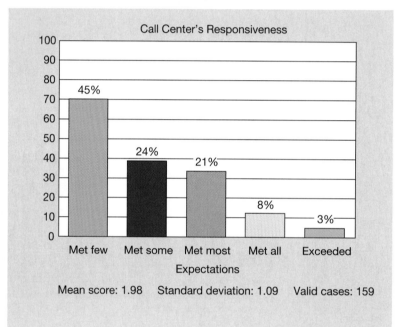

Mean score: 1.98   Standard deviation: 1.09   Valid cases: 159

respondents' overall impression of CompleteCare. It would be an ideal dependent variable for a regression study in which questions 1 through 5 were the independent variables (see Chapters 21 and 22).

Question 6. Overall Impression of CompleteCare's Effectiveness. CompleteCare has increased the number of truly satisfied respondents with 46 percent (versus 43 percent in November) in the *exceeded expectations* category. The top-box score has increased to 75 percent of respondents (against 70 percent in November).

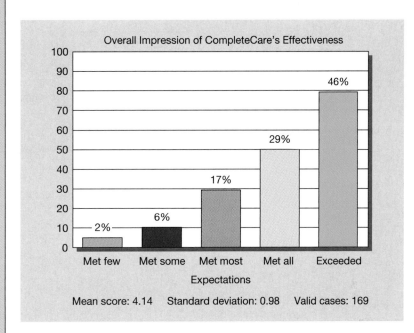

Overall Impression of CompleteCare's Effectiveness

Mean score: 4.14   Standard deviation: 0.98   Valid cases: 169

Question 8a is another question for more detailed research. It allows the researcher to connect the variables that describe the service/repair experience with repurchase intentions.
Using regression, it was

Question 8a. Likelihood of Repurchasing MindWriter Based on Service/Repair Experience.   Respondents' average scores (4.02) for this likelihood scale are the highest this month since measurement began. Improvement of the courier service's arrangements with customers and the resolution of the problem that prompted service appear to be the best predictors of repurchase at this time.

Using regression, it was possible to identify two key influences for this question.

Question 8b (not shown) is similar, asking about the relation of product performance to repurchase intention.

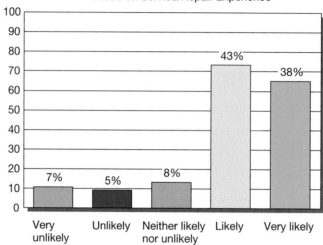

Likelihood of Repurchasing MindWriter
Based on Service/Repair Experience

Mean score: 4.02   Standard deviation: 1.10   Valid cases: 165

Patterns in the Open-Ended Questions

The following categories were found when the comments and suggestions were analyzed. The ratio of negative to positive comments was 1.7 to 1. Pickup problems continue to be "courier only" problems and coordination between MindWriter's telephone support and the courier. Customers complain of holding on the phone for long periods and being transferred between support people. Problems with service are split between large problems that have not been fixed and small, nuisance problems that customers are prepared to live with. Positive comments commend turnaround and service and also praise specific technical operators.

The questionnaire has one open-ended question that encourages respondents to make comments or suggestions.

Content analysis is used to distill the responses (see Chapter 18).

produces more than frequency counts of recurring themes, it is a labor-intensive process. The project's restrictive budget and the needs of the audience made this section of the report adequate for its purpose.

Negative Comments	Count
Shipping	19
Pickup problems (15)	
Delivery problems (2)	
Box damage (1)	
The courier charged customer (1)	
Call Center	19
Too long on hold (9)	
Transferred call too frequently/confusion (8)	
Untrained/hard to understand (2)	
Service	13
Problem continues (5)	
Small things not fixed/damaged (6)	
Took too long (2–7 weeks) (2)	
Product	6
Multiple repairs needed (3)	
Paint wears off (2)	
General dislike of product (1)	
Positive Comments	
General positive comment about the process	13
Quick response	12
Great service	7
Helpful phone personnel	6
Other Comments	
MindWriter shouldn't need to be repaired	4
Provide more information on what was done	2
Offer extended warranty	1
Won't use MindWriter Call Center again	1

>closeupcont'd

Appendix Contents
Sample Questionnaire

MindWriter personal computers offer you ease of use and maintenance. When you need service, we want you to rely on *CompeteCare,* wherever you may be. That's why we're asking you to take a moment to tell us how well we've served you.

	Met **few** expectations 1	Met **some** expectations 2	Met **most** expectations 3	Met **all** expectations 4	**Exceeded** expectations 5

1. Telephone assistance with your problem:
   - a. Responsiveness   1   2   3   4   5
   - b. Technical competence   1   2   3   4   5
2. The courier service's effectiveness:
   - a. Arrangements   1   2   3   4   5
   - b. Pickup speed   1   2   3   4   5
   - c. Delivery speed   1   2   3   4   5
3. Speed of the overall repair process.   1   2   3   4   5
4. Resolution of the problem that prompted service/repair.   1   2   3   4   5
5. Condition of your MindWriter on arrival.   1   2   3   4   5
6. Overall impression of CompleteCare's effectiveness.   1   2   3   4   5
7. Likelihood of using CompleteCare on another occasion.
   (1 = very unlikely 3 = neither likely nor unlikely 5 = very likely)   1   2   3   4   5
8. Likelihood of repurchasing a MindWriter based on:
   (1 = very unlikely 3 = neither likely nor unlikely 5 = very likely)
   - a. Service/repair experience   1   2   3   4   5
   - b. Product performance   1   2   3   4   5

Comments/Suggestions: _____

_____

_____

How may we contact you to follow up on any problems you have experienced?

_____   (_____) _____
Last Name   First Name   Phone

_____
City   State   Zip

Service Code

This report's appendix contains a copy of the questionnaire (see Chapter 15.)

Semitabular Presentation

When there are just a few figures, they may be taken from the text and listed. Lists of quantitative comparisons are much easier to read and understand than embedded statistics. An example of a semitabular presentation is shown below:

Wal-Mart's continued ascendancy to the ranks of super-business is clearly visible in a comparison between it and the Forbes 500 top-ranked business, General Electric:

- Wal-Mart's sales ($244.5 billion) are 85.6% greater than GE's sales ($131.6 billion).
- Wal-Mart's sales growth (12.3%) is 1.7 times greater than GE's sales growth (4.6%).

- Wal-Mart's profit growth (20.5%) is 2.9 times greater than GE's profit growth (7.1%).
- GE's profits ($15.133 billion), however, are 1.9 times greater than Wal-Mart ($8.039 billion).

Tabular Presentation

Tables are generally superior to text for presenting statistics, although they should be accompanied by comments directing the reader's attention to important figures. Tables facilitate quantitative comparisons and provide a concise, efficient way to present numerical data.

> Wal-Mart's continued ascendancy to the ranks of super-business is clearly visible in a comparison between it and the Forbes 500 top-ranked business, General Electric. Wal-Mart exceeds General Electric in sales, sales growth, and profit growth, but not in profits.

How Wal-Mart Compares	Rank	Sales ($, millions)	Sales Growth over Prior Yr.	Profits ($, millions)	Profit Growth over Prior Yr.
General Electric	1	$131,698	4.60%	$15,133.00	7.1%
Wal-Mart	6	$244,524	12.30%	$8,039.00	20.5%

Source: 2003 Forbes 500, http://www.forbes.com/2003/03/26/500sland.html.

Tables are either general or summary in nature. General tables tend to be large, complex, and detailed. They serve as the repository for the statistical findings of the study and are usually in the appendix of a research report.

Summary tables contain only a few key pieces of data closely related to a specific finding. To make them inviting to the reader (who often skips them), the table designer should omit unimportant details and collapse multiple classifications into composite measures that may be substituted for the original data.

Any table should contain enough information for the reader to understand its contents. The title should explain the subject of the table, how the data are classified, the time period, or other related matters. A subtitle is sometimes included under the title to explain something about the table; most often this is a statement of the measurement units in which the data are expressed. The contents of the columns should be clearly identified by the column heads, and the contents of the stub should do the same for the rows. The body of the table contains the data, while the footnotes contain any needed explanations. Footnotes should be identified by letters or symbols such as asterisks, rather than by numbers, to avoid confusion with data values. Finally, there should be a source note if the data do not come from your original research. Exhibit 23-5 illustrates the various parts of a table.

Graphics

Compared with tables, graphs show less information and often only approximate values. However, they are more often read and remembered than tables. Their great advantage is that they convey quantitative values and comparisons more readily than tables. With personal computer charting programs, you can easily turn a set of numbers into a chart or graph.

There are many different graphic forms. Exhibit 23-6 shows the most common ones and how they should be used. Statistical explanation charts such as boxplots, stem-and-leaf displays, and histograms were discussed in Chapter 19. Line graphs; area, pie, and bar charts; and pictographs and 3-D graphics receive additional attention here.

>**Exhibit 23-5** Sample Tabular Findings

Internet Access and Online Service Usage (2000)* ——————————————————————— Title

Item	Total adults	Any online Internet usage	Have Internet access			Used any online servce in the past 30 days
			Home or work	Home only	Work only	
Total Adults (1000)	199,438	90,458	112,949	77,621	50,476	75,409
PERCENT DISTRIBUTION						
Age						
18 to 34 years old	32.5	39.7	37.9	35.1	34.9	40.3
35 to 54 years old	39.9	47.7	46.0	49.4	55.4	47.4
55 years old or over	27.6	12.7	16.2	15.5	9.7	12.3
Gender						
Male	48	49.8	48.5	49.3	52.3	49.3
Female	52.0	50.2	51.5	50.7	47.7	50.7
Household Size						
1 to 2 persons	47.9	40.2	41.0	37.9	41.8	29.5
3 to 4 persons	36.9	44.4	43.3	45.9	44.6	44.5
5 or more persons	15.2	15.4	15.7	16.2	13.6	16.1
Any child in household	42.1	47.7	47.0	48.7	48.0	47.9
Marital status						
Single	23.7	27.5	26.0	23.4	22.6	28.4
Married	57.2	61.6	61.1	66.2	65.3	60.6
Other	19.1	10.9	12.9	10.3	12.0	10.9
Educational Attainment						
Graduated college plus	22.5	38.0	33.6	38.6	49.2	37.8
Attended college	26.5	34.8	33.7	34.0	30.6	35.0
Did not attend college	51.0	27.2	32.8	27.3	20.3	27.2
Household Income						
Less than $50,000	55.1	33.6	38.3	29.9	23.3	32.9
$50,000 to $74,000	20.7	26.2	25.7	26.9	27.4	26.0
$75,000 to $149,999	20.1	32.6	29.4	34.7	39.6	33.1
$150,000 or more	4.1	7.6	6.7	8.5	9.7	8.0

Column Heads — Banner — Title — Stub — Body

*For persons 18 years of age or older (199,438). As of spring.
Based on sample and subject to sampling error; see source for details.   **Footnote**
Source: Mediamark Research, Inc., New York, NY. CyberStats, © Spring 2000.   **Source Note**
Internet site http://www.mediamark.com (accessed 23 May 2000).

Line Graphs

line graph a statistical presentation technique used for time series and frequency distributions over time.

Line graphs are used chiefly for time series and frequency distribution. There are several guidelines for designing a line graph:

• Put the time units or the independent variable on the horizontal axis.

• When showing more than one line, use different line types (solid, dashed, dotted, dash-dot) to enable the reader to easily distinguish among them.

• Try not to put more than four lines on one chart.

• Use a solid line for the primary data.

It is important to be aware of perceptual problems with line diagrams. The first is the use of a zero baseline. Since the length of the bar or distance above the baseline indicates the statistic, it is important that graphs give accurate visual impressions of values. A good way to

>**Exhibit 23-6** Guide to Graphs

Column Compares sizes and amounts of categories usually for the same time. Places categories on *X* axis and values on *Y* axis.

Bar Same as the column but positions categories on *Y* axis and values on *X* axis. Deviations, when used, distinguish positive from negative values.

Stacked Bar In either bar or column, shows how components contribute to the total of the category.

Pie Shows relationship of parts to the whole. Wedges are row values of data.

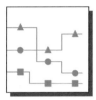

Stacked Pie Same as pie but displays two or more data series.

Multiple Pie Uses same data as stacked pie but plots separate pies for each column of data without stacking.

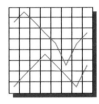

Line Compares values over time to show changes in trends.

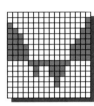

Filled Line Similar to line chart, but uses fill to highlight series.

Area (surface) Like line chart, compares changing values but emphasizes relative value of each series.

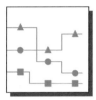

Step Compares discrete points on the value axis with vertical lines showing difference between points. Not for showing a trend.

Scatter Shows if relationship between variables follows a pattern. May be used with one variable at different times.

Bubble Used to introduce third variable (dots of different sizes). Axes could be sales, profits; bubbles are assets.

Spider (and Radar) Radiating lines are categories; values are distances from center (shows multiple variables—e.g., performance, ratings, progress).

Polar Shows relationship between a variable and angle measured in degrees (cyclical trends, pollution source vs. wind direction, etc.).

Open Hi Lo Close Shows fluctuating values in a given period (hour, day). Often used for investments.

Boxplot Displays distribution(s) and compares characteristics of shape (Chapter 19).

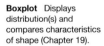

Pictograph Special chart that uses pictures or graphic elements in lieu of bars.

achieve this is to include a zero baseline on the scale on which the curves are plotted. To set the base at some other value is to introduce a visual bias. This can be seen by comparing the visual impressions in parts A and B of Exhibit 23-7. Both are accurate plots of cable television systems in the United States from 1985 through 2000. In part A, however, using the baseline of zero places the curve well up on the chart and gives a better perception of the relation between the absolute size of cable systems and the changes on a five-year interval. The graph in part B, with a baseline at 6 million, can easily give the impression that the growth was at a more rapid rate. When space or other reasons dictate using shortened scales, the zero base point should still be used but with a break in the scale as shown in part C of Exhibit 23-7. This will warn the reader that the scale has been reduced.

>**Exhibit 23-7** Cable TV Systems and Subscribers, 1985–2000

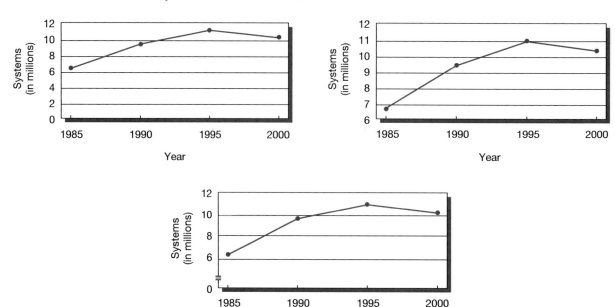

The balance of size between vertical and horizontal scales also affects the reader's impression of the data. There is no single solution to this problem, but the results can be seen by comparing parts B and C in Exhibit 23-7. In part C, the horizontal scale is twice that in part B. This changes the slope of the curve, creating a different perception of growth rate.

A third distortion with line diagrams occurs when relative and absolute changes among two or more sets of data are shown. In most charts, we use arithmetic scales, where each space unit has identical value. This shows the absolute differences between variables, as in part A of Exhibit 23-8, which presents the light- and heavy-truck sales in the United States from 1970 to 2000. This is an arithmetically correct way to present these data; but if we are interested in rates of growth, the visual impressions from a semi-logarithmic scale are more accurate. A semi-logarithmic scale uses a logarithm along one axis (usually the vertical or *Y* axis) and an arithmetic scale along the other axis (usually the horizontal or *X* axis). The *Y* axis shows quantity, and the *X* axis shows time. Arithmetic data are converted to natural logs by spreadsheet or statistical software and plotted. Semi-logarithmic graphics preserve percentage relationships across the scale.

A comparison of the line diagrams in parts A and B of Exhibit 23-8 shows how much difference a semi-logarithmic scale makes. Each is valuable, and each can be misleading. In part A, notice that sales of both light and heavy trucks have grown since 1970 but heavy-truck sales are only a small segment of U.S. sales of trucks and have a much flatter growth curve. One can even estimate what this proportion is. Part B gives insight into growth rates that are not clear from the arithmetic scale. It shows that while light trucks had a major growth spurt between 1980 and 1985, a spurt not shared by heavy trucks, since then their growth patterns have been more consistent with each other. From the calculated growth rate, in two of the last four five-year periods examined, the growth in heavy-truck sales actually exceeded the growth in light-truck sales, even while light-truck sales far exceeded heavy-truck sales.

Area (Stratum or Surface) Charts

area chart a graphical presentation for time series and frequency distributions over time.

An **area chart** is also used for a time series. Consisting of a line that has been divided into component parts, it is best used to show changes in patterns over time. The same rules apply to stratum charts as to line charts (see Exhibit 23-9).

>**Exhibit 23-8** U.S. Truck Sales 1970–2000 (in thousands)

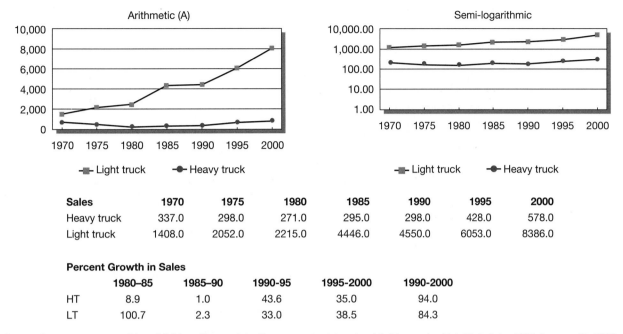

Sales	1970	1975	1980	1985	1990	1995	2000
Heavy truck	337.0	298.0	271.0	295.0	298.0	428.0	578.0
Light truck	1408.0	2052.0	2215.0	4446.0	4550.0	6053.0	8386.0

Percent Growth in Sales

	1980–85	1985–90	1990-95	1995-2000	1990-2000
HT	8.9	1.0	43.6	35.0	94.0
LT	100.7	2.3	33.0	38.5	84.3

Source: Data were extracted from Michigan Senate, http://www.senate.state.mi.us/sfa/Economics/RetailAutoSales.PDF, January 15, 2003.

>**Exhibit 23-9** Examples of Area Charts: A Stratum Chart and Two Pies

Notice the two pie charts seem to indicate a dramatic decrease in the "under 25" category. Now look at the stratum chart. The "under 25" category never decreased; it only changed relative to the entire population. It is important not to use pie charts alone in a time series, to avoid giving erroneous impressions.

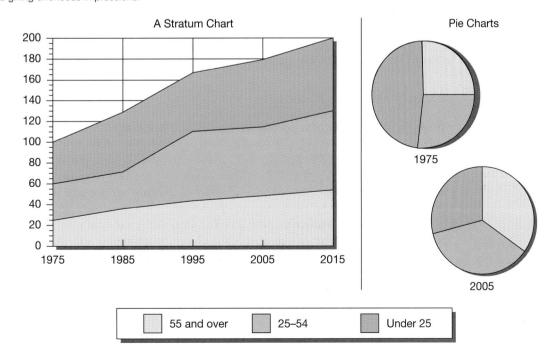

Pie Charts

pie chart graphical presentation using sections of a circle to represent 100 percent of a frequency distribution.

Pie charts are another form of area chart. They are often used with business data. However, they can easily mislead the reader or be improperly prepared. Research shows that readers' perceptions of the percentages represented by the pie slices are consistently inaccurate.[9] Consider the following suggestions when designing pie charts:

- Show 100 percent of the subject being graphed.
- Always label the slices with "call-outs" and with the percentage or amount that is represented. This allows you to dispense with a legend.
- Put the largest slice at twelve o'clock and move clockwise in descending order.
- Use light colors for large slices, darker colors for smaller slices.
- In a pie chart of black and white slices, a single red one will command the most attention and be memorable. Use it to communicate your most important message.[10]
- Do not show evolution over time with pie charts as the only medium. Since pie charts always represent 100 percent, growth of the overall whole will not be recognized. If you must use a series of pie charts, complement them with an area chart.

As shown in Exhibit 23-9, pie charts portray frequency data in interesting ways. In addition, they can be stacked to show relationships between two sets of data.

Bar Charts

bar chart graphical presentation technique that represents frequency data as horizontal or vertical bars.

Bar charts can be very effective if properly constructed. Use the horizontal axis to represent time and the vertical axis to represent units or growth-related variables. Vertical bars are generally used for time series and for quantitative classifications. Horizontal bars are less often used. If neither variable is time-related, either format can be used. A computer charting program (e.g., Excel, the newest version of SPSS) easily generates charts. If you are preparing a bar chart by hand, leave space between the bars equal to at least half the width of the bar. An exception to this is the specialized chart—the histogram—where continuous data are grouped into intervals for a frequency distribution (see Chapter 19). A second exception is the multiple-variable chart, where more than one bar is located at a particular time segment. In this case, the space between the groups of bars is at least half the width of the group. Bar charts come in a variety of patterns. In Chapter 19, Exhibit 19-3 shows a standard vertical bar graph. Variations are illustrated in Exhibit 23-6.

Pictographs and Geographs

pictograph bar chart using pictorial symbols rather than bars to represent frequency data.

These graphics are used in popular magazines and newspapers because they are eye-catching and imaginative. *USA Today* and a host of imitators are often guilty of taking this to the extreme, creating graphs that are incomprehensible. A **pictograph** uses pictorial symbols (an oil drum for barrels of oil, a stick figure for numbers of employees, or a pine tree for amount of wood). The symbols represent data volume and are used instead of a bar in a bar-type chart. It is proper to stack same-size images to express more of a quantity and to show fractions of an image to show less. But altering the scale of the symbol produces problems. Since the pictures represent actual objects, doubling the size will increase the area of the symbol by four (and the volume by more). This misleads the reader into believing the increase is larger than it really is. The exception is a graphic that is easily substituted for a bar, such as the pencils in Exhibit 23-6.

geographic chart uses a map to show regional variations in data.

Geographic charts use a portion of the world's map, in pictorial form, to show variations in regional data. They can be used for product sales, distribution status, media consumption, promotional response rates, per capita rates of consumption, demographics, or any of a number of other geographically specific variables.

>**Exhibit 23-10** 3-D Charts

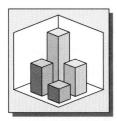  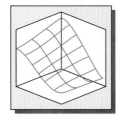 

3-D Column
A variation on column charts, they compare variables to each other or over time. Axes: *X* = categories, *Y* = series, *Z* = values. Other variations include 3-D area charts and connect-the-dots scatter charts.

3-D Ribbon This example is a one-wall plot showing columns of data (series) as ribbons. One or more columns are used. Axes: *X* = categories, *Y* = series, *Z* = values.

3-D Wireframe
A variation of a contour or response surface; suitable for changes in time and multivariate data. Axes: *X* = categories, *Y* = series, *Z* = values.

3-D Surface Line
Handles three columns of data and plots *XYZ* coordinates to show a response surface. Helpful for multivariate applications.

Stacked data sets produce variables of interest that can be aligned on a common geographic referent. The resulting pictorial display allows the user to "drill" through the layers and visualize the relationships. With better Windows-based software and government agencies providing geo-codes and reference points, geographic spatial displays are becoming a more common form of graphic.

> **See the example of mapped data in Chapter 19.**

3-D Graphics

With current charting techniques, virtually all charts can now be made three-dimensional. Although a **3-D graphic** adds interest, it can also obscure data. Care must be used in selecting 3-D chart candidates (see Exhibit 23-10). Don't confuse pie and bar charts that have achieved dimensionality simply by adding depth to the graphics; this is not 3-D. A 3-D column chart allows you to compare three or more variables from the sample in one bar chart–type graph. If you want to display several quarters of sales results for Hertz, Avis, Budget, and National, you have 3-D data. Surface charts and 3-D scatter charts are helpful for displaying complex data patterns if the underlying distributions are multivariate. Finally, be careful about converting line charts to ribbon charts, and area charts to 3-D area charts; these can be hard for a novice to read and your primary objective in graphical presentation is always data clarity.

3-D graphic a presentation technique that permits a graphical comparison of three or more variables.

> **Oral Presentations**

Researchers often present their findings orally. Such a presentation, sometimes called a **briefing,** has some unique characteristics that distinguish it from most other kinds of public speaking: Only a small group of people is involved; statistics normally constitute an important portion of the topic; the audience members are usually managers with an interest in the topic, but they want to hear only the critical elements; speaking time will often be as short as 20 minutes but may run longer than an hour; and the presentation is normally followed by questions and discussion.

briefing a short presentation to a small group where statistics constitute much of the content.

An internal, informal oral report of research findings (and often findings in process) is often a lively, interactive exchange of information. The researcher supports the discussion by sharing preliminary graphical and tabular displays of data and initial conclusions.

Preparation

A successful briefing typically requires condensing a lengthy and complex body of information. Since speaking rates should not exceed 100 to 150 words per minute, a 20-minute presentation limits you to about 2,000 to 2,500 words. If you are to communicate effectively under such conditions, you must plan carefully. Begin by asking two questions. First, how long should you plan to talk? Usually there is an indication of the acceptable presentation length. It may be the custom in an organization to take a given allotted time for a briefing. If the time is severely limited, then the need for topical priorities is obvious. This leads to the second question: What are the purposes of the briefing? Is it to raise concern about problems that have been uncovered? Is it to add to the knowledge of audience members? Is it to give them conclusions and recommendations for their decision making? Questions such as these illustrate the general objectives of the report. After answering these questions, you should develop a detailed outline of what you are going to say. Such an outline should contain the following major parts:

1. *Opening.* A brief statement, probably not more than 10 percent of the allotted time, sets the stage for the body of the report. The opening should be direct, get attention, and introduce the nature of the discussion that follows. It should explain the nature of the project, how it came about, and what it attempted to do.

2. *Findings and conclusions.* The conclusions may be stated immediately after the opening remarks, with each conclusion followed by the findings that support it.

3. *Recommendations.* Where appropriate, these are stated in the third stage; each recommendation may be followed by references to the conclusions leading to it. Presented in this manner, they provide a natural climax to the report. At the end of the presentation, it may be appropriate to call for questions from the audience.

Early in the planning stage you need to make two further decisions. The first concerns the type of audiovisuals (AVs) that will be used and the role they will play in the presentation. AV decisions are important enough that they are often made *before* the briefing outline and text are developed.

>**snap**shot

The Culture of Reporting

One of the few universally followed rules in presenting research results is to craft the message to fit the client. When the Team One/Lexus team ventured to Japan to share their early research findings, they knew they had to deliver any negatives with a polite, highly sensitive approach. The news was good. But to engineers who had crafted the Lexus SC 430 to be twice as good as the Jaguar XK8—more comfortable, quieter, and easier to handle—some of the findings would be puzzling. The team had held three static product clinics—where more than 250 luxury buyers were assembled to compare, but not drive, the Lexus SC 430 and its competitors. Shortly thereafter they had conducted numerous focus groups of the top tier of these interested luxury buyers, known as *acceptors*. Among the early findings the team learned that buyers expected the car to growl when the accelerator was depressed, to show exhaust, and to handle more like a

sports car. "Culturally, Japanese engineers have come to see themselves—and with justification—as entitled to make a car the way a car should be made," shared Arian Barrow, account manager for Lexus at Team One Advertising. This made telling them what they would consider negatives somewhat difficult. For example, buyers' expectations were that the car would zoom from zero to 60 in under five seconds, not arrive there in eight or nine seconds. "So we found ourselves sharing results in a less hard-hitting way than we would with a different client." How did they deliver the unexpected news? "People loved the car! But they would love it even more if it would go from zero to 60 in five seconds!"

www.teamoneadv.com; www.lexus.com.

Presenting your research findings using PowerPoint™ or other presentation software requires preparation similar to presenting with nonelectronic visual aids. The researcher must still determine his or her style of presentation, the order of findings, and which findings will be presented graphically, in tabular format, or verbally. As most visual aids are prepared using computer software, the key hyperlink files are already available. It might seem as though the presenter could bypass the costly printing of visual aids, which can be a time-consuming task. However, the electronic presenter must have a contingency plan for a malfunctioning computer. Color transparencies are the low-tech backup but clearly don't allow the full range of possibilities that electronic hyperlinks afford. Having a second laptop and projection system, as well as multiprong power cords and spare computer connection cords, is the usual high-tech insurance plan. The same general rule applied to all presentations is critical for electronic ones—practice, practice, practice—but a caveat is added: Practice *with your equipment* so that movement between files, hyperlinks, and your PowerPoint™ presentation seems effortless.

The second decision you must make as you plan for your presentation is what type it will be. Will it be memorized, read from your manuscript, or given extemporaneously? We rule out the impromptu briefing because impromptu speaking does not involve preparation. Your reputation and the research effort should not be jeopardized by "winging it."

Memorization is a risky and time-consuming course to follow. Any memory slip during the presentation can be a catastrophe, and the delivery sounds stilted and distant. Memorization virtually precludes establishing rapport with the audience members and adapting to their reactions while you speak. It produces a self- or speaker-centered approach and is not recommended.

Reading a manuscript is also not advisable, even though many professors seem to reward students who do so (perhaps because they themselves get away with it at professional meetings). The delivery sounds dull and lifeless because most people are not trained to read aloud, and therefore they do it badly. They become focused on the manuscript to the exclusion of the audience. This head-down preoccupation with the text is clearly inappropriate for management presentations.

**extemporaneous
presentation** a
conversational-style oral
presentation made from
minimal notes.

The **extemporaneous presentation** is audience-centered and made from minimal notes or an outline. This mode permits the speaker to be natural, conversational, and flexible. Clearly, it is the best choice for an organizational setting. Preparation consists of writing a draft along with a complete sentence outline and converting the main points to notes. In this way, you can try lines of argument, experiment with various ways of expressing thoughts, and develop phraseology. Along the way, the main points are fixed sequentially in your mind, and supporting connections are made.

Audiences accept speaker notes, and their presence does wonders in allaying speaker fears. Even if you never use them, they are there for psychological support. Many prefer to use 5-by-8-inch cards for their briefing notes because they hold more information and so require less shuffling than the smaller 3-by-5-inch size. Card contents vary widely, but here are some general guidelines for their design:

- Place title and preliminary remarks on the first card.
- Use each of the remaining cards to carry a major section of the presentation. The amount of detail depends on the need for precision and the speaker's desire for supporting information.
- Include key phrases, illustrations, statistics, dates, and pronunciation guides for difficult words. Include also quotations and ideas that bear repeating.
- Along the margin, place instructions and cues, such as SLOW, FAST, EMPHASIZE, TRANSPARENCY A, TURN CHART, and GO BACK TO CHART 3.
- Sequentially number your cards or notes, so you can return them quickly to order if they are accidentally shuffled.

After the outline and the AV aids comes the final stage of preparation—the rehearsal. Rehearsal, a prerequisite to effective briefing, is *too often slighted,* especially by inexperienced speakers. Giving a briefing is an artistic performance, and nothing improves it more than for the speaker to demonstrate mastery of the art. First rehearsal efforts should concentrate on those parts of the presentation that are awkward or poorly developed. After the problem areas have been worked out, there should be at least a few full-scale practices under simulated presentation conditions. All parts should be timed and edited until the time target is met. A videotape recorder is an excellent diagnostic tool.

Delivery

While the content of a report is the chief concern, the speaker's delivery is also important. A polished presentation adds to the receptiveness of the audience, but there is some danger that the presentation may overpower the message. Fortunately, the typical research audience knows why it is assembled, has a high level of interest, and does not need to be entertained. Even so, the speaker faces a real challenge in communicating effectively. The delivery should be restrained. Demeanor, posture, dress, and total appearance should be appropriate for the occasion. Speed of speech, clarity of enunciation, pauses, and gestures all play their part. Voice pitch, tone quality, and inflections are proper subjects for concern. There is little time for anecdotes and other rapport-developing techniques, yet the speaker must get and hold audience attention.

Speaker Problems

Inexperienced speakers have many difficulties in making presentations. They often are nervous at the start of a presentation and may even find breathing difficult. This is natural and should not be of undue concern. It may help to take a deep breath or two, holding each for a brief time before exhaling as fully as possible. This can be done inconspicuously on the way to the podium.

Overcoming the Jitters

The fear of public speaking ranks up there with the fear of death and/or public nudity. Whether you are a seasoned pro or this is your first speech, stage fright, the illogical fear of facing an audience, can be a paralyzing emotion. How do you handle those times when your mind starts going blank and your stomach is turning? Patricia Fripp, an award-winning keynote speaker and speech coach, provides some answers. She suggests that you "need to anticipate your speech mentally, physically, and logistically." Mental preparation is key and should be a six-to-one ratio: Invest three hours of preparation for a 30-minute speech. There is no substitute for rehearsal. Spend some time memorizing your opening and closing—three or four sentences each. Although you may speak from notes, knowing your opening and closing helps your fluency, allowing you to make the vital connection in rapport with your audience when you are likely to be most nervous.

Logistically, know the room. Go there as early as possible to get comfortable in the environment. Practice using the microphone and check the equipment. A quick review of your visual aids is also helpful. Then, during the presentation, you can focus on your audience and not be concerned with the environment.

The physical part of overcoming nervousness is varied and may be constrained by your setting. In a small-group setting, shake hands, exchange greetings, and make eye contact with everybody beforehand. In a larger meeting, at least connect with the people in the front row. Do so sincerely, and they'll be cheering for your success. They are not waiting for you to fail—they are far too worried about themselves—and they are there to listen to you. If possible, avoid sitting while you're waiting to speak. Find a position in the room where you can stand occasionally. The rear of the room gives you access to the bathroom and drinking fountain.

If your anxiety level is still high, then you need an outlet for your energy. Comedians and actors find that doing light exercises in their dressing rooms or in another private area can relieve the excess energy. Fripp adds, "Find a private spot, and wave your hands in the air. Relax your jaw, and shake your head from side to side. Then shake your legs one at a time. Physically shake the tension out of your body." The object is to release enough nervous energy to calm your anxieties—without becoming so stress-free that you forget your purpose and audience.
www.fripp.com

Several characteristics of inexperienced speakers may be summarized as questions. Even if you are an accomplished speaker, it is helpful to review them as you watch a videotape of your presentation.

1. *Vocal characteristics:*

    a. Do you speak so softly that someone cannot hear you well? It is helpful to have someone in the back of the room who can signal if your voice is not carrying far enough.

    b. Do you speak too rapidly? Remind yourself to slow down. Make deliberate pauses before sentences. Speak words with precision without exaggerating. However, some people talk too slowly, and this can make the audience restive.

    c. Do you vary volume, tone quality, and rate of speaking? Any of these can be used successfully to add interest to the message and engage audience attention. Speakers should not let their words trail off as they complete a sentence.

    d. Do you use overworked pet phrases, repeated *uhs, you know,* and *in other words?*

2. *Physical characteristics:*

    a. Do you rock back and forth, roll or twist from side to side, or lean too much on the lectern?

    b. Do you hitch or tug on clothing, scratch, or fiddle with pocket change, keys, pencils, or other devices?

    c. Do you stare into space? Lack of eye contact is particularly bothersome to listeners and is common with inexperienced speakers. Many seem to choose a spot above the heads of the audience and continue to stare at this spot except when looking at notes. *Eye contact is important.* Audience members need to feel that you are looking at them. It may be helpful to pick out three people in the audience (left, right, and center) and practice looking at them successively as you talk.

d. Do you misuse visuals by fumbling or putting them on in incorrect order or upside down? Do you turn your back to the audience to read from visuals?

Audiovisuals

Researchers can use a variety of AV media with good results. While there is need for computer-assisted media in many business applications, they will be mentioned here only briefly. Our emphasis is on visual aids that are relatively simple and inexpensive to make.

Low Tech

1. *Chalkboards and whiteboards.* Chalkboards are flexible and inexpensive, and they require little specific preparation. On the other hand, they are not novel and do not project a polished appearance. Whiteboards, both portable and installed, provide visual relief, particularly when color markers are used. Both varieties reduce speaking time while the speaker is writing. If you use either, write legibly or print, leave space between lines, and do not talk to the board with the audience to your back. If you are in an unfamiliar room, it is best to arrive prepared with erasable markers (or chalk) and erasure materials.

2. *Handout materials.* These are inexpensive but can have a professional look if done carefully. Handouts can include pictures and graphic materials that might be difficult to display otherwise. The disadvantages include the time needed to produce them and their distracting impact if not properly used. You may distribute them when the audience leaves, but a better use is to refer to them during your talk. If you use them this way, *do not hand them out until you are ready to refer to them.*

3. *Flip charts.* You can show color, pictures, and large letters with these. They are easy and inexpensive to make; they can focus listener attention on a specific idea. If not well made, they can be distracting. Unless they are large, they should be restricted to small groups and to types of material that can be summarized in a few words.

4. *Overhead transparencies.* These may be of different sizes, but the most common is about the same as an 8½-by-11-inch page. They are easily made with color markers or with a copy machine. Computer graphics can be plotted or printed directly to transparencies for a more accurate and professional look. Multiple-color and single-color renditions are available. You can also show overlays and buildups. In using transparencies, be sure they are in correct order and right side up when you place them on the projector.

5. *Slides.* Most slides are 35mm, but larger sizes are sometimes used. They are relatively inexpensive and colorful and present a professional-looking image if done well. They are somewhat more difficult to make but can be prepared with a personal computer and slide-construction software.

High Tech

6. *Computer-drawn visuals.* For transparencies and slides, the draw and paint programs for personal computers provide the presenter with limitless options for illustrating the message. Stored visuals can be teamed with a device for projecting the computer output to a screen, or the briefer can use the software to create the image at the moment a question is asked or a demonstration is appropriate. Be careful that the technology does not distract from the purpose of the message.

7. *Computer animation.* The development of larger and faster processors, memory chips, and disks has made it possible to store voice and image data in quantity in

As technology advances, the Internet has become a medium for oral presentations and videoconferences. As with other presentations, you need to be cautious with equipment and look for software glitches. Have a backup copy of your presentation on your laptop or your company's server. Test your external mouse as well as the one that is connected to your computer. Be certain that your screensavers are disabled. And most important, be prepared to give your presentation even if the technology fails.

personal computers. Technology permits multimedia presentations using videotape, videodisc, and CD-ROM elements that are integrated for the ultimate in image reproduction. For proposals, large contracts, or other business applications, the preparation and expense may be justifiable.

The choice of visual aids is determined by your intended purpose, the size of the audience, meeting room conditions, time and budget constraints, and available equipment.

Visual aids serve the presenter of a research presentation in several ways. They make it possible to present materials that cannot otherwise be communicated effectively. Statistical relationships are difficult to describe verbally, but a picture or graph communicates well. How better to describe some object or material than to show it or picture it?

Visual aids help the speaker to clarify major points. With visual reinforcement of a verbal statement, the speaker can stress the importance of points. In addition, the use of two channels of communication (hearing and sight) enhances the probability that the listener will understand and remember the message.

The continuity and memorability of the speaker's message are also improved with visual aids. Verbal information is so transient that any slight lapse of listener attention results in losing the information thread. The failure to fully comprehend a given point cannot be remedied by going back to hear it again, for the speaker has gone on. With a visual aid, however, there is more opportunity to review this point, relate it to earlier comments by the speaker, and improve retention.

>summary

1 A quality presentation of research findings can have an inordinate effect on a reader's or a listener's perceptions of a study's quality. Recognition of this fact should prompt a researcher to make a special effort to communicate skillfully and clearly.

2 Research reports contain findings, analysis, interpretations, conclusions, and sometimes recommendations. They may follow the short, informal format typical of memoranda and letters, or they may be longer and more complex. Long reports are of either a technical or a management type. In the former, the problem is presented and followed by the findings, conclusions, and recommendations. In the manage-

ment report, the conclusions and recommendations precede the findings. The technical report is targeted at the technically trained reader; the management report is intended for the manager-client.

3 The writer of research reports should be guided by four questions:

- What is the purpose of this report?

- Who will read it?

- What are the circumstances and limitations under which it is written?

- How will the report be used?

Reports should be clearly organized, physically inviting, and easy to read. Writers can achieve these goals if they are careful with mechanical details, writing style, and comprehensibility.

4 There is a special challenge to presenting statistical data. While some of these data may be incorporated in the text, most statistics should be placed in tables, charts, or graphs. The choice of a table, chart, or graph depends on the specific data and presentation purpose.

5 Oral presentations of research findings are common and should be developed with concern for the communication problems that are unique to such settings. Briefings are usually conducted under time constraints; good briefings require careful organization and preparation. Visual aids are a particularly important aspect of briefings but are too often ignored or treated inadequately.

Whether written or oral, poor presentations do a grave injustice to what might otherwise be excellent research. Good presentations, on the other hand, add luster to both the research and the reputation of the researcher.

>**key**terms

area chart 678	**letter of transmittal** 651	**readability index** 661
bar chart 680	**line graph** 676	**sentence outline** 659
briefing 681	**management report** 649	**technical report** 649
executive summary 652	**pace** 661	**3-D graphic** 681
extemporaneous presentation 684	**pictograph** 680	**topic outline** 659
geographic chart 680	**pie chart** 680	

>**discussion**questions

Terms in Review

1 Distinguish between the following:

   a Speaker-centered presentation and extemporaneous presentation.

   b Technical report and management report.

   c Topic outline and sentence outline.

Making Research Decisions

2 What should you do about each of these?

   a Putting information in a research report concerning the study's limitations.

   b The size and complexity of tables in a research report.

   c The physical presentation of a report.

   d Pace in your writing.

3 What type of report would you suggest be written in each of the following cases?

   a The president of the company has asked for a study of the company's pension plan and its comparison to the plans of other firms in the industry.

   b You have been asked to write up a marketing experiment, which you recently completed, for submission to the *Journal of Marketing Research.*

   c Your division manager has asked you to prepare a forecast of promotional budget needs for the division for the next 12 months.

   d The National Institutes of Health has given you a grant to study the relationship between advertising of prescription drugs and subsequent sales of those drugs.

4 There are a number of graphic presentation forms. Which would you recommend to show each of the following? Why?

   a A comparison of changes in average annual per capita income for the United States and Japan from 1990 to 2000.

   b The percentage composition of average family expenditure patterns, by the major types of expenditures, for families whose heads are under age 35 compared with families whose heads are 55 or older.

   c A comparison of the changes in charitable giving between December 31, 2000, and December 31, 2004.

5 Outline a set of visual aids that you might use in an oral briefing on these topics:

   a How to write a research report.

   b The outlook for the economy over the next year.

   c The major analytical article in the latest issue of *Business-Week*.

From Concept to Practice

6 Use Exhibit 23-2 and plan the structure of your course project or of a research study you have read about in one of the Snapshots or Cases in this text.

7 Choose any case containing data on your text DVD and prepare a findings page, similar to the one in Exhibit 23-3.

>**www**exercises

1 Visit Presentations.com (**www.presentations.com**) and navigate the site to find an article on using technology in presenting or building a clear presentation. How might the tips within the article help you with your project presentation?

2 Visit the Henry J. Kaiser Family Foundation Web site (**www.kff.org**), and study the layout of one of the written reports. Choose one statistical presentation and determine alternative ways the data could be presented.

3 Find a Web site that compares APA and MLA citation styles. Which is most appropriate for the type of report you are preparing for your class project? Hint: Both Columbia University and Bedford/St.Martins have excellent sites.

>**cases***

Inquiring Minds Want to Know—NOW!

 KNSD San Diego ( )

Mastering Teacher Leadership

NCRCC: Teeing Up and New Strategic Direction

* All cases, both written and video, are on the text DVD. The film icon indicates a video case. Check the DVD Index to determine whether a case has data, the research instrument, or other supplementary material.

>case abstracts

S. COME OUT SWI

> AgriComp

AgriComp, a supplier of computer systems for farmers, has surveyed its dealers on whether to change its procedure for settling warranty claim disputes. Currently local dealers handle warranty services for customers via local repair followed by a reimbursement claim to AgriComp. Denied claims follow an internal company appeal process. Dealers have been complaining about the fairness of the appeal process and in a recent survey were asked to respond to an alternative process, an impartial mediator. The student is asked to review survey results and determine whether the costly external mediator process would be worth implementing to keep the dealers happy.

> BBQ Product Crosses Over the Lines of Varied Tastes

This case asks students to assess measurement and scaling issues in the context of the introduction of a frozen, microwaveable BBQ product line into the Southeast by Rich Products, Buffalo, New York. Rich is a manufacturer of bakery and barbeque products for the food service and retail sectors of the food market. The new line is being introduced with commercials depicting Ruby, a fictitious waitress at Pork-O-Rama, who prefers the taste of the new frozen line. **www.richs.com**

> Calling Up Attendance

This case examines a study by Prince Marketing for TCS Management Group. TCS Management Group, Inc., part of Aspect Communications, is the leading provider of workforce management software, especially related to call center management. The study discusses measures of customer satisfaction and aims to predict attendance at a two-day educational event, Users Forum. **www.aspect.com**

> Campbell-Ewald Pumps Awareness into the American Heart Association

You wouldn't think that an organization that does as much good as the American Heart Association would have low awareness, but at the start of the described research program its unaided awareness level was just 16 percent. For a company reliant on contributions, low awareness is a major problem. This case profiles the research behind the American Heart Association's first-ever paid advertising campaign. **www.campbell-ewald.com; www.americanheart.org**

> Campbell-Ewald: R-E-S-P-E-C-T Spells Loyalty

Campbell-Ewald, the Detroit-based marketing communications company, part of the global Interpublic Group of Companies, is an award-winning consultancy. This case describes the research behind its effort to measure and improve customer loyalty and the development of its five respect principles that lead to enhanced customer commitment. **www.campbell-ewald.com**

> Can Research Rescue the Red Cross?

The American Red Cross seemed in its true element following September 11, 2001. It was flooded with donations to do its highly needed and regarded work. Most of those donations went to its Liberty Fund. But shortly after it started to disperse the funds, the media began asking questions. And the American Red Cross soon wore a patina of tarnish. Learn about the research that evaluated Americans' perception of the Red Cross and how research by Wirthlin Worldwide helped craft a new and highly effective donation solicitation process. **www.wirthlin.com; www.redcross.org**

> Covering Kids with Health Care

This video case describes the research done to increase enrollment in the federal government's SCHIP program. Managed at the state level, the State Children's Health Insurance Program provides basic health coverage for the children of the nation's working poor. Research by Wirthlin Worldwide revealed why families weren't enrolling, and findings were used by GMMB, Inc., to develop a major advertising and public relations initiative to increase enrollment. The research and campaign were sponsored by the Robert Wood Johnson Foundation. (Video duration: 16 minutes) **www.rwjf.org; www.wirthlin.com; www.gmmb.com**

> Cummins Engines

Cummins Engines makes advanced, fuel-efficient diesel power systems and engine-related components and specializes in customized diesel engine production. Shipping more than 1,000 engines per day to customers and dealers on every continent, Cummins has a long history of innovation, from winning performances at the Indianapolis 500 to the first natural gas–fueled engine to pass California's tough emissions regulations. This case focuses on the Signature 600 engine, the newest and most advanced diesel engine on the market. (Video duration: 14 minutes) **www.cummins.com**

> Data Development Corporation

This video case profiles Data Development Corporation (DDC), a leader in in-home and office personal interviewing. DDC has fielded more than 20,000 studies since 1960; it currently has four offices in the United States, with global capabilities in 80 countries worldwide. DDC WATS centers have 170 CATI (computer-assisted telephone interviewing) stations. The company offers a network of CAPI (computer-assisted personal interviewing) in more than 180 mall locations, as well as interactive software (STORE) simulations of store shelving, buildings, and so on, to develop and evaluate logos, signage, packaging, and the like. DDC's Internet Survey Group offers Web-based studies. (Video duration: 11 minutes) **www.datadc.com**

> Donatos: Finding the New Pizza

The pizza segment of the fast-food industry is very aggressive. As people's tastes change and new diets become the rage, restaurant chains must decide if and how to respond. This case focuses on the research behind the introduction of Donato's low-carbohydrate pizza, and how the company collapsed its normal product-development research process to take advantage of a current trend. **www.donatos.com**

> Endries International

In this video case the president of Endries Fasteners and Supply, Inc. (now Endries International), discusses the outcome of data collection, both internal and from customers, which resulted in the development of new, profitable customer services that provide significant cost savings for Endries' customers. Endries International has been a leader in inventory management solutions since the early 1980s. (Video duration: 6 minutes) **www.endries.com**

> Envirosell

Envirosell specializes in behavioral research, specifically in the retail environment. It has done this for Fortune 500 companies including banks, stores, and restaurant chains, as well as consumer product companies. In this video case, the managing director, research director, and senior analyst share information from several observational studies done in banks, as well as music, general-merchandise, and other retail environments. Envirosell, which has offices in the United States, Europe, Brazil, Japan, Mexico, and Turkey, strives to understand what people buy and how to get them to buy more. (Video duration: 10 minutes) **www.envirosell.com**

> Goodyear's Aquatred

This video case profiles the genesis of the Goodyear Aquatred tire. In 1993, the Aquatred tire, winner of more than a dozen awards, including Japan's prestigious "Good Product Design Award," reached 2 million units in sales in the United States. This revolutionary tire pumps away over 2 gallons of water per second as you drive at highway speeds. And a new tread rubber compound provides road-hugging traction and extends the tread life. The Aquatred tire segmented the market in a way that had not been done before. (Video duration: 14 minutes) **www.goodyear.com**

> HeroBuilders.com

Emil Vicale, president of BBC Design Group, used rapid prototyping technology (RPT) to build wax or plastic three-dimensional prototypes of his clients' designs. But this same technology can be used to custom manufacture dolls. Shortly after September 11, 2001, Vicale Corporation, BBC's parent company, purchased an e-commerce toy company. Vicale's first action figure was made to honor the heroes who emerged from that event. Using RPT, he crafted a doll with the head of George W. Bush and the body of Arnold Schwarzenegger. Other figures followed. This case is about a design firm that used exploratory research to define a niche in the action-figure business. **www.herobuilders.com**

> Inquiring Minds Want to Know—Now!

This case describes a multistage communication study undertaken by the research department of Penton Media, a publisher of business trade magazines, to determine the long-term viability of a reader and advertiser service, the *reader service card*, a postcard-size device used by readers to request additional information from a particular advertiser. **www.penton.com**

> John Deere & Company

John Deere has a rich 160-year history of serving the agricultural, construction, forestry, and lawn care markets. Its emphasis on helping its customers achieve better productivity has made it possible to successfully operate in more than 150 countries, in 50 currencies, and in every time zone of the world. During the 1970s, 1980s, and 1990s the company faced numerous challenges to its core businesses, yet its attention to environmental scanning and staying close to its customers permitted it to prosper when competitors abandoned whole segments of the business for industrial equipment or closed. This video traces the environmental influences on the company from the early 1970s through the late 1990s. The goal for John Deere was to double its mid-1990s sales by 2000. (Video duration: 12 minutes) **www.deere.com**

> KNSD San Diego

This video describes the "KNow San Diego" research project, undertaken so that advertisers purchasing time on this NBC-owned station would have a better understanding of which programs attracted which potential target audiences. It describes the use of VALS segmentation research, developed by SRI (now SRI Consulting Business Intelligence). According to its Web site, "In 1990, KNSD was awarded the Emmy for Outstanding News Station in San Diego. The station never lost this title, and has been awarded more Emmys this decade than all other stations in San Diego combined. On November 20, 1996, after a successful year as San Diego's most watched television station, KNSD was purchased by NBC. On January 1, 1997, it became known as NBC 7/39." (Video duration: 15 minutes) **www.nbcsandiego.com; www.sric-bi.com/**

> Lexus SC 430

This video case follows the research used to develop the newest Lexus, the SC 430, its hardtop convertible. From auto show interviews to Qual-Quant clinics and positioning analysis, learn about how Team One Advertising, Lexus's U.S. agency of record, used research to position this latest entry into the crowded sport coupe category. (Video duration: 8 minutes) **www.teamoneadv.com; www.lexus.com**

> Mastering Teacher Leadership

This case is about a multistage communication study of teachers by Wittenberg University's Department of Education to determine the viability of starting a Master of Education program for Ohio-certified teachers working within school districts serving a five-county area. **www.wittenberg.edu**

> McDonald's Tests Catfish Sandwich

This case describes the test marketing for McDonald's catfish sandwich in the southeastern United States. It asks students to assume they are the new product development team and to assess the research design described.

> NCRCC: Teeing Up a New Strategic Direction

The NCR Country Club started out as a benefit for thousands of National Cash Register employees. By the late 1990s, those employees were aging rapidly and the core membership needed to be increased. NCRCC offers two golf courses. One is an award-winning, championship-hosting course on the PGA tour. But it wasn't attracting new members, especially younger families. This case is about a membership study done as part of a larger management initiative to evaluate several strategic directions the club might take to expand its membership. **www.ncrcountryclub.com**

> NetConversions Influences Kelley Blue Book

Kelley Blue Book (KBB) is one of the most visited automotive sites on the Web. Visitors flock there to estimate the price of a car they might buy or sell. KBB needed to enhance its site's performance for advertisers, who had become a major source of revenue as sales of the printed *Kelley Blue Book* had declined. NetConversions is one of the new Web analytic services to evaluate Web site performance. This case reveals how Web sites are evaluated so that new design elements can be developed and tested. **www.netconversions.com; www.kelleybluebook.com**

> Open Doors: Extending Hospitality to Travelers with Disabilities

Eric Lipp started the Open Doors Organization (ODO) to help travelers with disabilities. In order to get the attention of the travel and hospitality industries, and to effect changes desired by people with disabilities, ODO undertook a major research project to estimate the expenditures of persons with disabilities and the accommodations that would be necessary to get them to travel more. Harris Interactive was chosen to field the multimethod survey. This case describes the methodology and the effects of the first round of a multiphase study. **www.opendoorsnfp.org**

> Outboard Marine Corporation

Outboard Marine Corporation (Waukegan, Illinois) is a leading manufacturer and marketer of internationally known boat brands, including Chris-Craft, Four Winns, Seaswirl, Javelin, Stratos, Lowe, Hydra-Sports, and Princecraft, as well as marine accessories and marine engines, under the brand names of Johnson and Evinrude. This video case discusses the evolution of a product and the importance of keeping competition off balance by continually "attacking" your own best product and developing replacements that the competition cannot match or cannot as cost-effectively produce. The example used is the standard for bass fisherman, the 150hp Evinrude Intruder 150. (Video duration: 12 minutes) **www.evinrude.com**

> Overdue Bills

This case is about testing a hypothesis related to collection on open accounts. The firm profiled is Quick Stab Collection Agency (QSCA). It is contemplating a change in its company slogan, or tagline. It needs research to substantiate the anticipated claim. The agency's accountant suspects that the amount of time to collect an account is determined by the size of the delinquent account and draws a sample of accounts to find out if he is correct. The student is asked to recommend a slogan to the marketing department based on an analysis of the results.

> Pebble Beach Co.

This case profiles the Pebble Beach Company, a 5,300-acre complex in Monterey, California, that offers three lodging options (Casa Palmero opened in September 1999, The Inn at Spanish Bay opened in 1989, and the Lodge at Pebble Beach opened in 1919), four golf courses, plus a new five-hole "golf links," eight restaurants, and an oceanside Beach and Tennis Club. Pebble Beach has repeatedly won awards as America's best travel resort and was host to the 2004 AT&T Pro-Amateur championship, the U.S. Open in 2000, the Callaway Golf Pebble Beach Invitational in 2004, and the newest tournament on the 2005 PGA Champions tour (First Tee Open). In January of 1999 The Inn at Spanish Bay was granted the coveted Mobil Five-Star Award from the 1999 *Mobil Travel Guide*. Pebble Beach achieves its quality status by focusing on seven core values. The company is land-locked, so it must develop ever-creative ways to make the facilities it has more intensively profit-generating. (Video duration: 11 minutes) **www.pebblebeach.com**

> Ramada Demonstrates Its *Personal Best*™

This case describes syndicated research in the hospitality industry that revealed trends in customer satisfaction and Ramada's proprietary research leading to the development of the *Personal Best*™ employee hiring, training, and motivation program. **www.ramada.com**

> Retailers Unhappy with Displays from Manufacturers

This case asks the student to design an experiment to test a new display design for Raid, following the release of survey results by a retail advisory board that revealed 60 percent dissatisfaction with current tracking systems provided to retailers by manufacturers.

> Starbucks, Bank One, and Visa Launch Starbucks Card Duetto™ Visa

In the very mature financial services industry, it is rare for a new financial product to garner much attention, let alone be named one of *BusinessWeek*'s outstanding products of the year. But what started as a way for Starbucks to add value to its existing Starbucks Card program developed into a financial product that many other institutions are interested in exploring. This case reveals the research that was done to develop this new payment option for Starbucks customers. (Video duration: 11 minutes) **www.starbucks.com; www.bankone.com; www.visa.com**

> State Farm: Dangerous Intersections

State Farm, the nation's largest auto insurer, distributed a list of the 10 most dangerous intersections in the United States based on crashes resulting in claims by its policyholders. What started as a study to reduce risk turned into an ongoing study that directs a major public relations effort: State Farm provides funds for communities to further research their dangerous intersections and initiate improvements based on the research. This case tells you how the State Farm Dangerous Intersections initiative got started and how it is done. **www.statefarm.com**

> Sturgel Division

This case profiles Martha, the manager of the Information Services division of Sturgel. She is trying to determine whether a survey of users should be conducted annually to assess the quality of service provided to the other divisions of the company, with the results used to make policy and procedural changes in her division. If a survey is deemed appropriate, the student is asked to design the survey.

> T-Shirt Designs

This case focuses on research done by Julio, a student who wants to raise money to pay off a portion of his student loans. The case provides a survey and data set and then asks the student to prepare a report recommending one of two prototype T-shirts Julio is considering.

> USTA: Come Out Swinging

The United States Tennis Association funded one of the most aggressive surveys ever undertaken about a single sport in order to revitalize tennis in the minds of consumers. The survey results were supplemented with qualitative research by Vigilante, a specialist in urban communication campaigns. What resulted was a full-scale marketing initiative involving the establishment of Tennis Welcome Centers and the Come Out Swinging advertising, merchandising, and public relations campaigns. This case reveals the research and how the marketing initiative developed. (Video duration: 11 minutes) **www.usta.com; www.vigilantenyc.com**

> Volkswagen's Beetle

This video case profiles the history of the original Beetle in the U.S. market from its introduction in 1949 to its demise in 1979 and then follows the initial two years of the New Beetle's rebirth, 1998 and 1999. The Beetle became a symbol of the 1960s rebelliousness, but it lost the love of a generation when it stressed engineering over style and low-cost operation, two factors that baby boomers considered crucial in the 1970s. By 1974, the Beetle had lost ground to its aggressive Japanese rivals for the value segment of the U.S. automobile market. In 1998, when the Beetle was reintroduced in the United States, it surpassed all sales estimates. The second year it doubled its sales. Historically, the Beetle is the world's best-selling car, having sold in more countries than any other automobile, with 21 million cars sold in its lifetime. (Video duration: 16 minutes) **www.vw.com**

> Yahoo!: *Consumer Direct* Marries Purchase Metrics to Banner Ads

As little as two years ago, many advertising pundits were bemoaning the inevitable demise of the banner ad on the Internet. But maybe they were too quick to judge. This case reveals how Yahoo!, in combination with ACNielsen's *Homescan*®, has developed a methodology (*Consumer Direct*) to evaluate the true effectiveness of banner ads, from ad exposure to shopping cart. It also reveals the role Dynamic Logic played in conducting postexposure ad evaluation. **www.yahoo.com; www.acnielsen.com; www.dynamiclogic.com**

>appendices

>appendixa

Focus Group Discussion Guide*

Background

What if your firm manufactures cleansing products in multiple forms—deodorant bar, beauty bar, cream body wash, gel body wash—and your customers are not using the best form for their skin types and activity levels? You might use exploratory focus groups to determine what drivers motivate customers to select the *form* they choose. Given the dramatic growth in this market, you want to hear from women aged 16 to 50 and also from men aged 16 to 25. Also, you need to understand their trade-offs when choosing a specific form.

You turn to a research specialist to conduct focus groups in three cities representative of the category market. Prior to meeting the six groups (two groups in each city; two consisting only of teens), researchers ask each participant to prepare two visual collages using pictures cut from magazines. One collage is to reflect the participant's perceptions and experiences with each form (regardless of personal use experience). A second collage is to depict a month in the participant's life. The Intro and Forms segments of the discussion guide below reference these creative exercises.

Personal Cleansing Form Drivers   Atlanta, Seattle, Phoenix

INTRO (15 min)

  A. ALL ABOUT ME—name, family info, work, play, activities, interests. SHOW LIFE IN THE MONTH COLLAGE
  B. AT SOME POINT ASK: How often shower / bathe?
                              Use fragrances / perfume? How often?
                              Use scented or unscented deodorant, lotions, etc?

FORMS (60 min)

  A. LISTED ON EASEL "DEODORANT BAR, BEAUTY BAR, CREAM BODY WASH, GEL BODY WASH" Here are the different forms of soaps available that we want to learn about.
     How many have ever used _____? Still using or moved on / rejected?
  B. EASEL RESPONSES (BE SURE PICTURES ARE LABELED) Show and describe your picture collage (from homework), as you tell what you like / not, what **associate** w/_____ form.
     What else **like**? / **why use**?
     What **not like** about _____? Why not using (more often)?
     How compare to other forms—advantages / disadvantages?
     What **wish for** this form . . . what would make it **better / perfect** for you?

---

*This discussion guide was developed by Pam Hay, an independent qualitative consultant for more than 24 years with a career focused on consumable goods (personal care products, health and beauty aids, and OTC drugs). Her experiences include conducting focus groups, individual depth interviews, ethnography home visits, and multifunctional consumer direct processes for the purposes of concept development, advertising evaluation, insight exploration, consumer segmentation, and product development.

How / why **begin** to use? Specifically, what **remember** about _____ form then?

How find out about it? (ads, TV commercial, friends) What details remember about the ad—what show, who in it?

REPEAT FOR ALL FORMS

C. LINE UP THE FORMS—When you think about these different forms, are they **basically the same**—just a different form or do you think of these as different products with **different results**? Describe.

D. EXPLAIN CHART—Line these attributes up in the order you think is **best to worst for each of the attributes** listed on the paper.

CLEANLINESS / SKIN CARE / GERM KILL / DEODORANCY / LATHER / SCENT / VALUE

Why put in this order? What experience / notice with this form for (*attribute above*)?

What about the form makes that difference?

How much do you care about (*attributes above*)? Why / not? Affect whether you'd buy it?

E. SHOW EXAMPLES OF BRANDS WITH BOTH BAR AND BODY WASH—

Oil of Olay / Dove / Lever 2000 / Dial

So to summarize with some specific brands, whether you have tried or not, what would you **expect to be the difference,** if any, when using the bar of _____ brand vs. the body wash?

What difference, if any, in how they make you feel emotionally after bathing with the bar vs. body wash?

BRANDS (30 min)

A. Now let's focus on different brands. Write your favorite on your name card.

LINE UP EXAMPLES OF THOSE COMMONLY USED.

B. How many of you have used _____ ? How often / long ago?

Why **use / choose** (at store)? What like (better) about _____ .

Why **NOT** use (more often)?

C. How many have **tried Oil of Olay / Dove / Lever 2000 / Dial**? Why / not (more recently)?

What associate with (brand above)? What stand for? What makes it different / unique vs. other brands?

SUMMARY (15 min)

A. There are 3 basic considerations when choosing a soap—**brand, form, price.** Put them in order of what matters most, 2nd, 3rd. For example you go to the store to buy, and your usual form isn't available in your usual brand, etc. What would you buy?

MAKE A CHART OF RESPONSES

B. Now think about 3 benefits we've discussed—**skin care, scent, cleanliness.** Put these in order of importance. Describe order.

Why is _____ more important than _____ ?

(MISC—TIME PERMITTING)

C. What do you see / notice in the store when shopping this aisle? New things? Switch around?

ADULTS—How many of you buy soap for other family members? Who? How do you decide which form / brand to choose for your husband / teen?

D. TEENS ONLY—Let's talk a bit more about how you learn about new types brands or versions of soaps. Where have you seen ads?

(Mall / locker room / Channel 1/ dressing rooms / etc.)

What do you remember about it? What show / say / what was the main idea?

What think of celebrity endorsements?

CONCLUSION

Direct Marketing Association Information Security Guidelines*

The protection of personally identifiable information is the responsibility of all marketers. Therefore, marketing companies should assume the following responsibilities to provide secure transactions for consumers and to protect databases containing consumers' personally identifiable information against unauthorized access, alteration, or dissemination of data:

- Marketers should establish information security policies and practices that assure the uninterrupted security of information systems.

- Marketers should create and implement staff policies, procedures, training and responsiveness measures to protect personally identifiable information handled in the everyday performance of duties.

- Marketers should employ and routinely reassess protective physical safeguards and technological measures in support of information security policies.

- Marketers should inform all business partners and service providers that handle personally identifiable information of their responsibility to ensure that their policies, procedures and practices maintain a level of security consistent with the marketer's applicable information security policies.

Comment:

- This guideline was developed for several reasons. Inasmuch as protecting privacy of personally identifiable information and maintaining security of information are closely intertwined, the DMA believed that it was important to specifically address the ethics of information security within the Guidelines for Ethical Business Practice. We also wanted to respond to challenges issued by the Federal Trade Commission and the Organization for Economic Cooperation and Development, which have been increasingly concerned with this issue globally, and have asked industry association leaders to be more involved in promoting security among industry members and encouraging them to factor security into the design of their systems. The DMA's guidelines are consistent with the OECD's revised security guidelines (see **www.oecd.org.**) (For more information on FTC business and consumer activities in this area that could be helpful to your company, check **www.ftc.gov/infosecurity.**)

- The ethics guidelines incorporate four main points that are baseline requirements for marketers:

  1. creating policies for an overall "culture of security"

  2. developing security standards and training employees

  3. incorporating the use of appropriate technologies, and

  4. informing business partners of their responsibilities to adhere to the same standards.

*Reprinted with permission, Direct Marketing Association, © Direct Marketing Association (http://www.the-dma.org/guidelines/informationsecurity.shtml).

You may also find it valuable to check the Direct Marketing Association Web site for the DMA's complete "Guidelines on Ethical Business Practice" (http://www.the-dma.org/guidelines/ethicalguidelines.shtml), especially as they relate to "Information From or About Children," the "Collection, Use, and Maintenance of Marketing Data," and "Online Information."

• Without a corporate standard of security ethics and the proper training, structure and technologies, it would be difficult to reassure consumers of your intentions and ability to keep personally identifiable information secure.

Questions to Ask:

1. In regard to **Establishing information security policies and practices:**

    • Have you established an internal culture of security and its supporting infra-structure, including a formal written plan?

    • Do you believe all employees understand the importance of keeping information secure?

    • Do you maintain confidentiality statements signed by employees when they are hired?

    • Do you regularly review your information security policies and practices?

    • Does your company maintain an adequate budget for security tools?

    • Have you considered employing network security specialists to assess your policies and practices, perform risk assessments and audits, and assist your company with compliance?

    • Have you considered liability insurance coverage in case of any security breaches?

    • Have you created and tested a data recovery plan in case of a natural disaster?

    • Has your company established a dispute resolution plan in case of disputes arising out of security breaches or alleged misuse of personally identifiable information?

    • Do you report cyber attacks to law enforcement agencies?

2. In regard to **Establishing staff policy and training measures:**

    • Have you designated responsible staff to design written information security policies and practices and ensured their implementation throughout your company? Do you feel confident that you have sufficient full-time staff available for your security program?

    • Have you developed documentation and training materials to educate appropriate staff on the importance of information security and their responsibilities related to it?

    • Do you perform background checks as necessary before hiring employees who would handle sensitive information, such as financial or medical data, or data about children?

    • Do you verify employee qualifications regarding information technology, to avoid security breaches due to employees' lack of technological ability?

    • Do you review your information security policy with appropriate employees, as indicated by their position or function, promptly upon their being hired, and regularly thereafter?

    • Do you routinely audit your information security practices or systems (including when changes to the practices or systems are made) to assure accurate execution and to assess vulnerabilities? Do you revise your practices as necessary?

    • Have you decided what information is sensitive and who has access to such information? Have you established a process for classifying data, and appropriate levels of security for each data class?

    • Do you routinely monitor employee access to and use of personally identifiable information?

- Have you set forth penalties for breaches of information security by employees and promptly implemented them upon discovery of any information security breach?
- Upon termination of employees, do you ensure that appropriate processes are changed?

3. In regard to **Employing technological measures to ensure security of consumer information:**

- Do you define information security specifications for all new technologies, products, and data uses, and for system developments?
- Have you considered diverse or redundant solutions for high-risk systems?
- Do you take steps to understand the security impact of any new technologies, products, or data uses?
- Do you use current virus protection programs to protect information and do you update them regularly?
- Do you pay attention to security "alerts" released by software vendors?
- Do you employ firewalls to protect personally identifiable information?
- Do you change passwords routinely and use passwords with multiple numbers and symbols?
- Do you put into place authentication measures, as they are available, in order to verify personnel and consumer use and access to personally identifiable information?
- Do you test information security systems to ensure that specifications are met and that data are secure in storage and in transit? Do you check with your software vendors to make sure they have tested their applications before public release?
- Do you compile and review audit logs for attempted intrusions?
- Are you able to identify potential security breaches before they occur? Do you use software patches as needed?
- Have you created an incident recovery/backup plan, including backup software and a secondary site to maintain data, in case of any breaches in your information security systems?
- Have you put into place a system to eradicate data from equipment prior to disposal?

4. In regard to **Informing business partners and vendors of their responsibility to ensure consistency with the marketer's own security policies:**

- Do you consider security ramifications before sharing networks with your business partners and vendors?
- Do you assure yourself that you understand the nature of any intended use of a list and that the list does not violate any of the ethical guidelines?
- Do you decoy and monitor the data practices of your business partners?
- Do you take steps to avoid unusual or suspicious list requests?
- Have you considered a sample notice to your business partners and vendors, for example: *[Marketer's] security policies are set forth below. [Marketer] expects [partner/vendor] to ensure that its security policies are consistent with and do not compromise [Marketer's] protection of personally identifiable information in any way.*

Nonparametric Significance Tests

This appendix contains additional nonparametric tests of hypotheses to augment those described in Chapter 20 (see Exhibit 20-7).

One-Sample Test

Kolmogorov-Smirnov Test

This test is appropriate when the data are at least ordinal and the research situation calls for a comparison of an observed sample distribution with a theoretical distribution. Under these conditions, the Kolmogorov-Smirnov (KS) one-sample test is more powerful than the χ^2 test and can be used for small samples when the χ^2 test cannot. The KS is a test of goodness of fit in which we specify the *cumulative* frequency distribution that would occur under the theoretical distribution and compare that with the observed cumulative frequency distribution. The theoretical distribution represents our expectations under H_0. We determine the point of greatest divergence between the observed and theoretical distributions and identify this value as D (maximum deviation). From a table of critical values for D, we determine whether such a large divergence is likely on the basis of random sampling variations from the theoretical distribution. The value for D is calculated as follows:

$$D = \text{Maximum } |F_0(X) - F_T(X)|$$

in which

$F_0(X)$ = the observed cumulative frequency distribution of a random sample of n observations. Where X is any possible score, $F_0(X) = k/n$, where k = the number of observations equal to or less than X.

$F_T(X)$ = The theoretical frequency distribution under H_0.

We illustrate the KS test, with an analysis of the results of the dining club study, in terms of various class levels. Take an equal number of interviews from each class, but secure unequal numbers of people interested in joining. Assume class levels are ordinal measurements. The testing process is as follows (see accompanying table):

1. *Null hypothesis.*

    H_0: There is no difference among student classes as to their intention of joining the dining club.

    H_A: There is a difference among students in various classes as to their intention of joining the dining club.

2. *Statistical test.* Choose the KS one-sample test because the data are ordinal measures and we are interested in comparing an observed distribution with a theoretical one.

3. *Significance level.* $\alpha = .05, n = 60$.

4. *Calculated value.* $D = \text{maximum } |F_0(X) - F_T(X)|$.

	Freshman	Sophomore	Junior	Senior	Graduate
Number in each class	5	9	11	16	19
$F_0(X)$	5/60	14/60	25/60	41/60	60/60
$F_T(X)$	12/60	24/60	36/60	48/60	60/60
$\lvert F_0(X) - F_T(X)\rvert$	7/60	10/60	11/60	7/60	0

$D = 11/60 = .183;$
$n = 60$

5. *Critical test value.* We enter the table of critical values of D in the KS one-sample test (see Appendix D, Exhibit D-5) and learn that with $\alpha = .05$, the critical value for D is

$$D = \frac{1.36}{\sqrt{60}} = .175$$

6. *Interpretation.* The calculated value is greater than the critical value, indicating we should reject the null hypothesis.

Two-Samples Tests

Sign Test

The sign test is used with matched pairs when the only information is the identification of the pair member that is larger or smaller or has more or less of some characteristic. Under H_0, one would expect the number of cases in which $X_A > X_B$ to equal the number of pairs in which $X_B > X_A$. All ties are dropped from the analysis, and n is adjusted to allow for these eliminated pairs. This test is based on the binomial expansion and has a good power efficiency for small samples.

Wilcoxon Matched-Pairs Test

When you can determine both *direction* and *magnitude* of difference between carefully matched pairs, use the Wilcoxon matched-pairs test. This test has excellent efficiency and can be more powerful than the *t*-test in cases where the latter is not particularly appropriate. The mechanics of calculation are also quite simple. Find the difference score (d_i) between each pair of values, and rank-order the differences from smallest to largest without regard to sign. The actual signs of each difference are then added to the rank values, and the test statistic T is calculated. T is the sum of the ranks with the less frequent sign. Typical of such research situations might be a study where husband and wife are matched, where twins are used, where a given subject is used in a before-after study, or where the outputs of two similar machines are compared.

Two types of ties may occur with this test. When two observations are equal, the d score becomes zero, and we drop this pair of observations from the calculation. When two or more pairs have the same d value, we average their rank positions. For example, if two pairs have a rank score of 1, we assign the rank of 1.5 to each and rank the next largest difference as third. When $n < 25$, use the table of critical values (see Appendix D, Exhibit D-4). When $n > 25$, the sampling distribution of T is approximately normal with

$$\text{Mean} = \mu_T = \frac{n(n + 1)}{4}$$

$$\text{Standard deviation} = \sigma_T \sqrt{\frac{n(n+1)(2n+1)}{24}}$$

The formula for the test is

$$z = \frac{T - \mu_T}{\sigma_T}$$

Suppose you conduct an experiment on the effect of brand name on quality perception. Ten subjects are recruited and asked to taste and compare two samples of a product, one identified as a well-known drink and the other as a new product being tested. In truth, however, the samples are identical. The subjects are then asked to rate the two samples on a set of scale items judged to be ordinal. Test these results for significance by the usual procedure.

1. *Null hypothesis.*

   H_0: There is no difference between the perceived qualities of the two samples.

   H_A: There is a difference in the perceived quality of the two samples.

2. *Statistical test.* The Wilcoxon matched-pairs test is used because the study is of related samples in which the differences can be ranked in magnitude.

3. *Significance level.* $\alpha = .05$, with $n = 10$ pairs of comparisons minus any pairs with a d of zero.

4. *Calculated value.* T equals the sum of the ranks with the less frequent sign. Assume we secure the following results:

Pair	Branded	Unbranded	d_i	Rank of d_i	Rank with Less Frequent Sign
1	52	48	4	4	
2	37	32	5	5.5*	
3	50	52	−2	−2	2
4	45	32	13	9	
5	56	59	−3	−3	3
6	51	50	1	1	
7	40	29	11	8	
8	59	54	5	5.5*	
9	38	38	0	*	
10	40	32	8	7	$T = 5$

*There are two types of tie situations. We drop out the pair with the type of tie shown by pair 9. Pairs 2 and 8 have a tie in rank of difference. In this case, we average the ranks and assign the average value to each.

5. *Critical test value.* Enter the table of critical values of T with $n = 9$ (see Appendix D, Exhibit D-4) and find that the critical value with $\alpha = .05$ is 6. Note that with this test, the calculated value must be smaller than the critical value to reject the null hypothesis.

6. *Interpretation.* Since the calculated value is less than the critical value, reject the null hypothesis.

Kolmogorov-Smirnov Two-Samples Test

When a researcher has two independent samples of ordinal data, the Kolmogorov-Smirnov (KS) two-samples test is useful. Like the one-sample test, this two-samples test is concerned with the agreement between two cumulative distributions, but both represent sample values. If the two samples have been drawn from the same population, the cumulative distributions of the samples should be fairly close to each other, showing only random deviations from the population distribution. If the cumulative distributions show a large enough maximum deviation D, it is evidence for rejecting the H_0. To secure the maximum deviation, one should use as many intervals as are available so as not to obscure the maximum cumulative difference.

The two-samples KS formula is

$$D = \text{maximum } |F_{N1}(X) - F_{N2}(X)| \text{ (two-tailed test)}$$

$$D = \text{maximum } |F_{N1}(X) - F_{N2}(X)| \text{ (one-tailed test)}$$

D is calculated in the same manner as before, but the table for critical values for the numerator of D, K_D (two-samples test) is presented in Appendix D, Exhibit D-6 when $n_1 = n_2$ and is less than 40 observations. When n_1 and/or n_2 is larger than 40, D from Appendix D, Exhibit D-7 should be used. With this larger sample, it is not necessary that $n_1 = n_2$.

Here we use a different sample from a tobacco industry advertising study. Suppose the smoking classifications represent an ordinal scale (heavy smoker, moderate smoker, nonsmoker), and you test these data with KS two-samples test for young and old age groups. Proceed as follows:

1. *Null Hypothesis.*

    H_0: There is no difference in ages of smokers and nonsmokers.

    H_A: The older the person, the more likely he or she is to be a heavy smoker.

2. *Statistical test.* The KS two-samples test is used because it is assumed the data are ordinal.

3. *Significance level.* $\alpha = .05$. $n_1 = n_2 = 34$.

4. *Calculated value.* See the one-sample calculation (KS test) and compare with the table below.

5. *Critical test value.* We enter Appendix D, Exhibit D-6 with $n = 34$ to find that $K_D = 11$ when $p \leq .05$ for a one-tailed distribution.

	Heavy Smoker	Moderate Smoker	Nonsmoker
$F_{n1}(X)$	12/34	21/34	34/34
$F_{n2}(X)$	4/34	10/34	34/34
$d_i = K_{D/n}$	8/34	11/34	0

6. *Interpretation.* Since the critical value equals the largest calculated value, we reject the null hypothesis.

Mann-Whitney U Test

This test is also used with two independent samples if the data are at least ordinal; it is an alternative to the t-test without the latter's limiting assumptions. When the larger of the two samples is 20 or less, there are special tables for interpreting U; when the larger sample exceeds 20, a normal curve approximation is used.

In calculating the U test, treat all observations in a combined fashion and rank them, algebraically, from smallest to largest. The largest negative score receives the lowest rank. In case of ties, assign the average rank as in other tests. With this test, you can also test samples that are unequal. After the ranking, the rank values for each sample are totaled. Compute the U statistic as follows:

$$U = n_1 n_2 + \frac{n_1(n_1 + 1)}{2} - R_1$$

or

$$U = n_1 n_2 + \frac{n_2(n_2 - 1)}{2} - R_2$$

in which

n_1 = number in sample 1

n_2 = number in sample 2

R_1 = sum of ranks in sample 1

With this equation, you can secure two U values, one using R_1 and the second using R_2. For testing purposes, use the smaller U.

An example may help to clarify the U statistic calculation procedure. Let's consider the sales training example with the t distribution discussion. Recall that salespeople with training method A averaged higher sales than salespeople with training method B. While these data are ratio measures, one still might not want to accept the other assumptions that underlie the t-test. What kind of a result could be secured with the U test? While the U test is designed for ordinal data, it can be used with interval and ratio measurements.

1. *Null hypothesis.*

   H_0: There is no difference in sales results produced by the two training methods.

   H_A: Training method A produces sales results superior to the results of method B.

2. *Statistical test.* The Mann-Whitney U test is chosen because the measurement is at least ordinal, and the assumptions under the parametric t-test are rejected.

3. *Significance level.* $\alpha = .05$ (one-tailed test).

4. *Calculated value.*

Sales per Week per Salesperson			
Training Method A	**Rank**	**Training Method B**	**Rank**
1,500	15	1,340	10
1,540	16	1,300	8.5
1,860	22	1,620	18
1,230	6	1,070	3
1,370	12	1,210	5
1,550	17	1,170	4
1,840	21	1,770	20
1,250	7	950	1
1,300	8.5	1,380	13
1,350	11	1,460	14
1,710	19	1,030	2
	$R_1 = 154.5$		$R_2 = 98.5$

$$U = (11)(11) + \frac{11(11 + 1)}{2} - 154.5 = 32.5 \qquad U = (11)(11) + \frac{11(11 + 1)}{2} - 98.5 = 88.5$$

5. *Critical test value.* Enter Appendix D, Exhibit D-9 with $n_1 = n_2 = 11$, and find a critical value of 34 for $\alpha = 0.5$, one-tailed test. Note that with this test, the calculated value must be smaller than the critical value to reject the null hypothesis.

6. *Interpretation.* Since the calculated value is smaller than the critical value ($34 > 32.5$), reject the null hypothesis and conclude that training method A is probably superior.

Thus, one would reject the null hypothesis at $\alpha = .05$ in a one-tailed test using either the t- or the U test. In this example, the U test has approximately the same power as the parametric test.

When $n > 20$ in one of the samples, the sampling distribution of U approaches the normal distribution with

$$\text{Mean} = \mu_U = \frac{n_1 n_2}{2}$$

$$\text{Standard deviation } \sigma_U = \sqrt{\frac{(n_1)(n_2)(n_1 + n_2 + 1)}{12}}$$

and

$$z = \frac{U - \mu_U}{\sigma_U}$$

Other Nonparametric Tests

Other tests are appropriate under certain conditions when testing two independent samples. When the measurement is only nominal, the Fisher exact probability test may be used. When the data are at least ordinal, use the median and Wald-Wolfowitz runs tests.

k-Samples Tests

You can use tests more powerful than χ^2 with data that are at least ordinal in nature. One such test is an extension of the median test mentioned earlier. We illustrate here the application of a second ordinal measurement test known as the Kruskal-Wallis one-way analysis of variance.

Kruskal-Wallis Test

This is a generalized version of the Mann-Whitney test. With it we rank all scores in the entire pool of observations from smallest to largest. The rank sum of each sample is then calculated, with ties being distributed as in other examples. We then compute the value of H as follows:

$$H = \frac{12}{N(N + 1)} \sum_{j=1}^{k} \frac{T_j^2}{n_j} - 3(N + 1)$$

where

T_j = sum of ranks in column j

n_j = number of cases in jth sample

$N = \Sigma w_j$ = total number of cases

k = number of samples

When there are a number of ties, it is recommended that a correct factor (C) be calculated and used to correct the H value as follows:

$$C = 1 - \left\{ \frac{\sum_{i}^{G}(t_i^3 - t_i)}{N^3 - N} \right\}$$

where

G = number of sets of tied observations

t_i = number tied in any set i

$$H' = H/C$$

To secure the critical value for H', use the table for the distribution of χ^2 (see Appendix D, Exhibit D-3), and enter it with the value of H' and d.f. $= k - 1$.

To illustrate the application of this test, use the price discount experiment problem. The data and calculations are shown in Exhibit C-1 and indicate that, by the Kruskal-Wallis test, one again barely fails to reject the null hypothesis with $\alpha = .05$.

> **Exhibit C-1** Kruskal-Wallis One-Way Analysis of Variance (price differentials)

One Cent		Three Cents		Five Cents	
X_A	Rank	X_B	Rank	X_C	Rank
6	1	8	5	9	8.5
7	2.5	9	8.5	9	8.5
8	5	8	5	11	14
7	2.5	10	11.5	10	11.5
9	8.5	11	14	14	18
11	14	13	16.5	13	16.5
	$T_j = 33.5$		60.5		77.0

$$T = 33.5 + 60.5 + 77$$

$$= 171$$

$$H = \frac{12}{18(18 + 1)} \left[\frac{33.5^2 + 60.5^2 + 77^2}{6} \right] - 3(18 + 1)$$

$$= \frac{12}{342} \left[\frac{1,122.25 + 3,660.25 + 5,929}{6} \right] - 57$$

$$= 0.0351 \left[\frac{10,711.5}{6} \right] - 57$$

$$H = 5.66$$

$$C = 1 - \left(\frac{3[(2)^3 - 2] + 2[(3)^3 - 3] + 4[(4)^3 - 4]}{18^3 - 18} \right)$$

$$= 1 - \frac{18 + 48 + 60}{5814}$$

$$= .978$$

$$H' = \frac{H}{C} = \frac{5.66}{.978} = 5.79$$

$$d.f. = k - 1 = 2$$

$$p > .05$$

>appendixd

Selected Statistical Tables

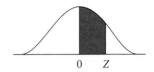

> **Exhibit D-1** Areas of the Standard Normal Distribution

	Second Decimal Place in z									
z	0.00	0.01	0.02	0.03	0.04	0.05	0.06	0.07	0.08	0.09
0.0	0.0000	0.0040	0.0080	0.0120	0.0160	0.0199	0.0239	0.0279	0.0319	0.0359
0.1	0.0398	0.0438	0.0478	0.0517	0.0557	0.0596	0.0636	0.0675	0.0714	0.0753
0.2	0.0793	0.0832	0.0871	0.0910	0.0948	0.0987	0.1026	0.1064	0.1103	0.1141
0.3	0.1179	0.1217	0.1255	0.1293	0.1331	0.1368	0.1406	0.1443	0.1480	0.1517
0.4	0.1554	0.1591	0.1628	0.1664	0.1700	0.1736	0.1772	0.1808	0.1844	0.1879
0.5	0.1915	0.1950	0.1985	0.2019	0.2054	0.2088	0.2123	0.2157	0.2190	0.2224
0.6	0.2257	0.2291	0.2324	0.2357	0.2389	0.2422	0.2454	0.2486	0.2517	0.2549
0.7	0.2580	0.2611	0.2642	0.2673	0.2704	0.2734	0.2764	0.2794	0.2823	0.2852
0.8	0.2881	0.2910	0.2939	0.2967	0.2995	0.3023	0.3051	0.3078	0.3106	0.3133
0.9	0.3159	0.3186	0.3212	0.3238	0.3264	0.3289	0.3315	0.3340	0.3365	0.3389
1.0	0.3413	0.3438	0.3461	0.3485	0.3508	0.3531	0.3554	0.3577	0.3599	0.3621
1.1	0.3643	0.3665	0.3686	0.3708	0.3729	0.3749	0.3770	0.3790	0.3810	0.3830
1.2	0.3849	0.3869	0.3888	0.3907	0.3925	0.3944	0.3962	0.3980	0.3997	0.4015
1.3	0.4032	0.4049	0.4066	0.4082	0.4099	0.4115	0.4131	0.4147	0.4162	0.4177
1.4	0.4192	0.4207	0.4222	0.4236	0.4251	0.4265	0.4279	0.4292	0.4306	0.4319
1.5	0.4332	0.4345	0.4357	0.4370	0.4382	0.4394	0.4406	0.4418	0.4429	0.4441
1.6	0.4452	0.4463	0.4474	0.4484	0.4495	0.4505	0.4515	0.4525	0.4535	0.4545
1.7	0.4554	0.4564	0.4573	0.4582	0.4591	0.4599	0.4608	0.4616	0.4625	0.4633
1.8	0.4641	0.4649	0.4656	0.4664	0.4671	0.4678	0.4686	0.4693	0.4699	0.4706
1.9	0.4713	0.4719	0.4726	0.4732	0.4738	0.4744	0.4750	0.4756	0.4761	0.4767
2.0	0.4772	0.4778	0.4783	0.4788	0.4793	0.4798	0.4803	0.4808	0.4812	0.4817
2.1	0.4821	0.4826	0.4830	0.4834	0.4838	0.4842	0.4846	0.4850	0.4854	0.4857
2.2	0.4861	0.4864	0.4868	0.4871	0.4875	0.4878	0.4881	0.4884	0.4887	0.4890
2.3	0.4893	0.4896	0.4898	0.4901	0.4904	0.4906	0.4909	0.4911	0.4913	0.4916
2.4	0.4918	0.4920	0.4922	0.4925	0.4927	0.4929	0.4931	0.4932	0.4934	0.4936
2.5	0.4938	0.4940	0.4941	0.4943	0.4945	0.4946	0.4948	0.4949	0.4951	0.4952
2.6	0.4953	0.4955	0.4956	0.4957	0.4959	0.4960	0.4961	0.4962	0.4963	0.4964
2.7	0.4965	0.4966	0.4967	0.4968	0.4969	0.4970	0.4971	0.4972	0.4973	0.4974
2.8	0.4974	0.4975	0.4976	0.4977	0.4977	0.4978	0.4979	0.4979	0.4980	0.4981
2.9	0.4981	0.4982	0.4982	0.4983	0.4984	0.4984	0.4985	0.4985	0.4986	0.4986
3.0	0.4987	0.4987	0.4987	0.4988	0.4988	0.4989	0.4989	0.4989	0.4990	0.4990
3.1	0.4990	0.4991	0.4991	0.4991	0.4992	0.4992	0.4992	0.4992	0.4993	0.4993
3.2	0.4993	0.4993	0.4994	0.4994	0.4994	0.4994	0.4994	0.4995	0.4995	0.4995
3.3	0.4995	0.4995	0.4995	0.4996	0.4996	0.4996	0.4996	0.4996	0.4996	0.4997
3.4	0.4997	0.4997	0.4997	0.4997	0.4997	0.4997	0.4997	0.4997	0.4997	0.4998
3.5	0.4998									
4.0	0.49997									
4.5	0.499997									
5.0	0.4999997									
6.0	0.499999999									

> **Exhibit D-2** Critical Values of *t* for Given Probability Levels

d.f.	Level of Significance for One-Tailed Test					
	.10	.05	.025	.01	.005	.0005
	Level of Significance for Two-Tailed Test					
	.20	.10	.05	.02	.01	.001
1	3.078	6.314	12.706	31.821	63.657	636.619
2	1.886	2.920	4.303	6.965	9.925	31.598
3	1.638	2.353	3.182	4.541	5.841	12.941
4	1.533	2.132	2.776	3.747	4.604	8.610
5	1.476	2.015	2.571	3.365	4.032	6.859
6	1.440	1.943	2.447	3.143	3.707	5.959
7	1.415	1.895	2.365	2.998	3.499	5.405
8	1.397	1.860	2.306	2.896	3.355	5.041
9	1.383	1.833	2.262	2.821	3.250	4.781
10	1.372	1.812	2.228	2.764	3.169	4.587
11	1.363	1.796	2.201	2.718	3.106	4.437
12	1.356	1.782	2.179	2.681	3.055	4.318
13	1.350	1.771	2.160	2.650	3.012	4.221
14	1.345	1.761	2.145	2.624	2.977	4.140
15	1.341	1.753	2.131	2.602	2.947	4.073
16	1.337	1.746	2.120	2.583	2.921	4.015
17	1.333	1.740	2.110	2.567	2.898	3.965
18	1.330	1.734	2.101	2.552	2.878	3.922
19	1.328	1.729	2.093	2.539	2.861	3.883
20	1.325	1.725	2.086	2.528	2.845	3.850
21	1.323	1.721	2.080	2.518	2.831	3.819
22	1.321	1.717	2.074	2.508	2.819	3.792
23	1.319	1.714	2.069	2.500	2.807	3.767
24	1.318	1.711	2.064	2.492	2.797	3.745
25	1.316	1.708	2.060	2.485	2.787	3.725
26	1.315	1.706	2.056	2.479	2.779	3.707
27	1.314	1.703	2.052	2.473	2.771	3.690
28	1.313	1.701	2.048	2.467	2.763	3.674
29	1.311	1.699	2.045	2.462	2.756	3.659
30	1.310	1.697	2.042	2.457	2.750	3.646
40	1.303	1.684	2.021	2.423	2.704	3.551
60	1.296	1.671	2.000	2.390	2.660	3.460
120	1.289	1.658	1.980	2.358	2.617	3.373
∞	1.282	1.645	1.960	2.326	2.576	3.291

Source: Abridged from Table III of Fisher and Yates, *Statistical Tables for Biological, Agricultural, and Medical Research,* 6th ed., published by Oliver and Boyd Ltd., Edinburgh, 1963. By permission of the publishers.

> **Exhibit D-3** Critical Values of the Chi-Square Distribution

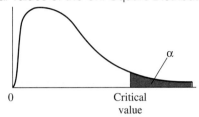

	Probability under H_0 That $\chi^2 \geq$ Chi-Square				
d.f.	.10	.05	.02	.01	.001
1	2.71	3.84	5.41	6.64	10.83
2	4.60	5.99	7.82	9.21	13.82
3	6.25	7.82	9.84	11.34	16.27
4	7.78	9.49	11.67	13.28	18.46
5	9.24	11.07	13.39	15.09	20.52
6	10.64	12.59	15.03	16.81	22.46
7	12.02	14.07	16.62	18.48	24.32
8	13.36	15.51	18.17	20.09	26.12
9	14.68	16.92	19.68	21.67	27.88
10	15.99	18.31	21.16	23.21	29.59
11	17.28	19.68	22.62	24.72	31.26
12	18.55	21.03	24.05	26.22	32.91
13	19.81	22.36	25.47	27.69	34.53
14	21.06	23.68	26.87	29.14	36.12
15	22.31	25.00	28.26	30.58	37.70
16	23.54	26.30	29.63	32.00	39.29
17	24.77	27.59	31.00	33.41	40.75
18	25.99	28.87	32.35	34.80	42.31
19	27.20	30.14	33.69	36.19	43.82
20	28.41	31.41	35.02	37.57	45.32
21	29.62	32.67	36.34	38.93	46.80
22	30.81	33.92	37.66	40.29	48.27
23	32.01	35.17	38.97	41.64	49.73
24	33.20	36.42	40.27	42.98	51.18
25	34.38	37.65	41.57	44.31	52.62
26	35.56	38.88	42.86	45.64	54.05
27	36.74	40.11	44.14	46.96	55.48
28	37.92	41.34	45.42	48.28	56.89
29	39.09	42.56	46.69	49.59	58.30
30	40.26	43.77	47.96	50.89	59.70

Source: Abridged from Table IV of Fisher and Yates, *Statistical Tables for Biological, Agricultural, and Medical Research,* 6th ed., published by Oliver and Boyd Ltd., Edinburgh, 1963. By permission of the publishers.

> **Exhibit D-4** Critical Values of T in the Wilcoxon Matched-Pairs Test

	Level of Significance for One-Tailed Test		
	.025	.01	.005
	Level of Significance for Two-Tailed Test		
n	.05	.02	.01
6	0	–	–
7	2	0	–
8	4	2	0
9	6	3	2
10	8	5	3
11	11	7	5
12	14	10	7
13	17	13	10
14	21	16	13
15	25	20	16
16	30	24	20
17	35	28	23
18	40	33	28
19	46	38	32
20	52	43	38
21	59	49	43
22	66	56	49
23	73	62	55
24	81	69	61
25	89	77	68

Source: Adapted from Table 1 of F. Wilcoxon, *Some Rapid Approximate Statistical Procedures* (New York: American Cyanamid Company, 1949), p. 13, with the kind permission of the publisher.

> **Exhibit D-5** Critical Values of D in the Kolmogorov-Smirnov One-Sample Test

Sample Size n	Level of Significance for $D = $ Maximum $\|F_0(X) - S_N(X)\|$				
	.20	**.15**	**.10**	**.05**	**.01**
1	.900	.925	.950	.975	.995
2	.684	.726	.776	.842	.929
3	.565	.597	.642	.708	.828
4	.494	.525	.564	.624	.733
5	.446	.474	.510	.565	.669
6	.410	.436	.470	.521	.618
7	.381	.405	.438	.486	.577
8	.358	.381	.411	.457	.543
9	.339	.360	.388	.432	.514
10	.322	.342	.368	.410	.490
11	.307	.326	.352	.391	.468
12	.295	.313	.338	.375	.450
13	.284	.302	.325	.361	.433
14	.274	.292	.314	.349	.418
15	.266	.283	.304	.338	.404
16	.258	.274	.295	.328	.392
17	.250	.266	.286	.318	.381
18	.244	.259	.278	.309	.371
19	.237	.252	.272	.301	.363
20	.231	.246	.264	.294	.356
25	.21	.22	.24	.27	.32
30	.19	.20	.22	.24	.29
35	.18	.19	.21	.23	.27
Over 35	$\dfrac{1.07}{\sqrt{N}}$	$\dfrac{1.14}{\sqrt{N}}$	$\dfrac{1.22}{\sqrt{N}}$	$\dfrac{1.36}{\sqrt{N}}$	$\dfrac{1.63}{\sqrt{N}}$

Source: F. J. Massey Jr., "The Kolmogorov-Smirnov Test for Goodness of Fit," *Journal of the American Statistical Association* 46, p. 70. Adapted with the kind permission of the publisher.

> **Exhibit D-6** Critical Values of K_D in the Kolmogorov-Smirnov
Two-Samples Test (small samples)

	One-Tailed Test		Two-Tailed Test	
n	a = .05	a = .01	a = .05	a = .01
3	3	–	–	–
4	4	–	4	–
5	4	5	5	5
6	5	6	5	6
7	5	6	6	6
8	5	6	6	7
9	6	7	6	7
10	6	7	7	8
11	6	8	7	8
12	6	8	7	8
13	7	8	7	9
14	7	8	8	9
15	7	9	8	9
16	7	9	8	10
17	8	9	8	10
18	8	10	9	10
19	8	10	9	10
20	8	10	9	11
21	8	10	9	11
22	9	11	9	11
23	9	11	10	11
24	9	11	10	12
25	9	11	10	12
26	9	11	10	12
27	9	12	10	12
28	10	12	11	13
29	10	12	11	13
30	10	12	11	13
35	11	13	12	
40	11	14	13	

Source: One-tailed test—abridged from I. A. Goodman, "Kolmogorov-Smirnov Tests for Psychological Research," *Psychological Bulletin* 51 (1951), p. 167, copyright (1951) by the American Psychological Association. Reprinted by permission. Two-tailed test—derived from Table 1 of F. J. Massey Jr., "The Distribution of the Maximum Deviation Between Two Sample Cumulative Step Functions," *Annals of Mathematical Statistics* 23 (1951), pp. 126–27, with the kind permission of the publisher.

> **Exhibit D-7** Critical Values of D in the Kolmogorov-Smirnov
>   Two-Samples Test for Large Samples (two-tailed)

Level of Significance	Value of D So Large as to Call for Rejection of H_0 at the Indicated Level of Significance, Where $D =$ maximum $|S_{n_1}(X) - S_2(X)|$
.10	$1.22\sqrt{\dfrac{n_1 + n_2}{n_1 n_2}}$
.05	$1.36\sqrt{\dfrac{n_1 + n_2}{n_1 n_2}}$
.025	$1.48\sqrt{\dfrac{n_1 + n_2}{n_1 n_2}}$
.01	$1.63\sqrt{\dfrac{n_1 + n_2}{n_1 n_2}}$
.005	$1.73\sqrt{\dfrac{n_1 + n_2}{n_1 n_2}}$
.001	$1.95\sqrt{\dfrac{n_1 + n_2}{n_1 n_2}}$

Source: Adapted from N. Smirnov, "Table for Estimating the Goodness of Fit of Empirical Distribution," *Annals of Mathematical Statistics* 18 (1948), pp. 280–81, with the kind permission of the publisher.

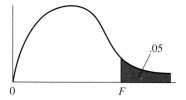

> **Exhibit D-8** Critical Values of the F Distribution for $\alpha = .05$

		Degrees of Freedom for Numerator							
n_2	1	2	3	4	5	6	7	8	9
1	161.4	199.5	215.7	224.6	230.2	234.0	236.8	238.9	240.5
2	18.51	19.00	19.16	19.25	19.30	19.33	19.35	19.37	19.38
3	10.13	9.55	9.28	9.12	9.01	8.94	8.89	8.85	8.81
4	7.71	6.94	6.59	6.39	6.26	6.16	6.09	6.04	6.00
5	6.61	5.79	5.41	5.19	5.05	4.95	4.88	4.82	4.77
6	5.99	5.14	4.76	4.53	4.39	4.28	4.21	4.15	4.10
7	5.59	4.74	4.35	4.12	3.97	3.87	3.79	3.73	3.68
8	5.32	4.46	4.07	3.84	3.69	3.58	3.50	3.44	3.39
9	5.12	4.26	3.86	3.63	3.48	3.37	3.29	3.23	3.18
10	4.96	4.10	3.71	3.48	3.33	3.22	3.14	3.07	3.02
11	4.84	3.98	3.59	3.36	3.20	3.09	3.01	2.95	2.90
12	4.75	3.89	3.49	3.26	3.11	3.00	2.91	2.85	2.80
13	4.67	3.81	3.41	3.18	3.03	2.92	2.83	2.77	2.71
14	4.60	3.74	3.34	3.11	2.96	2.85	2.76	2.70	2.65
15	4.54	3.68	3.29	3.06	2.90	2.79	2.71	2.64	2.59
16	4.49	3.63	3.24	3.01	2.85	2.74	2.66	2.59	2.54
17	4.45	3.59	3.20	2.96	2.81	2.70	2.61	2.55	2.49
18	4.41	3.55	3.16	2.93	2.77	2.66	2.58	2.51	2.46
19	4.38	3.52	3.13	2.90	2.74	2.63	2.54	2.48	2.42
20	4.35	3.49	3.10	2.87	2.71	2.60	2.51	2.45	2.39
21	4.32	3.47	3.07	2.84	2.68	2.57	2.49	2.42	2.37
22	4.30	3.44	3.05	2.82	2.66	2.55	2.46	2.40	2.34
23	4.28	3.42	3.03	2.80	2.64	2.53	2.44	2.37	2.32
24	4.26	3.40	3.01	2.78	2.62	2.51	2.42	2.36	2.30
25	4.24	3.39	2.99	2.76	2.60	2.49	2.40	2.34	2.28
26	4.23	3.37	2.98	2.74	2.59	2.47	2.39	2.32	2.27
27	4.21	3.35	2.96	2.73	2.57	2.46	2.37	2.31	2.25
28	4.20	3.34	2.95	2.71	2.56	2.45	2.36	2.29	2.24
29	4.18	3.33	2.93	2.70	2.55	2.43	2.35	2.28	2.22
30	4.17	3.32	2.92	2.69	2.53	2.42	2.33	2.27	2.21
40	4.08	3.23	2.84	2.61	2.45	2.34	2.25	2.18	2.12
60	4.00	3.15	2.76	2.53	2.37	2.25	2.17	2.10	2.04
120	3.92	3.07	2.68	2.45	2.29	2.17	2.09	2.02	1.96
∞	3.84	3.00	2.60	2.37	2.21	2.10	2.01	1.94	1.88

Degrees of Freedom for Denominator

Source: Reprinted by permission from *Statistical Methods* by George W. Snedecor and William G. Cochran, 6th edition, © 1967 by Iowa State University Press, Ames, Iowa.

	Degrees of Freedom for Numerator (cont'd)								
10	**12**	**15**	**20**	**24**	**30**	**40**	**60**	**120**	**∞**
241.9	243.9	245.9	248.0	249.1	250.1	251.1	252.2	253.3	243.3
19.40	19.41	19.43	19.45	19.45	19.46	19.47	19.48	19.49	19.50
8.79	8.74	8.70	8.66	8.64	8.62	8.59	8.57	8.55	8.53
5.96	5.91	5.86	5.80	5.77	5.75	5.72	5.69	5.66	5.63
4.74	4.68	4.62	4.56	4.53	4.50	4.46	4.43	4.40	4.36
4.06	4.00	3.94	3.87	3.84	3.81	3.77	3.74	3.70	3.67
3.64	3.57	3.51	3.44	3.41	3.38	3.34	3.30	3.27	3.23
3.35	3.28	3.22	3.15	3.12	3.08	3.04	3.01	2.97	2.93
3.14	3.07	3.01	2.94	2.90	2.86	2.83	2.79	2.75	2.71
2.98	2.91	2.85	2.77	2.74	2.70	2.66	2.62	2.58	2.54
2.85	2.79	2.72	2.65	2.61	2.57	2.53	2.49	2.45	2.40
2.75	2.69	2.62	2.54	2.51	2.47	2.43	2.38	2.34	2.30
2.67	2.60	2.53	2.46	2.42	2.38	2.34	2.30	2.25	2.21
2.60	2.53	2.46	2.39	2.35	2.31	2.27	2.22	2.18	2.13
2.54	2.48	2.40	2.33	2.29	2.25	2.20	2.16	2.11	2.07
2.49	2.42	2.35	2.28	2.24	2.19	2.15	2.11	2.06	2.01
2.45	2.38	2.31	2.23	2.19	2.15	2.10	2.06	2.01	1.96
2.41	2.34	2.27	2.19	2.15	2.11	2.06	2.02	1.97	1.92
2.38	2.31	2.23	2.16	2.11	2.07	2.03	1.98	1.93	1.88
2.35	2.28	2.20	2.12	2.08	2.04	1.99	1.95	1.90	1.84
2.32	2.25	2.18	2.10	2.05	2.01	1.96	1.92	1.87	1.81
2.30	2.23	2.15	2.07	2.03	1.98	1.94	1.89	1.84	1.78
2.27	2.20	2.13	2.05	2.01	1.96	1.91	1.86	1.81	1.76
2.25	2.18	2.11	2.03	1.98	1.94	1.89	1.84	1.79	1.73
2.24	2.16	2.09	2.01	1.96	1.92	1.87	1.82	1.77	1.71
2.22	2.15	2.07	1.99	1.95	1.90	1.85	1.80	1.75	1.69
2.20	2.13	2.06	1.97	1.93	1.88	1.84	1.79	1.73	1.67
2.19	2.12	2.04	1.96	1.91	1.87	1.82	1.77	1.71	1.65
2.18	2.10	2.03	1.94	1.90	1.85	1.81	1.75	1.70	1.64
2.16	2.09	2.01	1.93	1.89	1.84	1.79	1.74	1.68	1.62
2.08	2.00	1.92	1.84	1.79	1.74	1.69	1.64	1.58	1.51
1.99	1.92	1.84	1.75	1.70	1.65	1.59	1.53	1.47	1.39
1.91	1.83	1.75	1.66	1.61	1.55	1.50	1.43	1.35	1.25
1.83	1.75	1.67	1.57	1.52	1.46	1.39	1.32	1.22	1.00

> Exhibit D-9 Partial Table of Critical Values of U in the Mann-Whitney Test

Critical Values for One-Tailed Test at $a = .025$ or Two-Tailed Test at $a = .05$

$n_1 \backslash n_2$	9	10	11	12	13	14	15	16	17	18	19	20
1												
2	0	0	0	1	1	1	1	1	2	2	2	2
3	2	3	3	4	4	5	5	6	6	7	7	8
4	4	5	6	7	8	9	10	11	11	12	13	13
5	7	8	9	11	12	13	14	15	17	18	19	20
6	10	11	13	14	16	17	19	21	22	24	25	27
7	12	14	16	18	20	22	24	26	28	30	32	34
8	15	17	19	22	24	26	29	31	34	36	38	41
9	17	20	23	26	28	31	34	37	39	42	45	48
10	20	23	26	29	33	36	39	42	45	48	52	55
11	23	26	30	33	37	40	44	47	51	55	58	62
12	26	29	33	37	41	45	49	53	57	61	66	69
13	28	33	37	41	45	50	54	59	63	67	72	76
14	31	36	40	45	50	55	59	64	67	74	78	83
15	34	39	44	49	54	59	64	70	75	80	85	90
16	37	42	47	53	59	64	70	75	81	86	92	98
17	39	45	51	57	63	67	75	81	87	93	99	105
18	42	48	55	61	67	74	80	86	93	99	106	112
19	45	52	58	65	72	78	85	92	99	106	113	119
20	48	55	62	69	76	83	90	98	105	112	119	127

Critical Values for One-Tailed Test at $a = .05$ or Two-Tailed Test at $a = .10$

$n_1 \backslash n_2$	9	10	11	12	13	14	15	16	17	18	19	20
1											0	0
2	1	1	1	2	2	2	3	3	3	4	4	4
3	3	4	5	5	6	7	7	8	9	9	10	11
4	6	7	8	9	10	11	12	14	15	16	17	18
5	9	11	12	13	15	16	18	19	20	22	23	25
6	12	14	16	17	19	21	23	25	26	28	30	32
7	15	17	19	21	24	26	28	30	33	35	37	39
8	18	20	23	26	28	31	33	36	39	41	44	47
9	21	24	27	30	33	36	39	42	45	48	51	54
10	24	27	31	34	37	41	44	48	51	55	58	62
11	27	31	34	38	42	46	50	54	57	61	65	69
12	30	34	38	42	47	51	55	60	64	68	72	77
13	33	37	42	47	51	56	61	65	70	75	80	84
14	36	41	46	51	56	61	66	71	77	82	87	92
15	39	44	50	55	61	66	72	77	83	88	94	100
16	42	48	54	60	65	71	77	83	89	95	101	107
17	45	51	57	64	70	77	83	89	96	102	109	115
18	48	55	61	68	75	82	88	95	102	109	116	123
19	51	58	65	72	80	87	94	101	109	116	123	130
20	54	62	69	77	84	92	100	107	115	123	130	138

Source: Abridged from D. Auble, "Extended Tables from the Mann-Whitney Statistic," *Bulletin of the Institute of Educational Research at Indiana University* 1, no. 2, reprinted with permission. For tables for other-size samples, consult this source.

> **Exhibit D-10** Random Numbers

97446	30328	05262	77371	13523	62057	44349	85884	94555	23288
15453	75591	60540	77137	09485	27632	05477	99154	78720	10323
69995	77086	55217	53721	85713	27854	41981	88981	90041	20878
69726	58696	27272	38148	52521	73807	29685	49152	20309	58734
23604	31948	16926	26360	76957	99925	86045	11617	32777	38670
13640	17233	58650	47819	24935	28670	33415	77202	92492	40290
90779	09199	51169	94892	34271	22068	13923	53535	56358	50258
71068	19459	32339	10124	13012	79706	07611	52600	83088	26829
55019	79001	34442	16335	06428	52873	65316	01480	72204	39494
20879	50235	17389	25260	34039	99967	48044	05067	69284	53867
00380	11595	49372	95214	98529	46593	77046	27176	39668	20566
68142	40800	20527	79212	14166	84948	11748	69540	84288	37211
42667	89566	20440	57230	35356	01884	79921	94772	29882	24695
07756	78430	45576	86596	56720	65529	44211	18447	53921	92722
45221	31130	44312	63534	47741	02465	50629	94983	05984	88375
20140	77481	61686	82836	41058	41331	04290	61212	60294	95954
54922	25436	33804	51907	73223	66423	68706	36589	45267	35327
48340	30832	72209	07644	52747	40751	06808	85349	18005	52323
23603	84387	20416	88084	33103	41511	59391	71600	35091	52722
12548	01033	22974	59596	92087	02116	63524	00627	41778	24392
15251	87584	12942	03771	91413	75652	19468	83889	98531	91529
65548	59670	57355	18874	63601	55111	07278	32560	40028	36079
48488	76170	46282	76427	41693	04506	80979	26654	62159	83017
02862	15665	62159	15159	69576	20328	68873	28152	66087	39405
67929	06754	45842	66365	80848	15262	55144	37816	08421	30071
73237	07607	31615	04892	50989	87347	14393	21165	68169	70788
13788	20327	07960	95917	75112	01398	26381	41377	33549	19754
43877	66485	40825	45923	74410	69693	76959	70973	26343	63781
14047	08369	56414	78533	76378	44204	71493	68861	31042	81873
88383	46755	51342	13505	55324	52950	22244	28028	73486	98797
29567	16379	41994	65947	58926	50953	09388	00405	29874	44954
20508	60995	41539	26396	99825	25652	28089	57224	35222	58922
64178	76768	75747	32854	32893	61152	58565	33128	33354	16056
26373	51147	90362	93309	13175	66385	57822	31138	12893	68607
10083	47656	59241	73630	99200	94672	59785	95449	99279	25488
11683	14347	04369	98719	75005	43633	24125	30532	54830	95387
56548	76293	50904	88579	24621	94291	56881	35062	48765	22078
35292	47291	82610	27777	43965	31802	98444	88929	54383	93141
51329	87645	51623	08971	50704	82395	33916	95859	99788	97885
51860	19180	39324	68483	78650	74750	64893	58042	82878	20619
23886	01257	07945	71175	31243	87167	42829	44601	08769	26417
80028	82310	43989	09242	15056	48250	04529	96941	48190	69644
83946	46858	09164	18858	12672	55190	02820	45861	29104	75386
00000	41586	25972	25356	54260	95691	99431	89903	22306	43863
90615	12848	23376	29458	48239	37628	59265	50152	30340	40713
42003	10738	55835	48218	23204	19188	13556	06610	77667	88068
86135	26174	07834	17007	97938	96728	15689	77544	89186	41252
54436	10828	41212	19836	89476	53685	28085	22878	71868	35048
14545	72034	32131	38783	58588	47499	50945	97045	42357	53536
43925	49879	13339	78773	95626	67119	93023	96832	09757	98545

Source: The Rand Corporation, *A Million Random Digits with 100,000 Normal Deviates* (Glencoe, IL: Free Press, 1955), p. 225.

chapter 1

Reference Notes

1. Developed from official American Marketing Association definition and from Larry A. Constantineau, "Reengineering the Marketing Research Function," Quirk's *Marketing Research Review,* Article Number 0141, October 1995 (downloaded from quirks.com).

2. "AMA Adopts New Definition of Marketing," Chicago, IL: American Marketing Association press release, September 10, 2004 (http://wwww.marketingpower.com/live/content21257.php).

3. Steve Lohr and John Markoff, "You Call This a Midlife Crisis?" *New York Times,* August 31, 2003 (http://www.nytimes.com/2003/08/31/technology/31MICR.html).

4. http://www.haagen-dazs.com (downloaded August 23, 2002).

5. Peter D. Bennett, ed., *Dictionary of Marketing Terms,* 2d ed. (Chicago, IL: American Marketing Association, 1995).

6. Presentation by Larry Stanek, vice president, consumer and marketplace knowledge, Minute Maid, at AMA's Marketing Research Conference, Chicago, September 9, 2002.

7. Cited from *Sloan Management Review,* January 1996 (from "Soothsayer, Seer, and Sage: The Role of Research in an Information Economy," a presentation by Eileen Campbell, president and CEO, Millward Brown, Inc., at the AMA Marketing Research Conference, Chicago, September 9, 2002).

8. See, for example, Murray Levine, "Investigative Reporting as a Research Method: Analysis of Bernstein and Woodward's *All the President's Men," American Psychologist* 35 (1980), pp. 626–38.

9. See, for example, Elizabethann O'Sullivan and Gary R. Rassel, *Research Methods for Public Administrators* (New York: Longman, 1999).

10. Reprinted with permission of Macmillan Publishing Co., Inc., from *Theory Building,* rev. ed. 1978, by Robert Dubin. Copyright © 1969 by The Free Press, a division of Macmillan Co.

References for Snapshots, PicProfiles, Captions, and Pull Quotes

American Marketing Association

"Voice of the Marketer," *Marketing News,* February 1, 2004, p. 46.

Max Bazerman

An excerpt from "Ethical Leadership and the Psychology of Decision Making," *Sloan Management Review,* January 1996, as cited in Holman W. Jenkins Jr., "How Could They Have Done It?" *The Wall Street Journal,* August 28, 2002 (http://www.analects-ink.com/weekend/020830.htm).

Covering Kids

This and other Covering Kids Snapshots were developed through interviews with Stuart Schear, Robert Woods Johnson Foundation; Maury Giles, Wirthlin Worldwide; Annie Burns and Aimee Segal, GMMB; and Ellen Arkin, independent consultant to RWJF, during 2002 and 2003.

Mary Kay Inc.

Interview with Teri Burgess, director of marketing analysis, Mary Kay Inc., September 10, 2002.

Tom Peters

Consultant and author, TomPeters! Company (http://www.tompeters.com).

Classic and Contemporary Readings

Berry, Michael J. A., and Gordon Linhoff. *Data Mining Techniques: For Marketing, Sales, and Customer Support.* New York: Wiley, 1997. This is a practical guide to mining business data to help business managers focus their marketing and sales strategies.

Curry, David J., *The New Marketing Research Systems.* New York: Wiley, 1993.

Gibson, Lawrence D., "Quo Vadis, Marketing Research?" *Marketing Research,* Spring 2000, pp. 36–41.

Haas, Peter J., and J. Fred Springer. *Applied Policy Research: Concepts and Cases.* New York: Garland Reference Library of Social Science, No. 1051, 1998. Chapter 2 discusses policy research strategies and contributions.

Johannson, Johny K., and Ikujiro Nonaka, "Marketing Research the Japanese Way." *Harvard Business Review,* May–June 1987, pp. 16–22.

Kimball, Ralph, et al. *The Data Warehouse Lifecycle Toolkit: Expert Methods for Designing, Developing, and Deploying Data Warehouses.* New York: Wiley, 1998. A definitive work on the business dimensional life-cycle approach and data warehouse architecture.

Porter, Michael. *Competitive Strategy.* New York: The Free Press, 1980. The seminal work in strategy development.

Random, Matthew. *The Social Scientist in American Industry.* New Brunswick, NJ: Rutgers University Press, 1970. A research report of experiences of social scientists employed in industry. Chapter 7 presents a summary of findings.

Remenyi, Dan, et al. *Doing Research in Business and Management: An Introduction to Process and Method.* Thousand Oaks, CA: Sage Publications, 1998. Chapters 1 and 2 establish the business research perspective for management students.

Sutton, Howard. *Competitive Intelligence.* New York: The Conference Board, 1988.

chapter 2

Reference Notes

1. Peter F. Drucker, "Beyond the Information Revolution," *Atlantic Monthly,* October 1999, p. 47.

2. Brian W. Arthur, "Is the Information Revolution Dead? If History Is a Guide, It Is Not," *Business 2.0,* March 2002 (http://www.business2.com/articles/mag/0,1640,37570,00.html).

3. Martin H. Weik, *The ENIAC Story,* Ordnance Ballistic Research Laboratories, Aberdeen Proving Ground, MD, 1961. (http://ftp.arl.mil/~mike/comphist/eniac-story.html).

4. Donald R. Cooper, and Pamela S. Schindler, *Business Research Methods,* 8th ed. (New York: McGraw Hill/Irwin, 2003).

5. Robert C. Blattberg, Rashi Glazer, and John D. C. Little, eds., *The Marketing Information Revolution* (Boston: Harvard Business School Press, 1994).

6. Portions are adapted from a presentation by Larry P. Stanek, "Getting and Keeping a Seat at the Executive Table," 23d Annual AMA Marketing Research Conference, Chicago, September 9, 2002.

7. *INformed* 4, no. 2 (April 2001) (http://www.arfsite.org/webpages/informed/vol4-no2/page2.html).

8. Ibid.

9. Philip Kotler, "Bringing Marketing Research into the Board Room," 23d Annual AMA Marketing Research Conference, Chicago, September 9, 2002.

10. CASRO, http://www.casro.org.

11. NFO WorldGroup Web site, downloaded November 9, 2002 (http://www.nfow.com/default2.asp).

12. TNSI Web site, downloaded November 9, 2002 (http://www.intersearch.tnsofres.com/custom/).

13. Ibid.

14. Curt Coffman and Gabriel Gonzalez-Molina, *Follow This Path: How the World's Greatest Organizations Drive Growth by Unleashing Human Potential* (New York: Warner Books, Inc., October 2002); interviews with Larry Emond, CMO, The Gallup Organization, October 15–17, 2002.

15. Context-Based Research Group Web site, downloaded November 9, 2002 (http://www.contextresearch.com/context/index.cfm, http://www.contextresearch.com/context/clients_recent.cfm).

16. Survey Sampling Inc. Web site, downloaded November 9, 2002 (http://www.surveysampling.com/ssi_products.html).

17. Greenfield Online Web site, downloaded November 9, 2002 (http://www.greenfield.com/sampling/panel.htm, http://www.greenfield.com/sampling/msn.htm).

18. Qualtrics Labs materials from the AMA Marketing Research Conference, Chicago, September 9, 2002; interview with CIO, Qualtrics Labs, Chicago, September 9, 2002.

19. Training Technologies Inc. Web site (http://www.surveytracker.com).

20. Information Resources Inc. Web site, downloaded November 9, 2002 (http://www.infores.com/public/global/aboutiri/glo_abt_history.htm).

21. NOP World Web site, downloaded November 9, 2002 (http://www.nop.co.uk/omnibus/hp_omnibus.shtml).

22. Medical Marketing Research Inc. Web site, downloaded November 9, 2002 (http://www.mmrx.com/mmrx/sld026.htm); TNS Intersearch Web site, downloaded November 9, 2002 (http://www.tnsofres.com/consumeromnibus/phonebus/index.cfm).

23. POQ Web site, downloaded November 9, 2002 (http://www.journals.uchicago.edu/POQ/brief.html).

24. "What Is CASRO?" CASRO Web site, downloaded November 9, 2002 (http://www.casro.org/whatis.cfm).

25. MRA Web site, downloaded November 9, 2002 (http://www.mra-net.org/about/index.cfm).

26. ESOMAR Web site, downloaded November 9, 2002 (http://www.esomar.nl/what_is_esomar.html).

27. ESOMAR directory entry for ARF, downloaded November 9, 2002 (http://www.esomar.nl/assocs/111793.html).; "Mission of ARF," ARF Web site (http://www.thearf.org/Webpages/PrimaryPages/mission.htm).

28. ESOMAR directory entry for ANA, downloaded November 9, 2002 (http://www.esomar.nl/assocs/134419.html). "Marketing Research Committee," ANA Web site, downloaded November 9, 2002 (http://www.ana.net/com/com.htm).

29. "What Does the SRT Offer?" SRT Web site, downloaded November 9, 2002 (http://www.sales-research-trust.org/what.htm).

30. "About MPA," MPA Web site, downloaded November 9, 2002 (http://www.magazine.org/aboutMPA/membership.html).

31. "Research and Information," NAB Web site, downloaded November 9, 2002 (http://www.nab.org/Research/).

32. "Trends and Numbers," NAA Web site, downloaded November 9, 2002 (http://www.naa.org/artpage.cfm?AID=1565&SID=1022).

33. "Point-of-Purchase Advertising International Research and Information," POPAI Web site, downloaded November 9, 2002 (http://www.popai.com/frames/research_fr.html).

34. "RAB Research," RAB Web site, downloaded November 9, 2002 (http://www.rab.com/).

References for Snapshots, PicProfiles, Captions, and Pull Quotes

CourtTV

NielsenMedia, downloaded January 7, 2003 (http://www.nielsenmedia.com/).

Decision Analyst

"Concept Testing," Decision Analyst, Inc., downloaded January 7, 2003 (http://www.decisionanalyst.com/Services/concept.asp#conceptor).

Direct-to-Consumer Ads

Stuart Elliott, "The Fight to Keep Direct-to-Consumer Ads," *New York Times,* July 12, 2002, downloaded July 12, 2002 (http://www.nytimes.com/2002/07/12/business/media/12ADCO.html?tntemail)-&pagewan\The Fight to Keep 'Direct-to-Consumer Ads'.htm).

"PharmTrends," Ipsos-NPD, downloaded July 12, 2002 (http://www.ipsos-npd.com/index_pharm.cfm).

"Ad Aware Consumers Are Purchasing More Prescription Drug Scripts Than Those Not Aware of Direct-to-Consumer Advertising," Ipsos-NPD press release, June 27, 2002, downloaded July 12, 2002 (http://www.ipsos-npd.com/index_news.cfm?release=02_0626).

"Consumers Are Responding to Advertising for Prescription Medications," Ipsos-NPD press release, June 13, 2002, downloaded July 12, 2002 (http://www.ipsos-npd.com/index_news.cfm?release=02_0613).

Express

Interview with Brenda Edwards, vice president, marketing communications, TNS Intersearch, July 2001.

Rick Garlick

Director, consulting and strategic implementation, Maritz Research, Hospitality Research Group (http://www.maritzresearch.com/2002Fall/main.html).

Kodak

"Better! Faster! Cheaper!" *Marketing News,* American Marketing Association, February 1, 2004, pp. 1, 31–32.

Wal-Mart

Dana Blankenhorn, "100 Trillion Bytes of Customer Data: How Marketers' Database Muscle Is Growing," *AdAge.com Special Report,* Summer 2001 (http://adagespecials.com/data1.shtml).

"NCR More Than Doubles Warehouse for World's Leading Retailer to over 100 Terabytes," *Dsstar: Executive Journal for Data Intensive Decision Support,* Tabor Griffin Communications (http://hpcwire.com/dsstar/99/0824/1000966.html).

Betsy Spethman, "Wal-Mart Goes Private: Retailer Control Grows as Researchers Stop Getting Scanner Data This Month," *PROMO,* July 2001, pp. 39–40.

"Wal-Mart Buys World's Largest Decision-Support System from AT&T," AT&T press release, January 9, 1995 (http://www. att.com/press/0195/950109.nca.html).

"Wal-Mart's Purchasing Data Becomes Public," *InformationWeek.com,* August 27, 2001 (http://www.informationweek.com/ story/IWK20010824S0015).

Paul Westerman, *Data Warehousing: Using the Wal-Mart Model* (Morgan Kaufmann Publishers, 2001).

Yahoo!

Ken Mallon, director, Insights Products, Yahoo, interview February 17, 2004. SRI-Knowledge Networks, Media Scan—Spring 2003, shows that among women age 25 to 54, Internet consumption rose from 10 to 13% from fall 2000 to spring 2003.

Forrester Research, September 2003, shows decreases in radio (10%), newspaper (16%), TV (21%), and magazines (13%) by women 25 to 54 since going online.

"ACNielsen Homescan," ACNielsen, downloaded February 17, 2004 (http://www.acnielsen.com/products/reports/homescan/).

Phil Cara, "Online Market Research: Trends and Technology," American Marketing Association: WebEx event, February 5, 2004.

Classic and Contemporary Readings

Bartels, Robert. *The History of Marketing Thought.* 2d ed. Columbus, OH: Grid, 1976.

Blattberg, Robert C., Rashi Glazer, and John D. C. Little, eds. *The Marketing Information Revolution.* Boston, MA: Harvard Business School Press, 1994.

Converse, Jean M. *Survey Research in the United States: Roots and Emergence 1890–1960.* Berkeley, CA: University of California Press, 1987.

Miller, Thomas W. and Dana H. James. *Marketing Research and Information Services: 2003 Industry Report.* Madison, WI: Research Publishers, LLC, 2003.

chapter 3

Reference Notes

1. P. McC. Miller and M. J. Wilson, eds., *A Dictionary of Social Sciences Methods* (New York: Wiley, 1983), p. 27. Also see Benjamin B. Wolman, ed., *Dictionary of Behavioral Science,* 2d ed. (New York: Academic Press, 1989).

2. Thomas S. Kuhn, *The Structure of Scientific Revolutions* (Chicago: University of Chicago Press, 1970).

3. Based on John Dewey, *How We Think* (Boston: Heath, 1910), and John R. Platt, "Strong Inference," *Science,* October 16, 1964, pp. 347–53.

4. Howard Kahane, *Logic and Philosophy,* 2d ed. (Belmont, CA: Wadsworth, 1973), p. 3.

5. Dewey, *How We Think,* p. 79.

6. *Merriam-Webster's Collegiate Dictionary,* 10th ed. (Springfield, MA: Merriam-Webster, 1999), http://www.m-w.com/cgi-bin/dictionary.

7. Fred N. Kerlinger, *Foundations of Behavioral Research,* 3d ed. (New York: Holt, Rinehart & Winston, 1986), pp. 436–37.

8. Kenneth R. Hoover, *The Elements of Social Scientific Thinking,* 5th ed. (New York: St. Martin's Press, 1991), p. 71.

9. Bruce Tuckman, *Conducting Educational Research* (New York: Harcourt Brace Jovanovich, 1972), p. 45.

10. William Stephens, *Hypotheses and Evidence* (New York: Thomas Y. Crowell, 1968), p. 5.

11. Based on Roger A Kerin, Eric N. Berkowitz, Steven W. Hartley, and William Rudelius, *Marketing,* 7th ed. (New York: Irwin/McGraw-Hill, 2003), pp. 294–302.

12. Ibid., p. 298.

13. Scott M. Smith and William R. Swinyard, *Introduction to Marketing Models,* chap. 1 (Internet Text, 1999), http:// marketing.byu.edu/htmlpages/courses/693r/modelsbook.html.

14. Ibid., chap. 6, http://marketing.byu.edu/htmlpages/courses/693r/modelsbook/airjordan.html

References for Snapshots, PicProfiles, Captions, and Pull Quotes

Jeffrey Bradshow

"Futurespeak: Science's Potential to Create New Markets," *American Demographics,* April 2003, p. 44.

Forrester Research

"Making Auto Retail Lean," TechStrategy report, Forrester Research, downloaded January 5, 2004 (http://www.forrester.com/ER/Research/Report/Summary/0,1338,32782,00.html).

Mark Bunger, senior analyst, Forrester Research, interviewed January 22, 2004.

ITE

CBS Evening News with Dan Rather, June 30, 1999.

Dateline NBC, June 28, 1999.

Dateline NBC, July 1, 1999 (http://www.dateline.msnbc.com/news/284646.asp).

"Miami Area Intersection Tops State Farm List of Most Dangerous in the United States," State Farm press release, June 27, 2001.

"State Farm's Dangerous Intersection Initiative," Institute of Transportation Engineers press release, June 25, 2001 (http://www.ite.org/press_release.htm).

Marriott

Brenda Roth, manager of research, Marriott International, Inc., January 2000; http://www.marriott.com/milestone.asp; http://www.marriott.com/corporateinfo/98annual/about.asp.

Classic and Contemporary Readings

Beardsley, Monroe. *Practical Logic.* Englewood Cliffs, NJ: Prentice Hall, 1969. A lucid discussion of deduction and induction as well as an excellent coverage of argument analysis.

Hoover, Kenneth R., and Todd Donovan. *The Elements of Social Scientific Thinking.* 6th ed. New York: St. Martin's Press, 1995. A brief but highly readable treatise on the elements of science and scientific thinking.

Kaplan, Abraham. *The Conduct of Inquiry.* San Francisco: Chandler, 1964. A classic source for the philosophy of science and logical reasoning.

chapter 4

Reference Notes

1. Albert Einstein and L. Infeld, *The Evolution of Physics* (New York: Simon & Schuster, 1938), p. 95.

2. Walter B. Wentz, *Marketing Research: Management, Method, and Cases* (New York: Harper & Row, 1979), p. 35.

3. Robert D. Buzzell, Donald F. Cox, and Rex V. Brown, *Marketing Research and Information Systems* (New York: McGraw-Hill, 1969), p. 595.

4. Dik Warren Twedt, "What Is the 'Return on Investment' in Marketing Research?" *Journal of Marketing* 30 (January 1966), pp. 62–63.

5. Paul D. Leedy, *How to Read Research and Understand It* (New York: Macmillan, 1981), pp. 67–70.

6. "George W. Bush," Wikipedia (http://www.wikipedia.org/wiki/George_W._Bush).

7. "Bush Job Approval Falls," Reuters, September 8, 2003 (http://www.stuff.co.nz/stuff/0,2106,2652032a12,00.html).

8. Roger Cohen, "For U.S. Publishers, Awash in Red Ink, the Moment of Truth Looms," *International Herald Tribune,* March 6, 1990, p. 6.

9. "Johnson & Johnson Is Known for Its Handling of the Tylenol Crisis." Johnson & Johnson Information for Students (http://www.jnj.com/contact_us/info_for_students/index.htm#question03); "Was the Person Behind the Tylenol Poisonings in the 1980s Ever Caught?" Yahoo.com, Ask Yahoo (http://ask.yahoo.com/ask/20030130.html); "James Burke, Johnson & Johnson" transcript, *Phil Donahue Show,* 1982; "Diary of Product Tampering: Tylenol," *20-20,* ABC News, 1982.

10. The nine-dot and the traveling salesman problem are examples of ill-defined problems; see http://www.math.princeton.edu/tsp/ for further detail. See also David Reed, "The Use of Ill-Defined Problems for Developing Problem-Solving and Empirical Skills in CS1," *Journal of Computing in Small Colleges* 18, no. 1 (October 2002), p. 121; "Solving Traveling Salesman Problems," http://www.math.princeton.edu/tsp/; Walter B. Reitman, "Heuristic Decision Procedures, Open Constraints, and the Structure of Ill-Defined Problems," in *Human Judgments and Optimality,* ed. Maynard W. Shelly II and Glenn L. Bryan (New York: Wiley, 1964), p. 285.

11. Carl M. Moore, *Group Techniques for Idea Building*, 2d ed. (Thousand Oaks, CA: Sage Publications, 1994).

12. Fred N. Kerlinger, *Foundations of Behavioral Research*, 3d ed. (New York: Holt, Rinehart & Winston, 1986), pp. 436–37.

References for Snapshots, PicProfiles, Captions, and Pull Quotes

Walt Disney

http://www.brainyquote.com/quotes/quotes/w/waltdisney132637.html.

Donatos Pizza

Alexander Coolidge, "Hold the Carbs," *Cincinnati Post Online Edition,* posted January 22, 2004.

Spenser Research, downloaded February 26, 2003 (www.spencer-research.com).

The Atkins Diet is one of two often-followed low-carbohydrate eating plans; the other is the South Beach diet. For more information about both, visit http://atkins.com/ or http://www.southbeach.com.

Tom Krouse, chief concept officer, Donatos Pizza, interviewed February 26, 2004.

Kraft

"Cheese Please! Kraft Singles Talks to Moms about Kids and Calcium," *American Demographics,* March 2000, pp. s6–s7.

Lexus

"Lexus SC430 Case Study," submitted by Lexus and Team One Advertising to the David Ogilvy Research Committee, October 22, 2001.

Mark Miller, Team One Advertising, interviews on July 9, 2002, and October 5, 2002.

MarketVoice

Amy Davidoff, president, MarketVoice Consulting, interviewed September 10, 2002.

Rock the Vote

"Rock the Vote and Motorola Team to Mobilize Electorate," Motorola press release, March 2, 2004 (http://www.motorola.com/mediacenter/news/detailpf/0,,3935_3306_23,00.html).

Nat Ives, "Marketers Pitch to Young Voters," *New York Times,* March 22, 2004 (http://query.nytimes.com/mem/tnt.html?tntget=2004/03/22/business/media/22adco.html&tntemail0).

Anthony Newman, "Motorola Helps Rock the Vote," *InfoSync World,* March 2, 2004. downloaded March 21, 2004 (http://www.infosyncworld.com/news/n/4664.html).

Classic and Contemporary Readings

Fox, David J. *The Research Process in Education.* New York: Holt, Rinehart & Winston, 1969. Chapter 2 includes a research process model to compare with the one in this chapter.

Leedy, Paul D. *Practical Research: Planning & Design.* 6th ed. Englewood Cliffs, NJ: Prentice Hall, 1996. Practical and readable sections guide students through the research process.

Murdick, Robert G., and Donald R. Cooper. *Business Research: Concepts and Guides.* Columbus, OH: Grid, 1982. A supplementary text with a strong emphasis on problem identification and formulation.

Selltiz, Claire, Lawrence S. Wrightsman, and Stuart M. Cook. *Research Methods in Social Relations.* 3d ed. New York: Holt, Rinehart & Winston, 1976. Chapters 1 and 2 present a good research process example and discussion of formulating a research problem.

Tull, Donald S., and Del I. Hawkins. *Marketing Research: Meaning, Measurement, and Method.* 6th ed. New York: Macmillan, 1992. The authors provide good coverage of the valuation of research information through a Bayesian decision theory approach.

chapter 5

Reference Notes

1. *Online TDM Encyclopedia,* Victoria Transport Policy Institute, downloaded January 27, 2004 (http://www.vtpi.org/tdm/).

2. *Channel Encyclopedia,* Pittiglio Rabin Todd & McGrath, downloaded January 27, 2004 (http://www.prtm.com/channelstrategies/encyclopedia.html).

3. *Occupational Outlook Handbook,* U.S. Bureau of Labor Statistics (http://www.bls.gov/oco/ocoiab.htm).

4. *Commercial Potato Production in North America,* Potato Association of America, downloaded January 27, 2004 (http://www.ume.maine.edu/PAA/pubs.htm#America).

5. *North American Industry Classification System* (NAICS), U.S. Census Bureau, downloaded January 27, 2004 (http://www. census.gov/epcd/www/naics.html).

6. *Green Book, a Worldwide Directory of Marketing Research Companies and Services,* New York AMA Communications Services, Inc., downloaded January 27, 2004 (http://www.greenbook.org/); *Green Book, a Worldwide Directory of Focus Group Companies and Services,* New York AMA Communications Services, Inc., downloaded January 27, 2004 (http://www.greenbook.org/).

References for Snapshots, PicProfiles, Captions, and Pull Quotes

Covering Kids

About Us," Robert Wood Johnson Foundation, downloaded July 22, 2002 (http://www.rwjf.org/aboutRwjf/index.jhtml).

"Call for Proposals, Covering Kids and Families," Robert Wood Johnson Foundation.

"Call for Proposals, Covering Kids: A National Health Access Initiative for Low-Income Uninsured Children," Robert Wood Johnson Foundation.

"Covering Kids Communication Campaign—Target Market Summary: Phase I Market Research and Short-Term Evaluation Plans," Robert Wood Johnson Foundation, September 7, 2000.

Elaine Arkin, consultant to Robert Wood Johnson Foundation, interviewed October 4, 2002.

Stuart Schear, senior communication officer, Robert Wood Johnson Foundation, interviewed July 23, 2002.

Peter Drucker

Author and consultant (http://www.quotesandsayings.com/ finquoteframes.htm).

Marketing Intelligence

Andy Marken, CEO, Marken Communications, August 6, 2002. "Why Marken Com," Marken Communications Web site, downloaded August 6, 2002 (http://www.markencom.com/_frame.htm).

Political Marketing

Jon Gertner, "The Very, Very Personal Is the Political," *New York Times,* February 15, 2004, downloaded February 16, 2004 (http://query.nytimes.com/mem/tnt.html?tntget=2004/02/15/ magazine/15VOTERS.html&tntemail0).

Joshua Green, "In Search of the Elusive Swing Voter," *Atlantic Monthly,* January–February 2004, downloaded February 16, 2004 (http://www.theatlantic.com/issues/2004/01/green-voter.htm).

"Keeping High-Tech Tabs on Voters," CBSNews.com, October 20, 2003, downloaded February 16, 2004 (http://www.cbsnews.com/ stories/2003/10/20/politics/main578935.shtml).

"Kerry Web Ad Campaign Launched by Voter Interactive," PRNewswire.com, posted January 28, 2004.

Miles Benson, "'Demzilla' and 'Voter Vault' Are Watching You," Newshousenews.com, June 9, 2003, downloaded February 16, 2004 (http://www.newshousenews.com/archive/benson061003.html).

TARK, Inc.

Paul Vanderburgh, vice president, marketing, TARK, Inc., interviewed July 25, 2002.

Classic and Contemporary Readings

Berg, Bruce L. *Qualitative Research Methods for the Social Sciences.* 5th ed. Needham Heights, MA: Allyn & Bacon, 2003.

Blankenship, Albert, George Breen, and Alan Dutka. *State of the Art Marketing Research.* 2d ed. New York: McGraw-Hill Trade, 1998.

Stebbins, Robert A. *Exploratory Research in the Social Sciences.* Thousand Oaks, CA: Sage Publications, 2001.

Strauss, Anselm, and Juliet M. Corbin. *Basics of Qualitative Research: Techniques and Procedures for Developing Grounded Theory.* 2d ed. Thousand Oaks, CA: Sage Publications, 1998.

Yin, Robert K. *Applications of Case Study Research.* 2d ed. Thousand Oaks, CA: Sage Publications, 2002.

appendix 5a

Reference Notes

1. Good sources for Web size estimates are the studies by Steve R. Lawrence and C. Lee Giles, "Searching the World Wide Web," *Science* 280 (April 1998), pp. 98–100, and "Accessibility of Information on the Web," *Nature* 400 (July 8, 1999), pp. 107–109, with updated summary data at http://www.wwwmetrics.com.

2. Michael Dahm, "Counting Angels on a Pinhead: Critically Interpreting Web Size Estimates," *Online* 24 (January–February 2000), pp. 35–44. This article further interprets the pioneering research by authors Steve R. Lawrence and C. Lee Giles (op. cit.).

3. The May–June 1999 issue of *Online* focuses on search engine technology. See, for example, Danny Sullivan, "Crawling under the Hood: An Update on Search Engine Technology," *Online* 23 (May–June 1999), pp. 30–38. See also Danny Sullivan's "Search Engine Watch" (http://searchenginewatch.com/) and Greg Notess's "Search Engine Showdown" (http://www.notess.com/ search/) for current information about search engines and their features.

4. Greg R. Notess, "Duplicative Databases: Yellow Pages from infoUSA," *Database* 22 (February–March 1999), pp. 73–76.

5. See, for example, the June 22, 1999, issue of *PC Magazine* for a special report detailing "Ten Trends That Are Defining the Future" (Introduction, p. 100).

6. "Federal Register Online Via GPO Access" (http://www.access.gpo.gov/su_docs/aces/aces140.html).

7. "About the Code of Federal Regulations" (http://www. access.gpo.gov/nara/about-ctr.html#page1).

chapter 6

Reference Notes

1. Charles T. Brusaw, Gerald J. Alred, and Walter E. Oliu, *Handbook of Technical Writing,* 4th ed. (New York: St. Martin's Press, 1992), p. 375.

2. Paul D. Leedy, *Practical Research: Planning and Design,* 2d ed. (New York: Macmillan, 1980), p. 79.

3. R. Lesikar and John Pettit, *Report Writing for Business,* 9th ed. (Burr Ridge, IL: Irwin, 1995).

4. Ibid., p. 51.

5. William J. Roetzheim, *Proposal Writing for the Data Processing Consultant* (Englewood Cliffs, NJ: Prentice Hall, 1986), p. 106.

6. Brusaw, Alred, and Oliu, *Handbook,* p. 11.

7. Philip V. Lewis and William H. Baker, *Business Report Writing* (Columbus, OH: Grid, 1978), p. 58.

8. Robert G. Murdick and Donald R. Cooper, *Business Research: Concepts and Guides* (Columbus, OH: Grid, 1982), p. 112.

9. Roetzheim, *Proposal Writing*, pp. 67–68.

10. Many operations research and quantitative models texts cover project management and include details of scheduling and charting techniques such as Gantt charts and CPM charts, which are beyond the scope of this text.

11. See, for example, Kate L. Turabian, *A Manual for Writers of Term Papers, Theses, and Dissertations* (Chicago: University of Chicago Press, 1996); Joseph Gibaldi and Walter S. Achtert, *MLA Handbook for Writers of Research Papers* (New York: Modern Language Association of America, 1999); and the *Publication Manual of the American Psychological Association* (Washington, DC: APA, 1994).

References for Snapshots, PicProfiles, Captions, and Pull Quotes

Bissell

Interview with Ann Lamb, director of communications, Bissell, Inc., August 3, 2001.

"Research on a Shoestring: How Bissell Steamrolled Its Way to the Top of Its Category," *American Demographics,* April 2001, pp. 38–39.

Albert Einstein

http://www.quotesandjokes.com/3390.html.

Karastan

Susan Early, Austin Kelley Advertising, interviewed February 24, 2004.

Pebble Beach

"2001 Five-Star Award Winners List," *Mobil Travel Guide*, Exxon-Mobil Oil (http://www.mobil.com/mobil_consumer/travel/winners/winners_content.html).

"Inn at Spanish Bay Resort," Pebble Beach Resorts (http://www.pebblebeach.com/2b.html).

McGraw-Hill Video Library.

"Rating Criteria for Mobil Travel Guide" (http://www.maisonette.com/maisonette/fine-dining/5star.htm).

United States Tennis Association

Scott Staniar, independent marketing consultant to United States Tennis Association, interviewed April 27, 2004.

Danny Robinson, chief creative officer, Vigilante, interviewed April 30, 2004.

Through its *Urban Think Tank™,* Vigilante has a number of cutting-edge, proprietary products such as "Street Spies" and "Urban Passport" that keep the agency and its clients plugged into urban consumers, downloaded April 30, 2004 (http://www.vigilantenyc.com/vigilante.htm).

Classic and Contemporary Readings

Freed, R., J. Romanno, and S. Freed. *Writing Winning Business Proposals.* 2d ed. New York: McGraw-Hill, 2003.

Krathwohl, David R. *How to Prepare a Research Proposal.* 3d ed. Syracuse, NY: Syracuse University Press, 1988. A practical guide and framework for student projects.

Leedy, Paul D., and Jeanne Ellis Ormrod. *Practical Research: Planning and Design.* 7th ed. Englewood Cliffs, NJ: Prentice Hall, 2000. Practical and readable sections guide students through the research process.

Locke, Lawrence F., Waneen Wyrick Spiduso, and Steven J. Silverman. *Proposals That Work: A Guide to Planning Dissertations and Grant Proposals.* 4th ed. Thousand Oaks, CA: Sage Publications, 2000. An excellent guide for students and faculty advisers covering all aspects of the proposal process.

Porter-Roth, B. *Request for Proposal: A Guide to Effective RFP Development.* Boston: Addison-Wesley Professional, 2001.

appendix 6a

Covering Kids

Stuart Schear, senior communication officer, Robert Wood Johnson Foundation, interviewed July 23, 2002.

Elaine Arkin, consultant of Robert Wood Johnson Foundation, interviewed October 4, 2002.

Maury Giles, Wirthlin Worldwide, multiple interviews, 2002 and 2003.

chapter 7

Reference Notes

1. C. S. Benson, "Codes of Ethics," *Journal of Business Ethics* (1989), pp. 305–309.

2. *Code of Marketing Research Standards*, Marketing Research Association, May 12, 2003, downloaded January 27, 2004 (http://www.mra-net.org/codes/expanded_code.pdf).

3. Elizabethann O'Sullivan and Gary R. Rassel, *Research Methods for Public Administrators* (New York: Longman, 1999).

4. *Code of Marketing Research Standards*, Marketing Research Association, May 12, 2003, p. 9, downloaded January 27, 2004 (http://www.mra-net.org/codes/expanded_code.pdf).

5. American Psychological Association, *Ethical Principles of Psychologists and Code of Conduct* (Washington, DC: APA, 1997).

6. Exhibit 7-2 shows the standard procedures used for informed consent in surveys conducted by the Indiana University Center for Survey Research. Wording and protocol by CSR IU.

7. Paul Davidson Reynolds, *Ethics and Social Science Research* (Englewood Cliffs, NJ: Prentice Hall, 1982), pp. 103–108.

8. The Nuremberg Code is a set of 10 moral, ethical, and legal principles for medical experimentation on humans. It comes from the judgment of the Nuremberg Military Tribunal against doctors and scientists who committed World War II Nazi atrocities. For a full listing of the Nuremberg Code, see Jay Katz, *Experimentation with Human Beings* (New York: Russell Sage Foundation, 1972), pp. 305–306. See also Allan J. Kimmel, *Ethics and Values in Applied Social Research* (Newbury Park, CA: Sage Publications, 1988), pp. 54–56.

9. Reynolds, *Ethics and Social Science Research.*

10. Robert A. Baron and Donn Byrne, *Social Psychology: Understanding Human Interaction* (Boston: Allyn and Bacon, 1991), p. 36.

11. "In Brief: The Financial Privacy Requirements of the Gramm-Leach-Bliley Act," Federal Trade Commission, downloaded May 10, 2004 (http://www.ftc.gov/bcp/conline/pubs/buspubs/glbshort.htm).

12. "Children's Privacy: The Children's Online Privacy Protection Act," Federal Trade Commission, downloaded May 10, 2004 (http://www.ftc.gov/privacu/privacyinitiatives/childrens.html).

13. Floyd J. Fowler Jr., *Survey Research Methods,* rev. ed. (Beverly Hills, CA: Sage Publications, 1988), p. 138.

14. Jim Thomas, "Introduction: A Debate about the Ethics of Fair Practices for Collecting Social Science Data in Cyberspace," *Information Society* 12, no. 2 (1996).

15. "FAQs—Kroger Plus Shopper's Card," The Kroger Co., 2001 (http://www.kroger.com/faqs_shopperscard.htm).

16. "European Online Privacy Measures Up," *eMarketer,* October 26, 1998 (http://www.estats.com/news/102698_europri.html).

17. Robert O'Harrow, "Privacy Rules Send U.S. Firms Scrambling," *Washington Post,* October 20, 1998.

18. Robert Andrews, Mary Biggs, and Michael Seidel, eds, *The Columbia World of Quotations,* Bartleby.com, 2001, downloaded January 27, 2004 (http://www.bartleby.com/66/99/16799.html).

19. Fowler, *Survey Research Methods,* p. 139.

20. Thomas, "Introduction: A Debate About the Ethics of Fair Practices." The Belmont Report was produced by the National Commission for the Protection of Human Subjects of Biomedical and Behavioral Research under the title *Ethical Principles and Guidelines for the Protection of Human Subjects of Research* (Washington, DC: Department of Health, Education, and Welfare, 1979). The other source of ethical standards is the *Federal Register,* Part II: "Federal Policy for the Protection of Human Subjects: Notices and Rules" (Washington, DC: U.S. Government Printing Office, 1991).

21. R. Gorlin, ed., *Codes of Professional Responsibility,* 3d ed. (Washington, DC: BNA Books, 1994).

22. Jeff Allen and Duane Davis, "Assessing Some Determinant Effects of Ethical Consulting Behavior: The Case of Personal and Professional Values," *Journal of Business Ethics* (1993), p. 449.

23. Center for Business Ethics, Bentley College (Waltham, MA), http://ecampus.bentley.edu/dept/cbe/.

24. http://www.ethicsandbusiness.org/index3.htm.

25. Adapted from stories in the *Palm Beach Post* during September 1992.

References for Snapshots, PicProfiles, Captions, and Pull Quotes

Coca-Cola/Burger King

"Formal Investigation Opened in Coca-Cola Tampering Case," *PromoXtra,* January 20, 2004.

Sherri Day, "Coke Makes Up with Burger King over Rigged Frozen Drink Test," *New York Times,* August 2, 2003 (http://www.nytimes.com/2003/08/02/business/02SODA.html).

Google

Allan Hoffman, "It Had to Happen: Google Is Googled," *Star-Ledger of Newark,* November 13, 2002 (http://www.nola.com/archives/t-p/index.ssf?/livingstory/googled.html).

"Google's Technology Highlights," Google Press Center downloaded November 29, 2002 (http://www.google.com/press/highlights.html).

Jennifer 8 Lee, "Postcards from Planet Google," *New York Times,* November 28, 2002 (http://www.nytimes.com/2002/11/28/technology/circuits/28goog.html).

Hewlett-Packard

Ellen Tombaugh, "Refuge from Privacy Storms: Safe Harbor Principles," PricewaterhouseCoopers, downloaded November 30, 2002 (http://www.pwcglobal.com/extweb/manissue.nsf/DocID/773A677D05FE740E85256A64004CA3EB).

"Safe Harbor List" Export Portal, U.S. Department of Commerce, downloaded November 30, 2002 (http://web.ita.doc.gov/safeharbor/shlist.nsf/webPages/safe+harbor+list).

"HP Is First High-Tech Company to Join U.S.-E.U. Safe Harbor," Hewlett-Packard press release, February 12, 2001, downloaded November 30, 2002 (http://www.hp.com/hpinfo/newsroom/press/12feb01b.htm).

Jet Blue

Complaint filed with the FTC by Electronic Information Center, September 22, 2003, downloaded October 31, 2003 (http://209.157.64.200/focus/f-news/987420/posts).

Matthew L. Wald, "Airline Gave Government Information on Passengers," *New York Times,* January 18, 2004 (http://www.nytimes.com/2004/01/18/national/18NORT.html?ex=1075452528&ei=l&en=0077c1925e5acf3e).

Ryan Singel, "US: JetBlue Shared Passenger Data with Defense Contractor," *Wired,* September 18, 2003, downloaded October 31, 2003 (http://www.corpwatch.org/news/PND.jsp?articleid=8548).

Robert E. Litan

Director, AEI-Brookings Joint Center; former chairman, Federal Communications Commission, "The Data Paradox," *Gallup Management Journal,* March 15, 2001.

Procter & Gamble/Unilever

Julian Barnes, "Unilever Wants P&G Placed under Monitor in Spy Case," *New York Times on the Web,* September 1, 2001 (http://www.nytimes.com/2001/09/01/business/01soap.html).

Andy Serwer, "P&G Comes Clean on Spying Operation," *Fortune.com,* August 30, 2001 (http://www.fortune.com/indexw.jhtml?channel=artcol.jhtml&doc_id=203932).

TRUSTe

"The TRUSTe Program: How It Protects Your Privacy," TRUSTe, downloaded October 30, 2003 (http://www.truste.org/consumers/users_how.html).

Classic and Contemporary Readings

National Academy of Sciences. *On Being a Scientist: Responsible Conduct in Research.* 2d ed. Washington, DC: National Academy Press, 1995. Written for beginning researchers, this source describes the ethical foundations of scientific practices, personal and professional issues, and research applications for industrial, governmental, and academic settings.

Rosnow, Ralph L., and Robert Rosenthal. *People Studying People: Artifacts and Ethics in Behavioral Research.* New York: Freeman, 1997. A potent source of analysis and advice; particularly appropriate for Chapters 17 and 18 on observation and experimentation.

Stanley, Barbara H., et al., eds. *Research Ethics: A Psychological Approach.* Lincoln: University of Nebraska Press, 1996. Addresses important issues such as the discovery and neutralization of bias, sensitivity to the interests of experimental participants, and the counterweighing factors in rules, regulations, and enforcement.

Stern, Judy E., and Deni Elliott, eds. *Research Ethics: A Reader.* Hanover, NH: University Press of New England, 1997. An insightful review of ethical issues for managers and researchers.

chapter 8

Reference Notes

1. Reprinted with permission of Macmillan Publishing from *Social Research Strategy and Tactics,* 2d ed., by Bernard S. Phillips, p. 93. Copyright © 1971 by Bernard S. Phillips.

2. Fred N. Kerlinger, *Foundations of Behavioral Research,* 3d ed. (New York: Holt, Rinehart & Winston, 1986), p. 279.

3. Ibid.

4. The complexity of research design tends to confuse students as well as writers. The latter respond by forcing order on the vast array of design types through the use of classification schemes or taxonomies. Generally, this is helpful, but because the world defies neat categories, this scheme, like others, may either include or exclude too much.

5. Kerlinger, *Foundations of Behavioral Research,* p. 295.

6. Abraham Kaplan, *Conduct of Inquiry* (San Francisco: Chandler, 1964), p. 37.

7. W. Charles Redding, "Research Setting: Field Studies," in *Methods of Research in Communication,* ed. Philip Emmert and William D. Brooks (Boston: Houghton Mifflin, 1970), pp. 140–42.

8. John Van Maanen, James M. Dabbs Jr., and Robert R. Faulkner, *Varieties of Qualitative Research* (Beverly Hills, CA: Sage Publications, 1982), p. 32.

9. Catherine Marshall and Gretchen B. Rossman, *Designing Qualitative Research* (Newbury Park, CA: Sage Publications, 1989), pp. 78–108.

10. A comprehensive and detailed presentation may be found in Richard A. Krueger, *Focus Groups: A Practical Guide for Applied Research,* 2d ed. (Thousand Oaks, CA: Sage Publications, 1994), and David L. Morgan, *Successful Focus Groups: Advancing the State of the Art* (Thousand Oaks, CA: Sage Publications, 1993). Also see Thomas L. Greenbaum, "Focus Group Spurt Predicted for the '90s," *Marketing News* 24, no. 1 (January 8, 1990), pp. 21–22.

11. Morris Rosenberg, *The Logic of Survey Analysis* (New York: Basic Books, 1968), p. 3.

References for Snapshots, PicProfiles, Captions, and Pull Quotes

Alaris Media Network

Matt Richell, "New Billboards Sample Radios as Cars Go By," *New York Times,* December 27, 2002 (http://www.nytimes.com/2002/12/27/business/media/27ADCO.html).

Wally Balden

Director of Internet research, Maritz Research (http://research.report.sept03.mr-2.us/second2.phtml).

Boston Consulting Group/Hanover Brands

Alison Wellner, "A New Cure for Shoppus Interruptus," *American Demographics: The Marketing Tools Directory,* 2002, pp. D59–D61.

Cheskin

Cheskin ad: "What will spark your next evolution?" *American Demographics,* December 2001, p. 30.

"Pepsi Case Study," Cheskin, downloaded January 7, 2003 (http://www.cheskin.com/p/basic.asp?mlid=52).

Claria Corporation/Pepsi

"The Final Score: 2004 Big Game Ad Effectiveness Study," Claria Corporation, downloaded March 30, 2004 (http://www.claria.com/companyinfo/press/february04report/).

"Claria Corporation Overview," Claria Corporation, downloaded March 30, 2004 (http://www.claria.com/companyinfo/).

Kool-Aid

Joan Raymond, "All Smiles," *American Demographics,* March 2001, p. s18 (http://www.kraftfoods.com/kool-aid/ka_index.html).

Megan Nerz, MLN Research, July 2001.

Classic and Contemporary Readings

Babbie, Earl R. *The Practice of Social Research.* 9th ed. Belmont, CA: Wadsworth, 2000. Contains a clear and thorough synopsis of design.

Creswell, John W. *Qualitative Inquiry and Research Design.* 5th ed. Thousand Oaks, CA: Sage Publications, 1997. A creative and comprehensive work on qualitative research methods.

Krathwohl, David R. *Social and Behavioral Science Research: A New Framework for Conceptualizing, Implementing, and Evaluating Research Studies.* San Francisco: Jossey-Bass, 1985. Chapter 9 on causality is insightful, well reasoned, and highly recommended.

Mason, Emanuel J., and William J. Bramble. *Understanding and Conducting Research.* 2d ed. New York: McGraw-Hill, 1989. Chapter 1 has an excellent section on causation; Chapter 2 provides an alternative classification of the types of research.

Morgan, David L., and Richard A. Kruger, eds. *The Focus Group Kit.* Thousand Oaks, CA: Sage Publications, 1997. A six-volume set including an overview guidebook, planning, developing questions, moderating, involving community members, and analyzing results.

Selltiz, Claire, Lawrence S. Wrightsman, and Stuart M. Cook. *Research Methods in Social Relations.* 3d ed. New York: Holt, Rinehart & Winston, 1976. Chapters 4 and 5 discuss various types of research designs.

Strauss, Anselm, and Juliet Corbin. *Basics of Qualitative Research.* 2d ed. Thousand Oaks, CA: Sage Publications, 1998. A step-by-step guide with particularly useful sections on coding procedures.

chapter 9

Reference Notes

1. John Van Maanen, "Reclaiming Qualitative Methods for Organizational Research: A Preface," *Administrative Science Quarterly* 24 (December 1979), pp. 520–24.

2. Judith Langer, *The Mirrored Window: Focus Groups from a Moderator's Point of View* (Ithaca, NY: Paramount Market Publishing, 2001), p. 26.

3. Jennifer Mason, *Qualitative Researching,* 2d ed. (London: Sage Publications, 2002).

4. This list was developed from numerous sources including David Carson, Audrey Gilmore, Chad Perry, and Kjell Gronhaug, *Qualitative Marketing Research* (Thousand Oaks, CA: Sage Publications, 2001), pp. 67–68, which references Norman Denzin and Y. Lincoln, *Handbook of Qualitative Research* (London: Sage Publications, 1994); Y. Lincoln and E. Guba, *Naturalistic Inquiry* (Newbury, CA: Sage Publications, 1985); M. Q. Patton, *Qualitative Evaluation and Research Methods,* 2d ed. (Newbury Park, CA: Sage Publications, 1990); A. M. Pettigrew, "On Studying Organizational Cultures," *Administrative Science Quarterly* 24 (1979), pp. 570–81; Mellanie Wallendorf, Russel Belk, and John Sherry, "The Sacred and the Profane in Consumer Behavior: Theodicy on the Odyssey," *Journal of Consumer Research* 16 (June 1989), pp. 1–38.

5. Carson et al., *Qualitative Marketing Research,* p. 65.

6. Adrian Holliday, *Doing and Writing Qualitative Research* (London: Sage Publications, 2002), pp. 71–72, 99, 105.

7. Ibid.

8. Hy Mariampolski, *Qualitative Market Research: A Comprehensive Guide* (Thousand Oaks, CA: Sage Publications, 2001), p. 79.

9. *Making Connections,* AT&T (video).

10. Developed from material in Christine Daymon and Immy Holloway, *Qualitative Research Methods in Public Relations and Marketing Communications* (London: Sage Publications, 2002), pp. 223–25; and Mariampolski, *Qualitative Market Research,* pp. 206–19.

11. Mariampolski, *Qualitative Market Research,* pp. 31, 85.

12. Langer, *The Mirrored Window,* p. 41

13. "Services: Research: Case Studies: Cracking the Low-Involvement Ceiling," Primary Insights, downloaded January 1, 2003 (http://www.primaryinsights.com/services.cfm?cid=15&cscont=Cracking Ceiling.cfm).

14. Dennis W. Rook, "Out-of-Focus Groups," *Marketing Research* 15, no. 2 (Summer 2003), p. 13.

15. P. Hawe, D. Degeling, and J. Hall, *Evaluating Health Promotion: A Health Worker's Guide* (Artarmon, N.S.W.: MacLennan & Petty, 1990).

16. Rook, "Out-of-Focus Groups," pp. 10–15.

17. "Shoppers Speak Out in Focus Groups," *Discount Store News* 36, no. 5 (March 3, 1997), pp. 23–26.

18. Martin Bauer and George Gaskell, eds., *Qualitative Researching with Text, Image, and Sound: A Practical Handbook* (London: Sage Publications, 2000), pp. 48–51.

19. "How Nonprofits Are Using Focus Groups," *Nonprofit World* 14, no. 5 (September–October 1996), p. 37.

20. Carson et al., *Qualitative Marketing Research,* pp. 114–15.

21. Ibid., pp. 91–94, 100–106.

22. Tom Peters and Robert Waterman, *In Search of Excellence: Lessons from America's Best Run Companies* (New York: HarperCollins, 1982).

23. Carson et al., *Qualitative Marketing Research,* pp.159–63.

24. Uwe Flick, *An Introduction to Qualitative Research,* 2d ed. (London: Sage Publications, 2002), pp. 262–63.

References for Snapshots, PicProfiles, Captions, and Pull Quotes

Dreamworks

Greg Dean Schmitz, *Minority Report,* UpcomingMovies.com, June 9, 2002 (http://www.upcomingmovies.com/minorityreport.html).

Minority Report, Lee's Movie Info, downloaded September 14, 2003 (http://www.leesmovieinfo.net/wbotitle.php?t=78).

"The Movie: *Minority Report,*" *The Oprah Show*, June 10, 2002 (http://www.oprah.com/tows/pastshows/tows_2002/tows_past_20020610_b.jhtml), interviews conducted with both Stephen Spielberg and Tom Cruise.

William Arnold, "Spielberg and Cruise Dream Team Might Make *Minority Report* a Winner," *Seattle Post–Intelligencer,* June 7, 2002 (http://seattlepi.nwsource.com/movies/73591_cruise07.shtml).

Dynamic Survey

Peter MacKey, Invoke Solutions, interviewed October 22, 2004.

Melissa London, London Calling PR, agent of Invoke Solutions, e-mail contact from October 4, 2004, to November 5, 2004.

"Invoke Solutions Now Offers Elegant Answer to Order Bias Challenges," Invoke Solutions press release, London Calling PR, September 20, 2004.

"Dynamic Survey," Invoke Solutions, accessed October 15, 2004 (http://www.invoke.com/solutions_survey.html).

FocusVision

Debbie Robinson, senior account director, VideoMarker™ Services, FocusVision, interviewed September 10, 2002.

VideoMarker materials distributed at AMA Marketing Research Conference, Chicago, September 10, 2002.

Hallmark

Alison Wellner, "The Census Report," *American Demographics,* January 2002, p. S3.

"Cards Reflect Hispanic Culture and Heritage," Hallmark press release, downloaded January 7, 2003 (http://pressroom.hallmark.com/Caminos_al_alma.html).

"Facts about Hallmark en Español," Hallmark press release, downloaded January 7, 2003 (http://pressroom.hallmark.com/en_espanol_facts.html).

"Facts about Sinceramente Hallmark," Hallmark press release, downloaded July 29, 2004 (http://pressroom.hallmark.com/Sinceramente_Hallmark_facts.html).

Hamilton Beach

Joseph Rydholm, "Seeing the Right Mix," *Quirk's Marketing Research Review,* November 2001 (http://www.quirks.com/articles/article.asp?arg_ArticleID=728).

"The Company," Hamilton Beach/Proctor Silex, downloaded January 19, 2003 (http://www.hamiltonbeach.com/company/hbpsbio.html).

IBM

Steve Lohr, "Big Blue's Big Bet: Less Tech, More Touch," *New York Times on the Web,* January 25, 2004, downloaded January 27, 2004 (http://www.nytimes.com/2004/01/25/business/yourmoney/25ibm.html).

Daniel Yankelovich

"Demographic Diamonds (Market Researchers)," *American Demographics*, April 2003, p. 35.

Jerry Zaltman

S. Pink, *Doing Visual Ethnography* (London: Sage Publications, 2001), p. 214.

Classic and Contemporary Readings

Feagin, J. R. *A Case for the Case Study*. Chapel Hill: University of North Carolina Press, 1991. This book discusses the nature, characteristics, and basic methodological issues of the case study as a research method.

Langer, Judith. *The Mirrored Window: Focus Groups from a Moderator's Point of View*. (Ithaca, NY: Paramount Market Publishing, 2001). This book is written from the perspective of the moderator, and thus lets you get a perspective on focus groups you won't get elsewhere.

Mariampolski, Hy. *Qualitative Market Research: A Comprehensive Guide*. Thousand Oaks, CA: Sage Publications, 2001. This is a wonderful overview of qualitative research techniques, providing extensive detail on many methodologies that are only mentioned elsewhere.

A bibliography relating to the case study methodology can be found at http://writing.colostate.edu/references/research/casestudy/pop2e.cfm.

chapter 10

Reference Notes

1. Louise H. Kidder and Charles M. Judd, *Research Methods in Social Relations,* 5th ed. (New York: Holt, Rinehart & Winston, 1986), p. 292.

2. K. E. Weick, "Systematic Observational Methods," in *The Handbook of Social Psychology,* vol. 2, ed. G. Lindzey and E. Aronson (Reading, MA: Addison-Wesley, 1968), p. 360.

3. This section was developed from a variety of sources, including glossaries from About.com (http://marketing.about.com/library/glossary/Marketing_Terms), ESOMAR (http://www.esomar.org/content/pdf/GlossMaster.pdf), and Insight Express.com (http://insightexpress.com/ix/smalrtTag.asp?chapter=8). Also used were Robert S. Owen, "How to Build and Use a Tachistoscope," Sykronix.com (http://www.sykronix.com/researching/tscope.htm); John Caffyn, "Psychological Laboratory Techniques in Copy Research," *Journal of Advertising Research* 4, no. 4 (December 1964), pp. 45–50; and David Taylor, "A Study of the Tachistoscope," *British Journal of Marketing* 4 (Spring 1970), pp. 22–28. Much of the above was clarified in an interview with Jerry Thomas, president, Decision Analyst, on October 29, 2003.

4. Jerry Thomas, president, Decision Analyst, interviewed on October 29, 2003; "Packaging Research," Decisionanyalyst.com, downloaded October 25, 2003 (http://www.decisionanalyst.com/Services/package.asp).

5. Alan Brody, *Cigarette Seduction: How Cigarette Brands Work* (http://www.tobacco.org/gemera/9708cigsed.html).

6. Weick, "Systematic Observational Methods," p. 381.

7. "Method to the Madness: How FamilyFun Tests Toys for Toy of the Year," FamilyFun, downloaded February 8, 2003 (http://family.go.com/parties/holiday/feature/famf1002_toyproc/).

8. Kenneth D. Bailey, *Methods of Social Science,* 2d ed. (New York: Free Press, 1982), pp. 252–54.

9. Kidder and Judd, *Research Methods in Social Relations,* pp. 298–99.

10. Ibid., p. 291.

11. E. J. Webb, D. T. Campbell, R. D. Schwartz, L. Sechrest, and J. B. Grove, *Nonreactive Measures in the Social Sciences,* 2d ed. (Boston: Houghton Mifflin, 1981).

12. W. L. Rathje and W. W. Hughes, "The Garbage Project as a Nonreactive Approach: Garbage In ... Garbage Out?" in *Perspectives on Attitude Assessment: Surveys and Their Alternatives*, ed. H. W. Sinaiko and L. A. Broedling (Washington, DC: Smithsonian Institution, 1975).

13. William Grimes, "If It's Scientific, It's 'Garbology,'" *International Herald Tribune,* August 15–16, 1992, p. 17.

14. B. DePompe, "There's Gold in Databases," *CMP Publications,* January 8, 1996 (http://techweb.cmp.com/iwk).

15. Table adapted from DIG White Paper 95/01, "An Overview of Data Mining at Dun & Bradstreet," Data Intelligence Group, Pilot Software, Cambridge, MA (September 1995).

16. R. Srikant and R. Agrawal, "Mining Sequential Patterns: Generalizations and Performance Improvements," Proceedings, 5th International Conference on Extending Database Technology, Paris, France, March 1996.

17. DePompe, "There's Gold in Databases."

18. "Data Mining: Plumbing the Depths of Corporate Databases," *ComputerWorld Consumer Publication,* insert to *ComputerWorld,* April 21, 1997, pp. 6, 18.

19. "Data Mining," SAS Institute (http://www.sas.com).

20. Exhibit 10-9 was adapted from ibid.

References for Snapshots, PicProfiles, Captions, and Pull Quotes

Lexus

"Lexus SC 430 Case Study," submitted by Lexus and Team One Advertising to the David Ogilvy Research Commission, October 22, 2001.

Mark Miller, Team One Advertising, interviewed on July 9, 2002, and October 5, 2002.

NetConversions

Adrian Chiu, NetConversions, interviewed March 25, 2003, and March 28, 2003.

"Content Site Case Study: Kelley Blue Book," NetConversions, downloaded March 14, 2003 (http://www.netconversions/case_content.htm).

"Kelley Blue Book Serves 1 Billion Consumer Automotive Pricing Reports: Record Number of Consumers Flock to Trusted Resource kbb.com for Used and New Car Pricing," Kelley Blue Book, October 28, 2002 (http://www.kbb.com/media/).

"What Is True Usability?" NetConversions.com, downloaded March 14, 2003 (http://www.netconversions.com/true_usability.htm).

People Meters

"Arbitron and Nielsen Report Progress in Portable People Meter (PPM) Response Rate Testing," Abritron, October 21, 2003 (http://www.arbitron.com/portable_people_meters/home.htm).

"Nielsen Families," Nielsen Media Research (http://www.nielsenmedia.com/FAQ).

"NY Local People Meter 2003: A Super-Q Audit Process," Nielsen Media Research, March 29, 2004 (NY_LPM_Report_Nielsen.pdf).

"Our Research & Products," Nielsen Media Research (http://www.nielsenmedia.com/FAQ).

"Universe Estimates," Nielsen Media Research (http://www.nielsenmedia.com/FAQ).

"U.S. Market Trial Status," Arbitron, downloaded April 1, 2004 (http://www.arbitron.com/portable_people_meters/us_trial_status2.htm).

Tom Santor

Alexander Coolidge, "Hold the Carbs: Restaurants Try to Capitalize on New Diet Craze," *Cincinnati Post Online Edition,* January 22, 2004 (http://www.cincypost.com/2004/01/22/carb012204.html).

SizeUSA

"An Introduction to the Body Measurement System of Mass Customized Clothing," TechExchange, downloaded February 24, 2004 (http://www.techexchange.com/thelibrary/bmsdes.html).

"Background," SizeUSA, downloaded February 24, 2004 (http://www.sizeusa.com/background.html).

"Business Getting Squeezed Due to Poor Fitting Garments?" Tech Exchange, downloaded February 24, 2004 (http://www.techexchange.com/thelibrary/bmsades.html).

Dave Scheiber, "Whole Girth Catalog," *St. Petersburg Times,* October 18, 2003 (http://www.sptimes.com/2003/10/18/news_pf/Floridian/Whole_girth_catalog.shtml).

Rebecca Gardyn, "The Shape of Things to Come," *American Demographics* 25, no. 6 (July–August 2003), pp. 25–30.

"Sponsors," SizeUSA, downloaded February 24, 2004 (http://www.sizeusa.com/sponsors.html).

Teri Ross, "A Fitting Solution," *Apparel,* August 2003, downloaded February 24, 2004 (http://www.utexas.edu/centers/infic/NewCenNews/archives/2003/Oct.2003.ncn.html).

The US National Survey, TC2.com, downloaded February 24, 2004 (http://tc2.com/what/sizeusa/index.html).

"SizeUSA—The Consumer's Perspective," TC2, downloaded February 24, 2004 (http://www.tc2.com/what/sizeusa/consumer.html).

Trade Shows

Steve Jarvis, "MR Adds Value to Shows," *Marketing News* 36, no. 13, (June 24, 2002), p. 11.

Wal-Mart

"Goodyear Works with Wal-Mart to Bring RFID Supply Chain Technology to the Tire Industry," Goodyear Tire and Rubber Company press release, March 11, 2004 (http://www.goodyear.com/media/pr/22861ms.html).

Gerry Khermouch and Heather Green, "Bar Codes Better Watch Their Backs," *BusinessWeek Online*, July 14, 2003 (http://www.aol.businessweek.com/magazine/content/03_28/b3841063.htm).

Katherine Albrecht, "Supermarket Cards: The Tip of the Retail Surveillance Iceberg," *Denver University Law Review* 79, no. 4, (Summer 2002), pp. 534–39, 558–65.

"Overview of CASPIAN," CASPIAN, downloaded March 11, 2004 (http://www.nocards.org/press/overview.shtml).

"Press Releases," Trolley Scan (Pty) Ltd. (http://www.trolleyscan.com/pressrel.html).

"Radio Frequency ID: A New Era for Marketers?" *Consumer Insight,* ACNielsen, 2001 (http://acnielsen.com/pubs/ci2001/q4/features/radio.htm).

Vivek Agarwal, "Assessing the Benefits of Auto-ID Technology in the Consumer Goods Industry," Auto-ID Center, 2001 (http://www.autoidcenter.org/research/CAM-WWH-003.pdf).

Classic and Contemporary Readings

Bailey, Kenneth D. *Methods of Social Research.* 4th ed. New York: Free Press, 1994. Includes a thorough discussion of observational strategies.

Bales, Robert F. *Personality and Interpersonal Behavior.* New York: Holt, Rinehart & Winston, 1970. From a pioneer in interaction process analysis, a model for structured observation, checklists, and coding schemes.

Berry, Michael J., and Gordon Linoff. *Mastering Data Mining: The Art and Science of Customer Relationship Management.* New York: Wiley, 1999.

Denzin, Norman K., and Yvonna S. Lincoln. *Handbook of Qualitative Research.* 2d ed. Thousand Oaks, CA: Age Inc., 2000. Of particular interest is Part 3, on strategies of inquiry, and Part 4, on methods of collecting and analyzing empirical materials.

Fayyad, U. M., and G. Piatesky-Shapiro. *Advances in Knowledge Discovery and Data Mining.* Cambridge, MA: AAAI Press–MIT Press, 1996. An excellent text that provides an overview of knowledge discovery and data mining using statistical methods.

Hoyle, Rick H., Monica J. Harris, and Charles M. Judd. *Research Methods in Social Relations.* 7th ed. Belmont, CA: Wadsworth Publishing, 2001. Good overview of observational types and sampling plans.

Webb, Eugene J., Donald T. Campbell, Richard D. Swartz, and Lee B Sechrest. *Unobtrusive Measures.* Thousand Oaks, CA: Sage Publications, 1999. The revised edition of the classic source of information on all aspects of unobtrusive measures. Excellent examples and ideas for project planning.

chapter 11

Reference Notes

1. Floyd J. Fowler Jr., *Survey Research Methods* (Beverly Hills, CA: Sage Publications, 1988), p. 111.

2. B. W. Schyberger, "A Study of Interviewer Behavior," *Journal of Marketing Research,* February 1967, p. 35.

3. B. S. Dohrenwend, J. A. Williams Jr., and C. H. Weiss, "Interviewer Biasing Effects: Toward a Reconciliation of Findings," *Public Opinion Quarterly,* Spring 1969, pp. 121–29.

4. One of the top research organizations in the world is the Survey Research Center of the University of Michigan. The material in this section draws heavily on the *Interviewer's Manual,* rev. ed. (Ann Arbor: Survey Research Center, University of Michigan, 1976), and Fowler, *Survey Research Methods,* chap. 7.

5. Robert L. Kahn and Charles F. Cannell, *The Dynamics of Interviewing* (New York: Wiley, 1957), pp. 45–51.

6. D. Wallace, "A Case for and against Mail Questionnaires," *Public Opinion Quarterly,* Spring 1954, pp. 40–52.

7. Jon Krosnick, "The Art of Asking a Question: The Top 5 Things Researchers Need to Know about Designing Questionnaires," a seminar sponsored by SPSS and American Marketing Association, March 30, 2004.

8. Ibid.

9. "Gartner Dataquest Survey Shows 61 Percent of U.S. Households Actively Using the Internet," Gartner Inc. press release, August 30, 2001 (http://www4.gartner.com/5_about/press_ releases/2001/pr20010829b.html).

10. Edith de Leeuw and William Nicholls II, "Technology Innovations in Data Collection: Acceptance, Data Quality, and Costs," *Sociological Research Online* 1, no. 4. (1996) (http://www.socresonline.org.uk/1/4/leeuw.html).

11. Personal experience of the author, November 2002.

12. de Leeuw and Nicholls, "Technology Innovations in Data Collection."

13. Don A. Dillman, *Mail and Telephone Surveys* (New York: Wiley, 1978), p. 6.

14. de Leeuw and Nicholls, "Technology Innovations in Data Collection."

15. Dillman, *Mail and Telephone Surveys,* pp. 160–61.

16. Ibid., pp. 12, 22–24.

17. "Total Design Method" (http://survey.sesrc.wsu.edu/tdm.htm), February 4, 2000. Don Dillman is professor of sociology and rural sociology and deputy director of research and development of the Social and Economic Sciences Research Center at Washington State University.

18. Leslie Kanuk and Conrad Berenson, "Mail Surveys and Response Rates: A Literature Review," *Journal of Marketing Research,* November 1975, pp. 440–53; Arnold S. Linsky, "Stimulating Responses to Mailed Questionnaires: A Review," *Public Opinion Quarterly* 39 (1975), pp. 82–101.

19. Kanuk and Berenson, "Mail Surveys," p. 450. Reprinted from the *Journal of Marketing Research,* published by the American Marketing Association.

20. Nelson King, "[Web-Based Surveys] How They Work," *PC Magazine,* January 18, 2000 (http://www.pcmag.com).

21. Robert M. Groves and Robert L. Kahn, *Surveys by Telephone* (New York: Academic Press, 1979), p. 223.

22. Institute for Social Research, *ISR Newsletter* (Ann Arbor: University of Michigan, 1991–92), p. 3.

23. Michael J. Havice, "Measuring Nonresponse and Refusals to an Electronic Telephone Survey," *Journalism Quarterly,* Fall 1990, pp. 521–30.

24. "2003 CMOR Respondent Cooperation and Industry Image Study Topline Report," CMOR, downloaded November 23, 2003 (http://www.cmor.org/resp_coop_news1003_2.htm). CMOR, founded in 1992 as the Council for Marketing and Opinion Research, tries to improve access to consumers for its more than 150 member trade associations and research companies, to increase respondent awareness of the value of research, and to increase respondent cooperation rates.

25. See, for example, J. H. Frey Jr., *Survey Research by Telephone* (Beverly Hills, CA: Sage Publications, 1983).

26. "Chart 3-8: Percent of U.S. Households with a Telephone By Income By Rural, Urban, Central City Areas, and Total U.S.," downloaded December 15, 2003 (http://www.ntia.doc.gov/ntiahome/net2/presentations/slide5.html through slide8.html) See also U.S. Census Bureau, Census 2000 Summary File 3, Matrices H6 and H43.

27. U.S. Census Bureau, Census 2000 Summary File 3, Matrices H6 and H43.

28. J. Michael Brick, J. Waksberg, D. Kulp, and A. Starer, "Bias in List-Assisted Telephone Samples," American Association of Public Opinion Research, May 14, 1994 (http://www.genesys-sampling.com/reference/bias.htm).

29. The Cellular Telecommunications and Internet Association's annualized wireless industry survey results, June 1985–June 2002, downloaded February 15, 2003 (http://www.wow-com.com/images/survey/june2002/annual_Table_slide_3.gif).

30. "VocalTec Unveils Surf & CallTM Network Services," TechSourceNJ.com (http://www.techsourcenj.com/feature_articles/apr00/vocaltec.shtml).

31 "Wireless Local Number Portability," Federal Communications Commission, downloaded May 22, 2004 (http://www.fcc.gov/cgb/consumerfacts/wirelessportability.html).

32. A *block* is defined as an exchange group composed of the first four or more digits of a seven-digit number, such as 721-0, 721-1, and so forth.

33. G. J. Glasser and G. D. Metzger, "National Estimates of Nonlisted Telephone Households and Their Characteristics," *Journal of Marketing Research,* August 1975, p. 360.

34. G. J. Glasser and G. D. Metzger, "Random Digit Dialing as a Method of Telephone Sampling," *Journal of Marketing Research,* February 1972, pp. 59–64; Seymour Sudman, "The Uses of Telephone Directories for Survey Sampling," *Journal of Marketing Research*, May 1973, pp. 204–207.

35. Personal participation by the author, October 2002.

36. Seymour Sudman, *Reducing the Costs of Surveys* (Chicago: Aldine, 1967), p. 65.

37. J. J. Wheatley, "Self-Administered Written Questionnaires or Telephone Interviews," *Journal of Marketing Research,* February 1973, pp. 94–95.

38 Robert M. Groves and Robert L. Kahn, *Surveys by Telephone* (New York: Academic Press, 1979), p. 223.

39. Peter S. Tuckel and Barry M. Feinberg, "The Answering Machine Poses Many Questions for Telephone Survey Researchers," *Public Opinion Quarterly,* Summer 1991, pp. 200–17.

40. Paul J. Lavrakas, *Telephone Survey Methods: Sampling, Selection, and Supervision.* 2d ed. (Thousand Oaks, CA: Sage Publications, 1993), p. 16.

41. Marilyn Geewax, "FTC Scrubs Do-Not-Call Start Date," Cox News Service, posted September 27, 2003 (http://www.dfw.com/mld/dfw/news/nation/6875595.htm).

42. Ideas in this Close-Up are drawn largely from Seth Godin's *Permission Marketing: Turning Strangers into Friends and Friends into Customers* (Simon & Schuster, 1999) and *Unleashing the Idea Virus* (Hyperion, 2001). For a brief overview of the concepts within these books, see William Taylor, "Permission Marketing," *FastCompany* 14 (April 1998) (http://www.fastcompany.com/online/14/permission.html).

43. Kim B. Sheehan and S. J. McMillan, "Response Variation in E-Mail Surveys: An Exploration," *Journal of Advertising Research* 39, no. 4 (1999), pp. 45–54. Also see Kim Sheehan, "E-Mail Survey Response Rates: A Review," *Journal of Computer-Mediated Communication* 6, no. 2. (2001) (http://www.ascusc.org/jcmc/vol6/issue2/sheehan/html).

44. There are a number of sources for research services, some of which are annotated. For current listings, consult the latest edition of the *Marketing Services Guide* and the *American Marketing Association Membership Directory* (Chicago: American Marketing Association); *Consultants and Consulting Organizations Directory* (Detroit: Gale Research Corporation); or the research section of *Marketing News.*

45. A list of panel vendors is provided by Duane Davis, *Business Research for Decision Making,* 4th ed. (Belmont, CA: Wadsworth, 1996), p. 283. See also our Exhibit 2-4 on omnibus studies and Exhibit 2-3 on syndicated data providers in Chapter 2.

References for Snapshots, PicProfiles, Captions, and Pull Quotes

Aleve

Sara Eckel, "Road to Recovery," *American Demographics,* March 2001, p. s8.

Harris Interactive

The Harris Poll, September 4, 2003.

Perception Analyzer

David Paul, director of business development and marketing for Perception Analyzer, MSInteractive, interviewed September 10, 2002.

Radio

Lee Ann Obringer, "How Top 40 Radio Works," HowStuffWorks.com: Entertainment, downloaded May 21, 2004 (http://entertainment.howstuffworks.com/top-40.htm).

RTI International

Tim Gabel, director of computing, RTI International, interviewed December 17, 2001.

Alain Tessier

"Demographic Diamonds (Market Researchers)," *American Demographics,* April 2003, p. 34.

Zap-Attack

"Frequently Asked Questions," Privacy Technologies, January 3, 2001 (http://www.telezapper.com/faq.htm#3).

"Product Literature," Privacy Technologies, January 3, 2001 (http://www.privacytechnologies.com/product.asp).

Classic and Contemporary Readings

Arksey, Hilary, and Peter T. Knight. *Interviewing for Social Scientists: An Introductory Resource with Examples.* Thousand Oaks, CA: Sage Publications, 1999. Covers design, improvisation, success rates, specialized contexts, and transforming findings into results.

Dexter, Louis A. *Elite and Specialized Interviewing.* Evanston, IL: Northwestern University Press, 1970. Discusses the techniques and problems of interviewing "people in important or exposed positions."

Dillman, Don A. *Mail and Telephone Surveys.* New York: Wiley, 1978. A classic on mail and telephone surveys.

Dillman, Don A. *Mail and Internet Surveys: The Tailored Design Method.* New York: Wiley, 1999. The Tailored Design Method, which expands on the Total Design Concept of Dillman's classic work, takes advantage of computers, electronic mail, and the Internet to better our understanding of survey requirements.

Fowler, Floyd J., Jr. *Survey Research Methods.* 2d ed. Thousand Oaks, CA: Sage Publications, 1993. An excellent overview of all aspects of the survey process.

Groves, R. M., et al. *Telephone Survey Methodology.* New York: Wiley, 1989. An important reference on telephone data-collection techniques.

Lavrakas, Paul J. *Telephone Survey Methods: Sampling, Selection, and Supervision.* 2d ed. Thousand Oaks, CA: Sage Publications, 1993. This specialized work takes an applied perspective of interest to students and managers. Chapters 3, 5, and 6 on supervision are particularly useful.

Nesbary, Dale K. *Survey Research and the World Wide Web.* Needham Heights, MA: Allyn & Bacon, 2000. Screen shots from Windows and FrontPage, e-mail survey construction, and Internet orientation for survey research.

chapter 12

Reference Notes

1. Bibb Latane and J. M. Darley, *The Unresponsive Bystander: Why Doesn't He Help?* (New York: Appleton-Century-Crofts, 1970), pp. 69–77. Research into the responses of bystanders who witness crimes was stimulated by an incident in New York City where Kitty Genovese was attacked and killed in the presence of 38 witnesses who refused to come to her aid or summon authorities.

2. This section is largely adapted from Julian L. Simon and Paul Burstein, *Basic Research Methods in Social Science,* 3d ed. (New York: Random House, 1985), pp. 128–33.

3. For a thorough explanation of this topic, see Helena C. Kraemer and Sue Thiemann, *How Many Subjects? Statistical Power Analysis in Research* (Beverly Hills, CA: Sage Publications, 1987).

4. Kenneth D. Bailey, *Methods of Social Research,* 2d ed. (New York: Free Press, 1982), pp. 230–33.

5. The concept of a quota matrix and the tabular form for Exhibit 12–3 were adapted from Earl R. Babbie, *The Practice of Social Research,* 5th ed. (Belmont, CA: Wadsworth, 1989), pp. 218–19.

6. Donald T. Campbell and Julian C. Stanley, *Experimental and Quasi-Experimental Designs for Research* (Chicago: Rand McNally, 1963), p. 5.

7. Thomas D. Cook and Donald T. Campbell, "The Design and Conduct of Quasi-Experiments and True Experiments in Field Set-tings," in *Handbook of Industrial and Organizational Psychology,* ed. Marvin D. Dunnette (Chicago: Rand McNally, 1976), p. 223.

8. For an in-depth discussion of many quasi-experimental designs and their internal validity, see ibid., pp. 246–98.

9. Consumer Insight, Fifth Annual ACNielsen Consumer and Market Trends Report, 2001 (http://www.acnielsenbases.com/news/New%20Product%20Introductions.pdf).

10. http://www.iaea.or.at/icgfi/documents/dairy-queen.pdf.

11. Amy Forliti, "Shell Test Markets the First Robotic Gas Pump," Associated Press, March 9, 2000; http://www.canoe.ca/TechNews0003/09_pumps.html.

12. http://www.acnielsen.com/.

13. http://www.infores.com/public/us/prodserv/factsheet/us_fact_btnewproduct.htm.

14. http://www.infores.com/public/us/news/us_new_102901.htm.

15. Ibid.

16. Joseph Willke, "The Future of Simulated Test Markets: The Coming Obsolescence of Current Models and the Characteristics of Models of the Future," ESOMAR Conference Proceedings, September 2002, excerpted by permission for ACNielsen (http://www.acnielsenbases.com/news/news%20092002.html).

17. http://www.marcresearch.com/main.html.

18. Raymond R. Burke, "Virtual Shopping: Breakthrough in Marketing Research," *Harvard Business Review* 74, no. 2, (March–April 1996), p. 125.

19. Reg. No. 1,881,580, February 28, 1995, Allison Hollander Corporation of Atlanta, now Allison Research Technologies.

20. http://www.artechnology.com/.

21. Ely Dahan and V. "Seenu" Srinivasan, "The Predictive Power of Internet-Based Product Concept Testing Using Visual Depiction and Animation," *Journal of Product Innovation Management,* March 2000 (http://faculty-gsb.stanford.edu/ssrinivasan/rp1502.pdf).

22. John Gaffney, "How Do You Feel about a $44 Tooth-Bleaching Kit? Procter & Gamble Discovers What the Web Is Really Good For—Test Marketing," http://www.business2.com/articles/mag/0,1640,16977,FF.html (October 2001 issue).

23. Ibid.; Niall McKay, "What Test-Marketing? Why E-Tailers Are Testing the Waters after Jumping In," http://www.redherring.com/mag/issue78/mag-marketing-78.html (May 2000 issue).

References for Snapshots, PicProfiles, Captions, and Pull Quotes

FLOORad

Antonia DeMatto, FLOORgraphics, September 30, 1999.

"Raising the Roof with Floor Ads," *BusinessWeek,* September 16, 1999 (http://www.businessweek.com/smallbiz/news/coladvice/reallife/r1990916.htm?scriptFramed).

"Floor Show: Savvy Ideas to Boost Sales," *Entrepreneur* (http://www.entrepreneur.com/article/print/0,2361,227019,00.html).

Hill Top Research

Good Morning America, ABC News, March 3, 2000 (http://www.hill-top.com/consumer.html).

Magazine Publishers' Association

Lorraine Calvacca, "Making a Case for the Glossies," *American Demographics,* July 1999, pp. 36–37 (http://www.magazine.org/resources/downloads/Sales_Scan_Highlights.pdf).

Mark Sanborn

http://www.quotesandsayings.com/finquoteframes.htm.

Shell SmartPump

Amy Forliti, "Shell Test Markets the First Robotic Gas Pump," *Canoe CNews*, downloaded May 22, 2004 (http://www.canoe.ca/TechNews0003/09_pumps.html).

Test Marketing

Jack Neff, "White Bread, USA" *AdAge.com*, July 9, 2001 (http://adage.com/news.cms?newsllD=33487).

Unicast

This snapshot was developed from interviews with Annette Mullin, director of marketing, Unicast, on March 24, 2004, and after. Additionally, Unicast Web site and test result materials (*Unicast Communications White Paper, Research conducted by Dynamic Logic: A Look at the Superstitial 300v Ad Unit*), as well as materials about Dynamic Logic methodology, were provided by Unicast.

Classic and Contemporary Readings

Campbell, Donald T., and M. Jean Russo. *Social Experimentation.* Thousand Oaks, CA: Sage Publications, 1998. The evolution of the late Professor Campbell's thinking on validity control in experimental design.

Campbell, Donald T., and Julian C. Stanley. *Experimental and Quasi-Experimental Designs for Research.* Chicago: Rand McNally, 1963. A universally quoted discussion of experimental designs in the social sciences.

Cook, Thomas D., and Donald T. Campbell. "The Design and Conduct of Quasi-Experiments and True Experiments in Field Settings." In *Handbook of Industrial and Organizational Psychology,* 2d ed., ed. Marvin D. Dunnette and Leaetta M. Hough. Palo Alto, CA: Consulting Psychologists Press, 1990.

Cook, Thomas D., and Donald T. Campbell. *Quasi-Experimentation: Design and Analysis Issues for Field Settings.* Chicago: Rand McNally, 1979. Major authoritative works on both true and quasi-experiments and their design. Already classic references.

Edwards, Allen. *Experimental Design in Psychological Research.* 5th ed. New York: HarperCollins, 1985. A complete treatment of experimental design with helpful illustrative examples.

Green, Paul E., Donald S. Tull, and Gerald Albaum. *Research for Marketing Decisions.* 5th ed. Englewood Cliffs, NJ: Prentice Hall, 1988. A definitive text with sections on the application of experimentation to marketing research.

Kirk, Roger E. *Experimental Design: Procedures for the Behavioral Sciences.* 3d ed. Belmont, CA: Brooks/Cole, 1994. An advanced text on the statistical aspects of experimental design.

Krathwohl, David R. *Social and Behavioral Science Research: A New Framework for Conceptualizing, Implementing, and Evaluating Research Studies.* San Francisco: Jossey-Bass, 1985. Chapters 3, 4, and 5 present a convincing argument for reformulating internal and external validity into broader concepts.

chapter 13

Reference Notes

1. Fred N. Kerlinger, *Foundations of Behavioral Research,* 3d ed. (New York: Holt, Rinehart & Winston, 1986), p. 396; S. Stevens, "Measurement, Statistics, and the Schemapiric View," *Science,* August 1968, p. 384.

2. W. S. Torgerson, *Theory and Method of Scaling* (New York: Wiley, 1958), p. 19.

3. S. S. Stevens, "On the Theory of Scales of Measurement," *Science* 103 (1946), pp. 677–80.

4. We assume the reader has had an introductory statistics course in which measures of central tendency such as arithmetic mean, median, and mode have been treated. Similarly, we assume familiarity with measures of dispersion such as the standard deviation, range, and interquartile range. For a brief review of these concepts, refer to the "Descriptive Statistics" section in Chapter 18 or see an introductory statistics text.

5. While this might intuitively seem to be the case, consider that one might prefer *a* over *b, b* over *c,* yet *c* over *a.* These results cannot be scaled as ordinal data because there is apparently more than one dimension involved.

6. Parametric tests are appropriate when the measurement is interval or ratio and when we can accept certain assumptions about the underlying distributions of the data with which we are working (normality, independence, constant variance). Nonparametric tests usually involve much weaker assumptions about measurement scales (nominal and ordinal), and the assumptions about the underlying distribution of the population are fewer and less restrictive. More on these tests is found in Chapters 19 to 21 and Appendix C.

7. *Statistical power* is the probability of detecting a meaningful difference if one were to occur. Studies should have power levels of 0.80 or higher, i.e., an 80% chance or greater of discerning an effect if one was really there.

8. See Chapters 17 and 18 for a discussion of these procedures.

9. To learn more about Swatch's BeatTime, visit: http://www.swatch.com/internettime/internettime.php3.

10. The exception involves the creation of a dummy variable for use in a regression or discriminant equation. A nonmetric variable is transformed into a metric variable through the assignment of a 0 or 1 and used in a predictive equation.

11. Claire Selltiz, Lawrence S. Wrightsman, and Stuart W. Cook, *Research Methods in Social Relations,* 3d ed. (New York: Holt, Rinehart & Winston, 1976), pp. 164–69.

12. Robert L. Thorndike and Elizabeth Hagen, *Measurement and Evaluation in Psychology and Education,* 3d ed. (New York: Wiley, 1969), p. 5.

13. Examples of other conceptualizations of validity are factorial validity, job-analytic validity, synthetic validity, rational validity, and statistical conclusion validity.

14. Thomas D. Cook and Donald T. Campbell, "The Design and Conduct of Quasi Experiments and True Experiments in Field Settings," in *Handbook of Industrial and Organizational Psychology,* ed. Marvin D. Dunnette (Chicago: Rand McNally, 1976), p. 223.

15. *Standards for Educational and Psychological Tests and Manuals* (Washington, DC: American Psychological Association, 1974), p. 26.

16. Wayne F. Cascio, *Applied Psychology in Personnel Management* (Reston, VA: Reston Publishing, 1982), p. 149.

17. Thorndike and Hagen, *Measurement and Evaluation,* p. 168.

18. Cascio, *Applied Psychology,* pp. 135–36.

19. Emanuel J. Mason and William Bramble, *Understanding and Conducting Research,* (New York: McGraw-Hill, 1989), p. 268.

20. A problem with this approach is that the way the test is split may influence the internal consistency coefficient. To remedy this, other indexes are used to secure reliability estimates without splitting the test's items. The Kuder-Richardson Formula 20 (KR20) and Cronbach's coefficient alpha are two frequently used examples. Cronbach's alpha has the most utility for multi-item scales at the interval level of measurement. The KR20 is the method from which alpha was generalized and is used to estimate reliability for dichotomous items (see Exhibit 13–6).

21. Thorndike and Hagen, *Measurement and Evaluation,* p. 199.

References for Snapshots, PicProfiles, Captions, and Pull Quotes

Copyright Infringement

John Fetto, "Americans Voice Their Opinions on Intellectual Property Rights Violations," *American Demographics,* September 2000, p. 8.

Measurement instrument prepared by TaylorNelson Sofres Intersearch.

Data tabulation generated by TaylorNelson Sofres Intersearch.

Bob Donath

Bob Donath, "Despite Economic Shifts, Biz Marketers Still View ROMI as No.1 Concern," *Marketing News* 38, no. 4 (March 1, 2004), p. 6.

Eureka's Merwyn

http://www.eurekaranch.com.

Justin Beck, Merwyn Technology manager, Eureka!Ranch, interviewed September 6 and 8, 2002.

Surfing for the Perfect Measurement

Christopher Saunders, "Industry Players Seek to Distance Themselves from Click-Throughs," *InternetNews,* July 9, 2001 (http://www.internetnews.com/IAR/article/0,,12_797851,00.html).

"Interactive Advertising Bureau (IAB), DoubleClick, MSN, and CNET Networks Release Groundbreaking Online Brand Research Findings," IAB press release, July 18, 2001 (http://www.iab.net/news/content/brand_research.html).

Rob Walker, "System for Measuring Clicks Is under Assault," *New York Times on the Web,* August 27, 2001 (http://www.nytimes/2001/08/027/technology/27NECO.html?ex=1000139238&ei=1&en=c315615dca93ee07).

Terror Alert

"Gov. Ridge Announces Homeland Security Advisory System," Office of the Press Secretary, March 12, 2002.

"Junk Terror-Alert System or Get Message Straight," *Palm Beach Post* editorial, February 19, 2003.

http://www.whitehouse.gov/news/releases/2002/03/20020312-1.html.

http://www.gopbi.com/partners/pbpost/epaper/editions/wednesday/opinion_e3250bd7040a109c00a4.html.

Classic and Contemporary Readings

Cascio, Wayne F. *Applied Psychology in Personnel Management.* 4th ed. Englewood Cliffs, NJ: Prentice Hall, 1990.

Cook, Thomas D., and Donald T. Campbell. "The Design and Conduct of Quasi Experiments and True Experiments in Field Settings." In *Handbook of Industrial and Organizational Psychology,* ed. Marvin D. Dunnette. Chicago: Rand McNally, 1976, Chapter 7.

Embretson, Susan E., and Scott L. Hershberger. *The New Rules of Measurement.* Mahwah, NJ: Lawrence Erlbaum Associates, 1999. Bridges the gap between theoretical and practical measurement.

Guilford, J. P. *Psychometric Methods.* 2d ed. New York: McGraw-Hill, 1954.

Kelley, D. Lynn. *Measurement Made Accessible: A Research Approach Using Qualitative, Quantitative, and TQM Methods.* Thousand Oaks, CA: Sage Publications, 1999. Sections on bias, reliability, and validity are appropriate for this chapter.

Kerlinger, Fred N., and Howard B. Lee. *Foundations of Behavioral Research.* 4th ed. New York: HBJ College & School Division, 1999.

Newmark, Charles S. *Major Psychological Assessment Instruments.* 2d ed. Boston: Allyn and Bacon, 1996.

Nunnally, J. C., and Ira Bernstein. *Psychometric Theory.* 3d ed. New York: McGraw-Hill, 1994.

Thorndike, Robert M. *Measurement and Evaluation in Psychology and Education.* 6th ed. Upper Saddle River, NJ: Prentice Hall, 1996.

chapter 14

Reference Notes

1. E. Aronson, D. Wilson, and R. Akert. *Social Psychology* (Upper Saddle River, NJ: Prentice Hall, 2002); Robert J. Sternberg, *Cognitive Psychology,* 3d ed. (Reading, MA: Wadsworth Publishing, 2002); Richard E. Petty and John T. Cacioppo, *Attitudes and Persuasion: Classic and Contemporary Approaches* (Boulder, CO: Westview Press, 1996); Gordon W. Allport, "Attitudes," in *A Handbook of Social Pscychology,* ed. C. A. Murchison, vol. 2. (New York: Russell, 1935), 2 vols.

2. See, for example, Robert A. Baron and Donn Byrne, *Social Psychology,* 10th ed. (Boston: Pearson Allyn & Bacon, 2002), and David G. Myers, *Social Psychology*, 7th ed. (New York: McGraw-Hill, 2002).

3. Bernard S. Phillips, *Social Research Strategy and Tactics,* 2d ed. (New York: Macmillan, 1971), p. 205.

4. J. P. Guilford, *Psychometric Methods* (New York: McGraw-Hill, 1954), pp. 278–79.

5. H. H. Friedman and Taiwo Amoo, "Rating the Rating Scales," *Journal of Marketing Management* 9, no. 3 (Winter 1999), pp. 114–23.

6. Donald R. Cooper, "Converting Neutrals to Loyalists," unpublished paper prepared for the IBM Corporation, New York, 1996.

7. G. A. Churchill and J. P. Peter, "Research Design Effects on the Reliability of Rating Scales: A Meta-Analysis," *Journal of Marketing Research* 21 (November 1984), pp. 360–75.

8. See, for example, H. H Friedman and Linda W. Friedman "On the Danger of Using Too Few Points in a Rating Scale: A Test of Validity," *Journal of Data Collection* 26, no. 2 (1986), pp. 60–63; and Eli P. Cox, "The Optimal Number of Response Alternatives for a Scale: A Review" *Journal of Marketing Research* 17, no. 4 (1980), pp. 407–22.

9. A study of the historic research literature found that more than three-fourths of the attitude scales used were of the 5-point type. An examination of more recent literature suggests that the 5-point scale is still common but there is a growing use of longer scales. For the historic study, see Daniel D. Day, "Methods in Attitude Research," *American Sociological Review* 5 (1940), pp. 395–410. Single-versus multiple-item scaling requirements are discussed in Jum C. Nunnally, *Psychometric Theory* (New York: McGraw-Hill, 1967), chap. 14.

10. Guilford, *Psychometric Methods.*

11. P. M. Synods, "Notes on Rating," *Journal of Applied Psychology* 9 (1925), pp. 188–95.

12. This is adapted from Pamela L. Alreck and Robert B. Settle, *The Survey Research Handbook* (Burr Ridge, IL: Irwin, 1995), chap. 5.

13. One study reported that the construction of a Likert scale took only half the time required to construct a Thurstone scale. See L. L. Thurstone and K. K. Kenney, "A Comparison of the Thurstone and Likert Techniques of Attitude Scale Construction," *Journal of Applied Psychology* 30 (1946), pp. 72–83.

14. Allen L. Edwards, *Techniques of Attitude Scale Construction* (New York: Appleton-Century-Crofts, 1957), pp. 152–54.

15. Ibid., p. 153.

16. Charles E. Osgood, G. J. Suci, and P. H. Tannenbaum, *The Measurement of Meaning* (Urbana: University of Illinois Press, 1957).

17. Ibid., p. 49. See also James G. Snider and Charles E. Osgood, eds., *Semantic Differential Technique* (Chicago: Aldine, 1969).

18. Louis Guttman, "A Basis for Scaling Qualitative Data," *American Sociological Review* 9 (1944), pp. 139–50.

19. John P. Robinson, "Toward a More Appropriate Use of Guttman Scaling," *Public Opinion Quarterly* 37 (Summer 1973), pp. 260–67.

References for Snapshots, PicProfiles, Captions, and Pull Quotes

American Heart Association

Paul Herera, American Heart Association, interviewed April 12, 2004.

Arthur Mitchell, Campbell-Ewald, interviewed April 22, 2004.

Campbell-Ewald

David Lockwood, senior vice president and director of account planning, Campbell-Ewald, interviewed February 9, 2004.

Nortel Networks

Chrisin Nowakowski, senior manager of marketing communications, Informative, Inc., interviewed August 20, 2001.

Open Doors

"Research among Adults with Disabilities: Travel and Hospitality," final report prepared by Harris Interactive for Open Doors Organization, delivered January 2002.

Eric Lipp, executive director, Open Doors Organization, interviewed March 4, 2004.

Laura Light, research director for public policy and public relations, Harris Interactive, interviewed March 10, 2004.

Steve Struhl, Harris Interactive, interviewed March 10, 2004.

"About Harris Interactive," Harris Interactive, downloaded March 20, 2004 (http://www.harrisinteractive.com/about/). Headquartered in Rochester, New York, Harris Interactive combines proprietary methodologies and technology with expertise in predictive, custom, and strategic research. The company conducts international research through wholly owned subsidiaries—London-based HI Europe (http://www.hieurope.com) and Tokyo-based Harris Interactive Japan—as well as through the Harris Interactive Global Network of local market- and opinion-research firms.

Frank Schmidt

Jennifer Robison, "10,000 Managers Can't Be Wrong," *Gallup Management Journal,* March 11, 2004 (http://gmj.gallup.com/content/default.asp?ci=10882).

Classic and Contemporary Readings

Aiken, Lewis. *Attitudes and Related Psychosocial Constructs: Theories, Assessment, and Research.* Thousand Oaks, CA: Sage Publications, 2002. An overview for those involved in measuring, evaluating, and attempting to modify attitudes, especially Chapters 2 and 3.

Edwards, Allen L. *Techniques of Attitude Scale Construction.* New York: Irvington, 1979. Thorough discussion of basic unidimensional scaling techniques.

Kerlinger, Fred N., and Howard B. Lee. *Foundations of Behavioral Research.* 4th ed. New York: HBJ College & School Division, 1999.

Krebs, Dagmar, and Peter Schmidt, eds. *New Directions in Attitude Measurement.* Chicago: Walter De Gruyter, 1993.

Miller, Delbert C. *Handbook of Research Design and Social Measurement.* 5th ed. Thousand Oaks, CA: Sage Publications, 1991. Presents a large number of existing sociometric scales and indexes as well as information on their characteristics, validity, and sources.

Osgood, Charles E., George J. Suci, and Percy H. Tannenbaum. *The Measurement of Meaning.* Urbana: University of Illinois Press, 1957. The basic reference on SD scaling.

chapter 15

Reference Notes

1. "Technical Report: The How's and Why's of Survey Research," SPSS Inc., October 16, 2002.

2. Dorwin Cartwright, "Some Principles of Mass Persuasion," *Human Relations* 2 (1948), p. 266.

3. "What America Eats 2003," *Parade*, November 16, 2003. This is the ninth biennial survey of the food habits of the United States; 2,080 men and women, aged 18 to 65, were interviewed in March 2003 by Mark Clements Research.

4. More will be said on the problems of readability in Chapter 23, "Presenting Insights and Findings: Written and Oral Reports."

5. S. A. Stouffer et al., *Measurement and Prediction: Studies in Social Psychology in World War II,* vol. 4 (Princeton, NJ: Princeton University Press, 1950), p. 709.

6. An excellent example of the question revision process is presented in Stanley Payne, *The Art of Asking Questions* (Princeton, NJ: Princeton University Press, 1951), pp. 214–25. This example illustrates that a relatively simple question can go through as many as 41 different versions before being judged satisfactory.

7. Robert L. Kahn and Charles F. Cannell, *The Dynamics of Interviewing* (New York: Wiley, 1957), p. 132.

8. Hadley Cantril, ed., *Gauging Public Opinion* (Princeton, NJ: Princeton University Press, 1944), p. 31.

9. Jon A. Krosnick and Duane F. Alwin, "An Evaluation of a Cognitive Theory of Response-Order Effects in Survey Measurement," *Public Opinion Quarterly* 51, 2 (Summer 1987): 201–219.

10. Jean M. Converse and Stanley Presser, *Survey Questions: Handcrafting the Standardized Questionnaire* (Beverly Hills, CA: Sage Publications, 1986), pp. 50–51.

11. Ibid., p. 51.

12. Frederick J. Thumin, "Watch for These Unseen Variables," *Journal of Marketing* 26 (July 1962), pp. 58–60.

13. F. Cannell and Robert L. Kahn, "The Collection of Data by Interviewing," in *Research Methods in the Behavioral Sciences,* ed.

Leon Festinger and Daniel Katz (New York: Holt, Rinehart & Winston, 1953), p. 349.

14. Cantril, *Gauging Public Opinion,* p. 28.

15. Converse and Presser, *Survey Questions,* p. 52.

16. The MindWriter questionnaire used in this example is based on a pilot instrument by Cooper Research Group, Inc., 1993, for an unidentified client who shares the intellectual property rights. No part of the format, question wording, sequence, scale, or references to MindWriter © 2000 may be produced or transmitted in any form or by any means, electronic or mechanical, including photocopy, recording, or any information storage and retrieval system, without permission in writing from Cooper Research Group, Inc. Reprinted with permission.

References for Snapshots, PicProfiles, Captions, and Pull Quotes

Gordon Black

Demographic Diamonds (Market Researchers) *American Demographics,* April 2003, p. 34.

Direct Reponse

"Electronic Retailing Association Reveals DRTV Research Tracking Study Results," Electronic Retailing Association press release, February 24, 2003 (http://www.retailing.org/newsroom/ PressReleases/02-24-03.html).

"As seen on TV," *American Demographics,* June 2003, p. 11.

Ice Storm

"The North Carolina Ice Story: Who Lost What and for How Long," RTI International press release, January 8, 2003 (http://www.rti.org/ page.cfm?objectid=D3AF52E9-56E4-4478-875008F15123275F).

"The North Carolina Ice Storm: Lost Time at Work and Other Impacts," RTI International press release, January 16, 2003 (http://www.rti. org/printpg.cfm?objectid=D3AF52E9-56E4-4478- 875008F15123275F).

InsightExpress

Doug Adams and Bob Ferro, "Not as Easy as It Looks: Best Practices for Online Research," InsightExpress, March 11, 2004. This presentation was part of the American Marketing Association Online Seminar Series.

RTI International

Interview with Tim Gabel, director of research computing, RTI International, Inc., December 14, 2001.

Craig Tomashoff

Craig Tomashoff, "You Are What You Queue," *New York Times,* March 2, 2003 (http://www.nytimes.com/2003/03/02/movies/ 02TOMA.html).

VALS

"About VALS: The Proven Segmentation System," SRI Consulting Business Intelligence (http://future.sri.com/VALS/about.shtml).

"The VALS Segment Profiles," SRI Consulting Business Intelligence (http://future.sri.com/VALS/types.shtml).

"About Us," KNSD (NBC739) (http://www.knsd.com); (http://publish.nbc739.com/tvsd/email/index.shtml); (http://publish.nbc739.com/tvsd/about/.backup.history.shtml); (http://publish.nbc739.com/tvsd/about/.backup.marketing.shtml).

Classic and Contemporary Readings

Converse, Jean M., and Stanley Presser. *Survey Questions: Handcrafting the Standardized Questionnaire.* Beverly Hills, CA: Sage Publi-

cations, 1986. A worthy successor to Stanley Payne's classic. Advice on how to write survey questions based on professional experience and the experimental literature.

Dillman, Don A. *Mail and Internet Surveys: The Tailored Design Method.* New York: Wiley, 1999. A contemporary treatment of Dillman's classic work.

Fink, Arlene, and Jaqueline Kosecoff. *How to Conduct Surveys: A Step-by-Step Guide.* Thousand Oaks, CA: Sage Publications, 1998. Emphasis on computer-assisted and interactive surveys and a good section on creating questions.

Kahn, Robert L., and Charles F. Cannell. *The Dynamics of Interviewing.* New York: Wiley, 1957. Chapters 5 and 6 cover questionnaire design.

Payne, Stanley L. *The Art of Asking Questions.* Princeton, NJ: Princeton University Press, 1951. An enjoyable book on the many problems encountered in developing useful survey questions. A classic resource.

Sudman, Seymour, and Norman N. Bradburn. *Asking Questions: A Practical Guide to Questionnaire Design.* San Francisco: Jossey-Bass, 1982. This book covers the major issues in writing individual questions and constructing scales. The emphasis is on structured questions and interview schedules.

Appendix 15a

Reference Notes

1. Sam Gill, "How Do You Stand on Sin?" *Tide,* March 14, 1947, p. 72.

2. Stanley L. Payne, *The Art of Asking Questions* (Princeton, NJ: Princeton University Press, 1951), p. 18.

3. Unaided recall gives respondents no clues as to possible answers. Aided recall gives them a list of radio programs that played last night and then asks them which ones they heard. See Harper W. Boyd Jr. and Ralph Westfall, *Marketing Research,* 3d ed. (Homewood, IL: Irwin, 1972), p. 293.

4. Gideon Sjoberg, "A Questionnaire on Questionnaires," *Public Opinion Quarterly* 18 (Winter 1954), p. 425.

5. Robert L. Kahn and Charles F. Cannell, *The Dynamics of Interviewing* (New York: Wiley, 1957), p. 108.

6. Ibid., p. 110.

7. Payne, *The Art of Asking Questions,* p. 140.

8. Ibid., p. 141.

9. Ibid., p. 149.

10. Gertrude Bancroft and Emmett H. Welch, "Recent Experiences with Problems of Labor Force Measurement," *Journal of the American Statistical Association* 41(1946), pp. 303–12.

11. National Opinion Research Center, Proceedings of the Central City Conference on Public Opinion Research (Denver, CO: University of Denver, 1946), p. 73.

12. Hadley Cantril, ed., *Gauging Public Opinion* (Princeton, NJ: Princeton University Press, 1944), p. 48.

13. Payne, *The Art of Asking Questions,* pp. 7–8.

14. Barbara Snell Dobrenwend, "Some Effects of Open and Closed Questions on Respondents' Answers," *Human Organization* 24 (Summer 1965), pp. 175–84.

Appendix 15b

Reference Notes

1. The sections on methods and purposes of pretesting have been largely adapted from Jena M. Converse and Stanley Presser, *Survey Questions: Handcrafting the Standardized Questionnaire* (Beverly Hills, CA: Sage Publications, 1986), pp. 51–64, and Survey Research Center, *Interviewer's Manual,* rev. ed. (Ann Arbor: Institute for Social Research, University of Michigan, 1976), pp. 133–34. For an extended discussion of the phases of pretesting, see Converse and Presser, *Survey Questions,* pp. 65–75.

2. W. R. Belson, *The Design and Understanding of Survey Questions* (Aldershot, England: Gower, 1981), pp. 76–86.

3. Perceival White, *Market Analysis* (New York: McGraw-Hill, 1921).

chapter 16

Reference Notes

1. United States Department of Commerce, Press Release CB99-CN.22, June 2, 1999 (http://www.census.gov/Press-Release/www/1999/cb99.html).

2. W. E. Deming, *Sample Design in Business Research* (New York: Wiley, 1960), p. 26.

3. Henry Assael and John Keon, "Nonsampling versus Sampling Errors in Survey Research," *Journal of Marketing Research* (Spring 1982), pp. 114–23.

4. A. Parasuraman, *Marketing Research,* 2d ed. (Reading, MA: Addison-Wesley, 1991), p. 477.

5. Proportions are hypothetical. *Advertising Age* recognized Serta's "Counting Sheep 'Penalty'" ad as one of the campaign's most effective for brand recall. Serta ranked eighth, using rankings from more than 2.6 million surveys of TV viewers from January 2 to April 1, 2003. This same campaign won a prestigious Gold Effie award in June 2002. Serta spends $20 million annually on the sheep campaign. "Counting Sheep Scheme to Win Back Client in Serta's New TV Commercials," Serta press release, downloaded November 23, 2003 (http://www.serta.com/pressrelease/press_r2.pdf); "Ad Age Recognizes Serta," *Furniture Today* press release, downloaded November 23, 2003 (http://www.furnituretoday.com/cgi-bin/v2/showArchive.cgi?num=942&news=Ad%20Age%20recognizes%20Serta); *Advertising Age,* April 21, 2003.

6. Fred N. Kerlinger, *Foundations of Behavioral Research,* 3d ed. (New York: Holt, Rinehart & Winston, 1986), p. 72.

7. Amir D. Aczel, *Complete Business Statistics* (Burr Ridge, IL: Irwin, 1996), p. 180.

8. N. L. Rynolds, A. C. Simintiras, and A. Diamantopoulus, "Theoretical Justification of Sampling Choices in International Marketing Research: Key Issues and Guidelines for Researchers," downloaded May 28, 2004 (http://www.questia.com/PM.qst?a=o&d=5001902692).

9. Family Health International, "Sampling Approaches," and "Weighting in Multi-Stage Sampling," in *Guidelines for Repeated Behavioral Surveys in Populations at Risk of HIV* (Durham, NC: FHI, 2000), chaps. 4 and 5, pp. 29–65.

10. Standard international sampling systems are based on standards such as ISO 2859 and ISO 3951.

11. All estimates of costs are hypothetical.

12. Leslie Kish, *Survey Sampling* (New York: Wiley, 1965), p. 188.

13. Ibid., pp. 76–77.

14. Typically, stratification is carried out before the actual sampling, but when this is not possible, it is still possible to stratify after the fact. Ibid., p. 90.

15. W. G. Cochran, *Sampling Techniques,* 2d ed. (New York: Wiley, 1963), p. 134.

16. Ibid., p. 96.

17. Kish, *Survey Sampling,* p. 94.

18. For detailed treatment of these and other cluster sampling methods and problems, see ibid., pp. 148–247.

19. J. H. Lorie and H. V. Roberts, *Basic Methods of Marketing Research* (New York: McGraw-Hill, 1951), p. 120.

20. Kish, *Survey Sampling,* p. 156.

21. For specifics on these problems and how to solve them, the reader is referred to the many good sampling texts. Two that have been mentioned already are Kish, *Survey Sampling,* chaps. 5, 6, and 7, and Cochran, *Sampling Techniques,* chaps. 9, 10, and 11.

References for Snapshots, PicProfiles, Captions, and Pull Quotes

August Busch IV

Stuart Elliott "Anheuser-Busch Reconsiders Ads," *New York Times,* April 16, 2004 (http://query.nytimes.com/mem/tnt.html?tntget=2004/04/16/business/media/16adco.html).

Chinese Shoppers

"Change of Chinese People's Lives: Facts and Figures," *People's Daily,* September 16, 2002, http://english.peopledaily.com.cn.

IRI

Christopher T. Heun, "Information Resources Redesigns Its Market Research Data," *Informationweek.com,* CPM United Business Media, August 21, 2001.

"IRI Launches Proprietary InfoScan Advantage to Track Wal-Mart Sales Information," Information Resources, Inc., press release, August 21, 2001 (http://www.infores.com/public/global/news/glo_new_082101.htm).

SSI: Sampling

Linda Piekarski, senior vice president of database and research, Survey Sampling, Inc., interviewed June 10, 2002.

Truth

"Crispin Runs a Close Second for Agency of the Year: A Shop That Zigs as Everyone Else Zags," *Advertising Age* (*AdAge.com*) January 13, 2003 (http://www.adage.com/news.cms?newsId=36847).

"Data and Instruments," American Legacy Foundation, downloaded March 29, 2003 (http://www.americanlegacy.org/section.asp?location=content/programs/research/data.asp).

"Telling the Truth about Teen Smoking," Kaiser Family Foundation, downloaded March 29, 2003 (http://www.kkf.org/content/2002/20020221a/CaseStudy-4.pdf).

U.S. Census

2000 Census Questionnaire, U.S. Census Bureau, United States Department of Commerce.

John Fetto, "Lust for Statistics," *American Demographics,* March 2001, pp. 68–70.

James Heckman, "Polls Debate, Researchers Wait, Time's Short," *Marketing News,* March 29, 1999.

Joan Raymond, "The Multicultural Report," *American Demographics,* November 2001, p. s6.

The Census, U.S. Census Bureau, United States Department of Commerce (http://www.census.gov/census/).

Classic and Contemporary Readings

Deming, W. Edwards. *Sample Design in Business Research.* New York: Wiley, 1990. A classic by the late author, an authority on sampling.

Kalton, Graham. *Introduction to Survey Sampling.* Beverly Hills, CA: Sage Publications, 1983. An overview with particular attention to survey applications.

Kish, Leslie. *Survey Sampling.* New York: Wiley, 1995. A widely read reference on survey sampling, recently updated.

Namias, Jean. *Handbook of Selected Sample Surveys in the Federal Government.* New York: St. John's University Press, 1969. A unique collection of illustrative uses of sampling for surveys carried out by various federal agencies. Of interest both for the sampling designs presented and for the information on the methodology used to develop various government statistical data.

Yates, F. *Sampling Methods for Censuses and Surveys.* 4th ed. New York: Oxford University Press, 1987. A readable text with emphasis on sampling practices.

chapter 17

Reference Notes

This entire chapter was built from two examples developed for *Business Research Methods,* 8th ed. (New York: McGraw-Hill, 2003), by Donald Cooper and Pamela Schindler.

References for Snapshots, PicProfiles, Captions, and Pull Quotes

Alliance Research

Jim Lane, senior vice president, Alliance Research, interviewed September 8, 2002.

Materials presented at the AMA Marketing Research Conference, Chicago, September 8–11, 2002.

Henry J. Kaiser Family Foundation

"About the Henry J. Kaiser Family Foundation" (http://www.kff.org/about/).

"Sex Education in America: A View from Inside the Nation's Classrooms," Reproductive and Sexual Health: Henry J. Kaiser Family Foundation (http://www.kff.org/sections.cgi?section=repro&sub_section=re-sexed&disp=10).

"Summary of Findings: Sex Education in America: A Series of National Surveys of Students, Parents, Teachers, and Principals," Henry J. Kaiser Family Foundation, September 2000 (http://www.kkf.org/content/2000/3048/sexED.pdf).

Diana Jean Schemo, "Survey Finds Parents Favor More Detailed Sex Education," *New York Times on the Web,* October 4, 2000 (http://www.nytimes.com/2000/10/04/national/04SEX.html).

Frank Newport

Frank Newport, Lydia Saad, and David Moore in *Where America Stands* (New York: Wiley, 1997) (http://www.gallup.com/help/FAQs/poll1.asp).

Progressive

Chuck Salter, "Progressive Makes Big Claims," *FastCompany,* November 1998.

Progressive press kit, Progressive, December 1998.

Classic and Contemporary Readings

Deming, W. Edwards. *Sample Design in Business Research.* New York: Wiley, 1990. A classic by the late author, an authority on sampling.

Kish, Leslie. *Survey Sampling.* New York: Wiley, 1995. A widely read reference on survey sampling, recently updated.

Yates, F. *Sampling Methods for Censuses and Surveys.* 4th ed. New York: Oxford University Press, 1987. A readable text with emphasis on sampling practices.

chapter 18

Reference Notes

1. Jean M. Converse and Stanley Presser, *Survey Questions: Handcrafting the Standardized Questionnaire* (Beverly Hills, CA: Sage Publications, 1986), pp. 34–35.

2. B. Berelson, *Content Analysis in Communication Research* (New York: Free Press, 1952), p. 18.

3. Klaus Krippendorff, *Content Analysis: An Introduction to Its Methodology* (Beverly Hills, CA: Sage Publications, 1980), p. 22.

4. Based on the operation of the SPSS, Inc., product TextSmart.

5. Hans Zeisel, *Say It with Figures,* 6th ed. (New York: Harper & Row, 1985), pp. 48–49.

6. "Technology Overview," TraxUK, downloaded March 11, 2003 (http://www.trax-uk.co.uk./technology).

7. Ibid.

8. "Office XP Speaks Out: Voice Recognition Assists Users," Microsoft press release, April 18, 2001, downloaded March 11, 2003 (http://www.microsoft.com/presspass/features/2001/apr01/04-18xpspeech.asp).

9. Adapted from a history of bar-code development: http://www.lascofittings.com/BarCode-EDI/bc-history.htm.

References for Snapshots, PicProfiles, Captions, and Pull Quotes

Brawny

"Brawny Man Gets a Makeover: 30-Year Old Brand Debuts New Product and New Brawny Man," Georgia Pacific, Release No. C-1847, October 23, 2003 (http://www.gp.com/center/news/news.asp?NewsID=2637).

Liz Butler, DVC Worldwide, April 29, 2004.

CBS

"ACNielsen Entertainment Partners with CBS for Real-Time Audience Research," ACNielsen news release, April 18, 2001 (http://acnielsen.com/news/corp/2001/20010418.html).

"Tech Week: Entertainment's Creative Online Testing with Andy Wing, President, ACNielsen Entertainment," Washington Post.com, May 18, 2001 (http://discuss.washingtonpost.com/wp-srv/zform/01/washtech_wing0518.html).

"GES Builds Television City for CBS Television Network; Ambitious Research Facility Ingeniously Captures Opinions amidst Las Vegas Excitement," Viad Corp. news release, September 5, 2001 (http://www.businesswire.com/webbox/bw.090501/212480444.htm).

"CBS Television City Research Center," Vegas.com, downloaded April 16, 2004 (http://www.vegas.com/attractions/on_the_strip/televisioncity.html?f=m0at&t+stripat).

Kate Lynch

"Demographic Diamonds (Media Experts)," *American Demographics,* April 2003, p. 36.

Princess Cruises

"About Princess," P&O Princess Cruises plc., downloaded February 9, 2002 (http://www.princess.com/about).

J. Rydholm, "Scanning the Seas," *Quirk's Market Research Review,* May 1993 (http://www.quirks.com/articles/article_print.asp?arg_articleid=207).

VNS, Black Eye

"A Bad Day at the Exit Polls," *Savanna Morning News,* November 9, 2000 (http://www.savannamorningnews.com/sma/stories/110900/locsurvey.shtml).

"Antitrust Group Urges US to Break Up Voter News Service," Antitrust Institute, November 27, 2000 (http://www.antitrustinstitute.org/recent/90.cfm).

David M. Ewalt, "Web Sites Leaked Early Election Results," *Information Week,* November 8, 2000 (http://www.informationweek.com/story/showArticle.jhtml?articleID=6509999).

See poll results at http://www.cnn.com/election/2000/epolls/us/p000.html.

VNS, Knockout

"Politics: Voter News Service Shuts Down," *Washington Post,* January 13, 2003, downloaded March 22, 2003 (http://chblue.com/artman/publish/aricle_1522.shtml).

XSight

Interview with John Woolcott, vice president, American operations, QSR International, interviewed June 4, 2004.

"XSight: Your intuition. Our software," QSR International, product literature, © 2004.

"XSight," QSR International, demo software, © 2004.

chapter 19

Reference Notes

1. David C. Hoaglin, Frederick Mosteller, and John W. Tukey, eds., *Understanding Robust and Exploratory Data Analysis* (New York: Wiley, 1983), p. 2.

2. John W. Tukey, *Exploratory Data Analysis* (Reading, MA: Addison-Wesley, 1977), pp. 2–3.

3. Frederick Hartwig with Brian E. Dearing, *Exploratory Data Analysis* (Beverly Hills, CA: Sage Publications, 1979), pp. 9–12.

4. The exhibits in this section were created with statistical and graphic programs particularly suited to exploratory data analysis. The authors acknowledge the following vendors for evaluation and use of their products: SPSS, Inc., 233 S. Wacker Dr., Chicago, IL 60606; and Data Description, P.O. Box 4555, Ithaca, NY 14852.

5. Paul F. Velleman and David C. Hoaglin, *Applications, Basics, and Computing of Exploratory Data Analysis* (Boston: Duxbury Press, 1981), p. 13.

6. John Hanke, Eastern Washington University, contributed this section. For further references to stem-and-leaf displays, see John D. Emerson and David C. Hoaglin, "Stem-and-Leaf Displays," in *Understanding Robust and Exploratory Data Analysis,* pp. 7–31, and Velleman and Hoaglin, *Applications,* pp. 1–13.

7. This section is adapted from the following excellent discussions of boxplots: Velleman and Hoaglin, *Applications,* pp. 65–76; Hartwig, *Exploratory Data Analysis,* pp. 19–25; John D. Emerson and Judith Strenio, "Boxplots and Batch Comparison," in *Understanding Robust and Exploratory Data Analysis,* pp. 59–93; and Amir D. Aczel, *Complete Business Statistics* (Homewood, IL: Irwin, 1989), pp. 723–28.

8. Tukey, *Exploratory Data Analysis,* pp. 27–55.

9. Hoaglin et al., *Understanding Robust and Exploratory Data Analysis,* p. 2.

10. Several robust estimators that are suitable replacements for the mean and standard deviation we do not discuss here—for example, the trimmed mean, trimean, the M-estimators (such as Huber's, Tukey's, Hampel's, and Andrew's estimators), and the median absolute deviation (MAD). See Hoaglin et al., *Understanding Robust and Exploratory Data Analysis,* chap. 10, and SPSS, Inc., *SPSS Base 9.0 User's Guide* (Chicago: SPSS, 1999), chap. 13.

11. The difference between the definitions of a hinge and a quartile is based on variations in their calculation. We use Q_1, *25th percentile,* and *lower hinge* synonymously; and Q_3, *75th percentile,* and *upper hinge,* similarly. There are technical differences, although they are not significant in this context.

12. R. McGill, J. W. Tukey, and W. A. Larsen, "Variations of Box Plots," *The American Statistician* 14 (1978), pp. 12–16.

13. See J. Chambers, W. Cleveland, B. Kleiner, and John W. Tukey, *Graphical Methods for Data Analysis* (Boston: Duxbury Press, 1983).

14. Harper W. Boyd Jr. and Ralph Westfall, *Marketing Research,* 3d ed. (Homewood, IL: Irwin, 1972), p. 540.

15. SPSS, Inc., *SPSS Tables 8.0* (Chicago: SPSS, 1998), with its system file: Bank Data.

References for Snapshots, PicProfiles, Captions, and Pull Quotes

American Red Cross

Holly Ripans, manager of marketing research, American Red Cross, interviewed April 25, 2003.

"PR Week Awards 2003 Technique Award: Best Use of Research or Measurement," *PRWeek,* downloaded March 19, 2003 (http://www.prweek.com/events/botn.crf?sub=1529).

"PRWeek Awards 2003," *PRWeek,* downloaded March 19, 2003 (http://www.prweek.com/events/index.cfm?site=3).

"Wirthlin Wins PRWeek Award," Wirthlin Worldwide e-mail press release, March 19, 2003.

Digital Cameras

"Picture This: A Look at Where Americans Are Most Likely to Snap Up Digital Cameras," *American Demographics* 25, no 6 (July–August 2003), pp. 18–19.

Peter Drucker

businessThink NOW, e-newsletter, March 2004.

Forrester Research

Mark Bunger, senior analyst, Forrester Research, interviewed January 22, 2004.

"Tracking Carbuyers' Online Paths to Purchase Shows Their Likelihood to Buy, According to Forrester Research," Forrester Research press release, February 19, 2002.

"Who We Are," comScore Networks, downloaded January 22, 2004 (http://www.comscore.com/about/default.asp).

Media Outlook

Deborah Scruby, marketing director, PricewaterhouseCoopers, interviewed September 10, 2002.

Starbucks

Colette Courtion, director of Starbucks Global Card Services, interviewed April 26, 2004.

"Fast Facts," Duetto™ Card Press Kit jointly issued by Starbucks, Bank One and Visa, October 2003 (http://www.duettopressroom.com).

"Starbucks Coffee Company, Bank One and Visa Team Up to Develop the Next Evolution of the Starbucks Card," press release, February 21, 2003 (http://www.shareholder.com/one/news/20030221-102404.cfm?category).

This snapshot and the accompanying case were developed with the assistance of numerous people from Bank One: Jessica Iben; Hugh Bleemer, executive vice president of programming; Mike Bordner, relationship manager on the Starbucks account; and Ajay Gupta, primarily in charge of the research. All the above were interviewed by phone, with conversations supplemented by e-mail, during spring 2004.

Classic and Contemporary Readings

Aczel, Amir D., and Jayauel Sounderpandian. *Complete Business Statistics.* 5th ed. New York: Irwin/McGraw-Hill, 2001. Thorough coverage of exploratory and confirmatory data analysis.

Pallant, Julie. *SPSS Survival Manual: A Step by Step Guide to Data Analysis Using SPSS for Windows.* Maidenhead, UK: Open University Press, 2001.

Zeisel, Hans. *Say It with Figures.* 6th ed. New York: Harper & Row, 1985. The entire book is worth reading for its excellent discussion of numerical presentation.

chapter 20

Reference Notes

1. A more detailed example is found in Amir D. Aczel and Jayauel Sounderpandian, *Complete Business Statistics,* 5th ed. (New York: Irwin/McGraw-Hill, 2001).

2. The standardized random variable, denoted by Z, is a deviation from expectancy and is expressed in terms of standard deviation units. The mean of the distribution of a standardized random variable is 0, and the standard deviation is 1. With this distribution, the deviation from the mean by any value of X can be expressed in standard deviation units.

3. Procedures for hypothesis testing are reasonably similar across authors. This outline was influenced by Sidney Siegel, *Nonparametric Statistics for the Behavioral Sciences* (New York: McGraw-Hill, 1956), chap. 2.

4. Marija J. Norusis/SPSS, Inc., *SPSS for Windows Base System User's Guide,* Release 6.0 (Chicago: SPSS, 1993), pp. 601–606.

5. For further information on these tests, see ibid., pp. 187–88.

6. F. M. Andrews, L. Klem, T. N. Davidson, P. M. O'Malley, and W. L. Rodgers, *A Guide for Selecting Statistical Techniques for Analyzing Social Science Data* (Ann Arbor: Institute for Social Research, University of Michigan, 1976).

7. Statistical Navigator is a product from The Idea Works, Inc.

8. Exhibit 20-7 is partially adapted from Siegel, *Nonparametric Statistics,* flyleaf.

9. See B. S. Everitt, *The Analysis of Contingency Tables* (London: Chapman and Hall, 1977).

10. The critiques are represented by W. J. Conover, "Some Reasons for Not Using the Yates' Continuity Correction on 2 × 2 Contingency Tables," *Journal of the American Statistical Association* 69 (1974), pp. 374–76, and N. Mantel, "Comment and a Suggestion on the Yates' Continuity Correction," *Journal of the American Statistical Association* 69 (1974), pp. 378–80.

11. This data table and the analysis of variance tables and plots in this section were prepared with SuperANOVA™.

12. See, for example, Roger E. Kirk, *Experimental Design: Procedures for the Behavioral Sciences* (Belmont, CA: Brooks/Cole, 1982), pp. 115–33. An exceptionally clear presentation for step-by-step hand computation is found in James L. Bruning and B. L. Kintz, *Computational Handbook of Statistics,* 2d ed. (Glenview, IL: Scott, Foresman, 1977), pp. 143–68. Also, when you use a computer program, the reference manual typically provides helpful advice in addition to the setup instructions.

13. Kirk, *Experimental Design,* pp. 90–115. Alternatively, see Bruning and Kintz, *Computational Handbook of Statistics,* pp. 113–32.

14. For a discussion and example of the Cochran Q test, see Sidney Siegel and N. J. Castellan Jr., *Nonparametric Statistics for the Behavioral Sciences,* 2d ed. (New York: McGraw-Hill, 1988).

15. For further details, ibid.

References for Snapshots, PicProfiles, Captions, and Pull Quotes

Burrelle's

Sharon Miller, account executive, Burrelle's Information Services (Burrelle'sLuce), interviewed February 2003.

"Report on the Full Extent of Your Media Coverage," Burrelle's Media Analysis brochure, Burrelle's Information Services, Burrelle'sLuce, downloaded April 16, 2004 (http://www.burellesluce.com/images/mm/Bro_mediaana.pdf).

Colin Crook

"What's Behind the 4-Minute Mile, Starbucks and the Moon Landing? The Power of Impossible Thinking," *Knowledge at Wharton,* downloaded July 14, 2004 (http://www.knowledge.wharton.upenn.edu/article/1007.cfm).

Honda Insight

www.hondacars.com/models/model_overview.asp?ModelName= Insight.

Mediascope

"New Study Looks at Drugs in Movies and Songs," America Cares, Inc., April 1999 (http://www.americacares.org/drugs_in_movies.htm).

"Substance Use in Popular Movies and Music," Office of National Drug Control Policy, April 1999 (http://www.mediacampaign.org/publications/movies/movie_partIV.html).

PharmTrends

"Ad Aware Consumers Are Purchasing More Prescription Drug Scripts Than Those Not Aware of Direct-to-Consumer Advertising," Ipsos-NPD press release, June 27, 2002, downloaded July 12, 2002 (http://www.ipsos-npd.com/index_news.cfm?release=02_0626).

"Consumers Are Responding to Advertising for Prescription Medications," Ipsos-NPD press release, June 13, 2002, downloaded July 12, 2002 (http://www.ipsos-npd.com/index_news.cfm?release =02_0613).

"PharmTrends," Ipsos-NPD, downloaded July 12, 2002 (http://www.ipsos-npd.com/index_pharm.cfm).

Stuart Elliott, "The Fight to Keep Direct-to-Consumer Ads," *New York Times,* July 12, 2002, downloaded July 12, 2002 (http://www.aef.com/06/news/data/2002/2069).

Classic and Contemporary Readings

Aczel, Amir D., and J. Sounderpandian. *Complete Business Statistics.* 5th ed. New York: Irwin/McGraw-Hill, 2001. This excellent text is characterized by highly lucid explanations and numerous examples.

Cohen, Jacob. *Statistical Power Analysis for the Behavioral Sciences.* Mahwah, NJ: Lawrence Erlbaum Associates, 1990. A key reference on conducting power analysis.

DeFinetti, Bruno. *Probability, Induction, and Statistics.* New York: Wiley, 1972. A highly readable work on subjective probability and the Bayesian approach.

Kanji, Gopal K. *100 Statistical Tests.* Thousand Oaks, CA: Sage Publications, 1999. Coverage of the most commonly used statistics that students will encounter.

Kirk, Roger E. *Experimental Design: Procedures for the Behavioral Sciences.* 3d ed. Belmont, CA: Brooks/Cole, 1995. An advanced text on the statistical aspects of experimental design.

Levine, David M., Timothy C. Krehbiel, and Mark L. Berenson. *Business Statistics: A First Course.* Upper Saddle River, NJ: Prentice Hall, 1999. For students or managers without recent statistical coursework, this text provides an excellent review.

Siegel, Sidney, and N. J. Castellan Jr. *Nonparametric Statistics for the Behavioral Sciences.* 2d ed. New York: McGraw-Hill, 1988. The classic book on nonparametric statistics.

Winer, B. J .*Statistical Principles in Experimental Design.* 2d ed. New York: McGraw-Hill, 1971. Another classic source. Thorough coverage of analysis of variance and experimental design.

chapter 21

Reference Notes

1. Typically, we plot the *X* (independent) variable on the horizontal axis and the *Y* (dependent) variable on the vertical axis. Although correlation does not distinguish between independent and dependent variables, the convention is useful for consistency in plotting and will be used later with regression.

2. F. J. Anscombe, "Graphs in Statistical Analysis," *American Statistician* 27 (1973), pp. 17–21. Cited in Samprit Chatterjee and Bertram Price, *Regression Analysis by Example* (New York: Wiley, 1977), pp. 7–9.

3. Amir D. Aczel, *Complete Business Statistics,* 2d ed. (Homewood, IL: Irwin, 1993), p. 433.

4. This section is partially based on the concepts developed by Emanuel J. Mason and William J. Bramble, *Understanding and Conducting Research* (New York: McGraw-Hill, 1989), pp. 172–82, and elaborated in greater detail by Aczel, *Complete Business Statistics,* pp. 414–29.

5. Technically, estimation uses a concurrent criterion variable where prediction uses a future criterion. The statistical procedure is the same in either case.

6. Roz Howard and Jenny Stonier, "Marketing Wine to Generation X" for the 2000–2001 NSW Wine Press Club Fellowship. Reported in Murray Almond's "From the Left Island," May 25, 2002 (http://www.wineoftheweek.com/murray/0205genx.html).

7. Peter Passell, "Can Math Predict a Wine? An Economist Takes a Swipe at Some Noses," *International Herald Tribune*, March 5, 1990, p. 1; Jacques Neher, "Top Quality Bordeaux Cellar Is an Excellent Buy," *International Herald Tribune,* July 9, 1990, p. 8.

8. See Alan Agresti and Barbara Finlay, *Statistical Methods for the Social Sciences* (San Francisco: Dellen Publishing, 1986), pp. 248–49. Also see the discussion of basic regression models in John Neter, William Wasserman, and Michael H. Kutner, *Applied Linear Statistical Models* (Homewood, IL: Irwin, 1990), pp. 23–49.

9. We distinguish between the error terms $\varepsilon_1 = Y_i - EY_i$ and the residual $e_i = (Y_i - \hat{Y}_i)$. The first is based on the vertical deviation of Y_i from the true regression line. It is unknown and estimated. The second is the vertical deviation of Y_i from the fitted $\hat{Y}$ on the estimated line. See Neter et al., *Applied Linear Statistical Models,* p. 47.

10. For further information on software-generated regression diagnostics, see the most current release of software manuals for SPSS, MINITAB, BMDP, and SAS.

11. Aczel, *Complete Business Statistics,* p. 434.

12. This calculation is normally listed as the standard error of the slope (SE B) on computer printouts. For these data it is further defined as:

$$s(b_i) + \frac{8}{\sqrt{SS_x}} = \frac{538.559}{\sqrt{198.249}} = 38.249$$

where

$s = $ the standard error of estimate (and the square root of the mean square error of the regression)

$SS_x = $ the sum of squares for the *X* variable

13. Computer printouts use uppercase (R^2) because most procedures are written to accept multiple and bivariate regression.

14. The table output for this section has been modified from SPSS and is described in Marija J. Norusis/SPSS, Inc., *SPSS Base System User's Guide* (Chicago: SPSS, 1990). For further discussion and examples of nonparametric measures of association, see S. Siegel and N. J. Castellan Jr., *Nonparametric Statistics for the Behavioral Sciences,* 2d ed. (New York: McGraw-Hill, 1988).

15. Calculation of concordant and discordant pairs is adapted from Agresti and Finlay, *Statistical Methods for the Social Sciences,* pp. 221–23.

16. We know that the percentage of concordant plus the percentage of discordant pairs sums to 1.0. We also know their difference is $-.70$. The only numbers satisfying these two conditions are .85 and .15 (.85 + .15 = 1.0, .15 − .85 = −.70).

17. G. U. Yule and M. G. Kendall, *An Introduction to the Theory of Statistics* (New York: Hafner, 1950).

18. M. G. Kendall, *Rank Correlation Methods,* 4th ed. (London: Charles W. Griffin, 1970).

References for Snapshots, PicProfiles, Captions, and Pull Quotes

Business School Wine Clubs

E. Zelko, "Graduates of Wine," *Wine Spectator* 24, no. 15 (January 2000), pp. 88–90.

Envirosell

Live e-chat with Paco Underhill, July 8, 1999 (http://www.abcnews.go.com/sections/politics/DailyNews/chat_990511underhill.html).

David Singleton

David Singleton, "Basics of Good Research Involve Understanding Six Simple Rules," *Marketing News,* American Marketing Association, November 24, 2003, pp. 22–24.

Specialized MBAs

M. Rowe, "Learning the Business of Wine, Sports, and Music," *International Herald Tribune,* May 14, 2001, p. 18.

Speedpass

"McDonald's Accepts Speedpass for Fast Stomach Fill Up," press release (http://www.cardfrum.com/html/news/090800_1.htm).

"McDonald's Expands Cashless Test," *Promo Xtra!,* June 4, 2001.

"Speedpass Expands to More than 400 McDonald's Restaurants in Chicagoland Area," press release (http://biz.yahoo.com/bw/010531/0270.html).

Classic and Contemporary Readings

Aczel, Amir D., and Jayauel Sounderpandian. *Complete Business Statistics.* 5th ed. New York: Irwin/McGraw-Hill, 2001. The chapter on simple regression/correlation has impeccable exposition and examples and is highly recommended.

Agresti, Alan, and Barbara Finlay. *Statistical Methods for the Social Sciences.* 3d ed. Upper Saddle River, NJ: Prentice Hall, 1997. Very clear coverage of nonparametric measures of association.

Chatterjee, Samprit, and Bertram Price. *Regression Analysis by Example.* 3d ed. New York: Wiley, 1999. Updated version of widely used examples textbook.

Cohen, Jacob, and Patricia Cohen. *Applied Multiple Regression/Correlation Analysis for the Behavioral Sciences.* 2d ed. Mahwah, NJ: Lawrence Erlbaum Associates, 1983. A classic reference work.

Neter, John, Michael H. Kutner, Christopher J. Nachtsheim, and William Wasserman. *Applied Linear Statistical Models.* 4th ed. Burr Ridge, IL: Irwin, 1996. Chapters 1 through 10 and 15 provide an excellent introduction to regression and correlation analysis.

Siegel, S., and N. J. Castellan Jr. *Nonparametric Statistics for the Behavioral Sciences.* 2d ed. New York: McGraw-Hill, 1988.

chapter 22

Reference Notes

1. Jagdish N. Sheth, ed., *Multivariate Methods for Market and Survey Research* (Chicago: American Marketing Association, 1977), p. 3.

2. William Schneider, "Opinion Outlook," *National Journal,* July 1985.

3. Benson Shapiro, "Price Reliance: Existence and Sources," *Journal of Marketing Research,* August 1973, pp. 286–89.

4. For a discussion of path analysis, see Elazar J. Pedhazur, *Regression in Behavioral Research: Explanation and Prediction*, 2d ed. (New York: Holt, Rinehart & Winston, 1982), chap. 15, and Brian S. Everitt, Graham Dunn, and G. Dunn, *Applied Multivariate Data Analysis,* 2d ed. (London: Arnold Publishers, 2001).

5. Fred Kerlinger, *Foundations of Behavioral Research,* 3d ed. (New York: Holt, Rinehart & Winston, 1986), p. 562.

6. Joseph F. Hair Jr., Rolph E. Anderson, Ronald L. Tatham, and William C. Black, *Multivariate Data Analysis with Readings* (New York: Macmillan, 1992), pp. 153–81.

7. This section is based on the SPSS procedure MANOVA, described in Marija J. Norusis/SPSS, Inc., *SPSS Advanced Statistics Users Guide* (Chicago: SPSS, 1990), pp. 71–104.

8. This section was prepared by Jeff Stevens, School of Public Administration, Florida Atlantic University. For further information, see J. Hair, R. Anderson, R. Tatham, and W. Black, *Multivariate*

Data Analysis with Readings, 5th ed. (Upper Saddle River, NJ: Prentice Hall, 1998); J. Scott Long, *Covariance Structure Models: An Introduction to LISREL* (Thousand Oaks, CA: Sage Publications, 1984); J. Scott Long, *Confirmatory Factor Analysis: A Preface to LISREL* (Thousand Oaks, CA: Sage Publications, 1983); and Barbara M. Byrne, *A Primer of LISREL: Basic Applications and Programming for Confirmatory Factor Analytic Models* (New York: Springer-Verlag, 1989).

9. SPSS, Inc., *SPSS Categories* (Chicago: SPSS, 1990).

10. Product specifications adapted from Lewis Rothlein, "A Guide to Sun Protection Essentials," *Wind Rider,* June 1990, pp. 95–103.

11. The data for this example are hypothetical.

12. See the ALSCAL procedure in Marija J. Norusis/SPSS, Inc., *SPSS Base System User's Guide* (Chicago: SPSS, 1990), pp. 397–416.

References for Snapshots, PicProfiles, Captions, and Pull Quotes

Zora Neale Hurston

http://www.bartleby.com/66/45/29745.html.

NCR Country Club

"NCR Country Club McMahon Group Study Report, 1999," McMahon Group.

"NCR Country Club Membership Brochure, 1999," NCR Country Club Association.

Frank Vain, president of McMahon Group, interviewed July 2000.

PricewaterhouseCoopers LLP

B. Jordheim, "Building a Smarter Brand," *Sales and Marketing Management,* October 1999, p. 105.

Marla Sawasky, product manager for TelecomInsider, interviewed July 2000.

SuperLetter.com

Christopher Schultheiss, founder and CEO, SuperLetter.com, interviewed June 2004.

Classic and Contemporary Readings

Hair, Joseph F., Jr., Rolph E. Anderson, Ronald L. Tatham, and William C. Black. *Multivariate Data Analysis with Readings.* 5th ed. Upper Saddle River, NJ: Prentice Hall, 1998. A very readable book covering most multivariate statistics.

Sage Series in Quantitative Applications in the Social Sciences. Thousand Oaks, CA: Sage Publications. This monograph series includes papers on most multivariate methods.

Schumaker, Randall A., and Richard G. Lomax. *A Beginner's Guide to Structural Equation Modeling.* Mahwah, NJ: Lawrence Erlbaum Associates, 1996. An introduction to structural models.

Stevens, James P. *Applied Multivariate Statistics for the Social Sciences.* 3d ed. Mahwah, NJ: Lawrence Erlbaum Associates, 1999. Comprehensive coverage with computer examples.

chapter 23

Reference Notes

1. Paul E. Resta, *The Research Report* (New York: American Book Company, 1972), p. 5.

2. John M. Penrose Jr., Robert W. Rasberry, and Robert J. Myers, *Advanced Business Communication* (Boston: PWS-Kent Publishing, 1989), p. 185.

3. Ibid.

4. Most word processors contain dictionaries. All-purpose word processors such as MS Word, WordPerfect, WordPro, or Macintosh products contain a spelling checker, table and graphing generators, and a thesaurus. For style and grammar checkers, programs such as Grammatik, RightWriter, Spelling Coach, and Punctuation + Style are available. New programs are reviewed periodically in the business communication literature and in magazines devoted to personal computing.

5. Robert R. Rathbone, *Communicating Technical Information* (Reading, MA: Addison-Wesley, 1966), p. 64. Reprinted with permission.

6. Ibid., p. 72.

7. Penrose, Rasberry, and Myers, *Advanced Business Communication,* p. 89.

8. The material in this section draws on Stephen M. Kosslyn, *Elements of Graph Design* (San Francisco: Freeman, 1993); Delta-Point, Inc., *DeltaGraph User's Guide 4.0* (Monterey, CA: DeltaPoint, 1996); Gene Zelazny, *Say It with Charts* (Homewood, IL: Business One Irwin, 1991); Jim Heid, "Graphs That Work," *MacWorld,* February 1994, pp. 155–56; and Penrose, Rasberry, and Myers, *Advanced Business Communication*, chap. 3.

9. Marilyn Stoll, "Charts Other Than Pie Are Appealing to the Eye," *PC Week*, March 25, 1986, pp. 138–39.

10. Stephen M. Kosslyn and Christopher Chabris, "The Mind Is Not a Camera, the Brain Is Not a VCR," *Aldus Magazine,* September–October 1993, p. 34.

References for Snapshots, PicProfiles, Captions, and Pull Quotes

dataCAP

dataCAP, Opinion Search, downloaded June 1, 2004 (http://www.opinionsearch.com/en/services/index.asp?subsection=6&subsubsection=4).

Darcy Zwetko, director of research and systems, Opinion Search, interviewed June 2003.

Forrester Research

"Making Auto Retail Lean," TechStrategy report, Forrester Research, downloaded January 5, 2004 (http://www.forrester.com/ER/Reserach/Report/Summary/0,1338,32782,00.html).

Mark Bunger, senior analyst, Forrester Research, interviewed January 22, 2004.

Good Housekeeping Institute

"Good Housekeeping Institute," *Good Housekeeping,* July 2000 (http://goodhousekeeping.women.com/gh/institute/ghinstr1.htm).

"About the Good Housekeeping Institute," *Good Housekeeping,* February 2002 (http://magazines.ivillage.com/goodhousekeeping/consumer/institute/articles/0,12873,284511_290570,00.html).

"The GH Institute Report," *Good Housekeeping,* February 2002 (http://magazines.ivillage.com/goodhousekeeping/consumer/institute/articles/0,12873,284511_290570-4,00.html).

Lexus/Team One Advertising

Mark Miller, associate director, strategic planning, Team One Advertising, interviewed July 9 and October 5, 2002.

Dave Marcum

businessThink NOW, e-newsletter, March 2004.

Medical Radar International

"Medical Radar," SPSS, February 2002 (http://www.spss.com/spssatwork/template_view.cfm?Story_ID=24).

"Take Action with Organized, Interactive Analytic Information," SPSS, February, 2002 (http://www.spss.com/svws).

Public Speaking Jitters

Patricia Fripp, CSP, CPAE, award-winning keynote speaker and speech coach, author of *Get What You Want!,* and past president of the National Speakers Association (http://www.fripp.com/)

Classic and Contemporary Readings

Campbell, Steve. *Statistics You Can't Trust.* Parker, CO: Think Twice Publishing, 2000. An enjoyable and entertaining approach to interpreting statistical charts and arguments.

Kosslyn, Stephen M. *Elements of Graph Design.* San Francisco: Freeman, 1993. Fundamentals of graph and chart construction.

Lesikar, Raymond V., Marie E. Flatley, and John D. Pettit. *Lesikar's Basic Business Communication.* 8th ed. Burr Ridge, IL: Irwin/McGraw-Hill, 1999. Practical guidance for writing and presenting reports.

Penrose, John M., Robert W. Rasberry, and Robert J. Myers. *Advanced Business Communication.* 3d ed. Cincinnati, OH: South-Western Publishing, 1997. A presentation of all aspects of business communications from organization through final writing and oral presentation.

Strunk, William, Jr., and E. B. White. *The Elements of Style.* New York: Macmillan, 1959. A classic on the problems of writing style.

Tufte, Edward R. *The Visual Display of Quantitative Information.* New Haven, CT: Graphics Press, 1992. The book that started the revolution against gaudy infographics.

Tufte, Edward R. *Visual Explanations: Images and Quantities, Evidence and Narrative.* New Haven, CT: Graphics Press, 1997. Uses the principle of "the smallest effective difference" to display distinctions in data. Beautifully illustrated.

***a priori* contrasts** a special class of tests used in conjunction with the *F* test that is specifically designed to test the hypotheses of the experiment or study (in comparison to post hoc or unplanned tests).

accuracy the degree to which bias is absent from the sample—the underestimators and the overestimators are balanced among members of the sample (i.e., no systematic variance).

action research a methodology with brainstorming followed by sequential trial-and-error to discover the most effective solution to a problem; succeeding solutions are tried until the desired results are achieved; used with complex problems about which little is known.

active factors those independent variables (IV) the researcher can manipulate by causing the subject to receive one treatment level or another.

activity analysis see **process analysis.**

administrative question a measurement question that identifies the participant, interviewer, interview location, and conditions (nominal data).

alternative hypothesis (H_A) that a difference exists between the sample parameter and the population statistic to which it is compared; the logical opposite of the null hypothesis used in significance testing.

ambiguities and paradoxes a projective technique (imagination exercise) where participants imagine a brand applied to a different product (e.g., a Tide dog food or Marlboro cereal), and then describe its attributes and position.

analysis of variance (ANOVA) tests the null hypothesis that the means of several independent populations are equal; test statistic is the *F* ratio; used when you need *k*-independent-samples tests.

applied research research that addresses existing problems or opportunities.

arbitrary scales universal practice of ad hoc scale development used by instrument designers to create scales that are highly specific to the practice or object being studied.

area chart a graphical presentation that displays total frequency, group frequency, and time series data; a.k.a. *stratum chart* or *surface chart.*

area sampling a cluster sampling technique applied to a population with well-defined political or natural boundaries; population is divided into homogeneous clusters from which a single-stage or multistage sample is drawn.

argument statement that explains, interprets, defends, challenges, or explores meaning.

artifact correlations where distinct subgroups in the data combine to give the impression of one.

association the process used to recognize and understand patterns in data and then used to understand and exploit natural patterns.

asymmetrical relationship a relationship in which we postulate that change in one variable (IV) is responsible for change in another variable (DV).

attitude a learned, stable predisposition to respond to oneself, other persons, objects, or issues in a consistently favorable or unfavorable way.

audience characteristics and background of the people or groups for whom the secondary source was created; one of the five factors used to evaluate the value of a secondary source.

authority the level of data and the credibility of a source as indicated by the credentials of the author and publisher; one of five factors used to evaluate the value of a secondary source.

authority figure a projective technique (imagination exercise) where participants are asked to imagine that the brand or product is an authority figure and to describe the attributes of the figure.

automatic interaction detection (AID) a data partitioning procedure that searches up to 300 variables for the single best predictor of a dependent variable.

average linkage method evaluates the distance between two clusters by first finding the geometric center of each cluster and then computing distances between the two centers.

backward elimination sequentially removing the variable from a regression model that changes R^2 the least; see also *forward selection* and *stepwise selection.*

balanced rating scale has an equal number of categories above and below the midpoint or an equal number of favorable/unfavorable response choices.

band see **prediction and confidence bands.**

bar chart a graphical presentation technique that represents frequency data as horizontal or vertical bars; vertical bars are most often used for time series and quantitative classifications (histograms, stacked bar, and multiple-variable charts are specialized bar charts).

bar code technology employing labels containing electronically read vertical bar data codes.

basic research see **pure research**

Bayesian statistics uses subjective probability estimates based on general experience rather than on data collected. (See "Decision Theory Problem" on your DVD.)

benefit chain see **laddering.**

beta weights standardized regression coefficients where the size of the number reflects the level of influence *X* exerts on *Y*.

bibliography a secondary source that helps locate a book, article, photograph, etc.

bivariate correlation analysis a statistical technique to assess the relationship of two continuous variables measured on an interval or ratio scale.

bivariate normal distribution data are from a random sample where two variables are normally distributed in a joint manner.

blind when participants do not know if they are being exposed to the experimental treatment.

blocking factor a variable on which the researcher can only identify and classify a participant—not manipulate (e.g., gender, age, customer status); these factors are often the classification variables within a questionnaire.

Boolean logic the protocol used by many electronic databases for keyword searches.

boxplot an EDA technique; a visual image of the variable's distribution location, spread, shape, tail length, and outliers; a.k.a. *box-and-whisker plot.*

branched question a measurement question sequence determined by the participant's previous answer(s); the answer to one question assumes other questions have been asked or answered and directs the participant to answer specific questions that follow and skip other questions; branched questions determine question sequencing.

brand mapping a projective technique (type of semantic mapping) where participants are presented with different brands and asked to talk about their perceptions, usually in relation to several criteria. They may also be asked to spatially place each brand on one or more semantic maps.

briefing a short oral presentation to a small group, where statistics constitute much of the content.

buffer question a neutral measurement question designed chiefly to establish rapport with the participant (usually nominal data).

callback procedure involving repeated attempts to make contact with a targeted participant to ensure that the targeted participant is reached and motivated to participate in the study.

cartoons or **empty balloons** a projective technique where participants are asked to write the dialog for a cartoonlike picture.

case the entity or thing the hypothesis talks about.

case study (case history) a methodology that combines individual and (sometimes) group interviews with record analysis and observation; used to understand events and their ramifications and processes; emphasizes the full contextual analysis of a few events or conditions and their interrelations for a single participant; a type of preexperimental design (one-shot case study).

categorization for this scale type, participants put themselves or property indicants in groups or categories; also, a process for grouping data for any variable into a limited number of categories.

causal hypothesis see **explanatory hypothesis.**

causal study research that attempts to reveal a causal relationship between variables. (A produces B or causes B to occur).

causation situation where one variable leads to a specified effect on the other variable.

cell in a cross-tabulation, a subgroup of the data created by the value intersection of two (or more) variables; each cell contains the count of cases as well as the percentage of the joint classification.

census a count of all the elements in a population.

central limit theorem the sample means of repeatedly drawn samples will be distributed around the population mean; for sufficiently large samples (i.e., $n = 30+$), approximates a normal distribution.

central tendency a measure of location, most commonly the mean, median, and mode.

central tendency (error of) an error that results because the participant is reluctant to give extreme judgments, usually due to lack of knowledge.

centroid a term used for the multivariate mean scores in MANOVA.

checklist a measurement question that poses numerous alternatives and encourages multiple unordered responses; see *multiple-choice, multiple-response.*

chi-square-based measures tests to detect the strength of the relationship between the variables tested with a chi-square test: phi, Cramer's *V,* and contingency coefficient *C.*

chi-square (χ^2) test a test of significance used for nominal and ordinal measurements.

children's panel a series of focus group sessions where the same child may participate in up to three groups in one year, with each experience several months apart.

chronologic interviewing see **sequential interviewing.**

classical statistics an objective view of probability in which the hypothesis is rejected, or not, based on the sample data collected.

classification question a measurement question that provides sociological-demographic variables for use in grouping participants' answers (nominal, ordinal, interval, or ratio data).

closed question/response a measurement question that presents the participant with a fixed set of choices (nominal, ordinal, or interval data).

cluster analysis identifies homogeneous subgroups of study objects or participants and then studies the data by these subgroups.

cluster sampling a sampling plan that involves dividing the population into subgroups and then draws a sample from each subgroup, a single-stage or multistage design.

clustering a cluster analysis technique that assigns each data record to a group or segment automatically by clustering algorithms that identify the similar characteristics in the data set and then partition them into groups.

code of ethics an organization's codified set of norms or standards of behavior that guide moral choices about research behavior; effective codes are regulative, protect the public interest, are behavior-specific, and are enforceable.

codebook the coding rules for assigning numbers or other symbols to each variable; a.k.a. *coding scheme.*

coding assigning numbers or other symbols to responses so that they can be tallied and grouped into a limited number of categories.

coefficient of determination (r^2) the amount of common variance in *X* and *Y,* two variables in regression; the ratio of the line of best fit's error over that incurred by using the mean value of *Y.*

collinearity when two independent variables are highly correlated; causes estimated regression coefficients to fluctuate widely, making interpretation difficult.

communality in factor analysis, the estimate of the variance in each variable that is explained by the factors being studied.

communication approach a study approach involving questioning or surveying people (by personal interview, telephone, mail, computer, or some combination of these) and recording their responses for analysis.

communication study the researcher questions the participants and collects their responses by personal or impersonal means.

comparative scale a scale where the participant evaluates an object against a standard using a numerical, graphical, or verbal scale.

component sorts a projective technique where participants are presented with flash cards containing component features and asked to create new combinations.

computer-administered telephone survey a telephone survey via voice-synthesized computer questions; data are tallied continuously.

computer-assisted personal interview (CAPI) a personal, face-to-face interview (IDI) with computer-sequenced questions, employing visualization techniques; real-time data entry possible.

computer-assisted self-interview (CASI) computer-delivered survey that is self-administered by the participant.

computer-assisted telephone interview (CATI) a telephone interview with computer-sequenced questions and real-time data entry; usually in a central location with interviewers in acoustically isolated interviewing carrels; data are tallied continuously.

concealment a technique in an observation study where the observer is shielded from the participant to avoid error caused by observer's presence; this is accomplished by one-way mirrors, hidden cameras, hidden microphones, etc.

concept a bundle of meanings or characteristics associated with certain concrete, unambiguous events, objects, conditions, or situations.

conceptual scheme the interrelationships between concepts and constructs.

concordant when a participant that ranks higher on one ordinal variable also ranks higher on another variable, the pairs of variables are concordant.

confidence interval the combination of interval range and degree of confidence.

confidence level the probability that the results will be correct.

confidentiality a privacy guarantee to retain validity of the research, as well as to protect participants.

confirmatory data analysis an analytical process guided by classical statistical inference in its use of significance and confidence.

conjoint analysis measures complex decision making that requires multiattribute judgments; uses input from nonmetric independent variables to secure part-worths that represent the importance of each aspect of the participant's overall assessment; produces a scale value for each attribute or property.

consensus scaling scale development by a panel of experts evaluating instrument items based on topical relevance and lack of ambiguity.

constant-sum scale the participant allocates points to more than one attribute or property indicant, such that they total to 100 or 10; a.k.a. *fixed-sum scale.*

construct a definition specifically invented to represent an abstract phenomenon for a given research project.

construct validity see **validity, construct.**

content analysis a flexible, widely applicable tool for measuring the semantic content of a communication—including counts, categorizations, associations, interpretations, etc. (e.g., used to study the content of speeches, ads, newspaper and magazine editorials, focus group and IDI transcripts); contains four types of items: syntactical, referential, propositional, and thematic; initial process is done by computer.

content validity see **validity, content.**

contingency coefficient C a measure of association for nominal, nonparametric variables; used with any-size chi-square

table, the upper limit varies with table sizes; does not provide direction of the association or reflect causation.

contingency table a cross-tabulation table constructed for statistical testing, with the test determining whether the classification variables are independent.

control the ability to replicate a scenario and dictate a particular outcome; the ability to exclude, isolate, or manipulate the influence of a variable in a study; a critical factor in inference from an experiment, implies that all factors, with the exception of the independent variable (IV), must be held constant and not confounded with another variable that is not part of the study.

control dimension in quota sampling, a descriptor used to define the sample's characteristics (e.g., age, education, religion).

control group a group of participants that is not exposed to the independent variable being studied but still generates a measure for the dependent variable.

control situation questions a classification of management questions that includes monitoring or diagnosing various ways in which an organization is failing to achieve its established goals.

control variable a variable introduced to help interpret the relationship between variables.

controlled test market real-time test of a product through arbitrarily selected distribution partners.

controlled vocabulary carefully defined subject hierarchies used to search some bibliographic databases.

convenience sample nonprobability sample where element selection is based on ease of accessibility.

convenience sampling nonprobability sampling where researchers use any readily available individuals as participants.

convergent interviewing an IDI technique for interviewing a limited number of experts as participants in a sequential series of IDIs; after each successive interview, the researcher refines the questions, hoping to converge on the central issues in a topic area; sometimes called convergent and divergent interviewing.

correlation the relationship by which two or more variables change together, such that systematic changes in one accompany systematic changes in the other.

correlational hypothesis a statement indicating that variables occur together in some specified manner without implying that one causes the other.

Cramer's V a measure of association for nominal, nonparametric variables; used with larger than 2×2 chi-square tables; does not provide direction of the association or reflect causation; ranges from zero to $+1.0$.

creativity session qualitative technique where an individual activity exercise is followed by a sharing/discussion session, where participants build on one another's creative ideas; often used with children; may be conducted before or during IDIs or group interviews; usually consists of drawing, visual compilation, or writing exercises.

criterion-related validity see **validity, criterion-related.**

criterion variable see **dependent variable.**

critical incident technique an IDI technique involving sequentially asked questions to reveal, in narrative form, what led up to an incident being studied; exactly what the observed party did or did not do that was especially effective or ineffective;

the outcome or result of this action; and why this action was effective or what more effective action might have been expected.

critical path method (CPM) a scheduling tool for complex or large research proposals that cites milestones and time involved between milestones.

critical value the dividing point(s) between the region of acceptance and the region of rejection; these values can be computed in terms of the standardized random variable due to the normal distribution of sample means.

cross-sectional study the study is conducted only once and reveals a snapshot of one point in time.

cross-tabulation a technique for comparing data from two or more categorical variables.

cultural interview an IDI technique that asks a participant to relate his or her experiences with a culture or subculture, including the knowledge passed on by prior generations and the knowledge participants have or plan to pass on to future generations.

cumulative scale a scale development technique in which scale items are tested based on a scoring system, where agreement with one extreme scale item results also in endorsement of all other items that take a less extreme position.

custom-designed measurement questions questions formulated specifically for the project at hand.

custom researcher crafts a research design unique to the marketing decision maker's dilemma.

data information (attitudes, behavior, motivations, attributes, etc.) collected from participants or observations (mechanical or direct) or from secondary sources.

data analysis the process of editing and reducing accumulated data to a manageable size, developing summaries, looking for patterns, and applying statistical techniques.

data case see **record**.

data entry the process of converting information gathered by secondary or primary methods to a medium for viewing and manipulation; usually done by keyboarding or optical scanning.

data field a single element of data from all participants in a study.

data file a set of data records (all responses from all participants in a study).

data mart intermediate storage facility that compiles locally required information.

data mining applying mathematical models to extract meaningful knowledge from volumes of data contained within internal data marts or data warehouses; purpose is to identify valid, novel, useful, and ultimately understandable patterns in data.

data preparation the processes that ensure the accuracy of data and their conversion from raw form into categories appropriate for analysis; includes editing, coding, and data entry.

data visualization the process of viewing aggregate data on multiple dimensions to gain a deeper, intuitive understanding of the data.

data warehouse electronic storehouse where vast arrays of collected integrated data are stored by categories to facilitate retrieval, interpretation, and sorting by data mining techniques.

database a collection of data organized for computerized retrieval; defines data fields, data records, and data files.

debriefing explains the truth to participants and describes the major goals of the research study and the reasons for using deception.

deception when participants are told only part of the truth or the truth is fully compromised to prevent biasing participants or to protect sponsor confidentiality.

decision rule the criterion for judging the attractiveness of two or more alternatives when using a decision variable.

decision support system (DSS) numerous elements of data organized for retrieval and use in marketing decision making.

decision variable a quantifiable characteristic, attribute, or outcome on which a choice decision will be made.

deduction a form of reasoning in which the conclusion must necessarily follow from the reasons given; a deduction is valid if it is impossible for the conclusion to be false if the premises are true.

dependency techniques those techniques where criterion or dependent variables and predictor or independent variables are present (e.g., multiple regression, MANOVA, discriminant analysis).

dependent variable (DV) the variable measured, predicted, or otherwise monitored by the researcher; expected to be affected by a manipulation of the independent variable; a.k.a. *criterion variable*.

descriptive hypothesis states the existence, size, form, or distribution of some variable.

descriptive statistics display characteristics of the location, spread, and shape of a data array.

descriptive study attempts to describe or define a subject, often by creating a profile of a group of problems, people, or events, through the collection of data and the tabulation of the frequencies on research variables or their interaction; the study reveals who, what, when, where, or how much; the study concerns a univariate question or hypothesis in which the research asks about or states something about the size, form, distribution, or existence of a variable.

deviation scores displays distance of an observation from the mean.

dichotomous question a measurement question that offers two mutually exclusive and exhaustive alternatives (nominal data).

dictionary secondary source that defines words, terms, or jargon unique to a discipline; may include information on people, events, or organizations that shape the discipline; an excellent source of acronyms.

direct observation when the observer is physically present and personally monitors and records the behavior of the participant.

directory a reference source used to identify contact information (e.g., name, address, phone); many are free, but the most comprehensive are proprietary.

discordant when a subject that ranks higher on one ordinal variable ranks lower on another variable, the pairs of variables are discordant; as discordant pairs increase over concordant pairs, the association becomes negative.

discriminant analysis a technique using two or more independent interval or ratio variables to classify the observations in the categories of a norminal dependent variable.

discussion guide the list of topics to be discussed in an unstructured interview (e.g., focus group); a.k.a. *interview guide*.

disguised question a measurement question designed to conceal the question's and study's true purpose.

disk-by-mail (DBM) survey a type of computer-assisted self-interview, where the survey and its management software, on computer disk, are delivered by mail to the participant.

disproportionate sampling see **stratified sampling, disproportionate.**

distribution (of data) the array of value counts from lowest to highest value, resulting from the tabulation of incidence for each variable by value.

"don't know" (DK) response a response given when a participant has insufficient knowledge, direction, or willingness to answer a question.

double-barreled question a measurement question that includes two or more questions in one that the participant might need to answer differently; a question that requests so much content that it would be better if separate questions were asked.

double-blind study design when neither the researcher nor the participant knows when a subject is being exposed to the experimental treatment.

double sampling a procedure for selecting a subsample from a sample; a.k.a. *sequential sampling* or *multiphase sampling.*

"dummy" table displays data one expects to secure during data analysis; each dummy table is a cross-tabulation between two or more variables.

dummy variable nominal variables converted for use in multivariate statistics; coded 0, 1, as all other variables must be interval or ratio measures.

dyad (paired interview) a group interview done in pairs (e.g., best friends, spouses, superior-subordinate, strangers); used often with children.

EDA see **exploratory data analysis.**

editing a process for detecting errors and data omissions and correcting them when possible; certifies that minimum data quality standards are met.

eigenvalue proportion of total variance in all the variables that is accounted for by a factor.

electronic test market test that combines store distribution, consumer scanner panel data, and household-level media delivery.

empiricism observations and propositions based on sense experience and/or derived from such experience by methods of inductive logic, including mathematics and statistics.

encyclopedia a secondary source that provides background or historical information on a topic, including names or terms that can enhance your search results in other sources.

environmental control holding constant the physical environment of the experiment.

equal-appearing interval scale an expensive, time-consuming type of consensus scaling that results in an interval rating scale for attitude measurement; a.k.a. *Thurstone scale.*

equivalence when an instrument secures consistent results with repeated measures by the same investigator or different samples.

error discrepancy between the sample value and the true population value that occurs when the participant fails to answer fully and accurately—either by choice or because of inaccurate or incomplete knowledge.

error of central tendency see **central tendency (error of).**

error of leniency see **leniency (error of).**

error term the deviations of the actual values of Y from the regression line (representing the mean value of Y for a particular value of X).

ethics norms or standards of behavior that guide moral choices about research behavior.

ethnography interviewer and participant collaborate in a field-setting participant observation and unstructured interview; typically takes place where the behavior being observed occurs.

event sampling the process of selecting some elements or behavioral acts or conditions from a population of observable behaviors or conditions to represent the population as a whole.

ex post facto design after-the-fact report on what happened to the measured variable.

executive summary (final report) this document is written as the last element of a research report and either is a concise summary of the major findings, conclusions, and recommendations or is a report in miniature, covering all aspects in abbreviated form.

executive summary (proposal) an informative abstract providing the essentials of the proposal without the details.

experience survey (expert interview) semistructured or unstructured interviews with experts on a topic or dimension of a topic; an exploratory technique where knowledgeable experts share their ideas about important issues or aspects of the subject and relate what is important across the subject's range of experience; usually involves a personal or phone interview.

experiment (experimental study) study involving intervention (manipulation of one or more variables) by the researcher beyond that required for measurement to determine the effect on another variable.

experimental treatment the manipulated independent variable.

expert group interview group interview consisting of individuals exceptionally knowledgeable about the issues or topics to be discussed.

expert interview a discussion with someone knowledgeable about the problem or its possible solutions.

explanatory (causal) hypothesis a statement that describes a relationship between two variables in which one variable leads to a specified effect on the other variable.

explanatory study attempts to explain an event, act, or characteristic measured by research.

explicit attitude an expressed positive or negative evaluation.

exploration the process of collecting information to formulate or refine management, research, investigative, or measurement questions; loosely structured studies that discover future research tasks, including developing concepts, establishing priorities, developing operational definitions, and improving research design; a phase of a research project where the researcher expands understanding of the management dilemma, looks for ways others have addressed and/or solved problems similar to the management dilemma or management question, and gathers background information on the topic to refine the research question; a.k.a. *exploratory study* or *exploratory research.*

exploratory data analysis (EDA) patterns in the collected data guide the data analysis or suggest revisions to the preliminary data analysis plan.

exploratory research see **exploration.**

exploratory study see **exploration.**

exposition statement that describes without attempting to explain.

extemporaneous presentation a conversation-style oral presentation made from minimal notes or an outline.

external validity when an observed causal relationship can be generalized across persons, settings, and times.

extralinguistic observation the recording of vocal, temporal, interaction, and verbal stylistic behaviors of human participants.

extraneous variable (EV) variable to assume (because it has little affect or its impact is randomized) or exclude from a research study.

extranet a private network that uses the Internet protocols and the public telecommunication system to share a business's information, data, or operations with external suppliers, vendors, or customers.

F **ratio** *F* test statistic comparing measurements of *k* independent samples.

factor denotes an independent variable (IV) in an experiment; factors are divided into treatment levels for the experiment.

factor analysis a technique for discovering patterns among the variables to determine if an underlying combination of the original variables (a factor) can summarize the original set.

factor scales types of scales that deal with multidimensional content and underlying dimensions, such as scalogram, factor, and cluster analyses, and metric and nonmetric multidimensional scaling.

factors in factor analysis, the result of transforming a set of variables into a new set of composite variables; these factors are linear and not correlated with each other.

field conditions the actual environmental conditions where the dependent variable occurs.

field experiment a study of the dependent variable in actual environmental conditions.

filter question see **screen question.**

findings nondisclosure a type of confidentiality; when the sponsor restricts the researcher from discussing the findings of the research project.

five-number summary the median, the upper and lower quartiles, and the largest and smallest observations of a variable's distribution.

fixed-sum scale see **constant-sum scale.**

focus group the simultaneous involvement of a small number of research participants (usually 8 to 10) who interact at the direction of a moderator in order to generate data on a particular issue or topic; widely used in exploratory studies; usually lasts 90 minutes to 2 hours; can be conducted in person or via phone or videoconference.

forced-choice rating scale requires that participants select from available alternatives.

forced ranking scale a scale where the participant orders several objects or properties of objects; faster than paired comparison to obtain a rank order.

formal study research question–driven process involving precise procedures for data collection and interpretation; tests the hypothesis or answers the research questions posed.

format how the information is presented and how easy it is to find a specific piece of information within a secondary source; one of five factors used to evaluate the value of a secondary source.

forward selection in modeling and regression, sequentially adds the variables to a regression model that results in the largest R^2 increase; see also *backward elimination* and *stepwise selection.*

free-response question a measurement question where the participant chooses the words to frame the answer; a.k.a. *open-ended question* (nominal, ordinal, or ratio data).

frequency distribution ordered array of all values for a variable.

frequency table arrays category codes from lowest value to highest value, with columns for count, percent, valid percent, and cumulative percent.

full-service marketing researcher a firm with both quantitative and qualitative methodology expertise that conducts all phases of research from planning to insight development, often serving as both research firm and consultant.

funnel approach a type of question sequencing that moves the participant from general to more specific questions and is designed to learn the participant's frame of reference while extracting full disclosure of information on the topic (nominal, ordinal, interval, or ratio data).

gamma (γ) uses a preponderance of evidence of concordant pairs versus discordant pairs to predict association; the gamma value is the proportional reduction of error when prediction is done using preponderance of evidence (values from -1.0 to $+1.0$).

geographic chart uses a map to show regional variations in data.

Geographic Information System (GIS) system of hardware, software, and procedures that capture, store, manipulate, integrate, and display spatially referenced data for solving complex planning and management problems.

goodness of fit a measure of how well the regression model is able to predict *Y.*

graphic rating scale a scale where the participant places his or her response along a line or continuum; the score or measurement is its distance in millimeters from either endpoint.

grounded theory an IDI technique where analysis of the data takes place simultaneously with its collection, with the purpose of developing general concepts or theories with which to analyze the data.

group interview a data collection method using a single interviewer who simultaneously interviews more than one research participant.

halo effect error casued when prior observations influence perceptions of current observations.

handbook a secondary source used to identify key terms, people, or events relevant to the management dilemma or management question.

heterogeneous groups participant group consisting of individuals with a variety of opinions, backgrounds, and actions relative to a topic.

histogram a graphical bar chart that groups continuous data values into equal intervals with one bar for each interval; especially useful for revealing skewness, kurtosis, and modal pattern.

holdout sample the portion of the sample (usually ⅓ or ¼) excluded for later validity testing when the estimating question is first computed; the equation is then used on the holdout data to calculate R^2 for comparison.

homogeneous group participant group consisting of individuals with similar opinions, backgrounds, and actions relative to a topic.

hypothesis a proposition formulated for empirical testing; a tentative descriptive statement that describes the relationship between two or more variables.

hypothetical construct construct inferred only from data; its presumption must be tested.

ill-defined problem one that addresses complex issues and cannot be expressed easily, concisely, or completely.

imaginary universe a projective technique (imagination exercise) where participants are asked to assume that the brand and its users populate an entire universe; they then describe the features of this new world.

imagination exercises a projective technique where participants are asked to relate the properties of one thing/person/brand to another.

implicit attitude an attitude about one object that influences the attitude about other objects.

incidence the number of elements in the population belonging to the category of interest, divided by the total number of elements in the population.

independent variable (IV) the variable manipulated by the researcher, thereby causing an effect or change on the dependent variable.

index secondary data source that helps identify and locate a single book, journal article, author, etc., from among a large set.

indirect observation when the recording of data is done by mechanical, photographic, or electronic means.

individual depth interview (IDI) a type of interview that encourages the participant to talk extensively, sharing as much information as possible; usually lasts one or more hours; three types: structured, semistructured, and unstructured.

induction (inductive reasoning) to draw a conclusion from one or more particular facts or pieces of evidence; the conclusion explains the facts.

inferential statistics includes the estimation of population values and the testing of statistical hypotheses.

informed consent participant gives full consent to participation after receiving full disclosure of the procedures of the proposed survey.

intelligent mark recognition (IMR) software that applies a response template to scanned completed surveys to capture images that may be edited, saved, or processed.

interaction effect the influence that one factor has on another factor.

intercept (β_0) one of two regression coefficients; the value for the linear function when it crosses the Y axis or the estimate of Y when X is zero.

intercept interview a face-to-face communication that targets participants in a centralized location.

interdependency techniques techniques where criterion or dependent variables and predictor or independent variables are not present (e.g., factor analysis, cluster analysis, multidimensional scaling).

internal consistency characteristic of an instrument in which the items are homogeneous; measure of reliability.

internal database collection of data stored by an organization.

internal validity the ability of a research instrument to measure what it is purported to measure; when the conclusion(s) drawn about a demonstrated experimental relationship truly implies cause.

interquartile range (IQR) measures the distance between the first and third quartiles of a data distribution; a.k.a. *midspread;* the distance between the hinges in a boxplot.

interval estimate range of values within which the true population parameter is expected to fall.

interval scale scale with the properties of order and equal distance between points and with mutually exclusive and exhaustive categories; data that incorporate equality of interval (the distance between one measure and the next measure); e.g., temperature scale.

intervening variable (IVV) a factor that affects the observed phenomenon but cannot be seen, measured, or manipulated; thus its effect must be inferred from the effects of the independent and moderating variables on the dependent variable.

interview phone, in-person, or videoconference communication approach to collecting data.

interview guide see **discussion guide.**

interview schedule question list used to guide a structured interview; a.k.a. *questionnaire.*

interviewer error error that results from interviewer influence of the participant; includes problems with motivation, instructions, voice inflections, body language, question or response order, or cheating via falsification of one or more responses.

intranet a private network that is contained within an enterprise; access is restricted to authorized audiences; usually behind a security firewall.

investigative questions questions the researcher must answer to satisfactorily answer the research question; what the marketer feels he or she needs to know to arrive at a conclusion about the management dilemma.

item analysis scale development where instrument designers develop instrument items and test them with a group of participants to determine which highly discriminate between high and low raters.

judgment sampling a purposive sampling where the researcher arbitrarily selects sample units to conform to some criterion.

k-independent-samples tests significance tests when measurements are taken from three or more samples (ANOVA for interval or ratio measures, Kruskal-Wallis for ordinal measures, chi-square for nominal measures).

k-related-samples tests compares measurements from more than two groups from the same sample or more than two measures from the same subject or participant (ANOVA for interval or ratio measures, Friedman for ordinal measures, Cochran Q for nominal measures).

kinesics the study of the use of body motion communication.

kurtosis measure of a data distribution's peakedness or flatness (*ku*); a neutral distribution has a *ku* of 0, a flat distribution is negative, and a peaked distribution is positive.

laboratory conditions studies that occur under conditions that do not simulate actual environmental conditions.

laddering (benefit chain) a projective technique where participants are asked to link functional features to their physical and psychological benefits, both real and ideal.

lambda (λ) a measure of how well the frequencies of one nominal variable predict the frequencies of another variable; values (vary between zero and 1.0) show the direction of the association.

leading question a measurement question whose wording suggests to the participant the desired answer (nominal, ordinal, interval, or ratio data).

leniency (error of) a participant, within a series of evaluations, consistently expresses judgments at one end of a scale; an error that results when the participant is consistently an easy or hard rater.

letter of transmittal the element of the final report that provides the purpose of, scope of, authorization for, and limitations of the study; not necessary for internal projects.

level of significance the probability of rejecting a true null hypothesis.

life history an IDI technique that extracts from a single participant memories and experiences from childhood to the present day regarding a product or service category, brand, or firm.

Likert scale a variation of the summated rating scale, this scale asks a rater to agree or disagree with statements that express either favorable or unfavorable attitudes toward the object. The strength of attitude is reflected in the assigned score, and individual scores may be totaled for an overall attitude measure.

limiters database search protocol for narrowing a search; commonly include date, publication type, and language.

line graph a statistical presentation technique used for time series and frequency distributions over time.

linearity an assumption of correlation analysis, that the collection of data can be described by a straight line passing through the data array.

linguistic observation the observation of human verbal behavior during conversation, presentation, or interaction; may also include content analysis.

literature review recent or historically significant research studies, company data, or industry reports that act as the basis for the proposed study.

literature search a review of books, articles in journals or professional literature, research studies, and Web-published materials that relate to the management dilemma, management question, or research question.

loadings in principal components analysis, the correlation coefficients that estimate the strength of the variables that compose the factor.

longitudinal study the study includes repeated measures over an extended period of time, tracking changes in variables over time; includes panels or cohort groups.

mail survey a relatively low-cost self-administered study both delivered and returned via mail.

main effect the average direct influence that a particular treatment of the IV has on the DV independent of other factors.

management dilemma the problem or opportunity that requires a marketing decision; a symptom of a marketing problem or an early indication of a marketing opportunity.

management question the management dilemma restated in question format; categorized as "choice of objectives," "generation and evaluation of solutions," or "troubleshooting or control of a situation."

management report a report written for the nontechnically oriented manager or client.

management–research question hierarchy process of sequential question formulation that leads a manager or researcher from management dilemma to investigative questions.

mapping rules a scheme for assigning numbers to aspects of an empirical event.

marginal(s) a term for the column and row totals in a cross-tabulation.

marketing an organizational function and a set of processes for creating, communicating, and delivering value to customers and for managing customer relationships in ways that benefit the organization and its stakeholders.

marketing concept the primary strategy for achieving an organization's marketing goals is to satisfy its customers and establish lifetime customer-organization relationships.

marketing intelligence system (MkIS) a system of ongoing information collection about events and trends in the technological, economic, political and legal, demographic, cultural, social, and competitive arenas.

marketing research a systematic inquiry that provides information to guide marketing decisions; the process of determining, acquiring, analyzing and synthesizing, and disseminating relevant marketing data, information, and insights to decision makers in ways that mobilize the organization to take appropriate marketing actions that, in turn, maximize organizational performance.

marketing strategy the general approach an organization will follow to achieve its marketing goals.

marketing tactics specific, timed activities that execute a marketing strategy.

matching a process analogous to quota sampling for assigning participants to experimental and control groups by having participants match every descriptive characteristic used in the research; used when random assignment is not possible; an attempt to eliminate the effect of confounding variables that group participants so that the confounding variable is present proportionally in each group.

MDS see **multidimensional scaling.**

mean the arithmetic average of a data distribution.

mean square the variance computed as an average or mean.

measurement assigning numbers to empirical events in compliance with a mapping rule.

measurement questions the questions asked of the participants or the observations that must be recorded.

measures of location term for measure of central tendency in a distribution of data; see **central tendency.**

measures of shape statistics that describe departures from the symmetry of a distribution; a.k.a. *moments, skewness,* and *kurtosis.*

measures of spread statistics that describe how scores cluster or scatter in a distribution; a.k.a. *dispersion* or *variability* (variance, standard deviation, range, interquartile range, and quartile deviation).

median the midpoint of a data distribution where half the cases fall above and half the cases fall below.

method of least squares a procedure for finding a regression line that keeps errors (deviations from actual value to the line value) to a minimum.

metric measures statistical techniques using interval and ratio measures.

mini-group a group interview involving two to six people.

missing data information that is missing about a participant or data record; should be discovered and rectified during data preparation phase of analysis; e.g., miscoded data, out-of-range data, or extreme values.

mode the most frequently occurring value in a data distribution; data may have more than one mode.

model a representation of a system that is constructed to study some aspect of that system or the system as a whole.

moderating variable (MV) a second independent variable, believed to have a significant contributory or contingent effect on the originally stated IV-DV relationship.

moderator a trained interviewer used for group interviews such as focus groups.

multicollinearity when more than two independent variables are highly correlated.

multidimensional scaling (MDS) a scaling technique to simultaneously measure more than one attribute of the participant or object; results are usually mapped; develops a geometric picture or map of the locations of some objects relative to others on various dimensions or properties; especially useful for difficult-to-measure constructs.

multiphase sampling see **double sampling**.

multiple-choice, multiple-response scale a scale that offers the participant multiple options and solicits one or more answers (nominal or ordinal data); a.k.a. *checklist*.

multiple-choice question a measurement question that offers more than two category responses but seeks a single answer.

multiple-choice, single-response scale a measurement question that poses more than two category responses but seeks a single answer, or one that seeks a single rating from a gradation of preference, interest, or agreement (nominal or ordinal data); a.k.a *multiple-choice question*.

multiple comparison tests compare group means following the finding of a statistically significant *F* test.

multiple rating list scale a single interval or ordinal numerical scale where raters respond to a series of objects; results facilitate visualization.

multiple regression a statistical tool used to develop a self-weighting estimating equation that predicts values for a dependent variable from the values of independent variables; controls confounding variables to better evaluate the contribution of other variables; tests and explains a causal theory.

multivariate analysis statistical techniques that focus upon and bring out in bold relief the structure of simultaneous relationships among three or more phenomena.

multivariate analysis of variance (MANOVA) assesses the relationship between two or more dependent variables and classificatory variables or factors; frequently used to test differences among related samples.

narrative see **oral history**.

negative leniency (error of) an error that results when the participant is consistently a hard or critical rater.

nominal scale scale with mutually exclusive and collectively exhaustive categories, but without the properties of order, distance, or unique origin.

noncontact rate ratio of noncontacts (no answer, busy, answering machine, and disconnects) to all potential contacts.

nondisclosure various types of confidentiality involving research projects, including sponsor, findings, and purpose nondisclosures.

nonexpert groups participants in a group interview who have at least some desired information but at an unknown level.

nonmetric measures statistical techniques using ordinal and nominal measures (nonparametric).

nonparametric tests significance tests for data derived from nominal and ordinal scales.

nonprobability sampling an arbitrary and subjective procedure where each population element does not have a known nonzero chance of being included; no attempt is made to generate a statistically representative sample.

nonresistant statistics a statistical measure that is susceptible to the effects of extreme values; e.g., mean, standard deviation.

nonresponse error error that develops when an interviewer cannot locate the person with whom the study requires communication or when the targeted participant refuses to participate; especially troublesome in studies using probability sampling.

nonverbal observation observation of human behavior without the use of conversation between observers and participants (e.g., body movement, facial expressions, exchanged glances, eye blinks).

normal distribution a frequency distribution of many natural phenomena; graphically shaped like a symmetrical curve.

normal probability plot compares the observed values with those expected from a normal distribution.

null hypothesis (H_0) assumption that no difference exists between the sample parameter and the population statistic.

numerical scale a scale where equal intervals separate the numeric scale points, while verbal anchors serve as labels for the extreme points.

objects concepts defined by ordinary experience.

observation the full range of monitoring behavioral and nonbehavioral activities and conditions (including record analysis, physical condition analysis, physical process analysis, nonverbal analysis, linguistic analysis, extralinguistic analysis, and spatial analysis).

observation checklist a measurement instrument for recording data in an observation study; analogous to a questionnaire in a communication study.

observation playgroup an observation technique that involves observing children at play, often with targeted objects (toys or materials); observers are usually behind one-way mirrors.

observation study a monitoring approach to collecting data where the researcher inspects the activities of a subject or the nature of some material without attempting to elicit responses from anyone; a.k.a. *monitoring*.

observed significance level the probability value compared to the significance level (e.g., .05) chosen for testing and on this basis the null hypothesis is either rejected or not rejected.

observer drift a source of error affecting categorization caused by decay in reliability or validity of recorded observations over time.

OCR see **optical character recognition.**

omnibus researcher fields research studies, often by survey, at regular, predetermined intervals.

omnibus study combines the questions of several marketing decision makers who need information from the same population.

one-sample tests tests that involve measures taken from a single sample compared to a specified population.

one-tailed test a test of a null hypothesis that assumes the sample parameter is not the same as the population statistic, but that the difference is in only one direction.

online focus group a type of focus group where participants use the technology of the Internet, including e-mail, Web sites, Usenet newsgroups, or an Internet chat room, to approximate the interaction of a face-to-face focus group.

open-ended question see **free-response question.**

operational definition a definition for a variable stated in terms of specific testing criteria or operations, specifying what must be counted, measured, or gathered through our senses.

operationalized the process of transforming concepts and constructs into measurable variables suitable for testing.

optical character recognition (OCR) software programs that transfer printed text into a computer file in order to edit and use the information without rekeying the data.

optical mark recognition (OMR) software that uses a spreadsheet-style interface to read and process data from user-created forms.

optical scanning a data entry process whereby answers are recorded on computer-readable forms and then scanned to form a data record; reduces data handling and the errors that accompany such data handling.

oral history (narrative) an IDI technique that asks participants to relate their personal experiences and feelings related to historical events or past behavior.

ordinal measures measures of association between variables generating ordinal data.

ordinal scale scale with mutually exclusive and collectively exhaustive categories, as well as the property of order, but not distance or unique origin; data capable of determining greater-than, equal-to, or less-than status of a property or an object.

outliers data points that exceed +1.5 the interquartile range (IQR).

p **value** probability of observing a sample value as extreme as, or more extreme than, the value actually observed, given that the null hypothesis is true.

pace the rate at which the printed page presents information to the reader; it should be slower when the material is complex, faster when the material is straightforward.

paired-comparison scale the participant chooses a preferred object between several pairs of objects on some property; results in a rank ordering of objects.

paired interview see **dyad.**

panel a group of potential participants who have indicated a willingness to participate in research studies; often used for longitudinal communication studies; may be used for both qualitative and quantitative research.

parametric tests significance tests for data from interval and ratio scales.

Pareto diagram a graphical presentation that represents frequency data as a bar chart, ordered from most to least, overlayed with a line graph denoting the cumulative percentage at each variable level.

participant the subject, respondent, or sample element in a research study.

participant-initiated response error error that occurs when the participant fails to answer fully and accurately—either by choice or because of inaccurate or incomplete knowledge.

participant observation when the observer is physically involved in the research situation and interacts with the participant to influence some observation measures.

participants' perception the subtle or major changes that occur in participants' responses when they perceive that a research study is being conducted.

path analysis describes through regression an entire structure of linkages that have been advanced by a causal theory.

path diagram presents predictive and associative relationships among constructs and indicators in a structural model.

Pearson correlation coefficient the *r* symbolizes the estimate of strength of linear association and its direction between interval and ratio variables; based on sampling data and varies over a range of +1 to −1; the prefix (+, −) indicates the direction of the relationship (positive or inverse), while the number represents the strength of the relationship (the closer to 1, the stronger the relationship; 0 = no relationship); and the *p* represents the population correlation.

permission surveying the act of surveying prospects or customers who have given permission for such engagement, usually through panel membership.

personal interview a two-way communication initiated by an interviewer to obtain information from a participant; face-to-face, phone, or Internet.

personification a projective technique (imagination exercise) where participants are asked to imagine inanimate objects with the traits, characteristics and features, and personalities of humans.

phi (ϕ) a measure of association for nominal, nonparametric variables; ranges from zero to +1.0 and is used best with 2×2 chi-square tables; does not provide direction of the association or reflect causation.

physical condition analysis the recording of observations of current conditions resulting from prior decisions; includes inventory, signs, obstacles or hazards, cleanliness, etc.

physical trace a type of observation that collects measures of wear data (erosion) and accretion data (deposit) rather than direct observation (e.g., a study of trash).

pictograph a bar chart using pictorial symbols rather than bars to represent frequency data; the symbol has an association with the subject of the statistical presentation and one symbol unit represents a specific count of that variable.

pie chart uses sections of a circle (slices of a pie) to represent 100 percent of a frequency distribution of the subject being graphed; not appropriate for changes over time.

pilot test a trial collection of data to detect weaknesses in design and instrumentation and provide proxy data for selection of a probability sample; see also *pretesting.*

point estimate sample mean; our best predictor of the unknown population mean.

population the elements about which we wish to make some inferences.

population element the individual participant or object on which the measurement is taken; a.k.a. *population unit, sample element, sample unit.*

population parameter a summary descriptor of a variable of interest in the population; e.g., incidence, mean, variance.

population proportion of incidence the number of category elements in the population, divided by the number of elements in the population.

portal a Web page that serves as a gateway to more remote Web publications; usually includes one or more directories, search engines, and other user features such as news and weather.

power of the test 1 minus the probability of committing a Type II error (1 minus the probability that we will correctly reject the false null hypothesis).

practical significance when a statistically significant difference has real importance to the decision maker.

practicality a characteristic of sound measurement concerned with a wide range of factors of economy, convenience, and interpretability.

PRE see **proportional reduction in error.**

precision one of the considerations in determining sample validity: the degree to which estimates from the sample reflect the measure taken by a census; measured by the standard error of the estimate—the smaller the error, the greater the precision of the estimate.

precoding assigning codebook codes to variables in a study and recording them on the questionnaire; eliminates a separate coding sheet.

predesigned measurement questions questions that have been formulated and tested by previous researchers, are recorded in the literature, and may be applied literally or be adapted for the project at hand.

prediction and confidence bands bow-tie-shaped confidence intervals around a predictor; predictors farther from the mean have larger bandwidths in regression analysis.

predictive study attempts to predict when and in what situations an event, act, or characteristic will occur.

predictor variable see **independent variable.**

pretasking a variety of creative and mental exercises to prepare participants for individual or group interviews, such as an IDI or focus group; intended to increase understanding of participants' own thought processes and bring their ideas, opinions, and attitudes to the surface.

pretesting the assessment of questions and instruments before the start of a study; an established practice for discovering errors in questions, question sequencing, instructions, skip directions, etc.; see also *pilot test.*

primacy effect order bias where the participant tends to choose the first alternative.

primary data data the researcher collects to address the specific problem at hand—the research question.

primary sources original works of research or raw data without interpretation or pronouncements that represent an official opinion or position; include memos, letters, complete interviews or speeches, laws, regulations, court decisions, and most government data, including census, economic, and labor data; the most authoritative of all sources.

principal components analysis one method of factor analysis that transforms a set of variables into a new set of composite variables; these variables are linear and not correlated with each other; see also *factor analysis.*

probability sampling a controlled, randomized procedure that ensures that each population element is given a known nonzero chance of selection; used to draw participants that are representative of a target population; necessary for projecting findings from the sample to the target population.

probing techniques for stimulating participants to answer more fully and relevantly to posed questions.

process (activity) analysis observation by a time study of stages in a process, evaluated on both effectiveness and efficiency; includes traffic flow within distribution centers and retailers, paperwork flow, customer complaint resolution, etc.

project management the process of planning and managing a detailed project, though tables and charts with detail responsibilities and deadlines; details relationship between researchers, their assistants, sponsors, and suppliers; often results in a Gantt chart.

projective techniques qualitative methods that encourage the participant to reveal hidden or suppressed attitudes, ideas, emotions, and motives; various techniques (e.g., sentence completion tests, cartoon or balloon tests, word association tests) used as part of an interview to disguise the study objective and allow the participant to transfer or project attitudes and behavior on sensitive subjects to third parties; the data collected via these techniques are often difficult to interpret (nominal, ordinal, or ratio data).

properties characteristics of objects that are measured; a person's properties are his or her weight, height, posture, hair color, etc.

proportion percentage of elements in the distribution that meet a criterion.

proportional reduction in error (PRE) measures of association used with contingency tables (a.k.a *cross-tabulations*) to predict frequencies.

proportionate sampling see **stratified random sampling, proportionate.**

proposal a work plan, prospectus, outline, statement of intent, or draft plan for a research project, including proposed budget.

proposition a statement about concepts that may be judged as true or false if it refers to observable phenomena.

proprietary methodology a research program or technique that is owned by a single firm; may be branded.

proxemics the study of the use of space; the study of how people organize the territory around them and the discrete distances they maintain between themselves and others.

proximity an index of perceived similarity or dissimilarity between objects.

pure research (basic research) designed to solve problems of a theoretical nature with little direct impact on strategic or tactical decisions.

purpose the explicit or hidden agenda of the authors of the secondary source; one of five factors in secondary source evaluation.

purpose nondisclosure a type of confidentiality; when the sponsor camouflages the true research objective of the research project.

purposive sampling a nonprobability sampling process where researchers choose participants arbitrarily for their unique characteristics or their experiences, attitudes, or perceptions.

Q-sort participant sorts a deck of cards (representing properties or objects) into piles that represent points along a continuum.

qualitative research interpretive techniques that seek to describe, decode, translate, and otherwise come to terms with the meaning, not the frequency, of certain phenomena; a fundamental approach of exploration, including individual depth interviews, group interviews, participant observation, videotaping of participants, projective techniques and psychological testing, case studies, street ethnography, elite interviewing, document analysis, and proxemics and kinesics; see also *content analysis.*

qualitative techniques nonquantitative data collection used to increase understanding of a topic.

quantitative research the precise count of some behavior, knowledge, opinion, or attitude.

quartile deviation (*Q*) a measure of dispersion for ordinal data involving the median and quartiles; the median plus one quartile deviation on either side encompasses 50 percent of the observations and eight cover the full range of data.

questionnaire an instrument delivered to the participant via personal (intercept) or nonpersonal (computer-delivered, mail-delivered) means that is completed by the participant.

quota matrix a means of visualizing the matching process.

quota sampling purposive sampling where relevant characteristics are used to stratify the sample.

random assignment a process that uses a randomized sample frame for assigning sample units to test groups in an attempt to ensure that the groups are as comparable as possible with respect to the DV; each subject must have an equal chance for exposure to each level of the independent variable.

random dialing a computerized process that chooses phone exchanges or exchange blocks and generates numbers within these blocks for telephone surveys.

random error error that occurs erratically, without pattern; see also **sampling error.**

randomization using random selection procedures to assign sample units to either the experimental or control group to achieve equivalence between groups.

range the difference between the largest and smallest scores in the data distribution; a very rough measure of spread of a dispersion.

ranking question a measurement question that asks the participant to compare and order two or more objects or properties using a numeric scale.

ranking scale a scale that scores an object or property by making a comparison and determining order among two or more objects or properties; uses a numeric scale and provides ordinal data; see also **ranking question.**

rating question a question that asks the participant to position each property or object on a verbal, numeric, or graphic continuum.

rating scale a scale that scores an object or property without making a direct comparison to another object or property; either verbal, numeric, or graphic; see also **rating question.**

ratio scale a scale with the properties of categorization, order, equal intervals, and unique origin; numbers used as measurements have numeric value; e.g., weight of an object.

reactivity response the phenomenon where participants alter their behavior due to the presence of the observer.

readability index measures the difficulty level of written material; e.g., Flesch Reading Ease Score, Flesch Kincaid Grade Level, Gunning's Fog Index; most word processing programs calculate one or several of the indexes.

recency effect order bias where the participant tends to choose the last alternative.

reciprocal relationship when two variables mutually influence or reinforce each other.

record a set of data fields that are related, usually by subject or participant; represented by rows in a spreadsheet or statistical database; a.k.a. *data case, data record.*

record analysis the extraction of data from current or historical records, either private or in the public domain; a technique of data mining.

recruitment screener semistructured or structured interview guide designed to ensure the interviewer that the prospect will be a good participant for the planned research.

refusal rate ratio of participants who decline the interview to all potential/eligible contacts.

region of acceptance area between the two regions of rejection based on a chosen level of significance (two-tailed test) or the area above/below the region of rejection (one-tailed test).

region of rejection area beyond the region of acceptance set by the level of significance.

regression analysis uses simple and multiple predictions to predict *Y* from *X* values.

regression coefficients intercept and slope coefficients; the two association measures between *X* and *Y* variables.

relational hypothesis describes the relationship between two variables with respect to some case; relationships are correlational or explanatory.

relevant population those elements in the population most likely to have the information specified in the investigative questions.

reliability a characteristic of measurement concerned with accuracy, precision, and consistency; a necessary but not sufficient condition for validity (if the measure is not reliable, it cannot be valid).

reliability, equivalence a characteristic of measurement in which instruments can secure consistent results by the same investigator or by different samples.

reliability, internal consistency a characteristic of an instrument in which the items are homogeneous.

reliability, stability a characteristic of measurement in which an instrument can secure consistent results with repeated measurements of the same person or object.

replication the process of repeating an experiment with different subject groups and conditions to determine the average effect of the IV across people, situations, and times.

reporting study provides an account or summation of data, including descriptive statistics, on a particular topic, but requires little inference or conclusion drawing.

request for proposal (RFP) a formal bid request for research to be done by an outside supplier of research services.

research design the blueprint for fulfilling research objectives and answering questions.

research process various decision stages involved in a research project and the relationship between those stages.

research question(s) the hypothesis that best states the objective of the research; the answer to this question would provide the manager with the desired information necessary to make a decision with respect to the management dilemma.

research report the document that describes the research project, its findings, analysis of the findings, interpretations, conclusions, and, sometimes, recommendations.

research variable see **variable.**

residual the difference between the regression line value of Y and the real Y value; what remains after the regression line is fit.

resistant statistics statistical measures relatively unaffected by outliers within a data set; e.g., median and quartiles.

respondent a participant in a study; a.k.a. *participant* or *subject.*

response error when the participant fails to give a correct or complete answer.

return on marketing investment (ROMI) the calculation of the financial return for all marketing expenditures.

right to privacy the participant's right to refuse to be interviewed or to refuse to answer any questions in an interview.

right to quality the sponsor's right to an appropriate, value-laden research design and data handling and reporting techniques.

right to safety the right of interviewers, surveyors, experimenters, observers, and participants to be protected from any threat of physical or psychological harm.

rotation in principal components analysis, a technique used to provide a more simple and interpretable picture of the relationships between factors and variables.

sample a group of cases, participants, events, or records consisting of a portion of the target population, carefully selected to represent that population; see also **pilot test, data mining.**

sample statistics descriptors of the relevant variables computed from sample data.

sampling the process of selecting some elements from a population to represent that population.

sampling error error created by the sampling process; the error not accounted for by systematic variance.

sampling frame list of elements in the population from which the sample is actually drawn.

scaling the assignment of numbers or symbols to an indicant of a property or objects to impart some of the characteristics of the numbers to the property; assigned according to value or magnitude.

scalogram analysis a procedure for determining whether a set of items forms a unidimensional scale; used to determine if an item is appropriate for scaling.

scatterplot a visual technique that depicts both the direction and the shape of a relationship between variables

scientific method systematic, empirically based procedures for generating replicable research; includes direct observation of phenomena; clearly defined variables, methods, and procedures; empirically testable hypotheses; the ability to rule out rival hypotheses; and statistical rather than linguistic justification of conclusions.

scope the breadth and depth of topic coverage of a secondary source (by time frame, geography, criteria for inclusion, etc.); one of the five factors for evaluating the quality of secondary sources.

screen question question to qualify the participant's knowledge about the target questions of interest or experience necessary to participate.

search query the combination of keywords and connectors, operators, limiters, and truncation and phrase devices used to conduct electronic searches of secondary data sources; a.k.a. *search statement.*

search statement see **search query.**

secondary data results of studies done by others and for different purposes than the one for which the data are being reviewed.

secondary sources interpretations of primary data generally without new research.

self-administered questionnaire an instrument delivered to the participant via personal (intercept) or nonpersonal (computer-delivered, mail-delivered) means that is completed by the participant without additional contact with an interviewer.

semantic differential (SD) scale measures the psychological meanings of an attitude object and produces interval data; uses bipolar nouns, noun phrases, adjectives, or nonverbal stimuli such as visual sketches.

semantic mapping a projective technique where participants are presented with a four-quadrant map where different variables anchor the two different axes; they then spatially place brands, product components, or organizations within the four quadrants.

semistructured interview an IDI that starts with a few specific questions and then follows the individual's tangents of thought with interviewer probes; questions generally use an open-ended response strategy.

sensitive attitude one that a holder feels uncomfortable sharing with others.

sensory sorts participants are presented with scents, textures, and sounds, usually verbalized on cards, and asked to arrange them by one or more criteria as they relate to a brand, product, event, etc.

sentence completion a projective technique where participants are asked to complete a sentence related to a particular brand, product, event, user group, etc.

sentence outline report planning format; uses complete sentences rather than key words or phrases to draft each report section.

sequential interviewing an IDI technique where the participant is asked questions formed around an anticipated series of activities that did or might have happened; used to stimulate recall within participants of both experiences and emotions; a.k.a. *chronologic interviewing.*

sequential sampling see **double sampling.**

Simalto+Plus an advanced conjoint analysis technique.

simple category scale a scale with two mutually exclusive response choices; a.k.a. *dichotomous scale.*

simple observation unstructured and exploratory observation of participants or objects.

simple prediction when we take the observed values of X to estimate or predict corresponding Y values; see also *regression analysis.*

simple random sample a probability sample in which each element has a known and equal chance of selection.

simulated test market (STM) test of a product conducted in a laboratory setting designed to simulate a traditional shopping environment.

simulation a study in which the conditions of a system or process are replicated.

skewness a measure of a data distribution's deviation from symmetry; if fully symmetrical, the mean, median, and mode are in the same location.

skip interval interval between sample elements drawn from a sample frame in systematic sampling.

skip pattern instructions designed to route or sequence the participant to another question based on the answer to a branched question.

slope (β_1) the change in Y for a 1-unit change in X; one of two regression coefficients.

snowball sampling a nonprobability sampling procedure in which subsequent participants are referred by current sample elements; referrals may have characteristics, experiences, or attitudes similar to or different from those of the original sample element; commonly used in qualitative methodologies.

solicited proposal proposal developed in response to an RFP.

Somers's *d* a measure of association for ordinal data that compensates for "tied" ranks and adjusts for direction of the independent variable.

sorting participants sort cards (representing concepts or constructs) into piles using criteria established by the researcher.

sound reasoning the basis of sound research, based on finding correct premises, testing connections between facts and assumptions, and making claims based on adequate evidence.

source evaluation the five-factor process for evaluating the quality and value of data from a secondary source; see also *purpose, scope, authority, audience,* and *format.*

spatial observation the recording of human behavior and how humans physically relate to each other; see also **proxemics.**

Spearman's rho correlates ranks between two ordered variables; an ordinal measure of association.

specialty marketing researcher establishes expertise in one or a few research methodologies; these specialties usually are based on methodology, process, industry, participant group, or geographic region; often assist other research firms to complete projects.

specification error an overestimation of the importance of the variables included in a structural model.

sponsor nondisclosure a type of confidentiality; when the sponsor of the research does not allow revealing of its sponsorship.

spreadsheet a data-entry software application that arranges data cases or records as rows, with a separate column for each variable in the study.

stability a characteristic of a measurement scale if it provides consistent results with repeated measures of the same person with the same instrument.

standard deviation (*s*) a measure of spread; the positive square root of the variance; abbreviated *std. dev.;* affected by extreme scores.

standard error of the mean the standard deviation of the distribution of sample means.

standard normal distribution the statistical standard for describing normally distributed sample data; used with inferential statistics that assume normally distributed variables.

standard score (Z score) conveys how many standard deviation units a case is above or below the mean; designed to improve compatibility among variables that come from different scales yet require comparison; includes both linear manipulations and nonlinear transformations.

standard test market real-time test of a product through existing distribution channels.

standardized coefficients regression coefficients in standardized form (mean = 0) used to determine the comparative impact of variables that come from different scales; the X values restated in terms of their standard deviations (a measure of the amount that Y varies with each unit change of the associated X variable)

Stapel scale a numerical scale with up to 10 categories (7 positive, 7 negative) where the central position is an attribute. The higher the positive number, the more accurately the attribute describes the object or its indicant.

statistical significance an index of how meaningful the results of a statistical comparison are; the magnitude of difference between a sample value and its population value; the difference is statistically significant if it is unlikely to have occurred by chance (represent random sampling fluctuations).

statistical study a study that attempts to capture a population's characteristics by making inferences from a sample's characteristics; involves hypothesis testing and is more comprehensive than a case study.

stem-and-leaf display a tree-type frequency distribution for each data value, without equal interval grouping.

stepwise selection in modeling and regression, a method for sequentially adding or removing variables from a regression model to optimize R^2; combines *forward selection* and *backward elimination* methods.

stratified random sampling probability sampling that includes elements from each of the mutually exclusive strata within a population.

stratified sampling, disproportionate a probability sampling technique in which each stratum's size is not proportionate to the stratum's share of the population; allocation is usually based on variability of measures expected from the stratum, cost of sampling from a given stratum, and size of the various strata.

stratified sampling, proportionate a probability sampling technique in which each stratum's size is proportionate to the stratum's share of the population; higher statistical efficiency than a simple random sample.

stress index an index used in multidimensional scaling that ranges from 1 (worst fit) to 0 (perfect fit).

structural equation modeling (SEM) uses analysis of covariance structures to explain causality among constructs.

structured interview an IDI that often uses a detailed interview guide similar to a questionnaire to guide the question order; questions generally use an open-ended response strategy.

structured response participant's response is limited to specific alternatives provided; a.k.a *closed response.*

summated rating scale category of scales where participant agrees or disagrees with evaluative statements; the Likert scale is most known of this type of scale.

supergroup a group interview involving up to 20 people.

survey a measurement process using a highly structured interview; employs a measurement tool called a *questionnaire, measurement instrument,* or *interview schedule.*

symmetrical relationship when two variables vary together but without causation.

syndicated data provider tracks the change of one or more measures over time, usually in a given industry.

synergy the process at the foundation of group interviewing that encourages members to react to and build on the contributions of others in the group.

systematic error error that results from a bias; see also *systematic variance.*

systematic observation data collection through observation that employs standardized procedures, trained observers, schedules for recording, and other devices for the observer that mirror the scientific procedures of other primary data methods.

systematic sampling a probability sample drawn by applying a calculated skip interval to a sample frame; population (N) is divided by the desired sample (n) to obtain a skip interval (k). Using a random start between 1 and k, each kth element is chosen from the sample frame; usually treated as a simple random sample but statistically more efficient.

systematic variance the variation that causes measurements to skew in one direction or another; see also *systematic error.*

t **distribution** a normal distribution with more tail area than that in a Z normal distribution.

*t***-test** a parametric test to determine the statistical significance between a sample distribution mean and a population parameter; used when the population standard deviation is unknown and the sample standard deviation is used as a proxy.

target question measurement question that addresses the core investigative questions of a specific study; these can be structured or unstructered questions.

target question, structured a measurement question that presents the participant with a fixed set of categories per variable.

target question, unstructured measurement question that presents the participant with the context for participant-framed answers; a.k.a. *open-ended question, free-response question* (nominal, ordinal, or ratio data).

tau (τ) a measure of association that uses table marginals to reduce prediction errors, with measures from 0 to 1.0 reflecting percentage of error estimates for prediction of one variable based on another variable.

tau b (τ_b) a refinement of gamma for ordinal data that considers "tied' pairs, not only discordant and concordant pairs (values from -1.0 to $+1.0$); used best on square tables (one of the most widely used measures for ordinal data).

tau c (τ_c) a refinement of gamma for ordinal data that considers "tied' pairs, not only discordant and concordant pairs (values from -1.0 to $+1.0$); useful for any-size table (one of the most widely used measures for ordinal data).

technical report a report written for an audience of researchers.

telephone focus group a type of focus group where participants are connected to the moderator and each other by modern teleconferencing equipment; participants are often in separate teleconferencing facilities; may be remote-moderated or -monitored.

telephone interview a study conducted wholly by telephone contact between participant and interviewer.

tertiary sources aids to discover primary or secondary sources, such as indexes, bibliographies, and Internet search engines; also may be an interpretation of a secondary source.

test market a controlled experiment conducted in a carefully chosen marketplace (e.g., Web site, store, town, or other geographic location) to measure and predict sales or profitability of a product.

test unit an alternative term for a subject within an experiment (a person, an animal, a machine, a geographic entity, an object, etc.).

Thematic Apperception Test a projective technique where participants are confronted with a picture (usually a photograph or drawing) and asked to describe how the person in the picture feels and thinks.

theoretical sampling a nonprobability sampling process where conceptual or theoretical categories of participants develop during the interviewing process; additional participants are sought who will challenge emerging patterns.

theory a set of systematically interrelated concepts, definitions, and propositions that are advanced to explain or predict phenomena (facts); the generalizations we make about variables and the relationships among variables.

3-D graphic a presentation technique that permits a graphical comparison of three or more variables; types: column, ribbon, wireframe, and surface line.

time sampling the process of selecting certain time points or time intervals to observe and record elements, acts, or conditions from a population of observable behaviors or conditions to represent the population as a whole; three types include time-point samples, time-interval samples, and continuous real-time samples.

topic outline report planning format; uses key words or phrases rather than complete sentences to draft each report section.

treatment the experimental factor to which participants are exposed.

treatment levels the arbitrary or natural groupings within the independent variable of an experiment.

triad a group interview involving three people.

trials repeated measures taken from the same subject or participant.

triangulation research design that combines several qualitative methods or qualitative with quantitative methods; most common are simultaneous QUAL/QUANT in single or multiple waves, sequential QUAL-QUANT or QUANT-QUAL, sequential QUAL-QUANT-QUAL.

truncation a search protocol that allows a symbol (usually "?" or "*") to replace one or more characters or letters in a word or at the end of a word root.

two-independent-samples tests parametric and nonparametric tests used when the measurements are taken from two samples that are unrelated (Z test, t-test, chi-square, etc.).

two-related-samples tests parametric and nonparametric tests used when the measurements are taken from closely matched samples or the phenomena are measured twice from the same sample; (t-test, McNemar test, etc).

two-stage design a design in which exploration as a distinct stage precedes a descriptive or causal design.

two-tailed test a nondirectional test to reject the hypothesis that the sample statistic is either greater than or less than the population parameter.

Type I error error when one rejects a true null hypothesis (there is no difference); the alpha (α) value, called the level of significance, is the probability of rejecting the true null hypothesis.

Type II error error when one fails to reject a false null hypothesis; the beta (β) value is the probability of failing to reject the false null hypothesis; the power of the test $= 1 - \beta$ and is the probability that we will correctly reject the false null hypothesis.

unbalanced rating scale has an unequal number of favorable and unfavorable response choices.

unforced-choice rating scale provides participants with an opportunity to express no opinion when they are unable to make a choice among the alternatives offered.

unidimensional scale instrument scale that seeks to measure only one attribute of the participant or object.

unobtrusive measures a set of observational approaches that encourage creative and imaginative forms of indirect observation, archival searches, and variations on simple and contrived observation, including physical traces observation (erosion and accretion).

unsolicited proposal a suggestion by a contract researcher for research that might be done.

unstructured interview a customized IDI with no specific questions or order of topics to be discussed; usually starts with a participant narrative.

unstructured response where participant's response is limited only by space, layout, instructions, or time; usually free-response or fill-in response strategies.

utility score a score in conjoint analysis used to represent each aspect of a product or service in a participant's overall preference ratings.

validity a characteristic of measurement concerned with the extent that a test measures what the researcher actually wishes to measure; and that differences found with a measurement tool reflect true differences among participants drawn from a population.

validity, construct the degree to which a research instrument is able to provide evidence based on theory.

validity, content the extent to which measurement scales provide adequate coverage of the investigative questions.

validity, criterion-related the success of a measurement scale for prediction or estimation; types are predictive and concurrent.

variability term for measures of spread or dispersion within a data set.

variable (research variable) a characteristic, trait, or attribute that is measured; a symbol to which values are assigned; includes several different types: continuous, control, decision, dependent, dichotomous, discrete, dummy, extraneous, independent, intervening, and moderating variables.

variance a measure of score dispersion about the mean; calculated as the squared deviation scores from the data distribution's mean; the greater the dispersion of scores, the greater the variance in the data set.

videoconference focus group a type of focus group where researchers use the videoconference facilities of a firm to connect participants with moderators and observers; unlike telephone focus groups, participants can see each other; can be remotely moderated, and in some facilities can be simultaneously monitored by client observers via Internet technology.

virtual test market a test of a product using a computer simulation of an interactive shopping experience.

visitor from another planet a projective technique (imagination exercise) where participants are asked to assume that they are aliens and are confronting the product for the first time; they then describe their reactions, questions, and attitudes about purchase or retrial.

visual aids presentation tools used to facilitate understanding of content (e.g., chalkboards, whiteboards, handouts, flip charts, overhead transparencies, slides, computer-drawn visuals, computer animation).

voice recognition computer systems programmed to record verbal answers to questions.

Web-based questionnaire a measurement instrument both delivered and collected via the Internet; data processing is ongoing. Two options currently exist: proprietary solutions offered through research firms and off-the-shelf software for researchers who possess the necessary knowledge and skills; a.k.a. *online survey, online questionnaire, Internet survey.*

Web-enabled test market test of a product using online distribution.

word or **picture association** a projective technique where participants are asked to match images, experiences, emotions, products and services, and even people and places to whatever is being studied.

Z distribution the normal distribution of measurements assumed for comparison.

Z score see **standard score.**

Z test a parametric test to determine the statistical significance between a sample distribution mean and a population parameter; employs the *Z* distribution.

Photo #	Description	Page	Credit
chapter 1			
P1-1	Child getting checked by a doctor	5	© Corbis
P1-2	JRP Marketing Research Services ad	5	Courtesy of JRP Marketing Research Services, Inc.
P1-3	Bowl of Häagen-Dazs ice cream	13	Courtesy of Dreyer's Grand Ice Cream, Inc.
chapter 2			
P2-1	Decision Analyst ad	32	Courtesy of Decision Analyst
P2-2	Kodak disposable digital camera	35	Image Courtesy © Eastman Kodak Company. KODAK is a trademark.
P2-3	Court TV ad	36	Courtesy of Courtroom Television Network LLC
P2-4	Wal-Mart interior	44	Photo courtesy of www.walmart.com
chapter 3			
P3-1	Synovate ad	54	Courtesy of Synovate
P3-2	Boys flying paper airplanes	56	© Stephen S. T. Bradley/Corbis
P3-3	Marriott lobby	62	Courtesy of Marriott International, Inc.
P3-4	Lexus dealership	66	© Will & Deni McIntyre/Corbis
chapter 4			
P4-1	GreenfieldOnline ad—toaster	78	Courtesy of Greenfield Online
P4-2	Harris Interactive ad featuring man in plaid suit	80	© 2004, Harris Interactive Inc. All rights reserved.
P4-3	Red Lexus SC 430 hardtop convertible	82	Courtesy of Lexus
P4-4	Motorola camera phone	88	Courtesy of Motorola Inc.
P4-5	Focus group	89	© Spencer Grant/PhotoEdit
chapter 5			
P5-1	People working at white board	100	Getty Images
P5-2	Consumer Information Center ad	102	Reprinted with permission of the Federal Consumer Information Center
P5-3	Covering Kids ad	110	Produced for The Robert Wood Johnson Foundation's Covering Kids Initiative by GMMB
chapter 6			
P6-1	Luth Research ad	134	Courtesy of Luth Research
P6-2	Karastan ad featuring Andie MacDowell	139	Provided by Austin Kelly Advertising. Used with permission.
P6-3	USTA ad featuring Daisy Fuentes	141	Provided by USTA. Used with permission.
P6-4	Steam 'n Clean in use	148	Courtesy of BISSELL INC.
P6-5	STS ad: How much can you save at a nickle a number?	149	Courtesy of STS, Scientific Telephone Samples
chapter 7			
P7-1	Man washing hair	166	© Royalty-Free/CORBIS
P7-2	KidzEyes ad	169	Courtesy of C&R Research Services
P7-3	Money flying on Wall Street	178	© Royalty-Free/CORBIS
P7-4	Burger King exterior	179	© Cathy Melloan/PhotoEdit
chapter 8			
P8-1	GO snacks package	198	Courtesy of Frito-Lay, Inc.
P8-2	Teens with disposable camera	199	© The Image Bank/Getty Images
P8-3	Delve ad: Creating Connections	200	Courtesy of Delve

>company index

>subject index